The Impact of the Inter-American Human Rights System

The Impact of the Inter-American Human Rights System

Transformations on the Ground

Edited by
ARMIN VON BOGDANDY
FLÁVIA PIOVESAN
EDUARDO FERRER MAC-GREGOR
MARIELA MORALES ANTONIAZZI

Managing Editor
JULIA CORTEZ DA CUNHA CRUZ

OXFORD
UNIVERSITY PRESS

Oxford University Press is a department of the University of Oxford. It furthers the University's objective of excellence in research, scholarship, and education by publishing worldwide. Oxford is a registered trade mark of Oxford University Press in the UK and certain other countries.

Published in the United States of America by Oxford University Press
198 Madison Avenue, New York, NY 10016, United States of America.

© The multiple Contributors 2024

Some rights reserved. No part of this publication may be reproduced, stored in a retrieval system, or transmitted, in any form or by any means, for commercial purposes, without the prior permission in writing of Oxford University Press, or as expressly permitted by law, by licence or under terms agreed with the appropriate reprographics rights organization.

This is an open access publication, available online and distributed under the terms of a Creative Commons Attribution – Non Commercial – No Derivatives 4.0 International licence (CC BY-NC-ND 4.0), a copy of which is available at http://creativecommons.org/licenses/by-nc-nd/4.0/.

You must not circulate this work in any other form
and you must impose this same condition on any acquirer.

Library of Congress Cataloging-in-Publication Data
Names: Bogdandy, Armin von, 1960- author. | Piovesan, Flávia, author. | Mac-Gregor, Eduardo Ferrer, author. | Antoniazzi, Mariela Morales, author.
Title: The impact of the Inter-American human rights system : transformations on the ground / Armin von Bogdandy, Flávia Piovesan, Eduardo Ferrer Mac-Gregor, Mariela Morales Antoniazzi.
Description: New York : Oxford University Press, 2024. | Includes bibliographical references and index.
Identifiers: LCCN 2023036674 (print) | LCCN 2023036675 (ebook) | ISBN 9780197744161 (hardback) | ISBN 9780197744178 (epub) | ISBN 9780197744185 (updf)| ISBN 9780197744192 (digital-online)
Subjects: LCSH: Human rights—Latin America. | International and municipal law—Latin America. | International law and human rights—Latin America. | Inter-American Court of Human Rights.
Classification: LCC KG574 .B64 2024 (print) | LCC KG574 (ebook) | DDC 341.4/8098—dc23
LC record available at https://lccn.loc.gov/2023036674
LC ebook record available at https://lccn.loc.gov/2023036675

DOI: 10.1093/oso/9780197744161.001.0001

Printed by Integrated Books International, United States of America

Note to Readers
This publication is designed to provide accurate and authoritative information in regard to the subject matter covered. It is based upon sources believed to be accurate and reliable and is intended to be current as of the time it was written. It is sold with the understanding that the publisher is not engaged in rendering legal, accounting, or other professional services. If legal advice or other expert assistance is required, the services of a competent professional person should be sought. Also, to confirm that the information has not been affected or changed by recent developments, traditional legal research techniques should be used, including checking primary sources where appropriate.

(Based on the Declaration of Principles jointly adopted by a Committee of the American Bar Association and a Committee of Publishers and Associations.)

You may order this or any other Oxford University Press publication
by visiting the Oxford University Press website at www.oup.com.

Contents

List of Contributors   xxiii

Introduction   1
    Armin von Bogdandy, Flávia Piovesan, Eduardo Ferrer Mac-Gregor, and Mariela Morales Antoniazzi

PART I FRAMING THE IMPACT OF THE INTER-AMERICAN SYSTEM

I.1 Inducing Compliance as a Transformative Process: The Bright Side of a Dismal Record   17
    Armin von Bogdandy and René Urueña

I.2 Protecting Human Rights in the Americas: The Continuous Role of the Inter-American Commission on Human Rights   34
    Claudio Grossman

I.3 Inter-American Human Rights System: Sociopolitical, Institutional, and Cultural Dimensions of Its Transformative Impact   49
    Mariela Morales Antoniazzi, Flávia Piovesan, and Júlia Cortez da Cunha Cruz

I.4 Current Issues and Common Challenges for the Protection of Human Rights in Europe, the Americas, and Africa   76
    Rainer Grote

I.5 The Impact of the Inter-American Human Rights System beyond Latin America   100
    Par Engstrom

I.6 Conventionality Control: An Expression of the Basic Elements of the Judicial Function   122
    Miriam Lorena Henríquez Viñas and José Ignacio Núñez Leiva

I.7 Effectiveness of International Courts: From Compliance to Transformative Impact   138
    Gabriela C.B. Navarro

I.8 The Use of Transformative Provisional Measures by the Inter-American Court of Human Rights: Toward a Tangible Impact   153
    Clara Burbano-Herrera and Yves Haeck

I.9 Transformative Impact: A Framework for Analysis 176
    Mayra Ortiz Ocaña and Aníbal Pérez-Liñán

I.10 Creating the Narrative of Human Rights Impact in
    Latin America 199
    René Urueña and Stephania Yate Cortes

PART II IMPACT AND INTER-AMERICAN STANDARDS

II.1 Impact of the Inter-American Jurisprudence on Economic,
    Social, Cultural, and Environmental Rights 217
    Eduardo Ferrer Mac-Gregor

II.2 The Inter-American Human Rights System's Impact on the
    Protection of the Right to a Healthy Environment 237
    Henry Jiménez Guanipa and María Barraco

II.3 Indigenous Rights in the Inter-American System: The Application
    of Precautionary Measures from a Culturally Appropriate
    Perspective 254
    Antonia Urrejola and Elsy Curihuinca Neira

II.4 The Inter-American Human Rights System and Its Impact on the
    Human Rights of Women: The Issue of Sexual Violence 268
    Julissa Mantilla Falcón

II.5 The Transformative Impact of the *Artavia Murillo* Case on
    In Vitro Fertilization 285
    Silvia Serrano Guzmán

II.6 The Impact beyond Compliance of the Case of *Azul Rojas Marin*:
    Reflections around Strategic Litigation and the Inter-American
    Human Rights System 303
    *Chris Esdaile, Clara Sandoval, Alejandra Vicente,
    with Renata Politi and Nataly Sanchez*

II.7 The Rights of the Child According to the Inter-American Court
    of Human Rights: A Latin American Translation 326
    Mary Beloff

II.8 The *Riffo-Salinas* Case: Human Rights of Older Persons
    Consolidated in the Inter-American System 348
    Aída Díaz-Tendero

II.9 The Standards of the Inter-American Human Rights System
regarding Migration and Its Impact on the Region's States   366
Elizabeth Salmón and Cécile Blouin

II.10 The Human Right to Defend Human Rights in the Inter-American
System: Normative Enforcement and Transformative Impact
of the Case of *Escaleras Mejía and Others v. Honduras*   388
Melina Girardi Fachin

II.11 The Inter-American Human Rights System's/ICCAL's Impact
on Transitions to Democracy from the Perspective of
Transitional Justice   408
Christina Binder

II.12 Impact of the Inter-American Human Rights System in the
Struggle against Impunity   424
Oscar Parra Vera

II.13 The Independence of Justice as a Human Right and an
International Obligation in Inter-American Jurisprudence   449
Carlos Ayala Corao

II.14 Freedom of Expression: Inter-American Standards and Their
Transformative Impact   473
Catalina Botero-Marino

II.15 Impact of the IAHRS Principles on Freedom of Expression
and the Need for Their Expansion in the Digital Age:
Challenges to the IAHRS Principles on Freedom of Expression
in the Digital Age   495
Edison Lanza

PART III OPTIMIZING THE IMPACT OF THE INTER-AMERICAN SYSTEM

III.1 Proposals for the Improvement of the Work of the
Inter-American Commission on Human Rights   521
Joel Hernandez García

III.2 A Broader Look at the Transformative Impact of the
Inter-American Court of Human Rights' Decisions   537
Pablo Saavedra Alessandri

III.3 Addressing Conceptual Challenges: Compliance and Impact   564
Aníbal Pérez-Liñán, Kelly Morrison, and Luis L. Schenoni

III.4 Transformative Impact of the Inter-American Human Rights System: A Methodology to Think beyond Compliance   584
Viviana Krsticevic and René Urueña

III.5 Strategies of the Due Process of Law Foundation for the Promotion of New Standards and Expansion of the Impact of the Inter-American Human Rights System   603
Katya Salazar and Daniel Cerqueira

III.6 Activism Strategies Involving the Inter-American System: Reflections for the Field of Action and Perspectives from National Human Rights Organizations   625
Gabriela Kletzel

Conclusion   641
Armin von Bogdandy, Flávia Piovesan, Eduardo Ferrer Mac-Gregor, and Mariela Morales Antoniazzi

Index   649

Thematic Overview

List of Contributors	xxiii
Introduction Armin von Bogdandy, Flávia Piovesan, Eduardo Ferrer Mac-Gregor, and Mariela Morales Antoniazzi	1

PART I FRAMING THE IMPACT OF THE INTER-AMERICAN SYSTEM

I.1 Inducing Compliance as a Transformative Process: The Bright Side of a Dismal Record — 17
Armin von Bogdandy and René Urueña
  1. Introduction — 17
  2. Latin American Transformative Constitutionalism — 19
  3. The Latin American Human Rights Community — 22
  4. Compliance as a Transformative Practice — 26
  5. Transformative Constitutionalism beyond Compliance — 29
  6. Concluding Remarks — 32

I.2 Protecting Human Rights in the Americas: The Continuous Role of the Inter-American Commission on Human Rights — 34
Claudio Grossman
  1. Introduction — 34
  2. The Role of the Commission through Its Phases — 36
     2.1. Phase One: Maintaining a Human Rights Focus among Dictatorships — 36
     2.2. Phase Two: Individuals Bring Grievances against Their Nations — 37
     2.3. Phase Three: Greater Inclusion and Participation in the Political System — 39
  3. Challenges for the Commission in Executing Its Functions — 44
  4. Concluding Remarks — 47

I.3 Inter-American Human Rights System: Sociopolitical, Institutional, and Cultural Dimensions of Its Transformative Impact — 49
Mariela Morales Antoniazzi, Flávia Piovesan, and Júlia Cortez da Cunha Cruz
  1. Introduction — 49
  2. WHY Do We Need the Inter-American System? — 50
     2.1. Structural Challenges — 50
     2.2. Contemporary Challenges — 53
     2.3. The Aggravation of Challenges in Times of Crisis — 57

3. WHAT Are the Key Components of the
   Inter-American System? 62
   3.1. The Victim-Centric Approach 63
   3.2. Inter-American Standards 63
   3.3. Comprehensive Reparations 64
4. How Can One Understand IAHRS Transformative Impact,
   Taking into Account Its Sociopolitical, Institutional, and Cultural
   Dimensions? 65
   4.1. Institutional Dimension 67
   4.2. Sociopolitical Dimension 70
   4.3. Cultural Dimension 71
5. Concluding Remarks 74

I.4 Current Issues and Common Challenges for the Protection of
Human Rights in Europe, the Americas, and Africa 76
Rainer Grote
1. Introduction 76
2. The Expansion of Regional Human Rights Protection after the
   End of the Cold War 77
   2.1. Institutionalization 78
   2.2. Judicialization 80
   2.3. Diversification of Remedial Practice 82
   2.4. Embeddedness 86
3. The Backlash against the Increasing Scope and Intrusiveness of
   Regional Human Rights Jurisprudence 87
   3.1. Withdrawal from the Regional Human Rights System 88
   3.2. Institutional Reform 91
   3.3. Noncompliance with Individual Decisions 94
4. Responses to the Backlash 96
5. The Road Ahead 98

I.5 The Impact of the Inter-American Human Rights System
beyond Latin America 100
Par Engstrom
1. Introduction 100
2. The IAHRS and the Origins of Global Human Rights Governance 101
3. The IAHRS and International Human Rights Standards 105
4. The IAHRS and Transnationalized Human Rights Implementation 111
5. Human Rights Futures: A World of Regions and Experimental
   Governance 118

I.6 Conventionality Control: An Expression of the Basic
Elements of the Judicial Function 122
Miriam Lorena Henríquez Viñas and José Ignacio Núñez Leiva
1. Introduction 122
2. Methodology 124
3. The Meaning of Conventionality Control 125

	4. The Difference between Adjudication and Execution in Conventionality Control	129
	5. The Role of *Res Judicata* and *Res Interpretata*	131
	6. Conclusion	136

I.7 Effectiveness of International Courts: From Compliance to Transformative Impact — 138
Gabriela C.B. Navarro
   1. Introduction — 138
   2. Effectiveness as Compliance — 139
      2.1. Defining and Measuring Compliance — 139
      2.2. Evaluating Compliance with IACtHR Decisions — 141
   3. Impact beyond Compliance — 143
      3.1. Defining Impact and Effectiveness — 143
      3.2. The Effectiveness of the IACtHR — 147
   4. Illustrating Effectiveness: The Case of Indigenous Territorial Rights — 148
   5. Concluding Remarks — 152

I.8 The Use of Transformative Provisional Measures by the Inter-American Court of Human Rights: Toward a Tangible Impact — 153
Clara Burbano-Herrera and Yves Haeck
   1. Introduction — 153
   2. Human Rights Standards Applicable to Persons Deprived of Their Liberty in Latin America — 155
   3. Legal Basis of Provisional Measures in the Inter-American Human Rights System — 160
   4. Transformative Provisional Measures: Toward a Material Impact — 161
   5. Detention Conditions of Persons Deprived of Their Liberty in Latin America through the Lens of Transformative Provisional Measures — 163
   6. Case Study: Criminal Institute of *Plácido de Sá Carvalho v. Brazil* — 167
   7. Concluding Remarks — 175

I.9 Transformative Impact: A Framework for Analysis — 176
Mayra Ortiz Ocaña and Aníbal Pérez-Liñán
   1. Introduction — 176
   2. What Is Impact? — 177
   3. The Transformative Sequence: From Instruments to Outcomes — 180
      3.1. Time Zero: The System's Instruments — 180
      3.2. First Stage: Appropriation — 185
      3.3. Second Stage: Institutional Response — 187
      3.4. Third Stage: Transformations on the Ground — 190
   4. Strategies to Document Impact — 192
   5. Concluding Remarks — 196

I.10 Creating the Narrative of Human Rights Impact in Latin America 199
René Urueña and Stephania Yate Cortes
  1. Introduction 199
  2. Communities of Practice and Narratives of Human Rights Impact 200
  3. Creating Narratives: Cognitive Categories and Framing 201
    3.1. Description through Cognitive Categories 202
    3.2. Framing the Narrative of the Impact 204
  4. Narratives of Impact in Practice 207
    4.1. Deployment of Cognitive Categories to Define the Problem 208
    4.2. Diagnosis of Causes 210
    4.3. Definition of Remedies 211
    4.4. The Narrative of the Impact 212
  5. Conclusion 214

PART II IMPACT AND INTER-AMERICAN STANDARDS

II.1 Impact of the Inter-American Jurisprudence on Economic, Social, Cultural, and Environmental Rights 217
Eduardo Ferrer Mac-Gregor
  1. Introduction 217
  2. The Protection of ESCER through Civil and Political Rights 218
    2.1. Indirect Justiciability of Cases in Which a Violation of Article 26 Was Alleged 220
    2.2. Indirect Justiciability in Cases Relating to Groups in a Position of Vulnerability 221
    2.3 Cases Subject to the "Rereading" of ESCER from 1999 to 2017 223
  3. Direct Justiciability via the Protocol of San Salvador 225
  4. The New Model of Direct Justiciability 226
    4.1. A Chronicle of ESCER's Direct Justiciability through Article 26 226
    4.2. The Case of *Lagos del Campo* Approach 227
  5. Concluding Remarks 235

II.2 The Inter-American Human Rights System's Impact on the Protection of the Right to a Healthy Environment 237
Henry Jiménez Guanipa and Maria Barraco
  1. Introduction 237
  2. The Protection of Environmental Human Rights in the Inter-American Human Rights System 240
    2.1. The Protection of the Right to a Healthy Environment 245
    2.2. The Right to a Healthy Environment and Indigenous Communities 246
    2.3. The Right to Access Information Concerning and to Participate in Environmental Matters 248
  3. Transformative Impact: Recognition of Environmental Human Rights at the Domestic Level 249
  4. Concluding Remarks 252

II.3 Indigenous Rights in the Inter-American System:
The Application of Precautionary Measures from a
Culturally Appropriate Perspective   254
Antonia Urrejola and Elsy Curihuinca Neira
1. Introduction   254
2. Inter-American Human Rights System and General Standards
Regarding Indigenous Peoples   256
   2.1. The Right to a Cultural Identity   257
   2.2. The Right to the Lands, Territories, and Resources of
Indigenous Peoples   257
   2.3. Participatory Rights of Indigenous Peoples   259
3. MPMs and Cultural Pertinence   260
   3.1. Precautionary Measure No. 113/16: "Tres Islas" Native
Community of Madre de Dios Regarding Peru   261
   3.2. Precautionary Measure No. 395/18: Authorities and Members
of the Gonzaya (Buenavista) and Po Piyuya (Santa Cruz de
Piñuña Blanco) Reserves of the Siona Indigenous People
(ZioBain) Regarding Colombia   262
   3.3. Precautionary Measure No. 860/17: Indigenous Families of the
Chaab'il Ch'och' Community Regarding Guatemala   263
   3.4. Precautionary Measure No. 1014/17: U.V.O. Indigenous Girl
and Her Family Regarding Mexico   264
4. Progress and Challenges   264
5. Concluding Remarks   266

II.4 The Inter-American Human Rights System and Its Impact on
the Human Rights of Women: The Issue of Sexual Violence   268
Julissa Mantilla Falcón
1. Introduction   268
2. The IHRL Regulatory Framework for the Investigation
of Sexual Violence   268
3. Inter-American Standards and Their Role in the Recognition
and Condemnation of Sexual Violence   272
   3.1. Recognition of Sexual Violence as a Violation of Human Rights   272
   3.2. The Principle of Enhanced/Stringent Due Diligence   275
   3.3. The Intersectional Perspective when Approaching the Issue of
Sexual Violence   277
   3.4. Gender Stereotypes and Their Impact into the Investigation of
Sexual Violence   280
   3.5. Responsibility of the State for Sexual Violence as Torture   282
4. Concluding Remarks   284

II.5 The Transformative Impact of the *Artavia Murillo* Case
on In Vitro Fertilization   285
Silvia Serrano Guzmán
1. Introduction and Brief History of the Case   285
2. Transformative Impact in the Development of Inter-American
Jurisprudence   287

2.1. The Interpretation of the Protection of the Right to Life under
Article 4.1 of the Convention 287
2.2. The New Legal Standards Related to Reproductive Rights, Including
the Right to Reproductive Autonomy and Its Permissible Limitations . . . 292
2.3. Impact on the Decisions of Domestic Tribunals in Other
Countries of the Region 294
3. Nationwide and Structural Impact of the Reparations Ordered by
the Court 295
3.1. Training the Judiciary in Reproductive Rights 296
3.2. The Annulment of the Prohibition of the Practice of IVF in
Costa Rica 297
3.3. The Regulation of IVF and the Implementation of Systems of
Inspection and Quality Controls of Its Practice 300
3.4. The Inclusion of IVF in the State Healthcare System 301
4. Concluding Remarks 301

II.6 The Impact beyond Compliance of the Case of *Azul Rojas Marín*:
Reflections around Strategic Litigation and the Inter-American
Human Rights System 303
*Chris Esdaile, Clara Sandoval, Alejandra Vicente, with
Renata Politi and Nataly Sanchez*
1. Introduction 303
2. The Case of *Azul Rojas Marín and Other v. Peru*—Its Legal Significance . . 305
2.1. The Court Found that Arbitrary Detention of LGBTIQ+ Persons
Can Be Inferred When There Are Signs of Discrimination and
No Other Apparent Reason for the Detention 306
2.2. The Court Found that the Purposive Element of the Definition
of Torture Incorporates Discrimination Based on Sexual
Orientation and Gender Identity 307
2.3. The Court Found that States Have a Duty to Investigate
Violence Motivated by Discrimination against Members of
the LGBTIQ+ Community 308
2.4. The Court Tackled Structural Discrimination through Reparations . . . 309
3. The International Protection of LGBTIQ+ Rights before the Case of *Azul* . . 310
3.1. The European System 311
3.2. The UN System 312
3.3. The African System 314
3.4. The Inter-American System at the Forefront 314
3.5. Cross-Fertilization across Systems 316
4. Criteria to Assess the Impact of Strategic Litigation 317
5. The Impact of *Azul*'s Judgment 319
5.1. Justice, Truth, and Material Impacts for Azul, Her Mother, and Society . 320
5.2. Legal Impact of the Case in Other Supranational and National Bodies . 321
5.3. The Impact of the Case of *Azul* on the Community and the
LGBTIQ+ Movement 322
6. Reflection on the Impact of the Case 324
7. Concluding Remarks 325

II.7 The Rights of the Child According to the Inter-American Court
of Human Rights: A Latin American Translation   326
Mary Beloff
1. Introduction   326
2. The Recognition of the Existence of an International *Corpus Juris* on the Protection of the Rights of the Child   328
3. Defining "Child" in International Law: The Impact of the Convention on the Rights of the Child on the Inter-American Court Case Law   330
4. The Inter-American Court Jurisprudence on the Rights of Children   332
   4.1. Inter-American Court Advisory Opinions Related to Child Rights   333
   4.2. Provisional Measures Regarding Children outside the Framework of a Contentious Case   333
   4.3. The Inter-American Court Case Law Regarding the Rights of Children (ACHR Article 19)   334
5. The Right of the Child to Special Protection Measures in Conjunction with the Right to Life   337
6. The Right of the Child to Special Protection Measures in Relation to Other Rights   341
7. The Limits and Possibilities of the Inter-American System for Advancing the Rights of Children   343

II.8 The *Riffo-Salinas* Case: Human Rights of Older Persons Consolidated in the Inter-American System   348
Aída Díaz-Tendero
1. Introduction   348
2. *Riffo Salinas* Case Judgment   351
3. How Does the ICPHROP Go beyond the Bolivian Case?   354
   3.1. Equality and Nondiscrimination on the Basis of Age and the Right to Personal Freedom   355
   3.2. Rights to Safety, Life, and Health   356
4. In What Aspects Do the IACHR Court Cases on Older Persons Go Further than the Bolivian Case?   358
   4.1. Right to Life   358
   4.2. Right to Health   359
   4.3. Right to Liberty and Security   360
5. Social Constructions about Old Age and the Elderly   361
6. Concluding Remarks   363

II.9 The Standards of the Inter-American Human Rights System regarding Migration and Its Impact on the Region's States   366
Elizabeth Salmón and Cécile Blouin
1. Introduction   366
2. The Standards of the Inter-American Human Rights System for Migration Matters   367
   2.1. First Stage: Silence from the Inter-American Human Rights System   368
   2.2. Second Stage: Initial IAHRS Reactions   369

    2.3. Third Stage: Development and Expansion of Standards   372
    2.4. Pending Issues   377
3. The Transformative Impact of IAHRS Standards in Latin America: An Analysis in Light of the Legal Frameworks   378
    3.1. The Transformative Impact on the Normative Frameworks on Migration and Asylum in the Region   378
    3.2. The Recognition of the Standards of the IACHR in the Judicial and Constitutional Spheres   384
4. Concluding Remarks   387

II.10 The Human Right to Defend Human Rights in the Inter-American System: Normative Enforcement and Transformative Impact of the Case of *Escaleras Mejía and Others v. Honduras*   388
Melina Girardi Fachin

1. Introduction   388
2. Human Rights Defenders: Multilevel Approach   390
    2.1. Global System   391
    2.2. Regional Systems   393
    2.3. Domestic Systems   394
3. IACtHR Jurisprudence on Defenders   396
    3.1. *Luna López v. Honduras* (IACtHR)   398
    3.2. *Kawas Fernández v. Honduras*   398
    3.3. *Escaleras Mejía v. Honduras*   399
4. The Right to Defend Rights: The Legacy of *Escaleras Mejía*   401
    4.1. Right to Life (Article 4.1 of the American Convention)   402
    4.2. Right to Freedom of Association (Article 16 of the American Convention)   403
    4.3. Right to Participate in Government (Article 23.1.b of the American Convention)   403
    4.4. Rights to a Fair Trial and to Judicial Protection (Articles 8.1 and 25.1 of the American Convention)   404
    4.5. Right to Humane Treatment (Article 5.1 of the American Convention)   404
    4.6. Right to Freedom of Expression and Right of Assembly (Articles 13 and 15 of the American Convention)   404
    4.7. The Autonomous Right to Defend Rights   405
5. Concluding Remarks   406

II.11 The Inter-American Human Rights System's/ICCAL's Impact on Transitions to Democracy from the Perspective of Transitional Justice   408
Christina Binder

1. Introduction   408
2. Enabling Transitions to Democracy in Latin America: How to Deal with Past Human Rights Violations from the Perspective of Transitional Justice   409
3. Inter-American Human Rights Standards within a Multilevel Legal System of Law   411

4. Impact of the ICCAL/Inter-American Human Rights System on Transitions to Democracy	412
4.1. The Inter-American Court's Amnesty Jurisprudence: Standards and "Toolbox"	412
4.2. Domestic Reception of the IACtHR's Amnesty Jurisprudence	419
5. Concluding Remarks	422

II.12 Impact of the Inter-American Human Rights System in the Struggle against Impunity — 424
Oscar Parra Vera

1. Introduction	424
2. Some Details on the Scope of the Need to Investigate Serious Violations of Human Rights	426
2.1. Fraudulent Res Judicata and Admissible Weightings Surrounding the Principle of *Ne Bis In Idem*	426
2.2. Cooperative Interstate Obligations Regarding Investigation and Extradition	428
2.3. Qualification of Conduct as a Crime against Humanity to Determine the Scope of the Obligation to Investigate: Debates	431
2.4. Abuse of the Law and Other Procedural Irregularities Aimed at Hindering Due Diligence	432
2.5. Prevalent Formulation of Criminal Definition and Due Diligence	433
2.6. Due Diligence, Systemic Crimes, and "Transitional" Contexts	434
2.7. Limitations on the Intervention of the Military Criminal Jurisdiction	439
2.8. Impulse of Extraordinary International Supervisory Mechanisms	439
2.9. Due Diligence in the Investigation of Executions and Disappearances	441
2.10. Pardons for Humanitarian Reasons Should Not Affect the Proportionality of Punishment	442
3. Transformational Impact	443
4. Concluding Remarks	447

II.13 The Independence of Justice as a Human Right and an International Obligation in Inter-American Jurisprudence — 449
Carlos Ayala Corao

1. Introduction	449
2. Human Rights and the International Obligation of Effective Judicial Protection	450
2.1. The Essential Content of the Right/Obligation to Protect That Right	450
2.2. Protection via Independent Judges and Tribunals	451
3. Facets of the Independence of Judges	453
3.1. The Process of Selecting and Appointing Judges	453

3.2. The Political Right of Access to and Permanence in the
    Office of Judge under Equal Conditions 454
3.3. Guarantees against External Pressures: The Principle of
    Irremovability 456
4. The Stability and Exceptional Nature of Provisional Judges 458
5. The Exercising of Other Rights by Judges: Freedom of Expression
    and the Right to Association 459
6. The Disciplinary System and the System for Removing Judges
    from Office 462
7. Brief Reference to Impeachment Proceedings against Judges 465
8. Some Consequences of the Violation of Judicial Independence 467
    8.1. Full Reparation for Judges: Reinstatement and the Payment of
        Damages 468
    8.2. Reparation for Parties Subject to Trial 470
9. Concluding Remarks 472

II.14 Freedom of Expression: Inter-American Standards and
Their Transformative Impact 473
Catalina Botero-Marino
1. Introduction 473
2. The Creation of ICCAL Regarding Freedom of Expression
   and the Inter-American System's Transformative Mandate 474
3. Inter-American Standards within the Multilevel Legal System 477
    3.1. Special Protection of Public Interest Speech: The Rejection of
        Desacato and Criminal Defamation 479
    3.2. The Right of Access to Information 485
4. Concluding Remarks 493

II.15 Impact of the IAHRS Principles on Freedom of Expression and the
Need for Their Expansion in the Digital Age: Challenges to the
IAHRS Principles on Freedom of Expression in the Digital Age 495
Edison Lanza
1. Introduction 495
2. The Inter-American Legal Framework on Freedom of Expression
   and Its Impact on the Region's Legal Systems and Case Law 497
3. Challenges and Restrictions to the Exercise of Freedom of
   Expression on the Internet 501
4. Principles on Freedom of Expression and the Internet Developed
   by the Inter-American Human Rights System 503
    4.1. Universal Internet Access, Diversity, and Pluralism 504
    4.2. Principle of Net Neutrality 506
    4.3. Content Blocking and Filtering 509
    4.4. Intermediary Liability 510
    4.5. Subsequent Liability 511
    4.6. Hate Speech and Disinformation 512
    4.7. Cybersecurity, Privacy, and Surveillance 514
5. Concluding Remarks 516

PART III OPTIMIZING THE IMPACT OF THE INTER-AMERICAN SYSTEM

III.1 Proposals for the Improvement of the Work of the Inter-American Commission on Human Rights   521
Joel Hernandez García
   1. Introduction   521
   2. A Robust Inter-American Human Rights System   522
   3. Strengthening National Capacities   525
   4. Advancing Standards through the Selection of Cases to Remedy Structural Situations   530
   5. Promoting Compliance with the Decisions of the Commission   532
   6. Concluding Remarks   536

III.2 A Broader Look at the Transformative Impact of the Inter-American Court of Human Rights' Decisions   537
Pablo Saavedra Alessandri
   1. Introduction   537
   2. Structural Impact of Contention Cases   539
      2.1. General Considerations about Reparations   539
      2.2. Authorization and Access to In Vitro Fertilization—Transforming the Hope of Having Children   541
      2.3. Ensuring Effective Recourse—Transforming Access to Justice for Those Convicted by Councils of War   544
      2.4. Additional Reflections on the Transforming Impact of Contention Cases   547
   3. Consultative Opinions and Their Transformative Impact   548
      3.1. General Considerations   548
      3.2. The Consultative Opinion on Nondiscrimination against LGBTIQ+ People   550
   4. Provisional Measures: Avoiding Structural Setbacks, Providing Structural Protection   556
      4.1. Archivor Amnesty Bill: Avoiding Structural Retracement   557
      4.2. Immediate Protection and Adoption of Measures to Protect the Lives, Health, and Integrity of Migrants   560
   5. Concluding Remarks   562

III.3 Addressing Conceptual Challenges: Compliance and Impact   564
Aníbal Pérez-Liñán, Kelly Morrison, and Luis L. Schenoni
   1. Introduction   564
   2. Improving Inter-American Standards: Compliance in Time   567
   3. Why Time Matters   568
      3.1. Legal Outcomes   568
      3.2. The Causes of Compliance   569
   4. Four Metrics of Compliance   569

xx THEMATIC OVERVIEW

    5. Compliance with the IACtHR   571
        5.1. Rates of Compliance   574
        5.2. Average Time to Compliance   575
        5.3. Yearly Probability of Compliance   577
        5.4. Expected Time for Compliance   577
    6. The Compliance Life Cycle   578
    7. Concluding Remarks   580
        7.1. Direct Transformative Impact   581
        7.2. Indirect Transformative Impact   581
        7.3. Resistance   582
        7.4. Compliance Backlash   582

III.4 Transformative Impact of the Inter-American Human Rights System: A Methodology to Think beyond Compliance   584
Viviana Krsticevic and René Urueña
    1. Introduction   584
    2. Literature Review: Compliance with the Inter-American Court's Orders   585
    3. Dynamic Monitoring of Compliance   590
    4. A Methodology for Thinking beyond Compliance   595
        4.1. Accounting for Change over Time   595
        4.2. Improving the "Quality" of Compliance   596
        4.3. Institutional Impact   600
    5. Concluding Remarks   601

III.5 Strategies of the Due Process of Law Foundation for the Promotion of New Standards and Expansion of the Impact of the Inter-American Human Rights System   603
Katya Salazar and Daniel Cerqueira
    1. Introduction   603
    2. Impact of the IAHRS, beyond Compliance with Decisions Pertaining to Contentious Cases   604
    3. DPLF's Strategies for Increasing the Impact of the IAHRS Decisions   611
    4. Specific Strategies for the Development of Standards on the Part of the IAHRS   614
        4.1. Extraterritorial Responsibility of Countries of Origin of Companies Involved in Violations of Human Rights   614
        4.2. Corruption and Human Rights   619
    5. Concluding Remarks   623

III.6 Activism Strategies Involving the Inter-American System: Reflections for the Field of Action and Perspectives from National Human Rights Organizations   625
Gabriela Kletzel
    1. Introduction   625
    2. The Inter-American System as One Piece among More Complex Strategies   626

3. Toward a Genuine Strengthening of the Regional
    Protection System   631
    3.1. The Role of Civil Society in Generating Disruptive Tools   632
    3.2. Guardians of Mandate and Jurisdiction   635
    3.3. Broadening the Agenda and Scope   638
4. Concluding Remarks   639

Conclusion   641
Armin von Bogdandy, Flávia Piovesan, Eduardo Ferrer Mac-Gregor, and Mariela Morales Antoniazzi

Index   649

List of Contributors

Armin von Bogdandy is Director at the Max Planck Institute for Comparative Public Law and International Law in Heidelberg and Professor of Public Law at the University of Frankfurt/Main. He has been president of the OECD Nuclear Energy Tribunal as well as a member of the German Science Council and the Scientific Committee of the European Union Agency for Fundamental Rights. He has held visiting positions at the New York University School of Law, the European University Institute, the Xiamen Academy of International Law, and the National Autonomous University of Mexico, among others. Armin von Bogdandy is the recipient of the Leibniz Prize; the prize for outstanding scientific achievements in the field of legal and economic foundations by the Berlin-Brandenburg Academy of Sciences; the *Premio Internacional Fix-Zamudio*; and the gavel of the Inter-American Court of Human Rights. His research focuses on structural development in public law.

Flávia Piovesan is a Professor of Constitutional Law and Human Rights at the Pontifical Catholic University of São Paulo (PUC-SP). She was a human rights visiting fellow at the Human Rights Program at Harvard Law School in 1995 and 2000; a fellow at the Centre for Brazilian Studies, at the University of Oxford in 2005; and has been a visiting fellow at the Max Planck Institute for Comparative Public Law and International Law on numerous occasions. From 2009 to 2014, she was at the Institute as a Humboldt Foundation Georg Forster Research Fellow. She was also a Visiting Scholar at the David Rockefeller Center for Latin American Studies at Harvard University (DRLCAS) in 2018. Flavia Piovesan is a former member of the UN High Level Task Force on the implementation of the right to development and of the OAS Working Group working on the monitoring of the Protocol of San Salvador on social, economic, and cultural rights. In 2016, she was appointed Special Secretary for Human Rights in Brazil and President of the National Commission against Forced Labor. She was a Vice President and a Commissioner for the Inter-American Commission on Human Rights. She was the recipient of the Humboldt Georg Foster Research Award in 2022.

Eduardo Ferrer Mac-Gregor is judge of the Inter-American Court of Human Rights, as well as Professor at the National Autonomous University of Mexico and researcher at the Legal Research Institute of that university. He studied law at the Autonomous University of Baja California obtained his PhD in law from the University of Navarra. He is director of the Iberoamerican Journal of Procedural Constitutional Law (*Revista Iberoamericana de Derecho Procesal Constitucional*). Eduardo Ferrer Mac-Gregor has acted as visiting professor and/or lecturer at multiple universities and research centers in Europe, the United States, and Latin America, including Paris-Sorbonne University (*Panthéon París 1*) and the Max Planck Institute for Comparative Public Law and International Law.

Mariela Morales Antoniazzi is a senior research fellow at the Max Planck Institute for Comparative Public Law and International Law in Heidelberg. She studied law at Andrés Bello Catholic University, obtained her LLM at the University of Heidelberg, and earned her PhD at the University of Frankfurt/Main. Her doctoral thesis focuses on the supranational protection of democracy in South America and the *Ius Constitutionale Commune*. Mariela Morales Antoniazzi is a visiting professor at various Latin American universities and Vice President of the German section of the Iberoamerican Institute of Constitutional Law. She coordinates the *Ius Constitutionale Commune en América Latina* (ICCAL) project at the Max Planck Institute for Comparative Public Law and International Law.

Pablo Saavedra Alessandri is the Executive Secretary at the Inter-American Court of Human Rights. He has also worked as an attorney at the Inter-American Commission on Human Rights and at the National Corporation on Reparation and Reconciliation of Chile. He graduated from *Universidad Diego Portales* and obtained his master's degree in Law from the University of Notre Dame.

María Barraco is a former lawyer at the Argentine Human Trafficking Prosecutor's Office and visiting researcher at the Max Planck Institute for Comparative Public Law and International Law. She holds a law degree from the University of Buenos Aires and an LLM in Human Rights from Queen Mary University of London.

Mary Beloff received her law degree and a PhD from the University of Buenos Aires where she is Professor of Criminal Law and Criminal Procedure. She also holds a Master of Laws (LLM) from Harvard Law School. She is currently a member of the Committee on the Rights of the Child (2023–2027).

Christina Binder holds the Chair for International Law and Human Rights Law at the Bundeswehr University Munich. Previously, she was a Professor at the University of Vienna. She is member of the Executive Board and Vice President of the European Society of International Law.

Cécile Blouin is a Senior Researcher at the Instituto de Democracia y Derechos Humanos and a Professor at *Pontificia Universidad Católica del Perú*. She holds a degree in Law and Political Science from the University of Versailles *Saint-Quentin-en Yvelines* and a master's degree from Universidad Carlos III de Madrid.

Catalina Botero-Marino is the Dean of the law school at *Universidad de los Andes* and a founding partner of NGO DeJusticia. She served as the Special Rapporteur for Freedom of Expression for the Inter-American Commission on Human Rights, as well as Auxiliary Magistrate at the Constitutional Court of Colombia.

Clara Burbano-Herrera is Professor of International Human Rights Law and Director of the Programme for Studies on Human Rights in Context at the Ghent University Human Rights Centre. She has been awarded the Dutch Prince Bernhard Price for Innovative Research and holds a PhD in Law (Ghent University).

LIST OF CONTRIBUTORS XXV

Daniel Cerqueira is a Senior Program Officer at the Due Process of Law Foundation. He holds a master's degree from Georgetown University, a master's degree from the Universitá degli Studi di Genova, a law degree from the *Universidade Federal de Minas Gerais*, and a bachelor's degree in International Relations from the *Pontifícia Universidade Católica de Minas Gerais*.

Carlos Ayala Corao is a Professor and Head of the Constitutional Law Department at *Universidad Católica Andrés Bello* in Caracas. He is the former President of the Inter-American Commission on Human Rights and is also a Vice President of the International Commission of Jurists.

Stephania Yate Cortes is a PhD candidate at Universidad de los Andes, Colombia.

Júlia Cortez da Cunha Cruz holds a Master of Laws degree from Harvard Law School and a Master of International Law degree from *Universidade de Sao Paulo*. She has worked at the United Nations, the Organization of American States, and Brazilian human rights nongovernmental organizations.

Aída Díaz-Tendero is a Professor at *Universidad Nacional Autónoma de México* (UNAM). She holds a master's degree in Latin American Studies, as well as a doctorate from the *Universidad Complutense de Madrid*. She also holds a postdoctoral degree from the *Colegio de la Frontera Norte de México*.

Par Engstrom is Senior Lecturer in Human Rights at the Institute of the Americas, University College London. He was also a faculty member at the Paris School of International Affairs, at Sciences-Po. Dr. Engstrom holds a DPhil in International Relations from Oxford University.

Chris Esdaile is legal advisor at the human rights organization REDRESS. He studied law at Birmingham University (LLB) and has an LLM in International Human Rights Law from Queen Mary University of London.

Melina Girardi Fachin is a Professor at *Universidade Federal do Parana*. She holds a PhD in Constitutional Law and a master's degree in Human Rights, both from *Pontifícia Universidade Catolica de Sao Paulo*. She has also been a visiting researcher at Harvard Law School.

Julissa Mantilla Falcón has been elected a Commissioner at the Inter-American Commission on Human Rights (2020–2023). She is an adjunct Professor at the American University Washington College of Law, as well as a Professor at Pontificia Universidad Católica del Perú. She was an investigator in cases of sexual violence for the Truth and Reconciliation Commission of Peru.

Joel Hernandez García is a Commissioner of the Inter-American Commission on Human Rights. He holds a law degree from the Universidad Nacional Autónoma de Mexico and a master's degree in International Law from New York University. He is a member of the

Board of Trustees of the UN Interregional Crime and Justice Research Institute and was a member of the Inter-American Juridical Committee.

Claudio Grossman is Professor of Law, Dean Emeritus, and the Raymond Geraldson Scholar for International and Humanitarian Law at American University Washington College of Law, where he served as dean from 1995 to July 2016. He was also a member and President of the Inter-American Commission on Human Rights.

Rainer Grote is a senior research fellow at the Max Planck Institute for Comparative Public Law and International Law in Heidelberg. He holds a Master of Laws from the University of Edinburgh and a Doctoral degree from the University of Goettingen. His doctoral thesis was awarded the European Group of Public Law Thesis Prize.

Henry Jiménez Guanipa is a Venezuelan lawyer with over twenty years of experience in the energy industry, including power, natural gas, renewables, and energy conservation. He holds an LLB from University Santa Maria, an LLM from the University of Heidelberg 2001, and a PhD from Ruhr University Bochum 2010.

Silvia Serrano Guzmán is the Associate Director of the Healthy Families Initiative at Georgetown University. She holds a law degree from *Universidad Autónoma de Bucaramanga*, Colombia, a Master of Laws degree from Georgetown University, and a master's degree in Legal Argumentation from the University of Alicante.

Yves Haeck is Professor of International Human Rights Law and Director of the Programme for Studies on Human Rights in Context at the Ghent University Human Rights Centre. He is a PhD (Ghent University, 2007), Master, and Bachelor in Law (Ghent University, 1992).

Miriam Lorena Henriquez Viñas is the Dean at the *Universidad Alberto Hurtado* Law School, where she is also a Professor of Constitutional Law and Political Theory. She is a Doctor in Juridical Sciences (*Universidad de Santiago de Compostela*) and holds a master's degree in Public Law (*Pontificia Universidad Católica de Chile*).

Gabriela Kletzel is a lawyer specialized in international human rights law (*Universidad de Buenos Aires*) with a master's degree in law from New York University (NYU). She is the director of international work at the NGO CELS (*Centro de Estudios Legales y Sociales*).

Viviana Krsticevic is the Executive Director of the Center for Justice and International Law (CEJIL). Ms. Krsticevic received her law degree from *Universidad de Buenos Aires*, a master's degree in Latin American Studies from Stanford University, and an LLM from Harvard University. She is also a Professor at the American University Washington College of Law, where she teaches a course on litigation and activism.

Edison Lanza is the Special Rapporteur for Freedom of Expression of the Inter-American Commission on Human Rights. A Uruguayan lawyer, he graduated from the Faculty of Law of the *Universidad de la República*. He is also a PhD candidate at the Faculty of Social Sciences of the *Universidad de Buenos Aires*.

Kelly Morrison is a PhD student in Political Science at the University of Pittsburgh, with specializations in International Relations and Comparative Politics and a regional focus on Latin America. She graduated from Lee University with degrees in Political Science and Spanish.

Gabriela C.B. Navarro is an Assistant Professor at the Federal University of Lavras (Brazil). She obtained her PhD at Goethe University and her master's degree at the Federal University of Santa Catarina. She has researched in the fields of Indigenous rights and effectiveness of international courts.

Elsy Curihuinca Neira is a lawyer and holds a Bachelor of Laws degree from the Catholic University of Temuco, Chile. She has been a specialist for the Rapporteurship on the Rights of Indigenous Peoples at the Inter-American Commission on Human Rights.

José Ignacio Núñez Leiva is the Director of the Public Law Department at the University of Chile. He holds a master's degree in Public Law from the *Pontificia Universidad Católica de Chile* and a Doctor of Law degree from *Universidad Castilla La Mancha*.

Mayra Ortiz Ocaña is a doctoral student in Political Science and a member of the Reparations Design and Compliance Lab at the University of Notre Dame.

Aníbal Pérez-Liñán is Director of the Kellogg Institute for International Studies at the University of Notre Dame and a Co-Principal Investigator of the Reparations Design and Compliance Lab.

Renata Politi is Legal Officer at REDRESS.

Katya Salazar is the Executive Director of the Due Process of Law Foundation. Before joining DPLF, she was the Adjunct Coordinator of the Special Investigations Unit of the Truth and Reconciliation Commission of Peru. She has a master's degree from the University of Heidelberg and a bachelor's degree from *Pontificia Universidad Católica del Perú*.

Elizabeth Salmón is a Professor at Pontificia Universidad Católica del Perú. She holds a PhD in International Law from Universidad de Sevilla. Professor Salmón is currently Director of the *Instituto de Democracia y Derechos Humanos*, a member of the UN Human Rights Council Advisory Committee, and a Consulting Expert of the Colombian Special Jurisdiction for Peace.

Nataly Sanchez holds a Master of Laws from University of Essex.

Luis L. Schenoni is a research fellow at the Kellogg Institute for International Studies and a PhD student in Political Science at the University of Notre Dame. He holds an MSc in International Studies from the Torcuato Di Tella University and a BA in International Relations Catholic University of Argentina.

Antonia Urrejola is a Commissioner at the Inter-American Commission on Human Rights. She holds a law degree from the Universidad de Chile and a postgraduate degree in Human Rights and Transitional Justice. She has been a human rights advisor to the Chilean Presidency and a principal advisor to the OAS Secretary General.

René Urueña is a Professor and the Director of Investigations at *Universidad de los Andes* in Bogotá. He received his LLM (laudatur) and his Doctor of Law (eximia cum laude) from the University of Helsinki in Finland. He coordinates with the Max Planck Institute for Comparative Public Law and International Law the program on *ius commune* and international economic law, as well as the program on *ius commune* and the right to development.

Oscar Parra Vera is a Judge in the Special Jurisdiction for Peace in Colombia. He holds a master's degree in Criminal Justice from the University of Oxford and a Master of Laws degree from *Universidad Nacional de Colombia*. He was a senior lawyer at the Inter-American Court of Human Rights, as well as a consultant in the Inter-American Commission on Human Rights.

Alejandra Vicente is Head of Law at the human rights organization REDRESS and the former Legal Director at the Center for Justice and International Law. She holds an advanced degree in Conflict Resolution from the University of Zaragoza and an LLM in International Law and the Law of International Organisations from the University of Groningen.

Introduction

By Armin von Bogdandy, Flávia Piovesan, Eduardo Ferrer Mac-Gregor, and Mariela Morales Antoniazzi

1. The Inter-American System, *Ius Constitutionale Commune*, and the Focus on Impact

As legal scholars of and practitioners in the Inter-American Human Rights System (IAHRS), we have witnessed the emergence and growth of a robust transnational regime dedicated to the protection and advancement of human dignity in Latin America. This system is composed of domestic and international norms that interact to respect, protect, and fulfill human rights in the region. The IAHRS's main institutions are the Inter-American Commission on Human Rights (Inter-American Commission, or IACHR) and the Inter-American Court of Human Rights (Inter-American Court, or IACtHR), although domestic institutions dedicated to the human rights—in particular national courts, but also prosecutors or ombudspersons—are also crucial to the system's functioning. The interaction between domestic and international institutions has generated a regional *corpus iuris* in the field of human rights. Importantly, this system's operation relies not only on public institutions, but also on private actors, such as civil society organizations, lawyers, and academics. Their work has shaped human rights law in the Americas and has expanded its reach. One of our main concerns is to ensure that individuals, and in particular victims, have access to international institutions. Another concern, this book's very focus, is that IAHRS has a transformative impact on the rights of as many individuals as possible. To this end, the IAHRS is responsive to the context in which it operates, a context shaped by socioeconomic inequality, institutional instability, and the historic experience of authoritarianism, military dictatorship, and armed conflicts.

We have conceptualized this phenomenon as common Latin American constitutional law, or *Ius Constitutionale Commune en América Latina* (ICCAL). ICCAL has analytical, normative, and academic dimensions.[1] First, ICCAL

---

[1] We analyze these dimensions in more detail in Armin von Bogdandy et al., *Ius Constitutionale Commune en América Latina: A Regional Approach to Transformative Constitutionalism* (2016) MPIL Research Paper Series, No. 2016-21.

frames, and thereby creates, a specific subject of legal analysis, that is, a specific legal phenomenon that originates from interacting norms and institutional practices of various legal orders, united by their goal of bringing human rights to the social realities of Latin America. Second, as a normative concept, ICCAL provides a theoretically based justification of that goal as a specific, Latin American variant of transformative constitutionalism. Third, in terms of legal practices, ICCAL constitutes a working platform for the various actors who form the community of practice of human rights.[2] This is a broad community that extends beyond advocacy groups to include, for example, lawyers who defend their States before inter-American institutions.

ICCAL is a specific Latin American approach to transformative constitutionalism with distinctive characteristics.[3] The Latin American approach is, above all, unique because it is a regional phenomenon, as opposed to the country-specific approaches in South Africa and India, the two other main instances of transformative constitutionalism. As such, the Latin American approach has two specific dimensions. First, it integrates domestic and international law through many types of interaction. Second, it includes dense, horizontal interactions between the domestic legal orders in the region. At the heart of all these interactions lies the interpretation and application of inter-American standards and related domestic constitutional standards.[4] Additionally, the legal phenomenon identified by ICCAL is characterized by its continuous development.

Although ICCAL is distinctly Latin American, the phenomenon has implications beyond the region. ICCAL highlights Latin American contributions to constitutionalism as a global phenomenon, especially in the areas of violence; institutional instability and inequality; and economic, social, and cultural rights. Moreover, in a context where it is increasingly clear that power structures favoring the Global North did not vanish with the end of the colonial period,[5]

---

[2] Armin von Bogdandy and René Urueña, "International Transformative Constitutionalism in Latin America" [2020] 114 *AJIL* 403.

[3] For an introduction to this concept, see Daniel Bonilla Maldonado (ed.), *Constitutionalism of the Global South: The Activist Tribunals of India, South Africa, and Colombia* (Fordham University School of Law; Universidad de los Andes 2013); Philipp Dann, Michael Riegner, and Maxim Bönnemann (eds.), *The Global South and Comparative Constitutional Law* (Oxford University Press 2020).

[4] Viviana Krsticevic, "El derecho común transformador: el impacto del diálogo del sistema interamericano de derechos humanos con las víctimas en la consecución de justicia," in Armin von Bogdandy et al. (coords.), *Cumplimiento e impacto de las sentencias de la Corte Interamericana y el Tribunal Europeo de Derechos Humanos. Transformando realidades* (MPIL; Instituto de Estudios Constitucionales del Estado de Querétaro; IIJ; UANM 2019); Clara Burbano Herrera and Yves Haeck, "The Historical and Present-Day Role of Non-Governmental Organisations before the Inter-American Human Rights System in Documenting Serious Human Rights Violations and Protecting Human Rights and the Rule of Law Through Ensuring Accountability" [2021] 17 *Utrecht Law Review* 8.

[5] See, e.g., Philipp Dann and Felix Hanschmann, "Post-Colonial Theories and Law" [2012] 45 *Law and Politics in Africa, Asia and Latin America* 123.

ICCAL seeks to include voices from the Global South in the international conversation about the role and functions of public law. It also sheds light on how the human rights framework may be used to modify the structures of dominance that are embedded in traditional legal thinking. Additionally, due to Latin America's struggles with weak institutions and authoritarian governments, ICCAL might help to identify strategies for addressing the emergence of these challenges in other parts of the world.

In our 2017 volume *Transformative Constitutionalism in Latin America: The Emergence of a New Ius Commune*,[6] we brought together a group of scholars to present ICCAL to the English-speaking world. We acknowledge that voices critical to the ICCAL framework have helped us to refine our approach, as this volume will show.[7] Along these lines, this book will focus on ICCAL's impact on the ground in terms of transformative constitutionalism. This seems all the more important as Latin America continues to struggle against inequality, violence, and weak rule of law[8] and new difficulties have emerged, including a backlash against human rights and the rise to power of new leaders who threaten hard-fought achievements in human rights. Derogations from treaties might also signal the weakening of some States' commitment to human rights.[9]

---

[6] Armin von Bogdandy et al., (eds.), *Transformative Constitutionalism in Latin America: The Emergence of a New Ius Commune* (Oxford University Press 2017).

[7] Alberto Coddou Mc Manus, "A critical account of Ius Constitutionale Commune in Latin America: An intellectual map of contemporary Latin American constitutionalism" [2021] 11 *Global Constitutionalism* 110; for a mapping, see Juan C. Herrera, "La idea de un Derecho común en América Latina a la luz de sus críticas teóricas" [2020] MPIL Research Paper No. 2020–26; Ana Micaela Alterio and Francisca Pou Giménez, "Book Review: Transformative Constitutionalism in Latin America" (2018), <https://blog-iacl-aidc.org/blog/2018/10/21/book-review-transformative-constitutionalism-in-latin-america> (accessed February 5, 2022).

[8] Our Spanish language publications on these issues include Armin von Bogdandy, *Por un derecho común para América Latina: Cómo fortalecer las democracias frágiles y desiguales* (Siglo XXI Editores 2020); Armin von Bogdandy et al. (coords.), *Cumplimiento e impacto de las sentencias de la Corte Interamericana y el Tribunal Europeo de Derechos Humanos. Transformando realidades* (Instituto de Estudios Constitucionales del Estado de Querétaro 2019); Armin von Bogdandy and René Urueña, "International Transformative Constitutionalism in Latin America" [2020] 114 *American Journal of International Law* 403; Armin von Bogdandy, "El mandato transformador del sistema interamericano de derechos humanos. Legalidad y legitimidad de un proceso jurisgenerativo extraordinario" [2019] 9 *Revista del Centro de Estudios Constitucionales* 113; Armin von Bogdandy, Jesús María Casal Hernández, and Mariela Morales Antoniazzi, "La resistencia del Estado democrático de Derecho en América Latina frente a la pandemia de COVID-19. Un enfoque desde el ius commune" [2020] MPIL Research Paper No. 2020-35; Eduardo Ferrer Mac-Gregor, Mariela Morales Antoniazzi, and Rogelio Ángel Flores Pantoja (coords.), *Inclusión, Ius Commune y justiciabilidad de los DESCA en la jurisprudencia interamericana. El caso Lagos del Campo y los nuevos desafíos* (Instituto de Estudios Constitucionales del Estado de Querétaro 2018); Armin von Bogdandy, Mariela Morales Antoniazzi, and Franz Christian Ebert, "Human Rights versus Economic Law—The Case of Latin America", in Max Planck Society (ed.), *Highlights from the Yearbook 2019 of the Max Planck Society* (2020).

[9] Laurence R. Helfer, "Rethinking Derogations from Human Rights Treaties" [2021] 115 *American Journal of International Law* 20.

2. Moving toward Transformative Impact

The effectiveness of international human rights law has become the subject of heated debate among scholars. Some critics assert that there is a lack of evidence that human rights have led to relevant improvements in State behavior.[10] Proponents of international law and human rights question the adequacy of the empirical measures employed by critics[11] and assert that human rights law, institutions, and movements can be shown to have an impact beyond compliance,[12] an approach adopted in this book. Certainly, scholars should consider both the successes and the failures of human rights[13] and are right that human rights will not always be an appropriate or adequate means of addressing modern challenges.[14] This, however, is no reason to abandon the project. In the words of Anne Peters, human rights remain "a necessary and indeed indispensable legal instrument for protecting weak and vulnerable members of a society."[15] Moreover, they are key to constitutional democracy.

Analyses of effectiveness specific to the IAHRS have focused on the low rates of compliance with IAHRS decisions.[16] That the rates of compliance are low is

---

[10] See, e.g., Eric A. Posner and Alan O. Sykes, *Economic Foundations of International Law*, (Harvard University Press 2013), 207–208; Eric A. Posner, *The Twilight of Human Rights Law* (Oxford University Press 2014), 69–78.

[11] See, e.g., Robert Howse and Ruti G. Teitel, "Beyond Compliance: Rethinking Why International Law Really Matters" [2010] 1 *Global Policy* 127; Benedict Kingsbury, "The Concept of Compliance as a Function of Competing Conceptions of International Law" [1998] 19 *Michigan Journal of International Law* 345.

[12] See, e.g., Kathryn Sikkink, *Evidence for Hope: Making Human Rights Work in the 21st Century* (Princeton University Press 2017); Wayne Sandholtz, *Expanding Rights: Norm Innovation in the European and Inter-American Courts of Human Rights. Expanding Human Rights: 21st Century Norms and Gov Cheltenham* (Edward Elgar 2017).

[13] See, e.g., Makau Mutua, "Is the Age of Human Rights Over?," in Sophia A. McClennen and Alexandra Schultheis Moore (eds.), *The Routledge Companion to Literature and Human Rights* (Routledge 2015), 450.

[14] Samuel Moyn, *Not Enough: Human Rights in an Unequal World* (Harvard University Press 2018).

[15] Anne Peters, "The Importance of Having Rights" [2021] 81 *Heidelberg Journal of International Law* 7.

[16] See Juana Inés Acosta López and Diana Bravo Rubio, "El cumplimiento de los fines de reparación integral de las medidas ordenadas por la Corte Interamericana de Derechos Humanos: énfasis en la experiencia colombiana" [2008] 13 *Revista Colombiana de Derecho Internacional* 323; Sergio Iván Anzola, Beatriz Eugenia Sánchez, and René Urueña, *Después del fallo: el cumplimiento de las decisiones del Sistema Interamericano de Derechos Humanos. Una propuesta de metodología* (Universidad de los Andes; Documentos Justicia Global 2015); Cecilia M. Bailliet, "Measuring Compliance with the Inter-American Court of Human Rights: The Ongoing Challenge of Judicial Independence in Latin America" [2013] 31 *NJHR* 477; Fernando Basch et al., "The Effectiveness of the Inter-American System of Human Rights Protection: A Quantitative Approach to Its Functioning and Compliance with Its Decisions" [2010] 7 *Sur* 9; Helio Bicudo, "Cumplimiento de las sentencias de la Corte Interamericana de Derechos Humanos y de las recomendaciones de la Comisión Interamericana de Derechos Humanos," in Antônio Augusto Cançado Trindade (ed.), *El Sistema Interamericano de Protección de los Derechos Humanos en el umbral del siglo XXI* (UNAM 2001), 229; James Cavallaro and Stephanie Erin Brewer, "Reevaluating Regional Human Rights Litigation in the Twenty-First Century: The Case of the Inter-American Court" [2008] 102 *American Journal of International Law* 768; Elisa Mara Coimbra, "Inter-American System of Human Rights: Challenges to Compliance with the Court's Decisions in Brazil" [2013] 10 *Sur* 57; Vittorio Corasaniti, "Implementación de las

a sound and valuable observation. The Inter-American Commission itself has acknowledged that the States' lack of compliance with IAHRS decisions is a continuing challenge.[17] However, an exclusive focus on compliance, analyzed quantitatively, could lead to the erroneous conclusion that the IAHRS is of marginal legal, social, and political importance.[18] Yet, compliance is insufficient to achieve a full and nuanced understanding of the IAHRS's relevance and impact.[19]

With this volume, we aim to intervene in the debate about the relevance of international human rights in general and the IAHRS in particular by presenting a critical, contextualized, and systematic analysis of the IAHRS's transformative impact in the Americas. We adopt ICCAL as our conceptual framework and the centrality of the victim as our guiding principle. In doing so, we prove that the IAHRS's legal, political, and social relevance is far greater than the current literature suggests. We also indicate how that relevance might be increased in the years to come.

The core concept of our book is impact. We do not deny that compliance with the judgments of the IACtHR and with the IACHR's recommendations is an important indicator of the IAHRS's relevance. Indeed, one of the chapters in this volume suggests methods to improve measurements of compliance.[20] Nevertheless, we treat compliance as only one of several factors to consider when assessing the legal, social, and political relevance of the IAHRS.

We expand the notion of impact along three dimensions. First, we include as the subject of our analyses all tools of the IAHRS that might serve its

---

sentencias y resoluciones de la Corte Interamericana de Derechos Humanos: un debate necesario" [2009] 49 *Revista IIDH* 13; Damian A. Gonzalez-Salzberg, "Do States comply with the compulsory judgments of the Inter-American Court of Human Rights? An empirical study of compliance with 330 measures of reparation" [2013] 13 *Revista do Instituto Brasileiro de Direitos Humanos* 93; Damián A. González-Salzberg, "The Implementation of Decisions from the Inter-American Court of Human Rights in Argentina: An Analysis of the Jurisprudential Swings of the Supreme Court" [2011] 8 *Sur* 113; Darren Hawkins and Wade Jacoby, "Partial Compliance: A Comparison of the European and Inter-American Courts of Human Rights" [2010] 6 *Journal of International Law & International Relations* 35; Alexandra Huneeus, "Courts Resisting Courts: Lessons from the Inter-American Court's Struggle to Enforce Human Rights" [2011] 44 *Cornell International Law Journal* 493; César Rodríguez Garavito and Celeste Kauffman, "De las órdenes a la práctica: análisis y estrategias para el cumplimiento de las decisiones del sistema interamericano de derechos humanos," in Maia Camilo Barreto et al. (eds.), *Desafíos del sistema interamericano de derechos humanos. Nuevos tiempos, viejos retos* (Colección DeJusticia 2015), 276.

[17] Inter-American Commission on Human Rights, "Strategic Plan 2011–2015," 59, <https://www.oas.org/en/iachr/docs/pdf/iachrstrategicplan20112015.pdf> (accessed February 5, 2022).

[18] See Viviana Krsticevic and René Urueña's contribution to this volume.

[19] See, e.g., Clara Sandoval, "Two steps forward, one step back: Reflections on the jurisprudential turn of the Inter-American Court of Human Rights on domestic reparation programmes" [2018] 22 *The International Journal of Human Rights* 1192; Par Engstrom (ed.), *The Inter-American Human Rights System: Impact Beyond Compliance* (Palgave Macmillan 2019).

[20] Aníbal Pérez-Liñán, Kelly Morrison, and Luis L. Schenoni's contribution to this volume.

transformative mandate.[21] These tools encompass not only the processing of individual petitions and the issuance of judgments and recommendations in these cases but also the adoption of precautionary and provisional measures, the issuance of advisory opinions, the elaboration and publication of thematic and country reports, the convening of public hearings, and more. The IACtHR and, especially, the IACHR have a range of tools at their disposal. The decisions they issue in response to individual petitions, although undoubtedly important to their work, should not be viewed in isolation from their other activities. An assessment of the IAHRS's relevance that ignores its work outside of the individual petition system is markedly incomplete.

Second, we consider a wider range of actors than is reflected in compliance studies. Compliance studies mostly focus on the institution of the IAHRS issuing the decision and the State implementing, or failing to implement, the decision. To achieve a more accurate and nuanced picture of how the IAHRS's decisions—and other IAHRS activities—lead to change on the ground, we highlight the interactions of the IAHRS with a community composed not only of State governments and international and regional human rights institutions but also of victims, their lawyers, civil society organizations, and academic institutions, as well as various State institutions with their broad spectrum of mandates, interests, and practices. This broader *community of practice* is key to moving beyond compliance and toward a better understanding of transformative impact.[22]

Third, we argue that State compliance with a specific decision is not the only outcome the IAHRS seeks to achieve. Since its mandate is to transform the situation of human rights in the Americas, it aims not only to ensure that States remedy past violations of human rights but also to develop and consolidate human rights standards, to increase the capacity of civil society and States to respect, protect, and fulfill such standards, and to deepen transnational conversation and cooperation. Effectiveness and relevance thus become a question not only of States' implementation of specific IAHRS decisions but also of the extent to which inter-American standards have permeated education, culture, and politics, facilitating dialogue about and expansion of human rights in the Americas and beyond.

Fundamental to our understanding of the intended outcomes of the IAHRS's efforts is the concept of transformation. In line with the arguments advanced in our prior volume,[23] as well as in some of our independent scholarly

---

[21] On the transformative mandate of the IAHRS, see Armin von Bogdandy and René Urueña, "International Transformative Constitutionalism in Latin America" [2020] 114 *American Journal of International Law* 403.

[22] See Armin von Bogdandy and René Urueña's contribution to this volume.

[23] Armin von Bogdandy et al. (eds.), *Transformative Constitutionalism in Latin America: The Emergence of a New Ius Commune* (Oxford University Press 2017).

INTRODUCTION 7

undertakings,[24] we see the IAHRS as seeking not only to remedy individual wrongs but also to transform the social fabric, combatting oppressive structures in public and private institutions. For example, the IAHRS orders structural reforms in law, policy, and culture (generally classified as guarantees of nonrepetition), so that human rights will become deeply embedded in the domestic order. The IAHRS thus serves as a tool that like-minded domestic actors can use to effectuate systemic improvements in the human rights situation of the region, and enables inter-American standards to reach a far greater number of people than can directly gain individual access to inter-American institutions.

An important element of this transformative approach is the concept of substantive equality, which has recently been gaining ground in the Inter-American Court.[25] In the case of *Employees of the Fireworks Factory of Santo Antônio de Jesus and their families v. Brazil*, for example, the IACtHR built on its prior jurisprudence regarding the right to equality and nondiscrimination[26] by consolidating the notion that the States' obligation to ensure substantive equality includes a duty to actively combat situations of structural exclusion and marginalization.[27] The Court determined that States must adopt measures "to correct existing inequalities, to promote the inclusion and participation of historically marginalized groups, and to guarantee to disadvantaged individuals or groups the effective enjoyment of their rights."[28] Here, the IACtHR interprets the American Convention on Human Rights (American Convention, or ACHR) as requiring States to counteract structural inequalities, opening the door to further systemic transformations.

3. Guide to the Chapters

This volume maps, analyzes, and develops the key aspects of the IAHRS. The contributions span a wide range of perspectives, as the authors have diverse

---

[24] Armin von Bogdandy, "The Transformative Mandate of the Inter-American System," in Armin von Bogdandy et al. (coords.), *Cumplimiento e impacto de las sentencias de la Corte Interamericana y el Tribunal Europeo de Derechos Humanos. Transformando realidades* (MPIL; Instituto de Estudios Constitucionales del Estado de Querétaro; IIJ; UANM 2019); Flávia Piovesan, "Sistema Interamericano de Direitos Humanos, Impacto transformador, diálogos jurisdicionais e os desafios da reforma" [2014] 3 *Revista Direitos Emergentes na Sociedade Global* 76.

[25] *Case of the Employees of the Fireworks Factory of Santo Antônio de Jesus and their families v. Brazil* [2020] IACtHR, Ser. C No. 407; *Case of Members of the Miskitu Indigenous Peoples of the North Caribbean Coast regarding Nicaragua* [2021] IACtHR.

[26] *Case of the Employees of the Fireworks Factory of Santo Antônio de Jesus and their families v. Brazil* [2020] IACtHR, Separate Opinion of Judge Eduardo Ferrer Mac-Gregor. Judgment of July 15, 2020. Ser. C No. 407, paras. 83–96.

[27] *Case of the Employees of the Fireworks Factory of Santo Antônio de Jesus and their families v. Brazil* [2020] IACtHR, Ser. C No. 407, para. 199.

[28] Ibid.

backgrounds in academia, civil society, and State and human rights governance. The authors also approach the debate about the impact of the IAHRS through the lens of several disciplines, including constitutional law, international law, international relations, and some social sciences. The contributions often focus on a specific issue or country, but always refer back to ICCAL, the common analytical framework of this book. Additional recent cases are available in the database of the Inter-American Court of Human Rights.[29]

The book is organized in three parts. Part I situates the book's focus on impact within the ICCAL's general framework. It explores the history and theory of ICCAL, framing impact as central to understanding the IAHRS. It also situates the discussion on ICCAL within international human rights law in general, analyzing the IAHRS's impact beyond Latin America and discussing common challenges for the protection of human rights across regions.

Part II discusses specific inter-American standards. The contributions contained in this part span the main issue-areas that the IACtHR and the IACHR have addressed throughout their history. It includes analyses of the IAHRS's impact in the context of Latin America's dictatorial past, most notably in the chapters on transitional justice and judicial independence. This part also discusses issues that have recently gained attention within inter-American jurisprudence, such as the rights of people in situations of vulnerability and social rights. With an eye to the future, Part II also includes emerging topics like private accountability, the environment, and digital rights.

Part III looks even further ahead as the authors make evidence-based proposals for enhancing the impact of the IAHRS. It begins with recommendations on how to maximize the impact of the IAHRS, as well as on how to assess such impact. Part III then explores strategies that are already in use by three civil society organizations with extensive experience engaging with the IACHR and IACtHR, but that could be adopted more widely.

The individual contributions in Part I, "Framing the Impact of the Inter-American System," begin with the contribution of Armin von Bogdandy and René Urueña (Chapter I.1), who "explore[] the apparent paradox between the dismal record of compliance with Inter-American Court decisions and the central role that this Court plays in controversies in the Americas as states, victims, and civil society continue to ask it for judgments." Von Bogdandy and Urueña argue that compliance is too limited a measure to account for the transformative effects of the IACtHR's judgments and encourage us to consider among the IACtHR's most important contributions its reframing of important sociopolitical conflicts as human rights issues and its fostering of a community of practice around these issues.

---

[29] https://jurisprudencia.corteidh.or.cr/

Claudio Grossman's contribution (Chapter I.2) turns to the IACHR, considering the impact it has had on human rights practices in the Americas over the course of its existence. Grossman highlights the ways in which the IACHR has adapted its approach to focus on the activities that will be most useful in a given historical moment (e.g., fact-finding and denunciations in an era of dictatorships, individual petitions in an era of democratization). Given the current range of regimes and their accompanying challenges, he suggests that the IACHR requires full use of the tools at its disposal to promote and protect human rights effectively today.

The chapter by Mariela Morales Antoniazzi, Flávia Piovesan, and Júlia Cortez da Cunha Cruz (Chapter I.3) is structured around three key questions: (1) why do we need the IAHRS; (2) what are the key structuring components of the IAHRS; and (3) how can the IAHRS's transformative impact be understood. In answering these questions, the authors contextualize and holistically analyze the IAHRS's impact, identifying three constitutive elements of this impact: institutional, sociopolitical, and cultural. Ultimately, they argue that the IAHRS "reflects a regional substantive commitment to human rights norms and standards that works as a complementary tool to national mechanisms and therefrom derives its emancipatory role and impact."

Rainer Grote's chapter (Chapter I.4) describes the development of the institutions, standards, and practices of the European, African, and interAmerican human rights systems as well as the pushback and even backlash that these systems have faced. The core question Grote addresses in this chapter is "how the resilience of regional human rights institutions can be strengthened in an increasingly adverse environment."

Par Engstrom's input (Chapter I.5) explores the impact of the IAHRS on the theory and practice of global human rights governance. Engstrom highlights the IAHRS's institutional development, standard-setting, and operation to argue not only that the IAHRS has had a central role in global human rights governance but also that the IAHRS's innovative approaches to and resilience in the face of noncompliance have "the potential to offer human rights scholarship and advocacy significant insights into how human rights may continue to matter even in adverse political circumstances."

Miriam Lorena Henríquez Viñas and José Ignacio Núñez Leiva's contribution (Chapter I.6) offers a theory of conventionality control, an IACtHR doctrine establishing that the ACHR imposes an obligation on all public officials in States parties to the Convention to harmonize their interpretation of domestic law with the ACHR as well as with the IACtHR's interpretation of the ACHR.[30] Henríquez

---

[30] Laurence Burgorgue-Larsen, "Conventionality Control: Inter-American Court of Human Rights (IACtHR)," in Anne Peters (ed.), *Max Planck Encyclopedias of International Law* (Oxford

Viñas and Núñez Leiva argue that, to understand the full impact of conventionality control, it is necessary not only to examine an individual State's compliance with a specific IACtHR judgment against it but also to analyze the role of conventionality control in requiring all States to anticipate and thereby to prevent human rights violations.

Gabriela C.B. Navarro's chapter (Chapter I.7) considers the effectiveness of international courts. Navarro argues that studies of effectiveness have shifted away from a narrow focus on compliance by expanding to assess these courts' contributions in setting standards, promoting democracy, and empowering domestic social movements. She illustrates this broader notion of effectiveness using inter-American jurisprudence on the territorial rights of indigenous peoples and ethnic minorities as an example.

Clara Burbano-Herrera and Yves Haeck's input (Chapter I.8) assesses the transformative impact of the IACtHR's provisional measures, with a focus on detention. In this context, Burbano-Herrera and Haeck introduce the term "transformative provisional measures," which they characterize as "(i) [. . .] target[ing] structural problems; (ii) [. . .] aim[ing] to protect several persons in situations of extreme gravity and urgency; and (iii) [. . .] contain[ing] orders that must be complied with by more than one State organ."

Mayra Ortiz Ocaña and Aníbal Pérez-Liñán address the doctrine-void regarding the definition of impact. Their chapter (Chapter I.9) puts forward "a framework to conceptualize and measure the effects of the IAHRS," proposing a three-stage process that enables the identification of actors and outcomes. They also discuss empirical approaches to documenting and analyzing the effects of the IAHRS.

René Urueña and Stephania Yate Cortes further develop the discussion on the concept of impact, proposing the adoption of a mindset focused on narrative. In their contribution (Chapter I.10) they argue that impact is a "continuously evolving description of reality," bridging facts and their normative interpretation.

Part II, "Impact and Inter-American Standards," begins with Eduardo Ferrer Mac-Gregor's chapter (Chapter II.1), which addresses the development of economic, social, cultural, and environmental rights in the IAHRS. Ferrer Mac-Gregor highlights the transformative impact that these standards have in Latin America and asserts that the IAHRS's jurisprudence is even more essential today due to contemporary challenges in the region.

Henry Jiménez Guanipa and María Barraco's article (Chapter II.2) concerns the right to a healthy environment. Jiménez Guanipa and Barraco examine the development of inter-American standards in this area and describe the

University Press 2018) <https://opil.ouplaw.com/view/10.1093/law-mpeipro/e3634.013.3634/law-mpeipro-e3634> (accessed February 5, 2022).

incorporation of these norms into domestic jurisprudence. They argue that there is an emerging *ius commune* in the field of environmental human rights that stems from this multilevel jurisprudential dialogue and results in minimum standards of protection across the region.

Antonia Urrejola and Elsy Curihuinca Neira's input (Chapter II.3) reviews the IAHRS's standards on Indigenous rights through the lens of precautionary measures granted by the IACHR. In addition to reviewing the inter-American approach to territorial rights, cultural identity, and participation, Urrejola and Curihuinca Neira assess the effectiveness of precautionary measures in protecting the rights of indigenous peoples to life and physical integrity.

Julissa Mantilla Falcón's contribution (Chapter II.4) reviews the contributions of the IAHRS to the definition of the term sexual violence as well as to the investigation of it. Mantilla Falcón discusses the most relevant developments in the IAHRS's approach to sexual violence and highlights their transformative impact on prevention, investigation, and punishment in sexual violence cases. She specifically highlights the IAHRS's treatment of State responsibility, its analyses of intersectionality and gender stereotyping, and its determination that sexual violence can constitute torture.

Silvia Serrano Guzmán's chapter (Chapter II.5) analyzes the many impacts of the IACtHR's judgment in the case of *Artavia Murillo et al. ("In Vitro Fertilization") v. Costa Rica*. Serrano Guzmán argues that this case not only addressed the claims of individual victims but also developed inter-American standards on the right to life and reproductive rights, triggered structural reform in Costa Rica, and served as the basis for the decisions of domestic courts in other countries. She also observes that, when monitoring Costa Rica's compliance with the judgment in this case, the IACtHR issued an unprecedented holding that could be used when States attempt to impede the implementation of structural reparations in the future.

The chapter by Chris Esdaile, Clara Sandoval, Alejandra Vicente, Renata Politi, and Nataly Sanchez (Chapter II.6) concerns the case of *Azul Rojas Marín v. Peru*. They explain the path leading to the decision as well as the significance of the case as a means of advancing the protection of the rights to human treatment, personal liberty, reparation, and access to justice for the LGBTIQ+ community in the Americas and beyond. They discuss both the impact this case has had thus far and the potential impact it might have in the future.

Mary Beloff's input (Chapter II.7) examines the impact of the Convention on the Rights of the Child on the IAHRS, revealing the interdependence of international and regional human rights systems in this area. Beloff also observes that the IACtHR can be effective in cases brought in the interest of broad, structural change, but that child victims as individuals often require quicker relief than the IAHRS's individual petition system can provide. With this in mind, she suggests that greater use should be made of precautionary and provisional measures.

Aída Díaz-Tendero's contribution (Chapter II.8) assesses the impact of the IAHRS's standards on the rights of older persons, as reflected in the Inter-American Convention on Protecting the Human Rights of Older Persons as well as in the IACtHR's jurisprudence, on a judgment of the Plurinational Constitutional Court of Bolivia. Díaz-Tendero argues that this case is evidence of the impact of the IAHRS because it illustrates the convergence of domestic and inter-American legal norms in the direction of a more respectful treatment of the rights of older persons.

Elizabeth Salmón and Cécile Blouin's chapter (Chapter II.9) analyzes the progress of the IAHRS in protecting and guaranteeing the rights of migrants and considers the impact that the IAHRS has had in this area. Salmón and Blouin argue that the IACHR has played a crucial role both in developing human rights standards on migration in general and in responding to specific instances in which migrants' rights have been violated. They also note that States' receptiveness of and contributions to the IAHRS's work could generate transformative impacts in this area.

Melina Girardi Fachin's chapter (Chapter II.10) concerns human rights defenders. Fachin reviews the development and scope of the right to defend rights not only in the IAHRS but also at the State and international levels. She then analyzes the case of *Escaleras Mejía v. Honduras*, emphasizing both the structural challenges that endanger human rights defenders and the standards applied by the Inter-American Court.

Christina Binder's input (Chapter II.11) discusses the impact of the IACtHR's jurisprudence on transitional justice in Argentina, Chile, Peru, and Uruguay. Binder observes that the IACtHR's cases finding that amnesty laws violated the ACHR facilitated transitional justice by operating directly on domestic law, thus alleviating pressure on an executive or legislature to act, and in others by legitimizing a domestic judiciary's decision. She also suggests that the most important, transformative, and lasting impact of the IAHRS in the context of transitional justice has been its strengthening of domestic institutions, particularly domestic courts.

Oscar Parra Vera's contribution (Chapter II.12) analyzes the development of the IACtHR's jurisprudence on access to justice and its transformative impact on the struggle against impunity in the Americas. Parra Vera observes that, in cases concerning access to justice, there is a particular need for the IACtHR to cooperate with and, indeed, to strengthen the domestic institutions that cause the initial violations of rights.

Carlos Ayala Corao's chapter (Chapter II.13) provides an overview of the IAHRS's approach to judicial independence. Ayala Corao emphasizes the connection between the right of every person to access to justice, which includes the right to be tried before independent and impartial judges, and the procedural guarantees that enable judges to exercise their functions without undue external pressures. He also discusses the reparations that the IACtHR has granted to remedy State violations of the right to judicial independence.

Catalina Botero-Marino's chapter (Chapter II.14) assesses the transformative impact of the IAHRS's standards on freedom of expression. Botero-Marino argues that some of these standards either have become or have the potential to become part of the structural transformation of public law in the region of Latin America (ICCAL). Botero-Marino also emphasizes that inter-American standards on freedom of expression have developed through exchange between international and domestic mechanisms.

Edison Lanza's input (Chapter II.15) focuses on the right to freedom of expression in the digital age. Lanza flags that, although the IAHRS has begun to adapt its standards in the face of new technologies, more needs to be done to address the challenges these technologies present.

Part III, "Optimizing the Impact of the Inter-American System," begins with Joel Hernández García's contribution (Chapter III.1) providing an overview of the impact of the IACHR as well as proposals for increasing the IACHR's effectiveness. Hernández García generally emphasizes the need to cooperate with States and more specifically suggests that the Inter-American Commission to "(i) strengthen [. . .] national capacities; (ii) advanc[e] standards through the selection of cases to remedy structural situations and (iii) promot[e] compliance of the decisions of the Commission."

Pablo Saavedra Alessandri's chapter (Chapter III.2) focuses on the transformative impact of the IACtHR's advisory opinions and structural measures. Saavedra Alessandri argues that, to understand and assess the effectiveness of the Inter-American Court, it is insufficient to consider only contentious cases.

Aníbal Pérez-Liñán, Kelly Morrison, and Luis L. Schenoni's chapter (Chapter III.3) proposes that time be factored into measurements of compliance with the IAHRS's decisions to improve assessments of legal outcomes and to account for State behavior. Specifically, the authors introduce new metrics that can be used to measure compliance: the yearly probability of a State complying with a Court's decision and the expected duration of the implementation. They assert that these metrics provide a more reliable and perhaps even more optimistic picture of the impact of the IAHRS.

Viviana Krsticevic and René Urueña's input (Chapter III.4) rejects compliance as a monolithically defined analytical category, seeking instead to extend the scope of compliance analysis. Krsticevic and Urueña argue that institutions would be able to increase compliance with international norms if their institutional design and practice considers their wider impact. They suggest that the wider impact of an international order and compliance with that order are linked: compliance with an international order is facilitated by the wider impact of the decision, which feeds into its compliance processes.

Katya Salazar and Daniel Cerqueira's contribution (Chapter III.5) presents the Due Process of Law Foundation's strategies to enhance the IAHRS's effectiveness, including raising awareness of the IAHRS's standards and contributing to the development of those standards. Salazar and Cerqueira argue that the closer the IAHRS works with civil society organizations the greater the impact of the IAHRS will be.

Gabriela Kletzel's chapter (Chapter III.6) examines how civil society organizations in Argentina engaged with the IAHRS over the course of decades to transform the human rights situation in their country. Kletzel also notes the contributions of civil society actors throughout the Americas to the defense and improvement of the institutions of the IAHRS themselves.

We invite the reader to engage critically with our exploration of the IAHRS, which considers both its advances and setbacks, potential and limitations, strengths and weaknesses. We are confident that this volume will help readers to increase their understanding of ICCAL's multidimensional, transformative impact. They will be better placed to engage with and contribute to future research on the IAHRS's impact in the context of emerging challenges, such as digital rights, climate change, and freedom from violence, including cyberviolence. As this volume demonstrates, the IAHRS's community of practice is capable of overcoming unprecedented obstacles, guided by a victim-centric approach that prioritizes the protection of human rights and relying on a wide variety of tools to achieve not only individual reparations but also structural transformations affecting the entire region.

PART I
FRAMING THE IMPACT OF THE INTER-AMERICAN SYSTEM

I.1
Inducing Compliance as a Transformative Process
The Bright Side of a Dismal Record

By Armin von Bogdandy and René Urueña

1. Introduction

While much admired for its groundbreaking decisions, the Inter-American Court of Human Rights (Inter-American Court, or IACtHR) seems rather ineffective.[1] States particularly fail to implement full reparations on issues such as forced disappearances, amnesties, or socioeconomic rights. Many quantitative studies have evidenced low rates of compliance with IACtHR judgments.[2]

---

[1] This chapter is drawn from sections of Armin von Bogdandy and René Urueña, "International Transformative Constitutionalism in Latin America" [2020] 114 *American Journal of International Law* 403.

[2] One of us has contributed to this body of quantitative studies, with a study on the possible reasons behind Colombia's low level of compliance. See René Urueña, Beatriz Sanchez, and Sergio Anzola, *Después del fallo: El cumplimiento de las decisiones del sistema interamericano de derechos humanos. Una propuesta de metodología* (Universidad de los Andes 2015). While these kinds of quantitative studies on compliance provide a valuable and necessary starting point to think about the IACtHR's impact, they leave many issues of the wider dynamic of impact unexplained. The present chapter is an effort to fill that scholarly gap. For further quantitative work on low levels of compliance in the region, see, e.g., Fernando Basch et al., "The effectiveness of the Inter-American system of human rights protection: a quantitative approach to its functioning and compliance with its decisions" [2010] 12 *SUR-International Journal of Human Rights* 9. Cecilia M. Bailliet, "Measuring compliance with the Inter-American Court of Human Rights: The ongoing challenge of judicial independence in Latin America" [2013] 31 *Nordic Journal of Human Rights* 477. David C. Baluarte, "Strategizing for Compliance: The Evolution of a Compliance Phase of Inter-American Court Litigation and the Strategic Imperative for Victims' Representatives" [2011] 27 *American University International Law Review* 263. Damian A. Gonzalez-Salzberg, "Do States comply with the compulsory judgments of the Inter-American Court of Human Rights? An empirical study of the compliance with 330 measures of reparation" [2014] 13 *Revista do Instituto Brasileiro de Direitos Humanos* 93.). Celeste Kauffman and Cesar Rodriguez-Garavito, "De las órdenes a la práctica: análisis y estrategias para el cumplimiento de las decisiones del sistema interamericano de derechos humanos," in Camilla Barreto Maia et al., *Desafíos del Sistema Interamericano de Derechos Humanos. Nuevos tiempos, viejos retos* (Colección De Justicia 2015). Helio Bicudo, "Cumplimiento de las sentencias de la Corte Interamericana de Derechos Humanos y de las recomendaciones de la Comisión Interamericana de Derechos Humanos," in Antônio Augusto Cançado Trindade (ed.), *El Sistema Interamericano de Protección de los Derechos Humanos en el umbral del siglo XXI* (UNAM 2003). Juana Inés Acosta López and

At the same time, it is evident that States do not simply ignore the Inter-American Court. Unlike the Andean Tribunal of Justice (its regional economic integration peer, which exerts little influence on decision makers[3]), the IACtHR plays a key role in many important controversies in the Americas. Victims, civil society organizations, but also States continuously bring cases seeking to have rulings that deeply affect millions.

In this chapter, we explore the apparent paradox between low levels of compliance with the Inter-American Court's orders and high levels of engagement with the Court on key regional issues. We argue that "compliance" is too narrow a prism to understand the true impact, and indeed the transformative effects of the IACtHR's activities. Focusing solely on compliance risks overlooking the social relevance of its orders and interpretations. To see the full picture, it takes studying the Court's role in the Latin American community of human rights. This community consists of a dynamic process of interaction between many actors who trigger the transformative impacts of the decisions.

We begin our argument by briefly describing Latin American transformative constitutionalism, a regional iteration of the broader theory of transformative constitutionalism that emerged in South Africa in the 1990s.[4] We then introduce the concept of the Latin American community of human rights practice, a group of actors that organize around the American Convention on Human Rights (American Convention, or ACHR) to promote their agendas and fulfill their mandates. This community is key to the impact of the Inter-American Court, as we show in the fourth section of this chapter.

Diana Bravo Rubio, "El cumplimiento de los fines de reparación integral de las medidas ordenadas por la Corte Interamericana de Derechos Humanos: énfasis en la experiencia colombiana" [2008] 6 *International Law: Revista Colombiana de Derecho Internacional* 13. Ezequiel Gonzalez-Ocantos and Wayne Sandholtz, "Constructing a regional human rights legal order: The Inter-American Court, national courts, and judicial dialogue, 1988–2014" [2021] 19 *International Journal of Constitutional Law* 1559. For a critical review, see Par Engstrom, "Reconceptualising the impact of the Inter-American human rights system" [2017] 8 *Revista Direito e Práxis* 1250; Estrada Vargas and Eduardo Andrés, "Variación en el cumplimiento de las sentencias emitidas por la Corte Interamericana de Derechos Humanos" [2022] 33(2) *Revista Latinoamericana de Derechos Humanos* (II Semestre 2022) 85–105. González-Salzberg, Damián, "Complying (Partially) with the Compulsory Judgments of the Inter-American Court of Human Rights," in Borges Fortes et al. (eds.), *Law and policy in Latin America. Transforming Courts, Institutions, and Rights* (MacMillan 2017), 39–51.

[3] See Karen J. Alter and Laurence R. Helfer, *Transplanting international courts: the law and politics of the Andean Tribunal of Justice* (Oxford University Press 2017).

[4] On the concept of iteration Human Rights, Sovereignty and Democratic Iterations by Professor Dr. Seyla Benhabib Eugene Meyer Professor of Political Science and Philosophy, Yale University Session 6, Keynote Lectures: "Human Rights—Global Culture—International Institutions" Our Common Future, Hannover, November 4, 2010, Lecture manuscript.

2. Latin American Transformative Constitutionalism

Transformative constitutionalism describes the practice of interpreting and applying constitutional norms in a way that seeks to promote deep social change. US scholar Karl Klare initially proposed the notion in the context of South African constitutional adjudication in the late 1990s.[5] We do not fully endorse his concept, as Klare sees transformative constitutionalism as part of "post-liberal law," giving it a Critical Legal Studies bend. We rather follow the South African scholar Theunis Roux, who considers transformative constitutionalism as compatible with liberal constitutionalism.[6] Indeed, around the same time, many Latin American judges, activists, and academics started using policy-oriented techniques of legal interpretation from the liberal mainstream (such as the principle of proportionality) to transform political and distributive realities in the region, an approach often labeled "neo-constitutionalism."[7]

We understand transformative constitutionalism as an approach to legal interpretation that takes as one of its paramount goals the effective transformation of deeply entrenched structures toward a more democratic society that fully respects, protects, and fulfills human rights. The phenomenon has special relevance for Latin America, which particularly suffers from violence, exclusion, and weak institutions. In the next section, we argue that the judicial practice of the IACtHR displays characteristics of transformative constitutionalism in its response to these conditions.

To frame transformative constitutionalism in more theoretical terms, the notion of "responsive law" is helpful, introduced by Nonet and Selznick in the late 1970s.[8] In their seminal work, the authors identify various forms of legal

---

[5] Karl E. Klare, "Legal Culture and Transformative Constitutionalism" [1998] 14 *South African Journal on Human Rights* 146; "By transformative constitutionalism," says Klare, "I mean a long-term project of constitutional enactment, interpretation, and enforcement committed (not in isolation, of course, but in a historical context of conducive political developments) to transforming a country's political and social institutions and power relationships in a democratic, participatory, and egalitarian direction. Transformative constitutionalism connotes an enterprise of inducing large-scale social change through nonviolent political processes grounded in law." Ibid. at 150.

[6] See Theunis Roux, "A Brief Response to Professor Baxi," in Oscar Vilhena, Upendra Baxi, and Frans Viljoen (eds.), *Transformative Constitutionalism: Comparing the Apex Courts of Brazil, India and South Africa* (PULP 2013), 48–52; for Francois Venter, by contrast, the notion of transformation in South Africa has become "pliable, and ideologically compromised." See Francois Venter, "The Limits of Transformation in South Africa's Constitutional Democracy" [2018] 34 *South African Journal on Human Rights* 143, 165.

[7] See generally Paolo Comanducci, "Formas de (neo)constitucionalismo: Un análisis metateórico," in Miguel Carbonell (ed.), *Neoconstitucionalismo(s)* (Trotta-UNAM 2013), 159; Roberto Gargarella, Piazzolla, 'Dworkin, y el Neoconstitucionalismo' (*Seminario de teoría constitucional y filosofía*, August 25, 2011), <http://seminariogargarella.blogspot.com/2011/08/piazzolla-dworkin-y-el.html> (accessed February 5, 2022).

[8] Philippe Nonet and Philip Selznick, *Law & Society in Transition: Toward Responsive Law* (Harper Torch Books 1978). Making the explicit link of how Selznick's responsive law inspired some of the early thinking on new constitutionalism in Latin American in the 1990s, see Manuel José Cepeda Espinosa, "Responsive Constitutionalism" [2019] 15 *Annual Review of Law and Social Science* 21.

ordering. The first is "repressive law," in which the ultimate goal of the legal system is order; legal reasoning is ad hoc, expedient, and particularistic; coercion is expanded and weakly restrained; and law is generally subordinated to power politics. The second is "autonomous law," in which the legal system serves the development of modern market societies. Here, legal reasoning adheres strictly to legal authority (but is susceptible to excessive formalism), legal restraints control coercion, and law is generally not at the whim of politics.[9]

These two archetypes, which can exist side by side in one legal order, accurately depict the context in which transformative constitutionalism emerged in Latin America. In some respects, scholars, politicians, and activists have regarded law as a continuation of the politics of repression that characterized much of the region. From this perspective, constitutionalism could not work as a viable platform for social change, which would only be brought about by electoral politics, social mobilization, or armed revolution. At the same time, the archetype of autonomous law reflects the strand of formalistic legal thought that also characterized constitutionalism in the region, as it turned a blind eye to the structural problems of social life.

Nonet and Selznick argue a third archetype: a "responsive" law in which the legal system, building on the premise of an autonomous law, responds to social needs and aspirations. A key case in that respect has been the US Supreme Court's *Brown v. Board of Education* decision. It addressed the most serious deficiency in American society: racially motivated discrimination against citizens.[10] *Brown v. Board of Education* became the most famous transformative decision in legal history, and perhaps the most celebrated of all judicial decisions worldwide. This decision and the ensuing case law inspired what would emerge as transformative constitutionalism in Latin America a generation later: many of its protagonists had studied the US Rights Revolution.[11] Because it is evident that systemic racial discrimination persists in the United States, it is clear to all that judgments alone cannot transform society. But they can contribute to such transformation.[12] In other words, courts can transcend their customary role of settling individual cases and stabilizing the *status quo*. *Brown v. Board of Education*

---

[9] Nonet and Selznick (n. 8), at 16.
[10] USSC, *Brown v. Board of Education*, 347 U.S. 483 (1954); on its transformative thrust: John Seigenthaler, "Brown v. Board of Education: Making a More Perfect Union" [2005] 34 *Stetson Law Review* 457.
[11] Yves Dezalay and Bryant G Garth, *The Internationalization of Palace Wars: Lawyers, Economists, and the Contest to Transform Latin American States*, The Chicago Series in Law and Society (University of Chicago Press 2002), 110 ff.
[12] Samuel Moyn, *Not Enough: Human Rights in an Unequal World* (Belknap Press of Harvard University Press 2018), esp. at 173 ff.; Steven Levitsky and Daniel Ziblatt, *How Democracies Die* (Crown 2018), at 251 ff.

highlights that the law, with its many actors and institutions, can play its role in social transformations, notwithstanding its limits, paradoxes, and failures.

In this archetype, legal actors test "alternative strategies for the implementation of mandates and reconstruct (. . .) those mandates in the light of what is learned."[13] Such a process also implies a redistribution of resources within society that "transforms" social structures. Hence, what Nonet and Selznick call "responsive law" undergirds a transformative approach to the legal system that regards law as separate from politics, but remains concerned with the effects of law on society.

What we describe as "transformative constitutionalism," therefore, is an approach to constitutional texts composed of a set of empirical assumptions, argumentative tools, and normative goals that coalesce around the notion that legal interpretation should strive toward being responsive to societal problems. Such an approach can have both critical and pragmatic modes. In its critical mode, transformative constitutionalism identifies the social consequences of purely formal or technical questions of constitutional adjudication. In its pragmatic mode, transformative constitutionalism interprets legal texts to achieve constitutional objectives, which often implies changing or transforming current structures.[14]

Thus understood, the notion of transformative constitutionalism describes both the experience and the ambitions of the inter-American human rights project. Indeed, the admittedly charged concept of "constitutionalism" is useful in accounting for the inter-American regime's close connection to domestic constitutional law: the transformative thrust of the interpretations by the IACtHR is triggered and supported by features of domestic constitutions.[15] Moreover, the Court's interpretation of the American Convention reflects the Latin American approach to "transformative constitutionalism," as one of its interpretive objectives is to transform realities in the region, including by addressing structures of violence, exclusion, and weak institutions. Finally, the Court operates much like a domestic constitutional court, not least because it has declared that parliamentary statutes contrary to the ACHR are void, a power usually reserved for constitutional adjudication.

---

[13] Nonet and Selznick (n. 8), at 109.
[14] Karin van Marle, "Transformative Constitutionalism as/and Critique" [2009] 20 *Stellenbosch Law Review* 286; Javier Couso, "Latin American New Constitutionalism. A Tale of Two Cities," in Conrado Hübner Mendes, Roberto Gargarella, and Sebastián Guidi (eds.), *The Oxford Handbook of Constitutional Law in Latin America* (Oxford University Press 2022), 354–365.
[15] Paola Andrea Acosta Alvarado, *Diálogo judicial y constitucionalismo multinivel: el caso interamericano*, Primera edición (Bogotá: Universidad Externado de Colombia 2015).

3. The Latin American Human Rights Community

To show how such legal decisions can influence social reality, we conceive transformative constitutionalism as a practice: it is relevant in the region because numerous actors apply this approach in their legal work on the ground, thus turning an interpretive mindset into a social practice common to the region. We then consider these actors to form a Latin American human rights community. This latter concept helps develop the approach of Latin American transformative constitutionalism that posits a new common law of human rights in Latin America.[16]

The Latin American human rights community organizes around the American Convention on Human Rights. It is composed of various actors: of course, the judges and clerks of the Court, the commissioners, and staff of the Commission, but also transnational NGOs and lawyers that bring cases before the Inter-American System, grassroots organizations that use human rights to find and to protect victims on the ground, law school clinics that file amicus briefs, domestic courts that interpret and apply the Convention and IACtHR jurisprudence, civil servants that work on human rights for domestic governments, scholars writing and teaching inter-American human rights law, and, last, but certainly not least, politicians with human rights agendas.

The concept of a community of practice is derived from educational research. In 1991, anthropologist Jean Lave and computer scientist Etienne Wenger proposed the notion of situated learning. Learning, they argued, is fundamentally a social process and implies socialization.[17] A community of practice, then, denotes a group of people defined by mutual engagement, a joint enterprise, and a shared repertoire, meaning "routines, words, tools, ways of doing things, stories, gestures, symbols, genres, actions, or concepts that the community has produced or adopted in the course of its existence and which have become part of its practice."[18] This notion was later taken up by international relations scholar Emanuel Adler, who suggests that "there is no reason . . . why we should not be able to identify transnational or even global communities of practice. The closer we get to the level of practices, in fact, the more we can take the international system as a collection of communities of practice—for example, communities of diplomats, traders, environmentalists, and human rights activists. Communities of practice

---

[16] See generally Armin von Bogdandy et al. (eds.), *Transformative constitutionalism in Latin America: the emergence of a new Ius Commune* (Oxford University Press 2017).

[17] The seminal text is Jean Lave and Etienne Wenger, *Situated Learning: Legitimate Peripheral Participation* (Cambridge University Press 1991).

[18] Etienne Wenger, *Communities of practice: learning, meaning, and identity* (Cambridge University Press 1998), 83.

cut across state boundaries and mediate between states, individuals, and human agency, on one hand, and social structures and systems, on the other."[19]

Scholars of international law have already discussed communities of practice. Most importantly, Jutta Brunnée and Stephen Toope have used the notion to analyze the issue of international legal obligation.[20] For Brunnée and Toope, the interactions of transnational communities of practice enabled the emergence of such obligations: "Legal obligation, then, is best viewed as an internalized commitment and not as an externally imposed duty matched with a sanction for non-performance."[21] This notion applies to the workings of transformative constitutionalism in Latin America.

A community of practice is not homogeneous.[22] Its members often have different and even conflicting projects and views. A community of practice is constituted not by a single goal, but instead by common practices as well as a shared understanding of the social meaning of those practices.[23] These practices relate to a framework composed of inter-American institutions, inter-American law, actors in the Inter-American System, and distinct, regional challenges, which lend the community a sense of purpose. This is not to say that all actors in the community of practice agree on all issues. Members of the community might reject the Court's transformative approach;[24] they might reject the outcome of a particular case, or the remedies ordered by the Court, that reflect its transformative approach; they might also disagree that the Inter-American Court's activities should be framed in terms of transformative constitutionalism.[25] Such disagreements do not undermine the claim that a community has emerged around the transformative interpretative. On the contrary, they confirm

---

[19] Emanuel Adler, *Communitarian International Relations: The Epistemic Foundations of International Relations* (Routledge, 2005), at 15.

[20] Stephen J. Toope and Jutta Brunnée, *Legitimacy and Legality in International Law: An Interactional Account* (Cambridge University Press 2010).

[21] Ibid 115.

[22] Emanuel Adler, *Communitarian International Relations*, at 22. The notion of communities of practice has been criticized for remaining silent on the issue of power imbalances; for example, in Alessia Contu and Hugh Willmott, "Re-embedding Situatedness: The Importance of Power Relations in Learning Theory" [2013] 14 *Organization Science* 283. However, our reading of the Latin American community of human rights practice takes into account differences in power differences, as it considers many actors and not only States and international organizations.

[23] *Community* is a term that has many meanings, see Steven Brint, "Gemeinschaft Revisited: A Critique and Reconstruction of the Community Concept" [2001] 19 *Sociological Theory* 1.

[24] For example, by arguing that the transformative approach could result in an unjustifiable expansion of the Court's powers. See Jorge Contesse, "The Final Word? Constitutional Dialogue and the Inter-American Court of Human Rights" [2017] 15 *International Journal of Constitutional Law* 414.

[25] For example, when conservative Evangelical groups reject the Court's case law expanding LGBTIQ+ rights. See René Urueña, "Evangelicals at the Inter-American Court of Human Rights" [2019] 113 *American Journal of International Law* 360. Pro-family groups have also responded negatively to the Court's rulings on reproductive rights, see Julieta Lemaitre and Rachel Sieder, "The Moderating Influence of International Courts on Social Movements" [2017] 19(1) *Health and Human Rights* 149.

its existence, in the sense that actors compete to give meaning to the American Convention thereby feeding the community of practice. These disagreements thus reaffirm the relevance of the transformative constitutional approach and clarify its legal framework. The framework can accommodate many differing views concerning inter-American human rights, but continuous interaction settles the meaning of an international norm in any given case. National judges' engagement with decisions of the IACtHR, as members of the community of practice, is of particular importance.[26] Hence, it is of utmost relevance when national judges self-identify as "inter-American judges" even while expressly disagreeing with the Court on issues that affect them.[27]

The notion of a community implies that there are insiders and outsiders. Among outsiders, there are, first, and most obviously, those who simply are not engaging with Inter-American human rights law. Secondly, some seek to undermine the common practices of the community or the shared understanding of their social meaning.[28] In that respect, the governments of Nicaragua or Venezuela are clearly outsiders. An interesting border case is provided by the presidents of Argentina, Brazil, Chile, Colombia, and Paraguay when they sent a letter to the Inter-American Commission of Human Rights in April 2019 that strongly suggested the regional institutions show greater respect for the principle of subsidiarity, apply more restrained methods of interpretation, and operate with "due knowledge and consideration of the political, economic, and social realities of States by the organs of the ... System."[29] The president's letter reveals the politically motivated concern of governments that are often criticized by inter-American institutions but also reflects wider wariness with what critics perceive to be an illegitimate expansion of the Inter-American System's powers.

---

[26] See Gonzalez-Ocantos y Sandholtz (n. 2), 1559; Manuel Góngora Mera, "Interacciones y convergencias entre la Corte Interamericana de Derechos Humanos y los tribunales constitucionales nacionales," in Armin von Bogdandy, Flávia Piovesan, and Mariela Morales Antoniazzi (eds.), *Direitos humanos, democracia e integração jurídica: Emergência de um novo direito público* (Elsevier 2013), 312; Diana Guarnizo-Peralta, "¿Cortes pasivas, cortes activas, o cortes dialógicas?: Comentarios en torno al caso Cuscul Pivaral y otros v. Guatemala," in Mariela Morales Antoniazzi, Liliana Ronconi, and Laura Clérico (eds.), *Interamericanización de los DESCA. El caso Cuscul Pivaral de la Corte IDH* (MPIL 2020), 429.

[27] See the contributions by Arturo Zaldívar Lelo de Larrea (Mexico), Carmen María Escoto (Costa Rica), and Dina Ochoa Escribá (Guatemala) at the Inter-American Court in occasion of the fortieth anniversary of the American Convention, to be published on the Court's website.

[28] The letter by the presidents of Argentina, Brazil, Chile, Colombia, and Paraguay provides a borderline case.

[29] See República Argentina, la República Federativa del Brasil, la República de Chile, la República de Colombia y la República del Paraguay, *Declaración Sobre el Sistema Interamericano de Derechos Humanos* (2019), at https://www.mre.gov.py/index.php/noticias-de-embajadas-y-consulados/gobiernos-de-argentina-brasil-chile-colombia-y-paraguay-se-manifiestan-sobre-el-sistema-interamericano-de-derechos-humanos (visited October 23, 2023). On the backlash against the Inter-American tribunal, see Ximena Soley and Silvia Steininger, "Parting ways or lashing back? Withdrawals, backlash and the Inter-American Court of Human Rights" [2018] 14 *International Journal of Law in Context* 237–257.

On the one hand, the letter engages with the System, expresses support for its aims, and deploys legitimate arguments for its development. On the other hand, the letter could be part of a strategy to dismantle the System or to change its basic outlook.

Analyzing the Inter-American Court's transformative interpretation of the ACHR with a focus on the Latin American human rights community of practice also reveals the perception of many actors in the community that the IACtHR's case law allows them to better fulfill their mandates. Both the American Convention and most national constitutions task all public authorities, not only judges, with addressing, within the scope of their powers and procedures, the challenges of violence, social exclusion, and weak institutions. For example, Article 3 of the Ecuadorian Constitution states that the State's prime duties are, among others, "planning national development, eliminating poverty, and promoting sustainable development and the equitable redistribution of resources and wealth to enable access to good way of living," and "guaranteeing its inhabitants the right to a culture of peace, to integral security and to live in a democratic society free of corruption." Article 3 of the Brazilian Constitution similarly states that the fundamental objectives of the Federative Republic of Brazil are, among others, to "guarantee national development" and "to eradicate poverty and substandard living conditions and to reduce social and regional inequalities." As such, interaction with the Inter-American Court has become an important dimension of the mandate of national human rights institutions in the region. It is now common for such institutions to adopt the IACtHR's evolutive interpretation of the ACHR and to promote human rights in their respective States in accordance with this method of interpretation.[30]

The Inter-American Court, in turn, construes expansively its powers to foster this community for example by gathering information (Article 69(2) of its Rules).[31] The IACtHR depends on national human rights institutions to induce State compliance with the Court's orders. Sometimes such institutions can be mobilized against the respective government. To this end, the Inter-American Court draws those institutions into the community of practice. Such has occurred in the context of *Artavia Murillo v. Costa Rica*, a case concerning *in vitro* fertilization (IVF) in which Costa Rica's Public Defender's Office intervened in the public hearing of monitoring compliance, and *Velez Loor v. Panama*, a

---

[30] Thomas Innes Pegram, "National Human Rights Institutions in Latin America: Politics and Institutionalization," in Ryan Goodman and Thomas Innes Pegram (eds.), *Human Rights, State Compliance, and Social Change: Assessing National Human Rights Institutions* (Cambridge University Press 2012), 210.

[31] IACtHR Rules, Procedure for Monitoring Compliance with Judgments and Other Decisions of the Court, art. 69(2) ("The Court may require from other sources of information relevant data regarding the case in order to evaluate compliance therewith. To that end, the Tribunal may also request the expert opinions or reports that it considers appropriate.").

case concerning an Ecuadorian migrant, tortured and mistreated in Panama, in which the Panamanian Defender's Office intervened in a private hearing of compliance.[32]

4. Compliance as a Transformative Practice

Skeptics of the transformative impact of inter-American adjudication often highlight States' lack of compliance with the IACtHR's orders.[33] This lack might appear to undermine international transformative constitutionalism: if the Inter-American Court is unable to produce results at the level of an individual case, it might be assumed that it fails, even more, to produce social transformations. This conclusion, however, is incorrect. Focusing solely on case-specific compliance overlooks the transformative effects of the IACtHR's compliance activities. Moreover, a focus on compliance disregards the wider impact of the Inter-American Court's orders and interpretations,[34] which is more clearly seen if we consider the Court in the broader context of the Latin American community of human rights.[35]

The IACtHR considers inducing compliance to be part of its core mandate, unlike the European Court of Human Rights (ECtHR), as the European Convention on Human Rights (ECHR) delegates this task to the Committee of Ministers. The IACtHR's monitoring of compliance is mostly dialogical and informational. It is less concerned with swiftly enforcing certain orders than it is with creating cognitive frameworks and domestic political dynamics that will guide other actors toward implementing the Court's orders. Some of the relevant tools at the IACtHR's disposal are the country reports produced by the Inter-American Commission on Human Rights (Inter-American Commission, or IACHR), informational requirements, and *in loco* visits,[36] as well as the Court's decentralized compliance hearings.[37] Both the Court and the Commission use

---

[32] See *Case of Artavia Murillo* [2012] IACtHR, Ser. C No. 257; *Vélez Loor v. Panama* [2010] IACtHR, Ser. C No. 218.
[33] See note 1.
[34] See in this volume Chapter I.3, Mariela Morales Antoniazzi, Flávia Piovesan, and Júlia Cortez da Cunha Cruz; III.2, Pablo Saavedra; III.4, Viviana Krsticevic and René Urueña.
[35] The Inter-American Court is both part of the community of practice and also provides a forum for the other actors to interact. In certain contexts, the Court is an actor of the community (for example, when it interacts with domestic courts, with the Commission, or with other international courts and tribunals). However, in other contexts, the Court is a structure: it provides a space in which other actors meet and debate their own interpretations of the common law of human rights.
[36] Bertha Santoscoy Noro, "Las visitas in loco de la Comisión Interamericana de Protección de los Derechos Humanos," in Antonio Augusto Cançado Trindade (ed.), *El sistema interamericano de protección de los derechos humanos en el umbral del siglo XXI* (UNAM 2003), 606.
[37] See Felipe González, "La Comisión Interamericana de Derechos Humanos: Antecedentes, funciones y otros aspectos" [2009] 5 *Anuario de Derechos Humanos* 35, 39–41, 54.

these tools to create cognitive and political frameworks that will empower domestic civil society groups to exert pressure on States.[38] The Inter-American System also provides space for meetings between national authorities and domestic stakeholders, and it works in tandem with civil society to create the conditions needed for compliance. Compliance monitoring is thus geared to foster a wider process of transformation.

The inter-American approach differs greatly from traditional understandings of compliance. Traditionally, both the judicial decision and the context of implementation are viewed as static, and compliance is understood as a mechanical process in which "leverages" are activated to achieve the demanded behavior from the addressees. The paradigmatic example comes from domestic private law: compliance with a judicial decision is achieved by activating certain sociopolitical mechanisms (judicial enforcement, for instance) to "force" the addressee of the decision to do something (comply with an obligation). This notion informs the dominant understanding of compliance in international legal scholarship,[39] in which the key problem seems to be how to incentivize compliance when there is little political leverage to compel States to change their behavior.[40] Given the scarcity of enforcement mechanisms, compliance appears an almost discretionary choice for States, particularly in the context of human rights.[41]

Our characterization of compliance diverges from the traditional understanding of the concept in two ways. First, we reject the idea that a judicial decision is static. These decisions are neither fully crystallized nor carved in stone. Indeed, orders by international courts are often vague, and their precise contours only become apparent in the process of implementation through dialogue with the relevant State authorities. In other words, a judicial order is just one step, albeit an essential one, in a long process of transformation. The order defines the scope and direction of possible implementation but usually does not detail concrete policies.

---

[38] See Celeste Kauffman and César Rodríguez-Garavito, "De las órdenes a la práctica: Análisis y estrategias para el cumplimiento de las decisiones del sistema interamericano de derechos humanos," in Camilla Barreto Maia et al., *Desafíos del Sistema Interamericano de Derechos Humanos. Nuevos tiempos, viejos retos* (Colección De Justicia 2015), 276; Clara Burbano Herrera and Yves Haeck, "The Historical and Present-Day Role of Non-Governmental Organisations before the Inter-American Human Rights System in Documenting Serious Human Rights Violations and Protecting Human Rights and the Rule of Law Through Ensuring Accountability" [2021] 17 *Utrecht Law Review* 8.

[39] For a mapping of this issue, see Benedict Kingsbury, "The Concept of Compliance as a Function of Competing Conceptions of International Law" [1998] 19 *Michigan Journal of International Law* 345. For a critique, see Robert Howse and Ruti Teitel, "Beyond Compliance: Rethinking Why International Law Really Matters" [2010] 1(2) *Global Policy* 127–136.

[40] Eric A. Posner and Alan O. Sykes, *Economic Foundations of International Law* (Harvard University Press 2013), 198–208.

[41] See, e.g., Eric A. Posner, *The Twilight of Human Rights Law* (Oxford University Press 2014), 69–78.

Second, we observe that the context of implementation is rarely static. The Inter-American Court often drafts a decision in light of the conditions for its implementation. It understands that the political leverage for compliance often changes over time, including in response to the issuance of the decision itself. Thus, when the IACtHR adopts an order, compliance is a question not merely of whether tools needed to coerce the State into compliance exist but also of how the decision can be used to mobilize and even generate such tools and push the State toward compliance. It will reflect if there is an active domestic judiciary or civil society, and how these can use this decision to achieve compliance and to mobilize support.

Even incidents of open resistance to inter-American decisions are part of this long, transformative process in the direction of compliance. Consider the *Fontevecchia* case, in which the IACtHR ordered Argentina to render a Supreme Court decision ineffective because it violated the right to freedom of expression of two journalists who had been ordered by a domestic court to pay compensation to a former president.[42] The Supreme Court of Argentina, however, decided that the inter-American decision could not be implemented: while inter-American decisions were, "in principle,"[43] binding, they could not be complied with if the international tribunal had exceeded its powers or if its decision contradicted "basic principles of Argentinean public law."[44] The Supreme Court of Argentina was thus not only retreating from its precedent that had accepted inter-American decisions as binding under Argentinean law[45] but also positioned itself in direct opposition to the IACtHR.

The Inter-American Court, however, continued monitoring compliance with its *Fontevecchia* decision and signaled alternative mechanisms of compliance available to Argentina. It determined that Argentina could comply with the inter-American decision by removing the prior, domestic decision "from the web pages of the Supreme Court of Justice and the Judicial Information Center" or by adding to the decision "some type of annotation is made indicating that this sentence was declared in violation of the American Convention by the

---

[42] *Fontevecchia and D'amico v. Argentina* [2011] IACtHR, Ser. C No. 238, para. 137.

[43] Corte Suprema de Justicia de la Nación, *Ministerio de Relaciones Exteriores y Culto s/informe sentencia dictada en el caso "Fontevecchia y D'Amico vs. Argentina" por la Corte Interamericana de Derechos Humanos*, February 14, 2017, consideration 6 (Arg.).

[44] Corte Suprema de Justicia de la Nación, *Ministerio de Relaciones Exteriores y Culto s/informe sentencia dictada en el caso "Fontevecchia y D'Amico vs. Argentina" por la Corte Interamericana de Derechos Humanos*, February 14, 2017, consideration 16 (Arg.).

[45] See Víctor Abramovich, "Comentarios Sobre 'Fontevecchia', La Autoridad de Las Sentencias de La Corte Interamericana y Los Principios de Derecho Público Argentino" [2017] 10 *Pensar En Derecho* 9–25. See further Corte Suprema de Justicia de la Nación, *Espósito, Miguel Ángel s/ incidente de prescripción de la acción penal promovido por su defensa*, December 23, 2004, "considering" 6, 10 (Arg.); Corte Suprema de Justicia de la Nación, *Derecho, René Jesús s/ incidente de prescripción de la acción penal – causa n° 24.079*, November 29, 2011, "considering" 4, 5 (Arg.).

Inter-American Court."[46] The Argentinean court decided to accept the IACtHR's proposal, and added the following sentence to the official text of its decision: "This judgment was declared incompatible with the American Convention on Human Rights by the Inter-American Court (judgment of November 21, 2011)."[47]

To some critics, this outcome may seem insufficient, since Argentina did not comply with the IACtHR's initial order that the domestic decision be revoked. To us, however, the *Fontevecchia* saga reveals that an initial act of noncompliance can prompt a dynamic process of interaction that ultimately generates concrete results. In the face of the Argentinean tribunal's open rejection of its order, the Inter-American Court adapted its position, offering alternatives for compliance that were accepted by the State. Neither the specific mechanism of compliance, nor the Argentinean context, was carved in stone: both the international tribunal and its domestic counterpart engaged in a process of interaction and adaptation that resulted in an unanticipated outcome that both found satisfactory.

The IACtHR's monitoring compliance is not a political process largely outside the Court's bailiwick but rather forms an integral part of its adjudication. Importantly, monitoring compliance stretches over time and involves many stakeholders. Thereby, compliance in a given case morphs smoothly into the much larger process of transformation that strengthens the domestic community of practice, including civil society organizations, national human rights institutions, domestic tribunals, and even actors that oppose a particular decision of the Court.

5. Transformative Constitutionalism beyond Compliance

Compliance should not be fetishized as a proxy for real-life impact. While compliance studies are relevant, they are only one factor in determining the impact of inter-American institutions on the protection and advancement of human rights,[48] particularly when structural problems are at

---

[46] *Fontevecchia and D'Amico v. Argentina*, [2017] IACtHR, Ser. C No. 238, para. 21.
[47] Corte Suprema de Justicia de la Nación, Resolution No. 4015 (Arg.), December 5, 2017.
[48] On the impact of domestic adjudication, see César Augusto Rodríguez Garavito and Diana Rodríguez Franco, "Más allá del desplazamiento: Políticas, derechos y superación del desplazamiento forzado en Colombia [Beyond displacement: Politics, rights, and overcoming forced displacement in Colombia]" (Ediciones Uniandes 2010); Cesar Rodriguez-Garavito, "Beyond the Courtroom: The Impact of Judicial Activism on Socioeconomic Rights in Latin America" [2011] 89(7) *Texas Law Review* 1669, 1683. On the wider impacts of inter-American adjudication, see Oscar Parra, "The Impact of Inter-American Judgments by Institutional Empowerment," in Armin von Bogdandy et al. (eds.), *Transformative Constitutionalism in Latin America: The Emergence of a New Ius Commune* (Oxford University Press 2017), 357–376. Viviana Krsticevic, "El derecho común transformador: el impacto del diálogo del sistema interamericano de derechos humanos con las víctimas en la consecución de justicia," in Armin von Bogdandy, Eduardo Ferrer Mac-Gregor, Mariela Morales Antoniazzi, and Pablo Saavedra Alessandri (coords.), *Cumplimiento e impacto de las sentencias de la Corte Interamericana y el Tribunal Europeo de Derechos Humanos. Transformando*

stake.[49] Following its mandate of supporting transformative constitutionalism, the IACtHR orders reparations difficult to comply with, such as the prosecution of individuals who belong to powerful social groups. If the Inter-American Court considered full compliance its primary objective, it would have to renounce its mandate to help profound change.

"Impact," a wider analytical prism than "compliance," allows for a better understanding of the dynamics of human rights protection.[50] Domestic civil society groups often use inter-American decisions to promote domestic human rights agendas.[51] This creates "compliance partnerships," that is a cooperation between inter-American institutions and civil society groups.[52] The System's decisions, moreover, amplify the voices of those who have been systematically ignored. Inter-American reparations, for example, often include symbolic measures in which monuments are built to honor victims of atrocities. In *19 Merchants*, the Court ordered Colombia to "erect a monument in memory of the victims and, in a public ceremony in the presence of the next of kin of the victims, [. . .] place a plaque with the names of the 19 tradesmen" that were killed.[53]

In addition, the Inter-American System empowers domestic institutions that are committed to human rights to use inter-American decisions in their disputes with other domestic actors. For example, in 2009, three Colombian Supreme Court justices who were investigating the links of the right-wing paramilitary with both the presidency and Congress asked the Inter-American Commission for precautionary measures to protect the Supreme Court against threats that came from within the State.[54] The Commission granted the measures and the investigations could continue. The System's orders are also useful for breaking through institutional barriers that impede the protection of human rights.

---

realidades (MPIL; Instituto de Estudios Constitucionales del Estado de Querétaro; IIJ; UNAM 2019). For a review of the relevant literature, see Par Engstrom, "Introduction: Rethinking the Impact of the Inter-American Human Rights System," in Par Engstrom (ed.), *The Inter-American Human Rights System: Impact Beyond Compliance* (2019), 1.

[49] See James L. Cavallaro and Stephanie Erin Brewer, "Reevaluating Regional Human Rights Litigation in the Twenty-First Century: The Case of the Inter-American Court," [2008] 102(4) *American Journal of International Law* 768–827. Ximena Soley, "The Transformative Dimension of Inter-American Jurisprudence," in Armin von Bogdandy et al. (eds.), *Transformative Constitutionalism in Latin America: The Emergence of a New Ius Commune* (Oxford University Press 2017), 337–355; Howse and Teitel (n. 39).

[50] See René Urueña and Stephania Yate Cortes, in this volume.

[51] Burbano Herrera and Haeck (n. 38), 8; Cavallaro and Brewer (n. 49).

[52] Alexandra Huneeus, "Compliance with International Judgments," in Yuval Shany, Karen J. Alter, and Cesare P.R. Romano (eds.), *The Oxford Handbook of International Adjudication* (Oxford University Press 2013), 437. For the effect of the Inter-American System on the relative strength of domestic constituencies of constitutional lawyers, see Alexandra Huneeus, "Constitutional Lawyers and the Inter-American Court's Varies Authority" [2016] 79 *Law & Contemporary Problems* 179.

[53] See *Case of the 19 Merchants v. Colombia* [2004] IACtHR, Ser. C No. 109, at 132 (English translation).

[54] Parra (n. 48).

Bureaucracies are path-dependent and often lack empathy with marginalized individuals. Domestic civil society actors or public institutions might seek orders from the Inter-American System to combat institutional inertia or bypass institutional gatekeepers, spurring to-action bureaucracies that may otherwise be reluctant to protect human rights.[55]

Through this strategic interaction, inter-American institutions profoundly affect domestic legal systems and their operation.[56] Building on the domestic constitutional provisions explored in the first section of this chapter, inter-American norms penetrate the reasoning of domestic courts, parliaments, and administrative agencies, thus creating an expanding inter-American legal space in which the human rights community of practice can operate.[57]

Of course, that community cannot on its own effectuate profound social change. Transformations of that magnitude require a strong commitment from many more actors throughout society as well as great political will.[58] Most actors of the Latin American human rights community is aware of this. They are usually sophisticated repeat players who understand the possibilities for transformation, but also the limitations of international human rights law.

The ubiquity of inter-American norms, decisions, and institutions throughout the region creates a cognitive framework shared by civil society, courts, academics, and even State institutions that are responsible for human rights violations. In this process, many important sociopolitical conflicts are reframed as distinctive human rights issues, as opposed to problems of an economic or political nature that are beyond the law. This, we propose, is the crux of transformative constitutionalism: apparently intractable social problems, once understood as amenable to nothing but sheer political force or raw power, are reframed as legal issues and, indeed, as human rights violations. Effectively expanding the frontiers of what can be framed as a human rights issue is essential

---

[55] Clara Burbano Herrera and Yves Haeck, "The Innovative Potential of Provisional Measures Resolutions for Detainee Rights in Latin America Through Dialogue Between the Inter-American Court and Other Courts," in Eva Rieter and Karin Zwaan (eds.), *Urgency and Human Rights: The Protective Potential and Legitimacy of Interim Measures* (The Hague: T.M.C. Asser Press 2021), 223; Mónica Arango Olaya, "Medidas provisionales adoptadas por la Corte Interamericana de Derechos Humanos en el asunto B. vs El Salvador y el fortalecimiento de la protección de los derechos reproductivos en el sistema interamericano" [2014] 10 *Anuario de Derechos Humanos* 177; Rodríguez Garavito and Rodríguez Franco (n. 48).

[56] Acosta Alvarado, "Diálogo judicial y constitucionalismo multinivel," in Ezequiel A. González-Ocantos, *Shifting Legal Visions: Judicial Change and Human Rights Trials in Latin America* (1st ed., Cambridge University Press 2016).

[57] René Urueña, "Double or Nothing: The Inter-American Court of Human Rights in an Increasingly Adverse Context" [2017] 45 *Wisconsin International Law Journal* 398.

[58] Alexandra Huneeus, "Courts Resisting Courts: Lessons from the Inter-American Court's Struggle to Enforce Human Rights" [2011] 44 *Cornell International Law Journal* 493; Ariel E. Dulitzky, "El impacto del control de convencionalidad. Un cambio de paradigma en el sistema interamericano de derechos humanos?," in Julio César Rivera (ed.), *Tratado de los derechos constitucionales* (Abeledo Perrot 2014), 533; González-Ocantos (n. 56), 21; Soley (n. 49), 338, 344.

to transformative constitutionalism. Arguably, the Inter-American Court's most profound impact stems from this framing and its fostering of the respective Latin American community of practice.

6. Concluding Remarks

Transformative constitutionalism does not provide a blueprint for a better world. It is flexible and situational, not least because it depends on cases for its evolution. It requires relatively little in terms of "hardware" (e.g., institutional or financial infrastructure), but quite a lot in terms of "software" (e.g., a legal mindset). As for hardware, transformative constitutionalism requires the basic infrastructure of constitutional democracy: a constitution with basic rights that operates as a higher law, basic institutions of democratic representation, and a reasonable and somewhat independent judiciary. As for software, transformative constitutionalism requires a supportive public as well as a community of practice: several legal actors whose approach to legal interpretation, first, responds to the perception that a particular society is structurally failing on its constitutional principles and, second, understands those structural deficiencies as issues that can be meaningfully addressed—though not fully solved—through the adjudication of individual cases representative of such deficiencies. This transformative mindset rests on the hope that the interpretation and application of law to such cases might inch the entire society closer to the basic social compact. This, crucially, is a contribution only lawyers can make.

Part of transformative constitutionalism's strength, however, lies in its flexibility, which is evidenced by how the Inter-American Court is developing and adapting its crucial link with the domestic judiciary: the conventionality control doctrine. Given that it needs a community of practice that engages with its decisions, the IACtHR makes strategic efforts not to alienate some key community insiders, such as important national courts. In the face of critiques from scholars and domestic courts, the Inter-American Court has relaxed some elements of the conventionality control doctrine. At one point, the IACtHR seemed to require that conventionality control was an obligation of all State organs, not only of the top judicial authorities.[59] This interpretation, however, created major risks in domestic systems where the rule of law is often weak and also threatened the position of top judicial authorities in their domestic systems.[60]

---

[59] *Cabrera García and Montiel-Flores v. Mexico* [2010] IACtHR, Ser. C No. 220, para. 225.

[60] For an insider's view of the Court's shift, see Diego García-Sayán, *Cambiando el futuro* (Lápix 2017). García-Sayán was a judge at the Inter-American Court from 2004 to 2015 and served as President of the Court from 2010 to 2014, when the main shift took effect. For a scholarly overview of the critiques, see Ariel E. Dulitzky, "An Inter-American Constitutional Court-The Invention

When these concerns were raised, the Inter-American Court promoted a more limited understanding of the doctrine, clarifying that conventionality control should be exercised by State authorities "evidently within the framework of their respective jurisdictions and the corresponding procedural rules."[61] As such, conventionality control represents the duty of domestic institutions to apply international law, as long as this is compatible with domestic norms of jurisdictions and procedure—a doctrine much less radical than how it initially appeared.[62] Nevertheless, the IACtHR's flexibility is principled. In other words, its flexibility is not merely tactical but is a function of the pursuit of its transformative mandate. Thus, the Inter-American Court has not retreated with respect to its substantive case law, which has drawn no less criticism. In comparison with the ECtHR, the IACtHR has proven steadfast.[63]

Summing up, we reconstruct compliance as one component for understanding the IACtHR's transformative impact. It is helpful, not least because it can be measured. Yet interest in compliance should be integrated with an interest in the Inter-American Court's broader impact in Latin America. To see that impact, the concept of the Latin American community of human rights practice is useful. Moreover, in that broader picture, we have reframed compliance as an iterative process that helps expand the Court's impact by strengthening such a community. The Latin American community of human rights practice, for all the depth and breadth it has acquired over the last four decades, is only one of many forces that compete to shape the future of the Americas.

---

of the Conventionality Control by the Inter-American Court of Human Rights" [2015] 50 *Texas International Law Journal* 45, 60–64, 71–79.

[61] *Gelman v. Uruguay*, Merits and Reparations [2011] IACtHR, Ser. C No. 221, para. 193.
[62] The discussion of this dimension of conventionality control is based on René Urueña, "Domestic Application of International Law in Latin America," in Curtis A. Bradley, *The Oxford Handbook of Comparative Foreign Relations Law* (Oxford University Press 2019), 565.
[63] On refugee rights, compare *Hirsi Jamaa et al. v. Italy* App. No. 27765/09 (ECHR, Feb. 13, 2012), with *ND and NT v. Spain* App. Nos. 8675/15 and 8697/15 (ECHR, Feb. 12, 2020). On the ECtHR and the challenges to its decisions, see Mikael Rask Madsen, "The Challenging Authority of the European Court of Human Rights: From Cold War Legal Diplomacy to the Brighton Declaration and Backlash" [2016] 79 *Law & Contemporary Problems* 141.

I.2
Protecting Human Rights in the Americas
The Continuous Role of the Inter-American Commission on Human Rights

By Claudio Grossman

1. Introduction

This chapter's purpose is to explore the role of the Inter-American Commission on Human Rights (the Commission, or IACHR) throughout its history in the Americas. Created in 1959, the Commission's primary function is to advise the Organization of American States (OAS) on the promotion and protection of human rights and to ensure compliance by member States. The Commission exercises its compliance role at three levels: addressing individual complaints, assessing the human rights conditions of member States, and analyzing general thematic areas. As an advisory organ for the OAS, the Commission provides human rights input on political decision-making processes that have an impact on human rights at the individual, member State, and thematic levels. The Commission's uniquely broad mandate allowed it to adapt its role to various challenges throughout its history.

Moreover, the Commission pursues its human rights goals through several mechanisms. It documents general or specific violations occurring in member States through country reports and *in loco* country visits, then publishes and presents its reports to the Permanent Council and General Assembly of the OAS. The Commission has visited twenty-three member States in about one hundred on-site visits and published over seventy country reports since it began using this instrument in 1961.[1] The Commission also creates Rapporteurships on topics that, in its view, deserve particular attention. Currently, these topics include the rights of Indigenous peoples; the rights of women; the rights of migrants; freedom of expression; the rights of the child; human rights defenders; the rights of persons deprived of liberty; the rights of Afro-descended peoples and

---

[1] See IACHR, "Country Reports," <https://www.oas.org/en/IACHR/jsForm/?File=/en/iachr/reports/country.asp> (accessed January 5, 2022); and "Country Visits," https://www.oas.org/en/iachr/activities/countries_all.asp> (accessed January 5, 2022).

freedom from racial discrimination; the rights of LGBTI persons; and economic social, cultural, and environmental rights.[2] Additionally, through the cases in its reporting system, the Commission can determine if one or more rights in the inter-American System have been violated.

While the Inter-American Commission and the Inter-American Court of Human Rights (the Court) are both involved in handling petitions by those claiming that a violation of human rights has taken place, individuals are only able to petition the Commission, and only the Commission can refer a case to the Court. After a review of its standards, the Commission amended its rules to require consultation with the victims to determine whether a case should be sent to the Court, thereby ensuring rights-holders would have a voice in the IACHR's decision.[3] Additionally, once the case is presented to the Court, the victims are entitled to appoint their own representatives.[4]

Those claims can be made either under the American Convention on Human Rights[5] (American Convention) or under the American Declaration on the Rights and Duties of Man (American Declaration).[6] Claims under the American Convention allow the Commission to receive individual petitions, ipso facto, once a State ratifies it. Under the American Declaration, the Commission accepts claims from individuals against those nations by the mere fact of OAS membership. The Commission's decision on claims under the American Declaration is final. In the case of the American Convention, if a country has accepted the compulsory jurisdiction of the Court, the Commission is free to decide if it will publish its decision or, in the case of noncompliance, will send a case to the Court.

This chapter will look at the human rights impact of the Commission's functions and methods of work throughout its history. Across three general historical phases, the Commission adapted and focused its role when necessary according to the region's particular historical moment. The individual, State, and thematic levels of the Commission's work played a greater or lesser role throughout these phases, depending on their capacity to produce positive change.

---

[2] See IACHR, "Thematic Rapporteurships and Units," <https://www.oas.org/en/iachr/mandate/rapporteurships.asp> (accessed January 5, 2022).
[3] IACHR, "Annual Report of the Inter-American Commission on Human Rights 2000," OEA/Ser./L/V/II.111, Doc. 20, para. 26 (rev. April 16, 2001), <https://www.cidh.oas.org/annual.eng.htm> (accessed January 5, 2022).
[4] IACtHR, "Rules of Procedure of the Inter-American Court of Human Rights," November 18–28, 2009, arts. 25, 37, which asserts the right of victims and their representatives and allows for the Court to appoint a representative if a victim does not have adequate representation, <https://www.corteidh.or.cr/sitios/reglamento/nov_2009_ing.pdf> (accessed January 5, 2022).
[5] ACHR, November 22, 1969, 1144 U.N.T.S. 143.
[6] American Declaration of the Rights and Duties of Man, OEA/Ser.L/V.II.23, Doc. 21, rev. 6 (1948).

2. The Role of the Commission through Its Phases

2.1. Phase One: Maintaining a Human Rights Focus among Dictatorships

Until the beginning of the 1980s, the Commission operated against the backdrop of several dictatorships committing mass and gross human rights violations. These regimes sought to inscribe an authoritarian narrative onto the region as an alternative to human rights discourses. Under the guise of the National Security Doctrine, dictators sought to eliminate internal opposition. Viewing their opponents at worst as active agents in the destruction of "Western Civilization," or at best as naïve—by allowing themselves to be used by those who desired said destruction—anyone who opposed these dictators were vulnerable to persecution.[7] As a result, governments resorted to forced disappearances, torture, and the withholding of due process while simultaneously denying the existence of any human rights violations in an attempt to maintain their status in the international community.

All over the region, authoritarian regimes resorted to mass and gross human rights violations to eliminate or control any form of dissent. For instance, Chile's military dictatorship led by General Augusto Pinochet resorted to political repression through mass arbitrary imprisonment, killings, torturing, and forced disappearances numbering at least three thousand people. In Argentina, up to thirty thousand people disappeared throughout the country from systematic torture and extrajudicial executions.[8] These types of human rights violations were widespread throughout the region, including in the Central American States of Guatemala, El Salvador, and Honduras.[9]

Considering that there were no internal opportunities to expose and seek redress for human rights violations, the Commission played an important role in denouncing and documenting the scope and gravity of the crisis. The adoption of the American Convention, signed in 1969 and entering into force in 1978, gave the Commission further authority to identify specific human rights and the concomitant obligations of the State parties.[10] The Commission could easily

---

[7] See Hal Brands, *Latin America's Cold War* (Harvard University Press 2010), 70–78: he uses the examples of Peru, Brazil, and Argentina to show how the military and government sought to defeat threats to maintain their ideology under the National Security Doctrine.

[8] See Amnesty International's elaboration of their work on "Enforced Disappearances," https://www.amnesty.org/en/what-we-do/enforced-disappearances/.

[9] On the other side of the political spectrum is Cuba. The Cuban government under Fidel Castro codified repression into Cuban law, executed political opponents, and forced many others into labour camps. For more details, see BBC News, "Fidel Castro: las muertes, desapariciones y detenciones que se le atribuyen al líder de la Revolución Cubana" [2016], <https://www.bbc.com/mundo/noticias-america-latina-38153673> (accessed January 5, 2022).

[10] See Fernando Volio, "The Inter-American Commission on Human Rights Symposium: The American Convention on Human Rights" [1980] 30 *American University Law Review* 65, 70.

articulate violations, and its primary instrument for manifesting this role was using country reports. It developed extensive fact-finding investigations to prove gross and mass violations that governments were denying.[11]

Country reports served as useful tools for the regional human rights system by providing accurate information for the international community to create pressure against perpetrators of violations, support victims, and push for the denunciation of dictatorships. In this phase of its history the Commission published reports on the human rights situations in Cuba, Haiti, the Dominican Republic, El Salvador, Honduras, Uruguay, Argentina, Suriname, Paraguay, Chile, Nicaragua, Colombia, Bolivia, and Guatemala.[12] Exposing violations contributed to the international isolation of these regimes, which in turn provided a basis for condemning them, supporting domestic opponents, and helping to catalyze their eventual collapse.[13]

2.2. Phase Two: Individuals Bring Grievances against Their Nations

The Commission and its role changed direction with the ushering in of newly elected governments in the 1980s. These administrations inherited "normative constraints" from the previous regimes, including amnesty and contempt laws designed to stifle criticism against public figures. Moreover, jurisdiction to adjudicate human rights violations continued to be granted to military tribunals.[14] Despite struggling to create spaces for domestic justice and to address past human rights violations, the new administrations generally did not have the legislative majorities to change these old norms[15] For the citizens of these regimes looking to have their grievances redressed, the domestic system still did not fully serve their needs because the governments' hands were tied.

However, the new political dynamic of democratization generated new opportunities for the Commission. Elected governments allowed for greater accountability and compliance with human rights standards. Civil society now had a space to ask for compliance with these standards, and a multitude of organizations came into existence as a result. Building on the fact-finding missions of

---

[11] IACHR, "Country Reports" (n.1).
[12] Ibid.
[13] Cesar Sepulveda, "The Inter-American Commission on Human Rights (1960–1981)" [1982] 12 *Israeli Yearbook on Human Rights* 51, 52.
[14] See John J. Moore, "Problems with Forgiveness: Granting Amnesty under the Arias Plan in Nicaragua and El Salvador" [1991] 43 *Stanford Law Review* 733–735.
[15] Tina Rosenberg, "Overcoming the Legacies of Dictatorship" [1995] 74 *Foreign Affairs* 141–142: she argues that dictatorships never stay dead because the Latin American civilian governments could not prevent human rights violations by security forces or continued threats from military coups d'état.

"phase one" that documented mass and grave violations, the Commission now found a legal role through its petition system. All stakeholders now operated through a system that allowed for the identification of individual violations. This moved the human rights narrative from phase one, where the Commission mostly documented mass and gross human rights violations, to a regional legal system capable of individualizing specific violations. At this time, newly elected governments, rejecting their predecessors' dictatorial ideology, generally valued participation in the Commission's supervisory procedures, and individuals seeking to confront the legacies of dictatorship brought cases to the Commission that dealt with forced disappearances, military tribunals, amnesty laws, reparations, and freedom of expression.

A representative example of the successes of the individual petition system is *Barrios Altos v. Peru*, decided by the Inter-American Court in 2001.[16] Peru had carried out extrajudicial killings in its fight against terrorism and then protected its perpetrators through amnesty laws. On November 3, 1991, six members of the Peruvian military indiscriminately opened fire on a fundraising party in Lima, killing fifteen and injuring four.[17] The perpetrators were linked to a division of the army called *Grupo Colina*, which acted as a death squad.[18] Peru suspended investigations into the incident after passing Law No. 26479, the amnesty law exonerating human rights violators from 1980 to 1995.[19] The case was then brought to the Commission in 1995, where it rejected Peru's argument that amnesty was an allowable extraordinary measure used to support the fight against terrorism.[20] Having rejected the argument, the Commission sent the case to the Court, which held that Peru had violated the American Convention and the rights to life (Article 4), personal integrity (Article 5), due process (Article 8), and access to justice (Article 25).[21] The Commission's actions catalyzed a fight against impunity in Peru and rejected the idea that the most atrocious crimes can be shielded from investigation or punishment.

This phase in the Commission's history evolved its mandate and built a legal framework into the human rights narrative. For the first time, a variety of stakeholders created a community of practice in which civil society, public interest lawyers, activists, victims, and States could resolve domestic issues on an international platform. The Commission continued to fight amnesty laws and create regional precedents for the *obligation to investigate*.[22] While the rejection

---

[16] *Barrios Altos v. Peru* [2001], IACtHR, Ser. C No. 75, para. 2 (b).
[17] Ibid.
[18] Ibid., para. 2 (d).
[19] Ibid., para. 2 (i).
[20] Ibid., para. 41: rejecting all amnesty provisions as inadmissible because "they are intended to prevent the investigation and punishment of those responsible for serious human rights violation."
[21] Ibid., para. 42.
[22] See Lisa J. Laplante, "Outlawing Amnesty: The Return of Criminal Justice in Transitional Justice Schemes" [2009] 49 *Virginia Journal of International Law* 915, 938: citing *Garay Hermosilla v. Chile*

of amnesty did not immediately result in complete accountability for every human rights abuse, it did create a legal platform for the peaceful resolution of violations and the legitimacy of human rights concerns that continued in other Commission cases. States such as Chile, Peru, Argentina, and Colombia eventually abolished, or reinterpreted in different degrees, their positions on amnesty.[23]

2.3. Phase Three: Greater Inclusion and Participation in the Political System

The third and current phase once again refocused the Commission's goals and functions toward democracy, participation, and inclusion. The Commission still struggles to both expand democracy for all people and prevent existing democracies from backsliding into authoritarianism.[24] Notwithstanding the progress in the region, serious issues remain in the Americas: inequality, corruption, lack of economic opportunities, and access to quality healthcare and education.[25] Exclusion and discrimination on the basis of ethnicity, gender, or sexual

---

[1996], Case 10.843, IACtHR, Report No. 36/96, OEA/Ser.L/V/II.95, Doc. 7, para. 105; *Herrera v. Argentina*, Cases 10.147, 10.181, 10.240, 10.262, 10.309, 10.311, IACtHR, Report No. 28/92, OEA/Ser.L/V/II.83, Doc. 14, para. 50 (1992–1993): "[C]oncluding that amnesty laws violate the judicial guarantees embodied in Articles 8 and 25 of the American Convention"; *Mendoza v. Uruguay*, Cases 10.029, 10.036, 10.145, 10.305, 10.372, 10.373, 10.374, 10.375, IACtHR, Report No. 29/92, OEA/Ser.L/V/II.83, Doc. 14, para. 54 (1992–1993); *Massacre Las Hojas v. El Salvador* [1992–1993], Case 10.287, IACtHR, Report No. 26/92, OEA/Ser.L/V/II.83, Doc. 14, para. 83: "[D]eclaring that amnesty laws in El Salvador contravene the American Convention"; IACHR, "Report on the Situation of Human Rights in Peru," March 12, 1993, OEA/Ser.L/V/II.83, Doc. 31: One element that has been particularly disturbing to the Commission is that up until 1990, no member of the security forces had been tried and punished for involvement in human rights violations, <http://iachr.org/countryrep/Peru93eng/background.htm#f.%20Impunity> (accessed January 5, 2022); IACHR, "Annual Report of the Inter-American Commission on Human Rights 1985–1986," OEA/Ser.L/V/II.68, Doc. 8, rev. 1, Chapter IV: "[A]ddressing political transitions in the region and attempting to strike a balance between peace and the state's obligation to investigate," <http://cidh.org/annualrep/85.86eng/chap.4.htm> (accessed January 5, 2022).

[23] See Louise Mallinder, "The End of Amnesty or Regional Overreach: Interpreting the Erosion of South America's Amnesty Laws" [2016] 65(3) *International and Comparative Law Quarterly* 645, 650–653: She shows the legal strategies used to reinterpret amnesty laws to enforce the obligation to investigate. However, there are some cases in which issues of amnesty are still ambiguous or conflicting. For example, Uruguay passed Law 18.831 in 2011 to restrict amnesties for crimes committed during its dictatorship, yet the Uruguay Supreme Court repealed key provisions of the law in 2013, reviving the issue of amnesty; see Jo-Marie Burt and Francesca Lessa, "Recent Sentence by Uruguayan Supreme Court Obstructs Search for Truth and Justice" [2013], Washington Office on Latin America, <https://www.wola.org/analysis/recent-sentence-by-uruguayan-supreme-court-obstructs-search-for-truth-and-justice/> (accessed January 5, 2022).

[24] Guillermo O'Donnel, "Delegative Democracy" [1994] 5 *Journal of Democracy* 55, 56: he discusses the phenomenon where charismatic figures assume presidency through free elections that governs without the traditional counterweights of representative democracies.

[25] See Moisés Naím and Brian Winter, "Why Latin America Was Primed to Explode" [2019] *Foreign Affairs*, <https://www.foreignaffairs.com/articles/central-america-caribbean/2019-10-29/why-latin-america-was-primed-explode> (accessed January 5, 2022): they highlight the ways many

orientation permeate the region.[26] Facing these serious challenges alongside a general disenchantment toward political institutions has been made harder as alternative narratives have arisen, including authoritarian and populist claims to be better prepared to solve the challenges facing the region than democratic and human rights approaches.[27]

This struggle to maintain the human rights narrative plays out differently across Latin American. Venezuela's Nicolás Maduro regime questions the human rights position by using the language of inequality to delegitimize the American Convention, presenting an alternative narrative to economic disparities by pushing for a vanguardist ideology of centralization and populism in governmental power.[28] Similarly, upheavals in Bolivia and Nicaragua stem from disputes around political power and authoritarian actions.[29] In Brazil, Jair Bolsonaro's regime utilizes extreme nationalist and authoritarian language to discredit human rights approaches to societal ills.[30] Equally, President Nayib Bukele in El Salvador has resorted to similar measures.[31]

In 2019, Colombia, Ecuador, and Chile witnessed a number of explosive episodes of social unrest of varying magnitudes relating to issues about pensions,

---

Latin American nations faced economic inequality, corruption, failures of healthcare, security, infrastructure, and education, which created the conditions for the social upheavals seen today.

[26] See IACHR, "Advances and Challenges Towards the Recognition of the Rights of LGBTI persons in the Americas," December 7, 2018, OEA/Ser.L/V/II.170, Doc. 184, 127–128: noting the expansion of anti-LGBTI groups threatens regression of LGBTI rights and reiterates States' lack of reliable statistics reflecting the true nature of discrimination against these individuals, which further facilitates their discrimination; María Victoria Murillo, "Why Is South America in Turmoil? An Overview" [2019] *Americas Quarterly*, <https://www.americasquarterly.org/content/why-south-america-turmoil-overview> (accessed January 5, 2022): redistribution in Latin America led to social polarization on class, ethnicity, or gender, then disenchantment rose with corruption scandals throughout the region.
[27] See Naím and Winter (n.25).
[28] See "Venezuela Denounces American Convention on Human Rights as IACHR Faces Reform" [2019] International Justice Resource Center, <https://www.ijrcenter.org/2012/09/19/venezuela-denounces-american-convention-on-human-rights-as-iachr-faces-reform/> (accessed January 5, 2022).
[29] See Gremaud Angee and Joshua Berlinger, "Bolivia's Death Toll Rises as Protests Continue" [2019] CNN World, <https://www.cnn.com/2019/11/20/americas/bolivia-unrest-intl-hnk/index.html> (accessed January 5, 2022); see also UN News, "Repression, Use of Force Risk Worsening Bolivia Crisis: UN Human Rights Chief" [2019], <https://news.un.org/en/story/2019/11/1051531> (accessed January 5, 2020); and "UN Calls on Nicaragua to End 'Persistent Repression of Dissent'" [2019] *The Guardian*, <https://www.theguardian.com/world/2019/nov/19/un-nicaragua-persistent-repression-hunger-strike?fbclid=IwAR0_ls6WieW9ngAiqAqJM44AdnL95QrxJayKIKKy3ygBwOnhw1UI1Xlflxo> (accessed January 5, 2020).
[30] See David Miranda, "Bolsonaro Wants to End Democracy in Brazil. Here's One Way He Could Do It" [2019] *The Guardian*, <www.theguardian.com/commentisfree/2019/nov/21/bolsonaro-brazil-military-dictatorship-violence> (accessed January 5, 2022).
[31] See Natalie Kitroeff, "Young Leader Vowed Change in El Salvador but Wields Same Heavy Hand" [2020] *New York Times*, <https://www.nytimes.com/2020/05/05/world/americas/el-salvador-nayib-bukele.html> (accessed January 5, 2022).

access to healthcare, and quality education.[32] In those States, the legitimacy of human rights institutions, norms, and procedures have not been disputed. These States have functioning judiciaries and democratically elected governments but have not completely fulfilled their human rights obligations, including those concerning social inclusion. The present goal is for the inter-American System to present a human-rights-grounded alternative to the various types of authoritarian and populist approaches that are challenging the rule of law. Social and economic inclusion and the prohibition of discrimination, including on the basis of gender and sexual orientation, are essential components of this new phase in the protection of human rights in the region.

To address these various kinds of serious human rights challenges, the Commission maintains its legacy by resorting to the instruments developed in the three separate phases of its existence. Country reports and *in loco* visits are now used to ensure democracies do not backslide toward the authoritarianism of the past or toward various manifestations of populism. Country reports allow for a general analysis of the ongoing internal processes impacting human rights. For example, the Commission has broken down the human rights situation in Venezuela into the facts and their impact on several facets of Venezuelan life, including the democratic–institutional system, social protest and the freedom of expression, violence and citizen security, poverty, and economic, social, cultural, and environmental rights (with recommendations for each).[33] The accompanying websites for these reports illustrate the Commission's push for change by highlighting particularly alarming human rights situations and its recommendations to create change.[34] For human rights violations that stem from economic based social unrest (as in Chile) States, with few exceptions, consent to *in loco* visits where the Commission will meet with representatives from civil society and government officials to understand the human rights situation

---

[32] See Steven Grattan, "'We'll Continue Until Duque Listens': Colombians Hold 3rd Strike" [2019] *Al Jazeera*, <https://www.aljazeera.com/news/2019/12/continue-duque-listens-colombians-hold-3rd-strike-191204132527178.html> (accessed January 5, 2022): "Protesters are angry over a wide range of issues from the poor health system, inadequate pensions, violence, inequality, corruption and the weak implementation of the 2016 peace deal"; Jimmy Langman, "From Model to Muddle: Chile's Sad Slide into Upheaval" [2019] *Foreign Policy*, <https://foreignpolicy.com/2019/11/23/chile-upheaval-protests-model-muddle-free-market/> (accessed January 5, 2022): "From Santiago to other cities and towns such as Concepción and Valparaiso, anger over long-festering economic inequality issues, low wages, meager pensions, and a rising cost of living have Chileans pouring into the streets in protest."

[33] IACHR, "Situation of Human Rights in Venezuela: Democratic Institutions, the Rule of Law and Human Rights in Venezuela," December 31, 2017, OEA/Ser.L/II, Doc. 2017.

[34] See IACHR, "Situation of Human Rights in Venezuela," <https://cidhoea.wixsite.com/venezuela/; and IACHR, "Nicaragua," https://www.oas.org/en/iachr/activities/visits/nicaragua2018.asp> (accessed January 5, 2022).

in the country.[35] This cooperation demonstrates the Commission's legitimacy and monitoring role for member States.

Beyond the maintenance of the human rights narrative, the Commission also moves democracies forward by pushing for expansive equality and inclusion measures.[36] Ensuring the participation and equal treatment of every person in the region requires connecting the human rights situations of each State with that of their neighbors. The Commission accomplishes this goal through thematic reports by Special Rapporteurs. The Commission thus far has created thirteen Rapporteurships to address specific human rights challenges in the Western Hemisphere.[37] Moreover, while most Rapporteurships operate under a member of the Commission, the Commission itself has two Special Rapporteurships that operate as autonomous offices led by independent experts: the Special Rapporteurship for Freedom of Expression and the Special Rapporteurship on Economic, Social, Cultural, and Environmental Rights.

The Rapporteurships provide in-depth analyses on important challenges and recommend public policies for the region in thematic areas, as well as sometimes participating in individual cases. Each thematic report publishes standards for the region to follow while bringing to light systems of discrimination, oppression, and human rights violations. They conduct extensive investigations, meet with affected groups, establish legal and policy standards, educate the public, and encourage the implementation of best practices. Working in conjunction with individual petitions, the Commission helps catalyze change in domestic systems through landmark decisions and by keeping the human rights narrative on the agenda of each State in the region.[38]

Specifically, the Commission's thematic reports and related individual petitions improve the human rights situations of targeted groups of people. For example, the Commission strengthened Indigenous rights in the region through a combination of individual cases and thematic reports pressuring States to

---

[35] IACHR, Press Release No. 312/19, "IACHR Completes Preliminary Visit to Chile," November 29, 2019, https://www.oas.org/en/iachr/media_center/PReleases/2019/312.asp> (accessed January 5), 2022: acknowledging the value of the Chilean government's cooperation with the Commission's efforts.

[36] Lopes Olsen, Ana Carolina, and Katya Kozicki, "The Role Played by the Inter-American Court of Human Rights in the Dialogical Construction of an Ius Constitutionale Comune in Latin America" [2019] 9 *Brazil Journal of Public Policy* 307.

[37] See IACHR, "Thematic Rapporteurships and Units," <https://www.oas.org/en/iachr/mandate/rapporteurships.asp> (accessed January 5, 2022).

[38] See Jorge E. Taiana, "The Legacy and Current Challenges of the Inter-American Commission on Human Rights" [2013] 20 *Human Rights Brief* 42, 43, 44: demonstrates the strengthening of rule of law, gender equality, and Indigenous rights with examples; legislation adopted after the Commission's report on domestic violence in Brazil; marriage rights recognition in Guatemala; training on gender discrimination and violence against women in Bolivia; tens of thousands of hectares awarded in title to Indigenous communities in Nicaragua and Paraguay; and Ecuador's acceptance of international responsibility for violating Indigenous rights.

make changes. The push is reflected in *Mayagna (Sumo) Awas Tingni Community v. Nicaragua*, in which the Commission brought a case to the Court when the Nicaraguan government refused to implement the titling and demarcation of community land.[39] The decision of the Court was the first to recognize a communal property right and Indigenous law as providing for enforceable rights and obligations.[40] The Commission's decision, and decisions like it, coupled with the Commission's creation of a Special Rapporteur on the Rights of Indigenous Peoples (its first Rapporteurship) set a standard for human rights and fought against the social exclusion of Indigenous populations by addressing the high rate of poverty and illiteracy. Additionally, the Commission investigates country-specific situations and the general rights of Indigenous populations through *in loco* visits and by investigating more narrowly defined groups of people, such as Indigenous women or those in voluntary isolation.[41] For example, the Commission recently published a report on the human rights situation of the Indigenous and tribal peoples of the Pan-Amazon region.[42] The Commission's role in the situation of Indigenous rights in the Americas demonstrates how each of the Commission's available instruments are used together to promote human rights during the current phase of its work.[43]

As shown in the third phase, the individual petitions and country report mechanisms are valuable tools for encouraging and enforcing human rights and democratic standards that seek to address the challenges facing the region. Issues relating to gender, discrimination, social and economic exclusion, sexual orientation, the freedom of expression and assembly, Indigenous populations, and the identification of States' positive duties all go through the petition system. In fact, the petition system has continued to grow: in 1997, the Commission received 435 petitions, compared to the 3,034 it received in 2019.[44] Petitioners seek both the abstention of the State from violating human rights and positive action to contribute to a situation where everyone would count as a full member of society.

---

[39] *The Mayagna (Sumo) Awas Tingni Community v. Nicaragua* [2001], IACtHR, Ser. C No. 79; see also S. James Anaya and Claudio Grossman, "The Case of Awas Tingni v. Nicaragua: A Step in the International Law of Indigenous Peoples" [2002] 19 *Arizona Journal of International and Comparative Law* 1.
[40] Ibid.
[41] See IACHR, "Indigenous Peoples: Thematic Reports/Studies," <https://www.oas.org/en/iachr/indigenous/reports/thematic.asp> accessed January 5, 2022.
[42] IACHR, "Situation of Human Rights of the Indigenous and Tribal Peoples of the Pan-Amazon Region," September 29, 2019, OAS/Ser.L/V/II, Doc. 176.
[43] See IACHR, "Missing and Murdered Indigenous Women in British Columbia, Canada," December 21, 2014, OEA/Ser.L/V/II, Doc. 30/14: demonstrates an example outside of Latin America of the Commission's role examining the situation of the Indigenous, in this case the murder of Indigenous women.
[44] See IACHR, "Annual Report 2019," Chapter II: The Petitions, Cases, and Precautionary Measures System, 62, <http://www.oas.org/en/iachr/docs/annual/2019/docs/IA2019cap2-en.pdf> (accessed January 5, 2022).

The decisions that come out of the petition system are crucial for the protection of and compliance with human rights by individualizing situations and deciding on reparations, including material and moral compensation, measures of satisfaction, and guarantees of nonrepetition.[45] The Commission and the Court's comprehensive reparations system not only takes into account the nature of the human rights violation and the victims and society's interest in full compliance with the rule of law but also expands the definition of victim to encompass direct and indirect as well as collective and societal victims.[46] This is a process that is currently ongoing and is not immune from controversy by those who would like to stick with the classic method of solely addressing civil and political rights.

It is important to note that the phases identified in this chapter represent general trends in the Commission's role throughout its existence. Historical events affecting the Commission can lead to reversions and the intermingling of phases since different States may be at different stages in the development of human rights norms and practices.

3. Challenges for the Commission in Executing Its Functions

It is essential for the execution of its functions that the Commission maintains its independence. This independence is vital for the Commission's legitimacy and ensures its ability to pursue its broad mandate. As a body of the OAS, the Commission is bound by rules dictated by member States and their funding, and member States have the ability to limit the Commission's resources.[47] During the second phase, the Commission enjoyed a higher willingness from States to participate in its processes as newly elected governments saw the value of the Commission in assisting them with dismantling the legacies of dictatorship. Now there is more tension, as the Commission's work toward the full realization of human rights intersects with elected governments that value their own sovereign prerogatives.[48] An example of this disagreement is the application of human

---

[45] Douglass Cassel, "The Expanding Scope and Impact of Reparations Awarded by the Inter-American Court of Human Rights" [2007] 7 *Revista do Instituto Brasilerio de Direitos Humanos* 92–93.

[46] See key developments in case law: *Lhaka Honat Association v. Argentina* [2020], IACtHR, Ser. C No. 400; *Artavia Murillo v. Costa Rica* [2012], IACtHR, Ser. C No. 257; *Rosendo Cantú v. Mexico* [2010], IACtHR, Ser. C No. 216; *Fernández Ortega v. Mexico* [2010], IACtHR, Ser. C No. 215; *Gonzalez v. Mexico* [2009], IACtHR, Ser. C No. 205; *Raxcacó Reyes v. Guatemala* [2005], IACtHR, Ser. C No. 133; *Olmedo Bustos v. Chile* [2001], IACtHR, Ser. C No. 73.

[47] See IACHR, "Strategic Plan: 2017–2021," March 20, 2017, OEA/Ser.L/V/II.161, Doc. 27/17, 22: "The autonomy and independence of the Commission are compromised when they depend on voluntary contributions each year, as this affects its possibilities for stability and predictability."

[48] Ximena Soley and Silvia Steininger, *Parting Ways or Lashing Back? Withdrawals, Backlash and the Inter-American Court of Human Rights*, MPIL Research Paper No. 2018-01, <https://ssrn.com/abstract=3103666> (accessed January 5, 2022).

rights norms by the inter-American System's supervisory organs to address social and economic problems in the region.[49]

The tension existing in the System touches upon the Commission's mandate to issue precautionary measures, which allow it to rapidly respond to situations with immediate risk of irreparable harm. The need for expedited processing to avoid irreparable harm has resulted in tensions with governments that believe that expedited processes, to a certain extent, limit their ability to fully express their views.[50] Another source of tension is the need for full compliance with the Commission's and the Court's decisions. Although there are positive levels of compliance in most cases of human rights violations, achieving the investigation, prosecution, and punishment of those involved remains a fundamental challenge. However, while these tensions have an impact on the Commission's tasks, they have not deterred it from continuing to fulfill its mandate by accepting individual cases at an increasing rate, expanding the topics of its thematic reports, and demanding that States fully comply with human rights obligations.[51]

Additionally, the constraints and challenges existing in the System have resulted in a significant backlog and delays. On average, cases in front of the Commission can take six and a half years from the submission of the petition to a final merits decision.[52] While the Commission has not set time limits on cases, it has implemented measures to combat this challenge by deciding to dedicate special attention and resources to the backlog. Especially in the last several years, it has achieved notable advances in addressing delays in the initial evaluation of petitions determining whether they meet the requirements for processing. In December 2014, the Commission formed a Procedural Delay Group to review and evaluate 6,405 petitions.[53] At the same time, the Commission introduced the

---

[49] IACHR, "Report on Poverty and Human Rights in the Americas," September 7, 2017, OEA/Ser.L/V/II.164, Doc. 147, 151–169: addressing the key successes and challenges in reducing poverty within states in the region; see also *Urrutia Laubreaux v. Chile* [2020], IACtHR, Request for Provisional Measures: deciding on provisional measures for Chile after the Chilean courts penalized judge Daniel Urrutia Laubreaux for declaring arrests of some protestors illegal.

[50] See IACHR, "Reform Process 2012—Consultation on Module II: Precautionary Measures," <https://www.oas.org/en/iachr/consultation/2_measures.asp> (accessed January 5, 2022).

[51] See IACHR, "Annual Report 2018," Chapter II: System of Individual Petitions and Cases, 73: petitions approved for reports on the merits fluctuated from a height of thirty-eight in 1999 to its lowest of twelve in 2012, and rose to forty-three in 2018, <https://www.oas.org/en/iachr/multimedia/statistics/statistics.html> (accessed January 5, 2022); IACHR, "Thematic Rapporteurships and Units": topics both extended to various areas such as freedom of expression and the internet to more specific reports on internal displacement in the Northern Triangle of Central America, <https://www.oas.org/en/iachr/mandate/rapporteurships.asp> (accessed January 5, 2022); and IACHR, "Country Reports": there have been twelve country reports in the last decade, available at <https://www.oas.org/en/iachr/reports/country.asp> (accessed January 5, 2022).

[52] Human Rights Clinic, University of Texas School of Law, "Maximizing Justice, Minimizing Delay: Streamlining Procedures of the Inter-American Commission on Human Rights" [2011], <https://law.utexas.edu/wp-content/uploads/sites/11/2015/04/2012-HRC-IACHR-Maximizing-Justice-Report.pdf> (accessed January 5, 2022).

[53] IACHR Press Release, No. 257/18, "IACHR completes 2 years of its Procedural Backlog Reduction Program and announces new actions approved following a second round of its

Registration Group to review petitions within a year of their filing. Furthermore, the Commission joins petitions and cases together, when permitted, to conserve resources. Additionally, the Commission streamlined and simplified some procedural phases, such as its admissibility report process, to remove repetitions and unnecessary delays.[54] An important step to address these challenges is the Commission's Strategic Plan for 2017–2021, including the need to deal with admissibility and merits.[55] Following the completion of the plan, the Commission undertook a detailed monitoring of its results and found that, over the five years of implementing the plan, the IACHR "improved and modernized institutional management, furthered the results-based approach, obtained historic gains in each of its objectives, and attained results that had a significant impact on the countries of the region."[56] During the relevant period, the Commission saw a 412 percent increase in the number of admissibility reports were approved, a 324percent increase in the number of merits reports approved, and a 181percent increase in the number of cases referred to the Inter-American Court.[57]

An example of the Commission's ability to rapidly respond to new challenges was its response to the COVID-19 pandemic. The Commission instituted its Rapid and Integrated Response Coordination Unit, known by its Spanish acronym SACROI, to address its institutional capacity during the crisis. The group's work plan included monitoring and analyzing State measures, precautionary measures, the coordination of petitions and cases relevant to the crisis, training of State officials to strengthen capacity, public communication vis-à-vis the international community, and information exchanges with international and civil society organizations.[58] The Commission issued weekly statements and resolutions addressing key concerns as the crisis continued to develop, and switched to hosting its meeting online. Webinars on issues such as the right to health and national institutions helped provide information to the region and build conversations around the pandemic.[59] The crisis created by COVID-19 laid

---

participatory process of consultations," 8 December 2019: (describing two-year long review process and measures implemented as a result, available at <https://www.oas.org/en/iachr/media_center/PReleases/2018/257.asp> (accessed January 5, 2022).

[54] Ibid.
[55] See IACHR, "Strategic Plan: 2017–2021" (n.46), 23: acknowledges the need to rethink how far the Commission's recommendations go towards member states' compliance and creating measurable, uniform methods to evaluate compliance; the 2019 annual report shows progress: 151 admissibility reports and 62 merits reports, but not enough to anticipate a timely response to current numbers. As of that report, there were 4,757 cases pending.
[56] IACHR, "Strategic Plan 2023–2027", OAE/Ser.L/V/II.185 at 18 (October 31, 2022).
[57] Id. at 19.
[58] See IACHR, "SACROI Covid-19," <https://www.oas.org/en/IACHR/jsForm/?File=/en/iachr/sacroi_covid19/default.asp> (accessed January 5, 2022).
[59] See IACHR Webinars, <https://www.oas.org/es/cidh/sacroi_covid19/webinars.asp> (accessed January 5, 2022).

bare the issues of social inequality and exclusion that the System has attempted to address from a human rights perspective. The rapid reaction by the Commission established the presence of the human rights System and reaffirmed the value of human rights norms during emergencies and crises.

However, another continuing challenge is the region's struggle to combat increasing levels of violence and authoritarian tendencies, which makes the Commission's regional legitimacy paramount. Accordingly, the different measures the Commission has taken to respond to the human rights needs of the region and improve its procedures are essential. It is important to recognize that this effort does not rely entirely on the Commission. The Commission has been and continues to be an important player, but it does not operate in a vacuum: the behavior of States; the role of civil society, non-governmental organizations (NGOs), and academia; and ideological trends concerning the value of human rights and democracy continue to affect the Commission and the inter-American System as a whole.

4. Concluding Remarks

The Inter-American Commission on Human Rights has played various roles throughout its history. Its three interrelated phases display an evolution of human rights as the Commission has confronted dictatorships, embraced new democracies, and searched for a human rights solution to the challenges facing the region. As stated before, there are elements of those phases that continue to be present in region. This is illustrated, for instance, in a possible reversion to authoritarianism in some countries. To confront those challenges, the Commission is able resort to all the mechanisms it developed in its history, including country and thematic reports, *in loco* observations, and individual petitions.

By centering itself on human rights obligations acquired by States, the Commission has consistently promoted and protected human rights standards in each phase of its history by employing different instruments appropriate for the historical moment. First, it began a forceful effort to maintain and secure notions of human rights in the region during a period plagued by dictatorships and mass human rights violations. In this phase, there were generally no domestic legal avenues for victims of dictatorial regimes.[60] Accordingly, the Commission in the main resorted to country reports. Second, as the Western Hemisphere moved from dictatorships to democracies, a space opened up to allow the Commission to address individual complaints through its case system.[61] Its

---

[60] See *supra*, section 2.1.
[61] See *supra*, section 2.2.

decisions catalyzed change domestically by bringing forth direct consequences for violations of human rights. The case system was essential in dealing with the legacy of dictatorships, as well as with the need to create more inclusive societies. Today, the Commission is countering the resurgence of authoritarian and populist ideologies through country reports and individual petitions.[62] Additionally, the Commission wields the powerful instrument of thematic reports to formulate general observations and influence public policies for the promotion and protection of human rights in the region.[63]

The challenges to the Commission's independence and the limited State cooperation in certain areas conspire against the full realization of the Commission's goals of protecting and promoting human rights.[64] The case system is underfunded[65] and it suffers from unacceptable delays,[66] leading to justifiable criticisms from victims and NGOs. The Commission's broad range of functions led to arguments that these roles are too broad and contradict each other. However, as seen during 2019, when comparing the different intensities of social protests in Venezuela, Bolivia, and Nicaragua with protests in Chile, Ecuador, and Colombia,[67] a broad mandate appears to be justified. The reality for human rights violations in the region requires an adaptable mandate and narrowing the Commission's operational capacity would contradict that goal.

The scope and character of the Commission is important to allow for changing domestic circumstances. This chapter presented the three historical phases, with each demonstrating the variety of the Commission's roles and necessary techniques used to tackle the historical changes in the region. Derived from its mandate to observe and protect human rights, the Commission helped foster social, cultural, and legal change in the human rights conditions throughout the region. However, the future of the Inter-American System is not guaranteed. The threats posed by ideologies that deny the value of human rights cannot be underestimated. Yet vibrant civil societies, existing State support within the region, and the Commission's adaptability, validity, and resilience create an important space and legitimacy for the human rights system.

---

[62] See *supra*, section 2.3.
[63] Ibid.
[64] Flávia Piovesan, "Ius Constitutionale Commune latinoamericano en derechos humanos e impacto del Sistema Interamericano: rasgos, potencialidades y desafíos," in Armin von Bogandy, Héctor Fix Fierro, and Mariela Morales Antoniazzi (eds.), *Ius Constitutionale Commune en América Latina. Rasgos, potencialidades y desafíos* (IIJ-UNAM-MPIL-IIDC 2014), 61–84.
[65] See IACHR, "Strategic Plan: 2017–2021" (n.46), 22.
[66] ibid.
[67] See *supra* section 2.3.

I.3
Inter-American Human Rights System
Sociopolitical, Institutional, and Cultural Dimensions of Its Transformative Impact

By Mariela Morales Antoniazzi, Flávia Piovesan, and Júlia Cortez da Cunha Cruz

1. Introduction

The purpose of this chapter is to analyze the sociopolitical, institutional, and cultural dimensions of the transformative impact of the Inter-American Human Rights System (Inter-American System, or IAHRS). Three main questions guide our analysis:

1. Why do we need the Inter-American System?
2. What are the key structuring components of the Inter-American System?
3. How can one understand transformative impact, taking into account sociopolitical, institutional, and cultural dimensions?

The WHY question prompts our in-depth analysis of the unique regional context, in order to understand the structural and contemporary challenges facing the Americas, which have been aggravated during the COVID-19 pandemic. The WHAT question leads us to describe the central structuring components of the Inter-American System. We emphasize the "victim-centric approach," inter-American standards (the inter-American *corpus juris*), and comprehensive reparations. Finally, the HOW question requires us to address the sociopolitical, institutional, and cultural elements that enable the Inter-American System to foster structural transformations in the national societies that adhere to it.[1]

---

[1] According to Par Engstrom, "Analytically, there is an important distinction between 'compliance' and 'effectiveness' that is often glossed over in human rights and international law scholarship. Effectiveness, rather than a limited focus on rule compliance, generally refers to the degree to which the international human rights institutions work to improve human rights conditions and decrease the likelihood of the repetition of abuses, while also providing satisfactory recourse to the victims."

These driving questions enable us to approach the issue of the IAHRS's impact from a holistic perspective, placing it in context with the challenges and tensions of the region. We argue that the Inter-American System reflects a regional substantive commitment to human rights that serves as a complementary tool for national mechanisms, and therefrom derives its emancipatory role and impact. Three constitutive elements drive this impact: institutional, sociopolitical, and cultural.

The institutional element refers to institutions and norms involved in the implementation of inter-American standards, for example, procedures for the implementation of Inter-American Court of Human Rights (the Court, or IACtHR) decisions or for Inter-American Commission on Human Rights (the Commission, or IACHR) engagement with situations requiring attention. The sociopolitical element highlights the actions of relevant stakeholders who mobilize institutions from within or pressure them from outside. The cultural element provides the social basis that catalyzes—or impedes—actions related to the IAHRS. These three elements interact continuously, in a dynamic process that varies according to the context. Sometimes, impact will appear to be a direct result of effective implementation mechanisms. At other times, the sociopolitical and cultural dimensions will appear to have a more definitive role. In any case, however, understanding the impact of the IAHRS requires an analysis of how all three elements, institutions, politics and culture, interacted.

2. WHY Do We Need the Inter-American System?

2.1. Structural Challenges

In Latin America, 30.8 percent of the population lives in poverty and 11.5 percent in extreme poverty.[2] The region has some of the highest levels of inequality in the world.[3] Systematic, historical, and structural patterns of discrimination, exclusion, and violence affect Afro-descendant and Indigenous peoples in the region.

We see the political, institutional, and cultural dimensions of impact as the different components that can be used to identify the "effectiveness" of the Inter-American Human Rights System; Par Engstrom, *The Inter-American Human Rights System: Impact Beyond Compliance* (Springer 2019).

[2] ECLAC, "Social Panorama of Latin America" (2019), <https://repositorio.cepal.org/bitstream/handle/11362/44989/1/S1901132_en.pdf> (accessed February 22, 2022(.

[3] In 2017, seven of the twenty countries with the highest Gini coefficient were in Latin America: Costa Rica, Panama, Brazil, Colombia, Bolivia, Guatemala, and Honduras. The Gini coefficient is the measure of the deviation of the distribution of income among individuals or households within a country from a perfectly equal distribution. A value of zero represents absolute equality, whereas a value of 100 indicates absolute inequality. For more details, see <http://hdr.undp.org/en/composite/IHDI> (accessed February 22, 2022).

Indigenous peoples and Afro-descendants are disproportionately represented among the poor and the extremely poor.[4] Women are also overrepresented in these groups due to the feminization of poverty.[5]

The region is also the most violent in the world. Latin America represents 8 percent of the world's population and 33 percent of the world's homicides, with an average homicide rate that corresponds to three times the global average. Eight of the world's ten countries with the highest homicide rates are located in Latin America, as well as forty-three of the fifty most homicidal cities.[6] These endemic levels of violence include not only criminal violence but also acts committed by repressive State forces and selective political violence against human rights defenders, political opponents, and independent journalists.[7]

At the same time, the region faces persistent challenges relating to the rule of law. Over half of the countries in the region are placed in the bottom half of Transparency International's Corruption Perception Index (2018),[8] the Worldwide Governance Indicators Project (2018),[9] and the Rule of Law Index (2020).[10] The 2018 Latinobarómetro survey found that Latin Americans generally classify corruption as the fourth biggest problem in the region and that it was thought to be the first or second most serious problem in seven[11] out of eighteen countries. Weak governance structures are associated not only with violations of

---

[4] According to the World Bank, Indigenous peoples are overrepresented among those living in extreme poverty in several countries in Latin America. Individuals in Indigenous households also have lower chances of completing primary and secondary education, leading Indigenous peoples to extreme underrepresentation in high-skill jobs (The World Bank, *Indigenous Latin America in the Twenty-First Century* [World Bank 2015]). At the same time, Afro-descendants are overrepresented among those subject to poverty and under-represented among those who have access to higher education (The World Bank, *Afro-descendants in Latin America: Toward a Framework of Inclusion* [World Bank 2018]).

[5] This term was coined by sociologist Diane Pearce in 1978, in an article entitled "Feminization of Poverty: Women, Work and Welfare." Pearce used empirical data to demonstrate that US women suffered higher degrees of poverty and dependence on the welfare system in comparison with US men. Diane Pearce, "The Feminization of Poverty: Women, Work and Welfare" [1978] 11 *Urban Social Change Review* 28.

[6] Data available in the Igarapé Institute report entitled "Citizen Security in Latin America: Facts and Figures," released in April 2018. Igarapé Institute, Strategic Paper 33, 2015.

[7] Sabine Kurtenbach, "The Limits of Peace in Latin America" [2019] 7 *Peacebuilding* 284.

[8] In the 2018 index, only seven Latin American countries (Costa Rica, Chile, Uruguay, Cuba, Suriname, the Bahamas, and Jamaica) obtained a score higher than 40, on a scale from 0 to 100.

[9] The 2018 Worldwide Governance Indicators Project looks at several categories, namely, Voice and Accountability, Political Stability and Absence of Violence/Terrorism, Government Effectiveness, Regulatory Quality, Rule of Law, and Control of Corruption. On a scale of 0 to 100, most Latin American countries have obtained scores under 50 in all categories, with the exception of Voice and Accountability.

[10] Of the ten countries that had the lowest scores in the 2020 Rule of Law Index, two (Bolivia and Venezuela) are in Latin America. Furthermore, fourteen countries in the region (Venezuela, Bolivia, Nicaragua, Honduras, Mexico, Guatemala, Dominican Republic, Belize, Ecuador, El Salvador, Peru, Colombia, Suriname, and Guyana) had scores of 0.50 or lower (in a scale from 0.0 to 1.0) in terms of adherence to the rule of law.

[11] Colombia, Peru, Brazil, Mexico, Paraguay, Dominican Republic, and Bolivia (see 59).

civil and political rights—such as the rights to access information and to effective participation in public affairs, for example—but also indirectly affect the enjoyment of social and economic rights.[12]

Crucially, historical experience demonstrates that many countries in the region tend toward the centralization of power, which in some cases has generated the phenomenon known as hyper-presidentialism.[13] Ignoring the structure of checks and balances, many Latin American presidents have usurped functions belonging to the legislative or judicial branches (for example, governing through executive decrees and abusing the prerogatives of special judicial fora) or have intervened directly in the structure of these branches.[14] This trend is not unique to Latin America. Both historical analyses and recent research demonstrate that similar structural deficits are present in other regions.[15] Nevertheless, it is crucial to highlight that although the democratization process that took place in several Latin American countries in the past few decades strengthened the protection of rights,[16] it failed to achieve the in-depth institutional reforms necessary to consolidate democracy and strengthen the rule of law. The region still struggles with the legacy of past dictatorial regimes, a culture of violence and impunity,[17] weak rule of law, and a precarious tradition of respect for human rights.

---

[12] With regard to corruption, the IACHR has observed that "states are unable to meet their human rights obligations when corruption is widespread. On the contrary, the denial of rights such as the rights to health, food, education and housing are some of the terrible consequences that corruption in Latin American countries causes. Corruption also encourages discrimination and deprives historically excluded and discriminated-against persons of income, which also prevents them from exercising their rights, whether civil and political rights, or ESCER." *Report on the Situation of Human Rights in Venezuela* [2017] IACtHR, OEA/Ser.L/V/II, para. 412; *Corruption and Human Rights in the Americas: Inter-American Standards* [2019] OEA/Ser.L/V/II.

[13] Santiago Basabe-Serrano, "The Different Faces of Presidentialism: Conceptual Debate and Empirical Findings in Eighteen Latin American Countries" [2017] 157 *Revista Española de Investigaciones Sociológicas* 3.

[14] Ibid.

[15] See, e.g., the research on systemic deficiencies in the rule of law in Europe by Armin von Bogdandy, "Principles of a systemic deficiencies doctrine: How to protect checks and balances in the Member States" [2020] 3 *Common Market Law Review* 705.

[16] An analysis conducted by Par Engstrom and Peter Low ("Mobilizing the Inter-American Human Rights System: Regional Litigation and Domestic Human Rights Impact in Latin America," in Par Engstrom (ed.), *The Inter-American Human Rights System: Impact Beyond Compliance* [Springer 2019]); shows that litigation was three times as frequent in 2014 as it had been in 1999, an increase that could be attributed to, among other factors, the democratization that took place in several Latin American countries during this period and allowed for greater access to human rights bodies.

[17] According to the 2017 Global Impunity Index (available at https://www.udlap.mx/cesij/files/IGI-2017_eng.pdf), which evaluated the structural and functional dimensions of their justice and security systems of sixty-nine countries, twelve out of the twenty countries with the worst impunity are in Latin America (Guatemala, Ecuador, Panama, El Salvador, Honduras, Paraguay, Nicaragua, Colombia, Brazil, Venezuela, Peru, and Mexico).

2.2. Contemporary Challenges

In addition to the structural challenges mentioned previously—deep inequality, epidemic violence, and weak rule of law—Latin America confronts contemporary challenges, such as the rise of populism, re-militarization and strengthened anti-rights movements.

In the past decade, there has been an increase in the number of democratically elected presidents who have steered their countries toward authoritarian populism, nationalism, unilateralism, and a restrictive concept of State sovereignty. One of these leaders' particularly worrying tactics is scapegoating groups in situations of vulnerability. Many populist leaders, for example, blame socio-economic minorities and immigrants for economic deterioration, claiming that the solution for these problems is an "absolute democracy" in which only the voice of the majority would be heard. They state that institutions and systems of checks and balances that protect minorities and marginalized groups need to be abolished so that the will of the people can prevail.[18] This is part of a global trend of democracies being weakened from within.[19]

Along with the rise of populist leaders, there has been a constant decrease in support for democracy. In 2018, the Latinobarómetro survey[20] on support for democracy in Latin America found that only 48 percent of interviewees considered democracy to be preferable to any other form of government.[21] Eight years before, 61 percent of interviewees supported democracy.[22] At the same time, an increase was reported among those "indifferent to the type of regime"[23]—rising from 16 percent in 2010 to 28 percent in 2018. According to the Pew Research Center, in 2017, nondemocratic alternatives[24] were supported by 23 percent of interviewees in Brazil, 27 percent in Mexico, and 18 percent in Argentina.[25]

---

[18] Yascha Mounk, *The People v. Democracy* (Harvard University Press 2018), 8.

[19] See Steven Levitsky and Daniel Ziblatt, *How Democracies Die* (Crown 2018); David Runciman, *How Democracy Ends* (Profile Books 2018); Jason Brennan, *Against Democracy* (Princeton University Press 2018); Mounk (n. 18); Tom Ginsburg and Aziz Z. Huq, *How to Save a Constitutional Democracy* (University of Chicago Press 2018).

[20] Corporación Latinobarómetro, *Informe 2018* (Santiago, 2018).

[21] This survey was conducted between July 15 and August 2, 2018, with 20,204 persons from eighteen Latin American countries and an estimated margin of error of 3 percent per country.

[22] Corporación Latinobarómetro (n. 20), 14.

[23] According to the survey (p. 14), individuals who identify themselves as "indifferent" to the type of regime usually do not identify themselves with either the left or the right, do not belong to a political party, and might eventually alienate themselves from politics altogether by, for example, choosing not to vote.

[24] The nondemocratic alternatives suggested in the study were "rule by experts," "rule by a strong leader," and "rule by the military."

[25] Pew Research Center, "Globally, Broad Support for Representative and Direct Democracies—but many also endorse nondemocratic alternatives" (October 2017), <https://www.pewresearch.org/global/2017/10/16/globally-broad-support-for-representative-and-direct-democracy> (accessed February 3, 2022).

Across the seven Latin American countries included in the survey,[26] only one in every five interviewees reported a commitment to representative democracy. As for trust in public institutions, Latin Americans' trust in legislatures and political parties had decreased significantly: these institutions were supported by 21 percent and 13 percent of interviewees, respectively, as opposed to 34 percent and 23 percent in 2010.[27]

The trends toward populism and decreasing support for democracy pose a direct challenge to the belief that the end of dictatorships would pave the way for the long-term consolidation of democracies oriented around human rights.[28] Although there have been improvements in human rights protection and some strengthening of democratic institutions, these advances are threatened by the growth of authoritarian populism in a highly polarized context, characterized by hate speech, political violence, and ideologies of superiority based on differences. It should be noted that these ideologies are not restricted to one end of the political spectrum.

Additionally, after a long history of militarized politics in Latin America, democratization brought the hope of reduced military influence over civilian affairs. In recent years, however, there have been signs of re-militarization in several aspects of civilian life.

At the request of seventeen organizations from ten different countries, the Inter-American Commission on Human Rights (Inter-American Commission, or IACHR) hosted a public hearing in December 2018 on the increase in militarization across the region, especially in Argentina, Honduras, Guatemala, El Salvador, Brazil, the United States, and Mexico.[29] This trend is apparent not only

---

[26] Brazil, Chile, Mexico, Argentina, Venezuela, Colombia, and Peru.

[27] It is important to note that support for democracy decreased at the same time as frustrations relating to socioeconomic development increased. As indicated by Laura Chinchilla, "[b]etween 2003 and 2011, overall per capita income in the region rose by 3 percent on average (World Bank 2011). Our share in the world economy rose from 5 percent to 8 percent in that period (World Bank 2011). However, since 2013 the tide has turned, and optimism and euphoria have transformed into caution and concern. Ever since Latin America's boom came to a sudden end, some countries have struggled to avoid negative growth rates while others have faced modest to minimal growth." Laura Chinchilla, "Latin America: A Pending Assignment," in Michael Shifter and Bruno Binetti (eds.), *Unfulfilled Promises: Latin America Today* (The Dialogue 2019), 4.

[28] These challenges to democracy should be understood in context. As indicated by Dieter Nohlen, "if we situate the challenges of democracy in Latin America in a broader context, the interdependence of the different sets of problems becomes clear. Therein lies, first of all, the democratic institutional framework as such, its structure and capacity to function, including that of the elites that compete politically with each other and run the institutions; then the political culture, the attitude of the population and the different social sectors towards the institutions and the political elites, and, finally, the economic and social results of the democratic system. The relationship between these three sets of problems is established through the concept of legitimacy and, at the operational level, the concept of governance." Dieter Nohlen, "Democracia, Transición y Gobernabilidad en América Latina" (UNAM 2016), 42 [translation by the authors].

[29] The video of the public hearing is available at <https://www.youtube.com/watch?v=dqURO4UprCs>.

in political rhetoric, as political leaders frequently use military language to describe policies to "combat" drugs and terrorism, but also in the use of military tactics in public security and the formal militarization of police forces (meaning that certain sectors of the police are considered as part of the military or that the military performs public security roles).

According to a report by Argentina's Center for Legal and Social Studies (CELS), the legacy of military dictatorships in Latin America contributes to a high level of trust in military forces as agents of domestic policing.[30] At the same time, a "new threats" military ideology advocates increased involvement of the military in efforts to counter transnational crime networks, as well as to address other issues, such as poverty and migration. The resulting militarization of police forces in countries such as Mexico has led to increased police violence and lethality, a trend exacerbated by the passage of laws that remove safeguards against police brutality.[31] Military laws, moreover, are often lenient on the use of violence, and military personnel often are subject neither to regular courts nor to the accountability and information duties of regular police forces.

The broad jurisdiction of military courts in Latin America is a recurrent theme in the work of the IAHRS. The IACtHR has issued several decisions recommending that States abolish military courts' jurisdiction over crimes committed against civilians.[32] Those decisions, however, have had a low rate of compliance. In recent years, the Inter-American Commission has expressed concern[33] about the expansion of the jurisdiction of military courts in certain countries. In Brazil, for example, the Military Criminal Code was amended to grant military courts jurisdiction over homicides committed by members of the military against the civilian population.[34]

In several countries, the strong presence of the military in politics dates back to before the dictatorships and, even where their protagonism has been more discreet since democratization, they still influence public debates, especially those related to public security.[35] Several countries, including Brazil, Chile, Peru, and Colombia, have elected political leaders supported by the military in the

---

[30] Center for Legal and Social Studies, "Internal War—How the War on Drugs has been Militarizing Latin America." Spanish version available at <https://www.cels.org.ar/militarizacion/>.

[31] Denisse Legrand, "La militarización de la seguridad y la política en América Latina," *La Diaria* (Montevideo, November 16, 2019), <https://ladiaria.com.uy/articulo/2019/11/la-militarizacion-de-la-seguridad-y-la-politica-en-america-latina/> (accessed January 4, 2022).

[32] E.g., *Loayza Tamayo v. Peru* [1997] IACtHR, Ser. C No 33; *Lori Berenson-Mejía v. Peru* [2004] IACtHR, Ser. C No 119; *Radilla Pacheco v. Mexico* [2009] IACtHR, Ser. C No 209.

[33] IACHR, "UN Human Rights and IACHR categorically reject bill expanding jurisdiction of military courts in Brazil" (October 13, 2017), <https://www.oas.org/es/cidh/prensa/comunicados/2017/160.asp> (accessed January 4, 2022).

[34] Law n. 13.491/2017.

[35] Elvira Cuadra, "Primer Congreso de Seguridad Incluyente y Sostenible," *La Diaria* (Montevideo. November 16, 2019), <https://ladiaria.com.uy/articulo/2019/11/la-militarizacion-de-la-seguridad-y-la-politica-en-america-latina/> (accessed January 4, 2022).

past few years. Meanwhile, in Bolivia, the armed forces responded to popular demonstrations against the government by asking then President Evo Morales to step down.[36]

In several countries throughout Latin America there has also been an increase in the influence of groups that advocate against human rights. In many cases, these anti-rights movements are associated with religious leaders who oppose reproductive rights, LGBTIQ+ rights, and gender equality.[37] The growth of evangelical groups in a historically Catholic region has added to the influence of religion on politics.[38] For example, several current presidents are supported by strong evangelical leaders.

One of the effects of the increase in the power of religious and anti-rights groups has been setbacks in LGBTIQ+ rights. Although they have made substantial progress since the late 2000s, LGBTIQ+ rights recently have come under attack from religious groups even in the context of the IACtHR, where evangelical groups have used strategic litigation to challenge rights such as same-sex marriage, arguing that freedom of religion allows individuals and institutions to refuse services to same-sex couples. Religious and conservative groups also have organized anti-LGBTIQ+ marches in several Latin American countries (including Brazil, Chile, Colombia, Dominican Republic, Mexico, and Peru),[39] and have protested several LGBTIQ+-related advances, such as marriage equality and LGBTIQ+ representation in political institutions.[40] Some religious and anti-rights groups have also fought policies intended to curb discrimination, especially within educational institutions. In many cases, these groups claim that they are fighting so-called "gender ideology," an umbrella term used to cast a negative light on policies and actions that seek to protect women and LGBTIQ+ people from discrimination.

---

[36] The protests began after the Organization of American States (OAS) published the results of an audit conducted during the elections of October 20, 2019. The OAS concluded that there had been striking irregularities in the election process. The population then took to the streets to demand new elections and continued to do so for eighteen days.

[37] René Urueña has analyzed the growth of evangelicalism as a political force in Latin America as a shift from a "private" to a "public" mindset in terms of faith and religious practice. For a full exploration of this change, as well as its consequences for human rights in the region, see Rene Urueña, "Reclaiming the Keys to the Kingdom (of the World): Evangelicals and Human Rights in Latin America" [2019] *Netherlands Yearbook of International Law* 175.

[38] Pew Research Center, *Religion in Latin America: Widespread Change in Historically Catholic Region*, 2014.

[39] Javier Corrales, "The Expansion of LGBT Rights in LA and the Backlash," in Michael J. Bosia, Sandra M. McEvoy, and Momin Rahman (eds.), *The Oxford Handbook of Global LGBT and Sexual Diversity Politics* (Oxford University Press 2020), 190.

[40] As described by René Urueña: "Ever since 2010, the recognition of new LGBTI rights has been systematically met with a backlash from Evangelical groups, who discredit and resist such advances in the region. This process has created a dynamic of action and reaction that often features, first, an achievement often pushed by progressive civil society organizations (such as same-sex marriage), which is met by the reaction by a network of religious conservative activists, who put pressure on public institutions to scale back the achievement gained in the first place." Urueña (n. 37), 21.

These anti-rights movements have resulted in concrete actions and omissions by States of the region. In 2017, for example, Paraguay's Ministry of Education and Sciences issued Resolution No. 29.664, which prohibits the dissemination and use of educational materials referring to "gender theory and/or ideology." The State thus prevented its educational institutions from teaching and discussing gender inequality, raising awareness about discrimination, and fostering a non-violent, rights-based culture. As highlighted by the IACHR in a press release, this decision contradicted the right to equality and non-discrimination.[41]

Past, current, and potential future setbacks in the protection of LGBTIQ+ rights are especially worrisome because, despite recent progress, there is still much work to be done to consolidate LGBTIQ+ rights in the hemisphere.[42] Of particular concern is the fact that nine countries in the region still criminalize homosexuality (Guyana, Grenada, Barbados, Saint Vincent and the Grenadines, Saint Lucia, Dominica, Antigua and Barbuda, Saint Kitts and Nevis, and Jamaica).[43]

2.3. The Aggravation of Challenges in Times of Crisis

This context of shared challenges and tensions sheds light on why the region still needs the Inter-American Human Rights System. Times of crisis make these challenges even more acute, reinforcing the necessity of human rights mechanisms. The COVID-19 pandemic has been a strong reminder of this. Human rights violations were hidden among legitimate efforts to fight the pandemic in many countries. From a human rights perspective, Latin America entered a regional state of emergency.

The pandemic is the biggest global health emergency in at least a century and perhaps the most challenging global crisis since the creation of international human rights systems. Its immediate impacts on the rights to health and life are severe. At the same time, the indirect impacts of the virus and the measures to contain it have affected the economic security of millions of individuals, creating enormous risks to a wide range of economic, as well as social, cultural and environmental, rights. Moreover, global experience demonstrates that fighting the virus effectively—and therefore protecting the economic, social, and cultural rights threatened by it—depends on the full protection of civil and political

---

[41] IACHR, "IACHR Regrets Ban on Gender Education in Paraguay" (December 15, 2017), <https://www.oas.org/en/iachr/media_center/PReleases/2017/208.asp> (accessed January 4, 2022).

[42] For more information, see *Advances and Challenges towards the Recognition of the Rights of LGBTI Persons in the Americas* [2018] IACHR, OEA/Ser.L/V/II.170 Doc. 184.

[43] See ILGA, "Sexual Orientation Laws in the World" (2019), <https://ilga.org/downloads/ILGA_World_map_sexual_orientation_laws_December2019.pdf> (accessed January 4, 2022).

rights, such as access to information and freedom of expression. As such, the pandemic reinforces the interdependence and indivisibility of all human rights. Interestingly, it does so by demonstrating that the enjoyment of civil and political rights is necessary for the full protection of economic, social, cultural, and environmental rights (ESCER), an inversion of the usual argument that ESCER must be judicialized as necessary components of the enjoyment of civil and political rights.[44]

Although the virus does not discriminate, high levels of inequality in Latin America lead to disproportionate impacts on groups in situations of vulnerability.[45] In addition to difficulties in accessing adequate healthcare, those living in poverty and extreme poverty are less able to implement prevention measures—such as washing hands and social distancing—due to insufficient access to water, sanitation, and housing. At the same time, a substantial number of families living in poverty rely on informal labor, which means they are most exposed to the economic impacts of the crisis. Because poverty affects Afro-descendant and Indigenous groups disproportionately, there is also a racial and ethnic dimension to the impacts of the pandemic. In Brazil, the rate of COVID-19 deaths is higher among Black individuals across all segments of the population. The deadly impact of inequality becomes even more apparent when intersectionality is considered. According to the Health Intelligence and Operations Center, a Black illiterate person who is hospitalized in Brazil due to COVID-19 has a 76 percent chance of dying, a rate 3.8 times higher than the likelihood of a White, college-educated patient dying (19.6%).[46]

Noting the particularities of the COVID-19 crisis in a region plagued by systemic inequality, the Inter-American Commission adopted a resolution on human rights in the pandemic[47] and a resolution on the human rights of people with COVID-19.[48] These resolutions provide general recommendations to

---

[44] Flavia Piovesan and Mariela Morales Antoniazzi, "COVID-19 and the Need for a Holistic and Integral Approach to Human Rights Protection" (*VerfBlog*, April 25, 2020), <https://verfassungsblog.de/covid-19-and-the-need-for-a-holistic-and-integral-approach-to-human-rights-protection/> (accessed January 4, 2022).

[45] As noted by the UN Secretary General, "We have seen how the virus does not discriminate, but its impacts do—exposing deep weaknesses in the delivery of public services and structural inequalities that impede access to them." United Nations, "We are all in this together: UNSG delivers policy brief on COVID-19 and human rights." Statement by UN Secretary-General António Guterres (April 23, 2020), <https://www.ohchr.org/EN/NewsEvents/Pages/UNSG_HumanRights_COVID19.aspx> (accessed January 4, 2022).

[46] Amanda Batista et al., "Análise socioeconômica da taxa de letalidade da COVID-19 no Brasil. Núcleo de Operações e Inteligência em Saúde," *Nota Técnica* 11 (May 27, 2020), <https://sites.google.com/view/nois-pucrio/publica%C3%A7%C3%B5es?authuser=0> (accessed January 4, 2022).

[47] Resolution no. 1/2020: Pandemic and Human Rights in the Americas [2020] IACHR, <http://www.oas.org/en/iachr/decisions/pdf/Resolution-1-20-en.pdf> (accessed January 4, 2022).

[48] In Resolution 4/20, the IACHR stressed that the rapid spread of COVID-19 in the Americas was due in part conditions that predated the pandemic, including discrimination, poverty, and inequality, as well as fragile institutions. With this in mind, the Commission reminded States that measures to protect the human rights of individuals with COVID-19 must be intersectional and

protect the rights of all individuals and the democratic system itself, as well as targeted recommendations to protect groups in situations of vulnerability. In addition to observing the aforementioned impacts on the poor,[49] the Commission discusses other groups subject to increased risks. The elderly,[50] persons deprived of liberty,[51] women,[52] Indigenous peoples,[53] migrants,[54] children,[55] LGBTIQ+

multidisciplinary, addressing not only the disease itself but also the differentiated impacts it may have on different groups and fine-tuning measures to their specific needs. The resolution takes a comprehensive approach, highlighting the indivisibility of human rights by approaching the issue from different angles, including the rights to health, consent, equality, privacy, and access justice. See Human Rights of Persons with COVID-19 [2020] IACHR, Resolution No. 4/2020, <http://www.oas.org/en/iachr/decisions/pdf/Resolution-4-20-en.pdf> (accessed January 4, 2022).

[49] See also IACHR, "IACHR and OSRESCER Urge States to Provide Effective Protection for People Living in Poverty and Extreme Poverty in the Americas during the COVID-19 Pandemic" (June 2, 2020), available at <http://www.oas.org/en/iachr/media_center/PReleases/2020/124.asp>.

[50] See also IACHR, "IACHR Urges States to Guarantee the Rights of Older People during the COVID-19 Pandemic" (April 23, 2020), <http://www.oas.org/en/iachr/media_center/PReleases/2020/088.asp> (accessed January 4, 2022). Several UN agencies have also addressed the particularities of protecting the human rights of refugees, migrants, and stateless persons as part of the response to COVID-19. See United Nations, "The rights and health of refugees, migrants and stateless must be protected in COVID-19 response: A joint statement by UNHCR, IOM, OHCHR and WHO" (November 30, 2020), <https://www.ohchr.org/EN/NewsEvents/Pages/DisplayNews.aspx?NewsID=25762&LangID=E> (accessed January 4, 2022)..

[51] See also IACHR, "The IACHR urges States to guarantee the health and integrity of persons deprived of liberty and their families in the face of the COVID-19 pandemic" (March 31, 2020), available at <http://www.oas.org/en/iachr/media_center/PReleases/2020/066.asp> (accessed January 4, 2022); several UN agencies have also addressed the vulnerability of people deprived of liberty during the COVID-19 pandemic. See UNODC, "WHO, UNAIDS and OHCHR joint statement on COVID-19 in prisons and other closed settings," <https://www.ohchr.org/Documents/Events/COVID-19/20200513_PS_COVID_and_Prisons_EN.pdf> (accessed January 4, 2022).

[52] See also IACHR, "The IACHR calls on Member States to adopt a gender perspective in the response to the COVID-19 pandemic and to combat sexual and domestic violence in this context" (April 11, 2020), <http://www.oas.org/en/iachr/media_center/PReleases/2020/074.asp> (accessed January 4, 2022).

[53] See also IACHR, "IACHR Warns of the Specific Vulnerability of Indigenous Peoples to the COVID-19 Pandemic, Calls on States to Adopt Targeted, Culturally Appropriate Measures that Respect These Peoples' Land" (May 6, 2020), <http://www.oas.org/en/iachr/media_center/PReleases/2020/103.asp> (accessed January 4, 2022).

[54] See also IACHR, "The IACHR urges States to protect the human rights of migrants, refugees and displaced persons in the face of the COVID-19 pandemic" (April 27, 2020), <http://www.oas.org/en/iachr/media_center/PReleases/2020/077.asp> (accessed January 4, 2022); the UN High Commissioner for Human Rights has also addressed the specificities of protecting the human rights of older persons during the pandemic. See United Nations, Virtual debate "Human Rights of older persons in the age of COVID-19 and beyond": Statement by the United Nations High Commissioner for Human Rights (May 12, 2020), <https://www.ohchr.org/EN/NewsEvents/Pages/DisplayNews.aspx?NewsID=25879&LangID=E> (accessed January 4, 2022).

[55] See also IACHR, "IACHR Warns of the Effects of the COVID-19 Pandemic on Children and Adolescents" (April 27, 2020), <http://www.oas.org/en/iachr/media_center/PReleases/2020/090.asp> (accessed January 4, 2022); several UN agencies have also drawn attention to the impact of COVID-19 on children, developing an agenda for action to ensure a child rights and multisectoral response to COVID-19. See Inter-Agency Working Group on Violence against Children, "Agenda for Action," <https://www.ohchr.org/Documents/Events/COVID-19/Agenda_for_Action_IAWG-VAC.pdf> (accessed January 4, 2022).

individuals,[56] Afro-descendants,[57] people with disabilities,[58] and human rights defenders[59] all face specific challenges in the context of the pandemic, and States must therefore act in the particular interest of their protection. The Inter-American Court has also issued a statement highlighting the disproportionate impact of the pandemic on some groups:

> Given the nature of the pandemic, the economic, social, cultural and environmental rights must be guaranteed, without discrimination, to every person subject to the State's jurisdiction and, especially, to those groups that are disproportionately affected because they are in a more vulnerable situation, such as older persons, children, persons with disabilities, migrants, refugees, stateless persons, persons deprived of liberty, the LGBTI community, pregnant or post-partum women, indigenous communities, Afro-descendants, those who work in the informal sector, the inhabitants of underprivileged districts or areas, the homeless, those living in poverty, and the health care personnel who are responding to this emergency.[60]

States have a broad obligation to adopt urgent measures to protect the rights to life and health of the whole population, employing the maximum available resources to prevent and mitigate harm associated with the pandemic. This general obligation includes access to water and sanitation, adequate housing, and economic support measures.[61] Given the special risks experienced by the above-mentioned groups, States also have an enhanced duty to protect them. That is

---

[56] See also IACHR, "On the eve of the International Day against Homophobia, Biphobia and Transphobia, the IACHR and various international experts call attention to the suffering and resilience of LGBT people during the COVID-19 pandemic" (May 14, 2020), <http://www.oas.org/en/iachr/media_center/PReleases/2020/110.asp> (accessed January 4, 2022); IACHR, "The IACHR calls on States to guarantee the rights of LGBTI people in the response to the COVID-19 pandemic" (April 20, 2020), <http://www.oas.org/en/iachr/media_center/PReleases/2020/081.asp> (accessed January 4, 2022).

[57] See also IACHR, "IACHR and its Special Rapporteurship on ESCER calls on the States to guarantee the rights of Afro-descendant Persons and prevent racial discrimination in the context of the COVID-19 pandemic" (April 28, 2020), <http://www.oas.org/en/iachr/media_center/PReleases/2020/092.asp> (accessed January 4, 2022).

[58] See also IACHR, "The IACHR Calls on States to Provide Comprehensive Protection for the Lives of People with Disabilities During the COVID-19 Pandemic" (April 8, 2020), <http://www.oas.org/en/iachr/media_center/PReleases/2020/071.asp> (accessed January 4, 2022).

[59] See also IACHR, "IACHR Calls on States to Protect and Preserve the Work of Human Rights Defenders During the COVID-19 Pandemic" (May 5, 2020), <http://www.oas.org/en/iachr/media_center/PReleases/2020/101.asp> (accessed January 4, 2022).

[60] IACtHR, "Covid-19 and human rights: the problems and challenges must be addressed from a human rights perspective and with respect for international obligations," Statement 1/20 (April 9, 2020), <http://www.corteidh.or.cr/docs/comunicados/cp_27_2020_eng.pdf> (accessed January 4, 2022).

[61] Flavia Piovesan, "Rol y Medidas de la CIDH para el combate contra la Covid-19," *Konrad Adenauer Stiftung: Dialogo Derechos Humanos*, <https://dialogoderechoshumanos.com/rol-y-medidas-de-la-cidh-para-el-combate-contra-la-covid-19> (accessed January 4, 2022).

why the IACHR drafted targeted recommendations that, if implemented, would enable States to address the pandemic in light of the particular vulnerabilities of these groups. For example, the IACHR has recommended that States make information available in Indigenous languages, strengthen programs against domestic violence, reconsider cases of pretrial detention, and substitute incarceration for alternative measures.[62] All actions and measures, both general and targeted, must be based on the best scientific evidence and be adopted through transparent, participatory, and inclusive processes.

Nevertheless, human rights, such as the right of assembly, have been restricted in the context of the pandemic. While many of these restrictions are legitimate means of protecting public health, a region facing challenges related to weak rule of law, authoritarianism, and populism is prone to implementing abusive restrictive measures. In its resolution about the pandemic, the Inter-American Commission reiterated that all States must follow international law when designing and applying public health measures. This means that any restrictions must be provided by law, necessary in a democratic society, and strictly proportional to the legitimate purpose of protecting health.[63] States of emergency must also follow strict international law requirements, including temporality and proportionality.

If regional challenges become more acute in times of crisis, the role of human rights protection mechanisms also becomes more salient. During the pandemic, the IAHRS has monitored the situation of human rights in the region and has provided timely responses, centering its operations in the Rapid and Integrated Response Coordination Unit of the IACHR (SACROI-COVID-19).[64] From its inception in March 2020 until mid-May 2020, the SACROI not only drafted the above-mentioned IACHR resolutions, which contain eighty-five recommendations to States about how to implement a human rights–centered response to the pandemic but also analyzed eighty-four precautionary measure requests, requested information from States on twenty-one cases, strengthened channels for direct dialogue with States, held five social forums with civil society, and developed a robust public communication strategy to disseminate information about the pandemic and related human rights topics, which

---

[62] Resolution no. 1/2020: Pandemic and Human Rights in the Americas [2020] IACHR, <http://www.oas.org/en/iachr/decisions/pdf/Resolution-1-20-en.pdf> (accessed January 4, 2022).

[63] According to the Court: "All the measure that States may adopt to address this pandemic and that may impair or restrict the enjoyment and exercise of human rights must be temporarily limited, legal, adjusted to well-defined aims based on scientific criteria, reasonable, absolutely necessary and proportional and in accordance with other requirements developed in Inter-American human rights law." IACtHR, "Covid-19 and human rights: the problems and challenges must be addressed from a human rights perspective and with respect for international obligations," Statement 1/20 (April 9, 2020), <http://www.corteidh.or.cr/docs/comunicados/cp_27_2020_eng.pdf> (accessed January 4, 2022).

[64] See <http://www.oas.org/en/iachr/SACROI_COVID19/>.

included seventeen press releases, thirty-three newsletters, one multimedia website, and three webinars.[65] The impact of these actions can be seen in a series of judicial rulings, policy decisions, and regulations implementing IAHRS recommendations across the region. The IAHRS is expressly cited as a basis for measures implemented in a number of countries, including Argentina, Bolivia, Costa Rica, El Salvador, and Brazil.[66]

In the aftermath of the pandemic, a similar effort will be required to ensure that the medium- and long-term impacts of the crisis are also addressed through a human rights–centered approach. The IAHRS will be called upon to ensure accountability and to order reparations for possible human rights abuses committed during the pandemic.

In post-pandemic times, the imperative to fulfill the mandates of the System by addressing structural inequalities will be more evident than ever. Indivisibility and interdependency of all human rights must continue to be a cornerstone of the work of the IAHRS, as well as of the actions of the human rights community in the region. At the same time, for all stakeholders to come back stronger from COVID-19, they must recognize the all-encompassing impact of structural inequalities on the enjoyment of the human rights of all. Addressing structural inequalities is essential for furthering human rights.

3. WHAT Are the Key Components of the Inter-American System?

Now that we have addressed the question concerning why we need the Inter-American System in present-day Latin America, we turn, in this section, to the structuring components that have oriented the actions and decisions of the IAHRS throughout its existence. We focus on three key elements: the victim-centric approach, IAHRS standards, and comprehensive reparations.

These components are involve different tools and working methods. In addition to the advisory and contentious cases of the Inter-American Court, the Inter-American Commission has developed a hybrid "toolbox" encompassing both political and judicial methods. This includes the case system, precautionary measures, public hearings, friendly settlements, thematic reports, country reports, and *in loco* visits. The three elements explored below are present in each of these different tools, which have been used extensively throughout the Commission's history. On the IACHR's sixtieth anniversary, it had completed

---

[65] IACHR, "IACHR presents balance, impacts and results achieved by its Coordination and Timely Integrated Crisis Response Room for the COVID-19 Pandemic" (May 16, 2020), <http://www.oas.org/en/iachr/media_center/PReleases/2020/114.asp> (accessed January 4, 2022).
[66] Ibid.

172 periods of sessions, 2,335 public hearings, 81 thematic reports, 71 country reports, and 98 *in loco* visits.

3.1. The Victim-Centric Approach

The IAHRS aims to prevent human rights violations and, when these occur, to provide effective remedies that safeguard human dignity. The dialogue between the IAHRS and victims—through *in loco* visits, litigation, or any of its other tools—has been fundamental in shaping the work of the Court and the Commission toward this objective. Often acting as facilitators of the dialogue between the IAHRS and other stakeholders, civil society organizations have guaranteed that victims are heard and have access to the System.

The right of victims to approach the IAHRS and request protection is, by itself, a demonstration of the centrality of the victim in the System. From this starting point, the constant dialogue and engagement with victims and their representatives has led to the creation of institutes that further strengthen the position of the victim as the central stakeholder in the IAHRS. Examples of such improvements include precautionary measures and the creation of inter-American public defenders.

The victim-centric approach is also demonstrated by the types of reparations ordered by the Court, which include not only direct redress but also symbolic reparations and guarantees of nonrepetition. For example, symbolic reparations, such as memorials and commendations,[67] respond to victims' requests that States recognize their suffering and acknowledge their place in society.

3.2. Inter-American Standards

The IAHRS is charged with protecting and promoting human rights in the region with independence and impartiality. The American Declaration of the Rights and Duties of Man (American Declaration) and the American Convention provide the grounds for and delineate the boundaries of this work. Additional protocols and special conventions further expand the inter-American *corpus juris*, as do inter-American standards derived from the work of the Court and the Commission. These standards are present in the statutes of the Court and the Commission, judgments, advisory opinions, reports, and recommendations.[68]

---

[67] E.g., *González et al. ("Cotton Field") v. Mexico* [2009] IACtHR, Ser. C No. 205; *Rio Negro Massacres v. Guatemala* [2012] IACtHR, Ser. C No. 250.

[68] Sergio García Ramirez, "La "Navegación Americana" de los Derechos Humanos: Hacia un Ius Commune," in Armin von Bogdandy et al. (eds.), *Ius Constitutionale Commune en América Latina. Rasgos, Potencialidades y Desafíos* (IIJ-UNAM-MPIL-IIDC 2014), 459–500.

The Inter-American Court considers the *corpus juris* of international human rights law to be comprised of "international instruments of varied content and juridical effects (treaties, conventions, resolutions and declarations)," which should be interpreted in light of their dynamic evolution.[69] According to the Court, the constant evolution of human rights standards has had a positive impact on international law and must be considered in the interpretation and application of inter-American norms.[70] The evolutionary interpretation of inter-American standards has played a significant role in ensuring that the System is able to respond to changing times and contemporary challenges, both in cases involving new aspects of human relations (such as reproduction techniques or digital communications) and in situations in which the law itself has evolved (for example, as related to the justiciability of economic, social, and cultural rights).

Soft law, although not binding, often plays a key role in the evolution of international human rights law. Since it is more flexible, soft law enables the creation of dynamic solutions to complex problems in the region. Procedural and institutional innovations have also helped to guarantee effective protection that goes beyond the original provisions of the American Convention. Examples include special follow-up mechanisms and precautionary measures.[71]

3.3. Comprehensive Reparations

The Inter-American System has ordered comprehensive reparations (*reparación integral*) throughout its history. In its first case, *Velásquez Rodríguez v. Honduras*, the Court assessed material and nonmaterial damages.[72] Since then, the Court has ordered several types of symbolic reparations, the provision of services of the most diverse types to affected populations, and measures of prevention.[73]

The Court typically orders several different kinds of reparations, including: (a) payment of economic compensation for the victims or their

---

[69] Mariela Morales Antoniazzi, "The Rights of Persons Deprived of Liberty in Latin America: From the perspective of an *ius constitucionale commune*," in Clara Burbano and Yves Haeck, *Human Rights Behind Bars* (2022), 118, con referencia a *Advisory Opinion OC-16/99* [1999] IACtHR, §115.

[70] Ibid.

[71] It is worth noting that precautionary measures, one of the key mechanisms for the protection of human rights in Latin America, is not provided for in the American Convention but in the Commission's Rules of Procedure. This does not diminish their binding nature, which has been recognized by the OAS and several member States.

[72] In this opportunity, the Court stated: "Reparation of harm brought about by the violation of an international obligation consists in full restitution (restitutio in integrum), which includes the restoration of the prior situation, the reparation of the consequences of the violation, and indemnification for patrimonial and nonpatrimonial damages, including emotional harm." *Velásquez-Rodríguez v. Honduras* [1989] IACtHR, Ser. C No. 7.

[73] See Claudio Grossman, Agustina del Campo, and Mina Trudeau, *International Law and Reparations: The Inter-American System* (Clarity Press 2018).

families;[74] (b) investigation, prosecution, and punishment of perpetrators, with the adoption of due diligence measures by the State;[75] and (c) adoption of structural changes (such as legal reforms and new public policies) based on guarantees of nonrepetition, including measures directed at protecting the rights of groups in situation of vulnerability[76] and at furthering the effectiveness of economic, social, cultural, and environmental rights.[77] A wide range of measures may be ordered within each category to repair the complex individual and collective damages caused by human right violations.

Comprehensive reparations are so fundamental that they are often incorporated into friendly settlements.[78] The fact that friendly settlements, agreements entered into voluntarily by States and victims, include State commitments to preventive measures, guarantees of nonrepetition, and investigations shows how important comprehensive reparations are to all stakeholders within the IAHRS.

Through comprehensive reparations, the Inter-American System can compensate for States' failures to protect human rights and alter the power dynamics among States, victims, and civil society. The System can also complement the work of national human rights mechanisms, collaborating to strengthen human rights, democracy, and rule of law in the region.

4. How Can One Understand IAHRS Transformative Impact, Taking into Account Its Sociopolitical, Institutional, and Cultural Dimensions?

The Inter-American System has saved and continues to save lives all over Latin America. It has enabled the destabilization of dictatorial regimes;[79] it has

---

[74] The Court ordered payment of economic reparations for victims of human rights violation in its first case. See *Case of Velásquez Rodríguez v. Honduras* [1989] IACtHR, Ser. C No. 7, para. 60.

[75] See, e.g., *Case of Gomes Lund et al. ("Guerrilha do Araguaia") v. Brazil* [2010] IACtHR, Ser. C No. 219, paras. 253–257.

[76] See, e.g., *Case of Azul Rojas Marín et al. v. Peru* [2020] IACtHR, Ser. C No. 402, paras. 238-255.

[77] See, e.g. ,*Case of Cuscul Pivaral et al. v. Guatemala* [2018] Ser. C No. 359, paras. 224–230.

[78] *Natalia Saltalamacchia Ziccardi* et al., "Friendly Settlements in the Inter-American Human Rights System: Efficiency, Effectiveness and Scope," in Par Engstrom (ed.), *The Inter-American Human Rights System: Impact Beyond Compliance* (Springer 2019), 59–88.

[79] The Commission has issued numerous reports condemning the military dictatorships in the region and the human rights violations committed by them, especially after early *in loco* visits, which resulted in reports that primarily emphasized the relationship between democracy, human rights, and political participation. The 1974 report on Chile accused the Pinochet government of several grave violations of human rights, such as the rights to life, personal freedom, and due process. The 1980 report on Argentina formally established the existence of forced disappearances perpetrated by the State. The 2000 report on Peru questioned the legitimacy of the election of Fujimori.

Another strategy is the creation of programs of cooperation among States or State entities to share best practices. A good example is SIMORE (*Sistema de Monitoreo de Recomendaciones Internacionales de Derechos Humanos*). SIMORE is an online platform, created by Paraguay, that allows the State and its citizens to systematize and monitor compliance with decisions from international human rights bodies. The system is used by Paraguay, Chile, Costa Rica, the Dominican Republic, Guatemala, Honduras, and Uruguay. In 2017, Paraguay and the Inter-American Commission entered into an agreement to make SIMORE available to all States.[86]

Inspired by this experience, the IACHR has adopted a similar initiative. In June 2020, the Commission launched the inter-American SIMORE, which builds on the experience of national SIMOREs and aims to enhance monitoring of the Commission's recommendations by increasing the exchange of information with a wide range of stakeholders.[87] Embracing a participatory approach to monitoring, the system makes information available to the public, which enables outside actors to incorporate IACHR recommendations to their human rights work, while at the same time providing the opportunity for all actors to upload their own data on implementation.[88] Moreover, the tool increases the visibility of recommendations made by the IACHR, which may create additional pressure for their implementation. States, eager to avoid gaining a reputation as having too many pending obligations with the international community, may become more willing to facilitate compliance with IAHRS decisions. This may even build momentum for the creation of institutional mechanisms of implementation at

---

The Inter-American Human Rights System [Springer 2019]) describes Latin American States as "disaggregated" or "heterogeneous" (as opposed to "monolithic" or "homogeneous"), meaning that there are tensions between governmental bodies on several issues, including the implementation of human rights, that generate uncoordinated application and even internal conflicts. According to Parra-Vera, interaction with the IAHRS might mitigate those conflicts and disconnects. Even when there are no apparent conflicts, IAHRS standards empower intragovernmental actors to push for human rights–based policies within government structures, navigating complicated frameworks that often involve separate branches governments, federal systems, and various government agencies. National mechanisms for implementation of IAHRS standards institutionalize these processes, enhancing implementation by creating mechanisms that enable internal actors to overcome tensions and to catalyze constructive interactions.

[86] On December 5, 2017, during the Inter-American Human Rights Forum in Washington, the Inter-American Commission, and the State of Paraguay signed a Memorandum of Understanding with the goal of developing a "regional SIMORE" (Sistema de Monitoreo de Recomendaciones), as an effective instrument for systematizing the recommendations and decisions adopted by the Commission, as well as monitoring them in the region. <https://www.oas.org/es/cidh/docs/acuerdos/Memorandum-Paraguay-2017.pdf> (accessed January 4, 2022).

[87] IACHR, "IACHR Launches Inter-American SIMORE to Monitor Its Recommendations" (June 10, 2020), <http://www.oas.org/en/iachr/media_center/PReleases/2020/132.asp> (accessed January 4, 2022).

[88] See <https://www.oas.org/ext/en/human-rights/simore/> (accessed January 4, 2022).

the country level, as well as for the adoption of national SIMOREs by more States in the region.

In addition to the inter-American SIMORE, the Follow-Up of Recommendations Section (*Sección de Seguimiento de Recomendaciones*), established in 2017 as a special division at the Organization of American States (OAS), is also a promising initiative. The section monitors compliance with IACHR decisions. The IACHR has also launched an Impact Observatory, which identifies the impact of recommendations in promoting social change and consolidates lessons learned.[89] In 2019, the IACHR also launched the Specialized Academic Network of Cooperation with the IACHR, aiming to strengthen the Commission's ties with academic institutions through the provision of technical support to thematic Rapporteurships.[90] These institutional arrangements complement one another, as each pursues a different avenue to increase the impact of the IAHRS. These new institutional arrangements also have comprehensive thematic mandates that can adapt to match the challenges facing the region. For example, the Commission has updated the objectives of the first cycle of the academic network, which will now focus on the impact of the IACHR in the protection of human rights in the region, including measures taken within the context of the COVID-19 pandemic.[91] When updating the objectives of the network, the Commission made clear that these initiatives are interconnected and are supposed to complement each other. The academic network, for example, could work on SIMORE data and provide inputs to the Impact Observatory.

In the past few years, the IACHR has also created innovative special mechanisms for monitoring its recommendations in cases of severe human rights violations, such as the Interdisciplinary Group of Independent Experts of Ayotzinapa[92] and the Special Monitoring Mechanism for

---

[89] See IACHR, "Creation of the Inter-American Commission on Human Rights Impact Observatory," Resolution 2/19 (September 22, 2019), <https://www.oas.org/en/iachr/decisions/pdf/Resolution-2-19-en.pdf> (accessed January 4, 2022); see also Flavia Piovesan and Julia Cortez da Cunha Cruz, "Measuring Transformation: At the 50th anniversary of the American Convention on Human Rights, a move to maximize its structural impact," *Harvard International Law Journal*, <https://harvardilj.org/2019/02/measuring-transformation-at-the-50th-anniversary-of-the-american-convention-on-human-rights-a-move-to-maximize-its-structural-impact/> (accessed January 4, 2022).

[90] See IACHR, "Call for the Academic Network of Cooperation with the IACHR," <https://www.oas.org/en/iachr/activities/academic-network/docs/ConvocatoriaRedAcademica-en.pdf> (accessed January 4, 2022).

[91] IACHR, "La CIDH actualiza los objetivos de la Red Académica Especializada y avanza one l Observatorio de Impacto" (July 22, 2020), <http://www.oas.org/es/cidh/prensa/comunicados/2020/172.asp> (accessed January 4, 2022).

[92] In September 2014, the police from the city of Iguala (Mexico) attacked students of Rural School of Ayotzinapa, who were accused of illegally taking the bus. Forty-three students disappeared, nine were killed, and twenty-seven were injured. Following a request for precautionary measures, the IACHR created a mechanism to guarantee the implementation of the measures ordered by the IACHR. The mechanism created the Interdisciplinary Group of Independent Experts of Ayotzinapa, which was charged with overseeing the execution of Precautionary Measures by drawing up search

Nicaragua.[93] The work of these mechanisms builds on the tools of the Inter-American System, following up and coordinating action on precautionary measures, friendly settlements, working meetings, visits, and public hearings.

These institutional innovations at the country level and within inter-American institutions are promising because they strengthen the engagement of States, victims, and civil society with the System. The potential for impact increases institutions also contribute to sociopolitical changes that lead to human rights transformations. Recognizing that the mandate to protect human rights is not fulfilled through the mere publication of a decision, in recent years the IACtHR and the IACHR have increased their proactive role in the implementation process, which involves and depends on various stakeholders.

4.2. Sociopolitical Dimension

For the IAHRS to have an impact requires not only institutions and legal provisions but also actors who mobilize for the implementation of inter-American standards. Bogdandy and Urueña argue that a human rights *community of practice* is a fundamental element in opening domestic constituencies to IAHRS standards and to regional transformative constitutionalism, meaning that NGOs, grassroots organizations, clinics at law schools, domestic courts, civil servants, scholars, the commissioners and judges of the Inter-American system, and also politicians with a human rights agenda are key in transforming domestic contexts in a manner that advances IAHRS standards.[94]

Indeed, the most emblematic cases of IAHRS impact, many of them discussed in this book, involve local actors promoting the implementation of inter-American standards as part of a broad campaign to achieve a specific human rights objective. IAHRS tools and mechanisms are used to document violations, legitimize the claims of the victims, and provide leverage over decision makers. These actions affect the coalition of forces within the State, shifting

---

plans for missing persons, analyzing investigations and the attention given to victims and their families, and drafting recommendations of public policies related to forced disappearances.

[93] In 2018, the Inter-American Commission on Human Rights launched this Special Monitoring Mechanism and sent employees to Nicaragua to monitor the implementation of the IACHR's recommendations in the report "Serious human rights violations in the context of social protests in Nicaragua," as well as compliance with precautionary measures.

[94] Armin von Bogdandy and Rene Urueña, "International Transformative Constitutionalism in Latin America" [2020] 3 *American Journal of International Law* 403. According to the authors, this community of practice "has created a new legal phenomenon that comprises elements of different legal orders connected by a common thrust. A wave of new constitutionalism has created domestic legal settings for a region-wide transformative constitutional project. A community of practice brought such legal standards to life by attributing a core role to the IACtHR. The resulting body of law, in turn, strengthens the broader Latin American human rights community."

key stakeholders from a position of opposition or indifference to human rights obligations toward support for or openness to the implementation of IAHRS standards.

Civil society organizations are fundamental to make this shift happen.[95] Since they are immersed in local realities, they can connect the IAHRS to victims of human rights violations all over the region. Civil society is composed of NGOs, social movements, association of victims and their family members, and more. The roles civil society plays and the strategies it adopts are as diverse as the organizations themselves, meaning that the demands that reach the System and their place in grassroots campaigns are increasingly diverse. The IAHRS is no longer viewed as a mere forum in which to denounce violations but as a tool that can be used by civil society to raise awareness of new issues and to push for social change at the national or regional levels. In general, the work of civil society to transform a human rights situation begins long before these organizations begin to advocate before the IAHRS and finishes long after the IACHR or the IACtHR acts. Institutions provide the basic architecture of the IAHRS, but civil society brings people to these institutions and ensures that the institutions serve their purposes effectively.

Many civil society organizations, however, do not have the capacity to engage with the IAHRS, due to financial constrains or knowledge barriers. To address this problem, some organizations have created transnational issue networks and other types of coalitions. By pooling their resources (drawing on the financial, technical, and even geographical advantages of different organizations), these coalitions improve access to the System and therefore should be encouraged. Nevertheless, more needs to be done to address the systemic challenges that grassroots movements and smaller civil society organizations face when seeking access to the IAHRS.

4.3. Cultural Dimension

The impact of the IAHRS also depends on the degree to which domestic constituencies are open to inter-American standards. In addition to legal provisions that establish the status of international norms within domestic law, the legal culture is a key factor influencing the permeability of inter-American

---

[95] On the participation of civil society in the activities of the Inter-American Commission, see IACHR, "IACHR Expands and Deepens Civil Society Participation in Efforts to Fulfil its Mandate" (February 9, 2019), <https://www.oas.org/en/iachr/media_center/PReleases/2019/031.asp> (accessed January 4, 2022). For a broader approach to human rights mobilization and the role played by civil society, see Beth Simmons, *Mobilizing for Human Rights: International Law in Domestic Politics* (Cambridge University Press 2009); for a more recent take, see Kathryin Sikkink, *Evidence for Hope: Making Human Rights Work in the 21st Century* (Princeton University Press 2017), 211–219.

norms. Studies have shown that, even in countries where there is no legal obligation to adopt the decisions and recommendations of the IAHRS, countries that choose to engage with the System might have higher compliance rates. On the other hand, in countries where there is an express obligation to comply with the decisions of the IAHRS, but the legal culture influences national decisions against implementation, inter-American decisions tend not to be respected.[96] A similar logic may apply beyond the legal system, reaching the conduct of public authorities and the terms of the public debate.

One way to encourage a human rights culture is to integrate human rights into educational systems. Human rights–based educational programs should occur at every level, including primary education, but are especially relevant in legal curricula. Law schools play a defining role in the future of legal systems, as well as in the mindset of public authorities. Therefore, the integration of inter-American standards into legal curricula may prove to be an important means of achieving the transformative impact of the IAHRS. Likewise, the integration of the IAHRS within research agendas encourages knowledge of and engagement with inter-American institutions.

In addition, academic institutions may directly engage with the System, providing technical expertise to the IACHR and the IACtHR, producing knowledge about the IAHRS, and creating communities of dialogue. Think tanks, research institutes, and legal clinics are active participants of the System, playing hybrid roles that mobilize the Commission and the Court and, at the same time, contribute to a culture of engagement with the IAHRS.

States also play a fundamental role in shaping domestic attitudes toward human rights. In accordance with the principles of good faith and *pacta sunt servanda*, State officials should refrain from promoting narratives that are hostile to human rights, adopting instead a language of rights and duties that emphasizes States' legal obligations to guarantee the free and full exercise of human rights. Capacity-building programs and training for officials in all branches of the government can also generate long-term effects that permeate different forms of State action.[97] Recognizing this, the IAHRS has partnered with

---

[96] In the chapter "From Compliance to Engagement: Assessing the Impact of the Inter-American Court of Human Rights on Constitutional Law in Latin America" (in Par Engstrom (ed.), *Inter-American Human Rights System* [Springer 2019]), Marcello Torelly examines the different approaches of four countries (Brazil, Uruguay, Chile, and Mexico) to incorporation of and compliance with decisions of the IAHRS. Torelly concludes that constitutional provisions ordering the implementation of decisions are not as effective in countries where the legal culture does not value human rights and international law. In countries where the legal culture is more open, however, international law can "be used as an *interpretative tool* in a reflective process, and as a *normative source* alongside domestic law" (p. 119), even where international norms and decisions do not enjoy constitutional status.

[97] See *Paloma Angélica Escobar Ledezma et al. V. Mexico* [2013] IACHR, Report No. 51/13, Case 12.551. In this case, the Commission included the following recommendation: "Continue

various stakeholders to promote capacity-building programs, some of which target State authorities.

One example of an academic endeavor encouraging a culture of constructive engagement with the IAHRS is the *Ius Constitutionale Commune en América Latina* (ICCAL) project of the Max Planck Institute for Comparative Public Law and International Law. The ICCAL project is based on continuous cooperation among IAHRS experts who are or have been involved with the System through their work in academia, civil society, government, or IAHRS institutions themselves. The project's conceptual framework is based on the existence of a shared regional experience among Latin American countries, which encompasses IAHRS standards, fundamental rights embedded in national constitutions, and norms and practices that enable human rights frameworks to permeate the national and international law.[98] Described as a "legal but also a cultural and political project steeped in the structural transformation of public law,"[99] the project aims to strengthen the ICCAL phenomenon. It promotes research, learning, and cooperation among experts in the region with the goals of increasing the opening of domestic legal systems to the IAHRS and enhancing the effectiveness and legitimacy of IAHRS institutions.[100]

---

adopting public policies and institutional programs aimed at restructuring stereotypes concerning the role of women in the state of Chihuahua and promoting the eradication of discriminatory sociocultural patterns that impede their full access to justice, including training programs for public officials in all of the branches of the administration of justice and the police, and comprehensive prevention policies." As an example of capacity building program for national judges on human rights and conventionality control, see the National Pact for Human Rights in the Judiciary, adopted by the Brazilian National Council for Justice in 2022.

[98] For more information on ICCAL and its conceptual framework, see Armin von Bogdandy et al. (eds.), *Transformative Constitutionalism in Latin America: The Emergence of a New Ius Commune* (Oxford University Press 2017); Armin von Bogdandy et al., "Ius Constitutionale Commune in América Latina: A Regional Approach to Transformative Constitutionalism" (2016) MPIL Research Paper No. 2016-21, <https://ssrn.com/abstract=2859583 or http://dx.doi.org/10.2139/ssrn.2859 583> (accessed January 4, 2022).

[99] Max Planck Institute for Comparative Public Law and International Law, "Ius Constitutionale Commune en América Latina," <https://www.mpil.de/en/pub/research/areas/comparative-public-law/ius-constitutionale-commune.cfm> (accessed January 4, 2022).

[100] Some of the research stemming from the ICCAL project includes: Armin von Bogdandy, Flávia Piovesan, and Mariela Morales Antoniazzi (eds.), *Constitucionalismo transformador, inclusão e direitos sociais: desafios do Ius Constitutionale Commune Latino-Americano à luz do Direito Econômico Internacional* (Juspodivum 2019); Armin von Bogdandy et al. (eds.), *La jurisdicción constitucional en América Latina: un enfoque desde el Ius Constitutionale Commune*, (MPIL-U. Externado 2019); Eduardo Ferrer Mac-Gregor, Mariela Morales Antoniazzi, and Rogelio Flores (eds.), *Pantoja Inclusión, Ius Commune y justiciabilidad de los DESCA en la jurisprudencia interamericana El caso Lagos del Campo y los nuevos desafíos* (IECQ 2019); Armin von Bogdandy et al. (eds.), *El constitucionalismo transformador en América Latina y el derecho económico internacional: de la tensión al diálogo* (UNAM-IIJ-MPIL 2018); Armin von Bogdandy and Franz Christian Ebert, "El Banco Mundial frente al constitucionalismo transformador latinoamericano: panorama general y pasos concretos" (2018) MPIL Research Paper Series 2018-32; René Urueña, "Después de la fragmentación: ICCAL, derechos humanos y arbitraje de inversiones" (2018) MPIL Research Paper Series 2018-30; Manuel Gongora Mera, "El constitucionalismo interamericano y la fragmentación

5. Concluding Remarks

The Inter-American System has established itself as an important and effective instrument for the protection of human rights. It has made visible the struggles for rights and justice in Latin America, revealing the region's main challenges and aspirations by providing a forum where States, victims, civil society, the IACHR, and the IACtHR interact within the OAS framework. Mobilized by civil society, the System has advanced the protection of human rights in Latin America.

Transformative impact involves three dimensions. First, transformative impact is facilitated by conducive institutional frameworks. Adopting an implementation architecture could increase the impact of the IAHRS at the regional and national levels. Such architecture should include monitoring mechanisms (including mechanisms of implementation, platforms, indicators, and national laws), as well as a network of institutional arrangements to monitor compliance. At the same time, the IACHR and the IACtHR should continuously improve their own mechanisms with a view to increasing their transformative impact.

Second, transformative impact involves sociopolitical change. IAHRS decisions alter the power dynamics among social actors by empowering civil

---

del derecho internacional: posicionando al ICCAL en el debate sobre colisiones entre regímenes normativos" (2018) MPIL Research Paper Series 2018-29; Jose Gustavo Prieto Muñoz, "El Ius Constitutionale Commune frente al derecho internacional de inversiones. Desafíos en la construcción de principios comunes" (2018) MPIL Research Paper Series 2018-14; Armin von Bogdandy, Mariela Morales Antoniazzi, and Eduardo Ferrer Mac-Gregor (eds.), *Ius Constitutionale Commune en América Latina: textos básicos para su comprensión* (IECQ y MPIL 2017); Juan C. Herrera, "The Right of Cultural Minorities to Binding Consent: Case Study of Judicial Dialogue in the Framework of a Ius Constitutionale Commune en América Latina" (2017) MPIL Research Paper Series 2017-11; Armin von Bogdandy, Mariela Morales Antoniazzi, and Flávia Piovesan (eds.), *Ius Constitutionale Commune Na América Latina, Volume I: Marco Conceptual* (Juruá Editora 2016), Tomo I; Armin von Bogdandy, Mariela Morales Antoniazzi, and Flávia Piovesan (eds.), *Ius Constitutionale Commune Na América Latina, Volume II: Pluralismo e Inclusão* (Juruá Editora 2016), Tomo II; Armin von Bogdandy, Mariela Morales Antoniazzi, and Flávia Piovesan (eds.), *Ius Constitutionale Commune Na América Latina, Volume III: Diálogos Jurisdicionais e Controle de Convencionalidade* (Juruá Editora 2016); Armin von Bogdandy, Mariela Morales Antoniazzi, and Eduardo Ferrer Mac-Gregor (eds.), *Construcción de un ius constitutionale commune en América Latina: contexto, estándares e impacto a la luz de la Corte Interamericana de Derechos Humanos* (BUAP, UNAM-IIJ, CIDH y MPIL 2016); Armin von Bogdandy, "Ius Constitutionale Commune en América Latina: una mirada a un constitucionalismo transformador" [2015] 4 *Revista Derecho del Estado* 3; Mariela Morales Antoniazzi, *Protección supranacional de la democracia en Suramérica: un estudio sobre el acervo del ius constitutionale commune* (UNAM-IIJ 2014); Armin von Bogdandy, "Ius constitutionale commune," in Eduardo Ferrer Mac-Gregor, Fabiola Martínez Ramírez, and Giovanni A. Figueroa Mejía (coords.), Diccionario de Derecho Procesal Constitucional y Convencional (2. edn, II-J UNAM 2014); Armin von Bogdandy, Héctor Fix-Fierro, and Mariela Morales Antoniazzi (eds.), *Ius constitutionale commune en América Latina. Rasgos, potencialidades y desafíos* (IIJ-UNAM-MPIL-IIDC 2014); Armin von Bogdandy, Mariela Morales Antoniazzi, and Eduardo Ferrer Mac-Gregor (eds.), *Ius Constitutionale Commune en Derechos Humanos en América Latina* (MPIL-Porrúa 2013); Armin von Bogdandy et al. (eds.), *Construcción y papel de los derechos sociales fundamentales: hacia un ius constitutionale commune en América Latina* (UNAM-IIJ 2011); Armin von Bogdandy, Eduardo Ferrer Mac-Gregor, and Mariela Morales Antoniazzi (eds.), *La justicia constitucional y su internacionalización. ¿Hacia un ius constitucionale commune en América Latina?*, II (MPIL-UNAM 2010), Tomos I y II.

society,[101] pressuring States, and generating political will to effect human rights change. In other words, IAHRS decisions change the political equation as they open spaces of dialogue with State authorities,[102] provide tools for grassroots actors, and more.

Third, transformative impact requires cultural transformation. An often-neglected aspect of implementation is the creation of a human rights culture. This culture can be fostered through training programs for public authorities and the media, as well as human rights–based educational programs and academic engagement with the IAHRS. These actions can go a long way toward promoting human rights within domestic culture.

The ability of the IAHRS to impact realities on the ground depends on the dynamic interaction of these three dimensions. There might be cases of transformative impact in which one of these elements stands out, and even cases in which the different dimensions work in opposition to each other. In many cases examined in this book, however, the three dimensions strengthen each other. These positive interactions catalyze transformations, enabling the IAHRS to advance the protection of human rights in the region. Understanding these interactions may enable the System to have an even greater impact of the future, strengthening its ability to deliver on its mandate and to transform the situation of human rights throughout the hemisphere.

---

[101] Par Engstrom and Peter Low (n. 16) emphasized the role of NGOs in litigation before the IAHRS. Due to the highly specialized nature of the system and the costs associated with litigation, most cases are brought before the Inter-American Commission by a coalition of two or more NGOs, including at least one international organization with experience in human rights litigation and one domestic organization that is closer to the affected communities.

[102] According to Oscar Parra-Vera (n. 85), the decisions and recommendations of the IAHRS can have great impact in intra-State conflicts, that is, when two entities from the same State are in disagreement regarding the implementation of certain rights, especially when these conflicts are between national and subnational entities. Tom Pegram and Nataly Herrera Rodriguez, "Bridging the Gap: National Human Rights Institutions and the Inter-American Human Rights System," in Par Engstrom (ed.), *Inter-American Human Rights System* (Springer 2019), 167–198 also emphasize the need for dialogue between the institutions of the IAHRS and national human rights institutions, such as ombudsmen and human rights commissions, which would help bridge the gap between the international system and local realities.

I.4
Current Issues and Common Challenges for the Protection of Human Rights in Europe, the Americas, and Africa

By Rainer Grote

1. Introduction

Until a decade ago, the trends toward an ever more expansive protection of human rights at the regional level seemed unstoppable in Europe, the Americas, and Africa. In the 1990s, regional human rights systems gained in membership and political salience, the jurisprudence of European and American human rights courts increasingly permeated the domestic legal systems of member States, and the African Commission of Human Rights became more assertive in its interpretation of the African Charter on Human and Peoples' Rights (ACHPR), while the Protocol on the establishment of an African Court on Human and Peoples' Rights (ACtHPR) presented in 1998 immediately won the adherence of the quasi-totality of the Organisation of African Unity (OAU) membership, although it would take almost another decade before the Court became operational.[1] However, over the last decade these positive dynamics have fundamentally changed: member States have started to question and even reject the rulings of regional human rights courts, reforms have been promoted that no longer aim to strengthen and improve the powers of regional human rights bodies but instead try to limit their scope in favor of preserving a central role for national politicians and judges, and some member States have even partially or totally ended their participation in the regional system (see section 3). Some scholars see in these developments the twilight[2] or perhaps the end[3] of the human rights era, an era proclaimed after the end of the Cold

---

[1] See Alexandra Huneeus and Mikael Rask Madsen, "Between Universalism and Regional Law and Politics: A Comparative History of the American, European, and African Human Rights Systems" [2018] 16 *International Journal of Constitutional Law* 151–159.
[2] Eric A. Posner, *The Twilight of Human Rights Law* (Oxford University Press 2014).
[3] Makau Mutua, "Is the Age of Human Rights Over?," in Sohia A. McClennen and Alexandra Schultheis Moore (eds.), *The Routledge Companion to Literature and Human Rights* (Routledge 2016), 450.

War.[4] While this pessimism may be overblown,[5] it can hardly be denied that international human rights protection, and regional rights protection in particular—which has been in its vanguard for most of the last thirty years—have entered a new phase marked by the twin challenges of neo-sovereigntism and nationalism.[6] The size and significance of these challenges can only be understood if they are set against the advances in human rights protection that were achieved in the preceding "golden age of human rights" and the resulting strengths and weaknesses of regional human rights systems (section 2). The pushback against international human rights protection has taken a variety of forms, from total or partial withdrawal from regional human rights systems and reform efforts aimed at curbing the powers of international human rights bodies to selective noncompliance with unpopular rulings by international human rights bodies (section 3). Recent reform debates in the Americas and Europe have seen the proponents of a vigorous international human rights protection go on the defensive (section 4). This raises the question of how to strengthen the resilience of regional human rights institutions in an increasingly adverse international environment (section 5). Any such discussion must take into account the similarities as well as the differences between regional systems. While they have been shaped by the central ideas and practices of the global liberal order, which came into being in the 1990s,[7] they also present important variations with regard to the speed and depth of institutionalization and legalization, as well as the geopolitical context in which they are operating. All of these factors are likely to influence the way in which they confront the new challenges.

2. The Expansion of Regional Human Rights Protection after the End of the Cold War

The dynamic evolution of regional human rights protection in the late twentieth and early twenty-first century was marked by four interrelated developments: institutionalization, judicialization, diversification of remedial practice, and embeddedness. Together they have transformed the character of regional human rights systems from the human rights diplomacy that was their dominant mode of functioning during much of the Cold War era to the

---

[4] Most notably: Louis Henkin, *The Age of Rights* (Colombia University Press 1990).
[5] See Mutua (n. 4), 455–456, who, despite arguing that the human rights era has ended, nevertheless concedes that this does not necessarily signify the impotence of human rights norms and values: "The internationalization–universalization of human rights tenets and principles is so deeply embedded in the psyches of states and cultures around the world that it is irreversible."
[6] Huneeus and Madsen (n. 1), 157.
[7] Ibid., 136–137.

progressive development and enforcement of international human rights law that characterized their activities in the following decades.

2.1. Institutionalization

The institutionalization of international human rights protection has been taken to its most advanced level in Europe. The first system to provide for a full set of institutions to monitor human rights on the international plane with both a Commission and a Court was the regional system created by the European Convention on Human Rights (ECHR). This European System did not initially make judicial supervision over the implementation of obligations under the Convention by the State parties mandatory. Instead, the acceptance of both the jurisdiction of the European Court of Human Rights (ECtHR) and the right to individual petition before the Commission, which would later become emblems of the European human rights regime, were optional in the 1950 Convention.[8] It was only in the 1990s, when the end of the Cold War had completely transformed the geopolitical landscape, that an opportunity presented itself for a far-reaching overhaul of the European human rights machinery. The Council of Europe (CoE) welcomed practically all Central and Eastern European countries into the System. Between 1990 and 2007, twenty new member States, including Ukraine, Russia, and the successor States of the former Yugoslavia, joined the CoE and the ECHR. At the same time a major institutional reform streamlined the ECHR System. Protocol No. 11, which entered into force in 1998, abandoned the dual system of Commission and Court and created a unified structure of human rights reviews centered on the ECtHR. Both its compulsory jurisdiction and the rights of individuals in all member States to file applications for violations of their Convention rights after the exhaustion of domestic remedies were made mandatory and no longer depended on their acceptance via separate declarations by member States. The Court itself was transformed into a two-tier structure, consisting of three- and seven-member panels that deal with the admissible applications on the merits, and a seventeen-member Grand Chamber that hears appeals against panel rulings that raise issues of fundamental importance to the development of the Convention.

In the Americas, on the other hand, the development of regional human rights institutions have followed a more protracted path. While the Organization of American States (OAS) called for the creation of an Inter-American Court dedicated to the protection of human rights as early as 1948—when the American Declaration of Human Rights (ADHR) was adopted—the dynamics

---

[8] Ibid., 141.

of the unfolding Cold War meant that the judicial model of international rights protection was quickly set aside.[9] It would take another decade before the Inter-American Commission for Human Rights was created, with a limited mandate that gave it powers to educate and provide consultation only. It was the Commission itself that decided to move beyond these narrow limits and began asserting its authority not only to study and promote human rights in the abstract, but to protect them in specific situations and conduct in-country visits (with State consent) to this effect. In 1967, the OAS wrote the powers that the Commission had been claiming in practice into its mandate and promoted the Commission to the status of a principal organ of the OAS.[10] Two years later the American Convention on Human Rights (ACHR) was adopted, which also provided for the establishment of an Inter-American Court of Human Rights (IACtHR) whose jurisdiction was subject to the acceptance by member States through a separate declaration. As in the early European System there is no direct petition to the Court. Individual petitions can only be referred to it by the Commission, and the Commission will do so only if its efforts to reach a non-adjudicative resolution have failed. The Commission used this power after the entry into force of the Convention in 1978 to withhold cases from the Court for several more years, confining the Court's activity to requests for advisory opinions by States until the end of the following decade. By then, only nine States had accepted its jurisdiction, with important States like Brazil and Mexico notably absent.[11]

The way toward a fully fledged regional human rights system was even longer in Africa. When the ECHR was adopted in 1950, large parts of Africa were still under the control and jurisdiction of European colonial powers.[12] It was only in 1981 that the foundations of an autochthonous African system of human rights protection, with a heavy emphasis on the rights of decolonized African peoples supplementing the traditional focus on the rights of the individual, were put in place through the adoption of the African Charter on Human and Peoples' Rights. The African Commission on Human and Peoples' Rights was created one year after the ACHPR went into effect in 1986, and the establishment of a regional human rights court took even longer. As in the other regional systems, African States opted for a system that allowed States to choose their level of commitment, resulting in a protracted institutionalization process. The Protocol on the establishment of the African Court on Human and Peoples' Rights (ACtHPR) signed by fifty-two member States in 1998 made individual access to the Court optional and set the number of ratifications required for the Court to come into

[9] Ibid., 143.
[10] Ibid., 145.
[11] Ibid., 146.
[12] Ibid., 141.

existence at fifteen. The Protocol finally entered into force in 2004, and it took another three years before the Court became fully operational. By that time, the enthusiasm for powerful international human rights institutions had already slowed considerably, in Africa and elsewhere: of the thirty States that ratified the Protocol on the establishment of the ACtHPR, only nine have ever made the optional declaration under Article 34(6) to accept direct referral to the Court by an individual or an NGO.[13]

2.2. Judicialization

The work of the European human rights bodies took the form of legal diplomacy rather than human rights adjudication proper in the early stages of their existence. This was not surprising in the case of the Commission, whose mandate expressly covered and even favored efforts to reach a friendly settlement with member States charged with a violation of Convention rights. The same approach also applied to the early jurisprudence of the Court: while emphasizing its position as the final arbiter on the meaning of the Convention's rules, the Court also signaled its readiness to accommodate the security and other legitimate concerns of member States and sought solutions that did not alienate existing or prospective member States. This changed only after the big Western European States like the United Kingdom, France, and Italy accepted the optional clause on ECtHR jurisdiction and individual petition. The geopolitical context changed decisively as the major European powers shed their colonial empires and the Cold War *détente* created an opening for a new, more progressive European human rights law.[14] The Court seized this opportunity vigorously by issuing its first landmark decisions and in doing so set out the key legal features of the Convention: that it (1) imposes binding obligations on member States, (2) is a dynamic legal instrument to be interpreted in light of present-day conditions and not the conditions that existed at the time of its drafting,[15] and (3) intends to guarantee rights that are not merely theoretical or illusory but practical and effective.[16]

Not surprisingly, the IACtHR followed a different trajectory that—like the developments in Europe—reflected the rapidly changing geopolitical context in the region. When the IACtHR handed down its first judgment in the *Velasquez Rodriguez* case in 1988, the region was in the midst of a dramatic transformation,

---

[13] Tom Gerald Daly and Micha Wiebusch, "The African Court on Human and Peoples' Rights: Mapping Resistance Against a Young Court" [2018] 14 *International Journal of Law in Context* 294, 300.
[14] Huneeus and Madsen (n. 1), 148.
[15] *Tyrer v. United Kingdom* [1978], ECtHR, Application No. 5856/72, A/26, para. 31.
[16] *Airey v. Ireland* [1979], ECtHR, Application No. 6289/73, A/32, para. 24.

as the authoritarian regimes still in office had already started to lose their grip on power. In this context, the IACtHR established itself as a locus for rights protection and political integrity, accepting the rule of prior exhaustion of domestic remedies in principle but quickly rebutting that preference in favor of its own authority.[17] This started to change in the mid-1990s, when pressure increased from civil society actors to shift focus from the mere promotion of human rights to the effective protection and enforcement of the rights of individuals and those groups within the newly established democracies that had historically suffered from exclusion and systemic discrimination, like Latin America's Indigenous peoples.[18] It was also during this phase that the IACtHR embraced the ECtHR's living instrument doctrine, stressing that "[h]uman rights treaties are living instruments whose interpretation must consider the changes over time and present-day conditions."[19] However, it did so in a characteristic manner: refusing to countenance any "margin of appreciation" doctrine for governments, legislatures, and courts as partners in the progressive development of Convention rights, as the ECtHR had done, on the grounds that is was unsuitable to the specific Latin American context of weak rule of law principles.[20]

The African Commission and the African Court have not made explicit reference to the living instrument doctrine in their decisions.[21] However, that does not mean that the organs of the African Charter apply a fundamentally different methodology in the interpretation and application of the provisions of the African Charter. On the contrary, their case law indicates that they also follow the requirement laid down in Article 31 of the Vienna Convention: a treaty shall be interpreted in good faith in accordance with the ordinary meaning to be given to the terms of the treaty in their context and in light of their object and purpose. The object and purpose of a human rights treaty suggest that its provisions have to be interpreted so as to give real, effective protection to the rights and freedoms it guarantees. In accordance with this principle, the African Commission has held that the scope of a protected right (for example, the right to life) must not be construed narrowly,[22] whereas the limitations to a right should be given a narrow interpretation.[23] In the *Zongo* case, the ACtHPR adopted a similarly broad approach to the protection offered by the African Charter, in particular with regard to the concepts of moral damages and victims.[24] Unlike the IACtHR, the African

---

[17] Jorge Contesse, "Contestation and Deference in the Inter-American Human Rights System" [2016] 79 *Law & Contemporary Problems* 123, 130.
[18] Contesse (n. 17), 123.
[19] *Sánchez v. Honduras* [2003], IACtHR, Ser. C No. 102, para. 56.
[20] Contesse (n. 17), 134, quoting the former President of the IACtHR, Antonio Cançado Trindade.
[21] Magnus Killander, "Interpreting Regional Human Rights Treaties" [2010] 7(13) *SUR* 145, 150.
[22] *Aminu v. Nigeria* [2000], ACHPR, Communication No. 225/1997, para. 18.
[23] *Legal Resources Foundation v. Zambia* [2001], ACHPR, Communication No. 211/1998, para. 70.
[24] *Zongo and Others* [2011], ACtHPR, Ruling on Reparations, Application No. 013/2011.

Commission has expressly endorsed the margin of appreciation doctrine in the meaning given to it by the ECtHR.[25]

2.3. Diversification of Remedial Practice

A key factor in what member States increasingly came to view as the growing intrusiveness of international human rights bodies in the domestic sphere has been the diversification of their remedial practices. For more than three decades after becoming operative in 1959, the ECtHR followed the least intrusive remedy approach by sticking to declaratory judgments stating that a violation of Convention rights by the defendant State party had indeed been found, but leaving the choice of the appropriate remedy to the member State concerned, subject to the supervision of the Committee of Ministers—the body competent to monitor the execution of judgments under the Convention.[26] While the Convention expressly authorizes the ECtHR to afford just satisfaction to the injured party if the internal law of the High Contracting Party concerned allows only partial reparation, the ECtHR opted for a narrow interpretation and repeatedly regarded the finding of a violation to be a strong form of moral satisfaction in and of itself.[27] For its part, the Committee of Ministers has usually shown deference to member States in the exercise of its supervisory functions, viewing them as primarily responsible for deciding how to remedy defects in their legal system identified in a ruling by the ECtHR.[28]

The dominance of the declaratory model of human rights adjudication under the ECHR started to change when the Court was increasingly confronted with grave human rights problems of a structural character following the expansion of the Convention system toward Central and Eastern Europe in the 1990s; but even then change occurred only gradually and within certain limits. The Court first moved cautiously beyond the declaratory model in a number of cases concerning the unlawful seizure of property. Court held that in these cases priority had to be given to the restitution of the property concerned.[29] In a second phase, the Court developed a test of "logical requirement or necessity" with respect to *restitution ad integrum* to order nonmonetary remedies in cases concerning other rights than the right to property.[30] At the same time, the Court became

---

[25] Killander (n. 22), 152.
[26] Başak Çalı, "Explaining Variation in the Intrusiveness of Regional Human Rights Remedies in Domestic Orders" [2018] 16 *International Journal of Constitutional Law* 214, 220.
[27] Çalı, (n. 26), 220.
[28] Alexandra Huneeus, "Reforming the State from Afar: Structural Reform Litigation at the Human Rights Courts" [2015] 40 *Yale Journal of International Law* 1, 8.
[29] *Papamichadoupoulos and Others v. Greece* [1995], ECtHR, Application No. 14556/89; *Çakıcı v. Turkey* [1999], ECtHR Application No. 23657/94.
[30] Çalı (n. 26), 222.

bolder with regard to general remedies, no longer shying away from directly addressing the causes of abusive State behavior and practices in domestic legislation, calling openly for the amendment of the provisions and statutes on which the unlawful practices were based.[31] The trend toward more intrusive remedies received a further boost with the introduction of the pilot judgment procedure in 2004. Pilot judgments were introduced in response to the large number of repeated cases often coming from new member States in Central and Eastern Europe, which are rooted in systemic defects in the legal systems concerned: either the existence of poorly drafted legislation or the absence of any appropriate legislation, which give rise to a large number of similar applications concerning the same structural problem. By declaring one of the many cases a pilot case, the ECtHR is able to identify the structural problem at the root of many cases and order its removal through the introduction of the appropriate domestic legislation. However, the pilot judgment procedure is less intrusive than it seems at first sight, as the ECtHR under this procedure first informally consults with the respondent State about whether a pilot judgment is seen as helpful to address the systemic defect and only goes ahead with it if the latter signals its willingness to implement the legislative remedy framed by the Court.[32]

In contrast to the European Court, the Inter-American Court began life in 1979 by overseeing a region haunted by military dictatorships and civil wars.[33] In this environment, the IACtHR felt that it had to tread cautiously, focusing on determining whether there had been a violation of the Convention and the granting of monetary remedies, although Article 63 of the ACHR gives the Inter-American Court a broader remedial mandate than its European counterpart.[34] It also suggested specific actions that the defendant State should undertake to come into compliance with the ACHR. In the *Velásquez Rodriguez* case, the IACtHR suggested that Honduras had to investigate and punish forced disappearances.[35] However, this was not included in the remedial section of the judgment, with the consequence that Honduras was deemed to have complied with the judgment

---

[31] See *Ürper and Others v. Turkey* [2009], ECTHR, Application Nos. 14526/07 et al., (Second Section), in which the Court traced the violations of the journalists' rights under Article 10 ECHR, which it had identified expressly and directly to specific provisions in Law No. 3713 of Turkey.

[32] Çalı (n. 26), 224, who therefore speaks with regard to these cases of "negotiated intrusiveness."

[33] Huneeus (n. 28), 9.

[34] Ibid., 8: According to Article 63 ACHR: "If the Court finds that there has been a violation of a right or freedom protected by this Convention, the Court shall rule that the injured party be ensured the enjoyment of his right or freedom that was violated. It shall also rule, if appropriate, that the consequences of the measure or situation that constituted the breach of such right or freedom be remedied and that fair compensation be paid to the injured party." By contrast, Article 41 ECHR merely stipulates: "If the Court finds that there has been a violation of the Convention or the protocols thereto, and if the internal law of the High Contracting Party concerned allows only partial reparation to be made, the Court shall, if necessary, afford just satisfaction to the injured party."

[35] *Velásquez Rodríguez v. Honduras* [1989], IACtHR, Ser. C No. 7, para. 34.

once it had paid compensation to the victims, even if the State continued to deny and cover up State-sponsored forced disappearances.[36]

However, with the return to democracy for the vast majority of member States, the space for a more exacting jurisprudence increased. In 1996, the IACtHR issued several reparatory rulings addressing State-sponsored violence, ordering the defendant States to pay monetary compensation to the victims, as it had done in earlier cases, but in addition requiring them to undertake certain acts to remedy the violation of Convention rights it had identified. Rather than letting the respondent State choose for itself the manner of righting the wrong, the Court demanded specific remedial measures, including measures that were designed to bring about structural change,[37] such as derogating amnesties and grappling with the complex power structure underlying impunity.[38] As it went on, the IACtHR diversified its remedial practice still further, enumerating a substantive list of measures that must be taken by States and often adding to this list of orders "creative" noncompensatory remedies, that is, remedies not normally available under domestic law and that seek to recognize the humanity and the dignity of the victim.[39] Since the 2000s, the IACtHR has further deepened the intrusiveness of its judgments by attaching fixed time limits for compliance with the specific remedies it has ordered.[40]

Unlike the ECtHR, the Inter-American Court has claimed for itself a central role in supervising compliance with its remedial orders.[41] Although no provision in the ACHR expressly refers to the power of the IACtHR to monitor the compliance of its orders, the Court has held that its monitoring powers are inherent in Articles 67 and 68(1) of the Convention, which require States to comply fully and promptly—using all necessary means and mechanisms—with the decisions of the Court.[42] It has developed an increasingly intricate system of tracking compliance through a succession of judgments up to the time when the respondent State has complied to the satisfaction of the Court with all its remedial orders. Member States have accepted the practice, submitting compliance reports and taking part in special compliance hearings at the Court's request.[43]

Similar to the other regional bodies, the initial practice of the organs of the ACHPR followed a cautious approach in the development of remedies. In the

---

[36] Huneeus (n. 28), 9.
[37] Flávia Piovesan, "Ius Constitutionale Commune latinoamericano en derechos humanos e impacto del Sistema Interamericano: rasgos, potencialidades y desafíos," in Armin von Bogdandy, Héctor Fix Fierro, and Mariela Morales Antoniazzi (coords.), *Ius Constitutionale Commune en América Latina. Rasgos, potencialidades y desafíos* (IIJ-UNAM-MPIL-IIDC 2014), 61–84.
[38] Ibid., 10.
[39] Çalı (n. 26), 218.
[40] Ibid., 218.
[41] Huneeus (n. 28), 10.
[42] *Baena-Ricardo v. Panama* [2003], IACtHR, Competence, Ser. C No. 104, para. 131.
[43] Huneeus (n. 28), 11.

early years, the decisions of the African Commission simply had a declaratory function and contained no remedial section.[44] This changed in 2000, when for the first time the Commission specified a wide variety of nonmonetary remedies, including the opening of an independent inquiry to clarify the fate of persons thought to have disappeared and the prosecution of the authors of the violations.[45] Since then the Commission has increasingly focused on remedies and guarantees of nonrepetition tailored to the specific needs of the victims of violations, like the release of those wrongfully detained, the transfer of accused persons from one part of the country to another, or the establishment of a commission to determine the level of compensation required.[46] The African Court, on the other hand, has so far only delivered a limited number of violation judgments and reparation orders. The decisions it has issued, however, seem to indicate that it is prepared to order a diverse range of remedies based on the specific facts of the individual cases. In particular, it has adopted a broad interpretation of moral damages, recognizing that they do not only cover nonmaterial changes in the living conditions of the victims themselves but also include the suffering and emotional distress of family members.[47] The Court has also been prepared to order individual measures in politically charged cases, like the stay of the arrest warrant against the presidential candidate Guillaume Soro in Côte d'Ivoire pending the Court's final decision on the merits, a decision which immediately triggered the respondent State's decision to withdraw its declaration recognizing the right of individual petition to the Court.[48]

The basic design of the African system on human rights with regard to monitoring compliance is closer to the European than to the American system. Responsibility to ensure proper implementation of the decisions issued by the Court and the Commission rests primarily with the political bodies, the Executive Council, and the Assembly of the African Union. However, on the basis of a provision in the Protocol on the African Court of Human Rights, which requires the Court to specify cases of noncompliance in its regular activity report to the policy organs, the Court itself has to ensure that information is provided to it on the status of compliance by member States, although the details of such a follow-up mechanism were still under consideration in early 2020.

---

[44] Çalı (n. 26), 224.
[45] *Malawi African Association, Amnesty International, Ms. Sarr Diop, and Other v. Mauritania* [2010], ACHPR, Communication Nos. 54/91, 61/91, 98/93, 164/97, to 196/97, and 210/98.
[46] Çalı (n. 26), 224.
[47] ACtHPR, *Zongo and Others*, paras. 45–50.
[48] Tetevi Davi and Ezéchiel Amani, "Another One Bites the Dust: Côte d'Ivoire to End Individual and NGO Access to the African Court" (2020), *EJIL Talk!*, https://www.ejiltalk.org/another-one-bites-the-dust-cote-divoire-to-end-individual-and-ngo-access-to-the-african-court/ (accessed April 6, 2022).

2.4. Embeddedness

Another important development strengthening the role of regional human rights bodies, and regional courts in particular, has been the growing embeddedness of regional human rights law in domestic legal systems. In Europe, all member States of the CoE have incorporated the ECHR into national law. While some countries have limited themselves to giving the ECHR the same rank as ordinary (federal) statutes, others have opted to place them above the (federal) statutes but below their national constitutions. In exceptional cases, the Convention enjoys the rank of formal constitutional law (Austria) or is at least part of substantive constitutional law (Switzerland).[49] A similar development took place in Latin America. As part of the transition to democracy, since the end of the 1980s countries have adopted new constitutions or amended existing constitutions. A key feature of this reform movement was States' commitment to international human rights principles. Many of the reforming countries included provisions in their new or amended constitutions that accorded the international human rights treaties, foremost among them the ACHR, precedence either over ordinary (statutory) law or even constitutional rank.[50]

This had the immediate effect of enhancing the role of regional human rights courts as the final arbiters on the meaning and scope of the treaty provisions. As references by domestic lawyers and judges to the regional human rights treaties increased, regional courts moved to the center of the transnational networks integrating national and international law on human rights ever more closely. The growing role of fundamental rights in the jurisprudence of newly established or reformed national constitutional courts meant that regional human rights courts started to act as de facto constitutional courts once they became the last fora in which human rights claims that had failed at the national level could be argued.[51] While this shift happened gradually in Europe, it occured rather suddenly in the Inter-American System with the introduction of the conventionality control doctrine by the IACtHR in 2006. In the *Almonacid* judgment, the Court held that all courts in States under its jurisdiction are obligated to examine the compatibility between the domestic law they are supposed to apply to a case before them with the provisions of the ACHR, and to discard any domestic regulations that fail to conform to its clauses as authoritatively interpreted by the IACtHR.[52] This

---

[49] Frank Hoffmeister, "Germany: Status of European Convention on Human Rights in Domestic Law" [2006] 4 *International Journal of Constitutional Law* 722.

[50] Jorge Contesse, "Resisting the Inter-American Human Rights System" [2019] 44 *Yale Journal of International Law* 179, 186.

[51] Huneeus and Madsen (n. 1), 155.

[52] *Almonacid Arellano and Others v. Chile* [2006], IACtHR, Ser. C No. 154, para. 124.

was a controversial decision for several reasons. The first objection was that the doctrine lacks an actual basis in law as the American Convention does not contain any rule requiring national judges to carry out this review.[53] Secondly, the ruling seemed to imply that *all* national courts have to exert a judicial review of legislation, ignoring the considerable differences between the various national systems of judicial review within the Inter-American System, where countries with a concentrated system exist alongside others following the model of diffuse control.[54] Finally, the judgment could be understood as suggesting that the ACHR is self-executing in all States that have ratified it and that not only the Convention but the decisions of the IACtHR interpreting it are directly binding on domestic courts.[55]

3. The Backlash against the Increasing Scope and Intrusiveness of Regional Human Rights Jurisprudence

In the last decade, however, the dynamic expansion of human rights protection has largely ground to a halt. In all regional systems there have been various forms of pushback and even backlash.[56] As regional human rights law increasingly permeated the domestic legal systems of member States and the remedial practice of the regional human rights bodies and the courts in particular grew more intrusive in the 1990s and 2000s, this change in the dynamics of human rights protection has not been totally unexpected. It received a strong boost from the changing geopolitical context in the wake of the global financial crisis of 2008–2009, which paved the way in many places for the rise of populist and neo-authoritarian political regimes and a corresponding shift from a commitment to common values, foremost among them human rights and the international rule of law, toward a new emphasis on the defense of national sovereignty. The pushback against the expansion of international human rights law has taken various forms, from the total or partial withdrawal from regional human rights systems to institutional reforms designed to emphasize the limits of the jurisdiction and powers of regional bodies, as well as noncompliance with particularly unpopular or intrusive decisions issued by those bodies.

---

[53] Contesse (n. 50), 138.
[54] Huneeus and Madsen (n. 1), 153.
[55] Ibid., 153.
[56] Ximena Soley and Silvia Steininger, "Parting Ways or Lashing Back? Withdrawals, Backlash and the Inter-American Court of Human Rights" [2018] MPIL Research Paper No. 2018-01, https://papers.ssrn.com/sol3/papers.cfm?abstract_id=3103666 (accessed January 8, 2022).

3.1. Withdrawal from the Regional Human Rights System

Full exit from the regional human rights system, the most extreme form of resistance, has so far only been implemented by two members States of the Inter-American System, namely, Trinidad and Tobago, which withdrew its ratification of the ACHR in 1998, and Venezuela, which did the same fourteen years later. However, only in the latter case did dissatisfaction with the practice of the organs of the American Convention play a decisive role, whereas the decision of the government of Trinidad and Tobago was triggered by the case law of the British Judicial Committee of the Privy Council—at the time still Trinidad and Tobago's highest appellate court—on the use of the death penalty.[57]

In contrast, Venezuela's withdrawal from the Inter-American System was a direct response to the Commission and Court's alleged lack of impartiality and respect for Venezuelan national sovereignty. Withdrawal followed a prolonged period of confrontation between the Convention bodies and the Venezuelan authorities, particularly its Supreme Court, over the implementation of IACtHR judgments in Venezuela. The confrontation went back as far as 2000 when the newly established Constitutional Chamber of the Supreme Court of Venezuela opposed the precautionary measures of the Commission as an "unacceptable" interference in the competence and independence of Venezuelan judges on the grounds that the Commission had not made sure that all domestic remedies

---

[57] In a case concerning Jamaica, the Privy Council held that the prolonged time that inmates were on death row was a form of inhuman and degrading treatment that violated both constitutional norms and international treaties, and that inmates on death row ought not to wait for more than five years between their sentences and their executions, *Pratt v. Attorney General for Jamaica* [1994] 2 AC 1, 85 (PC). However, the Council's expectation that the review of death penalty cases carried out by international bodies, namely, the UN Human Rights Committee and the Inter-American Commission, would not require more than eighteen months and thus not add significantly to the prolongation of the waiting time proved far too optimistic, all the more so as complainants were allowed to petition both the Human Rights Committee and the Commission. As a result, review times added up, leading to a situation in which convicted prisoners, by lodging petitions before international bodies, could effectively delay their executions for more than the five years allowed by the Privy Council, thus often forcing Caribbean countries to commute their death sentences to lifelong imprisonment, coming close to a de facto abolition of the death penalty. It was in order to end this unhappy situation, which in the government's view allowed convicted murderers to escape the death penalty due to the delays and the inertia of international human rights bodies, that Trinidad and Tobago decided to withdraw its ratification from the American Convention and the International Covenant on Civil and Political Rights. This should not obscure the fact that the initial trigger of the withdrawal decision had not been a practice by the Court or the Commission, which was seen as overly intrusive, but jurisprudence by the Privy Council, which took its central concept—i.e., the definition of inhumane and degrading treatment—from the practice of ECHR bodies and not from that of ACHR institutions—in particular from the ECtHR's *Soering* decision, which had ruled that the delay in executing prisoners held on death row for six to eight years amounted to inhuman and degrading treatment within the meaning of Article 3 of the ECHR; see Jane Hearn, "New Legal Breakthrough for Death Row Prisoners: Pratt v Attorney General for Jamaica" [1994] 1 *Australian Journal of Human Rights* 392, 396.

had been exhausted before it ordered the measures.[58] Three years later, the Constitutional Chamber went further still by holding, with special reference to the IACtHR, that the judgments handed down by international courts can only be implemented in the Venezuelan legal system if they conform to the provisions of the national Constitution and the requirement of prior exhaustion of domestic remedies has been respected. For judgments handed down by international courts to be implemented, they must first be given the green light by the Constitutional Chamber, which will only be granted if they do not violate constitutional principles and rules.[59] While the primacy of the national constitution over decisions by international courts had thus been established in principle, it was given its first application five years later in the *Apitz Barbera et al v. Venezuela* case. In this instance, the IACtHR had required the Venezuelan State to reinstate three judges who had been dismissed arbitrarily from their posts. The Supreme Court ruled that implementation of the IACtHR judgment would lead to institutional chaos and affect the autonomy of the judiciary and the judicial disciplinary system, as well as violate the principle of *res judicata*, and therefore declared it unenforceable. In addition, the Supreme Court stated that with the *Apitz Barbera* judgment the IACtHR had attempted to engaged in an evident "usurpation of powers" and requested the executive branch to proceed to denounce the ACHR in order to remove it from the Venezuelan legal system.[60] Venezuela finally notified the OAS's Secretary General of its decision to withdraw from the ACHR on September 10, 2012.[61]

To support the argument that IACtHR rulings were unenforceable, the Supreme Court referred to several decisions handed down by the military courts in Peru during the Fujimori presidency, which had sought to exempt the State of Peru from the decisions of the IACtHR with respect to serious violations of human rights.[62] Indeed, Peruvian military courts had been the first to openly challenge the execution of IACtHR judgments for their lack of impartiality and their violation of the national constitution in a series of decisions in the late 1990s.[63] These decisions had been part of a wider effort of the Fujimori regime

---

[58] *Faitha Nahmens and Ben Ami Fishman "Excess" Magazine*, TSJ/SC, Judgment No. 386, 17-5-2000, http://historico.tsj.gob.ve/decisiones/scon/mayo/386-170500-00-0216.HTM (accessed January 8, 2022).

[59] *Rafael Chavero Gazdik*, TSJ/SC, Judgment No. 1942, July 15, 2003, <http://historico. tsj.gob.ve/decisiones/scon/julio/1942-150703-01-0415.HTM (accessed January 8, 2022).

[60] *Leopoldo López Mendoza*, TSJ/SC, Judgment No. 1939, December 18, 2008, <http://historico.tsj.gob.ve/decisiones/scon/diciembre/1939-181208-2008-08-1572.HTML (accessed January 8, 2022).

[61] See Carlos Ayala Corao, "Inconstitucionalidad de la Denuncia de la Convención Americana sobre Derechos Humanos por Venezuela" [2012] 20 *Revista Europea de Derechos Fundamentales* 45, 48.

[62] *Leopoldo López Mendoza*, TSJ/SC, Judgment No. 1939, December 18, 2008, <http://historico.tsj.gob.ve/decisiones/scon/diciembre/1939-181208-2008-08-1572.HTML (accessed January 8, 2022).

[63] Contesse (n. 50), 197.

to block the Inter-American human rights regime's intromission in Peru's national security affairs, particularly the ruthless methods used by the government in its fight against the brutal terrorism of *Sendero Luminoso* and other groups. In July 1999, this effort culminated in Peru withdrawing its declaration consenting to the optional clause in the American Convention recognizing the contentious jurisdiction of the IACtHR.[64] While this amounted only to a partial withdrawal from the Inter-American System, as it left the country's membership of the ACHR intact, it nevertheless constituted an attempt to break free from those of its elements that have the most direct and restricting effect on a member State's national sovereignty. While the IACHR declared the withdrawal inadmissible, arguing that a State may disengage from its obligations under the ACHR only by fully denouncing it,[65] the Peruvian government did not correct or amend its decision. It was only in 2001, after Fujimori had stepped down from office and the country had started to rebuild its democratic institutions under a newly elected leadership that Peru reinstated its recognition of the IACtHR's contentious jurisdiction.

However, the Peruvian precedent would not be forgotten. It played a major role in the struggle of the Venezuelan courts to escape from supervision of the Inter-American System: by looking at the Peruvian experience, Venezuela obviously concluded that they would only be able to successfully escape if they were prepared to fully denounce the ACHR. But it may also have taught the Constitutional Court of the Dominican Republic a valuable lesson when it considered how to neutralize the most troubling effects of ACHR membership without mounting a direct challenge to the system as such. It went back to the argument of unconstitutionality already used by the Peruvian and Venezuelan courts, but used it in a more sophisticated way. In a judgment in 2014, the Dominican Constitutional Court found that the Instrument of Recognition of the Inter-American Court's jurisdiction was unconstitutional, as it had only been signed by the President of the Republic and lacked the constitutionally required approval of Congress.[66] This meant that the decision handed down by the IACtHR a few weeks earlier on the highly sensitive issue of the right to citizenship of individuals of Haitian descent born in the Dominican Republic, which had requested that the country amend its constitution, lacked a proper constitutional basis to produce any domestic legal effects.[67]

---

[64] *Ivcher Bronstein v. Peru, Jurisdiction* [1999], IACtHR, Ser. C No. 54, at 28.
[65] Ibid., No. 54, at 40.
[66] Tribunal Constitucional de la República Dominicana, November 4, 2014, Sentencia TC/0256/14, https://www.tribunalconstitucional.gob.do/content/sentencia-tc025614 (accessed January 8, 2022).
[67] *Expelled Dominicans and Haitians v. Dominican Republic* [2014], IACtHR, Ser. C No. 282.

It is in the African human rights system, however, where the Peruvian precedent has been used most widely and to crippling effect in recent years. In just six months, three out of only ten member States that had initially made a declaration allowing individuals and NGOs to directly submit applications against them at the ACtHPR withdrew the declaration: Tanzania (the host State of the African Court), Benin, and Côte d'Ivoire. This brought the number of member States that still recognize the right to individual petition to just six: Burkina Faso, Gambia, Ghana, Malawi, Mali, and Tunisia (Rwanda already submitted its withdrawal note in 2016). The most recent case of Côte d'Ivoire illustrates clearly that withdrawal is a course of action deliberately chosen in response to a ruling considered too intrusive, and as the most convenient and efficient means to cut short any further meddling of the Court in domestic matters. The decision to withdraw its declaration was a direct response to an Order for Interim Measures issued against Côte d'Ivoire by the ACtHPR on April 22, 2020. In it the Court had ordered a stay of the arrest warrants of twenty Ivorians, most of them politicians, who had been indicted on charges of embezzling public funds and plotting against the authority of the State in the run-up to the presidential elections. Almost immediately following the Court's Order, Côte d'Ivoire withdrew its declaration, citing the African Court's "grave and intolerable actions," which violate its sovereignty and "undermine the foundations of the rule of law by weakening its justice system."[68]

In contrast, a partial withdrawal from the regional system is no longer possible in Europe, where member States can end the compulsory jurisdiction of the ECtHR and the right to individual petition only if they leave the Convention (or the CoE) altogether.[69] This has meant that in the ECHR System the debate has only in rare cases (the United Kingdom, for example) been about the withdrawal of dissatisfied members from the ECHR; the focus has instead been on the reform of the Convention and the limits of member States' duty to comply with decisions of the ECtHR.

3.2. Institutional Reform

Institutional reforms to regional human rights systems have been a major part of the pushback against international human rights supervision in Europe, America, and Africa. Reforms do not necessarily weaken a human rights regime; on the contrary, they can have the express goal of improving and strengthening

---

[68] Davi and Amani (n. 48).
[69] According to Article 58(3), a contracting party that ceases to be a member of the CoE shall also cease to be a party to the Convention under the same conditions.

it. Perhaps the most striking example of a reform process of the latter kind is the reform of the ECHR brought about by the adoption of the Eleventh Protocol. This marked the high tide of human rights law in Europe, and international human rights protection more generally, by making both the right of individual petition and the jurisdiction of the competent regional court (the ECtHR) to hear and decide those petitions a mandatory condition of membership for the first time in an international human rights regime. However, depending on the motivation that underlies the reform process, the arguments and rhetoric used by State representatives in the negotiations, and the ultimate results achieved by the reform process, reform debates can also be an effective tool to weaken rather than strengthen a regional human rights system.[70] The reforms adopted in the regional systems during the last decade fall largely into the latter category.

In Europe, reforms to the ECHR System in the last decade have been the result of two strongly divergent imperatives: (1) the necessity to reduce the caseload of the ECtHR in order to avoid its collapse under the sheer weight of the tens of thousands of petitions reaching the Court every year, and (2) the need to respond to the increasingly vigorous pushback by some member States, foremost among them the United Kingdom and Russia, against what they perceive as the excessive interference of the ECtHR's jurisprudence with domestic legal and political processes. The Brighton Declaration of 2012 was the first major response to thesecond demand. The Declaration seeks to redefine the balance between the Court and member States by giving more power to national institutions.[71] The Declaration led directly to the adoption of Protocol No. 15, which introduces an explicit reference to the principle of subsidiarity and the doctrine of the margin of appreciation into the Convention law. It also reduces the time limit within which an individual application may be made to the Court following the date of a final domestic decision from six to four months. While it has not yet entered into force, its influence can already be seen in the greater willingness of the ECtHR to give more deference to national decisions in its recent case law. Some observers have interpreted this development as the Court turning away from the rights-oriented jurisprudence that had become the ECtHR's hallmark since the late 1970s, and supplementing, or replacing, it with new forms of strategic judging reminiscent of the legal diplomacy of its early period.[72]

In the Inter-American system, the powers and procedures of the Commission became the target of a reform process conducted between 2011 and 2013 by the OAS Permanent Council. The consultation process in which the Commission,

---

[70] Contesse (n. 50), 210.
[71] Mikael Rask Madsen, "The Challenging Authority of the European Court of Human Rights: From Cold War Legal Diplomacy to the Brighton Declaration and Backlash" [2016] 79 *Law and Contemporary Problems* 141, 175.
[72] Ibid., 171.

States, and civil society organizations addressed the need to reform the Commission was a direct response to States' discomfort with the Commission's practices and procedures, and particularly its alleged expansive use of precautionary measures, the absence of precise guidelines for the admissibility of petitions, and the lack of transparent criteria for the inclusion in Chapter IV of the Commission's Annual Report of States in the "black list" of countries that violate human rights in a systematic manner. The process resulted in a much stricter framework for the Commission's activities, forcing it to adopt new rules and regulations with specific and detailed guidelines, amounting to a covert pushback by member States in diplomatic disguise.[73]

A similar development has taken place in Africa. At the summit of the African Union (AU) in July 2018 the Executive Council of the AU adopted Decision EX.CL/Dec.1015(XXIII), which severely undermines the African Commission.[74] According to the Decision, the independence of the Commission is merely functional in nature and thus not independent from the (political) organs of the AU that created it.[75] Among other things, the Decision limits the access of NGOs to the Commission by extending the already existing and more restrictive AU criteria on the accreditation of NGOs to the Commission. This means that the Commission has to close its doors to many of its partners who have supported its work for decades, thereby fatally harming the transnational civil society network that is central to promoting and defending a pan-African human rights culture. Another disingenuous decision is the directive to review the interpretative mandate of the African Commission in light of a similar mandate exercised by the ACtHPR. While African citizens can directly file complaints for violation of their rights to the Commission under the African Charter, which has been ratified by all AU member States with the exception of Morocco, access to the African Court is limited to citizens of those member States that have made the declaration under Article 34(6) to allow individuals and NGOs to directly file cases before the Court, a number which has never been very high (see section 3.1) and has been dwindling rapidly in the recent past.[76] This raises the specter that before

---

[73] Contesse (n. 50), 209–210.

[74] Japhet Biegon, "The Rise and Rise of Political Backlash: African Union Executive Council's Decision to Review the Mandate and Working Methods of the African Commission" [2018] *EJIL Talk!*, www.ejiltalk.org/the-rise-and-rise-of-political-backlash-african-union-executive-councils-decision-to-review-the-mandate-and-working-methods-of-the-african-commission/ (accessed January 8, 2022).

[75] Executive Council of the African Union, 33rd Ordinary Session, June 28–29, 2018, Decision on the Report on the Joint Retreat of the Permanent Representatives' Committee (PRC) and the African Commission on Human and Peoples' Rights (ACHPR), DOC.EX.CL/1089(XXXIII) I, para. 5, https://au.int/sites/default/files/decisions/34655-ex_cl_dec_1008_-1030_xxxiii_e.pdf (accessed January 8, 2022).

[76] Biegon (n. 74), 3.

long the great majority of Africans will be left without any direct access to the region's principal human rights bodies.

3.3. Noncompliance with Individual Decisions

Another important form of resistance to the perceived intrusiveness of regional human rights bodies is noncompliance, partial compliance, or selective compliance with the decisions and recommendations issued by these bodies. While compliance levels have historically been low in the Inter-American system,[77] compliance rates are also declining in Europe where most ECHR member States are now subject to compliance monitoring by the Committee of Ministers.[78] The situation in Africa is even worse. Baring two notable exceptions—namely, the *Zongo*[79] and *Konaté*[80] cases, in which there has been full compliance with the sixteen remedial orders issued by theACtHPR—the situation looks almost uniformly bleak.[81] It underscores the Court's own view that noncompliance is one of its major challenges.[82]

The problem of low compliance rates, which points not only to deficiencies in the regional systems monitoring but to structural problems as well, including the heterogeneity of member States in terms of rule of law standards and the growing complexity of remedial orders, has to be distinguished from cases of principled noncompliance, that is, cases in which the national authorities refuse to implement decisions in accordance with the criteria they have previously defined in the abstract. In both the European and Inter-American systems, such "principled" non-compliance is usually based on Constitutional primacy, or at least certain parts of the Constitution, notably its unamendable provisions or principles. This has been the position adopted by the Russian Constitutional Court in 2014 and later codified in national legislation.[83] In developing its arguments,

---

[77] Alexandra Huneeus, "Courts Resisting Courts: Lessons from the Inter-American Court's Struggle to Enforce Human Rights" [2011] 44 *Cornell International Law Journal* 493, 504: Huneeus notes that at the time of writing there had been full compliance only in one out of every ten cases in which the Court had handed down a final judgment; Contesse (n.50), 232: "structural lack of enforcement."

[78] Madsen (n. 71), 172.

[79] *Zongo v. Burkina Faso* [2014], ACtHPR, Application No. 3/2011.

[80] *Konaté v. Burkina Faso* [2014], ACtHPR, Application No. 004/2013.

[81] See 2018 Mid-Term Activity Report of the African Court on Human and Peoples' Rights, EX.CL/1088(XXXIII), June 2018, https://archives.au.int/handle/123456789/8868?locale-attribute=pt (accessed January 8, 2022).

[82] See 2017 Activity Report of the African Court on Human and Peoples' Rights, EX.CL/1057, January 2018, para. 52, https://archives.au.int/handle/123456789/8940?locale-attribute=fr (accessed January 8, 2022).

[83] Russian Constitutional Court, Judgment of July 14, 2015 No. 21-P; for the analysis of the ruling, see, e.g., Lauri Mälksoo, "Russia's Constitutional Court Defies the European Court of Human Rights: Constitutional Court of the Russian Federation Judgment of 14 July 2015, No. 21-P/2015" [2016] 12 *European Constitutional Law Review* 377.

the Russian Constitutional Court could point to a decision by Germany's Federal Constitutional Court that stated that while German courts are obliged to take into account the relevant judgments of the ECtHR, they can nevertheless arrive at a different conclusion, as the factual or legal issues before the national court may differ from those under scrutiny before the ECtHR.[84]

A similarly restrictive position has been gaining ground in countries that only a few years ago had advocated for a particularly broad interpretation of the domestic effects of international human rights law, including the rulings of the competent regional human rights court. A particularly striking example is Argentina. In 2005, the Argentine Supreme Court ruled that the constitutional rank that Article 75 of the national Constitution accords to international human rights treaties not only applies to the provisions of the ACHR but also to the decisions of the IACtHR, which determine the meaning and scope of these provisions regardless of whether Argentina had been a party to the relevant case or not.[85] However, a few years later when the Inter-American Court held that the freedom of expression under the ACHR of two Argentine journalists had been violated as a result of a civil judgment that found the pair liable to defamation for publishing stories about an illegitimate child of a former president and ordered the Supreme Court to revoke the judgment in its entirety,[86] the latter demurred, arguing that the IACtHR lacked the authority to order the squashing of a domestic judgment.[87]

Even in the absence of a written constitution as the basis for confronting the authority of a regional human rights court, compliance—whether fully or in part—is no longer a foregone conclusion, as the *Hirst* saga in the United Kingdom has shown. In 2005, the Grand Chamber judgment in *Hirst v. UK (No. 2)*[88] held by 12-5 that the "blunt" and "indiscriminate" nature of the ban on the right of convicted prisoners to vote under Section 3 of the 1983 Representation of the People Act breached Article 3 of ECHR Protocol No.1.[89] Five years later, when no measures had been taken to implement *Hirst*, the Court issued the *Greens and MT* pilot judgment,[90] which stipulated that the UK government within six months of the judgment becoming final had to "bring forward . . . legislative proposals" to render the law Convention-compliant.[91] It was following

---

[84] *Görgülü* [2004], BVerfG, 2 BvR 1481/04, para. 50.
[85] *Caso Simon* [2005] Suprema Corte de la Nación Argentina.
[86] *Fontevecchia and D'Amico v. Argentina* [2011], IACHR, Ser. C No. 238, 105.
[87] Corte Suprema de Justicia de la Nacion [CSJN] 5/12/2017, "Ministerio de Relaciones Exteriores y Culto s/ informe sentencia dictada en el caso 'Fontevecchia and D'Amico v. Argentina' por la Corte Interamericana de Derechos Humanos," CSJ 368/1998 (34-M)/CS1 (Arg.).
[88] *Hirst v. United Kingdom (No. 2)* [2006], ECtHR, 42 EHRR, para. 41 (GC).
[89] Ibid., para. 82.
[90] In pilot judgments, the Court identifies structural or systemic problems underlying repetitive cases and imposes an obligation on States to address those problems.
[91] *Greens and MT v. United Kingdom* [2011], ECtHR, 53 EHRR 21, para. 6(a).

Greens that the political storm in the United Kingdom reached its height, centering on the alleged judicial activism of the Strasbourg Court.[92] The governing Conservative Party issued a document proposing fundamental reforms of human rights law, including making judgments of the ECtHR merely advisory with respect to the United Kingdom. The document stated that, should it be unable to secure the CoE's agreement for reform, the United Kingdom would be left with no alternative but to withdraw from the Convention.[93] The Conservative Party manifesto for the May 2015 general election pledged to scrap the 1998 Human Rights Act, which had incorporated the ECHR into British law, and introduce a British Bill of Rights in order to break the formal link between British courts and the ECtHR, thus making Britain's "Supreme Court the ultimate arbiter of human rights matters in the UK."[94] Ironically, the outcome of the Brexit referendum in June 2016, in which a narrow majority voted to leave the European Union, had the effect of putting on hold Conservative plans to repeal the Human Rights Act or withdraw from the Convention during the long and complicated negotiations about the modalities of Brexit.

4. Responses to the Backlash

The responses by regional human rights organizations and institutions to the various forms of pushback from countries irritated by a human rights jurisprudence they consider as intrusive and disrespectful of national sovereignty has been mainly defensive. In Europe, the United Kingdom and similarly minded countries were able to include their grievances in the agenda of the ongoing reform process of the ECHR, which had originally been conceived as a way to prevent the collapse of the system under the excessive caseload of the ECtHR. In the process the opponents of an overexpansive Court were able to shift the parameters of the discussion away from technical issues to the crucial question of the adequate balance between the Court and national institutions. They did so by re-emphasizing the principles of subsidiarity and margin of appreciation and incorporating them into the text of the Convention itself, thus potentially changing the basic *modus operandi* of the Court in a more conservative direction. Protocol No. 15 may already have induced a certain shift in the ECtHR's

---

[92] Jonathan Sumption, "The Limits of Law," in N.W. Barber, Richard Ekins, and Paul Yowell (eds.), *Lord Sumption and the Limits of Law* (Hart Publishing 2016), 15.
[93] The Conservative Party, "Protecting Human Rights in the UK: The Conservatives' Proposals for Changing Britain's Human Rights Laws," October 2014, at 8.
[94] The Conservative Part, "Conservative Party Manifesto 2015," 60.

jurisprudence which more recently leaves greater space to diligent national authorities in the application of the proportionality assessment.[95]

Similarly, the reforms carried out in the Inter-American System over the last decade have been designed not to consolidate but reduce the powers of regional human rights bodies. The reform of Commission procedures and practices was driven by the dissatisfaction of important member States with the expansive way in which the Commission had interpreted its mandate, and the outcome of the evaluations and debates held between 2011 and 2013 reflected this motivation.[96] The States imposed on the Commission the adoption of clear guidelines and criteria for the Commission's annual reports and for the processing of precautionary measures and individual complaints. The new Rules of Procedure contain strict and detailed guidelines for when the Commission may grant precautionary measures, along with the duty to publish the opinions of all the members of the Commission, especially if some of them disagree with the measures issued.[97]

By contrast, the Court has not yet been the object of broader reform measures that will have to be incorporated into the ACHR in order to produce legal effects. But resistance has come in other forms, including through judicial decisions by domestic courts. As the Argentinian example illustrates, domestic courts have grown more restive, especially regarding attempts by the IACtHR to directly interfere with the operation of domestic legal and judicial systems through its remedial orders. As the IACtHR has never developed a doctrine of national margin of appreciation, it lacks the doctrinal tools that would allow it to accommodate member States' concerns in the application of the Convention. This has increased the risk of direct confrontation with member States during the implementation phase, with the latter ignoring or openly refusing to implement decisions they deem too intrusive. Unlike the ECtHR which can shift the burden of confronting member States in the implementation phase to the Committee of Ministers, the IACtHR has no easy way out as it has early on claimed full responsibility for supervising the implementation process itself. However, the Court is ill equipped for such bargaining processes with national governments since hard power, including the power to determine the resources put at the disposal of the Court,

---

[95] Oddny Mjöll Arnardottir, "The Brighton Aftermath and the Changing Role of the European Court of Human Rights" [2018] 9 *Journal of International Dispute Settlement* 223, 237: Arnardottir characterizes this development as a "procedural turn" in the ECtHR's application of the proportionality requirement.

[96] Namely, by the confrontation between the Commission and the Brazilian government over the treatment of the Indigenous communities of the Xingu River Basin, which ended up changing the relationship between Brazil and the Inter-American System from one of benign neglect to outright animosity; see Contesse (n. 50), 216.

[97] See OAS General Assembly, AG/Res. 1 (XLIV-E/13), Results of the Process of Reflection on the Workings of the Inter-American Commission of Human Rights with a View to Strengthening the Inter-American Human Rights System (July 23, 2013).

rests with the member States. The resolution to the standoff with Argentina illustrates how limited the Court's chances are of convincing a member State determined to assert its national sovereignty.[98]

5. The Road Ahead

The way ahead looks different for the three regional systems, reflecting each system's respective strengths and weaknesses. The ECHR system looks the best equipped to weather the storm of pushback and backlash, as its institutionalization is the most advanced of the three systems. In addition, it disposes of doctrinal tools that enable readjustments in the relationship between the Strasbourg Court and member States' institutions. The most important of such tools is the margin of appreciation, which allows for considerable flexibility in the application of the Convention, depending on the rule of law standards and democratic practices of the member State concerned. Leaving the supervision of the implementation of Court judgments to a peer-pressure mechanism also helps to stabilize the system, since it reduces the prospect of a direct confrontation between the Court and uncooperative member States, which could undermine the Court's authority. These institutional and doctrinal resources should allow the Court and the other Convention organs to steer the Strasbourg system through the present troubled period, all the more since they make the cost–benefit analysis for member States toying with the idea of a total withdrawal from the ECHR much more difficult.

Most of these considerations do not apply to the Inter-American system. For perfectly understandable reasons the IACtHR missed its opportunity to forge a partnership with national human rights institutions—and particularly national judiciaries—through the introduction of some form of margin of appreciation doctrine adapted to the region's peculiarities. The window of opportunity for such a move was open during the period that democratic governments were in power (1990s and 2000s) and credibly committed to democracy, human rights, and the rule of law.[99] With populism, neo-authoritarianism, and neo-sovereigntism

---

[98] The compliance monitoring hearing in April 2017 between the Court and the national government, in which lawyers for the victims and the Inter-American Commission took part as well, ended with a Resolution by the IACtHR acknowledging that revoking the judicial decision of 2001, which was found to have violated the Convention, was not the only possible remedy to comply, and that alternative mechanisms included the removal of the decision from all electronic websites or an annotation on the margins of the decision stating that the IACtHR had declared it incompatible with the ACHR; see Contesse (n.50), 223.

[99] See Leiv Marsteintredet, "The Inter-American Court of Human Rights and the Mobilisation of Parliaments," in Matthew Saul, Andreas Follesdal, and Geir Ulfstein (eds.), *The International Human Rights Judiciary and National Parliaments* (Cambridge University Press 2017), 248, 258: Marsteintredet emphasizes that there is basically no discursive space for parliamentarians to

rearing their heads again in the region, this opportunity has probably vanished, and the IACtHR risks sliding gradually into irrelevance. This seeming impasse in the Inter-American System has led to calls for further reform. Not surprisingly, these calls tend to revolve around the absence of a suitable doctrine on the degree of deference to be granted to national institutions in the application of the ACHR, exhorting the Court to adopt a more deferential approach when dealing with a national judiciary that enjoys, according to the documentation provided by the Commission and NGOs, a substantial measure of independence.[100] In addition, the IACtHR's self-asserted compliance–monitoring jurisdiction is increasingly being questioned, as it forces the Court to spend scarce resources on interactions with member States that often prove unproductive. There are proposals to replace judicial compliance monitoring with political supervision mechanisms. However, these mechanisms should not be left solely in the hands of OAS political bodies but ought to involve those Latin American civil society organizations that were crucial to the development of regional human rights law in the pastthrough permanent consultation processes during the implementation phase of the IACtHR's rulings.[101]

The short-term prospects for a recovery of regional human rights law seem bleakest in the case of Africa. Having developed more recently than the European and American systems, its central institutions were just starting to deploy their potential when the dynamics of international human rights protection started to falter.[102] As they were still in a fragile condition, the Commission—and particularly the Courthave been dealt devastating blows by the accelerated backlash that emerged in the wake of the repression of the Arab Spring. It is unlikely that they will be in a position to reinitiate their march toward a dynamic and progressive human rights regime for the whole of Africa any time soon. It is more likely that in Africa the subregional level will play the leading role in the development of international human rights law in the coming years. For instance, the Court of Justice of the Economic Community of West African States (ECOWAS and the East African Court of Justice are creatively carving out a space for rule of law litigation and may grow to include an express human rights jurisdiction in the future.[103]

---

explore and little room to discuss the interpretation of the ACHR; the same argument would seem to apply to the relationship between the IACtHR and domestic courts.

[100] Contesse (n. 50), 230.
[101] Ibid., 235.
[102] Daly and Wiebusch (n. 13), 298.
[103] Huneeus and Madsen (n. 1), 158.

I.5
The Impact of the Inter-American Human Rights System beyond Latin America

By Par Engstrom

1. Introduction

Global human rights governance is at a critical juncture. International politics has become distinctly hostile to human rights. Major powers in the current multipolar world have embraced a transactional and anti-liberal foreign policy, with little salience given to human rights concerns. The European Union is consumed with disintegrating and nationalistic forces on its own continent, with the so-called populist resurgence underpinning a political vision that is overtly anti-rights. The international human rights regime appears powerless when confronted with entrenched rights-abusive regimes. Even within some scholarly ivory towers the international human rights project is being dismissed as elitist, rigid, and inflexibly imposing a universalizing morality at the expense of local customs and standards of behavior.[1] Confronted with dramatic global inequalities and accelerating climate emergencies, international human rights are criticized for offering little, or no, practical assistance in efforts to bring about a more just and equal world, and for being underpinned by minimalist ambitions regarding the possibilities of an otherwise sustainable and just world.[2]

It is precisely in relation to these overlapping political, socioeconomic, and intellectual challenges that I hope to offer in this chapter a partial corrective to the disparate and gloomy assessments of the present state and possible future trajectories of international human rights. I will do so through a series of reflections on the contributions of the Inter-American Human Rights System (IAHRS) to the theory and practice of global human rights governance. More specifically, the chapter highlights three areas of contributions. First, by adopting a historical perspective on the institutional development of the IAHRS, we are reminded of the global and interconnected character of the evolution of the modern international human rights regime. Far from a straightforward narrative

---

[1] Stephen Hopgood, *The Endtimes of Human Rights* (Cornell University Press 2013).
[2] Samuel Moyn, *Not Enough: Human Rights in an Unequal World* (Harvard University Press 2018).

of international human rights resulting from Western imposition, the origins and early developments of the IAHRS demonstrate the important protagonism of the Global South in the emergence and consolidation of global human rights governance. Second, the IAHRS has played a central role in the normative construction and evolving interpretations of international human rights standards. And third, the IAHRS has made important contributions to the theory and practice of human rights governance as an exemplar of how international law and institutions can advance the realization of rights even in the absence of robust enforcement mechanisms and in often inhospitable political conditions.

These distinct contributions of the IAHRS are often overlooked in discussions on the evolution and impact of international human rights. This is partly due to the relative marginalization of regional systems in much human rights scholarship, and to the historical sidelining of the Global South from the history of the modern international human rights regime. The combined result is often a distinct sense of distortion in the analysis of international human rights, whether past, present, or future. It is important, therefore, not just for the IAHRS but for international human rights more broadly to better understand how the IAHRS fits within and has contributed to the development of global human rights governance.

2. The IAHRS and the Origins of Global Human Rights Governance

Since its origins, the IAHRS has been a central part of the modern international human rights regime. The American Declaration of the Rights and Duties of Man (ADHR) from April 1948 predates the Universal Declaration of Human Rights (UDHR), which was adopted in December of that year. More significantly, however, these founding documents of the modern international human rights regime were shaped by similar world historical influences prevailing at the moment in which they were created. In particular, as has been widely documented, there was significant Latin American engagement during the origins of the modern international human rights regime. As a result, there was notable cross-fertilization and interaction between the regional and global regimes, which left a noticeable imprint on both the institutional design and substantive contents of global human rights governance.

Support for democracy and human rights has historically figured prominently on the regional agenda in the Americas. Regional cooperation initiatives have often derived their legitimating rationales from the idea that the universal recognition of fundamental rights is a necessary condition for international life and the establishment of democratic societies. Such regional developments tended to reflect national developments through which newly independent republics adopted constitutions incorporating an ambitious range of rights principles and protections.[3] This is certainly not to deny the politically contested character of regional understandings of human rights. Regional rights traditions in the Americas encompass multiple strands of thought and political practice ranging from liberal definitions of individual rights as inherent and inalienable to those associated with a socialized rights tradition, most notably expressed in the 1917 Mexican Constitution.[4] Moreover, regional rights traditions have developed in a distinctly transnational context since the outset. For example, Kathryn Sikkink has recently highlighted the role of Alejandro Álvarez in the early development of the modern international human rights regime. As early as 1917, Álvarez—a Chilean professor of international law, founding member of the American Institute of International Law, and judge at the International Court of Justice between 1946 and 1955—proposed the idea of the international rights of the individual to the American Institute of International Law; an idea that was subsequently adopted by his peers in the burgeoning transnational legal epistemic communities at the time. In short, the 1948 adoption of the founding Charter of the Organization of American States (OAS) and the accompanying ADHR both need to be seen in light of over a century of inter-American and transnational relations that shaped the norms and principles enshrined in these foundational documents.[5]

It is also important to note Latin American efforts in pushing for an explicit human rights mandate for the United Nations.[6] When the great powers convened at Dumbarton Oaks (August–October 1944), they were manifestly reluctant to include human rights in the draft UN Charter. In contrast, at the Inter-American Conference on Problems of War and Peace at Chapultepec Castle in Mexico City in February 1945, Latin American countries endorsed a report prepared by the Inter-American Juridical Committee that called for a full range of rights to be included in the UN Charter. David Forsythe, for example, highlights:

> [A] small number of Latin states in the 1940s tried to exert moral leadership in support of precise legal obligations and a capacity for regional action on human rights. This handful of Latin states—Panama, Uruguay, Brazil, Mexico, the

---

[3] Paolo G. Carozza, "From Conquest to Constitutions: Retrieving a Latin American Tradition of the Idea of Human Rights" [2003] 25 *Human Rights Quarterly* 281.

[4] Greg Grandin, "The Liberal Traditions in the Americas: Rights, Sovereignty, and the Origins of Liberal Multilateralism" [2012] 117 *American Historical Review* 68.

[5] Louise Fawcett, "The Origins and Development of Regional Ideas in the Americas," in Louise Fawcett and Mónica Serrano (eds.), *Regionalism and Governance in the Americas: Continental Drift* (Palgrave Macmillan 2005).

[6] Mary Ann Glendon, "The Forgotten Crucible: The Latin American Influence on the Universal Human Rights Idea" [2003] 16 *Harvard Human Rights Journal* 13.

Dominican Republic, Cuba, and Venezuela—also pushed for binding human rights commitments at the San Francisco conference which led to the establishment of the United Nations.[7]

Moreover, at the San Francisco conference (April–June 1945), which led to the adoption of the UN Charter, the twenty Latin American countries participating constituted not only the largest regional grouping but also the most important voting bloc. As each part of the Charter required a two-thirds majority to pass, Latin American countries were instrumental in ensuring that the UN Charter eventually contained seven references to human rights, including listing the promotion of human rights as one of the basic purposes of the United Nations.

Latin American lawyers and diplomats also contributed to the expansion of the modern human rights canon. The ADHR's comprehensive directory of rights proved influential in shaping the incorporation of social and economic rights into the UDHR. This combined attention to civil and political *as well as* economic and social rights reflected the often eclectic mix of socialist, liberal, and Catholic traditions that had characterized Latin American intellectual thought and constitutional practice since the independence era. Moreover, while the ADHR's attention to human duties was eventually not reflected in the UDHR, its insistence on the "right to justice" (drawing from Latin American *amparo* laws) was translated into the UDHR's Article 8. The role of the pan-American feminist movement was also significant,[8] reflecting burgeoning transnational influences. Several prominent Latin American women delegates, such as Brazil's Bertha Lutz, the Dominican Republic's Minerva Bernardino, and Chile's Ana Figueroa, played instrumental roles in advocating for the inclusion of equal rights for women and men in the UDHR, as well as the use of explicit language calling for the defense of the rights of women.

In addition to their insistence on a full range of rights, including socioeconomic rights, Latin American government representatives also drew on a rich tradition of regional political debates concerning the scope of legitimate international intervention in the domestic affairs of States. Arguably, this was most notable at the 1945 Inter-American Conference on Problems of War and Peace, when the Inter-American Juridical Committee was requested to draft a human rights declaration. The Conference discussed the "Larreta Proposal"—named after the Uruguayan Minister of Foreign Affairs, Eduardo Rodríguez Larreta—which proposed to suspend or restrict the principle of nonintervention in the internal affairs of another country and called for multilateral action to defend

---

[7] David Forsythe, "Human Rights, the United States and the Organizations of American States" [1991] 13 *Human Rights Quarterly* 75.

[8] Katherine M. Marino, *Feminism for the Americas: The Making of an International Human Rights Movement* (UNC Press Books 2019).

democracy and human rights. Larreta argued that the principles of sovereignty and nonintervention could be misused to shield abusive governments, and that nonintervention had to be "harmonized" with other foundational principles of the Inter-American System, most notably the protection of fundamental human rights. While the proposal was never formally approved, it reflected a willingness to lobby for regional institutions having intrusive human rights mandates and foreshadowed more contemporary notions of conditional sovereignty and global intervention duties in response to mass atrocities.[9] Similarly, the notion of popular sovereignty also figured prominently in debates concerning the right of peoples to self-government. The 1948 Bogotá Conference adopted a resolution on the "Preservation and Defence of Democracy in America," and governments agreeing to the resolution resolved to take any necessary measures to ensure that "the free and sovereign right of their peoples to govern themselves in accordance with their domestic aspirations" would not be violated.[10]

However, it should be recognized that while many of the States participating in the simultaneous construction of the United Nations and Inter-American System endorsed human rights in principle, they nonetheless remained reluctant to accept any precise legal obligations that could legitimate international action to enforce these principles. For example, as documented by Forsythe: "In 1948, only six of twenty-one states, not including the United States, wanted the American Declaration to be part of the OAS Charter and hence binding international law. And only eight of twenty voting states, again not including the United States, wanted a binding convention on human rights."[11] That is, the American Declaration, though providing a wide-ranging directory of rights, was clearly not intended to be binding on signatory States.[12] Moreover, given the historical and regional power disparities in which American States were formed, certain principles—most notably self-determination, the right to independence, and freedom from intervention—came to guide their attempts at regional cooperation. Indeed, the emergence of the IAHRS vividly illustrates the challenges inherent in the tensions between human rights promotion and concerns about intervention in a regional context of longstanding power asymmetries.[13]

Nonetheless, the key point to note is that the early development of the IAHRS simultaneously nourished and was shaped by the flourishing of human rights

---

[9] Tom Long and Max Paul Friedman, "The Promise of Precommitment in Democracy and Human Rights: The Hopeful, Forgotten Failure of the Larreta Doctrine" [2020] 18 *Perspectives on Politics* 1088.

[10] Ninth International Conference of American States, held at Bogotá, Colombia, March 30–May 2, 1948, Resolution XXXII, <https://history.state.gov/historicaldocuments/frus1948v09/pg_1> (accessed February 17, 2022).

[11] Forsythe (n. 7), 77.

[12] Thomas Buergenthal and Dinah Shelton, *Protecting Human Rights in the Americas: Cases and Materials* (International Institute of Human Rights 1995), 39.

[13] Andrew Hurrell, "Security in Latin America" [1998] 74 *International Affairs* 531.

ideas and debates in the years leading up to and following the parallel adoptions in 1948 of the American Declaration and the Universal Declaration. The inclusion of human rights language in the founding text of the United Nations, with distinct Latin American contributions and influences, channeled the history of postwar global governance, with implications beyond the confines of the international human rights regime—such as in contemporary debates concerning the notion of the Responsibility to Protect. Recognizing the interrelated genesis of the UN and IAHRS regimes is part and parcel of ongoing efforts to bring to light the role of the Global South in the origins and early development of the international human rights regime. Latin American lawyers, diplomats, and activists were key protagonists in shaping the emergence of global human rights governance. These contributions are not only significant as a matter of historical accuracy, they also offer an important corrective to prevailing critiques of human rights as created and imposed by powerful countries of the Global North. The institutional origins of the IAHRS offer an important reminder that some of the central ideas of modern international human rights did not originate in the Global North. Rather, while not denying the pivotal role great powers played in the design of the postwar international order, human rights principles and law emerged to a very significant extent from the Global South, and from Latin America in particular.[14] Equally significant for the purposes of this chapter, these institutional origins also point to a distinctly regional story underpinning the development of the modern international human rights regime. Clearly, the emergence of human rights as part of regional governance structures in the Americas is not a simple story of hegemonic imposition. Rather, this emergence resulted from a lengthy and complex transnational history of interaction between external and local political forces and ideas about political organization. Recognizing these early institutional contributions from the Global South has important implications for thinking about the present and possible future trajectories of global human rights politics.

3. The IAHRS and International Human Rights Standards

A second major contribution of the IAHRS to global human rights governance is evident in its role as a human rights standard-setter. The IAHRS has been at the forefront of normative developments in international human rights law and in the process has contributed to progressive legal and institutional change. Both the Inter-American Commission on Human Rights (IACHR) and the

---

[14] Kathryn Sikkink, *Evidence for Hope: Making Human Rights Work in the 21st Century* (Princeton University Press 2019), 56.

Inter-American Court of Human Rights (IACtHR) perform crucial functions in the continued development of human rights standards. Specifically, the Court has developed progressive human rights jurisprudence through its rulings, while the Commission contributes to the development of soft law through its thematic reports and adoption of policy guidelines. This section summarizes four particularly distinctive and illustrative areas of international human rights law in which the IAHRS has been a prominent norm protagonist, with significant ramifications for the region and beyond.

First, the System's distinctive approach to transitional justice (TJ) and reparations to victims of mass atrocities has had a particularly significant set of influences on global legal and policy developments. The IAHRS's dealings with TJ have given rise to a broad set of State obligations. In particular, the IAHRS has played a particularly prominent role in the strengthening of anti-impunity norms: confirming that States have an international obligation to ensure accountability for human rights violations, establish the truth, and repair harms in the aftermath of mass atrocities.[15] The System has also engaged in expansive interpretations of States' international obligations, which in the process has both drawn on and contributed to the development of international criminal law. For example, the IACtHR has argued that forced disappearances are prohibited by *ius cogens* and declared them a continuous crime. These normative and legal developments have exerted important influences on judicial and legal changes in a range of Latin American countries, which in turn have facilitated ongoing criminal prosecutions of perpetrators of past violations in the region.[16] But the IAHRS has also been an instrumental force in the global shift "away from a state's general duty to guarantee rights and toward the victim's individual right to have the government investigate and punish."[17] Most prominently, the IACtHR's rulings on amnesty laws have widened the space for judicial proceedings against alleged human rights violators in national courts, and the Court's amnesty jurisprudence has influenced accountability pressures beyond the region.[18] In the process, the System has developed a victim-oriented jurisprudence and practice, emphasizing the right to effective judicial remedy—namely, the right to a

---

[15] Diego Rodriguez-Pinzon, "The Inter-American Human Rights System and Transitional Processes," in Antoine Buyse and Michael Hamilton (eds.), *Transitional Jurisprudence and the ECHR: Justice, Politics and Rights* (Cambridge University Press 2011).

[16] Ezequiel A. Gonzáles-Ocantos, *Shifting Legal Visions: Judicial Change and Human Rights Trials in Latin America* (Cambridge University Press 2016).

[17] Alexandra Huneeus, "International Criminal Law by Other Means: The Quasi-Criminal Jurisdiction of the Human Rights Courts" [2013] 107 *American Journal of International Law* 8.

[18] Louise Mallinder, "The End of Amnesty or Regional Overreach? Interpreting the Erosion of South America's Amnesty Laws" [2016] 65 *International and Comparative Law Quarterly* 645; Christina Binder, "The Prohibition of Amnesties by the Inter-American Court of Human Rights" [2011] 12 *German Law Journal* 1203; Gerald L. Neuman, "The External Reception of Inter-American Human Rights Law" [2011] *Quebec Journal of International Law* 99.

fair trial and judicial protection—in other words, access to justice, as well as an increasingly comprehensive, integral, and "holistic" set of reparation policies.[19] The IACtHR's policies of reparations now include monetary compensation to victims, symbolic reparations (for example memorials), demands for State reforms, and criminal prosecutions of individual perpetrators. Moreover, the IACtHR's activist remedial regime has led it to restrict the scope of State discretion regarding remedies and to boost its institutional efforts to monitor State implementation.[20] As a result, the IAHRS's TJ-related jurisprudence emphasizing criminal accountability, the right to individual judicial redress, the right to truth, and comprehensive reparations have had significant normative influences on global TJ policy and law. For example, at the normative and jurisprudential level, globally recognized human rights norms such as those concerning forced disappearances, the right to truth, and the right to an identity can be traced back to efforts by Latin American human rights actors, supported by the IAHRS, to confront pervasive violations in the region.[21]

Second, the IAHRS has been at the forefront of international efforts at reconceptualizing gender-based violence, not least since the 1994 adoption of the Inter-American Convention on the Prevention, Punishment, and Eradication of Violence against Women (the Belém do Pará Convention). The System's approach to violence against women (VAW) has had a significant impact by defining the concept of femicide, expanding the scope of State obligations, and adopting a gender perspective on reparations. The IAHRS has been particularly robust in highlighting the discriminatory character of VAW, including rape. Since the mid-1990s, the IAHRS has qualified rape (on the basis of the serious effects and the irreparable damage it causes) as torture under international law. In addition to the moral and psychological suffering caused by rape, the IACtHR has also highlighted the serious social and cultural effects such violations can have on victims, particularly, but not exclusively, in terms of the relationship between the victim and her community. Moreover, the Court has addressed the targeted nature of VAW in the context of armed conflict. Most noteworthy has been the IAHRS's conceptualization of VAW as "femicide." The 2009 ruling by the IACtHR in the so-called Cotton Field cases was a landmark in the judicial struggle against gender-based violence. The Cotton Field cases (concerning the

---

[19] Clara Sandoval, "Two Steps Forward, One Step Back: Reflections on the Jurisprudential Turn of the Inter-American Court of Human Rights on Domestic Reparation Programmes" [2018] 22 *International Journal of Human Rights* 1192.

[20] Alexandra Huneeus, "Reforming the State from Afar: Structural Reform Litigation at the Human Rights Courts" [2015] 40 *Yale Journal of International Law* 1.

[21] Reed Brody and Felipe Gonzalez, "Nunca Mas: An Analysis of International Instruments on 'Disappearances'" [1997] 19 *Human Rights Quarterly* 365; Ariel E. Dulitzky, "The Latin-American Flavor of Enforced Disappearances" [2019] 19 *Chicago Journal of International Law* 423; Thomas M. Antkowiak, "Truth as Right and Remedy in International Human Rights Experience" [2002] 23 *Michigan Journal of International Law* 977.

murder of three women in Ciudad Juárez, Mexico) highlighted the discriminatory character of lethal VAW, the social context in which such violence takes place, and the special vulnerability of the victims. The Court stressed the gender-based nature of the disappearances and killings and emphasized the fact that these violations took place in the context of structural discrimination against women, which extended to the Mexican authorities' distinct lack of adequate responses to the cases, leading to a pervasive state of impunity. In addition, the IAHRS has held that States have a responsibility to not only investigate, adjudicate, and sanction crimes of VAW but to act with due diligence to prevent such crimes from occurring, including scenarios where the perpetrators are private actors, as in domestic violence cases. The IACtHR has elaborated on the specific aspects of States' positive obligations to investigate instances of gender-based violence and to comprehensively assess the conditions that prevent women from accessing justice in contexts of widespread impunity. It is also worth noting how the IACtHR has increasingly developed what some observers refer to as a "holistic gender approach" to reparations.[22] This generally refers to the ways that the Court both identifies relevant facts, violations, and victims in the cases before it and to the extent that it adopts appropriately gender-sensitive reparations measures, including remedies that aim at transforming the sexual hierarchies at the root of gender-based violence and discriminatory practices.

A third example of innovative IAHRS jurisprudence is the concept of the right to a dignified life (*vida digna*), which also illustrates the potential of the IAHRS to feed into global human rights debates.[23] As highlighted in the previous section, the ADHR includes a full range of rights, encompassing civil and political, as well as economic, social, and cultural rights. However, in transforming the ADHR's provisions into legally binding obligations in the American Convention, OAS member States clearly prioritized the former over the latter. Despite the adoption of the San Salvador Protocol in 1988, much of the IAHRS caseload and institutional attention have focused primarily on civil and political rights. Historically, these normative priorities reflected the political and ideological context of the Cold War in the Americas, during which the IAHRS was institutionally consolidated.[24] The relative marginalization of socioeconomic rights notwithstanding, the pervasive realities of poverty and material inequalities in

---

[22] Ruth Rubio-Martin and Clara Sandoval, "Engendering the Reparations Jurisprudence of the Inter-American Court of Human Rights: The Promise of the Cotton Field Judgment" [2011] 33 *Human Rights Quarterly* 1062.

[23] Thomas M. Antkowiak, "A 'Dignified Life' and the Resurgence of Social Rights" [2020] 18 *Northwestern Journal of Human Rights* 1.

[24] Par Engstrom, "The Inter-American Human Rights System and US-Latin American Relations," in Juan Pablo Scarfi and Andrew R. Tillman (eds.), *Cooperation and Hegemony in US-Latin American Relations: Revisiting the Western Hemisphere Idea, Studies of the Americas* (Palgrave Macmillan 2016), 209–247; Patrick William Kelly, *Sovereign Emergencies: Latin America and the Making of Global Human Rights Politics* (Cambridge University Press 2018).

the region have still left their mark on the IAHRS's activities and caseload. Most notably, the IACtHR has advanced a particularly innovative understanding of the centrality of a range of social rights for human welfare. The IACtHR's jurisprudence on the right to life includes the notion of a "dignified and decent existence," which necessarily encompasses the obligation to ensure basic economic, social, and cultural rights.[25] This interpretation of the fundamental right to life advanced by the Court emphasizes the right of individuals and groups not to be denied access to the material conditions that guarantee a dignified life. This jurisprudential interpretation is in line with what some would call "the indivisibility and interdependence of rights approach."[26] Similarly, the Court has interpreted the fundamental civil rights notions of equal protection and nondiscrimination in conjunction with a range of socioeconomic rights to include the right to social security and the right to a healthy environment, as well as access rights to basic public services. In short, the Court's notion of a dignified life consists of an integrated understanding of the protection of rights and follows from its engagement with the lived realities of people in the region, in particular traditionally vulnerable and marginalized groups. As an illustration of the normative diffusion of the IACtHR's jurisprudence in this regard, it should be noted that the concept of the right to a dignified life was recently recognized by the UN Human Rights Committee in its General Comment No. 36 on the right to life, considered by some as a significant breakthrough in efforts to promote the justiciability of socioeconomic rights.[27] The IACtHR's recent jurisprudential turn has also lent additional support to advocates for the justiciability of socioeconomic rights, with an increasing number of its rulings recognizing the direct justiciability of Article 26 of the American Convention.[28] These are all potentially significant developments for global efforts to promote the international justiciability of socioeconomic rights.

Fourth, the IAHRS has also been in the vanguard of the international development of Indigenous rights. Since the adoption of the landmark ruling in the case of the Mayagna (Sumo) Awas Tingni community, the IACtHR

---

[25] Jo M. Pasqualucci, "The Right to a Dignified Life (Vida Digna): The Integration of Economic and Social Rights with Civil and Political Rights in the Inter-American Human Rights System" [2008] 31 *Hastings International and Comparative Law Review* 1.

[26] Mónica Feria Tinta, "Justiciability of Economic, Social, and Cultural Rights in the Inter-American System of Protection of Human Rights: Beyond Traditional Paradigms and Notions" [2007] 29 *Human Rights Quarterly* 431.

[27] Lucy McKernan and Bret Thiele, "UN Human Rights Committee Brings New Vitality to the Right to Life" (*OpenGlobalRights*, February 13, 2019), <www.openglobalrights.org/un-human-rights-committee-brings-new-vitality-to-the-right-to-life/> (accessed January 22, 2022).

[28] Daniel Cerqueira, "Jurisprudencia de la Corte IDH en casos sobre DESCA: entre lo retorico y lo impredecible" (*Justicia en las Américas*, January 7, 2020), <https://dplfblog.com/2020/01/07/jurisprudencia-de-la-corte-idh-en-casos-sobre-desca-entre-lo-retorico-y-lo-impredecible/> (accessed January 22, 2022).

has developed extensive Indigenous rights jurisprudence. The IAHRS has recognized the collective rights of Indigenous communities to ancestral lands and natural resources on the basis of their importance for the distinct cultural identities of these communities. By interpreting the right to property (Article 21 of the American Convention) to include a right of Indigenous people to communal property, the IAHRS has essentially advanced a communitarian understanding of human rights. Moreover, the IACtHR has also recognized the right of Indigenous communities to consultation and participation in all matters that could directly affect them. The IACtHR has argued that the right to free, prior, and informed consent to any administrative or legal measure affecting the livelihoods of Indigenous people is directly related to the general State obligation to guarantee the free and full exercise of Convention rights. As such, States have duties to take positive measures to promote and protect Indigenous rights. In addition, the IACtHR has generally adopted a broad interpretation of these rights and corresponding State duties to include the protection of the right of members of Indigenous communities to enjoy their own cultural and traditional practices. The Court has argued that the rationale for these special protections of Indigenous communities is to protect traditional ways of life, customs and beliefs, distinct cultural identities, and distinctive social and economic structures. In short, the IACtHR has highlighted the importance of the effective protection and preservation of the physical and cultural survival of Indigenous peoples through the protection of their cultural diversity. The Court has argued that the value of cultural diversity expands the scope of protection of Convention rights, most notably the right to property, in order to protect the specific rights of Indigenous peoples.

These jurisprudential developments notwithstanding, there have been recurrent tensions between, on the one hand, preserving the cultural identities and traditional values of Indigenous peoples through protecting their right to lands and natural resources, and on the other hand, economic development projects and extractive industries. There have also been critiques of the Court's tendency to connect Indigenous rights to the right of property.[29] Moreover, for some, Indigenous-rights claims raise questions regarding the applicability of universal conceptualizations of individual rights as advanced in the liberal tradition, which has tended to dominate the evolution of the modern international human rights regime, including the development of the IAHRS. Nonetheless, the IAHRS's expansive and path-breaking jurisprudence on Indigenous rights—most notably the notion of collective land rights—has stimulated practices of cross-regional

---

[29] Thomas M. Antkowiak, "Rights, Resources, and Rhetoric: Indigenous Peoples and the Inter-American Court" [2013] 35 *University of Pennsylvania Journal of International Law* 113.

judicial dialogue with other regional human rights systems, particularly with the African human rights system.[30]

Overall, the IAHRS's normative contributions to global human rights are extensive and go beyond these illustrative examples. The IAHRS has responded institutionally to the changing regional human rights landscape in ways that underline the potential for normative and institutional change and adaptation in human rights governance. In its practice, the IAHRS has shifted from its focus on TJ-related human rights challenges toward dealing with issues related to structural and ongoing violence. Whether it is gender-based violence committed by police and security forces or the rights of Indigenous groups to ancestral lands, the IAHRS's emphasis on accountability, victims' rights, and reparations builds on its decades-long engagement with TJ. The IAHRS is increasingly ambitious not only in terms of the types of human rights challenges it deals with but also in terms of what it demands from States. The IAHRS is pushing the normative boundaries of international human rights, not least beyond the liberal minimalist definitions of human rights—most clearly illustrated in the System's Indigenous rights jurisprudence—as well as in its continually evolving and expanding interpretation of the scope of State obligations, manifested, for example, with respect to cases of femicide and its incipient engagement with environmental rights standards. As a result, through the diffusion of its normative contributions the IAHRS has emerged as a central actor in global human rights governance. Hence, while it is true that the IAHRS has adopted global common human rights scripts and adapted them according to regional circumstances,[31] the System has also significantly contributed to the evolution of global human rights standards in multiple ways, some of which were outlined in this section.

4. The IAHRS and Transnationalized Human Rights Implementation

As illustrated in the previous section, the IAHRS has undergone significant normative and institutional changes since its creation. Most notably, the IAHRS has developed highly transnationalized structures of regional human rights

---

[30] Mauro Barelli, "The Interplay Between Global and Regional Human Rights Systems in the Construction of the Indigenous Rights Regime" [2010] 32 *Human Rights Quarterly* 951; Jérémie Gilbert, "Indigenous Peoples' Human Rights in Africa: The Pragmatic Revolution of the African Commission on Human and Peoples' Rights" [2011] 60 *International & Comparative Law Quarterly* 245; Lucy Claridge, "The Approach to UNDRIP within the African Regional Human Rights System" [2019] 23 *International Journal of Human Rights* 267.

[31] Alexandra Huneeus and Mikael Rask Madsen, "Between Universalism and Regional Law and Politics: A Comparative History of the American, European, and African Human Rights Systems" [2018] 16 *International Journal of Constitutional Law* 136.

governance. As I have documented elsewhere,[32] three features of this trend toward the transnationalization of the IAHRS in recent decades are particularly significant: (1) as already noted in the previous section, the expansion and increased intrusiveness of regional human rights norms and legal standards; (2) the increased pluralism of actors and stakeholders engaging with the System; and (3) the consolidation of decentralized implementation structures. This section elaborates on the significance of the latter two features of the contemporary IAHRS: the multiplicity of actors interacting with the System and its evolving practices of decentralized modalities of human rights implementation. In a nutshell, the patterns of institutional change that the IAHRS has undergone are significant not only for the System itself but also for the theory and practice of global human rights governance more broadly, particularly in light of persistent State resistance to human rights and the absence of robust and authoritative political enforcement structures.

The IAHRS has over the years developed from a "classical" intergovernmental regime into a transnational political space with a far-reaching human rights mandate. From its roots as a government-run diplomatic entity with a vaguely defined mandate to promote respect for human rights in the region, the System has emerged as a legal regime formally empowering citizens to challenge their own governments' human rights records. An independent regional human rights Court and an autonomous Commission are regularly judging whether regional States are in compliance with their international human rights obligations. The access of individuals and human rights organizations to the IAHRS has strengthened over time as the System has become increasingly judicialized with a procedural focus on legal argumentation and the generation of regional human rights jurisprudence.[33] Undeniably, these are all fundamental institutional changes hardly envisaged by the State representatives responsible for the initial creation of the IAHRS. The gradual erosion of State control over the IAHRS is clearly uneven and patchy, as the continuing reliance of the IAHRS on US funding illustrates. Nonetheless, the System has developed an increasingly extensive set of human rights norms and practices that legitimate both international concern for the general welfare of individuals and action regarding the internal human rights practices of States.[34]

---

[32] Par Engstrom and Andrew Hurrell, "Why the Human Rights Regime in the Americas Matters," in Mónica Serrano and Vesselin Popovski (eds.), *Human Rights Regimes in the Americas* (United Nations University Press 2010).

[33] Par Engstrom, "Reconceptualizing the Impact of the Inter-American Human Rights System" [2017] 8(2) *Revista Dereito & Práxis* 1250–1285, 1253.

[34] David Harris, "Regional Protection of Human Rights: The Inter-American Achievement," in David Harris and Stephen Livingstone (eds.), *The Inter-American Human Rights System* (Clarendon Press 1998).

The IAHRS has also developed important accountability functions. Both the Commission and the Court regularly monitor and evaluate the human rights performance of States. As a result, the IAHRS has established itself as an important advocacy actor in its own right. The Commission has developed a set of tools in addition to its role as a quasi-judicial organ processing individual cases, which range from public diplomacy in the form of press releases, public hearings, on-site visits, and interim measures (precautionary mechanisms), to behind-the-scenes negotiations with State officials and individual petitioners (through so-called friendly settlement proceedings).[35] Moreover, the IAHRS performs an important indirect advocacy role by providing a platform for human rights NGOs, some of which have been very adept at integrating the IAHRS into their domestic and transnational advocacy strategies.[36] Admittedly, these are weak accountability mechanisms when seen exclusively from a top-down enforcement perspective. There are no enforcement mechanisms in place to hold States responsible for implementation. For example, there is no clearly mandated political compliance mechanism—like the one assumed by the Committee of Ministers in the European human rights system. Nonetheless, the IAHRS amply illustrates how accountability can operate through various channels, including primarily domestic accountability mechanisms.[37] Most notably, the set of accountability functions provided by the IAHRS demonstrate how the System has become increasingly inserted into domestic policy and legislative debates on specific human rights issues across the region.

The normative and institutional evolution of the IAHRS has led to an increased interaction between the IAHRS, domestic political processes, and national legal orders. The internalization of IAHRS mechanisms and norms in domestic political and legal systems has significantly altered the character of human rights implementation. Human rights implementation has traditionally been dominated by the political branches of government and largely controlled by the executive and the Ministry of Foreign Affairs in particular. Although these entities remain central to State compliance with IAHRS rulings and decisions, a broader range of actors are now involved in implementation processes, accentuating the shift toward decentralized human rights enforcement. As I have examined in more detail elsewhere,[38] the IAHRS affects and shapes political relationships in relation to three main set of actors.

---

[35] Engstrom (n. 33) 1250–1285, 1257.
[36] Par Engstrom and Peter Low, "Mobilising the Inter-American Human Rights System: Regional Litigation and Domestic Human Rights Impact in Latin America," in Par Engstrom (ed.), *The Inter-American Human Rights System: Impact Beyond Compliance* (Springer 2019), 23–58.
[37] Engstrom (n. 33), 1250–1285, 1258.
[38] Engstrom (n. 33), 1250.

First, the IAHRS provides opportunities for domestic and transnational human rights actors to bring pressure for change in their domestic political and legal systems. The use of the IAHRS by human rights organizations across the region has increased dramatically in recent decades. Human rights groups use the IAHRS to expose systemic human rights violations, negotiate with State institutions, frame social and political debates on the basis of IAHRS norms and jurisprudence, promote the interests of vulnerable groups, boost human rights litigation before domestic courts, and to strengthen regional human rights networks through the use of the IAHRS in strategic supranational litigation. While the capacity of actors to access and mobilize the IAHRS is highly unequal, organized civil society groups have become the lifeblood of the IAHRS. The availability of the IAHRS for human rights groups has the potential to strengthen the domestic position of those groups engaging with the System, particularly when faced with resistance and obstacles at home. Moreover, at various critical conjunctures the System has found allies in regional human rights movements. However, it needs to be recognized that from efforts to hold perpetrators to account for gender violence in Mexico to mobilization around LGBTIQ+ or land rights in Brazil, human rights groups face regular harassment, political vilification, and violence. In the face of these realities, the IAHRS's often slow-moving procedures are of little direct or immediate help. The IAHRS has attempted to respond to these realities by developing specific institutional mechanisms aimed at supporting human rights defenders, such as its use of precautionary measures (*medidas cautelares*) to respond quickly to situations of acute risks. This illustrates that human rights actors tend not to remain passive recipients of international human rights norms, and important feedback mechanisms are generated as these actors influence the development of international norms and institutions.[39]

Second, with the expansion of international human rights standards, domestic court systems have come to play an increasingly prominent role as arenas of human rights implementation. In the countries of the IAHRS, as in many other States, a wide range of human rights treaties and conventions have become embedded in domestic legal systems.[40] The constitutional incorporation of international human rights treaties has made domestic courts key actors with a potential to activate human rights treaties and interpret international norms in light of domestic conditions.[41] While there is significant variation not just in the

---

[39] Ibid., 1261 ff.
[40] Armin von Bogdandy et al., *Transformative Constitutionalism in Latin America: The Emergence of a New Ius Commune* (Oxford University Press 2017).
[41] Marcelo Torelly, "Transnational Legal Process and Fundamental Rights in Latin America: How Does the Inter-American Human Rights System Reshape Domestic Constitutional Rights?," in Pedro Fortes et al. (eds.), *Law and Policy in Latin America: Transforming Courts, Institutions, and Rights* (Palgrave Macmillan 2017), 21–38.

effective enforcement of human rights within domestic legal systems but also in the willingness and ability of judges to engage in the transnational legal culture of human rights, domestic judges have become important political actors shaping the ways in which international human rights are applied domestically. Moreover, the IAHRS has been an active participant in these efforts at activating domestic judiciaries as enforcers of regional norms and standards. A unique aspect of the IACtHR's relationship with domestic judiciaries is the doctrine of "conventionality control," which states that all State actors must review laws under the American Convention and not apply laws found to be in violation of it. Through this doctrine, the Court seeks to enlist all State actors in monitoring compliance with the Convention, as interpreted by the Court. Hence, the Inter-American Court has sought to expand the role of domestic judiciaries in enforcing the American Convention and the rulings of the Court itself. Conventionality control has the potential to extend the shadow of the Court far beyond its relatively small docket. In so doing, however, it also seeks to harmonize judicial interpretations of the American Convention. This has led some legal scholars to suggest that the IACtHR has been transformed into a "supranational human rights constitutional court," whose role is to standardize the interpretation of rights enshrined in the American Convention.[42] While some legal scholars have quite sharply criticized the Court's attempts to extend its authority[43]—on the grounds of both its alleged limited effectiveness and shaky legitimacy—regional jurisprudential interaction and legal dialogues have intensified in recent years.[44] There has also been an incipient yet increasing trend toward extraregional judicial dialogues.[45] It is clearly the case that regional human rights systems, including the IAHRS, operate in a fertile environment of interlegality, one characterized by a plurality of domestic and international legal and judicial systems. This provides ample scope for judicial dialogue and exchange, as evidenced, for example, in rapidly evolving human rights jurisprudence on issues such as sexual orientation rights and the applicability of amnesties—both areas in which the IAHRS has made significant normative contributions.

Third, the domestic internalization of IAHRS mechanisms and norms has also shifted the ways in which the System engages with States. With the IAHRS no longer concerned primarily with "naming and shaming" repressive

---

[42] E.g., Ariel E. Dulitzky, "An Inter-American Constitutional Court? The Invention of the Conventionality Control by the Inter-American Court of Human Rights" [2015] 50 *Texas International Law Journal* 45; Engstrom (n. 33), 1266.

[43] Jorge Contesse, "Contestation and Deference in the Inter-American Human Rights System Subsidiarity in Global Governance" [2016] 79 *Law and Contemporary Problems* 123.

[44] Ezequiel Gonzalez-Ocantos, "Communicative Entrepreneurs: The Case of the Inter-American Court of Human Rights' Dialogue with National Judges" [2018] 62 *International Studies Quarterly* 737.

[45] See Neuman (n. 18).

authoritarian regimes, it instead engages with a variety of nominally democratic regimes through a quasi-judicial process that assumes at least partially responsive State institutions. This broader point underlines the potential for State actors and institutions to act as "compliance constituencies" and conduits for domestic implementation, linking international human rights norms to domestic political and legal institutions and actors. Different State institutions are now engaging with the System, which has led to the "disaggregation" of the relationship between countries and the IAHRS. This increasingly means that States no longer interact with the System solely through their respective Ministry of Foreign Affairs but through a number of different institutional channels including Ministries of Justice, *Ministerios Públicos*, and subnational authorities. The IACHR's friendly settlement procedures, for example, are frequently used to facilitate negotiations between different State institutions and petitioners. Furthermore, due to the IACtHR's creative remedial regime, the Court frequently issues orders that require action from State actors other than the executive. The impact of the IAHRS on the formulation and implementation of public policy is to a large extent a function of its embeddedness, or institutionalization, in State institutions and depends on whether a State has effectively organized its institutions in ways that provide effective remedies for human rights violations. Interestingly, a more strategic vision of the IAHRS appears to be increasingly recognized within some State bureaucracies across Latin America. State prosecutors' offices in several countries (for example, Argentina and Brazil) have created dedicated human rights units to actively petition the Inter-American Commission. Few Latin American States, however, have formal institutional mechanisms in place to ensure consistent implementation of IAHRS decisions and recommendations. Nonetheless, the IAHRS can provide a political space for discussions and negotiations between the key actors involved in human rights reforms (including different parts of the State): it provides an authoritative set of norms and standards to regulate the specific issue-area subject to the reforms, and it adds an additional layer of political pressure, momentum, and urgency to the resolution of human rights problems.[46]

In short, these illustrations of the transnational dynamics of human rights implementation in the context of the IAHRS offer important insights into how international law and institutions might operate against the odds or when confronted with inhospitable conditions. It is precisely in this way that the IAHRS stands out as an exemplar of contemporary human rights governance. The IAHRS is able to exert influence on human rights outcomes from a position of relative weakness. The System has limited leverage and highly inadequate resources at its disposal, particularly when considered in relation to the scale and number of human rights

---

[46] Engstrom (n. 33), 1268 ff.

challenges it confronts. It has no consistent backing from powerful States and there are no formal sanction mechanisms underpinning the System's rulings and decisions; the IAHRS is disconnected from regional political and economic governance structures; and there is no equivalent of EU accession incentives in the Americas. Moreover, the regional context in which the IAHRS operates displays limited normative convergence around values of human rights and democracy; civil society spaces are restricted in many places, and there are both material and political obstacles to the construction of influential epistemic communities that could support the System when most needed.

Despite these significant limitations and institutional obstacles to effective human rights implementation, the IAHRS has continually evolved and developed innovative mechanisms to remedy its inherent enforcement deficits. As such, the IAHRS has the potential to offer human rights scholarship and advocacy significant insights into how human rights may continue to matter even in adverse political circumstances. Indeed, in some important ways global human rights politics has started to increasingly resemble the political conditions in which the IAHRS emerged, developed, and currently operates. While the politics surrounding the IAHRS demonstrates that sustained human rights activism has strengthened processes of socialization in many societies, rule-consistent behavior as predicted by earlier human rights scholarship has quite clearly not materialized.[47] This should draw our attention to the continuing political contestation over human rights in the Americas and elsewhere. The domestic impact of international human rights norms is invariably mediated by their broader normative salience in local contexts.[48] This reminds us of the risks that the reification of the "the lens of rule-compliance" poses to advancing our knowledge on local understandings of international human rights.[49] As Robert Howse and Ruti Teitel argue, "Interpretation is pervasively determinative of what happens to legal rules when they are out in the world; and yet 'compliance' studies begin with the notion that to look at effects, we start with an assumed stable and agreed meaning to a rule, and whether it is complied with or obeyed, so understood."[50] In a global context of human rights contention, the IAHRS offers an important reminder that resistance has tended to be the norm in the history of international human rights. It is important, therefore, to recognize that the IAHRS, as part of a complex institutional network of international human rights institutions,

---

[47] Thomas Risse-Kappen, Steve C. Ropp, and Kathryn Sikkink (eds.), *The Power of Human Rights: International Norms and Domestic Change*, Cambridge Studies in International Relations (Cambridge University Press 1999), 66.

[48] Mark Goodale and Sally Engle Merry (eds.), *The Practice of Human Rights Tracking Law between the Global and the Local Cambridge Studies in Law and Society* (Cambridge University Press 2007).

[49] Engstrom (n. 24).

[50] Robert Howse and Ruti Teitel, "Beyond Compliance: Rethinking Why International Law Really Matters: Beyond Compliance" [2010] 1 *Global Policy* 135.

provides a crucial exemplar of how these institutions can still make a difference, even in a world of increasing hostility to both the idea and practice of human rights.

5. Human Rights Futures: A World of Regions and Experimental Governance

The central message of this chapter is that the IAHRS offers crucial insights into the past, present, and potential futures of global human rights governance. From its origins as a declaratory regime governed by States, the institutional evolution of the IAHRS into a transnational human rights system has been remarkable. And yet there has never been anything inevitable in how the IAHRS has developed over the years. The present conjuncture of multiple and interlocking political challenges facing the System is clearly a powerful reminder in this regard. Such challenges notwithstanding, the IAHRS also demonstrates that human rights institutions are more resilient than may be immediately apparent. Against this background, and in lieu of a conventional conclusion, I would like to end this chapter with some reflections on what the possible futures of global human rights might look like when informed by the varied experiences of the IAHRS.

The first point to note is that regional systems have emerged as central actors in global governance and are pivotal for the future of international human rights. After all, it is precisely in regional systems that much if not most of human rights action takes place. As this chapter illustrates, this has been true since the birth of modern international human rights. This is also one of the main reasons why regional human rights systems are crucial for understanding future human rights trajectories. However, most of the now dominant critiques of human rights—whether Stephen Hopgood's "endtimes" narrative, Eric Posner's "twilight" diagnosis, or Samuel Moyn's insufficiency thesis—focus nearly exclusively on *global* accounts of human rights.[51] These accounts tend to marginalize, or entirely ignore, regional systems: their attention is turned toward the UN-based system, the role of Western States, and the human rights politics of global NGOs. Furthermore, their emphasis is almost exclusively on the role of the West in the genesis, historical development, and future of human rights law, institutions, and policy. As a result, with the ongoing sovereigntist and nationalist turn in US and European politics, these scholarly accounts forecast the imminent demise of human rights. And yet, while not dismissing the central role of the United States and the nominally liberal West in the development of international

---

[51] Hopgood (n. 1); Eric Posner, *The Twilight of Human Rights Law* (Oxford University Press 2014); Moyn (n. 2).

human rights, its history and future is more plural and diverse than these accounts claim. As this chapter highlights, other actors than Western governments have been central protagonists in the development of international human rights law, policy, and practice; and they are likely to continue playing that role, with or without US and European leadership.

Moreover, regional perspectives on human rights tell us something important about institutional resilience even in adverse geopolitical contexts. The IAHRS is exemplary of the fact that human rights have never been a consensus project. Its institutional history is ripe with conflict and resistance to ambitious human rights norms and practices. The System also amply illustrates the potential of institutionally expanding human rights in a historically unstable region of the world. It offers an example of institutional survival despite dramatic adverse political shifts. Put differently, the case of the IAHRS offers insights into processes of institutional adaptation and resilience in illiberal or hostile political contexts.

As I have argued elsewhere,[52] the IAHRS is institutionally more resilient than generalized narratives of a human rights "end-times" suggest. After all, despite the rise of anti-rights politics in the region, human rights norms developed by the IAHRS remain formally embedded in national constitutions and domestic legislation. The formal embedment of human rights norms in domestic law provides crucial opportunities for individuals and groups to claim, define, and struggle over human rights. The institutional "stickiness" of the IAHRS is particularly noteworthy when compared to global human rights institutions. As this chapter highlights, the IAHRS is regularly engaged in dense interactions with domestic courts and State bureaucracies and is becoming far more deeply embedded in national systems than the UN System. This domestic institutionalization of regional human rights also highlights some intriguing, persistent puzzles: the IAHRS is subjected to chronic underfunding, is generally perceived to be characterized by an ongoing compliance crisis, and is facing strident resistance and backlash. And yet the demands on the IAHRS are ever increasing. A steadily rising number of cases are submitted to the Inter-American Commission. There are indications that a greater proportion of national high courts in the region are more consistently engaging with the jurisprudence of the Inter-American Court. Furthermore, even backlash could be understood as a specific response to the increasing impact or relevance of the IAHRS. After all, why spend so much political capital and attention on an irrelevant international human rights institution?

Similarly, regional systems are also important alternatives to the universal systems increasingly under strain. The UN human rights system is currently rocked by yet another budget crisis, which, for example, has led to the reduction

---

[52] Par Engstrom, "Between Hope and Despair: Progress and Resilience in the Inter-American Human Rights System" [2019] 113 *American Journal of International Law Unbound* 370.

of the monitoring activities of UN treaty bodies. In the case of the International Criminal Court (ICC), it is subject to increasingly strident criticisms, including from many human rights advocates who despair at the ICC's perceived double standards and lack of bite. From this perspective, regional systems may seem quite attractive when pursuing human rights accountability. This is particularly the case in regional contexts characterized by widespread and persistent impunity, including for gross and systematic human rights violations. It is striking, therefore, that the ICC is subject to such sustained political and scholarly attention despite its limited reach and narrow caseload. Indeed, the IAHRS has developed what Alexandra Huneeus refers to as a quasi-criminal jurisdiction that pushes States to prosecute human rights criminals in domestic courts.[53] The IAHRS offers, in this sense, an important alternative to international criminal justice strategies, which requires more attention.

In short, a fuller recognition of the regional character of global human rights is both analytically and normatively essential. In the first instance, it captures something empirically important about how global human rights governance actually works. The IAHRS and other regional human rights systems are part of a global *network* of human rights governance. There are important, yet still poorly understood, interactive effects, institutional feedback loops, and structural complementarity between existing institutional mechanisms within this networked global governance system. There are reasons to expect that the potential impact of human rights standards and institutions is greatest when they are deployed in a coordinated fashion. For example, specific rulings or awareness-raising activities can generate human rights changes in and by themselves, but their impact may be amplified if they occur within a broad and coordinated strategy. In many human rights areas, there are a plethora of instruments that may range from international treaties, Special Rapporteurships conducting in-country visits, individual petition mechanisms and litigation opportunities, and international court rulings. Where used strategically and in tandem, the mechanisms can be mutually reinforcing and augment the impact of one another. However, impact is likely to be more limited when mechanisms are used in isolation.

A more diffused, multilayered, and networked global human rights politics is also normatively desirable, as captured in experimentalist approaches to human rights governance.[54] It is clearly the case that international human rights institutions need to develop more sustained and collaborative relationships with a range of relevant stakeholders and actors at the local level, not least in order to strengthen the likelihood of effective and sustainable human rights

---

[53] Huneeus (n. 17).
[54] Gráinne de Búrca, "Human Rights Experimentalism" [2017] 111 *American Journal of International Law* 277.

implementation. The multifaceted contributions of the IAHRS outlined in this chapter point to the crucial role that the System has played in the development of global human rights governance. All human rights institutions share similar sets of challenges, whether limited State compliance with rulings and decisions, States seeking to reduce institutional mandates and undermine their legitimacy, or increasing case backlogs combined with increasingly squeezed resources. Despite the many political, institutional, and legal differences between the various human rights systems, important insights gained from any given institution can inform approaches and practices elsewhere. It is precisely in this respect that the IAHRS stands as an exemplar of the highly imperfect, often messy and contested, yet impactful and deeply meaningful human rights politics, especially for the many people who continue to struggle for the realization of their rights.

I.6
Conventionality Control
An Expression of the Basic Elements of the Judicial Function

By Miriam Lorena Henríquez Viñas and José Ignacio Núñez Leiva

1. Introduction

In September 2006, the Inter-American Court of Human Rights (Inter-American Court, or IACtHR) issued a ruling in the case of *Almonacid Arellano v. Chile*. In Paragraph 124 of the judgment, the Court coined the term "conventionality control," stating that domestic legislation must conform with the American Convention of Human Rights (American Convention, or ACHR). The Court also noted that the domestic judges must apply "a kind of control of conventionality" when legislators do not comply with this doctrine.

In judgments that followed, the Inter-American Court asserted that conventionality control is a compatibility test. In domestic cases, the adjudicator must either interpret the applicable norms in a way that is compatible with the obligations derived from the American Convention as elaborated in IACtHR jurisprudence or, if such interpretation is impossible, invalidate or decline to enforce the domestic law.

Studies of constitutional law and international human rights law, as well as inter-American jurisprudence, have differentiated between external and internal conventionality control,[1] between concentrated and diffuse

---

[1] This distinction was introduced by Sergio García Ramírez, who stated: "The control of the own, original or external conventionality falls on the supranational court called to exercise the confrontation between domestic acts and conventional dispositions, in this case, to appreciate the compatibility between the former and the latter—under the rule of international human rights law—and to solve the conflict through the corresponding declarative and condemnatory judgment. Ultimately, this control is incumbent, originally and officially, on the IACHR when it comes to examining cases of which it is aware and to which it applies standards in accordance with its own material jurisdiction. That is why the Court has referred to its own, original or external control."
Internal control, on the other hand, García Ramírez defined as "the power conferred or recognized to certain courts—or to all courts, as we will see below—to verify the consistency between internal acts—thus, essentially, domestic provisions of general scope: Constitutions, laws, regulations, etc.— with the provisions of international law (which, in the hypothesis that interests me, I will reduce to one of its expressions: international human rights law, and more strictly the inter-American law on

control,[2] and, more recently, between conventionality control as *res judicata* and as *res interpretata*. Instead of clarifying the concept, these distinctions have raised doubts about the nature of conventionality control as well as questions about the coherence of the content and scope of each category.

In this chapter, we argue that conventionality control consists of the three elements inherent to the judicial function: (1) to know, (2) to judge, and (3) to enforce judgments. From this, we develop a more precise understanding of conventionality control and a broader, more comprehensive conception of its distinctive forms.

Accordingly, we propose the following general hypothesis: the praetorian development of conventionality control by the Inter-American Court involves the essential elements of the judicial function: to know, to judge, and to enforce judgments. Our first sub-hypothesis states that external and concentrated control and internal conventionality control complement each other in examining compatibility between domestic acts and the inter-American *corpus juris* (i.e., all inter-American treaties and jurisprudence). The second sub-hypothesis states that conventionality control also constitutes *res judicata*, because an IACtHR judgment will later be executed by the competent domestic institutions, while the Court monitors their compliance. The third sub-hypothesis states that internal conventionality control coincides with diffuse control and applies *res interpretata*, as well as complements and prevents external control.

---

this subject)"; see Sergio García Ramírez, "El control judicial interno de convencionalidad" [2011] 5(28) *Revista Ius* 123.

[2] Eduardo Ferrer Mac-Gregor differentiated between concentrated and diffuse control of conventionality: "In this sense, the 'concentrated control of conventionality' had been carried out by the IACHR since its first judgments (...) Now, this 'control' has been extended as an obligation of action in the internal sphere to all national judges (hence its 'diffuse' character)." Eduardo Ferrer Mac-Gregor, "El control difuso de convencionalidad en el Estado Constitucional," in Héctor Fix-Zamudio and Diego Valadés (coords.), *Formación y perspectiva del Estado en México* (El Colegio Nacional-UNAM 2010).

Ferrer Mac-Gregor also considered distinct intensity levels of conventionality control: "[T]he intensity level of the diffuse conventionality control will decrease in those systems where the 'diffuse constitutionality control' is not allowed and, therefore, not all judges have the faculty to stop applying a law to the specific case. In these cases, it is clear that judges who lack such competence will exercise 'diffuse conventionality control' with less intensity, but this does not mean that they cannot do so 'within their respective competences.' The preceding implies that they may not fail to apply the rule (since they do not have that power), and they must, in any case, make a 'conventional interpretation' of it, that is to say, make a 'conforming interpretation,' not only of the national Constitution but also of the American Convention and the conventional jurisprudence." Eduardo Ferrer Mac-Gregor, "Reflexiones sobre el control difuso de convencionalidad," in *Opus Magna Constitucional Guatemalteco*, Tomo III (Instituto de Justicia Constitucional 2011).

For the purposes of this chapter, "diffuse control" refers to the fact that all national judges must exercise the conventionality control. Its greater or lesser intensity depends on the power that the judge must disregard or invalidate a rule that is incompatible with inter-American standards, which varies according to the dictates of the constitutional justice system.

This chapter thus seeks to provide a framework for understanding all aspects of conventionality control. In doing so, it emphasizes the regulatory nature of the activity of the Inter-American Court and the role of domestic courts in the enforcement of IACtHR decisions. This emphasis addresses the domestic impact of conventionality control, as well as the less studied areas of implementation and enforcement of judgments and monitoring of compliance.

2. Methodology

To test the hypothesis, we review compliance monitoring resolutions issued by the Inter-American Court from 2006 (i.e., beginning with the case of *Almonacid Arellano and others v. Chile*, or the first time the IACtHR mentioned conventionality control) to January 2019. Except for the introductory remarks in section 2, our analysis does not delve into judgments in contentious cases, which are already discussed in detail in the literature on internal conventionality control.[3]

We consider each of the judgments from this period as a unit of analysis in which we searched for the term "conventionality control." We then categorized these judgments. We identified those rulings that expressly contain the term "conventionality control" in the body of the judgment (as opposed to in the quotations or the footnotes) and we extracted the relevant paragraph. We dispensed with judgments that merely referred to conventionality control and did not further specify different categories of control;[4] judgments that mentioned conventionality control only in reference to the judgment of the contentious case that had given rise to the current monitoring of compliance;[5] judgments that quoted inter-American decisions in contentious cases in which a single category of conventionality control was discussed;[6] and judgments that assessed

---

[3] For a complete list of relevant judgments in contentious cases, see Miriam Henríquez, "El control de convencionalidad interno. Su conceptualización en la jurisprudencia de la Corte Interamericana de Derechos Humanos" [2019] 19 *XIX Anuario Mexicano de Derecho Internacional* 327.

[4] *Zambrano Vélez et al. v. Ecuador* [2009], Oversight of Judgment Compliance, Resolution, Inter-American Court of Human Rights, provision 42; *Barrios Altos v. Peru* [2012], Oversight of Judgment Compliance, Resolution of the Inter-American Court of Human Rights, provision 24; *Radilla Pacheco v. Mexico* [2013], Oversight of Judgment Compliance, Resolution of the Inter-American Court of Human Rights provisions 5, 19, 26, 31; *Gonzalez et al. (Campo Algodonero) Mexico* [2013], Oversight of Judgment Compliance, Resolution of the Inter-American Court of Human Rights, provision 78; *Cabrera García and Montiel Flores v. Mexico* [2015], Oversight of Judgment Compliance, Resolution of the Inter-American Court of Human Rights, provision 16, 21; *Radilla Pacheco, Fernández Ortega et al., and Rosendo Cantú et al. v. Mexico* [2015], Resolution of the Inter-American Court of Human Rights, provision 16; *Guatemalan Cases* [2015], Oversight of Judgment Compliance, Resolution of the Inter-American Court of Human Rights, provision 68.

[5] *Radilla Pacheco v. Mexico* [2012], Oversight of Judgment Compliance, Resolution of the Inter-American Court of Human Rights, provision 17.

[6] *Fermín Ramírez v. Guatemala, Raxcacó Reyes v. Guatemala* [2008], Oversight of Judgment Compliance, Resolution of the Inter-American Court of Human Rights, provision 63; *"Cinco Pensionistas" v. Peru* [2009], Oversight of Judgment Compliance, Resolution of the Inter-American

compliance with reparation measures involving a course, program, or seminar on conventionality control.[7] We then grouped the judgments that differentiated between different categories of conventionality control based on their target and purpose. We proceeded with our examination of each judgment in chronological order.

3. The Meaning of Conventionality Control

To understand conventionality control, it is necessary to answer some specific questions: What is conventionality control? What is the object and scope of the control? What is the purpose of control? Which authority has the power to control? Considering the first question, the conventionality control is an analysis of the compatibility between domestic standards, on the one hand, and the standards of the American Convention as well as the interpretation of the ACHR by the Inter-American Court, on the other.

What is the object and scope of control? The object of conventionality control is "internal legal standards" or "internal standards," such as regulations, legislation, and constitution. The scope of this control is determined by the American Convention,[8] as well as other treaties over which the Inter-American Court has

Court of Human Rights, provision 35; *Bámaca Velásquez v. Guatemala* [2010], Oversight of Judgment Compliance, Resolution of the Inter-American Court of Human Rights, recital 33; *Loayza TaMay v. Peru* [2011], Oversight of Judgment Compliance, Resolution of the Inter-American Court of Human Rights, provision 35; *Castillo Petruzzi et al. v. Peru* [2011], Oversight of Judgment Compliance, Resolution of the Inter-American Court of Human Rights, provision 20; *Lori Berenson Mejía s. Peru* [2012], Oversight of Judgment Compliance, Resolution of the Inter-American Court of Human Rights, provision 18; *Barrios Altos v. Peru* [2012], Oversight of Judgment Compliance, Resolution of the Inter-American Court of Human Rights, provision 24; *Castañeda Gutman v. Mexico* [2013], Oversight of Judgment Compliance, Resolution of the Inter-American Court of Human Rights, provision 23; *11 cases against Guatemala regarding the obligation to investigate, prosecute and, if applicable, punish those responsible for human rights violations* [2014], Oversight of Judgment Compliance, Resolution of the Inter-American Court of Human Rights, provision 17.

[7] *Atala Riffo and daughters v. Chile* [2013], Oversight of Judgment Compliance, Resolution of the Inter-American Court of Human Rights, provision 31; *Rochac Hernández et al. v. El Salvador* [2017], Oversight of Judgment Compliance, Resolution of the Inter-American Court of Human Rights, provision 17.

[8] The American Convention on Human Rights was said to determine the scope of conventionality control in 28 of the 36 cases decided by the Inter-American Court under the conditions outlined in the introduction to this chapter. See (1) CIDH, *Almonacid Arellano et al. v. Chile*, provision 124; (2) *The Dismissed Congressional Employees (Aguado-Alfaro et al.) v. Peru*, provision 128; (3) *La Cantuta v. Peru*, provision 173; (4) *Boyce et al. v. Barbados*, provision 78; (5) *Radilla Pachecho v. Mexico*, provision 339; (6) *The Xákmok Kásek indigenous community v. Paraguay*, provision 311; (7) *Fernández Ortega et al. v. Mexico*, provision 236; (8) *Rosendo Cantú et al. v. Mexico*, provision 219; (9) *Ibsen Cárdenas and Ibsen Peña v. Bolivia*, provision 202; (10) *Vélez Loor v. Panamá*, provision 287; (11) *Gomes Lund et al. ("Guerrilha do Araguaia") v. Brasil*, provision 176; (12) *Cabrera García and Montiel Flores v. México*, provision 225; (13) *Gelman v. Uruguay*, provision 193; (14) *Chocrón Chocrón v. Venezuela*, provisions 164 and 171; (15) *López Mendoza v. Venezuela*, provision 226; (16) *Fontevecchia and D'Amico v. Argentina*, provision 93; (17) *Atala Riffo and daughters v. Chile*, provision

subject matter jurisdiction and the inter-American treaties to which the State is a party.[9] The Inter-American Court has ruled that the scope of conventionality controls also extends to encompass the IACtHR's interpretations of these treaties since the Court is the ultimate authority on the American Convention.[10]

The specific standards subject to control are those applicable to each case. In the above-mentioned case of *Almonacid Arellano v. Chile*, the Inter-American Court explained that "the Judiciary must exercise a sort of 'conventionality control' between the domestic legal provisions which are applied to specific cases and the American Convention on Human Rights." The Court repeated this explanation in the cases of *La Cantuta v. Peru* (2006)[11] and *Boyce v. Barbados* (2007).[12] Beginning with the judgment in the case of *Radilla Pacheco v. Mexico*

282; (18) *Furlan and family v. Argentina*, provision 303; (19) *The Massacres of El Mozote and nearby places v. El Salvador*, provision 318; (20) *The Santo Domingo Massacre v. Colombia*, provision 142; (21) *J. v. Peru*, provision 407; (22) *Liakat Ali Alibux v. Surinam*, provision 151; (23) *Expelled dominicans and haitians v. República Dominicana*, provision 311; (24) *Rochac Hernández et al. v. El Salvador*, Merits, reparations and costs, Judgment of the Inter-American Court of Human Rights (October 14, 2014), provision 213; (25) *López Lone et al. v. Honduras*, provision 307; (26) *The Punta Piedra Garifuna Community and its members v. Honduras*, provisions 211, 255, and 346; (27) *Chinchilla Sandoval v. Guatemala*, provision 242; and (28) *The Hacienda Brasil Verde Workers v. Brazil*, provision 408.

[9] In the case of *Ibsen Cardenas v. Bolivia* (2010), the Inter-American Court stated: "The Court recalls that the purpose of its mandate is the application of the American Convention and other treaties that grant it jurisdiction." *Ibsen Cárdenas and Ibsen Peña v. Bolivia*, provision 199. Then, in the case of *The Río Negro Massacres v. Guatemala*, the Court referred to the inter-American *corpus juris* as determining the scope of conventionality control. The IACtHR also expressly stated that the *corpus juris* consists of the American Convention and the other treaties of the Inter-American System. *The Río Negro Massacres v. Guatemala*, paras. 142, 262; see also (1) *Gudiel Álvarez et al. ("diario militar") v. Guatemala*, provision 330; (2) *Members of the Chichupac Village and neighboring communities of the Municipality of Rabinal v. Guatemala*, provision 289; and (3) *Mendoza et al. v. Argentina*, provision 221. In *Mendoza et al. v. Argentina*, the Inter-American Court stated that the scope of conventionality controls is defined by "the human rights treaties to which the State is a party," and then specified that the domestic actors "must take into account not only the American Convention and other inter-American instruments."

[10] The Court confirmed that inter-American jurisprudence sets the scope of control in 26 of the 36 judgments issued by the IACtHR under the conditions outlined in this chapter's introduction. See (*1) *Almonacid Arellano et al. v. Chile*, provision 124; (2) *La Cantuta v. Peru*, provision 173; (3) *Boyce et al. v. Barbados*, provision 78; (4) *Radilla Pachecho v. Mexico*, provision 339; (5) *The Xákmok Kásek indigenous community v. Paraguay*, provision 311; (6) *Fernández Ortega et al. v. Mexico*, provision 236; (7) *Rosendo Cantú et al. v. Mexico*, provision 219; (8) *Ibsen Cárdenas and Ibsen Peña v. Bolivia*, provision 202; (9) *Gomes Lund et al. ("Guerrilha do Araguaia") v. Brasil*, provision 176; (10) *Cabrera García and Montiel Flores v. México*, provision 225; (11) *Gelman v. Uruguay*, provision 193; (12) *Chocrón Chocrón v. Venezuela*, provisions 164 and 171; (13) *López Mendoza v. Venezuela*, provision 226; (14) *Fontevecchia and D'Amico v. Argentina*, provision 93; (15) *Atala Riffo and daughters v. Chile*, provision 282; (16) *Furlan and family v. Argentina*, provision 303; (17) *The Río Negro Massacres v. Guatemala*, provision 262; (18) *Gudiel Álvarez et al. ("diario militar") v. Guatemala*, provision 330; (19) *The Santo Domingo Massacre v. Colombia*, provision 142; (20) *Mendoza et al. v. Argentina*, provision 221; (21) *J. v. Peru*, provision 407; (22) *Expelled dominicans and haitians v. República Dominicana*, provision 311; (23) *López Lone et al. v. Honduras*, provision 307; (24) *The Punta Piedra Garifuna Community and its members v. Honduras*, provisions 211, 255, and 346; (25) *Chinchilla Sandoval v. Guatemala*, provision 242; and (26) *The Hacienda Brasil Verde Workers v. Brazil*, provision 408.

[11] *La Cantuta v. Peru*, provision 173.

[12] *Boyce y otros v. Barbados*, provision 78.

(2009), however, the Inter-American Court left aside the mention that such the standards of conventionality control are those that apply to specific cases in favor of a wide statement.[13]

Nevertheless, the IACtHR's language leaves no doubt that conventionality control must be applied in concrete terms and in relation to a clear and specific set of norms and circumstances. These paragraphs indicate that: (1) the Inter-American Court is aware that the goals of conventionality control are subject to the rule of law and, therefore, obliged to apply the provisions in force in the domestic legal system; and (2) when a State has ratified an international treaty such as the American Convention, all government authorities are obligated to ensure the effects of the Convention's provisions are not undermined by the application of laws contrary to its object and purpose. As such, conventionality control requires not an abstract but a specific review of challenged domestic norms.

What is the purpose of control? We can additionally infer from the previously cases cited that the purpose of the conventionality control is to ensure that domestic standards do not contradict the object and purpose of the American Convention as interpreted by the Inter-American Court. It aims to achieve compatibility and consistency of domestic and inter-American standards. In the case of *Gomes Lund v. Brazil* (2010), conventionality control required the IACtHR "to assess the alleged non-compatibility of [a domestic] law with Brazil's international obligations under the American Convention."[14] Similarly, in the case of *Atala Riffo v. Chile* (2012), the Inter-American Court expanded on the formulation of conventionality control in *Radilla Pacheco v. Mexico* by stating that "based on the treaty control mechanism, legal and administrative interpretations, and proper judicial guarantees should be applied under the principles established in the jurisprudence of this Court in the present case."[15] The cases of *López Mendoza v. Venezuela* (2011)[16] and *Furlan v. Argentina* (2012)[17] include similar language. At the same time, the Inter-American Court decided in the case of *Andrade Salmón v. Bolivia* (2016) that this category of control requires that inconsistencies be resolved.[18]

There are two possible ways to comply with the doctrine of conventionality control. First, domestic actors, primarily judges, can interpret the domestic

---

[13] This sentence indicates that the conventionality control must be exercised between the controlled object and the control parameter, leaving behind the mention that such controlled norms are those that "apply in specific cases." *Radilla Pachecho v. Mexico*, provision 339.

[14] *Gomes Lund et al. ("Guerrilha do Araguaia") v. Brasil*, provision 49.

[15] *Atala Riffo and Daughters v. Chile*, provision 284.

[16] *López Mendoza v. Venezuela*, provision 228.

[17] *Furlan and family v. Argentina*, provision 303.

[18] According to the Court, "recent jurisprudence has recognized that all authorities of a State Party to the Convention must exercise 'conventionality control' in such a way that the interpretation and application of domestic law are consistent with the State's international human rights obligations." *Andrade Salmón v. Bolivia*, provision 93.

standards applicable to the specific case in accordance with the relevant inter-American standards. Constitutional provisions establishing that the domestic law must conform to international declarations and treaties facilitate this method of compliance. Following this method, conventionality control does not result in the invalidation of domestic law but in a specific interpretation of domestic law consistent with inter-American standards. Second, when it is not possible conciliation between the interpretation of domestic standards with inter-American standards, conventionality control requires that the domestic standard be invalidated. The inter-American standard could even directly preempt domestic standard if a State's constitution attributes supra-legal hierarchy to international human rights norms. However, a legal or supra-legal hierarchy is not enough when the internal standard is based on constitutional provisions.

As for the targets of conventionality control, the jurisprudence of the Inter-American Court has gradually expanded to encompass all State authorities. At first, the IACtHR focused on the judiciary or, more specifically, on judges.[19] The Court later expanded its analyses to include "the bodies linked to the administration of justice at all levels," which encompasses not only the judiciary but also other bodies such as the public prosecutor's office.[20] Eventually, the Inter-American Court clarified that every entity and authority is obligated to exercise conventionality control.[21]

---

[19] The following judgments referred to the judicial branch, or to each judge or judicial authority, as obligated to carry out conventionality control: (1) CIDH, *Almonacid Arellano y otros v. Chile*, 26 de September de 2006, provision 124; (2) *The Dismissed Congressional Employees (Aguado-Alfaro et al.) v. Peru*, provision 128; (3) *La Cantuta v. Peru*, provision 173; (4) *Boyce y otros v. Barbados*, provision 78; (5) *Heliodoro Portugal v. Panamá*, provision 180; (6) *Radilla Pachecho v. Mexico*, provision 339; (7) *Comunidad Indígena Xákmok Kásek v. Paraguay*, provision 311; (8) *Fernández Ortega y otros v. Mexico*, provision 236; (9) *Rosendo Cantú y otros v. Mexico*, provision 219; (10) *Ibsen Cárdenas e Ibsen Peña v. Bolivia*, provision 202; (11) *Gomes Lund et al. ("Guerrilha do Araguaia") v. Brasil*, provision 176; (12) *Cabrera García and Montiel Flores v. México*, provisions 225 a 232; (13) *Norín Catrimán et al. (leaders, members and activist of the mapuche indigenous people) v. Chile*, Merits, reparations, and costs (May 29, 2014), provision 464.

[20] This was expressed in the following judgments: (1) *Cabrera García and Montiel Flores v. México*, provisions 225 a 232; (2) *Chocrón Chocrón v. Venezuela*, provision 164; (3) *López Mendoza v. Venezuela*, provision 226; (4) *Fontevecchia and D'Amico v. Argentina*, provision 93; (5) *Atala Riffo and daughters v. Chile*, provisions 282 a 284; (6) *Furlan and family v. Argentina*, provision 303 and 304; (7) *The Río Negro Massacres v. Guatemala*, provision 262; (8) *Gudiel Álvarez et al. ("diario militar") v. Guatemala*, provision 330; (9) *The Santo Domingo Massacre v. Colombia*, provision 142; (10) *Mendoza et al. v. Argentina*, provision 221; (11) *J. v. Peru*, provision 407; (12) *Expelled dominicans and haitians v. República Dominicana*, provision 311; (13) *López Lone et al. v. Honduras*, provision 307; (14) *The Punta Piedra Garifuna Community and its members v. Honduras*, provision 346; (15) *Chinchilla Sandoval v. Guatemala*, provision 242; (16) *Members of the Chichupac Village and neighboring communities of the Municipality of Rabinal v. Guatemala*, provision 289.

[21] *Gelman v. Uruguay*, provision 239; (2) *The Massacres of El Mozote and nearby places v. El Salvador*, provision 318; (3) *Expelled dominicans and haitians v. República Dominicana*, provision 311; (4) *Rochac Hernández et al. v. El Salvador*, provision 213; (5) *Liakat Ali Alibux v. Surinam*, provision 151; (6) *García Ibarra et al. v. Ecuador*, Preliminary objections, merits, reparations, and costs, Judgment of the Inter-American Court of Human Rights (November 17, 2015), provision 306; (7) *The Hacienda Brasil Verde Workers v. Brazil*, provision 408; and (8) *Andrade Salmón v. Bolivia*, provision 93.

The Inter-American Court is aware that, in some States, courts beyond the constitutional court do not have the power to invalidate or to decline to enforce a domestic law in the event of a conflict between domestic and inter-American standards. The IACtHR responded to this situation, in the case of *The Dismissed Congressional Employees v. Peru* (2006), by clarifying that the judiciary must carry out the control of conventionality "*ex officio* [. . . and] in the context of their respective spheres of competence and the corresponding procedural regulations."[22] It follows that in States in which a constitutional court has the sole power of judicial review, the other courts are still obligated to interpret the domestic law in accordance with inter-American standards where feasible, but do not have the power, and thus do not have the duty, to invalidate or decline to enforce domestic law when such an interpretation is impossible.

4. The Difference between Adjudication and Execution in Conventionality Control

In 2012, in the case of *Apitz Barbera v. Venezuela*, the Inter-American Court used the same definition of conventionality control as in previous cases, stating that "judges and organs involved in the administration of justice at all levels are obliged to exercise *ex officio* a control of the conformity of domestic laws with the American Convention, within their respective terms of reference and the corresponding procedural regulations. In this task, the judges and organs involved in the administration of justice should consider not only the treaty but also its interpretation by the Inter-American Court, the ultimate interpreter of the American Convention."[23] The Court added that conventionality control is "a mechanism by which the judicial organs can prevent potential human rights violations."[24]

In the same paragraph, the Inter-American Court also indicated that conventionality control may play a role in the implementation of an inter-American judgment that establishes the international responsibility of a State:

[T]his "control of conformity with the Convention" also plays an important role in compliance with or implementation of a specific judgment of the Inter-American Court, especially when a judicial organ is responsible for this

---

[22] *The Dismissed Congressional Employees (Aguado-Alfaro et al.) v. Peru*, provision 128.
[23] *Apitz Barbera et al. ("First Court of Administrative Disputes") v. Venezuela* [2012], Oversight of Judgment Compliance, Resolution of the Inter-American Court of Human Rights, provision 26. In 2013, in the case of *Anzualdo v. Peru*, the Inter-American Court reaffirmed, without additional explanation, that conventionality control would have "an important role in the compliance or implementation of a judgment of the Inter-American Court." *Anzualdo Castro v. Peru* [2013], Oversight of Judgment Compliance, Resolution of the Inter-American Court of Human Rights, provision 24.
[24] *Apitz Barbera et al. ("First Court of Administrative Disputes") v. Venezuela*, provision 26.

compliance. In this situation, the judicial organ has the function of ensuring that the American Convention and the rulings of this Court prevail over domestic laws that obstruct compliance with the provisions in any specific case.[25]

This provision outlines internal control of conventionality, emphasizing its complementary and preventive role to external control, which aims to avoid human rights violations. Although it did not expressly state that these are different categories of conventionality control, the Court did suggest that different actors are responsible for implementation and the purposes for doing this differentiation.

Internal conventionality control thus consists of an assessment of compatibility between domestic regulations and the inter-American *corpus juris*, which is carried out by judges and organs linked to the administration of justice at all levels. The emergence of internal/diffuse conventionality control complicates domestic adjudication, which already involves the consideration of all domestic law, by requiring that the inter-American *corpus iuris* prevails in cases of incompatibility. External/concentrated conventionality control, on the other hand, is the assessment of compatibility carried out by the Inter-American Court.

The criterion for distinguishing between internal and external control, and between diffuse and concentrated control, is thus the authority that carries out conventionality control: judges and bodies involved in the administration of justice at all levels and the Inter-American Court, respectively. Regardless, according to the IACtHR, in all cases, State authorities have an obligation of conventionality control. They must identify domestic laws that contravene the inter-American *corpus juris* and to invalidate or decline to enforce those laws. We should also clarify that the function of the Inter-American Court is to determine whether the State has violated its obligations under international law. The IACtHR can find that domestic law if at issue, violates the American Convention, but it cannot directly invalidate that domestic law, nor can it assess the validity of domestic laws that are not involved in a specific proceeding before the Court.

In the case of internal control, the domestic tribunal that analyses the case may, according to its competencies, invalidate or decline to enforce an incompatible domestic law or provide an interpretation of the law compatible with inter-American standards following the concept of concentrated or diffuse control. In these cases, the adjudication has an immediate impact on domestic law because domestic courts have the power to know, judge, and enforce judgments. In cases of external conventionality control, on the other hand, the Inter-American Court lacks these powers. Although in several cases it issued sentences that resolved the

---

[25] *Apitz Barbera et al. ("First Court of Administrative Disputes") v. Venezuela*, provision 26.

unconventionality of the internal law, the IACtHR is not empowered to enforce its judgment directly by invalidating or declining to apply domestic law[26].

Compliance with IACtHR decisions depends on the cooperation of State entities, especially courts. The judgments on monitoring compliance demonstrate this. For example, when the Inter-American Court questions that the State has not introduced the legal reforms ordered by it or that the legal modifications ordered were carried out, at least partially, thus complying with the ruling. In both cases, the action of State bodies is necessary for the sentence to take effect in the condemned State. If the external conventionality control could directly invalidate, invalidate, modify, or repeal norms incompatible with the criteria of the Inter-American Court, the internal conventionality control would lack reason and the monitoring of compliance would not make sense either.

As part of the Inter-American Court's monitoring compliance with judgments, State parties are required to inform domestic judges about the international proceedings. Judges, in turn, are expected to comply with and enforce the IACtHR ruling by ensuring that the American Convention and inter-American jurisprudence prevail over domestic law when the latter is invoked as an excuse for noncompliance with the judgment the Inter-American Court issued against the State.

5. The Role of *Res Judicata* and *Res Interpretata*

Conventionality control is a complex doctrine, which describes a variety of different phenomena. Conventionality control can be internal and external, depending on whether it is exercised by a domestic or international actor. Conventionality control serves several purposes, from sanctioning violations of human rights and ensuring the implementation of inter-American judgments to preventing human rights violations and thus eliminating the need for international adjudication.

---

[26] Just as an example, some authors such as Max Silva Abbott maintain: "Whatever the action that the Court orders the condemned State to be, the unconventional norm incompatible with its criteria continues to exist while these bodies do not act." Max Silva Abbot, "¿Qué efectos produce el control de convencionalidad decretado por la Corte Interamericana en un ordenamiento jurídico?" [2020] 18(2) *Estudios Constitucionales* 272.

Hitters affirms: "This means that from this aspect the inter-American decision does not mean an automatic abrogation of the local precept, since it is the country that must comply with the regional pronouncement." Juan Carlos Hitters, "Control de constitucionalidad y control de convencionalidad. Comparación (Criterios fijados por la Corte Interamericana de Derechos Humanos)" [2009] 7(2) *Estudios Constitucionales* 123.

Juan Ibañez explains: "Despite the declaration of unconventionality made by the Court, the internal norm continues to exist, therefore, that unconventionality also continues to apply." Juana Ibáñez, *Control de convencionalidad* (México, Instituto de Investigaciones Jurídicas UNAM/Comisión Nacional de los Derechos Humanos 2017).

For example, in the monitoring of compliance with the judgment decision issued by the Inter-American Court in 2013 regarding the case of *Gelman v. Uruguay*, the IACtHR expressly introduces implementation as a component or phase of conventionality control. The context behind this monitoring compliance with judgment decision is the Supreme Court of Uruguay's having presented an obstacle to full compliance with the judgment in the case of *Gelman v. Uruguay*. In this decision, the Inter-American Court introduced the element of "enforcing judgments" as the final stage of conventionality control (the other elements being "knowing" and "judging," as discussed in the previous section).

First, the Inter-American Court states in this decision that it has, "in several judgments," developed the concept of conventionality control, which it describes as the obligation of State authorities "to exercise *ex officio* a 'control of conventionality' between domestic standards and the American Convention, within the framework of their respective spheres of competence and the corresponding procedural rules. Both the treaty and its interpretation by the Inter-American Court, the ultimate authority on the American Convention, must be considered in this task."

The IACtHR then refers to different categories of conventionality control, which differ depending on whether the State was a party to the proceedings. When the State was a party to the proceedings, the judgment has the character of *res judicata* as well as *res interpretata* with respect to that State.[27] When the State was not a party to proceedings, but is a party to the American Convention, the judgment does not have the character of *res judicata* but does have the character of *res interpretata*.[28]

According to the Inter-American Court, a State must comply with and strictly apply judgments that have the character of *res judicata* with respect to that State. The IACtHR explains *res judicata* in the case of *Gelman v. Uruguay* as "simply a matter of using it [conventionality control] to comply in its entirety and in good faith with what the Court ordered in the judgment it issued in the specific case."[29] This illustrates that the effects of *res judicata* operate only between parties. But the effects of *res interpretata* are *erga omnes*, which means they affect all parties.

---

[27] *Gelman v. Uruguay* [2013], Oversight of Judgment Compliance, Resolution of the Inter-American Court of Human Rights, provision 68.

[28] *Gelman v. Uruguay*, provision 69.

[29] *Gelman v. Uruguay*, provision 68; see also Juana Ibáñez, *Manual auto-formativo para la aplicación del control de convencionalidad dirigido a operadores de justicia* (Instituto Interamericano de Derechos Humanos 2015); Eduardo Ferrer Mac-Gregor, "Eficacia de la sentencia interamericana y la cosa juzgada internacional: vinculación directa hacia las partes (res judicata) e indirecta hacia los Estados Parte de la Convención Americana (res interpretata) (Sobre el cumplimiento del Caso Gelman v. Uruguay)" [2013] 11 *Estudios Constitucionales*; Sofía Sagüés, "Diálogo jurisprudencial y control de convencionalidad a la luz de la experiencia en el caso argentino," in Miriam Henríquez Viñas and Mariela Morales Antoniazzi (coords.), *El control de convencionalidad: Un balance comparado a 10 años de Almonacid Arellano V. Chile* (DER Ediciones 2017).

The IACtHR's decision also reiterates the elements of conventionality control that appear in the judgments of contentious cases, reaffirming that it concerns the compatibility of domestic regulations with the inter-American *corpus juris*:

> [A]ll public authorities and all the organs [of the State], including democratic bodies, judges, and other organs involved in the administration of justice at all levels, are bound by the treaty, which obliges them to exercise control of conventionality, within the framework of their respective spheres of competence and the corresponding procedural rules, both in the enactment and enforcement of laws, as regards their validity and compatibility with the Convention, and in fact-finding, trying, and deciding particular situations and specific cases, bearing in mind the treaty itself and, as appropriate, the precedents or lines of the jurisprudence of the Inter-American Court.[30]

In the same ruling, the Inter-American Court repeated its statement from the case of *Apitz Barbera v. Venezuela*, namely, that conventionality control first arises in the context of the implementation of a given IACtHR judgment and "is the responsibility of domestic judges." The Inter-American Court also explained that conventionality control means that "the judicial body functions so as to uphold the American Convention and the rulings of this Court, over and above domestic regulations, interpretations, and practices that impede compliance with its decision in a specific case."[31]

A couple of months later, in its monitoring compliance with the judgment decision in the case of the *Ituango Massacres v. Colombia*, the Inter-American Court reiterated the statements it had made in the case of *Gelman v. Uruguay*.[32] The Court differentiated the two categories of conventionality control, with an emphasis on the doctrine's effects, and noted that their differences depend on whether the State was a party to the proceedings. The decision then defined the first category and once again highlighted its effects:

> Thus, when an international judgment has been delivered that constitutes res judicata with regard to a State that has been a party to the case submitted to the Court's jurisdiction, all its bodies, including its judges and the organs concerned with the administration of justice, are also subject to the treaty and this Court's judgment, which obliges them to ensure that the effects of the provisions of the Convention and, consequently, the decisions of the Inter-American Court are not adversely affected by the application of norms contrary to their object

---

[30] *Gelman v. Uruguay*, provision 69.
[31] *Gelman v. Uruguay*, provision 73.
[32] *Ituangó Massacres v. Colombia* [2013], Oversight of Judgment, Resolution of the Inter-American Court of Human Rights, provisions 29 and 30.

and purpose or by judicial or administrative decisions that make total or partial compliance with the judgment illusory. In other words, in this case, an international res judicata exists based on which the State is obliged to comply with and execute the judgment.

The IACtHR then added:

> As a result of the legal force of the American Convention in all the States Parties to it, dynamic and complementary control of conformity with the Convention also plays an important role in compliance with or execution of specific judgments of the Inter-American Court, especially when this execution is the responsibility of the national judges. In this case, the function of the judicial organ is to ensure the prevalence of the American Convention and the rulings of this Court over domestic laws, interpretations, and practices that prevent compliance with what the Court has ordered in a specific case.

This judgment referred once again to *res judicata* conventionality control, within the scope of the implementation of the international judgment, addressed to the judges, requiring them to comply with and respect the decision or, in other words, to execute the judgment. In this context, the IACtHR reiterated that the judicial body must ensure that the American Convention and its jurisprudence prevail over internal obstacles that prevent compliance with the ruling against the State.

In 2014, in monitoring compliance with the judgment decision in the case of *Gomes Lund v. Brazil*,[33] the Inter-American Court repeated its position from previous judgments:

> The Court insists on the obligation of domestic judges and courts to carry out a control of conventionality, especially when there is international res judicata, since judges and courts have an important role in the fulfilment or implementation of the judgment of the Inter-American Court. The judicial body functions so as to uphold the American Convention and the rulings of this Court, over and above domestic regulations, interpretations, and practices that impede compliance with its decision in a specific case.

Thus, in the case of *Gomes Lund v. Brazil*, the Inter-American Court reaffirmed its jurisprudence on conventionality control in the face of a series of domestic

---

[33] *Gomes Lund et al. ("Guerrilha do Araguaia") v. Brazil* [2014], Oversight of Judgment, Resolution of the Inter-American Court of Human Rights, provision 19.

judicial decisions that ignored an IACtHR decision, despite its character of international *res judicata*, as well as international human rights law in general.

Additionally, in its 2014 monitoring compliance with judgment decisions in the cases of the *Rio Negro Massacres* and *Gudiel Álvarez et al. v. Guatemala*,[34] the Inter-American Court refers to the international and binding nature of its decisions in contentious cases. It also stated: "[I]t is contrary to the treaty obligations of the State of Guatemala for domestic entities to question the binding nature of the Court's decisions." In the face of the State of Guatemala's open defiance of both judgments, the Inter-American Court, referring to the monitoring compliance with judgment decisions in the case of *Gelman v. Uruguay*, stated that "[c]onventionality control an institution that functions as a tool for the application of international law." The IACtHR also reiterated that "when there is international *res judicata*, 'conventionality control' has an important role in the fulfilment or implementation of the judgment of the Inter-American Court, especially when such compliance is entrusted to national judges."[35]

In 2017, in monitoring compliance with judgment decision in the case of *Fontevecchia v. Argentina*,[36] the Inter-American Court discussed the close link between the mandatory nature of IACtHR judgments and conventionality control in the context of the implementation of these judgments, as well as how this link enabled the Supreme Court of Argentina to invalidate the decisions not only of lower courts but also of the Supreme Court itself. The Inter-American Court said:

> The position assumed on this occasion by the Supreme Court of Justice of the Nation, which questioned the obligatory nature of the judgments of the Inter-American Court under certain circumstances differs greatly from its previous line of jurisprudence, which this Court had highlighted it as a positive example as regards the acknowledgment that highest courts in the region have given of the binding nature of the judgments of the Inter-American Court and the application of conventionality control, taking into account the IACtHR's interpretations. This jurisprudence of the Supreme Court of Justice of the Nation also recognized the important role that the highest domestic court in Argentina has, within the scope of its competence, in the fulfilment or implementation of the judgments of the Inter-American Court.

---

[34] *Rio Negro Massacre and Gudiel Álvarez et al. v. Guatemala* [2014], Oversight of Compliance with Judgment, Resolution of the Inter-American Court of Human Rights.

[35] *The Río Negro Massacres v. Guatemala*, provision 16.

[36] *Fontevecchia and D'Amico v. Argentina* [2017], Oversight of Compliance with Judgment, Resolution of the Inter-American Court of Human Rights, provision 25.

More recently, the Inter-American Court has articulated a definition of conventionality control informed by its judgments discussing *res interpretata* and *res judicata*. In the monitoring compliance with judgment decision in the case of *Barrios Altos v. Peru* (2018),[37] the Inter-American Court mentioned both *res interpretata* and *res judicata* and reiterated the definition of conventionality control, quoting its monitoring compliance with judgment decision in the case of *Gelman v. Uruguay*:

> [T]his Court has indicated that, with respect to the implementation of a particular judgment of the Inter-American Court, "the function of the judicial organ is to ensure the prevalence of the American Convention and the rulings of this Court over domestic laws, interpretations, and practices that prevent compliance with what the Court has ordered in a specific case."

The two categories of conventionality control considered by the Inter-American Court point to separate moments. On the one hand, the internal and diffuse conventionality control coincides with the *res interpretata* and *erga omnes* aspects of IACtHR decisions. On the other hand, the control as monitoring compliance coincides with the *res judicata* and *inter-partes* aspects of these decisions.

6. Conclusion

Conventionality control is a complex doctrine, which contains a variety of different phenomena. In this chapter, we tried to prove that the praetorian development of conventionality control by the Inter-American Court involves the essential elements of the judicial function—to know, to judge, and to enforce judgments—thereby providing the doctrinal basis for impact on the ground.

The first sub-hypothesis of this chapter indicated that the external and concentrated control and the internal control of conventionality complement each other when examining the compatibility between the internal acts and the inter-American *corpus juris*.

The second sub-hypothesis states that conventionality control also constitutes *res judicata*, because an IACtHR judgment will later be executed by the competent domestic institutions, while the Court monitors their compliance. In this sense, we infer that conventionality control as *res judicata* relates to the third element of the judicial function, enforcing judgments. The Inter-American Court seeks to ensure through monitoring compliance with

---

[37] *Barrios Altos Case and La Cantuta v. Peru* [2018], Oversight of Judgment Compliance, Resolution of the Inter-American Court of Human Rights, provision 65.

judgment decisions that State entities, mainly courts, implement specific IACtHR orders.

And the third sub-hypothesis stated that internal conventionality control coincides with diffuse control and applies *res interpretata*, as well as complements and prevents external control.

According to those sub-hypotheses, we conclude both the Inter-American Court and domestic courts know and judge in a specific case by examining the compatibility between domestic law and the inter-American *corpus juris*. Here, internal and diffuse conventionality control requires the application of inter-American standards as *res interpretata*. This is complementary and preventive to external control: it prevents human rights violations.

The two categories of conventionality control considered by the Inter-American Court point to separate moments: the internal and diffuse conventionality control coincides with the *res interpretata* and *erga omnes* aspects of IACtHR decisions, and the control as monitoring compliance coincides with the *res judicata* and *inter-partes* aspects of these decisions.

Finally, analyzing conventionality control in the framework we have provided also enables us to observe where this doctrine has had an effect. We can demonstrate with greater accuracy the impact that inter-American jurisprudence has on domestic legal systems. Thus understood, conventionality control increases the relevance of domestic actors in the protection of human rights.

I.7
Effectiveness of International Courts
From Compliance to Transformative Impact

By Gabriela C.B. Navarro

1. Introduction

In 2007, the Inter-American Court of Human Rights (Inter-American Court, or IACtHR) decided the case of *Saramaka v. Suriname*. This was the first time that an international tribunal recognized the right to free, prior, and informed consent for the extraction of natural resources in indigenous and tribal peoples' territories. The Saramaka, a tribal community, brought the case against Suriname as part of their fight against the devastating deforestation of their lands by a mining company. The result was a groundbreaking decision on environmental conservation and recognition of indigenous and tribal peoples' rights. It was recognized worldwide as a landmark case and by the victims as a crucial symbolic victory. The State, however, has taken few steps toward compliance. On the contrary, mining activities and their destructive effects have increased in Suriname's tribal lands. How can the impact of this paradigmatic case be assessed and explained? What is the relationship among compliance, impact, authority, and effectiveness in the implementation of this decision?

Saramaka v. Suriname is not an unusual case in this regard, but rather illustrates the varied impacts of international litigation, which extend beyond compliance with measures of reparation. Although most significant in Latin America and the Caribbean, the transformation of the role of international courts is occurring globally. This trend has generated an intense academic debate on the functions of international courts and how to assess these courts' effectiveness. This chapter reviews the literature on the effectiveness of international courts and, in doing so, demonstrates how scholars have conceptualized the relationship between international litigation and changes in the domestic sphere. The chapter focuses on the Inter-American Human Rights System (Inter-American System, or IAHRS), particularly on the peculiarities of the Inter-American Court of Human Rights (Inter-American Court, or IACtHR) and how such peculiarities affect evaluations of its effectiveness. The chapter provides illustrative examples of its

Gabriela C.B. Navarro, *Effectiveness of International Courts* In: *The Impact of the Inter-American Human Rights System.*
Edited by: Armin von Bogdandy, Flávia Piovesan, Eduardo Ferrer Mac-Gregor, and Mariela Morales Antoniazzi,
Oxford University Press. © Gabriela C.B. Navarro 2024. DOI: 10.1093/oso/9780197744161.003.0008

broader points in its analyses the effectiveness of the IACtHR in the recognition of indigenous territorial rights.

The chapter is divided in three sections. The first section describes the theoretical approaches that equate effectiveness and compliance. It also provides a brief overview of studies concerning compliance with the IACtHR. The second section analyzes theoretical frameworks that expand the concept of effectiveness to include other forms of impact beyond compliance. It discusses theories specific to the impact and effectiveness of the IAHRS. The third section illustrates the different conceptions of effectiveness with IACtHR cases concerning Indigenous territorial rights. The chapter concludes by emphasizing the importance of studies about the transformative impact of international courts.

2. Effectiveness as Compliance

2.1. Defining and Measuring Compliance

One of the first studies regarding the effectiveness of international courts was published by Laurence R. Helfer and Anne-Marie Slaughter in 1997. Helfer and Slaughter defined effectiveness as a tribunal's "ability to compel compliance with its judgments by convincing domestic government institutions, directly and through pressure from private litigants, to use their power on its behalf."[1] In an attempt to understand why the European Court of Justice and the European Court of Human Rights were effective courts, the authors compiled a list of factors that influenced effectiveness. Later, in 2005, the authors clarified that their concept of effectiveness was closer to being relative than to being absolute.[2] In the same year, Eric Posner and John Yoo published an article in which they treated compliance as the primary measure for effectiveness, although they clarified that this measure should be complemented by assessments of the level of usage of the tribunal and success of the respective treaty regime. Overall, Posner and Yoo were skeptical of the ability of international courts to foment transformative change, describing them instead as mere problem-solving devices.[3]

In 2017, Helfer revisited the relationship between compliance and effectiveness with co-author Karen J. Alter. Alter and Helfer argued that, while both compliance and effectiveness involve conformity between State behavior and

---

[1] Laurence R. Helfer and Anne-Marie Slaughter, "Toward a Theory of Effective Supranational Adjudication" [1997] 107 *Yale Law Journal* 273.

[2] Laurence R. Helfer and Anne-Marie Slaughter, "Why States Create International Tribunals: A Response to Professors Posner and Yoo" [2005] 93 *California Law Review* 899.

[3] Eric Posner and John Yoo, "Judicial Independence in International Tribunals" [2005] 93 *California Law Review* 1.

a specified legal rule, only effectiveness involves desired changes in behavior that are attributable to that rule. In cases of compulsory jurisdiction, however, effectiveness could be fully captured by State compliance because there would be no meaningful difference between the two. Alter and Helfer also proposed recognizing effects beyond compliance and, while analyzing the Court of Justice of the Andean Community, pointed out the following effects: strengthened rule of law, opposition to corruption, and impacts on States that were not parties.[4]

Measuring compliance is, undoubtedly, fundamental to evaluating effectiveness. Understanding the time it takes for States to comply, the extent to which they comply and their reasons for compliance are central to assessing judicial power and patterns of judicial politics.[5] Compliance is also a central concern for victims because, to reach compliance, States must redress past human rights violations and guarantee their nonrepetition.[6] A recent study, however, suggested that IAHRS stakeholders should focus on implementation instead of compliance because measuring compliance fails to "capture the complexities of the necessary time, procedures and actors that may need to be involved in implementing a decision."[7] Compliance merely means the State's law and practice meet the requirements of a judgment. Implementation denotes the process by which domestic actors acknowledge, incorporate, and take ownership over the judgment.

The distinction between compliance and effectiveness is blurred when a tribunal orders reparations that affect an entire society, such as nonrepetition measures. Even for these measures, however, merely determining whether compliance exists could not explain all issues related to a judgment's effectiveness, such as a State's delayed compliance or partial compliance and the court's reasons for ordering those measures.[8] Compliance also does not capture the varied and innovative strategies courts have adopted, including promoting dialogue with State actors, civil society, and victims. Focusing exclusively on compliance disregards this complex network and its effects on domestic politics. International courts' functions should not be reduced to problem-solving, especially not the IACtHR,

---

[4] Karen J. Alter and Laurence R. Helfer, *Transplanting International Courts: The Law and Politics of the Andean Tribunal of Justice* (Oxford University Press 2017); see also Kal Raustiala, "Compliance & Effectiveness in International Regulatory Cooperation" [2000] 32 *Case Western Reserve Journal of International Law* 387.

[5] Diana Kapiszewski and Matthew M Taylor, "Compliance: Conceptualizing, Measuring, and Explaining Adherence to Judicial Rulings" [2013] 38 *Law & Social Inquiry* 803, 829–830.

[6] Carlos Martín Beristaín, *Diálogos sobre la Reparación: qué Reparar en los Casos de Violaciones de Derechos Humanos* (Instituto Interamericano de Derechos Humanos 2009).

[7] Rachel Murray, "Addressing the Implementation Crisis: Securing Reparation and Righting Wrongs" [2020] 21 *Journal of Human Rights Practice* 1, 10.

[8] Shai Dothan, "International Adjudication as Governance," in Helene R. Fabri (ed.), *Max Planck Encyclopedia of International Procedural Law* (Max Planck Institute Luxembourg for Procedural Law 2019).

whose nonrepetition reparation measures expand the reach of its judgments beyond the parties.

2.2. Evaluating Compliance with IACtHR Decisions

Many scholars have published quantitative analyses of compliance with IACtHR decisions, most of which concern all of the Inter-American Court's jurisprudence,[9] but some of which focus on specific countries[10] or specific measures.[11] Other studies have researched the factors that influence the extent to which States comply, suggested strategies for increasing compliance,[12] and analyzed the actors involved in reaching compliance, from civil society to State institutions.[13] Several studies analyze compliance with accountability and nonrepetition measures in the context of transitional justice.[14] There are, however, no studies that

---

[9] Darren Hawkins and Wade Jacoby, "Partial Compliance: A Comparison of the European and Inter-American American Courts for Human Rights" [2010] 6 *Journal of International Law and International Relations* 35; Fernando Basch et al., "The Effectiveness of the Inter-American System of Human Rights Protection: a Quantitative Approach to its Functioning and Compliance with its Decisions" [2010] 7 *SUR* 9; Cecilia M Bailliet, "Measuring Compliance with the InterAmerican Court of Human Rights: The Ongoing Challenge of Judicial Independence in Latin America" [2013] 31 *Nordic Journal of Human Rights* 477; Courtney Hillebrecht, *Domestic Politics and International Human Rights Tribunals: the Problem of Compliance* (Cambridge University Press 2014); Damián González-Salzberg, "The Effectiveness of the Inter-American Human Rights System: A Study of the American States' Compliance with the Judgments of the Inter-American Court of Human Rights" [2010] 16 *Revista Colombiana Derecho Internacional* 115; Aníbal Pérez Liñán, Luis Schenoni, and Kelly Morrison, "Time and Compliance with International Rulings: The Case of the Inter-American Court of Human Rights" [2019] *SSRN Electronic Journal*.

[10] Sergio Anzola, Beatriz Eugenia Sánchez, and Rene Urueña, "Después del Fallo: El Cumplimiento de las Decisiones del Sistema Interamericano de Derechos Humanos. Una Propuesta de Metodología," in Laurence Burgorgue-Larsen (ed.), *Derechos Humanos y Políticas Públicas: Manual* (Universidad Pompeu Fabra 2014); Damián González-Salzberg, "A Implementação das Sentenças da Corte Interamericana de Direitos Humanos na Argentina: uma Análise do Vaivém Jurisprudencial da Corte Suprema de Justiça da Nação" [2011] 8 *SUR* 115.

[11] Alexandra Huneeus, "Courts Resisting Courts: Lessons From the Inter-American Court's Struggle to Enforce Human Rights" [2011] 44 *Cornell International Law Journal* 493; María C Londoño-Lázaro, *Las Garantías de no Repetición en la Jurisprudencia Interamericana: Derecho Internacional y Cambios Estructurales del Estado* (Tirant lo Blanch México 2014).

[12] Viviana Krsticevic and Liliana Tojo (eds.), *Implementación de las Decisiones del Sistema Interamericano de Derechos Humanos: Jurisprudencia, Normativa y Experiencias Nacionales* (CEJIL 2007); James L. Cavallaro and Stephanie E. Brewer, "O Papel da Litigância para a Justiça Social no Sistema Interamericano" [2008] 5 *SUR—International Journal on Human Rights* 84; Jeffrey K. Staton and Alexia Romero, "Rational Remedies: The Role of Opinion Clarity in the Inter-American Human Rights System" [2019] *International Studies Quarterly* 1.

[13] James L. Cavallaro and Stephanie E. Brewer, "Reevaluating Regional Human Rights Litigation in the Twenty-First Century: The Case of the Inter-American Court" [2008] 102 *American Journal of International Law* 768; Huneeus (n. 11); Hillebrecht (n. 9).

[14] Kathryn Sikkink and Carrie B. Walling, "The Impact of Human Rights Trials in Latin America" [2007] 44 *Journal of Peace Research* 427; Bruno B. Bernardi, "O Sistema Interamericano de Direitos Humanos e o Caso da Guerrilha do Araguaia: Impactos no Brasil" [2017] 22 *Revista Brasileira de Ciência Política* 49; Elin Skaar, "Wavering Courts: From Impunity to Accountability in Uruguay" [2013] 45 *Journal of Latin American Studies* 483.

analyze compliance with one set of rights, with exception of my recent article on indigenous territorial rights.[15] There are also very few studies analyzing the amount of time it takes to achieve full compliance, even though delayed compliance is common among Latin American countries.[16]

Quantitative research on compliance with the IACtHR has adopted the Court's classification system for measures and cases. The Inter-American Court supervises its own decisions, a task that has become more and more demanding as the number of cases the IACtHR has decided grow. When this chapter was written, the Court was monitoring compliance with 223 of its judgments. For comparison, only 43 cases before the IACtHR are pending final judgment. In 2019, the Court issued 51 supervision orders and 21 merits decisions in contentious cases, as well as held 18 hearings in contentious cases and 16 for monitoring compliance.[17] Monitoring compliance is thus an important and time-consuming aspect of the Inter-American Court's work. Even though American Convention of Human Rights (American Convention, or ACHR) Article 68(1) provides that States are obligated to comply with final judgments issued by the IACtHR, it does not establish procedures for monitoring compliance. Monitoring compliance is instead regulated by the Inter-American Court's Rules of Procedure.[18] It mainly involves reports presented by the State, observations from the victims and their representatives, and observations from the Inter-American Commission on Human Rights (Inter-American Commission, or IACHR). The Inter-American Court reviews these materials and then determines that the State either has or has not complied with its measures, or else that the State has partially complied with the measures, although the criteria for partial compliance are not always clear.[19] The IACtHR has found partial compliance, for example, when a State paid a portion of the required compensation[20] and when a State published the judgment via one of the ordered outlets, but not in any of the others.[21] When a State complied with a measure after some delay, the Inter-American Court classifies this as compliance, without a separate distinction or category to reflect

---

[15] Gabriela C.B. Navarro, "The Struggle after the Victory: Non-compliance in the Inter-American Court of Human Rights' Jurisprudence on Indigenous Territorial Rights" [2021] 12 *Journal of International Dispute Settlement* 223.
[16] Pérez Liñán, Schenoni, and Morrison (n. 9).
[17] IACtHR, Annual Report 2019 (2020).
[18] A deeper analysis of the Inter-American Court's jurisdiction as it relates to the supervision of its own decisions can be found in *Baena Ricardo y otros v. Panamá* [2003] IACtHR, Ser. C No. 104. See also Edward J. Perez, "La Supervisión del Cumplimiento de Sentencias por Parte de la Corte Interamericana de Derechos Humanos y Algunos Aportes para Jurisdicciones Nacionales" [2018] 24 *Anuario de Derecho Constitucional Latinoamericano* 337.
[19] For a critical perspective on the use of the category of partial compliance, see Courtney Hillebrecht, "Rethinking Compliance: The Challenges and Prospects of Measuring Compliance with International Human Rights Tribunals" [2009] 1 *Journal of Human Rights Practice* 362.
[20] *Yakye Axa Indigenous Community v. Paraguay* [2019] IACtHR.
[21] *Yakye Axa, Sawhoyamaxa and Xákmok Kásek v. Paraguay* [2017] IACtHR.

the time elapsed. Overall, cases can be classified as in a state of compliance (the State has complied with all reparation measures), partial compliance (the State has complied with at least one reparation measure), or noncompliance (the State has yet to comply with any reparation measure).

Compliance studies are essential because they reveal how States react to the Inter-American Court's orders, identifying factors that enable, slow, or even impede compliance. This knowledge makes it possible to generate increased compliance in future cases through designing measures with greater precision, interacting with the most interested or most able domestic institutions, and finding ways for the IACtHR to engage more actively behavior in monitoring compliance. Compliance also matters for establishing the legitimacy and authority of the Inter-American Court, since lack of compliance could be seen as resistance to or even defiance against the Court. Nevertheless, evaluations of effectiveness should not be limited to assessments of compliance.

3. Impact beyond Compliance

3.1. Defining Impact and Effectiveness

Contemporary international relations involve a growing number of specialized international courts around the world, including the establishment of courts with new functions and means of access. The number of permanent international tribunals increased from six in 1989 to two dozen in 2014.[22] The growth is not only in numbers but also in importance, as international adjudication has increasingly influenced domestic politics on a wide range of issues, including environmental protection, gender equality, and access to justice. Human rights NGOs and movements have also increasingly pursued their agendas through strategic litigation before international courts. International courts are no longer viewed as mere resolvers of disputes and their expanded role enhances their effectiveness.

In the paradigm-changing book "The New Terrain of International Law," Alter analyzes the impact of "new-style international courts" on domestic politics. Alter suggests that certain features of new-style courts (e.g., compulsory jurisdiction and access by non-State litigators) facilitate the increased influence of international decisions on domestic politics. According to Alter, international courts have four functions: dispute settlement, administrative review,

---

[22] Karen J. Alter, "The Multiplication of International Courts and Tribunals After the End of the Cold War," in Cesare Romano, Karen J. Alter, and Yuval Shani (eds.), *The Oxford Handbook of International Adjudication* (Oxford University Press 2014).

constitutional review, and law enforcement. Alter also analyzes why some courts are more effective than others, arguing that effective courts rely on a coalition of compliance constituencies who support the rule of law.[23]

Yuval Shany, on the other hand, proposes that scholars adopt a goal-based approach in which effectiveness is assessed against predefined objectives contained in a court's stated mission and/or asserted by its constituencies. This approach is based on the normative assumption that international courts should be constrained by the expectations of their constituencies, focusing on States. Shany recognizes that the goals could have ambiguities and could change over time. He also identifies four general goals courts may have (norm support, resolving disputes, regime support, and legitimizing public authority), but does not clarify how to assess the idiosyncratic goals of international courts.[24] Shany also argues that analysis of a decision's outcomes requires consideration of compliance (effect on involved parties), the impact of jurisprudence (effect on the wider public), docket size, acceptance of jurisdiction, available budget, and legitimacy. These factors can, depending on the circumstances, indicate lower or higher rates of effectiveness. Lastly, Shany proposes that the evaluation of effectiveness be accompanied by a complementary assessment of cost-effectiveness that analyzes the relationship between structural attributes and effectiveness.[25]

Another similar approach analyzes the effectiveness of international tribunals by assessing their exercise of their functions. Armin von Bogdandy and Ingo Venzke argue that international courts can exercise three functions in addition to dispute settlement: asserting international law's validity and its enforcement; developing norms that have implications beyond the case under analysis; and controlling and affirming the legitimacy of domestic institutions.[26] Similarly, José E. Alvarez describes international courts as having four functions: dispute settlement, fact-finding, lawmaking, and governance.[27] For Bogdandy and Venzke, the expansion of the international courts' functions prompts a question relevant to their legitimacy: In whose name do these courts act? Bogdandy and Venzke suggest a need to move past the traditional, State-centered understanding of

---

[23] Karen J. Alter, *The New Terrain of International Law: Courts, Politics, Rights* (Princeton University Press 2014).
[24] Ibid.
[25] Yuval Shany, *Assessing the Effectiveness of International Courts* (Oxford University Press 2016).
[26] Armin von Bogdandy and Ingo Venzke, "In Whose Name? An Investigation of International Courts' Public Authority and its Democratic Justification" [2012] 23 *European Journal of International Law* 7; Armin von Bogdandy and Ingo Venzke, "On the Functions of International Courts: An Appraisal in Light of Their Burgeoning Public Authority" [2013] 26 *Leiden Journal of International Law* 49; Armin von Bogdandy and Ingo Venzke, *In Whose Name?: A Public Law Theory of International Adjudication* (Oxford University Press 2014).
[27] José E Alvarez, "What Are International Judges for?: The Main Functions of International Adjudication," in Cesare Romano, Karen J. Alter, and Yuval Shani (eds.), *The Oxford Handbook of International Adjudication* (Oxford University Press 2014).

international courts' legitimacy by viewing international courts as part of the international community or a particular legal regime and not only as State-created entities.[28]

Shai Dothan suggests that scholars analyze international courts in the context of global governance, demonstrating the manner in which tribunals produce long-term effects in the global arena. Dothan introduces two alternate ways of understanding the work of international courts: first, as existing in an international system of checks and balances, since an international decision rarely results in immediate State compliance with the decision's exact terms, instead the constant friction among contending actors eventually generates the implementation of policies informed by the many, varied opportunities for dialogue created by the international process; and, second, as part of networks composed of diverse actors (NGOs of various sizes, origins, and agendas; lawyers; activists; and government entities), in which the role of international courts is to make space for dialogue among key actors, disseminate information, and shame non-compliant States.[29]

In the field of legal sociology, César A. Rodríguez-Garavito has theorized the effects of litigation concerning social and economic rights in the Global South. Rodríguez-Garavito differentiates between enforcement (compliance with the court's measures) and impact (contribution to the fulfillment of the rights in question). He proposes four categories for the impacts of judicial decisions: material direct (leading to public policies), material indirect (increase in participation), symbolic direct, and symbolic indirect (reframing conflicts and socioeconomic realities). Rodríguez-Garavito has focused on domestic jurisprudence, specifically the rulings from the Constitutional Court of Colombia,[30] but other scholars have applied his theory to the decisions of international tribunals with some adaptation.[31]

Focusing on how domestic audiences react to international litigation, Alter, Helfer, and Mikael R. Madsen have theorized the *de facto* authority of international tribunals. Their theory offers a "yardstick to evaluate how a range of contextual factors shapes *de facto* authority of international courts via an analysis

---

[28] Bogdandy and Venzke, 2014 (n. 26).
[29] Dothan (n. 8); Shai Dothan, "A Virtual Wall of Shame: The New Way of Imposing Reputational Sanctions on Defiant States" [2017] 27 *Duke Journal of Comparative & International Law* 141.
[30] César A. Rodríguez-Garavito, "Beyond the Courtroom: The Impact of Judicial Activism on Socioeconomic Rights in Latin America" [2011] 89 *Texas Law Review* 1669; César A. Rodríguez-Garavito and Diana Rodriguez-Franco, *Juicio a la Exclusión: el Impacto de los Tribunales sobre los Derechos Sociales en el Sur Global* (Siglo 21 Editora Iberoamericana 2015); César A. Rodríguez-Garavito, "Beyond Enforcement: Assessing and Enhancing Judicial Impact," in Malcolm Langford, César A. Rodríguez-Garavito, and Julieta Rossi (eds.), *Social Rights Judgments and the Politics of Compliance: Making It Stick* (Cambridge University Press 2017).
[31] Joel E. Correia, Jeremie Gilbert, and Yogeswaran Subramaniam, *Strategic Litigation Impacts: Indigenous Peoples Land Rights* (Open Justice Society 2017).

of audiences' practices towards ICs."[32] Alter, Helfer, and Madsen analyze the interaction among legal, social, and political structures, as well as the behavior of actors situated within these structures. International courts thus reach an audience far greater than just the parties to a proceeding. Alter, Helfer, and Madsen's theory includes five types of *de facto* authority: no authority, narrow authority, intermediate authority, extensive authority, and popular authority. Narrow authority involves the practice of the litigants involved in the dispute. Intermediate authority extends to the behavior and decisions of similarly situated actors, including potential future litigants and compliance partners. A court has acquired extensive authority when it influences a broader range of legal actors, shaping both law and politics. Popular authority occurs when the general public is aware and accepting of the international court's decisions. It is important to note that courts do not progress linearly through the five levels of authority. Each authority can contract and expand independently and over time.[33]

In an attempt to consolidate the different conceptions of effectiveness, Helfer has divided the scholarship into four groups: case-specific effectiveness (closely linked to compliance), *erga omnes* effectiveness (systemic precedential effects for State parties not involved in the litigation), embedded effectiveness (influence on domestic legal orders), and norm-development effectiveness (lawmaking). Even though each type of effectiveness can be analyzed separately, these categories sometimes overlap, as, for example, when a State's compliance with nonrepetition measures ordered by an international court (an example of case-specific effectiveness) influences the State's domestic legal order more generally (an example of embedded effectiveness). In addition, these types of effectiveness interact with each other, alternately reinforcing and undermining each other.[34]

The Inter-American Court illustrates how an international court can expand its functions far beyond dispute settlement. For example, IACtHR decisions interpret rights broadly and affect States that are not parties to the proceedings. There are many examples of such decisions, including the ones that invalidate amnesty laws for mass atrocities committed during dictatorships, recognize the right of indigenous peoples to free, prior, and informed consent, and acknowledge incidents of intersectional discrimination against Indigenous women. The next section reviews recent studies that analyze the Inter-American Court's expanding influence.

---

[32] Karen J. Alter, Laurence R. Helfer, and Mikael R. Madsen (eds.), *International Court Authority* (Oxford University Press 2018).

[33] Ibid., 33.

[34] Helfer also acknowledges the existence of other functions exercised by international courts, but does not include them in his study. Laurence Helfer, "The Effectiveness of International Adjudicators," in Cesare Romano, Karen J. Alter, and Yuval Shani (eds.), *The Oxford Handbook of International Adjudication* (Oxford University Press 2014).

3.2. The Effectiveness of the IACtHR

A very prominent group of scholars has researched the *Ius Commune Constitutionale en América Latina* (ICCAL) in relation to the Inter-American System. ICCAL concerns the legal phenomenon of dialogue between domestic and international courts that aims to transform the situation of gross socioeconomic inequality in the region in the context of a transition from dictatorship to democracy. The concept promotes "the transformative potential of human rights, democracy and rule of law in Latin America," a region characterized by weak institutions and high rates of poverty. ICCAL provides a framework for understanding the interactions of comparative constitutional law and regional human rights law across a variety of institutions, stakeholders and actors. Within the ICCAL framework, scholars have researched topics such as the conventionality control, the "constitutional block," mechanisms through which inter-American norms are incorporated into domestic law (*interamericanización*), the impact of the reparations system, and institutional empowerment.[35]

Using a similar approach, the Inter-American Human Rights Network has analyzed the impact of the IAHRS on the implementation of human rights. Although its scholars avoid a narrow definition on impact, they "have developed a grounded and contextual understanding of how the IAHRS influences the politics and struggles between actors and institutions seeking to advance the realization of human rights and those who resist such social and political change," noting factors that could increase the positive effects of the system.[36] For example, Par Engstrom has criticized the equation of compliance and impact in analyses of the IACtHR's effectiveness and has proposed a broader view of impact that considers the role of the Inter-American System in the interpretation and expansion of human rights standards, the influence of the IAHRS on domestic political debates, and the IAHRS's creation of opportunities for domestic actors to pressure for change.[37] Engstrom defines effectiveness as "the degree to which international human rights institutions work to improve human rights conditions and decrease the likelihood of the repetition of abuses, while

---

[35] Armin von Bogdandy et al. (eds.), *Transformative Constitutionalism in Latin America: The Emergence of a New Ius Commune* (Oxford University Press 2017); Armin von Bogdandy, Héctor Fix Fierro, and Mariela Morales Antoniazzi (eds.), *Ius Constitutionale Commune en América Latina: Rasgos, Potencialidades y Desafíos* (Max Planck Institute of International Law 2014); Mariela Morales Antoniazzi and Laura Clerico (eds.), *Interamericanización del Derecho a la Salud: Perspectivas a la Luz del Caso Poblete de la Corte IDH* (Instituto de Estudios Constitucionales de Estado de Querétaro 2019).

[36] Par Engstrom et al., *Strengthening the Impact of the Inter-American Human Rights System Through Scholarly Research*, Inter-American Human Rights Network Reflective Report, 2016.

[37] Par Engstrom, "Reconceptualising the Impact of the Inter-American Human Rights System" [2017] 8 *Revista Direito e Práxis* 1251.

providing satisfactory recourse to the victims,"[38] a concept that includes but is not limited to compliance.

Other terms that refer to the effectiveness of international courts include engagement (the use of international human rights standards by domestic courts),[39] institutional empowerment (the use of the IAHRS by State officials to overcome institutional resistance and to promote the defense of human rights),[40] transconstitutionalism (the relationship between different legal orders in regard to a common constitutional problem, whether bilateral or multilateral),[41] and "efficacy chain" (a model that separates efficacy into five layers: observance, application, strengthening, implementation, and adequacy).[42]

4. Illustrating Effectiveness: The Case of Indigenous Territorial Rights

The Inter-American Court's jurisprudence on indigenous rights illustrates the inadequacy of compliance as the sole measure of effectiveness. These cases also demonstrate the wider impact the Court exerts in Latin America, which extends far beyond mere dispute settlement. This section provides examples of the many different theories of effectiveness drawn from the Inter-American System's unique approach to territorial rights. As of 2020, the IACtHR has decided fourteen cases in which it has recognized the rights of Indigenous and tribal peoples to their communal property.[43] Indigenous and tribal peoples brought cases in which they claimed demarcation of their traditional territory and full use and enjoyment of the natural resources thereon. The Inter-American Court responded by developing its jurisprudence in this area, especially as concerns the cultural

---

[38] Par Engstrom, "Introduction: Rethinking the Impact of the Inter-American Human Rights System," in Par Engstrom (ed.), *The Inter-American Human Rights System: Impact Beyond Compliance* (Palgrave Macmillan 2019).
[39] Marcelo Torelly, "From Compliance to Engagement: Assessing the Impact of the Inter-American Court of Human Rights on Constitutional Law in Latin America," in Par Engstrom (ed.), *The Inter-American Human Rights System: Impact Beyond Compliance* (Palgrave Macmillan 2019).
[40] Oscar Parra-Vera, "Institutional Empowerment and Progressive Policy Reforms: the Impact of the Inter-American Human Rights System on Intra-State Conflicts," in Par Engstrom (ed.), *The Inter-American Human Rights System: Impact Beyond Compliance* (Palgrave Macmillan 2019).
[41] Marcelo Neves, *Transconstitucionalismo* (WMF Martins Fontes 2013).
[42] Carina Calabria, *The Efficacy of the Inter-American Court of Human Rights: a Socio-legal Study Based on the Jurisprudence of the Inter-American Court of Human Rights Concerning Amnesty Laws, Indigenous Rights and Rights of Detainees* (University of Manchester 2018).
[43] *Mayagna (Sumo) Awas Tingni v. Nicaragua* [2001] IACtHR, *Moiwana v. Suriname* [2005], *Yakye Axa v. Paraguay* [2005] IACtHR, *Sawhoyamaxa v. Paraguay* [2006] IACtHR, *Saramaka v. Suriname* [2007] IACtHR, *Xákmok Kásek v. Paraguay* [2010] IACtHR, *Kichwa de Sarayaku v. Ecuador* [2012] IACtHR, *Kuna de Madungandí y Emberá de Bayano v. Panama* [2014] IACtHR, *Garífuna de Punta Piedra v. Honduras* [2015] IACtHR, *Garífuna Triunfo de la Cruz v. Honduras* [2015] IACtHR, *Kaliña y Lokono v. Suriname* [2015] IACtHR, *Xucuru v. Brazil* [2018] IACtHR, and *Lhaka Honhat v. Argentina* [2020] IACtHR.

adequateness of the reparation measures, transformation through implementation, and the innovative expansion of rights,[44] including recognition of the rights to collective property, cultural identity, and self-determination, as well as free, prior, and informed consent.

If effectiveness were solely a matter of compliance, the Court would be considered completely ineffective on indigenous rights. Only one case has reached full compliance (*Awas Tingni*), and the overall compliance rate is less than 30 percent. There are some cases that have been pending compliance, with very few steps taken in that direction, for more than fifteen years (i.e., *Moiwana* and *Yakye Axa*).[45] Some communities are living in the same conditions of displacement and poverty as they had been before the litigation.[46] Evaluations solely of compliance, however, obscure progress that has been made in the complex and costly domestic processes of implementation. In the case of *Sawhoyamaxa*, for example, the State has complied with only 25 percent of the measures ordered by the Inter-American Court. This number does not reflect that the State has already acquired the ancestral lands, started to pay the compensation, and built houses for the community, which it has done in response to the IACtHR's orders of the IACtHR but concerning which the Court has not yet declared compliance. Moreover, the victims from the case of *Sawhoyamaxa* have since formed a complex network of national and international NGOs that have pushed for compliance with this specific decision and have strengthened the domestic Indigenous movement more generally.[47]

A more full picture of effectiveness can be acquired through the consideration of each of the four categories Helfer identified: norm-development effectiveness, case-specific effectiveness, embedded effectiveness, and *erga omnes* effectiveness.[48] As for norm-development effectiveness, the standards developed by the Inter-American Court regarding the recognition of rights and the reparations system are a significant, original contribution to the protection of cultural specificities in the Americas. These norms also have contributed to the recognition of territorial rights globally and have been applied by other courts and

---

[44] Thomas Antkowiak, "Rights, Resources and Rhetoric: Indigenous Peoples and the Inter-American Court" [2014] 33 *University of Pennsylvania Journal of International Law* 113; Mariana Monteiro de Matos, *Indigenous Land Rights in the Inter-American System* (Brill Nijhoff 2021).

[45] Navarro (n. 15).

[46] Julie Wetterslev, *Surrounded by Settlers: The Creation and Fragmentation of Indigenous Territories in Nicaragua* (Annual Conference of the Latin American Studies Association 2020); Joel E. Correia, "Indigenous Rights at a Crossroads: Territorial Struggles, the Inter-American Court of Human Rights, and Legal Geographies of Liminality" [2018] 97 *Geoforum* 73.

[47] Joel E. Correia, "Unsettling Territory: Indigenous Mobilizations, the Territorial Turn, and the Limits of Land Rights in the Paraguay-Brazil Borderlands" [2019] 18 *Journal of Latin American Geography* 11; Maximiliano M. Miranda and Julia C. Alonso, *Advancing Indigenous Peoples' Rights Through Regional Human Rights Systems: The Case of Paraguay* (International Institute for Environment and Development 2017).

[48] Helfer (n. 34).

human rights mechanisms. As regards case-specific effectiveness, studying how and why States have complied with the reparation measures in Indigenous rights cases reveals the complex domestic political process that lead to implementation. Some State entities, including judiciaries, legislatures, and national human rights institutions, also have incorporate inter-American standards on Indigenous rights in ways that go beyond ordered reparation measures, contributing to the embedded effectiveness of the Inter-American Court. Lastly, even States that were not parties to IACtHR cases on Indigenous rights have incorporated the standards developed in this jurisprudence, contributing to the *erga omnes* effectiveness of the Court. For example, several constitutional courts have adopted the Court's standards on Indigenous rights,[49] as have many NGOs and national human rights institutions.

As for the *de facto* authority framework,[50] the Inter-American Court's authority has varied over time and by country. In the case of Nicaragua, the IACtHR exercises narrow authority, as evidenced by compliance with the *Awas Tingni* case and partial compliance with *Acosta et al.* (2017).[51] This narrow authority, however, has decreased over time, as shown by the State's overt defiance to some reparation measures in *Acosta et al.* and its insufficient response to the provisional measure *Pobladores de las Comunidades del Pueblo Indígena Miskitu de la Region Costa Caribe Norte* (2016). The Inter-American Court has also exercised intermediate authority in Nicaragua, revealed by the many victims who have brought petitions in the IAHRS in the hope of a favorable ruling to protect their rights. These petitions have increased since the 2018 coup.[52] Lastly, the Inter-American Court has extensive authority in Nicaragua, since it is recognized by civil society as creating binding law on Indigenous rights and because councilpersons have referred to the IACtHR's standards on consent when discussing bills concerning development projects (e.g., during discussion of Law 800 in 2012 and Law 840 in 2013, regarding the Nicaraguan Grand Canal).[53]

---

[49] Manuel E.G. Mera, "Judicialização da discriminação estrutural contra povos indígenas e afrodescendentes na América Latina: conceptualização e tipologia de um diálogo interamericano" [2015] 8 *Rev Quaestio Iuris* 826.

[50] Karen J. Alter, Laurence R Helfer, and Mikael R Madsen (eds.), *International Court Authority* (Oxford University Press 2018).

[51] *Acosta et al. v. Nicaragua* [2017] IACtHR, Ser. C No. 334; *Acosta et al. v. Nicaragua* [2019] IACtHR.

[52] See, e.g., the provisional measure 2019 *Matter of the Nicaraguan Centre for Human Rights and the Permanent Commission of Human Rights*; petition P912-14, proposed in 2014 by the NGO CALPI regarding the violation of territorial rights and the precautionary measure MC 495-14a, also proposed in 2014 by the NGO CALPI.

[53] Law N°. 840, Special Law for the Development of Nicaraguan Infrastructure and Transport Relating to the Canal, Free Trade Zones and Associated Infrastructure (Assembly of Nicaragua, June 13, 2013), <http://legislacion.asamblea.gob.ni/Diariodebate.nsf/xpMain.xsp> (accessed January 23, 2022).

Rodríguez-Garavito's framework of impact, meanwhile, has been applied to the three Paraguayan Indigenous cases by Joel E. Correia, Jeremie Gilbert, and Yogeswaran Subramaniam.[54] One of the cases Correia, Gilbert, and Subramaniam analyzed had not been fully implemented, but was nevertheless effective in increasing the political tools used by the Indigenous movement, building the capacities of grassroots groups, raising awareness about human rights, prompting the reoccupation of traditional lands, and shifting the balance of political power between Indigenous peoples and State and private companies. As the Xákmok Kásek leader stated, "The resolution from the court was important and it made us stronger. It spoke of a truth."[55]

Finally, the IACtHR's jurisprudence on Indigenous rights fits within the ICCAL approach. The Argentinian Supreme Court of Justice,[56] the Peruvian Constitutional Court,[57] the Bolivian Plurinational Constitutional Court,[58] and the Colombian Constitutional Court[59] have all applied the conventionality control to recognize the Indigenous right to free, prior and informed consent. The Inter-American Court also influenced the creation and strengthening of State entities focused on Indigenous peoples and the adoption of domestic legal standards that protect Indigenous and tribal peoples' rights. There is thus a clear process of *interamericanización* of the standards for protection of Indigenous peoples' territories that includes increasing recognition of Indigenous and tribal peoples' rights. There are, however, three limitations to this process. First, it is not linear and progressive, as revealed by the recent setbacks in the Brazilian protection of territorial rights.[60] Second, the IACtHR is not the only international organization promoting Indigenous and tribal peoples' territorial rights but is instead joined in these efforts by several UN entities and also financial institutions such as the World Bank.[61] Third, and unfortunately, the transformation of legal standards is not necessarily accompanied by transformation of realities on the

---

[54] Correia, Gilbert, and Subramaniam (n. 31).
[55] Ibid., 17.
[56] *Comunidad Indígena Eben Ezer c/ provincia de Salta—Ministerio de Empleo y la Producción s/ amparo*, [2008] Suprema Corte Argentina, Interno C2124XLI.
[57] *Gonzalo Tuanama Tuanama and others* [2011] Tribunal Constitucional de Peru, Pleno, Lima, Exp. N. 24-2009-PI.
[58] Sentence 0079/2015 (Bolivian Plurinational Constitutional Court, September 9, 2015).
[59] Judgment T-307/2018 (Colombian Constitutional Court, July 27, 2018).
[60] HRC "Report of the Special Rapporteur on the rights of indigenous peoples on her mission to Brazil" (August 8, 2016) A/HRC/33/42/Add.1; Diogo F. da Rocha and Marcelo Firpo S. Porto, *A vulnerabilização dos povos indígenas frente ao COVID-19: autoritarismo político e a economia predatória do garimpo e da mineração como expressão de um colonialismo persistente* (Neepes/ENSP/Fiocruz, 2020).
[61] Karl H. Offen, "The Territorial Turn: Making Black Territories in Pacific Colombia" [2003] 2 *Journal of Latin American Geography* 43.

ground. There is a persistent gap between the acceptance of these norms and their enforcement.[62]

5. Concluding Remarks

As this chapter has demonstrated, scholars at first measured the effectiveness of international courts solely by assessing compliance with their decisions, although they sometimes counterbalanced this with considerations of usage rates and the success of treaty regimes. More recently, scholars have identified functions and objectives of international courts that go beyond dispute settlement, indicating that the effectiveness of these courts requires a broader, more nuanced evaluation. At the same time, some scholars have started to analyze the authority and legitimacy of international courts. Scholars researching the Inter-American System specifically have also studied the structural impact of litigation, which is related to nonrepetition measures and, more broadly, the influence of the IAHRS on civil society and States. Last but not least, a prominent group of scholars has argued that the IAHRS transforms the situation of rights in Latin America by make space for dialogue among domestic actors in the interest of alleviating poverty and eliminating discrimination.[63]

Although the terms and definitions vary, the most recent literature generally shares a concern about the effects of international litigation on domestic politics. This concern is even more present in studies conducted on the IAHRS, due to the nature of the IACtHR and transformative constitutionalism in Latin America. The Inter-American Court's jurisprudence on Indigenous rights shows the assessing only compliance is insufficient to achieve an accurate measure of the effectiveness of the IACtHR. The Court's function when faced with litigation on indigenous land rights is not merely dispute settlement. Its decisions have much broader impacts on civil society actors, within the State that is party to the proceedings and in other States as well. A similar pattern appears in other areas, including women's rights, LGBTIQ+ rights, and the right to health. Future research should further reveal the diverse ways the IACtHR has increased the protection of human rights in Latin America and determine factors that facilitate a transformative impact so the Inter-American Court can have even greater effect in future cases.

---

[62] Felipe G. Isa, "The Decision by the Inter-American Court of Human Rights on the Awas Tingni vs. Nicaragua Case (2001): The Implementation Gap" [2017] 8 *Age of Human Rights Journal* 67; Correia (n. 47).

[63] Bogdandy et al. (n. 35); Armin von Bogdandy, Mariela Morales Antoniazzi, and Eduardo Ferrer Mac-Gregor (eds.), *Ius constitutionale Commune en América Latina: Textos Básicos para su Commprensión* (Instituto de Estudios Constitucionales de Estado de Querétaro 2017).

I.8
The Use of Transformative Provisional Measures by the Inter-American Court of Human Rights

Toward a Tangible Impact

By Clara Burbano-Herrera[1] and Yves Haeck

1. Introduction

In 2017, the Inter-American Court of Human Rights (Inter-American Court, or IACtHR) ordered provisional measures to protect the life and integrity of all persons deprived of liberty at the Criminal Institute of Plácido de Sá Carvalho (the Institute), 3,820 detainees in total.[2] The detention facility faced serious challenges, including high levels of violence, lack of access to health services and medicine, spread of contagious infections, and deaths. Overpopulation at the Institute had reached an approximate density of 200 percent.[3] Only one doctor attended to the medical needs of the 3,820 prisoners, and most other aspects of life at the Institute were controlled by the prisoners themselves. In its provisional measures, the Inter-American Court ordered Brazil to reduce overcrowding, assess the overall situation, and create a plan for the structural reform of the Institute.[4] In 2018, despite the provisional measures, the general situation at the Institute did not improve.

---

[1] This work was supported by the Research Fund Ghent University and the European Union. Views and opinions expressed are however of those of the authors only and do not necessarily reflect those of the European Union or the European Research Council. Neither the European Union nor the granting authority can be held responsible for them

[2] *Criminal Institute of Plácido de Sá Carvalho v. Brazil* [2017] IACtHR; see also precautionary measures adopted by the Inter-American Commission on Human Rights (Inter-American Commission, or IACHR) *Criminal Institute of Plácido de Sa Carvalho v. Brazil* [2016] IACHR. Precautionary measures had also been granted by the Inter-American Commission in 2016.

[3] International standards, such as those advanced by the Council of Europe, have established that a population density exceeding 120 percent means a prison is dangerously overcrowded. See *Criminal Institute of Plácido de Sá Carvalho v. Brazil* [2018] IACtHR, para. 78.

[4] *Criminal Institute of Plácido de Sá Carvalho v. Brazil* [2017] IACtHR, paras. 28, 70, and Resolutive, para. 3.

The situation at the Institute is far from an isolated case. On several occasions, the Inter-American Court has ordered provisional measures to protect persons deprived of liberty from degrading conditions in Brazilian prisons.[5] Since terrible prison conditions is a tragedy common not only in Brazil but also in other Latin American countries, this chapter aims to study the impact of *transformative provisional measures* granted by the IACtHR to address contexts of detention.[6] We suggest that the term *transformative provisional measures* refer to those provisional measures adopted by the Inter-American Court that address structural problems endangering many individuals (see section 4).

We will devote special attention to the transformative provisional measures adopted in the case of the Institute in November 2018 because, in this case, the IACtHR departed from its usual method of addressing detention cases. The provisional measures in this case are so revolutionary that they may eventually be considered a benchmark for studies of protective measures in international human rights law, at least in the context of prisons if not more generally. Furthermore, the unique qualities of this order of provisional measures could generate a debate about the legitimacy of the IACtHR's interventions in public policy as well as about its role and limitations. It is not yet clear whether the provisional measures ordered were appropriate to prevent human rights violations and protect detainees' human rights, as stipulated in Article 63(2) of the American Convention on Human Rights (American Convention, or ACHR), or whether the State will comply with these measures.[7]

This chapter is divided into six sections. The second section gives a general overview of the human rights standards developed by the IACtHR with respect to persons deprived of their liberty in Latin America. The third section introduces the concept of transformative provisional measures. The fourth

---

[5] See, e.g., *Matter of the Penitentiary Complex of Pedrinhas v. Brazil* [2019] IACtHR; *Matter of the Penitentiary Complex of Curado v. Brazil* [2018] IACtHR; *Matter of the Socio-Educational Internment Facility v. Brazil* [2017] IACtHR; *Socio-Educational Internment Facility of the Penitentiary Complex of Curado v. Brazil* [2017] IACtHR; *Matter of the Socio-Educational Internment Facility v. Brazil* [2015] IACtHR; *Matter of Urso Branco Prison v. Brazil* [2011] IACtHR; *Matter of the persons imprisoned in the "Dr Sebastião Martins Silveira" Penitentiary in Araraquara, São Paulo v. Brazil* [2008] IACtHR; *Matter of children deprived of liberty in the "Complexo do Tatuapé" of Fundação CASA v. Brazil* [2008] IACtHR; *Matter of the persons imprisoned in the "Dr Sebastião Martins Silveira" Penitentiary in Araraquara, São Paulo v. Brazil* [2008] IACtHR.

[6] See, e.g., *Criminal Institute of Plácido de Sá Carvalho v. Brazil* [2018] IACtHR; *Certain Penitentiary Centers of Venezuela, Penitenciaria Center of the Central Occidental Region (Uribana Prison) v. Venezuela* [2013] IACtHR and Order [2015]; *Capital Detention Center El Rodeo I and II v. Venezuela* [2011] IACtHR; *Convicted and tried inmates committed to the Penitentiary of Mendoza and its offices v. Argentina* [2004] IACHR; *108 inmates in the Maximum Security Prison at Kilometer 14 v. Colombia* [2004] IACHR; *Political prisoners in buildings 1 and 2 of the National Model Prison in Bogotá v. Colombia* [2000] IACHR; *Minors in the San Pedro de Sula Prison v. Honduras* [1996] IACHR.

[7] See Clara Burbano Herrera, Yves Haeck, and Alessandra Cuppini, "Transformative Provisional Measures and Prisons in the Americas: Protect the Invisible," in Clara Burbano Herrera and Yves Haeck (eds), *Human Rights Behind Bars. Ius Gentium: Comparative Perspectives on Law and Justice*, vol. 103 (Springer 2022), 143.

section then focuses on the current conditions in which detainees are kept in some Latin American countries. The fifth section analyzes conditions of detention through the lens of provisional measures ordered by the Inter-American Court. The sixth section returns to the case of the *Criminal Institute of Plácido de Sá Carvalho v. Brazil*, analyzing in greater detail the terrible conditions of the prison and the measures ordered by the IACtHR. The seventh section concludes with some reflections on the Inter-American Court's role in protecting human rights in the context of detention.

2. Human Rights Standards Applicable to Persons Deprived of Their Liberty in Latin America

Respect for human dignity is the guiding principle in the context of persons deprived of their liberty. American Convention Article 5(2) provides: "No one shall be subjected to torture or to cruel, inhuman, or degrading punishment or treatment. All persons deprived of their liberty shall be treated with respect for the inherent dignity of the human person." The Inter-American Court interprets ACHR Article 5(2) to mean that every person deprived of liberty has the right to be treated with respect for their dignity.[8] For example, in the case of *Montero Aranguren et al. (Detention Center of Catia) v. Venezuela*, the IACtHR found:

> [C]ertain inmates of the Detention Center of Catia not only had to defecate in the presence of their [cell]mates, but they also had to live amid excrements and even eat their food in these humiliating conditions. The Court consider[ed] that said detention conditions were absolutely unacceptable, [as] they involve[d] disdain for human dignity; cruel, inhuman and degrading treatment; high risk for health and life and a clear violation of Articles 5(1)[, which provides that "[e]very person has the right to have his physical, mental, and moral integrity respected,"] and 5(2) of the American Convention.[9]

The Inter-American Court, through its jurisprudence, has developed a set of human rights standards related to persons deprived of liberty. The IACtHR

---

[8] *Criminal Institute of Plácido de Sá Carvalho v. Brazil* [2018] IACtHR, para. 45; *Boyce and others v. Barbados* [2007] IACtHR, para. 88; *Lori Berenson Mejía v. Peru* [2004] IACtHR, para. 102; *De la Cruz Flores v. Peru* [2004] IACtHR, para. 124; *Bulacio v. Argentina* [2003] IACtHR, para. 126; *Durand and Ugarte v. Peru* [2000] IACtHR, para. 78; *Institute of Reeducation of the Minor "Panchito López" v. Paraguay* [1995] IACtHR, para. 151; *Neira Alegría and others v. Peru* [1995] IACtHR, para. 60.

[9] *Montero Aranguren and others v. Venezuela* [2006] IACtHR, para. 99. Similarly, the European Court of Human Rights (ECtHR) held that forcing a prisoner to live, sleep, and use sanitary facilities together with a large number of other prisoners was, per se, degrading treatment. See *Khudoyorov v. Russia* [2005] ECtHR, para. 107; *I.I. v. Bulgaria* [2005] ECtHR, para. 73; *Karalevicius v. Lithuania* [2005] ECtHR, para. 39.

recognizes that, in addition to presenting a potential violation of the right to personal liberty, the deprivation of liberty inevitably implicates other human rights. Nevertheless, the Court has held that imprisonment's direct impairment of the right to liberty and indirect impairment of other rights must be strictly minimized.[10] To that effect, the Inter-American Court has stated:

> [T]he State must ensure that the manner and method of any deprivation of liberty do not exceed the unavoidable level of suffering inherent in detention and that the detainee is not subjected to sufferings or hardships exceeding the unavoidable suffering inherent in detention, and that, given the practical requirements of incarceration, the detainee's health[11] and welfare are adequately warranted.[12]

At the same time, the Inter-American Court has asserted that the deprivation of liberty must not be accompanied by the dispossession of certain rights.[13] The rights of detainees to life,[14] personal integrity,[15] and fair trial,[16] for example, must be effectively respected and guaranteed just as they must be ensured to individuals who have not been deprived of liberty.[17] According to the IACtHR:

> [T]he poor physical and sanitary conditions existing in detention centres, as well as the lack of adequate lighting and ventilation, are per se violations to Article 5 of the American Convention, depending on their intensity, length of detention and personal features of the inmate, since they can cause hardship that exceed the unavoidable level of suffering inherent in detention, and because they involve humiliation and a feeling of inferiority.[18]

---

[10] *Montero Aranguren and others v. Venezuela* [2006] IACtHR, para. 86; *López Álvarez v. Honduras* [2006] IACtHR, para. 105; *"Juvenile Reeducation Institute" v. Paraguay* [2004] IACtHR, para. 154; *"Five Pensioners" v. Peru* [2003] IACtHR, para. 116.

[11] The UN Standard Minimum Rules for the Treatment of Prisoners ("Mandela Rules") provide that "[p]risoners should enjoy the same standards of health care that are available in the community, and should have access to necessary health-care services free of charge without discrimination on the grounds of their legal status." UN Standard Minimum Rules for the Treatment of Prisoners (the Mandela Rules), UN Doc. A/RES/70/175 (December 17, 2015), Rule 24(1).

[12] *Montero Aranguren and others v. Venezuela* [2006] IACtHR, para. 86.

[13] *Gómez Paquiyauri Brothers v. Peru* [2004] IACtHR, para. 108; *Maritza Urrutia v. Guatemala* [2003] IACtHR, para. 87.

[14] Art. 4 American Convention.

[15] Art. 5 American Convention.

[16] Art. 8 American Convention.

[17] *Institute of Reeducation of the Minor "Panchito Lopez" v. Paraguay* [2004] IACtHR, para. 155. See also the Inter-American Commission's Principles and Best Practices on the Protection of Persons Deprived of Liberty in the Americas, which declare that every person deprived of liberty shall have the right to health (Principle X). Similarly, the UN Standard Minimum Rules for the Treatment of Prisoners (Mandela Rules) adopted by the United Nations, General Assembly in Resolution A/RES/70/175, Rule 24.

[18] *Montero Aranguren and others v. Venezuela* [2006] IACtHR, para. 97.

The Inter-American Court has also found that States have a special obligation to protect detainees. It has reasoned that "the State is in a special position of guarantor to the persons deprived of their liberty, since prison authorities exercise a strong control or supervision over the persons under custody."[19] Moreover, in the case of persons deprived of their liberty who belong to vulnerable groups, such as persons with disabilities, women, and children, the IACtHR has established the need for a stricter scrutiny, given this added vulnerability.[20] Children are also protected under Article 19 of the American Convention, which provides: "Every minor child has the right to the measures of protection required by his condition as a minor on the part of his family, society, and the [S]tate." States therefore function as guarantors for children, which means they must adopt all the care that is required for their development.[21] In this context, States have two specific obligations: first, Articles 1 and 19 ACHR[22] obligate States to assume this special position as guarantor with particular care and responsibility, and, second, Article 19 ACHR obligates States to take special measures based on the principle of the best interests of the child.[23] With respect to the rights of children deprived of liberty, the State additionally must undertake to provide health and educational assistance in order to ensure that imprisonment will not destroy their life projects.[24]

The Inter-American Court's jurisprudence has also established that rape can constitute torture.[25] According to the IACtHR's interpretation of Article 5(2) ACHR, torture consists of any act of ill treatment that: (i) is intentional, (ii) causes severe physical or mental suffering, and (iii) is committed with an objective or purpose.[26] The Inter-American Court has found that rape is, under

---

[19] *Montero Aranguren and others v. Venezuela* [2006] IACtHR, para. 87; *Cantoral Benavides v. Peru* [2001] IACtHR, para. 87; *Neira Alegría and others v. Peru* [1996] IACtHR, para. 60.

[20] *Chinchilla Sandoval v. Guatemala* [2016] IACtHR, paras. 218–224; *Villagrán Morales and others v. Guatemala* [1999] IACtHR, paras. 146, 191.

[21] This obligation, as regards the conditions of juvenile detention, is therefore reinforced. See, e.g., *Servellón-García v. Honduras* [2006] IACtHR, para. 112; *Juvenile Reeducation Institute "Panchito Lopez" v. Paraguay* [2004] IACtHR, para. 16; *Gómez-Paquiyauri Brothers v. Peru* [2004] IACtHR, paras. 124, 163, 164, 171; *Bulacio v. Argentina* [2003] paras. 126, 134; *Villagrán Morales and others v. Guatemala* [1999] IACtHR, paras. 146, 191.

[22] *Institute of Reeducation of the Minor "Panchito Lopez" v. Paraguay* [2004] IACtHR, para. 160.

[23] *Gómez Paquiyauri Brothers v. Peru* [2004] IACtHR, paras. 124, 163–164, 171.

[24] IACtHR, Advisory Opinion OC-17/2002, "Juridical Condition and Human Rights of the Child," August 28, 2002, paras. 80, 81, 84, 86–88. The IACHR refers to Rule 13(5) of the UN Standard Minimum Rules for the Administration of Juvenile Justice (the Beijing Rules), adopted by the General Assembly in Resolution 40/33, November 28, 1985. See also the UN Rules for the Protection of Juveniles Deprived of their Liberty, adopted by the General Assembly in Resolution 45/113, December 14, 1990.

[25] *Women Victims of Sexual Torture in Atenco v. Mexico* [2018] IACtHR, para. 191.

[26] Ibid. See also *López Soto et al. v. Venezuela* [2018] IACtHR, para. 186; *Favela Nova Brasília v. Brazil* [2017] IACtHR, para. 252; *Río Negro Massacres v. Guatemala* [2012] IACtHR, para. 132; *Rosendo Cantú et al. v. Mexico* [2010] IACtHR, para. 118; *Fernández Ortega et al. v. Mexico* [2010] IACtHR, para. 128; *Bueno Alves v. Argentina* [2007] IACtHR, para. 79.

certain circumstances, an intentional act that causes intense suffering to the victim in order to intimidate, debase, humiliate, punish, or control the victim. For rape to constitute torture, the intentionality, the severity of the suffering, and the purpose of the act must be analyzed, taking into consideration the specific circumstances of each case.[27]

Additionally, Article 5(2) ACHR's prohibition of any injury or damage to the life, integrity, or health of a person deprived of liberty is complemented by the essential purpose of the deprivation of liberty, which is the rehabilitation of the prisoners.[28] Article 5(6) ACHR provides: "Punishments consisting of deprivation of liberty shall have as an essential aim the reform and social readaptation of the prisoners." Failure to comply with the duty to safeguard the health and welfare of detainees and ensure that the manner and method of deprivation of liberty does not exceed the inevitable level of suffering inherent in detention could result in a violation of the absolute prohibition against cruel, inhuman, or degrading treatment or punishment.[29] States cannot invoke economic hardships to justify conditions of detention that do not meet the minimum international standards in this area and do not respect human dignity.[30] As we mentioned earlier, every person deprived of liberty must be treated with respect for human dignity and must not be subjected to torture or cruel, inhuman, or degrading treatment or punishment.[31] Failure to respect the dignity of persons deprived of their liberty violates a basic principle of democratic societies.[32] As such, Article 5(2) ACHR can never be suspended, not even in cases of war, public danger, or other threats to the independence or the security of the State Parties,[33] and not when a person has committed a crime.[34]

As for prison conditions, the Inter-American Court has established that "imprisonment in overcrowded conditions, isolation in a reduced cell, with lack of ventilation and natural light, without a bed to lie in or adequate hygiene

---

[27] See *López Soto et al. v. Venezuela* [2018] IACtHR, paras. 186–187; *Rosendo Cantú et al. v. Mexico* [2010] IACtHR; *Fernández Ortega et al. v. Mexico* [2010] IACtHR, para. 127.

[28] *Penal Miguel Castro Castro v. Peru* [2006] IACtHR, para. 314; *García Asto and Ramírez Rojas v. Peru* [2005] IACtHR, para. 223; *Lori Berenson Mejía v. Peru* [2005] IACtHR, para. 101.

[29] *Lori Berenson Mejia v. Peru* [2005] IACtHR, para. 101; *Tibi v. Ecuador* [2004] IACtHR, para. 150; *Juvenile Reeducation Institute "Panchito López" v. Paraguay* [2004] IACtHR, para. 151; *Bulacio v. Argentina* [2003] IACtHR, para. 126.

[30] *Boyce and others v. Barbados* [2007] IACtHR, para. 88; *Montero Aranguren and others v. Venezuela* [2006] IACtHR, para. 85.

[31] *Durand and Ugarte v. Peru* [2000] IACtHR, para. 78; *Neira Alegría and others v. Perú* [1996] IACtHR, para. 86.

[32] *Lopez-Alvarez v. Honduras* [2006] IACtHR, para. 104; *Institute of Reeducation of the Minor "Panchito Lopez" v. Paraguay* [2004] IACtHR, para. 154.

[33] The right to personal integrity is included in the list of non-derogable rights in Article 27(2) of the American Convention on Human Rights.

[34] *Penal Miguel Castro Castro v. Peru* [2006] IACtHR, para. 274; *Institute of Reeducation of the Minor "Panchito Lopez" v. Paraguay* [2004] IACtHR, para. 157; *Montero Aranguren and others v. Venezuela* [2006] IACtHR, para. 85; *Ximenes Lopes v. Brazil* [2006] IACtHR, para. 126.

condition, and solitary confinement or unnecessary restrictions to visitation regimes constitute a violation to the right to humane treatment."[35] In the case of *Vélez Loor v. Panama*, the IACtHR held that "a population density higher than 120% [. . .] reaches dangerous levels."[36] Prison overcrowding is a factor the Court considers when determining whether a State has violated Article 5(2) ACHR. In the *Montero Aranguren* case, the Court relied on the European Committee for the Prevention of Torture's definition of an overcrowded prison and guidelines on the minimum size for each prisoner's cell.[37] The IACtHR has even held, as it did in the case of *Pacheco Teruel et al. v. Honduras*, that "[o]vercrowding is, in itself, a violation of personal integrity."[38] The prolonged isolation and coercive lack of communication experienced in prisons can also cause severe harm, such as moral suffering and mental stress, to any individual, which in turn creates a risk of aggression and abuse of authority.[39]

On the topic of preventive detention, the Inter-American Court has asserted that it is a precautionary and nonpunitive measure.[40] Preventive detention also must meet the essential requirements in a democratic society, that is, it must be exceptional and limited by the principles of legality, presumption of innocence, necessity, and proportionality.[41] Similarly, the IACtHR will find a custodial measure arbitrary unless it complies with the following standards: (i) its purpose must be compatible with the American Convention, (ii) it must be suitable to achieve the objective pursued, (iii) it must be necessary, and (iv) it must be proportional.[42] The Inter-American Court also has repeatedly stated that the only legitimate purpose for the deprivation of liberty of a criminal defendant is to ensure that the defendant will not impede the efficient development of an investigation or evade justice.[43]

---

[35] *Penal Miguel Castro Castro v. Peru* [2006] IACtHR, para. 315.

[36] *Vélez Loor v. Panama* [2010] IACtHR, para. 203.

[37] *Montero Aranguren and others v. Venezuela* [2006] IACtHR, para. 90, referring to CPT/Inf (92) 3 [EN] 2nd General Report, April 13, 1992, para. 43. The latest European Committee for the Prevention of Torture (CPT) minimum standard for personal living space in prison establishments is: $6m^2$ of living space for a single-occupancy cell + sanitary facility; $4m^2$ of living space per prisoner in a multiple-occupancy cell + fully-partitioned sanitary facility; at least 2m between the walls of the cell; and at least 2.5m between the floor and the ceiling of the cell (CPT, Living space per prisoner in prison establishments: CPT standards, CPT/Inf (2015) 44, Strasbourg, December 15, 2015, paras. 9–11.

[38] *Pacheco Teruel et al. v. Honduras* [2012] IACtHR, para. 67.

[39] *Lori Berenson Mejía v. Peru* [2005] IACtHR, para. 104; *Maritza Urrutia v. Guatemala* [2003] IACtHR, para. 87; *Cantoral Benavides v. Peru* [2001] IACtHR, para. 84; *Bamaca Velasquez v. Guatemala* [2000] IACtHR, para. 150.

[40] *Acosta Calderón v. Ecuador* [2005] IACtHR, para. 75; *Tibi v. Ecuador* [2004] IACtHR, para. 106.

[41] *García Asto and Ramírez Rojas v. Peru* [2005] IACtHR, para. 106.

[42] *Women Victims of Sexual Torture in Atenco v. México* [2018] IACtHR, para. 251; *Ricardo Canese v. Paraguay* [2004] IACtHR, para. 129.

[43] *Suárez Rosero v. Ecuador* [1997] IACtHR, para. 77; *Women Victims of Sexual Torture in Atenco v. Mexico* [2018] IACtHR, para. 251.

3. Legal Basis of Provisional Measures in the Inter-American Human Rights System

Article 63(2) of the American Convention expressly authorizes the Court to adopt provisional measures "in cases of extreme gravity and urgency, and when necessary to avoid irreparable damage to persons."[44] The Inter-American Commission on Human Rights (Inter-American Commission, or IACHR) can also request provisional measures from the IACtHR, even when the case has not been submitted to the Court.[45]

Provisional measures are both preventive and protective. They are preventive because they are issued to avoid violations of human rights.[46] Provisional measures prompt a State to act expeditiously to correct situations that may *prima facie* cause irreparable damage to individual rights. Related, when a State complies with provisional measures it will avoid being found legal responsible by an international mechanism because the State thereby corrects, in a timely manner, situations where violations of human rights could have occurred. Provisional measures are protective because they preserve the rights at issue during adjudication.[47] Due to their purpose and legal character, the adoption of provisional measures does not require the IACtHR to prejudge the merits of the case, nor does it represent a condemnation of the State.[48]

---

[44] American Convention, Article 63(2). The procedures for provisional measures have been further developed in the Rules of Procedure and the Statute of the IACHR as well as those of the Inter-American Court of Human Rights.

[45] When the case is under consideration before the Inter-American Commission, the Inter-American Court may adopt provisional measures at the request of the IACHR. The IACtHR cannot adopt measures *ex officio* at this stage. See Article 63(2) American Convention.

[46] Eva Rieter and Karin Zwaan (eds.), *Urgency and Human Rights, The Protective Potential and Legitimacy of Interim Measures* (Asser Press 2021), 229.

[47] For an in-depth study of provisional measures, see Clara Burbano Herrera, *Provisional Measures in the Case Law of the Inter-American Court of Human Rights* (Intersentia 2010), 227; see also Clara Burbano Herrera and Yves Haeck, "Letting States off the Hook? The Paradox of the Legal Consequences following State Non-compliance with Provisional Measures in the Inter-American and European Human Rights Systems" [2010] 28(3) *Netherlands Quarterly of Human Rights* 332–360; Clara Burbano Herrera and Yves Haeck, "The Impact of Precautionary Measures on Persons Deprived of Liberty in the Americas," in Par Engström (ed.), *The Inter-American Human Rights System: Impact Beyond Compliance* (Palgrave Macmillan 2018), 89–113; Antonio Cançado Trindade, "The Evolution of Provisional Measures Under the Case Law of the Inter-American Court" [2003] 24 *Human Rights Law Journal* 162–168; Felipe González, "Urgent Measures in the Inter-American Human Rights System" [2010] 7 *SUR* 51–73; Jo M. Pasqualucci, "Medidas provisionales en la Corte Interamericana de Derechos Humanos: una comparación con la Corte Internacional de Justicia y la Corte Europea de Derechos Humanos" [1994] 19 *Revista IIDH* 47–112; Eva Rieter, *Preventing Irreparable Harm: Provisional Measures In International Human Rights Adjudication* (Intersentia 2010), 1200.

[48] The Inter-American Court can order provisional measures in matters concerning States that have ratified the American Convention and accepted the IACtHR's contentious jurisdiction. As of 2019, only twenty-three of the thirty-five Member States of the Organization of American States have ratified the American Convention, and of these, only twenty have accepted the contentious jurisdiction of the Inter-American Court.

Provisional measures can be adopted in urgent situations involving serious danger, as is the case for harsh detention conditions that present an imminent risk to the right to life, the right to personal integrity, or the right to health.[49] In response to the terrible conditions of detention in some prisons in the Americas, the Inter-American Court has issued provisional measures to protect both individuals and groups of persons deprived of their liberty. Provisional measures have protected clearly identified persons, such as sick detainees and detainees condemned to death, as well as large groups up to and including all inmates in some prisons.[50]

Due to the urgency of the situation, the Inter-American Court responds to requests for provisional measures quickly. Sometimes the IACtHR adopts provisional measures on the same day it receives the request.[51] Although, by definition, the provisional measures ordered by the Court are temporary, in practice some provisional measures have remained in place for years. These measures last because cases with which they are associated are so grave that, in spite of the implementation of certain measures by State authorities, the situation of extreme gravity is not resolved. It is thus difficult to determine in advance how long the provisional measures will be in force. Some provisional measures have remained in place for less than a year, while others have been in force for more than ten years.[52]

4. Transformative Provisional Measures: Toward a Material Impact

The term *transformative provisional measures* has not previously been used by international courts or scholars, but we would like to introduce and use it in this

---

[49] *Wong Ho Wing v. Peru* [2006] IACtHR, and *Boyce and Joseph v. Barbados* [2007] IACtHR.
[50] See, e.g., *Criminal Institute Plácido de Sá Carvalho v. Brazil* [2018] IACtHR; *Curado Complex (in Recife) v. Brazil* [2016] IACtHR; *Inmates in the Urso Branco Prison v. Brazil* [2002] IACHR.
[51] In the *Boyce and Joseph v. Barbados* case, the Inter-American Court granted provisional measures to protect four individuals who had been sentenced to death. The orders for execution had already been read out and the executions were scheduled four days after the request. Due to the urgency of the matter, the IACtHR issued the provisional measures on the same day that they were requested. See *Boyce and Joseph v. Barbados* [2004] IACtHR, para. 4, decides para. 1. The Inter-American Court's time frame depends on the circumstances of the case. See Clara Burbano Herrera, *Provisional Measures in the Case Law of the Inter-American Court of Human Rights* (Intersentia 2010), 96.
[52] For example, in the Matter of Certain Venezuelan Prisons, the provisional measures that were adopted in 2006 have been maintained through 2020. See *Matter of Certain Venezuelan Prisons v. Venezuela* [2007] IACtHR and Order November 13, 2015. Similarly, provisional measures were adopted in 2002 to protect the inmates in the Urso Branco Prison in Brazil, and they were only lifted in 2011. See *Inmates in the Urso Branco Prison v. Brazil* [2002] IACtHR and Order August 25, 2011. Provisional measures were also adopted to protect Humberto Prado in 2009, and they are still maintained in 2020. See *Matters of Certain Penitentiary Centers of Venezuela. Humberto Prado. Marianela Sánchez Ortiz and family v. Venezuela* [2020] IACtHR, para. 3.

context. We define transformative provisional measures as provisional measures that have the following characteristics:[53] (i) they target structural problems, (ii) they aim to protect several persons in situations of extreme gravity and urgency, and (iii) they contain orders that must be complied with by more than one State entity. Transformative provisional measures aim to protect the rights of several people who are collectively in danger while also preventing human rights violations. Transformative provisional measures arise out of structural problems, that is, situations in which State authorities have consistently failed to respect, protect, and fulfill the rights of historically marginalized groups. As in Claudio Nash and Constanza Núñez's research on structural judgments, in this context, cultural norms maintain dominant political and legal structures and obscure the experiences of vulnerable groups.[54] Finally, coordinated action and participation of various State authorities is required to comply with transformative provisional measures. The human rights situation cannot be addressed with a single provisional measure targeting a single authority or requesting a single public policy, because a complex institutional framework has generated, enabled, and perpetuated the structural problems involved.[55]

The conditions of detention in some Latin American prisons illustrate structural problems which transformative provisional measures can address and potentially alleviate. As reports and decisions adopted by the UN Special Rapporteurs and regional human rights mechanisms reveal, some Latin American prisons do not comply with the minimum international human rights standards.[56] These deplorable detention conditions are not the result of isolated

---

[53] Clara Burbano Herrera, Yves Haeck, and Alessandra Cuppini, "Transformative Provisional Measures and Prisons in the Americas: Protect the Invisible," in Clara Burbano Herrera and Yves Haeck (eds.), Human Rights Behind Bars. Ius Gentium: Comparative Perspectives on Law and Justice, vol. 103 (Springer 2022), 146 ff.

[54] According to Nash and Núñez, there are two reasons for State inaction: (a) States that do not act for ideological reasons, for which the establishment of fundamental rights has not been sufficient to mobilize internal political decisions; and (b) States that do not have the capacity to act because they do not have territorial control or economic resources, or are captured by interest groups. See Claudio Nash and Constanza Nunez, "Sentencias Estructurales Momento de Evaluacion, Sobre los Derechos Sociales" [2015] *Revista de Ciencias Sociales (Volumen Monografico Extraordinario)*, 267–289. The authors refer to Jonathan Di John, "Conceptualización de las causas y consecuencias de los Estados fallidos: una reseña crítica de la literatura" [2010] 37 *Revista de Estudios Sociales* 46–86; Daniel Kaufmann et al., *Captura del Estado, Corrupción, e Influencia en la Transición, Trabajo de Investigación de Políticas* (Banco Mundial 2000), 1–39.

[55] Ibid., Nash and Nunez, 284.

[56] See, for example, Preliminary observations and recommendations, UN Special Rapporteur on torture and other cruel, inhuman, or degrading treatment or punishment, Mr. Nils Melzer on the official visit to Argentina, April 9–20, 2018: the Rapporteur mentions that the conditions of detention in Argentina severely contravene international standards and are incompatible with human dignity, <https://www.ohchr.org/EN/NewsEvents/Pages/DisplayNews.aspx?NewsID=22974&LangID=E> (accessed November 10, 2021). See also UN Report of the Special Rapporteur on torture and

incidents. They are instead the consequence of enduring, systemic problems with prison systems in the region.

Structural problems in prisons affect detainees collectively and have prompted them join together in their requests for provisional measures from the IACtHR. These requests for provisional measures enable detainees to demand that the State addresses detention conditions. The Inter-American Court similarly aims, when it responds to these requests with orders of provisional measures, to prompt the State toward the fulfillment of its international commitment to respect the human dignity of persons deprived of liberty. When State authorities implement the provisional measures ordered by the IACtHR, these measures are shown to be a legal (normative) tool and not a mere formality. The Inter-American Court also issue§s orders that not only seek to protect the detainees who made the request but also to transform detention conditions more broadly.

5. Detention Conditions of Persons Deprived of Their Liberty in Latin America through the Lens of Transformative Provisional Measures

For decades, the treatment of the prison populations in some Latin American countries, and in Brazil in particular, generally has been degrading and inhumane. In spite of Latin American countries' tradition of espousing human rights rhetoric in their engagement with the international community and even in spite of domestic legislation incorporating their international commitments to rights, State authorities often fail to respect, protect, and fulfill individuals' rights to equality and dignity of individuals. For example, States sometimes act as though the right to dignity belongs not to all individuals, but only to deserving individuals, among whom they do not include persons deprived of liberty.

Several Latin American prisons have structural problems that affect their entire populations. When detainees from these prisons have requested provisional measures, the ones the Inter-American Court has granted have been transformative. The IACtHR sees prisoners as a group that is at risk of human rights violations. These risks generally concern critical overcrowding, high levels of violence, lack of control by prison authorities, insalubrity, spread of contagious

---

other cruel, inhuman, or degrading treatment or punishment on his mission to Brazil, January 26, 2016, <https://digitallibrary.un.org/record/831519?ln=en#record-files-collapse-header> (accessed November 10, 2021); UN Report of the Special Rapporteur on torture and other cruel, inhuman, or degrading treatment or punishment, Juan E. Mendez. Follow-up to the recommendations made by the Special Rapporteur to previous country visits (with regard to Uruguay), February 28, 2013, paras. 80–81, <https://www.ohchr.org/Documents/HRBodies/HRCouncil/RegularSession/Session22/A.HRC.22.53.Add.3_ES.pdf> (accessed November 19, 2022).

infections, lack of access to health services, and death.[57] Several examples show the terrible conditions of prisons in Brazil. For example, in the case of the *Penitentiary Complex of Curado (Brazil)*, the Inter-American Court found that detention conditions had not improved between the time it had ordered an initial set of provisional measures in 2014 and the time it revisited the situation in 2018. The IACtHR observed that the prison remained overcrowded, with a density exceeding 200 percent.[58] Similarly, the Inter-American Commission granted precautionary measures in the case of the *Inmates at the Polinter Police Station in Rio de Janeiro (Brazil)*, where 1,000 detainees, including young offenders, were held even though the police station had a capacity of only 205 persons.[59] In the case of the *Criminal Institute of Plácido de Sá Carvalho (Brazil)*, the prison had a capacity of 1,699, but contained 3,820 detainees.[60] In the case of the *Urso Branco Prison (Brazil)*, the IACHR granted precautionary measures responding not only to the terrible detention conditions but also to the conflicts among the prisoners as well as a massacre resulting in the deaths of over 30 prisoners.[61]

Children deprived of liberty have also faced situations of extreme danger in Brazilian prisons.[62] Children are particularly vulnerable to violence in penitentiary circumstances. As a result, the Inter-American Court has granted provisional measures to protect all the children imprisoned in the case of the *Socio-Educational Internment Facility (Brazil)*[63] and the case of *Children and Teenagers Deprived of Liberty in the "Complexo de Tatuapé" of FEBEM (Brazil)*.[64] The Inter-American Commission had previously issued precautionary measures in the *Complexo de Tatuapé* case following allegations of violent acts, including

---

[57] *Criminal Institute of Plácido de Sá Carvalho v. Brazil* [2018] IACtHR, paras. 3, 37; *Detainees at Toussaint Louverture Police Station in Gonaïves v. Haiti* [2008] IACHR, 144/07; *Penitentiary Services Buenos Aires Province v. Argentina* [2012] IACHR, 104/12.

[58] *Penitentiary Complex of Curado v. Brazil* [2018] IACtHR, paras. 80–81. See also *Penitentiary Complex of Curado v. Brazil* [2014, 2015, 2016, 2017] IACtHR.

[59] *Men deprived of freedom in the cells located in the basement of Polinter Police District in Rio de Janeiro v. Brazil* [2005] IACHR.

[60] *Criminal Institute Plácido de Sá Carvalho v. Brazil* [2018] IACtHR, para. 17.

[61] The forty-seven survivors were at risk of being killed. See *Inmates in the Urso Branco Prison v. Brazil* [2002] IACHR.

[62] The American Declaration of the Rights and Duties of Man and the American Convention provide for the protection of children but do not define the term "child." The Inter-American Court and Inter-American Commission have established that the definition of a child is based on Article 1 of the UN Convention on the Rights of the Child. As such, "child" refers to any person who has not yet turned eighteen years of age. See IACtHR, Juridical Condition and Human Rights of the Child, Advisory Opinion OC-17/02, August 28, 2002, para. 42; *Villagran Morales (Street Children) v. Guatemala* [1999] IACtHR, para. 188; *Bulacio v. Argentina* [2003] IACtHR, para. 133.

[63] *Unidade de Internação Socioeducativa (la Unidad o la UNIS) v. Brazil* [2011, 2012, 2013] IACtHR. See also the Resolutions adopted by the President of the IACtHR on September 26, 2014, June 23, 2015, and November 15, 2017.

[64] The Court also ordered the State to protect the lives of all of the individuals within the compound. *Matter of Children and Adolescents Deprived of Liberty in the "Complexo do Tatuapé" of FEBEM v. Brazil* [2006] IACtHR.

the death of Roni César de Souza.[65] A continuous lack of security and control by the prison staff showed that the State had not satisfactorily fulfilled its obligation to prevent attacks against the life and personal integrity of imprisoned children.[66] Since the situation did not improve and the children faced increasing dangers, the Inter-American Court adopted provisional measures in 2005. The transformative provisional measures adopted by the Court in this case have remained in place through 2020.[67]

The problems with the Brazilian prison system have existed for decades. Overcrowding in the prison system dates back to at least the beginning of the nineteenth century.[68] Additionally, at the Twelfth UN Congress on Crime Prevention and Criminal Justice in 2010, the President of the Supreme Federal Court of Brazil said that Brazil's "prison system is on the brink of total collapse."[69]

Similar problems to those already described in Brazil can be found in other Latin American countries, including Argentina, Colombia, Honduras, Guatemala, and Venezuela. The Inter-American Court has also granted transformative provisional measures in response to requests from persons deprived of liberty in these countries. The petitioners have alleged deplorable prison conditions related to violence and overcrowding. One consequence of overcrowding is that it becomes difficult to separate inmates by gender, age, or the seriousness of their crimes. In some cases, a lack of separation between pre-trial and convicted detainees,[70] members of armed groups and common prisoners,[71] members of different armed groups (guerrilla and paramilitary),[72] children and adults,[73] non-LGBTIQ+ and LGBTIQ+ detainees,[74] non-elderly and elderly detainees,[75] and able-bodied detainees and detainees with a disability has resulted in conflict.[76]

---

[65] Ibid., para. 7.
[66] Ibid., para. 6.
[67] Ibid., and IACHR, *2005 Annual Report*, paras. 41–42. See also *Matter of Children and Adolescents Deprived of Liberty in the "Complexo do Tatuapé" of FEBEM v. Brazil* [2005, 2006, 2007, 2008] IACtHR.
[68] Clarissa Nunes Maia et al. (eds.), *História das prisões no Brasil*, vols. I and II (Rocco 2009).
[69] Website Consultor juridico, <https://www.conjur.com.br/2010-abr-15/deficiencia-sistema-carcerario-beira-falencia-total-peluso> (accessed January 2, 2022).
[70] *Convicted and tried inmates committed to the Penitentiary of Mendoza and its offices v. Argentina* [2004] IACHR.
[71] *108 inmates in the Maximum Security Prison at Kilometer 14 v. Colombia* [2004] IACHR.
[72] *Political prisoners in buildings 1 and 2 of the National Model Prison in Bogotá v. Colombia*, Precautionary Measures [2000] IACHR ("On April 27, 2000, prisoners belonging to paramilitary groups detained in cellblock 5 launched a violent attack on prisoners in cellblock 4, killing 47 inmates and injuring 17 others").
[73] *Minors in the San Pedro de Sula Prison v. Honduras* [1996] IACHR.
[74] *Criminal Institute Plácido de Sá Carvalho v. Brazil* [2018] IACtHR, para. 48.
[75] Ibid.
[76] *Curado Complex (in Recife) v. Brazil* [2016] IACtHR, para. 4.

In the case of the *Matters of Certain Venezuelan Penitentiary Centres (Venezuela)*,[77] for which the Inter-American Court ordered comprehensive provisional measures to a large number of beneficiaries, the IACtHR started to engage with the conditions of detention in a number of prisons in Venezuela.[78] In its orders, the Inter-American Court required the State to take immediate steps to ensure that no more detainees would be treated inhumanely or killed. At the same time, the IACtHR ordered more general measures, such as the separation of pre-trial and convicted detainees, healthcare to all persons deprived of liberty, reduction of overcrowding, adequately trained staff, and prison conditions that conform with applicable international standards. As of the end of 2020, the Inter-American Court is still monitoring this case and has observed the persistence of violent acts culminating in the deaths of persons deprived of liberty.[79]

Several factors contribute to the prison crisis in some Latin American countries. Although describing all of these problems comprehensively is beyond the scope of this chapter, one factor appears to be a tendency to expand the use of criminal law, incarceration, and preventive detention in the face of various societal issues.[80] For example, from 2000 to 2020, the incarcerated population increased by three times in Colombia, five times in Brazil, and six times in El Salvador.[81] Politicians in power have responded to the popular demand for

---

[77] On September 6, 2012, the Inter-American Court decided to combine the processing of some requests and established that the joint provisional measures would from then on be known as the "Matters of Certain Venezuelan Prisons." The Orders of the IACtHR, of November 24, 2009, in *Monagas Judicial Detention Center ("La Pica") v. Venezuela*, the *Penitentiary Center of the Capital Region Yare I and II (Yare Prison) v. Venezuela*, the *Penitentiary Center of the Central Occidental Region (Uribana Prison) v. Venezuela*, the *Capital Detention Center El Rodeo I and II v. Venezuela* of May 15, 2011, in the matters of the Penitentiary Center of Aragua "Tocorón Prison" and of the Ciudad Bolívar Judicial Detention Center "Vista Hermosa Prison," as well as of September 6, 2012, the Penitentiary Center of the Andean Region. See *Certain Penitentiary Centers of Venezuela, Penitenciaria Center of the Central Occidental Region (Uribana Prison) v. Venezuela* [2013] IACtHR and Order November 13, 2015.

[78] On February 4, 2020, members of the Inter-American Commission were denied entry into Venezuela. The Commissioners wished to conduct a visit *in loco* in order to have direct contact with the beneficiaries of precautionary measures. See <https://www.oas.org/en/IACtHR,/media_center/PReleases/2020/020.asp> (accessed January 2, 2022).

[79] Venezuela denounced the American Convention on September 10, 2012.

[80] For studies related to prison problems in the Americas, see Ely Aharonson, "Pro-Minority. Criminalization and the transformation of visions of citizenship in contemporary liberal democracies: A critique" [2010] 13 *New Criminal Law Review: An International and Interdisciplinary Journal* 286–308; Gerardo Ramírez Urosa, "Algunas reflexiones en relación con el 'Derecho penal del enemigo' dentro del contexto nacional" [2006] 61 *RDFM*; Eugenio Raúl Zaffaroni, *El enemigo en el derecho penal* (Dykinson 2006), 198; Douglas Husak, *Overcriminalization: The Limits of the Criminal Law* (Oxford University Press 2008), 248; David W. Garland, *The Culture of Control: Crime and Social Order in Contemporary Society* (University of Chicago Press 2001), 336; John Barry, "From drug war to dirty war: Plan Colombia and the US role in human rights violations in Colombia" [2002] 12 *Transnational Law & Contemporary Problems* 161.

[81] International Centre for Prison Studies, *World Prison Brief*, Institute for Crime and Policy Research, <https://www.prisonstudies.org/world-prison-brief-data> (accessed January 2, 2022); Mario Andrés Torres and Libardo José Ariza, "Jueces y prisiones en la era del encarcelamiento

security with repressive measures, such as harsher punishments and excessive and prolonged use of pre-trial detention.[82] These measures are ostensibly geared to prevent crimes, but, in the long term, the use of prison and preventive detention does not solve the problem of insecurity outside and inside prisons. In spite of their ineffectiveness, these measures enjoy great popularity with voters and strengthen the legitimacy of governments.

A repressive policy of criminalization results in the exclusionary treatment of the prison population, which becomes marginalized and stigmatized. This policy casts detainees as antisocial and inhuman. As a result, the interest of society is not aroused by the indignities, such as overcrowding, the many persons deprived of liberty face. The excessive and prolonged use of incarceration and pre-trial detention contributes greatly to overcrowding and its negative consequences. Preventive detention may also violate the principles of presumption of innocence, legality, necessity, and proportionality, as well as the fundamental principle that criminal law and criminal punishments, especially imprisonment, should be a last resort.[83] Another factor that contributes to the failure of detention centers to meet minimum international standards is that increases in prison populations are not accompanied by proportional increases in prison systems' budgets.[84]

6. Case Study: Criminal Institute of *Plácido de Sá Carvalho v. Brazil*

In 2017, the Inter-American Court granted transformative provisional measures to protect the life and integrity of all persons deprived of liberty at the Criminal Institute of Plácido de Sá Carvalho.[85] State authorities told the IACtHR that the challenges faced by the Institute were not unique but were instead shared by the entire penitentiary system of the State of Rio de Janeiro.[86]

---

masivo," in Jonathan Simon, Libardo José Ariza, and Mario Andrés Torres (eds.), *Encarcelamiento masivo, Derecho, raza y castigo* (Siglo del Hombre Editores 2020), 268.

[82] 6.3 average in the region, IACHR Report 2017 "Measures to Reduce Pretrial Detention," 22.

[83] Clara Burbano Herrera, Yves Haeck, and Alessandra Cuppini, "Transformative Provisional Measures and Prisons in the Americas: Protect the Invisible," in Clara Burbano Herrera and Yves Haeck, *Human Rights Behind Bars. Ius Gentium: Comparative Perspectives on Law and Justice*, vol. 103 (Springer 2022), 148.

[84] DeJusticia, "Sistemas Sobrecargados, Leyes de drogas y cárceles en América Latina" [2010], <https://www.dejusticia.org/publication/sistemas-sobrecargados-leyes-de-drogas-y-carceles-en-america-latina/> (accessed January 2, 2022).

[85] *The Socio-Educational Internment Facility of the Penitentiary Complex of Curado, of the Penitentiary Complex of Pedrinhas and the Criminal Institute of Plácido de Sá Carvalho v. Brazil* [2017] IACtHR.

[86] *Criminal Institute of Plácido de Sa Carvalho v. Brazil* [2018] IACtHR, para. 3.

In the transformative provisional measures, the Inter-American Court ordered Brazil to reduce overcrowding,[87] assess the overall situation, and create a plan for the structural reform of the Institute. The IACtHR requested permission from the State to conduct an on-site visit to the Institute[88] and to organize a public hearing[89] to monitor the implementation of its provisional measures. In the months that followed, in spite of the provisional measures issued, the situation of extreme gravity persisted.[90] The detention facility was confronted with serious problems, including overpopulation, lack of medical care, and absent services. Additionally, fifty-six detainees had died within two years and, in most of these cases, the cause of death was unknown.[91]

Since the persons deprived of their liberty in the Institute remained in a situation of extreme danger even after it had granted an initial set of provisional measures, the Inter-American Court issued another order of provisional measures in 2018.[92] The order showed that the IACtHR was aware it faced legal and practical limits, but also that it continued to seek concrete improvements in detention conditions. The Inter-American Court also noted that Brazil's prison crisis was not unique, comparing it to structural problems common to other prisons in the Americas. The IACtHR explained how the domestic courts of other States of the Organization of American States (OAS) and other international monitoring bodies had responded to prison crises and took into account domestic and international jurisprudence when designing provisional measures for the Institute.

In its 2018 order of transformative provisional measures, the Inter-American Court stated that the measures Brazilian authorities had adopted in 2017 had been ineffective.[93] The IACtHR emphasized that it was not enough for the State merely to adopt specific protection measures. In order to comply with its human rights obligations, the State must take effective action that generates positive results.[94] The Inter-American Court analyzed the situation of persons deprived of their liberty in the Institute alongside the jurisprudence of three supreme or

---

[87] *The Socio-Educational Internment Facility, of the Penitentiary Complex of Curado, of the Penitentiary Complex of Pedrinhas and the Criminal Institute of Plácido de Sa Carvalho v. Brazil* [2018] IACtHR, para. 3 and Provisional Measures August 31, 2017, para. 28.

[88] President of the IACtHR, *Seventeen Persons Deprived of Liberty v. Nicaragua*, Urgent Measures May 21, 2019, paras. 18 and 19.

[89] *The Socio-Educational Internment Facility, of the Penitentiary Complex of Curado, of the Penitentiary Complex of Pedrinhas and the Criminal Institute Plácido de Sa Carvalho v. Brazil* [2017] IACtHR, para. 4; President of the IACtHR, Seventeen Persons Deprived of Liberty v. Nicaragua, Urgent Measures, May 21, 2019, paras. 18 and 19.

[90] *Criminal Institute of Plácido de Sá Carvalho v. Brazil* [2017] IACtHR, para. 3.

[91] Ibid., para. 5; and *Criminal Institute of Plácido de Sa Carvalho v. Brazil* [2018] IACtHR, para. 40.

[92] *The Socio-Educational Internment Facility of the Penitentiary Complex of Curado, of the Penitentiary Complex of Pedrinhas and the Criminal Institute de Sá Carvalho v. Brazil* [2018] IACtHR, para. 1.

[93] Ibid., para. 84.

[94] Ibid., para. 63; *Criminal Institute Plácido de Sá Carvalho v. Brazil* [2017] IACtHR, para. 67.

constitutional courts of OAS States that had addressed similar situations, namely the Constitutional Court of Colombia,[95] the Supreme Court of the United States,[96] and the Supreme Federal Court of Brazil.[97] The IACtHR also took into account the jurisprudence of the European Court of Human Rights (European Court, or ECtHR);[98] Brazilian law[99] and policy;[100] the UN Standard Minimum Rules for the Treatment of Prisoners ("Mandela Rules");[101] and the IACHR's Principles and Best Practices on the Protection of Persons Deprived of Liberty in the Americas.[102]

The IACtHR refers extensively to the jurisprudence of the Colombian Constitutional Court for its finding that overcrowding is the first problem to be resolved in detention centers because of its terrible effects.[103] According to the Colombian Constitutional Court, overcrowding leads to increased health risks and the spread of diseases and infections, thus adding strain to an already overburdened healthcare system.[104] Overcrowding also increases the risk of violent conflicts and decreases the capacity of prison guards to maintain control. The Colombian Constitutional Court understands prison overpopulation to result from excessive incarceration. It has determined that the overuse of criminal law and imprisonment is unsustainable in a social and democratic State abiding by the rule of law due to the costs it imposes on fundamental rights, social cohesion, and scarce public resources.[105]

A solution to overcrowding, according to the Constitutional Court of Colombia, must strike a balance between individuals' right to due process of law, on the one hand, and a State's obligations to prevent crimes and respect for judicial decisions, on the other.[106] Overcrowding must be resolved with prudent judicial policies and individualized[107] (as opposed to

[95] *Criminal Institute of Plácido de Sá Carvalho v. Brazil* [2018] IACtHR, paras. 98–102.
[96] Ibid., paras. 103–107; *Edmund G. Brown Jr., Governor of California, et al., Appellants v. Marciano Plata et al.*, Supreme Court of the United States, No. 09–1233, On Appeal from the US District Courts for the Eastern District and the Northern District of California.
[97] *Criminal Institute of Plácido de Sá Carvalho v. Brazil* [2018] IACtHR, paras. 113–117.
[98] Ibid., paras. 108–112, referring to *Torregiani et al. v. Italia* [2013] ECtHR, para. 65.
[99] Resoluciones N14/1994, and 09/2011 of the CNPCP; Ley de Ejecución Penal (Ley No. 7.210/84); Ministerio de Salud y Ministerio de Justica, Portaria Interministerial, No. 1777, September 9, 2003; Consejo Nacional de Política Criminal y Penitenciaria (CNPCP), Resolutions No. 04/2014, July 18, 2014, and 02/2015, October 29, 2015; Consejo Nacional de Política Criminal y Penitenciaria (CNPCP).
[100] *Criminal Institute of Plácido de Sá Carvalho v. Brazil* [2018] IACtHR, paras. 8–13. The State submitted: "Diagnostico Tecnico y Plan de Contingencia para el Complejo de Curado."
[101] The UN Standard Minimum Rules for the Treatment of Prisoners (Mandela Rules), adopted by the United Nations, General Assembly in Resolution A/RES/70/175, May 18–22, 2015, Rules 19–21.
[102] IACHR, Principles and Best Practices on the Protection of Persons Deprived of Liberty in the Americas, OAS/Ser.L/V/II.131 Doc. 38, March 13, 2000, Principle XII.
[103] *Criminal Institute of Plácido de Sá Carvalho v. Brazil* [2018] IACtHR, paras. 98–102.
[104] Ibid., para. 98.
[105] Ibid., paras. 98–102.
[106] Ibid., para. 96.
[107] Ibid., para. 98.

automatic)[108] decisions to release detainees.[109] Relatedly, the State has to implement policies that facilitate these releases.[110] The terrible conditions in the detention centers do not create a right of automatic release, since this would prevent the State from considering its obligations to the victims of the prisoners' crimes as well as to society.[111]

The Constitutional Court of Colombia emphasizes that the solution to the problem of overcrowding not only requires the construction of new prisons but can also be addressed by reducing the number of people deprived of liberty.[112] The Court notes that there are persons who remain in prison despite there being constitutional and legal reasons for them to be released, such as age, serious terminal illness, or requests for release that have yet to be processed.[113] According to the Colombian Constitutional Court, the continued imprisonment of individuals who could be released[114] signals that building more prisons will not solve the problem of prison overpopulation.[115]

According to the IACtHR,[116] the most significant judgment concerning detention conditions in the Americas was issued by the Supreme Court of the United States in 2011 in response to grave rights violations in the Californian penitentiary system.[117] The California prison population had a 200 percent density during at least eleven years, with conditions of overcrowding similar to those of the Institute.[118] In that context, two class actions were submitted to the Federal District Courts: the *Coleman v. Brown* case, brought on behalf of prisoners with serious mental disorders, and the *Plata v. Brown* case, brought on behalf of prisoners with serious medical conditions.[119] The District Court ordered California to reduce its prison population to 137 percent over the course of two years. The State of California appealed the case to the Supreme Court of the United States. The majority (five to four) in the case said:

---

[108] Ibid., para. 100.
[109] Ibid., para. 99.
[110] Ibid., para. 101.
[111] Ibid., para. 101.
[112] Ibid., para. 99.
[113] Ibid., para. 98.
[114] Ibid. Individuals who should not be in custody include those detained without charge, those arbitrarily detained, and those detained for offenses that should not be criminalized. See Subcommittee on Prevention of Torture and Other Cruel, Inhuman, or Degrading Treatment or Punishment, Advice of the Subcommittee on Prevention of Torture to States Parties and National Preventive Mechanisms relating to the Coronavirus Pandemic (adopted on March 25, 2020), <https://www.ohchr.org/Documents/HRBodies/OPCAT/AdviceStatePartiesCoronavirusPandemic2020.pdf> (accessed January 2, 2022).
[115] Ibid., para. 96.
[116] Ibid., para. 103.
[117] *Edmund G. Brown Jr., Governor of California, et al.; Appellants v. Marciano Plata et al.* US Supreme Court, No. 09–1233, On Appeal from the US District Courts for the Eastern District and the Northern District of California.
[118] *Criminal Institute of Plácido de Sa Carvalho v. Brazil* [2018] IACtHR, para. 104.
[119] Ibid.

For years, the medical and mental health care provided by California prisons has not met the minimum constitutional requirements and has not met the basic health needs of inmates. Unnecessary suffering and death have been well-documented. Throughout the years during which this litigation has been pending, no other sufficient resources have been found. Efforts to remedy the rape have been thwarted by severe overcrowding in the California prison system. The short-term benefits of care delivery have been eroded by the long-term effects of severe and widespread overcrowding.[120]

The IACtHR noted that the US Supreme Court also indicated that overcrowding was the primary cause of severe and illegal mistreatment of prisoners as a result of inadequate medical care. The Supreme Court held that, in order to protect the prisoners' constitutional rights, the state was required to limit the prison population. Additionally, in the case, many experts stated that overcrowding was the main cause of constitutional violations.[121]

The IACtHR also considered judgments from the European Court and the Supreme Federal Court of Brazil. In relation to the ECtHR, the Inter-American Court mentioned that in the case of *Torregiani et al. v. Italy*, the European Court determined that the detention conditions were incompatible with the European Convention on Human Rights (European Convention, or ECHR). The ECtHR ordered Italy to create a procedure with preventive and compensatory effects, as well as to guarantee an effective remedy for violations of the European Convention.[122] In relation to Brazil, the Inter-American Court discussed a case[123] concerning overcrowding.[124] In this case, the Supreme Federal Court of Brazil ruled that, in contexts of overcrowding and overpopulation, judges should consider ordering early release, probation, or house arrest.

Returning to the facts of the case before it, the *Criminal Institute of Plácido de Sá Carvalho v. Brazil*, the Inter-American Court determined that a situation

---

[120] Ibid.
[121] Ibid.
[122] *Torregiani and others v. Italy* [2013] ECtHR, para. 88 ("In general, these data reveal that the violation of the right of applicants to benefit from adequate detention conditions is not a consequence of isolated incidents, but is due to a systemic problem resulting from chronic malfunction of the Italian prison system, which affected and may still interest many people in the future [. . .]. According to the European Court, the situation established in this case is therefore constitutive of a practice incompatible with the European Convention on Human Rights"). See *Criminal Institute of Plácido de Sá Carvalho v. Brazil*, Provisional Measures November 22, 2018, Considering para. 106.
[123] Súmula Vinculante No. 56 of the Supreme Federal Court of Brazil, 2016.
[124] This decision is binding and mandatory for all judges, courts, and administrative entities. It can only be modified by the Supreme Federal Court of Brazil itself. *Criminal Institute of Plácido de Sá Carvalho v. Brazil* [2018] IACtHR, para. 110.

that risked causing irreparable damage to the personal integrity and life of the beneficiaries of the provisional measures persisted in the prison and required the IACtHR to order specific measures to preserve these rights.[125] According to the Inter-American Court, reducing the prison population of the Institute was the only way to end this situation of risk. The IACtHR also stated that the Supreme Federal Court of Brazil's binding judgment on this matter[126] applied to the prisoners in the Institute.[127] As such, judges are required to consider early release, probation, or house arrest for these prisoners.[128] Additionally, following the reasoning of the Constitutional Court of Colombia, the Inter-American Court stated that if, hypothetically, the conditions in the Institute violated ACHR Article 5(2), this violation could not be remedied through the construction of new prisons because, first, the State had no immediate plans to construct new prisons and, second, the State itself had claimed it lacked the resources to do so. The IACtHR also stated that the situation could not be resolved through transferring prisoners from the Institute to other prisons, since the other prisons did not have the capacity to receive more prisoners and would themselves be overcrowded.[129] The Inter-American Court thus determined that "the only way to stop the continuation of the situation that will eventually violate the American Convention is to seek to reduce the population of the Curado Complex."[130] This was the first time the IACtHR had asserted that building new detention centers or transferring detainees would not solve the problem at hand.

The Inter-American Court also stated that the poor conditions of detention make unlawful deprivations of liberty that might otherwise be lawful. Detainees are experiencing more harm than is inherent in a lawful deprivation of liberty. Given this, the IACtHR suggested that prisoners' sentences be reduced to account for the additional harm they undergo.[131] In the case of the Institute, the Inter-American Court reached the unprecedented conclusion that, given that the prison had a population density double its capacity, every day of deprivation of liberty in the Institute must be counted twice toward the completion of each prisoners' sentence. The IACtHR also did not exclude the possibility of early release, probation, and house arrest, alternatives

---

[125] Ibid., para. 116.
[126] Súmula Vinculante No. 56 of the Supreme Federal Court of Brazil, 2016.
[127] *Criminal Institute of Plácido de Sá Carvalho v. Brazil* [2018] IACtHR, paras. 110–114.
[128] Ibid., para. 115; Súmula Vinculante No. 56 of the Supreme Federal Court of Brazil, 2016.
[129] Ibid., paras. 115–116.
[130] Ibid., para. 120.
[131] Ibid., para. 97.

mentioned by the Supreme Federal Court of Brazil in the 2016 case discussed previously.[132]

According to the Inter-American Court, the situation at the Institute could also lead to a violation of Article 5(6) ACHR, since terrible detention conditions impede the reform and rehabilitation of individuals deprived of their liberty. Degrading conditions affect prisoners' self-esteem.[133] The fact that the Institute is controlled by dominant violent groups also results in the humiliation of detainees, a serious deterioration of their self-perception and self-esteem, and a high risk of recidivism.[134]

In sum, the Inter-American Court has determined that the conditions at the Institute make the punishment degrading[135] and that when the conditions in a prison deteriorate to this point as a result of overpopulation and its effects, the deprivation of liberty itself becomes unlawful.[136] This determination could be seen as the IACtHR prejudging the merits of the case. It could also be seen, however, as the Court searching for a way to order transformative provisional measures that will result in effective protection for detainees who live in deplorable conditions and have done so, in some cases, for many years. Concretely, the Inter-American Court ordered the measures listed in Table I.8.1.[137]

The Inter-American Court clarified that the potential release of prisoners convicted of, or charged with, crimes against life or physical integrity and sex crimes needed to be handled more carefully.[138] These cases require a technical criminological examination or examination of the cause of the detainees' conduct performed by experts.[139] The IACtHR also emphasized that its jurisdiction in this case was limited to the Institute and the persons deprived of liberty there, so the order of provisional measures does not have an *erga omnes* effect.[140]

---

[132] *Criminal Institute of Plácido de Sá Carvalho v. Brazil* [2018] IACtHR, enacting paras. 2, 4. See also the case of *Milagro Sala v. Argentina*, in which the Inter-American Court requested that the State replace Mrs. Sala's preventive detention with the alternative measure of house arrest to be carried out at her residence or the place where she usually lives, or by any other alternative measure to pretrial detention that is less restrictive of one's rights than house arrest. *Milagro Sala v. Argentina* [2017] IACtHR, para. 33.
[133] *Criminal Institute of Plácido de Sá Carvalho v. Brazil* [2018] IACtHR, para. 87.
[134] Ibid., paras. 87–88.
[135] Ibid., para. 87.
[136] Ibid., para. 92.
[137] Table elaborated by the authors.
[138] Ibid., para. 131.
[139] Ibid., para. 133.
[140] Ibid., paras. 121–122.

Table I.8.1 Measures ordered by the Inter-American Court of Human Rights in the case *Criminal Institute of Plácido de Sá Carvalho v. Brazil* [2018] IACtHR.

Structural problem		Measure ordered
Deaths	High number of deaths: 56 deaths in two years.	To take measures to prevent more deaths and to report what these specific measures are.
	Lack of information concerning the causes of the deaths.[a] Mortality higher than the free population. One doctor for over 3,000 prisoners.	To investigate the causes of the deaths and to inform the next of kin[b] and the IACtHR.
Infrastructure	Absence of a fire prevention and response plan. Nine people responsible for the safety of 3,800 detainees. Insufficient provision of mattresses, uniforms, footwear, bedding, and towels to detainees. Absence of adequate lighting and ventilation. Physical insecurity due to unforeseen fires. Insufficient funds.	To adapt the infrastructure conditions to those minimally necessary to provide a decent life.[c] To remodel all the prison pavilions. To install emergency lighting, a fire detection system, and an alarm system. To implement the provisions of Law No. 7.210/84.[d]
Overcrowding	Overpopulation with approximate density of 200%. Overcrowding in cells. Personal and physical insecurity resulting from the disproportionate ratio of personnel to prisoners.[e] Control of internal order in the hands of the prisoners themselves. The most violent generally organized for survival or self-defense. Insufficient number of judges. Only seven judges in the State of Rio de Janeiro oversaw the completion of sentences of more than 50,000 individuals deprived of liberty.[f]	To reduce the number of prisoners through counting each day of deprivation of liberty twice. To adjust the number of guards so it would be proportionate to the number of persons deprived of liberty. To subject persons deprived of their liberty for crimes against life or physical integrity, as well as sex crimes, to a criminological technical exam conducted by psychologists and social workers.

[a] Ibid., para. 61.
[b] Ibid., para. 62.
[c] Ibid., para. 68.
[d] Ibid., para. 69.
[e] Ibid., para. 79.
[f] Ibid., para. 72.

7. Concluding Remarks

Studying the IACtHR's transformative provisional measures concerning persons deprived of their liberty in Latin America reveals that countless individuals live in undignified conditions of detention that are incompatible with international human rights standards. The Inter-American Court is using these transformative provisional measures to prompt gStates to change decades-old policies and practices of criminalization and incarceration. The IACtHR's transformative provisional measures concerning detention centers also provide insight into a structural problem in Latin America, a prison crisis involving overcrowding, insalubrity, rapid spread of infections and diseases, high levels of violence, deaths, lack of control by State authorities, lack of access to medical services, lack of investigation and punishment, and a lack of funds.[141]

In its order of provisional measures in the case of the *Criminal Institute of Plácido de Sá Carvalho v. Brazil*, the Inter-American Court balances the right to dignified conditions of detention on the one hand, and States' obligation to punish those who commit crimes on the other. The IACtHR does not find that dire prison conditions create an automatic right to be released, but it does find that persons deprived of their liberty in such conditions undergo a harsher punishment than is inherent to a state of imprisonment and that their additional suffering must be taken into account by domestic judicial authorities. Judges can do this by reducing the length of prison sentences in proportion to the additional pain suffered by the detainees. In the case of the Institute, the Inter-American Court reasoned that since the population density of the prison had reached 200 percent (that is, the double of the prison's capacity), the suffering of detainees had also doubled and, as such, every day of deprivation of liberty should be counted twice. The IACtHR also clearly stated that in the case of Brazil and perhaps in the Americas as a whole, pretrial detention is not the solution to criminality, and building more prisons or transferring detainees to other prisons or detention centers is not the solution to overcrowding.[142]

To reach these conclusions, the Inter-American Court relied heavily on domestic jurisprudence, not only from Brazil but also from other OAS member States, as well as the jurisprudence of the European Court to detect a growing, global consensus about how to understand and solve the prison crisis.

---

[141] Burbano Herrera and Haeck, "The Innovative Potential of Provisional Measures Resolutions for Detainee Rights in Latin America Through Dialogue Between the Inter-American Court and Other Courts," in Rieter and Zwaan, *Urgency and Human Rights, The Protective Potential and Legitimacy of Interim Measures* (2021), 242.

[142] Ibid., 243.

I.9
Transformative Impact
A Framework for Analysis

By Mayra Ortiz Ocaña and Aníbal Pérez-Liñán

1. Introduction

This chapter advances a general framework to conceptualize and measure the impact of the Inter-American Human Rights System (IAHRS). Our definition of impact includes the intended and unintended effects of the IAHRS's instruments in three settings: practices, structures, and social outcomes. The framework presented in this chapter acknowledges that a broad set of IAHRS instruments have potential to generate impact and defines compliance as a (narrow) form of impact.

Understanding the role of the IAHRS requires moving beyond a focus on compliance to consider multiple ways in which the System affects a variety of actors and arenas. The authors of this book, as well as other students of the Inter-American Commission (IACHR)[1] and the Inter-American Court (IACtHR),[2] have increasingly observed that low levels of compliance with reparations ordered by the System have not precluded a transformative influence of the IAHRS across the region. A growing body of work thus analyzes the various forms of "impact" created by the IAHRS.[3]

Unfortunately, a clear definition of impact seems to be missing from the specialized literature. This void creates a challenge when researchers seek to assess transformative effects systematically. Moreover, the lack of a coherent definition complicates the empirical study of this subject. In the following section, we build on existing literature about national and international adjudication bodies to provide a definition of impact suitable for analyzing the IAHRS.[4]

---

[1] Natalia Saltalamacchia Ziccardi et al., "Friendly Settlements in the Inter-American Human Rights System: Efficiency, Effectiveness and Scope," in Par Engstrom (ed.), *The Inter-American Human Rights System Impact Beyond Compliance* (Palgrave Macmillan 2019).
[2] Patricia Zuloaga Palacios, "Judging Inter-American Human Rights: The Riddle of Compliance with the Inter-American Court of Human Rights" [2020] 42 *Human Rights Quarterly* 392.
[3] Par Engstrom, *The Inter-American Human Rights System: Impact Beyond Compliance* (Palgrave Macmillan 2019).
[4] Diana Kapiszewski and Matthew M. Taylor, "Compliance: Conceptualizing, Measuring, and Explaining Adherence to Judicial Rulings" [2013] 38 *Law & Social Inquiry* 803; Siri Gloppen,

In the third section, we identify the *transformative sequence* generating impact. This sequence begins at "moment zero," when the organs of the IAHRS deploy particular instruments at their disposal. The first stage of the sequence involves members of a community of practice appropriating the frames generated by those instruments to pursue demands about human rights.[5] This appropriation entails a transformation in their sociolegal *practices*. The second stage involves an institutional response to the new demands. If the response is positive, there is a transformation of institutional *structures*. After State institutions have embraced a particular interpretation of the frames generated by the instrument and redefined by the community of practice, the final stage is a transformation on the ground in the rights of the target population, reflected in *social outcomes*.

This theoretical framework allows us to think about impact comprehensively and systematically, across multiple analytical moments. However, any claim about the actual impact of the IAHRS requires an operationalization of this framework for empirical research. In the fourth section of the chapter, we provide examples of strategies to empirically test the three different forms of impact—and the mechanisms behind them. The last section summarizes our main conclusions.

2. What Is Impact?

There is broad agreement in the field, including the contributors to this volume, that the IAHRS has had significant impact in the Americas.[6] However, a clear definition of impact is missing in the specialized literature. To advance the systematic analysis of this issue, we conceptualize impact as *the intended or unintended effects on practices, structures, and social outcomes stemming from adjudicatory and non-adjudicatory actions by international bodies*.

This definition involves three components: an international body, which takes action through adjudicatory (e.g., court rulings) or non-adjudicatory (e.g., country reports) instruments; a sequence of effects, which can be intended or unintended; and a set of potential transformations (in sociolegal practices, institutional structures, or social outcomes).

Our definition encompasses the concept of compliance, but it also accommodates a broad range of indirect and unexpected effects created by the

---

"Litigating Health Rights: Framing the Analysis," in Alicia Ely Yamin and Siri Gloppen (eds.), *Litigating Health Rights: Can Courts Bring More Justice to Health?* (Harvard University Press 2011).

[5] Armin von Bogdandy and René Urueña, "International Transformative Constitutionalism in Latin America" [2020] 114 *American Journal of International Law* 403.

[6] Engstrom (n. 3).

IAHRS. The traditional notion of compliance refers to actions undertaken by the addressee of a court ruling in order to fulfill the measures ordered by such ruling.[7] Chiara Giorgetti notes that compliance takes place "when the obligated party acts accordingly to the ruling of a court, by either doing what the court asked to be done or by refraining from doing what the court prohibited it to do."[8] Thus, compliance refers to the intended behavior of actors involved in a controversy resulting from a legal decision with *inter partes* effects. In this sense, compliance is a particular form of impact, included in our definition as the intended effect of an adjudicatory instrument.

However, compliance is a narrow concept that prevents consideration of other actors (a community of practice beyond the parties in a case), non-adjudicatory instruments, and unintended transformations beyond the parameters of the controversy. By incorporating those aspects, our definition makes it possible to analyze impact beyond compliance.

Our approach is therefore similar to the one advanced by Sandra Botero, who describes impact as "changes in the ideational, discursive, legal, organizational and material realm that are attributable to the court ruling and the changes in life outcomes."[9] Like Botero, we acknowledge that a court order may prompt direct compliance, as well as indirect effects and changes in rights' effectiveness beyond the parties in the case. Unlike Botero, however, our characterization of impact transcends the adjudicatory role of judicial bodies and unpacks the process by which international bodies exert influence into a sequence of stages.

According to Botero, the literature on domestic courts has considered two forms of impact beyond compliance: indirect effects and rights effectiveness.[10] Indirect effects are the transformation of social relations or perceptions that are not ordered by the sentence but still happen as a consequence.[11] Thus, indirect effects are transformations that go beyond specific court orders in the case. Scholars addressing the IAHRS often analyze its impact in terms of indirect effects. For example, Viviana Krsticevic and René Urueña, in this volume, equate impact to the indirect effects of the standards created by the System's bodies. Under this notion, standards, not reparation measures, begin the path toward impact.

---

[7] Bogdandy and Urueña (n. 5).

[8] Chiara Giorgetti, "What Happens after a Judgment Is Given? Judgment Compliance and the Performance of International Courts and Tribunals," in Theresa Squatrito et al. (eds.), *The Performance of International Courts and Tribunals* (Cambridge University Press 2018), 325.

[9] Sandra Botero, *Courts that Matter: Judges, Litigants and the Politics of Rights Enforcement* (Cambridge University Press 2023).

[10] Botero (n. 9).

[11] César Rodríguez Garavito, "Beyond the Courtroom: The Impact of Judicial Activism on Socioeconomic Rights in Latin America" [2010] 89 *Texas Law Review* 1669.

Rights effectiveness, in turn, refers to the everyday fulfillment of human rights.[12] Under this notion, impact is related to the quality of life of a broad set of persons affected by the ruling. Prompted by a legal decision, State action leads to policy change, and eventually to a greater effectiveness of some rights for a larger population. Given the scope of such changes, the expected time for them to occur can be longer than the time for other types of transformations.[13]

In the IAHRS, the effect of most rulings transcends the specific controversy. The contributions in this volume consistently support this claim. Our definition thus incorporates the possibility of unintended consequences to accommodate indirect effects beyond the scope of the court's orders, and changes in social outcomes to accommodate the effectiveness of rights enjoyed by actors who are not parties in the case.

We differ from Botero in two crucial ways. First, our definition of impact, centered in the IAHRS, transcends the work of judicial bodies and thus contemplates non-adjudicatory instruments as potential sources of impact. Second, we conceptualize the process by which the System exerts transformative influence on domestic audiences as a sequence of stages.

The IAHRS is formed by two distinct bodies: a Commission entrusted with an individual petition system and with monitoring the human rights situation in the Continent,[14] and a Court with a jurisdictional function and an advisory role to member States.[15] Despite those differences, both bodies rely on adjudicatory instruments, such as the merits reports issued by the IACHR and the decisions issued by the IACtHR, and on non-adjudicatory instruments, like the country reports issued by the IACHR and the advisory opinions issued by the IACtHR.[16] Thus, the concept of impact needs to go beyond judicial sentences and include other instruments related to nonjurisdictional action.

As for the process of influence, we claim that the impact of the IAHRS can only be understood as a transformative sequence by which adjudicatory and non-adjudicatory instruments have an effect on practices, structures, and social outcomes. Effective instruments prompt changes in daily activities and

---

[12] Sandra Botero, "Judges, Litigants, and the Politics of Rights Enforcement in Argentina" [2018] 50 *Comparative Politics* 169.

[13] UN Office of the High Commissioner for Human Rights (OHCHR), *Human Rights Indicators: A Guide to Measurement and Implementation* (HR/PUB/12/5 2012), <https://www.refworld.org/docid/51a739694.html> (accessed November 26, 2022).

[14] Aníbal Pérez Liñán, Mariana Brocca, and Isabel Anayanssi Orizaga Inzunza, "Compliance Agreements in the Inter-American Human Rights System" [2021] Max Planck Institute for Comparative Public Law & International Law (MPIL Research Paper No. 2021-26).

[15] Jeffrey K. Staton and Alexia Romero, "Rational Remedies: The Role of Opinion Clarity in the Inter-American Human Rights System" [2019] 63 *International Studies Quarterly* 477.

[16] A.A. Cançado Trindade, "La Función Consultiva De La Corte Interamericana De Derechos Humanos: Naturaleza y Principios 1982–1987. By M.E. Ventura and D. Zovatto. San José, Madrid: Instituto Interamericano de Derechos Humanos/Editorial Civitas, 1989. Pp. 463" [1991] 85 *American Journal of International Law* 420.

discourses of certain groups or individuals in a broader community of practice. Such changes, in turn, drive shifts in formal rules inside State and non-State organizations. Lastly, social outcomes reflect the transformation of the population's living conditions as a result of this process.

The issues discussed in this section underscore that the IAHRS demands a capacious concept of impact encompassing compliance, acknowledging the importance of adjudicatory and non-adjudicatory instruments, and conceiving a broad range of effects as a sequential process. The following section describes the transformative sequence and its effect on practices, structures, and social outcomes.

3. The Transformative Sequence: From Instruments to Outcomes

The transformative sequence is the process by which the instruments of the IAHRS create a path toward impact. The sequence starts at "time zero" when the Commission or the Court employs an instrument, and it unfolds in three analytical moments: appropriation, institutional response, and transformations on the ground. The three moments of this sequence map into three levels of analysis where impact is manifested: practices, structures, and social outcomes. Arguably, each stage is necessary to advance to the next level of impact: a change in practices by relevant actors is needed to achieve structural change, and structural change is in turn necessary to achieve a transformation in social outcomes.

3.1. Time Zero: The System's Instruments

The onset of this sequence takes place when the Inter-American Commission or the Inter-American Court employs an instrument to address a particular situation and frame it as a human rights matter. As mentioned in the previous section, instruments can be adjudicatory or non-adjudicatory, and they may fulfill different functions depending on the context of the case. In this section, we discuss six functions performed the IAHRS' instruments: directing the State, building standards, documenting facts, positioning topics, reframing issues, and assisting local actors. By performing any of these functions, instruments can set in motion the transformative sequence.

By instruments, we refer to the official means by which international bodies exert their influence when addressing human rights issues. Adjudicatory instruments are those used to settle a legal dispute in specific cases.[17] In the

---

[17] Courtney Hillebrecht, *Saving the International Justice Regime: Beyond Backlash Against International Courts* (Cambridge University Press 2022).

IAHRS, adjudicatory instruments are distinctively employed in the individual petition system, and take the form of merits reports in the IACHR, precautionary and provisional measures, and sentences in the IACtHR. Non-adjudicatory instruments, in turn, transcend the dispute-resolution function, and they are tied to the system's advisory and monitoring functions.[18] Despite the lack of jurisdictional effects, non-adjudicatory instruments have great potential for impact because they develop general human rights principles and inform a community of practice. The Court's advisory opinions are an excellent example: as Pablo Saavedra Alessandri shows in his chapter in this volume, several Constitutional Courts have used advisory opinions as a central part of their reasoning to rule in domestic cases. The impact of non-adjudicatory instruments is here directly traceable, from the advisory opinion to the domestic judgment.

The range of possible instruments deployed by the System varies widely, from extensive court rulings to brief press releases. The common feature of all instruments is that they aim to influence human rights issues, but they do so in different ways. We have identified six functions performed by the system's instruments: directing, reframing, documenting, standard-building, positioning, and assisting. It is essential to point out that the same instrument can perform multiple functions. For instance, a judgment can give an order to the parties in the controversy and at the same time create a standard that will be appropriated by actors who are not involved in the case.

Directing. In the system of petitions and cases, the IACHR (through its merits reports) and the Inter-American Court (through its judgments) act as adjudicatory bodies.[19] Adjudication requires those bodies to direct the State on the actions necessary to address a human rights violation. Although merits reports present such directives as recommendations, and Court rulings do so as injunctions for reparations, their function is similar. Both instruments effectively command the State to honor its international obligations within the limits of a legal controversy. As a result, an identifiable actor is expected to comply with the directive, even though the responsible party can be identified as the overall State or pinpointed as a specific domestic institution.[20]

Instruments releasing orders or directives are the starting point of a sequence that potentially leads to compliance. Judgments and recommendations command a specific actor to fulfill an obligation; it is immaterial what actors beyond the controversy do. In this case, victims rely on the order to obtain an institutional response.

---

[18] Cançado Trindade (n. 16).
[19] Gerald L. Neuman, "Import, Export, and Regional Consent in the Inter-American Court of Human Rights" [2008] 19 *European Journal of International Law* 101.
[20] Rachel Murray and Clara Sandoval, "Balancing Specificity of Reparation Measures and States' Discretion to Enhance Implementation" [2020] 12 *Journal of Human Rights Practice* 101.

Different instruments express directives in distinctive legal ways. In the case of the Commission, directives are presented as recommendations. Even without them having binding effects, they indicate the expected action to take care of human rights violations. The Court's case is more straightforward because the judgments clearly order the State what to do. Also, precautionary and provisional measures are directing instruments because they require the State to act in accordance to their terms.

Standard-building. The IACHR and IACtHR, in their labor, develop general obligations about human rights and create guidelines regarding how States should conduct their activities. By employing instruments that order specific States how to act, the Commission and the Court indirectly construct a set of standards that show how States, in general, should behave. Instruments perform a standard-building function when they develop legal principles that can be reclaimed by parties who are not involved in the controversy. Standard-building thus differs from directing because there is no explicit target for compliance. The community of practice appropriates those standards, and leverages them to foster the legitimacy of particular legal claims. In this volume, Oscar Parra Vera illustrates how the Supreme Court of Chile used IACtHR's rulings to substantiate Alberto Fujimori's extradition.

When performing the standard-building function, the IAHRS bodies are at the vanguard of international human rights law. The inter-American standards have been adopted by domestic courts and other international bodies like the African Court on Human and Peoples' Rights or the European Court of Human Rights.[21] As Par Engstrom notes in this volume, the IAHRS is a "human rights standard-setter."

As with the directing function, the "time zero" of the transformative sequence often takes place when an instrument adjudicating a case articulates a novel human rights standard. In contrast to the directing function, however, the impact of the standard-building function manifests itself in parties beyond the case, like constitutional courts from other countries or other international courts. Moreover, non-adjudicatory instruments, like advisory opinions or country reports, may set standards and trigger this transformative sequence without targeting any State.

Positioning. Instruments can also highlight human rights issues that have not been discussed widely across the region or that have not been acknowledged as a pervasive problem. Thus, beyond setting legal standards, the IAHRS can position a topic, bringing it into a regional conversation and making it salient across the Americas. For example, the case *González and others v. Mexico* not

---

[21] Wayne Sandholtz, "Human Rights Courts and Global Constitutionalism: Coordination through Judicial Dialogue" [2021] 10 *Global Constitutionalism* 439.

only set up a paradigmatic standard about structural discrimination[22] but also established that Mexico had a systematic problem of violence against women. In constructing the instrument, the Court collected information from multiple actors and positioned the issue of violence against women as a pervasive problem in Ciudad Juárez.[23]

When performing the positioning function, the IAHRS's bodies do not come up with topics on their own. Most likely, the System's users have provided prior input for the Commission and the Court to realize the importance of the matter. On this basis, the positioning function involves the use of an authoritative instrument to highlight the topic's relevance for human rights beyond the specific case.

The positioning function differs from standard-setting because instruments are deployed for a discursive purpose, not a legal one. Therefore, press releases and country reports are valuable tools to position issues, even if they fail to convey specific orders or articulate new standards. In positioning a topic, the IACHR or the IACtHR delivers a platform for actors in the community of practice to back up the relevance of their claims about hitherto ignored issues.[24]

Reframing. The IAHRS plays a relevant function by recasting situations naturalized as "common problems" as pressing human rights issues. According to Armin von Bogdandy and René Urueña in this volume, considering the key features of transformative constitutionalism and the role of the IAHRS as part of this trend in Latin America, they argue that "the Inter-American Court's most profound impact stems from its enabling this reframing."

One of the best examples of reframing is the conceptualization of structural discrimination developed by the IACtHR. In its jurisprudence,[25] the Court has argued that the classic differentiation between direct and indirect discrimination is not enough to address situations based on indirect discrimination.[26] The Court thus advanced the concept of structural discrimination to recognize the historical domination and subordination suffered by some groups, and the actions reproducing such inequalities.[27] It further argued that the State

---

[22] Víctor Abramovich, "Responsabilidad estatal por violencia de género: comentarios sobre el caso Campo Algodonero en la Corte Interamericana de Derechos Humanos" [2010] 6 *Anuario de Derechos Humanos* 167.

[23] *Case of González et al. ("Cotton Field") v. Mexico. Preliminary Objection, Merits, Reparations and Costs* [2009] IACtHR, Ser. C No. 205.

[24] Eduardo Ferrer Mac-Gregor, "Lhaka Honhat y Los Derechos Sociales de Los Pueblos Indígenas" [2020] 39 *Revista Electrónica de Estudios Internacionales*, <https://doi.org/10.17103/reei.39.01> (accessed July 27, 2022).

[25] IACtHR (n. 23).

[26] *Trabajadores de la Hacienda Brasil Verde v. Brasil. Interpretación de la Sentencia de Excepciones Preliminares, Fondo, Reparaciones y Costas* [2017]. IACtHR, Ser. C No. 337. Separate Opinion Judge Eduardo Ferrer.

[27] Pedro Salazar and Mayra Ortiz Ocaña, "Libre expresión, universidad pública y mundo digital: reflexiones a propósito de los casos de Nicolás Alvarado y Marcelino Perelló," in Jesús Rodríguez Zepeda and Teresa González (eds.), *El prejuicio y la palabra: Los derechos a la libre expresión y a la no discriminación en contraste* (CONAPRED 2018).

has special obligations toward members of those groups. This concept offered a novel frame for a type of discrimination present in everyday life that seemed to do nothing with the State and, therefore, was not a human rights issue. Once it was "named" in the Court's instruments, structural discrimination became a human rights problem.

Like the positioning function, reframing serves a discursive purpose. The community of practice can appropriate the new frame and use it for legal and political demands. The main difference between positioning and reframing is that in the former, the IAHRS acts as a platform to amplify the discussion of a human rights topic. When reframing an issue, the IAHRS provides a new conceptualization of the issue as a human rights problem.

Documenting. A distinctive role played by the Commission, and to a certain extent by the Court, is documenting cases of widespread and systematic human rights violations. This documentation provides support to narratives that differ from the ones created by powerful actors and serves as evidence for future processes of justice. With this function, the system's bodies have assisted local actors in denouncing gross human rights violations and offered a forum where their stories are listened to and preserved.

In particular, as Gabriela Kletzel claims in this volume, the Commission had a prominent role during the military dictatorships in the Southern Cone, documenting gross human rights violations and echoing the victims' and their families' claims in a period when domestic institutions were not responsive. Moreover, the documentation about human rights violations that allowed the creation of counternarratives also served to generate evidence against authoritarian regimes. For instance, the IACHR's country reports were essential for collecting information about the human rights situation in countries like Argentina, Chile, Paraguay, and Uruguay during the 1970s. Claudio Grossman, in this volume, underscores that the Commission "developed extensive fact-finding investigations to prove gross and mass violations that governments were denying." Instruments performing a documentation function can initiate a transformative sequence if they are appropriated by domestic actors and leveraged in their demands for justice.

Assisting. The IAHRS often deploys non-adjudicatory instruments to provide direct assistance to member States, in order to strengthen local capabilities. Under this function, the System's organs engage directly with domestic actors and transfer knowledge or expertise to address human rights problems. The Commission and the Court offer guidance to a broad community of practice, including State officials, journalists, academics, and human rights activists.

As Joel Hernández Garcia shows in this volume, the Commission has provided technical aid to both States and civil society to improve capacities. A clear example of the Commission's assistance role is the Interdisciplinary Group of

Independent Experts' work in Mexico. The GIEI (for its acronym in Spanish) was built as an ad hoc body to help search for the forty-three missing students from the Rural Normal School "Raúl Isidro Burgos" in Ayotzinapa, Guerrero. It was entrusted to provide expertise in order to advance the investigations and to find and prosecute the perpetrators.[28] This configuration illustrates a form of hybrid prosecution in which an international organization collaborates with national institutions to perform a criminal investigation.[29] The GIEI elaborated reports with the evidence gathered from its work. Those instruments served the victims' families and the NGOs accompanying them to push their claims with domestic institutions.

When assisting State agents, the IAHRS appears to activate a straightforward transformative sequence because it is acting directly at the domestic level. However, as the example of the GIEI shows, instruments intended to assist domestic actors still need to be appropriated by the community of practice to initiate an effective transformative sequence.

3.2. First Stage: Appropriation

The first moment of the transformative sequence takes place when particular actors appropriate the instruments for their purposes. Those actors incorporate the IAHRS's directives, standards, positions, frames, documented facts, or technical guidance into their discourses and everyday practices and leverage them in their demands to advance human rights.

The notion of a "community of practice" helps us understand the wide variety of actors who can leverage the System's instruments. According to Bogdandy and Urueña, the community of practice "is a group of actors that interact, on the basis of the Inter-American Convention on Human Rights, to promote their agendas and to fulfill what they regard as their mandates."[30] This community includes State agents, like domestic courts, politicians, or civil servants, as well as non-State actors, such as NGOs, grassroots organizations, and scholars working on topics related to the IAHRS.

At the appropriation stage, the community of practice becomes the key player in the transformative sequence. Its members adopt and adapt the novel frames

---

[28] "Agreement between the Mexican State and the Inter-American Commission of Human Rights" [2014], <https://centroprodh.org.mx/GIEI/?wpdmpro=acuerdo-de-asistencia-tecnica-con-mexico> (accessed July 27, 2022).

[29] Guillermo Trejo and Camilo Nieto-Matiz, "Containing Large-Scale Criminal Violence Through Internationalized Prosecution: How the Collaboration Between the CICIG and Guatemala's Law Enforcement Contributed to a Sustained Reduction in the Murder Rate" [2023] *Comparative Political Studies*, forthcoming, <https://doi.org/10.1177/00104140221139386>.

[30] Bogdandy and Urueña (n. 5), 414.

advanced by the System's instruments and employ them to gain leverage in their legal and political disputes. During the appropriation phase, it is possible to grasp the System's impact on the community's discursive and everyday practices. The community of practice takes IAHRS instruments where they are most needed; it drives the tools on the ground, where they can make a difference.

This set of actors overlaps to some extent with Karen Alter's "compliance constituencies," but it is broader in scope.[31] For Alter, compliance constituencies are actors whose interests align with an international court's legal interpretation and use its rulings because they provide legitimacy to their claims. In addition, those constituencies can use the rulings as leverage for their domestic political disputes.[32] Compliance constituencies are crucial for compliance because they appropriate the court's ruling and push the State toward implementation.

Compliance constituencies include government officials as well as civil society actors. The State is not a unitary actor but a heterogeneous entity crossed by intra-State conflict.[33] Thus, public officials often start the transformative sequence when they invoke an instrument to advance a human rights issue within the State. Along those lines, Gabriel C.B. Navarro, in this volume, identifies how State officials can be empowered by IAHRS instruments and use them to overcome institutional resistance from other parts of the State.

Our discussion in this section, however, includes a broader set of actors and instruments than the ones implied by Alter's concept. Compliance constituencies mobilize for the implementation of court rulings. The concept does not easily describe the appropriation of instruments like country reports, press releases, or advisory opinions. Bogdandy and Urueña's notion of community of practice, in contrast, enables us to analyze an extended set of actors who may not be part of the litigation, and who may leverage "softer" instruments that do not perform a directing function.

At this stage, impact manifests itself as a transformation of actors' discourse and practices toward human rights topics. Actors incorporate ideas from an instrument into their discourse and use those ideas to provide new force to their arguments. In addition, the System's directives, standards, positions, frames, documented facts, or technical guidance may encourage attitudinal change and thus a new set of socio-legal behaviors. As noted by Botero, a court decision can

---

[31] Karen Alter, *The New Terrain of International Law: Courts, Politics, Rights* (Princeton University Press 2014).

[32] Daniel Naurin and Øyvind Stiansen, "The Dilemma of Dissent: Split Judicial Decisions and Compliance With Judgments From the International Human Rights Judiciary" [2020] 53 *Comparative Political Studies* 959.

[33] Jessica Rich, *State-Sponsored Activism* (Cambridge University Press 2019), https://doi.org/10.1017/9781108626453.

help with the "effective diffusion of policy ideas and new cognitive paradigms among governmental actors."[34]

In cases in which State officials embrace new ideas from IAHRS instruments, the analytical boundary between appropriation and structural change (the transformative stage discussed in the next section) may be hard to establish in practice. When public officials change their practices, it might appear that the State has changed its structures. Nevertheless, the difference between the transformation of practices and the transformation of structures is that the former only requires ideational change among State officials, while the latter also requires codification into formal institutions. As an example, consider the distinction between the legal culture of the judiciary and its jurisprudence.[35] Legal culture and jurisprudence may eventually converge. However, a sector of the judiciary may be open to the IAHRS—a form of impact verifiable in their attitudes and actions—while there is still no jurisprudence recognizing a particular instrument.

In conclusion, appropriation is the first mechanism of the transformative sequence, and it creates impact by producing change in discourses and sociolegal behaviors. The community of practice, which includes State and non-State actors, becomes the key player during this phase, as it adopts and adapts the System's instruments to gain leverage in ongoing disputes.

3.3. Second Stage: Institutional Response

The second moment in the transformative sequence is the institutional response to the actors in the community of practice who leverage IAHRS instruments in their demands. While most instruments target the State—e.g., they direct the State to provide reparations or protect vulnerable populations—non-State organizations may as well respond to those actors, for instance, by adopting new doctrines of frames.

We define the institutional response as an organizational transformation guided by the System's instruments invoked by the community of practice. The critical actors at this stage are State institutions, universities, human rights NGOs, and other organizations. The actors of the community of practice approach these organizations to present their demands, and the institutions regulate what proposals materialize into structural change.

The institutional response can be positive or negative. On the positive side, State officials or other institutions can provide space to the ideas or demands

---

[34] Botero (n. 12).
[35] Karina Ansolabehere, Sandra Botero, and Ezequiel Gonzalez-Ocantos, "Conceptualizar y medir la cultura legal: evidencia a partir de una encuesta a los jueces federales mexicanos" [2022] 29 *Política y Gobierno* 1.

articulated by the community of practice and spur organizational change. A positive response may translate into new legislation, jurisprudence, or educational curricula. This constitutes a second form of impact: structural transformation reshaping formal institutions. On the negative side, institutions may ignore the new demands even if the IAHRS legitimizes them. Moreover, legal mobilization invoking human rights instruments can incite different degrees of pushback, from resistance to backlash,[36] if there is an inhospitable environment or if the instrument addresses a sensitive topic.[37]

An assessment of impact at this level requires a displacement of the analysis from individual actors to collective institutional frameworks. For instance, the distinction between State officials acting individually and institutions acting as legal entities is crucial to understand the difference between impact in practices and impact in structures. While an individual official might be open to the IAHRS and incorporate the principles expressed by an instrument in her everyday practice, it is possible that her institution will not include the same principles in its regular functioning. However, if the official's diligence or civil society pressures lead the institution to incorporate those ideas into the administrative or legal framework, new principles will apply to all members of the institution. When impact spreads from individual officials to their organizations, it is possible to say that ideational change has bred structural transformation.

The chapters in this volume provide multiple examples of impact as structural change and allow us to identify five institutional arenas where transformations take place: legislation, jurisprudence, public policy, institutional designs, and curricular changes.

The adaptation of domestic legislation is a common measure of nonrepetition ordered by the IACtHR.[38] At the same time, this volume documents several instances in which States that were not part of a legal controversy preemptively changed their legislation to align with IAHRS standards. The behavior of States altering their domestic legal framework without being ordered to do so reflects our earlier distinction between directing and standard-building. The community of practice leverages an instrument directed to a different State and activates a positive institutional response leading to new legislation. This path of the transformative sequence is illustrated in this volume by Catalina Botero-Marino's analysis of the *Claude Reyes* case. The case triggered legislative reform

---

[36] Wayne Sandholtz, Yining Bei, and Kayla Caldwell, "Backlash and International Human Rights Courts," in Alison Brysk and Michael Stohl (eds.), *Contracting Human Rights: Crisis, Accountability, and Opportunity* (Edward Elgar 2018).
[37] Hillebrecht (n. 17).
[38] Damián González-Salzberg, "Do States Comply with the Compulsory Judgments of the Inter-American Court of Human Rights? An Empirical Study of the Compliance with 330 Measures of Reparation" [2013] 13 *Revista do Instituto Brasileiro de Direitos Humanos* 93.

in Chile but also started a domino effect across Latin America. The case led to an early wave of reforms codifying the right to access information in Honduras, Nicaragua, Guatemala, and Uruguay. After the Inter-American Court restated the principles in *Gomes Lund et al. v. Brazil*, a second legislative wave took place in El Salvador, Brazil, Colombia, Argentina, Paraguay, Guyana, and the Bahamas. Those examples show how the directing and standard-building functions activate the transformative sequence through different paths.

Jurisprudence is a second arena for structural change. The incorporation of an IAHRS instrument into local jurisprudence implies that the judiciary is bound by the terms of the instrument, and all cases decided afterward should follow the framework provided. There is a change in structures because the judiciary must collectively abide by new standards. Jurisprudential change may result from two processes: a unilateral decision directing the State to adopt the new framework, or a judicial dialogue resulting in standard-building.[39] The Inter-American Court might order domestic judges to exercise control of conventionality on a particular topic, but there is also the possibility that domestic courts will adopt and develop IAHRS standards on their own. Multiple contributors to this volume show how domestic courts have used inter-American standards to support a judicial decision. For example, Edison Lanza assesses how the standards about freedom of expression had an impact in the region and were crucial for the decisions of national tribunals on this matter.

Public policy is the third possible arena of structural transformation. Public policies involve State action to address social problems; they require allocation of public resources and regulation of a comprehensive set of actors.[40] The IAHRS promotes the adoption of programs that protect human rights and allocate national budgets to guarantee access to economic, social, cultural, and environmental rights. For example, in this volume, Silvia Serrano Guzmán demonstrates how the IACtHR's decision in *Artavia Murillo v. Costa Rica* led to the inclusion of in vitro fertilization (IVF) in the Costa Rican healthcare system. In response to the Court's decision, in early 2016 a series of executive decrees authorized two private healthcare facilities to practice IVF, and eventually led to the establishment of a Unit of Reproductive Medicine of High Complexity for the Social Security System in June 2019.

Additionally, there is a change in structures when States modify their institutional design. For example, the creation of specialized prosecution offices or

---

[39] Jorge Contesse, "The Final Word? Constitutional Dialogue and the Inter-American Court of Human Rights" [2017] 15 *International Journal of Constitutional Law* 414.

[40] Pierre Lascoumes and Patrick Le Gales, "Introduction: Understanding Public Policy through Its Instruments—From the Nature of Instruments to the Sociology of Public Policy Instrumentation" [2007] 20 *Governance* 1.

the reorganization of executive offices to address human rights issues show how IAHRS instruments have general implications for the design of State institutions. Parra Vera provides an illustrative example in this volume. Addressing the standards on the fight against impunity, the author claims that human rights instruments have prompted "readjustments of institutional designs, schemes, directives and other types of measures." In Colombia, after the ruling in the *Gutiérrez Soler* case, the Attorney General and the National Institute of Legal Medicine and Forensic Sciences issued domestic directives related to torture. Moreover, the Final Peace Agreement between the State and the FARC guerrilla group incorporated a Comprehensive System of Truth, Justice, Reparation and Guarantees of Non-Repetition, including the creation of a Special Jurisdiction for Peace.

A final, and often overlooked form of structural change is the transformation of academic curriculums. Bogdandy et al., in this volume, underscore the need to look at institutions of higher education to ponder impact. Universities play a vital role in the diffusion of ideas, which become particularly powerful when they are incorporated as part of regular teaching. When universities modify their study plans to include topics related to the IAHRS, they prompt ideational change for future generations of professionals. Educational reform qualifies as structural change because the new curriculum regulates the learning process for students and instructors in the institution of higher education.

The five above-mentioned arenas document the diversity of mechanisms by which inter-American instruments can shape structural change. But, as we argued earlier in this chapter, structural transformation only takes place after a previous appropriation of those instruments by the community of practice, which articulates new demands and prompts an institutional response. The effectiveness of those demands in promoting positive structural change depends on an array of contextual factors that require systematic empirical study.

3.4. Third Stage: Transformations on the Ground

The third stage in this complex causal sequence yields transformations on the ground, the final link in the transformative chain. Let us recapitulate: an IAHRS instrument aiming to influence a human rights situation is appropriated by the community of practice, which succeeds in prompting an institutional response. Once structural change is in place, the ultimate form of impact corresponds to the transformation of social outcomes, a sustained change in people's lives and in the enjoyment of rights.

Transformative processes that reach the third phase are the most successful ones because they change the way local populations experience rights. The relevant population in each case is defined by the function performed by the initial instrument. For example, if the instrument had a directing role and thus started a sequence toward compliance, the relevant population forms the victims in the case. If the instrument performed a standard-building role, the relevant population is a much broader segment of persons who will benefit from the new standard across the region.

Transformations in social outcomes reflect directly into rights-holders' living conditions. For example, in a case related to the violation of access to healthcare, a successful instrument will direct the State to address the individual situation, impacting the lives of patients who gain access to the care they need. Moreover, if the instrument performs a standard-building role, it will impact a larger population, as the community of practice promotes the new standard. In this volume, Saavedra Alessandri and Serrano Guzmán emphasize how the *Artavia Murillo* decision transformed the lives of Costa Ricans seeking in vitro fertilization. Between the ruling in 2012 and the time of their writing, 159 babies had been born by IVF treatment in Costa Rica.

The Inter-American System therefore has impact at multiple levels: in sociolegal practices, in institutions, and in social outcomes. Because transformations on the ground are the last stage of this transformative sequence, the time required to reach this form of impact might be lengthy. The process will require the completion of previous stages—appropriation and institutional change—before changes in social outcomes are feasible. In addition, the probability of change becomes more uncertain at each stage. It is relatively easy for the community of practice to appropriate a particular instrument, but it is much harder to succeed in achieving institutional reform. And even when institutions respond favorably, reforms do not guarantee that new institutions will properly achieve the desired outcomes.[41]

In brief, the last moment of the sequence refers to the transformation of people's lives, both objectively and subjectively. This stage corresponds to the most ambitious notion of impact as social transformation. For example, Cecilia Bailliet discusses how the Inter-American Court has set standards with potential to reduce structural violence across Latin America.[42] Only after this long transformative chain is it possible to observe actual change that is meaningful for the citizenry.

---

[41] Daniel M. Brinks, Steven Levitsky, and Maria Victoria Murillo, *Understanding Institutional Weakness: Power and Design in Latin American Institutions* (Cambridge University Press 2019).

[42] Cecilia Bailliet, *The Construction of the Customary Law of Peace: Latin America and the Inter-American Court of Human Rights* (Edward Elgar Publishing 2021), ch. 6.

4. Strategies to Document Impact

In the previous section, we theorized the transformative sequence, connecting each stage with a particular form of impact. In this section, we discuss empirical strategies to document impact. We outline common challenges to the identification of causality and illustrate empirical strategies based on their ability to assess the effect of the IAHRS on practices, structures, and social outcomes.

Claiming that a human rights instrument had an effect on the community of practice, on institutional change, or on the rights enjoyed by the population inevitably implies a statement about causation. To validate such claim, it is necessary to verify the consistency between the causal argument and the empirical evidence. In this regard, the transformative sequence poses three challenges. First, it is a complex causal process with multiple stages. Transitioning from each moment in the sequence to the next implies a distinct form of causality. Thus, analysts may require different empirical strategies to document the causal mechanisms operating at every step. Second, claiming causality at any stage requires isolating the effect of the IAHRS from the effect of many other factors that also shape practices, institutions, or social outcomes. Considering that the IAHRS is immersed in a context where both domestic and international forces are at play, any empirical strategy should account for alternative factors that might influence the outcome. Lastly, causal accounts may document impact at the level of individual cases, by tracing the process leading to a given transformation, or at the level of generalized patterns, by documenting the impact of IAHRS instruments across multiple cases.

The transformative sequence has three moments with their corresponding forms of impact. We have argued that a transformation in the earlier stages is necessary to allow for impact in the later stages. For instance, an appropriation of the instrument by the community of practice is necessary to achieve institutional change. It follows from this structure that strategies to document impact may focus on individual stages, on a combination of stages, or on the "long" transformative chain. An analyst might focus solely on the first stage, for example, documenting how Indigenous movements modified their strategies in response to a given decision by the Inter-American Court. Or she might document impact across all stages, showing that an IACtHR ruling empowered Indigenous communities to lobby for land reform, which in turn improved their living conditions. Research design choices, however, come at a cost. Focusing on any single stage provides greater clarity about the causal mechanisms involved, but it makes it more difficult to assess the overall impact. Focusing on a longer sequence, on the other hand, allows for a more comprehensive picture, but it makes it more difficult to advance plausible claims about causality.

A second challenge relates to the fact that human rights outcomes can be explained by factors other than the IAHRS influence. When an instrument directs the State to the creation of a new policy, other domestic processes also drive this transformation. The efforts of the community of practice might be helped by a timely change in the ruling party, or by mass mobilization that does not have the IAHRS as a source of inspiration. To the extent that any alternative explanations overlap with the transformative sequence, they will confound the effects of the IAHRS. Documenting the System's impact on social outcomes, the most distant form of impact, is particularly difficult because many variables— some of them not even under the State's control—affect the enjoyment of rights. Botero similarly notes that multiple factors determine how much any right is realized for a particular population, and that judicial intervention is only one of the possibilities.[43] An economic crisis or a bonanza may also affect to what extent the State succeeds in guaranteeing a right.

The third challenge is given by the trade-off between documenting impact in a particular case and documenting patterns of impact across cases. An exercise in process-tracing may establish, for instance, that a compliance agreement between Chile and representatives of the victims facilitated the implementation of reparation measures recommended by the IACHR in the case of Carmelo Soria Espinoza (2003). But a larger comparative study will be necessary to determine whether compliance agreements are, in general, effective instruments to prompt the adoption of the Commission's recommendations.[44] Focus on a single case may improve the internal validity of the conclusions (i.e., greater certainty on the mechanisms that produce impact), but a cross-sectional study will improve the external validity of the study (i.e., the generalizability of the conclusions across the Inter-American System).

In the rest of this section, we illustrate alternative strategies to study the IAHRS impact using selected examples beyond this volume. We follow the structure of the transformative sequence to organize the selected examples, focusing on distinctive outcomes at each stage.

Documenting change in practices. An empirical strategy to document impact in the first stage of the sequence requires analysts to assess if some members of the community of practice appropriate a particular instrument and incorporate it to their discourse and practices. The measurable outcomes at this stage are ideational changes and the incorporation of instruments to regular activities.

The study of ideational change can employ a wide range of methodologies, including surveys, text analysis, archival research, or ethnography. For instance, Karina Ansolabehere et al. administered an online survey to more than 1,100

---

[43] Botero (n. 12).
[44] Pérez Liñán, Brocca, and Orizaga Inzunza (n. 14).

Mexican judges to assess their legal culture.[45] About 52 percent of judges indicated that they rely on the jurisprudence of the IACtHR in a majority of their decisions, and 70 percent indicated they have exercised conventionality control. The authors placed the legal culture of judges in a continuum of "hermeneutic routines," with textualist judges less open, and interpretivist judges more open to the inter-American instruments.

Besides the use of surveys, it is also possible to assess the IAHRS's impact on practices through archival research and text analysis, determining whether documents issued by State agents, civil society organizations, or international bodies increasingly incorporate a particular instrument.[46] Wayne Sandholtz's analysis of citation networks, for instance, documents the emergence of a "global constitutionalism" by showing how the Inter-American Court, the European Court of Human Rights, the African Court of Human and People's Rights, and the UN Committee incorporate each other's instruments in their own work.[47] In turn, qualitative interviews and ethnography are useful to validate the impact of particular instruments on the community of practice's daily work and to understand how instruments are appropriated.[48] Process-tracing may help researchers to reconstruct the process by which the introduction of a novel instrument ultimately led to the transformation of collective practices in a particular case.[49]

Documenting change in structures. Impact at the level of structures requires a positive institutional response. The measurable outcomes at this stage are changes of legislation, jurisprudence, public policy, institutional design, or curricula.

Some of the analytical tools employed to assess appropriation can also be adapted to assess structural change. Studies using citations, for example, can easily document transformations in jurisprudence. In their analysis of citation patterns for thirteen national high courts in Latin America, Ezekiel González-Ocantos and Sandholtz show that citations to the IACtHR expanded in the twenty-first century, reaching more than a thousand citations across the region by 2012. The authors show that IACtHR decisions related to judicial guarantees (i.e., those referring to Article 8 of the American Convention on Human Rights), the duty to investigate human rights violations (Article 25), freedom of religion

---

[45] Ansolabehere et al. (n. 35).
[46] John Wilkerson and Andreu Casas, "Large-Scale Computerized Text Analysis in Political Science: Opportunities and Challenges" [2017] 20 *Annual Review of Political Science* 529.
[47] Sandholtz (n. 21).
[48] Diana Kapiszewski, Lauren M. MacLean, and Benjamin L. Read, *Field Research in Political Science: Practices and Principles* (Cambridge University Press 2015).
[49] Stuart S. Glennan, "Mechanisms and the Nature of Causation" [1996] 44 *Erkenntnis* 49.

(Article 12), and freedom of speech (Article 13) are the most cited by domestic courts.[50]

As for legislation and public policy, legislative bills and administrative regulations typically include whereases expounding the justifications for policy change. Using text analysis, researchers can conduct a systematic review of whether laws or policies invoke particular instruments. In turn, qualitative strategies based on process-tracing allow researchers to unveil the alliances between State actors and the community of practice to achieve institutional transformations. For example, Botero underscores the alliance between domestic courts and civil society in strategies of collaborative oversight,[51] and Jessica Rich underscores the alliance between the bureaucracy and social movements to adopt public policies in favor of marginalized groups.[52]

Documenting change in social outcomes. Impact at the level of social transformation is distinctively difficult to document. The measurable outcomes at this stage are changes in the living conditions of the target populations and their subjective enjoyment of rights. As we noted earlier, the challenges when analyzing the most distant outcomes result from the fact that researchers need to reconstruct the "long" transformative sequence to determine impact. Equally important, the long chain of causation also implies that many alternative explanations may account for aggregate social outcomes, confounding the effects of the Inter-American System. While qualitative process-tracing may be useful to reconstruct the long transformative chain in a single case, statistical analysis will be most useful to isolate the effect of international instruments vis-à-vis alternative explanations.

Careful qualitative research can reconstruct the long chain leading from instruments to social outcomes through case studies. It may also expose how the transformative chain is disrupted. Based on ethnographic fieldwork, Natalia Koper shows how the Mayangna and Miskito Indigenous peoples in Nicaragua appropriated the IACtHR's decision in the *Awas Tingni* case (2001) to defend their land rights. Initially, the State responded positively, adopting legislation (Law 445 of 2003) that established new demarcation mechanisms and procedures for granting property titles in Indigenous lands. In the end, however, structural change failed to produce the desired social outcomes, as an increasingly authoritarian regime used the new legislation to interfere in the election of communal

---

[50] Ezequiel González-Ocantos and Wayne Sandholtz, "Constructing a Regional Human Rights Legal Order: The Inter-American Court, National Courts, and Judicial Dialogue, 1988–2014" [2021] 19 *International Journal of Constitutional Law* 1559.

[51] Botero (n. 12).

[52] Rich (n. 33).

and territorial authorities, and failed to protect Indigenous territories from the violent incursions of non-Indigenous settlers.[53]

Careful quantitative research, in turn, can offer systematic measurement of social outcomes and account for alternative explanations. Cross-national indicators allow us to assess the enjoyment of rights through comparative indices,[54] which are typically based on expert and general population surveys.[55] Accounting for cross-national variation in those outcomes, moreover, requires multivariate analyses able to isolate the effect of human rights instruments from the effect of additional factors, such as institutional weakness,[56] economic development, and corruption.[57]

5. Concluding Remarks

Scholars and practitioners coincide in pointing out that the IAHRS has considerable impact throughout the region and beyond.[58] The chapters in this volume document multiple ways in which the System has influenced the work of the community of practice, legislation, public policy, and the enjoyment of citizen rights, among other outcomes. This chapter has offered a general theoretical framework to integrate and systematize all manifestations of impact. We articulated a comprehensive definition of impact and outlined the transformative sequence behind the various effects generated by the IAHRS. The usefulness of this framework was illustrated by a set of empirical strategies used to assess impact. In this concluding section, we summarize the four contributions advanced by our framework.

The first contribution of this chapter is the idea that compliance should be considered as a particular form of impact. Calls to investigate "impact beyond compliance" emerged from the realization that, despite its compliance problems,[59] the IAHRS had transformative effects across Latin America. Several authors distinguished compliance from impact, using the latter term to describe ill-defined but significant—and sometimes unexpected—consequences of the

---

[53] Natalia Koper, "The Inter-American Court of Human Rights and Indigenous Rights in Nicaragua: From Land to Empowerment?" [2022] 41 *Bulletin of Latin American Research* 608.

[54] UN Office of the High Commissioner for Human Rights (n. 13).

[55] Juan Carlos Botero and Alejandro Ponce, "Measuring the rule of law" [2011], available at SSRN 1966257.

[56] Brinks, Levitsky, and Murillo (n. 41).

[57] Luz Ángela Cardona, Horacio Ortiz Ríos, and Luis Daniel Vázquez Valencia, "Corrupción y derechos humanos" [2018] 80 *Revista Mexicana de Sociología* 577.

[58] Engstrom (n. 3).

[59] Fernando Basch et al., "The effectiveness of the Inter-American system of human rights protection: a quantitative approach to its functioning and compliance with its decisions" [2010] 7 *Sur—International Journal on Human Rights* 9.

System's actions. Our definition of impact covers the intended and unintended effects of adjudicatory and non-adjudicatory instruments. As such, the concept incorporates compliance as a special case of impact; compliance is the desired effect of an adjudicatory instrument among the parties in a controversy.

In addition, following relevant work in domestic judicial politics,[60] our definition provides an encompassing framework to include several types of impact: in practices, structures, and social outcomes. Along those lines, we developed a concept of impact that is useful to assess the effects, not only of judicial rulings but also of non-adjudicatory instruments such as country reports and press releases. We systematically mapped out the multiple functions performed by the IAHRS's instruments: directing State action, developing standards, documenting facts, positioning new topics, reframing issues as human rights problems, and assisting local actors in their human rights work.

In the third place, we contribute to the literature by advancing the idea of a transformative sequence. In our account, the System's organs create impact through a transformative process in which sequence matters. At the start of the sequence, the IAHRS deploys an instrument that can perform a number of roles. This instrument is first appropriated by the community of practice and leveraged in legal and political disputes. The community of practice utilizes this leverage to obtain a response from the State or other organizations. When the response is positive, we observe a transformation in structures, such as changes in jurisprudence or academic curricula. In the most successful cases, structural change leads to a transformation in the livelihood and the perception of rights among the target population. Thus, the transformations normally cited as examples of impact, such as changes in jurisprudence or legislation, cannot be understood without a previous stage, where the community of practice plays a crucial role.

By pinpointing the specific outcomes that define each stage in the transformative chain, our framework facilitates, in the fourth place, an empirical approach to the study of impact. The framework does not ignore the possibility of negative consequences, such as backlash against the IAHRS's actions.[61] But our analytical focus underscores transformations at each stage that alter the status quo in the direction of advancing human rights. Our proposed research program relies on the methodological tools of social sciences to assess how inter-American instruments activate such transformations. Future empirical studies should explain why the community of practice appropriates some instruments more effectively than others, and why some instruments are more effective at driving

---

[60] Botero (n. 12).
[61] Ximena Soley and Silvia Steininger, "Parting Ways or Lashing Back? Withdrawals, Backlash and the Inter-American Court of Human Rights" [2018] 14 *International Journal of Law in Context* 237.

structural change. Also, future research should trace the causal mechanisms behind the advancement in the transformative sequence in successful cases.

The ideas presented in this chapter underscore the role of the community of practice in bringing the instruments of the IAHRS to specific settings and using them to achieve palpable transformations in legal structures. Empirical studies of successful transformative sequences can provide important insights into effective strategies and inspire lessons to achieve new transformations on the ground across the region.

I.10
Creating the Narrative of Human Rights Impact in Latin America

By René Urueña and Stephania Yate Cortes

1. Introduction

The practical relevance of a *Ius Constitutionale Commune en América Latina* (ICCAL) is deeply intertwined with the impact of the Inter-American Court of Human Rights (IACtHR). A regional court with little societal impact would seem to be in tension with the idea of *transformative* constitutionalism in Latin America—that is, a project of collective construction of legal meaning that seeks to transform society.[1] In this context, the body of literature arguing that the IACtHR is often but a toothless tiger, adopting orders with little expectation of actual State compliance, appears to be a powerful indictment of the transformative possibilities of the common law of human rights in Latin America.[2] And yet, in sharp contrast with that view, a second robust body of work has argued that observers should go "beyond compliance,"[3] and factor in the wider societal "impacts" of the Court's orders.[4]

This chapter intervenes in that discussion. It seeks to revisit the importance of the IACtHR by proposing a redefinition of the terms of the debate. It argues that "impact" is not a static fact but is rather a continuously evolving description of reality, performed by the community of human rights practice in Latin America. Specifically, participants of the community, including the IACtHR, construe reality through cognitive categories provided by law and then organize such descriptions in particular frameworks. Through such framing, the community of practice interprets national political, policy, and juridical events as the consequence of utterances from the IACtHR, thus creating a narrative about which

---

[1] On that project, see Armin von Bogdandy and René Urueña, "International Transformative Constitutionalism in Latin America" [2020] 114(3) *American Journal of International Law* 403–442.

[2] For a review of such literature, see Viviana Krsticevic and René Urueña in this volume.

[3] See the essays in Par Engstrom (ed.), *The Inter-American Human Rights System: Impact beyond Compliance* (Palgrave Macmillan 2019).

[4] See Viviana Krsticevic and René Urueña; René Urueña and Armin von Bogdandy in this same volume.

the assessment of "impact" makes sense. Ultimately, this chapter argues, the IACtHR's impact is a narrative built by the community of human rights practice through a particular framing, deploying a wide range of cognitive categories provided by law to describe "reality." This wider process is lost when observers focus solely on compliance with discrete inter-American orders as the relevant analytical unit to interrogate how the Court affects reality in the region. While such discrete data observations are of course relevant they must be understood in reference to the story that the community of practice is telling about the Court, and about itself. That narrative of impact helps explain the continued importance of the Court in the region, beyond compliance with its specific orders.

To make that argument, this chapter starts by introducing the role of communities of practice in creating narratives. It then moves on to describe how such narratives are developed through the deployment of cognitive categories that are organized in frameworks. The practice of such a process is then explored in reference to three inter-American cases: *González et al. v. Mexico* ("Cotton Field"); *Vardo dos Fogos v. Brazil* ("Fireworks Factory"); and *Lemoth Morris et al. v. Honduras* ("Miskito Divers"). The final section concludes.

2. Communities of Practice and Narratives of Human Rights Impact

International transformative constitutionalism is developed and sustained by a group of actors that coalesce around the development of a common law of human rights in Latin America—a *Ius Constitutionale Commune en América Latina* (ICCAL).[5] This common law creates, in Robert Cover's pathbreaking rendering, a "world of law" (a "nomos") that "entails the application of human will to an extant state of affairs as well as toward our visions of alternative futures."[6] This common law (this ICCAL) is, however, not enough to sustain the community. To that effect, though, the community requires normative guidance in its interpretation of texts. As Cover explains, a legal tradition includes "not only a corpus juris but also a language and a mythos—narratives in which the corpus juris is located by those whose wills act upon it."[7] Ultimately, the community of practice creates a world of human right law—but also a need to inhabit it, which is only possible through the development of a narrative that connects the harsh reality of continuing human rights violations in Latin America with the normative horizon of transformative constitutionalism. This gap between a

---

[5] This definition is drawn from Bogdandy and René Urueña (n. 1). See further Armin von Bogdandy and René Urueña in this volume
[6] Robert M. Cover, "Nomos and Narrative" [1983] 97(4) *Harvard Law Review* 4–68, at 9.
[7] Ibid., 9.

transformative ambition and the reality of human rights violations is, from this perspective, not a problem of compliance (or lack thereof), but is a crucial part of the dynamic process of creating the "world of law" that is ICCAL. As Cover explains, narratives "build relations between the normative and the material universe, between the constraints of reality and the demands of an ethic," which operate at different levels, and are connected by narrative.

Narratives are crucial to understanding the dynamic construction of "impact" in that they imply the collapse of the "is," the "ought," and, as Cover explains, the "what might have been." By constantly contrasting the descriptive "is" of human rights violations in Latin America (or the incipient advances in protection in certain States), with the normative "ought" of ICCAL's transformative ambitions, the community of human rights practice creates a narrative of "impact" that actualizes the IACtHR's relevance. This tension gives sense to the Court's mandate: always struggling, but never defeated—a tension in which the community of practice operates. The narrative of "impact" therefore introduces a constant normative irritation to reality, as it provides the link that connects the factual representation of domestic reality (say, the prosecution of an alleged perpetrator of human rights violations) and the normative goals of the Court.

Such narratives allow us to explain why focusing on just compliance misses the mark. Compliance puts the spotlight on discrete orders by the Court, which in turn trigger certain domestic actions. However, tying together such discrete events is a wider fabric narrative—in this case, a narrative in reference to which it is possible to speak of "impact." As historian and literary critic Hayden White explains, narrative as a meta code is the key difference between the historical document of the annals and the chronicles: while the annals (a list of events) are "fact," the chronicle is narrative. Similarly, the quantitative "fact" about compliance are the annals of the IACtHR, while impact implies a narrative, a connection between such discrete "facts" and an overall normative mindset—in White's words, the impact is not the "real," but a "discourse of the real."[8] Thus, when quantitative studies show extremely low levels of compliance with the Court's orders, they are also creating a narrative—that of the System as an ineffectual institution of a largely symbolic role. That is also a "discourse of the real."

3. Creating Narratives: Cognitive Categories and Framing

How is the narrative of impact created and sustained? In this section, we highlight two strategies. First, the common law of human rights provides the community

---

[8] Hayden White, "The Value of Narrativity in the Representation of Reality" [1980] 7(1) *Critical Inquiry* 5–27, at 23.

of practice with a set of cognitive categories that allow it to describe its reality and the position of each actor within that reality. However, cognitive categories in themselves are not enough to build a narrative. In a way, they risk remaining as vignettes within a wider framework of meaning. Hence, the community of practice needs to appeal to framing, as a second strategy to give sense and texture to the narrative of impact.

3.1. Description through Cognitive Categories

Narratives are built on descriptions that allow us to understand reality, particularly when such descriptions are shared, told, and retold by the members of a community of practice. When a narrative becomes broadly known and part of a canon, "it appears to be an inevitable, necessary and natural impulse to narrate, so that those narratives that correspond to the dominant cultural expectations are not problematic."[9]

In the case of the community of human rights practice in Latin America, the descriptive work is performed through law.[10] Indeed, the law provides the community of practice with cognitive categories, by which we mean a concept, created by the community of practice, which may help its participants to organize their perception of their reality, as well as their role in it.[11] As Julieta Lemaitre has suggested when describing the role of law in grassroots activism, we understand the world through concepts and networks of concepts that, in turn, refer to other concepts, hence a part of social reality has no necessary materiality outside of this constructed network of meanings.[12]

All actors in the community of practice use cognitive categories to describe a particular reality. Elsewhere, one of us has explored how the concept of "victim" in the Inter-American System provides a key cognitive category that organizes

---

[9] Julia Otten, "Narratives in International Law" [2016] 99(3) *KritV, CritQ, RCrit. Kritische Vierteljahresschrift Für Gesetzgebung Und Rechtswissenschaft / Critical Quarterly for Legislation and Law / Revue Critique Trimestrielle de Jurisprudence et de Législation* 187–216, http://www.jstor.org/stable/44504923.

[10] Otten (n. 9). To take an example outside of Latin America, the narrative behind Article 51 of the UN Charter, which recognizes the right to self-defense, provides the cognitive tools to narrate use of force and is necessary to describe the "reality" of those who engage in self-defense See Gina Heathcote, "Article 51 Self-Defense as a Narrative: Spectators and Heroes in International Law" [October 2005] 12(1) *Texas Wesleyan Law Review* 131–153, https://doi.org/10.37419/TWLR.V12.I1.6.

[11] For further discussion about this set of concepts, see René Urueña's work on cognitive categories in "International Law as Expert Knowledge: Exploring the Changing Role of International Lawyers in National Contexts," in Jean d'Aspremont et al. (eds.), *International Law as a Profession* (Cambridge University Press 2017), 389–410.

[12] Julieta Lemaitre, *El derecho como conjuro: fetichismo legal, violencia y movimientos sociales* (Siglo del Hombre 2009), 394.

how civil society gets to know its realities, and eventually itself. It offers the building blocks to describe reality—the actors, structures, and the representation of a process—the criminal process whereby the "perpetrator" creates the victim. All this influences strategy on the ground.[13]

Among all other participants of the community, the IACtHR is a crucial provider and user of such cognitive categories. Many of the cognitive categories deployed by the Court are expressed in the language of rights, which implies an inherent claim to legal bindingness. However, their legal status as legal obligations is neither necessary nor sufficient for them to work categories to describe reality. Beyond their legal status, it is only through the constant practical use by the community that rights become cognitive categories useful for the construction of narratives.

Consider the right of Indigenous peoples to prior consultation.[14] Since its recognition through the IACtHR's evolutive interpretation of the rights to property and culture,[15] prior consultation has prompted the development of a wide portfolio of categories describing geographical and ethnographic realities that have allowed the community of human rights practice to make sense of their environment, create a mental image of their geographical reality, and plan their strategies accordingly.

An example of this process is the notion of "ancestral territory."[16] Of course, such territories do exist in "reality." Indigenous communities do have a geographical area where they have been traditionally located. However, the cognitive category of "ancestral territory" mobilizes legal language to go beyond mere historical or geographical data, and creates a geographical, cultural, and spiritual reality "on the ground" that exists, however, only in reference to the law. That

---

[13] Bogdandy and Urueña (n. 1).

[14] See Corte IDH. Caso del Pueblo Saramaka v. Surinam; Corte IDH. Caso Pueblo Indígena Kichwa de Sarayaku v. Ecuador; among others.

[15] See generally Sorily Carolina Figuera Vargas and Meylin Heleana Ortiz Torres, "El Derecho a La Consulta Previa a Los Pueblos Indígenas En El Sistema Interamericano de Derechos Humanos. Casos de Estudio: Ecuador y Colombia" [2019] 19(36) *Civilizar Ciencias Sociales y Humanas* 59–76.

[16] See, e.g., the rich Inter-American case law on the protection of "ancestral territory" in Comisión Interamericana de Derechos Humanos, "Derechos de Los Pueblos Indígenas y Tribales Sobre Sus Tierras Ancestrales y Recursos Naturales: Normas y Jurisprudencia Del Sistema Interamericano de Derechos Humanos" (OEA/Ser.L/V/II Doc. 56/09, diciembre 2009). The Inter-American Court has also often used the category of "ancestral land" or "ancestral territory," for example, in Caso de la Comunidad Moiwana v. Surinam. Excepciones Preliminares, fondo, Reparaciones y Costas. Sentencia de 15 de junio de 2005. Ser. C No. 124, paras. 131–133; Caso Comunidad Indígena Yakye Axa v. Paraguay. Fondo Reparaciones y Costas. Sentencia 17 de junio de 2005, paras. 96, 124, 167, 225; Caso Comunidad Indígena Sawhoyamaxa v. Paraguay. Fondo, Reparaciones y Costas. Sentencia de 29 de marzo de 2006 paras. 164, 212, 235; Pueblo Saramaka. v. Surinam. Excepciones Preliminares, Fondo, Reparaciones y Costas. Sentencia de 28 de noviembre de 2007, para. 85 (quoting Moiwana); Caso Comunidad Indígena Xákmok Kásek. v. Paraguay. Fondo, Reparaciones y Costas. Sentencia de 24 de agosto de 2010, paras. 309–310; Caso de los Pueblos Indígenas Kuna de Madungandí y Emberá de Bayano y sus Miembros v. Panamá. Excepciones Preliminares, Fondo, Reparaciones y Costas. Sentencia de 14 de octubre de 2014, paras. 121–122, among others.

is, it creates a space with a particular type of inhabitants, around which litigation strategies of both claimants and respondents gravitate, and has to be dealt with by both, which exists however only in reference to that shared cognitive category.[17]

Similarly, the law of prior consultation also provides cognitive categories that describe the communities that are protected by such a right. In a veritable process of interpellation, a particular notion of Indigenous community emerges in reference to the category "ancestral territory," which is defined through the bundle of legal relations created by the right to prior consultation.[18] But the process is not only top-down; that is, it is not only a bestowing of identity through cognitive categories from international institutions. The Indigenous community is not passive and, as an agent of its politics, in turn, puts forward its definition of the geographical and ethnographic reality where the right to prior consultation is to be applied—and, by doing so, defines crucial dimensions of its very own identity as a community. Through this process of interpellation by institutions and continuous redefinition of the community itself, the law of prior consultation shapes a particular subject of protection and, as this constant description of reality becomes stabilized, it guides the range of possible reactions by national and international institutions to the problem triggered of "prior consultation."

3.2. Framing the Narrative of the Impact

Cognitive categories, though, are not enough to give sense to the narrative of impact. A wider framework is needed for discrete cognitive categories to coalesce into a narrative. Any given fact or event, as part of an interpretative process, can

---

[17] Anthropologist and Indigenous rights activist Efraín Jaramillo has argued that the very notion of "indigenous territory" is "a concept that arises from the relations of ethno-territorial groups with the State" as, first, it "was not in the nature of indigenous peoples to determine territories to define the spaces of their social being and to establish relations or differences with or differences with other peoples" and, second, "the primary relationship of an indigenous group with its habitat is based on the supply of resources for the subsistence of the group." "Many of its myths and legends," Jaramillo explains, "revolve around a fertile and generous nature. From there arises the notion that the earth is the mother of all that exists. But these cosmovisions were not limited to a delimited physical space, outside of which their religious beliefs about nature were not valid." Therefore, for Jaramillo "the notion of indigenous territory as we know it today, arises from conflicting relations with the surrounding society. It arises more from the political needs (of political affirmation) of indigenous peoples, rather than from cultural imperatives, at a time when their habitat was invaded, during the Spanish conquest and subsequent colonization." (Efraín Jaramillo, "Territorio, Identidad Étnica y Estado" [2003] 4(3) *Revista Asuntos Indígenas* 44–49, at 44–45). We argue, however, that regardless of its historical or ethnographic origin, the cognitive category of "ancestral territory" does its contemporary work of describing reality for the community of practice, in accordance with the contemporary consensus around its use. This cognitive role is not affected, but rather confirmed, by Jarmillo's valuable insight.

[18] On interpolation in the Althusseian sense used here, see Ntina Tzouvala, *Capitalism as Civilisation: A History of International Law* (Cambridge University Press 2020), at 61

be described in different terms or focus, narrowly or broadly—that is, in regard to different "frames," or "schemas of interpretations that transform a succession of events into something meaningful."[19]

When the IACtHR intervenes in a particular situation, it translates context into human rights frameworks, which it then uses to organize its interpretation of "reality." The first intervention is therefore to understand social relations as distinctively *legal* and, most importantly, to understand complex social problems (such as inequality or violence) as legal challenges that can be processed through legal reasoning.[20] However, framing theory relies on acknowledging that definitions of a situation are built up under a set of principles of organization that govern social events and our subjective involvement in them.[21] Frames are not randomly given, or spontaneously constructed. The construction of a frame can be a conscious process, led by certain actors of a particular community of practice. Thus, to frame is, as Robert Entman has put it, "to select some aspects of perceived reality and make them more salient in a communicating text, in such a way as to promote a particular problem definition, causal interpretation, moral evaluation, and/or treatment recommendation for the item described."[22]

Such a framing process plays a key role in organizing the description of reality performed through cognitive categories. Together, frames and cognitive categories allow the construction of the narrative of the IACtHR's impact in Latin America. A particular framing of the issue will imply a particular version of impact, beyond the specifics of compliance with a discrete Court order. Thus, while cognitive categories provide the building blocks to describe the reality of the Court, framing provides a blueprint to organize facts to build a narrative— with "impact" being a necessary part of such narratives, one that indeed gives them closure, as it helps organize events toward a conclusion of changed lives by the Court's action.

Framing is competitive. Participants of the community of practice put forward particular frames to interpret the "reality" where ICCAL operates.[23] In that process, there will be conflict among different framings, some of which will become dominant, and others less so. However, once a framework becomes dominant, it constrains the future interpretation of ICCAL's "reality," setting the baseline for the next interpretation of said reality.[24] In social movements literature, this temporarily dominant frame is often labeled as a "master frame," which

---

[19] Erving Goffman, *Framing Analysis: An Essay on the Organization of Experience* (Northeastern University Press, 1986).
[20] See Bogdandy and Urueña (n. 1).
[21] Goffman (n. 19), 11.
[22] Robert M. Entman, "Framing: Toward Clarification of a Fractured Paradigm" [December 1, 1993] 43(4) *Journal of Communication* 52, https://doi.org/10.1111/j.1460-2466.1993.tb01304.x.
[23] See Bogdandy and Urueña (n. 1).
[24] Otten (n.9), 195.

implies a broad scope and works as a "master algorithm" that influences and constrains the orientation of many social movements.[25] Such a master frame is organized in terms of a wide range of ideas; it is "syntactically flexible and lexically universalistic" and "provides flexible modes of interpretation; consequently, it works as an inclusive system."[26]

The IACtHR plays a crucial role in defining what the dominant framework will be at a particular time. While not the only actor by any means, the Court's role in this framing process is salient, due to its unique position as the only regional institution with a transnational mandate. While domestic constitutional courts or universal human rights institutions do as much framing as the Court, the latter's framing is more likely to be adopted as a shared point of reference by actors throughout the region, for at least two reasons: first, because, in a context where many participants are putting forward their frames, the Court is particularly influential, as it has the mandate to evaluate the frameworks proposed by others and legally validate those frameworks as a particular violation of human rights. And second, because due to its prior successes in adopting dominant framings, the Court can constrain future frames, both implicitly by foreclosing the horizon of possible alternative framings and, explicitly, by demanding as a legal obligation that its prior framing, as expressed through prior interpretations of legal texts (that is, its case law) be followed.

This is not to say that the Court's framing is indisputable. The fact that a particular framework is influential at a given moment does not mean that there is a uniform or unique interpretation of reality.[27] As with any piece of literature, in which the author plays with points of view that build up the overall structure, the Court's intervention foregrounds a particular frame that is just one part of the story as a whole.[28] However, the Court's framing does set the terms for the narrative of its impact: it is in the context of a particular framework that "impact" makes sense. Ultimately, "impact" tells the story of a reality (described through cognitive categories) organized around a particular framework (or contestation of frameworks), that narrates a Court intervention that is more, or less, effective in its task of transforming society.

---

[25] Robert D. Benford and David A. Snow, "Framing Processes and Social Movements: An Overview and Assessment" [2000] 26 *Annual Review of Sociology* 618.

[26] David A. Snow and Robert D. Benford, "Master Frames and Cycles of Protest," in *Frontiers in Social Movement Theory* (Yale University Press 1992), 140.

[27] See Gwendolyn Leachman, "Legal Framing," in Austin Sarat, *Studies in Law, Politics, and Society*, vol. 61 (Emerald 2013), 25–59.

[28] Jerome Bruner, "What Is a Narrative Fact?" [1998] 560 *Annals of the American Academy of Political and Social Science* 17–27.

4. Narratives of Impact in Practice

The IACtHR creates and sustains narratives through all of its legal utterances—most importantly through its decision. This section discusses three instances of inter-American adjudication that illustrate how narratives of impact are created through the deployment of cognitive categories, organized around a particular framing. In each of these cases, the Court: (a) used cognitive categories to define a particular problem, (b) diagnosed its causes, and (c) suggest remedies, thus creating a complete frame of intervention.[29] It is only with regards to such a frame that it becomes possible to (d) start thinking about "impact."[30]

The first case is *González et al. v. Mexico* ("Cotton Field"). Its facts are well known: in Juárez (Mexico), three young women disappeared in 2001, later to be found dead in a cotton field with signs of sexual violence. After the disappearance had been reported and criminal proceedings activated, local authorities failed to give an appropriate response to the victims' families, failing also to investigate or sanction those responsible.[31] The second case is *Vardo dos Fogos v. Brazil* ("Fireworks Factory"), which addresses the events around a fireworks factory in Santo Antônio de Jesus that exploded in 1998, killing sixty people (forty women, nineteen girls, and one boy).[32] Finally, the third case is *Lemoth Morris et al. v. Honduras* ("Miskito Divers"), concerning forty-two victims of the Miskito Indigenous community living in the department of Gracias a Dios, who worked in deep-sea dive fishing. The free-diving practice was traditionally used

---

[29] The two aspects were selected using Entman's framing functions, considering the affinity with the work of the Court and the qualitative method it implies. See Robert M. Entman, "Framing: Toward Clarification of a Fractured Paradigm" [December 1, 1993] 43(4) *Journal of Communication* 51–58, https://doi.org/10.1111/j.1460-2466.1993.tb01304.x. Other approaches and methodologies available, see Dafrizal Samsudin, "Understanding the Models of Framing Analysis Approaches in Media Framing Studies," in *Proceedings of the Second International Conference on Social, Economy, Education and Humanity* (The Second International Conference on Social, Economy, Education, and Humanity, Riau, Indonesia: SCITEPRESSScience and Technology Publications 2019), 385–389, https://doi.org/10.5220/0009159503850389. In particular, framing theory is currently interested in empirical verification and measuring the effects of framing, a concern that goes beyond the scope of this chapter, but might prove an interesting venue of ICCAL future research. See Dietram A. Scheufele and Shanto Iyengar, *The State of Framing Research*, ed. Kate Kenski and Kathleen Hall Jamieson, vol. 1 (Oxford University Press 2014), https://doi.org/10.1093/oxfordhb/9780199793471.013.47.

[30] Equivalency frames will not be discussed; this means frames that present different but logically equivalent words or phrases and reflect an interest in the method of communication, mainly focusing on framing effects research. See Irwin P. Levin, Sandra L. Schneider, and Gary J. Gaeth, "All Frames Are Not Created Equal: A Typology and Critical Analysis of Framing Effects" [November 1, 1998] 76(2) *Organizational Behavior and Human Decision Processes* 149–188, https://doi.org/10.1006/obhd.1998.2804; Hillary C. Shulman and Matthew D. Sweitzer, "Advancing Framing Theory: Designing an Equivalency Frame to Improve Political Information Processing" [April 1, 2018] 44(2) *Human Communication Research* 155–175, https://doi.org/10.1093/hcr/hqx006.

[31] *González y otras (Campo Algodonero) v. México*. Preliminary Objection, Merits, Reparations and Costs (Inter-American Court of Human Rights, November 16, 2009).

[32] *Case of the Workers of the Fireworks Factory in Santo Antônio de Jesus and their families v. Brazil* (Inter-American Court of Human Rights, June 21, 2021).

for family consumption with safe limits regarding the depth of the immersion. However, due to the increased commercialization of this activity, it started to be practiced by Miskito boys outside the labor legislation with serious consequences for their health and life.

4.1. Deployment of Cognitive Categories to Define the Problem

The first move to develop a narrative is the definition of the problem to be addressed. To do so, as was discussed earlier, the Court uses cognitive categories, provided by law, to describe the reality in which its decision will intervene, thus defining the possible scope of its "impact." Ultimately, the "impact" of the Court has to be understood with regard to a particular reality. However, this reality is not given—it has to be construed through the interpretation of the community of practice.

In *Cotton Field*, the question was whether the problem that these killings posed pertained to the individual victims, or whether to adopt a wider prism that included all three acts of violence (and others) as part of a larger reality. In this case, the Court's key move was one of scale. The scale at which the Court analyzes the facts varies from the scale in which local actors initially portray them.[33] On a purely descriptive basis, the facts in *Cotton Field* will look very different when read through the cognitive categories provided by international law to an international judge, as opposed to the same facts read through the cognitive categories provided by domestic law to domestic authorities. States, in turn, might want to resist such use of international cognitive categories and put forward their interpretation of the relevant "reality" of the case. That was the case in *Cotton Field*, where the three women's cases were treated by Mexico as discrete occurrences, each following an individual track in the Mexican criminal system. That is, the "reality" of each killing was disconnected from the "reality" of the other cases and, of course, disconnected from the wider "reality" of structural gender discrimination. The concurrence of patterns of criminality was not considered at the national level and only after entering into the Inter-American System did the relevant scale description change, and it became a structural case of violence against women.

In *Fireworks Factory*, the Court uses the category of intersectionality to present the reality of Santo Antônio de Jesus. The key issue was not only that victims suffered structural discrimination based on their situation of poverty

---

[33] Boaventura de Sousa Santos, "Law: A Map of Misreading. Toward a Postmodern Conception of Law" [1987] 14(3) *Journal of Law and Society* 287, https://doi.org/10.2307/1410186.

but that at the same time this situation was intersected by gender, race, and age, generating a particular type of discrimination against them.[34] The Court thus describes in detail the context of Santo Antônio de Jesus, including its historical background,[35] the victims' socioeconomic profile,[36] and the conditions after the tragedy. Workers in this sector are mostly Afro-descendant women who did not finish elementary school and started working between the ages of ten and thirteen as a way of increasing their income and because they have no one with whom to leave their children during working hours.[37] The key cognitive intervention is, therefore, to describe the reality of the workers around their identity as Afro-descendants, women, *and* workers. The problem, thus described, becomes less about industrial safety as such (a classic labor union and social rights issue) and more an issue of intersectionality.

A similar move can be observed in *Miskito Divers*, this time on the perpetrators' end of the description.[38] In that case, the Court deployed different cognitive categories to new subjects in its description of the case. Even though it acknowledges that it lacks jurisdiction to determine the responsibility of private parties under international human rights law,[39] the Court does include such private parties in its description of the "reality" it is studying—in this case, the fishing industry, who were of course crucial actors in the political economy of diving.[40] Framing the case around private companies transforms it into a business and human rights case, taking the opportunity to tackle this issue from a different perspective.[41]

---

[34] *Case of the Workers of the Fireworks Factory in Santo Antônio de Jesus and their families v. Brazil*, paras. 190–197.

[35] The Court considered that Santo Antônio de Jesus is in a region historically known for having a significant presence of Afro-descendants. The receding was partly because, during the sixteenth century, it received many slaves brought in to work on the cane sugar plantations and in tobacco farming. Discrimination against them continued even after the abolition of slavery, since the exercise of citizenship and the rights to housing and property were restricted, and entry into the labor market was obstructed. See *Case of the Workers of the Fireworks Factory in Santo Antônio de Jesus and their families v. Brazil*, paras. 57–58.

[36] Around the time of the events, poverty affected 65% of the population and 25,52% of children lived in extreme poverty. *Case of the Workers of the Fireworks Factory in Santo Antônio de Jesus and their families v. Brazil*, para. 60.

[37] *Case of the Workers of the Fireworks Factory in Santo Antônio de Jesus and their families v. Brazil*, para. 65.

[38] *Miskitos* was settled, but the parties asked the Court to analyze the content and scope of the rights that were affected and provide elements to the States of the region regarding their obligations to respect and guarantee human rights when companies and Indigenous peoples are involved. *Case of the Miskito Divers (Lemonth Morris et al.) v. Honduras* (Inter-American Court of Human Rights, August 31, 2021).

[39] Ibid., para. 46.

[40] Ibid., para. 104.

[41] See "Justice for Miskito Divers: A Turning Point for Business and Human Rights Standards from the Inter-American Court of Human Rights," *OpenGlobalRights*, https://www.openglobalrights.org/justice-for-miskito-divers-a-turning-point-for-business-and-human-rights-standards/ (accessed June 10, 2023).

This may initially seem to be a trivial observation: all courts define the "reality" as part of their adjudication. But this role of the Inter-American Court is anything but trivial. The whole point in *Cotton Field*, *Fireworks Factory*, and *Miskito Divers* was precisely that domestic authorities had been unable (or unwilling) to "see" the wider reality of the systematic victimization that the Court identified and validated. In *Cotton Field*, the Court introduced its scale to the description of the problem, while in *Fireworks Factory*, it introduced a new description of the victims' plight, and in *Miskitos*, a new actor was introduced in the description. In each of these cases, one key transformative intervention was to describe a wider reality—a transformation that was not achieved by developing new legal standards or by offering legal interpretation or "naming and shaming" strategies, but by using different cognitive categories.

4.2. Diagnosis of Causes

The definition of the reality of the problem is followed by an implicit or explicit diagnosis of its causes. In *Cotton Field*, the IACtHR put into sharp relief the social context of victimization based on gender. To do so, the complainants emphasized a general pattern of violence in Ciudad Juárez, and a specific pattern of femicide, that turned the three deaths into part of a wider context of gender-based violence that had existed since the 1990s in the city and its surrounding areas. This diagnosis of causes was accepted by the Court. Rejecting the Mexican Prosecutor's Office's initial approach, according to which most of the murders of women in Ciudad Juárez had been committed under different circumstances, time, manner, and occasions,[42] the Court developed a framework that explained the facts more broadly and unveiled a phenomenon that Mexican authorities had been reluctant to see—the systematic victimization of women—identified and validated by inter-American institutions.

Similarly, in *Fireworks Factory*, including intersectionality allowed the Court to reorganize the narrative about causes and effects. For the Court, the leading cause of the problem in this case was the pattern of structural and intersectional discrimination the victims faced. Accordingly, those patterns (i) forced the victims to work in the firework factory because their situation prevented them from finding alternatives in the commercial sector or even in domestic service,[43] and (ii) facilitated the factory's operation without adequate occupational health and safety conditions.[44].

---

[42] *González y otras (Campo Algodonero) v. México. Preliminary Objection, Merits, Reparations and Costs*, para. 127.
[43] *Case of the Workers of the Fireworks Factory in Santo Antônio de Jesus and their families v. Brazil*, para. 71.
[44] Ibid., para. 203

This diagnosis of causes was in sharp contrast with that of Honduras. For example, the State's agents argued that there were "reasonable limitations" to conducting actions to verify and oversee the different economic activities considering the size of the territory.[45] However, the Court's reading through the prism of intersectionality shifted the emphasis of the case, as it became not only a matter of supervising and overseeing hazardous activities but of overcoming those patterns of structural and intersectional discrimination.

Lastly, in *Miskito Divers*, the role of private fishing companies was highlighted as one of the main causes of the divers' dire conditions. The private buyers of fish did not meet the minimum standards required to engage labor in dive-fishing, have a formal employment contract or fair wage payments, or provide compensation for those who suffered accidents or diseases associated with this work. Moreover, they forced divers to work for long periods (ten or twelve days) and gave them drugs that allow divers to remain underwater for as long as possible.[46]

The Court emphasized that Gracias a Dios was one of Honduras's poorest and most isolated areas and that the Miskito population had limited formal employment opportunities—a combination of facts that allowed the (relatively small) fishing company to have an outside influence on people in the area.[47] This analysis proved crucial for the Court's framing of the case. While the Court was careful not to attribute direct responsibility to these private parties, its diagnosis of the case's causes is mostly focused on them.[48]

4.3. Definition of Remedies

Finally, framing includes suggesting remedies. In *Cotton Field*, changing the scale in the definition of a problem also changed the scale of possible solutions. In cases with a wide framing, such as *Cotton Field*, reparation has become a veritable exercise of governance, aiming to modify and guide public policy and channel resources for that purpose. Thus, on top of individual reparations, the Court ordered Mexico to continue standardizing all the institutional materials used for investigating all the crimes relating to the disappearance, sexual abuse, and murders of women from a gender perspective, adapting the Protocol for Reception, Reaction and Coordination between municipal, State, and federal authorities in cases of missing women and girls in the Municipality of Juárez and to implement education and training programs and courses for public officials on human rights and gender and on a gender perspective to ensure due diligence.

---

[45] Ibid., paras. 136
[46] *Case of the Miskito Divers (Lemonth Morris et al.) v. Honduras*, paras. 33–38.
[47] Ibid., paras. 30–31.
[48] Ibid., paras. 42–53.

In *Fireworks Factory*, the framing of the problem and the diagnosis of its causes also provided different types of remedies, targeting the Court's intersectional reading of the case. On the one hand, the Court required Brazil to implement a systematic policy of inspecting fireworks factories, both to verify the health and safety conditions of the workplace and to oversee compliance with the regulations on the storage of the materials involved.[49] At this level, the focus was the State's due diligence in regulating, supervising, and overseeing the performance of private or public entities. Following more closely its intersectional framing, though, the Court imposed guarantees of nonrepetition, ordering Brazil to develop a socioeconomic development program, especially for the population of Santo Antônio de Jesus, in coordination with the victims and their representatives.[50] The purpose of these measures was to provide better employment opportunities in the area and to prevent, eradicate, and penalize child labor.

Similarly, in *Miskito Divers*, the Court accepted the remedies previously agreed upon by Honduras and the representatives of the victims in their settlement agreement. In terms of structural measures, the State agreed to ensure the inclusion of Miskito divers and their families in existing social programs; to implement measures to ensure the adequate regulation, control, and supervision of the activities of industrial fishing companies in Miskito territory; and to strengthen the health and education systems in La Mosquitia. The parties' settlement, though, did not fully account for the Court's framing, in which private parties (in this case, the fishing companies) were a crucial part of the problem— and hence, part of the solution. Thus, following its framing of the case as a business and human rights issue, the Court brought the private party back to the picture by imposing direct obligations upon them as part of the remedies, and ordered that "businesses should adopt, at their own expense, preventive measures to protect the human rights of their workers, as well as measures aimed at preventing their activities from harming the communities in which they operate or on the environment."[51]

4.4. The Narrative of the Impact

Through the deployment of cognitive categories to define a particular "reality" of a problem, then diagnosing its causes, and finally proposing remedies, the IACtHR sets the narrative in reference to which its impact can be assessed. In each of these cases, the Court adopted orders that are subject to evaluation

---

[49] *Case of the Workers of the Fireworks Factory in Santo Antônio de Jesus and their families v. Brazil*, para. 287.
[50] Ibid., para. 298
[51] *Case of the Miskito Divers (Lemonth Morris et al.) v. Honduras*, paras. 42–53.

of compliance.[52] However, it is clear that each of these cases is often understood to have had an "impact" in the respective target State, beyond the (low) levels of compliance; for example, on Mexico's gender policy,[53] or on policies for preventing work accidents and treating diseases linked to dive fishing in Honduras.[54]

It is not possible to think about such an impact outside the Court's definition of the reality of the problem of the case, its causes, and the appropriate remedies—that is, outside the Court's narrative. In each of these cases, the Court deployed a particular set of cognitive categories and chose among a variety of possible frameworks and created a particular narrative for each case. In that narrative, the Court adopts a decision that is intended to affect the reality that the same Court defined as relevant—often by adopting remedies prescribed by the Court that are to tackle the causes of the problem, again as defined by the Court. The evaluation of "impact" only exists within such a narrative; that is, an evaluation of "impact" outside the basic narrative put forward by the Court (for example, by evaluating whether *Cotton Field* had an impact on, say, the environment) would seem nonsensical.

The Court is only one producer/user of narratives. While, as discussed earlier, its framings are particularly influential, it might be the case that other actors of the community of practice resist the Court's narrative and propose a different one. For example, it could happen that a case like *Cotton Field* could be framed to include violence against LGBTIQ+ people, or that a case like *Miskitos* could be framed in terms of Indigenous peoples or children's rights. The Court's decisions presented here, therefore, work as the baseline for discussing possible alternative framing, and hence possible alternative narratives. Each of these narratives will include its horizon of impact.

---

[52] The Inter-American Court of Human Rights monitors compliance with its orders. Levels of compliance can be reviewed at https://www.corteidh.or.cr/casos_en_supervision_por_pais.cfm.

[53] See Gloria de los Ángeles Suárez Escoffié, "Situación Actual de La Violencia de Género En México," in *Género, Derechos Humanos e Interseccionalidad*, ed. Andrea Carolina Subía and Seyedeh Sougand Hessamzadeh (Universidad de Otavalo 2021), 88–108.

[54] See "Reglamento de Seguridad y Salud Ocupacional de La Pesca Submarina Por Buceo," Pub. L. No. Acuerdo Nº STSS-577-2020 (2020). Considering this case is recent, the public act of acknowledgment of international responsibility took place on March 2023. The State started to work on a census of the situation of divers, the process for buying three hyperbaric chambers for the treatment of decompression syndrome, and a permanent office in Puerto Lempira to monitor the condition of divers and the various problems in the region. See "Buzos Miskitos: Autoridades Hondureñas Asumen Compromisos y Expresan Disculpas Ante Problemática de Buceo En La Región," CEJIL, https://cejil.org/comunicado-de-prensa/buzos-miskitos-autoridades-hondurenas-asumen-compromisos-y-expresan-disculpas-ante-problematica-de-buceo-en-la-region/ (accessed June 9, 2023).

5. Conclusion

Adopting a narrative mindset regarding the impact of the IACtHR implies shifting gears and focusing on cognitive processes. Narratives are necessary for organizing and controlling knowledge and have an impact on how and where interpretations take place in the community of practice. At the same time, the framing process determines how reality is grasped and described to participants of the community and those outside it.

Narratives are a potent way of describing reality. All participants of the community of practice, including the IACtHR, have the responsibility to consider the role and representation of those who have suffered human rights violations in the construction of such narratives. To do so, it seems important to begin by acknowledging the role of the participants of the community of practice in the creation of such a narrative. Denying the crucial role of narratives by appealing to an alleged objective "reality" of compliance risks obscuring the crucial cognitive works that are at play in human rights adjudication. It is crucial to strive for epistemic justice—that is, narratives should not become technocratic obstacles for recognition, justice, and reparations. The mobilization of the performative aspect of IAHRS narratives should consider first and foremost the dignity of the specific individuals that present their cases and their representation.

Of course, this is not the whole picture: the IAHRS's sole function is not to narrate events, and all of its activities cannot be reduced to their performative aspect. And yet, as this chapter shows, it is important to include such a narrative dimension in our vocabulary of "impact," as it has an effect on cognitive processes and potentially changes how reality is perceived. "Impact" is not a static fact but is rather a continuously evolving description of reality, performed by the community of human rights in Latin America—beyond the mere compliance with its specific orders.

PART II
IMPACT AND INTER-AMERICAN STANDARDS

II.1
Impact of the Inter-American Jurisprudence on Economic, Social, Cultural, and Environmental Rights

By Eduardo Ferrer Mac-Gregor

1. Introduction

The Inter-American jurisprudence relating to economic, social, cultural, and environmental rights (ESCER) is becoming an essential part of a *Ius Commune* in Latin America in the context of *transformative constitutionalism*[1] oriented toward human rights, the rule of law, and democracy, which is particularly important in the most unequal region in the world, with worrying rates of poverty and social exclusion.[2]

This chapter aims to characterize how this rich inventory of jurisprudence has been created and to analyze the various topics and how the judicial protection of ESCER has been carried out by the Inter-American Court of Human Rights (Inter-American Court, or IACtHR).[3] The chapter also aims at recognizing advances within the Organization of American States (OAS),[4] in particular the far-reaching work that the Inter-American Commission on Human Rights (Inter-American Commission, or IACHR) has achieved under its mandate, which in the last few years has been revitalized through the creation of the Special Rapporteurship on Economic, Social, Cultural, and Environmental Rights.[5]

---

[1] *Cf.* Armin von Bogdandy et al. (eds.), *Transformative Constitutionalism in Latin America. The Emergence of a New Ius Commune* (Oxford University Press 2017).

[2] See also recent annual reports of the Economic Commission for Latin America and the Caribbean (ECLAC), *Social Panorama of Latin America*, Santiago de Chile, United Nations, 2017, 2018, and 2019.

[3] The jurisprudence on ESCER evolves continuously. Since the conclusion of this article, the Inter-American Court has issued decisions that expand its precedents on Article 26 of the American Convention on Human Rights.

[4] For example, see the *Social Charter of the Americas*, approved by the OAS General Assembly in Cochabamba, Bolivia, in 2012, and the *Standards for the Preparation of Periodic Reports pursuant to Article 19 of the Protocol of San Salvador*, as well as the working group created to draft documents on progress indicators on the ESCER rights discussed in the said Protocol through a review of submitted national reports.

[5] In 2012, the Inter-American Commission agreed upon the creation of the *Unit on Economic, Social and Cultural Rights*. From 2014, this became the *Special Rapporteurship on Economic, Social,*

Thus, we will analyze the channels and settings within which the Inter-American Human Rights System has performed its supervisory function on ESCER through the connection with civil and political rights from 1999 to 2017. Subsequently, we will refer to ESCER's justiciability, which, according to the Additional Protocol to the American Convention on Human Rights in the area of Economic, Social, and Cultural Rights (Protocol of San Salvador), can be accomplished through the individual petitions' mechanism. In addition, we will address developments based on the precedents *Acevedo Buendía* (2009) and *Lagos del Campo* (2017), which marked a "before" and an "after" in this subject matter that had a profound impact on the Inter-American System. In relation to the direct justiciability of Article 26 of the American Convention on Human Rights (American Convention, or ACHR), we will address the following topics: the used identification methodology, the derived obligations of the State, and the rights and issues covered to date. Finally, we provide recent examples from the perspective of ensuring nonrecurrence through transformative impact.

2. The Protection of ESCER through Civil and Political Rights

The ACHR does not list ESCER expressly in its text. Like other international documents of the time,[6] the rights enshrined in the 1969 American Convention are the so-called "civil and political rights" or "rights of freedom." However, one of the differences between the ACHR and its contemporaneous European Convention on Human Rights[7] is that the former includes a general provision dedicated to economic, social, and cultural rights (Chapter III, Article 26). Albeit in 1988, the Protocol of San Salvador covered ESCER in a similar way to the provisions of the International Covenant on Economic, Social and Cultural Rights. The Protocol stated that only trade union rights and rights relating to education were subject to the system of direct individual petitions to the Inter-American Commission and, when applicable, the IACtHR.[8] These generated an interesting decades-long debate within the Inter-American System relating to

Cultural, and Environmental Rights (SRESCER), with the first Special Rapporteur being appointed in 2017.

[6] For example, the International Covenant on Civil and Political Rights and the European Convention on Human Rights.
[7] We should not forget that the African Charter on Human and Peoples' Rights was adopted in 1981.
[8] Art. 19.6 of the Additional Protocol to the American Convention on Human Rights in the Area of Economic, Social and Cultural Rights, concluded on November 17, 1998, and entering into force on November 16, 1999, having been signed, ratified, and acceded to by sixteen States parties by that date.

the interpretation of Article 26 of the American Convention on ESCER and were not considered justiciable through the mechanism of individual petitions in the Protocol of San Salvador.

The initial interpretative step of Article 26 took place in 1999 in the case of *Street Children (Villagrán Morales et al.) v. Guatemala*. The IACtHR analyzed violations not only from the perspective of the duty of the State to abstain from specific actions but also adding positive obligations (the duty to act or to guarantee a particular right). Although, in the case of *Street Children*, ESCER rights were not—strictly speaking—analyzed, and although the facts of the case did not concern this issue, the case established the bases for what would subsequently be called "positive obligations in relation to rights" in those cases where, given the particular circumstances, the State would be expected to take a series of actions to prevent the violation of rights.[9]

Based on this line of jurisprudence, for many years, the IACtHR applied the "connection theory" or "indirect justiciability by connectivity." In other words, the IACtHR would analyze ESCER indirectly, whereas finding States internationally responsible for the violation of civil and political rights enshrined in the ACHR.[10] One explicit example of this theory and how the IACtHR applied it can be found in the 2004 *Juvenile Reeducation Institute* case.[11] In this case, the IACtHR established:

> 149. The examination of the State's possible failure to comply with its obligations under Article 19 of the American Convention should take into account that the measures of which this provision speaks go well beyond the sphere of strictly civil and political rights. The measures that the State must undertake, particularly given the provisions of the Convention on the Rights of the Child, encompass economic, social and cultural aspects that pertain, first and foremost, to the children's right to life and right to humane treatment.

In this case, the representatives of the victims alleged that Article 26 of the American Convention had been violated. However, the IACtHR did not deem it necessary to pronounce upon the matter, considering that the issues pertaining to a life with dignity, health, and recreation had already been analyzed in the decision's section on the rights to life and personal integrity concerning the rights of the child.[12]

---

[9] In general, the IACtHR indicated that failure to act on the part of the State impacted upon standards for a "dignified life." *Case of the Street Children (Villagrán Morales et al.) v. Guatemala* [1999] IACtHR, Ser. C No. 63, para. 191.
[10] *Cf. Case of the "Juvenile Reeducation Institute" v. Paraguay* [2004] IACtHR, Ser. C No. 112.
[11] *Cf. Case of the "Juvenile Reeducation Institute" v. Paraguay* [2004] IACtHR, Ser. C No. 112.
[12] Ibid., para. 255.

In the period between 1999 and 2017, the IACtHR applied the connection theory through three major strands:[13] (a) via substantive rights (such as the right to life and personal integrity); (b) via procedural rights[14] (such as legal safeguards, the right to an effective remedy, and the right to access information); and (c) via the right to equality and nondiscrimination (particularly with regard to the obligations in Articles 1.1 and 24 of the ACHR).

The IACtHR applied the connection theory mentioned above in three different scenarios: (a) toward direct allegations relating to Article 26 of the ACHR, whether on the part of the Inter-American Commission or by representatives of the victims; (b) toward acts relating to vulnerable groups; and (c) in those cases in which, through rereading the decisions made by the Inter-American Court between 1999 and 2017, it was possible to derive the content of certain ESCER. It is worth noting that only in the case of scenarios "a" and "b" did a classification take place concerning the three manners in which indirect connectivity was applied (via procedural rights, substantive rights, or via rights of equality and nondiscrimination); in the case of scenario "c", a different classification was chosen since the specifics of the cases required a different approach.

2.1. Indirect Justiciability of Cases in Which a Violation of Article 26 Was Alleged

2.1.1. Substantive Rights

With regard to the first scenario and the application of substantive rights, we find cases such as the case of the *Juvenile Reeducation Institute v. Paraguay* from 2004 and the case of the (year) *Girls Yean and Bosico v. Dominican Republic* from 2005 concerning the alleged violation of the right of two girls to education. In the latter, the IACtHR found that the facts characterized a violation of the rights of the children to juridical personality (Article 3 of the ACHR) and to a name (Article 18 of the ACHR), as a result of which—since they had no identity documents—they were not able to access primary education.[15] It must also be noted that this was all associated—like in the 2004 *Juvenile Reeducation Institute* case—with Article 19 of the ACHR interpreted in accordance with the 1989 UN Convention on the Rights of the Child. With regard to the Indigenous communities in the cases of *Yakye Axa* (2005) and *Sarayaku* (2012), both against

---

[13] See also Tara Melish, *Protecting Economic, Social, and Cultural Rights in the Inter-American Human Rights System: A Manual on Presenting Claims* (Orville H. Schell, Jr. Center for International Human Rights, Yale University and the Center for Economic and Social Rights 2003).

[14] Similarly, in Advisory Opinion No. 23, the IACtHR identified procedural rights such as the right to access information.

[15] *Cf. The case of the Girls Yean and Bosico v. Dominican Republic* [2005] IACtHR, Ser. C No. 130, paras. 175, 185.

Paraguay, the IACtHR subsumed the alleged violations relating to the right to health, education, housing, and food (in the first case) and to the right to culture (in the second case) under the right to a dignified life and the right to personal integrity.

2.1.2. Procedural Rights

With regard to the focal point of procedural rights, we encounter the cases of *Five Pensioners* (2003), *Acevedo-Jaramillo et al.* (2006), *Dismissed Congressional Employees* (2006), and *Acevedo Buendía et al.* (2009), all against Peru, where the IACtHR found Peru internationally responsible mainly for the violation of procedural rights relating to legal safeguards—failure to execute domestic judgments guaranteeing the right to an adjustable pension, which by association affects the right to property and the enforcement of sentences (Articles 21 and 25.2.c of the ACHR).

In addition, the IACtHR stated that the long passage of time could affect certain social rights, thus declaring a violation of the right to a hearing within a reasonable time as per Article 8.1 of the American Convention. In this type of case, the IACtHR has applied the guiding principle that exceptional due diligence was required in the handling of cases due to what was at stake, "given that the victims were persons in a vulnerable situation," as occurred in the case of *Furlan et al. v. Argentina* (2012)[16] and *Gonzales Lluy et al. v. Ecuador* (2015).[17]

2.2. Indirect Justiciability in Cases Relating to Groups in a Position of Vulnerability

2.2.1. Substantive Rights

Regarding most cases pertaining to the second scenario, that is, cases dealing with groups in positions of vulnerability, the application of connectivity via substantive rights prevails. Although technically, the IACtHR adopted this approach for the first time in the case of the *Juvenile Reeducation Institute*, it was in the case of *Ximenes Lopes v. Brazil* (2006) that the Inter-American Court expressed particular concern with the vulnerability of certain groups and their enjoyment of ESCER, referring to the circumstances in which a person might find himself or herself in such a situation of vulnerability (whether due to their personal

---

[16] In this case, the Inter-American Tribunal declared that the right to a hearing within a reasonable time (Article 8.1 of the ACHR) had been violated due to the excessive duration of the processing of damages, which would have enabled the victim to access the rehabilitation required for her disability.

[17] The Court found that the delay in concluding criminal proceedings (which, in accordance with Ecuadorian law, was required to establish responsibility for the payment of damages in civil proceedings) had an impact on the life (health) of the victim, since she was a child and was living with HIV in poor economic conditions.

condition or due to a specific situation).[18] In this way, the IACtHR protected the rights of Indigenous communities,[19] conditions of people deprived of their liberty,[20] the rights of migrants,[21] the rights of persons with a disability,[22] and the rights of persons in a situation of poverty.[23]

2.2.2. Procedural Rights

In *Claude Reyes et al. v. Chile* (2006), the IACtHR used the right of access to information to protect the right to the environment indirectly.[24] Equally, in the case of *I.V. v. Bolivia* (2016), access to sexual and reproductive health was addressed in terms of the right to access information (informed consent).[25]

2.2.3. Equality and Nondiscrimination

With regard to equality and nondiscrimination, the IACtHR has ruled cases where it drew upon the clauses of equality and nondiscrimination enshrined in Articles 1.1. and 24 of the American Convention. In particular, the IACtHR has reiterated its jurisprudence that while the nondiscrimination clause contained in Article 1.1 (self-contained clause) is violated through the discriminatory infringement of any provision of the American Convention, Article 24 is violated if a domestic regulation is applied in a differentiated manner without objective

---

[18] *Case of Ximenes Lopes v. Brazil* [2006] IACtHR, Ser. C No. 149, para. 103.

[19] For example, in the cases of the *Sawhoyamaxa* and *Xákmok Kásek* communities, the Court subsumed the content of rights such as the right to education, health, housing, food, and water under the content of the right to a dignified life.

[20] See also the following cases among others: *Montero-Aranguren et al. (Detention Center of Catia) v. Venezuela*, *Pacheco Teruel et al. v. Honduras*, and *Mendoza et al. v. Argentina*. In such situations, the IACtHR evaluated, through Articles 4 and 5 of the ACHR, conditions relating to health, food, and water, for example.

[21] For example, in the cases of *Vélez Loor v. Panama* and *Nadege Dorzema et al. v. Dominican Republic*, the IACtHR analyzed the lack of medical attention suffered by the victims in these cases during their time in the custody of the State. In the referenced cases, the IACtHR connected the content of the right to health with the content of the right to personal integrity.

[22] In the case of *Chinchilla Sandoval et al. v. Guatemala*, the IACtHR analyzed the impact of insufficient medical attention, resulting in the victim's acquisition of a physical limitation while deprived of her liberty. In this case, the content of the right to health of a person deprived of her liberty was analyzed from the particular point of view of the content of the right to life and to personal integrity.

[23] In the case of the *Hacienda Brasil Verde Workers v. Brazil*, the IACtHR declared that Article 6 (Freedom from Slavery) of the American Convention had been violated since it found that the working conditions were comparable with contemporary forms of slavery.

[24] In the case of *Claude Reyes*, in the light of the State's refusal to furnish the victims of the case with all of the information they required in relation to a deforestation project that was to take place in Chile and that could be harmful to the environment, the Inter-American Tribunal ruled that the violated right was the right to access information as per Article 13 of the American Convention.

[25] In the case of *I.V. v. Bolivia*, the IACtHR discussed the violation of the right to sexual and reproductive health of the victim through the State obligation of active transparency. In this case, the referenced allegation was associated with the violation of the content of the parameters that must be used when obtaining informed consent in medical practice.

or reasonable justification.[26] Furthermore, we should point out that in those cases, the IACtHR developed the notions of "suspect categories" and "conditions of vulnerability," which single out groups that enjoy enhanced protection under IAHRS standards.[27]

In certain cases, the application of domestic regulations discriminates who is entitled to access certain social rights and who is not, as in the case of the regulation of social security in which same-sex couples are often deprived of such a right.[28] The IACtHR has used this approach to assess similar situations related to the enjoyment of sexual and reproductive rights, such as in the case of *Artavia Murillo et al. v. Costa Rica* (2012), where the IACtHR pronounced a judgment of "indirect discrimination" that took into account the victim's disability, gender, and financial situation in a context of general prohibition of in vitro fertilization in Costa Rica.[29]

2.3. Cases Subject to the "Rereading" of ESCER from 1999 to 2017

This section addresses a series of cases in which the categories mentioned previously, and their subclassifications are not applicable. Instead, the section focuses on the "rereading" of the categories explored previously under an ESCER language. According to this perspective, we can identify three degrees in which the IACtHR recognizes ESCER in several thematic threads: (a) rights from an ESCER perspective; (b) rights with a certain degree of social rights; and (c) emerging phenomena that involve ESCER.

The first of the aforementioned thematic threads that the jurisprudence of the IACtHR has addressed is the right to work in the context of the dismissal of judges.[30] Furthermore, in cases of sexual violence, the IACtHR has addressed—albeit not explicitly—standards relating to women's sexual and reproductive

---

[26] Cf. *Proposed Amendments to the Naturalization Provision of the Constitution of Costa Rica* [1984], Advisory Opinion OC-4/84, Ser. A No. 4, paras. 53, 54, and the case of *Ramírez Escobar et al. v. Guatemala* [2018] IACtHR, Ser. C No. 351, para. 272.
[27] For example, with regard to disability, sexual orientation, and asylum.
[28] In the case of *Duque v. Colombia*, the IACtHR found that the State had not presented an objective and reasonable justification for the restriction established in Law 54 of 1990 and Decree 1889 of 1994 based on sexual orientation for access to a survivor's pension, thus violating Article 24 of the ACHR.
[29] Cf. *Case of Artavia Murillo et al. (In Vitro Fertilization) v. Costa Rica* [2012] IACtHR, Ser. C No. 257, paras. 288–317.
[30] See also (among others): *Case of Reverón Trujillo v. Venezuela* [2009] IACtHR, Ser. C No. 197; *Case of Chocrón Chocrón v. Venezuela* [2011] IACtHR, Ser. C No. 227; *Case of the Constitutional Tribunal (Camba Campos et al.) v. Ecuador. Preliminary Objections* [2013] IACtHR, Ser. C No. 268; and *Case of the Supreme Court of Justice (Quintana Coello et al.) v. Ecuador. Preliminary Objection* [2013] IACtHR, Ser. C No. 266.

health.[31] In cases concerning Indigenous communities (specifically the ones regarding the lack of prior consultation), other elements beyond communal property have been protected.[32] Finally, in another thread of cases that includes medical malpractice cases, the IACtHR defined rights based on the settings in which the events occurred.[33]

In a second group, we encounter cases where the victims were trade unionists seeking protection under Article 16 (Freedom of Association) of the American Convention.[34] Although, in these cases, the IACtHR did not find that States violated Article 8.1.a of the Protocol of San Salvador, which protects freedom of association in that instrument, these judgments referred to the Article 8.1.a provision of the Protocol of San Salvador. Moreover, the case of the *Río Negro Massacres v. Guatemala* (2012) dealt with the violation of the right of Maya Achí communities to "bury the dead" by association with Article 12 (Freedom of Conscience and Religion) of the ACHR.[35] In this sense, the religiousness of the Mayan communities can be considered a form of cultural manifestation; however, the IACtHR did not judge the case based on the right to culture; instead, it linked the right "to bury the dead" with the right to personal integrity and the right to religion.

Finally, regarding the third category, we can refer, on the one hand, to the macro phenomena involving the violation of various ESCER and, on the other, to cases where the violations observed have impacted a vulnerable group. Regarding the first scenario, some cases relating to massacres have also addressed forced internal displacement. In such cases, the inter-American jurisprudence has focused its analysis on the infringement of the freedom of movement (Article 22 of the ACHR). However, national jurisprudence indicates that, for example, the phenomenon of forced internal displacement is associated with a violation of social rights such as the right to education, work, health, and food.[36]

In some of these cases concerning forced internal displacement, such as *Yarce et al.* (2016) and *Vereda la Esperanza* (2017), both against the State of Colombia, the IACtHR took into account the damages caused to the homes of some of the

---

[31] See also (among others): *Case of Fernández Ortega et al. v. Mexico* [2010] IACtHR, Ser. C No. 215; *Case of Rosendo Cantú et al. v. Mexico* [2010] IACtHR, Ser. C No. 216; *Case of V.R.P., V.P.C. et al. v. Nicaragua* [2018] IACtHR, Ser. C No. 350.

[32] See also (among others): *Case of the Saramaka People v. Suriname* [2007] IACtHR, Ser. C No. 172; *Case of the Garífuna Punta Piedra Community and its Members v. Honduras* [2015] IACtHR, Ser. C No. 304; *Case of the Kaliña and Lokono Peoples v. Suriname* [2015] IACtHR, Ser. C No. 309.

[33] *Case of Suárez Peralta v. Ecuador* [2013] IACtHR, Ser. C No. 261; *Case of Albán Cornejo et al. v. Ecuador* [2007] IACtHR, Ser. C No. 171.

[34] See also, for example: *Case of Huilca Tecse v. Peru* [2005] IACtHR, Ser. C No. 121, and *Case of Baena Ricardo et al. v. Panama* [2001] IACtHR, Ser. C No. 72.

[35] Cf. *Case of the Río Negro Massacres v. Guatemala* [2012] IACtHR, Ser. C No. 250, para. 155.

[36] In this respect, see the decision of the Constitutional Court of Colombia: T-025/2004.

victims through Article 21 of the ACHR (Right to Property). Regarding the second scenario, the impact of violations of the rights of a vulnerable group, the case of *Florencio Chitay Nech v. Guatemala* (2010) showed that the forced disappearance of the victim influenced the displacement suffered by some of his family members and, in particular, caused the disruption of the cultural life of his children, since their displacement resulted in the impossibility of rekindling their cultural practices.

3. Direct Justiciability via the Protocol of San Salvador

As already mentioned, the Protocol of San Salvador grants direct justiciability to victims of trade union rights and the right to education. With regard to the former, although the IACtHR has not so far declared the violation of trade union rights as covered by the Protocol of San Salvador in an individual case, in its Advisory Opinion No. 22 on the *Entitlement of legal entities to hold rights under the Inter-American Human Rights System*, the IACtHR found that "those rights are afforded to trade unions, federations and confederations, given that they represent their members and seek to safeguard and protect their rights and interests,"[37] meaning that the IACtHR could eventually declare a violation of the trade union rights of both physical persons and legal entities.

With regard to the right to education, in the case of *Gonzales Lluy et al.*, the IACtHR declared that Ecuador was responsible for the violation of this right as provided by the Protocol of San Salvador. In the case in question, the IACtHR recognized that the victim had been expelled from school and denied entry to other schools because of the discrimination suffered by the victim due to her condition as HIV positive which, according to her teachers, imposed a risk to the other students. As a result, the victim suffered intersectional discrimination due to her condition as a person with a disability (social attitude barriers), but also for her condition as a female, a child, and because of her economic status.[38] In 2020, in the case of *Guzmán Abarracín et al. v. Ecuador*, the IACtHR again declared that the right to education as per Article 13 of the Protocol of San Salvador had been violated when determining the right of the victim, as a female and a child, to a life free from sexual violence in the educational sphere.[39]

---

[37] *Entitlement of Legal Entities to Hold Rights under the Inter-American Human Rights System.* Advisory Opinion OC-22/16 of February 26, 2016. Ser. A No. 22, para. 97.
[38] *Case of Gonzales Lluy at al. v. Ecuador* [2015] IACtHR, Ser. C No. 298, para. 290.
[39] *Case of Guzmán Albarracín et al. v. Ecuador* [2020] IACtHR, Ser. C No. 405.

4. The New Model of Direct Justiciability

4.1. A Chronicle of ESCER's Direct Justiciability through Article 26

The IACtHR's jurisprudence on the direct justiciability of ESCER began with the case of the *Five Pensioners v. Peru* (2003).[40] However, the landmark case in this area was the case of *Acevedo Buendía et al.* (2009), also against Peru. In this latter case, although the IACtHR did not establish the violation of Article 26 of the American Convention (in this case, the violation of the right to a leveled pension was alleged), the IACtHR restated its jurisdiction over Article 26[41] as well as the interdependence between civil and political rights and economic, social, and cultural rights. The IACtHR also recognized the progressive development of and the nonregression obligation associated with such rights, which could be claimed before competent human rights bodies called upon to resolve potential violations of human rights.[42]

In the cases of *Furlan et al. v. Argentina* (2012) and *Suárez Peralta et al. v. Ecuador* (2014),[43] the IACtHR resumed the debate over the direct justiciability of ESCER through Article 26 of the American Convention,[44] both cases concerning the right to health and based on the *Acevedo Buendía* precedent. In the cases *Canales Huapaya et al. v. Peru* and *Gonzales Lluy et al. v. Ecuador*, both from 2016, the IACtHR considered the possibility of direct justiciability of the right to work and the right to health, respectively. The IACtHR used these cases to revitalize its argumentative threads on the topic. In particular, it is worth highlighting that, in the case of *Gonzales Lluy*, the IACtHR declared that the right to education had been autonomously violated through the Protocol of San Salvador. As such, the Inter-American Court's interpretation pointed toward the possible materialization of the justiciability of ESCER.

---

[40] It should be noted that the Inter-American Commission on Human Rights had already issued judgments on ESCER before the IACtHR was asked to rule on this case. For example, the *Case of the Yanomami Community v. Brazil* [1985] Case No. 7615, Resolution No. 12/85, *Case of Jorge Odir Miranda Cortez v. El Salvador* [2009] Case No. 12.249, Admissibility Report No. 29/01, *Case of Amilcar Menéndez, Juan Manuel Caride et al. v. Argentina* [2001] Case No. 11.67, Report No. 03/01, and *Case of Milton García Fajardo et al. v. Nicaragua* [2000] Report No. 100/01, Case No. 11.381.

[41] *Case of Acevedo Buendía et al. ("Discharged and Retired Employees of the Office of the Comptroller") v. Peru* [2009] IACtHR, Ser. C No. 198, paras. 12–19, 97.

[42] Cf. *Case of Acevedo Buendía et al. ("Discharged and Retired Employees of the Office of the Comptroller") v. Peru* [2009] IACtHR, Ser. C No. 198, paras. 101–103.

[43] This case, which addressed medical malpractice, expressed the need to declare a violation of the right to health via Article 26 of the American Convention, illustrating various interpretative options and their implications. See also my Concurring Opinion in the *Case of Suárez Peralta v. Ecuador*, para. 27.

[44] In this respect, see the opinions given in the cases in question.

A series of later cases and the opinions given by the judges between 2016 and 2017[45] provided a fertile argumentative background against which the IACtHR, in 2017, decided that ESCER could be directly justiciable via Article 26 of the ACHR.

4.2. The Case of *Lagos del Campo* Approach

The first time that the IACtHR declared a direct violation of Article 26 of the ACHR was in the case of *Lagos del Campo v. Peru*, from 2017, where the IACtHR sought to protect the right to employment stability and the right of workers to associate themselves freely for the defense and promotion of their interests (via a combination of Articles 16 and 26 of the American Convention). In this case, the Inter-American Court reiterated the existing interdependence and indivisibility between civil and political rights and economic, social, and cultural rights since they *should be understood comprehensively and collectively, without any hierarchy, and enforceable in all cases before the competent authority.*[46]

Since then, the IACtHR has declared the violation of ESCER based on Article 26 in eleven contentious cases and has referred to it explicitly in one advisory opinion. To give an overview of the general aspects of Article 26's direct justiciability, in the following we briefly discuss the methodology used to determine the content of Article 26 and the set of mandatory obligations associated with the analysis of ESCER cases as well as the topics and rights that have been addressed to date. We also provide examples of the reparations that have been ordered.

4.2.1. Methodology

In general, the IACtHR has applied the following four methodological steps: (a) the identification of the standards contained in the Charter of the Organization of American States (Charter of the OAS), (b) the verification of whether the right is covered by the American Declaration of the Rights and Duties of Man, (c) the verification of the existence of the right in national and international *corpus iuris*, and (d) the verification of whether the right is recognized in the domestic system. To a great extent, this methodology has been limited by the content of Article 29 of the ACHR through the application of Sections b, c, and d of said article.[47]

---

[45] In the cases of *Chinchilla Sandoval et al. v. Guatemala*, *I.V. v. Bolivia*, *Yarce et al. v. Colombia*, and *Vereda la Esperanza v. Colombia*.

[46] *Cf. Case of Lagos del Campo v. Peru* [2017] IACtHR, Ser. C No. 340, para. 141.

[47] The article in question states the following: "Article 29. Restrictions Regarding Interpretation. No provisions of this Convention shall be interpreted as: [. . .]; b. restricting the enjoyment or exercise of any right or freedom recognized by virtue of the laws of any State Party or by virtue of another convention to which one of the said states is a party; c. precluding other rights or guarantees that are inherent in the human personality or derived from representative democracy as a form of

According to the mandate established in Article 26 of the American Convention, initially, the IACtHR must determine whether the provision of Article 26 covers a specific ESCER. At this first step, it is necessary to assess whether the ESCER—as Article 26 requires—makes a direct reference to the Charter of the OAS insofar as the rights are derived from economic and social norms and norms relating to education, science, and culture.

The second step is to refer to the 1948 American Declaration of the Rights and Duties of Man (American Declaration). According to the argument of the IACtHR in its Advisory Opinion OC-10/89 that "the member states of the Organization have signaled their agreement that the Declaration contains and defines the fundamental human rights referred to in the Charter. Thus the Charter of the Organization cannot be interpreted and applied as far as human rights are concerned without relating its norms, consistent with the practice of the organs of the OAS, to the corresponding provisions of the Declaration."[48]

Thirdly, the Inter-American Court stated that, to define *the content of the right*, it is also important to turn to other international instruments for the protection of human rights, including the Protocol of San Salvador itself, as well as other "general" treaties (such as the International Covenant on Economic, Social and Cultural Rights) or treaties concerning certain vulnerable groups (such as the UN Convention on the Elimination of All Forms of Discrimination against Women, the UN Convention on the Rights of the Child, and the UN Convention on the Rights of Persons with Disabilities). It is noteworthy that the IACtHR has also drawn upon *soft law* when determining what comprises part of the *international corpus iuris*.[49] Furthermore, the IACtHR has taken into consideration whether the right in question is recognized by a domestic constitution.

4.2.2. Obligations of the State

Similarly to the rights covered by Articles 3 to 25 of the American Convention, the IACtHR has indicated that the general obligations to respect and guarantee rights contained in Article 1 and the adaptation of domestic law stipulated in Article 2 of the American Convention also apply to ESCER. Likewise, the nondiscrimination clause in Article 1.1 should be taken into account. Furthermore, the Court has stated that three types of obligations can be identified

---

government; or d. excluding or limiting the effect that the American Declaration of the Rights and Duties of Man and other international acts of the same nature may have."

[48] *Interpretation of the American Declaration of the Rights and Duties of Man in the context of Article 64 of the American Convention on Human Rights* [1989], Advisory Opinion, OC-10/89, Ser. A No. 10, para. 43.
[49] For example, in the case of the *Lhaka Honhat*, the IACtHR took into account—as part of international law—the UN Declaration on the Rights of Indigenous Peoples and the American Declaration on the Rights of Indigenous Peoples.

as a manifestation of the special features of ESCER: (a) obligations of immediate enforceability, (b) the obligation of progressive development, and (c) the obligation to prevent regression.

In the case of the first type, the content of these obligations are associated with requirements that, *in themselves*, do not require economic resources, such as the prohibition of discrimination.[50] As for the *obligation of progressive development*, the Court has interpreted this obligation as the gradual advancement of a right—taking available resources into account—in order to achieve the full realization of that right. Because this obligation implies action, it can be considered a projection of the general obligation to guarantee rights. Finally, the *obligation of nonregression* means that the State must refrain from actions that might damage the achieved level of enjoyment of a right. This obligation implies a duty to refrain from action, which classifies regression prevention as an obligation to respect rights.[51]

4.2.3. Rights and Topics Addressed[52]
4.2.3.1. Right to Work

The first three cases that the IACtHR resolved by recognizing the direct justiciability of ESCER via Article 26 of the ACHR concerned different aspects of the right to work. The first of these cases, the case of *Lagos del Campo v. Peru* (2017), was set in a context of work relationships between private individuals. In this case, the IACtHR declared that the dismissal of the victim due to complaints he had made within the company where he worked was not justified. In this regard, the IACtHR also found that, among other things, the victim's defense arguments were not adequately examined and that this flaw was not remedied by the various attempts of recourses, including a writ of amparo in which the judge did not examine Mr. Lagos del Campo's allegations on substantive rights under the justification that the matter was *res iudicata*. In its turn, the IACtHR declared that the State had violated Articles 8.1 and 25.1 of the ACHR concerning Article 1.1 of the ACHR. In this case, when the IACtHR protected the right to stability

---

[50] In this sense, for example, the preceding interpretation of the IACtHR reflects to a great extent the stipulations of General Comment No. 3 of the ESCER Committee and has been reiterated in various subsequent general comments.

[51] Even though, in the case of *Acevedo Buendía et al.*, the IACtHR conceived the notion of progressive development and of the prohibition of regression—greatly inspired by the General Comment of the ESCER Committee—it was not until the case of *Cuscul Pivaral et al.* that the actual content was developed and applied to a specific case. In particular, see paras. 147, 148.

[52] In addition to the cases mentioned in this section, the IACtHR has found a violation of Article 26 of the ACHR in many subsequent cases (2021–2023). It has also recognized the justiciability of the rights to freedom of association, collective bargaining, and strike (Advisory Opinion OC-27/21), as well as the rights to health, water, food, and culture (Advisory Opinion OC-29/22). There is also a highly relevant environmental case on the agenda of the IACtHR (*La Oroya v. Peru*), as well as two advisory opinions on climate emergency and human rights (requested by Chile and Colombia) and on the right to health care (requested by Argentina).

of employment due to the lack of justification for Mr. Lagos del Campo's dismissal, it did so from a perspective of the State's obligation to guarantee that legal remedies protect substantive rights such as, in this case, the right to work.[53]

Some months later, the IACtHR again declared the violation of Article 26 of the ACHR in the case of the *Dismissed Employees of Petroperu et al. v. Peru* (2017). Unlike in the case of *Lagos del Campo*, this time, the IACtHR found that the victims were dismissed by the public sector. In addition, and similar to *Lagos del Campo*, the IACtHR found a lack of judicial response to the unfair dismissals of the victims, analyzing the right from the perspective of an obligation to guarantee rights.[54]

Subsequently, the IACtHR examined the dismissal of the three victims for political discrimination reasons in the case of *San Miguel Sosa et al. v. Venezuela* (2018) (specifically because they had signed the recall petition against the then President Hugo Chávez). In this case—unlike in the previous ones—the IACtHR found that the violations observed in the sentence (particularly the discrimination due to political views and the impact on political rights) "had a shared operative event," that being the dismissal of the three victims from the public sector.[55]

In 2020, the IACtHR pronounced a judgment in the cases of *Spoltore v. Argentina* (2020) and *Employees of the Santo Antônio de Jesus Fireworks Factory and their Family Members v. Brazil* (2020), which dealt with another aspect of the right to work, related to the right to just and favorable conditions of work. The first case addressed how the delay in labor proceedings impacted the victim and his access to justice, aiming to win damages for an alleged occupational disease. The case analysis considered the State's acceptance of its responsibility on the delay in legal proceedings and the fact that the victim had a disability.

The second case, concerning an explosion at a fireworks factory in which mainly women and children died or were injured, focused on the substantial and obligational content of the "just and favorable conditions" that ensured the "safety, health, and hygiene conditions at work." In its sentence, the IACtHR held the State internationally responsible since the events occurred without the State's "*monitoring or scrutiny* with the intention of verifying the *working conditions* of those working at the fireworks factory and without any action to *prevent accidents* despite the activity conducted at the factory being classified by the regulations as especially dangerous."[56]

---

[53] *Cf. Case of Lagos del Campo v. Peru* [2017] IACtHR, Ser. C No. 340, paras. 141–154.

[54] *Cf. Case of Dismissed Employees of Petroperu et al. v. Peru* [2017] IACtHR, Ser. C No. 344, para. 193.

[55] *Cf. Case of San Miguel Sosa et al. v. Venezuela* [2018] IACtHR, Ser. C No. 348, paras. 108–109.

[56] This case is also important in the context of the topic of businesses and human rights. In this respect, see the *United Nations Guiding Principles on Businesses and Human Rights* [2011], UN Doc. A/HRC/17/31, and IACHR/SRESCER, *Report on Business and Human Rights: Inter-American Standards* [2019], OAS/Ser.L/V/II IACHR/SRESCER/REP.1/19.

4.2.3.2. Right to Health
The first case in which the IACtHR ruled that the right to health had been violated was the case of *Poblete Vilches et al. v. Chile* (2018). The Inter-American Court analyzed the violation of *obligations of immediate effect* in the light of the urgent situation faced by Mr. Poblete when admitted to a public Chilean hospital in two occasions. The IACtHR found that his right to health was also violated due to the failure in obtaining the consent of a representative on his behalf and added that rights such as the right to access information are rights which, in the presence of a social right, can change from a right to a guarantee in order to embody the social right in question—in this case, the right to health of Mr. Vinicio Poblete.[57]

The second case in which the IACtHR declared a violation of the right to health was *Cuscul Pivaral et al. v. Guatemala* (2018). In this case, the right to health was examined in a context where forty-nine people were living or had lived with HIV and in association with attacks on the personal integrity of their family members. In this case, the IACtHR examined the right to health based on two main strands: the lack of medical care and the impact that insufficient healthcare had in the case of pregnant women with HIV. The sentence broke down the analysis of the first issue into two time periods: before and after 2004. In the first period, the IACtHR found that, given that before 2004 the State had not provided treatment despite the existence of domestic legislation ordering it to do so, the obligation of progressive development covered by Article 26 of the ACHR had been violated due to inaction on the part of the State. After 2004, on the other hand, when the State began to provide medical treatment to patients with HIV, the Inter-American Court found that essential and interrelated elements of the right to health had not been guaranteed (i.e., accessibility, availability, acceptability, and quality). Regarding the impact of insufficient healthcare for pregnant women with HIV, the IACtHR analyzed the referenced violation from a perspective of intersectional discrimination due to the coexistence of various factors since some of the women were not given treatments to prevent the transmission of HIV to their children.[58]

Finally, in the case of *Hernández v. Argentina* (2019), the Court held the State internationally responsible because it had not guaranteed adequate medical attention to Mr. Hernández for conditions associated with his tuberculosis whilst deprived of his liberty; even after his mother's complaints and court orders (which were not adequately executed) requiring the State's prompt attention in order to protect the victim's right.[59]

---

[57] *Cf. Case of Poblete Vilches et al. v. Chile* [2018] IACtHR, Ser. C No. 349, paras. 100 et seq.
[58] *Cf. Case of Cuscul Pivaral et al. v. Guatemala* [2018] IACtHR, Ser. C No. 359, paras. 103 et seq.
[59] *Cf. Case of Hernández v. Argentina* [2019] IACtHR, Ser. C No. 395, paras. 62 et seq.

4.2.3.3. Right to Social Security

In the case of *Muelle Flores v. Peru* (2019), the IACtHR analyzed the impact of the failure to execute two amparo judgments that recognized the right of the victim. This constituted a violation of the obligation to guarantee the right in question. The IACtHR found that the failure of the State to execute the judgments represented not only an impact of "alimentary and income-substituting nature" but also a violation of the victim's right to dignity and personal integrity.[60] The case of the *National Association of Discharged and Retired Employees of the National Superintendence of Tributary Administration (ANCEJUB-SUNAT) v. Peru* (2019) was analyzed similarly, with the difference that this case involved the right to a pension of 598 people.[61]

4.2.3.4. Right to a Healthy Environment

In Advisory Opinion No. 23, the IACtHR declared that the right to a healthy environment could be understood as a justiciable right under Article 26 of the American Convention. Further, it also stipulated that the obligations of respect, guarantee, and nondiscrimination applied when interpreting this right content. The IACtHR added that given the relationship between the right to a healthy environment and other rights, certain rights are vulnerable to environmental degradation (such as the right to life, personal integrity, and health) and that some rights have an instrumental nature when it comes to guaranteeing the right to a healthy environment (such as the right to access information and the right to political participation).[62]

The Court found that the right to a healthy environment was also violated in the *Case of the Community of Lhaka Honhat v. Argentina*, which is addressed in the following section due to its implications for other rights.

4.2.3.5. The Right of Indigenous Peoples to Land and ESCER (Food, Environment, Water, and Cultural Identity)

The case of the *Community of Lhaka Honhat v. Argentina* (2020) is worthy of special attention since the IACtHR found that various ESCER protected by Article 26 of the American Convention were jointly violated in the case.

We should highlight two differences with regard to previous cases related to Indigenous peoples, where the Inter-American Court subsumed the protection of ESCER under the content of the right to collective property. First, in the *Lhaka Honhat* case, an implicit distinction was made between "land" and "territory."

---

[60] Cf. *Case of Muelle Flores v. Peru* [2019] IACtHR, Ser. C No. 375, paras. 167 et seq.
[61] Cf. *Case of the National Association of Discharged and Retired Employees of the National Superintendence of Tributary Administration (ANCEJUB-SUNAT) v. Peru* [2019] IACtHR, Ser. C No. 394, paras. 151 et seq.
[62] See OC-23/17, *The Environment and Human Rights*, November 15, 2017.

· Secondly, the right to the territory was protected explicitly via Article 26 of the American Convention, declaring and refining—for the first time in a contentious case—the rights to a healthy environment, adequate food, water, and cultural identity.

Regarding the first aspect, one of the prior limitations in this matter was that the violation of rights linked with the territory (for example, the right to water) was confined to the concept of "land," therefore attached to a notion of production. Although the IACtHR had already indicated that the concept of *lands* must also include the concept of *territories*, this subsumption of concepts meant that when the international responsibility was determined, the remedies were restricted to the restitution of "land" or were aimed at rectifying possible shortfalls in previous consultation processes. In the case of *Lhaka Honhat*, the IACtHR found a violation of the right to property in Article 21 of the American Convention because the guarantee of the right to communal property was insufficient since the State did not implement adequate mechanisms for titling and demarcation, thus failing to guarantee the right of communal ownership.

Concerning the second aspect, which is concerned with the protection of the social, cultural, and environmental rights of the territory via Article 26 of the American Convention, the IACtHR isolated the elements that it had previously subsumed under the concept of communal property to give substance to and individualize violations of the said rights.

It is worth noting that this would not have been possible without the jurisprudence on the separate and direct justiciability of ESCER that the IACtHR has developed since the case of *Lagos del Campo*. The separate violation of concerning social, cultural, and environmental rights was alleged by the representatives of the victims in their petition to the IACtHR, invoking the precedents of the Court in this area with respect to labor rights and the right to health, to a healthy environment, and to social security mentioned previously. Similarly, the numerous *amicus curiae* briefs presented in the case, some of which linked direct justiciability to the United Nations' 2030 Agenda and its objectives for sustainable development, are also important. Thus, in *Lhaka Honhat*, a series of relevant precedents already existed, supporting the separate analysis of civil and political rights and ESCER.

As well as declaring the separate violation of the rights to participate in cultural life (in relation to cultural identity), a healthy environment, and sufficient food and water and giving substance to these rights, from our standpoint the IACtHR addressed the actual magnitude of the violations suffered by members of these peoples and communities, being considered collective subjects with rights, when they cannot fully dispose of and use the land and the elements linked with the territory (natural resources). All in all, this interpretation constitutes a holistic vision when it comes to the protection of Indigenous peoples' rights.

4.2.4. Reparation Measures

Among reparation measures, those aiming to prevent similar events from perpetuating the violation of rights stand out. To that end, it is important to highlight certain reparations cases that aim to have a transformative impact in ESCER.

In the case of *Poblete Vilches et al. v. Chile* (2018), the IACtHR included as guarantees of nonrepetition: (i) the adoption of permanent education and training programs for medical students and medical professionals, as well as all the personnel of the healthcare and social security systems, including mediation bodies, on the appropriate treatment of the older person in health-related matters from the perspective of human rights and differentiated impacts, referring to the right to health, the right of access to information, and judicial decisions; (ii) the duty to report to the Court on the progress made in relation to the Sotero del Río Hospital; (iii) designing a publication or booklet outlining the rights to health of older persons; and iv) the adoption of the necessary measures to design an overall policy for comprehensive protection of older persons.[63]

Secondly, in the case of *ANCEJUB-SUNAT v. Peru* (2019), the IACtHR found that insofar as it warned that other members of the association could find themselves in similar situations to those analyzed in the case, given the possible lack of execution of court rulings about the adjustment of their pensions, the IACtHR found appropriate to order the creation of a register identifying: (a) other members of ANCEJUB-SUNAT who were not listed as victims in the case; and (b) other persons who were not members of the association but were discharged and retired employees of the National Superintendence of the Tributary Administration facing similar conditions to the victims in the case.[64]

Thirdly, in *Cuscul Pivaral et al. v. Guatemala* (2018), the IACtHR ordered that the State designed a mechanism to guarantee the accessibility, availability, and quality of health services for persons living with HIV. The Inter-American Court specified that the design of this mechanism must involve the participation of the medical community and other sectors.[65] This measure aimed to impel government institutions to use deliberation and discussion to—together with other medical care sectors—design strategies and actions for providing adequate medical attention. In this sense, the measure attempts to create effective mechanisms for the materialization of ESCER on the ground so that they become a medium through which stakeholders participate in decision-making processes that will affect them rather than only remaining confined in judicial decisions.

---

[63] *Cf. Case of Poblete Vilches et al. v. Chile* [2018] IACtHR, Ser. C No. 349, paras. 232 et seq.

[64] *Cf. Case of the National Association of Discharged and Retired Employees of the National Superintendence of Tributary Administration (ANCEJUB-SUNAT) v. Peru* [2019] IACtHR, Ser. C No. 394, paras. 225, 226, 227.

[65] *Cf. Case of Cuscul Pivaral et al. v. Guatemala* [2018] IACtHR, Ser. C No. 359, para. 226.

In the above-mentioned *Lhaka Honhat* case, the IACtHR ordered—although not as a nonrepetition measure—the identification of critical situations of lack of access to water and food and the formulation of a plan of action with measures to mitigate situations of this kind. The sentence specified a series of concrete objectives that the plan had to cover. In the same case, the IACtHR ordered the creation of a *community development fund* that was innovative to regenerate Indigenous identity. Accordingly, the IACtHR ordered that this fund be "earmarked for actions addressed at the recovery of the indigenous culture, including among its uses, without prejudice to any others, the implementation of programs relating to food security, and the documentation, teaching and dissemination of the history of the traditions of the indigenous communities that are victims."[66]

Lastly, in the recent case of the *Employees of the Fireworks Factory v. Brazil* (2020), the Inter-American Court ordered that the State adopted a *systematic policy of periodic inspections in premises for the production of fireworks* with the aim of verifying occupational health and safety conditions and supervising compliance with fireworks storage standards, meaning that the inspectors must possess knowledge about occupational health and safety and that the State can turn to organizations such as the International Labour Organization and UNICEF to seek advice or support when complying with the Inter-American Court's measure. The IACtHR also ordered, as a nonrepetition measure, that the State must design and execute a socioeconomic program for the population of Santo Antônio de Jesus in order to confront the lack of alternative types of work, particularly for children under the age of sixteen and for women of African descent living in conditions of poverty.[67]

5. Concluding Remarks

The challenges relating to implementing ESCER and making them effective in Latin America and the Caribbean are increasing. The region remains the most unequal on Earth, with high poverty, inequality, and social exclusion.[68] Linking the analysis of ESCER presented in this chapter to the challenges engendered by the

---

[66] *Cf. Case of the Indigenous Communities of the Lhaka Honhat Association (Our Land) v. Argentina* [2020] IACtHR, Ser. C No. 400, para. 339.

[67] The sentence states that this program must include the creation of professional and/or technical training courses that enable workers to enter other labor markets, such as commerce, farming, IT, and other important economic activities in the region, as well as measures aiming to confront school dropout rates due to minors entering the workforce and campaigns raising awareness about working rights and the risks involved in the production of fireworks. Moreover, this program must take into account the main economic activities in the region, the possible need to promote other economic activities, the need to ensure the adequate training of workers to undertake certain professional activities, and the obligation to eradicate child labor in accordance with standards of international law.

[68] See also the ECLAC reports on the *Social Panorama of Latin America* (n. 2), years 2017, 2018, and 2019.

COVID-19 pandemic, it is worth highlighting that, according to the Economic Commission for Latin America and the Caribbean, scenarios resulting from the effects of the pandemic are discouraging, and "poverty, extreme poverty and inequality will increase in all countries of the region."[69] This UN body estimates that, in 2020, poverty in Latin America will rise by at least 4.4 percentage points in comparison to the previous year, "bringing the total number of people living in poverty to 214.7 million (34.7% of the region's population)."[70]

In this vein, the Inter-American Commission on Human Rights[71] and the Inter-American Court of Human Rights[72] have expressed their concern and highlighted the scenarios and impacts of the pandemic on different human rights, not only the rights to life and personal integrity but also—with a particular intensity and with differential and intersectional impacts—the rights to health, work, social security, education, the environment, food, water, and housing, among other ESCER.[73] They are also consistent in indicating the impact on persons and groups in a particular situation of vulnerability, which, historically, have found themselves in a situation of social exclusion or disadvantage.[74]

Today, more than ever, the rich and growing standards on ESCER promoted by the Inter-American System—and tuned with the United Nation's 2030 Agenda and its objectives of sustainable development[75]—are essential for constitutional democracies to face the challenges they currently encounter in the region.

---

[69] Economic Commission for Latin America and the Caribbean (ECLAC), *The Social Challenge in Times of COVID-19* [2020] Santiago de Chile, United Nations, 1.

[70] Among these persons, extreme poverty will rise by 2.6 percentage points (15.9 additional people compared with 2019, to affect a total of 83.4 million people). *Cf.* ibid., 2.

[71] *Pandemic and Human Rights in the Americas* [2020] IACHR, Resolution 1/2020.

[72] *COVID-19 and Human Rights: The problems and challenges must be addressed from a human rights perspective and with respect for international obligations* [2020], Statement of the Inter-American Court of Human Rights 1/20.

[73] *Cf.* Statement of the Inter-American Court of Human Rights 1/20. *COVID-19 and Human Rights* (n. 72), 2 and 3, and Resolution 1/2020 of the IACHR *Pandemic and Human Rights in the Americas* (n. 71), 7.

[74] Older people, children, adolescents, women, persons deprived of their liberty, Indigenous and tribal peoples, persons in a situation of human mobility (migrants, stateless persons, victims of human trafficking, and victims of forced internal displacement), LGBTIQ+ persons, persons of African descent, persons with a disability, persons living in poverty, persons living from the proceeds of informal work, persons living on the street, defenders of human rights, social leaders, healthcare professionals, and journalists.

[75] For example, ending hunger (goal 2), health and well-being (goal 3), quality education (goal 4), clean water and sanitation (goal 6), decent work (goal 8), reducing inequality (goal 10), combating climate change, conserving oceans and marine resources, and protecting ecosystems (goals 13–15), and promoting peace, justice, and solid institutions (goal 16). In this regard, the Inter-American Commission has stated: "The 2030 Agenda is a global agenda and therefore all the States of the Americas have committed to attaining the targets thereof. This Agenda constitutes a strategic opening for working with States in the implementation of ESCER." and "Overcoming the poverty and exclusion that exist in the region is an ongoing challenge. In this regard, it bears highlighting that the intervening factors that keep people in poverty are interrelated and encompass economic, social, cultural, and environmental rights, in addition to civil and political rights. [...]. Undoubtedly, work on the 2030 Agenda is essential in this regard [...]." *Annual Report of the Inter-American Commission on Human Rights 2017, Annual Report of the Office of the Special Rapporteur on Economic, Social, Cultural and Environmental Rights (SRESCER)* [2017] IACHR, OAS/Ser.L/V/II, paras. 130, 131.

II.2
The Inter-American Human Rights System's Impact on the Protection of the Right to a Healthy Environment

By Henry Jiménez Guanipa and María Barraco

1. Introduction

The right to a healthy environment was first recognized in 1972 in the Declaration of the UN Conference on the Human Environment, also known as the Stockholm Declaration.[1] Since then, more than one hundred countries have included this right in their constitutions.[2] Additionally, in 1992, the Rio Declaration on Environment and Development provided—in its first principle—that "[h]uman beings are at the centre of concerns for sustainable development" and that "[t]hey are entitled to a healthy and productive life in harmony with nature."[3] Similarly, Christopher Weeramantry, while serving as vice president of the International Court of Justice in 1997, issued a separate opinion in the case of *Gabčikovo-Nagymaros Project (Hungary/Slovakia)*, in which he stated that "[t]he protection of the environment is [...] a vital part of contemporary human rights doctrine, for it is a *sine qua non* for numerous human rights such as the right to health and the right to life itself."[4]

International environmental law and international human rights law are separate bodies of law and impose distinct obligations on States.[5] The "environmental rule of law" (the state of affairs in which "laws are widely understood, respected, and enforced and the benefits of environmental protection are enjoyed by people

---

[1] David Boyd, "The Effectiveness of Constitutional Environmental Rights" (Yale School of the Environment, April 26–27, 2013), <https://environment.yale.edu/> (accessed October 3, 2021).

[2] Marcos Orellana, "The Case for a Right to a Healthy Environment" (HRW Website, March 1, 2018), at <https://www.hrw.org/news/2018/03/01/case-right-healthy-environment> (accessed October 3, 2021).

[3] Rio Declaration on Environment and Development, First principle.

[4] *Gabcikovo-Nagymaros Dam (Hungary v. Slovakia)* [1997], ICJ Rep. 9, 91.

[5] Their differences and similarities are explained in Gonzalo Aguilar Cavallo, "Los derechos ambientales en el Sistema Interamericano de Protección de los Derechos Humanos," in Gonzalo Aguilar Cavallo (ed.), *Los derechos fundamentales como inspiración y marco del cambio constitucional* (Editorial Jurídica de chile 2017), 148–150.

and the planet"),[6] however, is undoubtedly related to human rights.[7] Even though environmental rights were incorporated relatively late into human rights systems,[8] several regional instruments on human rights recognize the right to a healthy environment, including the African Charter on Human and Peoples' Rights Article 24[9] and the International Covenant on Economic, Social and Cultural Rights Article 12. None of the main treaties in the European Human Rights System expressly recognize the right to a healthy environment, but the right is nevertheless protected through other rights, such as the right to life and the right to respect for private and family life.[10]

In 2011, the Human Rights Council adopted Resolution 16/11 on Human rights and the environment, in which it stated that "environmental damage can have negative implications, both direct and indirect, for the effective enjoyment of human rights" and that "environmental damage is felt most acutely by those segments of the population already in vulnerable situations."[11] Additionally, in 2012, the Human Rights Council issued the Resolution 19/10, which emphasized that "certain aspects of human rights obligations relating to the enjoyment of a safe, clean, healthy and sustainable environment require further study and clarification."[12] In 2018, John H. Knox, former Special Rapporteur on human rights and the environment, said that "[t]here can no longer be any doubt that human rights and the environment are interdependent"[13] and that "[t]he full enjoyment of human rights [. . .] depends on biodiversity, and the degradation and loss

---

[6] UNEP, "Environmental Rule of Law: First Global Report" (UNEP Website, January 24, 2019), <https://www.unep.org/resources/assessment/environmental-rule-law-first-global-report> (accessed October 3, 2021).

[7] Ibid., 25.

[8] UNGA, *Report by Special Rapporteur John H. Knox* (December 24, 2012), UN Doc. A/HRC/22/43, para. 7.

[9] An important case in the jurisprudence of the African Human Rights System is *Social and Economic Rights Action Centre (SERAC) and the Centre for Economic and Social Rights (CESR) v. Nigeria*, Communication No. 155-96 (ACHPR, October 27, 2001), concerning oil contamination in the region where the Ogoni community lived. In this case, the African Commission on Human and Peoples' Rights recognized the strong relationship between the environment and human rights, detailed States' obligations to protect the environment, and concluded that Nigeria had violated Article 24 of the African Charter on Human and Peoples' Rights, among other provisions.

[10] Clarissa Castillo Cuibillo, "El derecho a un ambiente sano y su relación con el cambio climático," in Henry Jiménez Guanipa and Javier Tous Chimá (eds.), *Cambio Climático, energía y derechos humanos: Desafíos y Perspectivas* (Ediciones Ántropos 2017), 40. Among the cases of the ECtHR are the following: *Fadeyeva v. Russia* [2005], ECtHR, App. No. 55723/00; *Okyay et al. v. Turkey* [2005], ECtHR, App. No. 36220/97; *Giacomelli v. Italy* [2006], ECtHR, App. No. 59909/00; *Marangopoulos Foundation for Human Rights (MFHR) v. Greece* [2006], European Committee of Social Rights, Complaint No. 30/2005.

[11] Human Rights Council, *Resolution 16/11: Human rights and the environment* (2011), UN Doc. A/HRC/RES/16/11, Preamble.

[12] Human Rights Council, *Resolution 19/10: Human Rights and the environment* (2012), UN Doc. A/HRC/RES/19/1.

[13] OHCHR, "UN expert calls for global recognition of the right to safe and healthy environment" (OHCHR Website, March 5, 2018), <https://www.ohchr.org/EN/NewsEvents/Pages/DisplayNews.aspx?NewsID=22755&LangID=E> (accessed November 19, 2021).

of biodiversity undermine the ability of human beings to enjoy their human rights."[14] Also in 2018, the UN General Assembly adopted the Declaration on the Rights of Peasants and Other People Working in Rural Areas, which contains several provisions related to environmental protection. Article 18, for example, provides that "[p]easants and other people working in rural areas have the right to the conservation and protection of the environment and the productive capacity of their lands, and of the resources that they use and manage."

The inextricable link between the environment and the full enjoyment of human rights is widely recognized. A clean, healthy, and functional environment is integral to the enjoyment of the rights to life, human dignity, health, food, and more. The Inter-American Court of Human Rights (Inter-American Court, or IACtHR) acknowledged this in its Advisory Opinion OC-23/17,[15] and so did the Inter-American Commission on Human Rights (Inter-American Commission, or IACHR) in its report on "Business and Human Rights."[16] The IACtHR also recently established, in the case of *Lhaka Honhat Association (Our Land) v. Argentina*, that Article 26 of the American Convention on Human Rights (American Convention, or ACHR) encompasses the right to a healthy environment.

There is also a general agreement that climate change poses the gravest threat toward the environment and all living species, as it will restrict access to the resources necessary to life. In 2019, UN High Commissioner for Human Rights Michelle Bachelet said "[w]e are burning up our future" to underscore the negative impact that climate change has on human rights.[17] The international community has issued warnings about this phenomenon for almost fifty years and, at the same time, has contributed to the development of a normative framework to combat climate change and to prevent a global temperature increase of more than two degrees. Profound change, however, is required for these efforts to succeed.[18]

---

[14] UNGA, "Report by Special Rapporteur John H. Knox" (February 7, 2018), UN Doc. A/HRC/37/58/Add.1, para. 78.

[15] See Advisory Opinion 23/17: Environment and Human Rights, Ser. A No. 23 (IACtHR, November 15, 2017).

[16] IACHR, "Business and Human Rights: Inter-American Standards" (IACHR Website, November 1, 2019), <http://www.oas.org/en/iachr/reports/pdfs/Business_Human_Rights_Inte_American_St andards.pdf> (accessed November 19, 2022), para. 46.

[17] Michelle Bachelet, "Global update at the 42nd session of the Human Rights Council" (OHCHR Website, September 9, 2019), <https://www.ohchr.org/en/NewsEvents/Pages/DisplayNews. aspx?NewsID=24956&LangID=E> (accessed November 15, 2022).

[18] IPCC, "Global Warming of 1.5°C—An IPCC Special Report on the impacts of global warming of 1.5°C above pre-industrial levels and related global greenhouse gas emission pathways, in the context of strengthening the global response to the threat of climate change, sustainable development, and efforts to eradicate poverty" (IPCC Website, 2019), <https://www.ipcc.ch/site/assets/uploads/sites/2/2019/06/SR15_Full_Report_High_Res.pdf> (accessed November 15, 2022).

The 2030 Agenda for Sustainable Development, adopted in 2015 by the UN General Assembly through Resolution 70/1, was a significant step toward the protection of the environment.[19] The resolution recognizes that climate change is one of the greatest contemporary challenges and includes as one of its objectives "[t]ak[ing] urgent action to combat climate change and its impacts." The resolution also states that one of the three dimensions to achieve sustainable development is the environmental dimension and establishes specific actions related to the environment in other goals to eliminate poverty, to ensure decent work and economic growth, and to promote responsible consumption and production.

Civil society has played an active role in the development of the right to a healthy environment, especially by using domestic and international instruments that protect the right to participate in environmental issues, such as the UN Economic Commission for Europe's Convention on Access to Information, Public Participation in Decision-Making and Access to Justice in Environmental Matters (Aarhus Convention) and the Regional Agreement on Access to Information, Public Participation and Justice in Environmental Matters in Latin America and the Caribbean (Escazú Agreement).[20] The rights of access to information, participation, and access to justice in environmental matters are key to the environmental rule of law, since individuals are affected by the environment and advocate to ensure that States comply with their obligations to protect the environment.[21]

This chapter is structured into two main sections. The first section presents inter-American instruments and standards that recognize and protect the right to a healthy environment as well as other, related human rights. These contribute to an international *corpus juris* on environmental protection and human rights. The second section examines examples in which domestic courts apply inter-American standards to protect environmental human rights. Finally, the chapter concludes that a *ius commune* on environmental rights is emerging and that it will continue to be strengthened by both the international human rights mechanisms and domestic courts.

2. The Protection of Environmental Human Rights in the Inter-American Human Rights System

Even though the Inter-American Human Rights System (Inter-American System, or IAHRS), during the first several decades of its existence, did not

---

[19] UNGA, *Resolution 70/1: Transforming our world: the 2030 Agenda for Sustainable Development* (2015), UN Doc. A/RES/70/1.
[20] Adopted on March 2018 within the framework of the Economic Commission for Latin America and the Caribbean (ECLAC), the Escazú Agreement entered into force in April 2021. It is a key instrument for the protection of environmental rights in Latin America.
[21] UNEP (n. 6), 21.

consider the relation between human rights violations and environmental damage,[22] it has since recognized the right to a healthy environment as protected by its normative framework. The IAHRS *acquis* is composed of the American Declaration of the Rights and Duties of Men (American Declaration), the Charter of the Organization of American States (OAS Charter), the Inter-American Democratic Charter, and the American Convention and its subsequent protocols, as well as the IACtHR and the IACHR's interpretations of these instruments. Additionally, with the entry into force of the Escazú Agreement in April 2021, the region now has a specific treaty that contains guiding principles on human rights and the environment.

The preamble of the American Declaration states that "[t]he American peoples have acknowledged the dignity of the individual, and their national constitutions recognize that juridical and political institutions, which regulate life in human society, have as their principal aim the protection of the essential rights of man and the creation of circumstances that will permit him to achieve spiritual and material progress and attain happiness." In the case of *Kawas Fernández v. Honduras*, the IACtHR determined that there is an undeniable link between the environment and the enjoyment of other human rights, which are negatively affected by the environmental degradation and climate change.[23] The preamble of the American Declaration should be read in light of the Inter-American Court's interpretation in *Kawas Fernández*, since it would be impossible to achieve spiritual and material progress and happiness in a contaminated environment. Moreover, even if the American Declaration does not mention in particular the right to a healthy environment, it includes rights related to the environment, such as the rights to life, property, health, and work.[24]

The OAS Charter establishes the obligation of member States to ensure the "integral development" of their peoples, which the Executive Secretariat for Integral Development of the OAS has defined as "the general name given to a host of policies that work in tandem to foster sustainable development."[25] Additionally, the preamble of the Inter-American Democratic Charter recognizes that the integral development of human beings depends on a safe environment, and Article

---

[22] Daniel Cerqueira, "Derechos Humanos y Ambiente: Contribuciones al Sistema Interamericano," in Henry Jiménez Guanipa and Marisol Luna Leal (eds.), *Crisis climática, transición energética y derechos humanos. Tomo II. Protección del medio ambiente, derechos humanos y transición energética* (Ediciones Ántropos 2020), 157.

[23] *Kawas Fernández v. Honduras* [2009], IACtHR, Ser. C No. 196, para. 148.

[24] Dinah Shelton, "Derechos ambientales y obligaciones en el sistema interamericano de derechos humanos" [2010] 6 *Anuario de Derechos Humanos*, 114; "Indigenous an Tribal Peoples' Rights over their Ancestral Lands and Natural Resources" (IACHR, 2009), <https://www.oas.org/en/iachr/indigenous/docs/pdf/ancestrallands.pdf> (accessed November 19, 2021), 191.

[25] OAS, "Integral Development," <http://www.oas.org/en/topics/integral_development.asp> (accessed November 22, 2021).

15 establishes that "[t]he exercise of democracy promotes the preservation and good stewardship of the environment."

On June 2001, the General Assembly of the OAS adopted Resolution 1819 on "Human Rights and the Environment," which states that the effective enjoyment of human rights can improve environmental protection, thereby recognizing the importance of promoting both environmental protection and the enjoyment of human rights.[26] Subsequently, in June 2008, the OAS General Assembly adopted Resolution 2429 on "Human Rights and Climate Change in the Americas," which recognizes the negative impact that climate change might have on human rights and instructs the IACHR to contribute "to the efforts to determine the possible existence of a link between adverse effects of climate change and the full enjoyment of human rights."[27] The General Assembly also adopted, in June 2015, the American Declaration on the Rights of Indigenous Peoples, Article 19 of which recognizes the right to a healthy environment.

As for the ACHR, Article 4 protects the right to life, which includes the right to a dignified life (*vida digna*).[28] The latter has to be analyzed in light of other human rights, such as the right to a healthy environment.[29] American Convention Article 26, for example, provides for "the full realization of the rights implicit in the economic, social, educational, scientific, and cultural standards set forth in the Charter of the Organization of American States," which the Inter-American Court interpreted to include the right to a healthy environment in the recent *Lhaka Honhat v. Argentina* case.[30]

Notwithstanding the provisions of the ACHR, the main instrument protecting the right to a healthy environment is the Additional Protocol to the American Convention on Human Rights in the Area of Economic, Social and Cultural Rights (Protocol of San Salvador). Article 11 of the Protocol of San Salvador expressly recognizes the right to a healthy environment, providing that "[e]veryone shall have the right to live in a healthy environment and to have access to basic public services" and that "[t]he States Parties shall promote the protection, preservation, and improvement of the environment."

The Inter-American Commission has also developed standards related to the environment in various reports and cases. In its 1997 "Report of the Human Rights Situation in Ecuador," the IACHR analyzed the impact of the oil extraction on the rights to life and health of Indigenous communities living in areas

---

[26] Inter-American Forum on Environmental Law, *Human Rights and the Environment* (2011), AG/RES. 1819 (XXXI-O/01).

[27] OAS General Assembly, *Human Rights and Climate Change in the Americas* (2008), AG/RES. 2429 (XXXVIII-O/08).

[28] "*Instituto de Reeducación del Menor*" v. Paraguay [2004], IACtHR, Ser. C No. 112, para. 159.

[29] *Yakye Axa Indigenous Community v. Paraguay* [2005], IACtHR, Ser. C No. 125, para. 163.

[30] *Lhaka Honhat (nuestra tierra) v. Argentina* [2020], IACtHR, Ser. C No. 400, para. 202.

with oil fields. The Inter-American Commission emphasized that Ecuador must protect the environment against contamination, as well as the lives of the region's inhabitants, because "where environmental contamination and degradation pose a persistent threat to human life and health, the foregoing rights [to life and to physical security and integrity] are implicated."[31] Similarly, the IACHR stated that "[s]evere environmental pollution may pose a threat to human life and health, and in the appropriate case give rise to an obligation on the part of a [S]tate to take reasonable measures to prevent such risk, or the necessary measures to respond when persons have suffered injury."[32]

Additionally, in its thematic report on "Indigenous and Tribal Peoples' Rights over their Ancestral Lands and Natural Resources," the Inter-American Commission stated that "State members of the OAS must prevent the degradation of the environment in order to comply with their human rights obligations in the framework of the Inter-American system."[33] In its thematic report on "Business and Human Rights," the IACHR established that corporations must also respect the right to a healthy environment by taking into consideration all relevant international standards and principles, guaranteeing access to information and effective reparation for victims of environmental degradation, and more.[34] In the report, the Inter-American Commission also emphasized the importance of the ratification of the Escazú Agreement. Moreover, the IACHR published the Resolution on Climate Emergency and Human Rights in the Americas,[35] with a section on "Human rights in the context of environmental deterioration and the climate emergency in the Americas" developing various state obligations related to the right to a healthy environment. The Resolution also has a section that develops the rights of Indigenous peoples.

With respect to the IACtHR, it has examined the right to a healthy environment in several cases concerning Indigenous peoples' rights to their communal lands.[36] The Inter-American Court also recognized the existence of the right to access information about matters of public interest in the case of *Claude Reyes v. Chile*, in which part of the information requested was related to the environmental impact of a potential industrialization project.

---

[31] IACHR, "Report on the situation of human rights in Ecuador" (1997), < http://www.cidh.org/countryrep/ecuador-eng/index%20-%20ecuador.htm> (accessed October 3, 2021).
[32] Ibid.
[33] *Kawas Fernández v. Honduras* (n. 23), para. 193.
[34] Advisory Opinion 23/17 (n. 15), para. 46.
[35] IACHR, "Resolution No. 3/2021. Climate Emergency: Scope of Inter-American Human Rights Obligations" (2021), <https://www.oas.org/en/iachr/decisions/pdf/2021/resolucion_3-21_ENG.pdf> (accessed October 25, 2023).
[36] *Pueblos Kaliña y Lokono v. Surinam* [2015], IACtHR, Ser. C No. 309; *Comunidad Indígena Xákmok Kásek v. Paraguay* [2010], IACtHR Ser. C No. 214, para. 313; *Pueblo Saramaka v. Surinam* [2007], IACtHR, Ser. C No. 172; *Kichwa de Sarayaku v. Ecuador* [2012], IACtHR, Ser. C No. 245.

In addition, in its Advisory Opinion OC-23/17 on "The Environment and Human Rights," the Inter-American Court recognized that the right to a healthy environment has both a collective and an individual dimension.[37] The IACtHR also emphasized that "as an autonomous right, the right to a healthy environment, unlike other rights, protects the components of the environment, such as forests, rivers and seas, as legal interests in themselves, even in the absence of the certainty or evidence of a risk to individuals."[38] At the same time, the Inter-American Court stated that "adequate protection of the environment is essential for human well-being, and also for the enjoyment of numerous human rights, particularly the rights to life, personal integrity and health, as well as the right to a healthy environment itself."[39]

When determining the scope of the right to a healthy environment, the Inter-American Court considered the domestic laws of States of the region that recognize this right, establish the obligation to carry out environmental impact assessments, provide for public participation, and incorporate the precautionary principle. The IACtHR's approach to environmental issues thus evolved through dialogue with domestic legal systems.

In the case of *Lhaka Honhat v. Argentina*, the Inter-American Court found, for the first time, that a State had violated the right to a healthy environment. The IACtHR concluded that Argentina had failed to fulfill its due diligence obligation to prevent third parties from interfering in the Indigenous communities' right to a healthy environment and that the environmental degradation had also affected other human rights (to food, water, and cultural identity).

The Inter-American Human Rights System thus has recognized the right to a healthy environment and has theorized its interdependence with the enjoyment of other human rights. The following sections examine this right in further detail, with a focus on: (a) the protection of the right to a healthy environment, (b) the right to a healthy environment and Indigenous communities, and (c) the right to access information concerning and to participate in environmental matters.

---

[37] Advisory Opinion 23/17 (n. 15), para. 59 ("The human right to a healthy environment has been understood as a right that has both individual and also collective connotations. In its collective dimension, the right to a healthy environment constitutes a universal value that is owed to both present and future generations. That said, the right to a healthy environment also has an individual dimension insofar as its violation may have a direct and an indirect impact on the individual owing to its connectivity to other rights, such as the rights to health, personal integrity, and life. Environmental degradation may cause irreparable harm to human beings; thus, a healthy environment is a fundamental right for the existence of humankind.").
[38] Ibid., para. 64.
[39] Ibid., para. 124.

2.1. The Protection of the Right to a Healthy Environment

The first cases in which the IACtHR discussed the right to a healthy environment concerned the rights of Indigenous communities. For example, in the case of the *Kaliña and Lokono Peoples v. Suriname*, the Inter-American Court decided that the protection, conservation, and improvement of the environment is "an essential human right related to the right to a dignified life derived from Article 4 of the [American] Convention."[40]

In 2017, the Inter-American Court took important steps toward filling gaps in the law relating to the right to a healthy environment in its Advisory Opinion OC-23/17.[41] First, the IACtHR established that States have extraterritorial jurisdiction over environmental problems that cause transboundary harm, which means that "States must ensure that activities within their jurisdiction or control do not cause damage to the environment of other States or of areas beyond the limits of their jurisdiction."[42] The Inter-American Court also dedicated a section of the Advisory Opinion to the obligations stemming from the right to a healthy environment, in which it established that States have a due diligence obligation "to take 'all appropriate measures' to achieve, progressively, the full effectiveness" of the right to a healthy environment.[43] Due diligence encompasses four main duties:

1. The duty to prevent, which includes the obligations to safeguard human rights and to ensure accountability and reparations when they are violated. According to the IACtHR, this duty encompasses the above-mentioned obligation not to cause damage to the environment in other States. It also encompasses the obligations to regulate, supervise, and monitor activities that might cause environmental damage; to require environmental impact assessments; and to establish contingency and mitigation plans.[44] Similarly, the IACHR has interpreted the duty to prevent to require States to supervise and regulate activities that could harm the environment.[45]
2. The duty to act in accordance with the precautionary principle by taking measures to protect the environment "in cases where there is no scientific certainty about the impact that an activity could have."[46]

---

[40] *Pueblos Kaliña y Lokono v. Surinam* (n. 36), para. 172.
[41] Daniel Cerqueira, "El derecho a un medio ambiente sano en el marco normativo y jurisprudencial del Sistema Interamericano de Derechos Humanos" (DPLF Fundación para el Debido Proceso, 2020), <http://www.dplf.org/sites/default/files/el_derecho_a_un_medio_ambiente_sano.pdf> (accessed November 12, 2022), 22.
[42] Advisory Opinion 23/17 (n. 15), para. 97.
[43] Ibid., para. 123.
[44] Ibid., para. 145.
[45] Ibid., para. 174; para. 92.
[46] Ibid., para. 175.

3. The duty to cooperate to protect the environment, in good faith,[47] including the obligations to notify, to consult and negotiate, and to share information.
4. Procedural duties, including the obligation to respect, protect, and fulfill the rights of access to information, public participation, and access to justice as they relate to environmental matters.[48]

In the case of *Lhaka Honhat v. Argentina*, the Inter-American Court expanded on its discussion of States' obligations stemming from the right to a healthy environment. The IACtHR emphasized that the obligations to respect and guarantee, contained in ACHR Article 1.1, apply to this right. As such, States must prevent third parties from violating the right to a healthy environment and to treat a violation of the right, should one occur, as illegal. The Inter-American Court also highlighted that the rights of vulnerable groups are disproportionally harmed by environmental damage.[49] Accordingly, States have an added obligation to address those vulnerabilities.

In February 2020, the IACHR granted precautionary measures in favor of inhabitants of the areas near the Santiago River, in Mexico, whose rights to life, health, and personal integrity were threatened by contamination caused by industrial activity.[50] In its decision, the Inter-American Commission took into account States' obligations to "regulate and control activities under their jurisdiction that may cause significant damage to the environment" and to "mitigate significant environmental damage."

2.2. The Right to a Healthy Environment and Indigenous Communities

The right to a healthy environment is crucial for Indigenous communities, who have a strong connection with their lands and who are particularly vulnerable to environmental degradation.[51] The Inter-American Court has decided that "members of tribal and indigenous communities have the right to own the natural resources they have traditionally used within their territory for the same reasons that they have a right to own the land they have traditionally used and

---

[47] Ibid., para. 185.
[48] Ibid., para. 212.
[49] *Lhaka Honhat (nuestra tierra) v. Argentina* (n. 30), para. 209.
[50] *Inhabitants of the areas near the Santiago River regarding Mexico* [2020], IACHR, Precautionary Measure No. 708-19.
[51] IACHR, "Pueblos indígenas y tribales de la Panazmazonía" (IACHR Website, September 29, 2019), <https://www.oas.org/es/cidh/informes/pdfs/panamazonia2019.pdf> (accessed November 12, 2021); Advisory Opinion 23/17 (n. 15), para. 121.

occupied for centuries. Without them, the very physical and cultural survival of such peoples is at stake."[52] Accordingly, the IACtHR and the IACHR have recognized the importance of guaranteeing the right to a healthy environment for securing Indigenous communities' human rights, as well as the need to conduct environmental impacts assessments before undertaking projects that would affect their lands.

When analyzing the link between a healthy environment and the protection of Indigenous communities' human rights, the IACtHR has taken into consideration the fact that the right to collective property entails protection of the lands and access to the natural resources located within the territories since these are necessary for Indigenous peoples' survival as well as the development of their traditional way of life.[53] Similarly, the IACHR recognized in its thematic report on "Indigenous and Tribal Peoples' Rights over their Ancestral Lands and Natural Resources" the importance of protecting the natural resources on Indigenous communities' lands in order to secure their fundamental rights, including the rights to life, dignity, health, and property. The IACHR stated that "the State must undertake preventive and positive action aimed at guaranteeing an environment that does not compromise indigenous persons' capacity to exercise their most basic human rights."[54]

The Inter-American Commission has also determined that effective protection of the natural resources in Indigenous peoples' territories requires access to justice, access to information, and participation in decision-making. In connection with this last obligation, the Inter-American Court has decided that the right to property, contained in ACHR Article 21, creates an obligation to conduct an environmental impact assessment[55] so that Indigenous communities who might be affected by a project can evaluate the risks and decide whether to give their consent.[56]

The IACHR has also issued various recommendations in cases relating to Indigenous communities and the environment. In the case of the *Yanomami Community v. Brazil*,[57] which concerned the construction of a motorway within Yanomami territories that had resulted in diseases and even deaths of community members, the Inter-American Commission concluded that the State had violated the victims' right to the preservation of health and well-being, among others, and recommended the delimitation of Yanomami territories. In the case of *Mercedes Julia Huenteao Beroiza v. Chile*,[58] concerning the construction of a

---

[52] *Pueblo Saramaka v. Surinam* (n. 36), para. 121.
[53] *Yakye Axa Indigenous Community v. Paraguay* (n. 29), para. 137.
[54] *Kawas Fernández v. Honduras* (n. 23), para. 194.
[55] *Pueblo Saramaka v. Surinam* (n. 36), para. 129.
[56] *Pueblo Saramaka v. Surinam* (n. 36), para. 40; *Kichwa de Sarayaku v. Ecuador* (n. 36), para. 205.
[57] *Yanomami v. Brasil* [1985], IACHR, Case No. 7615.
[58] *Mercedes Julia Huenteao Beroiza v. Chile* [2004], IACHR, Friendly Settlement Petition No. 4617/02.

hydroelectric plant in the Mapuche-Pehuenche's territories against their will, the parties reached a friendly settlement agreement in which the State committed to implementing mechanisms that would guarantee the development and environmental conservation of the territories. Additionally, in the case of the *Maya Indigenous Communities of the Toledo District v. Belize*, the IACHR found that the State violated the victims' right to property by failing to recognize and protect their territories, as well as by granting logging and oil concessions on their lands to third parties. The Inter-American Commission recommended that the State provide reparations for the environmental damage that resulted from the concessions. Finally, in the case of the *Indigenous Communities of the Xingú River Basin v. Brazil*, the IACHR granted a precautionary measure in which it ordered the State to halt the construction of the *Belo Monte* hydroelectric plant until Indigenous communities had been consulted.

2.3. The Right to Access Information Concerning and to Participate in Environmental Matters

The right to a healthy environment is closely related to the right of access to information concerning environmental matters, which in turn enables public participation in these issues.

As previously mentioned, in the case of *Claude Reyes v. Chile*, the Inter-American Court found that the State had violated its international obligations when it did not guarantee the right of access to information concerning environmental matters.[59] The IACtHR expanded on this right on its Advisory Opinion OC-23/17, in which it stated that "access to information on activities and projects that could have an impact on the environment is a matter of evident public interest."[60] The Court also emphasized the direct relation between the right of access to information and the right to public participation in matters of sustainable development and environmental protection.[61]

Finally, Articles 5 and 6 of the Escazú Agreement protect the right of access to information concerning environmental matters, and Article 7 protects the right to public participation in the decision-making processes related to the environment. The ratification of the Escazú Agreement by States is therefore pivotal to the consolidation of these rights in the Americas.

---

[59] *Claude Reyes et al. v. Chile* [2006], IACtHR, Ser. C No. 151, para. 174.
[60] Advisory Opinion 23/17 (n. 15), para. 214.
[61] Ibid., para. 217.

3. Transformative Impact: Recognition of Environmental Human Rights at the Domestic Level

Twenty Latin American constitutions recognize the right to a healthy environment. The incorporation of the right to a healthy environment into a constitution significantly affects a country's legal system.[62] According to David Boyd, the impacts of this incorporation are twofold: stronger environmental legislation and judicial decisions defending the right from violations.[63] This section focuses on domestic judicial decisions, especially on constitutional matters, that acknowledge the relationship between human rights and the environment.

Among the twenty Latin American countries whose constitutions recognize environmental rights, eighteen have constitutional provisions that directly protect the right to a healthy environment of the population as a whole. These countries are: Argentina (art. 41), Bolivia (art. 33), Brazil (art. 225), Chile (art. 19.8), Colombia (art. 79), Costa Rica (art. 50), Cuba (art. 75), Ecuador (arts. 14, 66), Guyana (art. 149J(1)), Honduras (art. 145), Jamaica (art. 13), Mexico (art. 4.5), Nicaragua (art. 60), Panama (art. 118), Paraguay (art. 7), Peru (art. 2.22), the Dominican Republic (art. 67), and Venezuela (art. 127). The other two countries, Belize and El Salvador, refer to environmental protection only in its preamble and provide environmental protection only to a particular, vulnerable group (girls and boys), respectively.

Antigua and Barbuda, Guyana, Saint Vincent and the Grenadines, Saint Kitts and Nevis, Saint Lucia, and Uruguay do not recognize the right to a healthy environment in their constitutions. Nevertheless, these countries have ratified the Escazú Agreement and proclaimed the right to access information and participate in public affairs as a constitutional right. Article 4(1) of the Escazú Agreement establishes that "[e]ach Party shall guarantee the right of every person to live in a healthy environment and any other universally-recognized human right related to the present Agreement." Therefore, these countries have indirectly incorporated into their constitutions the right to a healthy environment.

Eight countries do not have the right to a healthy environment in their constitutions, directly or indirectly. These countries are the Bahamas, Barbados, Dominica, Granada, Guatemala, Haiti, Suriname, and Trinidad and Tobago.

---

[62] The case of *Future Generations v. Ministry of the Environment and others* [2018] Colombian Supreme Court 11001-22-03-000-2018-00319-01 demonstrates the importance of having the right to a healthy environment in constitutions. The Supreme Court of Justice of Colombia orders the executive branch to reverse the negative effects of deforestation in the Amazon by implementing a plan to combat climate change. The Court takes into consideration that the Colombian constitution is an "Ecological Constitution" that declares the right to a healthy environment to be a fundamental right. The Court also finds that various provisions within the constitution form a "national ecological public order."

[63] Boyd (n. 1).

In addition to the constitutional recognition of the right to a healthy environment, many States have integrated into their domestic legal systems inter-American treaties, jurisprudence, and standards concerning environmental human rights, as required by conventionality control.[64] These States implement public policies in line with inter-American norms related to the environment and apply these norms in judicial decisions.

For example, in 2016, the Constitutional Court of Colombia adjudicated a case concerning illegal mining that had contaminated the Atrato River, where various Indigenous and Afro-descendant communities reside.[65] When recognizing the right to water, the Colombian court referred to several IACtHR cases, such as the case of the *Yakye Axa Indigenous Community v. Paraguay*, in which the Inter-American Court had recognized the right of Indigenous communities to use the natural resources of their ancestral lands. The Constitutional Court of Colombia also cited the IACHR's report on the "Human Rights Situation in Ecuador," which described human rights violations caused by oil extraction.

In Mexico, the National Human Rights Commission issued Recommendation No. 32 on violations of the human rights to health, an adequate standard of life, a healthy environment, and public information. The recommendation describes the negative impact of urban air pollution, and highlights State obligations and rights violations associated with the phenomenon.[66] The recommendation derives State obligations to protect the right to a healthy environment from international human rights law, including the IACtHR's Advisory Opinion OC-23/17 and the IACHR's definition of what constitutes a healthy environment.

Similarly, in two landmark cases, domestic Courts relied on the work of the IAHRS when drawing connections between Indigenous communities and the right to a healthy environment. In 2007, the Supreme Court of Belize determined that the Maya community's customary rights, recognized in the country's constitution, obligated the government to give the community title to their territories. In this case, the Belizean court expressly references the standards elaborated by the Inter-American Court in the case of the *Mayagna (Sumo) Awas Tingni Community v. Nicaragua* regarding the close connection Indigenous communities have with their lands.[67] In *Mayagna (Sumo) Awas Tingni Community*, the IACtHR also found that the State had a duty to obtain

---

[64] Advisory Opinion 23/17 (n. 15), para. 28.

[65] *Centro de Estudios para la Justicia Social "Tierra Digna" v. Presidencia de la República et al.* [2016] Colombian Constitutional Court Decision T-622-16.

[66] For a detailed analysis of this Recommendation, see Jorge Ulises Carmona, "Derecho humano a la salud, a un nivel de vida adecuado, a un medio ambiente sano, y a la información pública. Recomendación No. 32 de la CNDH de México," in Henry Jiménez Guanipa and Marisol Luna Leal (eds.), *Crisis climática, transición energética y derechos humanos. Tomo II. Protección del medio ambiente, derechos humanos y transición energética* (Ediciones Ántropos 2020), 399–424.

[67] *Aurelio Cal et al. v. The attorney general of Belize et al* [2007] Supreme Court of Belice Claim No. 171/2007, 59-60.

informed consent from indigenous communities before authorizing leases or extractive licenses on their lands. In 2015, the Caribbean Court of Justice (CCJ) also analyzed the human rights situation of Indigenous communities in Belize and found that Q'eqchi', Mopan Maya, and other Indigenous communities' right to property obligates the government to delimit and register their traditional lands.[68] In its decision, the CCJ refers to the IACHR's standards regarding the right of access to information and participation in decision-making about industrial and mining projects. The CCJ also mentioned the IACtHR case *Claude Reyes v. Chile* when recognizing the right of access to information concerning environmental matters.

In another, more recent case, the Supreme Federal Court of Brazil ordered protective measures for Indigenous communities in the context of the COVID-19 pandemic, including a measure to prevent third parties from entering their territories and illegally extracting natural resources. The Brazilian court's decision emphasizes the relation between the right to a healthy environment and the rights of Indigenous communities, as well as the State obligation to implement the necessary measures to protect Indigenous territories. In reaching its conclusions, the Brazilian court relied on inter-American standards, especially the IACtHR case *Lhaka Honhat* and the IACHR Resolution 1/2020, in which the Inter-American Commission recommended, among other things, that States "[t]ake utmost measures to protect the human rights of indigenous peoples in the context of the COVID-19 pandemic."[69]

The right to participate in decision-making concerning environmental matters has also been recognized at the domestic level, as in the case of Rio Blanco in Ecuador.[70] Mining had begun without the prior, free, and informed consultation of the local population. In May 2018, various nongovernmental organizations (NGOs) representing rural and Indigenous communities requested an injunction that would suspend the mining. The lower court granted the injunction, preventing the mining in Rio Blanco from continuing until local communities had been duly consulted, in accordance with international standards. On appeal, a higher court determined that the communities' right to prior consultation had been violated and affirmed the lower court's decision.

---

[68] *The Maya Leaders Alliance et al. v. The attorney general of Belize* [2015] The Caribbean Court of Justice BZCV2014/002.

[69] IACHR, "Resolution No. 1/2020. Pandemic and Human Rights in the Americas" (2020), <https://www.oas.org/en/iachr/decisions/pdf/Resolution-1-20-en.pdf> (accessed November 12, 2022), 15.

[70] For more cases that demonstrate the *interamericanización* of the right to participate in decision-making concerning environmental matters, see Mariela Morales Antoniazzi and María Barraco, "Aproximación al ius commune: Interamericanización en los derechos de participación y defensa del medio ambiente," in Henry Jiménez Guanipa and Marisol Luna Leal (eds.), *Crisis climática, transición energética y derechos humanos. Tomo II. Protección del medio ambiente, derechos humanos y transición energética* (Ediciones Ántropos 2020), 31–41.

Domestic judicial decisions have also recognized the right of access to information concerning environmental matters. In February 2015, the Constitutional Court of Colombia adjudicated a case concerning a chemical spill in Cartagena that contaminated water sources.[71] When analyzing standards on reparations for environmental damage, the Colombian court referenced the IACtHR case *Claude Reyes v. Chile*, which recognized the right of to access information concerning the environment. The Colombian court also decided that the affected community has the right to participate in the design of measures to restore the environment to its previous conditions.

Most recently, an Argentine court found that the energy company YPF had an obligation to provide information to an NGO regarding activity taking place in the Vaca Muerta oil deposit. In so doing, the court referenced the right of access to information concerning environmental matters contained in the Escazú Agreement. This was the first time that the Escazú Agreement had served as the basis for a judicial decision.[72]

These cases illustrate domestic courts' reception of the standards on the right to a healthy environment developed by the IACtHR and the IACHR and consolidated in the Escazú Agreement. Additionally, considering that the interaction between and the confluence of domestic and international law is characteristic of the *ius constitutionale commune* in Latin America,[73] these cases signal the emergence of an *ius commune* on environmental rights, with a particular focus on the right to a healthy environment and the rights of participation in and access to information concerning environmental matters.

4. Concluding Remarks

In the past decades, global efforts to protect the environment have grown and evolved. These efforts include strengthening the environmental rule of law, as has been seen in Latin America. This international environmental movement has been accompanied and reinforced by an emerging *ius commune* on environmental rights. The development of this environmental *ius commune* results from standard-setting by the Inter-American Court and the Inter-American

---

[71] *Fundación para la Defensa del Interés Público -Fundepúblico- y Carmenza Morales Brid v. Sala Civil y de Familia del Tribunal Superior del Distrito Judicial de Cartagena* [2015] Colombian Constitutional Court Decision T-080/15.

[72] Henry Jiménez Guanipa, "El acuerdo de Escazú y el derecho de acceso a la información dan a luz una nueva jurisprudencia" [2019], 44 *Revista Derecho del Estado*.

[73] Armin von Bogdandy et al., "Ius Constitutionale Commune En América Latina: A Regional Approach to Transformative Constitutionalism," MPIL Research Series, October 28, 2016, <https://papers.ssrn.com/sol3/papers.cfm?abstract_id=2859583> (accessed November 13, 2022), 3.

Commission, combined with the incorporation of these norms in domestic legal systems.

The IACtHR and IACHR's standards have clarified State obligations stemming from the right to a healthy environment. The Inter-American Court's Advisory Opinion OC-23/17 and its judgment in the *Lhaka Honhat* case explain in detail the content of the right to a healthy environment and the corresponding obligations of the State. This chapter has focused on the protection of the right to a healthy environment, the enhanced obligation to guarantee the environmental rights of Indigenous communities, and the rights of access to information and to participate in decision-making concerning environmental matters.

Inter-American standards on environmental rights and obligations have been invoked by domestic tribunals, signaling the emergence of a *ius commune* on the environment in Latin America. This environmental *ius commune* has been strengthened by the entry into force on April 22, 2021, of the Escazú Agreement, which could catalyze additional judicial decisions that reinforce the environmental rule of law in the region.

II.3
Indigenous Rights in the Inter-American System
The Application of Precautionary Measures from a Culturally Appropriate Perspective

By Antonia Urrejola and Elsy Curihuinca Neira

1. Introduction

The Inter-American Human Rights System (IAHRS) has increasingly strengthened the recognition of the individual and collective rights of Indigenous peoples. Both the Inter-American Court of Human Rights (IACtHR) and the Inter-American Commission on Human Rights (IACHR) have developed important standards that are applied in a cross-cutting manner throughout all their mechanisms.[1] One such mechanism is the system of precautionary measures (PMs), whereby the IACHR has the power to request States take urgent action to protect the human rights of people living in the thirty-five countries under their jurisdiction.[2] This power is established in Article 18(b) of the Statute of the Commission and Article 41(b) of the American Convention on Human Rights (ACHR).[3]

Since the 1980s, the Commission has systematically spoken about the rights of Indigenous peoples through the case system, in special reports, in admissibility reports, in country reports, in reports on friendly settlements, in the mechanism

---

[1] In this regard, see IACHR, "Indigenous and Tribal Peoples' Rights over their Ancestral Lands and Natural Resources: Norms and Jurisprudence of the Inter-American Human Rights System," December 30, 2009, OAS/Ser.L/V/II, English translation is available at http://cidh.org/countryrep/Indigenous-Lands09/TOC.htm; IACHR, "Indigenous Peoples, Afro-Descendant Communities and Natural Resources: Protection of Human Rights in the Context of Extraction, Exploitation and Development Activities," December 31, 2015, OEA/Ser.L/V/II. Doc. 47/15, www-cdn.law.stanford.edu/wp-content/uploads/2017/09/ExtractiveIndustries2016.pdf (accessed January 2, 2022).

[2] This Mechanism is part of the IACHR's function of supervising compliance with human rights obligations established in Article 106 of the Charter of the Organization of American States (OAS).

[3] This power rests on the general obligation that States have to respect and guarantee human rights (Art. 1 ACHR), to adopt the necessary measures to ensure those rights (Art. 2), and to fulfill in good faith the obligations contracted under the Convention and the OAS Charter.

Antonia Urrejola and Elsy Curihuinca Neira, *Indigenous Rights in the Inter-American System* In: *The Impact of the Inter-American Human Rights System*. Edited by: Armin von Bogdandy, Flávia Piovesan, Eduardo Ferrer Mac-Gregor, and Mariela Morales Antoniazzi, Oxford University Press. © Antonia Urrejola and Elsy Curihuinca Neira 2024.
DOI: 10.1093/oso/9780197744161.003.0014

for precautionary measures (MPMs), as well as through requests for orders and provisional measures filed with the IACtHR. The Commission has insisted that the right of Indigenous peoples to their lands and resources needs to be specially protected because the full exercise of that right not only implies the protection of an economic unit but the protection of the human rights of a community whose economic, social, and cultural development is based on its relationship to the land. When analyzing petitions dealing with cases in which the victims are Indigenous peoples, the Inter-American System has stressed that human rights violations affecting these groups also have implications for their collective rights as communities, societies, and cultures with their own values and ways of living. This is applicable also when dealing with PMs.

The recognition of the right of Indigenous peoples to a cultural identity and to have their sociocultural context taken into account during the different procedural stages to grant a PM in the IACHR—from studying the application to its granting and subsequent follow-ups—can generate more effective joint strategies among Indigenous communities and States, and may go beyond the conventional ways in which the latter have been operating these mechanisms for Indigenous people. We believe that an intercultural perspective and consideration of the collective rights of Indigenous peoples will improve the impact of PMs on protecting Indigenous communities' rights to health, life, and personal integrity.

In that context, regarding Indigenous people who are beneficiaries of PMs, it is worth asking about how the standards developed by the Inter-American System have been interpreted and applied. Is there an intercultural approach when analyzing a PM request? And once the PM has been granted, what challenges exist for its effective implementation? Seeking to answer these questions, the objective of this chapter is to provide an overview of the main inter-American standards regarding Indigenous peoples and how they have been applied through MPMs. Our methodological approach is qualitative, the type of study is descriptive, and our analysis will be based primarily on resolutions issued by the IAHRC.

The first section of the chapter provides an overview of the IAHRS, its constituent bodies, and its mandate. In addition, we discuss three inter-American standards developed on the subject of Indigenous peoples: (1) territorial rights, (2) cultural identity, and (3) participatory rights, all of which must be respected and guaranteed by States when preparing and implementing their laws, policies, and programs. The second section focuses on the MPMs and provides a description of how the IACHR, through the analysis of PM requests, has interpreted and applied the referred standards. The PMs we analyze illustrate the main Indigenous issues addressed by the Commission between 2013 and 2018, with the understanding that there are other issues and cases still to be addressed.

Finally, the third section of the chapter mentions some progress and challenges encountered regarding the implementation of PMs by States and the monitoring carried out by the IACHR in this regard.

2. Inter-American Human Rights System and General Standards Regarding Indigenous Peoples

The IAHRS is a regional system for the promotion and protection of human rights. It was created by the member States of the Organization of American States (OAS). It consists of two bodies: the IACtHR, whose objective is the jurisdictional application and interpretation of the ACHR, and the IACHR, whose main function is to promote the observance and defense of human rights and to serve as an advisory body of the OAS on this matter.

Moreover, the System is based on three international instruments: the Charter of the OAS, the American Declaration of the Rights and Duties of Man, and the ACHR. The American Convention establishes, among other matters, the obligation of States to respect the rights and freedoms recognized therein, as well as the duty to adopt domestic law provisions that are necessary to ensure the enjoyment of such rights.[4] In this sense, States are obligated to adapt national procedures and substantive norms to the rights established in the Inter-American System, as well as to design norms, mechanisms, guidelines, and institutions for the full execution of their decisions.[5] The Inter-American Court and the Commission have the power to decide whether the conduct of a State is in violation of the Convention and other inter-American instruments and, consequently, once the violation has been established, to determine the corresponding remedies.[6] In accordance with the provisions of the American Convention, the decisions of these supervisory bodies are binding on States: they must comply with the judgments of the Court and comply in good faith with the decisions of the IACHR.[7] In fulfilling their mandate, both bodies of the Inter-American System have developed extensive international standards applicable to Indigenous peoples. Among these standards, it is possible to mention the following.

---

[4] Art. 1 of the American Convention on Human Rights ("Pact of San Jose, Costa Rica"), adopted November 22, 1969, and entered into force on July 18, 1978.
[5] Center for Justice and International Law (CEJIL), "Implementation of the decisions of the Inter-American Human Rights System," 2009, https://cejil.org/wp-content/uploads/pdfs/implementacion_aportes_para_los_procesos_legislativos_2.pdf (accessed January 2, 2022).
[6] Arts. 63 and 49 American Convention on Human Rights.
[7] Ibid., art. 14.

2.1. The Right to a Cultural Identity

In accordance with the provisions of Article 1 of the American Convention, States must guarantee on equal terms the full exercise and enjoyment of the rights of persons who are subject to their jurisdiction. In the case of Indigenous peoples, this norm has special significance since Indigenous peoples represent native and diverse societies with their own identity.[8] As such, the right to a cultural identity is a fundamental and collective right of Indigenous communities and must be respected in a multicultural, pluralistic, and democratic society.[9] Under this right, States have a duty to recognize the aspirations of Indigenous peoples to "exercise control over their own institutions, ways of life and economic development and to maintain and develop their identities, languages and religions, within the framework of the States in which they live."[10] This implies that States must adopt the necessary preventive and corrective measures for the full and effective protection of this right.[11] In that sense, the Inter-American Court has established that States must grant "effective protection that takes into account their own particularities, their economic and social characteristics, as well as their situation of special vulnerability, their customary law, values, uses and customs."[12]

2.2. The Right to the Lands, Territories, and Resources of Indigenous Peoples

The jurisprudence of the IAHRS has repeatedly recognized the proprietary rights of Indigenous peoples over their territories and the duty of protection that emanates from Article 21 of the American Convention.[13] Both the Commission and the Court have indicated that Indigenous territorial property is a form of property not based on official State recognition but on the traditional use and possession of the land and its resources.[14] In virtue of this distinction, it has been affirmed that "the traditional possession of the indigenous people on their lands

---

[8] Ibid., Preamble.
[9] *Kichwa Indigenous People of Sarayaku v. Ecuador* [2012], IACtHR, para. 217.
[10] International Labour Organization (ILO), *Indigenous and Tribal Peoples Convention No. 169, 1989*, adopted June 27, 1989 and entered into force on September 5, 1991, Preamble.
[11] Art. 12 American Declaration on the Rights of Indigenous Peoples.
[12] *Case of the Yakye Axa indigenous community v. Paraguay* [2005], IACtHR, Ser. C No. 125, paras. 51, 63.
[13] "Indigenous and Tribal Peoples' Rights over their Ancestral Lands and Natural Resources" (n. 1), para. 55; additionally, see *Case of the Mayagna (Sumo) Awas Tingni Community v. Nicaragua* [2001], IACtHR, Ser. C No. 79, para. 148.
[14] Ibid., para. 140 (a); *Case of the Saramaka People v. Suriname* [2007], IACtHR, Ser. C No. 172, para. 96.

has effects equivalent to the title of full domain granted by the State."[15] Thus, the IAHRS bodies have provided specific content to the right to Indigenous property: on repeated occasions they have emphasized that the territory and natural resources traditionally used by these groups are necessary for their physical and cultural survival.[16] The Court has expressly recognized the right of Indigenous peoples to live freely in their own territories, adding:

> [T]he culture of the members of the indigenous communities corresponds to a particular way of life of being, seeing and acting in the world, constituted from their close relationship with their traditional territories and the resources that are there, not only because they are their main means of subsistence, but also because they constitute an integral element of their worldview, religiosity and, therefore, of their cultural identity.[17]

Recently, the Court reiterated its jurisprudence regarding the collective ownership of the lands and territories of Indigenous peoples by indicating that: (1) the traditional possession that Indigenous peoples have over their lands has effects equivalent to the title of full domain granted by the State; (2) traditional possession gives Indigenous peoples the right to demand official recognition of property and registration; (3) the members of Indigenous communities who, for reasons beyond their control, have left or lost possession of their traditional lands maintain the right of ownership over them, even in the absence of legal title, except when the lands have been legitimately transferred to third parties in good faith; (4) the State must define, demarcate, and grant collective ownership titles over lands claimed by members of Indigenous communities; (5) members of Indigenous communities who have involuntarily lost possession of their lands, and have been legitimately transferred to third parties in good faith, have the right to recover them or obtain other lands of equal size and quality; (6) the State must guarantee the effective ownership of Indigenous peoples to their land and refrain from performing acts that may lead to agents of the State itself, or third parties acting with their acquiescence or tolerance, to affect the existence, value, use, or enjoyment of the respective territory; (7) the State must guarantee the right of Indigenous peoples to effectively control and own their own territory without any external interference from third parties; and (8) the State must

---

[15] *Case of the Mayagna (Sumo) Awas Tingni Community v. Nicaragua* (n. 13), para. 151; *Case of the Sawhoyamaxa Indigenous Community v. Paraguay* [2006], IACtHR, Ser. C No. 146, para. 128; and *Case of the Xákmok Kásek Indigenous Community v. Paraguay* [2010], IACtHR, Ser. C No. 214, para. 109.

[16] *Case of the Yakye Axa Indigenous Community v. Paraguay* (n. 12), paras. 124, 135, 137; *Case of the Sawhoyamaxa Indigenous Community v. Paraguay* (n. 15), paras. 118, 121.

[17] *Case of the Yakye Axa Indigenous Community v. Paraguay* (n. 12), para. 135.

guarantee the right of Indigenous peoples to control and use their territory and natural resources.[18]

2.3. Participatory Rights of Indigenous Peoples

The IAHRS has a vast jurisprudence on the participatory rights of Indigenous peoples. Both the Court and the Commission have recognized that these groups hold the right to consultation as well as free, informed, prior, culturally appropriate, and in-good-faith consent.[19] Likewise, it has been specified that these processes must be carried out beforehand, that is, before the execution of actions that could significantly affect the interests of Indigenous peoples, such as the exploration, exploitation, or extraction of Indigenous peoples lands and resources.[20] In this regard, the Commission has warned that one of the complaints most frequently reported by Indigenous peoples relates to consultation processes occurring after the concession for a given project had been granted.[21] This matter is particularly relevant for the IACHR because Indigenous peoples must have prior and sufficient awareness of the possible risks involved in such projects, including health and environmental risks, in order to voluntarily accept the proposed development or investment plan in an informed way.[22] Specifically regarding the right to consent, the IACHR has expressly stated that the objective of any consultation process must be to reach an agreement or obtain consent. Accordingly:

> [I]ndigenous and tribal peoples must be able to significantly influence the process and the decisions made in it, which includes the accommodation of their perspectives and concerns, for example, through provable and verifiable changes regarding the project objectives, parameters and design, as well as any concerns they may have about the acceptance of the project itself.[23]

---

[18] *Case of the Xucuru Indigenous People and their members v. Brazil* [2018], IACtHR, Ser. C No. 346, para. 117.
[19] In this regard, the IACHR has highlighted the need for the consultation processes to have an advisory mechanism or procedure developed with the participation, collaboration, and coordination of the Indigenous peoples themselves; see *Indigenous Peoples, Afro-Descendant Communities and Natural Resources* (n. 1), para. 195. Additionally, see *Case of the Saramaka People v. Suriname* (n. 14), para. 133; and *Case of the Kichwa Indigenous People of Sarayaku v. Ecuador* (n. 9), para. 186.
[20] *Case of the Kaliña and Lokono Peoples v. Suriname* [2015], IACtHR, Ser. C No. 309, para. 207.
[21] *Indigenous Peoples, Afro-Descendant Communities and Natural Resources* (n. 1), para. 196.
[22] Ibid., para. 179; and IACtHR, *Case of the Saramaka People v. Suriname* (n. 14), para. 134.
[23] *Indigenous Peoples, Afro-Descendant Communities and Natural Resources* (n. 1), para. 179; and IACtHR, *Case of the Saramaka People v. Suriname* (n. 14), para. 134.

3. MPMs and Cultural Pertinence

Much has been written about the inter-American jurisprudence on the rights of Indigenous peoples through the judgments of the IACtHR and the recommendations of the IACHR.[24] However, it seems to us that analyzing MPMs and the effects that they have had on the rights of the Indigenous peoples provides a new perspective.

MPMs were established in Article 25 of the Rules of Procedure of the IACHR,[25] which provides that in grave and urgent situations the Commission may, at its own initiative or at the request of a party, "request that a State adopt precautionary measures. Such measures, whether related to a petition or not, shall concern serious and urgent situations presenting a risk of irreparable harm to persons or to the subject matter of a pending petition or case before the organs of the inter-American system."[26] These measures may be of a collective nature in order to prevent irreparable harm to persons due to their link with an organization, group, or community of determined or determinable persons.[27]

It should be added that the analysis carried out by the IACHR relates only to the requirements of severity, urgency, and the risk of irreparable harm and therefore can be resolved without entering into substantive determinations that are typical when analyzing a case. In that sense, the current Rules of Procedure provide that the granting of the PM will not constitute a prejudgment about the violation of the rights protected in the ACHR and other applicable instruments, and that the decisions on granting, extending, modifying, and lifting them must be issued by informed resolutions.[28]

---

[24] See, e.g., Gonzalo Aguilar Cavallo, "Emergencia de un derecho constitucional común en materia de pueblos indígenas," in Armin von Bogdandy et al. (eds.), *La justicia constitucional y su internacionalización: hacia un Ius constitutionale commune en América Latina? T. II* (UNAM, Instituto de Investigaciones Jurídicas, MPIL, Instituto Iberoamericano de Derecho Constitucional, 2010), 3–84.

[25] This Mechanism has remained in the Commission's Rules of Procedure for more than three decades, and the last regulatory reform came into force on August 1, 2013.

[26] IACHR, "Rules of Procedure of the Inter-American Commission on Human Rights" (approved by the Commission at its 137th regular session, held from October 28, 2009, to November 13, 2009; and modified on September 2, 2011, and at its 147th regular session, held from March 8 to 22, 2013, for its entry into force on August 1, 2013), Article 25.2. In accordance with the provisions of Article 25.2, the Commission, when assessing the origin of a PM, evaluates compliance with the following requirements: "a. the 'seriousness of the situation' means the serious impact that an action or omission may have on a protected right or on the eventual effect of a pending decision in a case or petition before the organs of the Inter-American System; b. The 'urgency of the situation' is determined by the information that indicates that the risk or threat is imminent and can be materialized, thus requiring preventive or protective action; and c. The 'irreparable damage' means the affectation on rights that, by their very nature, are not susceptible to repair, restoration or adequate compensation."

[27] Ibid., art. 25.3.

[28] Ibid, art. 25.7.

PMs fulfill two functions related to the protection of fundamental rights enshrined in the norms of the IAHRS: a "precautionary" function, in the sense of preserving a legal situation under consideration by the IACHR, and a "guardianship" function because they seek to avoid irreparable harm and preserve the exercise of human rights. These considerations have led to the granting of PMs in a wide range of situations. Section 3.1 provides some examples of cases in which the beneficiaries have been Indigenous peoples and where it is possible to note the inclusion of inter-American standards regarding territorial rights, cultural identities, and participation.

3.1. Precautionary Measure No. 113/16: "Tres Islas" Native Community of Madre de Dios Regarding Peru[29]

In Precautionary Measure No. 113/16, the request indicated that the proposed beneficiaries were in a dangerous situation due to a lack of effective, comprehensive, and continuous medical care in relation to the presence of unsafe levels of mercury in their ecosystem as a result of mining activities in their territory. Based on the case background, the IACHR requested that the State, in consultation with the beneficiaries or their representatives, adopt the necessary measures to preserve the life and personal integrity of the members of the community, including carrying out necessary medical diagnoses to determine contamination levels—mercury or other substances—and ensuring that community members have access to nutritionally and culturally adequate food and within levels acceptable to international organizations like the World Health Organization and the Pan American Health Organization.

The Commission noted that the applicants had submitted information on various studies conducted over a number of years that indicated several community members had mercury in their bodies, some exceeding levels considered acceptable. Although these reports referred only to some members of the community, the IACHR considered that "the situation of alleged health risk would extend to the rest of the population, given the relationship that it would have, among other aspects, with the intake of fish allegedly contaminated by mercury, which would constitute one of the main food sources of the community."[30]

This decision is an important advancement, as it is one of the first PMs to recognize an Indigenous community as a collective beneficiary. In its decision, the IACHR indicated that the proposed beneficiaries, despite not being

---

[29] IACHR, Resolution 38/17, Precautionary Measure 113/16, "Tres Islas" Native Community of Madre de Dios, Peru.
[30] Ibid., para. 34.

individualized, were members of the "Tres Islas" Native Community of Madre de Dios, and therefore determinable under the terms of Article 25.6.(b) of the Rules of Procedure of the IACHR.

3.2. Precautionary Measure No. 395/18: Authorities and Members of the Gonzaya (Buenavista) and Po Piyuya (Santa Cruz de Piñuña Blanco) Reserves of the Siona Indigenous People (ZioBain) Regarding Colombia[31]

The proposed beneficiaries of Precautionary Measure No. 395/18 indicated that they were subjected to threats, harassment, and other acts of violence by armed actors in their territory who sought to impose themselves on the native authorities. Additionally, they reported the presence of antipersonnel mines and explosive devices in the area, as well as the problem of Indigenous youth being recruited into armed groups. In this case, the Commission requested the State to adopt the necessary measures to safeguard the life and personal integrity of identified Siona leaders so that the families of the Siona Gonzaya and Po Piyuya Reserves could live safely in their territory. To this end, Precautionary Measure No. 395/18 established measures aimed at enabling the members of the Indigenous communities to move in a safe manner and allowing for the exercise of their cultural and subsistence activities; removing the explosive material; preventing and avoiding the recruitment of young people into armed groups; and strengthening communications to deal with emergencies. The Commission also requested that culturally appropriate measures be taken to protect the life and integrity of the Siona leaders, so that they could fulfill their mandate according to their own norms. Likewise, it indicated that the measures should be adopted with the beneficiaries and/or their representatives in accordance with their own forms of decision-making and systems of self-government.

It should be noted that in this instance the IACHR highly valued the special relationship that Indigenous peoples had with their territory, indicating that the lack of free access to various areas could impede their use, enjoyment, and effective control of it, and exposing them to greater vulnerability and precarious living conditions. Likewise, the IACHR noted that the alleged existence of forced or voluntary recruitment into armed groups, in addition to putting their rights to life and integrity at risk, could lead to the collective community becoming disarticulated and thus deprived of an important demographic

---

[31] IACHR, Resolution 53/18, Precautionary Measure 395/18, Authorities and Members of the Gonzaya (Buenavista) and Po Piyuya (Santa Cruz de Piñuña Blanco) Reserves of the Siona Indigenous People (ZioBain), Colombia.

for the transmission of their values, norms, and culture.[32] In addition, the Commission noted that due to the presence of armed groups, members of the Siona people would have limited mobility, restricting their ability to freely conduct cultural and subsistence activities. These restrictions specifically affected the Siona authorities, who were unable to comply with the mandate granted by their people. Furthermore, the Commission warned that the presence of armed groups could undermine forms of Indigenous organization and leadership, affecting the community's life and future.

3.3. Precautionary Measure No. 860/17: Indigenous Families of the Chaab'il Ch'och' Community Regarding Guatemala[33]

According to the PM request, the Chaab'il Ch'och' community was formed by various families who fled the internal armed conflict from various places in Alta Verapaz, where they had been persecuted and stripped of their lands by armed groups. The complaint alleges that the community became vulnerable as a result of being evicted from an area called Santa Isabel farm. The Commission warned that the fact that families were dispersed—as a consequence of the evictions—into various communities and villages beyond the area where they previously lived could affect the social cohesion of the collective and impact its cultural identity. In this context, the IACHR requested the State to adopt the necessary and culturally appropriate measures to protect the rights to life and personal integrity of the Indigenous families of the Chaab'il Ch'och' community. These measures were aimed at improving, inter alia, sanitary conditions and health and food standards, especially for children, women, and the elderly. In addition, it indicated that these measures should be taken in consultation with the beneficiaries and their representatives.

In addition to recognizing the beneficiaries as a collective subject—namely, those evicted families—the resolution specified the effects the forced eviction could generate on community members, including a breakdown of the social fabric and the weakening and fragmentation of the community. Likewise, the IACHR reiterated that the forced displacement of Indigenous peoples may place them in a situation of special vulnerability, generating a risk of cultural and physical extinction.[34]

---

[32] Ibid., paras. 20–34.
[33] IACHR, Resolution 3/18, Precautionary Measure 860/17, Indigenous Families of the Chaab'il Ch'och' Community, Guatemala.
[34] Ibid., para. 27.

3.4. Precautionary Measure No. 1014/17: U.V.O. Indigenous Girl and Her Family Regarding Mexico[35]

According to the complaint, the proposed beneficiaries suffered threats, intimidation, and accusations from within their own community after having reported the alleged sexual violation of a girl from the community who, as a result of the violation, suffered health problems. The Commission requested the State to adopt the necessary measures to protect the life, personal integrity, and health of the girl and her family. It also requested that culturally appropriate and gender-based measures be adopted that would consider what was in the girl's best interest: to ensure that she had access to necessary medical and psychological care, could study in a protective environment, and live safely in her community. The Commission also stressed the importance of these measures being adopted in consultation with the beneficiaries and their representatives, taking into consideration the opinion of the girl and her best interests.

This case stands out for the intersectional analysis the IACHR made in its reasoning, that is, when establishing that the proposed beneficiary was a girl who, due to her status as a growing person, deserved special, adapted, and reinforced protection and that her best interests and personal development needed to be considered and guaranteed.[36] Furthermore, the Commission added that because she was an Indigenous person, there were specific impacts in the context of the culture of which she is part, referring to the ideas that women in her community have of their own rights and what they consider "good living."[37]

4. Progress and Challenges

States, in compliance with their international obligations, must provide effective protection to the beneficiaries of PMs in order to avoid the materialization of the presented risk. These responses are varied; in some cases they have consisted of granting bodyguards and direct means of communication with authorities, among others. However, despite the efforts made by States, in the case of PMs granted to Indigenous peoples, there have been several implementation challenges.

Recently, during the 172nd Period of Sessions of the IACHR, the Commission highlighted the importance of States being able to develop and strengthen their

---

[35] IACHR, Resolution 27/18, Precautionary Measure 1014/17, U.V.O. Indigenous Girl and family, Mexico.
[36] Ibid., para. 25.
[37] Ibid.

inter-institutional coordination at national, regional, and municipal levels to implement PMs. Likewise, it emphasized that these coordination measures should be adopted not only with due participation but alongside differential, ethnic, and gender and age approaches, as well as within the framework of an intercultural dialogue.[38] During the same occasion, Indigenous representatives from Colombia expressed their concerns that:

> [T]he State [of Colombia] emphasizes the individual scope of the measures and there is little consultation with the indigenous authorities for their implementation and there is no clarity regarding the scope of the collective contained in the precautionary measures [...] All stages of consultation and implementation of precautionary measures must be carried out in the territories, unless the beneficiaries themselves consider otherwise in response to the uses, customs and proper governance of indigenous peoples as well as the specificities of the territories and their geography.[39]

In addition, at the 174th Period of Sessions of the IACHR, various civil society organizations denounced the increase in acts of violence in the Cauca Department of Colombia. In particular, they referred to an increase in retaliatory murders and threats perpetrated by organized armed groups against ancestral authorities and Indigenous guards[40] who have made formal attempts to claim their rights. They stressed that the Cauca Department is the second most militarized area in Colombia and expressed concern about a military deployment announced by the State. They also highlighted the lack of compliance by the Columbian State with various points established in the Peace Agreement, including on matters of ethnicity and the guarantees proposed in the framework on the voluntary substitution of illegal crops. The State, for its part, referred to the deployment of a comprehensive strategy to address the situation in Cauca, which would have a social and a security dimension.[41]

This context is the background for several PMs relating to Indigenous people in Colombia, especially in the Cauca Department, and reveals some of the problems in the implementation of effective, systematic, and culturally appropriate measures to safeguard territorial rights and protect the life and

---

[38] UN, "Implementation of Precautionary Measures with a Differential and Collective Ethnic Approach in Colombia (Indigenous Peoples)," May 9, 2019.

[39] IACHR, Hearing "Implementation of Precautionary Measures with a differential and collective ethnic approach in Colombia," Jamaica, 172 Period of Sessions, May 9, 2019.

[40] The Indigenous Guard is conceived by many Indigenous people in the region as an ancestral body; an instrument of unity, autonomy, and resistance, which acts both in the defense of the territory and the future of the Indigenous community. It is not a police structure but a humanitarian and civil resistance mechanism.

[41] IACHR, Hearing Violence and situation of indigenous peoples in the Department of Cauca in Colombia, Ecuador, 174 Period of Sessions, November 12, 2019.

integrity of Indigenous peoples in Colombia. Meanwhile, the murder rate for Indigenous leaders is on the rise and their precarious situation is intensifying daily. In a public statement, the IACHR expressed its strong condemnation of the attacks and murders committed against persons, leaders, and members of the Indigenous Guard, as well as of the spike in violence in the Cauca Department. According to publicly available information, on Sunday, November 3, 20193 two armed men shot at the Indigenous leader Jesús Mestizo. That same night, Toribío Alexander Vitonas Casamachin was killed by armed men. The Commission also learned of the murder of Cristina Bautista, a leader of the Nasa community, and José Gerardo Soto, James Wilfredo Soto, Eliodoro Uniscue, and Asdruval Cayapu, who were ambushed by a group of unidentified subjects on October 29, 2019, in this same municipality. As a result of this latter attack, Matías Montaño Noscué, José Norman Montano Noscué, Crescencio Peteche Mensa, Dora Rut Mesa Peteche, Rogelio Tasquinas, and Alver Cayapú were also injured.[42]

One of the challenges related to the implementation of PMs by States is the lack of State bodies to oversee compliance and implementation of PMs from an intercultural approach. For the protection and integrity of Indigenous peoples, it is essential to strengthen their autonomy and self-government, including Indigenous security personnel, who have knowledge of their own territory, unlike, in most cases, external State agents. PMs with a differentiated approach are essential to the protection of Indigenous peoples as well as the implementation of inter-American standards, which regard Indigenous peoples as subjects of collective rights.

However, and despite the efforts of the IACHR to monitor compliance with these measures, challenges remain. Although the Commission has a variety of tools to facilitate the follow-up of granted PMs—such as calls for work meetings or hearings in the framework of the IACHR sessions, press releases, thematic reports, or country reports—and there is a "Program to Strengthen Precautionary Measures,"[43] the current context demands greater monitoring efforts in each case. In this regard, a useful precedent is the IACHR Special Mechanism to Follow Up on the Ayotzinapa Matter regarding Precautionary Measure 409-14.

5. Concluding Remarks

The recognition by both the IACtHR and the IACHR of the individual and collective rights of Indigenous peoples can be seen in their various working

---

[42] IACHR, Press Release No. 292/19, "IACHR strongly condemns attacks and murders against persons, authorities and members of the Indigenous Guard in Colombia," November 12, 2019, https://www.oas.org/en/iachr/media_center/PReleases/2019/292.asp (accessed December 16, 2021).

[43] IACHR, "IACHR presents its semi-annual balance sheet report on the implementation of the 2017–2021 Strategic Plan and the results of its work during the first half of 2019," July 31, 2019.

mechanisms, including the system of PMs. In the four cases described, the Commission applied the existing standards on territorial rights, cultural identity, and intersectional and inter-institutional participation: requesting States to adopt culturally appropriate measures to protect the life and integrity of the beneficiaries, valuing the special relationship that Indigenous peoples have with their territory, and expressly requiring that the measures adopted be agreed upon with the beneficiaries or their representatives. However, despite the progress made by the Court and the Commission in these areas, considerable challenges remain. Regarding States in general, there is a lack of State bodies to oversee compliance and the implementation of PMs, especially when they are required to be culturally relevant. The IACHR, for its part, also presents challenges linked to the monitoring of compliance with these PMs by States.

The foregoing issues reveal the need for the different actors to join forces in order to make fulfilling the precautionary and supervisory function of the IAHRS more effective with regards to the human rights of Indigenous peoples living in grave and urgent situations. In the current regional context, this situation gains a higher priority every day. Ombudsmen and national human rights institutions in different countries in the region, as well as the IACHR itself, have found that preventive and protective measures via PMs are increasingly relevant in guaranteeing the rights of Indigenous peoples to life and physical integrity. Their implementation has a real impact on safeguarding the lives of Indigenous beneficiaries.

Despite the preceding, both the IACHR and nongovernmental organizations report an alarming upsurge in violent actions, including murders of Indigenous people and their authorities and leaders, and a growing stigmatization of Indigenous peoples by public officials in the region. Hence, it is essential that States complying with these PMs do so through intercultural dialogue; this way the affected peoples also agree to the measures. The measures should also enable the strengthening of the Indigenous communities' own protection and prevention mechanisms, especially regarding those peoples who have an Indigenous Guard. This is essential when we talk about PMs with Indigenous beneficiaries: the measures must be agreed upon with due participation and with differentiated approaches within the framework of an intercultural dialogue. This is undoubtedly a challenge for States, as well as for the Inter-American System.

II.4
The Inter-American Human Rights System and Its Impact on the Human Rights of Women

The Issue of Sexual Violence

By Julissa Mantilla Falcón

1. Introduction

The importance of the Inter-American Human Rights System (IAHRS)'s recognition of sexual violence as a violation of human rights and formulation of sexual violence criminal investigation guidelines is undeniable. Although this recognition has arrived only recently due to the absence of a gender perspective in the traditional vision of international human rights law (IHRL), it is clear that the input and guidelines of the IAHRS are now making a long-lasting contribution to the fight against impunity concerning the various forms of sexual violence. In this chapter, we present some of the most relevant developments in this topic, highlighting their transformative impact on preventing such occurrences and guaranteeing the adequate punishment thereof.

2. The IHRL Regulatory Framework for the Investigation of Sexual Violence

In recent years, the introduction of a gender perspective into law and, particularly, IHRL has allowed the human rights community to realize how, traditionally, certain forms of gender violence have been neglected. The most prominent example of this is violence against women. In fact, even though equality and nondiscrimination have been recognized as fundamental aspects of human rights since the Universal Declaration of Human Rights (1948), the issue of women's rights and the rights of the LGBTIQ+ community were not a priority in the development of human rights standards. This influenced the late recognition of human rights violations that affect these groups, such as femicide, obstetric violence, sexual violence, and hate-based violence.

The first human rights treaty to specifically address women's rights was the Convention on the Elimination of All Forms of Discrimination against Women (CEDAW, 1979). This treaty defines discrimination against women as "any distinction, exclusion or restriction made on the basis of sex which has the effect or purpose of impairing or nullifying the recognition, enjoyment or exercise by women, irrespective of their marital status, on the basis of equality of men and women, of human rights and fundamental freedoms in the political, economic, social, cultural, civil or any other field" (Article 1).[1] This treaty constituted a critical milestone since, until then, there had been no precise definition of discrimination against women and, in addition, the content of the treaty established obligations on the part of the States to modify the social and cultural patterns of conduct of men and women "with a view to achieving the elimination of prejudices and customary and all other practices which are based on the idea of the inferiority or the superiority of either of the sexes or on stereotyped roles for men and women" (Article 5). In other words, it acknowledges the importance of a vision of the transformation of social reality to eliminate discrimination. Furthermore, it recognizes that the gender stereotypes and roles that are replicated through socialization from childhood contribute to the subordination suffered by women.

In 1989, the CEDAW Committee published General Recommendation No. 12,[2] which recommends that the States report upon their legislation in force to protect women against violence against women, including sexual violence, and upon the support measures for victims, statistical data, and any other measures being taken with the aim of eradicating violence.

In 1992, the CEDAW Committee issued General Recommendation 19, stating that "[g]ender-based violence, which impairs or nullifies the enjoyment by women of human rights and fundamental freedoms under general international law or under human rights conventions, is discrimination within the meaning of Article 1 of the Convention."[3] As can be seen, this document establishes a clear link between violence against women and discrimination. This link has a

---

[1] Convention on the Elimination of All Forms of Discrimination against Women (CEDAW) (1979), <https://www.ohchr.org/EN/ProfessionalInterest/Pages/CEDAW.aspx> (accessed January 14, 2022).

[2] Committee on the Elimination of Discrimination against Women, "Violence against women," General Recommendation No. 12 (1989), <https://conf-dts1.unog.ch/1%20SPA/Tradutek/Derechos_hum_Base/CEDAW/00_4_obs_grales_CEDAW.html#GEN12> (accessed January 14, 2022).

[3] Committee on the Elimination of Discrimination against Women, "Violence against women," General Recommendation No. 19 (January 29, 1992), para. 7, <https://tbinternet.ohchr.org/Treaties/CEDAW/Shared%20Documents/1_Global/INT_CEDAW_GEC_3731_E.pdf> (accessed January 14, 2022).

significant impact because the principle of nondiscrimination is a peremptory norm (*ius cogens*) of IHRL.

In 2017, the CEDAW Committee published General Recommendation 35, stating that "prohibition of gender-based violence against women has evolved into a principle of customary international law."[4] This includes sexual violence, an aspect of extreme relevance, since it enshrines the prohibition of this type of violence in the sphere of international practice, which constitutes a source of international law.

The approval of the CEDAW and the first recommendations of the CEDAW Committee formed the background against which, in 1993, the UN General Assembly—on the occasion of the Second World Conference on Human Rights in Vienna—approved the Declaration on the Elimination of Violence Against Women (the Declaration).[5] The Declaration defines violence against women as "any act of gender-based violence that results in, or is likely to result in, physical, sexual or psychological harm or suffering to women, including threats of such acts, coercion or arbitrary deprivation of liberty, whether occurring in public or in private life" (Article 1).

Additionally, the Declaration includes in its definitions "[p]hysical, sexual and psychological violence occurring in the family, including battering, sexual abuse of female children in the household, dowry-related violence, marital rape, female genital mutilation and other traditional practices harmful to women, non-spousal violence and violence related to exploitation; Physical, sexual and psychological violence occurring within the general community, including rape, sexual abuse, sexual harassment and intimidation at work, in educational institutions and elsewhere, trafficking in women and forced prostitution; Physical, sexual and psychological violence perpetrated or condoned by the State, wherever it occurs" (Article 2). The Declaration would be the precedent for the creation of the UN post of Special Rapporteur on violence against women, its causes and consequences.[6]

In the inter-American sphere, in 1994, the Inter-American Convention on the Prevention, Punishment and Eradication of Violence against Women (Convention of Belém do Pará)[7] was approved. The Convention of Belém do

---

[4] Committee on the Elimination of Discrimination against Women, "Violence against women," General Recommendation No. 35 (July 14, 2017), para. 2, <https://tbinternet.ohchr.org/Treaties/CEDAW/Shared%20Documents/1_Global/CEDAW_C_GC_35_8267_E.pdf> (accessed January 14, 2022).

[5] United Nations General Assembly, "Declaration on the Elimination of Violence Against Women" (1993), <https://www.ohchr.org/EN/ProfessionalInterest/Pages/ViolenceAgainstWomen.aspx> (accessed January 14, 2022).

[6] Commission on Human Rights, Resolution 1994/45 (March 4, 1994).

[7] Inter-American Convention on the Prevention, Punishment and Eradication of Violence against Women (Convention of Belem do Para) (1994), <http://www.cidh.org/Basicos/English/basic13.Conv%20of%20Belem%20Do%20Parahtm> (accessed January 14, 2022).

Pará is the first international treaty that directly focuses on this topic. This treaty conceptualizes violence against women as a violation of human rights, defining it as "any act or conduct, based on gender, which causes death or physical, sexual or psychological harm or suffering to women, whether in the public or the private sphere" (Article 1) and including physical, sexual, and psychological violence that occurs within the family or domestic unit or within any other interpersonal relationship or in the community as well as such violence that is perpetrated or condoned by the State or its agents regardless of where it occurs (Article 2).

Furthermore, Article 7 of the Convention of Belém do Pará stipulates that the States parties agree to pursue, by all appropriate means and without delay, policies to prevent, punish, and eradicate violence against women. One extremely relevant provision of the Convention of Belém do Pará is found in Article 6, which provides for the right of every woman to a life free from violence, including the right of women to be free from all forms of discrimination and the right of women to be valued and educated free of stereotyped patterns of behavior and cultural practices based on concepts of inferiority or subordination. In addition, the Convention addresses the topic through an intersectional approach, indicating that—when adopting measures to prevent, eradicate, and punish violence—the States parties shall "take special account of the vulnerability of women to violence because of, among others, their race or ethnic background or their status as migrants, refugees or displaced persons. Similar consideration shall be given to women subjected to violence while pregnant or who are disabled, of minor age, elderly, socioeconomically disadvantaged, affected by armed conflict or deprived of their freedom" (Article 9). Moreover, the Convention of Belém do Pará establishes the possibility of submitting petitions to the IAHRS when the States parties fail to comply with their obligations (Articles 7 and 12). In this context, the Inter-American Commission on Human Rights (IACHR) established the Rapporteurship on the Rights of Women, also in 1994. The work of this Office has been invaluable concerning the development of standards and reporting on this topic.

In this way, a general international framework for increasing awareness about the human rights of women and for protecting these rights is being gradually consolidated, which in turn will help to enable the denormalization of violence against women and the analysis of violence against women as a human rights issue in the context of State international responsibility. In this regard, we are seeing an increase in the awareness of sexual violence in its various forms and within the framework of the inter-American standards, which we will consider in more detail in the following.

3. Inter-American Standards and Their Role in the Recognition and Condemnation of Sexual Violence

Jurisprudence and advances relating to the IAHRS have contributed to both the definition of sexual violence and to the investigation of sexual violence. Although initial developments did not specifically increase factual awareness, we now have precise, clear standards that have allowed national jurisdictions and local policy development to establish clear action frameworks. In this respect, the first thing to highlight here is that the Inter-American Court of Human Rights (IACtHR) has established through its case law that both CEDAW and the Convention of Belém do Pará supplement international *corpus iuris* with regard to the protection of the personal integrity of women, which forms part of the American Convention on Human Rights (ACHR).[8] In Advisory Opinion 16/99,[9] the IACtHR already stressed the importance of the IHRL *corpus iuris*, establishing that it was composed of international legal instruments with varied content and legal effect (treaties, declarations, and resolutions) and that its dynamic evolution enabled an understanding of the development of fundamental rights. In this sense, the recognition of the conventions mentioned previously as part of this *corpus iuris* has significant consequences for protecting women's rights and, specifically, for the prevention, investigation, and sanctioning of sexual violence and the provision of reparations for victims.

3.1. Recognition of Sexual Violence as a Violation of Human Rights

An initial contribution of extreme importance in this process can be found in the report on the case of *Raquel Martín de Mejía v. Peru* (1996)[10] by the Inter-American Commission on Human Rights, analyzing the sexual violence suffered by the victim in the context of the arbitrary detention of her husband Fernando Mejía Egocheaga, a lawyer, journalist, and political activist, in 1989.

In this report, the IACHR resolves to acknowledge as true the events relating to the rape of Ms. Martín de Mejía by members of the Peruvian army, considering a series of reports from various intergovernmental and nongovernmental organizations documenting "numerous rapes of women in Peru by members

---

[8] *Castro Castro v. Peru* [2006] IACtHR, Ser. C No. 160, para. 276.
[9] *The right to information on consular assistance in the framework of the guarantees of the due process of law* [1999], IACtHR, Advisory Opinion 16, para. 115, <https://corteidh.or.cr/docs/opiniones/seriea_16_ing.pdf> (accessed January 14, 2022).
[10] *Report on Raquel Martin de Mejía v. Peru* [1996], Case 10.970, IACHR, Report No. 5/96, OAS/Ser.L/V/II.91, Doc. 7, at 168.

of the security forces in emergency areas and in which the specific case of Raquel Mejía is mentioned and described as representative of this situation."[11] Additionally, the IACHR recognized the nonexistence of effective domestic legal remedies for Raquel and her husband, taking into account the fact that she did not report the sexual abuse because she was afraid of reprisals and because the available domestic resources were not sufficient to enable the events to be reported.[12] In its analysis, the IACHR concluded that the rape that occurred constituted a violation of the State's international responsibility to prohibit torture as established in Article 5 of the American Convention on Human Rights.[13] To this effect, the IACHR identified elements of physical and mental suffering and the intention of the perpetrator to punish and intimidate, and it found that the act was realized by a member of State forces. Although this case was not referred to the IACtHR, it can be considered as a landmark report with regard to the forcefulness of the conclusions of the IACHR in characterizing rape as a form of torture.

That said, if we take a look at the judgments of the IACtHR at this time, this jurisprudence did not specifically include sexual violence and did not incorporate a gender perspective in its analysis. For example, in the judgment on the case of *María Elena Loayza Tamayo v. Peru* (1997),[14] referring to the detention and subsequent mistreatment of the victim, the IACHR claimed that the right to a humane treatment of the petitioner as per Article 5 of the ACHR had been violated, since she had suffered torture and mistreatment during detention, including rape. Nevertheless, the sentence of the IACtHR stated:

> Although the Commission contended in its application that the victim was raped during her detention, after examination of the file and, *given the nature of this fact, the accusation could not be substantiated*. However, the other facts alleged, such as incommunicado detention, being exhibited through the media wearing a degrading garment, solitary confinement in a tiny cell with no natural light, blows and maltreatment, including total immersion in water, intimidation with threats of further violence, a restrictive visiting schedule, all

---

[11] Ibid.
[12] Ibid.
[13] American Convention on Human Rights, Article 5 Right to Humane Treatment. "1. Every person has the right to have his physical, mental, and moral integrity respected. 2. No one shall be subjected to torture or to cruel, inhuman, or degrading punishment or treatment. All persons deprived of their liberty shall be treated with respect for the inherent dignity of the human person. . . .," <https://www.oas.org/dil/treaties_B-32_American_Convention_on_Human_Rights.pdf> (accessed January 14, 2022).
[14] *Case of María Elena Loayza v. Peru* [1997] IACtHR, Ser. C No. 33, para. 58.

constitute forms of cruel, inhuman or degrading treatment in terms of Article 5(2) of the American Convention. (Emphasis added.)

The IACtHR does not provide further information about the criteria that caused it to accept all the allegations of mistreatment and torture but not those of rape, nor does it give further detail about what the phrase "the nature of this fact" means. Although the IACtHR condemns the State for violations of due process and the infringement of the right to personal integrity in this case, it is clear that the sexual aggression was rendered invisible and that, through its sentence, the IACtHR established a different standard of truth for rape than for other violations of human rights.

Subsequently, the IACtHR's jurisprudence was amended, and in the case of *Plan de Sánchez Massacre v. Guatemala* (2004), the sentence mentioned that "the rape of the women was a common practice designed to destroy one of their most intimate and vulnerable aspects of a person's dignity,"[15] concluding that the victims were stigmatized in their communities.[16]

However, in 2006, with the sentence in the case of the *Miguel Castro Castro Prison v. Peru* (2006),[17] that the IACtHR consolidated a jurisprudential tendency to recognize the existence of sexual violence, clearly identifying it as a violation of human rights and including a gender-based focus in its analysis.

Thus, in this case, the IACtHR states that "during the armed conflicts women face specific situations that breach their human rights, such as acts of sexual violence, which in many cases is used as 'a symbolic means to humiliate the other party.'"[18]

Additionally, the IACtHR analyzes different types of sexual violence and "considers that sexual violence consists of actions with a sexual nature committed with a person without their consent, which besides including the physical invasion of the human body, may include acts that do not imply penetration or even any physical contact whatsoever."[19]

Furthermore, the IACtHR identified the vaginal inspection suffered by one inmate at the Hospital of National Police at the hands of a group of hooded persons as a sexual rape constituting torture, putting aside traditional interpretations limiting rape to sexual relations without consent and establishing that "sexual rape must also be understood as [an] act of vaginal or anal penetration, without the victim's consent, through the use of other parts of the aggressor's body or objects, as well as oral penetration with the virile member."[20]

---

[15] *Case of Plan de Sánchez Massacre v. Guatemala* [2004] IACtHR, Ser. C No. 116, para. 38.
[16] Ibid., para. 49.
[17] *Castro Castro v. Peru* [2006] IACtHR, Ser. C No. 160.
[18] Ibid., paras. 223, 224.
[19] Ibid., para. 306.
[20] Ibid., paras. 309 and 310.

Both the definition of sexual violence and that of rape would serve as references for the analysis of subsequent cases in the region and as a point of reference for the development of national regulations.

In subsequent cases, the IACtHR established important precedents with regard to the concept of rape, the investigation of violent acts, the role of legal practitioners, and gender stereotypes as an element affecting the investigation and punishment of such acts. In this sense, the IACtHR established that rape is a particular type of aggression which, in general, is characterized through the fact that it takes place in the absence of persons other than the victim and the aggressor, which means that there is no visual or documentary evidence, meaning that the word of the victim becomes crucial evidence. Moreover, the IACtHR stressed that acts of sexual aggression constitute a type of crime that victims do not tend to report due to the stigma generally associated with doing so.[21]

In the wake of these advances, the IAHRS has consolidated the concept of sexual violence as a violation of human rights and has made other important contributions to combating impunity in this area.

3.2. The Principle of Enhanced/Stringent Due Diligence

As of the precedent of *Castro Castro v. Peru* (2006), the IACtHR continued to develop its jurisprudence in matters of sexual violence. In 2009, it published the well-known sentence in the case of *González et al. ("Cotton Field") v. Mexico* (2009), dealing with the disappearance and death of Claudia Ivette Gonzáles, Esmeralda Herrera Monreal, and Laura Berenice Ramos Monárrez.[22] In this case, identified as an incidence of violence against women, the IACtHR concluded that the murders of the three women featured high levels of violence, including sexual violence, and identified the existence of a culture of discrimination against women—recognized by the State and by various national and international organizations—which was evident in the motives and methods of the crimes and in the prevailing impunity.[23]

---

[21] In this respect, see *Case of Rosendo Cantú et al. v. Mexico* [2010] IACtHR, Ser. C No. 216; *Case of J. v. Peru* [2013] IACtHR, Ser. C. No. 275.

[22] For an analysis of this decision within a transformative constitutionalism paradigm, see Katrin Tiroch and Luis E. Tapia Olivares, "La Corte Interamericana de Derechos Humanos y la protección transnacional de la mujer: análisis de la sentencia González y otras vs. México (Campo Algodonero)," in Armin von Bogdandy, Eduardo Ferrer Mac-Gregor, and Mariela Morales Antoniazzi (coords.), *La Justicia Constitucional y su Internacionalización:¿ Hacia un Ius Constitutionale Commune en América Latina?* T. II (UNAM 2010), 497–531; Eduardo Ferrer Mac-Gregor and Fernando Silva García, "Homicidios de mujeres por razón de género. El Caso Campo Algodonero," in Armin von Bogdandy, Eduardo Ferrer Mac-Gregor, and Mariela Morales Antoniazzi (coords.), *La justicia constitucional y su internacionalización: ¿Hacia un Ius Constitutionale Commune en América Latina?* T. II (UNAM 2010), 259–333.

[23] *Case of Gonzáles et al. ("Cotton Field") v. Mexico* [2009] IACtHR, Ser. C No. 205, para. 164.

What is interesting here is how the IACtHR analyzes the State's duty of prevention and establishes that, in the specific instance of cases of violence against women, the States "also have the general obligation established in the American Convention on Human Rights, an obligation reinforced since the Convention of Belem do Para came into force."[24] This means that, once again, the IACtHR reinforced the idea of the Convention of Belém do Pará forming part of international *corpus iuris* on the rights of women, reinforcing a jurisprudential tendency in this field that is increasingly progressive.

After analyzing the context of the events of the case, the IACtHR found that the State was aware that there was a real and imminent risk that the victims would be sexually abused, subjected to ill-treatment, and killed and that therefore "an obligation of strict due diligence arises in regard to reports of missing women, with respect to search operations during the first hours and days."[25] This is a fundamental aspect since, in addition to the principle of due diligence that the IACtHR had already recognized since the precedent of *Velásquez Rodríguez v. Honduras* (1987), the Tribunal established a higher threshold for evaluating the diligence of the State with regard to compliance with international obligations, also finding that impunity in such cases contributes to tolerance in general toward violence against women.

Recently, in 2018, the IACtHR ruled on the case of *Linda López Loayza v. Venezuela*,[26] which concerns the deprivation of liberty suffered by the victim in 2001, lasting almost four months. During that time, the victim was subjected to various acts of violence and mistreatment, including sexual violence, to the extent that she subsequently had to spend almost a year in hospital, undergoing numerous surgical interventions.

In this case, and although one individual committed the acts, the IACtHR again stressed that—in addition to the general obligations of the ACHR—States have particular obligations arising from the Convention of Belém do Pará and established that since the acts concerned violence against a woman, this constituted "a circumstance that required an enhanced due diligence that transcended the particular context of this case and resulted in the need to adopt a range of different measures intended, in addition to preventing specific acts of violence, to eradicate any act of gender-based violence in future."[27] As can be seen, the IACtHR again raises the existence of an enhanced/stringent form of due diligence and places it within the framework of the objectives of the Convention of Belém do Pará with regard to the eradication of violent acts.

---

[24] Ibid., para. 258.
[25] Ibid., para. 283.
[26] *Case of Linda López Loaiza v. Venezuela* [2018], IACtHR.
[27] Ibid., para. 136.

Also, in this case, the IACtHR revises its previous jurisprudence and mentions the various elements and indications used to determine whether the State was aware of the inherent risk in cases of violence against women, evaluating the manner in which the State became aware of the facts, the relevant context, and the reports filed or the real possibility of persons connected to the victims filing reports.[28]

Another essential aspect when assessing the due diligence of the States concerns the specific risk of women suffering sexual violence in cases of the kidnapping or disappearance of women, as occurred in the case of *Linda López*. This aspect is highly relevant since it consolidates the idea of the examination of a backdrop of violations of human rights that facilitates the perpetration of sexual violence and that, at the same time, enables an understanding of the failure to report such acts considering the high incidence of disappearances of women and of femicide in the region. This context analysis realized by the IACtHR is an extremely valuable tool for understanding the particular risk of women of suffering sexual violence, allowing us to understand the need for the training and education of agents of the State and legal practitioners to take the complexity of the facts into account as part of compliance by the States with their international obligations with enhanced due diligence.

3.3. The Intersectional Perspective when Approaching the Issue of Sexual Violence

The concept of intersectional analysis arose primarily from the work of Kimberlé Crenshaw who, having studied the situation of Black women and their subordination on the basis of race and gender, highlighted the need to analyze their experiences in a multidimensional way, raising awareness of the complexities of discrimination and the heterogeneity of the groups of people affected by it.[29] In this regard, the concept of intersectionality is a tool enabling awareness to be raised about the "interaction between various forms and sources of systems of power and discrimination,"[30] an aspect that needs to be taken into consideration in the analysis of human rights.

---

[28] Ibid., para. 143.
[29] Suggested further reading on this topic: Kimberlé Crenshaw, "Demarginalizing the Intersection of Race and Sex: A Black Feminist Critique of Antidiscrimination Doctrine, Feminist Theory and Antiracist Politics," 1989 University of Chicago Legal Forum, Article 8, <http://chicagounbound.uchicago.edu/uclf/vol1989/iss1/8> (accessed January 14, 2022); Ben Smith, "Intersectional Discrimination and Substantive Equality: A Comparative and Theoretical Perspective" [2016] 16 *The Equal Rights Review* 73.
[30] United Nations, "Report of the Special Rapporteur on extrajudicial, summary or arbitrary executions on a gender-sensitive approach to arbitrary killings, Human Rights Council," Thirty-fifth Session 2017, para. 21.

In this regard, the inter-American standards incorporate an intersectional perspective when analyzing the human rights of women that allows discrimination to be understood from a structural and historical viewpoint and that, rather than being limited to the sum of individual acts, has a general impact upon the enjoyment of human rights and fundamental freedoms.

In the inter-American sphere, the IACHR has asserted an intersectional approach in its work on promoting and protecting human rights. Without going too far back, in its recent Resolution 1/2020, "Pandemic and Human Rights in the Americas," the IACHR insists that the States parties apply an intersectional perspective in all measures adopted in this context and, in the specific case of women, recommends to the States parties that their response to the pandemic should incorporate the perspective of gender based on an intersectional approach, "taking into account the different contexts and conditions that could increase the vulnerability to which women are exposed, such as, *inter alia*, economic difficulties, age, status as a migrant or displaced person, disability, incarceration, ethnic or racial origin, sexual orientation and gender identity and/or expression."

For the specific case of sexual violence, the IACHR, in its various declarations and reports, has established a series of guidelines with this intersectional perspective for studying and raising awareness of such acts. Thus, for example, in its report on access to justice for women who have been victims of sexual violence, the IACHR highlighted the particular risk that girls, Indigenous women, women with a disability, and women affected by armed conflict have of their human rights being violated.[31]

Additionally, in its report on Indigenous women, the IACHR expressed its concern that forensic medical and legal expert examinations do not ensure respect for Indigenous customs in cases of sexual offenses, establishing that the States have an obligation to realize culturally appropriate expert examinations in cases involving Indigenous women.[32]

Recently, the IACHR published a report on violence toward girls and adolescents, highlighting the impact of this type of violence upon their life plans, as occurs in the case of maternity and forced marriages as a result of rape and in the case of stigmatization suffered in schools, for example, focusing in particular on cases of girls and adolescents of Indigenous or African descent.[33] All of these reports contribute to a better understanding of the specific situations of human

---

[31] IACHR, "Report on Access to Justice for Women Victims of Sexual Violence: Education and Health" (2011), 19, <https://www.oas.org/en/iachr/women/docs/pdf/SEXUALVIOLENCEEducHealth.pdf> (accessed January 14, 2022).

[32] IACHR, "Report on Indigenous Women and Their Human Rights in the Americas" (2017), 104, <http://www.oas.org/en/iachr/reports/pdfs/IndigenousWomen.pdf> (accessed January 14, 2022).

[33] Ibid., paras. 231, 238.

rights violations and the complex impact of sexual violence in the various affected groups.

In the scope of the jurisprudence of the IACtHR, the Tribunal had already revealed its hand from this perspective in the sentences in the cases of *Valentina Rosendo Cantú* and *Inés Fernández Ortega*, both versus Mexico (2010), relating to rape committed on Indigenous women by members of the armed forces. One of the victims was seventeen years old when the acts were committed. In its judgments, the IACtHR highlighted aspects such as the situation of particular vulnerability of the victims as members of Indigenous communities, difficulties in reporting the acts to authorities who did not speak their language, and possible rejection by their community. It also stressed the need to take this situation into account for remedial measures.[34]

Recently, the IACtHR has issued meaningful sentences incorporating an intersectional approach. Firstly, the case of *V.R.P., V.P.C. et al. v. Nicaragua*,[35] concerning irregularities in the judicial process regarding a rape committed on a nine-year-old girl by her father. In the face of the complaints made by the girl's mother (V.P.C.), complaints were filed against her for slander and libel, and she felt obliged to flee the country with her two children for the United States, where they were granted asylum. Applying an intersectional approach, the IACtHR established that, according to Article 19 of the ACHR on the rights of the child, the States parties should adopt special measures for cases of sexual violence in which the victims are children or adolescents over and above the established standards for cases where the victims are adult women, in the context of the obligation of the State to exercise enhanced due diligence.

The IACtHR, therefore, applied the principles of the Convention on the Rights of the Child, referring to the principle of nondiscrimination, the principle of the best interest of the child, the principle of respect for the right to life, survival, and development, and the principle of respect for the opinion of the child.[36] It is worthwhile to underline how the IACtHR consolidates the idea of different standards in this case, guiding the way for the adoption of specific measures by the States for cases relating to children and adolescents, which will consequently result in the adaptation of investigation processes in line with their situation. As is already known, these processes were not conceived with children and adolescents in mind and can bring about their revictimization. This is why the stringent diligence required to avoid the perpetrator's presence and interaction between the perpetrator and the victims is vital.

---

[34] *Case of Fernández Ortega et al. v. Mexico* [2010] IACtHR, Ser. C No. 215; *Case of Rosendo Cantú et al. v. Mexico* [2011], IACtHR, Ser. C No. 47.
[35] *Case of V.R.P. and V.P.C.** et al. v. Nicaragua* [2018] IACtHR, Ser. C No. 350.
[36] Ibid., para. 115.

In this case, the IACtHR recommended that the professionals in charge of the investigation and victim assistance should have training that takes the perspectives of gender and children into account. In its sentence, the IACtHR analyzed each of the procedures and examinations to which the victim was subjected, concluding that these did not respect human rights standards and, furthermore, in many cases constituted discriminatory acts and renewed aggression toward the girl, stating that her participation "was conceived only in terms of evidence and not taking into consideration her situation as a titleholder of rights, whose opinions should have been taken into account."[37]

In March 2020, the IACtHR pronounced sentence in the case of *Azul Rojas Marín et al. v. Peru* (2020),[38] relating to the torture suffered by a transgender woman in 2008 after being detained by the police on her way home. During her arrest and at the police station where she was held, the victim suffered homophobic insults, was forcefully stripped, and subjected to torture and rape.

In this case, the IACtHR stressed the structural and historical discrimination suffered by the LGBTIQ+ population and highlighted the fact that sexual orientation, gender identity, and gender expression are categories that are protected by the ACHR, further establishing that violence against LGBTIQ+ persons has a symbolic purpose since "the victim is chosen in order to communicate a message of exclusion or subordination."[39]

An intersectional approach to cases of sexual violence and other violations of human rights is of the utmost importance to recognize the victims' specific situations and, further, to determine proposals for reparation. In other words, incorporating this approach in inter-American advances relating to sexual violence enables improved and increased awareness of such acts along with specific analysis for the prevention of future, similar acts and the recognition of diversity and nondiscrimination.

3.4. Gender Stereotypes and Their Impact into the Investigation of Sexual Violence[40]

International human rights standards have identified gender stereotypes as a cause of violations of human rights and, in particular, of violence against women, since such stereotypes contribute to the perpetuation of situations of

---

[37] Ibid., para. 189.
[38] *Case of Azul Rojas Marín et al. v. Peru* [2020] IACtHR, Ser. C No. 402.
[39] Ibid., para. 93.
[40] This section has been drafted on the basis of the expert reports presented by the author to the Inter-American Court of Human Rights in her capacity as an expert appraiser for the Inter-American Commission on Human Rights in 2016 and 2017.

subordination and inequality between men and women. In their well-known work, Cook and Cusack define stereotypes as generalized or preconceived views of the personal attributes of men and women, including personality traits, behavioral characteristics, roles, physical characteristics, and social functions.[41]

In this respect, we talk of "gender stereotypes" when certain characteristics, attitudes, and roles are attributed to persons simply because they belong to the female or male social grouping and when it is expected that persons will act accordingly and will not violate the rules and regulations of behavior that have been assigned to them by society. Such stereotypes limit autonomy and personal development since when people do act in a way that contradicts these stereotypes, they are faced with social condemnation that jeopardizes their autonomy, human rights, and fundamental freedoms and which can result in situations of violence.

At the IAHRS level, the jurisprudence of the IACtHR has enabled the challenging of the gender stereotypes present in the investigation of violence against women and in the punishment of perpetrators; these stereotypes have contributed to the widespread impunity in this area. In the specific case of sexual violence, in the *Cotton Field* case, the IACtHR established that stereotypes are one of the causes and one of the consequences of gender violence toward women.[42] Similarly, throughout its jurisprudence, the IACtHR stresses that one of the prerequisites for access to justice on the part of victims of sexual violence is establishing rules for assessing evidence that avoids gender stereotypes[43] that could encourage impunity.

Moreover, in the case of *Claudina Velásquez Paiz v. Guatemala* (2017),[44] concerning the disappearance and death of a young Guatemalan woman, the IACtHR noted that the absence of a gender-based approach in the criminal investigation—so an investigation based in preconceived ideas and stereotypes—would render invisible prior events and the circumstances in which the death occurred as well as the sexual violence suffered by the victim. In other cases, the IACtHR has established that gender stereotypes contribute to undermining the credibility of the victims and to making them feel responsible for the violence they have suffered—due to their sexual conduct, occupation, or way of dressing—and that this affects the lines of investigation that the State should follow in such cases.[45]

---

[41] Rebecca J. Cook and Simone Cusack, "Gender Stereotyping: Transnational Legal Perspectives" [2010] *Profamilia* 11.
[42] *Case of Gonzáles et al. ("Cotton Field") v. Mexico* [2009] IACtHR, Ser. C No. 205.
[43] *Case of Espinosa Gonzáles v. Peru* [2014] IACtHR, Ser. C No. 283, para. 278.
[44] *Case of Velásquez Paiz et al. v. Guatemala* [2017] IACtHR, Ser. C No. 307, para. 197.
[45] *Case of Gutiérrez Hernández v. Guatemala* [2017] IACtHR, Ser. C No. 339, para. 170.

3.5. Responsibility of the State for Sexual Violence as Torture

Although the IAHRS has recognized various kinds of sexual violence, in this section, we will focus on the development of sexual violence as torture and the standards for the responsibility of the State, since this is an issue where inter-American jurisprudence has made extremely recent contributions.

As pointed out previously, with the case of *Raquel Martín de Mejía v. Peru* (1996), the IACHR started to analyze rape as a form of torture, a precedent which was reflected in subsequent IAHRS developments, in addition to the aforementioned case of *Castro Castro v. Peru* (2006).

In its jurisprudence,[46] the IACtHR has analyzed certain acts of sexual violence in the light of the Inter-American Convention to Prevent and Punish Torture, identifying intent, the severe physical and mental suffering resulting from such acts, and the fact that the acts are committed for a specific purpose or end as prerequisites for classification as torture. In its jurisprudential development, the IACtHR has stated that severe suffering on the part of the victim is inherent to sexual violence even if there is no evidence of injury or physical harm, recognizing the fact that victims experience psychological and social damage and consequences, and listing standards of international criminal courts. With regard to the purpose of sexual violence as torture, the IACtHR has stated that it has the objective to intimidate, degrade, humiliate, punish, or control the person subjected to it.

About the responsibility of the State, the IACtHR has stressed in its jurisprudence that sexual violence committed by agents of the State while the victims are in custody constitute serious and reprehensible acts where the agent abuses his power and takes advantage of the vulnerability of the victim, which can cause serious psychological consequences for the victim.[47] In this context, in the recent sentence in the case of *Women Victims of Sexual Torture in Atenco v. Mexico* (2018),[48] the IACtHR resolved that the sexual violence—besides constituting torture—was used by agents of the State as a strategy of control and dominance that entailed using the detained women to transmit a message of repression. Similarly, the IACtHR found that the absence of a gender

---

[46] In this respect, see *Case of Inés Fernández Ortega v. Mexico* [2010] IACtHR, Ser. C No. 215, paras. 120 et seq., *Case of Rosendo Cantú et al. v. Mexico* [2010] IACtHR, Ser. C No. 216; *Case of Espinoza Gonzáles v. Peru* [2014] IACtHR, Ser. C No. 289.

[47] The Inter-American Court of Human Rights pronounced accordingly in the case of *Favela Nova Brasília v. Brazil*, 2017, para. 255, <https://www.corteidh.or.cr/docs/casos/articulos/seriec_333_esp.pdf>, and in the case of *Women Victims of Sexual Torture in Atenco v. Mexico*, 2018, para. 196, <https://www.corteidh.or.cr/docs/casos/articulos/seriec_371_ing.pdf> (accessed January 14, 2022).

[48] *Case of Women Victims of Sexual Torture in Atenco v. Mexico* [2018] IACtHR, Ser. C No. 371.

perspective in the investigation of torture and sexual violence violated the special obligations imposed by the Convention of Belém do Pará and the obligation to respect and guarantee the rights contained in the ACHR without discrimination.

Furthermore, in the case of *Linda López Soto et al. v. Venezuela*, the IACtHR made reference to the Convention of Belém do Pará, confirming that this text "should permeate the evolutive interpretation of conducts and acts of violence against women that may be categorized as torture."[49] As mentioned previously, the victim was kidnapped and subjected to a series of abusive and aggressive acts, including rape constituting violations of her right to personal integrity, these being analyzed by the IACtHR. In conclusion, the IACtHR stated that "intentional acts perpetrated by a private individual that cause a woman severe physical, sexual or psychological suffering may constitute acts of torture and deserve a punishment adapted to their severity to achieve the goal of their eradication."[50]

However, since the acts were not committed by public officials, the State questioned their classification as torture. Despite this, the IACtHR found that classification as torture was not limited only to "its perpetration by public officials, and the State's responsibility is not engaged merely by the direct action of its agents,"[51] thus setting an important precedent with regard to the scope of the State's responsibility in this matter. Moreover, making use of the evolutive interpretation for analyzing acts of violence against women that might constitute torture and making reference to the Convention of Belém do Pará, the IACtHR concluded that "acts of violence against women perpetrated by private individuals cannot be excluded, when they are committed with the State's tolerance or acquiescence because it has deliberately failed to prevent them,"[52] condemning the State in that its failure enabled the acts of torture against the victim.

This case represents a milestone in this field. It opens up the possibility of the State being held responsible for sexual violence committed by individuals, which is essential because many acts of gender violence toward women and girls take place in the private sphere and not necessarily only by agents of the State. This analysis of the IACtHR, developing the notion of State responsibility, without a doubt enables the consolidation of improved protection standards for the victims of sexual violence.

---

[49] *Case of Linda López Soto et al. v. Venezuela* [2018] IACtHR, Ser. C No. 362, para. 197.
[50] Ibid., para. 194.
[51] Ibid., para. 192.
[52] Ibid., para. 197.

4. Concluding Remarks

While prior to the turn of the millennium, as in particular reflected in the case of *María Elena Loayza Tamayo v. Peru* (1997), the IACtHR did not yet include a gender perspective in its interpretations and even rendered sexual aggression invisible, subsequent jurisdiction adapted to a trend which already had been paved by the IACHR and its landmark report on the case of *Raquel Martín de Mejía v. Peru* (1996). Forthcoming, an inter-American *corpus iuris*, with the Convention of Belém do Pará at its heart, was consolidated and contributed both to a more precise definition and to the investigation of sexual violence. As such, the sentence in the case *González et al. ("Cotton Field") v. Mexico* (2009) specified the obligations of States and their duty of prevention. In 2018, the IACtHR ruled on the case of *Linda López Loayza v. Venezuela* and thereby placed due diligence within the framework of the objectives of the Convention of Belém do Pará to further promote and guarantee the eradication of violent acts.

Both the Court's intersectional approach and the challenging of gender stereotypes—present in the investigation of violence against women and in the punishment of perpetrators—complement the *corpus iuris*. The intersectional approach has led to an acknowledgment of the increased vulnerability and discrimination of certain groups as rooted in structural and historical conditions. This has helped to determine proposals for reparation and enforces a recognition of diversity and nondiscrimination. Likewise, gender stereotypes have been revealed to be present in the investigation of violence against women and in the punishment of perpetrators. Finally, over the past decades, the IACtHR has analyzed certain acts of sexual violence in the light of the Inter-American Convention to Prevent and Punish Torture, thereby both defining sexual violence as a form of torture as well as reminding of the State obligations in this regard, in particular when it comes to violent acts on behalf of agents of the State.

In sum, the definition of sexual violence as gender violence and violation of human rights coincides with a process of international standards development in which the IAHRS has played an important role. States in the region have a necessary set of legal tools that enables them to comply with international obligations and reduce impunity in such cases. Further, in the IAHRS, victims have a means of access to justice in which they can have their dignity recognized and—above all—recover the full enjoyment of their human rights and freedom.

II.5
The Transformative Impact of the *Artavia Murillo* Case on In Vitro Fertilization

By Silvia Serrano Guzmán

1. Introduction and Brief History of the Case

On January 19, 2001, an individual petition was filed before the Inter-American Commission on Human Rights (IACHR) against the Republic of Costa Rica in representation of nine infertile couples who were affected by the general prohibition against the practice of assisted reproduction known as in vitro fertilization (IVF). The number assigned to the petition was 12,361, and it had different denominations during the proceedings before the Commission.[1] The Inter-American Court of Human Rights (IACtHR) named the case *Artavia Murillo and others—In Vitro Fertilization ("Artavia Murillo") v. Costa Rica*. The basic facts of the case can be summarized as follows. On March 15, 2000, the Constitutional Chamber of the Supreme Court of Justice of Costa Rica (the Constitutional Chamber) issued a judgment with general effects in which it declared that Executive Decree 24029-5 of February 3, 1995, was unconstitutional. This Executive Decree authorized IVF treatment for married couples and included a regulation for its practice.

The substantive argument of the Constitutional Chamber was related to its interpretation of the scope of the protection of the right to life. The Constitutional Chamber first established that, given the stage of scientific development at the moment of the judgment, the practice of IVF necessarily encompassed the loss of embryos. A reference was then made to the right to life being enshrined in the Costa Rican Constitution and the American Convention on Human Rights (ACHR) and concluded that both normative instruments impose an absolute protection of the embryos that result from the fertilization of an egg by sperm outside the womb and are not implanted into the uterus.[2] On March 11, 2004, the

---

[1] Gretel Artavia Murillo et al. ("In Vitro Fertilization") [2010] IACHR, "Report No. 85/10," Case 12.361.
[2] Constitutional Chamber of the Supreme Court of Justice, Costa Rica, Judgment No. 2000-02306 of March 15, 2000, Case file No. 95-001734-007-CO.

Silvia Serrano Guzmán, *The Transformative Impact of the* Artavia Murillo *Case on In Vitro Fertilization* In: *The Impact of the Inter-American Human Rights System*. Edited by: Armin von Bogdandy, Flávia Piovesan, Eduardo Ferrer Mac-Gregor, and Mariela Morales Antoniazzi, Oxford University Press. © Silvia Serrano Guzmán 2024. DOI: 10.1093/oso/9780197744161.003.0016

Commission approved its Admissibility Report No. 25/2004, which established its competence to decide the petition and declared that it was admissible under the requirements of Articles 46 and 47 of the ACHR.[3] The Commission received the additional allegations on the merits from the petitioners and the State, as well as several additional submissions. It also held a public hearing on the merits during its 133º period of sessions on October 28, 2008. The Commission received a relevant number of amici curiae briefs in support of the arguments of both parties.[4]

According to Article 50 of the ACHR, on July 14, 2010, the IACHR approved its Merits Report No. 85/10, in which it established the international responsibility of Costa Rica for the violation of Articles 11.2 (right to privacy), 17.2 (rights of the family), and 24 (right to equal protection) of the Convention in relation to the general obligations established in Articles 1.1 and 2 of the same treaty, to the detriment of the eighteen persons named on the initial petition. The Commission also recommended that Costa Rica (1) lift the domestic prohibition on the practice of IVF, (2) guarantee that the regulation of IVF after lifting the prohibition is compatible with its international obligations, and (3) provide integral reparations for the victims.[5] The Commission notified its Merits Report to the parties and requested Costa Rica to provide information within two months regarding compliance with the recommendations. After granting three extensions at this stage, the IACHR considered that Costa Rica did not report substantial compliance with the recommendations. Therefore, on July 29, 2011, the Commission submitted the case to the Court.[6]

The case was processed by the Court as established in its Rules of Procedure. Consequently, the representatives of the victims presented their autonomous Briefs containing Pleadings, Motions, and Evidence on December 19 2011,[7] and the State presented its Answer on April 30, 2012[8]. Given that the State filed preliminary objections, the Court granted to both the Commission and the representatives of the victims an additional opportunity for written allegations regarding those objections.[9] A few months later, the Court held a public hearing on September 5–6, 2012, in which victims, witnesses, and expert witnesses presented their declarations and the parties presented their oral allegations.[10]

---

[3] *Ana Victoria Sánchez Villalobos and others* [2004] IACHR, "Report No. 25/04," Petition 12.361.
[4] *Gretel Artavia Murillo et al. ("In Vitro Fertilization")* (n. 1).
[5] *Gretel Artavia Murillo et al. ("In Vitro Fertilization")* (n. 1).
[6] IACHR, Submission Note to the IACtHR, https://www.corteidh.or.cr/docs/casos/articulos/seriec_257_ing.pdf (accessed December 29, 2022).
[7] IACtHR, Article 40 of the Rules of Procedure.
[8] IACtHR, Article 41 of the Rules of Procedure.
[9] IACtHR, Article 42 of the Rules of Procedure.
[10] For the complete hearing, see https://vimeo.com/48921880 (accessed December 29, 2022).

After receiving the final written allegations, the IACtHR issued its judgment on the preliminary objections, merits, reparations, and costs on November 28, 2012.

The *Artavia Murillo* judgment is paradigmatic for several reasons. First, considering the judgment itself, it was the first opportunity to develop in various directions the case law of the Inter-American System. The interpretation of the Court has been used by a number of domestic tribunals in other States and functions as the basis for the recognition of reproductive rights.[11] Second, although the case was presented in favor of eighteen individualized victims, it has had a nationwide impact in Costa Rica. Third, during the process of compliance supervision, the Court played an unprecedented role in safeguarding the effectiveness of its decision. This chapter is intended to describe and comment on each component of the widespread and multilevel impact of this case.

2. Transformative Impact in the Development of Inter-American Jurisprudence

The evolution of the case law of the Inter-American System in the wake of the *Artavia Murillo* case can be presented in two main topics: (1) the interpretation of the protection of the right to life under Article 4.1 of the Convention, and (2) the legal standards related to reproductive rights, including the right to "reproductive autonomy" and its permissible limitations.

2.1. The Interpretation of the Protection of the Right to Life under Article 4.1 of the Convention[12]

The IACtHR noted that the Constitutional Chamber interpreted Article 4.1 of the Convention to establish the absolute protection of the right to life and subsequently justified the prohibition of IVF on these grounds. Therefore, it deemed it necessary to analyze, as the authoritative interpreter of the Convention, whether such an interpretation was admissible. In order to do so, the Court resorted to the methods of interpretation provided in the Vienna Convention on the Law of Treaties, as well as the parameters set forth in Article 29 of the Convention.

---

[11] For a broader analysis of how Inter-American precedents generate transformative impact: Ximena Soley, "The transformative dimension of inter-American jurisprudence," in Armin von Bogdandy et al. (eds.), *Transformative Constitutionalism in Latin America: the emergence of a new ius commune* (Oxford University Press 2017), 337–355.

[12] *Artavia Murillo et al. ("In Vitro Fertilization") v. Costa Rica* [2012], IACtHR, Ser. C No. 257. The contents of the Judgment quoted under this subheading can be found in paras. 171–264.

In this section, I will summarize the result of the interpretation according to each method and the final conclusion of the Court.

2.1.1. Interpretation in Accordance with the Ordinary Meaning of the Terms

As the start, the IACtHR recalled the literal content of Article 4.1 of the ACHR: "Every person has the right to have his life respected. *This right shall be protected by law and, in general, from the moment of conception.* No one shall be arbitrarily deprived of his life [emphasis added]." Based on such wording, the Court underlined the relevance of assessing the terms "conception" and "in general." The following were the main considerations of the Court with respect to those terms:

- According to the scientific evidence and the expert declarations received during the processing of the case, IVF transformed the understanding of the term "conception" because it showed the possibility that some time frame passes between the union between the egg and the sperm and the actual implantation of the embryo in the uterus. In 1969 (the year the Convention was signed), the Royal Spanish Academy defined "conceive" as "the female getting pregnant," and "fertilize" as "join[ing] together the male reproductive element to the female one." These definitions remain almost identical for the Royal Spanish Academy. The scientific evidence coincides in stating that only when the moment of implantation ends is it possible to speak of conception because there is no chance of development without implantation of the embryo. When Article 4 of the Convention was drafted, neither the Royal Spanish Academy nor the Convention mentioned the moment of fertilization when referring to conception.
- Regarding the expression "in general," the literal interpretation indicates that the norm involves the possibility of considering exceptions.

The conclusion of the IACtHR under this method of interpretation was that (1) the term "conception" is related to the moment of implantation inside the woman's body and, therefore, before that event the protection of the right to life established in Article 4 of the Convention is not applicable; and (2) the expression "in general" entails exceptions to the rule.

2.1.2. Systematic and Historical Interpretation

The Court then proceeded to the systematic and historic methods of interpretation, recalling that norms should be interpreted as part of a whole and their meaning and scope must be established on the basis of the legal system to which they belong. In the *Artavia Murillo* case, the relevant legal system is international human rights law. Consequently, the IACtHR considered the approach of (1) the Inter-American System, (2) the Universal System, (3) the European System, and (4) the African System. The Court also explained that Article 32 of the Vienna Convention on the Law of Treaties provides the *travaux preparatoires* of a treaty may be used to confirm the result of the interpretation based in Article 31 (in accordance with the ordinary meaning of the terms), or when such interpretation leads to an ambiguous or unclear result, or when the result is manifestly absurd or unreasonable. Article 31.4 of the same Convention states that a term can be afforded a special meaning if it appears that it was the intent of the parties. On that basis, the Court deemed it pertinent to use the *travaux preparatoires* when analyzing the approach in each system. The considerations of the Court with respect to each system are summarized in the following paragraphs.

With respect to the Inter-American System, the *travaux preparatoires* of the American Declaration of the Rights and Duties of Man do not offer a definitive conclusion. The *travaux preparatoires* of the Convention show that the proposal eliminating the expression "and, in general, from the moment of conception," as well as the proposal eliminating only "in general," were unsuccessful. Both the Declaration and the Convention refer to "every person" in numerous articles. From the analysis of such articles, it is not feasible to hold that the embryo is the holder and can exercise the rights that they enshrine. Therefore, the systematic and historic interpretation of the precedents of the Inter-American System confirms that the status of "person" cannot be granted to the embryo.

Regarding the Universal System, the *travaux preparatoires* of the Universal Declaration of Human Rights show that the drafters expressly rejected the proposal of eliminating the term "born," which aimed to exclude the unborn child form the rights established in the Declaration. In that sense, the expression "human being" used in the Declaration has not been understood to include the unborn. The *travaux preparatoires* of Article 6 of the International Covenant on Civil and Political Rights (establishing the right to life) indicate that the States did not intend on giving to the unborn the treatment of a person nor granting it the same level of protection accorded to children already born. Also, none of the General Comments of the Human Rights Committee refer to the right to life of the unborn child. In that sense, the Covenant does not entail an absolute protection of the embryo, or prenatal life. The decisions and observations of the Committee on the Elimination of Discrimination against Women—that is, the authoritative interpreter of the Convention on the Elimination of All Forms of Discrimination against Women—point to the argument that the principle of equality and nondiscrimination requires that the rights of the pregnant woman are privileged over the interest of protecting the life of her unborn child. Finally, the Convention on the Rights of the Child defines "child" as "every human being below the age of eighteen years, unless under the laws applicable to the child majority is attained earlier." The Preamble of this treaty noted the need to grant protection to the child "before as well as after birth." The *travaux preparatoires* indicate that this phrase did not have the intention of extending the provisions of the Convention to the unborn child. Indeed, there was a compromise for the inclusion of said reference in the Preamble, but the *travaux preparatoires* clarify that the Preamble would not define the interpretation of the Convention.

With respect to the European System, the provision establishing the right to life in the European Convention on Human Rights states that "everyone's right to life shall be protected by law." The former European Commission on Human Rights and the European Court of Human Rights have interpreted this provision in the sense that the protection of prenatal life is not absolute. This interpretation has been made in the context of cases involving abortion and medical treatments like IVF. Finally, in the African System, the provision of the Charter on Human and People's Rights establishes that "every human being shall be entitled to respect for his life and for the integrity of his person." The drafters of the Charter expressly disregarded terminology that implied the protection of life from the moment of conception.

Based on the foregoing, the IACtHR concluded that under the systematic and historical interpretation none of the international treaties quoted by the Constitutional Chamber and by Costa Rica in its defense can be used as the basis for considering the embryo a person in terms set out in Article 4 of the Convention. Neither the *travaux preparatoires* nor the systematic interpretation of the Convention and the American Declaration lead to such a finding.

2.1.3. Evolutive Interpretation

The Court recalled that international treaties are living instruments and their interpretation must be consistent with current living conditions, as per Article 29 of the Convention. The IACtHR underlined that an evolutive interpretation is particularly pertinent in this case, considering that by the moment the Convention was signed IVF treatment did not exist. The Court analyzed two topics in terms of an evolutive interpretation: (1) the legal status of the embryo, and (2) the regulations and practices in comparative law in relation to IVF. The Court gave consideration to both topics. With respect to the *legal status of the embryo*, from the decisions of the European Court of Human Rights and the Court of Justice of the European Union, as well as the Oviedo Convention for the Protection of Human Rights and Dignity of the Human Being with regard to the Application of Biology and Medicine, the IACtHR concluded that the regulatory tendencies of international law do not lead to the conclusion that the embryo is accorded the same treatment as a person or that it is afforded a right to life. Regarding the *regulations and practices in comparative law*, Costa Rica is the only country that has a prohibition in place. Although there are not many regulations on IVF, most States in the region permit its practice. That means that from the perspective of the practice of most of the State parties, IVF treatment has been understood to be permissible under the Convention. Such general practice is linked to the principle of gradual and incremental (rather than absolute) protection of prenatal life. It is also linked to the conclusion that the embryo cannot be understood as a person.

2.1.4. The Principle of the Most Favorable Interpretation, and the Object and Purpose of the Treaty (Teleological Interpretation)

The Court recalled that the teleological interpretation consists of analyzing the intention of the interpreted norms, its object and purpose, and, when pertinent, the aims of the regional system of protection. In the opinion of the Court, the systematic and teleological interpretations are closely related. The IACtHR considered that the position taken by Costa Rica denied the existence of other rights that could be subjected to disproportionate limitations as a result of the absolute protection of the right to life. This position is contrary to the protection of human rights, which constitute the purpose and object of the treaty. Furthermore, the Court mentions that some judgments of constitutional tribunals show that it is possible to strike an adequate balance between the possible rights at stake, which is a relevant reference to interpret the sentence "in general, from the moment of conception" as established in Article 4.1 of the Convention.[13] In sum, the IACtHR considered that the most favorable interpretation of such a provision (in line with its object and purpose) is to allow an adequate balance between the rights and interests in tension. According to the Court, this interpretation implies that it is not acceptable to argue for an absolute protection of the embryo, which would have the effect of nullifying other possible rights involved.

2.1.5. Conclusion on the Interpretation of Article 4.1 of the Convention

Based on the foregoing, the Court reached the conclusion, expressed in Paragraph 264 of the judgment that the different methods of interpretation lead to consistent results. First, the embryo cannot be understood as a person for the purposes of Article 4.1 of the Convention, and the scientific evidence shows that "conception" in the meaning of the provision takes place from the moment the embryo is implanted into the uterus, which means that before implantation Article 4 of the Convention is not applicable. Moreover, the words "in general" mean that the protection of the right to life established in the provision

---

[13] The IACtHR here quotes the German Constitutional Court, the Constitutional Court of Spain, the US Supreme Court, the Constitutional Court of Colombia, the Argentine Supreme Court of Justice, and the Supreme Court of Justice of Mexico.

is not absolute, that such protection entails exceptions, and that it is "gradual and incremental."

2.2. The New Legal Standards Related to Reproductive Rights, Including the Right to Reproductive Autonomy and Its Permissible Limitations[14]

Artavia Murillo was the first case related to reproductive rights decided by the IACtHR. The main legal issue was the determination on whether the prohibition against IVF arbitrarily affected the rights to personal integrity (Article 5), personal liberty (Article 7), a private life (Article 11), and to a family (Article 17), as well as the prohibition against discrimination (Article 1.1). The process was to first assess whether there was an interference in the exercise of those rights and, if so, to establish whether such interference was arbitrary or disproportionate. In the analysis of the first step, the Court had the opportunity to set forth for the first time a number of legal standards:

- The decision on whether or not to become a parent is part of the right to a private life and the right to a family, protected by Articles 11 and 17 of the Convention and includes the decision on whether or not to become a mother or a father in the genetic or biological sense. This decision is protected from the perspective of the individual and that of the couple.
- The right to personal liberty established in Article 7 of the Convention should be read in a broad sense, that is, as the ability to do and not do all that is lawfully permitted. This includes the possibility of all human beings to self-determination and to choose freely the options and circumstances that give meaning to their life, according to their own choices and beliefs, in keeping with the law.
- The right to a private life enshrined in Article 11 of the Convention, and also the right to personal liberty protected by Article 7 of the same treaty, is related to reproductive autonomy and to have access to reproductive services, which includes the right to have access to the medical technology necessary to exercise this right. For the first time, the IACtHR mentioned the existence of a right to "reproductive autonomy" protected by the Convention as a derivation of the right to a private life and to personal liberty. Moreover, the Court (also for the first time) referred to access to scientific progress as a means of realizing the right to reproductive autonomy.

---

[14] *Artavia Murillo et al. ("In Vitro Fertilization") v. Costa Rica* (n. 12): the contents of the judgment that are quoted under this subheading can be found in paras. 141–151 and 272–316.

- Reproductive autonomy is also related to healthcare. The lack of legal safeguards that take reproductive health into consideration can result in a serious impairment to the right to reproductive autonomy. Consequently, there is a connection between personal autonomy, reproductive freedom, and physical and mental integrity. The right to reproductive health entails the rights of men and women to be informed about, be free to choose, and have access to methods of fertility regulation that are safe, effective, easily accessible, and acceptable.

After considerations on the substantive rights affected by the prohibition of IVF, the Court recalled that such rights can be subjected to limitations, as long as they are not arbitrary or abusive. According to the case law of the Court, in order to be compatible with the Convention such limitations need to (1) be established by law in the formal and material sense, (2) pursue a legitimate aim, and (3) comply with the requirements of suitability, necessity, and proportionality *strictu sensu*. In *Artavia Murillo*, the IACtHR stated that there was no need to analyze each requirement, given that—as a consequence of the determinations above with respect to the scope of the right to life—the absolute protection of the life of the embryo has no basis under the Convention. The Court implied that the State had not pursued a legitimate aim and considered that this fact was enough to conclude the arbitrary and abusive nature of the limitation of rights and the consequent international responsibility of the State.

The Court deemed it pertinent to explain the extent to which the rights at stake in the case were sacrificed and that this outcome was not offset by the advantages allegedly obtained via the absolute protection of the embryo. In other words, even though the Court determined that the prohibition against the practice of IVF did not comply with the basic requirement of pursuing a legitimate aim, it proceeded to the analysis of the last requirement, the proportionality *strictu sensu* to carry out a balancing exercise for pedagogic purposes. The Court emphasized that for the limitation to be proportional *strictu sensu* in the specific case, it must satisfy to a significant degree the protection of prenatal life without nullifying the rights involved. The balancing was achieved according to three issues: (1) the degree of impact to the rights at stake (grave, intermediate, or moderate); (2) the importance of the satisfaction of the interest pursued by the limitation; and (3) whether the satisfaction of the latter justifies the limitation of the former.

With respect to the *degree of interference in the exercise of the rights involved*, the Court affirmed that it was severe, particularly with respect to the couples whose only option to have a biological child was through IVF. It mentioned, among other aspects, the psychological impact derived from the lack of access to an existing procedure that enabled their desired reproductive liberty. The Court also took into account (in establishing the severity of the limitation) the fact that infertility can be considered a disability, with distinct consequences related to gender and class, in the sense that not all infertile couples have the economic resources to travel to another country where IVF is permitted. Regarding the *importance of the satisfaction of the interest to protect embryonic life*, the Court indicated that the evidence indicates that embryonic loss takes place in the context of both natural and IVF-assisted pregnancies. It considered it disproportionate to claim an absolute protection of the embryo with respect to a risk that is not only common but inherent to the natural process of conception.

Based on those findings, the Court reached the conclusion that the prohibition against IVF created a severe limitation to the rights to personal integrity, personal liberty, privacy, reproductive autonomy, access to reproductive health services, and to start a family. In contrast, the impact on the protection of the embryo is very low, given that embryonic loss occurs in IVF and natural pregnancy. Therefore, the Court affirmed that the protection of embryonic life had no basis under the American Convention and the limitation of the rights at stake was disproportionate.

2.3. Impact on the Decisions of Domestic Tribunals in Other Countries of the Region

The impact of the *Artavia Murillo* case is not limited to Costa Rica. The judgment not only established legal standards applicable to all the States parties to the American Convention but those standards have also been used by domestic tribunals in different countries.[15]

For example, on June 22, 2016, the Constitutional Court of Colombia issued Judgment C 327-16 on the constitutionality of Article 90 of the Civil Code. According to this provision, the legal existence of the person begins at the moment of birth. The Constitutional Court of Colombia, taking into consideration the standards set forth in *Artavia Murillo* considered the scope that the IACtHR gave to the right to life and its non-absolute character was consistent with the provision of the Civil Code that had been challenged.[16] Additionally, on August 28, 2017, the Constitutional Tribunal of Chile issued a decision on the constitutionality of the statute that decriminalized abortion in three circumstances: when the life of the mother is at risk, when a genetic illness with the fetus makes life

---

[15] For a broader analysis on how Inter-American judgments impact the Latin-American region: Flávia Piovesan, "Ius Constitutionale Commune latinoamericano en derechos humanos e impacto del Sistema Interamericano: rasgos, potencialidades y desafíos," in Armin von Bogdandy, Héctor Fix Fierro, and Mariela Morales Antoniazzi (eds.), *Ius Constitutionale Commune en América Latina. Rasgos, potencialidades y desafíos* (IIJ-UNAM-MPIL-IIDC 2014), 61–84.

[16] Constitutional Court of Colombia, Judgment C-327/16, June 22, 2016, https://www.corteconstitucional.gov.co/RELATORIA/2016/C-327-16.htm (accessed January 7, 2022).

outside the uterus impossible, and when the pregnancy is the result of rape. In its decision, the Constitutional Tribunal of Chile quoted the *Artavia Murillo* case when establishing that the protection of life from the moment of conception was not absolute.[17]

3. Nationwide and Structural Impact of the Reparations Ordered by the Court[18]

The reparations ordered by the IACtHR were:

(i) To provide the victims with the psychological treatment they require, immediately and free of charge, for up to four years. The psychological treatment must be provided by State institutions and personnel specialized in attending to victims of events such as those that occurred in the case at hand. When providing this treatment, the specific circumstances and needs of each victim should also be considered, so that they are provided with family and individual treatment, as agreed with each of them, after an individual assessment. The treatments must include the provision of medicines and, if appropriate, transportation and other expenses that are directly related and strictly necessary.

(ii) As compensation for pecuniary damage, to pay the sum of USD 5,000 in favor of the victims of the case who had to travel abroad to obtain access to IVF treatment. As compensation for nonpecuniary damage, to pay the sum of USD 20,000 to each victim.

(iii) To publish, within six months of notification of the judgment (1) the official summary of the judgment prepared by the Court in the Official Gazette, and (2) in a newspaper with a wide national circulation, as well as (3) the full text of the judgment, available for one year, on an official judiciary website.

(iv) To ensure that the prohibition against IVF is annulled as rapidly as possible so that those who wish to use this assisted reproductive technique may do so without encountering any impediments to exercising the rights that the judgment has found to have been violated.

(v) To regulate those aspects necessary for the implementation of IVF, taking into account the principles established in the judgment. This reparation includes the gradual establishment of systems for the inspection

---

[17] Constitutional Tribunal of Chile, Judgment of August 28, 2017, https://www.csjn.gov.ar/dbre/verNoticia.do?idNoticia=2166 (accessed January 4, 2022).

[18] *Artavia Murillo et al. ("In Vitro Fertilization") v. Costa Rica* (n. 12), paras. 318–373.

and quality control of qualified professionals and institutions that perform this type of assisted reproduction technique.
(vi) To gradually make IVF a part of healthcare infertility treatments and programs of the Costa Rica Social Security Institute.
(vii) To implement permanent education and training programs and courses on human rights, reproductive rights, and nondiscrimination for judicial employees in all areas and at all echelons of the judiciary.

These seven reparations can be divided in two groups. In the first group, the individual reparations in favor of the eighteen victims of the case, which include the measures of rehabilitation (i), compensation (ii), and satisfaction (iii). In the second group, the structural measures intended to revert the general situation of unconventionality caused by the persistence of the prohibition and to avoid repetition of the human rights violations that took place in the case (iv, v, vi, and vii). After receiving and processing several written submissions from the parties during the supervision on compliance procedure, the Court held a public hearing on compliance on September 3, 2015,[19] almost three years after the judgment on the merits and reparations. On February 26, 2016, the Court issued its Order on compliance, in which it declared that Costa Rica fully complied with the individual reparations related to compensation and satisfaction. With respect to rehabilitation, the Court considered that it should continue to supervise its compliance.[20]

Considering that the purpose of this chapter is to focus on the transformative impact of the case, I will comment on the situation of compliance (and the concrete impact) of the second group of reparations, that is, the general structural measures described previously. The information will be presented in four sections: training the judiciary in reproductive rights (section 3.1), the annulment of the prohibition against IVF in Costa Rica (3.2), the regulation of IVF and the implementation of systems of inspection and quality control regarding its practice (3.3), and the inclusion of IVF in the State healthcare system (3.4).

3.1. Training the Judiciary in Reproductive Rights[21]

In compliance with this order, in January 2013 the Supreme Court of Justice of Costa Rica issued a resolution establishing the obligation of the *Escuela Judicial*

---

[19] It is relevant to mention here that the usual practice of the Court is to hold private hearings on compliance. An important feature of the process of compliance with the judgment in the *Artavia Murillo* case was the public character of this hearing, which took place under exceptional circumstances.

[20] *Artavia Murillo et al. ("In Vitro Fertilization") v. Costa Rica* [2016], IACtHR, Monitoring Compliance with Judgment.

[21] *Artavia Murillo et al. ("In Vitro Fertilization") v. Costa Rica* (n. 20): the contents of the Monitoring Compliance Order quoted under this subheading can be found in paras. 58–65.

to implement permanent training programs mainly with respect to reproductive rights and nondiscrimination. The *Escuela Judicial* created a working group with the participation of the *Defensoría de los Habitantes de Costa Rica* (the Ombudsperson institution). The working group designed a forty-hour workshop named "Human, sexual and reproductive rights." The Court analyzed four aspects of the workshop, consistent with the parameters set forth in its judgment: the contents of the courses, its implementation, the type of officials to whom it was directed, and its permanence.

The contents of the workshop were designed to include "the development of sexual and reproductive rights in light of human rights and gender perspective[s]," "assisted reproductive techniques," the "description, legal implications and scientific aspects of IVF as an assisted reproductive technique," the "reasoning used by the Court to establish that the prohibition of IVF is a human rights violation," and the "relevant case-law of the Court in the area of sexual and reproductive rights." The Court underlined the transversal approach of these topics under "non-discrimination," "gender perspective," "prohibition of violence," "access to scientific progress," and "access to justice." With respect to implementation, the Court noted that the workshop has happened three times and that a fourth was already scheduled. And in relation to permanence, the Court noted that the resolution of the Supreme Court of Justice stated that the training must be permanent.

Regarding the type of officials, the Court pointed to the participation of judges—of different levels of authority and areas of the judiciary—public defenders, other Public Defence institution officials, prosecutors, other *Ministerio Público* officials, and academic personnel of the *Escuela Judicial*. The Court mentioned that training should be mandatory. However, the Court did not establish this mandatory character as an obligation imposed by the judgment, which would have helped it to attain a greater and broader impact. Based on the foregoing, the Court concluded that Costa Rica fully complied with this reparation.

3.2. The Annulment of the Prohibition of the Practice of IVF in Costa Rica[22]

The annulment of the prohibition against IVF was the primary and basic measure of nonrepetition established in the judgment. As a result of the different possible paths available to ensure compliance with this measure and its obstacles, the Court issued an unprecedented holding during the supervision of the

---

[22] *Artavia Murillo et al. ("In Vitro Fertilization") v. Costa Rica* (n. 20): the contents of the Monitoring Compliance Order quoted under this subheading can be found in paras. 4–27.

compliance process. After the judgment of the Court (November 2012), three possible mechanisms of compliance were opened at the domestic level: (1) the approval of legislation by the Legislative Assembly (legislative branch), (2) the adoption of a judicial decision by the Supreme Court of Justice leaving without effect its 2000 decision, which established the prohibition in the first place (judicial branch), and (3) the decision of the constitutional actions (*amparos*) that were filed in order to lift the prohibition, with *erga omnes* effects, by the Supreme Court of Justice (judicial branch).

By the time of the public hearing on compliance three years after the judgment (September 2015), the different draft laws pending at the Legislative Assembly had accrued hundreds of objections presented by members of the Assembly that needed to be processed and decided. The perspective supporting a prompt approval of legislation with the effect of lifting the prohibition was minimal. Also, the contents of those draft laws were highly criticized by the parties before the IACtHR during the compliance process—including the State of Costa Rica as a whole—and by the Ombudsperson institution.

For its part, the Constitutional Chamber not only refused to show any willingness to issue a decision, and thus leaving its previous judgment without effect, but rejected the constitutional actions (*amparos*) under arguments that did not take into consideration two aspects of the order of the Court: that it had to be fulfilled "as soon as possible" and that the lack of regulation could not be opposed as an obstacle to authorize the practice of IVF. Furthermore, the decisions of the *amparos* included arguments reiterating the protection of the right to life of embryos in clear contradiction to the reasoning of the IACtHR.

In these circumstances, the State expressed in the public hearing that compliance with this fundamental order of the Court could be reached by means of an Executive Decree (executive branch) that had already been drafted. The purpose of the decree was to authorize the practice of IVF and to approve its regulation. About a week after the public hearing, the State informed the Court about the entry into force of Executive Decree No. 39210-MP-S: "Authorization for the practice of In Vitro Fertilization and Embryo Transfer assisted reproductive technique." However, a few days after the entry into force of the Decree it was challenged before the Constitutional Chamber under the arguments that it encompassed a violation of the "fundamental right to life of the unborn" and that it was contrary to the constitutional mandate that fundamental rights could only be regulated by the legislative branch. In February 2016, five months after the public hearing on compliance, the Constitutional Chamber annulled the Executive Decree.

Based on the sequence described in the previous paragraphs, the IACtHR faced a challenging supervision of compliance process: State representatives claimed that IVF had already been authorized by an Executive Decree, although it was further annulled by the Supreme Court of Justice, and established that fulfilling the order of the Court was the competence of the Legislative Assembly, which after three years proved to be incapable of promptly doing so. In its paradigmatic compliance Order of February 26, 2016, the Court had the opportunity to consolidate important principles regarding compliance with its judgments. At least three aspects deserve to be underlined here. First, States have the conventional obligation of fully and promptly implementing the decisions of the Court, and when such obligations are unfulfilled they incur in an international violation. Second, the conventional obligations of the State parties to the Convention are mandatory for all the branches and institutions of the State, including the highest tribunals, which must in good faith comply with international law. And third, States cannot use domestic law arguments to avoid an international responsibility that has been already established.

After noting that in Costa Rica domestic law affirms that IACtHR decisions can be directly executed, the Inter-American Court made the strong statement that the Supreme Court of Justice had actively hindered compliance with the Order authorizing IVF in Costa Rica. Specifically, it did so when omitting to leave its own 2000 judgment without effect, then with the rejection of the *amparos* and finally with the annulment of the Executive Decree that constituted the only concrete and effective measure adopted by the State in order to comply with the judgment. Based on the preceding, the IACtHR included the following historic paragraph in its Order of Compliance:

> By maintaining the prohibition to practice IVF in Costa Rica ... the State has unfulfilled its international obligations perpetuating a situation of violation of rights ... that could create grave and irreversible effects in those persons that need access to the assisted reproductive technique. According to the judgment of this Tribunal, the prohibition to practice IVF is manifestly incompatible with the American Convention ... and, therefore, it cannot produce legal effects nor constitute an obstacle in the exercise of the rights protected by the Convention. In consequence, in light of the American Convention and the reparation ordered in the Judgment, it must be understood that IVF is authorized in Costa Rica and, with immediate effects ... without the need of a further legal state act that acknowledges such possibility or regulated the implementation of the technique. No sanction can be imposed due to the fact of practicing IVF.

With this decision, the Court not only consolidated the scope of its authority in the context of the supervision on compliance processes but also faced a complex challenge created by the different branches of the State involved. The innovative manner in which the IACtHR approached this challenge had the direct consequence of authorizing IVF in Costa Rica with its correlative structural and nationwide impact. Between the Order of compliance of the Court and March 2019, 159 babies were born with the help of IVF treatment.

3.3. The Regulation of IVF and the Implementation of Systems of Inspection and Quality Controls of Its Practice

The judgment of the Court included an order to regulate the practice of IVF and to implement systems of inspection and quality controls. In the same context described previously regarding the lack of compliance on the part of the legislative and judicial branches, the executive branch complied with this obligation via the same Decree No. 39210-MP-S, which served to lift the ban, authorize IVF in Costa Rica, and regulate its practice. The Decree contains four chapters: general provisions with respect to IVF; competent authorities including the responsibilities and functions of the Ministry of Health, the *Caja Costarricense del Seguro Social*, and the Association of Doctors and Surgeons of Costa Rica in relation to the practice of IVF; the rights of the patients; and the treatment of the gametes. In its compliance Order of February 26, 2016, the Court noted that Decree No. 39210-MP-S was the only measure adopted by Costa Rica to comply with the judgment and, therefore, determined that the Decree must remain in force without harming the possibility that the legislative body will issue subsequent regulations in conformity with the standards set forth in the judgment.

According to the information available, by March 2019 Decree No. 39210-MP-S was still in force and the executive branch issued two additional Decrees. The first, Decree No. 39616-S of March 11, 2016, constitutes the technical norm for healthcare facilities performing IVF and embryo transfer. The second, Decree No. 39646-S of April 8, 2016, regulates the authorization of healthcare facilities practicing IVF treatment.[23] These three Decrees constitute the normative basis for the implementation of IVF in Costa Rica and for the inspection procedures of the Ministry of Health. The other legislative proposals within the Legislative Assembly were archived.[24] In terms of the concrete impact of the regulation, by March 2019 two private healthcare facilities had been authorized to practice IVF: Centro FECUNDAR Costa Rica—Panamá (authorized in May 2016) and Centro Fertilización In Vitro La California (authorized in February

---

[23] *Caso Artavia Murillo y otros (Fecundación in Vitro) y Caso Gómez Murillo y otros v. Costa Rica* [2019], IACtHR, Supervisión de Cumplimiento de Sentencias. Resolución de la Corte Interamericana de Derechos Humanos.
[24] Ibid.

2017).²⁵ Furthermore, the Ministry of Health performed inspection visits and determined that both facilities fully comply with the technical norms.

3.4. The Inclusion of IVF in the State Healthcare System

One of the most important and innovative reparations ordered by the Court was the gradual inclusion of IVF in the public healthcare system. It is relevant to briefly mention that this reparation is directly related to the conclusion of the Court that the State breached the principle of nondiscrimination because of the disproportionate impact of the IVF prohibition in the case of couples with scarce economic resources. *Artavia Murillo* was the first case in the history of the Court's case law to declare a violation of Article 1.1 of the Convention using the notion of indirect discrimination and disparate impact. It is worth underlining that in this particular case, such an historic determination had its correlative impact in the unprecedented reparation ordered by the Court.²⁶ In compliance with this reparation, in June 2019 the Unit of Reproductive Medicine of High Complexity of the Caja Costarricense del Seguro Social, located in the Womens Hospital Dr. Adolfo Carit, San José, started to operate. In its Compliance Order of November 22, 2019, the Court declared that the State of Costa Rica had fully complied with the judgment and archived the case.

4. Concluding Remarks

Although the petition and case system were conceived as mechanisms to provide individual justice and reparation to victims of human rights violations that had not received an adequate response at the domestic level, the *Artavia Murillo* judgment serves as an example of the transformative impact that can result from an individual case in the Inter-American Human Rights System. The transformative impact in this particular case had multiple elements, and each deserves individual consideration. Firstly, *the case law of the Inter-American System* developed in various directions:

- with respect to the scope of the protection of the right to life, after using all the methods of interpretation in international law, the Court concluded that (1) an embryo cannot be understood as a person for the purposes of the Convention; (2) the protection of the right to life is not applicable prior

---

[25] Ibid.
[26] *Artavia Murillo et al. ("In Vitro Fertilization") v. Costa Rica* (n. 12), paras. 285–303.

to conception; and (3) the words "in general" should be interpreted in the sense that such protection is not absolute, entails exceptions, and is "gradual and incremental." A number of domestic tribunals in the region have used these standards.
- with respect to reproductive rights and their permissible limitations, the Court established that (1) the decision of whether or not to become a parent (in both the biological and genetic sense) is protected by the Convention; and (2) the rights to personal liberty and a private life read in conjunction enshrine a right to reproductive autonomy that includes access to advances in medical treatment.

Secondly, *the reparations ordered by the Court had a nationwide impact in Costa Rica*. In addition to compensation and rehabilitation in favor of the eighteen victims, the Court ordered structural changes intended to reverse the general situation of unconventionality caused by the persistence of the prohibition against IVF from the moment of the judgment and to avoid a repetition of the human rights violations that took place in the case. Up to now, Costa Rica has fully complied with its obligations: the training of the judiciary in reproductive rights, the annulment of the prohibition against IVF in Costa Rica, and the regulation of IVF and the implementation of systems of inspection and quality control. Also, the State has adopted effective steps toward full compliance with the inclusion of IVF in the public healthcare system. Between the Court's Compliance Order and March 2019, 159 babies were born with the assistance of IVF treatment. Moreover, two private healthcare facilities have been authorized to practice IVF treatment and in June 2019 the Unit of Reproductive Medicine of High Complexity started to function.

And lastly, the situation that emerged with respect to the different possible paths available to ensure compliance with the judgment led the Court to issue *an unprecedented holding during a supervision process*, which can also be used in other contexts in which State institutions create obstacles that impede the implementation of structural reparations. As a result of the proactive approach of the Court, reparations were fully implemented.

II.6
The Impact beyond Compliance of the Case of *Azul Rojas Marin*

Reflections around Strategic Litigation and the Inter-American Human Rights System

By Chris Esdaile, Clara Sandoval, Alejandra Vicente, with Renata Politi and Nataly Sanchez

1. Introduction

Violence against LGBTIQ+ people is a persistent and often systematic practice around the world.[1] They are often punished for transgressing gender roles when expressing non-normative sexual and gender identities.[2] Violence takes different forms, including arbitrary killings, death threats, beatings, corporal punishment, arbitrary detention, sexual violence, verbal abuse, harassment, forced medical procedures, and "conversion therapy" practices.[3] In some instances, this violence is legitimized by legislation or by the pronouncements of political leaders and other authority figures. The COVID-19 pandemic saw a marked increase in LGBTIQ+ violence worldwide.[4] Discrimination is often an underlying cause of this violence.

Equally, the investigation of such violence—when it takes place—is frequently characterized by prejudice, stigma, and disbelief of the victim's story, which discourages victims from coming forward and results in high rates of underreporting[5] and impunity.[6] Survivors of such violence are therefore often

---

[1] This chapter was written by three of the legal representatives of Azul during the litigation of the case before the Inter-American System: Chris Esdaile (Legal Advisor at REDRESS), Alejandra Vicente (Head of Legal at REDRESS), and Clara Sandoval (Professor, University of Essex/consultant at REDRESS). Renata Politi (REDRESS) and Nataly Sanchez (University of Essex) provided invaluable research during the writing of this chapter.

[2] IACHR, "Violence against LGBTI persons in The Americas," OEA/Ser.L/V/II.Doc.36/15 Rev.2, November 12, 2015, para. 25.

[3] Report of the Independent Expert on protection against violence and discrimination based on sexual orientation and gender identity A/HRC/38/43 (SOGI Report), May 11, 2018, paras. 27–28; ACHPR Resolution 275, April 28, 2014.

[4] Report on the impact of the COVID-19 pandemic on the human rights of LGBTIQ+ persons, A/75/258, July 28, 2020, para. 14.

[5] IACHR (n. 2), para. 97.

[6] IACHR (n. 2), para. 479.

unable to access justice and commonly suffer revictimization as a result of the flaws in the investigation and any subsequent judicial processes.

Some of these forms of violence, along with a lack of diligent investigation, were present in the case of *Azul Rojas Marin and Other v. Peru*. Azul is a transgender woman, who at the time of the events identified as a gay man. She was detained late at night on February 25, 2008, by members of the Peruvian police when she was walking home. Some of the officers knew who Azul was. They insulted her and made derogatory remarks about her sexual orientation. She was forcibly taken to a police station and kept there for almost six hours, although her detention was not officially registered. During her detention, Azul was stripped naked, beaten repeatedly, and anally raped with a police baton. The insults and derogatory remarks about her sexual orientation continued throughout. She was released early the next day.

Azul reported the crime to the authorities, but they did not believe her and did not investigate properly. Different members of the justice system revictimized Azul. During the reconstruction of the crime scene, Azul was forced to face her perpetrators while they made fun of her. The prosecutor was present during her medical examination, without Azul's consent, and kept making comments to influence the findings of the forensic doctor. Azul's complaint was eventually dismissed. To date, no one has been held to account or punished for what happened.

The case, culminating in the March 2020 judgment of the Inter-American Court of Human Rights (IACtHR), was the first to be decided by a supranational body recognizing that torture can be carried out with the intent to discriminate a person on the grounds of sexual orientation. This is an important step in a world where discrimination based on sexual orientation and gender identity continues to take place daily. The significance of this judgment merits careful reflection: What positive impacts could the case have beyond the importance of the legal decision itself? Can a judgment like this trigger structural changes and have impact in the life of Azul and many others in her situation?

The argument that we put forward is that even if discrimination and violence against LGBTIQ+ people persists and compliance with the judgment remains a challenge, the judgment itself, and the stakeholders engaged in the case, including the Inter-American Commission on Human Rights (IACHR) and the Inter-American Court, have triggered important dynamics. We argue that the judgment advances the development of a world where LGBTIQ+ people live free of violence and are able to exercise their rights without discrimination. We understand impact in this context to be the ability of strategic litigation, and the judgment, to unleash social dynamics capable of changing the structures that enable violence, going beyond the specific forms of reparation ordered by the

Court (even though we recognize that they too can become a vehicle for impact and societal change).

Therefore, this chapter will look at the case of *Azul*, considering how the case came about, what was achieved with it, but also, and importantly, what has been the impact of the case since it was decided in March 2020. To this end, section 2 of the article explores the legal significance of the *Azul* judgment. Section 3 analyzes the development of the LGBTIQ+ protection framework by the universal and regional human rights systems, as well as the cross-fertilization and dialogue between these bodies. Section 4 proposes a methodology to assess the impact of human rights litigation that can be used in the case of *Azul* and other strategic litigation cases. Section 5 applies this methodology to the case of *Azul*, highlighting the various forms of impact achieved since the judgment was issued. Section 6 offers some reflections on the significance of the case of *Azul* beyond compliance with the IACtHR judgment. The chapter concludes with some reflections about what is needed to ensure that cases such as that of *Azul* and others trigger changes to reduce the discrimination that—all too often—surrounds the lives of LGBTIQ+ people.

This chapter is written by some of the lawyers involved in the litigation of the case, using primary and secondary data on the case and available information that serves as evidence of the impact the case has had so far.

2. The Case of *Azul Rojas Marín and Other v. Peru*—Its Legal Significance

REDRESS[7] joined forces with two Peruvian civil society groups, the *Coordinadora Nacional de Derechos Humanos* (CNDDHH)[8] and PROMSEX,[9] and filed a complaint before the IACHR in April 2009 to assist Azul in obtaining justice. The case raised significant issues of law and practice that provided a unique opportunity to advance protection of the rights of LGBTIQ+ persons, particularly in relation to the prohibition of discrimination on sexual orientation grounds, the prohibition of torture, the obligation to investigate with due diligence, and the right to reparations. The case lasted more than a decade

---

[7] REDRESS is a UK-based NGO which delivers justice and reparation for survivors of torture, challenges impunity for perpetrators, and advocates for legal and policy reforms to combat torture: <https://redress.org> (accessed October 22, 2023).

[8] The National Coordinator for Human Rights is a coalition of civil-society organisms that work toward the defense, promotion and education of human rights in Peru: <http://derechoshumanos.pe> (accessed October 22, 2023).

[9] PROMSEX is a Peruvian feminist NGO that, through political advocacy, knowledge generation and partnerships, helps people make decisions about their sexuality and reproduction with autonomy, dignity, justice, and equality: <https://promsex.org/> (accessed October 22, 2023).

before the Inter-American System. The IACHR decided the merits of the case in February 2018.[10] Given that Peru did not comply with the recommendations made by the IACHR, the case was referred to the Inter-American Court in August 2018. The Commission noted this would be the first case before the IACtHR dealing with violence against LGBTIQ+ persons.[11] The Court held a hearing in August 2019[12] and decided the case in March 2020,[13] making significant findings of fact and law.

The Court declared the State of Peru internationally responsible for the violation of the right not to be subjected to torture, and the rights to personal liberty, personal integrity, privacy, judicial guarantees and the judicial protection of Azul, all in connection with the prohibition of discrimination. Peru was also found to be responsible for the violation of the right to personal integrity of Azul's mother, Juana Rosa Tanta Marín, who died in 2017, and who suffered greatly due to what happened to Azul. The key issues decided by the Court are summarized in the remainder of this section.

2.1. The Court Found that Arbitrary Detention of LGBTIQ+ Persons Can Be Inferred When There Are Signs of Discrimination and No Other Apparent Reason for the Detention

Peru argued that the detention of Azul took place to carry out an identity check as she did not have her ID with her.[14] Peru disputed the length of the detention. However, the Court found that the detention was not carried out in accordance with domestic law, that one of the officers who detained Azul knew who she was, and that derogatory comments about her sexual orientation were made. The Court, following the views of the UN Working Group on Arbitrary Detention[15] and those of the expert Maria Mercedes Gómez,[16] considered that the lack of a legal basis for Azul's detention and the existence of discriminatory elements,

---

[10] *Azul Rojas Marín et al. v. Peru* [2018] Case 12.982, IACHR, Report No. 24/18.

[11] Letter from IACHR to Pablo Saavedra Alessandri (Secretary of the IACtHR) (August 22, 2018): <https://www.oas.org/es/cidh/decisiones/corte/2018/12982NdeREs.pdf> (accessed October 22, 2023).

[12] Public Hearing in the Case of *Rojas Marín and another v. Perú* (August 27, 2019): <https://vimeo.com/347339620> (accessed October 22, 2023).

[13] *Case of Azul Rojas Marín et al. v. Peru* (hereinafter *Azul*) [2020] IACtHR, Ser. C No. 402.

[14] Ibid., para. 124.

[15] UNGA, "Report of the Working Group on Arbitrary Detention" (July 19, 2017) UN Doc. A/HRC/36/37, [48].

[16] Assistant professor of Criminology at Saint Mary's University in Halifax, Canada; called as an expert by the IACHR.

together, inferred that she was detained based on her sexual orientation, which automatically rendered the arrest arbitrary.[17]

2.2. The Court Found that the Purposive Element of the Definition of Torture Incorporates Discrimination Based on Sexual Orientation and Gender Identity

Peru alleged that it was not proven that sexual violence took place, because the domestic courts were unable to establish it due to the lack of direct evidence of the crime.[18] It also argued that torture did not take place because two elements of the crime were missing: the intent and the purpose.

The IACtHR concluded Azul was anally raped while in detention. In contrast to the domestic courts' approach, the IACtHR reached this conclusion by assessing various pieces of evidence, including Azul's statements, medical examination reports, and the forensic analysis of the clothes she wore at the time of the events.[19] The IACtHR considered that what happened to Azul amounted to torture as the intentionality, severity, and purposive elements were met.[20] Further, the Court expanded the list of specific purposes by which sexual violence can constitute torture, to include the motive of discrimination based on the sexual orientation of the victim. Following the expert opinions of Juan Méndez[21] and Maria Mercedes Gómez, the Court found that sexual violence that involves anal rape, especially when carried out with a tool of authority such as a police baton, all while derogatory remarks were made, shows that the specific motive of the crime was to discriminate against Azul.[22]

The Court went further to label it as a hate crime given that it was the result of prejudice and stated that the crime not only breached Azul's rights but also the freedom and dignity of the whole LGBTIQ+ community.[23] This finding constitutes a major development under international law as this is the first case decided by an international tribunal to conclude that torture can take place with the specific purpose of discriminating against a person because of their sexual orientation.

---

[17] IACtHR, *Azul* (n. 13), paras. 127–128.
[18] Ibid., para. 138.
[19] Ibid., para. 157.
[20] Ibid., paras. 161–163.
[21] Professor of Human Rights Law, American University, Washington School of Law; former UN Special Rapporteur on Torture and Other Cruel, Inhuman or Degrading Treatment or Punishment; called as an expert by Azul's legal representatives.
[22] IACtHR, *Azul* (n. 13), paras. 163–164.
[23] Ibid., para. 165.

2.3. The Court Found that States Have a Duty to Investigate Violence Motivated by Discrimination against Members of the LGBTIQ+ Community

Peru argued that as soon as it learned about Azul's allegations, it opened an investigation that was carried out with due diligence,[24] although this was disputed by Azul's legal representatives. Given the prevailing levels of impunity for such crimes in the Americas, the IACtHR made a careful assessment of the facts in this regard.

The IACtHR reiterated its case law regarding due diligence in cases of sexual violence,[25] but extended its application to violence against LGBTIQ+ persons, adding new dimensions to its existing standards. Notably, the Court found that when investigating violence States have a duty to take all necessary steps to clarify if it was motivated by prejudice and discrimination.[26] The Court said that this implies that the State should collect all the required evidence, provide full reasons for its decisions, and decide in an impartial and objective manner. The authorities should not ignore any facts that could establish that the violence was motivated by discrimination.[27] In the case of *Azul*, the Peruvian authorities never considered discrimination as a motivating factor and did not pursue this line of investigation. This finding by the Court demonstrates its ongoing dialogue with the European Court of Human Rights (ECtHR), as it took note of the ECtHR's decision in *Identoba* (which set a similar precedent but in relation to ill treatment).[28]

The Court also noted that investigations should avoid the use of stereotypes. In this case, local prosecutors undermined the declaration of Azul by stating, "but if you're a homosexual, how am I going to believe you?,"[29] and by inquiring about her past sex-life. The Court noted that such stereotypical lines of inquiry should not be used in cases of sexual violence, including when that violence is committed against members of the LGBTIQ+ community.[30] This is another important contribution of the Court to the protection of LGBTIQ+ people under international law, which does not exist under ECtHR jurisprudence.

---

[24] Ibid., para. 172.
[25] *Case of Fernández Ortega et al. v. Mexico* [2010] IACtHR, Ser. C No. 215.
[26] IACtHR, *Azul* (n. 13), para. 196, citing *Identoba and Others v. Georgia* (hereinafter *Identoba*) [2014] ECtHR, App. No. 73235/12, para. 67.
[27] IACtHR, *Azul* (n. 13), para. 196.
[28] ECtHR, *Identoba* (n. 26), para. 67. Note that, in contrast to the ECtHR, the IACtHR does not make any reference to the difficulty of the task or the fact that it is, in the views of the ECtHR, "an obligation of best endeavours, and is not absolute."
[29] IACtHR, *Azul* (n. 13), para. 200.
[30] Ibid para. 202.

2.4. The Court Tackled Structural Discrimination through Reparations

The IACtHR ordered holistic forms of reparation for both individual as well as societal harm. From an individual perspective, the Court recognized Azul and her mother as victims in the case and awarded them compensation for pecuniary and nonpecuniary damage[31] and ordered that the State "facilitate and continue" the investigation into the facts, to identify, prosecute, and punish those responsible for the sexual violence and torture which Azul suffered.[32] The Court also ordered that there should be a public ceremony, where senior government figures recognize the State's international responsibility.[33] It also required the State to provide rehabilitation to Azul for physical and psychological harm, including access to medicines and transport expenses necessary to undergo treatment.[34]

But what is most remarkable about this judgment, and which Peru challenged during the litigation, are the measures requested by Azul and awarded by the Court to address structural discrimination as a cause of hate crimes. The Court ordered Peru to adopt a protocol for the effective criminal investigation of violence against members of the LGBTIQ+ community.[35] The protocol shall be binding under domestic law, instruct State representatives to abstain from applying stereotypes, and include due diligence standards developed by the Court in the judgment. The Court instructed the State to provide training to members of the justice system and the police on LGBTIQ+ rights and diligent investigations.[36] Additionally, Peru was ordered to implement a data collection system to officially register all cases of violence against members of the LGBTIQ+ community, including disaggregated information.[37]

Finally, the Court ordered Peru to eliminate from its local/regional security plans the reference to the "eradication of homosexuals and transvestites" since this exacerbates discrimination against members of the LGBTIQ+ community and "promotes the possibility of violence based on prejudice."[38]

Unfortunately, as of October 2023, more than a three and a half years after the judgment was handed down, Peru has fully complied with very few of the reparatory measures ordered by the Court. None of the deadlines imposed by the Court have been met. It is in this context that questions about impact become so crucial, as will be noted in the forthcoming sections. In any case, to fully address

---

[31] Ibid., paras. 260, 267.
[32] Ibid., para. 229.
[33] Ibid., paras. 233–234.
[34] Ibid., para. 236.
[35] Ibid., paras. 242–244.
[36] Ibid., paras. 248–249.
[37] Ibid., para. 252.
[38] Ibid., para. 255.

the impact of the judgment, it is essential to consider the case of *Azul* as part of international efforts, at various levels, to ensure the protection of LGBTIQ+ persons. The next section of this chapter turns to this point, aiming to establish the significance of the case of *Azul* in the context of international developments in this area.

3. The International Protection of LGBTIQ+ Rights before the Case of *Azul*

Successful litigation on LGBTIQ+ violence in Latin America, the region with the highest rate of Sexual Orientation and Gender Identity (SOGI)-based violence,[39] has only been possible as a result of the significant work undertaken by civil society organizations to draw the attention of regional and international political and human rights bodies to the issue.[40] For instance, the work of the Coalition of LGBTIQ+ Organizations of Latin America and the Caribbean before the Organization of American States (OAS) laid the foundations for the "historic resolution on human rights, sexual orientation and gender identity in 2008."[41] This then encouraged the IACHR to adopt a strategy to deal with SOGI issues, after which the first cases of litigation started to emerge.[42]

Strategies adopted by LGBTIQ+ movements worldwide include public education, documenting human rights violations, lobbying, and legislative campaigns.[43] These have been essential tools used before, during, and after any litigation, without which the litigation will lack the secure footing, or the follow-up required, to achieve the desired impact. At the same time, LGBTIQ+ movements have stressed that their demands for protection under the human rights framework are not new, but rather that well-established principles, such as the right to freedom from torture and ill treatment, should be applied irrespective of sexual orientation and gender.[44]

---

[39] Monica Malta et al., "Sexual and gender minorities rights in Latin America and the Caribbean: a multi-country evaluation" [2019] 19 *BMC International Health Human Rights* 1, 3.

[40] Victor Madrigal, "Protecting LGBT+ Persons in Africa from Torture: Challenges, Opportunities and Comparative Experiences," REDRESS [Video]: <https://youtu.be/UFe6g1Esl8Y> (accessed November 30, 2021).

[41] IACHR (n. 2), para. 3.

[42] SOGI Report (n. 3).

[43] Ryan Thoreson, "An International LGBT Movement" (October 27, 2020) Oxford Research Encyclopedia of Politics: <https://oxfordre.com/politics/view/10.1093/acrefore/9780190228637.001.0001/acrefore-9780190228637-e-1214> (accessed October 22, 2023); Amnesty International, "Speaking Out, Advocacy experiences and tools of LGBTI activists in sub-Saharan Africa" (2014).

[44] Anthony J. Langlois, "Making LGBT Rights into Human Rights," in Michael J. Bosia et al. (eds.), *The Oxford Handbook of Global LGBT and Sexual Diversity Politics* (Oxford University Press 2020).

Positive developments in the Americas are not isolated. Cases like that of *Azul* have been possible partly because a conducive international human rights protection environment has enabled this type of litigation. Important litigation in Europe and the United Nations helped to pave the way for the case of *Azul*.

3.1. The European System

Initially, the ECtHR and former European Commission appeared reluctant to deal with cases of SOGI-based violence, having ruled inadmissible the five applications filed between 1959 and 1962 under Article 3 of the European Convention on Human Rights (ECHR—prohibition of torture and ill treatment), which challenged the criminalization of sexual acts between men.[45] However, in *Dudgeon v. United Kingdom* in 1980, the ECtHR found that criminalizing consensual same-sex relations violates the right to respect for private life (Article 8 ECHR).[46] In the 1990s, there was successful litigation on discrimination against sexual minorities under Article 8 ECHR,[47] and in 1999, the ECtHR ruled that discrimination on the grounds of sexual orientation was covered by the prohibition of discrimination under Article 14 ECHR.[48]

It was not until the late 1990s, in *Smith and Grady v. the United Kingdom*, that the ECtHR took its first step toward recognizing discriminatory torture or ill treatment of LGBTIQ+ persons.[49] Despite concluding that Smith's humiliating interrogation by police officers—with intimate questions about her sexual orientation and partners—did not amount to torture or ill treatment, the ECtHR noted that it would not rule out the possibility that treatment "grounded upon a predisposed bias on the part of a heterosexual majority against a homosexual minority" could fall within the scope of Article 3 ECHR.[50] Subsequently, the ECtHR has increasingly approached the issue of LGBTIQ+ violence within the framework of the prohibition of torture and ill treatment. For example, in *X v. Turkey* in 2012, the ECtHR found a State in breach of its obligations under Article 3

---

[45] Paul J. Johnson and Silvia Falcetta, "Sexual Orientation Discrimination and Article 3 of the European Convention on Human Rights: Developing the protection of sexual minorities" [2018] 43 *ELR* 167, 168.

[46] *Dudgeon v. the United Kingdom* [1980] Commission Report, App. 7525/76.

[47] See, e.g., *Norris v. Ireland* App. 10581 (1988); *Modinos v. Cyprus* App. 259 (1993). See also Laurence R. Helfer and Erik Voeten, "International Courts as Agents of Legal Change: Evidence from LGBT Rights in Europe" (2014) 68 *International Organization* 77, 86

[48] *Mouta v. Portugal* App. 33290 (December 21, 1999); Council of Europe, "Discrimination on grounds of sexual orientation and gender identity" (2nd ed., Council of Europe Publishing, September 2011), 37.

[49] Its earlier reluctance to explore this issue is shown in, for example, *S v. the Federal Republic of Germany* App. 10686 (Commission decision, October 5, 1984).

[50] *Smith and Grady v. the United Kingdom* Apps. 33985/96 and 33986/96 (ECtHR, December 27, 1999). See also *Stasi v. France* App. 25001/07 (ECtHR, January 20, 2012).

ECHR due to discrimination based on sexual orientation, when the applicant had been detained in conditions which caused him mental and physical suffering and stripped him of his dignity.[51]

Subsequently, in *Identoba and others v. Georgia*[52] and *MC and AC v. Romania*,[53] both of which were brought by victims of attacks on activists during (or after) LGBTIQ+ demonstrations, the ECtHR further developed its views on States' obligations to prevent and investigate LGBTIQ+ violence. The decisions made clear that, in addition to the nature and context of the insults, the general hostile environment toward LGBTIQ+ persons is a relevant factor in the examination of the discriminatory purpose behind the attacks. The Court concluded that authorities had failed to protect adequately the victims, since, in light of the negative attitudes toward LGBTIQ+ persons, the "authorities knew or ought to have known of the risks associated with any public event concerning that vulnerable community, and were consequently under an obligation to provide heightened State protection."[54] The ECtHR also ruled that authorities have a duty to investigate effectively violent incidents against LGBTIQ+ persons, which includes acting promptly and taking all reasonable measures to "unmask possible discriminatory motives."[55] Such an obligation is not absolute but requires the use of "best endeavours."

These standards have been confirmed by the ECtHR in more recent rulings, including the January 2021 judgment in *Aghdgomelashvili and Japaridze v. Georgia*, issued almost a year after the judgment of *Azul*, which marked the first time the ECtHR found a substantive violation of Article 3 ECHR in a case of LGBTIQ+ violence.[56]

3.2. The UN System

As in the European System, progress on the protection of LGBTIQ+ persons before UN bodies can be identified from the 1990s onward. In 1994, in *Toonen v. Australia*, the Human Rights Committee (HRC) recognized sexual orientation as a protected ground under the category of "sex" of the International Covenant

---

[51] *X v. Turkey* App. 14626/09 (ECtHR, October 9, 2012). Jurist Legal News & Commentary, Paul J Johnson, "The Impact of X v. Turkey: Homosexuality and the ECHR" (October 9, 2012): <https://www.jurist.org/commentary/2012/10/paul-johnson-echr-turkey/> (accessed October 22, 2023).
[52] ECtHR, *Identoba* (n. 26).
[53] *MC and AC v. Romania* [2016] ECtHR, App. 12060/12.
[54] ECtHR, *Identoba* (n. 26), para. 72.
[55] Ibid., para. 67; *MC and AC v. Romania* (n. 53), para. 113.
[56] *Aghdomelashvili and Japaridze v. Georgia* (hereinafter *Aghdomelashvili and Japaridze*) [2021] ECtHR, App. 7224/11. See also *Sabalić v. Croatia* [2021] ECtHR, App. 50231/13, *Association ACCEPT and Others v. Romania* [2021] ECtHR, App. 19237/16, *Beizarras and Leivickas v. Lithuania* [2020] ECtHR, App. 41288/15, and *Maksim Grigoryevich Lapunov v. Russia* [2023] ECtHR, App. 28834/19.

on Civil and Political Rights (ICCPR). It further established that "adult consensual sexual activity in private is covered by the concept of privacy [under Article 17]," hence criminalization of same-sex sexual acts between consenting adults constitutes an unreasonable interference by the State on the rights of individuals.[57]

Later, other UN treaty bodies followed the trend of treating sexual orientation as a protected category under various treaty provisions. In General Comments 14,[58] 15,[59] 18,[60] and 20,[61] the Committee on Economic, Social and Cultural Rights (CESCR) specified that the prohibition of discrimination based on sexual orientation or gender identity is covered by the International Covenant on Economic, Social and Cultural Rights (ICESCR).

Although UN bodies have developed doctrine on the discriminatory purpose of certain acts of torture, they have not gone as far as the ECtHR on setting standards on LGBTIQ+ violence. In *Cacho Ribeiro v. Mexico*, the HRC found that the torture inflicted on the victim by police officers—including sexual violence—had a discriminatory purpose based on the sex of the victim. As in ECtHR's cases and in *Azul*, this assessment took into account "the nature of the sexual comments made" by the perpetrators.[62] However, in *D.C. and D.E. v. Georgia*, the Committee against Torture (CAT), whilst referring to "the risks that arise for prisoners who raise allegations of sexual assault, as they are likely to be labelled as homosexuals and exposed to a high risk of abuse by other prisoners," did not address the discriminatory motive behind such increased risks.[63]

The CAT has also refrained from setting standards on the duty to investigate with due diligence acts of violence potentially motivated by discrimination on grounds of sexual orientation. In *Mamatkarim Ernazarov v. Kyrgyzstan*, decided in 2011, while the CAT referred to the risks faced by the victim—who had been killed in prison following his conviction of a sexual offence against another man—it did not take into account these risks as a factor that should have led to an investigation into the discriminatory purpose behind such violence.[64] Future decisions of the CAT, to be adopted after *Azul*'s judgment, could develop important standards in relation to nondiscrimination, torture, and due diligence investigations in such cases.

---

[57] *Toonen v. Australia* [1994] HRC Communication No. 488/1992 [8.7], [8.2], [8.5].
[58] CESCR, "General Comment 14" [August 11, 2000] E/C.12/2000/4 [18].
[59] CESCR, "General Comment 15" [January 20, 2003] E/C.12/2002/11 [13].
[60] CESCR, "General Comment 18" [February 6, 2006] E/C.12/GC/18 [12].
[61] CESCR, "General Comment 20" [July 2, 2009] E/C.12/GC/20 [32].
[62] *Lydia Cacho Ribeiro v. Mexico* [2018] CCPR Communication No. CCPR/C/123/D/2767/2016 [10.3], [3.7].
[63] *D.C. and D.E. v. Georgia* [2017] CAT Communication No. CAT/C/60/D/573/2013 [5.3].
[64] *Mamatkarim Ernazarov v. Kyrgyzstan* [2011] CAT Communication No. 2054/2011 [9.6].

3.3. The African System

Despite the prevalence of *de jure* and *de facto* discrimination of LGBTIQ+ people in Africa, it is very telling that the African Human Rights System has not yet dealt with cases concerning equality or discrimination based on sexual orientation and gender identity. As of October 2023, there has not been litigation of cases of SOGI-based violence before the African Commission on Human and Peoples' Rights (ACHPR). The only case relating to the rights of LGBTIQ+ persons ever brought to the ACHPR was a communication filed back in 1994, which challenged the criminalization of sexual conduct between men and the legal status of homosexuals in Zimbabwe.[65] However, the ACHPR did not have the opportunity to express its view on the matter as the complainant withdrew the case.

Despite the lack of litigation, the ACHPR's Resolution No. 275 of 2014 condemns SOGI-based violence and, although not binding on member States, calls upon them to introduce effective legislative and judicial mechanisms to prevent and respond to such violence. Notwithstanding the significance of Resolution 275, the subsequent withdrawal of the observer status of the organization Coalition of African Lesbians before the African Union[66] is a sign of continued tension on LGBTIQ+ rights in Africa and reinforces the need to develop a strategy to engage African human rights bodies in the fight against SOGI-based violence.[67]

3.4. The Inter-American System at the Forefront

Although its jurisprudence protecting LGBTIQ+ persons started to develop slightly later than in Europe, the Inter-American Human Rights System has now gone further than the other supranational mechanisms in terms of protecting LGBTIQ+ persons from violence, placing the Americas at the forefront of these efforts. Since 2003, the IACtHR has highlighted the essential role that the principle of equality and nondiscrimination plays into effectively safeguarding the rights protected both under international and domestic law.[68] Nonetheless it was not until 2012, in *Atala Riffo and daughters v. Chile*, that the IACtHR ruled

---

[65] *William Courson v. Zimbabwe* [2000] Communication No. 136/94 (8th Annual Activity Report of the ACHPR).

[66] African Court on Human and Peoples' Rights, Advisory Opinion No. 002/2015, September 28, 2017.

[67] Sibongile Ndashe and Ayodele Sogunro, "Protecting LGBT+ Persons in Africa from Torture: Challenges, Opportunities and Comparative Experiences," *REDRESS* [Video]: <https://youtu.be/UFe6g1Esl8Y> (accessed November 30, 2021).

[68] IACtHR, "Juridical Condition and Rights of Undocumented Migrants," Advisory Opinion 18, September 17, 2003, Ser. A No. 18, 88.

that discrimination on the basis of sexual orientation and gender identity was prohibited under Article 1(1) of the American Convention on Human Rights (ACHR).[69]

As in Europe, the protection of sexual minorities from discrimination was initially approached by the IACtHR as an aspect of private and family life (Article 11 ACHR). In *Atala Riffo and daughters v. Chile* and *Ramírez Escobar et al. v. Guatemala*, the IACtHR ruled on custodial rights of LGBTIQ+ parents and caregivers;[70] *Duque v. Colombia* tackled the right to equal access to social benefits for same-sex couples;[71] while *Flor Freire v. Ecuador* dealt with the discriminatory discharge from military service based on the perception of nonconforming sexual orientation.[72]

Whilst the question of SOGI-based violence remained unaddressed by the IACtHR until its decision in *Azul* in 2020,[73] other bodies of the Inter-American Human Rights' System had earlier recognized the high rates of violence against LGBTIQ+ populations in the Americas and, between 2008 and 2017, the OAS General Assembly adopted nine resolutions condemning violence against LGBTIQ+ people and calling on States to prevent and investigate these violent acts and ensure victims' right to judicial redress.[74]

Additionally, in 2015, the IACHR published its report on *Violence against LGBTI persons*, which documented a context of systemic violence based on SOGI prejudice in the Americas and established regional standards on how OAS States should prevent, investigate, and punish these human rights violations. This standard-setting process paved the way for the IACtHR to assess the case of *Azul* in terms of due diligence in investigations concerning hate crimes against LGBTIQ+ persons. For instance, the report puts together a list of nonexhaustive elements that serve to identify when a crime is motivated by SOGI prejudice,[75] and these elements were pivotal to determine the discriminatory intent of the torture suffered by Azul.[76] It also demonstrates the catalyzing role of supranational human rights bodies, developing not only new jurisprudence but also elements that trigger social change. A diverse group of actors in the Americas,

---

[69] *Atala Riffo and daughters v. Chile* [2012] IACtHR; Ser. C No. 239, para. 91.
[70] Ibid.; *Ramírez Escobar et al. v. Guatemala* [2018] IACtHR, Ser. C No. 351.
[71] *Duque v. Colombia* [2016] IACtHR, Ser. C No. 310.
[72] *Flor Freire v. Ecuador* [2016] IACtHR, Ser. C No. 315.
[73] The IACtHR briefly acknowledged the issue of LGBTIQ+ violence in IACtHR, "Gender identity, and equality and non-discrimination of same-sex couples," Advisory Opinion OC-24, November 25, 2017, Ser. A No. 22, paras. 33–35, which concerned the obligations of States' to legally recognize same-sex couples' and transgender people accordingly with their self-perceived gender expression. However, the opinion does not address specific State obligations regarding SOGI-based violence.
[74] OAS, General Assembly AG/RES. 2908 (XLVII-O/17); AG/RES. 2887 (XLVI-O/16); AG/RES. 2863 (XLIV-O/14); AG/RES. 2807 (XLIII-O/13); AG/RES. 2721 (XLII-O/12); AG/RES. 2653 (XLI-O/11); AG/RES. 2600 (XL-O/10); AG/RES. 2504 (XXXIX-O/09); AG/RES. 2435 (XXXVIII-O/08).
[75] IACHR (n. 2), 504.
[76] IACtHR, *Azul* (n. 13), paras. 163–166.

including the IACHR, victims, and civil society, paved the way for the Court to decide on the case of Azul the way it did.

The path to *Azul* was, therefore, shaped by an ongoing dialogue between the IACtHR and other OAS bodies. The developing understanding of the links between gender and SOGI-based prejudice allowed the Court in *Azul* to rely on its rich jurisprudence on gender-based violence as a lens through which to understand the structural nature of the discrimination. Recently, this was reaffirmed in *Vicky Hernández v. Honduras*,[77] the second case decided by the IACtHR on LGBTIQ+ violence—concerning the killing of a trans woman—which already showcases the promise of *Azul* for the Inter-American System and its leading role on this issue.

3.5. Cross-Fertilization across Systems

The first cases relating to SOGI before the ECtHR, the HRC, and the IACtHR were framed in terms of privacy and respect for family life. However, the focus shifted. The ECtHR started issuing rulings about the discriminatory nature of SOGI-based violence, whilst the OAS started recognizing the issue through its resolutions condemning acts of violence against LGBTIQ+ persons. Then, a year after the ACHPR issued Resolution No. 275, in 2015 the IACHR published its report on *Violence against LGBTI Persons* and held a joint dialogue with the ACHPR and the UN mechanisms to share recent developments regarding violence against LGBTIQ+ people.[78]

This cross-fertilization across systems was one key factor which made the *Azul* judgment possible. The findings of the IACtHR relied on some of the ECtHR's standards concerning due process when investigating acts of violence against LGBTIQ+ persons, as well as the developments regarding discriminatory grounds for arbitrary detention put forward by the UN Working Group on Arbitrary Detention. Nonetheless, the IACtHR went further by assessing SOGI-based discrimination as a purposive element of torture for the first time and addressing, with a comprehensive set of reparations, the various root causes of LGBTIQ+ violence and impunity.

---

[77] *Vicky Hernández and others v. Honduras* [2021] IACtHR, Ser. C No. 422.
[78] ACHPR, "Ending violence and other human rights violations based on sexual orientation and gender identity: A joint dialogue of the African Commission on Human and Peoples' Rights, Inter-American Commission on Human Rights and United Nations," University of Pretoria (2016): <https://www.ohchr.org/Documents/Issues/Discrimination/Endingviolence_ACHPR_IACHR_UN_SOGI_dialogue_EN.pdf> (accessed October 22, 2023).

Having explored the milestones that led to the IACtHR decision in the case of *Azul*, the following section proposes a methodology to assess the impact of the judgment in this and other human rights strategic litigation cases.

4. Criteria to Assess the Impact of Strategic Litigation

Strategic litigation is an effective tool to achieve several goals, including justice and reparation to the direct victims as well as policy and legal reform, and social change. Yet evaluating the impact of strategic litigation is not always an easy task. Victims and those assisting them might have different expectations on the impact of litigation, and therefore might measure it differently. For example, direct victims of gender- and sexual-based violence may be seeking reparations focused on satisfaction (for example, the prosecution of those responsible), while those assisting them may be focused on legislative impact. In some cases, it can also be challenging to identify a causal relationship between a specific case and any possible outcomes, in part because strategic litigation is usually a lengthy process. In the procedural lifetime of a case, political elections may have occurred, legal reforms may have been adopted, social norms may have changed, or other factors could have resulted in improved protection for human rights, independently of the litigation.[79]

The impact also transcends strategic litigation, and the case of *Azul* is a good example of this. The case was possible thanks to an ecosystem of actors that included the Inter-American System, both the IACHR and the Court, which were also key agents of social change. So reflecting on impact not only requires looking at strategic litigation but also at the magnifying role played by key actors that "work to improve human rights conditions and decrease the likelihood of the repetition of abuses, while also providing satisfactory recourse to the victims."[80]

Given the diverse forms of impact and actors involved in strategic litigation, it is possible to identify a variety of factors or criteria to evaluate the impact of a case, both as a case-planning exercise prior to the instigation of a case, as well as after the litigation has ended. REDRESS, one of the co-litigant organizations behind the case of *Azul*, has developed an impact matrix that considers various criteria to measure the impact of strategic litigation. While there are competing or complementary views on measuring impact, the criteria suggested here to

---

[79] See Open Society Justice Initiative, "Strategic Litigation Impacts: Insights from Global Experience" (2018), 28: <https://www.justiceinitiative.org/uploads/fd7809e2-bd2b-4f5b-964f-522c7c70e747/strategic-litigation-impacts-insights-20181023.pdf> (accessed October 22, 2023).

[80] Par Engstrom (ed.), *The Inter-American Humans Rights System, Impact Beyond Compliance* (Palgrave 2019), 4.

consider the impact of litigation are comprehensive and permit us to assess the outcomes so far in the case of *Azul*.[81]

- *Justice*: The impact on the victim(s) through (i) the declaratory element of the litigation (such as greater public awareness of what has occurred, including an acknowledgment of wrongdoing by the relevant authorities), and (ii) adequate punishment or sanctions (such as a public apology by the wrongdoer and/or the authorities being compelled to take affirmative action to repair damage).
- *Truth*: Definitive findings of fact that can be of crucial importance to victims and in campaigns against impunity.
- *Legal*: Changes in international and/or national normative standards brought about by the litigation, whether through treaty, case law, legislation, or decrees.
- *Policy and Governance*: Commitments by State authorities to change policy as a result of the litigation, as well as to concrete changes to technical procedures necessary to implement any policy changes.
- *Material*: Specific benefits to the victim(s) stemming from the litigation, including material reparations (such as psychosocial support, rehabilitation, and compensation for harms suffered).
- *Community*: Benefits of the litigation to others in a similar situation, going beyond the victim(s) in the case itself (e.g., collective reparations, public education campaigns, paving the way for other claimants).
- *Movement*: The impact the litigation has on the relevant social movements, both in the country where the litigation took place and globally, and the role of human rights systems which may both impact the litigation and be impacted by it.
- *Attitudes*: Shifts in the attitudes of decision makers and stakeholders (such as judges, diplomats, journalists, and law enforcement officials) as a result of the litigation.
- *Social*: Changes in the acceptability or tolerance of the particular issue in the country or region concerned.

These criteria, though broadly framed, reflect the kinds of results that can stem from strategic litigation—including both discrete outcomes such as reparations for the individual victim(s) in the case and broader, systemic changes, including legislative changes or other essential reforms (such as abolishing impunity measures that prevent accountability for grave human rights violations).

---

[81] Open Society Justice Initiative, *Strategic Litigation Impacts: Insights from Global Experience* (OSJI 2018), 27.

Additionally, some of these criteria are intended to assess the extent to which the case has contributed to changing the attitudes of relevant stakeholders, including lawmakers, journalists, judges, or law enforcement officials (for example, whether strategic litigation and advocacy efforts have sensitized judges to apply human rights standards in cases related to violence against the LGBTIQ+ community), as well as the effect that the process itself may have in terms of empowering and rehabilitating the victim.

Some of these criteria may be more relevant in some contexts than others, or suitable only for evaluating strategic litigation at certain phases. In this regard, while "truth"-related outcomes may emerge relatively early in the litigation process, policy and governance impacts may take much longer to materialize (often after years of ongoing advocacy and community organizing).

In assessing material impacts, it is important to recognize that a court judgment does not necessarily ensure that a victim will receive the necessary reparations. Our litigation experience shows that the implementation of reparations orders in human rights cases is slow, and many victims wait years before the reparations to which they are entitled finally materialize, while some orders are never implemented.[82]

In addition, a slightly different approach might be taken when evaluating national litigation as compared to regional or international litigation. The policy changes sought at regional and international human rights mechanisms (such as the UN treaty bodies, for example) differ from those sought through national courts, in part because the decisions in the former fora are not always considered to have the same legal weight that national decisions do, whereas national decisions will often not contain orders for State actors to implement measures of nonrepetition.

The following section uses the preceding criteria to assess the impact of the *Azul* judgment so far, since the decision was issued in March 2020.

5. The Impact of *Azul*'s Judgment

In the case of *Azul*, the IACtHR ordered important reparation measures, including key guarantees of nonrepetition, as well as comprehensive reparations for both individual and community harms. More than three and a half years has passed since the decision was issued, and the implementation of reparations by Peru has been hugely disappointing. As of October 2023, the only measures in

---

[82] "Righting Wrongs: The Dynamics of Implementing International Human Rights Decisions" [2020] 12(1) *Journal of Human Rights Practice*; Clara Sandoval, Philip Leach, and Rachel Murray, "Monitoring, Cajoling and Promoting Dialogue: What Role for Supranational Human Rights Bodies in the Implementation of Individual Decisions" [2020] 12 *Journal of Human Rights Practice* 71.

respect of which there has been full compliance are the publication of the judgment, and the staging of a public ceremony of apology and acknowledgment of international responsibility. Yet the IACtHR decision has had a significant impact on Azul, as well as on others within the continent and beyond.

5.1. Justice, Truth, and Material Impacts for Azul, Her Mother, and Society

The IACtHR ordered comprehensive individual reparations aimed at recognizing the material and moral damage caused by the violations to Azul and her mother. From a justice and truth perspective, the judgment acknowledges Azul and her mother as victims of all the violations alleged by them in the case.[83] The decision recognizes the facts as reported by the victim, and in doing so it vindicates Azul's account of what happened to her, denying the false narrative of those that committed, supported, and tried to cover up the violations.

Given the existing violence and stigmatization of LGBTIQ+ victims in the Americas,[84] the "truth" and "justice" impacts of the decision should not be underestimated. Upon learning of the IACtHR judgment, Azul stated: "I have no words to describe how I feel. I thank God above all. After all that I have been through, finally a court believes me. I only wish I could have been able to share this joy with my mother, who was always by my side in my efforts to report the crime and find justice."[85]

Since the judgment was issued, Azul's personal situation has changed. Even though the Peruvian State has still only paid a small proportion of the monetary compensation due to Azul, her situation of vulnerability and exclusion has improved, and she is starting studies to become a lawyer.

Furthermore, the judgment has also impacted positively on the empowerment of Azul and her fight for justice. In August 2021, Azul was invited as a speaker to an event organized by the IACHR on the eradication of violence against women and girls in the Americas. Azul was able to share what happened to her and the challenges and progress made in her case.[86] She spoke powerfully at the ceremony at which the State apologized to her, and has also been invited

---

[83] IACtHR, *Azul* (n. 13), para. 289.

[84] IACHR, "Recognition of the Rights of LGBTI Persons," OEA/Ser.L/V/II.170, December 7, 2018, para. 240.

[85] REDRESS Press Release, "Groundbreaking ruling: Inter-American Court finds Peru responsible for discriminatory torture against an LGBTI person and orders the State to combat discrimination": <https://redress.org/news/groundbreaking-ruling-inter-american-court-finds-peru-responsible-for-discriminatory-torture-against-an-lgbti-person-and-orders-the-state-to-combat-discrimination/> (accessed October 22, 2023).

[86] See <https://www.youtube.com/watch?v=PP9qOI7HKtw> (accessed October 22 2023).

to give media interviews and attend other events in Peru. In many ways, she has become an active player in the fight against SOGI violence. This shows the impact that litigation can have in empowering victims to be mobilizers for broader social change.

5.2. Legal Impact of the Case in Other Supranational and National Bodies

Given that *Azul* set an unprecedented standard on discriminatory torture, the decision has had a significant legal impact worldwide.

As mentioned previously, since the ruling in the case of *Azul*, the ECtHR has taken a more forceful approach to expand the protection of LGBTIQ+ people. In *Aghdgomelashvili and Japaridze*,[87] the tribunal found for the first time a substantive violation of Article 3 of the ECHR due to ill treatment by the police when carrying out a search in the premises of an LGBTIQ+ organization. Subsequently, in *B. and C. v. Switzerland*,[88] the tribunal ruled for the first time in a case of non-refoulement that the failure of the State to consider the risk of torture and inhumane treatment of LGBTIQ+ people in the country of origin can result in a violation of Article 3.

Furthermore, during the litigation and following the *Azul* case, civil society organizations submitted several joint *amicus curiae* briefs, encouraging the ECtHR to develop further its case law on LGBTIQ+ discriminatory torture and ill treatment under Article 3 of the Convention.[89]

At the UN and regional level, the Group of Eminent International and Regional Experts on Yemen, mandated by the Human Rights Council to investigate violations in that country, referred to the concept of violence "motivated by prejudice" developed by the IACtHR in *Azul* (citing the case), when referring to instances of violence against LGBTIQ+ people in the context of the conflict in Yemen.[90] Similarly, the case was featured in the report of the UN Independent Expert on SOGI, which focuses on Gender Theory, referring to the decision as "a remarkable example of judicial recognition of the fluid nature of gender identity."[91]

---

[87] ECtHR, *Aghdomelashvili and Japaridze* (n. 56).

[88] *Case of B and C v. Switzerland* [2020] ECtHR, App. Nos. 889/19 and 43987/16.

[89] See, e.g., *A v. Azerbaijan and 24 others* [2019] ECtHR, App. No. 17184/18; and *Maxim Grigoryevich Lapunov v. Russia* (n. 56), the judgment in respect of which was issued in September 2023.

[90] UN HRC, "Situation of human rights in Yemen, including violations and abuses since September 2014—Detailed findings of the Group of Eminent International and Regional Experts on Yemen," UN Doc. A/HRC/45/CPR.7, September 29, 2020, at 214.

[91] UN Independent Expert on SOGI. Report on Gender Theory. A/HRC/47/27 and A/76/152, of June and July 2021, respectively, para. 33.

At the national level, in November 2020 the Mexican Supreme Court of Justice adopted a Protocol for the Adjudication of Cases with a Gender Perspective that incorporates some of the standards developed in *Azul*,[92] for example, by noting that discriminatory violence can be committed against certain social groups, such as the LGBTIQ+ community, as well as the duty to investigate acts motivated by prejudice. In Argentina, in 2021 the Prosecutors Office released a casebook containing key international decisions on gender at the international and regional level. The case of *Azul* is included, but the volume is especially notable for not treating gender in a binary manner (men and women) but rather rejecting this artificial distinction.[93]

5.3. The Impact of the Case of *Azul* on the Community and the LGBTIQ+ Movement

The case of *Azul* has contributed to shedding light on a key issue that until a few years ago was invisible in the Americas and given only minimal attention globally. The IACtHR recognized explicitly that in Peruvian society, strong prejudices against the LGBTIQ+ population existed both at the time of the events in question and continue today, resulting, in some cases, in violence.[94] In this regard, the decision has had an important impact by recognizing elements of "justice" and "truth" in relation to violence against the LGBTIQ+ community in Peru, which, according to the IACtHR, had been effectively invisible due to the lack of official data.[95]

The judgment in the *Azul* case also contributes to the nurturing of synergies among the community working on LGBTIQ+ violence on the continent, with initiatives such as the creation in 2019 of the LGBTIQ+ Litigants Network of the Americas, set up by Promsex (co-litigants in the *Azul* case), *Colombia Diversa*, and other regional organizations.[96]

The case of *Azul* is an important precedent for the feminist movement conducting strategic litigation on gender violence, as it includes important standards on the due diligence required to investigate violence with a gender

---

[92] Mexico, Suprema Corte de Justicia de la Nación. Protocolo para Juzgar con Perspectiva de Género, November 2020.

[93] Ministerio Publico, República de Argentina, Perspectiva de género en los sistemas de protección regional y universal de derechos humanos: Compendio sobre las decisiones e informes de los órganos y mecanismos internacionales de derechos humanos en materia de género, 2021: <https://www.mpf.gob.ar/direccion-general-de-politicas-de-genero/files/2021/03/DGPG_Ebook_2021_9-3.pdf> (accessed November 30, 2021).

[94] IACtHR, *Azul* (n. 13), para. 51.

[95] Ibid., para. 48.

[96] Red de Litigantes LGBT de las Américas: < https://litiganteslgbt.org/quienes-somos/> (accessed October 22, 2023).

perspective.[97] Yet among the feminist and LGBTIQ+ movements, the *Azul* and the *Vicky Hernández* cases have also generated legal debate on the concept of gender and the application of treaties on the protection of women's rights to trans women. The dissenting votes of IACtHR Judges Vio Grossi and Odio Benito in the *Vicky Hernández* case, by which the two Judges disagreed with the majority in asserting that the Convention of Belém do Pará protects the rights of trans women, has generated controversy in this respect.[98]

At the international level, the significance of the *Azul* decision has been recognized both in relation to the anti-torture movement[99] and by the LGBTIQ+ rights movement.[100]

Likewise, civil society organizations like Equal Rights Trust or *De-Justicia* have used the findings in *Azul* to argue key points of law and fact at national and international levels and to continue advocating for full protection of members of the LGBTIQ+ community. For example, Equal Rights Trust cited *Azul* as a precedent in its submission to the UN Special Rapporteur on torture and other cruel, inhuman or degrading treatment or punishment on psychological dynamics conducive to torture and ill treatment,[101] and *De-Justicia* in Colombia did the same before the Colombian Constitutional Court in a case where the rights of a trans woman to access her pension were at stake.[102] Finally, the case has energized the LGBTIQ+ movement in other regions of the world. For example, in Africa, the case has been debated publicly among the organizations working on LGBTIQ+ rights, learning from the litigation experience of colleagues in the Americas.[103] Debate over the significance of Azul's case in the African context

---

[97] The case was featured by the *Red Latinoamericana de Litigio Estratégico en Género*. See Alejandra Vicente, "Sexual orientation-based torture: one year since the judgement of the Inter-American Court case of Azul Rojas Marín": <https://www.releg.red/blog-eng/blog-azul> (accessed October 22, 2023).

[98] Carlos J. Zelada, "Vicky Hernández et al. V. Honduras: A Landmark Victory with a Bitter Aftertaste" (August 27, 2021) *EJIL*: < https://www.ejiltalk.org/vicky-hernandez-et-al-v-honduras-a-landmark-victory-with-a-bitter-aftertaste/> (accessed October 22, 2023).

[99] Former UN Special Rapporteur on Torture, Juan Méndez, has recognized the importance of the Azul judgment of the anti-torture movement: <https://www.youtube.com/watch?=hmc03pDRmSA> (accessed October 22, 2023).

[100] Victor Madrigal, "UN Independent Expert on Protection against violence and discrimination based on sexual orientation and gender identity, has highlighted the significance of the judgement for the LGBTIQ+ movement": https://www.facebook.com/watch/?v=760455034952166> (accessed October 22, 2023).

[101] Equal Rights Trust (June 2020), paras. 20–21: <https://www.ohchr.org/Documents/Issues/Torture/Call/NGOs/EqualRightsTrust.pdf> (accessed October 22, 2023).

[102] Dejusticia, "Respuesta invitación por Oficio OPT-A-2318/2021 al Centro de Estudios de Derecho, Justicia y Sociedad" (August 5, 2021), 15: <https://www.dejusticia.org/wp-content/uploads/2021/09/20210906-Intervencio%CC%81n-Dejusticia-ra%CC%81d.-T-7.987.537-1.pdf> (accessed October 22, 2023).

[103] See, e.g., event of July 1, 2021, with ISLA, the University of Pretoria, Promsex, REDRESS, and the UN Independent Expert on SOGI.

has also taken place in events organized by the Pan-African Reparation Initiative and the African Moot Court Conference organized by the University of Pretoria.

6. Reflection on the Impact of the Case

In recent years, important literature has emerged showing the importance of the implementation of, and compliance with, international decisions.[104] At the same time, there is a push to look beyond that, considering the impact of such international decisions, as well as the key role played by the Inter-American System in dynamics that enable societal change. In the Americas, it is argued, despite limited compliance with international decisions, the impact of the System is hard to deny when considering the various decisions, reports, and positions taken by the IACHR and the IACtHR to facilitate and promote the reinforcement of human rights protection.

The case of *Azul* allows us to situate the discussion between three key concepts: compliance, implementation, and impact. Compliance here means the actual execution of orders given by supranational bodies in individual cases (for example, the payment of the compensation ordered, the restitution of land, or reforms of legal norms). Implementation, on the other hand, refers to the processes and dynamics that make compliance possible. Clearly, as has been pointed out,[105] looking only at compliance misses the opportunity to understand the real impact of actors and/or decisions beyond a specific case, but looking only at impact without taking into account the various dynamics that are unleashed through the process of implementing decisions also misses the opportunity to understand the correlation that exists between these three concepts. The case of *Azul* allows us to argue that, while compliance with both the individual and collective measures ordered by the Court has been poor, the case has generated dynamics of implementation both to achieve compliance and also to ensure impact. These are mutually reinforcing dynamics.

These dynamics have been the result of diverse factors, but there are two that stand out: first, the organizations behind the case have generated pathways to impact through multiple meetings, conferences, and workshops to promote the findings of the case and help such standards to penetrate legal consciousness at various levels (nationally, regionally, and internationally). To this end, they are

---

[104] "Righting Wrongs: The Dynamics of Implementing International Human Rights Decisions" (n. 82), 71; Society Justice Initiative, "Implementing Humans Rights Decisions: Reflection, Successes and New Directions" (OSJI 2021): <https://www.justiceinitiative.org/uploads/3e398a5e-0b10-4fa4-ba28-275bc909a8f8/implementing-human-rights-decisions-20210721.pdf> (accessed October 22, 2023).

[105] Ibid.

part of key networks and communities of practice in this area as exemplified by the LGBT Network of Litigants in the Americas, or as demonstrated by their partnering with key civil society organizations such as Colombia Diversa to write a report about violence against the LGBTIQ+ community in the Americas region.

Second, these organizations have not acted alone. The Inter-American Human Rights System, both Commission and Court, have been essential to their strategy, and clearly, as this chapter demonstrates, there are reinforcing positions taken by both institutions that paved the way for the judgment and that allowed them to develop new standards in key policy and legal spaces in the region and beyond. As indicated by Engstrom and others, "the IASHR is likely to be most effective where its various mechanisms are employed in a coordinated fashion [and] where domestic actors utilise its rulings and precedents to further their own efforts to bring about national-level policy change...".[106]

Importantly, this network has facilitated work in the region but also beyond, including in Africa, which, as already noted in this article, is lagging behind in the protection of the rights of LGBTIQ+ persons. Therefore, a key element to consider when exploring impact, are the networks of action that exist, and the ecosystem of change that develops as a result of strategic litigation, as well as the dynamics that predate, exist alongside, and follow such international litigation.

7. Concluding Remarks

The criteria to assess impact utilized in this chapter, including justice, truth, the social movement, legal, policy, material, and other forms of impact, show that while it is still too early to analyze the full impact of the case of *Azul*, the reach of this judgment is undeniable, even despite poor implementation thus far of the orders given by the Court.

It is also clear that key dynamics have been unleashed to ensure implementation of the judgment, as shown by the work of Azul, REDRESS, and Promsex, aiming to secure compliance but also to ensure that broader social change is achieved. On this point, the ecosystem of actors, including the IAHRS, UN bodies and special procedures, and the ECtHR, alongside civil society organizations and State authorities, have all played a key role. Hopefully, the case of *Azul* and subsequent judgments like that of *Vicky Hernández*, will prompt effective change in Africa and other regions, thus representing a significant contribution to ensuring that, worldwide, there is broad acceptance that no one should suffer violence and discrimination based on sexual orientation or gender identity.

[106] Ibid., 1.

II.7
The Rights of the Child According to the Inter-American Court of Human Rights

A Latin American Translation[*]

By Mary Beloff

1. Introduction

The rights of the child were recognized early on both in the Universal[1] and Inter-American human rights systems.[2] These rights were originally framed as positive

---

[*] I am deeply grateful to Virginia Deymonnaz (UBA) for her outstanding research assistance and to Ana Horowitz for her patient and thoughtful reading and comments on the text.

[1] International Labour Organization: *Convention fixing the minimum age for admission of children to industrial employment* (1919); *Convention concerning the night work of young personas employed in industry* (1919); *Convention fixing the minimum age for admission of children to employment at sea* (1920); *Convention concerning the age for admission of children to employment in agriculture* (1921); *Convention on the medical examination of young persons—sea—*(1921); *Convention fixing the minimum age for the admission of children to employment at sea* (revised 1936); *Convention concerning the Night Work of Young Persons Employed in Industry* (revised 1948); *Convention concerning the prohibition and immediate action for the elimination of the worst forms of child labour* (1999). United Nations: (a) Declarations: *Declarations of the Rights of the Child* (1924 and 1959); *Universal Declaration of Human Rights*, article 25.2 (1948); *Declaration on the Protection of Women and Children in Emergency and Armed Conflict* (1974), *Declaration on Social and Legal Principles relating to the Protection and Welfare of Children, with special reference to Foster Placement and Adoption Nationally and Internationally* (1986); (b) Conventions and Covenants: *Geneva Convention* (IV) relative to the Protection of Civilian Persons in Time of War articles 14, 17, 23, 24, 38, 50, 76, 89, 94, and 132 (1949); *International Covenant on Economic, Social and Cultural Rights* articles 10.3 and 12.2.a (1966); *International Covenant on Civil and Political Rights* articles 6.5, 10, 14.4, and 24 (1966); *Protocol Additional to the Geneva Conventions of 12 August 1949, and relating to the Protection of victim of International Armed Conflicts—Protocol I* (1977) articles 70, 77, and 78; *Protocol Additional to the Geneva Conventions of 12 August 1949, and relating to the Protection of Victims of Non-International Armed Conflicts—Protocol II* (1977) articles 4.3, and 6.4; *Convention on the Elimination of All Forms of Discrimination against Women*, articles 5, 9, 11, 12, and 16 (1979); *Hague Convention on the Civil Aspects of International Child Abduction* (1980); *Convention on the Rights of the Child* (1989) and its Optional Protocols (*Optional Protocol to the Convention on the Rights of the Child on the sale of children, prostitution and child pornography* (2000), *Optional Protocol to the Convention on the Rights of the Child on the involvement of children in armed conflict* (2000), and *Optional Protocol to the Convention on the Rights of the child on a communications procedure* (2011); *Hague Convention on Protection of Children and Cooperation in respect of Intercountry Adoption* (1993); and *Hague Convention on Jurisdiction, Applicable Law, Recognition, Enforcement and Co-operation in respect to Parental Responsibility and Measures for the Protection of Children* (1996).

[2] *American Declaration of the Rights and Duties of Man* (1948), articles VII and XXX [hereinafter American Declaration, or ADHR]; *American Convention on Human Rights* (1969), article 19

State obligations under the legal definition of "special protection measures," and they were generally understood to be inextricably linked to the principle of the "best interest" of the child. In Latin America this normative structure associated with the then-in-force inquisitorial procedural norms occasionally gave rise to an unjustified paternalism in administrative and judicial practices that could go to the extreme of making the child invisible as a subject of rights. Only after the ratification of the Convention on the Rights of the Child (CRC) in 1989 did the general understanding of child rights shift in its approach in favor of a more complex appreciation of childhood that seeks to balance protection and autonomy, and that reasonably combines positive and negative State obligations toward this age group that is defined by its essential vulnerability.[3]

This development brought together two fields that had remained separate until the early 1990s in the region: human rights and child protection activism. Legal academia has, in turn, just recently begun to consider the rights of the child, especially as these have evolved in the jurisprudence of the Inter-American Court of Human Rights (IACtHR).[4]

The Inter-American Human Rights System's (IAHRS's)[5] relative omission of child rights cannot be explained as a matter of law, since its main instruments—the American Declaration on the Rights and Duties of Man in 1948 and the American Convention on Human Rights in 1969—explicitly recognized the rights of children.

The motives for the IAHRS's delay in processing cases related to children's rights are not analyzed here. This chapter instead examines one possible reason for why it began to pay attention to the rights of the child. The thesis adopted here is that it was not the legal but the political and cultural impact of the CRC which explains the changes in perspective and practices in this field among different actors of the Inter-American system.[6] Only after the CRC was adopted and was subsequently ratified by all countries in less than two years did the IAHRS begin to systematically frame child protection cases in human rights terms.

---

and also articles 4.5, 5.5, 13.4, 17, and 27; and *Additional Protocol to the American Convention on Human Rights in the Area of Economic, Social and Cultural Rights* (*Protocol of San Salvador*), article 16 (1988) [hereinafter American Convention, or ACHR]. Also *Inter-American Convention on Conflict of Laws concerning the Adoption of Minors* (1984); *Inter-American Convention on Support Obligations* (1989); *Inter-American Convention on the International Return of Children* (1989); and *Inter-American Convention on International Traffic in Minors* (1994). The *Inter-American Convention on the Prevention, Punishment and Eradication of Violence against Women* (*Convention of Belem do Pará*), article 9 (1994) contains a reference to the vulnerability due to a girl's minority in relation to protection measures in contexts of violence.

[3] Mary Beloff, *Derechos del niño. Su protección especial en el sistema interamericano* (2nd ed., Hammurabi 2019), ch. 1, at 39.
[4] Hereinafter Inter-American Court or IACtHR
[5] Hereinafter Inter-American System, or IAHRS.
[6] See Mary Beloff, *Derechos del niño. Su protección especial en el sistema interamericano* (2nd ed., Hammurabi 2019), Introduction and chs. 1–3.

This chapter outlines the evolution in the Inter-American Court's interpretation of the content of child rights (ACHR, art. 19). It aims to comprehensively analyze the Court's decisions concerning this article, as well as to provide some clues as to why the rights of the child remains an unsettled issue in the region.

2. The Recognition of the Existence of an International *Corpus Juris* on the Protection of the Rights of the Child

The three general inter-American instruments for the protection of human rights (the American Declaration, the American Convention, and the Additional Protocol to the American Convention on Economic, Social, and Cultural Rights, or "Protocol of San Salvador") recognize the right of the child to special protection measures.

The American Declaration contains two provisions concerning children's rights: Article VII, which provides that "all children have the right to special protection, care and aid," and Article XXX, which establishes "the duty of every person to aid, support, educate and protect his minor children," as well as "the duty of children to honor their parents always and to aid, support and protect them when they need it."

The American Convention contains five provisions related to children: Articles 4.5, 5.5, 13.4, 17.4–5, and, most importantly, Article 19. Article 4.5 states that "[c]apital punishment shall not be imposed upon persons who, at the time the crime was committed, were under 18 years of age"; Article 5.5. establishes that "minors, while subject to criminal proceedings, shall be separated from adults and brought before specialized tribunals, as speedily as possible, so that they may be treated in accordance with their status as minors"; Article 13.4 states that "public entertainments may be subject by law to prior censorship for the sole purpose of regulating access to them for the moral protection of childhood and adolescence"; and Article 17, which provides for the protection of the family, requires that "[i]n case of dissolution [of a marriage], provision shall be made for the necessary protection of any children solely on the basis of their own best interests" (17.4) and also states that "[t]he law shall recognize equal rights for children born out of wedlock and those born in wedlock" (17.5).[7]

Only ACHR Article 19, however, refers directly to the rights of the child in its title and content. The provision states: "Every minor child has the right to the measures of protection required by his condition as a minor on the part of his family, society, and the state." This article serves as the backbone of the Inter-American System's approach to the protection of children.

In addition, Article 16 of the Protocol of San Salvador provides that "[e]very child, whatever his parentage, has the right to the protection that his status as

---

[7] The relevance of children's rights in the system of protection created by the American Convention is also reflected in Article 27 of this treaty, which establishes that Articles 4 (Right to Life), 5 (Right to Humane Treatment), 17 (Rights of the Family), 18 (Right to a Name), *and Article 19 (Rights of the Child)* cannot be suspended even in the event of war, public danger, or other emergency.

a minor requires from his family, society and the state"; that he or she has "the right to grow under the protection and responsibility of his parents"; that "save in exceptional, judicially-recognized circumstances, a child of young age ought not to be separated from his mother; and that "[e]very child has the right to free and compulsory education, at least in the elementary phase, and to continue his training at higher levels of the educational system."

Although the aforementioned article develops some content of the general right to special protection, the fact is that, in the inter-American sphere, there are no other rules and principles that assign further content to it. For this reason, the adjudication of cases on the basis of Article 19 of the American Convention and other articles included in regional treaties over which the IACtHR has jurisdiction becomes more complex due to the considerable lack of precision regarding what content these special protection measures must have.

For that reason, the Inter-American Court's recognition that "[b]oth the American Convention and the Convention on the Rights of the Child form part of a very comprehensive international *corpus juris* for the protection of the child that should help this Court establish the content and scope of the general provision established in Article 19 of the American Convention" was decisive.[8]

It was not until 1999, when the Court first decided a case on the basis of ACHR Article 19 (*Villagrán Morales et al.*—case of the *"Street Children"*—v. *Guatemala*), that it began to draw on this *corpus juris* and continued to do so in later decisions concerning children in different situations of vulnerability due to socioeconomic deprivation, gender, ethnicity, and disabilities, among others.[9]

According to the Court, the very comprehensive *corpus juris* in question includes not only Article 19 of the *American Convention* but it also extends beyond the IAHRS to incorporate the UN Declarations of the Rights of the Child (1924 and 1959), the Convention on the Rights of the Child, the UN Standard Minimum Rules for the Administration of Juvenile Justice ("The Beijing Rules," 1985), the UN Standard Minimum Rules for Non-custodial Measures ("The

---

[8] IACtHR, *Case of the "Street Children" (Villagrán Morales et al.) v. Guatemala*, Merits, November 19, 1999, Ser. C. No. 63, 8para. 194.

[9] The Inter-American Court has recognized the existence of several international *corpora juris*: "[R]egarding the special protection required by the members of the indigenous communities" (IACtHR, *Case of the Yakye Axa Indigenous Community v. Paraguay*, Merits, Reparations, and Costs, June 15, 2005, Ser. C No. 125, para. 163); of "human rights of migrants" (IACtHR, *Case of the Pacheco Tineo family v. Bolivia*, Preliminary objections, Merits, Reparations, and Costs, November 25, 2013, Ser. C No. 272, para. 129), and "for the protection of human rights of children that are asylum seekers and refugees in the American continent" (IACtHR, Advisory Opinion OC-21/14, *Rights and guarantees of children in the context of migration and/or in need of international protection*, August 19, 2014, Ser. A No. 21, para. 249); "of protection of the personal integrity of women" and "as regards the prevention and punishment of violence against women" (IACtHR, *Case of González et al. ("Cotton Field") v. Mexico*, Preliminary Objection, Merits, Reparations, and Costs, November 16, 2009, Ser. C No. 205, paras. 225 and 248); "for the protection of the human rights of persons with disabilities" (IACtHR, *Case of Chinchilla Sandoval et al. v. Guatemala*, Preliminary objection, Merits, Reparations, and Costs, February 29, 2016, Ser. C No. 312, concurring opinion of Judge FERRER MAC-GREGOR, para. 9); and "of human rights related to the prohibition of discrimination based on sexual orientation" (IACtHR, *Case of Atala Riffo and daughters v. Chile*, Merits, Reparations, and Costs, February 24, 2012, Ser. C No. 239, para. 272).

Tokyo Rules," 1990), and the UN Guidelines for the Prevention of Juvenile Delinquency ("The Riyadh Guidelines," 1990), in addition to other, general international human rights instruments.

It also resorted to the Convention on the Rights of the Child when developing its interpretation of the best interests of the child as a "regulating principle regarding children's rights [...] based on the very dignity of the human being, on the characteristics of children themselves, and on the need to foster their development, making full use of their potential, as well as on the nature and scope of the Convention on the Rights of the Child."[10]

The Inter-American Court's reliance on UN instruments and resolutions through the wide notion of *corpus juris* reveals its intention to initiate a sort of dialogue with the Universal human rights protection system. This tendency was striking at first given that it had no *a priori* legal basis for doing so nor did the Universal system include bodies with adjudicative competence. With the passage of time and the sustained issuing of rulings by the IACtHR, the question has become naturalized to the point that, currently, both the Court and the different treaty monitoring bodies of the Universal system (in this case, the Committee on the Rights of the Child), reciprocally invoke decisions of the other.[11]

3. Defining "Child" in International Law: The Impact of the Convention on the Rights of the Child on the Inter-American Court Case Law

Although human rights instruments recognized that children have rights under international law since the beginning of the twentieth century, the content and scope of these rights remained associated with unjustified paternalistic criteria until recently.

---

[10] IACtHR, Advisory Opinion OC-17/2002, *Juridical Condition and Human Rights of the Child*, August 28, 2002, Ser. A No. 17, para. 56; *Case of Bulacio v. Argentina*, Merits, Reparations, and Costs, September 18, 2003, Ser. C No. 100, para. 134; *Case of the Gómez Paquiyauri Brothers v. Peru*, Merits, Reparations, and Costs, July 8, 2004, Ser. C No. 110, para. 163; *Case of Fornerón and daughter v. Argentina*, Merits, Reparations, and Costs, April 27, 2012, Ser. C No. 242, para. 49; *Case of Atala Riffo and daughters v. Chile* (n. 9) para. 108; *Case of Gonzales Lluy et al. v. Ecuador*, Preliminary Objections, Merits, Reparations, and Costs, September 1, 2015, Ser. C No. 298 para. 268; *Case of Ramírez Escobar et al. v. Guatemala*, Merits, Reparations, and Costs, March 9, 2018, Ser. C No. 351, para. 152; among others.

[11] The Committee on the Rights of the Child frequently cites the Inter-American Court, and vice versa. For example, in General Comment No. 8 on "The right of the child to protection from corporal punishment and other cruel or degrading form of punishment," the CRC refers to the Advisory Opinion OC-17/02 when it asserts that the States "are under the obligation . . . to adopt all positive measures required to ensure protection of children against mistreatment, whether in their relations with public authorities, or in relations among individuals or with nonstate entities." (para. 24). The CRC also systematically evaluates compliance with decisions adopted by regional bodies when monitoring country situations.

The Inter-American Court has played a decisive role in bringing about change by weighing positive State obligations and negative freedoms in relation to children without making the mistake of adopting a liberationist approach that places them *par conditio* with adults. To this end, the Court has relied heavily on the Convention on the Rights of the Child. This illustrates the aforementioned dialogue and the current interdependence of regional and Universal human rights systems on issues related to the scope and content of the protection of children.

The fact that neither of the four specific regional instruments related to minors[12] that regulate matters of private international law, nor general inter-American human rights instruments that establish State, community, and family duties to secure the rights of children, define "child" for purposes of international human rights law, explain why the Convention on the Rights of the Child and the decisions of its treaty body, the Committee on the Rights of the Child,[13] have become so crucial for the development of the scope of children's rights in IACtHR case law.

In the aforementioned *Villagrán Morales et al. v. Guatemala* case, the Court adopted the Convention's age-based definition of "child."[14] It stated that although "Article 19 of the American Convention does not define what is meant by 'child' [. . .], the Convention on the Rights of the Child (Article 1) considers every human being who has not attained 18 years of age to be a child."[15] Shortly after, in Advisory Opinion OC-17/02, the Court again established that "taking into account international norms [. . .], 'child' refers to any person who has not yet turned 18 years of age" and also decided that the term child "*obviously* [. . .] encompasses boys, girls, and adolescents."[16]

---

[12] Art. 2 *Inter-American Convention on support obligations* (1989): "For the purposes of this Convention, a child shall be any person below the age of eighteen years"; art. 2 *Inter-American Convention on the International return of children* (1989): "For the purposes of this Convention, a child shall be any person below the age of sixteen years."; and art. 2, a), *Inter-American Convention on International traffic in minors* (1994): "For the purpose of the present Convention: a) "Minor" means any human being below the age of eighteen."

[13] Hereinafter CRC.

[14] Article 1, *Convention on the Rights of the Child*. The last part of this article allows the States to retain the ability to establish in their domestic law that the age of majority can be reached prior to eighteen years, but in Latin America this second provision has not been used to challenge the rule that one is a child until the age of eighteen. Even the United States, which did not ratify the CRC, upholds the same criterion in its Supreme Court rulings. On the other hand, the Human Rights Committee has established that "the ages for protection" should not be "unreasonably brief" and that in no case may a State fail to comply with its obligations of protection of children and adolescents, even if they attained legal age prior to eighteen years under national legislation. See Human Rights Committee, General Comment 17, Article 23 Rights of the Child, para. 4. Additionally, *Convention 182 concerning the Prohibition and Immediate Action for the Elimination of the Worst Forms of Child Labour*, establishes in its Article 2 that the term "child" refers to "every person under 18 years of age" as does the *Protocoto Prevent, Suppress and Punish Trafficking in Persons, Especially Women and Children*, supplementing the *United Nations Convention against Transnational Organized Crime* (art. 3).

[15] IACtHR, *Case of the "Street Children" (Villagrán Morales et al.) v. Guatemala* [1999], Ser. C No. 63, para. 188.

[16] IACtHR, *Juridical Condition and Human Rights of the Child* (n. 10) para. 42 and fn. 45, italics added.

The *Villagrán Morales et al. v. Guatemala* case involved five victims; only three were under eighteen years of age. Nevertheless, the Inter-American Court referred to all five victims as "street children."[17] In subsequent cases, it reiterated its understanding that "'child' refers to any person who has not yet turned 18 years of age"[18] and did not modify its definition even when considering issues such as the scope of the right to special protection measures when dealing with adults serving jail time for crimes committed when they were minors. This was recently decided in the *Mota Abarullo et al. v. Venezuela* case, where the Court extended the right to special protection to persons beyond the age of eighteen years serving a custodial sentence by determining:

> (...) the relevant obligations of the State (...) started from the time they came into contact with the system of justice and their deprivation of liberty when they were juveniles, corresponded to those relating to the rights of the child, pursuant to Article 19 of the Convention. Accordingly, in order to comply with the socio-educational objective inherent in measures adopted in the case of children who have committed criminal offenses, even when such offenses entail the deprivation of liberty, it is necessary to extend the special juvenile regime to those who turn 18 while they are complying with those measures. Thus, the mere fact of turning 18 does not remove young people subject to deprivation of liberty in facilities for juveniles from the special protection that should be provided by the State. (...).[19]

This precise definition of "child" is associated with the person's essential vulnerability, which has also led the Court to consistently highlight the positive obligations that this condition imposes on the adult world. These duties constitute the clearest expression of justified paternalism in international human rights law: according to the Court, children have "special rights corresponding to specific obligations of the family, society, and the State."[20]

4. The Inter-American Court Jurisprudence on the Rights of Children

The Court has addressed the rights of the child in: (1) advisory opinions; (2) provisional measures; and (3) contentious cases.

---

[17] Beloff (n. 3), ch. IV.
[18] IACtHR, *Case of Bulacio v. Argentina*, (n. 10) para. 133.
[19] IACtHR, *Case of Mota Abarullo et al. v. Venezuela*, Merits, Reparations, and Costs, November 18, 2020, Ser. C No. 417, para. 85.
[20] Among others, IACtHR, *Case of the Girls Yean and Bosico v. Dominican Republic*, Merits, Reparations, and Costs, September 8, 2005, Ser. C No. 130, para. 133; *Case of the Xákmok Kásek Indigenous Community v. Paraguay*, Merits, Reparations, and Costs, August 24, 2010, Ser. C No. 214, para. 257; *Case of the Dos Erres Massacres v. Guatemala*, para. 184; and *Case of González et al. ("Cotton Field") v. Mexico* (n. 9) para. 408.

4.1. Inter-American Court Advisory Opinions Related to Child Rights

The Inter-American Court has issued two advisory opinions related to the rights of children: OC-17/02 "Juridical Condition and Human Rights of the Child"[21] and OC-21/14 "Rights and Guarantees of Children in the Context of Migration and/or in Need of International Protection."[22] It issued a third advisory opinion OC-29/22 "Differentiated Approaches with respect to Certain Groups of Persons Deprived of Liberty" that includes one section regarding "children living in detention centers with their mothers or primary caregivers."[23]

Among them, the most relevant document is, however, the Advisory Opinion OC-17/02 where the Court determined "the reach of special measures of protection for children (Article 19 of the Convention) in relation to the legal and judicial guarantees of the Convention." Despite some lack of conceptual clarity, OC-17/02 constitutes a milestone in the field because it is the one inter-American document containing the most comprehensive set of legal standards pertaining to children.

4.2. Provisional Measures Regarding Children outside the Framework of a Contentious Case

The Inter-American Court has intervened in matters related to the rights of the child not only by issuing judgments in individual proceedings but also by adopting provisional measures according Article 63.2 of the ACHR and Article 27 of the Rules of Procedure of the Inter-American Court "[i]n cases of extreme gravity and urgency, and when necessary to avoid irreparable damage to persons (...) in matters it has under consideration."

This article also empowers the Court to issue provisional measures in cases not yet submitted before it, at the request of the Commission. This happened in the context of two juvenile detention centers in Brazil[24] and in connection with adoption proceedings in Paraguay.[25]

---

[21] IACtHR, *Juridical Condition and Human Rights of the Child* (n. 10), para. 56.

[22] IACtHR, Rights and guarantees of children in the context of migration and/or in need of international protection. Advisory Opinion OC-21/14 of August 19, 2014. Series A No.21.

[23] IACtHR, Differentiated approaches with respect to certain groups of persons deprived of liberty (Interpretation and scope of Articles 1(1), 4(1), 5, 11(2), 12, 13, 17(1), 19, 24, and 26 of the American Convention on Human Rights and other human rights instruments), Advisory Opinion OC-29/22, May 30, 2022, Ser. A No. 29.

[24] IACtHR, *Matter of children deprived of liberty in the "Complexo do Tatuapé" of Fundação CASA* Provisional Measures regarding Brazil; and *Matter of the Socio-Educational Internment Facility* [Provisional Measures regarding Brazil].

[25] IACtHR, *Matter of L.M. regarding Paraguay.*

4.3. The Inter-American Court Case Law Regarding the Rights of Children (ACHR Article 19)

In its jurisprudence, the Inter-American Court has focused primarily on ACHR Article 19. It does not apply a uniform approach when analyzing State practice in relation to this provision. In some cases, the Court analyzes ACHR Article 19 autonomously, while in others it analyzes this provision in conjunction with other norms. It similarly varies in its application of ACHR Article 19 in determining reparations.

In the following paragraphs, I present all sixty-three contentious cases in which, as of September 2023, the Court found a violation of ACHR Article 19. In fifty-three cases, the Court analyzed the content of ACHR Article 19 and found that a State had violated this provision; in the remaining ten cases, it found that a State had violated ACHR Article 19 without analyzing its content.[26] Additionally, there are two cases where it analyzed the content of ACHR Article 19, but did not determine its violation for procedural reasons.[27]

I classify the sixty-three decisions into two main groups: one set of decisions concerns violations of the rights of individuals and the other set concerns attacks on the rights of communities.

There are fifty-one cases regarding violations of the rights of individuals, which I in turn categorize into six categories: (1) institutional violence; (2) juvenile justice; (3) discrimination; (4) health, education, and special needs; (5) forced labor and trafficking; and (6) child soldiers. Some of these categories are in turn divided into subcategories:

(1) *Institutional violence* includes: (a) summary executions (two cases),[28] (b) institutional/urban violence (four cases),[29] (c) institutional violence in

---

[26] IACtHR, *Case of Molina Theissen v. Guatemala*, Reparations and Costs, July 3, 2004, Ser. C No. 106; *Case of Carpio Nicolle et al. v. Guatemala*, Merits, Reparations, and Costs, November 22, 2004, Ser. C No. 117; *Case of Tiu Tojín v. Guatemala*, Merits, Reparations, and Costs, November 26, 2008, Ser. C No. 190; *Case of Human Rights Defender et al. v. Guatemala*, Preliminary Objections, Merits, Reparations, and Costs, August 28, 2014, Ser. C No. 283; *Case of Yarce et al. v. Colombia*, Preliminary Objection, Merits, Reparations, and Costs November 22, 2006, Ser. C No. 325; *Case of Vereda La Esperanza v. Colombia*, Preliminary Objections, Merits, Reparations, and Costs, November 21, 2017, Ser. C No. 341; *Case of Carvajal Carvajal et al. v. Colombia*, Merits, Reparations, Court Costs, and Legal Fees, March 13, 2018, Ser. C No. 352; *Case of Omeara Carrascal et al. v. Colombia*, Merits, Reparations, and Costs, November 21, 2018, Ser. C No. 368; *Case of Deras García et al. v. Honduras*, Merits, Reparations, Costs, and Expenses, August 25, 2022, Ser. C No. 482; and *Case of Tabares Toro et al. v. Colombia*, Merits, Reparations, and Costs, May 23, 2023, Ser. C No. 491.

[27] IACtHR, *Case of Serrano Cruz Sisters v. El Salvador*, Merits, Reparations, and Costs, March 1, 2005, Ser. C No. 120; and *Case of Vargas Areco v. Paraguay*, September 26, 2006 Ser. C No. 155.

[28] IACtHR, *Case of the "Street Children" (Villagrán Morales et al.) v. Guatemala* (n. 8); and *Case of Servellón García et al. v. Honduras*, Merits, Reparations, and Costs, September 21, 2006, Ser. C No. 152.

[29] IACtHR, *Case of Bulacio v. Argentina* (n. 10); *Case of García Ibarra et al. v. Ecuador* Preliminary Objections, Merits, Reparations, and Costs, November 17, 2015, Ser. C No. 306; *Case of Carpio Nicolle et al. v. Guatemala* (n. 26); and *Case of Valencia Campos et al. v. Bolivia*, Preliminary Objections, Merits, Reparations, and Costs, October 18, 2022, Ser. C No. 469.

the context of political crises and political instability (eight cases),[30] (d) violence against human rights defenders (two cases),[31] and (e) forced disappearance (ten cases).[32]

(2) *Juvenile justice* includes three cases.[33]

(3) *Discrimination* includes: (a) discrimination due to migrant or refugee status (three cases),[34] (b) discrimination due to gender stereotypes and gender-based violence (six cases),[35] and (c) discrimination in the context of the family (five cases).[36]

(4) *Health, education, and special needs* includes four cases.[37]

---

[30] IACtHR, *Case of the Gómez Paquiyauri Brothers v. Peru*, Merits, Reparations, and Costs, July 4, 2004, Ser. C No. 110; *Case of the Barrios family v. Venezuela*, Merits, Reparations, and Costs, November 24, 2011, Ser. C No. 237; *Case of Uzcátegui et al. v. Venezuela*, Merits and Reparations, September 3, 2012, Ser. C No. 249; *Case of Vélez Restrepo and family v. Colombia*, Preliminary Objection, Merits, Reparations, and Costs, September 3, 2012, Ser. C No. 248; *Case of Landaeta Mejías Brothers et al. v. Venezuela*, Preliminary Objections, Merits, Reparations, and Costs, August 27, 2014, Ser. C No. 281; *Case of Carvajal Carvajal et al. v. Colombia* (n. 26); *Case of Omeara Carrascal et al. v. Colombia* (n. 26); and *Case Deras García et al. v. Honduras*, Merits, Reparations, Costs, and Expenses, August 25, 2022, Ser. 482.

[31] IACtHR, *Case of Human Rights Defender et al. v. Guatemala* (n. 26); and *Case of Yarce et al. v. Colombia* (n. 26).

[32] IACtHR, *Case of Molina Theissen v. Guatemala* (n.26); *Case of Tiu Tojín v. Guatemala* (n. 26); *Case of Chitay Nech et al. v. Guatemala*, Preliminary Objections, Merits, Reparations, and Costs, May 25, 2010, Ser. C No. 212; *Case Gelman v. Uruguay*, Merits and Reparations, February 24, 2011, Ser. C No. 221; *Case of Contreras et al. v. El Salvador*, Merits, Reparations, and Costs, August 31, 2011, Ser. C No. 232; *Case of Gudiel Álvarez et al. ("Diario Militar") v. Guatemala*, Merits, Reparations, and Costs, November 20, 2012, Ser. C No. 253; *Case of Rochac Hernández et al. v. El Salvador*, Merits, Reparations, and Costs, October 14, 2014, Ser. C No. 285; *Case of Vereda La Esperanza v. Colombia* (n. 26); *Case of Movilla Galarcio et al. v. Colombia*, Merits, Reparations, and Costs, June 22, 2022, Ser. C No. 452; and *Case of Tabares Toro et al. v. Colombia* (n. 26).

[33] IACtHR, *Case of the "Juvenile Reeducation Institute" v. Paraguay*, Preliminary Objections, Merits, Reparations, and Costs, September 2, 2004, Ser. C No. 112; *Case of Mendoza et al. v. Argentina*, Preliminary Objections, Merits, and Reparations, May 14, 2013, Ser. C No. 260; *and Case of Mota Abarullo et al. v. Venezuela*, Merits, Reparations, and Costs, November 18, 2020, Ser. C No. 417.

[34] IACtHR, *Case of the Girls Yean and Bosico v. Dominican Republic* (n. 20); *Case of the Pacheco Tineo family v. Bolivia* (n. 9); and *Case of expelled Dominicans and Haitians v. Dominican Republic*, Preliminary Objections, Merits, Reparations, and Costs, August 28, 2014, Ser. C No. 282.

[35] IACtHR, *Case of González et al. ("Cotton Field") v. Mexico* (n. 9); *Case of Rosendo Cantú et al. v. Mexico* Preliminary Objections, Merits, Reparations, and Costs, August 31, 2010, Ser. C No. 216; *Case of Véliz Franco et al. v. Guatemala*, Preliminary Objections, Merits, Reparations, and Costs, May 19, 2014, Ser. C No. 277; *Case of V.R.P., V.P.C. et al. v. Nicaragua*, Preliminary Objections, Merits, Reparations, and Costs, March 18, 2018, Ser. C No. 350; *Case of Guzmán Albarracín et al. v. Ecuador*, Merits, Reparations, and Costs, June 24, 2020, Ser. C No. 405; and Case *Angulo Losada v. Bolivia*, Preliminary Objections, Merits, and Reparations, November 18, 2022, Ser. C No. 475.

[36] IACtHR, *Case of Atala Riffo and daughters v. Chile* (n. 9); *Case of Fornerón and daughter v. Argentina* Merits, Reparations, and Costs, April 27, 2012, Ser. C No. 242; *Case of Ramírez Escobar et al. v. Guatemala* Merits, Reparations, and Costs, March 9, 2018, Ser. C No. 351; *Case of López et al. v. Argentina*, Preliminary Objections, Merits, Reparations, and Costs, November 25, 2019, Ser. C No. 396; and *Case María et al. v. Argentina*, Merits, Reparations, and Costs, August 22, 2023. Ser. C No. 494.

[37] IACtHR, *Case of Furlan and family v. Argentina*, Preliminary Objections, Merits, Reparations, and Costs August 31, 2012, Ser. C No. 246; *Case of Gonzales Lluy et al. v. Ecuador*, Preliminary Objections, Merits, Reparations, and Costs, September 1, 2015, Ser. C No. 298; *Case Vera Rojas et al. v. Chile*, Preliminary Objections, Merits, Reparations, and Costs, October 1, 2021, Ser. C No. 439; and *Case of Brítez Arce et al. v. Argentina*, Merits, Reparations, and Costs, November 16, 2022, Ser. C No. 474.

(5) *Forced labor and trafficking* includes three cases.[38]
(6) *Child soldiers* includes one case.[39]

The remaining twelve cases concern massive violations of the rights of Indigenous or Afro-descendant communities. I classify these decisions by country for the purpose of facilitating a better understanding of the issue and to avoid repetition due to nature of the rights that have been violated and the similarity of the sociopolitical contexts in which these violations took place: Paraguay (two cases);[40] Colombia (four cases);[41] Guatemala (four cases);[42] El Salvador (one case);[43] and Peru (one case).[44]

If all sixty-three cases were to be sorted by country, the breakdown would be: Argentina, seven cases;[45] Bolivia, three cases;[46] Brazil, two cases;[47] Chile, two cases;[48] Colombia, eleven cases;[49] the Dominican Republic, two cases;[50] Ecuador,

---

[38] IACtHR, *Case of the Hacienda Brasil Verde Workers v. Brazil*, Preliminary objections, Merits, Reparations, and Costs, October 20, 2016, Ser. C No. 318; *Case of the Workers of the fireworks factory in Santo Antônio de Jesus and their families v. Brazil*, Preliminary Objections, Merits, Reparations, and Costs, July 15, 2020, Ser. C No. 407; and *Case of Buzos Miskitos (Lemoth Morris et al.) v. Honduras*, August 31, 2021, Ser. C No. 432.

[39] IACtHR, *Case of Noguera et al. v. Paraguay*, Merits, Reparations, and Costs, March 9, 2020, Ser. C No. 401.

[40] IACtHR, *Case of the Sawhoyamaxa Indigenous Community v. Paraguay*, Merits, Reparations, and Costs, March 29, 2006, Ser. C No. 146; *Case of the Xákmok Kásek Indigenous Community v. Paraguay*, Merits, Reparations, and Costs, August 24, 2010, Ser. C No. 214.

[41] IACtHR, *Case of the Mapiripán Massacre v. Colombia*, Merits, Reparations, and Costs, September 15, 2005, Ser. C No. 134; *Case of the Ituango Massacres v. Colombia*, Preliminary Objections, Merits, Reparations, and Costs, July 1, 2006, Ser. C No. 148; *Case of the Santo Domingo Massacre v. Colombia*, Preliminary objections, Merits, and Reparations, November 30, 2012, Ser. No. 259, and *Case of the Afro-descendant Communities displaced from the Cacarica River Basin (Operation Genesis) v. Colombia*, Preliminary Objections, Merits, Reparations, and Costs, November 20, 2013, Ser. C No. 270.

[42] IACtHR, *Case of the "Las Dos Erres" Massacre v. Guatemala*, Merits, Reparations, and Costs, September 15, 2009, Ser. C No. 211; *Case of the Río Negro Massacres v. Guatemala*, Preliminary Objection, Merits, Reparations, and Costs, September 4, 2012, Ser. C No. 250; *Case of Coc Max et al. (Massacre of Xamán) v. Guatemala*, Merits, Reparations, and Costs, August 22, 2018, Ser. C No. 356; and *Case of the Village of Los Josefinos Massacres v. Guatemala*, Preliminary objection, Merits, Reparations, and Costs, November 3, 2021, Ser. C No. 442.

[43] IACtHR, *Case of the Massacres of El Mozote and Nearby Places v. El Salvador*, Merits, Reparations, and Costs, October 25, 2012, Ser. C No. 252.

[44] IACtHR, *Case of Peasant Community of Santa Barbara v. Peru*, Preliminary Objections, Merits, Reparations, and Costs, September 1, 2015, Ser. C No. 299.

[45] IACtHR, *Case of Bulacio v. Argentina* (n. 10); *Case of Fornerón and daughter v. Argentina* (n. 10); *Case of Furlan and family v. Argentina* (n.37); *Case of Mendoza et al. v. Argentina* (n. 33); *Case of López et al. v. Argentina* (n. 36); *Case of Brítez Arce et al. v. Argentina* (n. 37); and *Case of María et al. v. Argentina* (n. 36).

[46] IACtHR, *Case of the Pacheco Tineo family v. Bolivia* (n. 9); *Case of Angulo Losada v. Bolivia* (n. 35); and *Case of Valencia Campos et al. v. Bolivia* (n. 29).

[47] IACtHR, *Case of the Hacienda Brasil Verde Workers v. Brazil* (n. 38); and *Case of the Workers of the fireworks factory in Santo Antônio de Jesus and their families v. Brazil* (n. 38).

[48] IACtHR, *Case of Atala Riffo and daughters v. Chile* (n. 9); and *Case of Vera Rojas et al. v. Chile* (n. 37).

[49] IACtHR, *Case of the Mapiripán Massacre v. Colombia* (n. 41); *Case of the Ituango Massacres v. Colombia* (n. 41); *Case of Vélez Restrepo and family v. Colombia* (n. 30); *Case of the Santo Domingo Massacre v. Colombia* (n. 41); *Case of the Afro-descendant Communities displaced from the Cacarica River Basin (Operation Genesis) v. Colombia* (n. 41); *Case of Yarce et al. v. Colombia* (n.26); *Case of Vereda La Esperanza v. Colombia* (n. 26); *Case of Carvajal Carvajal et al. v. Colombia* (n. 26); *Case of Omeara Carrascal et al. v. Colombia* (n. 26); *Case of Movilla Galarcio et al. v. Colombia* (n. 32); and *Case of Tabares Toro et al. v. Colombia* (n. 26).

[50] IACtHR, *Case of the Girls Yean and Bosico v. Dominican Republic* (n. 20); and *Case of expelled Dominicans and Haitians v. Dominican Republic* (n. 34).

three cases;[51] El Salvador, three cases;[52] Guatemala, thirteen cases;[53] Honduras, three cases;[54] Mexico, two cases;[55] Nicaragua, one case;[56] Paraguay, four cases;[57] Peru, two cases;[58] Uruguay, one case;[59] and Venezuela, four cases.[60]

5. The Right of the Child to Special Protection Measures in Conjunction with the Right to Life

The Inter-American Court has interpreted the right of children to special protection in order to address children's vulnerability[61] by requiring States to take measures additional to those which would be called for in an equivalent case concerning an adult.[62]

---

[51] IACtHR, *Case of Gonzales Lluy et al. v. Ecuador* (n. 10); *Case of García Ibarra et al. v. Ecuador* (n. 29); and *Case of Guzmán Albarracín et al. v. Ecuador* (n. 35).

[52] IACtHR, *Case of Contreras et al. v. El Salvador* (n. 32); *Case of the Massacres of El Mozote and Nearby Places v. El Salvador* (n. 43); and *Case of Rochac Hernández et al. v. El Salvador* (n. 32).

[53] IACtHR, *Case of the "Street Children" (Villagrán Morales et al.) v. Guatemala* (n. 8); *Case of Molina Theissen v. Guatemala* (n. 26); *Case of Carpio Nicolle et al. v. Guatemala* (n. 26); *Case of Tiu Tojín v. Guatemala* (n. 26); *Case of the Las Dos Erres Massacre v. Guatemala* (n. 20); *Case of Chitay Nech et al. v. Guatemala* (n. 32); *Case of the Río Negro Massacres v. Guatemala* (n. 42); *Case of Gudiel Álvarez et al. ("Diario Militar") v. Guatemala* (n. 32); *Case of Human Rights Defender et al. v. Guatemala* (n. 26); *Case of Véliz Franco et al. v. Guatemala* (n. 35); *Case of Coc Max et al. (Massacre of Xamán) v. Guatemala* (n. 42); *Case of Ramírez Escobar et al. v. Guatemala* (n. 36); and *Case of the Village of Los Josefinos Massacres v. Guatemala* (n. 42).

[54] IACtHR, *Case of Servellón García et al. v. Honduras* (n. 28); *Case Buzos Miskitos (Lemoth Morris et al.) v. Honduras* (n. 38); and *Case of Deras García et al. v. Honduras* (n. 26).

[55] IACtHR, *Case of González et al. ("Cotton Field") v. Mexico* (n. 9); and *Case of Rosendo Cantú et al. v. Mexico* (n. 35).

[56] IACtHR, *Case of V.R.P., V.P.C. et al. v. Nicaragua* (n. 35).

[57] IACtHR, *Case of the "Juvenile Reeducation Institute" v. Paraguay* (n.33); *Case of the Sawhoyamaxa Indigenous Community v. Paraguay* (n. 40); *Case of the Xákmok Kásek Indigenous Community v. Paraguay* (n. 20); and *Case of Noguera et al. v. Paraguay* (n. 39).

[58] IACtHR, *Case of the Gómez Paquiyauri Brothers v. Peru* (n. 10); and *Case of Peasant Community of Santa Barbara v. Peru* (n. 44).

[59] IACtHR, *Case of Gelman v. Uruguay* (n. 32).

[60] IACtHR, *Case of the Barrios family v. Venezuela* (n. 30); *Case of Uzcátegui et al. v. Venezuela* (n. 30); *Case of Landaeta Mejías Brothers et al. v. Venezuela* (n. 30); and *Case of Mota Abarullo et al. v. Venezuela* (n. 33).

[61] "The point becomes more complex when in addition to its sensitivity due to the subject matter—irregularity, extravagance, marginality, dangerousness, crime—members of an especially vulnerable human group are involved, often lacking the personal abilities to adequately face certain problems, due to lack of experience, immaturity, weakness, lack of information or of training; or when they do not meet the requirements of the law to freely manage their own interests and exercise their rights in an autonomous manner [. . .]. Such is the situation of children or minors, who on the one hand generally and in a relative manner—as different factors generate diverse situations—lack those personal requirements, and on the other hand exercise of their rights is restricted or halted, ope legis. It is natural that in this 'mine-strewn terrain' abuse may appear and thrive, often shrouded by paternal discourse or one of redemption, which can hide the severest authoritarianism." IACtHR, *Juridical Condition and Human Rights of the Child* (n. 10), Judge GARCÍA RAMÍREZ concurring opinion, para. 8.

[62] "The ultimate objective of protection of children in international instruments is the harmonious development of their personality and the enjoyment of their recognized rights. It is the responsibility of the State to specify the measures it will adopt to foster this development within its own sphere of

It has established that States must consider the particular situation of the child when adopting special protection measures.[63] In other words, if other critical factors—such as family context,[64] extreme social exclusion,[65] ethnicity,[66] gender,[67] State custody,[68] and/or a special need (for example, one derived from a disability)[69]—further augment the child's vulnerability, the State's obligations toward this child likewise increase due to the intersecting circumstances affecting him or her.

The right to life contained in ACHR Article 4 is thus foundational for the exercise of other rights.[70] The Inter-American Court stated that "Article 4 of the [American] Convention guarantees not only the right of every human being not to be arbitrarily deprived of life, but also the obligation of the State to take the necessary measures to establish an adequate legal framework to dissuade any threat to the right to life."[71] It was in *Villagrán Morales et al. v. Guatemala* where the Court began to develop the content of the right to a "dignified life"

---

competence and to support the family in performing its natural function of providing protection to the children who are members of the family. [. . .] it is important to highlight that children have the same rights as all human beings—minors or adults—and also special rights derived from their condition, and these are accompanied by specific duties of the family, society, and the State." IACtHR, Advisory Opinion OC-17/02, *Juridical Condition and Human Rights of the Child* (n. 10) paras. 53, 54, 60, and 62); also *Case of the "Street Children" (Villagrán Morales et al.)* (n. 8), para. 146; *Case of Vélez Restrepo and family v. Colombia* (n. 30), para. 226; *Case of González et al. ("Cotton Field") v. Mexico* (n. 9), para. 408; *Case of the Girls Yean and Bosico v. Dominican Republic* (n. 20), para. 133; *Case of the Xákmok Kásek Indigenous Community v. Paraguay* (n. 20), para. 257; and *Case of Véliz Franco et al. v. Guatemala* (n. 35), para. 133; among others.

[63] IACtHR, Advisory Opinion OC-17/02, *Juridical Condition and Human Rights of the Child* (n. 10), para. 61. The Court stressed in the same decision that the protection of children must take into account "the characteristics of children themselves, and [. . .] the need to foster their development, making full use of their potential," para. 56.

[64] IACtHR, *Case of Ramírez Escobar et al. v. Guatemala* (n. 36).

[65] IACtHR, *Case of Servellón García et al. v. Honduras* (n. 28), para. 116; and *Case of the "Juvenile Reeducation Institute" v. Paraguay* (n. 33); and *Case of Mendoza et al. v. Argentina* (n. 33), para. 262.

[66] IACtHR, *Case of the Girls Yean and Bosico v. Dominican Republic* (n. 20), among others.

[67] *Ibidem*, para. 134; *Case of Rosendo Cantú et al. v. Mexico* (n. 35); *Case of González et al. ("Cotton Field") v. Mexico* (n. 9); *Case of Véliz Franco et al. v. Guatemala* (n. 35); among others.

[68] IACtHR, *Case of the "Juvenile Reeducation Institute" v. Paraguay* (n. 33); *Case of Mendoza et al. v. Argentina* (n. 33); *Case Mota Abarullo et al. v. Venezuela* (n. 33), *Matter of children deprived of liberty in the "Complexo do Tatuapé" of Fundação CASA* (n. 24); and *Matter of the Socio Educational Internment Facility* (n. 10).

[69] In *Furlan and family v. Argentina*, the Inter-American Court decided that the rights violations should be analyzed in the light of (1) the international *corpus juris* for the protection of children, and (2) the international standards on the protection and guarantee of the rights of persons with disabilities, IACtHR, *Case of Furlan and family v. Argentina* (n. 37), para. 124; and in *Gonzales Lluy et al. v. Ecuador*, the Court's found that multiple factors of vulnerability and risk of discrimination associated with a child's conditions of gender, extreme poverty, and HIV status had converged in a cross-cutting manner, IACtHR, *Case of Gonzales Lluy et al. v. Ecuador* (n. 10), paras. 193, 290, 291, among others.

[70] IACtHR, *Case of the "Street Children" (Villagrán Morales et al.) v. Guatemala* (n. 8), para. 144; *Case of the Gómez Paquiyauri Brothers v. Peru* (n. 10), para. 128; *Case of the Barrios family v. Venezuela* (n. 30), para. 48; among many others.

[71] IACtHR, *Case of Gonzales Lluy et al. v. Ecuador* (n. 10), para. 169; among others.

(*vida digna*) as the right to the material conditions that are necessary for leading a dignified existence.

Following this interpretation, the Court indicated that the right to life should not only be interpreted as a negative right that requires States to refrain from interfering with and arbitrarily depriving individuals of life but also as a positive right that obligates States to guarantee the conditions in which children lives meet basic standards of dignity and to provide them with opportunities to realize their life projects.[72]

Although the Inter-American Court has not specified how States can guarantee children's right to a dignified life, it has asserted that education and healthcare "require various measures of protection and are the key pillars to ensure enjoyment of a decent life by the children, who in view of their immaturity and vulnerability often lack adequate means to effectively defend their rights."[73] The Court has also characterized States' systematic violence against children as particularly serious and has established that the rights of children who are "at risk" can be violated by omission as well as by action.[74]

Its understanding of ACHR Article 19 in conjunction with Article 4 thus reveals States' positive duties toward children who are at risk, particularly in the area of economic, social, environmental, and cultural rights.[75]

The Court has also analyzed the right to a dignified life in cases involving children deprived of their liberty,[76] members of Indigenous communities (particularly in cases also addressing the right to cultural identity),[77] minors who are victims of massive human rights violations in contexts of political or institutional violence,[78] and children with special needs.[79]

In a decision concerning a juvenile detention center, the Inter-American Court linked the State's obligation to guarantee the conditions necessary for

---

[72] "We believe that the project of life is consubstantial with the right to existence, and requires for its development conditions of dignified life, security and integrity of the human person," ibid., Judges CANÇADO TRINDADE and ABREU BURELLI, para. 8.

[73] IACtHR, *Juridical Condition and Human Rights of the Child* (n. 10), para. 86; and *Case of the Xákmok Kásek Indigenous Community v. Paraguay* (n. 20), para. 258; among others.

[74] IACtHR, *Case Gelman v. Uruguay* (n. 32), para. 130; and *Case of Contreras et al. v. El Salvador* (n. 32), para. 90.

[75] According to the concurring vote, the right to protection of street children is derived from their vulnerability and is inextricably linked to the right to life. Later, the Inter-American Court applied this reasoning in other decisions relating to vulnerable groups: "The protection needs of the weakest, such as street children, ultimately require an interpretation of the right to life that includes the minimum conditions for a dignified life. Hence the inexorable link that we find, in the circumstances of the present case, between Articles 4 (Right to Life) and 19 (Rights of the Child) of the American Convention," ibid., Judges CANÇADO TRINDADE and ABREU BURELLI concurring opinion, para. 7.

[76] IACtHR, *Case of the "Juvenile Reeducation Institute" v. Paraguay* (n. 33).

[77] IACtHR, *Case of the Xákmok Kásek Indigenous Community v. Paraguay* (n. 20); *Case of the Sawhoyamaxa Indigenous Community v. Paraguay* (n. 40); and *Case of the Río Negro Massacres v. Guatemala* (n. 42); among others.

[78] IACtHR, *Case of the Mapiripán Massacre v. Colombia* (n. 41), among others.

[79] IACtHR, *Case of Furlan and family v. Argentina* (n. 37); and *Case of Gonzales Lluy et al. v. Ecuador* (n. 10).

children to lead a dignified life to the special position of guarantor that the State has in connection with persons in detention:

> The State has a special role to play as guarantor of the rights of those deprived of their freedom, as the prison authorities exercise heavy control or command over the persons in their custody. So there is a special relationship and interaction of subordination between the person deprived of his liberty and the State; typically the State can be rigorous in regulating what the prisoner's rights and obligations are, and determines what the circumstances of the internment will be; the inmate is prevented from satisfying, on his own, certain basic needs that are essential if one is to live with dignity.[80]

In another case, the Court noted that the State's duty is enhanced if the arrested person is a child:

> State authorities exercise total control over persons under their custody. The way a detainee is treated must be subject to the closest scrutiny, taking into account the detainee's vulnerability; this guarantee function of the State is especially important when the detainee is a minor. This circumstance gives the State the obligation to exercise its function as guarantor taking all care required by the weakness, the lack of knowledge, and the defenselessness that minors naturally have under those circumstances.[81]

It has also invoked the principle of the best interests of the child when discussing the right of children to special protection measures and the right to life:

> In the case of the right to life, when the person the State deprives of his or her liberty is a child [. . .], it has the same obligations it has regarding to any persons, yet compounded by the added obligation established in Article 19 of the American Convention. On the one hand, it must be all the more diligent and responsible in its role as guarantor and must take special measures based on the principle of the best interests of the child. On the other hand, to protect a child's life, the State must be particularly attentive to that child's living conditions while deprived of his or her liberty, as the child's detention or imprisonment does not deny the child his or her right to life or restrict that right.[82]

In other cases, however, the Court does not refer to the duty that States have to ensure dignified living conditions but instead to their duty to prevent acts

---

[80] IACtHR, *Case of the "Juvenile Reeducation Institute" v. Paraguay* (n. 33), para. 152; *Case of Mendoza et al. v. Argentina* (n. 33), para. 188; *Case of Mota Abarullo et al. v. Venezuela* (n. 33) a, para. 88.
[81] IACtHR, *Case of Bulacio v. Argentina* (n. 10), para. 126.
[82] IACtHR, *Case of the "Juvenile Reeducation Institute" v. Paraguay* (n. 33), para. 160.

threatening children's right to life.[83] In the case of *Juvenile Reeducation Institute v. Paraguay*, it added a requirement to the right to decent living conditions[84] when the vulnerable population consists of children who are deprived of liberty.

Additionally, in the case of *Xákmok Kásek Indigenous Community v. Paraguay*, the Court evaluated measures the State had adopted to comply with its duty to guarantee the right to life of the members of the Xákmok Kásek Indigenous community. It considered both the positive and negative obligations of the State relating, on the one hand, to the right to a dignified life, and, on the other, to the right not to be arbitrarily deprived of life.[85] It also interpreted the right to a dignified life to require the State to provide water,[86] food,[87] healthcare,[88] and education.[89]

Finally, in a case involving a girl with HIV, the Inter-American Court found that the harm to her health that had resulted from the disease and the danger it posed to her life impaired the child's right to life.[90] It also found that the State had violated the negative obligation not to interfere with the girl's life even though the girl's blood had been contaminated by a private actor.[91]

6. The Right of the Child to Special Protection Measures in Relation to Other Rights

The Inter-American Court has analyzed the right of the child to special protection measures in connection with various other rights. It has considered the scope of the right to personal integrity and the right to health in cases of children deprived of their liberty[92] and of children with special needs.[93] It has also

---

[83] Thus, compliance with ACHR Article 4 ACHR "not only requires that a person not be deprived arbitrarily of his or her life (negative obligation) but also that the States adopt all the appropriate measures to protect and preserve the right to life (positive obligation) [...] not only to prevent, try and punish those responsible for deprivation of life as a consequence of criminal acts, in general, but also to forestall arbitrary executions by its own security agents." IACtHR, *Case of the Gómez Paquiyauri Brothers v. Peru* (n. 10), para. 129; also *Case of the "Street Children" (Villagrán Morales et al.) v. Guatemala* (n. 8), paras. 139, 144, and 145.

[84] IACtHR, *Case of the "Juvenile Reeducation Institute" v. Paraguay* (n. 33), para. 164, also para. 161; and *Case of the "Street Children" (Villagrán Morales et al.) v. Guatemala* (n. 8), para. 196.

[85] IACtHR, *Case of the Xákmok Kásek Indigenous Community v. Paraguay* (n. 20), para. 193.

[86] *Ibid.*, para. 194/196.

[87] *Ibid.*, para. 258, also 197/202.

[88] IACtHR, *Case of the Sawhoyamaxa Indigenous Community v. Paraguay* (n. 40), para. 171; also *Case of the Xákmok Kásek Indigenous Community v. Paraguay* (n. 20), para. 260.

[89] IACtHR, *Case of the Xákmok Kásek Indigenous Community v. Paraguay* (n. 20), para. 209/213. The Court linked the right to life to the stay on ancestral land (*Case of the Sawhoyamaxa Indigenous Community v. Paraguay* (n. 40), Judge Cançado Trindade concurring opinion, para. 28).

[90] IACtHR, *Case of Gonzales Lluy et al. v. Ecuador* (n. 10), para. 190.

[91] *Ibid.*, para. 191.

[92] IACtHR, *Case of the "Juvenile Reeducation Institute" v. Paraguay* (n. 33); and *Case of Mendoza et al. v. Argentina* (n. 33).

[93] IACtHR, *Case of Furlan and family v. Argentina* (n. 37); and *Case of Gonzales Lluy et al. v. Ecuador* (n. 10).

evaluated whether a State violated the right of the child to be heard vis-à-vis the right to personal integrity and to health.

The Court has analyzed ACHR Article 19 extensively in relation to the right to family protection in cases involving discrimination and arbitrary interference with privacy, family life, and child custody,[94] and it has established that these violations can occur in contexts such as intercountry adoption[95] and contact with parents deprived of liberty.[96]

It has also considered the rights of Indigenous children to special measures and to family protection[97] by recognizing "(...) the special significance that the coexistence of the family has in the context of an indigenous family, which is not limited to the familial nucleus, but also includes the distinct generations that make up the family and includes the community of which the family forms a part."[98] In addition, the Court has also discussed the right of Indigenous children to their cultural identity.[99]

In other cases, the Inter-American Court has applied ACHR Article 19 when children have been separated from their parents, which has occurred in contexts of armed conflict,[100] institutional violence and political crises,[101] enforced disappearances,[102] and discrimination on the basis of their migrant or asylum-seeker status.[103]

It has also ruled on the rights of the child to special protection with respect to privacy and private property,[104] the best interests of the child,[105] residential care,[106] the right to be heard, the right to movement and residence,[107] the right to

---

[94] IACtHR, *Case of Atala Riffo and daughters v. Chile* (n. 9); and *Case of Fornerón and daughter v. Argentina* (n. 10).

[95] IACtHR, *Case of Ramírez Escobar et al. v. Guatemala* (n. 36).

[96] IACtHR, *Case of López et al. v. Argentina* (n. 36).

[97] IACtHR, *Case of the Las Dos Erres Massacre v. Guatemala* (n. 20); and *Case of the Río Negro Massacres v. Guatemala* (n. 42).

[98] IACtHR, *Case of Chitay Nech et al. v. Guatemala* (n. 32), para. 159.

[99] IACtHR, *Case of Chitay Nech et al. v. Guatemala* (n. 32); *Case of the Río Negro Massacres v. Guatemala* (n. 42); *Case of the Sawhoyamaxa Indigenous Community v. Paraguay* (n. 40); *Case of the Xákmok Kásek Indigenous Community v. Paraguay* (n. 20); and *Case of the Río Negro Massacres v. Guatemala* (n. 42).

[100] Among others, IACtHR, *Case of Rochac Hernández et al. v. El Salvador* (n. 32); *Case of the Las Dos Erres Massacre v. Guatemala* (n. 20); and *Case of the Río Negro Massacres v. Guatemala* (n. 42).

[101] Among others, IACtHR, *Case of Vélez Restrepo and family v. Colombia* (n. 30); and *Case of the Barrios family v. Venezuela* (n. 30).

[102] Among others, IACtHR, *Case of Contreras et al. v. El Salvador* (n. 32), para. 116; *Case Gelman v. Uruguay* (n. 32); and *Case of Gudiel Álvarez et al. ("Diario Militar") v. Guatemala* (n. 32).

[103] IACtHR, *Case of expelled Dominicans and Haitians v. Dominican Republic* (n. 34); *Case of the Pacheco Tineo family v. Bolivia* (n. 9); and Advisory Opinion OC-21/14 (n. 42).

[104] IACtHR, *Case of Furlan and family v. Argentina* (n. 37); *Case of the Massacres of El Mozote and Nearby Places v. El Salvador* (n. 43); and *Case of Peasant Community of Santa Barbara v. Peru* (n. 44).

[105] IACtHR, *Case of Atala Riffo and daughters v. Chile* (n. 9); *Case of Fornerón and daughter v. Argentina* (n. 10); and *Case of Ramírez Escobar et al. v. Guatemala* (n. 36).

[106] IACtHR, *Case of Atala Riffo and daughters v. Chile* (n. 9); *Case of Ramírez Escobar et al. v. Guatemala* (n. 36).

[107] Among others, IACtHR, *Case of the Barrios family v. Venezuela* (n. 30); *Case of Vélez Restrepo and family v. Colombia* (n. 30); *Case of the Girls Yean and Bosico v. Dominican Republic* (n. 20); *Case of the Mapiripán Massacre v. Colombia* (n. 41); *Case of expelled Dominicans and Haitians v. Dominican Republic* (n. 34); and IACtHR, *Case of the Santo Domingo Massacre v. Colombia* (n. 41).

physical, mental, and moral integrity,[108] the right to honor and dignity,[109] the right to identity,[110] the right to legal personality,[111] the right to a name,[112] and the right to nationality.[113]

As for the right to education, although several cases related to children's education had previously reached the Court,[114] it was not until the 2015 case of *Gonzales Lluy et al. v. Ecuador* that the Inter-American Court held a State directly responsible for the violation of Article 13 (Right to Education) of the Protocol of San Salvador. This decision implies a significant advance in the Court's jurisprudence on children's right to special protection.[115]

The Inter-American Court has also analyzed the right of children to special protection in relation to the rights to liberty, judicial guarantees, and judicial protection, as well as in relation to the right to protection and access to justice in a reasonable time.[116]

It most important achievement in the context of juvenile justice has been to derive from the right of children to special protection (ACHR Article 19) the need for a differentiated comprehensive criminal response for juveniles, the content of which was developed in subsequent rulings.[117]

Finally, the Court has also analyzed several cases concerning the right to special protection of child victims of sexual violence[118] and child refugees, migrants, and asylum seekers.[119]

7. The Limits and Possibilities of the Inter-American System for Advancing the Rights of Children

Having reviewed the Inter-American Court's contentious cases, advisory opinions, and provisional measures related to child rights under Article 19 of the

---

[108] IACtHR, *Case of the Barrios family v. Venezuela* (n. 30); *Case of Rosendo Cantú et al. v. Mexico* (n. 35); *Case of Véliz Franco et al. v. Guatemala* (n. 35); and *Case of Contreras et al. v. El Salvador* (n. 32).

[109] IACtHR, *Case of Rosendo Cantú et al. v. Mexico* (n. 35); *Case of V.R.P., V.P.C. et al. v. Nicaragua* (n. 35); *Case of Contreras et al. v. El Salvador* (n. 32); *Case of Atala Riffo and daughters v. Chile* (n. 9); and *Case of the Hacienda Brasil Verde Workers v. Brazil* (n. 38).

[110] IACtHR, *Case Gelman v. Uruguay* (n. 32); and *Case of Serrano Cruz Sisters v. El Salvador* (n. 24), dissenting opinion of Judges CANÇADO TRINDADE and VENTURA ROBLES.

[111] IACtHR, *Case of the Girls Yean and Bosico v. Dominican Republic* (n. 20); *Case of expelled Dominicans and Haitians v. Dominican Republic* (n. 34); and *Case Gelman v. Uruguay* (n. 32).

[112] IACtHR, *Case of the Girls Yean and Bosico v. Dominican Republic* (n. 20); *Case Gelman v. Uruguay* (n. 32); *Case of the Las Dos Erres Massacre v. Guatemala* (n. 20); *Case of expelled Dominicans and Haitians v. Dominican Republic* (n. 34); and *Case of Ramírez Escobar et al. v. Guatemala* (n. 36).

[113] Among others, IACtHR, *Case of the Girls Yean and Bosico v. Dominican Republic* (n. 20); *Case of expelled Dominicans and Haitians v. Dominican Republic* (n. 34); and *Case Gelman v. Uruguay* (n. 32).

[114] Among others, IACtHR, *Case of the Girls Yean and Bosico v. Dominican Republic* (n. 20); and *Case of the Xákmok Kásek Indigenous Community v. Paraguay* (n. 20).

[115] IACtHR, *Case of Guzmán Albarracín et al. v. Ecuador* (n. 35).

[116] See (n. 33).

[117] See (n. 33).

[118] See (n. 35).

[119] See (n. 34).

American Convention, I now turn to the question of to what extent the Court's legal developments have effectively advanced the recognition and protection of children's rights in practice.

Clearly, the Court's development of legal standards concerning the protection of children does not prevent their rights and guarantees from ever being violated. However, there are areas where the impact of its decisions can be more clearly seen, such as the field of juvenile justice.

In order to evaluate the repercussion of an Inter-American Court's decision, it is crucial to first identify the reason why the case was brought before the Inter-American System. Consequently, when assessing the effectiveness (or ineffectiveness) of the Inter-American System in advancing children's rights, it should be determined whether litigators at the supranational level conceive their practice as an end in itself to secure justice and reparations for victims which were not granted to them at the domestic level, or if they conceive it as a means to achieve ulterior ends. These additional purposes may be specific or structural, focused or comprehensive, narrow or ambitious. They may also include legal or institutional reforms that among other things may change public policies, budget allocation, or even the structure of government itself.

Failure to achieve the objectives that these actors set out to accomplish with the presentation of a claim can produce criticism and/or generate frustration among those who promoted it and/or among those who observe the functioning of the system from academia or politics. These dynamics may occur even when the Inter-American Court issues a decision that is favorable to children's rights. This may be the case when it comes to rulings related to violence against children in the context of the fight against organized crime in Central America. Despite these decisions of the Inter-American Court that determined the international responsibility of States for violation of ACHR Article 19 in these cases, violence against children in situations of marginalization and exclusion in Guatemala, El Salvador, and Honduras has worsened, and tolerance for practices that violate child rights by the security forces and the army has been reinforced. Another example is the increased discrimination in the Dominican Republic against the Haitian or Haitian-descendant population, including children, that persisted after the Court decision that recognized the gravity of the issue in the country.

Frustration with the lack of effectiveness of cases that do determine the responsibility of the State for the violation of children's rights is due to an expectation of structural impact, as opposed to an approach that aims at victims obtaining a judgment that recognizes that the State violated their rights and that establishes reparations. Both viewpoints respond to a substantially different conception of the functions and legitimate activities of jurisdictional bodies.

Given that the strategies and actions to be implemented differ depending on what is expected from a supranational adjudicative system, it could be useful to return to the question of what petitioners submitting cases before the Inter-American System seek to accomplish. In terms of achieving the purpose of justice, it is of the utmost importance that victims obtain sentences that determine the international responsibility of the State for unlawful acts committed against them and order reparations. The mere fact that a supranational court such as the Inter-American Court declares a State responsible for the violation of the rights of *one* child and orders reparations is of extraordinary value. It provides individual (or collective) justice at the same time that it recognizes the human dignity of the victim(s).

A different scenario would take place if a case was litigated with a strategic purpose and achievements were evaluated in that regard. Here progress is less noticeable, to put it mildly: the last two decades of litigation for the rights of children have proven that an Inter-American Court judgment alone is unlikely to have a transformative impact in the lives of the continent's children, especially those in the most disadvantaged situations.

An additional problem arises in connection with the instrumentalization of child victims (or their families or communities) who may not share this broader vision of change, instead seeking simply to obtain justice at the individual level. In order to avoid a conflict of interests and expectations, it is essential for organizations to consider the opinions of the victim(s) and their families. This poses a unique dilemma: children are either universally considered to be moral agents without competence or, once they grow up, persons with reduced competence until they reach adulthood. How to determine the best way to claim a child's right and how to hear his or her opinion freely and without manipulation of any kind constitutes the greatest challenge facing any international mechanism created to protect his or her rights today. It is also crucial that adults evaluate whether bringing a case before the Inter-American System is the best option available to effectively protect the rights at stake. Other faster and potentially more effective means can provide more suitable solutions for the enforcement of the rights of the children involved in a given case.

Another important element to consider when assessing the Inter-American Court's transformative impact on the development of children's rights is time. As the cases of *Fornerón and daughter v. Argentina* and *Furlan and family v. Argentina* demonstrate, the timeline of the Inter-American System differs from that of child victims. It is an undisputed fact that children do not experience time as adults do. The Court's proceedings and legal reasoning often does not coincide with the needs of child victims. If the Court were more sensitive to time in child's rights proceedings, it could more effectively ensure the right of children to special protection.

Tensions between procedural requirements and the satisfaction of the best interests of the child—recognized as a guiding principle in any decision involving a child—have been thoroughly discussed. Litigating children's rights cases before the Inter-American System appears counterintuitive because by the time a decision is obtained, the victim will almost inevitably have become an adult. For this reason, other mechanisms that might be more effective in advocating for children's rights should be explored. The Inter-American Court could prove that it takes children's rights seriously by finding alternatives to the traditional, slow methods of processing of individual petitions.

One mechanism that could be reinterpreted or redesigned to make the IAHRS more sensitive to the rights of children could be a more intensive use of precautionary or provisional measures. These measures could serve as an efficient alternative to the litigation of individual petitions. Precautionary and provisional measures respond to grave and urgent situations, aim to avoid irreparable harm, and have a more immediate effect.

Eligio RESTA[120] argues that when judging cases involving children, one is always wrong or, at the least, one cannot be sure if one is right, because only time will tell if the resolution reached in a child's case was the right decision. Simultaneously, one cannot stand still in the face of violations of the human rights of the most vulnerable among us. Children whose rights are violated cannot wait. They need urgent answers in ultra-fast times.

To avoid the drawn-out individual petitions procedure, the use of precautionary or provisional measures in serious, urgent children's rights cases should be reconsidered and reformulated. In order to evaluate whether a case is serious and urgent, all the circumstances of the child and his or her vulnerability should be assessed. Vulnerability is derived from the condition of being a child, as well as from family or social context, ethnic origin, special needs, gender, extreme social exclusion, lack of care, and state custody, among other things. All these factors should enter the analysis of a child's right to special protection.

Another aspect to consider when evaluating the Inter-American System's effectiveness in the promotion and protection of children's rights is the relationship between substance and procedure. The IAHRS's individual petitions mechanism, which is its traditional and primary method of addressing rights violations, is so inadequately designed for the defense of children's rights that it is almost incompatible with ACHR Article 19. The individual petition mechanism requires domestic remedies to be exhausted, and itself involves lengthy proceedings, during which time the child becomes an adult. The procedure thus weakens the ability of the Inter-American System to handle the substance of these cases.

For this reason, the IAHRS's restrictions on the issuance of precautionary and provisional measures concerning economic, social, environmental, and cultural

---

[120] Eligio Resta, *La infanzia ferita* (Laterza, Bari 1998).

rights are unjustifiable in relation to cases involving child victims. The immediate protection of children at risk requires that criteria to adopt precautionary measures be differentiated from general criteria governing adult cases. Applying the same rule for adults and for children here would empty the right to special protection of its content.

In order to fairly balance protection and autonomy, freedom and development, the IAHRS must indicate not only what States should stop doing in order not to interfere with or harm children (negative obligations) but also what States should do to guarantee children dignified living conditions (positive obligations).

Comprehensively analyzing both inter-American and UN human rights treaties that provide for children's rights, as the Inter-American Court has done in its jurisprudence on ACHR Article 19, led to the articulation of obligations that reach beyond the mere defense of negative rights, as these new understandings require States to establish public policies for groups that demand special protection. Nevertheless, ACHR Article 19 does not establish the content nor the limits of special protection measures, the methodology of their implementation, or the branch of the State (judicial, legislative, or executive) that should enact and enforce them. As such, the jurisprudence of the Inter-American Court on the rights of the child is at the moment an abstract, unfulfilled promise. To begin to fulfill the promise—by means of an original and robust hermeneutic—the Inter-American System must strengthen its institutional mechanisms for effectively guaranteeing children's rights.

II.8

The *Riffo-Salinas* Case

Human Rights of Older Persons Consolidated in the Inter-American System

By Aída Díaz-Tendero

1. Introduction

According to the Inter-American Convention on the Protection of the Human Rights of Older Persons (ICPHROP)[1] and the dominant trend in gerontology, aging is a gradual process that develops during the course of life and involves biological, physiological, psychosocial, and functional changes of various consequences, which are associated with dynamic and permanent interactions between the subject and his or her environment. For its part, old age is a social construction[2] referring to the last stage of the life course in the sense that both old age and the problems faced by the elderly[3] are socially constructed. In other words, aging is a verifiable or objective fact, while old age is a subjective concept.[4]

The culture of old age, the individual and collective perceptions and ideas about what it is to be an older person are under permanent construction and deconstruction, and the age groups and generations that today are older people have an impact on the paradigm of old age that subsequent age groups and generations will experience through their reproduction or rupture of the stereotype.

---

[1] Organization of American States (OAS), *Inter-American Convention on the Protection of the Human Rights of Older Persons* (A-70), General Assembly, forty-fifth regular session, Washington, DC, June 15, 2015.

[2] Peter Berger and Thomas Luckmann, *The Social Construction of Reality* (Anchor 1967).

[3] In more developed countries, the lower age limit is sixty-five years of age, while in developing countries it is sixty years of age. Thus, in the ICPHROP, the age limit is sixty years or older, unless domestic law determines a lower or higher base age, provided that it does not exceed sixty-five years. This concept includes, among others, the concept of elderly person, which is the concept used in the Bolivian legislation (Article 2 of the *General Law for the Elderly* reads: "[B]eing holders of the rights expressed therein the elderly persons of sixty years of age or older, in the Bolivian territory" (Law No. 369 General Law for the Elderly Persons, Supreme Decree 1807, May 1, 2013)).

[4] For a dissident position with respect to the aforementioned dominant criterion, see Aída Díaz-Tendero, "Epílogo," in Aída Díaz-Tendero (coord.), *Un pacto con la soledad. Envejecimiento y vejez en la literatura en América Latina y el Caribe* (Tirant Lo Blanch 2019).

Aída Díaz-Tendero, *The* Riffo-Salinas *Case* In: *The Impact of the Inter-American Human Rights System*. Edited by: Armin von Bogdandy, Flávia Piovesan, Eduardo Ferrer Mac-Gregor, and Mariela Morales Antoniazzi, Oxford University Press. © Aída Díaz-Tendero 2024. DOI: 10.1093/oso/9780197744161.003.0019

The treatment of the elderly by the law, or in other words, the legal formulations[5] on the elderly, reflect the social constructs on old age of previous cohorts and generations. It is for this reason that there is a gap between public policies and legal frameworks that were designed for a short old age[6] that was conceived as one of physical, economic, and social deprivation and the needs of today's older persons, who in many cases live their old age in conditions of health, productivity, autonomy, and well-being during a stage that extends over decades.[7] It should be noted that this new paradigm does not contradict the recognition of the existence of frail and vulnerable older persons for different reasons and circumstances,[8] nor their corresponding need for protection.

The adoption of an inclusive perspective, encompassing the multiple forms of old age, is an essential part of the human rights approach to older persons, which has shown itself to be notably more agile in adapting to the new realities and new paradigms of old age. The visibility of older persons as subjects of rights is the result of certain phenomena such as the increase in the relative and absolute number of older persons in the world, an irrefutable fact also in the case of Latin America and the Caribbean.[9] At the same time, the evolution in the development of human rights, after normatively consolidating the rights of citizens, led to the creation of instruments of various kinds for specific groups, including those dedicated to the elderly.

Before the Protocol of San Salvador, there were few inter-American norms directly protecting the rights of older persons. Those were limited to the right to social security (American Declaration on the Rights and Duties of Man, art. XVI) and the prohibition of the death penalty (American Convention on Human Rights, art. 4.5). The Protocol introduced broader protection, determining that "[e]veryone has the right to special protection in old age" and establishing the duty to progressively take the necessary steps to ensure proper housing, food, medical care, work, and quality of life (art. 17). After the Protocol,

---

[5] Riccardo Guastini, "Interpretation and legal construction" [2015] 43 *Isonomia* 11–48.

[6] Life expectancy in the Latin American and Caribbean region was 51.4 years in the five-year period 1950–1955 (ECONOMIC COMMISSION FOR LATIN AMERICA AND THE CARIBBEAN, *Observatorio Demográfico 2019. Proyecciones de población*, Santiago de Chile, ECLAC 2020).

[7] Life expectancy in the Latin American and Caribbean region is 76.1 years in the five-year period 2020–2025 (ibid.).

[8] Antonio Martínez Maroto, "Aspectos legales y consideraciones éticas básicas relacionadas con las personas mayores," in Rocío Fernández-Ballesteros (dir.), *Gerontología social* (Ediciones Pirámide 2009).

[9] Latin American and Caribbean aging is characterized by the high speed at which the aging process will occur in relation to the pioneer countries in the demographic transition (such as the European countries), although each country within the subset of the sample will carry out these changes with a different chronology, with decades of difference between them. In the coming years, the proportion of older persons in the total population of the countries of the region will double and even triple (ECONOMIC COMMISSION FOR LATIN AMERICA AND THE CARIBBEAN, *Demographic Observatory 2015. Population projections*, Santiago de Chile, ECLAC 2016).

other inter-American treaties also introduced direct protections for the rights of older persons (Inter-American Convention on the Prevention, Punishment, and Eradication of Violence against Women, art. 9; Inter-American Convention against All Forms of Discrimination and Intolerance, art. 1.1).

The year 2015 marked a shift regarding the rights of older persons in the Inter-American System. The adoption of the ICPHROP was a milestone, not only in the region but also the world. The treaty places the Inter-American System at the vanguard of international human rights law, in so much as it establishes biding obligations specifically targeted at protecting the rights of older persons, adopting a holistic and inclusive approach. It has catalyzed the protection of the rights of older persons even for States that are yet to ratify the ICPHROP, fostering holistic protection. For example, in *Poblete Vilches et al. v. Chile*, the Inter-American Court relied on the ICPHROP to interpret the American Convention on Human Rights, concluding that the right to nondiscrimination applies to discriminatory conduct based on older age.

In this context, this chapter focuses on the analysis of the *Riffo Salinas* case, judged on February 28, 2018, by the Plurinational Constitutional Court of Bolivia. This chapter questions some aspects of the protection of the human rights of older persons[10] in the Inter-American System, aiming to demonstrate how inter-American jurisprudence and norms impact on our national courts of justice.

Section 2 assesses the relevance of this judgment in several ways: first, in the dimension of its significance for the jurisprudence on older persons as subjects of law; second, in terms of whether it integrates or excludes the ad hoc instrument available to the Inter-American System for the protection of the human rights of older persons, the ICPHROP;[11] third, by the degree of integration or exclusion of the inter-American standards established by the Inter-American Court and Commission on Human Rights; fourth, by the degree to which it constitutes evidence of the multilegal system, converging national and inter-American norms; and fifth, by the type of social constructions on old age and the elderly that derive from the case.

Section 3 is devoted to an in-depth examination of the articles of the ICPHROP that are used in the *Riffo Salinas* judgment, in order to determine how they go beyond, or not, the interpretations of these articles made in the judgment.

---

[10] In Bolivian legislation, the concept used is that of an elderly person (Article 2 of the *General Law of the Elderly* reads: "[B]eing holders of the rights expressed therein the elderly persons of sixty or more years of age, in the Bolivian territory" (Law No. 369 General Law of the Elderly Persons, Supreme Decree 1807, May 1, 2013)).

[11] Organization of American States, Inter-American Convention on Protecting the Human Rights of Older Persons, June 15, 2015, T.S. No. A-70.

Section 4 addresses the cases on older persons in which the Inter-American Court of Human Rights established the violation of the same rights violated in the *Riffo Salinas* case.

Section 5 focuses on identifying the social constructions on old age and the elderly in the judgments of the Inter-American Court. Some of these social constructions will also be indicated in a cross-cutting manner throughout the sections.

Section 6 summarizes the contributions of the chapter, although the final assessment of whether the *Riffo Salinas* case represents a good practice for the countries that are part of the Inter-American System will be made by the reader after reviewing this chapter and, of course, the judgment itself.[12]

In general, this judgment shows the coexistence, antagonism, and/or overlapping of two phenomena: on the one hand, the permanent updating of international law on the protection of rights and in this case, the adaptation to the subjects of law that are the elderly today; and on the other hand: the permanence of jurisprudential interpretations that obey social constructions on old age that correspond to previous stages of history.

2. *Riffo Salinas* Case Judgment

Marco Antonio Riffo Salinas, a seventy-eight-year-old man prosecuted for material and ideological falsehood and others, was granted by the Eighth Criminal Sentencing Court of the Department of La Paz, Bolivia, the cessation of his preventive detention. The cessation was appealed by the plaintiff and the Second Criminal Chamber of the Departmental Court of Justice of La Paz, which ordered the enforcement of the detention.

In February 28, 2018, the Plurinational Constitutional Court's Second Chamber annulled the challenged resolutions, ordering the issuance of a new resolution, which should respect his constitutional rights and guarantees, and provided for the immediate release of Mr. Riffo Salinas.

The legal grounds essentially revolved around the error of not taking into account that the subject was an elderly person. The decision is based on the following arguments: differential and intersectional approach to the rights of the elderly; exceptionality of the preventive detention of elderly persons; the principle or test of proportionality in the application of preventive detention based

---

[12] Plurinational Constitutional Ruling 0010/2018-S2, Sucre, February 28, 2018, La Paz, file 21259-2017-43-AL, https://jurisprudenciaconstitucional.com/sentencias/19232-sentencia-constitucional-0010-2018-s2 (accessed December 29, 2022).

on an intersectional approach; criteria for the application of preventive detention of elderly persons; and analysis of the specific case.

On all points, except for the *criteria*, the ruling is based on the ICPHROP, as well as on Bolivian domestic law.[13] In the *differential and intersectional approach*[14] of the legal grounds as well as in the *exceptionality of the preventive detention of older adults*, reference is made to Article 5 (equality and nondiscrimination on grounds of age) of the aforementioned ICPHROP to underline the importance of intersection and multiple discrimination:

> The States Parties shall develop specific approaches in their policies, plans and legislation on aging and old age, in relation to older persons in vulnerable conditions and those who are victims of multiple discrimination (...) persons deprived of their liberty.

The right to liberty and security of person of the elderly is upheld on the basis of Article 13 (right to personal liberty) of the aforementioned instrument, which mentions:

> States Parties (...) shall promote alternative measures to deprivation of liberty, in accordance with their domestic legal systems.

Regarding Bolivian legislation, although there are rules such as the General Law on Older Persons (2013) that guarantee and protect the rights of this age group, and where special protection is established, the fact is that the interpretation of these rules by the Plurinational Constitutional Court of Bolivia is based primarily on the ICPHROP and complementarily on domestic law.[15] As for the *analysis of the specific case*, the ruling is based on Article 13 of the aforementioned instrument, which promotes the adoption of criminal precautionary measures other than those involving deprivation of liberty.

The judgment does not refer to any of the Inter-American Court judgments related to older persons that predate *Riffo Salinas* (*Five Pensioners v. Peru* (2001); *Yakye Axa v. Paraguay* (2005); *Acevedo Buendía et al. v. Peru* (2009); and *García*

---

[13] Constitución Política del Estado Plurinacional (2009), Ley General de las Personas Adultas Mayores (2013), Código De Procedimiento Penal (1999).

[14] Intersectionality describes micro processes with respect to how each individual and group occupies a social position in interlocking structures of oppression. The dimensions and relationships of class, gender, and race/ethnicity must be studied together (Paula Dressel et al., "Gender, Race, Class, and Aging: Advances and Opportunities," in Meredith Minkler and Carroll L. Estes, *Critical Gerontology: Perspectives from Political and Moral Economy* (Baywood 1999).

[15] The ruling cites Articles 3, 5.b. and c., 67.I, and 68 of the *General Law on Older Persons* (2013); Articles 13.I and 125 of the *Political Constitution of the State* (2009); and Articles 233.2 and 234 of the *Code of Criminal Procedure* (1999).

Lucero et al. v. Chile (2013).[16] However, other rulings and votes issued by that international tribunal are present. In relation to the argument of the *exceptionality of the preventive detention of elderly people*, there is the intersectional approach that was introduced in the Inter-American System as an interpretation criterion on violence against women, whose application was later extended to the analysis of discrimination of other groups in vulnerable situations. In the *principle or test of proportionality in the application of pretrial detention based on an intersectional approach*, the Inter-American Commission established the following in its Report on the Use of Pretrial Detention:

> When courts resort to pretrial detention without considering the application of other less burdensome precautionary measures, given the nature of the facts under investigation, pretrial detention becomes disproportionate.[17]

In turn, the Inter-American Court in its 2016 judgment on Merits, Reparations and Costs in the *Andrade Salmón v. Bolivia* case, reiterates what was mentioned in the *Chaparro Álvarez and Lapo Íñiguez v. Ecuador* case (2007):

> That the purpose of the measures that restrict this right (...) will not impede the development of the procedure or evade the action of justice . . . that they are absolutely indispensable (...) and that they are measures that are strictly proportional in such a way that the sacrifice inherent to the restriction of the right is not exaggerated or disproportionate to the advantages obtained through such restriction and the fulfillment of the purpose pursued.[18]

Proportionality is also upheld in the Bolivian ruling in the reasoned opinion of Judge Sergio García Ramírez in relation to the judgment of the IACHR Court in the aforementioned case versus Ecuador, which states:

> Criminal precautionary measures, like any other restriction of fundamental rights, should be: a) exceptional and not ordinary (...) b) justified within a precise framework of reasons and conditions that give them legitimacy and rationality; c) agreed upon by an independent jurisdictional authority (...); d) indispensable; e) proportional; f) limited; g) periodically reviewable;

---

[16] These cases will be reviewed in section 4, "In What Aspects Do the IACHR Court Cases on Older Persons Go Further than the Bolivian Case?," *infra*.

[17] IACHR, *Report on the Use of Pretrial Detention in the Americas*, OEA/SER.L/V/II, Doc. 46/13, December 30, 2013, para. 162.

[18] *Caso Andrade Salmón v. Bolivia* [2016], IACtHR, Ser. C No. 330, para. 147.

h) revocable or replaceable (...) All this (...) has special emphasis if one thinks of the most severe of these: the precautionary deprivation of liberty.[19]

An important aspect that forms a central part of the grounds of the ruling of the Bolivian Plurinational Constitutional Court in the *Riffo Salinas* case is the right to health, which had been ignored by the Second Criminal Chamber of the Departmental Court of Justice of La Paz.

3. How Does the ICPHROP Go beyond the Bolivian Case?

The ICPHROP was signed on June 15, 2015, within the OAS and entered into force on January 11, 2017. To date, it has been ratified by Uruguay, Costa Rica, Bolivia, Chile, Argentina, El Salvador, and Ecuador and requires three more ratifications for the follow-up mechanisms established therein to become operational. Just as well, the Inter-American Convention on the Prevention, Punishment, and Eradication of Violence against Women (Belém do Pará Convention) requires special consideration for elderly women (art. 9), while the Inter-American Convention against All Forms of Discrimination and Intolerance prohibits age-based discrimination (art. 1.1).

The ICPHROP is a cutting-edge instrument that introduces new concepts on aging and includes the civil, political, and social rights of the elderly.[20] It takes inequality into account—Latin America and the Caribbean is the most unequal region on the planet—as well as multiculturalism and multiple forms of aging. By determining that States must take awareness-rising measures, the treaty aims to target the root causes of discrimination against older persons. It also includes a progressive agenda,[21] recognizes the right to palliative care,[22] and adopts a

---

[19] *Case of Chaparro Álvarez and Lapo Íñiguez v. Ecuador Bolivia* [2007], IACtHR, Ser. C No. 170, reasoned opinion of Judge Sergio Ramírez, para. 7.

[20] For a review of the civil, political and social dimensions of the ICPHROP, see Aída Díaz-Tendero, "Dimensiones civil, política y social de la Convención Interamericana sobre la Protección de los Derechos Humanos de las Personas Mayores," in Eduardo Ferrer Mac-Gregor and Luis Raúl Guerrero (coords.), *Derechos del Pueblo Mexicano: México a través de sus Constituciones*, vol. V, *Transversalidad constitucional con prospectiva convencional* (Instituto de Investigaciones Jurídicas/ Miguel Ángel Porrúa 2016), 187–202.

[21] Suffice it to mention the inclusion in the right to equality and nondiscrimination on grounds of age (art. 5) of victims of multiple discrimination, such as persons of diverse sexual orientations and gender identities (see section 3.1 *infra*); the inclusion in the right to health (art. 19) of public policies on sexual and reproductive health of the elderly (see section 3.2 *infra*); the inclusion in the right to life and dignity in old age (art. 6) of palliative care and palliative care for the elderly (see section 3.3 *infra*); and the inclusion in the right to life and dignity in old age (art. 6) of palliative care and other measures to avoid unnecessary suffering and futile and useless interventions, in accordance with the right of the elderly person to express informed consent (art. 11) in the field of health (see section 3.2 *infra*).

[22] See Tamar Ezer, Diederik Lohman, and Gabriela B. de Luca, "Palliative Care and Human Rights: A Decade of Evolution in Standards" [2018] 55 *Journal of Pain & Symptom Management* 163,

concept of "older person."[23] Although there is room for improvement,[24] there is also a gender perspective.[25]

This section will specifically review in what sense Articles 5 (equality and nondiscrimination on grounds of age) and 13 (right to personal liberty) go beyond their use in the *Riffo Salinas* judgment, and what other dimensions of the ICPHROP do the rights to liberty, life, health, and security that the judgment considers to have been violated appear in the ICPHROP.

3.1. Equality and Nondiscrimination on the Basis of Age and the Right to Personal Freedom

The broadening of the criteria for discrimination[26] in the ICPHROP is very notable: gender, disability, sexual orientation, gender identity, migration, poverty, marginalization, Afro-descent, and Indigenous origin, but also discrimination against homeless people, people in prison, people belonging to traditional peoples or ethnic, racial, national, linguistic, and religious and rural groups, as well as the multiplying effect of discrimination when several of these conditions or characteristics are added together. Article 5 (equality and nondiscrimination) represents a recognition of regional multiculturalism, responding to the vast cultural richness and heterogeneity and to the claims of the Indigenous peoples.[27] It also strongly emphasizes the gender perspective in the instrument.

164, 166; Francesco Seatzu, "Constructing a Right to Palliative Care: The Inter-American Convention on the Rights of Older Persons" [2015] 1 *Ius et Scientia* 25.

[23] See Francesco Seatzu, "Sulla convenzione dell'organizzazione dell'organizzazione degli stati americani sui diritti delle persone anziane" [2015] 31 *Anuario Espanol de Derecho Internacional* 349, 358.
[24] See Caitlin R. Williams, Erin C. Bennett, and Benjamin Mason Meier, "Incorporating a Gender Perspective to Realise the Health and Human Rights of Older Persons," in Allyn Taylor and Patricia Kuzler (eds.), *Ageing, Health and International Law: Towards an International Legal Framework to Advance the Health and Human Rights of Older Persons* (2010), https://ssrn.com/abstract_id=3790125 (accessed December 13, 2021).
[25] Preamble and art. 3 (I), 12 Inter-American Convention on Protecting the Human Rights of Older Persons.
[26] Discrimination is understood as any distinction, exclusion, or restriction that has the purpose or effect of nullifying or impairing the recognition, enjoyment, or exercise, on an equal footing, of human rights and fundamental freedoms in the political, economic, social, cultural, or any other sphere of public and private life (ICPDHPM definition).
[27] On Indigenous Peoples and the *Convention*, see Aída Díaz-Tendero, "La *Convención Interamericana sobre la Protección de los Derechos Humanos de las Personas Mayores* y los Pueblos Originarios," in Jorge Olvera, Julio César Olvera, and Ana Luisa Guerrero, *Los Pueblos Originarios en los debates actuales de los Derechos Humanos* (Universidad Autónoma del Estado de México/CIALC/UNAM and MA Porrúa 2017), 237–254.

At the same time, Article 5 constitutes one of the most avant-garde elements of the ICPHROP. It incorporates sexual orientation[28] and gender identity[29] in the *corpus* of human rights of the elderly, thus breaking the homogeneous and stereotyped vision about this population.

The *Riffo Salinas* sentence also refers to Article 13, the promotion of alternative measures to the deprivation of liberty by the States. This article is particularly interesting because it establishes the guarantee by the States of access by the elderly person deprived of liberty to rehabilitation mechanisms for their reintegration into society. Underlying the spirit of the norm is the consideration of life after the period of deprivation of liberty, discarding the idea that for an incarcerated elderly person there is no future in society after the end of his or her sentence.

In the ICPHROP, freedom also appears in Article 12 dedicated to the rights of the elderly person receiving long-term care services, establishing in one of the subparagraphs of Paragraph c) on the operation of the services that "the exercise of the freedom and mobility of the elderly person shall be protected." Other specific freedoms that appear in the ICPHROP are the right to freedom of expression (art. 14), the right to freedom of movement and the freedom to choose one's residence (art. 15).

3.2. Rights to Safety, Life, and Health

The right to security is present in the ICPHROP in other articles in addition to the aforementioned Article 13. The "right to safety and to a life free from violence" (art. 9) refers to multiple types of violence and mistreatment.

> Violence against the elderly includes, among others, different types of abuse, including financial and patrimonial, physical, sexual, psychological, labor exploitation, expulsion from their community and all forms of abandonment

---

[28] Sexual orientation is independent of biological sex or gender identity; it refers to the capacity of each person to feel a deep emotional, affective and sexual attraction to persons of a gender different from his or her own, of the same gender or of more than one gender, as well as the capacity to maintain intimate and sexual relations with people. It is a complex concept whose forms change over time and differ among different cultures. (United Nations, Sexual Orientation and Gender Identity in International Human Rights Law. South America, Office of the United Nations High Commissioner for Human Rights, 2012, 3).

[29] The internal and individual experience of gender as each person deeply experiences it, which may or may not correspond to the sex assigned at birth, including the personal experience of the body (which may involve modification of bodily appearance or function through medical, surgical, or other techniques, provided it is freely chosen) and other expressions of gender, including dress, speech, and manners (ibid.).

or neglect that take place within or outside the family or domestic unit or that are perpetrated or tolerated by the State or its agents wherever they occur.

Again, multiculturalism is reflected in the expulsion of the elderly from their community, a customary practice of certain native peoples.

Safety is also reinforced in the rights of the elderly person receiving long-term care services[30] in Article 12, which determines the establishment of a regulatory framework for the operation of long-term care services, including the adoption of measures to "protect the personal safety and the exercise of freedom and mobility of the elderly person."

The right to life occupies a prominent place in Article 6 "Right to life and dignity in old age" and relates especially to the end of life, palliative care, appropriate management of problems related to the fear of death of the terminally ill, pain, unnecessary suffering, and futile and useless interventions, in accordance with the right of the elderly person to express informed consent. This article affirms life and considers death as a normal process, which should neither be accelerated nor delayed.

The right of the elderly person to make decisions and to define his or her life plan, as well as to develop an autonomous life (art. 7, right to independence and autonomy), is also a dimension of the right of the life.

The right to health enshrined in Article 19 is one of the broadest and most comprehensive of the ICPHROP. It takes into account regional socioeconomic inequality as well as multiculturalism.

The instrument's emphasis on multiculturalism is also evident in the special attention it pays to traditional, alternative, and complementary medicine. The right to provide free and informed consent—in the field of health—in accordance with the communication needs of the elderly person and the fact that the information provided must be presented in accordance with the level of education (art. 11) shows sensitivity to regional socioeconomic inequity. Likewise, the inclusion of sexual and reproductive health and the treatment of sexually transmitted diseases in the right to health of the elderly (art. 19), as well as the right to give free and informed consent (art. 11, to accept, refuse to receive or voluntarily interrupt medical or surgical treatment and to receive clear and timely information on the possible consequences and risks of such decision), may be considered a progressive agenda in the area of health.

---

[30] Elderly person receiving long-term care services: a person who resides temporarily or permanently in a regulated facility, whether public, private, or mixed, in which he/she receives quality comprehensive social and health services, including long-stay residences, that provide these long-term care services to the elderly person with moderate or severe dependency who cannot receive care at home (CIPDHPM definition).

4. In What Aspects Do the IACHR Court Cases on Older Persons Go Further than the Bolivian Case?

This section will analyze cases of the Inter-American Court of Human Rights on the elderly in relation to the *Riffo Salinas* case, in order to find some coincidences, differences, and/or complementarities. The analysis focuses on freedoms and rights that were violated in *Riffo Salinas* (to life, to health, and to liberty and security).

4.1. Right to Life

In the case *Yakye Axa v. Paraguay*[31] (2005), the Court analyzes Article 4 (right to life) of the American Convention in relation to Article 1.1, concluding that it "includes not only the right of every human being not to be arbitrarily deprived of life, but also the right not to be subjected to conditions that prevent or hinder access to a dignified existence."

This can be understood as a special relationship of the right to life with other rights, that is, the factors that intervene in the attainment of a dignified life such as health. Similarly, the *Riffo Salinas* case (Point III.5) sheds light into the health-life binomial: "[T]he rights to life and health must take precedence when making a determination." The *Yakya Axa* case also calls attention to factors that hinder a dignified life, specially the extreme poverty generated by the lack of access to land ownership and natural resources. It even goes much further in this same case, and the Commission's arguments relate the right to life to social rights, in an interpretation of Article 26 of the American Convention:

> Paraguay has the duty to guarantee the conditions necessary for the attainment of a life in dignity, a duty that is underlined by the commitment contained in Article 26 of the Convention to adopt appropriate measures to achieve the full realization of social rights.[32]

In the same sense, the Court manifests itself in the case *Poblete-Vilches v. Chile*[33] (2018) when it establishes the right to life as a fundamental right for whose compliance and according to Article 4 of the American Convention:

---

[31] The lands of the Paraguayan Chaco, where the Yakye Axa Indigenous community used to live, were sold to British businessmen at the end of the nineteenth century for cattle ranching, and the Indigenous people worked for these companies in very poor conditions. In 1986, they moved to another tract of land, which also brought no improvement in their quality of life. Since 1993, the Yakye Axa Indigenous community began the corresponding procedures to claim the lands they consider their traditional habitat. The case reached the Court on March 17, 2003 (*Case Yakye Axa v. Paraguay* [2005], IACtHR, Ser. C No. 123).

[32] *Case Yakye Axa v. Paraguay* [2005], Ser. C No. 123, para. 157, subpara. e).

[33] On January 17, 2001, Mr. Vinicio Antonio Poblete Vilches, seventy-six years old, was admitted to the Sótero del Río public hospital due to severe respiratory failure. He was hospitalized for four days in

States have the obligation to ensure the creation of the conditions required to prevent violations of this right.[34]

4.2. Right to Health

It is convenient to separate allusions to the right to health from those referring to the condition of lack of health.

In the *Riffo Salinas* case, health, or rather the lack thereof, is understood as an impediment to the exercise of rights in the general sense, that is, a deficit in the exercise of rights of a civil, political, or social nature whose origin is the lack of the right to health, a social right par excellence.

It is also "the lack of health" that appears as a conditioning factor for the analysis of the evidentiary elements from a different perspective in the *Riffo Salinas* ruling.

In the case *Yakye Axa v. Paraguay*, the right to health is protected by Article 10 of the Protocol of San Salvador, which "establishes the right of ethnic and cultural groups to use their own traditional medicines and health practices, as well as the right of access to health institutions and medical care provided to the rest of the population in order to preserve their physical, mental and moral integrity,"[35] and the protection is reinforced because they are elderly people. If in this ruling there is a social construction of old age as vulnerability, it certainly does not appear explicitly.

The *Poblete-Vilches v. Chile* case[36] is the first case in which the Inter-American Court of Human Rights ruled directly on the right to health of the elderly.[37]

---

the intensive care unit. He was then admitted to the Surgical Intensive Care Unit where he underwent surgery when the patient was unconscious, without having obtained the consent of his relatives. On February 2, he was discharged early, without further instructions, and his relatives had to hire a private ambulance to take him home, since the hospital had no ambulances available. Three days later, Mr. Poblete was admitted to the same public hospital, where he remained in the intermediate care unit, despite the fact that the medical record required him to be admitted to the intensive care ward. He also required a respirator, which was not provided. Mr. Poblete-Vilches died two days later, on February 7, 2001. The relatives filed a first criminal complaint in 2001 and a second one in 2005. On December 11, 2006, the First Civil Court ordered the dismissal of the case; it was dismissed in 2007. Again, on June 30, 2008, the case was dismissed and on August 5, 2008, the case was unsealed. It reached the Court in 2018 (*Case Poblete-Vilches v. Chile* [2018], IACtHR, Ser. C No. 372).

[34] Ibid., para. 145.
[35] *Case Yakye Axa v. Paraguay* [2005], IACtHR, Ser. C No. 123, partially dissenting opinion of Judge A. Abreu Burelli, para. 25.
[36] On the *Poblete-Vilches v. Chile case*, see Mariela Morales Antoniazzi and Laura Clericó (coords.), *Interamericanización del derecho a la salud. El caso Poblete de la Corte IDH bajo la lupa* (Instituto de Estudios Constitucionales del Estado de Querétaro 2019).
[37] The designation "elderly person" is used for the first time by the Court in the *Poblete-Vilches v. Chile case*, based on the ICPHROP, setting an important precedent. However, it cannot support its judgment on this instrument, due to the fact that it was ratified by the Chilean State on July 11, 2017.

The Court interprets that the protection of the right to health derives from the American Convention and relies—due to the impossibility of invoking the ICPHROP because the facts were prior to the date of when Chile ratified it (August 15, 2017)—on a multiplicity of instruments. It establishes that health is a fundamental and indispensable human right and that every human being has the right to the enjoyment of the highest attainable standard of health that enables him or her to live in dignity, health being understood not only as the absence of disease or infirmity but also as a complete state of physical, mental, and social well-being, derived from a lifestyle that allows individuals to achieve a comprehensive balance. This general obligation translates into the duty of the States to ensure people's access to essential health services, ensuring quality and effective medical care, as well as to promote the improvement of the population's health conditions.

The merits of the case state that the elderly are entitled to a reinforced protection of the right to health and, therefore, require the adoption of differentiated measures.

The Court valued the opportunity to rule for the first time specifically on the rights of the elderly in the area of health. It highlighted the importance of making the elderly visible as subjects of rights with special protection and therefore comprehensive care, with respect for their autonomy and independence. The Court considered that there is a reinforced obligation to respect and guarantee their right to health. The questioning of the social construction of old age behind this ruling should be repaired in that the exercise of the right to health is linked to the enforceability of the same by its holder, in this case, the elderly person; and in no way is it related to the fact that he or she is vulnerable or fragile. On the other hand, the immediate accompaniment of the principles of autonomy and independence reinforces the interpretation in the same sense.[38]

4.3. Right to Liberty and Security

The case of *García Lucero et al. v. Chile*[39] (2011) can be considered complementary to the Riffo Salinas case in relation to due process. The Bolivian case upholds

---

[38] IACtHR's more recent cases expanding social and economic rights of older persons were not yet decided at the time *Riffo Salinas* was ruled (e.g., *Muelle Flores v. Peru*, 2019). See Daniel Cerqueira, "Jurisprudencia de la corte IDH en casos sobre DESCA: entre lo retórico y lo impredecible. Justicia en Las Américas" (Blog de la Fundación para el Debido Proceso, July 1, 2020), https://dplfblog.com/2020/01/07/jurisprudencia-de-la-corte-idh-en-casos-sobre-desca-entre-lo-retorico-y-lo-impredecible/ (accessed January 5, 2022).

[39] The facts of this case take place during the Chilean dictatorship. On September 16, 1973, Mr. Leopoldo García Lucero was arrested by Carabineros in Santiago de Chile and was held incommunicado and tortured in various ways. He was then taken to a concentration camp "Chacabuco" where he remained for thirteen months. After Decree-Law 81 of 1973, Mr. García Lucero was expelled from Chile on June 12, 1975, and has been living in the United Kingdom ever since. In 1993, he sent a letter

the need to promote alternative measures to the deprivation of liberty of an elderly person (see section 2), and the *García Lucero* case raises the right to a simple and prompt recourse before competent judges or courts (art. 25(1) of the ICPHROP: judicial protection) in relation to Article 1(1) of that instrument (obligation to respect rights) on the basis of age.

In the *Poblete-Vilches* case, the right to personal liberty is interpreted in relation to the right to health, specifically, the freedom to give consent prior to surgery. The Chilean State had already accepted prior to the arrival of the case before the Inter-American Court the violation of Mr. Poblete's right to personal liberty[40] (art. 7, everyone has the right to liberty and security of person).

5. Social Constructions about Old Age and the Elderly

In the *Riffo Salinas* ruling, the social construction of old age is based on inactivity, a precarious state of health, economic scarcity, and limited social environments. It is counterintuitive to use the ICPHROP without rescuing the ideological part of the instrument, given that its leitmotif is the empowerment of the elderly, the recognition of the multiplicity of old age, and especially the breaking of the association between vulnerability and fragility, with old age.

Similarly, in the case of the IACtHR *García Lucero et al. v. Chile*, the characterization of Mr. Leopoldo García Lucero as a person in a situation of vulnerability due to the fact that he is seventy-nine years old and suffers from a permanent disability is emphasized. Regarding this characterization, it is explained that the Protocol of San Salvador indicates in its Articles 17 and 18 the relevance of "protection" to the "elderly" and "handicapped." Advanced age is also taken into account in the requirement of special diligence in the resolution of the process.

On the contrary, the construction around the elderly in the *Yakye Axa v. Paraguay* case is not monochromatic, since it has to do on the one hand with vulnerability, in that the State is expected to adopt measures aimed at maintaining their functionality and autonomy, guaranteeing the right to adequate food, access to clean water, and healthcare, but on the other hand it has to do with the

---

from London to the Program for the Recognition of the Politically Exonerated in Chile in which he referred to the injuries caused by the torture he received. He receives three types of monetary compensation under different laws. The case reaches the court in 2011 (*Case García Lucero et al. v. Chile* [2013], IACtHR, Ser. C No. 267).

[40] Of utmost interest is the Court's interpretation of liberty, defining it as "the capacity to do and not to do everything that is lawfully permitted, allowing every person to organize, in accordance with the law, his individual and social life according to his own choices and convictions" (*Case Poblete-Vilches v. Chile* [2018], IACtHR, Ser. C No. 372, para. 169).

empowerment of the elderly, visualizing them as the main oral transmitters of culture to the new generations. In other words, older persons are not only rights-holders but also duty bearers (in this sense, the specific reference to obligations in the African protection instrument is very relevant[41]).

This two-dimensional construction is also found in the *Poblete-Vilches v. Chile* case. The Commission constructs old age around vulnerability, specifically in relation to access to the right to health and the public health system, as well as taking into account people living in poverty. However, the Court highlights the importance of making the elderly visible as subjects of rights with special protection and therefore comprehensive care, with respect for their autonomy and independence. The empowerment of the elderly as subjects of rights and responsibilities can be seen in these principles. Of particular interest for the justiciability of Economic, Social and Cultural Rights (ESCR) is the location of the discourse of social construction. It would seem a priori that the enforceability of civil and political rights is strengthened by social constructions that empower older persons, while that of social rights is based on social constructions of old age based on vulnerability and fragility. However, this is a false dilemma. The ESCR are rights that can be demanded not on the basis of the vulnerability of those who are entitled to them but on the basis of their empowerment, in the same way that in the realm of public policies, social assistance is differentiated from social security.[42] Finally, social constructions based on the ownership of rights, empowerment, autonomy, and independence support the phenomena of interdependence and indivisibility of civil, political, and social rights.

On the occasions when health appears in the *Riffo Salinas* judgment, it is related to certain social constructions that relate the elderly to poor health, in accordance with the previous paradigm on old age. The following excerpt (Point III.1.) of the *Riffo Salinas* ruling shows the argument on the *differential and intersectional approach to the rights of older persons* based on certain social constructions:

> Given that old age implies the loss of means of subsistence, either due to the advent of diseases and the consequent loss of health, or because they become economically inactive and are therefore limited in the exercise of their rights.

---

[41] In the African instrument, the obligations of older persons, integrated in Article 20, consist of generating and transferring knowledge to younger generations, generating intergenerational solidarity and dialogue, and resolving conflicts as mediators (African Union, *Protocol to the African Charter on Human and People's Rights on the Rights of Older Persons in Africa*, General Assembly, Twenty Sixth Ordinary Session, Addis Ababa, January 31, 2016).

[42] Aída Díaz-Tendero, "The State and the economic security of older adults. Marco conceptual en torno a las dimensiones de la solidaridad económica" [2015] 85 *Papeles de Población Nueva Época* 79-108.

In other words, there is a social construction of old age as a stage of losses and vulnerabilities, which may be true for a specific case, but is not true for the generality of the elderly population.

The *criteria for the application of preventive detention of the elderly* in the *Riffo Salinas* ruling establish that it is also necessary to analyze the evidence from a differentiated perspective and without requiring formalities that are difficult to comply with for the elderly (Point III.4, Paragraph a.1):

> Most of them are sick, inactive at work, without patrimony and often without a family environment (...)

This is, once again, a construction of old age based on shortcomings and deficits, in this case in the health, economic, and even social spheres, which in some ways is contrary to the spirit of the ICPHROP.

In the arguments of the *analysis of the specific case in* the *Riffo Salinas* judgment, the right to health appears together with the right to life, and this time it is repeated categorically that "the elderly person has by nature a vulnerable health condition," that is, again a negative social construction of old age in the following context (Point III.5):

> Medical certifications and even a forensic medical expert report recommending the internment of the accused in a hospital due to his advanced age; (...) precisely when facing resolutions that impose precautionary measures on elderly people, the rights to life and health must take precedence when making a determination, since the elderly person has by nature a vulnerable health condition.

6. Concluding Remarks

The multilevel impact of the standards of the Inter-American System can be seen in the *Riffo Salinas* case in the application of the ICPHROP, in the integration of the inter-American standards established by the Court and the Commission in cases that do not involve elderly persons, and in the convergence of national and inter-American norms. Regarding its significance for the jurisprudence on the elderly as subjects of law, it is clear that the case is based on the preferential and special treatment to which the defendant is entitled because he is an elderly person.

The answer to the question of whether the case integrates the ad hoc instrument of the Inter-American System for the protection of the human rights of the elderly, the ICPHROP is affirmative and is based, specifically, on the use of

Articles 5 (equality and nondiscrimination on grounds of age) and 13 (right to personal liberty).

In relation to the degree of integration or exclusion of the inter-American standards established by the Court and the Commission, the *Riffo Salinas* judgment includes judgments and votes issued by the Inter-American Court in cases that, although they are not about older persons, are substantive for its legal argumentation, such as the Report of the Inter-American Commission on the use of pretrial detention based on the *intersectional approach*; and the cases *Lapo Íñiguez v. Ecuador* (2007) and *Andrade Salmón v. Bolivia* (2016) on *indispensability* and *proportionality*.

To answer the question of whether the case constitutes evidence of the multilegal system, converging national and inter-American regulations, it is noted in the legal grounds that both the ICPHROP and Bolivian domestic regulations are used, especially the General Law on Older Adults (2013), but also the Political Constitution of the Plurinational State (2009) and the Code of Criminal Procedure (1999).

Regarding the conclusions on the social constructions of old age and the elderly that emerge from the judgment, the ruling does reinforce a negative construction of old age and the elderly, associated with losses and vulnerabilities in different dimensions. Although it is appropriate to portray these circumstances in the characterization of specific cases, it is not correct to generalize them as a definition of old age and/or older persons. In this sense, the *Riffo Salinas* ruling goes against the spirit of the ICPHROP.

Other conclusions that emerge from the analysis of the *Riffo Salinas* case and that were not established in the initial questions are, on the one hand, the interdependence (of civil, political, and social rights) and, on the other hand, the multidimensionality of rights, specifically the right to health. The main right violated in the *Riffo Salinas* case belongs to the civil sphere (right to life), but its link with the right to health (social right), echoing *Poblete-Vilches v. Chile*, a case based on the violation of the right to health in its social dimension but which irremediably brings with it the violation of civil rights such as the right to give informed consent.

A new era in the protection of the human rights of the elderly begins, based on the instrument created specifically for this purpose and which constitutes the vanguard at the global level. The ICPHROP deepens the content and applicability of human rights to the daily reality of the elderly, as evidenced in the possibilities of Articles 5 and 13 and in the magnitude of the rights to security, freedom, life, and health.

Likewise, evidence has been presented to support the assertion that the Court's jurisprudence on the human rights of older persons has established interesting standards in relation to the right to life (*Yakye Axa v. Paraguay* and

Poblete-Vilches v. Chile cases, 2018), the right to health (*Yakye Axa v. Chile* and *Poblete Vilches v. Chile* cases), and the rights to liberty and security (*García Lucero et al. v. Chile* and *Poblete-Vilches v. Chile* cases).

A judge's knowledge of the human rights approach applied to aging opens his or her eyes to how his or her jurisdictional task can be strengthened with regional instruments, standards, and jurisprudence that allow understanding the phenomenon of aging and the elderly as subjects of law.

Finally, one of the pending tasks in the *Ius Constitutionale Commune en América Latina* is the inclusion of social constructions on old age and older persons that embrace the multiplicity, plurality, and heterogeneity of old age, without weakening the need for protection, the existence of intersections that enhance the vulnerability of certain older persons, and, in general, the application gap (as recognized by the European Recommendation of 2014[43]) of the regulations that a good number of older persons suffer to a greater extent than other age groups. Positive and plural social constructions about old age and older people have a considerable impact in the legal sphere and beyond, as recognized in the line of jurisprudence classified as therapeutic[44] in Anglo-Saxon gerontological law. Likewise, the way in which older people live and think about their old age today will shape the social—and legal—constructions of old age that will contextualize the lives of older people and the gerontological legal praxis of the next generation.

---

[43] Council of Europe, *Recommendation on the promotion of the human rights of older persons*, CM/Rec(2014)2, 2014.

[44] David B. Wexler, "Therapeutic jurisprudence in clinical practice" [1996] 153 *American Journal of Psychiatry* 455.

II.9
The Standards of the Inter-American Human Rights System regarding Migration and Its Impact on the Region's States

By Elizabeth Salmón and Cécile Blouin

1. Introduction

The complexity of the issues explored in this chapter and the unfinished character of the applicable inter-American standards poses a series of difficulties for researchers.[1] The first difficulty lies in the dialectical tension between sovereignty and the rights of migrants. Control over the entry, residence, and exit of foreigners or non-nationals within a sovereign territorial area has traditionally been understood as part of the "reserved domain" of the State.[2] However, since there are no vetoed spaces for human rights, such rights have been able to enter into this privileged area of State regulation.[3] Thus, human rights have risen as a limit to an otherwise strictly sovereign realm. Additionally, the evolution of legislation, together with the dynamic or relative nature of "reserved domain," has progressively transformed human rights into an unavoidable issue in the development of legal regimes and the framing of public policies on migration.

---

[1] This chapter is part of a Pontificia Universidad Católica del Perú (PUCP) research project entitled "Migrant Trajectories: An Approach to the Factors that Structure the Migratory Projects and Strategies of Young Venezuelan People in Peru" (2019–2021). This PUCP Project was presented by the Interdisciplinary Research Group on Human Rights and International Humanitarian Law (GRIDEH) and won PUCP's Annual Research Project Contest. We would like to thank Crisbeth Vigo and Lucero Ibarra, both GRIDEH research assistants, for their help in reviewing literature review and jurisprudence.

[2] See *Case Concerning Military and Paramilitary Activities in and Against Nicaragua (Nicaragua against v. United States of America)* [1986] International Court of Justice (ICJ), para. 205; and United Nations General Assembly (UNGA), Resolution No. 2625 (XXV), "Declaration on Principles of International Law concerning Friendly Relations and Co-operation among States in accordance with the Charter of the United Nations," October 24, 1970, A/RES/2625(XXV).

[3] For a broader analysis on the impact of international human rights law on the paradigm of "Open State": Mariela Morales Antoniazzi, "El Estado Abierto como objetivo del Ius Constitutionale Commune. Aproximación desde el impacto de la Corte Interamericana de Derechos Humanos," in Armin von Bogdandy et al. (eds.), *Ius constitutionale commune en América Latina: rasgos, potencialidades y desafíos* (UNAM; IIJ; MPIL; IIDC 2014), 277–278.

Another difficulty arises from the conceptualization of migration. There is no legal consensus on the definition of "migrant." Nevertheless, different instruments characterize the various groups of people who move, each granting them a specific protection regime.[4] In this chapter, we choose to start from a broad concept of migration in order to address the totality of the standards of the Inter-American Human Rights System (IAHRS) developed in this field. Therefore, when we refer to migrants we include refugees, migrants, and stateless persons in situations of displacement. Detailing each one of these figures does not correspond to the aims of this chapter, but it is worth emphasizing that they share a common trait: they all refer to non-nationals. Moreover, it is important to recognize human mobility as an intricate phenomenon where legal categories are increasingly discussed.[5]

This chapter has two objectives: (1) analyzing the progress made by the IAHRS in terms of the protection and guarantees of migrant rights, and (2) understanding the magnitude of the impacts of these standards in the region. Each objective will be explored consecutively in the two following sections.

2. The Standards of the Inter-American Human Rights System for Migration Matters

One needs to consider that there is no normative reference to explain the notion of "standard" within the IAHRS. Instead, there is a reference model guiding the effective fulfillment of contracted obligations: an unavoidable interpretive paradigm for the attainment of international obligations and a permanent enrichment mechanism that ensures international courts contribute to the essential content of human rights.[6] From the perspective of the national enforcer, according to César Landa a standard would be a criterion shaping the interpretations of national judges and a reference point for the validation of the national laws of a State.[7]

---

[4] Cécile Blouin, "Antes de la llegada: migración (forzada) de personas venezolanas," in Cécile Blouin (ed.), *Después de la llegada Realidades de la migración venezolana* (Themis IDEHPUCP 2019).

[5] See Roger Zetter, "More Labels, Fewer Refugees: Remaking the Refugee Label in an Era of Globalization" [2007] 20 *Journal of Refugee Studies* 172, <https://academic.oup.com/jrs/article-abstract/20/2/172/1539814> (accessed February 5, 2022); Jane McAdam, "Swimming Against the Tide: Why a Climate Change Displacement Treaty Is Not the Answer" [2011] 23 *International Journal of Refugee Law* 2, <https://papers.ssrn.com/sol3/papers.cfm?abstract_id=1714714> (accessed February 5, 2022).

[6] Elizabeth Salmón and Cristina Blanco, *El derecho al debido proceso en la jurisprudencia de la Corte Interamericana de Derechos Humanos* (4th ed., Fondo Editorial de la Pontificia Universidad Católica del Perú 2021), 13.

[7] César Landa, *Control of Conventionality: The Peruvian Case* (Editorial Academia Española 2017), 122.

Within this framework, one can distinguish between at least three precise stages in the relationship between the IAHRS and the issue of migration. These stages can be explained by the evolution of the jurisprudence of the Inter-American Court of Human Rights (IACtHR) and the work of the Inter-American Commission on Human Rights (IACHR).

2.1. First Stage: Silence from the Inter-American Human Rights System

The Economic Commission for Latin America and the Caribbean (CEPAL) and the International Organization for Migration (IOM) have pointed out that since the end of the twentieth century migratory flows[8] have increased throughout the region, and primarily in North America.[9] Nonetheless, efforts to develop human rights standards in the IAHRS were not initially focused on the human rights of migrants. Hence, we can speak of an initial stage in the IAHRS consideration of migration as characterized by silence. This silence could be explained by the upheavals taking place during that period, which was marked by a number of dictatorships and systematic human rights violations and meant that priority issues, such as torture and enforced disappearances, demanded the greatest attention. As is already known, the IACtHR began its work in a convulsed Latin America. This is reflected by its first judgments on cases involving "enforced disappearances and other serious human rights violations related to this crime."[10] The first judgment by the Inter-American Court, the *Velásquez Rodríguez* case against Honduras, responded to the need to confront the phenomenon of forced disappearance of persons and, therefore, established the constituent elements of such crime.[11] The following two cases were also from Honduras, which is understandable due to the numerous complaints of missing persons and the inaction of the State in the face of such a crisis.[12] This jurisprudential line is also evidenced later in the cases of *Godínez Cruz v. Honduras* (1989), *Blake v. Guatemala* (1998),

---

[8] Carlos Maldonado Valera, Jorge Martínez Pizarro, and Rodrigo Martínez, *Protección social y migración: una mirada desde las vulnerabilidades a lo largo del ciclo de la migración y de la vida de las personas* (CEPAL 2018), 13, <https://repositorio.cepal.org/bitstream/handle/11362/44021/1/S1800613_es.pdf> (accessed February 5, 2022).

[9] International Organization for Migration (IOM), "Migration and Migrants: Regional Dimensions and Developments," in Maire McAuliffe and Martin Ruhs (eds.), *World Migration Report 2018* (IOM 2017), 91, <https://publications.iom.int/system/files/pdf/wmr_2018_sp.pdf> (accessed February 5, 2022).

[10] Elizabeth Salmón, *Introducción al Sistema Interamericano de Derechos Humanos* (PUCP Fondo Editorial 2019), 289.

[11] IACtHR, *40 años protegiendo derechos* (IACtHR 2018), 20, <https://www.corteidh.or.cr/sitios/libros/todos/docs/40anos_esp.pdf> (accessed February 5, 2022).

[12] Salmón (n. 10), 290.

and *Goiburú et al. v. Paraguay* (2006). In this way, the initial action of the IACtHR responded to the reality of a region suffering from severe and systematic human rights violations perpetrated mostly by State agents from the 1970s onward.[13]

Another reason for the silence during this stage is that following the inception of the Inter-American System there was no concerted focused on international migration, given that the region was mainly an origin for migration and not an area of transit, let alone a destination.[14] However, this situation has changed in recent years. Mobility trends between 2000 and 2010 indicate that the number of Latin American people living in countries other than those of their birth increased by 32 percent and by 35 percent in Central America.[15] Therefore, in the last decades "the intra-regional immigration increase in Latin America and the Caribbean is consistent with the processes of international mobility."[16]

These two circumstances bring to light the initial lack of response by the Inter-American System for the protection of the rights of migrants. However, the IACHR was able to rule, in specific but isolated cases, on certain obligations regarding the rights of migrants. In this regard, we have the Merits Report on the 1997 case of *Haitian Refugees v. the United States*,[17] which outlines protection guidelines on the prohibition of non-refoulement based on the rights to life, security, and personal integrity. Likewise, in the report on the case of *Loren Laroye Riebe Star, Jorge Barón Guttlein, and Rodolfo Izal Elorz v. Mexico* in 1999,[18] the IACHR sought to establish State obligations regarding judicial guarantees in administrative expulsion proceedings. These cases are only two incipient efforts that would be further developed in subsequent years.

2.2. Second Stage: Initial IAHRS Reactions

A foundational moment in the protection of the rights of migrants occurs with the release of the IACtHR's Advisory Opinion OC-18/03 on the legal status and rights of undocumented migrants. It is important to recall that in 2002 Mexico requested the opinion of the Inter-American Court mainly because the practices and interpretations of various States in the region were denying the labor rights of undocumented workers by using discriminatory criteria based on their immigration status.

---

[13] Ibid.
[14] Jorge Matínez Pizzaro and Cristián Oerrego Rivera, *Nuevas tendencias y dinámicas migratorias en América Latina y el Caribe* (CEPAL 2016), 12, <https://repositorio.cepal.org/bitstream/handle/11362/39994/1/S1600176_es.pdf> (accessed February 5, 2022).
[15] Ibid.
[16] Ibid.
[17] *Haitian Boat People (United States)* [1997] Case 10.675, IACHR, Merits Report No. 51/96.
[18] *Loren Laroye Riebe Star, Jorge Barón Guttlein and Rodolfo Izal Elorz (Mexico)* [1999] Case 11.610, IACHR, Report No. 49/99.

In this Advisory Opinion, the IACtHR explicitly refers to the rights of migrants and thus places migration as an axis of concern for human rights.[19] It also states that the objectives of migration policies must bear in mind the respect for human rights.[20] In other words, the power of the State to exercise its migration policies was recognized, considering it lawful for States to establish measures on the entry, permanence, or exit of migrants as workers in specific areas of production within their territory. However, this competency must follow measures for the protection of the human rights of all persons and, in particular, the human rights of workers.[21]

Regarding the main standards developed by the IACtHR, it is noteworthy that they established an unbreakable tie between the respect for the principle of equality and nondiscrimination and the obligation to guarantee and respect human rights. They even determined that this principle has *ius cogens* status.[22] Concerning the effects of the principle, the Court recognizes the vulnerability of migrants. It establishes that States cannot discriminate or tolerate discriminatory situations to the detriment of migrants, but they can grant a different treatment to documented compared to undocumented migrants. A State can differentiate between migrants and nationals as long as the differential treatment is reasonable, objective, proportional, and does not harm human rights.[23] It is relevant to stress that on this occasion the IACtHR established for the first time that the right to due process[24] must be recognized within the framework of the minimum guarantees provided to all migrants, regardless of their immigration status.[25] Regarding the rights of undocumented migrant workers, the IACtHR emphasized that having an immigration status cannot be a justification for depriving people of the enjoyment and exercise of their human rights, including labor rights.[26]

---

[19] Lila García, "Migraciones, Estado y una política del derecho humano a migrar: ¿hacia una nueva era en América Latina?" [2016] 88 *Colombia Internacional* 113. It should be recognized that before Advisory Opinion 18/03, the Inter-American Court in 1999 adopted Advisory Opinion 16/99, which recognizes the right of effective access to consular assistance for foreign persons deprived of liberty. This pronouncement, although of crucial importance, focuses mainly on the obligations of the States of origin. In that sense, we do not detail it in this chapter; see IACtHR, "The Right to Information on Consular Assistance within the Framework of the Guarantees of Due Process of Law," Advisory Opinion OC-16/99, October 1, 1999, Ser. A No. 16.

[20] IACtHR, "Juridical Condition and Rights of Undocumented Migrants," Advisory Opinion OC-18/03, September 17, 2003, para. 168.

[21] Ibid., para. 169.

[22] Ibid., paras. 85, 97.

[23] Ibid., para. 119.

[24] The Court considers it as "the list of minimum guarantees of due process is applied in the determination of rights and obligations of a 'civil, labor, tax or any other nature,'" therefore revealing that due process affects all these spheres and not just the criminal aspect, ibid., para. 124.

[25] Ibid., para. 122.

[26] Helena María Olea Rodríguez, *Los derechos humanos de las personas migrantes: Respuestas del Sistema Interamericano* (Instituto Interamericano de Derechos Humanos 2004), 77. IACtHR,

In summary, the IACtHR addresses the rights of migrants in the framework of the general obligations of nondiscrimination embodied in the American Convention on Human Rights (ACHR). These pronouncements and decisions laid the foundations for the protection of the human rights of migrants at the Latin American level. The jurisprudence and specialized doctrine that we will examine later reflects this.

Regarding its contentious jurisdiction, the IACtHR in 2010 issued its ruling on the case of *Vélez Loor v. Panama*. The process began after Mr. Jesús Vélez, who was from Ecuador, was arrested and held in a Panamanian prison and subsequently deported because he allegedly did not have with him the necessary documentation to remain in the country. This judgment is especially relevant because it was the first time the IACtHR ruled on the deprivation of liberty for migratory reasons.[27] The Court made it clear that detention for migratory reasons cannot have a punitive purpose. In this sense, the judgment marks an advance in the prohibition of the criminalization of irregular migration in the region, and it establishes that in cases involving migrants, detention and deprivation of liberty due to irregular migratory situations are only admissible when necessary and proportionate to the specific case, for the shortest possible time, and in response to the legitimate purposes alleged.[28] Additionally, where appropriate, migrants should be detained in establishments specifically intended for that purpose and following their legal situation, and not in common prisons or other places where they may be held together with persons accused or convicted of criminal offenses.[29] The IACtHR also established clear elements and guidelines concerning judicial guarantees in immigration procedures and regarding the sanctions that could be imposed for the violation of its provisions. Among these guarantees it is worth mentioning legal representation, the right to be notified of your rights under the Vienna Convention on Consular Relations, the right to communicate with a consular officer and to receive consular assistance within a reasonable timeframe, and the judicial guarantees contemplated in Article 8.1 of the ACHR.[30]

"Juridical Condition and Rights of Undocumented Migrants," Advisory Opinion OC-18/03, September 17, 2003, paras. 133–160.

[27] For a complete analysis of the sentence, see Romina Sijniensky, "Limitaciones al uso de medidas privativas de libertad para el control de los flujos migratorios: comentario al caso Vélez Loor Vs. Panamá de la Corte Interamericana de Derechos Humanos," in Opus Magna Constitucional Guatemalteco, Tomo IV (Instituto de Justicia Constitucional 2011), 71–97, <https://www.corteidh.or.cr/tablas/28053-4.pdf> (accessed February 5, 2022).
[28] Ibid.
[29] Ibid.
[30] Helena María Olea Rodríguez, "Migración (en la jurisprudencia de la Corte Interamericana de Derechos Humanos)" [2015] 9 *Revista en Cultura de la Legalidad* 249–272.

Another substantial contribution of this judgment is that it reaffirms the categorization of migrants as a "vulnerable group."[31] According to the IACtHR, the condition of vulnerability has an ideological dimension, and it differs depending on the different historical contexts of each State. It is maintained de jure (inequalities between nationals and foreigners within the law) and de facto (structural inequalities).[32] This vital recognition places migrants in a jurisprudential and interpretive category of the highest order, establishing reinforced protection for people on the move. Such jurisprudential development is one of the particularities of the Inter-American jurisprudence on the topic.

We can say, therefore, that there is now a coexistence between the recognition regarding the applicability of general obligations, such as the commitment to guarantee and respect human rights without discrimination, and what is explicitly applicable to migrants as a vulnerable group.

2.3. Third Stage: Development and Expansion of Standards

The IACtHR has developed robust jurisprudence on people on the move, which includes and is based upon the adoption of measures aimed at the protection of migrants.[33] In this regard, the IACtHR has developed standards based on the protection of the right to life, personal integrity, freedom of movement, and residence for refugees and asylum seekers, as well as irregular migrants, and it has also provided for the protection of family members and migrant children.[34] A list of these precedents is provided in Table II.9.1.

This development is first evidenced in the 2012 case of *Nadege Dorzema et al. v. the Dominican Republic*. This case involved the death of several individuals resulting from the use of force by military agents. The incident took place when a truck carrying a group of Haitian people entered Dominican Republic territory and Dominican military agents engaged in a high-speed pursuit that resulted in the truck overturning.[35] In this regard, the Court declared that the Dominican State was responsible for the events, particularly for violating their obligation to respect and guarantee the rights of all persons, as well as the obligation of normative adequacy (Articles 1 and 2 ACHR). Likewise, it is important to point out that the Court referred to indirect discrimination resulting from "norms, actions,

---

[31] Case *Vélez Loor v. Panama* [2010] IACtHR, Ser. C No. 218, para. 207.
[32] Ibid., para. 98.
[33] Belen Olmos, "Assessing the Evolution of the Inter-American Court of Human Rights in the Protection of Migrants' Rights: Past, Present, and Future" [2017] 21 *International Journal of Human Rights* 1483.
[34] Ibid.
[35] *Nadege Dorzema et al. v. the Dominican Republic* [2012] IACtHR, Ser. C No. 251, paras. 41–65.

Table II.9.1 Summary table of IACtHR contentious cases on rights of migrants.

Contentious cases	Rights provided in the ACHR	Group
The case of *Vélez Loor v. Panama* (2010)	• Due process in administrative procedures, access to justice: procedural guarantees (Arts. 8 and 25 ACHR) • The deprivation of liberty for migratory reasons (Art. 7.5 ACHR)	Migrants in an irregular situation
The case of *Nadege Dorzema and others v. Dominican Republic* (2012)	• Equality, nondiscrimination, and regulatory compliance obligation (Arts. 1 and 2 ACHR) • Prohibition of collective expulsions due to the principle of non-refoulement (Art. 22.9 ACHR)	Migrants
The case of *Familia Pacheco Tineo v. Bolivia* (2013)	• Principle of non-refoulement (Art. 22.9 ACHR) • Due process and access to justice within the framework of the refugee status determination (Arts. 8, 22.7, and 25 ACHR)	Asylum seekers and children
Case of expelled Dominicans and Haitians v. the Dominican Republic (2014)	• The obligation of normative adequacy (Art. 2 CADH) • Duty to prevent, avoid, and reduce statelessness (Arts. 1.1 and 27 ACHR)	Stateless persons

policies, or measures"[36] that in practice may produce negative effects for specific groups of people, in this case, migrants. The Court also referred to the prohibition of collective expulsions derived from the principle of non-refoulement (Article 22.9 ACHR). Expulsion proceedings are to be evaluated individually and according to the particular circumstances of each case.[37] Additionally, the Court refers to the standards of legality, necessity, and proportionality in the use of force, which must be applied in contexts of migratory operations as well.[38]

Another relevant case is *Pacheco Tineo family v. Bolivia*, in which the Court for the first time analyzed the situation of refugees. The Pachecos were a Peruvian family who were expelled from Bolivia, despite their refugee status, solely on the basis of their irregular entrance into the country as migrants. The Court developed standards regarding procedural guarantees in processes to determine

---

[36] Ibid., para. 235.
[37] Ibid., para. 175.
[38] Ibid., paras. 85–91.

refugee status through the joint interpretation of the right to seek and receive asylum, and the right to due process and access to justice (Articles 8, 22.7, and 25 ACHR).[39] Specific obligations were established[40] for States toward applicants, such as providing a competent interpreter and guidance concerning the procedure to be followed, legal advice and representation, and the opportunity to contact a UNHCR representative. The Court also established that the examination of the request would be performed by a competent and identified authority that duly substantiates its decisions, as well as respecting the personal information of applicants at all stages. Likewise, in case the request is rejected, the pertinent information needed to appeal the decision must be granted within a reasonable period. The State must also allow the applicant to remain in the country for as long as the appeal is reviewed.[41]

In 2014, the IACtHR achieved a third milestone when it had the opportunity to rule on statelessness. In the case of the *Expelled Dominicans and Haitians v. the Dominican Republic*, the Court established the duty of States to prevent, avoid, and reduce statelessness. The Dominican Republic had violated the rights of a group of Haitian and Dominican people by expelling them from their territory. Moreover, by applying these discriminatory measures, the State had hindered the access of the Haitian people to identification documents, which led the Court to affirm the existence of a systematic discriminatory pattern of expulsions against Haitian people and people of Haitian descent.[42]

In the case of *Expelled Dominicans and Haitians v. the Dominican Republic*, the Court established the obligation not to adopt practices or legislation concerning nationality that in practice leads to the increase of stateless persons.[43] Additionally, the right to nationality must be understood from two perspectives. On the one hand, the right to nationality endows the individual with essential legal protection to establish a connection with a specific State; on the other hand, the right to nationality protects the individual against arbitrarily being deprived of all political rights and civil rights.[44] Thus, when legislating on nationality, States should not only consider the duty to reduce statelessness but also the obligation to adopt an appropriate legal framework under the principle of equality and nondiscrimination.[45]

---

[39] *Case of the Pacheco Tineo Family v. Plurinational State of Bolivia* [2013] IACtHR, Ser. C No. 272, para. 154.
[40] Ibid., para. 159.
[41] Ibid.
[42] *Case of expelled Dominicans and Haitians v. the Dominican Republic* [2014] IACtHR, paras. 192–198.
[43] Salmón (n. 10), 318.
[44] IACtHR, *Case of expelled Dominicans and Haitians v. the Dominican Republic* (n. 42), para. 254.
[45] Ibid., para. 256.

Table II.9.2 Summary table of IACtHR advisory opinions on rights of migrants.

Advisory Opinion	Rights provided in the ACHR	Group
Advisory Opinion 18/03 (2003)	• Obligation to respect and guarantee human rights (Art. 1.1 CADH) • Principle of equality and nondiscrimination (Arts. 1 and 24 CADH) • The obligation of normative adequacy (Art. 2 CADH)	Migrants in an irregular situation
Advisory Opinion 21/14 (2014)	• Due process guarantees applicable in migratory processes involving girls and boys (Arts. 8, 19, and 25 CADH) • Guarantees for asylum applications (Arts. 19, 22.7, and 22.8 CADH) • Principle of nondeprivation of the freedom of children due to their immigration status (Arts. 7 and 19 CADH) • Right to family life (Arts. 11.2 and 17 CADH)	Children
Advisory Opinion 25/18 (2018)	• Right to seek and receive asylum (Art. 22.7 CADH)	Refugees and asylum seekers

The Court has also set standard within its consultative role, as shown in Table II.9.2. The IACtHR in 2014 issued Advisory Opinion 21/14 on "Rights and Guarantees of Children in the Context of Migration and/or in Need of International Protection."[46] In this ruling, the IACtHR referred to the particular vulnerability of this group and recognized that children are entitled to the right to seek and receive asylum and may, in consequence, submit applications for recognition of refugee status in their capacity, whether accompanied or not.[47] Among others, the IACtHR developed four main rights: (1) guarantees of due process applicable to migratory processes involving girls and boys, (2) guarantees for asylum applications, (3) the principle of nondeprivation of liberty of boys girls because of their migration status, and (4) the right to family life.

Another IACtHR pronouncement came in 2018: Advisory Opinion 25/18 on "The Institution of Asylum and its Recognition as a Human Right in the Inter-American System of Protection."[48] Indeed, the institution of asylum includes

---

[46] At the request of the States of Brazil, Argentina, Paraguay, and Uruguay.

[47] IACtHR, "Rights and Guarantees of Children in the Context of Migration and/or in Need of International Protection," Advisory Opinion OC-21/14, August 19, 2014, para. 80.

[48] At the request of the State of Ecuador, on the interpretation of asylum (Art. 22 CADH and Art. XXVII DADDH).

all guarantees[49] associated with the international protection of people who are forced to leave their country of nationality or habitual residence.[50] The primary purpose of the institution is to preserve: (i) the protection that a State offers to a person who is not of its nationality or who does not habitually reside in its territory; and, (ii) the principle of non-refoulement, or in others words the obligation not to deliver said person to a different State where his or her rights to life, security, freedom, and integrity are under imminent risk.[51] This principle requires the host State to carry out an individual and preliminary assessment of the risk of return, granting the opportunity for the person to express their reasons for fleeing, and deploy all necessary measures to protect the person in case a genuine risk is proven. Furthermore, this principle must be understood in conjunction with the prohibition of torture, since the duty of non-refoulement implies determining whether there is a well-founded presumption that a person is in danger of being subjected to torture or cruel, inhuman, or degrading treatment.

Likewise, the IACtHR notes that the right to seek and receive asylum goes beyond a State prerogative and must be recognized as such, with legislative measures that allow the effective exercise of such a right under Article 22.7 of the ACHR.[52] In both advisory opinions, the Inter-American Court specifies that the right to seek and receive asylum applies to refugees under the traditional rationale and according to the expanded definition of the Cartagena Declaration.[53]

In short, the Court has recognized the precarious position of migrants. It has also provided rights such as due process in administrative procedures and access to justice.[54] Additionally, in a more concrete specification process, the

---

[49] Refugee status, territorial asylum, diplomatic asylum, and equal protection.

[50] IACtHR, "The Institution of Asylum and its Recognition as a Human Right in the Inter-American System of Protection," Advisory Opinion OC-25/28, May 30, 2018, Ser. A No. 25, para. 65.

[51] IDEHPUCP, *Documento resumen de la OC25/18: La institución del asilo y su reconocimiento como derecho humano en el SIDH* (IDEHPUCP 2018), 2, <https://cdn01.pucp.education/idehpucp/wp-content/uploads/2018/10/01223946/dr-oc-25-18.pdf> (accessed February 5, 2022).

[52] IACtHR, *The Institution of Asylum and its Recognition as a Human Right in the Inter-American System of Protection* (n. 50), paras. 122–123.

[53] Article 3 of Cartagena Declaration established : "Hence the definition or concept of a refugee to be recommended for use in the region is one which, in addition to containing the elements of the 1951 Convention and the 1967 Protocol, includes among refugees persons who have fled their country because their lives, safety or freedom have been threatened by generalized violence, foreign aggression, internal conflicts, massive violation of human rights or other circumstances which have seriously disturbed public order." The Cartagena Declaration seeks to complement the conventional definition in order to ensure greater protection for people who have experienced any of its five key determinants of displacement. Cartagena Declaration on Refugees, Colloquium on the International Protection of Refugees in Central America, Mexico and Panama. Adopted by the Colloquium on the International Protection of Refugees in Central America, Mexico and Panama, held at Cartagena, Colombia from November 19 to 22, 1984.

For more information, see Luisa Feline Freier, Isabel Berganza, and Cécile Blouin, *The Cartagena Refugee Definition and Venezuelan Displacement in Latin America* (International Migration 2020).

[54] Procedural guarantees, detention and deprivation of liberty, equality and nondiscrimination, an obligation of normative adequacy, prohibition of collective expulsions, the principle of

Inter-American System has addressed with particular interest the situation of migrant children, both in its contentious cases and in its advisory opinions. Nevertheless, it is appropriate to mention some pending issues on this matter. See Tables II.9.1 and II.9.2.

2.4. Pending Issues

The rights of migrants in the region are still a matter of study and discussion for the IAHRS. The central bodies of the System have undoubtedly given answers to the protection and guarantee of migrant rights. However, the response has not always been timely and has focused on the protection of some rights rather than others. The reinforced protection of vulnerable groups in the IAHRS is at an early stage. While State obligations concerning migrant children have been recognized, there is little or no jurisprudence on other vulnerable groups that also move across borders, such as women, the disabled, Indigenous populations, and victims of human trafficking. The European and UN human rights systems have greater jurisprudential and soft law development for these groups.

Attention to the particular needs and vulnerabilities of these groups has resulted in reinforcing the content of the right to non-refoulement to serve as an additional tool for the protection of the specific human rights enjoyed by these people.[55] This interpretation comes from the jurisprudence of the IAHRS, from pronouncements by UN human rights bodies, and from precedents set by the European Court of Human Rights (ECtHR).[56] In the last three years the IACHR has not submitted any substantive merits reports on alleged violations of migrant rights to the IACtHR. However, in 2018 the IACHR granted a precautionary measure to a Venezuelan woman with HIV who was at risk of deportation from Panama.[57] This decision demonstrates the level of interest and concern that the IACHR has for the situation of migrants in the region.[58]

---

non-refoulement, due process and access to justice within the framework of refuge request procedures, obligation of normative adequacy, duty to prevent, avoid, and reduce statelessness.

[55] Crisbeth Vigo, *Estándares jurídicos para garantizar el derecho a la no devolución en el sistema interamericano de derechos humanos: especial atención a algunos grupos en situación de vulnerabilidad* (PUCP 2019).

[56] See *M.S.S. v. Belgium and Greece* [2011] ECtHR App. no. 30696/09; *Sufi and Elmi v. the United Kingdom* [2011] ECtHR App. nos. 8319/07 and 11449/07; *Yoh-Ekale Mwanje v. Belgium* [2011] ECtHR App. no. 10486/10; *N. v. United Kingdom* [2008] App. no. 26565/05; and *D. v. the United Kingdom* [1997] ECtHR App. no. 30240/69.

[57] IACHR, Resolution 81/18, Precautionary Measure 490/18—M.B.B.P., regarding Panama, October 15, 2018, <https://www.oas.org/es/cidh/decisiones/pdf/2018/81-18MC490-18-PN.pdf> (accessed February 5, 2022).

[58] See also IACHR, Resolution 2/18, "Forced Migration of Venezuelan People," March 14, 2018. The IACHR grants precautionary measures to protect migrant children separated from their families

Finally, despite the contribution of the IACHR to the justiciability of economic, social, and cultural rights,[59] there is still a long road ahead regarding the development of these rights in relation to the protection of migrant populations.

3. The Transformative Impact of IAHRS Standards in Latin America: An Analysis in Light of the Legal Frameworks

In this section we seek to identify how the standards of the Inter-American System influence and transform the legal frameworks of Latin American States. The normative framework on migration and asylum matters in the region is complex and heterogeneous; therefore, it is difficult to identify the overall impact of the IAHRS on this matter. Additionally, domestic judgments are increasingly heeding IAHRS standards. All this translates into a complicated relationship between the IAHRS and States on this pressing regional issue.

3.1. The Transformative Impact on the Normative Frameworks on Migration and Asylum in the Region

The normative frameworks of the countries in the region do not treat migration uniformly. Most South American countries—with the exception of Chile, Colombia, and Paraguay—have liberalized their regulatory framework to include more protective provisions for foreigners and have thus become one of the areas with the most considerable discourse in favor of the rights of migrants.[60] Yet these reforms have taken place at different times and coexist with regulatory frameworks based on the doctrine of national security. Additionally, regulation does not always move towards improving the protection of migrants' rights. There have also been some setbacks, as was the case in Argentina.[61]

---

in the United States, <https://www.oas.org/es/cidh/prensa/comunicados/2018/186.asp> (accessed February 5, 2022).

[59] Christian Courtis, "El aporte de los sistemas internacionales de derechos humanos internacionales a la justicibilidad de los derechos económicos, sociales y culturales," in Magdalena Cervantes Algayde et al. (eds.), ¿Hay justicia para los derechos económicos, sociales y culturales? Debate abierto a propósito de la reforma constitucional en materia de derechos humanos (Suprema Corte de Justicia de la Nación 2014).

[60] Diego Acosta Arcarazo and Luisa Feline Freier, "Turning the Immigration Policy Paradox Upside Down? Populist Liberalism and Discursive Gaps in South America" [2018] 49 *International Migration Review* 659–696.

[61] Pablo Ceriani Cernadas, *Migration Policies and Human Rights in Latin America: Progressive Practices, Old Challenges, Worrying Setbacks, and New Threats*, Policy Brief (2018) Global Campus of Human Rights, <https://repository.gchumanrights.org/bitstream/handle/20.500.11825/629/PoliencyBrief_LatinAmerica_ok.pdf?sequence=4&isAllowed=y> (accessed February 5, 2022).

According to Pablo Ceriani, there are three types of normative migration frameworks in the region:[62] (1) regulatory frameworks derived from military dictatorships, (2) recent regulatory frameworks, and (3) those that are undergoing a reform process.[63] The first category includes those with the least degree of incorporation of IAHRS standards, while those in the second group incorporate most of them. In the first group, Chile—and to a lesser extent Paraguay[64]—offers the most worrying case. For example, Chile has the oldest migration law: Decree 1094, adopted by Pinochet in 1975 and based on the doctrine of national security, is still in force.[65] To date, Chile has not adopted a new normative migration framework despite a legislative proposal with a clear restrictive approach presented by President Sebastián Piñera.[66] Another case worth mentioning is Colombia, which does not have a law regarding migration but only specific provisions adopted by the executive.[67] According to Donna Cabrera, Gabriela Cano, and Alexandra Castro, these norms do not establish a

---

[62] Pablo Cernadas only analyzes the strict census migration regulation frameworks. We decided to incorporate asylum rules into this classification based on our definition of migration and the importance of international protection standards.

[63] Pablo Ceriani Cernadas, "Luces y sombras en la legislación migratoria latinoamericana" [2011] 233 *Revista Nueva Sociedad* 75. At the time of writing, Chile and Colombia were in the process of reforming their migration law. In the case of Chile, after many years of inertia, a bill was presented in April 2018 with a restrictive approach. In the case of Colombia, a reform was presented in 2019 that, according to the analysis made by a group of universities and civil society organizations, must be modified to include the IHRL standards on migration. See Ministerio del Interior y Seguridad Pública, "Minuta: Reforma Migratoria y Política Nacional de Migraciones y Extranjería" (April 8, 2018), <https://cdn.digital.gob.cl/filer_public/b0/09/b0099d94-2ac5-44b9-9421-5f8f3 7cf4fc5/nueva_ley_de_migracion.pdf> (accessed February 5, 2022); Carolina Stefoni, Claudia Silva, and Sebastián Brito, "Migración venezolana en Chile: La (des)esperanza de los jóvenes," in Luciana Gandini, Victoria Prieto Rosas, and Fernando Lozano-Ascencio (eds.), *Crisis y migración de población venezolana: Entre la desprotección y la seguridad jurídica en Latinoamérica* (UNAM 2019); Victoria Finn and Sebastian Umpierrez de Reguero, "Inclusive Language for Exclusive Policies: Restrictive Migration Governance in Chile, 2018" [2020] 11 *Latin American Policy* 42–61; CODHES, Servicio Jesuita a Refugiados Colombia, Programa de asistencia legal a población con necesidad de protección internacional y víctimas del conflicto armado—Corporación Opción Legal, Universidad Nacional de Colombia, Universidad de los Andes, Universidad Externado de Colombia y Pastoral Social-Caritas Colombia, "Document for analysis of bill number Senate 036 through which principles and regulatory framework of the comprehensive immigration policy of the Colombian state are established" (March 20, 2020), <https://col.jrs.net/wp-content/uploads/sites/14/2020/06/AnálisisProyLeyMigraciones2020.pdf> (accessed February 5, 2022).

[64] The Migration Law, Law No. 978/96, 1996, <https://www.bacn.gov.py/leyes-paraguayas/3211/ley-n-978-migraciones> (accessed February 5, 2022).

[65] Francisca Vargas Rivas, "Una Ley de migraciones con un enfoque de derechos humanos," in Tomás Vial (ed.), *Informe Anual sobre Derechos Humanos en Chile 2018* (Universidad Diego Portales 2018), 488, <https://derechoshumanos.udp.cl/cms/wp-content/uploads/2020/12/Vargas-Ley-Migraciones-2.pdf> (accessed February 5, 2022).

[66] Carolina Stefoni, Claudia Silva, and Sebastian Brito, "Migración venezolana en Chile: La (des)esperanza de los jóvenes," in Luciana Gandini, Victoria Prieto Rosas, and Fernando Lozano-Ascencio (eds.), *Crisis y migración de población venezolana: Entre la desprotección y la seguridad jurídica en Latinoamérica* (UNAM 2019).

[67] Decree 1067 of 2015 and Resolution 6045 of 2017.

protective legal framework for all migrants. On the contrary, they grant broad discretionary powers to immigration authorities.[68]

We have found that most States in the second group have adopted new regulatory frameworks in the last ten years. It is difficult to categorically affirm that these normative frameworks respond to the development of the IAHRS.[69] However, it is clear that the general concern about migration and the specific concern regarding migration as a human rights matter have a lot to do with the expansion of these normative frameworks. Therefore, we propose looking into the normative frameworks of the region according to the developmental stages of the IAHRS.

A chronological list of norms adopted in the Americas is found in Table II.9.3.

Table II.9.3 demonstrates that the most productive periods of reforms to normative migration and asylum frameworks correspond to the two most fruitful stages of the IAHRS.[70] This development can be explained by the significant concern of those States that were traditionally considered origin sites for migration, such as Peru, Ecuador, and Bolivia, but later became transit and destination sites. Regional States also became more concerned about the human rights of foreigners due to changes in migration dynamics. In addition, the obligations imposed by the IAHRS by themselves generate the need to adapt national normative frameworks.

Recent regulatory frameworks are adopting a human rights approach based on the right to equality and nondiscrimination as a basis for the recognition of the rights of foreigners.[71] Throughout the region, we find in these norms a range of standards related to the end of migration criminalization, the right to non-refoulement, and guarantees of due process.[72] Likewise, despite its nonbinding nature, the expanded definition of the Cartagena Declaration has been incorporated into the laws of fifteen countries in the region.[73] Additionally, there is a trend whereby regulatory frameworks now recognize these standards to a larger extent (in the last stage), especially in the last four years. For instance, this is the

---

[68] Donna Catalina Cabrera Serrano, Gabriela M. Cano Salazar, and Alexandra Castro Franco, "Procesos recientes de movilidad humana entre Venezuela y Colombia 2016–2018," in Luciana Gandini, Victoria Prieto Rosas, and Fernando Lozano-Ascencio (eds.), *Crisis y migración de población venezolana: Entre la desprotección y la seguridad jurídica en Latinoamérica* (UNAM 2019).

[69] Pablo Ceriani Cernadas comments that the normative changes in the area of migration regarding the countries of the region toward a human rights approach can be explained in part by the approval of the Mercosur Residence Agreement in 2002. Cernadas (n. 63).

[70] We refer here to the third and fourth moment in the development of standards of the IAHRS.

[71] All regulatory frameworks refer to this principle in their national regulations on migrants and refugees, except Belize.

[72] Cernadas (n. 63).

[73] Cécile Blouin, Isabel Berganza, and Luisa Feline Feier, "The spirit of Cartagena? Applying the extended refugee definition to Venezuelans in Latin America" [2020] 63 *Forced Migration Review* 64–66, <https://www.fmreview.org/cities/blouin-berganza-freier> (accessed February 5, 2022).

Table II.9.3 Adoption of the normative frameworks on migration and asylum matters according to the development stage of the IACHR.

State	Normative framework
Normative frameworks adopted during the stage of silence (until 2002)	
Chile	Decree 1094 (1975)
Paraguay	Law No. 978/96, Migration Law (1996)
Brazil	Refugee Act (1997)
Belize	Immigration Act, Chapter 156 (2000) Refugees Act, Chapter 165 (2000)
Venezuela	Organic Law on Refugees or Refugees and Asylum Seekers (2001)
Peru	Law No. 27891, Refugee Law (2002)
Paraguay	Law No. 1938, General Law on Refugees (2002)
El Salvador	Decree No. 918 (2002)[a]
Normative frameworks adopted during the initial IAHRS reactions stage (2003–2010)	
Argentina	Migration Law No. 25871 (2003)
	General Law on Refugee Recognition and Protection Law No. 26165 (2006)
Venezuela	Immigration Law, Law No. 37944 (2004)
Honduras	Decree No. 208-2003, Migration and Foreigners Law (2004)
Uruguay	Law No. 18076, Refugee Status Law (2006)
	Law 18250 Migration (2008)
Panamá	Decree Law No. 3 On the National Migration Service, the Immigration Career and Other Provisions (2008)
Costa Rica	Law 8764 Law on Migration and Foreigners (2009)
México	Law on Refugees and Complementary Protection (2011)
	Migration Law (2011)
Normative frameworks adopted during the standards development stage (2011 onward)	
Chile	Law No. 20430, establishes provisions on refugee protection (2010)
Nicaragua	Law No. 761, General Law on Migration and Aliens (2011)
Bolivia	Refugee Protection Law No. 251 (2012)
	Migration Law No. 370 (2013)
Colombia	Decree No. 2840, Whereby the Procedure for the Recognition of the Status of Refugee, rules on the Advisory Commission for the Determination of the Refugee Status and other provisions (2013)

(continued)

Table II.9.3 Continued

State	Normative framework
Guatemala	Migration Code (2016)
Brazil	Migration Law 13445 (2017)
Ecuador	Human Mobility Law (2017)[b]
Peru	Legislative Decree No. 1350, Migration Law (2017)
Panama	Executive Decree No. 5 (2018)[c]
El Salvador	Decree No. 286: Special Law on Migration and Foreigners (2019)

[a] Regulates the protection of refugees.
[b] It is an integral framework on migrants, refugees, stateless persons, and victims of human trafficking.
[c] It regulates the protection of refugees.

case for Ecuador's 2017 Human Mobility Law, which recognizes all the standards of the IAHRS.[74]

There is also a tendency in some countries to set higher standards than those established by the IAHRS. Argentina and Uruguay, for example, recognize the right to migration in their national migration laws.[75] Ecuador, however, is the most paradigmatic case, recognizing the right to migrate and universal citizenship within its Constitution,[76] rights not yet developed within the framework of the IAHRS. However, there have been some setbacks. In 2017, Argentina adopted the National Emergency Decree (DNU) No. 70/2017,[77] which restricts the rights of migrants previously granted by Law 25871. Additionally, Peru, following an influx of migration from Venezuela,[78] adopted temporary norms characterized

---

[74] The right to non-refoulement for any person and the guarantees of due process in migratory administrative procedures and in the framework of the refugee status determination; the duty to prevent, avoid, and reduce statelessness, the guarantees of due process applicable in migratory processes (boys and girls), the principle of nondeprivation of liberty of children by their family unit situation.
[75] Art. 4 of Argentina Migration Law and Art. 1 of Uruguayan Migration Law.
[76] Constitution of Ecuador, 2008, Art. 40 raises, among others, the right to migrate, and 416.6, universal citizenship.
[77] Claudia Pedone et al., "De la estabilidad económica y la regularidad jurídica al ajuste socioeconómico y la precariedad del trabajo: migración venezolana en la Ciudad Autónoma de Buenos Aires," in Luciana Gandini, Victoria Prieto Rosas, and Fernando Lozano-Ascencio (eds.), *Crisis y migración de población venezolana: Entre la desprotección y la seguridad jurídica en Latinoamérica* (UNAM 2019).
[78] Almost 5.7 million Venezuelans had fled from their country. Colombia and Peru are the main destination countries. UNHCR and IOM. R4V official website (2021), <https://www.r4v.info/es/refugiadosymigrantes> (accessed February 5, 2022).

by their lack of coherence or clear legal grounds.[79] Furthermore, Ecuador has been increasing the entry barriers for Venezuelan people, marking a setback to its constitutional framework.[80]

The complexity and heterogeneity of the adaptation process of regulatory reform—unfinished and many times more de jure than de facto—can be explained by three main reasons. The first is linked to the migratory profile of the countries that are both expellers and receivers of migrant populations. Colombia, for example, receives the largest amount of Venezuelans and continues to be a country that expels people in need of international protection.[81] In countries, such as Colombia and Peru, that are facing new realities such as Venezuelan migration, we observe the fragility of this opening trend in migration policies. Although both countries offer new possibilities to protect Venezuelan migrants this trend coexists with setbacks, inconsistencies, and instabilities.[82] Another reason has to do with the relationship between States and the IAHRS in general. Different States in the region are questioning the IAHRS in an attempt to weaken the System.[83] The number of cases and the number of public hearings before the IACHR are signs, among others, of the level of contact between States and the System. This can also influence how States receive these standards. Third, the general situation of human rights and the rule of law in a given country are key elements to consider when understanding progress and setbacks. Thus, political changes, the use of migrants as scapegoats, and other violations of rights shed some light onto this process of regulatory reform.

---

[79] Cécile Blouin and Luisa Feline Freier, "Población venezolana en Lima: entre la regularización y la precariedad," in Luciana Gandini, Victoria Prieto Rosas, and Fernando Lozano-Ascencio (eds.), *Crisis y migración de población venezolana: Entre la desprotección y la seguridad jurídica en Latinoamérica* (UNAM 2019). Cécile Blouin et al., *Estudio sobre el perfil socio económico de la población venezolana y sus comunidades de acogida: una mirada hacia la inclusión* (PUCP 2019), <http://idehpucp.pucp.edu.pe/lista_publicaciones/estudio-sobre-el-perfil-socio-economico-de-la-poblacion-venezolana-y-sus-comunidades-de-acogida-una-mirada-hacia-la-inclusion-2/> (accessed February 5, 2022).

[80] Ramírez Jacques, Yoharlis Lináres, and Emilio Useche, "(Geo)políticas migratorias, inserción laboral y xenofobia: Migrantes venezolanos en Ecuador," in Cécile Blouin (ed.), *Después de la llegada: Realidades de la migración venezolana* (Themis-PUCP 2019); Diego Acosta, Cécile Blouin, and Luisa Feline Freier, "La emigración venezolana: Respuestas latinoamericanas" [2019] 3 *Documentos de trabajo*, <https://www.fundacioncarolina.es/wp-content/uploads/2019/04/DT_FC_03.pdf> (accessed February 5, 2022).

[81] Liliana Lyra Jubilut and Rachel de Oliveira Lopes, "Forced Migration and Latin America: Peculiarities of a Peculiar Region in Refugee Protection" [2018] 56 *Archive des Völkerrechts* 131–154.

[82] Ibid. Cécile Blouin, "Complejidades y contradicciones de la política migratoria hacia la migración venezolana en el Perú" [2021] 106 *Colombia Internacional* 141–164.

[83] Salmón (n. 10).

3.2. The Recognition of the Standards of the IACHR in the Judicial and Constitutional Spheres

This section analyzes the judicial and constitutional spheres of the regional States and their use of IAHRS standards on migration matters.[84] It should be mentioned that this development is still in its initial stages and differs depending on the country or subregion. This can be explained by the difficulties that foreigners encounter—as a generally excluded demographic—when attempting to access justice and by the diversity of the existing judicial control mechanisms in migration matters. In recent years, however, we have observed an increasing number of pronouncements on migration that develop human rights standards for migrants. In this section, we present the most relevant judgments from different subregions to make visible the importance of the IAHRS in the development of standards.[85]

The Argentine case is the most obvious place to start. Unlike in other countries where judicial review comes by exception through *amparos* or habeas corpus, Argentine judges exercise control over immigration measures.[86] This has generated extensive jurisprudence on immigration control. In a recent 2018 judgment, the Federal Contentious Administrative Chamber indicated that Argentina's immigration policy must consider the special vulnerability of migrants, since their situation can become extremely fragile, as stressed by Advisory Opinion 03/10 and the Case of *Dominican and Haitian People v. Dominican Republic*. Additionally, the court reaffirmed its standards on the minimum guarantees of due process that should be applied to the immigration procedures established in the *Vélez Loor* case against Panama and in the IACHR's report on human mobility.[87]

Mexico offers a further elaboration of this dynamic. In relation to a 2013 case on immigration detention and due process, the Mexican Supreme Court made

---

[84] For a broader look on transformative constitutionalism: Armin von Bogdandy, "Ius Constitutionale Commune en América Latina: una mirada a un constitucionalismo transformador" [2015] 34 *Revista Derecho del Estado* 3.

[85] Due to difficulties in accessing complete information, this is not an exhaustive review of all the judgments on this matter in Latin America but an initial approach to the subject.

[86] Lila García Emilse, "Decisiones de la Corte Suprema de Justicia de la Nación (Argentina) sobre control migratorio (2004–2018)" [2019] 3 *Périplos: Revista Las Políticas Migratorias* 84.

[87] Federal Contentious-Administrative Chamber—Chamber V, Judicial Power of the Nation of Argentina. File No. 3061/2017. Judgment of March 22, 2018, <https://www.cels.org.ar/web/wp-content/uploads/2018/03/fallo-camara-migrantes.pdf> (accessed February 5, 2022). Another relevant decision is Attorney General's Office, "Zhang, Peili" Cause No. FMP 81048271/2009. Judgment of April 27, 2016, <https://www.mpf.gob.ar/dictamenes/2016/VAbramovich/abril/Z_FMP_81048271_2009.pdf> (accessed February 5, 2022). For an analysis of the judgments in immigration matters in Argentina, see also Diego Morales, "Derechos humanos de los migrantes en Argentina: Apuntes sobre nuevas perspectivas jurisprudenciales" [2012] 1 *Revista Derecho Público* 345.

express reference to Advisory Opinion OC-16/99.[88] A more recent case on immigration detentions before the Eighth District Court of Amparo concerning administrative matters in Mexico City draws on different IACHR standards contained in Advisory Opinion 18/03, *Vélez Loor v. Panama* and the *Pacheco Tineo Family v. Bolivia* cases of the Inter-American Court.[89]

The Andean region of Chile is interesting for our purposes because the country's Supreme Court has generated a systematization of immigration cases brought to this Court between 2010 and 2018.[90] It reveals that the Chilean Supreme Court has been willing to rule on the guarantees of due process in the context of migration and is following the jurisprudence of the Inter-American Court, though without mentioning it explicitly.[91] Similarly, in relation to cases about the right to nationality, the Chilean Supreme Court makes direct reference to the ACHR.[92] Additionally, the Santiago Court of Appeals analyzed the case of migrants living in an irregular situation, making express reference to the provisions of the Inter-American Court in the Advisory Opinion on the legal status and rights of undocumented migrants.[93]

In Ecuador, one can identify different judgments of its Constitutional Court regarding international protection, which take into account the standards of the IAHRS.[94] A recent case involves an appeal for precautionary measures filed against the imposition of passport requirements for Venezuelan people entering Ecuadorian territory. The Constitutional Court of Ecuador declared this measure inadmissible, arguing that border controls that deny Venezuelan people entry and then return to their point of departure would imply a violation of the right to non-refoulement. To this end, the Court made direct references to the

---

[88] Supreme Court of Justice of the Nation. Direct protection under review 517/2011. Judgment of January 23, 2013, <https://www2.scjn.gob.mx/ConsultaTematica/PaginasPub/DetallePub.aspx?AsuntoID=125754> (accessed February 5, 2022).

[89] Eighth District Court of Amparo in administrative matters of Mexico City. Judgment No. 357/20188 June 2018, <http://cmdpdh.org/wp-content/uploads/2018/07/sentencia.pdf> (accessed February 5, 2022).

[90] Supreme Court of Chile. Legal Collections Magazine: "Migrantes" (Dirección de Estudios de la Corte Suprema: Santiago 2019), <http://decs.pjud.cl/download/revista-colecciones-juridicas-migrantes/> (accessed February 5, 2022).

[91] Miriam Henriquex Viñas, "La jurisprudencia de la Corte Suprema como agente transformador en la protección de la libertad personal de los migrantes" (2020) MPIL Research Paper Series No. 2020-04, 12, <https://papers.ssrn.com/sol3/papers.cfm?abstract_id=3545196> (accessed February 5, 2022).

[92] For instance: Supreme Court File 10.897/2013, Judgment of January 14, 2014.

[93] Court of Appeals of Santiago, Cuartel Borgoño Case. File 351-2013. Judgment of March 9, 2013, <https://studylib.es/doc/5048594/sentencia-de-la-corte-de-apelaciones--santiago—cuatro> (accessed February 5, 2022).

[94] Constitutional Court of Ecuador. Judgment No. 002-14-SIN-CC. Case No. 0056-12-IN and 0003-12-IA, August 14, 2014, <https://www.uasb.edu.ec/documents/62017/1489475/002-14-SIN-CC/91d0c9de-a640-4c0a-a8dc-50efe2e4db0e?version=1.0.> (accessed February 5, 2022). Constitutional Court of Ecuador. Judgment No. 090-15-SEP-CC. Case No. 1567-13-EP, March 25, 2015.

ACHR, particularly Article 22.8, as well as several of the precedents mentioned in this chapter, such as the *Nadege Dorzema et al. v. the Dominican Republic* and the *Pacheco Tineo Family v. the Plurinational State of Bolivia* cases.[95]

When considering the situation in Peru, it is important to mention a recently adopted judgment from the country's Constitutional Court.[96] The Court cited the *Vélez Loor v. Panama* and the *Pacheco Tineo Family v. Bolivia* cases in order to determine that Peru must respect at all times the standards of due process, as well as the guarantees derived from it, even if the migrant person is in an irregular situation. Another compelling case from Peru is the habeas corpus petition granted in 2018 against the decision of the National Superintendence of Migration to impose mandatory passports for Venezuelan people entering Peru. Although the request was declared partially founded, the National Superintendency of Migration and the Ministry of Interior appealed the judgment and obtained a new ruling that completely revoked the previous judgment.[97] Now the Constitutional Court must determine, as was the case for Ecuador, the limits of migration policy concerning the rights of Venezuelan migrants, especially concerning the right to non-refoulement.

Additionally, we find in the jurisprudence of the Constitutional Court of Colombia some progress regarding standards that go beyond those laid out by the IAHRS. The Columbian Constitutional Court has recently set standards for the right to health of Venezuelan migrants by using standards from the Universal System of Human Rights. On that basis, the Court ordered that the right to health of a Venezuelan woman who was denied radiotherapy and chemotherapy treatments be guaranteed, as well as to a minor who needed an operation. This judgment sets standards not yet established in the IAHRS and addresses some of the pending problems mentioned previously.[98]

In short, this quick review shows that the IACHR has played a crucial role in the adoption of new normative frameworks and in responses to a number of specific cases put before several of the region's domestic justice systems that determine and specify the content of the rights of migrants. Additionally, the region

---

[95] Constitutional Court of Ecuador. Sentence relapsed in Case No. 0014-19-IN, March 27, 2019, <http://doc.corteconstitucional.gob.ec:8080/alfresco/d/d/workspace/SpacesStore/327ea82c-7604-4a52-8261-8a189c85b1bf/0014-19-in-auto> (accessed February 5, 2022).

[96] Peruvian Constitutional Court File No. 02744-2015-PA/TC. Judgment from November 8, 2016, <https://www.tc.gob.pe/jurisprudencia/2016/02744-2015-AA.pdf> (accessed February 5, 2022).

On the award see the following note: <http://idehpucp.pucp.edu.pe/notas-informativas/una-sentencia-galardonada-lo-establece-tc-derechos-los-migrantes/> (accessed February 5, 2022).

[97] Superior Court of Lima. File No. 06488-2018-0-1801-JR-PE-05. Judgment of October 5, 2018, <https://static.legis.pe/wp-content/uploads/2018/10/Exp.-06488-2018-0-1801-JR-PE-05-2-32-Legis.pe_.pdf>.

[98] Colombian Constitutional Court, Judgment T-500/18, Guardianship action presented by Luisa Alejandra Bravo Sainea and Lázaro Valdés Carrillo, through a legal representative, against the Special Administrative Unit for Migration Colombia-Regional Andina, Judgment of December 9, 2018.

has proven to be open to the development of standards related to what in this chapter we have called pending issues. With this, mutual feedback and possible transformative impacts are observed between the IAHRS and a number of States in the region. In this sense, these national developments can help to consolidate a protection framework for migrants in the region and inspire the IAHRS to further develop standards on issues still pending.

4. Concluding Remarks

It can be said that despite the identified progress, the protection of the rights of migrants is still a relatively new issue for the IAHRS. As yet there is no consolidation of standards on the matter of migration within the IAHRS. Given the regional migration dynamics, it is likely that in the following years standards will have addressed some of the pending issues mentioned above.

With regards to transformative impacts, we have seen that the majority of the States in the region have adopted increasingly protective internal normative frameworks that guarantee the rights of migrants. However, numerous gaps persist between the regulation and its implementation. Likewise, when facing specific crises—such as the Venezuelan one—there have been some setbacks regarding the construction of normative frameworks. Regarding these setbacks, it is vital to remember the standards of the IAHRS. On the other hand, however, the IAHRS standards have influenced the judicial and constitutional work of Latin American States, particularly Chile, Ecuador, Argentina, and Colombia. In some cases, national courts have set standards that go beyond those raised by the IAHRS. Nonetheless, significant challenges remain concerning the transformative impacts linked to the still incipient role of national courts in defending the rights of migrants in the region and their possible setbacks. We should finally note that the recent rulings in Ecuador and Peru following Venezuelan migration suggest the relevance of strategic litigation in this field, a point that should not be neglected.

II.10
The Human Right to Defend Human Rights in the Inter-American System
Normative Enforcement and Transformative Impact of the Case of *Escaleras Mejía and Others v. Honduras*

By Melina Girardi Fachin

1. Introduction

This chapter examines how the Inter-American Human Rights System (Inter-American System, or IAHRS) responds to violations of the rights of human rights defenders in the framework of the *right to defend rights*. Focusing primarily on the case of *Escaleras Mejía and Others v. Honduras*, decided by the Inter-American Court of Human Rights (Inter-American Court, or IACtHR) in 2018, the chapter addresses common challenges in the implementation of protections for human rights defenders in Latin America.

Defending human rights in Latin America has always been risky due to the region's high rates of violence. The Inter-American System began to address this challenge in 2000 in response to demands from civil society. The IAHRS developed and started to enforce standards specific to human rights defenders.[1]

Violence against human rights defenders has also increased alongside the spread of the democratic setbacks and authoritarianism throughout Latin America in recent years. For example, city councilor Marielle Franco, a Brazilian human rights defender who spoke out against the police's deadly raids in densely populated favelas, was assassinated in 2018. Her murdered remains unresolved, although some suspect the involvement of high-level Brazilian political authorities.

All violations of the rights of human rights defenders, including those of the rights of defender Carlos Escaleras Mejía, are attempts to silence those who draw

---

[1] See, e.g., IACHR, "Report on the situation of human rights defenders in the Americas" (2006); IACHR, "Second Report on the situation of human rights defenders and defenders in the Americas" (2012).

attention to rights violations and impunity in the face of these violations. The recent IACtHR case of *Escaleras Mejía and others v. Honduras*, the focus of this chapter, further examines the normative grounds of the right to defend rights in the inter-American *corpus juris*.[2]

Escaleras Mejía concerns the killing of Carlos Escaleras Mejía, a mayoral candidate and environmental activist, in 1997. Before his death, Escaleras Mejía was threatened, pressured, and offered bribes to withdraw his candidacy. Escaleras Mejía has been recognized as a human rights defender because he publicly denounced many illegal activities that harmed the environment.

This chapter is divided into three sections. The first section explains who human rights defenders are and how global, regional, and domestic legal systems protect them. The second section analyzes both the procedure and the substance of the IACtHR's judgment in the case of *Escaleras Mejía*. Finally, the third section examines the transformative impact of the Inter-American System on human rights defenders' work in Latin America, especially at the current moment.

This subject was selected to demonstrate the gap between inter-American standards and human rights practices in the region. The specific case, *Escaleras Mejía*, will be analyzed in detail not only because it is one of the Inter-American Court's most recent judgments on the subject but also because it contributes significantly to the elaboration of the right to defend rights. The line of jurisprudence leading up to this case will also be analyzed, as will this jurisprudence's impact on the IAHRS, States, and, most importantly, victims.

The chapter focuses on the transformative potential of the Inter-American System and its impact about human rights in the Americas. The IAHRS has succeeded in elaborating and disseminating norms related to the respect for human dignity through strengthening the inter-American *corpus juris*.[3] Inter-American standards have enabled reductions in national deficits, encouraged advances in legislative frameworks and public policies on human rights, and prevented setbacks in the protection of human rights.

The standards on human rights defenders developed by the IACtHR have facilitated the protection of defenders themselves and of those on whose behalf the defenders advocate, as the analysis of *Escaleras Mejía* will demonstrate. The

---

[2] Sérgio García Ramirez, "La 'navegación americana' de los derechos humanos: hacia un Ius Commune," in Armin von Bogdandy, Mariela Morales Antoniazzi, and Eduardo Ferrer Mac-Gregor (coords.), *Ius Constitutionale Commune en América Latina: textos básicos para su comprensión* (Instituto de Estudios Constitucionales del Estado de Querétaro; MPIL 2017).

[3] Daniel O'Donnel, *Derecho Internacional de los Derechos Humanos. Normativa, jurisprudencia y doctrina de los sistemas universal e interamericano* (Oficina en Colombia del Alto Comisionado de las Naciones Unidas para los Derechos Humanos 2004), 57–59.

Inter-American Court has recognized that protecting human rights defenders is not only a matter of securing their right to defend rights but also essential for the operation of the IAHRS. Human rights defenders drive the work of the Inter-American System because they are the ones who alert the IAHRS to rights violations not only against themselves but against all victims.

2. Human Rights Defenders: Multilevel Approach

This section introduces international law's multilevel approach to the protection of human rights defenders.[4] It emphasizes the importance of dialogue between the different protective levels to protect human rights effectively. Institutions with distinct mandates coexist and complement each other in ways that strengthen respect for human dignity. The interactions of plural institutions create a larger regime that protects individuals and their rights.

Out of the contemporary framework of human rights has arisen a "new public order"[5] that impacts the entire international community by making international human rights principles a condition and limit on State practices. The articulation of this new order and its relationship with domestic law is based on the principles of a *pro personae* principle[6] (i.e., a victim-centered approach) and subsidiarity.[7]

This is the essence of common Latin American constitutional law, or *Ius Constitutionale Commune en América Latina* (ICCAL).[8] The coexistence of global, regional, and domestic legal systems has established a new paradigm of human rights based on mutual dialogue that not only enhances protection for individual victims but also the situation of human rights throughout the region. This chapter examines the rights of human rights defenders within the ICCAL framework.

---

[4] Ingolf Pernice, *Constitutional law implications for a state participating in a process of regional integration. German Constitution and "multilevel constitutionalism"* (German Rapport to the XV International Congress on Comparative Law 1998), 2-3.

[5] Armin von Bogdandy, Flávia Piovesan, and Mariela Morales Antoniazzi (coords.), *Estudos avançados em direitos humanos: democracia e integração jurídica: emergência de um novo direito público* (Campus 2012), xiv/xv.

[6] Alejandro Rodiles, "The Law and Politics of the Pro Persona Principle in Latin America," in Armin von Bogdandy et al. (eds.), *Transformative Constitutionalism in Latin America* (Oxford University Press 2017), 153-174.

[7] Simon Hentrei, *Complementary Adjudication: Legitimating International Judicial Authority in the Americas* (DPhil thesis, University of Frankfurt am Main 2018), 79.

[8] Armin von Bogdandy, "Ius Constitutionale Commune en América Latina: observations on Transformative Constitutionalism," in Armin von Bogdandy et al. (eds.), *Transformative Constitutionalism in Latin America* (Oxford University Press 2017), 27-48.

2.1. Global System

Since 1948, the UN human rights system has served as the foundation for the promotion of the international rights of the individual. The United Nations adopted a minimalist set of standards and obligations concerning a variety of rights, including the rights of human rights defenders.

The Declaration on the Right and Responsibility of Individuals, Groups and Organs of Society to Promote and Protect Universally Recognized Human Rights and Fundamental Freedoms (UN Declaration on Human Rights Defenders, or Declaration), enacted in 1998,[9] was the set of international principles to focus on the right to defend rights. Since then, it has served as a model for domestic and regional systems. Although the UN Declaration on Human Rights Defenders is not binding, States are nevertheless obligated to enforce its content because it has been approved by consensus in the UN General Assembly and because it concerns rights contained in binding international treaties.[10]

The Declaration comprehensively articulates defenders' rights and corresponding State's responsibilities. Articles 2, 9, 12, 14, and 15 concern the State obligations, including the duty to protect, promote, and implement all human rights and to ensure that all persons under their jurisdiction are able to enjoy all social, economic, political, and other rights and freedoms in practice.[11] Additionally, Article 4 of the UN Declaration on Human Rights Defenders clarifies that the Declaration should not be used to impair, contradict, restrict, or derogate from other international instruments such as the International Covenants on Human Rights, which contain standards recognized by most of the international community.

The Declaration provides minimum standards for the UN system and beyond. It also seeks to answer three fundamental questions about human rights defenders: Who are they? What are their rights? Who is obliged to protect their rights?

In response to the first question, *Who are human rights defenders?*, the Declaration defines defenders broadly and inclusively as all individuals who advocate for human rights. Article 1 of the Declaration provides: "Everyone has the right, individually and in association with others, to promote and to strive for the protection and realization of human rights and fundamental freedoms at the national and international levels."[12] In other words, advocating for human rights is all that is required to make someone a human rights defender.

---

[9] General Assembly, General Resolution No. 53/144 UN A/RES/53/144, "Declaration on the Right and Responsibility of Individuals, Groups and Organs of Society to Promote and Protect Universally Recognized Human Rights and Fundamental Freedoms" (March 8, 1999).
[10] OHCHR 2011.
[11] Article 2 UN Declaration on Human Rights Defenders 1999.
[12] OHCHR 1999.

As for the second question, *What are their rights?*, the Declaration includes many. Some, however, stand out as particularly relevant for the work of human rights defenders: the right to meet or assemble peacefully; the right to form, join, and participate in nongovernmental organizations, associations, or groups;[13] the right to communicate with nongovernmental or intergovernmental organizations; the right to know, seek, obtain, receive, and hold information about all human rights and fundamental freedoms;[14] the right to develop and discuss new human rights ideas and principles; the right to have adequate access, on a nondiscriminatory basis, to participation in their State's government;[15] the right to benefit from an effective remedy and to be protected in the event of the violation of their rights;[16] the right to exercise their occupation or profession;[17] and the right to participate in peaceful activities protesting violations of human rights and fundamental freedoms.[18] This set of rights constitutes the core of legal protection for human rights defenders and their activities. Identifying this core is essential to understand the content of the right to defend rights.

Finally, in response to the question of *Who is obliged to protect the rights of defenders?*, the UN Declaration on Human Rights Defenders focuses—as most of international human rights law does—on States. The Declaration provides that States have the "prime responsibility and duty to protect, promote and implement all human rights and fundamental freedoms" and that, to comply with their obligations, States should "adopt[] such steps as may be necessary to create all conditions necessary in the social, economic, political and other fields, as well as the legal guarantees required to ensure that all persons under its jurisdiction, individually and in association with others, can enjoy all those rights and freedoms in practice."[19] Additionally, the Declaration provides that States are obligated to promote and facilitate education in human rights for everyone, but especially for lawyers, law enforcement, the armed forces, and public servants.[20]

The Declaration also highlights the importance of the role individuals, nongovernmental organizations, and relevant institutions play in the protection of human rights. It emphasizes that not only State, but also non-State actors contribute to the promotion and protection of human rights in the interest of strengthening, among others things, "understanding, tolerance, peace and friendly relations among nations and among all racial and religious groups."[21]

---

[13] Article 5 UN Declaration on Human Rights Defenders 1999.
[14] Article 6 UN Declaration on Human Rights Defenders 1999.
[15] Article 7 UN Declaration on Human Rights Defenders 1999.
[16] Article 9 UN Declaration on Human Rights Defenders 1999.
[17] Article 11 UN Declaration on Human Rights Defenders 1999.
[18] Article 12 UN Declaration on Human Rights Defenders 1999.
[19] Article 2 UN Declaration on Human Rights Defenders 1999.
[20] Article 15 UN Declaration on Human Rights Defenders 1999.
[21] Article 16 UN Declaration on Human Rights Defenders 1999.

Although the UN Declaration on Human Rights Defenders does not expressly include a right to defend rights, one can be inferred from the Declaration's grouping together of civil, political, economic, social, and cultural rights and accompanying State obligations. The right to defend rights can thus be reached through an "umbrella" approach[22] that unifies different human rights. UN standards concerning human rights defenders have also greatly influenced regional and domestic articulations of the right to defend rights, which will be discussed in the next sections.

2.2. Regional Systems

Regional systems also have recognized the work of human rights defenders. Operating in more homogeneous contexts that enable innovations suited to their regional specificities, these systems have had the opportunity to advance the protection of human rights defenders in ways that complement global standards. Each regional human rights system has developed its own approach to the topic of human rights defenders. The African System, like the UN System, adopted a declaration, while the American and European Systems issued resolutions and guidelines.

In 2009, the European Union adopted guidelines about human rights defenders with the goal of improving their protection. The European Union based its guidelines on the commitments of the Organization for Security and Cooperation in Europe (OSCE) and on universally recognized human rights standards. The guidelines expressly stated that they "do not set new standards or seek to create 'special' rights for human rights defenders but concentrate on the protection of the human rights of those who are at risk as a result of their human rights work."[23] The guidelines' aim was thus not to establish new rights but "to contribute to promoting equal protection of human rights for all."[24] In line with the mandate of the OSCE Office for Democratic Institutions and Human Rights (ODIHR), which prepared the document, the guidelines were framed as a tool "to support participating States in the implementation of their human dimension commitments related to the protection of human rights defenders."[25]

The General Assembly of the Organization of American States (OAS) has issued a resolution on human rights defenders every year since 1999.[26] Mirroring

---

[22] Katarina Tomasevski, *Development Aid and Human Rights Revisited* (Pinter Publishers 1993), 48.
[23] ODIHR 2016, 6.
[24] ODIHR 2016, 6.
[25] ODIHR 2016, 6.
[26] OAS General Assembly, AG/RES.1671 (XXIX-O/99), "Human rights defenders in the Americas, support for the individuals, groups, and organizations of civil society working to promote and protect human rights in the Americas," Res. 2 (June 7, 1999).

the principles embodied in the UN Declaration on Human Rights Defenders, the OAS resolutions recognize the work of human rights defenders and call on States to ensure the ability of human rights defenders to do that work.[27] Notably, in Resolution No. 2941 on "Promotion and Protection of Human Rights," the OAS General Assembly asserted that its motivation for adopting a resolution on human rights defenders was "member states' historic concern for situations that prevent or hamper the work of human rights defenders at the national and regional levels in the Americas."[28]

In 1999, the African Union adopted the Grand Bay Declaration and Plan of Action, which underlines the importance of protecting human rights defenders and calls on African States to act. The declaration also reaffirms the African Union's commitment to the purpose and principles stated in the Charter of the Organization of African Unity (OAU), in the Charter of the United Nations, the Universal Declaration of Human Rights, and the African Charter on Human and Peoples' Rights. The First OAU Ministerial Conference on Human Rights in Africa, which prepared the declaration, called it a historic milestone, and encouraged African States to implement it.[29]

Although the primary instruments of the regional systems do not expressly refer to human rights defenders, the resolutions, guidelines, and declaration mentioned here provide a basis from which regional human rights mechanisms can extract the right to defend rights using systematic and evolutive interpretation. This also illustrates the working methods of the regional systems. They develop human rights norms both through interpreting human rights treaties as living instruments[30] and through jurisdictional tools or *quasi* jurisdictional tools, as in the case of the Inter-American Commission on Human Rights (Inter-American Commission, or IACHR) and the African Commission on Human and Peoples' Rights. The section on the inter-American standards on human rights defenders will return to this point.

2.3. Domestic Systems

The global and regional standards mentioned previously concentrate on States' obligations to promote and protect human rights. As per the subsidiarity principle, the State has the primary responsibility for the protection of human

---

[27] OAS General Assembly, AG/RES. 2941 (XLIX-O/19), "Promotion and Protection of Human Rights" (June 28, 2019), 134–135.
[28] Ibid., 133–135.
[29] Grand Bay (Mauritius) Declaration and Plan of Action 1999.
[30] *Villagran Morales et al. v. Guatemala (The Street Children Case)* [1999] IACtHR, Ser. C No. 63.

rights.[31] International systems act when States fail to comply with their human rights obligations.

Domestic law and international law affect each other. Due to the rich dialogue between international and domestic legal systems, many Latin American countries have incorporated international standards for the protection of human rights defenders into domestic law and policy.

In the Inter-American System, Honduras is the State against which the highest number of cases concerning defenders' rights violations have been brought, even though Honduras has expressly recognized the existence of the right to defend human rights at the domestic level in Article 1 of the Law on the Protection of Human Rights Defenders, Journalists, Social Communicators, and Justice Officials. Similarly, Mexico has passed legislation that protects human rights defenders and journalists.[32]

Other countries in the IAHRS, such as Brazil and Colombia, have created administrative programs to protect human rights defenders. Brazil set up the National Program for the Protection of Human Rights Defenders (PPDDH) within the Secretariat for Human Rights of the Presidency of the Republic. The National Policy of Protection for Human Rights Defenders was created in 2009. Decree No. 9937/2019 established the PPDDH to coordinate measures to protect people who work protecting human rights.[33] Colombia has protected human rights defenders through the nongovernmental program *Somos Defensores*, created in 1999. In 2011, Decree No. 4065 established the *Unidad Nacional de Protección*.

This landscape of legislation and administrative programs concerning human rights defenders appears, to a greater or lesser extent, in most States of the region. Nevertheless, States often fail to protect human rights defenders as required by domestic and international law.

Latin America experiences high rates of violence against human rights defenders, which has been increasing in recent years.[34] A wave of conservative populism touting anti-human rights discourses in the region has threatened human rights defenders by framing them as enemies of the State.[35] The assassination of Brazilian councilwoman Marielle Franco, mentioned in the introduction to this chapter, illustrates how important it is to promote the protection of human rights defenders in this violent context.

---

[31] César Rodríguez Garavito, *El derecho en América Latina. Un mapa para el pensamiento jurídico del siglo XXI* (Siglo Veintiuno Editores 2011).

[32] For more information on protection policies at Colombia and Mexico, Global Justice, see "Guia de Proteção para Defensoras e Defensores de Direitos Humanos," <http://www.global.org.br/wp-content/uploads/2016/09/guia-DDHs-final.pdf> (accessed February 5, 2022).

[33] Decree No. 9937/2019.

[34] Ibid.

[35] Esther Solano Gallego, "La bolsonarización de Brasil" [2019] 121 *Documentos de Trabajo* (IELAT, Instituto Universitario de Investigación en Estudios Latinoamericanos), 1, 18.

The Inter-American System addresses this situation with ICCAL, through which domestic and international courts share responsibilities in accordance with the principle of subsidiarity and the idea that transformative constitutionalism can be a driving force for social change in Latin America. The connections ICCAL draws between the Inter-American Court and national courts enables the latter to confront the threat to human rights posed by authoritarian populism.[36]

Due to its transformative mandate, the IAHRS plays a crucial role in strengthening domestic protections for human rights defenders and unifying movements that advocate on behalf of human rights defenders.

3. IACtHR Jurisprudence on Defenders

This section reviews the IACtHR's jurisprudence on human rights defenders, culminating in the *Escaleras Mejía* case. The Inter-American System engages with emancipatory struggles for rights and justice specific to Latin America. The IAHRS aims to encourage State compliance with human rights obligations by, among other things, setting in motion cooperative efforts that facilitate each State's implementation of its commitments and consider States' diversity and pluralism. Collaboration and dialogue are among the IAHRS's tools for generating a transformative impact based on common standards of human rights in the region.

Cooperation between regional and local systems advances transformative constitutionalism in Latin America, giving momentum to human rights–oriented social change. The IACtHR develops and disseminates the standards of the inter-American *corpus juris*, which provide a baseline of protection for human rights. These protective standards have encouraged the adoption of legislation and public policies that protect human rights defenders, prevented backlashes, and strengthened the capacities of human rights defenders in the struggle for rights and justice. The Inter-American Court has done this through its jurisprudence on human rights defenders. The IACtHR proclaimed the existence of a *right to defend rights* through its interpretation of international norms and despite the absence of an express provision containing this right in the American Convention on Human Rights (American Convention, or ACHR).[37] This *vis expansiva*[38] of the IACtHR is especially important because Latin America is

---

[36] Cristóbal Rovira Kaltwasser et al. (eds.), *The Oxford Handbook of Populis* (Oxford University Press 2017).
[37] Flávia Piovesan, "Direitos Humanos e diálogos entre jurisdições" 19 [2012] *Revista brasileira de Direito Constitucional* 68.
[38] Eduardo Ferrer Mac-Gregor, "What Do We Mean When We Talk About Judicial Dialogue? Reflections of a Judge of the Inter-American Court of Human Rights" [2017] 30 *Harvard Human Rights Journal* 89.

characterized by a high degree of social exclusion, inequality, and threats to democracy. In this context, those who choose to fight against injustice and defend human rights are particularly vulnerable.

When domestic institutions fail to respect, protect, and fulfill human rights, the human rights defenders turn to the IAHRS for protection. The Inter-American Court protects human rights defenders in two ways. First, the IACtHR strengthens respect for the Rule of Law and human rights.[39] Second, the IACtHR aims to address structural challenges as well as individual violations, facilitating a transformative impact. As Armin von Bogdandy[40] has explained, the decisions of international courts shape international law in ways that affect domestic law. International standards become legal reference points for domestic legal actors and generate ICCAL through cooperation and dialogue.

Much of the Inter-American System's jurisprudence on human rights defenders involves the State of Honduras, but as explained previously, these cases are of regional interest. Honduras's experience is relevant to the Americas as a whole. Since the beginning of the 1990s, Honduran environmental activists have defended nature. Their efforts have been met with harassment, threats, assault, and murder.

In 2012, the UN Special Rapporteur on the situation of human rights defenders (UN Special Rapporteur) issued a report about her visit to Honduras in which she expressed concern about "the degree of violence affecting people claiming their economic, social and cultural rights, including land rights, by peaceful means."[41] In response to the report, the State of Honduras created a special group to investigate the deaths of environmental activists. Nevertheless, as the Inter-American Court confirmed in the case of *Kawas Fernández v. Honduras*, the State did "not implement[] an overall public policy aimed at protecting the supporters of human rights, in particular environmental activists."[42] In 2016, the UN Special Rapporteur and the IACHR's Rapporteur on the Rights of Human Rights Defenders and Justice Operators noted that Honduras had become one of the most dangerous countries in the Americas for human rights defenders.

This section analyzes the impact of the cases of *Luna López v. Honduras*, *Kawas Fernández v. Honduras*, and *Carlos Escaleras Mejía and others v. Honduras* on the protection of human rights defenders in the IACtHR.

---

[39] This forms what Dworkin has called a "chain novel." Ronald Dworkin, *Uma questão de princípio* (Luís Carlos Borges tr., Martins Fontes 2000), 236.
[40] Armin von Bogdandy, "Ius Constitutionale Commune in América Latina: observations on Transformative Constitutionalism," in Armin von Bogdandy et al. (eds.), *Transformative Constitutionalism in Latin America* (Oxford University Press 2017).
[41] A/HRC/22/47Add.1, para. 73.
[42] *Kawas Fernández v. Honduras* [2009] IACtHR, para. 70.

3.1. *Luna López v. Honduras* (IACtHR)

On October 10, 2013, the IACtHR declared the State of Honduras internationally responsible for violating its obligation to guarantee Carlos Antonio Luna López's right to life and his family's right to humane treatment.

Carlos Antonio Luna López was a city councilor in the town of Catacamas, Honduras, who denounced and introduced policies against illegal tree logging in the area. Since his investigations and political actions had affected the interests of local politicians, Luna López began to receive threats. Then, on May 18, 1998, he was shot while leaving the city after a town council meeting. He died while on his way to the hospital.

The petitioners claimed that there had been an unwarranted delay in the investigation and prosecution of those responsible for the murder of Luna López. In its analysis of Article 4 of the American Convention, which contains the right to life, the Inter-American Court reiterated that the States' obligations to human rights defenders, including environmental activists, becomes more relevant in countries where these defenders are targeted with threats, acts of violence, and killings.

When considering the right to humane treatment, contained in Article 5 of the ACHR, the IACtHR found that the State's failure to guarantee Luna López's right to life caused psychological and emotional trauma to his family. The situation of continuous risk to which his family was exposed (which was further aggravated by threats and irregularities that occurred during the investigation) inflicted suffering, anguish, and feelings of insecurity, frustration, and helplessness on Luna López's family members.

3.2. *Kawas Fernández v. Honduras*

On April 3, 2003, the IACtHR issued its judgment in the case of *Kawas Fernández v. Honduras*. It declared that the State was partially responsible for the extrajudicial execution of Blanca Jeannette Kawas Fernández because it had hindered investigations and legal proceedings related to her execution. Specifically, the Inter-American Court found that the State had violated the rights to a fair trial and judicial protection, enshrined in ACHR Articles 8(1) and 25(1), respectively, in conjunction with ACHR Article 1.1's general obligation to respect and guarantee human rights, to the detriment of Kawas Fernández, as well as Jacobo Roberto Kawas Cury, Selsa Damaris Watt Kawas, Jaime Alejandro Watt Kawas, Jacobo Roberto Kawas Fernández, Jorge Jesús Kawas Fernández, and Carmen Marilena Kawas Fernández.

Kawas Fernández was well known in Honduras as a defender of the environment. On February 6, 1995, while working at home with her assistant in the city of Tela, Kawas Fernández was shot in the neck and died instantly.

The State began a criminal investigation. Nevertheless, when the IACtHR heard the case, the domestic criminal proceedings were still in a preliminary phase. The Inter-American Court held that the authorities in charge of investigating Kawas Fernández's death delayed the collection of relevant testimony for so long that they impeded the fact-finding process.

The IACtHR explained that States have a duty to respect and to ensure the right to life and that the duty to ensure rights requires States to take positive action. The Inter-American Court held that the State had violated its obligation to take positive action regarding Kawas Fernández's right to life by failing to punish those responsible for the death of Kawas Fernández. Fourteen years had passed since Kawas Fernández was murdered and the State had not identified the perpetrator. The IACtHR concluded that evidence indicated that State agents, including those charged with investigating the case, had been involved in the events that led to Kawas Fernández's death, a conclusion which the State has not disproved.

The Inter-American Court additionally said that "[r]eaching any other conclusion would entail allowing the State to resort to its own negligence or inefficacy for the criminal investigation to release itself from responsibility for the violation of Article 4(1) of the [American] Convention."[43]

The IACtHR developed its jurisprudence on human rights defenders in *Luna López* and *Kawas Fernández*. These cases then provided a foundation for the Inter-American Court's judgment in the case of *Escaleras Mejía* in 2018.[44]

3.3. *Escaleras Mejía v. Honduras*

Before arguing that the *Escaleras Mejía* case illustrates the transformative impact of the Inter-American System, this section describes the facts of the case and the proceedings before the Inter-American Commission.

At approximately 6:30 p.m. on October 18, 1997, Carlos Escaleras Mejía was returning from a political meeting when two men emerged from the shadows and shot him in the back. Escaleras Mejía was taken to the hospital but did not survive surgery. Escaleras Mejía was one of the most distinguished political leaders of the Aguán Valley. He led several human rights organizations, which mainly focused on environmental issues. Escaleras Mejía denounced and

---

[43] *Kawas Fernández v. Honduras* [2009] IACtHR, para. 97.
[44] Ronald Dworkin, *Uma questão de princípio* (Luís Carlos Borges tr., Martins Fontes 2000).

opposed the companies that dumped toxic substances in local rivers. Due to his activism, Escaleras Mejía received death threats and eventually was killed. Like the cases of *Kawas Fernández* and *Luna López*, the case of *Escaleras Mejía* illustrates the atmosphere of insecurity and the persecution of environmental activists in Honduras.

Impunity aggravates this situation. The State's investigation into the facts surrounding Escaleras Mejía's death was not exhaustive, impartial, or effective. On January 13, 2003, the Center for Justice and International Law (CEJIL) filed a petition with the Inter-American Commission alleging that Honduras had violated ACHR Articles 1(1), 4, 8, and 25 by failing to undertake an exhaustive and effective investigation and to punish those responsible for Escaleras Mejía's death, as well as by failing to adopt effective measures to prevent crimes against human rights defenders.

CEJIL also alleged that Honduras had violated Article 5 of the American Convention with respect to Escaleras Mejía's family members by failing to hold those responsible for the crime accountable, to undertake a serious and effective investigation, and to provide effective domestic legal remedies. The Inter-American Commission declared the case admissible on February 24, 2005,[45] and issued a report on the merits in June 2014. In the merits report, the IACHR concluded that the State was responsible and made recommendations to Honduras.[46] The Inter-American Commission relied on prior decisions against Honduras when establishing the State's responsibility in the case of *Escaleras Mejía*.

Following the Inter-American Commission's recommendations, the petitioners and the State signed a friendly settlement agreement.[47]

In this agreement, the State recognized that it had violating Escaleras Mejía's rights to life, freedom of association, and participation in government (ACHR Articles 4.1, 16.1, and 23, in conjunction with Article 1.1), as well as his family members' rights to humane treatment, a fair trial, and judicial protection (ACHR Articles 5, 8, and 25, in conjunction with Article 1.1).

Although the State made significant progress toward compensating the victims and complying with the measures of satisfaction, the State did not make significant progress in its criminal investigations. For this reason, the IACHR decided the case should proceed to the IACtHR.

On September 22, 2017, the Inter-American Commission submitted the case of *Escaleras Mejía* to the Inter-American Court. The IACHR requested that the

---

[45] *Carlos Escaleras Mejía* [2005] IACHR, Report No. 15/05.
[46] *Carlos Escaleras Mejía and Family Honduras* [2014] Case 12.492, IACtHR, Report No. 43/14, OEA/Ser. L/V/II. 151, Doc. 8.
[47] "Friendly Agreement in Compliance with the recommendations of the Inter-American Commission on Human Rights in the Report on the Merits No. 43/14."

IACtHR find the State internationally responsible and to consider the measures already adopted by the State as a result of the friendly settlement agreement. Afterward, the parties filed a joint request to the Court to approve the agreement, in which the State acknowledged its responsibility for the events and committed to providing reparations. The victims requested that the Inter-American Court develop the content of the right to defend human rights in its judgment. The friendly settlement did not foreclose the possibility of consideration of the merits by the IACtHR.

The Inter-American Commission itself highlighted: "[T]he pertinence of the joint request of the parties concerning the development of the content of the right to defend human rights is an important element to strengthen the [Inter-American] Court's line of jurisprudence [...] on this subject."

Now that this section has reviewed the case's facts and procedure, the following section will explain how the IACtHR used *Escaleras Mejía* to transform the protection of human rights defenders in the Americas.

4. The Right to Defend Rights: The Legacy of *Escaleras Mejía*

The cases against Honduras described in the previous section form an important part of the Inter-American Court's jurisprudence on the right to defend rights. The IACtHR's jurisprudence on human rights defenders begins with the premise that their work is essential to strengthening democracy and the rule of law. In this way, the right to defend rights grows out of earlier IACtHR jurisprudence concerning rights violations that hinder the consolidation of the rule of law,[48] including decisions regarding the strengthening of institutions and the limitations on States' use of force. The first case ruled by the Inter-American Court, *Velásquez Rodríguez v. Honduras*, concerns enforced disappearance and the State's duties to prevent, investigate, and sanction any violation of the rights contained in the American Convention.

Similarly, in the case of *Godínez Cruz v. Honduras*, the IACtHR held the State responsible for leaving enforced disappearances in impunity and thus creating conditions under which they would continue. The Inter-American Court reiterated this reasoning in *La Cantuta v. Peru*, in which it found the State responsible for systematic enforced disappearances. The IACtHR has established that States must initiate serious, impartial, and effective investigations *ex officio* and without delay in the event of serious human rights violations.

---

[48] Flávia Piovesan, "Ius constitutionale commune latino-americano em Direitos Humanos e o Sistema Interamericano: perspectivas e desafios" [2017] 8 *Revista Direito e Práxis* 1362.

The IACtHR's cases on the protection of human rights defenders also form part of its jurisprudence concerning the consolidation of the rule of law. According to inter-American standards, the protection of human rights in a democratic society depends on effective and appropriate guarantees that human rights defenders will be free to do their work.[49] Human rights defenders are essential to ensuring States' compliance with human rights norms and complement the role of the Inter-American System.

Latin America, which has long had a poor record on the protection of human rights defenders, has recently experienced an increase in violence against and criminalization of defenders, especially environmental activists like those in the Honduran cases.[50]

The case of *Escaleras Mejía* is important because it consolidates the IACtHR's prior jurisprudence in the umbrella concept of the right to defend rights.[51] The IACtHR has determined that the rights relevant to the work of human rights defenders are ACHR Articles 4, 5, 8, 16, 23, and 25, in conjunction with Article 1.1. Together, these rights obligate States to ensure that human rights defenders enjoy the protection they need to do their work. The Inter-American Court has not, however, expressly recognized the right to defend rights as a stand-alone right, preferring to treat it as an umbrella concept. In *Escaleras Mejía*, the IACtHR derived the right to defend rights from the following rights.

4.1. Right to Life (Article 4.1 of the American Convention)

ACHR Article 4(1) provides that all individuals have a right to life. Often, violence against human rights defenders results in death, a violation of their right to life.

Murders, assaults, forced disappearances, threats, persecution, and other forms of violence target and impede the work of human rights defenders. State agents frequently participate in this violence or enable it through a failure to investigate violent acts with due diligence, as in the case of Escaleras Mejía, Marielle Franco, and many others.

---

[49] IACHR, "Report on the Situation of Human Rights Defenders in the Americas" (2006), para. 124

[50] Global Witness Report (July 2020), <https://www.globalwitness.org/en/press-releases/pior-ano-da-história-para-ativistas-do-meio-ambiente-e-da-terra-pelo-menos-200-assassinados-em-2016-enquanto-crise-se-espalha-ao-redor-do-mundo/> (accessed February 5, 2022).

[51] Katarina Tomasevski, *Development Aid and Human Rights Revisite* (Pinter Publishers 1993).

4.2. Right to Freedom of Association (Article 16 of the American Convention)

The Inter-American Court has interpreted ACHR Article 16.1 to contain both negative and positive obligations. The State not only must respect the freedom of individuals to associate without interference, but it also must protect those who exercise this right from non-State interference as well as investigate any violation of this right.[52]

The State thus is obligated not only to refrain from interfering with human rights defenders' freedom of association but also to ensure that human rights defenders can exercise this right freely and without fear of violence.

The Inter-American Court has also found that the right to freedom of association is closely connected to the exercise of other rights, including the right to a healthy environment derived from Article 26 of the American Convention.[53] The IACtHR has established that the right to a healthy environment is a fundamental human right and that degradation of the environment negatively affects the enjoyment of this right. Moreover, the Inter-American Court has clearly stated that States have an obligation to ensure that their actions do not impair the enjoyment of fundamental rights. In the case of *Escaleras Mejía*, there was evidence that Escaleras Mejía was targeted due to his defense of the environment, a legitimate exercise of the freedom of association.

4.3. Right to Participate in Government (Article 23.1.b of the American Convention)

Participation in government is one of the rights that enables the defense of human rights, as illustrated by the case of city councilor Marielle Franco, who was shot dead, along with her driver, in March 2018 due to her criticism of police violence in Rio's favelas.

Similarly, the harassment and threats suffered by Escaleras Mejía were connected not only to his defense of human rights in general but also more specifically to his running for office. In the weeks leading up to his death, Escaleras Mejía was harassed, threatened, and even offered money in exchange for withdrawing his candidacy.

---

[52] IACHR, "Report on the Situation of Human Rights Defenders in the Americas" (2006), para. 50.
[53] IACtHR, Advisory Opinion OC-23/17, "State obligations in relation to the environment in the context of the protection and guarantee of the rights to life and to personal integrity: interpretation and scope of Articles 4(1) and 5(1) in relation to articles 1(1) and 2 of the American Convention on Human Rights," November 15, 2017.

As in its prior jurisprudence,[54] the Inter-American Court explained that the right to defend human rights involves the exercise of a combination of other rights, which, like all human rights, are interdependent and indivisible.

4.4. Rights to a Fair Trial and to Judicial Protection (Articles 8.1 and 25.1 of the American Convention)

When a human rights defender is harmed, the State has an obligation to ensure impartial and timely justice. This implies an exhaustive collection of the relevant information and an exploration of all relevant lines of investigation to identify the perpetrators of the attack.

The obligation to investigate the impairment of human rights defenders' rights is reinforced by the fact that the defense of human rights can only be freely exercised when the defender is not subject to threats, harassment, or physical or psychological assault. In the case of *Escaleras Mejía*, shortcomings, irregularities, and omissions in the investigation contributed to a considerable delay in identifying and punishing the perpetrators. The failure to clarify the motive behind the attack on Escaleras Mejía resulted in impunity.

The Inter-American Court also held the State responsible for violating the rights of Escaleras Mejía's family, since the domestic investigations and proceedings had not been effective in ensuring access to justice, establishing the facts, investigating, and punishing those responsible, or redressing the consequences of the attack.

4.5. Right to Humane Treatment (Article 5.1 of the American Convention)

The IACtHR also found a violation of the family's right to humane treatment because of the anguish caused by the lack of adequate protection and the profound suffering that stemmed from it.

4.6. Right to Freedom of Expression and Right of Assembly (Articles 13 and 15 of the American Convention)

Although the Inter-American Court did not discuss the right to freedom of expression or the right of assembly in *Escaleras Mejía*, the IACtHR had analyzed

---

[54] H. *Case of Human rights defender et al. v. Guatemala* [2014] IACtHR, Ser. C No. 283, para. 129.

these rights in prior cases concerning human rights defenders. According to the Special Representative of the UN Secretary-General on the situation of human rights defenders, violations of defenders' right to freedom of expression leads to self-censorship.[55] ACHR Article 13 thus has not only an individual dimension but also a collective dimension, affecting how entire societies share and receive ideas and information.[56]

The freedom of assembly is also an important element of the right to defend human rights. In the case of *López Lone v. Honduras*, the Inter-American Court found the freedom of expression and the freedom of assembly to be necessary components of the "right to defend democracy." The Inter-American Court also established in that case that the right to defend rights "involves . . . the joint exercise of other rights, such as freedom of expression and freedom of assembly."[57]

The list of rights that the IACtHR has discussed thus far in relation to the right to defend rights is not exhaustive. Depending on the circumstances of the case involving human rights defenders, other rights may be relevant.

The right to defend human rights is thus an umbrella concept that encompasses many rights. Although there is no single, established formula for the right to defend rights, the IACtHR has identified a set of essential attributes. This right represents a complex synthesis of rights that bring together values such as political participation, social justice, and sustainability, and that require international cooperation as well as State action.

4.7. The Autonomous Right to Defend Rights

In the *Escaleras Mejía* case, the Inter-American Court expressly decided not to examine the existence of an autonomous right to defend the rights, despite the parties' request that it did so. Previously, in the case of *Human Rights Defender and others v. Guatemala*, the IACtHR states that "there is an international consensus regarding the activities carried out by human rights defenders to promote and protect human rights, among others." There, also, the Inter-American Court stopped short of identifying an autonomous right to defend rights.

Although the IACtHR could have gone further in recognizing the right to defend rights, the *Escaleras Mejía* case represents a step in this direction, especially when compared to the previous cases against Honduras highlighted previously. The scope of the umbrella concept of the right to defend rights was better

---

[55] UN, "Report of the Special Representative Hina Jilani on the situation of human rights defenders," para. 20.
[56] *López Lone et al. v. Honduras case* [2015] IACtHR, Ser. C No. 302, para. 166.
[57] *López Lone et al. v. Honduras case* [2015] IACtHR, Ser. C No. 302, para. 164.

defined, and the Inter-American Court mentioned the existence of the right to defend rights even though it did not analyze it independently from other rights.

In the *Escaleras Mejía* case, the IACtHR missed a significant opportunity to establish the existence of an autonomous right to defend rights in the inter-American *corpus juris*. This right is especially important to Latin America given the prevalence of violence against human rights defenders in the region. The defense of human rights in Latin America is a dangerous activity that has endangered the lives and liberties of thousands of defenders like Escaleras Mejía.

5. Concluding Remarks

Challenges to human rights demand that courts, especially the international courts, create a common law (ICCAL) that sets shared standards oriented toward the adequate protection of human rights in the framework of a democratic society. Through an analysis of *Escaleras Mejía and others v. Honduras*, this chapter has reviewed inter-American standards on human rights defenders, while emphasizing shared regional challenges and the impact of the Inter-American System, as well as interaction among global, regional, and domestic standards.

This chapter focused on the case of *Escaleras Mejía v. Honduras*, one of the most recent IACtHR cases and the one that made the most significant advances in developing the law around the protection of human rights defenders.

More recently, in June 2022, the case of Gabriel Salles Pimenta versus Brazil[58] was ruled by the IACtHR. The Court considered the State responsibility in the death of Gabriel Salles Pimenta, a rural workers' rights advocate, in 1982. He was murdered amidst violence linked to land and agrarian reform demands in the State of Pará. Pimenta had received multiple threats related to his work and had sought protection from the State, but his pleas went unheeded. He was fatally shot in 1982. The subsequent investigation, which concluded in 2006 due to a statute of limitations decision, was marred by numerous State omissions.

The Inter-American Court of Human Rights found that the Brazilian State violated various human rights, including the right to life, justice, and association. It recommended comprehensive reparations for the victim's family, a diligent investigation, and measures to prevent such incidents in the future, including strengthening the protection for human rights defenders.

In its Merits Report, the Court made several recommendations to the Brazilian State, including implementing measures of non-repetition, strengthening the Program for the Protection of Human Rights Defenders with a focus on preventing violence against defenders of the rights of rural workers, conducting

---

[58] *Sales Pimenta v. Brazil case* [2022] IACtHR, Ser. C No. 454.

an independent and thorough assessment of the situation of human rights defenders in the context of land conflicts to detect and eradicate risk factors they face (including land distribution disparities), and enhancing the capacity to investigate crimes against human rights defenders in line with the guidelines outlined in the report.

Human rights defenders play a crucial role in advocating for the protection of human rights and ensuring that governments adhere to international human rights standards. When cases involving human rights defenders are brought before the Inter-American Human Rights System, it serves as a significant platform to highlight and address violations against these individuals. Such cases can set important precedents, emphasizing the importance of protecting those who work tirelessly to uphold human rights and hold governments accountable. These cases underscore the necessity of safeguarding freedom of expression, association, and assembly for all citizens and reinforce the importance of a robust, effective, and impartial human rights protection mechanism within the region.

The recognition of the right to defend rights is necessary to strengthen the protection of defenders and prevent their being killed, criminalized, harassed, and threatened as part of efforts to halt the progress of their vital work. This recognition is especially important in many Latin American countries, which struggle with high levels of repression, inequality, and violence.

Although the Inter-American Court did not expressly recognize the right to defend rights as a stand-alone right in *Escaleras Mejía*, it defined the right's contours by emphasizing its umbrella quality and examining the political, social, and environmental dimensions of the defense of rights. In addition to this, the IACtHR underlined the importance of the Court's function to protect both individual defenders and the broader community. Similarly, the Inter-American Commission has stated that "when a person is kept from defending human rights, the rest of society is directly affected."[59]

The Inter-American System saves lives.[60] There is, of course, room for improvement. The IAHRS has not, for example, prevented the murders of Carlos Escaleras Mejía, Marielle Franco, and many other defenders. Nevertheless, the standards that the IAHRS has developed in response to these tragic events will help to protect many human rights defenders and other victims in the region. This will be achieved through the interaction of domestic, regional, and international standards culminating in the regional transformative constitutionalism we call ICCAL.

---

[59] IACHR, "Report on the situation of human rights defenders in the Americas" (2006), para. 34.
[60] Flávia Piovesan, "Ius constitutionale commune latino-americano em Direitos Humanos e o Sistema Interamericano: perspectivas e desafios" [2017] 8 *Revista Direito e Práxis* 1362.

II.11
The Inter-American Human Rights System's/ICCAL's Impact on Transitions to Democracy from the Perspective of Transitional Justice

By Christina Binder

1. Introduction

In Latin America, transitions to democracy have often involved an engagement with major human rights violations committed by former regimes (frequently military dictatorships).[1] The question of how to deal with past crimes is thus crucial for developing and consolidating new democratic norms and institutions in Latin American States. It is a test of practice for the Inter-American Human Rights System and, more particularly, the *Ius Constitutionale Commune en América Latina* (ICCAL).[2] The impact of the Inter-American Human Rights System (and of ICCAL) on transitions to democracy will indeed relate to its ability to deal with these violations at the domestic level and its corresponding support for domestic institutions. Still, what are parameters to measure this impact?

This chapter argues that the concept of Transitional Justice provides relevant parameters and will thus draw on the concept for guidance. According to the definition contained in a report by the UN Secretary-General, Transitional Justice is "the full range of processes and mechanisms associated with a society's attempts to come to terms with a legacy of large scale past abuses, in order to ensure accountability, serve justice and achieve

---

[1] An earlier iteration of this chapter was published under the title "The Prohibition of Amnesties by the Inter-American Court of Human Rights," in Armin von Bogdandy and Ingo Venzke (eds.), *International Judicial Lawmaking: On Public Authority and Democratic Legitimation in Global Governance* (Springer 2012), 295–328. The author wishes to thank Verena Jackson for her valuable research assistance.

[2] In this chapter, ICCAL refers to the transformative potential of the Inter-American Human Rights System, most importantly to the Inter-American Court of Human Rights (IACtHR), which has unfolded—as will be argued—as a set of regional constitutional laws based on human rights.

reconciliation."[3] Transitional Justice, therefore, concerns the question of how to deal with past human rights violations and is central to transitions toward a more peaceful, democratic society. It provides the parameters to measure both success and scale of democratic transitions as well as the impact of the Inter-American Human Rights System on these transitions.

Transitional Justice has three dimensions: retributive, restorative, and distributive. Retributive justice refers to forms of reparations that primarily aim to criminally prosecute perpetrators; restorative and distributive justice, however, put the victims at center stage and aim to make good the harm that occurred. Restorative justice does this by giving a voice to victims, by establishing the truth through an official historical record of what happened, by hearing confessions of guilt by perpetrators, and through institutional reforms. Distributive justice instead focuses on (monetary) compensation. As will be shown, all these components are of relevance in Latin America.

Since many Latin American States passed amnesty laws in the course of their transitions to democracy, the question of how to qualify these amnesties for past human rights violations arose. As will be shown, blanket amnesties run against the very idea of Transitional Justice. Amnesty laws were subject to a rich case law of the Inter-American Court of Human Rights (IACtHR) and were found to violate key provisions in the American Convention on Human Rights (ACHR).[4] Accordingly, the IACtHR's case law on amnesties is of crucial importance for democratic transitions. More particularly, the Inter-American Human Rights System and the Inter-American Court have contributed to the realization of all three aspects of Transitional Justice when dealing with amnesty laws that contravene the ACHR.

2. Enabling Transitions to Democracy in Latin America: How to Deal with Past Human Rights Violations from the Perspective of Transitional Justice

In the course of democratic transitions, the question of amnesties proved a major concern in Latin America. Domestic amnesty laws in many countries, such as

---

[3] UN Security Council, Report of the Secretary-General, "The rule of law and transitional justice in conflict and post-conflict societies," August 23, 2004, UN Doc. S/2004/616, para. 8. See also Anja Seibert-Fohr, "Transitional Justice in Post-Conflict Situations," in Anne Peters and Rüdiger Wolfrum (eds.), *The Max Planck Encyclopedia of International Law* (Oxford University Press 2008), para. 1: "Transitional justice describes a field of international law which is concerned with the question how to confront a situation of past large-scale human rights violations and humanitarian abuses in a period of transition to peace and democracy."

[4] See *Barrios Altos v. Peru* [2001] IACtHR, Ser. C No. 75; *La Cantuta v. Peru* [2006] IACtHR, Ser. C No. 162; *Almonacid Arellano v. Chile* [2006] IACtHR, Ser. C No. 154; *Gelman v. Uruguay* [2011] IACtHR, Ser. C No. 221; *Case of the massacre of El Mozote and nearby places v. El Salvador* [2012] IACtHR, Ser. C No. 252; *Gomes Lund et al. v. Brazil* [2010] IACtHR, Ser. C No. 219.

Argentina, Chile, and Uruguay,[5] de facto established impunity for past violations. In Peru, then President Alberto Fujimori passed a number of amnesty laws in 1995, shielding himself and other human rights perpetrators against prosecution for crimes committed in the context of their fight against left-wing guerrilla fighters in the early 1990s.[6] Thus, the three dimensions of Transitional Justice—retributive, restorative, and distributive—were set aside at the domestic level. In Latin America, therefore, transitions to democracy often came "at a price": it proved difficult for the nascent and still fragile democracies to struggle against impunity as many of the human rights perpetrators remained in influential positions.[7] At the same time, the "quality" of the respective amnesty laws diverged significantly. In countries like Peru and Chile, quasi self-amnesties were passed by the former regimes. Similarly, in Argentina the previous regime exercised sufficient pressure in favor of the provision of amnesty laws.[8] In other parts of the region, amnesties seemed to be the result of a national deliberation process. In Uruguay, for example, the amnesty deal was brokered between the political parties and the armed forces, subsequently passed by Parliament, and upheld twice by popular referenda in 1989 and 2009.[9,10]

---

[5] See, for instance, the notorious *Punto Final* and *Obediencia Debida* Acts in Argentina, which were passed in 1986 and 1987, respectively, and brought investigations on human rights violations committed by the military junta between 1976 and 1983 to a practical halt. See also the 1978 Chilean amnesty decree law (Decreto Ley No. 2191, April 19, 1978; *Diario Oficial* No. 30.042), which established the nonresponsibility for crimes committed between September 11, 1973 (the military coup by Pinochet) and March 10, 1978. For Uruguay, see the Law Nullifying the State's Claim to Punish Certain Crimes/Limitations Act/Law of Expiry, Law No. 15848, December 22, 1986.

[6] Law (Ley) No. 26479, "Conceden amnistía general a personal militar, política y civil para diversos casos," June 14, 1995, published in Normas Legales, No. 229 (1995), 200; modified by Ley No 26492 "Precisan interpretación y alcances de amnistía otorgada por La Ley No 26479," June 28, 1995, published in Normas Legales, No. 230, 1995, 8.

[7] See, e.g., Argentina, where President Carlos Menem, in view of the danger of a new military coup, pardoned around thirty top junta leaders in 1989 who had been imprisoned for human rights abuses (Decree 1002/89). The Decree was recently declared unconstitutional by the Argentine Supreme Court; see *Mazzeo Julio Lilo y otros*, Judgment of July 13, 2007, in Jurisprudencia Argentina 2007-III-573).

[8] Ibid.

[9] The Expiry Law was approved on December 22, 1986, by the Uruguayan parliament, and according to Article 1: "It is recognized that, as a consequence of the logic of events stemming from the agreement between the political parties and the Armed Forces signed in August 1984, and in order to complete the transition to full constitutional order, the State relinquishes the exercise of penal actions with respect to crimes committed until March 1, 1985, by military and police officials either for political reasons or in fulfillment of their functions and in obeying orders from superiors during the de facto period." See Wayne Sandholtz, unpublished paper, "Juggling Rights, Juggling Politics: Amnesty Laws and the Inter-American Court," 33: "The *Gelman v Uruguay* case was the first in which the IACtHR ruled expansively in a case that did not involve a self-amnesty. The Uruguayan amnesty law (the 'Expiry Law') was subject to a democratic process by which a majority of the population chose to uphold it on two occasions, first in a referendum held in 1989 and two decades later through a plebiscite in 2009."

[10] Note that also the Supreme Court of Justice of Uruguay captioned orders "Detta, Josefina; Menotti, Noris; Martínez, Federico; Musso Osiris; Burgell, Jorge s/ unconstitutionality of the Law 15.848. Arts. 1, 2, 3 and 4," Judgment No. 112/87, resolution of May 2, 1988, evidence, folios 2256 to 2318 upheld in a first judgment the constitutionality of the law. In a second judgment on October

While the procedural legitimacy of the various amnesty laws differs—with self-amnesties being the most problematic—the result is the same: impunity for major human rights violations in disregard of the different dimensions of Transitional Justice. A key issue when discussing the impact of the Inter-American System on democratic transitions, therefore, relates to the System's contribution to realizing the different dimensions of Transitional Justice at the domestic level and its support for national efforts in the fight against impunity. Indeed, the Inter-American System has eased transitions by pushing States to uphold certain minimum requirements. So what were the requirements set by the Inter-American Court's amnesty jurisprudence for the domestic level, and what was their impact?

The following layers can be distinguished: Firstly, there are substantive standards that focus on ending impunity for major human rights violations and the right of victims and their family members to truth, due process, and compensation. Secondly, there are supportive strategies and techniques of norm control that give a maximal effect to standards and jurisprudence at the domestic level, namely, the nullification of amnesty laws and the Inter-American Court's conventionality control. And thirdly, when discussing the impact of the ICCAL on democratic transitions, there are broader democratic considerations like strengthening domestic institutions, the separation of powers, and the rule of law; the independence and impartiality of domestic tribunals vis-à-vis the executive seems especially crucial in societies emerging from a violent and often authoritative past. These layers will be examined in turn to determine the impact of the Inter-American Human Rights System on democratic transitions.

3. Inter-American Human Rights Standards within a Multilevel Legal System of Law

A preliminary question relates to the position that the inter-American human rights standards occupy in the multilevel system of law present in Latin American States. Indeed, this position is a decisive factor in determining the potential impact of the inter-American standards on democratic transitions.

So how does the Inter-American System work, and what is its place in the internal order of States, as well as, more generally, in the multilevel system of law? With regards to the international level, the ACHR is a treaty binding on the States parties to it. The ACHR establishes international obligations and

---

19, 2009 the Supreme Court of Uruguay rendered Judgment No. 365 in the case of "Sabalsagaray Curuchet Blanca Stela," where it declared the unconstitutionality of Articles 1, 3, and 4 of the Law and resolved the inapplicability in the specific case at hand. See also *Gelman* (n. 4), paras. 145 et seq. Also, the impact of the ICCAL varies, as will be shown, depending, inter alia, on the different "qualities" of adoption of the amnesty laws.

sets human rights standards applicable to the domestic sphere.[11] A violation of these standards entails the international responsibility of the State in question in accordance with the International Law Commission's (ILC) Articles on State Responsibility.[12] However, even though the international responsibility of a State in breach of its obligations is at stake in such situations, there are no automatic consequences at the domestic level. Rather, the consequences at the domestic level depend on the legal and constitutional system of the respective State. A State's constitutional order determines the incorporation of international obligations—including, therefore, the ACHR—and is thus of importance for the ACHR's domestic effect. The ACHR has been given a high rank in the internal constitutional hierarchy of most Latin American States, commonly with a self-executing character attributed to the rights enshrined in the Convention.[13] This considerably facilitates the reception of the ICCAL and the Inter-American Court's jurisprudence.[14] Thus, the domestic impact of the ACHR—and the case law of the IACtHR in the interpretation of the ACHR—is considerable. As will be shown, this impact is also supported by the Inter-American Court's techniques of norm control: the nullification of amnesty laws and the conventionality control.

The constitutional setup in most Latin-American countries is thus primed to give a maximum effect to the ICCAL and its standards. It also supports the Inter-American Human Rights System's impact on democratic transitions.

4. Impact of the ICCAL/Inter-American Human Rights System on Transitions to Democracy

4.1. The Inter-American Court's Amnesty Jurisprudence: Standards and "Toolbox"

The amnesty jurisprudence of the inter-American human rights institutions has a considerable history, reaching back several decades. Already in the 1980s the

---

[11] The ACHR is a treaty that has to be complied with by the States party to it (Art. 26 Vienna Convention on the Law of treaties (VCLT): *pacta sunt servanda*; and Art. 27 VCLT).

[12] ILC, "Draft Articles on Responsibility of States for Internationally Wrongful Acts" [2001] 2 Yearbook of the International Law Commission (Part Two).

[13] See Allan Brewer Carías, "La interrelación entre los Tribunales Constitucionales de America Latina, la Corte Interamericana de Derechos Humanos, y la Cuestión de la inejecutabilidad de sus decisiones en Venezuela" [2009] unpublished paper 6 et seq. and 13. This is of particular importance for the conventionality control explained later. In fact, norm control regarding the constitutionality of laws or decrees exercised by domestic judges often automatically includes a conventionality control, since the ACHR is incorporated with a constitutional rank. See, e.g., María Angélica Gelli, "El Liderazgo Institucional de la Corte Suprema y las Perplejidades del Caso 'Mazzeo,'" La Ley of 7 December 2007, Buenos Aires, 1.

[14] See, e.g., ibid.

question of amnesty laws came up in the Inter-American System. In 1992, the Inter-American Commission stated that the Argentine and Uruguayan amnesty laws contradicted those States' human rights obligations.[15] The Inter-American Court, asked by Argentina and Uruguay to render an advisory opinion on the Commission's competence to decide on the validity of domestic legislation, upheld the Commission's competence in this regard.[16] Nevertheless, "the political climate in the relevant countries remained hostile to the [inter-American human rights] system's views on amnesty laws,"[17] and no immediate reaction at the national level gave effect to the Court's findings. It was only with the Inter-American Court's landmark decision in the 2001 *Barrios Altos* case,[18] and later with the 2006 *La Cantuta v. Peru*[19] and *Almonacid v. Chile*[20] decisions, that the issue of amnesty legislation was brought back onto the regional human rights agenda.[21] Since then the question of amnesties has been at stake in numerous cases brought before the Court.[22]

In its amnesty jurisprudence, the Inter-American Court addressed all three dimensions of Transitional Justice: retributive, restorative, and distributive. It did so first by establishing substantive standards. For example, in the *Barrios Altos* case, the Inter-American Court found that impunity for human rights violations, which were recognized as *ius cogens* under international human rights law because of their seriousness, was inadmissible and those responsible ought to be punished.[23] Accordingly, the Court established that the 1995 Peruvian amnesty

---

[15] See IACHR, Cases 10.147, 10.181, 10.240, 10.262, 10.309, 10.311; IACHR, Report No. 28/92, OEA/Ser.L/V/II.83, Doc. 14, corr.1 (1992–93) (Argentina); IACHR, Cases 10.029, 10.036, 10.145, 10.305, 10.372, 10.373, 10.374, 10.375, Report No. 29/92, (Uruguay). See James Cavallaro and Stephanie Brewer, "Reevaluating Regional Human Rights Litigation in the Twenty-First Century: The Case of the Inter-American Court" [2008] 102 *American Journal of International Law* 768, 819 et seq.

[16] IACtHR, "Certain Attributes of the Inter-American Commission on Human Rights (Arts. 41, 42, 44, 46, 47, 50, and 51 of the American Convention on Human Rights)," Advisory Opinion OC-13/93, July 16, 1993, Ser. A No. 13, paras. 30, 37, 57(1).

[17] See Cavallaro and Brewer (n. 15), 820.

[18] IACtHR, *Barrios Altos v. Peru* (n. 4).

[19] IACtHR, *La Cantuta v. Peru* (n. 4).

[20] IACtHR, *Almonacid v. Chile* (n. 4).

[21] The *Barrios Altos* and *La Cantuta* cases against Peru concerned massacres in 1991 and 1992 that were committed by the paramilitary death squad *La Colina* and ordered by then President Albero Fujimori. Those responsible were shielded from prosecution by amnesty laws passed by the Fujimori government in 1995: Laws No. 26479 and 26492 (n. 6). See also the following cases concerning self-amnesties: IACtHR, *Castillo-Páez v. Peru* [1998] IACtHR Ser. C No. 43; *Loayza Tamayo v. Peru* [1998] IACtHR, Ser. C No. 60.

[22] See IACtHR, *Barrios Altos v. Peru*, IACtHR, *La Cantuta v. Peru*, IACtHR, *Almonacid Arellano v. Chile*, IACtHR, *Gelman v. Uruguay*, IACtHR, *Case of the massacre of El Mozote and nearby places v. El Salvador*, IACtHR, *Gomes Lund et al. v. Brazil* (n. 4).

[23] IACtHR, *Barrios Altos v. Peru* (n. 4), para. 41: "This Court considers that all amnesty provisions, provisions on prescription and the establishment of measures designed to eliminate responsibility are inadmissible, because they are intended to prevent the investigation and punishment of those responsible for serious human rights violations such as torture, extrajudicial, summary or arbitrary execution and forced disappearance, all of them prohibited because they violate non-derogable rights recognized by international human rights law."

laws violated the rights of the survivors and victims' families to be heard by a judge and to judicial protection, as established in Article 8.1 and Article 25 ACHR, respectively. The Court stated further that these amnesty laws impeded the investigation, capture, prosecution, and conviction of those responsible for the human rights violations in the *Barrios Altos* massacre, in contravention of Article 1.1 ACHR, and obstructed the clarification of the facts of the case. Finally, the Inter-American Court held that the respective laws contributed to the defenselessness of victims and the perpetuation of impunity and were thus "manifestly incompatible with the aims and spirit of the [American] Convention."[24] The Inter-American Court established in relation to the 2001 Peruvian amnesty laws that they lacked legal effects in internal Peruvian legislation.[25] The survivors and the next of kin of victims of massacres involving perpetrators who had not been prosecuted due to the effect of the amnesty laws implemented between 1995 and 2001 were to be indemnified monetarily and given adequate psychological support, and investigations and prosecutions holding responsible those who were accountable for the massacre had to proceed.

Similar findings were reached in *Almonacid v. Chile*, which concerned the extrajudicial killing of a professor—and a supporter of the Communist Party—in September 1973 by State police forces acting under the instructions of the Pinochet regime. The Inter-American Court found that the killing constituted a crime against humanity,[26] which as a non-derogable right under the ACHR could not remain unpunished.[27] The Court reasoned similarly to the *Barrios Altos* case: it established that the nonprosecution of those responsible in application of the 1978 amnesty decree law (*Decreto Ley*)[28] constituted a violation of Articles 8.1 and 25 together with Articles 1.1 and 2 of the ACHR.[29] The Court, as in *Barrios Altos*, stated that the respective decree law was devoid of legal effects.[30] What is more, the IACtHR ordered the indemnification and satisfaction of the victims, including the prosecution of those responsible, and the publication of the established facts in the *Diario Oficial* of Chile and in another widely circulated newspaper, as well as other measures. Furthermore, the Court found with effect *erga omnes* that the Chilean State was obliged to ensure that the respective amnesty decree law hindered neither the continued investigations on

---

[24] IACtHR, *Barrios Altos v. Peru* (n. 4), para. 43.
[25] The IACtHR extensively listed Peruvian measures and jurisprudence to reach this conclusion.
[26] See, e.g., IACtHR, *Almonacid v. Chile* (n. 4), para. 115.
[27] Ibid., para. 111: "Los crímenes de lesa humanidad producen la violación de una serie de derechos inderogables reconocidos en la Convención Americana, que no pueden quedar impunes."
[28] Chilean Amnesty Decree Law No. 2.191 (n. 5).
[29] IACtHR, *Almonacid v. Chile* (n. 4) para. 2.
[30] Ibid., para. 3. The fact that the amnesty laws had not been applied by Chilean courts in various cases since 1998 was not considered sufficient to comply with the requirements of Article 2 ACHR, as the implementing authorities could change their approach (ibid., para. 121).

the extrajudicial execution of the victim and similar situations nor the identification and punishment of those responsible in that case and similar cases.[31]

In *Gelman v. Uruguay*,[32] the Inter-American Court found Uruguay in violation of its obligations under the American Convention by letting crimes go unpunished through the country's amnesty law. While taking into consideration the democratic approval of the Uruguayan law, the Court ultimately considered this immaterial[33] and found that the law was lacking legal effects.[34] The Court stated that the democratic legitimacy of a law had no effect on its general compatibility with human rights law. Even in cases like the one before it, the conventionality control could not be spared and was therefore not only a task for judicial authorities but for every public authority.[35]

In the above-mentioned cases, the Inter-American Court adopted a similar approach to domestic amnesty laws[36] that shield perpetrators of grave human rights violations from prosecution. Interestingly, the Court was less concerned about the method of adoption, that is, whether the respective law was an act of self-amnesty or an amnesty passed by a subsequent regime or national parliament transitioning toward democracy.[37] Rather, the Court based its decision on the amnesty laws' *ratio legis*: that they shield perpetrators of grave human rights violations from prosecution. In so doing, the Court explicitly referred to the *ius cogens* character (non-derogable nature) of the prohibition of torture and extrajudicial killings.[38] Consequently, the respective amnesty laws were found to violate the rights of survivors and the family members of victims to a fair trial and judicial protection;[39] the laws' very existence, according to the Court, constituted a violation of a State's obligation under the ACHR.[40] While not of immediate relevance for the Court's reasoning, the procedural legitimacy of the amnesty law's adoption, as will be shown, is important for the reception and effects of the Court's amnesty jurisprudence at the domestic level.[41]

---

[31] Ibid., paras. 5 and 6.
[32] IACtHR, *Gelman v. Uruguay* (n. 4).
[33] Ibid., para. 229, 238; see also Sandholtz, (n. 9), 35 *et seq.*
[34] IACtHR, *Gelman v. Uruguay* (n. 4) para. 232.
[35] Ibid., para. 238.
[36] As mentioned, the criteria for the incompatibility of amnesty laws are most clearly established in *Almonacid v. Chile* (n. 4), para. 120: it is the *ratio legis*—i.e., to shield perpetrators of grave human rights violations from prosecution—rather than how the law was adopted—e.g., a self-amnesty—which is decisive.
[37] Ibid., para. 120. The Inter-American Court seems to make a distinction as regards amnesty laws that are adopted to end an armed conflict. See IACtHR, *Massacre of El Mozote and nearby places v. El Salvador* (n. 4).
[38] See, e.g., IACtHR, *Barrios Altos v. Peru* (n. 4), para. 41; *Almonacid v. Chile* (n. 4), para. 111.
[39] ACHR, arts. 8.1 and 25.
[40] ACHR, arts. 1.1 and 2.
[41] See section 4.2 *infra*.

With its jurisprudence, the Inter-American Court obliges States to give effect to the different dimensions of Transitional Justice, which are important for democratic transition processes of societies emerging from a violent past. Therefore, the retributive dimension of Transitional Justice is accomplished via the required criminal prosecution of perpetrators; the restorative dimension is accomplished by defending the right of victims to the truth and to a fair process, as well as the necessary psychological aid and help when instances of torture are involved; and the distributive dimension is realized by awarding monetary compensation to victims. The standards and human rights conditions set up by the Inter-American Court for domestic democratic transition processes are thus stringent and comprise all three dimensions of Transitional Justice.

What is more, the Inter-American Court has also developed especially two innovative types of norm control to facilitate the reception and increase the impact of its judgments at the domestic level: first, the nullification of unconventional amnesty laws and second, the conventionality control. As regards the former, the Inter-American Court in its amnesty jurisprudence—for example, *Barrios Altos*, *La Cantuta*, *Gelman*, and *Almonacid*—does not task domestic authorities with amending or repealing deficient legislation. Rather, the Court itself determines whether the respective amnesty laws are "without effect" *ab initio* as a result of contravening the ACHR.[42] The wording chosen by the Inter-American Court—"lack legal effect," *carecen efectos jurídicos*—demonstrates that the Court does not consider an additional national legal act—for example, a repeal of the amnesty law—necessary to give effect to its determination.[43] This is explicitly confirmed in the *voto razonado* of Judge García Ramírez in *La Cantuta*.[44] When stating that national laws "are without effect" when contravening the ACHR, the Inter-American Court attributes supranational force to its determinations and acts like a national constitutional court.[45] This direct norm control exercised by the

---

[42] This was stated most clearly in *La Cantuta v. Peru* (n. 4), para. 187: "[D]ichas leyes no han podido generar efectos no los tienen en el presente ni podrán generarlos en el future."

[43] While the Court's findings in *La Cantuta* indicate that the Inter-American Court's statement is declaratory and not constitutive, such an establishment would have been up to the competent institution at the domestic level (e.g., the constitutional court).

[44] See *voto razonado* by Judge Sergio García Ramírez, IACtHR, *La Cantuta v. Peru* (n. 4), paras. 4 and 5: "En suma, la ineficacia de esos mandamientos resulta inmediatamente—y sin necesidad de actos especiales que lo dispongan y que, en todo caso, se limitarían a declararlo—de su colisión con la Convención Americana."

[45] See Néstor Sagüés, "El 'Control de Convencionalidad' en particular sobre las Constitucionales Nacionales," La Ley, February 19, 2009, Buenos Aires, 3: "[E]n ciertos veredictos ... la Corte Interamericana habría incluso nulificado normas nacionales, como leyes de amnistía, con efectos *erga onmnes*, comportándose así como un verdadero Tribunal Constitucional nacional." Note that, especially when establishing the nullity of amnesty laws and decrees, the Court refers explicitly to the particularly serious character of human rights violations the amnesty laws are providing impunity for: the respective human rights guarantees being recognized as non-derogable (*ius cogens*) in international human rights law. The IACtHR thus seems to introduce a certain hierarchy of norms. This is evidenced by the fact that with respect to other laws that violated the ACHR but did not provide

Inter-American Court maximizes the impact of its findings, since no additional national act is necessary to give effect to the Inter-American Court's judgments.

Likewise, the conventionality control (*control de convencionalidad*) increases the effects of the Inter-American Court's jurisprudence. Indeed, in *Almonacid v. Chile*, the Inter-American Court established for the first time that national courts were obliged not to apply national norms that were in violation of the ACHR and, what is more, of the ACHR in the interpretation given by the Inter-American Court (*control de convencionalidad*).[46] According to the IACtHR:

> 124. The Court is aware that domestic judges and courts are bound to respect the rule of law, and therefore, they are bound to apply the provisions in force within the legal system. But when a State has ratified an international treaty such as the American Convention, its judges, as part of the State, are also bound by such Convention. This forces them to see that all the effects of the provisions embodied in the Convention are not adversely affected by the enforcement of laws which are contrary to its purpose and that have not had any legal effects since their inception. In other words, the Judiciary must exercise a sort of "conventionality control" between the domestic legal provisions which are applied to specific cases and the American Convention on Human Rights. To perform this task, the Judiciary has to take into account not only the treaty, but also the interpretation thereof made by the Inter-American Court, which is the ultimate interpreter of the American Convention.[47]

Such decentralized conventionality control tasks national courts not to apply (provisions of) laws that are in contravention of the ACHR.[48] This obligation applies to all States parties to the ACHR and without the necessity of a prior judgment by the Inter-American Court against the respective State. The

---

for amnesty in cases of serious human rights violations, the IACtHR tasked national authorities to modify/amend the respective laws. See *Fermín Ramires v. Guatemala* [2005] IACtHR, Ser. C No. 126: the Court established that a provision of the Guatemalan penal legislation that contravened the ACHR should be amended in a reasonable time and not be applied as long as it was not amended. Likewise in *La Última Tentación de Cristo* (Case of *Olmedo Bustos y otros (La última Tentacion de Cristo) v. Chile* [2001] IACtHR, Ser. C No. 73, para. 4: the Court asked Chile to amend a provision of its constitution as the preliminary censorship established there violated Article 13 (freedom of thought and expression) of the ACHR; the Court did not declare the latter norms "without effect" itself, and it seems that only in reliance on non-derogable rights, in cases concerning *ius cogens* norms violations, the Court resorts to the drastic sanction to nullify a law.

[46] Sagüés (n. 45); see also Juan Carlos Hitters, "Control de Constitucionalidad y Control de Convencionalidad. Comparación (Criterios fijados por la Corte Interamericana de Derechos Humanos)" [2009] 7 *Estudios Constitucionales*, <https://www.scielo.cl/scielo.php?pid=S0718-52002009000200005&script=sci_arttext> (accessed February 5, 2022).

[47] IACtHR, *Almonacid v. Chile* (n. 4), para. 124.

[48] In the interpretation of the IACtHR.

Inter-American Court bases the duty to exercise the conventionality control, inter alia, on Article 27 of the Vienna Convention on the Law of Treaties (VCLT), which holds that a State cannot justify noncompliance with a treaty with reference to internal law.[49] Put differently, the Inter-American Court asks domestic courts to exercise a conventionality control comparable to the constitutionality control in constitutional law. The standard of review is not only the ACHR but also "the interpretation thereof made by the Inter-American Court, which is the ultimate interpreter of the American Convention."[50] The Inter-American Court thus tasks national judges to exercise their review with reference to its own case law. According to the Inter-American Court, national judges have to engage in such controls not only when requested by a party to the case but also "*ex officio*,"[51] and abstain from applying it to the concrete case when an internal norm or law contravenes the ACHR.[52] In situations where the national legislator has failed to amend the deficient law,[53] it is domestic courts and judges that have to give effect to the human rights guarantees in the ACHR. After being applied first in the 2006 *Almonacid* case, the doctrine was consolidated in subsequent jurisprudence, including *Trabajadores Cesados del Congreso (Aguado Alfaro y otros) v. Peru*,[54] and more recently in *Heliodoro Portugal v. Panama*.[55]

In sum, both forms of norm control—the nullification of national laws and the conventionality control—enable an effective implementation of a State's human rights obligations and give maximum effect to the ACHR. The Inter-American Court's supranational determination that national laws, or decrees, are "without effect" bypasses the need for an additional national legal act.[56] The conventionality control especially has far reaching consequences for the inter-American human rights protection system, as it makes national judges guardians of the human rights guarantees enshrined in the ACHR[57] and thus provides for the latter's effective implementation at a decentralized level. The conventionality

---

[49] IACtHR, *Almonacid v. Chile* (n. 4), para. 125.
[50] Ibid., para. 124.
[51] See also *Trabajadores Cesados del Congreso (Aguado Alfaro y otros) v. Peru* [2006] IACtHR, Ser. C No. 158, para. 128.
[52] IACtHR, *Almonacid v. Chile* (n. 4), paras. 123–125: the effect of such control by national judges is *inter partes*, see Sagüés (n. 45), 2. The IACtHR has not pronounced itself on what happens when the respective national tribunal is competent to invalidate norms *erga omnes*. Still, according to Sagüés, it might do so.
[53] See, in this sense, IACtHR, *Almonacid v. Chile* (n. 4), para. 123.
[54] IACtHR, *Trabajadores Cesados del Congreso* (n. 51), para. 128.
[55] *Heliodoro Portugal v. Panamá* [2008] IACtHR, Ser. C No. 186, paras. 180–181. See also IACtHR, *La Cantuta v. Peru* (n. 4), para. 173; *Boyce y otros v. Barbados* [2007] IACtHR, Ser. C No. 169, para. 78.
[56] This facilitates the work of national institutions, especially when the nullification of amnesty laws may be met with domestic resistance (see *infra* section 4.2).
[57] The IACtHR seems to leave open whether such control might be exercised with respect to other human rights treaties; see IACtHR, *Almonacid v. Chile* (n. 4), para. 124: "[A]n international treaty, *such as* the American Convention."

control in particular, if properly implemented, would counterbalance the limited number of cases brought before the IACtHR, as domestic judges are required to ensure the effectiveness of the guarantees contained in the ACHR at the national level. Such effectiveness seems crucial in the field of amnesties and, more broadly, in the Latin American context of democratic transitions and serious human rights violations. The "toolbox" of the IACtHR, therefore, is highly developed. What remains to be seen is the domestic reception and the impact of the Inter-American Human Rights System "on the ground."

4.2. Domestic Reception of the IACtHR's Amnesty Jurisprudence

To truly measure the IACtHR's impact on democratic transitions, a domestic-oriented analysis seems warranted. As will be shown, the reception of the Court's jurisprudence at the national level was generally positive, with the judiciary (domestic tribunals and judges) turning out to be the IACtHR's best allies. It did not make a difference whether States were parties to a specific case or not, which illustrates the acceptance of the Court's doctrine of conventionality control. What somehow mattered, conversely, was the method with which the respective amnesty law was adopted, namely, its procedural legitimacy—self-amnesty versus an amnesty passed by parliamentary approval—and the degree of societal consensus on which the amnesty was based. Peru, Chile, Argentina, and Uruguay will be discussed by way of example.

Peru fully complied with the Inter-American Court's *Barrios Altos* decision, which concerned an act of self-amnesty passed by Alberto Fujimori. As the Peruvian national legal system does not provide for a "nullification of laws," this was done on the basis of the incorporation of the ACHR into the domestic legal system[58] and national legal provisions, making it possible to give effect to international decisions.[59] According to the Peruvian Constitutional Court (*Tribunal Constitucional*),[60] the Inter-American Court's interpretative authority

---

[58] Arts. 55–57 of the Peruvian Constitution. While the 1993 Peruvian Constitution does not provide for an incorporation of international (human rights) treaties at a certain rank in its legal hierarchy, Article 55 provides that international treaties are "part of national law"; its final provisions establish that constitutional rights and freedoms have to be interpreted in accordance with treaties on human rights ratified by Peru.

[59] See, e.g., La Ley No 27.775, "Regula el procedimiento de ejecución de Sentencias emitidas por Tribunales Supranacionales"; art. 115 Código Procesal Constitucional.

[60] The Peruvian Constitutional Court acts as the final interpreter of the constitution and may derogate, with *erga omnes* effects, unconstitutional legislation. In addition, normal judges may decide not to apply or enforce unconstitutional laws with effects *inter partes* (system of judicial diffuse norm control in combination with a concentrated control in a specialized extra court; see arts. 138, 201, 202, and 204 of the Peruvian Constitution). See also Sagüés, "Regional Report Latin America"

in accordance with Article 62.3 ACHR made the Court's interpretations binding upon all national authorities, including Peru's Constitutional Court. More particularly, the Peruvian Constitutional Court found that not only the resolutive part of the judgments but also the Inter-American Court's reasoning had binding force.[61] The Peruvian Constitutional Court accordingly followed the IACtHR's determination that the 1995 amnesty laws were devoid of legal effect.[62] In short, the Inter-American Court's position on the nullity of amnesty laws contravening the ACHR was given effect in Peru.[63]

The implementation of *Almonacid* in Chile was more indirect. At first, no direct effect was attributed to the Inter-American Court's judgments.[64] Furthermore, a bill promoted by the Chilean government to amend the Chilean criminal code so that serious human rights violations were not subject to amnesties or statutes of limitation, such as foreseen in the 1978 amnesty decree law, had not been passed as of April 2019.[65] Still, the 1978 amnesty decree law is not applied in practice as the Chilean Supreme Court has ruled consistently that the amnesty decreed by the military government was inapplicable to war crimes or crimes against humanity, and that these crimes were not subject to the statute of limitations.[66] The Chilean Supreme Court referred inter alia to the Inter-American Court's *Almonacid* decision—as well as to *Barrios Altos*—when establishing that domestic legal norms could not be used as obstacles for the prosecution of perpetrators of gross human rights violations.[67] Thus, national authorities complied with the Inter-American Court's findings, although on a case-by-case basis. Given that legislation to repeal the controversial 1978 amnesty decree law

[2009] VII. Konrad Adenauer Stiftung Conference on International Law: The Contribution of Constitutional Courts in Safeguarding Basic Rights, Democracy and Development, 10.

[61] This even in cases where Peru was not a party to the dispute.
[62] See Peruvian Constitutional Court, *Caso Santiago Martín Rivas*, November 29, 2005, Expediente No. 4587-2004, AA/TC, para. 63.
[63] See, e.g., the findings of the IACtHR in *La Cantuta v. Peru*, where the Court establishes that Peru had fully implemented the *Barrios Altos* Judgment: IACtHR, *La Cantuta v. Peru* (n. 4), para. 186.
[64] The 2005 reforms of the Chilean Constitution introduced a system of centralized norm control located at the Constitutional Court with a monopoly to control the constitutionality of legislation with *erga omnes* effects (art. 82 of the Chilean Constitution). Still, the Chilean Supreme Court is tasked to exercise the system of diffuse norm control until the end of its term of office (*Cuadragesimacuarta*, Chilean Constitution). Article 5 of the Chilean Constitution establishes the obligation to respect the fundamental rights of persons recognized in the Constitution and relevant international human rights treaties. Thus, international human rights treaties arguably have a constitutional rank.
[65] See the Office of the High Commissioner on Human Rights, "Committee on Enforced Disappearances Examines Report of Chile," Geneva April 10, 2019, <https://www.ohchr.org/en/NewsEvents/Pages/Display News.aspx?NewsID=24469&LangID=E> (accessed February 5, 2022).
[66] See Ibid.
[67] Supreme Court of Chile, Criminal Chamber, *Molco Case* (No. 559-2004) of December 13, 2006, paras. 19-20. See also the IACtHR's findings in *Almonacid v. Chile* (n. 4), para. 121.

had not been passed, Chilean courts only chose in practice not to apply the 1978 amnesty decree law.

The case of Argentina demonstrates that, in States that are not party to a case, the reception of the Inter-American Court's judgments is generally good and the Court's impact on transitions to democracy are considerable, from a Transitional Justice perspective. The Inter-American Court's doctrine of *control de convencionalidad* was explicitly accepted by the Argentine Supreme Court.[68] For example, the Argentine Supreme Court relied extensively on the *Barrios Altos* decision of the Inter-American Court when stating that Argentina's amnesty laws (*Punto Final* and *Obediencia Debida*) were unconstitutional. The Argentine Supreme Court drew on the Inter-American Court's reasoning especially when finding that the Argentine amnesty laws had the same deficiencies as the Peruvian ones: being "self-amnesties," ad hoc, and intended to prevent the prosecution of grave human rights violations.[69] The impact of the Inter-American Court's jurisprudence thus seems considerable: domestic amnesty legislation is not applied to specific cases or declared unconstitutional among others in reliance on the criteria established in the judgments of the Inter-American Court.

In sum, the Inter-American Court's amnesty jurisprudence was met with acceptance in Peru, Chile, and in Argentina. In all three countries, the Court's case law seems to have supported transitions by alleviating domestic institutions. In Peru and Chile the nullification of amnesty laws through the Inter-American Court "facilitated" the work of Chilean and Peruvian domestic authorities insofar as it dispensed with the need for an additional national act. In Argentina, the Inter-American Court's amnesty jurisprudence provided standards and increased the legitimacy of the findings of Argentine tribunals by requiring them to engage in the *control de convencionalidad*. This support for democratic transitions seems especially important in cases where it is difficult—due to internal resistance—to formally amend or repeal the respective amnesty laws at the domestic level. It also points to the crucial role of domestic judges where the implementation of human rights obligations and transitions to democracy are concerned. Therewith, the domestic rule of law is strengthened through the case law of the IACtHR.

---

[68] See the Argentine Supreme Court cases *Mazzeo Julio Lilo y otros* (n. 7), para. 21; and *Recurso de hecho deducido por la defensa de Julio Héctor Simón en la causa Simon, Julio Hector y otros s/ privación ilegitima de la libertad, etc.*, June 14, 2005, the Argentine Supreme Court relied extensively on the *Barrios Altos* decision of the IACtHR when stating that Argentina's amnesty laws (*Punto Final* and *Obediencia Debida*) were unconstitutional. See the questioning of constitutionality control in Acosta by the Argentine Prosecutor General, Walter Carnota, "The Inter-American Court of Human Rights and 'Conventionality Control'" [2015] unpublished paper, 25 et seq. See also the Argentine Supreme Court in *Rodríguez Pereyra v. Ejército Nacional*, November 27, 2012.

[69] Argentine Supreme Court, *Rodríguez Pereyra v. Ejército Nacional* (n. 68), para. 24; see also *Mazzeo Julio Lilo y otros* (n. 7).

Tellingly, the reception of the Inter-American Court's case law at the domestic level is particularly good in cases where the amnesty laws at stake lack procedural legitimacy: when they are self-amnesties or were adopted under the pressure of the former regime, as was the case in Peru, Chile, and Argentina. The Court's jurisprudence is especially welcome in these instances. Conversely, the reception of the Inter-American Court's amnesty jurisprudence is more critical in countries where the amnesty is combined with a broad societal consensus, as was the case in Uruguay. Indeed, the reception of the *Gelman* case at the domestic level was controversial: the Uruguayan vote on a law doing away with the Expiry Law in October 2011 resulted in a 49–49 deadlock. Until 2019, Uruguay had not fully complied with the Inter-American Court's judgment in the *Gelman* case. There seemed to be a lack of effective prosecution from judicial bodies, a general unwillingness to recognize crimes as crimes against humanity, and a certain opposition to the conventionality control.[70] This indicates how influential the method with which an amnesty law is adopted at the domestic level can be in determining the reception of the Inter-American Court's case law. The Inter-American Court's authority is questioned to a further reaching extent in relation to amnesties that were adopted by parliament or backed by a broad societal consensus, as in Uruguay, and thus in a process with increased domestic procedural legitimacy.[71] Conversely, it proved to be of minor relevance whether a particular State was party to a case: Peru, Chile, and Argentina complied equally well with the Court's judgments even though not all were party to a case and followed the interpretative guidance provided by the Inter-American Court.

5. Concluding Remarks

To deal with past human rights violations is a challenge for any society moving from a violent past to a hopefully more peaceful future. The success of these transitions will largely depend on a society's ability to address this past. This has proved true for many Latin American States. As was shown throughout this chapter, the Inter-American Court has accompanied domestic democratic transition processes remarkably well through its "amnesty jurisprudence," overruling the impunity extended to perpetrators of violations. The Court's transformative impact is thus considerable, as illustrated in Peru, Chile, and Argentina.

---

[70] Center for Justice and International Law, "Uruguay reconoció ante la Corte Interamericana de Derechos Humanos el incumplimiento de la sentencia del caso Gelman," September 19, 2019, <https://www.cejil.org/es/uruguay-reconocio-corte-interamericana-derechos-humanos-incumplimiento-sentencia-del-caso-gelman> (accessed February 5, 2022).

[71] Another challenge may arise in relation to amnesties that are part of a peace process (as in Colombia).

Different dimensions, however, can be distinguished. First, the Inter-American Court has set up clear substantive standards, which guide democratic transitions at the domestic level and set limits on State action from a human rights perspective—especially in terms of the rights of victims. These standards cover the three dimensions of Transitional Justice—retributive, restorative, and distributive. Domestic transitions to democracy, therefore, are facilitated along these lines. Second, innovative techniques of norm control make the implementation of the respective human rights standards easier at the domestic level. The nullification of amnesty laws without the need for an additional domestic act helps to overcome national obstacles in implementation—for example, internal resistance—and contributes to giving maximum effect to the respective standards. The conventionality control disperses the impact of the Inter-American Court's jurisprudence throughout the Americas. Thus, the *inter partes* effect of judgments—which, in view of the limited number of IACtHR judgments, could be an impediment to transformative impact—is overcome.

Overall, the Inter-American Court's case law on amnesties has been well received in Latin American States, as shown in Peru, Chile, and Argentina. Domestic tribunals especially have given effect to the Inter-American Court's jurisprudence and made themselves allies of the Court. Indeed, the references to the Court's jurisprudence seem to support domestic tribunals in their fight against impunity and inadmissible amnesties at the domestic level, as it gives their decisions moral, political, and legal authority. Domestic tribunals are relieved from carrying the burden of dealing with past human rights violations alone. The Inter-American Court thus supports domestic judiciaries vis-à-vis the executive and possibly the legislative branch, strengthens the separation of powers, and furthers domestic checks and balances. Notably, the Inter-American Court's amnesty jurisprudence is best received in relation to amnesty laws that were passed by the former executive branch responsible for or involved in human rights violations, and therefore lack internal domestic legitimacy.

In sum, the transformative impact of the Inter-American Human Rights System appears most lasting through its strengthening of domestic tribunals. This is not only of relevance for the question of how to deal with *past* human rights violations. A strong and independent domestic judiciary is also a firm promise for a peaceful and democratic society in the future, which is perhaps the most important and most durable impact of the ICCAL in Latin America.

II.12
Impact of the Inter-American Human Rights System in the Struggle against Impunity

By Oscar Parra Vera

1. Introduction

In 1994, Juan Méndez[1] indicated that the Inter-American System involved "a promise that the community of nations of the Hemisphere made to its victims: that if the State institutions did not respond to the violations of human rights, the international authorities would be there to listen to their grievances and to re-establish the observance of law." An analysis of the jurisprudential evolution of the Inter-American Court of Human Rights in the form of "due diligence" in combating impunity helps illustrate the transformational impact the Inter-American System has triggered in making possible said promise.

For example, the first stage of this process[2] corresponds to the 1970s and 80s, when the System played a significant role in denouncing and documenting the systematic, large-scale violations of human rights, especially in the context of military dictatorships and abuse of states of emergency. The system of individual petitions was then at a very early stage. The emphasis was placed on *in loco* visits by the Inter-American Commission and on the corresponding country reports. Significant examples of the latter are the Commission's visits and reports concerning Chile (1974, 1976, and 1977) and Argentina (1980). These reports and visits dealt with military dictatorships in which there was no domestic institution for confronting State repression. Therefore, the international community provided the only answer. One difficulty the Inter-American Court faced in this

---

[1] Juan E. Méndez, "Prólogo," en *ILSA. Sistema Interamericano para la Protección de los Derechos Humanos: Aportes para una evaluación* (ILSA 1994), 9.

[2] I elaborate on this historical description of the regional system as of, inter alia, in Víctor Abramovich, "De las violaciones masivas a los patrones estructurales. Nuevos enfoques y clásicas tensiones en el sistema interamericano de derechos humanos" [2010] 11 *Sur, Revista Internacional de Derechos Humanos* 7–39 and Cecilia Medina Quiroga, "Los 40 años de la Convención Americana sobre Derechos Humanos a la luz de cierta jurisprudencia de la Corte Interamericana" [2009] *Anuario de Derechos Humanos* 15–34.

phase was the fact that the system of individual petitions had not yet crystallized for dealing with systematic, large-scale violations. In other words, the System presupposed States governed by the rule of law whereby domestic remedies were exhausted before subsequently tackling the situation of regional protection. In its first contentious cases, the Court established standards of procedure and evidence to allow it to confront such obstacles.

A second aspect of this process is connected to the so-called "transitions to democracy" and the problems associated with impunity caused by past abuse. Reports and disputes surfaced of cases relating to restrictions on amnesties and on the rights to truth, justice, and reparation. At the same time, emphasis was placed on removing the loopholes of repressive systems such as the abuse of states of emergency, the restrictions on *habeas corpus*, and the arbitrary use of military criminal justice. During this period, institutional forms emerged in some countries (constitutional courts, ombudsman offices, supervisory bodies, etc.) to report current and past arbitrariness. However, the real power the oppressors still managed to maintain, along with other forces and factors, weakened the activity of these bodies and nullified their impact. The international community was beginning to support the efforts being made in domestic law, and assumed a more active role—via inter-American litigation of strategic cases—in such cases where progress is much too limited.

Taking into account the previous framework, in the present chapter, I analyze several paradigmatic issues concerning the evolution of jurisprudence in accessing justice in the context of the battle against impunity. I shall begin by highlighting some details and supplements made in the standards of due diligence, aimed at greater accountability of the efforts that States bring forward in this matter. In this respect, whereas twenty years ago, the main battle was to document an international consensus on the impossibility of pardoning serious violations of human rights, in the last few years, the Inter-American Court has had to analyze more complex institutional circumstances which have generated case law in aspects such as inter-State judicial cooperation, prevalent criminal offenses, the "criminality of the system," and due diligence in investigating violence toward women as a form of discrimination.

I shall continue by analyzing some of these circumstances and examples in order to later consider their impact. There are, of course, other interesting issues and cases I have not included in this selection. Nonetheless, the focus on these cases aims to best explain the advances and challenges the inter-American case law faces in its battle against impunity.[3]

---

[3] I do not include in these examples the significant progress in due diligence concerning the investigation of abuse of women and gender-based violence, aspects which are analyzed in other chapters of this book. Because this book also includes a chapter on transitional justice, I make very little mention of this topic.

2. Some Details on the Scope of the Need to Investigate Serious Violations of Human Rights

In 1988, in its first contentious case concerning forced disappearance, the Inter-American Court indicated that the duty to guarantee the rights recognized by the Convention involves the duty of preventing, investigating, and sanctioning all violation of human rights.[4] Subsequently, in 2001, in the judgment on the massacre of *Barrios Altos v. Peru*,[5] the Court established that the self-amnesty laws were incompatible with the American Convention along the following lines:

> [...] all amnesty provisions, provisions on prescription and the establishment of measures designed to eliminate responsibility are inadmissible, because they are intended to prevent the investigation and punishment of those responsible for serious human rights violations such as torture, summary, extrajudicial or arbitrary executions and forced disappearance, all of them prohibited because they violate non-derogable rights recognised by international human rights law.

Another chapter of the present book[6] analyzes in detail the impact of the *Barrios Altos* case regarding various amnesties adopted in the Americas. Thus, in this segment, I merely concentrate on describing how in recent years the Court has issued various rulings which complement and clarify the criteria indicated in the *Velásquez* and *Barrios Altos* cases.

2.1. Fraudulent Res Judicata and Admissible Weightings Surrounding the Principle of *Ne Bis In Idem*

First of all, the Court developed the concept of *fraudulent res judicata*. In the case of *Carpio Nicolle et al. v. Guatemala*,[7] in association with extrajudicial executions and attacks on personal integrity, the Court considered that "the courts of law [acted] without independence and impartiality, applying legal standards and provisions contrary to due diligence, and omitting the implementation of corresponding ones." Additionally, the Court established that there had been "continual obstruction of the investigations by State agents and the so-called 'parallel groups' in power, and also a lack of diligence in conducting the investigations, all of which [established] total impunity," it had missed the "guarantees needed

---

[4] *Case of Velásquez Rodríguez v. Honduras* [1988], IACtHR, Ser. C No. 4.
[5] *Case of Barrios Altos v. Peru. Merits* [2001], IACtHR, Ser. C No. 75.
[6] See Christina Binder in Chapter II.11 of this anthology.
[7] *Case of Carpio Nicolle et al. v. Guatemala* [2004], IACtHR, Ser. C No. 117, paras. 76.23, 76.34, and 133.

to start investigating and evaluate all evidentiary material," and claimed that the "prevailing general situation of the legal system [...] [indicated] its inability to maintain its independence and impartiality in the face of pressure which [may have been] exercised on its members." The Court alluded to the "fraudulent res judicata," and considered that "it [had been] established that systematic obstruction of the administration of justice and of due diligence [had] prevented the identification, judgement and punishment of the material and intellectual perpetrators" the victims were subjected to.

The *Carpio* case tends to equate fraudulence with a seriously irregular global situation in the developed overall legal proceedings. Subsequently, the notion of fraudulence was applied in a manner closely associated with the intervention of military jurisdiction. In fact, in the case of *Gutiérrez Soler v. Colombia*, which relates to acts of torture, the Court stated that the case had been brought forward to the military criminal justice authorities "where it was decided to stop all proceedings," thus disqualifying, for no apparent reason, the victim's legal claim. At the same time, a disciplinary investigation was filed by applying the *non bis in idem* principle. The Court determined that a "fraudulent res judicata" was evident because the national proceedings were "contaminated by [v]ices" connected with a lack of respect for the rules of due diligence, and, because of this, "the State, exonerating itself from its investigation and punishment obligations, shall not invoke judgements emanating from proceedings which do not comply with the standards of the American Convention, since legal decisions which originate in internationally wrongful circumstances are not res judicata."[8] This phrasing in the *Gutierrez* case is somewhat complex for an understanding of the scope of "fraudulent res judicata" when associated with all abuse of the Convention.

Nevertheless, the subsequent application of the standard is associated with situations in which impunity is clearly promoted. In the *Almonacid* case,[9] the Court indicated that the *ne bis in idem* was not an absolute right and was therefore inapplicable when: (i) the action of the court presiding over the case was aimed at waiving or suspending responsibility for an abuse of human rights or international law or at shielding the person concerned from criminal responsibility; (ii) the proceedings were not conducted independently or impartially in conformity with the due procedural guarantees, or (iii) there was no proper intention of bringing the perpetrators to justice. When presented with these situations, the Court indicated that either an "apparent" or "fraudulent" res judicata arises, as well as what was stated in the aforementioned *Carpio Nicolle* case. In addition, the Court indicated:

---

[8] *Case of Gutiérrez Soler v. Colombia* [2005], IACtHR, Ser. C No. 132.
[9] *Case of Almonacid Arellano et al. v. Chile* [2006], IACtHR, Ser. C No. 154.

If new facts or evidence [appeared] that make it possible to ascertain the identity of those responsible for human rights violations, particularly for crimes against humanity, investigations can be reopened, even if the case ended in an acquittal with the authority of a final judgement, since the dictates of justice, the rights of the victims, and the spirit and the wording of the American Convention supersedes the protection of the *ne bis in idem* principle.[10]

2.2. Cooperative Interstate Obligations Regarding Investigation and Extradition

Furthermore, the Court specified obligations derived from international law in terms of inter-State cooperation in investigating and possibly extraditing alleged perpetrators in cases of serious violation of human rights. Thereon, in the *Case of Goiburú et al v. Paraguay*,[11] the Court issued a ruling on the forced disappearance of several persons within the context of the so-called Operation Condor. The Court reasoned that thousands of citizens of the Southern Cone had tried to escape repression in their countries of origin during the 1970s and 80s, seeking refuge in neighboring countries. As a result, the dictatorships developed a strategy called "Operation Condor" (a key name given to the alliance uniting the security forces and intelligence services of the Southern Cone dictatorships in combating and subjugating persons designated as "subversive elements").

In the face of the prosecution of the perpetrators of Operation Condor, the Court considered that Paraguay had "a compulsory obligation to have requested the extradition of the accused, promptly and with due diligence"[12] as well as "the necessary measures, of a diplomatic and judicial nature, to prosecute and punish all those responsible for the violations committed, which includes furthering the corresponding extradition requests by all possible means."[13] The Court found that "the inexistence of extradition treaties does not constitute a motive or justification for failing to institute a request of this type"[14] and that "the need to eradicate impunity establishes an obligation for the international community to ensure interstate cooperation to this end."[15] With that in mind, the Court alluded to a "collective guarantee" within the system, whereby the States had an

---

[10] Ibid., para. 154.
[11] *Case of Goiburú et al. v. Paraguay* [2006], IACtHR, Ser. C No. 153.
[12] Ibid., para. 130.
[13] Ibid.
[14] Ibid.
[15] Ibid., para. 131.

obligation to exercise "their jurisdiction to apply their domestic law and international law to prosecute and, if applicable, punish those responsible"[16] or by collaborating "with other States which do so or attempt to do so."[17] Hence, extradition is an important instrument to this end.

The foregoing was reiterated and deepened in the *Case of La Cantuta v. Peru*.[18] The events, which occurred in 1992, are connected with the disappearance of eight persons (one professor and seven university students) and the execution of two students. The soldiers responsible for these actions were pardoned under an amnesty law until the legal decisions applied in the said law were annulled. The Court stated that "since it was a matter of systematic violation of human rights, it presented, before the international community, the need to eradicate impunity as an obligation of interstate cooperation," to the extent that a State exercises its jurisdiction or collaborates with other States to prompt investigation of the events. These standards of inter-State cooperation had the important effect of creating building blocks permitting the extradition to Peru of Alberto Fujimori, ex-president of that country, on whom the Peruvian judiciary placed criminal responsibility for the massacre of Barrios Altos and the disappearances in La Cantuta. The rulings adopted by the Inter-American Court substantiated, to a large extent, the ruling of the Supreme Court of Chile in permitting the extradition of the latter ex-politician. Subsequently, the Special Chamber, specially created by the Supreme Court of Justice of Peru for the trial of Fujimori, found that even though the proven facts, the penal-judicial relevance of the latter, the interpretation and implementation of the pertinent penal standards and the individualization of the penalty were exclusive domestic court powers,[19] one could not disconnect this from the interpretation and application of international law performed by the Inter-American Court.

Another projection of these inter-State cooperation obligations can be found in a significant order on the monitoring compliance issued in 2009 in the *Case of the Mapiripán Massacre v. Colombia*, whose judgment on merits was issued in 2005.[20] This case refers to a massacre committed by Colombian paramilitary groups, which occurred in 1997.

---

[16] Ibid.
[17] Ibid.
[18] *Case of La Cantuta v. Peru* [2006], IACtHR, Ser. C No. 162.
[19] Special Chamber of the Supreme Court of Justice of Peru, Judgment of April 7, 2009. For this and other types of impact on the jurisprudence of the Inter-American Court in Peru, see Clara Sandoval, "The Challenge of Impunity in Peru: The Significance of the InterAmerican Court of Human Rights" [2008] 1(5) *Essex Human Rights Review* 97–118.
[20] *Case of the "Mapiripán Massacre" v. Colombia* [2005], IACtHR, Ser. C No. 134.

The Inter-American Court demanded a detailed investigation of the events. Years later, one of the commanders of the paramilitary group that committed the atrocities was extradited to the United States to face drug-trafficking charges. It was alleged, however, that the extradition was a response to the government's intention to prevent the person from telling the truth about what had occurred, particularly the extent to which State authorities were involved in the said events. The Inter-American Court then issued an order in which it stated that "the implementation of entities such as extradition shall not serve as a mechanism to favour, seek or secure impunity."[21]

Bearing in mind that extradition had occurred on drug-trafficking charges, the Court pointed out that "the prevailing consideration must be that of imputation of serious violations of human rights."[22] Furthermore, it demanded that the State of Colombia "clarify the mechanisms, instruments and legal entities applied to ensure that the extradited person collaborates in the investigation of the acts [and] to ensure that he is duly tried."[23] The Court took into account the obstacles that the said extradition might present for truth, justice, and reparations of the serious violations of human rights attributable to State paramilitarism. The Court mentioned the "lack of agreement in legal cooperation"[24] between Colombia and the United States in "ensuring that the proceedings taking place outside of Colombia do not interfere with or jeopardise the investigations into the serious violations which occurred."[25] This order was later used by the Criminal Chamber of the Supreme Court of Justice of Colombia as one of the grounds for refusing the extradition of a paramilitary leader until the latter had done his duty concerning truth, justice, and reparations in accordance with a "Justice and Peace" law adopted in the said country.[26]

The IACtHR reiterated this criterium in the case of *Manuel Cepeda Vargas v. Colombia*,[27] regarding the extrajudicial execution of a left-wing party leader, within the context of a pattern of assassinations of leaders of the said party. In this case, one of the perpetrators had been extradited to the United States. The Court reiterated that the entity of extradition must not pose an obstacle to due diligence in the investigations nor be used as a mechanism to secure impunity.

---

[21] *Case of the "Mapiripán Massacre" v. Colombia* [2009], para. 41.
[22] Ibid.
[23] Ibid.
[24] Ibid.
[25] Ibid.
[26] Supreme Court of Justice of Colombia, Criminal Appeals Chamber, Judgment of August 19, 2009.
[27] *Case of Manuel Cepeda Vargas v. Colombia* [2010], IACtHR, Ser. C No. 213.

2.3. Qualification of Conduct as a Crime against Humanity to Determine the Scope of the Obligation to Investigate: Debates

The Inter-American Court is not a criminal court. Nevertheless, in some cases it has been considered pertinent to consider certain acts as crimes pursuant to international criminal law with the aim of determining the scope of international responsibility or to specify the scope of due diligence in the investigation of the acts. In the aforementioned case of *Almonacid v. Chile*,[28] the amnesty law dealing with crimes by the military dictatorship suffered in said country was analyzed. The Court reviewed the elements that constitute a crime against humanity and assessed what had occurred based on the said elements. It found that the assassination of the victim, which occurred in 1973, was part of a widespread or systematic attack on segments of the civilian population. It indicated that there could be no amnesty for this offense according to the current dictates of international law since it constituted a crime against humanity. Thus, the Court found that the State did not meet its obligation of adapting its national law for the purpose of guaranteeing the rights established in the American Convention, because it kept in force the Decree Law, which in Chile does not exempt crimes against humanity from the general amnesty it grants.

It is possible to consider that the Court qualifies the extrajudicial execution that occurred as a crime against humanity, bearing in mind that its jurisdiction *ratione temporis* could only have been exercised since 1990. The Inter-American Court took into account that the European Court had established that if, at the time of the events, these acts were considered crimes against humanity by international law (as was indeed the case in 1973), it did not matter if national legislation did not penalize them. Therefore, its investigation, judicialization, and penalties are lawful and respect the international principles established to safeguard the guarantees of the defendants. In 1973, the year of the death of Mr. Almonacid Arellano, the commissioning of crimes against humanity, including the murder committed in the context of a widespread and systematic attack on sections of the civilian population, was a violation of an imperative standard of international law. The Court emphasized that the said ban on committing crimes against humanity was a standard of *ius cogens*, and that the punishment of these crimes was an obligation in line with general international law. It concluded that the States could not shirk the duty of investigating, establishing, and sanctioning those responsible for

---

[28] *Case of Almonacid Arellano et al. v. Chile* [2006], IACtHR, Ser. C No. 154.

crimes against humanity, implementing amnesty laws or other types of internal regulation.[29]

The *Almonacid* judgment triggered various debates on whether the Inter-American Court had the competence to declare that certain actions constituted crimes against international criminal law. In fact, in the *Cepeda* case, the State presented a preliminary exception relating to a lack of competence in that matter stating that the Inter-American Court could not declare that a particular right constituted an offense or that a State was responsible for a crime. The Court rejected the allegation, stating that in cases of serious violation of human rights the Court had taken into account that such violations could also be characterized or qualified as crimes against humanity for the purpose of clearly explaining the scope of State responsibility within the Convention in that specific case and assess the respective legal consequences, without these having to imply, in any way, an imputation or offense to any natural person.[30]

Subsequently, within the context of monitoring compliance of the *Barrios Altos* case, the Court determined that the domestic court decision of not considering the facts to be a crime against humanity was contrary to the State's recognition of responsibility and in contradiction with judgments of high domestic authorities (such as the Supreme Court and the Truth and Reconciliation Commission), which is why it failed to comply with Court orders and impaired the right to truth.[31] As can be seen, the qualification of an offense as a crime against humanity by the Inter-American Court should not necessarily be understood as a determination of individual criminal responsibility, but rather, in a complementary manner, be used by an international court or by national institutions to specify the scope of due diligence in the respective investigations and for aspects needed to overcome impunity in a particular case.

2.4. Abuse of the Law and Other Procedural Irregularities Aimed at Hindering Due Diligence

Apart from the impunity built on exclusion from responsibility or forms of amnesty and pardons, the Inter-American Court has had to assess obstacles to due diligence built on irregular abuse of procedural institutions of domestic law belonging to the respective States. In the case of the *"Las Dos Erres" Massacre v. Guatemala*, the use by the defense of those charged with the massacre of at

---

[29] The Court emphasized that said ban on committing crimes against humanity was a standard of *ius cogens*, and that the punishment of these crimes was an obligation in line with general international law.
[30] *Case of Manuel Cepeda Vargas v. Colombia* (n. 27).
[31] *Case of Barrios Altos v. Peru* [2012], IACtHR.

least thirty-three appeals for protection was analyzed, some of which took up to four years to be resolved.[32] The Court considered that "the appeals for legal protection submitted in the internal proceedings exceeded their processing within the terms established by the law,"[33] and that "the provisions which [regulated] the appeal of protection, the lack of due diligence and tolerance of the courts when processing as well as the lack of effective judicial protection, [...] [permitted] the abuse of the writs of protection as a delaying tactic in the proceeding"[34] and the said abuse was transformed "into an element of impunity."[35]

Similarly, in the case of *Ibsen Cárdenas and Ibsen Peña v. Bolivia*, concerning forced disappearance, the Court established that in the course of nine years of domestic crime proceedings, around 111 excuses had been made by various judges of differing hierarchy and specialization of whom 59 suspended instruction, judicial debates, or the prosecution of the same. The Court concluded that the due diligence of the investigation had been impaired, because

> the constant filing of abstentions affected the seriousness of the conduction of the domestic law proceedings. And that those abstentions affected the processing of this case due to the delays brought as a result of the judicial system's minimal control, which, as a consequence of the legislation applied, left to the judges' discretion the referral of abstentions to superior authorities for consultation as to their legality, all of this while threatened with a penalty if the abstentions were declared legal.[36]

2.5. Prevalent Formulation of Criminal Definition and Due Diligence

In cases such as *Heliodoro Portugal v. Panama*, *Tiu Tojín v. Guatemala*, *Ibsen Cárdenas*, and *Ibsen Peña v. Bolivia*, or *Gelman v. Uruguay*, the jurisprudence established that, in the framework of due diligence regarding the prosecution of forced disappearances, when domestic investigations had been opened only as homicide or kidnapping, excluding other offenses such as torture or forced disappearance, it is possible that the criminal case would reach its statute of limitations at the domestic courts. For this reason, it has been noted that

---

[32] *Cf. Case of the "Las Dos Erres" Massacre v. Guatemala* [2009], IACtHR, Ser. C No. 211, paras. 111, 113, 114, and 115.
[33] Ibid., para. 112.
[34] Ibid., para. 120.
[35] Ibid.
[36] *Case of Ibsen Cárdenas and Ibsen Peña v. Bolivia* [2010], IACtHR, Ser. C No. 217, para. 190.

when dealing with serious violations of human rights, in particular forced disappearances, authorities should investigate and prosecute cases based on the most stringent criminal norms. Additionally, as it pertains to a crime of a continuous execution, that is to say, one whose consummation extends over time, when the formulation of criminal definition of the offense of forced disappearance comes into force, the new law became applicable without it representing retroactive application or a violation of the principle of legality.[37] Also, the Court stressed that the formulation of criminal definition of forced disappearance of persons as an autonomous crime and the explicit definition of punishable conduct it included were of vital importance for effective eradication of this practice.

2.6. Due Diligence, Systemic Crimes, and "Transitional" Contexts

A large portion of the case law developments on due diligence are connected with countries which address the matter of how to tackle past atrocities, or what measures ought to be taken to cope with a situation of armed conflict or of large-scale systematic violations of rights. In this context, there is a significant debate as to the specific nature achieved by certain obligations relating to the investigation and punishment of these crimes.

Some of these debates have been raised in cases before the Inter-American Court which involve an analysis of "systemic crimes."[38] For example, in the case of *Rochela Massacre v. Colombia*, the ruling of which was issued in 2007,[39] the Court analyzed the execution, in 1989, of several members of a judicial committee who were investigating crimes committed by paramilitaries. Although Colombia's judiciary had convicted seven individuals and a noncommissioned officer of the army —for concealing information— the Court established that several relationship patterns between the paramilitary group that committed the massacre, and the senior military commanders, and civil authorities of the said zone had not been investigated.

The Court declared said State internationally responsible for the issuance of a legal framework through which it encouraged the creation of self-defense groups which developed into paramilitary ones.[40] Moreover, the Court declared that

---

[37] *Case of Gelman v. Uruguay. Merits and Costs* [2011], IACtHR, Ser. C No. 221.
[38] For more on the concept and implications of institutional design inherent to systemic criminality, see Michael Reed Hurtado (ed.), *Judicialización de crímenes de sistema. Estudios de caso y análisis comparado* (ICTJ 2008).
[39] *Case of the Rochela Massacre v. Colombia* [2007], IACtHR, Ser. C No. 163.
[40] *Case of the 19 Merchants v. Colombia* [2004], IACtHR, Ser. C No. 109.

Colombia had not adopted the necessary measures to effectively end the risky situation created by the same State by way of the aforementioned legal framework,[41] and had not adopted effective preventative and protective measures for the civilian population in a situation where attacks from paramilitary groups could likely be anticipated.[42] Also, the Court declared Colombia responsible for the support, acquiescence, participation, and collaboration between members of the armed forces and paramilitaries.[43]

In the case of the *Rochela Massacre*, the Court specifically analyzed a regulation and counter-guerrilla combat manual, which stated in great detail the functions and ties between the armed civilian groups and the security forces. The test in this case indicated that such regulations had fostered various institutional relationships between the State and the paramilitaries, including training, organization and patrols, and intelligence networks. Thereon, the Court specified:

[T]he State allowed the involvement and cooperation of private individuals in the performance of certain duties (such as the military patrol of public order areas, the employment of arms designed for the exclusive use of the armed forces or the performance of military intelligence activities), which, in general, are within the exclusive competence of the State and where the State has the special duty to act as a guarantor. Therefore, the State is directly responsible, either as a result of its acts or omissions, for all the activities undertaken by these private individuals in the performance of the foregoing duties, particularly if it is taken into consideration that private individuals are not subject to the strict control exercised over public officials regarding the performance of their duties. The situation in which private individuals cooperated in the performance of such duties reached such a magnitude that, when the State sought to adopt measures designed to address the lack of restraint in the actions undertaken by paramilitary groups, these groups themselves, with the support of State agents, attacked the judicial officers.[44]

Furthermore, the Court emphasized the particular gravity of the crimes. The Court took into account that the State was responsible for a massacre directed against its own judicial officers while they were performing their duty of investigating serious violations of human rights, and that members of the State armed forces had participated in the massacre. Furthermore, the Court stated that such a crime was part of a pattern of killings and acts of violence toward

---

[41] *Case of the Pueblo Bello Massacre v. Colombia* [2006], IACtHR, Ser. C No. 140.
[42] *Case of the Ituango Massacres v. Colombia* [2006], IACtHR, Ser. C No. 148.
[43] Ibid.; *Case of the "Mapiripán Massacre" v. Colombia* [2005], IACtHR, Ser. C No. 134.
[44] *Case of the Rochela Massacre v. Colombia* (n. 39), para. 102.

judicial officers with such responsibilities, the aim being to intimidate and frighten the justice system in order to achieve impunity for atrocities.

The Court observed that the State failed to conscientiously investigate the systematic patterns in which the actions of those responsible were incriminated. Instead, over a period of eighteen years in a criminal trial, the prosecution at the local level made at least seven failed attempts to identify and single out approximately one hundred persons who were indicated by an "alias" or whose role in a paramilitary group was clearly uncertain. Additionally, the attempts to identify members of the armed forces were confined to officers and subalterns of a low rank. The State failed to investigate the responsibility of high-ranking military officers in the zone. Furthermore, the disciplinary trials of civil authorities and other State agents had been completely inefficient. The Court found that all the foregoing "affected, in particular, the identification of possible responsible persons in charge of the military battalions involved in the field of activity of the paramilitary groups associated with the massacre."[45] Taking into account the dimensions of what had not been investigated, the Court highlighted the need to analyze patterns associated with the criminal execution structure and the responsibility of the military commanders of the zone.[46]

> In context of the facts of the present case, the principles of due diligence required that the proceedings be carried out taking into account the complexity of the facts, the context in which they occurred and the systematic patterns that explain why the events occurred. In addition, the proceedings should have ensured that there were no omissions in gathering evidence or in the development of logical lines of investigation. Thus, the judicial authorities should have borne in mind the factors [...] that denote a complex structure of individuals involved in the planning and execution of the crime, which entailed the direct participation of many individuals and the support and collaboration of others, including State agents, an organisational structure which existed before the crime and persisted after it had been perpetrated, because the individuals who belong to it share common goals.[47]

In a similar vein, concerning due diligence in the investigation of *systemic crimes* in the *Cepeda* case, the Court announced that army members and

---

[45] Ibid., para. 164.
[46] The Court indicated that "the judicial authorities should have borne in mind the factors [...] that denote a complex structure of individuals involved in the planning and execution of the crime, which entailed the direct participation of many individuals and the support and collaboration of others, including State agents, an organisational structure which existed before the crime and persisted after it had been perpetrated, because the individuals who belong to it share common goals." Ibid., para. 158.
[47] Ibid.

members of one or several paramilitary groups had participated in the planning and implementation of the killings. The Court established:

> [A]lthough the division of tasks makes it difficult to clarify the ties between the perpetrators, in complex cases, the obligation to investigate includes the duty to direct the efforts of the apparatus of the State to clarify the structures that allowed these violations, the reasons for them, the causes, the beneficiaries and the consequences, and not merely to discover, prosecute, and, if applicable, punish the direct perpetrators.[48]

In view of the foregoing, the IACtHR ordered as a redress to:

> identify the group of individuals involved in the planning and execution of the facts, including those who designed, planned or assumed control, decision or leadership of their implementation, and those who performed the necessary logistic functions to execute the decisions taken, even if senior civil authorities, high-ranking military officers or intelligence services are involved, avoiding omissions in following up on logical lines of investigation.[49]

It is possible to detect a certain complementarity between these standards and those developed in international criminal law regarding criminal participation such as the "joint criminal enterprise," perpetration-by-means, co-perpetration-by-means, command responsibility, and so forth. The use of these entities to allocate individual criminal responsibility can help toward giving effect to strict due diligence in the investigation depending on the details implemented by the Inter-American Court.[50]

On the other hand, in the *Rochela Massacre* case and in the *Cepeda* case, the IACtHR was informed of the implementation of standards of "transitional justice" in relation to the process of demobilization and bestowal of judicial benefits to paramilitary groups. In Colombia, "alternative sentencing" was incorporated as a "benefit consistent with suspending the issuance of the determined penalty in the respective sentence, replacing it with an alternative penalty" of between five and eight years duration, "conceded to allow the beneficiary to contribute to

---

[48] *Case of Manuel Cepeda Vargas v. Colombia* (n. 27), para. 118.
[49] Ibid., para. 216.
[50] In this context, concepts such as "collection of evidence," "relevant fact," the assessment of evidence, among other benchmarks for an investigative methodology, evolve according to the needs of the inquiry into systematization. For an analysis of this possible dynamic relationship, see Ward Ferdinandusse, *Direct Application of International Criminal Law in National Courts* (T.C.M., Asser Press 2006) and, in the case of Colombia, Alejandro Aponte, "Persecución nacional de crímenes internacionales: el caso colombiano," en K. Ambos y E. Malarino (eds.), *Persecución nacional de crímenes internacionales en América Latina y España* (Instituto MaxPlank para derecho penal internacional de Friburgo y Fundación Konrad Adenauer 2003), 201–258.

the achievement of national peace, collaborate with the law, and make amends to and adequately resocialise the victims."[51]

Concerning this type of law, in the case of the *Rochela Massacre*, the Court stated that "all the elements which prompt the effectivity of the penalty should return a verifiably sound objective and be compatible with the Convention."[52] The insistence on verifiable compliance of this objective, intended as a penal benefit, infers that the Court does not deny the possibility of granting such a benefit. Nevertheless, the Court correspondingly verifies—both normatively and empirically—that the State makes progress with the high legal constraint in its proposal of justice to the victims.

On the other hand, some of these standards on demobilization allow the acquisition of legal benefits (for example, suspension of the issuance of penalties) for persons who were not investigated for serious human rights violations, even though they belonged to a group responsible for systemic crimes (such as persons who claim to have participated only as logistical support or only carried illegal weapons). In the *Cepeda* case, the Court conceded that during the process of demobilization of one of the perpetrators of the crimes, the State did not adopt the due diligence required for his individualization and proper identification, so that he would not receive those benefits, which were intended for individuals not involved in serious violations of human rights.

At the end of 2010, the IACtHR issued a further significant precedent in the area of transitional justice: the case of *Gomes Lund et al. ("Guerrilha Do Araguaia") v. Brazil*.[53] The matter was the forced disappearance of the members of a resistance movement during the Brazilian military regime, and the implementation of an amnesty law which hindered the investigation and punishment of those responsible. The IACtHR reiterated its jurisprudence concerning access to justice in such cases. Concerning what was debated upon by the parties as to whether the Brazilian Amnesty Law was an amnesty, a self-amnesty or a "political agreement," the Court indicated that incompatibility with the American Convention included amnesties of serious violations of human rights and was not restricted solely to the so-called "self-amnesties." In addition, the Court indicated that incompatibility of the amnesty laws with the American Convention did not stem from its implementation process and from the authority which issued these (formal aspect), but from the material aspect of providing impunity from serious violations of international law committed by the military regime.

On the other hand, the IACtHR observed that the monitoring of conventionality had not been observed by the jurisdictional authorities of the State and that,

---

[51] *Case of the Rochela Massacre v. Colombia* (n. 39), para. 182.
[52] Ibid., para. 196.
[53] *Case of "Gomes Lund v. Brasil"* [2010], IACtHR, Ser. C No. 219.

on the contrary, a Federal Supreme Court judgment which had confirmed the validity of the amnesty law did not observe Brazil's international obligations stemming from international law. Also, in this case, the IACtHR issued important definitions on the scope of the right to truth. The Court established that in cases of violations of human rights, the State authorities were not permitted to use protective mechanisms like State secrecy, confidentiality of information, reasons of public interest, or national security, to withhold information required by the legal or administrative authorities in charge of the investigation or pending trials. Also, in cases where a punishable act is being investigated, the decision whether information qualifies as being secret, and refusal to submit the latter or refusal to determine if documentation still exists, may depend exclusively on a State authority whose members are delegated the task of performing wrongful acts.

2.7. Limitations on the Intervention of the Military Criminal Jurisdiction

The IACtHR indicated that "the military criminal jurisdiction is not the competent jurisdiction to investigate and, in its case, prosecute and punish the authors of violations of human rights but that instead the processing of those responsible always corresponds to the ordinary jurisdiction."[54] The Court also mentioned the problems of unconventionality of such "ample and imprecise" standards that prevented "the objective assessment as to whether the crimes could be legally classified as civil or military ones", or that extended "the competence of the military jurisdiction to crimes which do not have a strict connection with military discipline or with juridical rights characteristic of the military realm."[55] Furthermore, the Court addressed the incompetence of the military jurisdiction in investigating all events which constituted violations of civilian human rights.[56]

2.8. Impulse of Extraordinary International Supervisory Mechanisms

An extraordinary international supervisory mechanism was the *Grupo Interdisciplinario de Expertos Independientes* (GIEI (Interdisciplinary Group of Independent Experts)), which was agreed upon by the Inter-American

---

[54] *Case of Radilla Pacheco v. Mexico* [2009], IACtHR, Ser. C No. 209, para. 273.
[55] Ibid., para. 286.
[56] Ibid., paras. 273, 286, and 289. A further three cases versus Mexico, the judgments of which were issued in 2010, reiterated this type of rule.

Commission, the State of Mexico, petitionary human rights organizations, and the relatives of the forty-three students who were forcibly abducted in Ayotzinapa.[57] The mandate of the GIEI had three objectives: (1) to set up the students' search and rescue plans; (2) to technically analyze the lines of investigation to determine criminal responsibility; and (3) to conduct an analysis of the integrated care plan for the victims of the acts. The GIEI was established by five experts and independent experts (none of them of Mexican nationality), and supported by a technical team. Upon conclusion of their work, in April 2016, the GIEI left behind a series of lines of investigation to follow up on what had happened to the students and determine who was responsible for their forced disappearance.

This initiative emerged quite soon, only a few months after the shocking events and not decades later, as tends to be the case with many inter-American decisions. This helps improve the chances of success of the investigation, because much of the assessment of evidence can still be conducted without the passage of time affecting the availability of evidence. The GIEI activities were continued via transfer to the Special Follow-Up Mechanism as a Precautionary Measure of the Ayotzinapa case (established by IACHR staff), whose first report was issued in 2018 and which has been promoting IACHR hearings on the issue.

Another similar mechanism was established in 2018, following the subjugation of protests which flared up in Nicaragua against policies driven by the government of Daniel Ortega. For this reason, the Inter-American Commission began a working visit and registered the excessive use of force majeure /by State security bodies and armed third parties. Also, the IACHR received complaints concerning the death of 76 persons and a further 868 injured.[58] On June 25, 2018, the IACHR announced the establishment of the *Mecanismo Especial de Seguimiento para Nicaragua* (MESENI (Special Monitoring System for Nicaragua)), created by a technical team from the same Commission. The goal of the MESENI is to follow up on the fifteen recommendations issued by the IACHR following its working visit in May of 2018 and the recommendations arising from the Report on Serious Violations to Human Rights in the context of the social protests in Nicaragua.[59] The IACHR also announced the creation of the aforementioned Interdisciplinary Group of Independent Experts (GIEI) in the case of Nicaragua, set up by international experts to contribute to and support domestic investigations into acts of violence which occurred in Nicaragua. The GIEI was supplied with powers to technically analyze the lines of investigation

---

[57] Students of the rural school "Raúl Isidro Burgos," Mexico [2014], IACHR, Resolution 28/2014 Precautionary Measure No. 409-2014.
[58] Observaciones preliminares de la visita de trabajo de la CIDH a Nicaragua [2018] IACHR.
[59] Report on Serious Violations to Human Rights in the context of the social protests in Nicaragua [2018] IACHR.

and make recommendations to the State on the level of legal responsibility. In particular, reviewing whether adequate legal entities are being utilized for the framework of possible illicit deeds and those responsible for them. The group was supplied with the autonomy and independence to access investigative and security files.

2.9. Due Diligence in the Investigation of Executions and Disappearances

In 2019, the Inter-American Court had the opportunity to reiterate its consistent case law concerning its duty to investigate serious violations of human rights. In the case of *Diaz Loreto et al v. Venezuela*,[60] the Court held the State internationally responsible for the victims' detention and later extrajudicial execution by police officers.[61] Similarly, regarding the duty to investigate, it indicated:

> The Court has established that efficient determination of the truth within the context of the obligation to investigate a death must be evident as of the very first procedures. When investigating the violent death of a person, the first stages of investigation are of crucial importance, as is the negative impact that omissions and irregularities may have in such stages on the proper and effective prospects of clarifying the event. In this context, this Court has specified the guiding principles that require observation in an investigation concerning violent death, as is clear from the events of the present case. The State authorities who conduct an investigation of this type must try, at the very least, inter alia: i) to identify the victim; ii) to recover and preserve the probative material related to the death in order to assist in any potential criminal investigation of those responsible; iii) to identify possible witnesses and obtain their statements in relation to the death under investigation; iv) to determine the cause, manner, place and time of death, as well as any pattern or practice which could have caused the death, and v) to distinguish between natural death, accidental death, suicide and homicide. The autopsies as well as analyses of human remains must be rigorously performed by competent professionals, employing the most appropriate procedures.
>
> In addition, the Court indicated in its case-law regarding the scene of crime that the investigators must, at the very least: i) photograph the scene and any other physical evidence, and the body as it was found and after it has been moved; ii)

---

[60] The case referred to the extrajudicial execution perpetrated against three persons within the context of extrajudicial executions on the part of police officers in Aragua State, Venezuela. *Case of Díaz Loreto et al. v. Venezuela* [2019], IAtCHR, Ser. C No. 392.

[61] Ibid., para. 97.

gather and conserve all samples of blood, hair, fibres, threads and other clues; iii) examine the area to look for footprints or any other trace that could be used as evidence, and iv) prepare a detailed report with any observations regarding the scene, the measures taken by the investigators, and the assigned storage of all the evidence collected. The Court also ruled that when investigating a scene of crime, the latter shall be maintained with a view to protecting all evidence.[62]

In this case, the international responsibility of the State was determined, since it had been verified that "proceedings had not been initiated to monitor various aspects of the version offered by relatives and other witnesses, such as a reconstruction of events, the investigations of the victims' clothing, the evidence of the mud they had in their mucous membrane, lungs and digestive system, etc."[63] and that "it had not been proven whether the victims had fired the weapons which were collected at the scene of the crime since there had been no sampling of fingerprint or of traces of powder on the hands, none of which had been controverted by the State in its arguments."[64] The Court thus concluded that "the lack of implementation of proceedings and important samples, in particular concerning the scene of the crime and examination of bodies resulted in an infringement of the due diligence required in an investigation."[65]

2.10. Pardons for Humanitarian Reasons Should Not Affect the Proportionality of Punishment

On May 30, 2018, the Inter-American Court issued an order on the monitoring compliance of the aforementioned judgments of the *Barrios Altos* and *La Cantuta* cases, in which it assessed the compatibility of the presidential authority to issue a pardon for humanitarian reasons in favor of a perpetrator of serious violations of human rights. The specific case concerned Alberto Fujimori, the former president of Peru, who had been convicted for commissioning the said serious crimes.

To determine the compatibility of the humanitarian pardon with international human rights law, the Inter-American Court assessed whether it disproportionately affected the victims' right of access to justice. The Court indicated that the penalty imposed on the perpetrator of a serious violation of human rights "cannot be unduly affected or become illusive during enforcement of the judgement which imposed the punishment in adherence to the principle

---

[62] Ibid., paras. 104 and 105. See also *Case of Gómez Virula et al. v. Guatemala* [2019], IACtHR, Ser. C No. 393, paras. 73 and 74.
[63] Ibid., para. 108.
[64] Ibid., para. 106.
[65] Ibid., paras. 106 and 107.

of proportionality."[66] In this case, the Court then assessed (1) the existence of measures to safeguard the life and personal integrity of the persons deprived of their liberty, (2) the right of access to justice of the victims of serious violations of human rights, and (3) the possibility of jurisdictional monitoring of the Presidential Resolution through which the pardon for humanitarian reasons has been conceded. The Court concluded:

> [I]t would be up to the national authorities to determine if the Peruvian legal system were able to provide alternative measures which, without involving a pardon on the part of the Executive, would allow protection of the life and integrity of Alberto Fujimori, convicted of serious violations of human rights, assuming that his state of health and detention conditions really posed a threat to his life. One would have to consider which measure were most in line with the principle of proportionality and the right of access to justice of the victims.[67]

3. Transformational Impact

The various standards and criteria associated with due diligence in the battle against impunity have been projected in legal decisions in the domestic environment as readjustments of institutional designs, schemes, directives, and other types of measure adopted by human rights institutions.

For example, the inter-American standards boosted legal and constitutional reforms in the criminal military jurisdiction of Colombia, Peru, Argentina, and Mexico.[68] Another advance at an institutional level has been the implementation of the Istanbul Protocol in Colombia as of the *Gutiérrez Soler* case. In fact, the said case led to the issuance of domestic directives by the Attorney General and the National Institute of Legal Medicine and Forensic Sciences.[69]

In Colombia, the rulings of the Inter-American Court have been used in decisions of the High Courts of the country (Constitutional Court, Council of

---

[66] *Case of Barrios Altos and Case of La Cantuta v. Peru* [2018], IACtHR, Monitoring of Compliance with Judgment, para. 47.

[67] Ibid., "Whereas" Clause 68.

[68] Annabella Sandri Fuentes "La reforma integral del sistema de justicia militar argentino motivada por el cumplimiento de las obligaciones que surgen de la Convención Americana sobre Derechos Humanos" [2015] 61 *Revista IIDH* 319–356; Juan Rial (ed.), *La justicia militar. Entre la reforma y la permanencia* (RESDAL 2010); Julio Ríos-Figueroa, *Constitutional Courts as Mediators. Armed Conflict, Civil-Military Relations, and the Rule of Law in Latin America* (Cambridge University Press 2017).

[69] Mónica Trespalacios Leal, *El estado colombiano frente a las órdenes de investigar, juzgar y sancionar a los responsables de violaciones a los derechos humanos, dictadas por la Corte Interamericana de Derechos Humanos* (National University of Colombia 2018).

State, Supreme Court of Justice), the Office of the Attorney General, supervisory bodies (Ombudsman's Office, Office of the Inspector General), and even by branches of the executive and the legislative powers.[70]

The rulings of the IACtHR in the *Velásquez Rodríguez* and *Barrios Altos* cases had a strong effect on the determination of Judgment C-004 of 2003, in which the Constitutional Court verified the constitutionality of one of the causal factors for the origin of the extraordinary appeal for review in criminal matters. The Court found that this appeal was not only implemented in favor of the accused, and stated that it was possible to restrict the principle of *ne bis in idem* in cases of violations of human rights and of serious infringements of international humanitarian law. Taking as a foundation the inter-American jurisprudence, among other entities, the Court indicated that the duties of the State in investigating and punishing the violations of human rights are much more intensive than in the case of petty offenses and that, as a result, the rights of the victims become more prevalent. The High Court then explained that the decisions of international bodies could generate, under certain assumptions, the reopening of proceedings, and the modification of sentences which have been transferred to res judicata.[71] This transcendental decision had an impact on a later legislative debate which lead to the reform of the procedural code which incorporated this approach.[72] Also, this precedent has been used by the Criminal Chamber of the Supreme Court of Justice to reopen various cases concerning violations of human rights.[73]

---

[70] See Alejandro Ramelli, "Sistema de fuentes del derecho internacional público y 'bloque de constitucionalidad' en Colombia" [2004] 11 *Revista Mexicana de Derecho Constitucional* 157; Rodrigo Uprimny, *Uses and Abuses of Transitional Justice Discourse in Colombia* (PRIO 2007).

[71] The High Court stated that the appeal for review takes place when there is "a domestic court ruling or a decision from an international supervisory and monitoring authority on human rights, formally accepted by our country, which determines the existence of this new offence or of a test that was not known at the time of the debates." In the same manner, it indicated that the review process could not be appealed against the penal orders which declared termination of the investigation, the proceedings or of the judgment of acquittal, "invariably, and when a domestic court decision, the decision of an international court on supervision and monitoring of human rights, formally approved by our country, establishes a conspicuous breach of the obligations of the Columbian state, thoroughly and impartially to investigate said violations."

[72] Article 4 of Law 906 of 2004.

[73] Taking into account, among other entities what was ordered by the Inter-American Court in the *Case of the 19 Tradesmen*, the Criminal Appeals Chamber of the Supreme Court of Justice of Colombia approved an appeal for review and ordered the reopening of investigations against the senior military officers of the zone. *Cf.* Judgment issued on March 6, 2008, file 24841. A similar reopening of the investigations against several acquitted persons occurred in connection with the receipt, at a domestic level, of the judgments of the Inter-American Court on the extrajudicial execution of Jesús María Valle Jaramillo, a defender of human rights, and on the torture suffered by Wilson Gutiérrez Soler. *Cf.* Judgments of July 6, 2011, and September 17, 2008, respectively. See also the judgments of November 1, 2007 (relating to the decision of the Inter-American Commission in the Leydi Dayán Sánchez case) and of February 24, 2010 (concerning the decision of the Inter-American Commission in the Case of Collective 82).

On the other hand, as indicated by Góngora,[74] in other rulings it is possible to observe a co-evolutionary vision of a convergence of standards concerning the rights of victims between the Constitutional Court and the Inter-American Court. For example, in the *Mapiripán* case the litigants requested a specific declaration of the Inter-American Court disapproving of the aforementioned "Law of Justice and Peace" that had not yet been passed. The IACtHR abstained from a direct declaration in this respect, although it did reiterate the scope of its jurisprudence regarding the impossibility of amnesties for serious violations and of the principles of victims' access to justice. Subsequently, when the Constitutional Court had to review the Law of Justice and Peace, it referred to inter-American jurisprudence. The Constitutional Court identified several problems of the said law, and ordered various amendments to strengthen victims' rights.[75] When the controversy returned to the regional level, in the aforementioned cases of the *Massacres of La Rochela* and *Cepeda*, the Inter-American Court supported the jurisprudence of the Constitutional Court in insisting on the guidelines the law had to comply with and the due diligence required from the authorities charged with its implementation.

One expression of dialogues that goes beyond the judicial reception of inter-American standards can be witnessed in recent legal strategies in Colombia where the lessons learnt from the Inter-American System are projected. It consists of a Comprehensive System of Truth, Justice, Reparation and Guarantees of Non-Repetition established by the Final Peace Agreement negotiated between the State of Colombia and the former FARC guerrilla group in 2016. The Comprehensive System incorporates judicial and extrajudicial mechanisms to safeguard the rights of the victims. The judicial component of the system is incorporated into the Special Jurisdiction for Peace (JEP). The extrajudicial mechanisms are the Truth Commission, the Search Unit for Presumed Disappeared Persons, and the mechanisms of administrative reparation.

The JEP was conceived as a tribunal to end domestic armed conflict in Colombia,[76] leading to the creation of an institutional apparatus which aims to define the legal situation of all those who participated in the conflict and, at the same time, create incentives which satisfy and boost the rights of the victims. In

---

[74] Manuel Eduardo Góngora Mera, "Diálogos Jurisprudenciales Entre La Corte Interamericana de Derechos Humanos y La Corte Constitucional de Colombia: Una Visión Coevolutiva de La Convergencia de Estándares Sobre Derechos de Las Víctimas," *La Justicia Constitucional y su Internacionalización: ¿Hacia un Ius Constitutionale Commune en América Latina?*, vol II (UNAM, Instituto de Investigaciones Jurídicas, Max-Planck-Institut Für Ausländisches Offentliches Recht und Völkerrecht e Instituto Iberoamericano de Derecho Constitucional 2010).

[75] Judgment C-370 of 2006.

[76] Andrés Bermúdez Liévano, *Los debates de La Habana: una mirada desde adentro* (Institute for Integrated Transitions 2019), 234–235.

Colombia, these rulings have been making changes to concepts and the manner of investigation, judgment, and punishment.

It is worth mentioning that the inter-American criteria of due diligence in investigation are central to the design of the JEP, with special emphasis on the analysis of macro-criminality. On the matter of investigation, a constitutional reform has allowed the possibility of prioritizing and selecting cases to promote the elucidation of the most serious and representative crimes. Also, the principal focus of action is on criminal charges for the most responsible perpetrators and on the criminal structures which allowed the perpetration of the crimes. On the other hand, the proceedings of investigation and prosecution are strongly characterized by the contributions to the truth and reparations offered by those appearing in court. The accused submit themselves to a system of conditionality under the new Comprehensive System as a requirement for maintenance of benefits.

The special emphasis on analysis of context and on analysis of macro-criminality are effects of inter-American jurisprudence. In fact, from some of the judgments I have reviewed in this chapter, the IACtHR has pointed out that a certain type of serious violation of human rights are understood to be linked to other acts in a specific context, and to certain policies, patterns, criminal plans, and special practices. Investigations that analyze individual crimes in isolation fail to make various connections and often result in the impunity of the cases. Unveiling the criminal plans, patterns, and policies is crucial for obtaining the guarantees of non-repetition which the inter-American jurisprudence has insisted on concerning reparations.

One example of this type of judicial macro-case of the JEP is useful to understand the magnitude of the challenge. Case 03 on extrajudicial executions analyzes more than four thousand executions that occurred in every department of the country. The case is determining the main individuals responsible among around twenty-five hundred servicemen associated with the executions.[77] At the point of termination of this chapter, six hundred victims have been accredited, and more than twenty human rights organizations participate as legal representatives. The victims and their organizations have presented reports which file the atrocities. For example, one of the most recent reports listed 232 executions in a single region of the country. On the other hand, more than 80 of the crimes are currently being tried in international lawsuits before the Inter-American System. For this reason, the JEP Chamber for the Acknowledgment of Truth, currently in charge of the macro-case, has highlighted many of these crimes. Furthermore, the Chamber's dialogues with the inter-American authorities shall remain permanent.

---

[77] <https://www.jep.gov.co/Especiales/casos/03.html> (accessed December 13, 2022).

Finally, another field relevant to the interaction between the inter-American community and the national one can be seen in the connection of the Constitutional Court of Colombia with the implementation of several inter-American rulings. In fact, regarding several precautionary measures (of the Inter-American Commission) and provisional measures (of the Inter-American Court), the Constitutional Court has upheld its obligation in the domestic field and issued various orders to contribute to the compliance of the measures imparted by the Commission and the Court. These orders, particularly related to the thorough investigation of crimes, include the provision of specific types of information necessary for conducting the investigations with due diligence.[78]

4. Concluding Remarks

The legal developments analyzed in this chapter illustrate some advances and challenges in the case law of the Inter-American Court in the battle against impunity. The analyzed cases demonstrate several development routes toward a protective union building on the interaction between the national systems and the inter-American one.[79] This constitutes a dynamic process which has taken on a variety of forms depending on the institutional design of the respective countries. This protective union encourages a legal dialogue in which the positive aspect of one level is called upon to strengthen the other parallel level, in light of the principle of the most favorable interpretation. In this context, as Diego García-Sayán[80] has indicated, the legal standards arising from international law make no sense whatsoever without a State counterpart which applies them and abides by them, because "they [are] the most immediate national references the population has, and are the institutional structures and social structures capable of advancing or reversing the gains which can be achieved in terms of human rights."

The Inter-American Court has also made an effort to achieve a high level of efficiency in the battle against impunity in striving to implement its decisions by way of more precise orders and by trying to strengthen the initiatives of internal actors. The Court thus contributes to forms of institutional empowerment to try to break down the factors that generate impunity in a specific situation, and that

---

[78] See in this regard Judgments T-327 of 2004 (on the precautionary measures in support of the Peace Community of San José de Apartadó) and T-558 of 2003 (on precautionary measures issued by the Inter-American Commission).

[79] Manuel Eduardo Góngora Mera, *Inter-American Judicial Constitutionalism. On the Constitutional Rank of Human Rights Treaties in Latin America through National and Inter-American Adjudication* (IIDH 2011).

[80] Diego García-Sayán, *Una Viva Interacción: Corte Interamericana y Tribunales Internos Un Cuarto de Siglo* 1979-2004 (La Corte Interamericana de Derechos Humanos (IACtHR) 2005).

use legal means to hold authorities to account to the highest possible degree. The approaches from the Court demonstrate great interest in combining purely normative reasonings with empirical findings to boost justice in the best manner, generating improvement strategies that have proven to be effective when decreed by the Court.

In this sense, the cases analyzed also illustrate the great paradox surrounding the Inter-American System. These cases reach the Inter-American Court because decisions and internal institutions, in particular judicial ones, have not been effective in re-establishing the rule of law. Nonetheless, the efficacy of the Inter-American System depends on the ability of those national institutions, along with the bodies of the system, to implement inter-American standards. Despite the said paradox, on a path which is not free of unsatisfactory aspects, the Inter-American Court has been keeping the promise of the Inter-American System toward the victims by offering circumstances in which the rule of law is fully established where the local institutions have not responded adequately to their grievances. And, in this undertaking, the Court has come across various local actors who, by working together with it, have allowed the Inter-American System to continuously provide room for hope.

II.13
The Independence of Justice as a Human Right and an International Obligation in Inter-American Jurisprudence

By Carlos Ayala Corao

1. Introduction

The rights of all persons, as recognized in the American Convention on Human Rights (American Convention, or ACHR), are simultaneously obligations upon the States parties and must be respected, guaranteed, and protected. In other words, a human being is the holder of international human rights that are reflected in the international obligations of nation States. In this respect, Article 1 of the American Convention stipulates that the States parties undertake to respect the rights recognized in the Convention and to ensure that all persons subject to their jurisdiction can freely and fully exercise these rights without discrimination on the basis of race, color, sex, language, political opinion or any other opinion, national or social origin, economic status, position at birth, or any other social condition. This obligation upon the States parties is complemented by the obligation to adopt provisions in domestic law that commit the States parties to implement, in accordance with their constitutional procedures and the stipulations of the American Convention, the legislative measures or other measures required in order to give effect to the rights mentioned in Article 1 if the exercise of these rights is not already guaranteed by legislative provisions or provisions of another kind.

This treaty framework assumes that the States parties, as the addressees of the obligations relating to human rights, are those who directly take responsibility for effective compliance with international obligations to respect and ensure human rights within their domestic jurisdiction. Therefore, the States parties are responsible for enforcing human rights without any discrimination with regard to all persons under their jurisdiction.

According to the jurisprudence of the Inter-American Court of Human Rights (Inter-American Court, or IACtHR), these obligations to respect and ensure the

Carlos Ayala Corao, *The Independence of Justice as a Human Right and an International Obligation in Inter-American Jurisprudence* In: *The Impact of the Inter-American Human Rights System*. Edited by: Armin von Bogdandy, Flávia Piovesan, Eduardo Ferrer Mac-Gregor, and Mariela Morales Antoniazzi, Oxford University Press.
© Carlos Ayala Corao 2024. DOI: 10.1093/oso/9780197744161.003.0024

rights contained in Article 1 of the American Convention imply "an obligation upon the States Parties to organize the governmental apparatus and, in general, all the structures through which public power is exercised, so that they are capable of juridically ensuring the free and full enjoyment of human rights."[1]

2. Human Rights and the International Obligation of Effective Judicial Protection

2.1. The Essential Content of the Right/Obligation to Protect That Right

Human rights and the treaty obligation of the States parties to protect the rights of all human beings should be structured through the separation of powers and judicial independence.

The protection of the rights of all human beings is expressed in international treaties through the right to simple and prompt recourse, or any other effective recourse, to a competent, independent, and impartial judge or tribunal.[2]

The right to effective judicial protection of human and fundamental rights is accompanied by certain essential, intrinsic, substantial, and inseparable guarantees. These are the judicial guarantees of due process for the protection of human rights for all persons accessing justice:[3] the petitioner or appellant; the victim; and the defendant or accused. Of these judicial guarantees to which all persons are entitled, the right to be heard stands out first and foremost: (i) by a competent, *independent*, and impartial judge or tribunal; (ii) previously established by law; (iii) with due guarantees; (iv) within a reasonable time. The rights of persons accused of a crime are also noteworthy: (v) to be presumed innocent as long as his guilt has not been proven according to law; and (vi) with full equality, to the minimum guarantees of Article 8.2 of the ACHR.

In accordance with the aforementioned principles of international law as per Articles 1 and 2 of the American Convention, the States parties undertake to ensure effective judicial protection for all persons subject to their jurisdiction with the guarantees of due process and of the rights recognized in their constitution, laws, and the Convention itself without discrimination of any kind.

---

[1] IACtHR, "Exceptions to the exhaustion of domestic remedies (Art. 46(1), 46(2)(a), and 46(2)(b), American Convention on Human Right," Advisory Opinion OC-11/90, August 10, 1990, Ser. A No. 11, para. 23.
[2] Art. 25, ACHR.
[3] Art. 8, ACHR.

2.2. Protection via Independent Judges and Tribunals

The protection of rights in accordance with Article 25 of the Convention is not restricted to a requirement that the judges or tribunals be competent; instead—in accordance with Article 8.1 of the Convention—they must also be "independent and impartial."

Thus, the American Convention requires that the effective judicial protection of rights be guaranteed through independent judges and tribunals. The *Basic Principles on the Independence of the Judiciary* of the United Nations cited repeatedly in the reports and decisions of the IACHR and the IACtHR state the following:[4]

1. The independence of the judiciary shall be "guaranteed by the State" so that "it is the duty of all governmental and other institutions to respect and observe the independence of the judiciary." (Principle 1)
2. "The judiciary shall decide matters before them impartially, on the basis of facts and in accordance with the law, without any restrictions, improper influences, inducements, pressures, threats or interferences, direct or indirect, from any quarter or for any reason." (Principle 2)
3. "The judiciary shall have jurisdiction over all issues of a judicial nature and shall have exclusive authority to decide whether an issue submitted for its decision is within its competence as defined by law." (Principle 3)
4. "There shall not be any inappropriate or unwarranted interference with the judicial process" and judicial decisions by the courts shall be subject only to "judicial review" (or to mitigation or commutation by competent authorities of sentences imposed by the judiciary, in accordance with the law). (Principle 4)
5. "Everyone shall have the right to be tried by ordinary courts or tribunals using established legal procedures" and, accordingly, "tribunals that do not use the duly established procedures . . . shall not be created" to displace the jurisdiction normally belonging to the ordinary courts. (Principle 5)

---

[4] E.g., *Case of the Constitutional Court v. Peru* [2001] IACtHR, Ser. C No. 71, para. 73; *Case of López Lone et al. v. Honduras* [2015] IACtHR, Ser. C No. 302, para. 170. See also IACHR, "Guarantees for the independence of justice operators. Towards strengthening access to justice and the rule of law in the Americas," OAS/Ser.L/V/II. Doc. 445, December 2013, <http://www.oas.org/es/cidh/defensores/docs/pdf/Operadores-de-Justicia-2013.pdf> (English version <https://www.oas.org/es/cidh/defensores/docs/pdf/justice-operators-2013.pdf>) (accessed February 5, 2022). "Basic Principles on the Independence of the Judiciary," Adopted by the Seventh United Nations Congress on the Prevention of Crime and the Treatment of Offenders held at Milan from August 26 to September 6, 1985 and endorsed by General Assembly Resolutions 40/32 of November 29, 1985 and 40/146 of December 13, 1985, <https://www.ohchr.org/EN/ProfessionalInterest/Pages/IndependenceJudiciary.aspx> (accessed February 5, 2022).

6. "The principle of the independence of the judiciary entitles and requires the judiciary to ensure that judicial proceedings are conducted fairly and that the rights of the parties are respected." (Principle 6)
7. "It is the duty of each Member State to provide adequate resources to enable the judiciary to properly perform its functions."

In addition to these initial principles, the Basic Principles document also mentions principles relative to: freedom of expression and association (Principles 8 and 9), qualifications, selection, and training (Principle 10), conditions of service and tenure (Principles 11 to 14), professional secrecy and immunity (Principles 15 and 16), and discipline, suspension, and removal (Principles 17 to 20).

Judicial independence has two dimensions: (i) institutional or objective, relating to the judicial system as an organ of the State under the separation of powers; and (ii) individual or subjective, relating to the judge as a member of the judiciary. However, ultimately, judicial independence requires that "neither the judiciary nor the judges who compose it be subordinate to the other public powers."[5] In this sense, the Inter-American Court has affirmed that these two dimensions have the objective of protecting "the Judicial System in general and its members in particular, from finding themselves subjected to possible undue limitations in the exercise of their functions, by bodies alien to the Judiciary..."[6] The Inter-American Court has made an important clarification by affirming that the right of any person as enshrined in Article 8.1 of the American Convention to protection or to be judged by an independent judge must be analyzed not only with regard to the dimension of the defendant but also with regard to the dimension of the judge, who must enjoy the guarantees that make judicial independence possible. The latter dimension must be analyzed in the light of the treaty rights of *the judge as holder of the guarantees of judicial independence*, including cases in which a State decision arbitrarily affects the irremovability and stability of the judge.[7] To sum up, the Inter-American Court has established that

---

[5] International Principles on the Independence and Accountability of Judges, Lawyers and Prosecutors, Practitioners Guide No. 1, International Commission of Jurists (Geneva, 2007), 21, <https://www.icj.org/wp-content/uploads/2012/04/International-Principles-on-the-Independence-and-Accountability-of-Judges-Lawyers-and-Procecutors-No.1-Practitioners-Guide-2009-Eng.pdf> (accessed February 5, 2022).

[6] *Case of Apitz Barbera et al. ("First Court of Administrative Disputes") v. Venezuela* [2008] IACtHR, Ser. C No. 182, para. 55. Similarly: *Case of Reverón Trujillo v. Venezuela* [2009] IACtHR, Ser. C No. 197, para. 67; *Case of Chocrón Chocrón v. Venezuela* [2011] Ser. C No. 227, para. 97; *Case of Atala Riffo and Daughters v. Chile* [2012] IACtHR, Ser. C No. 239, para. 186; *Case of the Constitutional Tribunal (Camba Campos et al.) v. Ecuador* [2013] IACtHR, Ser. C No. 268, para. 188.

[7] *Case of the Supreme Court of Justice (Quintana Coello et al.) v. Ecuador* [2013] IACtHR, Ser. C No. 266, para. 153. Similarly: IACtHR, *Case of the Constitutional Tribunal (Camba Campos et al.) v. Ecuador* (n. 6), paras. 191 and 197.

judicial independence is an essential judicial guarantee of due process of which the judge is the holder and in which regard the judge has the right to have the State respect his or her stability in office. This guarantee also includes the subjective right of the judge for any removal of the judge from office to be based on expressly established grounds and via due process or, if applicable, because the term of the judge's mandate has come to an end. This means that when the State arbitrarily violates the tenure of a judge, it not only violates judicial independence as enshrined in Article 8.1 of the American Convention but also violates the right of a citizen to access to and continuity of the public service of their country under general conditions of equality as established in Article 23.1 of the American Convention.[8]

3. Facets of the Independence of Judges

The facets forming an integral part of the independence of judges are as follows: the process of selecting and appointing judges, guarantees against external pressures, the principle of irremovability, and the system for sanctioning and removing judges from office.

3.1. The Process of Selecting and Appointing Judges

In accordance with Basic Principle 10, persons selected for judicial office shall be "individuals of integrity and ability with appropriate training or qualifications in law." Any method of judicial selection shall "safeguard against judicial appointments for improper motives," and there shall be no discrimination.

Following this principle, the Inter-American Court has maintained that States must, when establishing procedures for appointing judges, take into account the fact that not just any procedure satisfies the conditions demanded by the Convention for the adequate implementation of a truly independent regimen, particularly if *basic parameters of objectivity and reasonability* are not respected and if the procedures are left open to a high level of discretionary consideration that does not necessarily enable the selection of the most suitable candidates.[9] At the same time, the Inter-American Court has declared that judges must be selected exclusively based on their *personal merits and professional qualifications*, ensuring *equal opportunities* in the access to the judicial power.[10]

---

[8] IACtHR, *Case of the Constitutional Tribunal (Camba Campos et al.) v. Ecuador* (n. 6), para. 199.
[9] IACtHR, *Case of Reverón Trujillo v. Venezuela* (n. 6), para. 74.
[10] Ibid., para. 72.

In this sense, the procedures for appointing judges must guarantee *equal opportunities* by means of an open competition so that any citizen who can prove it complies with the requirements determined in law may participate. This open competition in the selection process excludes any arbitrary inequality and may not include any privileges or advantages with regard, for example, to those provisionally occupying the office.[11]

3.2. The Political Right of Access to and Permanence in the Office of Judge under Equal Conditions

Open competition in the procedures for appointing judges under general conditions of equality through reasonable and objective means also shapes the political right of all citizens, recognized in Article 23.1c of the American Convention, "to have access, under general conditions of equality, to the public services of his country."

There is also another aspect to this right: the right of a judge to remain in the public office to which he or she was appointed under conditions of equality. Thus, if a judge is improperly dismissed for belonging to a certain group, this constitutes *arbitrary unequal treatment with regard to the right to remain in office in conditions of equality* (art. 23.1.c, ACHR) and if, in turn, the judge in question *is not reinstated, in conditions of equality, to the exercise of public functions* (as a judge), this shall also constitute a violation of the right recognized in Article 23.1.c of the American Convention.

In this regard, the Inter-American Court has confirmed the following:

> 138. According to the State's arguments, Article 23(1)c of the American Convention does not include the protection of the right to remain in the exercise of public service. In this sense, the Court points out that in the case of *Apitz Barbera et al.*, this Tribunal stated that **Article 23(1)c** does not establish the **right to access a public position**, but to do so in **"general conditions of equality"**. This means that **the respect and guarantee of this right are fulfilled when "the criteria and procedures for the appointment, promotion, suspension and dismissal [are] reasonable and objective" and when "the people are not object of discrimination" in the exercise of this right**. Likewise, the Human Rights Committee has interpreted that the guarantee of protection covers both the access and the continuance in equal conditions and non-discrimination with regard to the suspension and dismissal procedures. As observed, **the access in equal conditions would constitute an insufficient**

---

[11] Ibid., para. 73.

guarantee if it were not accompanied by the effective protection of the continuance in what is accessed.

[...]

140. [. . .]In synthesis, the Court observes that a titular judge, under circumstances of an annulled dismissal similar to that of Mrs. Reverón Trujillo could have been reinstated. On the contrary, in the present case, since it is a provisional judge, under the same factual assumptions, the reinstatement was not ordered.

141. This difference in the treatment of titular judges that enjoy a full guarantee of tenure and provisional ones who do not have any protection by that guarantee within the context of continuance that corresponds to them, does not respond to a reasonable criterion (*supra* para. 138) pursuant to the Convention (*supra* paras. 114 through 117 and 121). Therefore, the Tribunal concludes that Mrs. Reverón Trujillo suffered an **arbitrary unequal treatment regarding the right to remain, under equal conditions, in the exercise of public service, which constitutes a violation of Article 23(1)(c) of the American Convention** in connection to the obligations of respect and guarantee established in Article 1(1) of the same.[12] (Emphasis added by the author.)

In conclusion, when the permanence of judges in office is arbitrarily affected, the "right to judicial independence established in Article 8(1) of the American Convention is violated, in conjunction with the right of access to and permanence in public service, under general conditions of equality, established in Article 23(1)(c) of the American Convention."[13] This occurs, in the opinion of the Inter-American Court, not only in cases of the arbitrary removal of judges by judicial or disciplinary authorities but also in cases of the removal or dismissal of judges or magistrates as a result of impeachment proceedings in parliamentary instances if these are carried out arbitrarily in violation of the minimum guarantees of due process as established in Article 8 of the American Convention:

3.4. Conclusion of the Court on judicial guarantees and political rights

222. Consequently, the Court declares the violation of Article 8(1), and the pertinent parts of Article 8(2) and 8(4), in relation to Article 1(1) of the American Convention, owing to the **arbitrary termination and the impeachment proceedings that occurred, facts that gave rise to the violation of judicial guarantees** to the detriment of the eight victims in this case. Furthermore, the Court declares the **violation of Article 8(1), in relation to**

---

[12] Ibid., paras. 138, 140, and 141.
[13] IACtHR, *Case of the Constitutional Tribunal (Camba Campos et al.) v. Ecuador* (n. 6), para. 199.

Article 23(1)(c) and Article 1(1) of the American Convention, owing to the arbitrary effects on tenure in the exercise of the judicial function and the consequent harm to judicial independence and the guarantee of impartiality, to the detriment of the eight victims in this case.[14] (Emphasis added by the author.)

3.3. Guarantees against External Pressures: The Principle of Irremovability

The guarantee against external pressures is an essential element of the independence of judges and tribunals. Judges must enjoy the conditions necessary to hear, process, substantiate, decide upon, and execute cases freely, so without fear of suffering consequences for their actions. A judge who has been threatened or who has a justified fear of suffering reprisals in their position as a judge if he or she does not reach a certain decision is not a free or independent judge. Judges must be capable of resolving cases in accordance with the facts on record and on the basis of their reasoning in accordance with the law. Consequently, external pressures executed by political and governmental authorities against a judge and threats—including threats by judicial authorities of suspension or removal from office if a judge does not reach a certain decision—constitute a violation of the principles of judicial independence and impartiality.

In this regard, the Inter-American Court has invoked the Basic Principles, which state that the judges will decide the matters brought before them "on the basis of facts and in accordance with the law, without any restrictions, improper influences, inducements, pressures, threats or interferences, direct or indirect, from any quarter or for any reason" (Principle 2), and that the judiciary "shall have jurisdiction over all issues of a judicial nature and shall have exclusive authority to decide whether an issue submitted for its decision is within its competence as defined by law" (Principle 3), and that "[t]here shall not be any inappropriate or unwarranted interference with the judicial process" (Principle 4). The Court reached the conclusion that these guarantees reinforce the stability of the judges in their position in seeking to guarantee their independence with regard to the parties, society, and the State.[15]

---

[14] IACtHR, *Case of the Constitutional Tribunal (Camba Campos et al.) v. Ecuador* (n. 6), para. 222.

[15] IACtHR, *Case of Reverón Trujillo v. Venezuela* (n. 6), para. 80. Similarly: IACtHR, *Case of Chocrón Chocrón v. Venezuela* (n. 6), para. 100; IACtHR, *Case of Atala Riffo and Daughters v. Chile* (n. 6), para. 186; IACtHR, *Case of the Supreme Court of Justice (Quintana Coello et al.) v. Ecuador* (n. 7), para. 146; and IACtHR, *Case of the Constitutional Tribunal (Camba Campos et al.) v. Ecuador* (n. 6), para. 190.

Otherwise, if the irremovability of judges did not exist as a guarantee against external pressures, the States could remove judges and intervene in judicial power, bringing about a fear of being arbitrarily dismissed in other judges, and thus encouraging those judges to obey their instructions or refrain from challenging the appointing and sanctioning bodies.

Pressures exerted by political, economic, and social groups might also constitute external pressures in this sense, depending on their weight and importance. However, this is not the case if these pressures are manifestations of critical ideas or opinions as part of the legitimate exercise of freedom of expression. In this regard, the quotation made by the Inter-American Court in the case of *Apitz Barbera et al.* of the statement by Mr. Param Cumaraswamy (former Special Rapporteur of the United Nations on the Independence of Judges and Lawyers, between 1994 and 2003) is relevant. In his capacity as an expert witness proposed by the Commission in the case in question, Cumaraswamy confirmed that "[w]hile constructive public criticism of judgments or decisions in temperate language would be permissible even from political forces, when such criticism is couched in virulent, intemperate, threatening, and intimidating language and in bad faith, it will be considered a threat or interference with judicial independence."[16]

In conclusion, a judge must be free to decide upon a dispute in accordance with the law and his or her reasoning and legal awareness without fearing any kind of reprisal. Thus, the Inter-American Court has called attention to statements of public officials, particularly the top government authorities, which might constitute a form of interference with or pressure impairing judicial independence or that might induce or invite other authorities to engage in activities that may abridge the judge's independence or affect the judge's freedom of action.[17] The irremovability of judges therefore protects judicial independence, consisting of the following guarantees: continuance in the position, an adequate promotions process, and no unjustified dismissals or free removal. This means that if the State does not comply with one of these guarantees of irremovability, it violates its obligation to respect and guarantee judicial independence.[18] On the other hand, as we have seen, judicial independence transcends the individual dimension of the person of the judge and extends to the whole of society and to its institutional dimension as an essential element of the rule of law and democracy. Thus, there is a direct relationship between judicial independence and the

---

[16] IACtHR, *Case of Apitz Barbera et al. ("First Court of Administrative Disputes") v. Venezuela* (n. 6), footnotes 59 and 157.
[17] Ibid., para. 131.
[18] IACtHR, *Case of Reverón Trujillo v. Venezuela* (n. 6), para. 79.

right of judges to accede to and remain in their posts under general conditions of equality, as an expression of their guarantee of tenure.[19]

4. The Stability and Exceptional Nature of Provisional Judges

In some countries for reasons of necessity and in others for reasons of reckless political expediency, provisional judges are appointed. These may also be called temporary, interim, acting, substitute judges, and the like. Some of the States appointing judges of this kind have attempted to claim that there is no need to comply with any procedures or objective merit requirements for such provisional judges and that they are appointed "discretionally." But what is worse is that at least some of these States have also claimed that such provisional judges do not have any stability or, consequently, irremovability and that, as a result, they may be removed discretionally without any cause or procedure and, further, without any right to effective judicial recourse. In other words, they are freely appointed judges subject to discretionary removal.

It is not possible to conceive a judge without independence guarantees. Thus, even though it is not possible to equate the position of a permanent judge to that of a provisional one, even in the case of the latter, the irremovability of the judge is closely linked to the guarantee against external pressures. Indeed, if provisional judges do not have the security of permanence for a determined period, they are vulnerable to pressures from various sectors, primarily those that have the ability to decide upon dismissals or promotions within the judiciary.

As we saw previously, the appointment of judges must be governed by objective conditions that ensure the success of the best qualified candidates under general conditions of equality. Therefore, appointments of provisional judges must also be guaranteed to comply with these requirements through measures that are adapted to the special characteristics of such judges. Moreover, once provisional judges have been suitably appointed, they must enjoy the same minimum guarantees of stability as permanent judges. In the words of the Inter-American Court, the States must guarantee that provisional judges benefit from a suitable procedure for their appointment and a certain irremovability with regard to their position. This appropriate stability and irremovability of provisional judges is subject to a dissolving condition such as the completion of a predetermined term or the observance and conclusion of a public competitive tender governed by the principles of objectivity, transparency, and publicity. Therefore, provisional

---

[19] IACtHR, *Case of López Lone et al. v. Honduras* (n. 4), para. 194.

judges must enjoy all of the benefits characteristic of continuance until the dissolving condition that puts a legal end to their term of office occurs.[20]

A different situation might arise in the light of appointments that are openly irregular due to a violation of the rule of law and democracy on the part of a dictatorship or authoritarian regime with the aim of politically controlling the judiciary and suppressing society using party agents or a political movement.

In any case, it is important to stress that since provisional judges constitute significant obstacles to judicial independence, they must be an *exception* in two senses: both with respect to *duration* and with respect to the *rule* of judges in a country. In this sense, even if there are duly justified reasons for the appointment of provisional judges, this situation must be temporary, so it must last for the least time necessary to enable the regularization of normality with regard to judges. At the same time, the general rule with regard to judges in a country must be the appointment of permanent judges, and the appointment of a group of provisional judges must take place only as a justified exception that is limited in time.[21]

Lastly, as we have seen in the cases of *Reverón Trujillo* and *Chocrón Chocrón*, the Inter-American Court has confirmed that the exceptional nature of judges with a provisional character is a requirement for such judges to be compatible with the right of access to public service under conditions of equality. Thus, the Court has insisted on indicating the importance of the *right of judges to remain in office on general terms of equality in accordance with Article 23(1)(c) of the ACHR* since "the guarantee of stability or tenure of the judge is related to the right to remain in public office, on general terms of equality."[22]

5. The Exercising of Other Rights by Judges: Freedom of Expression and the Right to Association

One important element of the guarantees of the independence of judges in a democratic society is *freedom of expression*. This is defined in the Inter-American Democratic Charter (IADC) as one of the *essential components* of the exercise of democracy.[23] With regard to judges, the Basic Principles invoked by the Inter-American Court in its jurisprudence establish that "members of the judiciary are like other citizens entitled to freedom of expression, belief, association and assembly; provided, however, that in exercising such rights, judges shall always

---

[20] IACtHR, *Case of Reverón Trujillo v. Venezuela* (n. 6), paras. 116 and 117. Similarly: IACtHR, *Case of Chocrón Chocrón v. Venezuela* (n. 6), para. 106.

[21] IACtHR, *Case of Reverón Trujillo v. Venezuela* (n. 6), para. 118. Similarly: IACtHR, *Case of Chocrón Chocrón v. Venezuela* (n. 6), para. 107.

[22] IACtHR, *Case of López Lone et al. v. Honduras* (n. 4), para. 235.

[23] Art. 4, IADC.

conduct themselves in such a manner as to preserve the dignity of their office and the impartiality and independence of the judiciary" (Principle 8).[24]

Freedom of expression, recognized in Article 13 of the American Convention, has been broadly developed in the jurisprudence of the Inter-American Court as a cornerstone for the existence of a democratic society, both in its individual dimension, regarding who has the right to seek, receive, and disseminate information and opinions of all kinds without prior censorship, and in its social dimension, in relation to the collective right of society to receive information and opinions of all kind without prior censorship.[25]

Even if these rights are not absolute and are subject to restrictions, the Court has established in its jurisprudence that a right can be restricted only as long as any interference is not abusive or arbitrary, and such interference must therefore: (i) be enacted by law; (ii) serve a legitimate purpose; and (iii) meet the requirements of suitability, necessity, and proportionality.[26] Owing to their functions in the administration of justice, under normal conditions of the rule of law, judges may be "subject to different restrictions, and in different ways, that would not affect other individuals, including other public officials."[27] Thus, in accordance with these principles, the aim of protecting the independence and impartiality of justice as a right or freedom of others can justify "the restriction of certain conduct by judges."[28] In any case, "the power of the State to regulate or restrict these rights is not discretionary and any limitation of the rights recognized in the Convention must be interpreted restrictively."[29]

Notwithstanding even legitimate restrictions upon freedom of expression to which a judge might be subjected in normal conditions, in certain exceptional circumstances, the scope of this freedom is wider. The Inter-American Court, citing the Bangalore Principles of Judicial Conduct, has confirmed that there may be situations in which a judge, as a citizen who is a member of society, considers that he or she has a moral duty to speak out.[30] In this respect, in

---

[24] IACtHR, *Case of López Lone et al. v. Honduras* (n. 4), para. 170.

[25] *Cf.* IACtHR *Cuadernillo de Jurisprudencia de la Corte Interamericana de Derechos Humanos N° 16: Libertad de Pensamiento y de Expresión*, <https://www.corteidh.or.cr/sitios/libros/todos/docs/cuadernillo16.pdf> (accessed February 5, 2022).

[26] *Cf.* IACtHR, "The word 'Laws' in Article 30 of the American Convention on Human Rights" [1986] Advisory Opinion OC-6/86, paras. 35 and 37, and *Case of Artavia Murillo et al. ("In Vitro Fertilization") v. Costa Rica* [2012] IACtHR, Ser. C No. 257, para. 273. See also the following on the right to the freedom of speech: *Case of Herrera Ulloa v. Costa Rica* [2004] IACtHR, Ser. C No. 107, para. 120; *Case of Fontevecchia and D'Amico v. Argentina. Merits, Reparations, and Costs.* Judgment of November 29, 2011, Ser. C No. 238, para. 43; and *Case of Mémoli v. Argentina. Preliminary Objections, Merits, Reparations, and Costs.* Judgment of August 22, 2013, Ser. C No. 265, para. 127, cited in the judgment of IACtHR, *Case of López Lone et al. v. Honduras* (n. 4), para. 168.

[27] IACtHR, *Case of López Lone et al. v. Honduras* (n. 4), para. 169.

[28] Ibid., para. 171.

[29] Ibid., para. 172.

[30] *Cf.* United Nations, "Commentary on the Bangalore Principles of Judicial Conduct," compiled by the UN Office on Drugs and Crime (2013), paras. 65 and 140. In this respect, the Ibero-American

the *Case of López Lone et al.*, the IACtHR cited among the bases for its decision the statement of Leandro Despouy (former Special Rapporteur of the United Nations on the Independence of Judges and Lawyers, 2003–2009), an expert witness in this case, who indicated that it may constitute an obligation for judges to speak out "in a context in which democracy is being impaired, because they are the public officials[,] specifically the judicial agents, who are the guardians of the basic rights, in the face of abuses of power by other public officials or other power groups."[31] In the said case, the Inter-American Court concluded that "at times of grave democratic crises, as in this case, the norms that normally restrict the rights of judges to participate in politics are not applicable to their actions in defence of the democratic order," citing their rights as citizens to take part in politics, to freedom of expression, to the right of assembly and to protest.[32]

The preceding principles and guidelines for jurisprudential interpretation are also applicable to the *freedom of association* of judges. In this regard, the Basic Principles state that judges enjoy the right "to form and join associations of judges or other organizations to represent their interests, to promote their professional training and to protect their judicial independence" (Principle 9). This right implies an international obligation upon the States to guarantee the conditions necessary to allow the right to be exercised and, at the same time, to refrain from imposing obstacles or illegitimate restrictions upon this right.

Associations of judges have various legitimate ends, including those relating to the promotion of the values and principles of the judiciary, the rule of law, democracy and human rights, the training of judicial personnel, the fight for dignified conditions in the exercise of judicial function, and other similar ones. Thus, these associations of judges normally need to be composed of active judges, so judges who are currently exercising their functions. In other words, in such cases, the judges are exercising their right to association in their very capacity as judges. This means that once they are no longer judges, they are generally no longer active members of these associations, and they therefore also cease to exercise this right of the association of judges.

Consequently, the Inter-American Court has maintained that the arbitrary dismissal of a judge who is a member of an association of judges which, as such, also brings about an end to the judge's exercising of his or her condition as a member of the association in question also constitutes "an undue restriction of

---

Code of Judicial Ethics establishes that "[t]he judge has the right and the duty to denounce any attempt at disruption of his/her independence." Ibero-American Code of Judicial Ethics 2006, Article 6, <https://www.poderjudicial.es/cgpj/en/CIEJ/Ibero-American-Code-of-Judicial-Ethics/> (accessed February 5, 2022).

[31] IACtHR, *Case of López Lone et al. v. Honduras* (n. 4), para. 173.
[32] Ibid., para. 174.

the right to freedom of association," in violation of Article 16 of the American Convention."[33]

6. The Disciplinary System and the System for Removing Judges from Office

As we saw previously, stability as an essential guarantee of judicial independence entails the principle of the stability of judges and their consequent inviolability. Even if this principle is not absolute, it is subject to a series of guarantees and requirements. As a general principle, during their time in office, judges may not be removed or dismissed unless the following prerequisites are met: (i) previously established statutory grounds in accordance with the principles of determination of criminality ("tipicidad") and proportionality; (ii) a prior process that respects the guarantees of due process and defense; and (iii) the right to effective judicial recourse before competent, impartial, and independent judges and tribunals.

This gives rise to a need to conduct a high scrutiny test or rigorous examination of cases and procedures through which judges are removed from office, whether these procedures be disciplinary or of another kind.

Based on the cited Principles 17 and 18 as invoked by the Inter-American Court and on the interpretations of the Human Rights Committee of the United Nations in General Comment 32, the IACtHR has confirmed that judges may be dismissed only for "conduct that is clearly unacceptable" and for "reasons of serious misconduct or incompetence."[34] Thus, the possibility of dismissal must abide by the "principle of extreme gravity" given that the protection of judicial independence requires that the dismissal of judges "be considered as the la *ultima ratio* in judicial disciplinary matters."[35] In this regard, judges may be removed only "for serious disciplinary offenses or incompetence, and by proceedings with due guarantees or when their term of office has ended." This means that dismissal "cannot be an arbitrary measure, and must be analysed in light of the existing domestic framework and the circumstances of the specific case."[36]

Further, the Court has considered that, "based on the guarantee of judicial tenure, the grounds for removing judges from their posts must be clear and established by law." Thus, considering that "dismissal or removal from office is the most restrictive

---

[33] Ibid., para. 186.
[34] IACtHR, *Case of the Supreme Court of Justice (Quintana Coello et al.) v. Ecuador* (n. 7), para. 147. Similarly: IACtHR, *Case of the Constitutional Tribunal (Camba Campos et al.) v. Ecuador* (n. 6), para. 191; IACtHR, *Case of the Supreme Court of Justice (Quintana Coello et al.) v. Ecuador* (n. 7), para. 198; and *Case of López Lone et al. v. Honduras* (n. 4), paras. 196, 198, 199, and 259.
[35] IACtHR, *Case of López Lone et al. v. Honduras* (n. 4), para. 259.
[36] IACtHR, *Case of the Constitutional Tribunal (Camba Campos et al.) v. Ecuador* (n. 6), para. 200.

and severe disciplinary measure that can be adopted, the possibility of its application must be predictable, either because the punishable conduct is expressly and clearly established, precisely, clearly and previously, by law, or because the law delegates its imposition to the judge or to an *infra-legal* norm, under objective criteria that limit the scope of discretion."[37]

Likewise, citing the Principles and Guidelines on the Right to a Fair Trial and Legal Assistance in Africa,[38] the Court has referred specifically to the inadmissibility of removing judges from office only because their decisions have been overturned or even because they have been subjected to other disciplinary or administrative procedures solely because a decision made by them has been reversed on appeal or upon review by a higher judicial body.[39]

The IACtHR has developed the differences between the various sanctions applicable to judges depending on the gravity of the offense, citing other international standards such as those contained in Principle VI of the Recommendation of the Council of Europe on the Independence, Efficiency and Role of Judges.[40] Based on the principles and authoritative interpretations invoked by the Inter-American Court, the IACtHR has maintained that dismissal, as the maximum penalty, must be the result of "serious misconduct," whereas "other sanctions" that are less serious may be considered in the event of "negligence or incompetence."[41]

In the case of sanctions applied to judges, and particularly dismissals, the authority in charge must "act independently and impartially in the proceedings established for that effect and allow the exercise of a right to a defence."[42] Furthermore, the Court considers that for an investigation of a complaint against a judge to be effective, "those responsible for it must be independent, from a

---

[37] IACtHR, *Case of López Lone et al. v. Honduras* (n. 4), para. 259.

[38] *The Principles and Guidelines on the Right to a Fair Trial and Legal Assistance in Africa*, adopted as part of the African Commission's activity report at second summit and meeting of heads of State of AU held in Maputo from July 4–12, 2003, Principle A, Article 4, Clause n (2), published in *International Principles on the Independence and Accountability of Judges, Lawyers and Prosecutors* (2007), 213 to 223, <https://www.icj.org/wp-content/uploads/2012/04/International-Principles-on-the-Independence-and-Accountability-of-Judges-Lawyers-and-Procecutors-No.1-Practitioners-Guide-2009-Eng.pdf> (accessed February 5, 2022).

[39] IACtHR *Case of the Supreme Court of Justice (Quintana Coello et al.) v. Ecuador* (n. 7), para. 149. Similarly: IACtHR, *Case of the Constitutional Tribunal (Camba Campos et al.) v. Ecuador* (n. 6), para. 193.

[40] *Recommendation No. R (94) 12 of the Committee of Ministers to Member States on the Independence, Efficiency and Role of Judges* (adopted by the Committee of Ministers on October 13, 1994, at the 518th Meeting of the Ministers' Deputies), <https://www.euromed-justice.eu/en/system/files/20090123125232_recR%2894%2912e.pdf> (accessed February 5, 2022).

[41] IACtHR, *Case of the Supreme Court of Justice (Quintana Coello et al.) v. Ecuador* (n. 7), para. 148. Similarly: IACtHR, *Case of the Constitutional Tribunal (Camba Campos et al.) v. Ecuador* (n. 6), paras. 191 and 192.

[42] IACtHR, *Case of Reverón Trujillo v. Venezuela* (n. 6), para. 78. Similarly: IACtHR, *Case of Chocrón Chocrón v. Venezuela* (n. 6), para. 99; IACtHR, *Case of the Constitutional Tribunal (Camba Campos et al.) v. Ecuador* (n. 6), para. 189; and *Case of López Lone et al. v. Honduras* (n. 4), para. 196.

hierarchical and institutional point of view and also in the practice, from the individuals implicated in the events investigated."[43]

In accordance with the standards developed by the Inter-American Court, the IACtHR has fully rejected the free or arbitrary removal of judges (including provisional judges), since this violates judicial independence seeing that it foments an objective doubt regarding the "effective possibility they may have to decide specific controversies without fearing the retaliation."[44] Thus, the Court has endorsed the guarantees of judicial independence in the institutional and subjective sense in relation to the principle of the inviolability of tenure, confirming the following strict prerequisites of the disciplinary or punitive system for judges: (i) previously established statutory grounds in accordance with the principles of determination of criminality ("tipicidad") and proportionality; (ii) a prior process that respects the guarantees of due process and defense; and (iii) the right to effective judicial recourse before competent, impartial, and independent judges and tribunals. Therefore, when judicial independence is affected, it is not only a case of the guarantees of due process recognized in Article 8 of the American Convention and the right to access and remain in public office, on general terms of equality, as established in Article 23(1)(c) of the American Convention being violated with regard to the judge; in addition, the right to effective judicial protection as recognized in Article 25 of the Convention is also affected, with regard to the parties subject to trial and certainly with regard to the actual judge.[45] Lastly, the Inter-American Court, invoking its precedent in the *Case of Uzcátegui et al.*, has indicated that criminal proceedings can have "an intimidating or inhibiting effect" on the exercise of freedom of expression, "contrary to the State's obligation to guarantee the free and full exercise of this right in a democratic society,"[46] and has stated that the application of this consideration depends on the specific facts of each case.[47] Further, despite the fact that the case under consideration did not involve criminal proceedings, the Court has considered that "the mere fact of instituting disciplinary proceedings against the judges and the

---

[43] *Case of Gutiérrez and Family v. Argentina* [2013] IACtHR, Ser. C No. 271, para. 120.

[44] IACtHR, *Case of Reverón Trujillo v. Venezuela* (n. 6), para. 78. Similarly: IACtHR, *Case of Chocrón Chocrón v. Venezuela* (n. 6), para. 99; IACtHR, *Case of the Constitutional Tribunal (Camba Campos et al.) v. Ecuador* (n. 6), para. 189; and *Case of López Lone et al. v. Honduras* (n. 4), para. 196.

[45] IACtHR, *Case of the Supreme Court of Justice (Quintana Coello et al.) v. Ecuador* (n. 7), para. 155. Similarly: IACtHR, *Case of the Constitutional Tribunal (Camba Campos et al.) v. Ecuador* (n. 6), para. 191; *Case of López Lone et al. v. Honduras* (n. 4), para. 200; and *Case of Valencia Hinojosa et al. v. Ecuador* [2016] IACtHR, Ser. C No. 327, para. 105.

[46] *Case of Uzcátegui et al. v. Venezuela* [2012] IACtHR, Ser. C No. 249, para. 189, cited in *Case of López Lone et al. v. Honduras* (n. 4), para. 176.

[47] As an example, the IACtHR mentioned that in the *Case of Uzcátegui et al.*, criminal proceedings were taking place against Mr. Uzcátegui and the person who filed suit held a high position (Commander General of the Armed Police Forces of the State of Falcón) and that there was a context of violence in which the victim had been subject to threats, harassment, and unlawful arrest. *Cf.* IACtHR, *Case of Uzcátegui et al. v. Venezuela* (n. 46), para. 189, cited in *Case of López Lone et al. v. Honduras* (n. 4), para. 176.

justice based on their actions against the coup d'etat and in favor of the rule of law could have had this intimidating effect and, therefore, constituted an undue restriction of their rights."[48]

7. Brief Reference to Impeachment Proceedings against Judges

In some countries, the removal or dismissal of judges (magistrates or ministers) of high courts such as a supreme court of justice or constitutional tribunals or courts is the responsibility of the legislative body (parliament or congress), which acts through the process of impeachment. However, this process, despite taking place within the seat of political power, must still be governed by the general principles and guarantees of judicial independence, namely, legal cause, competence, due process, and the right to effective judicial recourse.

The Inter-American Court has had opportunity on two occasions to pronounce upon the use of impeachment proceedings for the dismissal of judges. By coincidence, both of these cases relate to the judges of constitutional courts. In the case of the *Constitutional Court of Peru*, the IACtHR established the following criteria, confirmed in the case of the *Constitutional Court of Ecuador*, in relation to the judicial guarantees applicable to impeachment proceedings in general and, in particular, to impeachment proceedings against judges:

1. The exercising of the State's sanctioning power must be carried out in full compliance with the legal order, which includes respecting the minimum guarantees of due process in accordance with the requirements established in the American Convention.
2. The application of Article 8 of the American Convention relating to judicial guarantees ("Right to a Fair Trial" in the English version) is not limited to judicial recourse in the strictest sense; instead, it relates to "the procedural requirements that should be observed in order to be able to speak of effective and appropriate judicial guarantees so that a person may defend himself adequately in the face of any kind of act of the State that affects his rights."
3. The list of minimum guarantees established in Article 8 Para. 2 of the Convention also applies to the determination of rights and obligations of a civil, labor, fiscal, or any other nature and, therefore, "in this type of matter, the individual also has the overall right to the due process applicable in criminal matters."

---

[48] IACtHR, *Case of López Lone et al. v. Honduras* (n. 4), para. 176.

4. The provision of the Convention proclaiming the right of a person to be heard by a competent judge or tribunal to determine their rights (Article 8.1) refers to "any public authority, whether administrative, legislative, or judicial, which, through its decisions determines individual rights and obligations." Thus, "any State organ that exercises functions of a materially jurisdictional nature has the obligation to adopt decisions that are in consonance with the guarantees of due legal process in the terms of Article 8 of the American Convention."
5. The independence of any judge requires an appropriate appointment process with a fixed term in the position and a guarantee against external pressures. This means that "under the rule of law, the independence of all judges and, in particular, that of constitutional judges, must be guaranteed owing to the nature of the matters submitted to their consideration."
6. Regarding the exercise of the authority of Congress to conduct impeachment proceedings, which engages the responsibility of a public official, the Court believes that "it should be recalled that any person subject to a proceeding of any nature before an organ of the State must be guaranteed that this organ is competent, independent and impartial and that it acts in accordance with the procedure established by law for hearing and deciding the case submitted to it."[49]

In relation to the right of judges as per Article 8.1 of the American Convention to a hearing and to exercise the right to defense in impeachment proceedings or sanctioning processes in the parliamentary context, the Inter-American Court has reiterated that the guarantees established in Article 8 of the Convention presume that "the victims should have extensive possibilities of being heard and acting in the respective proceedings so that they may submit their claims and present probative elements, and that these are analyzed completely and rigorously by the authorities before a decision is taken on the facts, responsibilities, sanctions, and reparations."[50]

Based on the application of the preceding principles and guarantees of due process applicable to impeachment proceedings against judges, the Inter-American Court concluded in the *Case of the Constitutional Court of Peru* that the State had violated the right to a fair trial embodied in Article 8 of the American Convention with regard to the magistrates (Manuel Aguirre Roca,

---

[49] IACtHR, *Case of the Constitutional Court v. Peru* (n. 4), paras. 68 to 71, 75, and 77; confirmed in IACtHR, *Case of the Constitutional Tribunal (Camba Campos et al.) v. Ecuador* (n. 6), para. 166.

[50] IACtHR, *Case of the Constitutional Tribunal (Camba Campos et al.) v. Ecuador* (n. 6), para. 181. The first part of the citation of the court, "The victims should have extensive possibilities of being heard and acting in the respective proceedings," was first expressed in IACtHR, *Case of the Constitutional Court v. Peru* (n. 4), IACtHR, para. 81.

Guillermo Rey Terry y Delia Revoredo Marsano) since "the impeachment proceeding to which the dismissed justices were submitted *did not ensure them guarantees of due legal process and did not comply with the requirement of the impartiality of the judge."* In addition, the Court observes that, in the context of this specific case, *the Legislature did not have the necessary conditions of independence and impartiality to conduct the impeachment proceeding against the three justices of the Constitutional Court."*[51] (Emphasis added by the author.)

Similarly, in the *Case of the Constitutional Tribunal of Ecuador*, the Inter-American Court concluded that the judges (members) of the said Tribunal: (i) were not notified in the first proceeding conducted by Congress in order to determine the termination of their positions and were not able to respond to the charges that were being made against them, given that it was necessary that their possibility of being heard was guaranteed in relation to the alleged irregularities in their appointment; and that (ii) in the subsequent impeachment trial conducted against them by Congress, which was a new proceeding, the judges were not notified of the new parliamentary session and had no opportunity to exercise their right of defense in order to intervene in this proceeding and to be heard.[52]

8. Some Consequences of the Violation of Judicial Independence

Failure to respect the guarantees of judicial independence, specifically through the arbitrary removal or dismissal of a judge, violates various provisions of the American Convention, including the guarantees of due process, the right to access and remain in public office on general terms of equality, and the right to effective judicial protection as recognized in Articles 9, 23(1)(c), and (25) of the Convention.

The victim of any such violation of judicial independence is the judge; but in addition, depending on the circumstances, the parties subject to trial may also be victims of the violation of judicial independence: the plaintiffs, defendants, accused, and victims of the violation of human rights. All the victims of the violation of the right to judicial independence must be fully compensated for the damages suffered.

---

[51] IACtHR, *Case of the Constitutional Court v. Peru* (n. 4), paras. 84 and 85.
[52] IACtHR, *Case of the Constitutional Tribunal (Camba Campos et al.) v. Ecuador* (n. 6), paras. 183, 187, and 222.

8.1. Full Reparation for Judges: Reinstatement and the Payment of Damages

Judges who have been the victims of arbitrary removal or dismissal from office have the right to be protected in domestic law through effective judicial recourse before competent, independent, and impartial judges with regard to the acts through which their judicial guarantees were violated, including their guarantee of judicial independence as recognized in Article 8 of the American Convention. For this protection, the judges have the right to simple and prompt recourse or any other effective recourse as enshrined in Article 25 of the Convention. In this regard, the Basic Principles establish that decisions in disciplinary, suspension, or removal proceedings relating to the office of judges should be "subject to an independent review" (Principle 20).

If the appeal is upheld, the judge must be protected and fully compensated, including being reinstated to the position of which he or she was arbitrarily deprived. In other words, this effective protection must enable the judge to again exercise his or her office due to the principle of irremovability. This means that the upholding of a judiciary appeal against the arbitrary dismissal of a judge must necessarily lead to the reinstatement of that judge to his or her office in addition to further compensation for material and moral damages caused.[53]

Nonetheless, in accordance with the rule established in the American Convention and once domestic recourses have been exhausted without full reparation having been obtained, a judge who has been subject to arbitrary removal or dismissal may appeal to the IACHR and, in turn, subsequently to the IACtHR, in order to obtain international protection for his or her violated treaty rights.

As we have seen, the Inter-American Court has had opportunity to become familiar with and decide upon various cases relating to the arbitrary removal or dismissal of judges in violation of judicial independence and other guarantees of due process and the right to effective judicial protection.

In some cases, given the arbitrary removal or dismissal suffered by the judges, the Inter-American Court has declared the State internationally responsible for the violation of Articles 8 and 25 with respect to the judge as the victim; further, as of the *Case of Reverón Trujillo*, it declared the violation of Article 23(1) (c) (political rights to have access, under general conditions of equality, to the public services of the country).[54] Given the specific characteristics of the *Case*

---

[53] IACtHR, *Case of Reverón Trujillo v. Venezuela* (n. 6), para. 81.
[54] *Case of the Constitutional Court v. Peru* [2001] IACtHR, para. 130.1 and 2; *Case of Apitz Barbera et al. ("First Court of Administrative Disputes") v. Venezuela* [2008] IACtHR, Operative Paragraphs, para. 267.7, 8, and 9; IACtHR, *Case of Reverón Trujillo v. Venezuela* (n. 6), Operative Paragraphs, para. 209.2, 3, and 4; IACtHR, *Case of Chocrón Chocrón v. Venezuela* (n. 6), Operative Paragraphs, para. 205.2 and 3; IACtHR, *Case of the Supreme Court of Justice (Quintana Coello et al.) v. Ecuador* (n. 7), Operative Paragraphs, para. 284.2, 3, and 4; IACtHR, *Case of the Constitutional Tribunal (Camba*

of *López Lone et al.* with regard to the vagueness of the measures and disciplinary sanctions, the declaration of the judges against the coup d'etat, and the association of judges to which they belonged, the Inter-American Court also declared the violation of Article 9 (Freedom from Ex Post Facto Laws), Article 13.1 (Freedom of Thought and Expression), Article 15 (Right of Assembly), and Article 16 (Freedom of Association) of the Convention.[55]

As of the *Case of Apitz Barbera et al.*, as a general rule, the Inter-American Court has provided in its sentences for the requirement, as part of full reparation, that the State reinstate the judges, "if they so desire," in a position in which "they have the same salaries, related benefits, and equivalent rank as they had prior to their removal from office."[56] This benefit, direct or in kind, must be replaced by a compensation payment if, due to legitimate reasons, the State is unable to reinstate the judges as required by the compensation provision.[57]

In cases the Inter-American Court has ascertained the "impossibility" of reinstating the judges "in their functions as judge," the Court has provided directly for the payment of substitutive compensation. This has occurred for reasons associated with amendments made to the Constitution, which modified the organ (Constitutional Tribunal), the new organ (Constitutional Court) not being equivalent in composition or powers to the previous organ,[58] or if a constitutional change has generated the subsequent restructuring of the organ (Supreme Court of Justice) including significant modifications in aspects such as the number of members making up the new organ (National Court of Justice), the new number being less than the old number of members, with some of the judges (magistrates) already having refused reinstatement.[59]

With regard to reparations for damaged caused, in all of the cases, the Inter-American Court provided in its judgments for the compensation of the victims for "pecuniary and non-pecuniary damages, and reimbursement of costs and expenses" in accordance with the stipulated conditions for each case. The Court included the lost salaries and related benefits not received by the judges along

---

Campos et al.) v. Ecuador (n. 6), Operative Paragraphs, para. 327.2, 3, and 4; and IACtHR, *Case of López Lone et al. v. Honduras* (n. 4), Operative Paragraphs, para. 341.2, 3, 4, 5, 7, and 8.

[55] IACtHR, *Case of López Lone et al. v. Honduras* (n. 4), Operative Paragraphs, para. 341.2 to 6 and 9.

[56] *Case of Apitz Barbera et al. ("First Court of Administrative Disputes") v. Venezuela* [2008] IACtHR, para. 267.17.

[57] *Case of Apitz Barbera et al. ("First Court of Administrative Disputes") v. Venezuela* [2008] IACtHR, Operative Paragraphs, para. 267.17. The State was given one (1) year to reinstate the arbitrarily removed or dismissed judge in IACtHR, *Case of Chocrón Chocrón v. Venezuela* (n. 6), para. 205.7, and in IACtHR, *Case of López Lone et al. v. Honduras* (n. 4), paras. 298 and 341.16.

[58] IACtHR, *Case of the Constitutional Tribunal (Camba Campos et al.) v. Ecuador* (n. 6), paras. 263 and 264; and Operative Paragraphs, para. 327.10.

[59] IACtHR, *Case of the Supreme Court of Justice (Quintana Coello et al.) v. Ecuador* (n. 7), paras. 214 and 215; and Operative Paragraphs, para. 284.10.

with other material and moral damages caused in addition to loss of profits after dismissal.[60]

Other additional full reparation measures stipulated by the IACtHR have referred to structural problems that caused the violations of the rights, such as laws, regulations, and jurisprudence. In these cases, with the aim of making the obligation of nonrepetition effective, the IACtHR has required the State to adopt general measures to prevent further violations. For example, in the Venezuelan cases relating to the fact that a majority of judges were provisional, freely appointed, and subject to discretionary removal without effective judicial recourse, the Court required the State to remedy the situation by adopting corrective legislative measures (Venezuelan Code of Judicial Ethics) and changing the jurisprudential policy of its Supreme Tribunal of Justice.[61]

8.2. Reparation for Parties Subject to Trial

Having been subjected to a "judge" without guaranteed independence, whether as the accused, plaintiff, or victim, is not only a violation of the right to access to justice with guarantees of due process (arts. 8 and 25 ACHR); in addition, it can be associated with a range of serious additional violations and damages.

In light of such situations, we must ask ourselves the following: What protection can persons who have been victim to decisions made by judges who are not independent, or who have been denied protection due to decisions made by judges who are not independent, seek at international level?

The *Case of Castillo Petruzzi et al.*, in which Chilean victims were tried and convicted for treason in Peru by military courts lacking independence in violation of their right to judicial guarantee, was heard by the IACrHR. In this case, the Inter-American Court determined that "the military tribunals that tried the alleged victims for the crimes of treason did not meet the requirements implicit in the *guarantees of independence* and impartiality that Article 8(1) of the American Convention recognizes as *essentials of due process of law*."[62] (Emphasis

---

[60] *Case of Apitz Barbera et al. ("First Court of Administrative Disputes") v. Venezuela* [2008] IACtHR, Operative Paragraphs, para. 267.16; IACtHR, *Case of Reverón Trujillo v. Venezuela* (n. 6), Operative Paragraphs, para. 209.12; IACtHR, *Case of Chocrón Chocrón v. Venezuela* (n. 6), Operative Paragraphs, para. 205.10; IACtHR, *Case of the Supreme Court of Justice (Quintana Coello et al.) v. Ecuador* (n. 7), Operative Paragraphs, para. 284.11; IACtHR, *Case of the Constitutional Tribunal (Camba Campos et al.) v. Ecuador* (n. 6) Operative Paragraphs, para. 327.11; and IACtHR, *Case of López Lone et al. v. Honduras* (n. 4), Operative Paragraphs, para. 341.18.

[61] IACtHR, *Case of Apitz Barbera et al. ("First Court of Administrative Disputes") v. Venezuela* (n. 6), Operative Paragraphs, para. 267.19; IACtHR, *Case of Reverón Trujillo v. Venezuela* (n. 6), Operative Paragraphs, para. 209.9 and 10; and IACtHR, *Case of Chocrón Chocrón v. Venezuela* (n. 6), Operative Paragraphs, para. 205.8.

[62] *Case of Castillo Petruzzi et al. v. Peru* [1999] IACtHR, Ser. C No. 52, para. 132.

added by the author.) The Court therefore determined that "the State violated Article 8(1) of the American Convention,"[63] finding the military proceedings against the victims "*invalid.*" Among the full reparation measures for the victims, the Court required that the State guarantee "*a new trial in which the guarantees of due process of law are ensured.*"[64] (Emphasis added by the author.)

Similarly, in the *Case of Palamara Iribarne*, the victim, who was a civilian and had published a book on topics concerning military intelligence, was tried and convicted by military courts lacking independence. In this case, the Inter-American Court, having first confirmed that "*the independence of the Judiciary from other State powers is essential for the exercise of judicial functions*"[65] (emphasis added by the author), concluded that the State "did not guarantee Mr. Palamara's right to be tried by an appropriate, impartial, and independent judge in the criminal proceedings brought against him, and therefore, it has violated Article 8(1) of the Convention to his detriment,"[66] and furthermore "violated the right to judicial protection consecrated in Article 25 of the American Convention"[67] to his detriment. Among the measures of full reparation for the victim, the Court required that the State "*must leave without effect*, in the term of six months and to every extent, the conviction"[68] passed by the Chilean military tribunals against Mr. Palamara Iribarne (emphasis added by the author).

In conclusion, in the case of the trial and conviction of victims by judges lacking judicial independence, the IACtHR has pronounced the violation of the essential guarantee of due process and the right to judicial protection as enshrined in Articles 8 and 25 of the American Convention. Further, among the full reparation measures for the victims, it has provided for the invalidity of the processes, requiring the State to leave without effect the convictions and guarantee a new trial with full observance of the due legal process.

In two of its cases, the Human Rights Committee of the United Nations, in a similar way to the IACtHR in the cases relating to the trial or failure to provide judicial protection to victims by judges lacking judicial independence, has declared the violation of the essential guarantee of due process and of judicial protection as enshrined in Article 14.1 of the International Covenant on Civil and Political Rights and, among the full reparation measures for the victims, has required that the State provide the victim with effective recourse, guaranteeing—among other

---

[63] Ibid., para. 226.4.
[64] Ibid., para. 226.4, Operative Paragraphs, para. 226.13.
[65] *Case of Palamara Iribarne v. Chile* [2005] IACtHR, Ser. C No. 135, para. 145.
[66] Ibid., para. 269.3.
[67] Ibid., para. 161; and Operative Paragraphs, para. 269.4.
[68] IACtHR, *Case of Palamara Iribarne v. Chile* (n. 65), para. 161; and Operative Paragraphs, para. 269.12; and IACtHR. *Case of Radilla Pacheco v. Mexico*. Preliminary Objections, Merits, Reparations, and Costs. Judgment of November 23, 2009. Series C No. 209, paras. 114, 115; Operative Paragraphs 5 and 8.

measures—a judicial proceeding that complies with the guarantees established by Article 14 of the Covenant.[69] Likewise, in these cases, the Committee, in a similar way to the ICHR, ordered the State to adopt general structural measures in order to avoid the future occurrence of similar violations.[70]

9. Concluding Remarks

Judicial independence is an essential element of the rule of law and constitutional democracy. This is why the constitutions of democratic States enshrine it in the chapters on the organization of justice, judges, and courts. Its classic role is to guarantee freedom and uphold the Constitution, through its supervisory functions.

At the same time, judicial independence has progressively developed as an essential constitutional and human right within the guarantees of due process. Indeed, the right of every person to have access to the protection of his or her rights and to be tried before independent and impartial judges has been enshrined in international human rights instruments as an international obligation of States.

For a judge to be independent and free from external pressures, he or she must in turn enjoy a series of guarantees relating to his or her appointment, tenure, stability, and termination of his or her function. Hence, if a judge is the victim of a violation of any of these judicial guarantees, he or she is a legitimate subject to claim effective protection and full reparation. If protection is not granted by national courts, the affected judge may bring an action before the competent international protection bodies in order to obtain such protection and reparation.

Thus, the right-obligation of every person to protection and trial before independent judges is also a right-obligation of all judges, both at the domestic (constitutional-legal) and international level (treaties and other human rights instruments).

---

[69] The Human Rights Committee of the United Nations has acted similarly to the ICHR. *Cf. Gabriel Osío Zamora v. Venezuela* [2018] UN Human Rights Committee, Opinion of Communication No. 2203/2012, CCPR/C/121/D/2203/2012; and *Marco Siervo Sabarsky v. Venezuela* [2019] UN Human Rights Committee, Opinion of Communication No. 2254/2013, CCPR/C/125/D/2254/2013.

[70] For a broader analysis on structural impact of Inter-American decisions: Pablo Saavedra Alessandri, "Algunas reflexiones en cuanto al impacto estructural de las decisiones de la Corte Interamericana de Derechos Humanos," in Armin von Bogdandy et al. (eds.), *Ius Constitucionale Commune en América Latina. Textos básicos para su compression* (MPIL; Instituto de Estudios Constitucionales del Estado de Querétaro 2017), 457–502.

II.14
Freedom of Expression

Inter-American Standards and Their Transformative Impact

By Catalina Botero-Marino

1. Introduction

Ius Constitutionale Commune en América Latina (ICCAL),[1] or the common Latin American constitutional law that involves the interaction of norms across domestic constitutions and the Inter-American Human Rights System (Inter-American System, or IAHRS) of the Organization of American States (OAS),[2] has played a substantial role in developing shared legal standards that drive constitutional transformation in the region.[3] Considering the severe democratic crisis Latin America currently face, the transformative impact of ICCAL might not seem believable. The available evidence, however, demonstrates the existence of a virtuous circle of social impact generated by a multilevel protection of human rights, democratic principles, and the rule of law. This multilevel

---

[1] On the original idea of a *Ius Constitutionale Commune en América Latina*, see Armin von Bogdandy, "The Transformative Mandate of the Inter-American System—Legality and Legitimacy of an Extraordinary Jurisgenerative Process" (2019) MPIL Research Paper No. 2019-16, https://ssrn.com/abstract=3463059 (accessed December 3, 2021).

[2] The Inter-American Human Rights System (Inter-American System, or IAHRS) of the Organization of American States (OAS) is composed by the Inter-American Commission on Human Rights (Inter-American Commission, or IACHR), the Inter-American Court of Human Rights (Inter-American Court, or IACtHR), and the Rapporteurships created by the IACHR. The Office of the Special Rapporteur for Freedom of Expression is a key player in promoting the right to freedom of expression.

[3] An earlier version of this chapter was written in 2018 for the Global Freedom of Expression Project of the University of Columbia and can be found at: Catalina Botero-Marino, "The Role of the Inter-American Human Rights System in the Emergence and Development of Global Norms on Freedom of Expression," in Lee C. Bollinger and Agnès Callamard (eds.), *Regardless of Frontiers: Global Freedom of Expression in a Troubled World* (Columbia University Press 2021), 185–206. I would like to thank my colleagues Julián Niño and Salomé Gómez for their invaluable support in the production of that article. This chapter also incorporates some of the decisions collected by the team of Los Andes University that works on the Spanish page of the Global Freedom of Expression Project. I would like to thank them for their dedicated work summarizing and synthesizing the most relevant regional jurisprudence on freedom of expression, https://globalfreedomofexpression.columbia.edu/espanol/?lang=es (accessed December 3, 2021).

Catalina Botero-Marino, *Freedom of Expression* In: *The Impact of the Inter-American Human Rights System*. Edited by: Armin von Bogdandy, Flávia Piovesan, Eduardo Ferrer Mac-Gregor, and Mariela Morales Antoniazzi, Oxford University Press. © Catalina Botero-Marino 2024. DOI: 10.1093/oso/9780197744161.003.0025

protection grows out of interactions among domestic courts, the IAHRS, and a broader community of practice.

This chapter explains the relationship between domestic and international institutions that has enabled the creation of human rights standards at multiple levels. These standards have transformed the understanding and application of the law at both the domestic and international levels. This chapter also argues that the Inter-American System has promoted and developed regional standards for the protection of the right to freedom of expression, some of which have become—or at the very least have the potential to become—ICCAL. To this end, the chapter explains the process through which existing standards on freedom of speech have been established; describes the content of these standards; and demonstrates the transformative impact that two of these standards have had in domestic legal systems: the standard regarding the limits of criminal law and the standard regarding the scope and nature of the right to access public information.

2. The Creation of ICCAL Regarding Freedom of Expression and the Inter-American System's Transformative Mandate

During the 1980s and 1990s, the Inter-American Commission on Human Rights (Inter-American Commission, or IACHR) produced a single thematic report[4] and decided only a few cases on freedom of expression.[5] Meanwhile, the Inter-American Court of Human Rights (Inter-American Court, or IACtHR) issued only two advisory opinions regarding this right, one of which had only a minor impact.[6] Nevertheless, by the late 1990s and the 2000s, the Inter-American Commission and the Inter-American Court had emerged as leaders in the promotion the right to freedom of expression in the Americas.

Three critical events characterize the Inter-American System's transition toward increased attention to the right of freedom of expression:[7] (i) the creation, in 1997, of the Office of the Special Rapporteur for Freedom of Expression (Office of the Special Rapporteur, or Office) at the IACHR; (ii) the publication, in 2000,

---

[4] IACHR, "Annual Report 1994," Chapter V: *Report on the Compatibility of "Desacato" Laws with the American Convention on Human Rights*, OEA/Ser.L/V/II.88, Doc. 9 rev., February 17, 1995.

[5] For a list of the most important IACHR cases concerning freedom of expression, see http://www.oas.org/en/iachr/expression/jurisprudence/decisions_iachr_merit.asp (accessed December 3, 2021).

[6] *Compulsory Membership in an Association Prescribed by Law for the Practice of Journalism* (Arts. 13 and 29 American Convention on Human Rights), IACtHR, Advisory Opinion OC-5/85 of November 13, 1985, Ser. A, No. 5; *Enforceability of the Right to Reply or Correction* (Arts. 14(1), 1(1) and 2 American Convention on Human Rights), IACtHR, Advisory Opinion OC-7/86 of August 29, 1986, Ser. A, No. 7.

[7] For more details on this issue, see Botero-Marino (n. 3), 185–206.

of the IACHR's Declaration of Principles on Freedom of Expression;[8] and (iii) the approval, in 2000, of the Inter-American Democratic Charter of the OAS,[9] which provided that freedom of expression is one of the "essential components for the exercise of democracy."

These events sparked an exponential increase in regional attention to the development of standards concerning freedom of expression. From 2001 until the date of completion of this chapter,[10] the IACtHR has decided fifty[11] cases related to freedom of expression and access to information.[12] These cases constitute slightly less than 15 percent of all rulings issued by the Inter-American Court (347).[13] Meanwhile, the IACHR has issued many admissibility, merits, thematic, and country reports on the subject and, through its Office of the Special Rapporteur, has produced twenty-two annual reports detailing progress and setbacks in the right to freedom of expression in every State of the Americas. During the same period, the Office also issued more than forty thematic reports analyzing broader trends concerning the right to freedom of expression.[14]

The Inter-American System's exponential increase in attention and contributions to legal norms concerning freedom of expression has provided a basis for hundreds of well-known cases from courts throughout the region and has given rise to significant constitutional and legislative reforms, as I will analyze here.[15] For example, Chile modified its constitution to eliminate prior censorship in response to one of the Inter-American Court's decisions. Chile, along with over twenty other countries in the region, also has created mechanisms that guarantee access to information in accordance with an IACtHR ruling. More than twelve Latin American countries repealed or modified criminal provisions due to the Inter-American Commission's reports and the Inter-American Court's

---

[8] The Declaration of Principles on Freedom of Expression, approved by the IACHR in October 2000.

[9] AG/RES. 1 (XXVIII-E/01), September 11, 2001.

[10] June 1, 2021.

[11] The Inter-American Court includes fifty-three cases related to freedom of expression in its jurisprudence search engine. In a study conducted together with Anderson Dirocie at Columbia Global Freedom of Expression, however, we found that five of these fifty-three cases have no relation to Article 13, and that two other cases concerning freedom of expression were not included among the fifty-three. We concluded that a total of fifty cases relate to freedom of expression. Most of these decisions are referenced in this chapter.

[12] For a list of judgments on the right to freedom of expression of the Inter-American Court, see http://www.oas.org/en/iachr/expression/jurisprudence/si_decisions_court.asp (accessed December 3, 2021).

[13] For a list of judgments of the IACtHR, see http://www.corteidh.or.cr/cf/Jurisprudencia2/busqueda_casos_contenciosos.cfm?lang=en (accessed December 3, 2021).

[14] For the annual and thematic reports concerning the right to freedom of expression from the Special Rapporteurship, see http://www.oas.org/en/iachr/expression/reports/annual.asp and http://www.oas.org/en/iachr/expression/reports/thematic.asp (both accessed December 3, 2021).

[15] For information on the most emblematic cases on this subject, see Global Freedom of Expression of the University of Columbia, Spanish Database: https://globalfreedomofexpression.columbia.edu/espanol/?lang=es (accessed December 3, 2021).

rulings.[16] Additionally, and as this chapter will show, the most emblematic domestic judgments that promote the right to freedom of expression in the region consistently cite decisions and other products of the Inter-American System.

The Inter-American System's influence in the region is not a one-way street, flowing only from the IAHRS to States. Instead, the construction of transformative standards has resulted from a virtuous circle in which domestic legal developments also enrich the work of the Inter-American System. For example, *Claude Reyes et al. v. Chile*, the first ruling issued by an international human rights court to safeguard access to information as a fundamental right, was made possible, in part, by the legislative progress that Mexico had made during the turn of the century with regard to access to information. The increase in criminal law restrictions that punished critical discourse regarding public affairs slowed after Argentina acknowledged, in *Kimel v. Argentina*, that it had violated the rights of investigative journalist Eduardo Kimel by sentencing him to a year in prison for denouncing a domestic judge's alleged collaboration with the dictatorship.[17] Similarly, at the end of the twentieth century, Colombia created the first domestic protection system for journalists, which was later acknowledged by the Inter-American Court in the case of *Vélez Restrepo and family v. Colombia*.[18] Before analyzing the Inter-American System's innovations concerning the right to freedom of expression and their impact on States, however, it is worth noting States' recurrent backlash against the development of these standards.

Inter-American standards on freedom of expression have not developed linearly or without contradictions. Since the beginning, these developments have encountered fierce opposition from illiberal governments and less democratic Latin American States, as well as OAS political bodies influenced by these States. From the Peruvian President Alberto Fujimori to the Venezuelan and Ecuadorian presidents Chavez, Maduro, and Correa, Latin American leaders have challenged the IAHRS's promotion of freedom of expression. Venezuela, for instance, started a campaign against the Inter-American System that, in September 2012, culminated in the State's withdrawal from the American Convention on Human Rights (American Convention, or ACHR). The Ecuadorian government under Rafael Correa was the subject of questions, concern, and condemnation in the Office of the Special Rapporteur's annual reports and press releases for

---

[16] This corresponds to the number of countries that have modified either their *desacato* or criminal defamation laws. Later in this chapter, I will mention which countries made modifications in one or both of those categories. See also Botero-Marino (n. 3), 185–206.

[17] *Kimel v. Argentina* [2008] IACtHR, Ser. C, No. 177.

[18] *Vélez Restrepo and family. v. Colombia* [2012] IACtHR, Ser. C, No. 248. To learn more about the influence of State developments on international standards regarding freedom of expression, see "The Role of the Interamerican Human Rights System in the Emergence and Development of Global Norms on Freedom of Expression, Botero Catalina, Columbia Freedom of Expression Project," currently in the process of being published.

imposing criminal sanctions on journalists, charging media companies large sums of money for alleged damages they had caused to the "person of the president," arbitrarily using State publicity, suspending the transmission of television channels critical of Correa's administration, monopolizing media ownership in the hands of the State, and more.[19] In the same year of Venezuela's withdrawal, Ecuador proposed a program to reform the IACHR to the Permanent Council of the OAS. The reform sought to hamper the Office of the Special Rapporteur's work by imposing technical and financial constraints.[20] Thanks to the strong opposition Ecuador faced at the Permanent Council, the reforms were eventually rejected.[21]

Even if these attacks have affected the IAHRS, and even if the conditions of political uncertainty in which the region currently finds itself do not favor expansive developments in the scope of the rights contained in the American Convention, inter-American standards regarding freedom of expression still have a notable impact, as shown in the following sections.

3. Inter-American Standards within the Multilevel Legal System

Over the last twenty years, the Inter-American System has advanced a set of legal standards on freedom of expression in the region. The IAHRS has developed and applied a three-part proportionality test to evaluate limitations on the right to freedom of expression. This test is based on the general notion that the right to freedom of expression enjoys special protection when it concerns matters of public interest. The three-part test requires that, for any limitation on freedom of expression on matters of public interest to be legitimate, the following must be demonstrated: (1) that the restrictions are contemplated in a clear and concise law; (2) that the law pursues a legitimate aim, that is, a purpose protected by international human rights law such as the American Convention; and (3) that the measure is useful, necessary, and proportionate to the end pursued.[22]

The IAHRS's jurisprudence also has developed relevant protective standards across the following main topics within the freedom of expression:[23]

---

[19] 2011 Annual Report of the OAS Special Rapporteur for Freedom of Expression, Catalina Botero-Marino, Chapter II(B)(9): *Ecuador*. OEA/Ser.L/V/II, Doc. 69, December 30, 2011.

[20] The proposals to reform the Office of the Special Rapporteur sought to prevent the Rapporteurship from acting autonomously and from acquiring funds from sources external to the OAS.

[21] For more on this, see Botero Marino (n. 3).

[22] For more on the three-part proportionality test, see *Kimel v. Argentina* (n. 17).

[23] The Office of the Special Rapporteur for Freedom of Expression has proposed the development of standards on other issues, such as: the scope of freedom of expression on the Internet; freedom

First, the IAHRS has determined that speech concerning matters of public interest, or public interest speech, requires special protection, which is reflected in the prohibition of the use of criminal law to limit expressions that may affect the reputations of public officials.[24]

Second, the Inter-American Court has been a pioneer on the right of access to public information.[25] The IACtHR has furthered the right of access to information in at least three key contexts: the right of access to information concerning serious human rights violations,[26] Indigenous peoples' right of access to information,[27] and the right of access to information as a requirement for obtaining informed consent in matters relating to an individual's health.[28]

Third, the Inter-American Court has ruled that the American Convention prohibits prior[29] and indirect censorship.[30]

Fourth, the IACtHR has determined that States must grant special protection to individuals who are threatened or harmed for exercising their right to freedom of expression.[31]

Fifth, the Inter-American Court has developed important standards on the limitations on, as well as duties[32] and rights[33] of, public officials with respect to freedom of expression.

---

of expression in electoral proceedings; freedom of expression and poverty; and standards on diversity and pluralism in the media; see http://www.oas.org/en/iachr/expression/index.asp (accessed December 7, 2021); see *Granier et al. (Radio Caracas Televisión) v. Venezuela* [2015], IACtHR, Ser. C, No. 293 (on pluralism); and 2016 Thematic Report of the OAS Special Rapporteur for Freedom of Expression, Edison Lanza: *Standards for a Free, Open and Inclusive Internet.* OEA/Ser.L/V/II, IACHR/RELE/INF.17/17, March 15, 2017.

[24] The two landmark cases of the Inter-American Court on this issue are *Kimel v. Argentina* (n. 17), and *Tulio Alvarez v. Venezuela.* The other eight cases are mentioned later in this chapter.

[25] The most significant case on this issue is *Claude-Reyes et al. v. Chile*.

[26] *Case of Myrna Mack Chang v. Guatemala*. Merits [2003], IACtHR, Ser. C No. 101; *Case of Gomes Lund et al. ("Guerrilha do Araguaia") v. Brazil* [2010], IACtHR, Ser. C No. 219; *Case of Maldonado Vargas et al. v. Chile* [2015], IACtHR, Ser. C No. 300.

[27] Two of the most emblematic cases in this area are probably *Kaliña and Locono v. Suriname*, and *Kichwa Indigenous People of Sarayaku v. Ecuador*.

[28] *Case of I. V. v. Bolivia* [2017], IACtHR, Ser. C No. 336.

[29] The most emblematic case on the matter is likely *Olmedo Bustos et al. v. Chile (The Last Temptation of Christ)* [2001], IACtHR, Ser. C, No. 73. The Inter-American Commission has also considered this issue in cases such as the *Francisco Martorell v. Chile*.

[30] The most emblematic cases on the issue are probably: *Ivcher Bronstein v. Peru* [2001], IACtHR, Ser. C, No. 74. And IACtHR *Granier et al. (Radio Caracas Televisión) v. Venezuela* [2015], IACtHR, Ser. C, No. 293.

[31] The emblematic case of the Inter-American Court in this matter is *Vélez Restrepo and family v. Colombia* (n. 18). Other significant cases on the subject are *Ríos et al. v. Venezuela*, *Perozo et al. v. Venezuela*, and *Carvajal Carvajal et al. v. Colombia*, IACtHR, and *Manoel Leal de Oliveira v. Brazil*, IACHR.

[32] The most emblematic cases on the limitations on freedom of expression for public officials are *Apitz Barbera v. Venezuela*, *Ríos et. al v. Venezuela*, *Perozo et al. v. Venezuela*, *Uzcátegui et al. v. Venezuela*, and *Granier et al. (Radio Caracas Television) v. Venezuela*, all cases IACtHR.

[33] On the right of public officials to question actions of other public authorities or to participate in the debate of matters of public interest, see cases *San Miguel Sosa et al. v. Venezuela*, *López Lone et al.*

The IACtHR's jurisprudence has also addressed media regulation,[34] the relation between freedom of expression and the right of association,[35] the limits of civil law as a means of restricting freedom of expression,[36] and special protection for speech that expresses essential elements of personal identity or dignity.[37]

Two of these topics are particularly relevant to this chapter, since the IAHRS's jurisprudence in these areas has had a remarkable transformative impact: the special protection of public interest speech, and more specifically the prohibition of contempt and criminal defamation; and access to public information. The IAHRS's approach to the other issues mentioned has also had a notable impact in some countries, but has not been as significant on a regional scale. For example, although inter-American standards on the prohibition of censorship have not had an impact on the entire region, they still have produced a transformative impact in some countries,[38] including constitutional reform in Chile.[39]

In the next section, I describe the content of inter-American standards related to the protection of public interest speech and the right to access information as well as these standards' impact on domestic legal systems.

3.1. Special Protection of Public Interest Speech: The Rejection of *Desacato* and Criminal Defamation

An issue of great concern to the Inter-American Commission and the Office of the Special Rapporteur for Freedom of Expression has been the application of criminal sanctions to punish those who express their opinions on matters of public concern. The IACHR and the Office of the Special Rapporteur have expressed this concern in the report on the crime of *desacato* (contempt),[40] the

---

v. Honduras, IACtHR, and *Urrutia Laubreaux v. Chile*, IACtHR, and, especially, the case *Adriana Beatriz Gallo et al. v. Argentina*, IACHR.

[34] *Case of Granier et al. (Radio Caracas Televisión) v. Venezuela* [2015], IACtHR, Ser. C No. 293; IACHR, Report No. 48/16, Case 12.799, Merits (Publication). Miguel Ángel Millar Silva and Others (Radio Estrella del Mar de Melinka) Chile, November 29, 2016.
[35] *Case of Lagos del Campo v. Peru* [2018], IACtHR, Ser. C No. 366; *Case of Yarce et al. v. Colombia* [2017], IACtHR, Ser. C No. 343.
[36] *Case of Fontevecchia and D'Amico v. Argentina* [2011], IACtHR, Ser. C No. 238; *Case of Tristán Donoso v. Panama* [2009], IACtHR, Ser. C No. 193.
[37] *Case of the Community Garífuna Triunfo de la Cruz and its members v. Honduras* [2015], IACtHR, Ser. C No. 305; *Case of Vicky Hernández et al. v. Honduras* [2021], IACtHR, Ser. C No. 422.
[38] See Supreme Court Justice of Brazil, Judgment of August 4, 2015; Supreme Court of Justice of Mexico, Judgment of May 2, 2012; Supreme Court of Justice of Costa Rica, Judgment of March 29, 2011; Constitutional Court of Colombia, Judgment of February 3, 2011, https://globalfreedomofexpression.columbia.edu/espanol/?lang=es (accessed December 11, 2021).
[39] Law No. 19.742 of August 8, 2001, *Boletín Oficial* of August 25, 2001.
[40] IACHR, "Annual Report 1994," Chapter V: *Report on the Compatibility of "Desacato" Laws with the American Convention on Human Rights*, OEA/Ser.L/V/II.88, Doc. 9 rev., February 17, 1995.

Declaration of Principles on Freedom of Expression,[41] and additional thematic and country reports, as well as in a number of cases the IACHR has brought before the IACtHR.

Thus far in the twenty-first century, the Inter-American Commission has brought ten cases before the Inter-American Court concerning the use of criminal law to restrict freedom of expression.[42] In nine of those cases, the IACtHR found that the use of criminal law constituted an unnecessary and disproportionate measure in violation of the right to freedom of expression. Only in one of these cases, *Mémoli v. Argentina*, did the Inter-American Court uphold the imposition of criminal sanctions as a consequence of speech. In *Mémoli*, the IACtHR decided that it would not be appropriate strictly to apply the three-part test because that the expression that had been subjected to criminal liability was not, in the Inter-American Court's view, public interest speech. The IACtHR reached this conclusion by noting that the offensive expression was directed not at a public official but at private individuals. The IACtHR decided that illegal use of public property leased to private individuals was not relevant. In the latest case on the matter, *Álvarez Ramos v. Venezuela*,[43] the IACtHR provided a detailed formulation of the jurisprudential rule on proportionality and the use of criminal law to punish criticism of public officials. Nevertheless, this judgment exclusively concerns speech that criticizes public officials in the exercise of their functions.

The IACtHR's jurisprudence rejecting the use of criminal law to punish those who have criticized public officials has given rise to at least three transformations. First, the development of this standard led most States of the region to repeal the crime of *desacato*. Second, this standard has restricted the concept of criminal defamation in several criminal codes. Third, the standard provides judicial protection for individuals who face charges after expressing criticism that "offends" public officials. In the following subsections, I discuss each of these three transformations.

3.1.1. Contempt Laws/*Leyes de Desacato*

At the beginning of the 1990s, as a legacy of Latin America's authoritarian past, many criminal codes in the region retained sanctions that enabled the imprisonment of anyone who, by any means, offended the honor or reputation of a public official.[44] *Desacato* (contempt), as this crime is called, should not be mistaken for

---

[41] Declaration of Principles on Freedom of Expression, approved by the IACHR in October 2000.

[42] *Cf. Herrera Ulloa v. Costa Rica* (n. 52); *Ricardo Canese v. Paraguay* (n. 52); *Palamara Iribarne v. Chile* [2005], IACtHR, Ser. C, No. 135; *Kimel v. Argentina* (n. 17); *Tristán Donoso v. Panamá* [2009], IACtHR, Ser. C, No. 193; *Usón Ramírez v. Venezuela* [2009], IACtHR, Ser. C, No. 207; *Mémoli v. Argentina* [2013], IACtHR, Ser. C, No. 265; *Álvarez Ramos v. Venezuela* [2019], IACtHR, Ser. C, No. 380; *Case of Norín Catrimán et al. (Leaders, Members and Activist of the Mapuche Indigenous People) v. Chile* [2014], IACtHR, Ser. C No. 279.

[43] *Álvarez Ramos v. Venezuela* (n. 42).

[44] Botero-Marino (n. 3).

criminal defamation. The victim of *desacato* is necessarily a public official, which is not true of criminal defamation. The punishment for *desacato* is also more severe than those crimes of defamation.

The IACHR first considered *desacato* laws in the 1992 case of *Verbitsky v. Argentina*.[45] After entering a friendly settlement agreement, Argentina removed the crime of *desacato* from its criminal code.[46] At the same time, the IACHR found that the crime of *desacato* was incompatible with Article 13 of the American Convention. According to the Inter-American Commission, *desacato* undermines a fundamental democratic principle: that, public officials should always be subject to public scrutiny.[47] In support of its position, the IACHR drew on the jurisprudence of the European Court of Human Rights.[48] The IACHR also observed that *desacato* remained a crime in at least fourteen Latin American countries and recommended that it be repealed. As a direct consequence of the IACHR's report, Paraguay repealed the crime of *desacato* in 1997.[49] Shortly after, the Inter-American Commission issued its Declaration of Principles on Freedom of Expression, which provides that "[l]aws that penalize offensive expressions directed at public officials, generally known as 'desacato laws,' restrict freedom of expression and the right to information." Following this, Costa Rica[50] and Peru[51] removed the crime of *desacato* from their criminal codes.

Later, three cases concerning the criminalization of public interest speech were brought before the IACHR: *Herrera Ulloa v. Costa Rica* (2004), *Ricardo Canese v. Paraguay* (2004), and *Palamara Iribarne v. Chile* (2005). In the third case, Palamara Iribarne was convicted for *desacato*. Cases decided by the IACHR between 2002 and 2003 were also brought before the Inter-American Court, which issued its rulings in 2004 and 2005.[52] In the *Palamara Iribarne* case, the IACtHR found that crimes of *desacato* are incompatible with the American Convention. Furthermore, it held that the use of criminal law to limit public interest speech is unnecessary and disproportionate in democratic societies. In response to these rulings, Panama,[53] Chile,[54] and Nicaragua[55] removed *desacato* from their criminal codes. Additionally, the constitutional courts of Honduras,[56]

---

[45] *Verbitsky v. Argentina* [1994], IACHR, "Report No. 22/94 (Friendly Settlement)," Case No. 11.012.
[46] Law 24.198 of May 12, 1993, Boletín Oficial No. 27.652.
[47] Inter-American Commission, "1994 Annual Report," Chapter V.
[48] *Lingens v. Austria* [1986], ECtHR, and *Castells v. Spain* [1992], ECtHR.
[49] Law No. 1.160 of November 26, 1997 (Criminal Code).
[50] Law No. 8.224 of March 13, 2002, La Gaceta No. 65.
[51] Law No. 27.975 of May 28, 2003, Diario Oficial El Peruano, 244.983.
[52] *Herrera Ulloa v. Costa Rica* [2004], IACtHR, Ser. C, No. 107; *Ricardo Canese v. Paraguay* [2004], IACtHR, Ser. C, No. 111; *Palamara Iribarne v. Chile* [2005], IACtHR, Ser. C, No. 135.
[53] Law No. 22 of June 29, 2005, Gaceta Oficial 25.336.
[54] Law No. 20.048 of August 22, 2005, Diario Oficial No. 38.250.
[55] Law No. 641 of November 16, 2007, La Gaceta No. 232.
[56] Supreme Court of Justice of Honduras, Chamber of Constitutional Affairs, Judgment of May 19, 2005. For case information of this and all other judgments handed down by national courts

Guatemala,[57] and Bolivia[58] held the crime of *desacato* unconstitutional based on the Inter-American Court's jurisprudence. Similarly, the Fifth Chamber of the Superior Court of Justice of Brazil[59] held that the crime of *desacato* is incompatible with the American Convention in a special appeal.[60]

The Guatemalan and Bolivian rulings that declared *desacato* laws to be contrary to these countries' respective constitutions illustrate the transformative impact of inter-American jurisprudence on constitutional law in Latin America.

The Constitutional Court of Guatemala declared unconstitutional the criminal provisions that severely sanctioned insult, defamation, and offenses that damaged the honor and reputation of public officials if they were related to the exercise of public functions.[61] In adopting this decision, the court interpreted Guatemala's constitutional right to freedom of expression in light of inter-American standards. Drawing on the IACtHR's Advisory Opinion OC-5/85 and the IACHR's *Report on the Compatibility of "Desacato" Laws with the American Convention on Human Rights*, the Guatemalan court concluded that contempt laws were, per se, contrary to the American Convention and the Guatemalan Constitution. According to the Guatemalan court, public officials in a democratic society have a duty to submit themselves to greater public scrutiny and not, through *desacato* laws, to greater protection of their right to personality, including the right to a good name. In response to the argument that the decriminalization of *desacato* would lead to an avalanche of unfair criticism of officials, the Guatemalan court held that the right to freedom of expression must protect not only inoffensive speech but also offensive, shocking, and disturbing ideas or information, as this is what pluralism, tolerance, and broadmindedness—the foundational values of democratic societies—demand.

A few years later, the Plurinational Constitutional Court of Bolivia declared unconstitutional the crime of *desacato*, while expressly relying on inter-American law.[62] The Bolivian court used the same formulation of the principle of proportionality as used by the Inter-American Court in cases concerning freedom of expression. The Bolivian court stated that restrictions on freedom of expression, according to the jurisprudence of the IACtHR, must: (i) be expressly provided for by law; (ii) be aimed at the protection of the rights and reputation

---

mentioned in this chapter, see https://globalfreedomofexpression.columbia.edu/casos/?lang=es (accessed December 1, 2021).

[57] Constitutional Court of Guatemala, Judgment of February 1, 2006.
[58] Constitutional Court of Bolivia, Judgment of September 20, 2012.
[59] Superior Tribunal de Justiça do Brasil (STJ), Recurso Especial No. 1.640.084 - SP (2016/0032106-0), Judgment of December 15, 2016.
[60] More on this same subject: Botero-Marino (n. 3), 185–206.
[61] Constitutional Court of Guatemala, Judgment of February 1, 2006.
[62] Constitutional Court of Bolivia, Judgment of September 20, 2012.

of individuals, national security, public order, public health, or morals; and (iii) be necessary in a democratic society to "achieve imperative public interests." On the one hand, the Bolivian court acknowledged that the crime of *desacato* pursued a legitimate aim, since it sought to protect the right to honor, which is held by all persons. On the other hand, the court indicated that government authorities or public servants carry out activities that are in the interest of society and, therefore, it is necessary that the way in which they exercise their functions be openly debated. If any information published for this purpose is false, officials can respond through rectification and reply, as provided in Article 106.II of the Bolivian Constitution. According to the Bolivian court, *desacato* impedes oversight of the administration of public funds and facilitates corruption, thereby failing to protect the collective rights of society as a whole. In support of this decision, the Bolivian court expressly cited the IACtHR case of *Herrera Ulloa v. Costa Rica* and the IACHR's *Report on the Compatibility of "Desacato" Laws with the American Convention on Human Rights*.

3.1.2. Criminal Defamation

The Office of the Special Rapporteur for Freedom of Expression has repeatedly asserted in its reports that criminal law is a disproportionate means of restricting public interest speech.[63] The Inter-American Commission reiterated this concern in its Declaration of Principles on Freedom of Expression.[64] The IACHR also has adopted all of the Office of the Special Rapporteur's reports and submitted cases concerning criminal defamation to the Inter-American Court that have given rise to the Inter-American System's jurisprudence on the matter.

According to IAHRS jurisprudence, the use of criminal law to limit freedom of expression violates Article 13.2 of the American Convention unless it meets these three conditions: (i) the limitation must be defined in a precise and clear manner by law, formally and materially; (ii) the limitation must be in the interest of compelling objectives that are enshrined in the American Convention; and (iii) the limitation must be necessary for a democratic society to achieve the compelling objectives pursued, strictly proportionate to the objectives, and appropriate to serve the objectives.[65]

Under the first requirement, the principle of legality (also known as strict legality, which applies to criminal provisions in the terms of Article 9 of the

---

[63] IACHR, Office of the Special Rapporteur on Freedom of Expression. *The Inter-American Legal Framework Regarding the Right to Freedom of Expression*, <http://www.oas.org/en/iachr/expression/docs/publications/INTER-AMERICAN%20LEGAL%20FRAMEWORK%20OF%20THE%20RIGHT%20TO%20FREEDOM%20OF%20EXPRESSION%20FINAL%20PORTADA.pdf> (accessed December 1, 2021).

[64] Declaration of Principles on Freedom of Expression, approved by the IACHR in October 2000.

[65] IACHR, *The Inter-American Legal Framework Regarding the Right to Freedom of Expression*, para. 67.

American Convention), the restriction must be formulated in a clear and precise manner, free of ambiguities or uncertainties. Under the second requirement, the principle of legitimate aim, the restriction must be oriented toward achieving a purpose enshrined in the American Convention. Finally, under the third requirement, the principle of necessity, the restriction must be essential to achieve the desired purpose; it must constitute the least onerous means, among all means available, for the achievement of that purpose; and it must be proportional to the degree of infringement of freedom of expression.

Applying this in the case of *Kimel v. Argentina*, the IACtHR concluded that Argentina's criminal libel and slander laws violated Articles 9 and 13 of the American Convention due to their extreme vagueness.[66] The Inter-American Court used this test to find that, in establishing liability, States must employ the measures least restrictive of freedom of expression.[67] The IACtHR additionally clarified that the principle of necessity is not met when a restriction is merely useful, reasonable, or timely. To be necessary, the restriction must be essential to achieve a legitimate purpose.[68] Moreover, in cases concerning public interest speech, restrictions must be strictly proportionate, meaning that the sacrifice of freedom of expression "is not exaggerated or disproportionate in relation to the advantages obtained from the adoption of such limitation."[69]

According to the IACtHR, critical speech directed at public officials and concerning matters related to their public functions enjoys special and reinforced protection for three fundamental reasons: first, public officials have voluntarily exposed themselves to public scrutiny, so they are obliged to tolerate a higher level of criticism and intrusion into their private lives; second, public officials, due to their social position, have a greater capacity than does the average individual to counter any criticism directed against them in the public arena; and, third, the existence of open public debate on the conduct and suitability of those who exercise or aspire to exercise public functions is indispensable for the functioning of democracy.[70]

As a result of these inter-American standards, a significant number of States party to the American Convention have repealed—completely or partially—the crime of defamation from their respective legal systems through either legislation or jurisprudence.

Drawing on arguments similar to those developed within the Inter-American System, Nicaragua,[71] Panama,[72]

---

[66] *Kimel v. Argentina* (n. 17).
[67] Ibid., para. 76.
[68] Ibid., para. 85.
[69] Ibid., para. 83.
[70] *Cf.* ibid.
[71] Law No. 641 of November 16, 2007, La Gaceta No. 232.
[72] Law No. 26 of May 21, 2008, Gaceta Oficial 26.045. See Supreme Court of Justice, Judgment of April 11, 2014.

Argentina,[73] and El Salvador[74] partially abolished the crimes of slander and libel. Meanwhile, the highest criminal courts in Peru[75] and Colombia[76] cited the Inter-American Court's jurisprudence when deciding that defamation crimes, although constitutional in principle, are disproportionate in practice when used to protect the honor of public officials. Mexico,[77] Grenada,[78] and Jamaica[79] fully removed defamation crimes from their legislation. Similarly, the Mexican Supreme Court[80] held that, where libel and/or slander remained crimes in local legislation, public officials' critics nevertheless could not be charged with these crimes to ensure the special protection of public interest speech.[81]

In total, eleven countries have repealed the crime of *desacato*, and nine have repealed the crime of defamation, in accordance with the evolving inter-American standards on freedom of expression. Unfortunately, some countries have lagged behind. In Venezuela, for example, domestic courts continue to convict journalists for publicly criticizing politicians and other public authorities. In response to these countries' behavior, the IACHR and the Office of the Special Rapporteur have issued public statements[82] that have produced strong political reactions from these States.[83]

3.2. The Right of Access to Information

The Office of the Special Rapporteur addressed the right of access to information in detail for the first time in its 2001 Annual Report.[84] In this document, the Office of the Special Rapporteur observes that ACHR Article 13 protects the right of access to information,[85] an interpretation supported not only by the text of that provision but also by the Inter-American Court's Advisory Opinion

---

[73] Law No. 26.551 of November 18, 2009, Boletín Oficial No. 31.790. See Supreme Court of Justice, Judgment of June 24, 2008.
[74] Decree No. 836 of December 7, 2011, Diario Oficial No. 299, Vol. 393.
[75] Supreme Court of Justice of Peru, Chamber of Criminal Affairs, Judgment of June 18, 2010.
[76] Supreme Court of Justice of Colombia, Chamber of Criminal Affairs, Judgment of July 10, 2013.
[77] Decree of April 13, 2007, Diario Oficial de la Federación of April 13, 2007.
[78] Criminal Code (Amendment) Act 2012.
[79] Defamation Act 2013.
[80] Supreme Court of Justice of the Nation of Mexico, Judgment of June 17, 2009.
[81] To further examine this topic: Botero-Marino (n. 3), 185–206.
[82] OAS Special Rapporteurship for Freedom of Expression, Press Release No. 96/11 (*Revista Sexto Poder v. Venezuela*), August 31, 2011; Press Release No. 93/15 (*La Nación, Tal Cual et al. v. Venezuela*), August 24, 2015. IACHR, Precautionary Measure No. 406/11 (*Palacio et al. v. Ecuador*), February 21, 2012; Precautionary Measure No. 30-14 (*Villavicencio v. Ecuador*), March 24, 2014; Report No. 66/2015 (Admissibility), Case No. 1436-11 (*Palacios v. Ecuador*), October 27, 2015.
[83] See Botero-Marino (n. 3), 185–206.
[84] 2001 Annual Report of the OAS Special Rapporteur for Freedom of Expression, Santiago Cantón, Chapter III: *Report on the Action with Respect to Habeas Data and the Right of Access to Information in the Hemisphere*.
[85] Ibid., para. 10.

OC-5/85[86] and Principle 4 of the Inter-American Commission's Declaration of Principles of Freedom of Expression.[87] Nonetheless, the Office expressed concern that only a few States in the Americas at the time had in place legislation concerning the right of access to information.

In 2006, in the case of *Claude Reyes et al. v. Chile*,[88] the IACtHR interpreted Article 13 of the American Convention to provide a right of access to information held by the State.[89] In its ruling, the Inter-American Court found that it is not necessary for an individual to prove they have a particular interest in order to access this information. The Inter-American Court also stated that any restriction on this right must be provided by law, pursue a legitimate aim, and be necessary to attain that purpose.[90] The IACtHR drew on many of the Office of the Special Rapporteur's arguments and products, especially in its 2003 Annual Report. The Office, in turn, had drawn inspiration from the Mexican law on access to information.

In addition to the pioneering developments in the right of access to information in the *Claude Reyes* case, the Inter-American Court has also addressed three specific aspects of the right of access to information that have had a less significant regional impact: the right of access to information concerning serious human rights violations;[91] Indigenous peoples' right of access to

---

[86] The Report draws from the Advisory Opinion, IACHR, OC 5/85, Ser. A. No. 5, para. 70, in paragraph 21 of the third chapter, the following conclusion: "[A]ccess to state-held information represents a fundamental individual right that states have the duty to uphold."

[87] The Report homes in on Principle 4 of the IACHR Declaration of Principles of Freedom in paragraph 22 of the third chapter: "Access to information held by the state is a fundamental right of every individual. States have the obligation to guarantee the full exercise of this right. This principle allows only exceptional limitations that must be previously established by law in case of a real and imminent danger that threatens national security in democratic societies." And paragraph 23: "Principle 4 of the IACHR Declaration of Principles of Freedom of Expression establishes the parameters the state must observe in denying information in its possession. Given the need to promote greater transparency in government as the basis for strengthening democratic institutions in the hemisphere, limitations with respect to the information contained in state archives must be exceptional. Such limitations must be clearly established in the law and applicable only in the case of substantial and imminent detriment to a legitimate pursuit of public policy, and when the protection of such information must take precedence over the public interest in being informed. Petitions in respect of any act restricting access to information should therefore be considered on a case-by-case basis." See also 2001 Annual Report of the OAS Special Rapporteur for Freedom of Expression, Santiago Cantón, Chapter III: *Report on the Action with Respect to Habeas Data and the Right of Access to Information in the Hemisphere*, ch. 3.

[88] For more details on the impact of the *Claude Reyes* decision, see Sofía Jaramillo-Otoya, "Claude Reyes et al v. Chile: A Global Trailblazer," in Lee C. Bollinger and Agnès Callamard (eds.), *Regardless of Frontiers: Global Freedom of Expression in a Troubled World* (Columbia University Press, 2021), 185-206.

[89] The European Court of Human Rights (European Court), in the case of *Guerra et al. v. Italy* [1998], had already recognized the existence of a right of access to information concerning environmental issues. The European Court, however, held that the right arose not from Article 10 of the European Convention on Human Rights but from Article 8; see *Guerra et al. v. Italy* [1998] ECtHR.

[90] *Claude Reyes*, IACtHR, paras. 88-91.

[91] *Case of Gomes Lund et al. ("Guerrilha do Araguaia") v. Brazil* [2010], IACtHR, Ser. C No. 219; *Case of Maldonado Vargas et al. v. Chile* [2015], IACtHR, Ser. C No. 300.

information;[92] and the right of access to information for the exercise of personal autonomy or as a requirement for obtaining informed consent in matters relating to an individual's health.[93] *Claude Reyes* is one of the IACtHR cases that has had the greatest transformative impact in the region.

In response to *Claude Reyes*, Chile passed a legislative reform that established a system of guarantees for the right of access to information.[94] In 2007, following this legislative reform, the Constitutional Court of Chile found that there is a fundamental right of access to information.[95] At the same time, Honduras,[96] Nicaragua,[97] Guatemala,[98] and Uruguay[99] enacted laws on access to information. These events constituted the first legislative wave concerning the right of access to information in the Americas. Later, after the OAS General Assembly approved the Inter-American Model Law on Access to Public Information,[100] the Inter-American Court restated the holding of *Claude Reyes* in the case of *Gomes Lund et al. v. Brazil*.[101] In so doing, the Inter-American System unleashed a second legislative wave, in which access to information laws were enacted in El Salvador,[102] Brazil,[103] Colombia,[104] Argentina,[105] Paraguay,[106] Guyana,[107] and the Bahamas.[108]

Although *Claude Reyes v. Chile* is probably the most cited judgment of the Inter-American Court concerning ACHR Article 13, the overall impact of the IACtHR's jurisprudence on access to information has also been remarkable. Promoting the right of access to information has not been easy, since access to information contradicts the culture of secrecy that has prevailed in Latin America and which in many cases has been protected by laws inherited from dictatorships. Legislative and judicial transformations in the field of access to information are critical. The regional transformations that have resulted from the development of IAHRS standards concerning access to information demonstrate the existence

---

[92] *Case of the Kaliña and Lokono Peoples v. Suriname* [2015], IACtHR, Ser. C No. 309; *Case of Kichwa Indigenous People of Sarayaku v. Ecuador* [2012], IACtHR, Ser. C No. 245.
[93] *Case of I. V. v. Bolivia* [2017], IACtHR, Ser. C No. 336.
[94] Law No. 20.285 of August 11, 2008, Boletín Oficial of August 20, 2008.
[95] Constitutional Court of Chile, Judgment of August 9, 2007.
[96] Decree No. 170-2006 of December 30, 2006, La Gaceta of December 30, 2006.
[97] Law No. 621 of May 16, 2007, La Gaceta No. 118 of June 22, 2007.
[98] Decree No. 57-2008 of October 23, 2008, Diario de Centro América No. 45, Vol. 285.
[99] Law No. 18.381 of October 17, 2008, Diario Oficial of November 7, 2008.
[100] AG/RES. 2607 (XL-O/10), June 8, 2010.
[101] *Gomes Lund et al. ("Guerrilha do Araguaia) v. Brazil* [2010], IACtHR, Ser. C, No. 219, paras. 196–199.
[102] Decree No. 534 of December 2, 2010, Diario Oficial No. 70, Vol. 391.
[103] Law No. 12.527 of November 18, 2011, Diário Oficial da União of November 18, 2011.
[104] Law No. 1.712 of March 6, 2014, Diario Oficial No. 49.084.
[105] Law No. 27.275 of September 14, 2014, Boletín Oficial No. 33.472, 1.
[106] Law No. 5.282 of September 18, 2015, Registro Oficial No. 180 of September 19, 2014.
[107] Access to information Act of 2011, The Official Gazette of Guyana of September 27, 2011.
[108] Freedom of information Act of 2017, Official Gazette of Bahamas of March 31, 2017.

of ICCAL. In the remainder of this section, I will discuss some of the most recent domestic court rulings on the subject.

In ruling 1306 (2013), the Supreme Court of Justice of Paraguay cited inter-American jurisprudence when determining that the public has a right to know the salary of public officials. According to the Paraguayan court, this information was not so confidential as to justify the restriction of the right of access to information under the test established by the IACtHR in *Claude Reyes v. Chile*.

The Costa Rican judiciary has repeatedly defended the right of access to public information. Even before the enactment of the Costa Rica's law on transparency and access to public information,[109] the Constitutional Chamber of the Supreme Court had developed important jurisprudence on access to information based on the jurisprudence of the IACtHR, which the Costa Rican court gradually expanded until it met the highest regional standards. For example, in one of its key judgments on the subject, the Costa Rican court held that, under the principle of maximum disclosure, the State should provide anyone who requested information with all the information the State was obligated to keep, regardless of how cumbersome the searching and systematization of this information might be. The Costa Rican court did, however, decide to impose the costs of digitization or copying on the individual, failing to establish an adequate method for differentiating between cases in which the costs should be borne by the State and those in which it could be passed on to the individual.[110] In a more recent case, after the adoption of the law on transparency and access to information, the Costa Rican court reiterated that there exists a right to receive complete, current, and orderly public information within a specified timeframe. The court also highlighted the progressive nature of the right of access to information, according to which the State should gradually implement measures to facilitate access, preferably by computerized means using freeware. In support of its decision, the Costa Rican court once again cited the case of *Claude Reyes et al. v. Chile*.[111]

The transformative impact of the Inter-American System's jurisprudence on access to information has been particularly striking in El Salvador. The Constitutional Chamber of the Supreme Court of Justice of El Salvador has frequently used inter-American standards to advance its jurisprudence and transform El Salvador's democracy, as the following four judgments demonstrate.

In 2012, the Supreme Court of Justice of El Salvador noted that, according to inter-American standards, a statutory provision could not introduce new categories of confidentiality of information into the legal system that were not originally encompassed in the law.[112] The Supreme Court determined that the

---

[109] Executive Order No. 40200 of April 27, 2017, Sistema Costarricense de Información Jurídica.
[110] Supreme Court of Justice of Costa Rica, Judgment of March 21, 2014.
[111] Supreme Court of Justice of Costa Rica, Judgment of June 30, 2017.
[112] Supreme Court of Justice of El Salvador, Chamber of Constitutional Affairs, Judgment of December 5, 2012.

right of access to public information may be subject to exceptions, but these must be enshrined in a "formal, prior, written and strict law" based on the principle of maximum disclosure. In support of its decision, the Salvadoran court cited *Claude Reyes et al. v. Chile* and the IACtHR's Advisory Opinion OC-6/86.

During the following year, the same Chamber relied on similar arguments to find that the public information officer of the Salvadoran legislature had violated an individual's rights of access to public information and petition by (i) refusing to provide a copy of the 2012 resolutions of the legislature's board of directors that authorized the purchases of works of art, Christmas gifts, and alcoholic beverages; (ii) failing to provide a list of the aforementioned goods, together with their invoices; and (iii) failing to rule on a request for information about the origin of the funds used to purchase these goods.[113]

In 2014, the Constitutional Chamber of the Supreme Court of Justice of El Salvador again interpreted the right of access to information in the light of inter-American standards, stating that the information contained in a criminal proceeding in which a former president was investigated is not necessarily confidential.[114] In this case, the Salvadoran court linked access to information to the right to truth, which implies "free access to objective information about events that have violated fundamental rights" as well as "the possibility and the actual capacity to investigate, search for, and receive reliable information that leads to the impartial and full clarification of the facts."[115]

Finally, in 2016, the Supreme Court of Justice of El Salvador established that a lower court's refusal to unseal a criminal case investigating a collective homicide from a 1982 military operation in "El Calabozo" violated the plaintiffs' right to know the truth.[116] The Salvadoran court established a link between the right to truth and the right of access to information based in part on the IACtHR case *19 Merchants v. Colombia*. According to the Inter-American Court's judgment in this case, the relatives of victims of serious human rights violations have a right to know the truth, which entails the right to request and obtain information held by the State. The Salvadoran court also referred to the IACHR report in the 1999 case of *Ignacio Ellacuría, S.J. et al. v. El Salvador*[117] to establish that victims have a right of access to information and that society as a whole has a right to know the truth about serious human rights violations.

In Argentina, domestic legislation does not adequately protect the right of access to information and so jurisprudence has become the most important

---

[113] Supreme Court of Justice of El Salvador, Chamber of Constitutional Affairs, Judgment of July 25, 2014.
[114] Supreme Court of Justice of El Salvador, Chamber of Constitutional Affairs, Judgment of June 13, 2014.
[115] Supreme Court of Justice of El Salvador, Judgment of June 13, 2014.
[116] Supreme Court of Justice of El Salvador, Chamber of Constitutional Affairs, Judgment of November 11, 2016.
[117] IACHR, "Report No. 136/99," Fondo: *Caso 10.488* of December 22, 1999.

means of guaranteeing this right, as the following four cases illustrate. In 2012, the Supreme Court of Argentina decided whether the National Institute of Social Services for Retirees and Pensioners was obligated to provide the Argentine Association for Civil Rights (Association, or ADC) with detailed information concerning its advertising budget. Even though the ADC was a private entity exercising public functions, the Argentine court ruled in favor of the Association, relying in part on the principle of maximum disclosure developed by the IACtHR. Indeed, the Argentine court cited *Claude Reyes et al. v. Chile* when it stated that "Article 13 of the American Convention, by expressly providing the right to 'seek,' 'receive,' and 'impart,' protects the right of everyone to request access to information under the control of the State, with the exceptions permitted under the American Convention regime of restrictions." The Supreme Court of Justice of Argentina also cited the Office of the Special Rapporteur for Freedom of Expression's 2003 Annual Report to establish the close relationship between the right of freedom of expression and thought and the right of access to public information.[118]

In 2014, the Supreme Court of Argentina determined whether the Center for the Implementation of Public Policies Promoting Equity and Growth (CIPPEC) had a right to access information concerning the beneficiaries of social assistance from the State.[119] In this case, the court held that the State could not invoke the beneficiaries' privacy protection to refuse CIPPEC this information, since the data was not sensitive and the purpose of the request was to exercise public control over the expenditure of public funds. Again, in support of its decision, the Argentine court cited inter-American standards. It used the case of *Claude Reyes et al. v. Chile* to explain the scope and nature of the right of individuals to request access to public information and the obligation of the State to guarantee the right to receive the requested information. The court also cited the IACtHR case *Gomes Lund et al. ("Guerrilha do Araguaia") v. Brazil*, the IACHR's 2007 *Report on Terrorism and Human Rights*, and the Office of the Special Rapporteur for Freedom of Expression's 2007 Special Study on the Right of Access to Information.[120]

The Supreme Court of Justice of Buenos Aires relied on the Supreme Court of Argentina's jurisprudence concerning access to information when it sought to determine whether the failure of the General Directorate of Culture and Education to respond to a request for information regarding the number of days that students in certain schools in the country had not had classes due to the absence of teachers violated the right of access to information.[121] The Buenos Aires court ordered the General Directorate of Culture and Education to provide the requested information, citing the Office of the Special Rapporteur for Freedom

---

[118] Supreme Court of Justice of the Nation of Argentina, Judgment of December 12, 2012.
[119] Supreme Court of Justice of the Nation of Argentina, Judgment of August 5, 2014.
[120] The Supreme Court ruled in the same way in cases such as *Rubén Héctor Giustiniani v. Y.P.F.* [2015], Arg., Sup., CAF37747/2013/1/RH1.
[121] Supreme Court of Justice of the Province of Buenos Aires, of December 29, 2014.

of Expression's 2004 Annual Report on the right of access to information and the IACtHR cases *Claude Reyes v. Chile* and *Gomes Lund v. Brazil* to support its argument that "Article 13 of the American Convention on Human Rights, by expressly providing the rights to 'seek' and 'receive' 'information,' protects the right of every person to request access to information under the control of the State" and that "[t]his information must be provided without the need to prove a direct interest in obtaining it or a personal interest, except in cases where a legitimate restriction applies. Providing information to a person may in turn allow it to circulate in society in such a way that all may become aware of it, access it, and assess it."

Finally, Court No. 18 of Buenos Aires relied on inter-American standards when determining whether the government of the City of Buenos Aires had violated an individual's right of access to information by providing incomplete information concerning the value allocated to official advertising in the media. The court ordered the City to provide the complete information, citing the IACtHR case *Claude Reyes v. Chile* and the IACHR Report on Terrorism and Human Rights in the same manner as the other Argentine courts.

Mexico, for its part, is the birthplace of the right of access to information in the region. The country's Federal Law on Transparency and Access to Public Government Information was the first of its kind[122] and the former Federal Institute of Access to Public Information (now the National Institute of Transparency, Access to Information, and Protection of Personal Data) was probably the most prominent institution in the field in Latin America. Nevertheless, in some exceptional cases, cases on access to information have reached the Mexican Supreme Court. In the judicial resolution of these cases, one can see the influence of the Inter-American System's jurisprudence on the matter, as shown by the two following examples.

In the 2011 case of *Radilla v. Procaduría General de la República*,[123] the Supreme Court of Justice of Mexico determined whether it was legitimate for the State to withhold information contained in preliminary investigations of crimes against humanity and/or serious human rights violations. The specific case referred to facts that had appeared in the IACtHR case *Radilla Pacheco v. Mexico*,[124] in which the Inter-American Court had recognized the right of the victims to know the results of criminal investigations. The Mexican court concluded its case by upholding the right of access to information, thereby complying with one aspect of the IACtHR ruling and, at the domestic level, opening the possibility of public control over the management of the prosecutors' offices in cases involving serious human rights violations and/or crimes against humanity.

---

[122] Federal Law on Transparency and Access to Public Government Information of June 11, 2002, Diario Oficial of June 11, 2002.
[123] *Radilla v. Procaduría General de la República* [2011], Mex. Sup., AR-168/2011.
[124] *Radilla Pacheco v. Mexico* [2009], IACtHR, Ser. C, No. 209.

In another case in which a petitioner requested access to information contained in previous investigations, the Supreme Court of Justice of Mexico determined that the right of access to information should prevail whenever the necessity for secrecy of the requested documents could not be demonstrated. According to the Mexican court, secrecy is allowed only when in the pursuit of a legitimate aim and necessary for a democratic society. Consequently, the court found that a rule withholding all documents that form part of the preliminary investigations, solely because they form part of these investigations, is a disproportionate restriction on the right of access to information. In support of its decision, the Mexican court referred to Article 13 of the American Convention and Article 19 of the International Covenant on Civil and Political Rights, to OC-5/85, as well as to the cases *Claude Reyes et al. v. Chile*, *Herrera Ulloa v. Costa Rica*, and *Palamara Iribarne v. Chile*. The inter-American jurisprudence helped the Mexican court to underline the importance of the right of access to public information, to apply the principle of maximum disclosure, and to formulate a proportionality test determining whether a given restriction is legitimate.

The Constitutional Court of Colombia shows how continual and comprehensive use of IAHRS jurisprudence can produce important democratic transformations. The Colombian court has invoked inter-American standards concerning access to information in dozens of cases in an attempt to break with the dominant culture of secrecy maintained by certain sectors of the State, such as the defense sector. In Judgment T-1025 of 2007, for example, the court determined whether, in a context of serious human rights violations, individuals could access the names, institutional codes, command lines, and units of security forces agents who had participated in allegedly irregular domestic military operations. The Colombian court found in favor of the individuals in part because of inter-American standards on access to information. In its judgment, the Colombian court quoted extensively from *Claude Reyes et al. v. Chile*, *Herrera Ulloa v. Costa Rica*, *Palamara Iribarne v. Chile*, and Advisory Opinion OC-5/85. The court also referred to the IACHR's Declaration of Principles on Freedom of Expression and the Office of the Special Rapporteur for Freedom of Expression's 2001 and 2003 reports.[125] The Colombian court concluded that secrecy is only legitimate when it is necessary for a democratic society, which requires that it conform to the principles of proportionality and reasonableness.

In Judgment T-511 of 2010,[126] the Constitutional Court of Colombia found that the National Police's refusal to provide two individuals with the information

---

[125] *Claude Reyes and others v. Chile* [2006], IACtHR; *Herrera Ulloa v. Costa Rica* [2004], IACtHR; *Palamara Iribarne v. Chile* [2005], IACtHR; *Compulsory Membership in an Association Prescribed by Law for the Practice of Journalism* (Arts. 13 and 29 American Convention on Human Rights), IACtHR, Advisory Opinion OC-5/85 of November 13, 1985, Ser. A, No. 5; The Declaration of Principles on Freedom of Expression [2000], IACHR; IACHR, 2001 Annual Report of the OAS Special Rapporteur for Freedom of Expression; CHR, 2003 Annual Report of the OAS Special Rapporteur for Freedom of Expression.

[126] Constitutional Court of Colombia, Eighth Chamber of Review, Judgment T-511/10 of June 18, 2010.

they had requested concerning the identity of police officers who had been present during the occurrence of several crimes violated the right of access to information. Once again, to support its decision, the Colombian court referred to inter-American standards on access to information and, in particular, to the IACHR's Declaration of Principles on Freedom of Expression and the Office of the Special Rapporteur for Freedom of Expression's Special Study on the Right of Access to Information of 2007.

As a final example from the Constitutional Court of Colombia, in Judgment T-608 of 2013,[127] the court interpreted inter-American standards to mean that the refusal to provide an individual with an explanation for why she was not granted compensation as a victim of the armed conflict violated her right of access to information. Again, the Colombian court cited the 2007 Special Study on the Right of Access to Information of the Office of the Special Rapporteur for Freedom of Expression.[128]

Last but not least, in an emblematic case,[129] the Supreme Court of the Dominican Republic relied on inter-American standards to find that the names and salaries of public officials constitute public information to which any individual may have access. In reaching this decision, the Dominican court explained that both ACHR Article 13 and Article 19 of the Universal Declaration of Human Rights form part of the domestic law of the Dominican Republic, since these instruments were ratified by the legislature. The Dominican court also specifically discussed the *Claude Reyes v. Chile* case as supporting the notion that access to public information is fundamental to strengthening democracy, since it enables the public to control the management of public resources.

4. Concluding Remarks

This chapter has shown the positive relationship and virtuous circle between domestic authorities and international bodies that strengthens the protection of human rights by highlighting progress on two issues within the right to freedom of expression: criminalization and access to information. Eleven countries have repealed *desacato* laws, nine countries have limited the use of criminal law in cases of criticism leveled against public officials, and more than twenty-four countries have recognized the right of access to information. These evolving inter-American standards on freedom of expression seem to have been consolidated into ICCAL.[130]

---

[127] Constitutional Court of Colombia, Eighth Chamber of Review, Judgment T-608/13 of September 2, 2013.
[128] IACHR, Office of the Special Rapporteur for Freedom of Expression, Special Study on the Right to Access to Information (2007).
[129] Constitutional Tribunal of Dominican Republic, Judgment of September 21, 2012.
[130] *Omar Humberto Maldonado Vargas et al. v. Chile* [2015], IACtHR, Ser. C, No. 300.

This chapter does not mean to suggest that progress is necessarily constant or permanent. The right to freedom of expression has encountered strong opposition in countries such as Venezuela.[131] There have already been significant setbacks in freedom of expression in Latin America and rising authoritarianism in the region has created additional threats to this right.

Notwithstanding those challenges, there is no doubt that the relationship between the Inter-American System and domestic legal systems, including constitutional courts, has generated a transformation in international law and constitutional law across the region. Although we might not expect to see major advances in freedom of expression in the coming years, due to the challenge of rising authoritarianism, we do know that in States in which the judiciary continues to enjoy sufficient autonomy inter-American standards have curbed authoritarian attacks on individual rights. International standards lend domestic courts the legitimacy they need to rebuff authoritarian advances in contexts of political polarization.

During the COVID-19 pandemic, for example, Brazilian and US courts have staved off restrictions on the rights of access to information and freedom of expression. In Brazil, the Supreme Federal Tribunal issued a provisional measure suspending legislation that limited freedom of information requests.[132] In the United States, the case of *Rodríguez-Cotto v. Vázquez-Garced* will determine whether imposing criminal penalties for the dissemination of false information related to COVID-19 is unconstitutional.[133] Similarly, an Argentine agency exempted requests for information from the executive branch's general suspension of administrative deadlines in response to COVID-19, expressly citing IACHR Resolution No. 1/2020 in its reasoning.[134]

The transformative impact of multilevel dialogue has enabled resistance, in no small number of cases, against government attempts to limit the right of access to information severely, thereby preserving fragile democratic institutions.

---

[131] A clear example of the way in which the different branches in Venezuela have limited the right of access to information can be found in the following judgment: Supreme Court of Justice of Venezuela, Judgments of June 15, 2010, and August 5, 2014.

[132] See Ruling from Brazil's Federal Supreme Tribunal suspending the efficacy of a law that limited the access to information, http://portal.stf.jus.br/processos/detalhe.asp?incidente=5881853 (accessed December 9, 2021).

[133] *Rodriguez-Cotto v. Vazquez-Garced* [2020], District Court, D. Puerto Rico—ongoing proceedings against 25 L.P.R.A §§ 3654(a) and (f), limiting freedom of expression, <https://www.courtlistener.com/docket/17179901/rodriguez-cotto-v-vazquez-garced/?filed_after=&filed_before=&entry_gte=&entry_lte=&order_by=desc> (accessed December 10, 2021).

[134] Argentina's public access to information agency, citing Resolution No. 1/2020 of the IACHR, stated that access to information administrative requests will not be subject to delays, <https://www.oas.org/es/cidh/expresion/showarticle.asp?artID=1173&lID=2> (accessed December 10, 2021).

II.15
Impact of the IAHRS Principles on Freedom of Expression and the Need for Their Expansion in the Digital Age

Challenges to the IAHRS Principles on Freedom of Expression in the Digital Age

By Edison Lanza

1. Introduction

This chapter provides an overview of the development of the right to freedom of expression in the Inter-American System and its impact on the region. It contains a systematization of the principles that the Inter-American Human Rights System (IAHRS) has helped to consolidate as minimum guarantees for the exercise of this right through the decisions of its main bodies: the Inter-American Commission on Human Rights (IACHR), its Office of the Special Rapporteur for Freedom of Expression, and the Inter-American Court of Human Rights (IACtHR).

In a region with a long history of dictatorships and authoritarianism rooted in different ideological leanings and doctrines, the liberties derived from the right to freedom of expression have been subject to manipulation and suppression in virtually every country in the hemisphere for much of the twentieth century. However, one of the major achievements of the Inter-American System over the past thirty years has been to build a common inter-American legal framework for the respect and promotion of rights linked to freedom of expression and the strengthening of democratic systems.

Perhaps the most perceptible impact is the expansion of these guarantees and principles in the different legal systems of Latin America and the Caribbean through national court decisions and their implementation through legislation—as described in a few specific cases in this chapter.[1] Although the region has not been spared the consequences of governments turning toward authoritarianism,

---

[1] For a broader analysis on how Inter-American decisions impact national contexts: Oscar Parra Vera, "El impacto de las decisiones interamericanas. Notas sobre la producción académica y una propuesta de investigación en torno al empoderamiento institucional." Armin von Bogdandy, Héctor

Edison Lanza, *Impact of the IAHRS Principles on Freedom of Expression and the Need for Their Expansion in the Digital Age* In: *The Impact of the Inter-American Human Rights System*. Edited by: Armin von Bogdandy, Flávia Piovesan, Eduardo Ferrer Mac-Gregor, and Mariela Morales Antoniazzi, Oxford University Press. © Edison Lanza 2024.
DOI: 10.1093/oso/9780197744161.003.0026

it is important to note that these principles have become the yardstick for progress and are used to denounce measures that governments have taken to undermine fundamental freedoms.

This chapter also examines how the fundamental principle of the right to freedom of expression developed by the Inter-American System has been adapted to the development of information and communication technologies, in particular with the advent of the so-called "digital arena" that the internet has created. The new virtual and cross-border space that characterizes communication between people dovetails perfectly with the wording of Article 13 of the American Convention, which states that freedom of expression can be exercised "regardless of frontiers" and "or through any other medium of one's choice."

The emergence of the internet and a new ecosystem of intermediaries—some of them driven by machines or intelligent software—have made it possible for millions of people to be connected and participate in the public sphere, but it has also forced the IAHRS to rethink its principles in a more challenging context.

The revolution in communication technologies is an inevitable factor that has radically changed the means of exercising the rights and freedoms to seek, receive, and impart information and ideas. When the IACHR and the IACtHR began to cut through the Gordian knot of the right to freedom of expression and the role of the media in the late 1980s, such a revolution had yet to take place. In the last decade, however, the Inter-American System has contributed its own interpretations and standards (considered international soft law) with the aim of providing content to the right to freedom of expression on the internet in general and on social media networks especially. Through the thematic reports on the enjoyment of these rights on the internet—two of which have been prepared by the Office of the Special Rapporteur for Freedom of Expression of the IACHR— and the Joint Declarations published by the Rapporteurs for Freedom of Expression from the United Nations, the IACHR, the Organization for Security and Co-operation in Europe (OSCE), and the African Commission on Human Rights, the IAHRS has had a significant influence on internet policy debates and on those national courts addressing these types of challenges.[2]

This chapter concludes by outlining a series of current challenges to the exercise of human rights in the digital arena and the questions that the System must begin to consider in order to help shape the constantly evolving inter-American legal framework in this field. Undoubtedly, the digital age is different from previous times, and the opportunities to affect freedoms and rights through

---

Fix-Fierro, and Mariela Morales Antoniazzi (coords.), *Ius Constitutionale Commune en América Latina. Rasgos, potencialidades y desafíos* (UNAM 2014), 383–420.

[2] Sejal Parmar, "The Significance of the Joint Declaration on Freedom of Expression" [2019], 37(2) *Netherlands Quarterly of Human Rights* 179.

technology have increased. The System, therefore, must begin to interpret inter-American instruments in order to address these new risks.

2. The Inter-American Legal Framework on Freedom of Expression and Its Impact on the Region's Legal Systems and Case Law

For the Inter-American System, freedom of expression is a fundamental right that is essential to the functioning of democratic political systems.[3] This is because this right serves three basic functions: it safeguards the primary function of communicating and thinking about the world from our own perspectives,[4] it plays a central and structural role in the functioning of democratic institutions,[5] and it is a critical tool for the exercise of other human rights.[6] As the IACtHR held its Advisory Opinion 5/85:

> Freedom of expression is a cornerstone upon which the very existence of a democratic society rests. It is indispensable for the formation of public opinion. It is also a *conditio sine qua non* for the development of political parties, trade unions, scientific and cultural societies and, in general, those who wish to influence the public. It represents, in short, the means that enable the community, when exercising its options, to be sufficiently informed. Consequently, it can be said that a society that is not well informed is not a society that is truly free.[7]

In the inter-American context, this right has a dual dimension: an *individual* dimension, consisting of the right of each person to express his or her own thoughts, ideas, and information; and a *collective* dimension, consisting of a society's right to seek and receive any information, to know the thoughts, ideas, and information of others, and to be well informed.[8] This dual dimension gives

---

[3] IACtHR, Compulsory Membership in an Association Prescribed by Law for the Practice of Journalism (Arts. 13 and 29 American Convention on Human Rights), Advisory Opinion OC-5/85 of November 13, 1985, Ser. A No. 5, para. 50; IACHR, "Annual Report 1994," Office of the Special Rapporteur for Freedom of Expression of the IACHR (1994), Chapter V.

[4] IACHR, "Inter-American Legal Framework Regarding the Right to Freedom of Expression," Office of the Special Rapporteur for Freedom of Expression de la IACHR (2010), para. 7.

[5] Ibid., para. 8.

[6] Ibid., para. 9.

[7] *Cf.* "Compulsory Membership in an Association Prescribed by Law for the Practice of Journalism" (n. 3), para. 70; for an affirmation of this point, see also *San Miguel Sosa, et al. v. Venezuela* [2018] IACtHR, Ser. C No. 348, para. 153.

[8] *Cf. Kimel v. Argentina* [2008] IACtHR, Ser. C No. 177, para. 53; *Claude-Reyes et al. v. Chile* [2006], IACtHR Ser. C No. 151, 2006, para. 75; *López Álvarez v. Honduras* [2006] IACtHR, Ser. C No. 141, para. 163; *Herrera Ulloa v. Costa Rica* [2004] IACtHR, Ser. C No. 107, para.108; *Ivcher Bronstein v. Peru* [2001] IACtHR, Ser. C No. 74, para. 146; *Ricardo Canese v. Paraguay* [2004] IACtHR, Ser. C

rise to the principle that both must be preserved: it is unacceptable under inter-American standards to undermine one of these dimensions while claiming to preserve the other.[9]

The importance of the right to freedom of thought and expression for the functioning of the system is reflected in the development of reinforced standards of protection for all speech *ab initio*. This includes all kinds of ideas, opinions, and information, including those that "offend, are unwelcome or shock the State or any sector of the population."[10] But the instrumental nature of the right has meant that certain types of speech are specially protected. This includes political speech and speech on matters of public interest,[11] speech about public officials in the exercise of their duties, speech about candidates for public office,[12] and speech expressing essential elements of someone's personal identity or dignity.[13]

Not all speech enjoys such special protection. Article 13.5 of the American Convention expressly allows for the penalization of a particular kind of speech: war propaganda and hate speech that constitutes incitement to lawless violence or to any other similar action against any person or group of persons on any grounds including those of race, color, religion, language, or national origin. The IACHR has stated:

> [T]he imposition of sanctions for the abuse of freedom of expression under the charge of incitement to violence (understood as the incitement to commit crimes, the breaking of public order or national security) must be backed up by actual, truthful, objective and strong proof that the person was not simply

No. 111, para. 77; *"The Last Temptation of Christ" (Olmedo Bustos et al.) v. Chile* [2001] IACtHR, Ser. C No. 73, 2001, para. 64; "Compulsory Membership in an Association Prescribed by Law for the Practice of Journalism" (n. 3), para. 30.

[9] *Cf.* ibid., para. 33.
[10] *Cf. Herrera Ulloa v. Costa Rica* (n. 8), para. 113; *"The Last Temptation of Christ" (Olmedo Bustos et al.) v. Chile*, (n. 8), para. 69; *Ríos et al. v. Venezuela* [2009] IACtHR, Ser. C No. 194, para. 105; *Perozo v. Venezuela* [2009] IACtHR, Ser. C No. 195, para. 116; see also *Kimel v. Argentina* (n. 8), para. 88: "In the domain of political debate on issues of great public interest, not only is the expression of statements which are well seen by the public opinion and those which are deemed to be harmless protected, but also the expression of statements which shock, irritate or disturb public officials or any sector of society. In a democratic society, the press must inform extensively on issues of public interest which affect social rights, and public officials must account for the performance of their duties."
[11] *Cf.* Inter-American Legal Framework Regarding the Right to Freedom of Expression (n. 4), paras. 33 et seq.; see also *Kimel v. Argentina* (n. 8), para. 57; *Claude Reyes et al. v. Chile* (n. 8), paras. 84–87; *Palamara Iribarne v. Chile* [2005] IACtHR, Ser. C No. 135, para. 83; *Herrera Ulloa v. Costa Rica* (n. 8), para. 127.
[12] *Kimel v. Argentina* (n. 8), paras. 86–88; *Palamara Iribarne v. Chile* (n. 11), para. 83; *"The Last Temptation of Christ" (Olmedo Bustos et al.) v. Chile* (n. 8), para. 69; *Ivcher Bronstein v. Peru* (n. 8), paras. 152, 155; *Ricardo Canese v. Paraguay* (n. 8), para. 83; *Herrera Ulloa v. Costa Rica* (n. 8), paras. 125–129; *Claude Reyes v. Chile* (n. 8), para. 87; *Tristán Donoso v. Panama* [2009] IACtHR, Ser. C No. 193, para. 115.
[13] *Cf.* "Inter-American Legal Framework Regarding the Right to Freedom of Expression" (n. 4), para. 53; see also *López Álvarez v. Honduras* (n. 8), para. 169.

issuing an opinion (even if that opinion was hard, unfair or disturbing), but that the person had the clear intention of committing a crime and the actual, real and effective possibility of achieving this objective.[14]

Child pornography is also prohibited in absolute terms by the Convention on the Rights of the Child (Article 34 (c)), the Optional Protocol to the Convention on the Rights of the Child on the sale of children, child prostitution, and child pornography, and International Labour Organization Convention No. 182 on the worst forms of child labor (Article 3 (b)).[15]

The protection that the Inter-American System affords to freedom of expression is not absolute. The inter-American standards allow for limitations or restrictions to this right, but they must meet strict requirements as these limitations are designed to be exceptional.[16] Thus, in order for a restriction on the right to freedom of expression to be admissible:

(1) the limitation must have been defined in a precise and clear manner by a law, in the formal and material sense; (2) the limitation must serve compelling objectives authorized by the Convention; and (3) the limitation must be necessary in a democratic society to serve the compelling objectives pursued, strictly proportionate to the objective pursued, and appropriate to serve said compelling objective.[17]

The system has also rejected *prior censorship* in near absolute terms and imposes an obligation on States not to take actions or measures that indirectly affect freedom of expression.

Finally, the inter-American standards highlight the importance of States to promote diversity and pluralism in the media ecosystem where democratic public debates occur.[18] In this regard, the Inter-American Commission has said that "States must prevent public or private monopoly of ownership and control over media outlets, and must promote different groups' access to radio and television frequencies and licenses, whichever the groups' technological means might be."[19] The IACtHR has held that States must:

---

[14] Ibid., para. 58.
[15] *Cf.* ibid., para. 60.
[16] *Cf. Lagos del Campo v. Peru* [2017] IACtHR, Ser. C No. 340, para. 98; *Tristán Donoso v. Panama* (n. 12), para. 110; *Usón Ramírez v. Venezuela* [2009] IACtHR, Ser. C No. 207, para. 48; *Kimel v. Argentina* (n. 8), para. 54.
[17] "Inter-American Legal Framework Regarding the Right to Freedom of Expression" (n. 4), para. 67; affirming this jurisprudence, see, e.g., *Lagos del Campo v. Peru* (n. 16), para. 102.
[18] "Inter-American Legal Framework Regarding the Right to Freedom of Expression" (n. 4), paras. 224 et seq.
[19] Ibid., para. 224.

minimize the restrictions to information and balance, as much as possible, the participation of the different movements present in the public debate, promoting informative pluralism. The protection of the human rights of whoever faces the power of the media, who must exercise the social task it develops with responsibility, and the effort to ensure structural conditions that allow an equal expression of ideas can be explained in these terms.[20]

The inter-American standards developed by the IACtHR and the IACHR are, as a whole, a powerful legal framework for the protection of freedom of expression—one of the rights without which democratic systems cannot flourish. According to the Court, Article 13 offers one of the most robust guarantees of this right in comparative terms, including Article 19 of the International Covenant on Civil and Political Rights and Article 10 of the European Convention on Human Rights.[21] These guarantees have been strengthened by local courts adopting the protection standards of the Inter-American System. One of the most visible impacts of the Inter-American System lies in the jurisprudential dialogue between national high courts and the standards of the Inter-American System, and vice versa. This has helped to broaden and strengthen the content of the constitutional norms and regional treaties related to this right.

The Office of the Special Rapporteur for Freedom of Expression systematized relevant national case law on freedom of expression, starting with the set of court decisions documented as best practice in its Annual Reports for the 2013–2016 period.[22] The region's courts have addressed a range of issues, including cases involving public officials and the judicial protection of specially protected speech, particularly political speech; protections against the criminalization of circulating information and opinions of public interest; developing the doctrine of actual malice to resolve conflicts between freedom of expression and the honor of public officials and persons involved in public debates; and protecting journalists against the pressure to reveal the identity of their sources, among others. With respect to emerging issues, the Office has reported the growing litigation of matters related to freedom of expression on the internet (including blocking, downloading, and de-indexing content), privacy, and digital surveillance, on which the case law is still in the early stages of development.

In one of the cases examined, upon considering a journalist's extraordinary petition for cassation, the Supreme Court of Colombia exhaustively examined the function of freedom of expression in its political dimension, citing the case law of the country's Constitutional Court. The judgment underscored

---

[20] *Ríos et al. v. Venezuela* (n. 10), para. 106.
[21] *Cf.* ibid., para. 50.
[22] *Cf.* IACHR, "National Case Law on Freedom of Expression and Access to Information," Office of the Special Rapporteur for Freedom of Expression of the IACHR (2017).

the importance of freedom of expression as a precondition for effective social participation, the improvement of public policies, and the guarantee of robust discussions on matters of general interest. It held that freedom of expression:

> promotes socio-political stability, by providing a safety valve for social dissent . . . protects the political minorities that are active at a given time, preventing them from being silenced by prevailing or majority forces . . . helps shape public opinion on political matters and the consolidation of a properly informed electorate.

The Chamber of Criminal Cassation of the Supreme Court of Colombia thus concluded that the "profound" constitutional and international protection of freedom of expression "is justified precisely because of those lofty goals of solidifying participatory democracy."[23]

An illustrative example of these kinds of national decisions regarding the protection of freedom of expression on the internet is the June 4, 2014[4] opinion (*voto-vista*) delivered by Judge Nancy Andrighi of the Superior Court of Justice (*Superior Tribunal de Justiça* (STJ)) of Brazil, in which the high court's majority ruled to set aside an injunction against an internet search service provider. Judge Andrighi held that guardianship of the virtual environment demands "increased care" and that as a consequence "any type of restriction must be carefully considered" so that it does not affect "the perfect functioning" of the Web. She added that "in the case of Internet search service providers, the imposition of implicit or subjective obligations would entail, potentially, the restriction of the search results, which would be to the detriment of all user[s]." She also highlighted the importance of online search services in a world in which the daily lives of millions of people depend on information that is on the internet and would be difficult to find without the search tools offered by search sites.[24]

3. Challenges and Restrictions to the Exercise of Freedom of Expression on the Internet

At the beginning of the twenty-first century, traditional mass media continue to play a crucial role in investigating and publishing information of public interest, promoting government accountability, and engendering debates on all kinds of issues. However, internet platforms and services now represent a massive conduit for public debate and information of interest to citizens. These services

---

[23] Ibid., para. 14.
[24] Ibid., para. 122.

facilitate the expression of individuals and social groups, allow for more horizontal communication, and promote open and robust public debate in general because the decentralized spaces into which everyone can pour information and opinions become more difficult to control. The online environment has also provided "ideal conditions for innovation and the exercise of other fundamental rights such as the right to education and free association."[25]

The flip side of this *positive* aspect of the internet, however, involves challenges linked both to the power of States to interfere in the circulation of information and to the growing role of private platforms that facilitate communication by moderating content. Unquestionably, challenges in the region include direct and indirect interference by some States to prevent the circulation of information and ideas that are not in their interest. There is also the difficulty of preventing or discouraging some governments, individuals, or groups from making abusive comments or using social media with the deliberate intent to deceive or promote violence. Some States have also increased their technological capacity to block entire websites, as well as ordering that internet access be suspended at certain times or in certain areas, or enacting disproportionate legislative measures to order the removal of specific content. Other challenges include the new role of private actors as intermediaries in the flow of information, the liability of intermediaries for content produced by third parties, and the viral spread of problematic speech on social networks, such as hate speech or mass disinformation campaigns. These are some of the issues modern democracies face in regulating their digital public sphere.

Second, there is a consensus in international law on the powerful role that private actors now play in the circulation of information. These private actors are companies that provide services or platforms that facilitate the exchange of information, ideas, and opinions among citizens, government officials, organizations, and so on. Indeed, with billions of people participating in the digital arena, the internet is providing a new way of circulating (or "sharing") information. Traditional media's own editorial selection, while not disappearing, has been largely replaced by the terms and conditions, or "community rules," that individuals agree to when they open an account on these websites. These community rules are also implemented through content-recommendation systems based on automated algorithms that operate on the basis of artificial intelligence. These automated tools analyze the information, allow or block content, and make recommendations to users about content that—according to data collected from their online activity—people follow based on their web browsing habits.

---

[25] IACHR, "Freedom of Expression and the Internet," Office of the Special Rapporteur for Freedom of Expression of the IACHR (2013), para. 2.

The decentralized network of the internet, which entails reciprocal communications between senders and receivers of communications, has been dominated by commercial actors whose investments have enabled the development of various public forums on a previously unimaginable scale but whose actions, for better or worse, shape public debate and in part determine what citizens consume, read, and watch.

A third, growing challenge is the ability to track "digital footprints," or data that people leave behind when they use the internet. As part of the very design of the internet (in the form of a network) the traffic users create, unlike analog communications, leaves traces that are stored and used by social networks in line with their business model, which consists of selling advertising through user preferences. This has created an advertising industry with highly targeted messages that depend largely on amassing and exploiting peoples' digital footprints; at least one result of this development concerns a number of novel challenges to privacy rights. Some recent cases show that the data stored by private actors have been used not only to sell commercial advertising but also to send targeted political messages and disinformation during election periods.[26]

This feature of the internet has also been exploited by State actors engaging in the surveillance or monitoring of journalists, activists, and dissidents, jeopardizing elements of Article 11 of the American Convention, which safeguards privacy from interference by both State and non-State actors—particularly when individuals are exercising fundamental rights such as the freedom to investigate, the freedom to contact others to seek and impart information, and in connection to the freedoms of association, assembly, and political participation.

4. Principles on Freedom of Expression and the Internet Developed by the Inter-American Human Rights System

Over the past ten years, the IACHR and the Office of the Special Rapporteur for Freedom of Expression have been developing interpretations and principles, especially in their thematic reports and decisions, applicable to violations and conflicts of rights in the digital arena. In addition, national courts in the Americas and Europe, the European Court of Human Rights, and to a lesser extent the Inter-American Case System, have established jurisprudential criteria (though not always uniform) on these issues.

---

[26] IACHR, "Guide to Guarantee Freedom of Expression Regarding Deliberate Disinformation in Electoral Contexts," Office of the Special Rapporteur for Freedom of Expression of the IACHR (2019).

In the following I discuss some of these principles that are best suited to respond to these challenges, and which have been developed within the paradigm of the decentralized network of the internet. It is important to emphasize that these principles are not only theoretical developments but are being actively articulated in dialogue with the best practices adopted by several States and promoted by civil society, in legislation and in court decisions. In this regard, and in light of the American Convention and other IAHRS instruments, there is a hemispheric consensus on the importance of maintaining a free, open, and inclusive internet. These principles are also tied to State obligations to prohibit prior censorship, to promote pluralism of information and the debating of ideas, and to encourage citizen participation required by democratic systems.

4.1. Universal Internet Access, Diversity, and Pluralism

All of the benefits to public debates that the internet has brought—that is, increased access, horizontal participation, and freedom to access and share information—can only be enjoyed if citizens have access to the internet. From the very beginning this has represented a major challenge in the Americas due to widespread social inequality. While internet access has expanded over the years, especially through the rise of mobile phone use, public policies are still needed to ensure equitable and affordable access for all citizens. In particular, the expansion of mobile telephony and smartphones in recent years have facilitated Internet access to sectors of the population that were previously excluded from enjoying, for example, the rights to information and expression and access to knowledge and education.

Nevertheless, when States' public policies for social inclusion are weakened, internet coverage is left to the private sector, which has tended to promote agreements between Internet service providers and telecommunication companies known in practice as "zero rating." These agreements typically offer the most disadvantaged sectors of the population an Internet experience limited to popular and mass services under privileged data usage conditions.

Principle 2 of the IACHR's Declaration of Principles on Freedom of Expression establishes:

> All people should be afforded equal opportunities to receive, seek and impart information by any means of communication without any discrimination for reasons of race, color, sex, language, religion, political or other opinions, national or social origin, economic status, birth or any other social condition.[27]

---

[27] IACHR, "Declaration of Principles on Freedom of Expression" (2000), Principle 2.

In addition, the IACtHR has underscored the obligations of *diversity* and *pluralism* that should guide States in regulating the communications ecosystem in which public debates take place, in relation both to the obligation to prevent public and private monopolies and to the promotion of access to that ecosystem by different groups "[whatever their] technological means [may] be."[28] The Court emphasized the obligation to foster information pluralism[29] and called attention to the need for the media to operate under conditions that meet the requirements of freedom of expression.[30]

The digital divide between those who can afford internet access and take advantage of the benefits of this technology and those who, for economic, generational, or geographical reasons, do not yet have full access to it, poses a major obstacle to the enjoyment of the freedoms and knowledge that the internet brings. For this reason, several countries in the region have moved forward with programs to include more people on the internet, from schools to remote rural areas.[31]

In this field, the question of access is governed by the general principle of nondiscrimination, according to which States must:

adopt affirmative measures (legislative, administrative, or [any other kind]), to reverse or change existing discriminatory situations that may [undermine] certain groups' effective enjoyment and exercise of the right to freedom of expression [under conditions of equality and non-discrimination].[32]

The Office of the Special Rapporteur considered that Principle 2 of the Declaration should be interpreted in such a way as to create consequences and positive obligations for States to take steps to promote universal access:

---

[28] *Cf.* "Inter-American Legal Framework Regarding the Right to Freedom of Expression" (n. 4), para. 224.

[29] *Cf. Ríos v. Venezuela* (n. 10), para. 106; *Granier et al. (Radio Caracas Television) v. Venezuela* [2015] IACtHR, Ser. C No. 293, para. 142: "the plurality of the media and news constitutes an effective guarantee of freedom of expression, and the State has a duty to protect and ensure this under Article 1(1) of the Convention, by minimizing restrictions to information and encouraging a balanced participation, and by allowing the media to be open to all without discrimination, because the idea is that 'no individuals or groups are, a priori, excluded.'"

[30] *Cf.* "Compulsory Membership in an Association Prescribed by Law for the Practice of Journalism," Advisory Opinion 5/85 (n. 3), para. 34.

[31] See the Constitution of the United Mexican States, Chamber of Deputies, February 5, 1917; most recent amendments published on December 27, 2013, Art. 7; Library of the National Congress of Chile. Law No. 20.435. Amending Law No. 17.336 on Intellectual Property of August 28, 1970. May 4, 2010. Arts. 85L to 85U and 71A to 71S; Congress of Argentina. Law 26.032. Internet Service. Establishes that searching for, receiving, and disseminating information and ideas through the Internet falls within the constitutional guarantee of freedom of expression. June 16, 2005. Art. 1; Congress of Brazil. Law No. 12.965/2014 (Civil Rights Framework for the Internet [*Lei do Marco Civil da Internet*]).

[32] IACHR, Annual Report of the Office of the Special Rapporteur for Freedom of Expression (2008), Chapter III, 230.

not only to infrastructure but also the technology necessary for its use and to the greatest possible amount of information available on the Internet; to eliminate arbitrary barriers to access to infrastructure, technology and information online, and to adopt measures of positive differentiation to allow for the effective enjoyment of this right for individuals or communities who face marginalization and discrimination.[33]

In addition, the principles of *diversity* and *pluralism* that the Inter-American System has developed are also related to the issue of access, since the open and decentralized architecture of the internet has made it possible to lower the entry barriers to participate in public debates; it is up to States to preserve "the Internet's ideal conditions for promoting and maintaining informational pluralism."[34]

4.2. Principle of Net Neutrality

The IACHR and its Office of the Special Rapporteur have documented numerous cases in which a State has ordered public and private telecommunications companies to remove specific content and even entire media outlets from the internet. Another censorship practice has led authoritarian governments to shut down, block, or reduce the intensity of the internet signal during certain protest periods or in response to messages that they consider critical or contrary to their policies. All of this must be interpreted in light of the prohibition against prior censorship established in Article 13.2 of the Convention. Similarly, civil society organizations in the hemisphere have warned of the possible violation of this principle by private sector internet service providers. The growing "bandwidth" demand for different services has led providers to prioritize traffic from certain packages over others in order to offer a better service. This technical possibility could be used, for example, for services that handle priority traffic, which in effect could result in a two-speed network: one that works faster but is limited to the most popular or powerful services, and a slower one through which all services can be accessed but at a lower speed. This would violate a fundamental principle of the network architecture.

One international law response to this new reality, also provided for in the Inter-American System, has been to develop the principle of *net neutrality*. This principle, aimed at preserving the free flow and plurality of information and opinions on the web, is in part an application of the principles of neutrality

---

[33] "Freedom of Expression and the Internet" (n. 25), para. 15; *cf.* "Annual Report 2017," para. 7.
[34] "Freedom of Expression and the Internet" (n. 25), para. 19; *cf.* "Annual Report 2017" (n. 33), para. 8.

and nondiscrimination required of States under international conventions regarding all kinds of ideas and speech.[35] One of the central pillars of freedom of expression is the principle that the State must be neutral toward the content of information and opinions: laws or measures must not seek to reward or punish people for speech acts based on their content.[36] This means, for example, that when adopting a restriction, the State would be unable to limit only some of the content involved in the message, such as religious or ideological elements; nor could it, in the words of the Court, use direct or indirect mechanisms to restrict freedom of expression, such as allocating government advertising or radio frequencies based on editorial decisions. States are bound by a general principle of nondiscrimination. Furthermore, in accordance with the social dimension of the law, which allows access to all kinds of ideas and information *ab initio*, States cannot engage in "discriminatory treatment [favoring] certain content [on] the Internet [over content] distributed by certain sectors of society."[37]

The horizontal nature of the network, the exponential multiplication of sources of information and the weakening of traditional gatekeepers have made public debates freer and more open but also more chaotic and difficult to control. This is partly a result of network design: being decentralized, "data packets" sent from one device to another seek the most efficient way to reach their final destination through the network.[38] This "maximizes the use of the networks."[39]

The value of this network design therefore is twofold: first, it is efficient in terms of traffic; and second, it offers freedom, since the principle of content *neutrality* allows for a more open and robust public debate. The circulation of ideas, information, and opinions is essential for citizens to freely choose their preferences under the "free marketplace of ideas" paradigm.[40] The Joint Declaration of 2011 reaffirmed this principle, stating that "there should be no discrimination in the treatment of Internet data and traffic, based on the device, content, author, origin and/or destination of the content, service or application."[41] The objective of this principle is to ensure that the internet is not "subject to conditions, or directed or restricted, such as blocking, filtering or interference."[42] Several countries in the region have established the general principle of *neutrality* in their legislation.

---

[35] *Cf.* ibid., para. 21.
[36] *Cf.* IACHR, "Inter-American Legal Framework Regarding the Right to Freedom of Expression" (n. 4), para. 30.
[37] "Freedom of Expression and the Internet" (n. 25), para. 21.
[38] *Cf.* "Freedom of Expression and the Internet" (n. 25), para. 27: "Net neutrality is part of the original design of the Internet. It facilitates access to and circulation of content, applications and services freely and without any distinction."
[39] "Annual Report 2017" (n. 33), para. 21.
[40] *Cf. Abrams v. United States*, 250 US 616 (1919), Holmes, J., dissenting.
[41] OSCE, *Joint Declaration on Freedom of Expression and the Internet* (2011), point 5.a.
[42] IACHR, "Freedom of Expression and the Internet" (n. 25), para. 25.

Thus, for instance, in Chile, Law 20.453 established that communication service providers cannot:

> arbitrarily block, interfere with, discriminate against, hinder or restrict the right of any Internet user to use, send, receive, or offer any content, application, or lawful service through the Internet, or to engage in any other type of lawful activity or use through the network. In this regard, they must offer every user a type of Internet access service or connectivity to the Internet access provider, as appropriate, that does not arbitrarily differentiate content, applications, or services based on the source of origin or ownership, taking into account the different configurations of the Internet connection according to the contract in force with the users.[43]

In 2014, the National Congress of the Argentine Republic passed Law 25.078 that guaranteed every user the right to "access, use, send, receive, or offer any content, application, service, or protocol through the Internet without any type of restriction, discrimination, distinction, blocking, interference, hindrance, or degradation."[44] For its part, in 2014 Brazil enacted the *Civil Framework for the Internet*, comprehensive legislation that (among other things) expressly safeguards net neutrality.[45] The United States did the same in a policy statement issued by the Federal Communication Commission and through State legislation. The Office of the Special Rapporteur considers it important "that authorities guarantee the validity of this principle through adequate legislation"[46] since it is "fundamental for guaranteeing the plurality and diversity of the flow of information."[47] As the IACtHR has held, "the State must not only minimize restrictions on the [flow] of information, but also [balance], to the greatest possible extent, [the inclusion of different perspectives] in the public debate, fostering [pluralism of information]. Consequently, [fairness must govern] the flow of information."[48] This general principle could give way when it is:

> strictly necessary and proportional in order to preserve the integrity and security of the network; to prevent the transmission of online content at the express request—free and not incentivized—of the user; and to temporarily and exceptionally manage network congestion. In this latter case, the measures employed should not discriminate between types of applications or services.[49]

---

[43] National Congress of Chile, Law No. 20.453, 2010, Art. 1.
[44] National Congress of the Argentine Republic, Law No. 25.078, 2014, Art. 56.
[45] *Cf.* National Congress of the Federative Republic of Brazil, Law No. 12.965 (Civil Rights Framework for the Internet), 2014, Art. 3. IV.
[46] Ibid., para. 26.
[47] Ibid., para. 28.
[48] *Kimel v. Argentina* (n. 8), para. 57; *Fontevecchia and D'Amico v. Argentina* [2017], IACtHR, para. 45.
[49] "Freedom of Expression and the Internet" (n. 25), para. 30.

4.3. Content Blocking and Filtering

The decentralized nature of the internet makes it very difficult to control the flow of information. Taking down a website does not prevent the content from being replicated on a different site within minutes. Removing a video from an online video-sharing platform does not guarantee that it will not (in a slightly modified form) be uploaded again or circulated on other platforms (such as encrypted messaging services) or information management systems (such as peer-to-peer networks). This difficulty in controlling what circulates on the internet has allowed citizens of closed societies to organize and demand their rights by breaking through official barriers to information. However, the flip side of this feature is that plainly illegal content such as child pornography or content inciting acts of terrorism can be distributed through channels that are difficult to control. This has triggered a variety of reactions: internet service providers have, for example, developed automated mechanisms to identify illegal content, and States and law enforcement agencies have deployed investigative teams that are constantly scanning the web to remove and prosecute disseminators of child pornography. The Special Rapporteurs for freedom of expression have stated that:

> forcing the blocking or suspension of entire websites, platforms, channels, IP addresses, domain name extensions, ports, network protocols, or any other kind of application, as well as measures intended to eliminate links, information and websites from the servers on which they are stored, all constitute restrictions that are prohibited and exceptionally admissible only strictly pursuant to the terms of Article 13 of the American Convention.[50]

In this regard, the *blocking* of online content is an act that very much resembles *prior censorship*, something that the Inter-American System has considered improper in near-absolute terms.[51]

Indeed, as the Inter-American Commission has maintained, the practice of content *blocking* or *filtering* is only acceptable in exceptional cases involving clearly illegal content or speech that is not covered by the right to freedom of expression.[52] The typical example of this kind of speech is child pornography. To combat the exploitative and abusive practices behind this type of material,

---

[50] "Freedom of Expression and the Internet" (n. 25), para. 84; *Joint Declaration on Freedom of Expression and the Internet* (n. 41), point 3.a.

[51] In OC5/85, the Court held that prior censorship is a violation that is "extreme not only in that it violates the right of each individual to express himself, but also because it impairs the right of each person to be well informed, and thus affects one of the fundamental prerequisites of a democratic society." The only exception to this general principle is provided for in Article 13(4) of the Convention, which states: "Notwithstanding the provisions of paragraph 2 above, public entertainments may be subject by law to prior censorship for the sole purpose of regulating access to them for the moral protection of childhood and adolescence."

[52] *Cf.* "Freedom of Expression and the Internet" (n. 25), para. 85.

most countries block websites that contain or disseminate it. In these cases, the measure must be subjected to a "strict balance of proportionality" to ensure that it does not "affect legitimate speech that deserves protection."[53] Speech that enjoys the presumption of protection cannot be subjected to this type of measure, which (by definition) would usually be considered draconian.[54] In this regard, the Office of the Special Rapporteur has expressed concern and found the practice of blocking specific websites or applications, sometimes under court order, to be disproportionate, with "little or no consideration for the impact of such measures on the right to freedom of expression online."[55]

4.4. Intermediary Liability

Before the internet, the mainstream media served as a highly influential vehicle in public debates, with the ability to select and edit the information they made available to the public. As defined in various Inter-American Court decisions, the media enable society to be informed and thus made the exercise of freedom of expression a reality. While that function has not disappeared in the age of the internet, it has migrated (at least partially) to large online platforms that were developed to facilitate the flow of information and ideas and enable anyone to disseminate and share content. Even though these intermediaries do not explicitly intervene in the editing of content, they have a growing influence on what we can access on it due to the requirements imposed by States and content moderation by social media companies, pursuant to their terms of service and community rules.

Indeed, major internet platforms, social networks, and intermediary services are having an ever-greater impact on online public discourse. Although there are different platforms, in general social networks have specialized particular functions, such as providing free access to content produced and shared by third parties, whether they are people close to users (family, friends, leaders, companies) or producers of information such as the media, artists, and so on. In the case of search engines, they facilitate users' search for information by indexing the millions of websites hosted on the internet. In return, these companies have captured the attention of three billion people and control a large part of the targeted advertising market through users' digital footprints.

Their central role in the flow of information has turned these intermediaries into *nodal points of control* that are targeted by State actors seeking to shape public debates by directing, restricting, or censoring public conversation.[56] The private

---

[53] Ibid., para. 85.
[54] *Cf.* ibid., para. 90.
[55] *Cf.* "Annual Report 2017" (n. 33), para. 86; IACHR, "Annual Report 2015," Office of the Special Rapporteur for Freedom of Expression (2015), para. 264.
[56] *Cf.* "Freedom of Expression and the Internet" (n. 25), para. 93.

decisions these services make in order to meet their objectives and contractual terms also have a significant impact on public discourse. This creates challenges from the standpoint of freedom of expression and the legal liability that applies to the online ecosystem. There is a consensus that the incentives created by a system that imposes subsequent liabilities on intermediaries for third-party content may be disproportionate or fail to respect international human rights protection standards. If the law imposes legal or financial penalties for harm arising from content distributed by third parties, intermediaries may approach the issue with excessive zeal and filter or exclude from public discourse more content than is strictly necessary. This problem of overreaching is a form of private censorship that adversely affects third parties who use these platforms to distribute their content.

Such dynamics would undermine the principle that public discourse should be open, robust, and uninhibited. For this reason, various countries in the world and in the region have chosen to limit the liability of intermediaries for content produced by third parties. In this respect, the 2011 Joint Declaration stated:

> No one who simply provides technical Internet services such as providing access, or searching for, or transmission or caching of information, should be liable for content generated by others, which is disseminated using those services, as long as they do not specifically intervene in that content or refuse to obey a court order to remove that content, where they have the capacity to do so ("mere conduit principle").[57]

The Office of the Special Rapporteur has maintained that extending this basic principle to the internet means (1) the absolute exclusion of any system of strict liability,[58] and (2) the exclusion of systems of fault-based liability that require intermediaries to exercise prior control or monitor the services they provide.[59]

4.5. Subsequent Liability

One point that warrants special attention is the *subsequent liability* contemplated in the digital context. As stated earlier, the right to freedom of expression is not absolute: when harm arises from the exercise of that right, subsequent liability can be established in clearly and precisely worded laws, provided that it is proportionate.[60] In particular, the Inter-American Commission (systematizing the case law of the

---

[57] *Joint Declaration on Freedom of Expression and the Internet* (n. 41), point 2.a.
[58] "Freedom of Expression and the Internet" (n. 25), paras. 95–100.
[59] Ibid., paras. 102, 105: arguing that "this type of mechanism puts private intermediaries in the position of having to make decisions about the lawfulness or unlawfulness of the content, and for the reasons explained above, create incentives for private censorship."
[60] *Cf.* "Inter-American Legal Framework Regarding the Right to Freedom of Expression" (n. 4), para. 67.

Inter-American Court) recommended that it consists of the exercise of the right of reply or, when that is insufficient, proportionate civil liability.[61] In the digital environment, the Office of the Special Rapporteur specified that the systemic dimensions of the Internet must be considered when addressing certain types of subsequent liability, since they must be precisely designed so as not to affect the exercise of the right to freedom of expression. As a general principle, the Rapporteurs for Freedom of Expression stated that, when assessing the necessity and proportionality of restrictive measures, it is essential to apply a digitally systemic perspective that considers the impact of such a measure on the functioning of the internet as a decentralized and open network.[62] In this regard, "the correction of erroneous information is the least costly measure for redressing damage related to it."[63]

It is imperative that the drafters of subsequent liability laws and the judges who apply them consider the impact of certain decisions. For instance, as noted previously, decisions to block access to certain websites are in general grossly disproportionate and therefore incompatible with the American Convention. It is also unacceptable to apply subsequent liability especially, or in an aggravated manner, to online speech, given the previously outlined principles of *neutrality* and *nondiscrimination*.[64]

4.6. Hate Speech and Disinformation

Hate speech and the dissemination of false information for the purpose of deliberately misleading the public are challenges that modern democracies have always faced. In general, legislative and judicial systems have sought proportionate responses to tackle the problem of speech that impoverishes public discourse without sacrificing the general principle that States must remain *neutral* in terms of content regulation. These problems, which have always existed, have been exacerbated by the speed and capacity of content to go viral, the center of a horizontal social media ecosystem. The oversight mechanisms that previously identified hate speech or disinformation practices appear to have lost their ability to influence. A more open and decentralized public discourse, such as that offered by the internet, is also by definition a more chaotic space and one in which this type of speech is likely to be more visible.

The ACHR strikes an appropriate balance on these issues. The Convention excludes hate speech from protection, but only in strictly exceptional circumstances, namely, when such speech incites violence or there is:

---

[61] Ibid., para. 79.
[62] *Cf. Joint Declaration on Freedom of Expression and the Internet* (n. 41), point 1.c; see also "Freedom of Expression and the Internet" (n. 25), para. 63.
[63] "Freedom of Expression and the Internet" (n. 25), para. 72.
[64] *Cf.* ibid., para. 74.

actual, truthful, objective and strong proof that the person was not simply issuing an opinion (even if that opinion was hard, unfair or disturbing), but that the person had the clear intention of committing a crime and the actual, real and effective possibility of achieving this objective.[65]

The digital environment and the perception that hate speech and disinformation are more widespread should lead not to a revision of the principles but to their reaffirmation. Indeed, subsequent liability, including criminal liability, can be adapted to address speech that incites violence based on discrimination. However, the Court could advance its case law on hate speech by establishing what elements and requirements both the law and the courts should consider in identifying speech that has the potential to incite violence on discriminatory grounds. In a recent report on hate speech and violence against LGBTIQ+ persons in the Americas, the IACHR and its Office of the Special Rapporteur recommended observing the Rabat Plan of Action on the prohibition against advocating for national, racial, or religious hatred. The Rabat Plan sets out criteria to make it easier for national authorities to discern when they are dealing with speech that may incite violence on discriminatory grounds.[66]

In its interpretation of Article 13.5 of the American Convention, the Commission held that States should pass legislation to punish the advocacy of hatred that constitutes "incitement to violence or any other similar unlawful action," and it referred to the limits for such penalties. On the other hand, under Article 13.2 of the American Convention, other intolerant expressions or remarks that do not strictly constitute an "incitement to violence" may be subject to the imposition of subsequent liability to ensure the rights to dignity and the nondiscrimination of particular groups in society, including LGBTIQ+ persons. The International Covenant on Civil and Political Rights (ICCPR) takes a similar approach. The Rabat Plan of Action adds a third type of speech that, although not punishable, raises concerns about tolerance and respect and clearly distinguishes between: (1) expressions that constitute a criminal offense, (2) expressions that are not criminally punishable but may justify a civil suit or administrative penalties, and (3) expressions that are not legally punishable "but still rais[e] a concern in terms of tolerance, civility and respect for the rights of others."[67]

---

[65] "Inter-American Legal Framework Regarding the Right to Freedom of Expression" (n. 4), para. 58.
[66] "Violence Against Lesbian, Gay, Bisexual, Trans and Intersex Persons in the Americas" (2015), paras. 227 et seq.
[67] United Nations Committee on the Elimination of Racial Discrimination, General recommendation No. 35, Combating racist hate speech, September 26, 2013, CERD/C/GC/35, paras. 20, 25.

4.7. Cybersecurity, Privacy, and Surveillance

The emergence of the internet has created a communication system that is more horizontal but also produces many more traces for identifying people than analog technologies. Under the previous paradigm, information could be accessed relatively anonymously. The technological capacity of others to know what we were reading, listening to, or watching was limited unless these actors invested in costly surveillance tactics or actions that contravened human rights. Today, surfing the internet means *leaving traces* of everything we do. The websites we visit know who we are, they know our patterns of consumption, what websites we visit, what newspapers we read, and who we vote for. Based on that information, they can create profiles that are used for commercial purposes. This knowledge has radically transformed the advertising market. Companies that wish to transmit their messages or advertisements can design precise and highly targeted strategies. This creates a message dissemination process that is more efficient and effective (while also far more invasive) than traditional advertising.

This feature of the internet has given rise to at least three consequences. First, the internet has been developing on the basis of an advertising scheme through which companies provide different types of services based on the advertising income they generate. These companies have acquired influential positions within the online communication ecosystem. Second, users—wary of the existence of highly personalized profiles that capture their consumption patterns, tastes, and social relationships—have demanded and are demanding technologies that give them greater control over their personal data and allow them to avoid some of the industry's practices, such as tracking on websites. In addition, States around the world have made efforts to strengthen and update their legal frameworks that protect personal data, which are considered essential to prevent the most abusive advertising practices.

Finally, some States have taken advantage of internet traffic in order to carry out mass surveillance, with not a few reported cases of unlawful intrusion (namely, surveillance or spying) into the digital communications of people exercising their fundamental rights as journalists, human rights advocates, judges, or members of opposition parties. This has also been aided by the inadequate or insufficient development of privacy-enhancing tools and technologies, such as default encryption, as well as by the absence of legislation and independent oversight of the surveillance activities of security agencies.[68] These activities have been called into

---

[68] *Cf.* OSCE, *Joint Declaration on Surveillance Programs and their Impact on Freedom of Expression*; SR/UN, *Report of the Special Rapporteur on the promotion and protection of the right to freedom of opinion and expression*. United Nations General Assembly, New York, NY, Office of the Special Rapporteur on Freedom of Opinion and Expression, 2013, para. 2. On this issue, a report by the University of Toronto's Citizen Lab found that State institutions in Mexico acquired Pegasus spyware

question and confirm the need for adequate and efficient mechanisms to protect privacy rights. The right to privacy is in fact one of the fundamental rights for a democratic political community. Without the adequate protection of a private sphere away from the gaze of others, human beings cannot develop full and free lives. A reasonable expectation of privacy is a prerequisite for democratic citizenship and is closely linked to the freedom of expression.[69]

The Office of the Special Rapporteur for Freedom of Expression of the IACHR has said that "[r]espect for online freedom of expression assumes that there is privacy for people's communications."[70] The IACtHR underscored the close connection between the right to privacy and the right to personal liberty guaranteed by Article 7 of the Convention.[71] The protection of privacy extends to areas such as the home, forms of correspondence, and family life.[72] In addition, the IACHR has stated that the right to privacy encompasses four legally protected interests "that are closely related to the exercise of other fundamental rights such as freedom of thought and expression," including:

> the right to have an individual sphere impervious to the arbitrary interference of the State or third parties ... the right to govern oneself, in that solitary space, by one's own rules defined autonomously according to one's individual life plan. ... the confidentiality of all the data produced in that private space—in other words, it prohibits the disclosure or circulation of information captured, without the consent of their owner, in that space of private protection reserved to the individual ... and the right to one's own image, meaning the right to not have one's image used without consent.[73]

This renewed concern for the right to privacy is intimately linked to the emergence of the internet. The world has moved away from a focus on the initial promise of the Internet as a profoundly democratizing, horizontal space toward a realization of its complications and dangers, in which that equalizing element coexists with a global surveillance network built on the massive and selective

---

and unlawfully used it to intercept communications from journalists and human rights defenders. See J. Scott-Railton et al., "Reckless VI: Mexican Journalists Investigating Cartels Targeted with NSO Spyware Following Assassination of Colleague" (2018). Retrieved from Citizen Lab at the University of Toronto website: <https://citizenlab.ca/2018/11/mexican-journalists-investigating-cartels-targeted-nso-spyware-following-assassination-colleague/> (accessed February 5, 2022).

[69] *Cf.* SR/UN, *Report of the Special Rapporteur on the promotion and protection of the right to freedom of opinion and expression*. General Assembly United Nations, New York, NY. Office of the Special Rapporteur on Freedom of Opinion and Expression, 2011, para. 11.

[70] "Freedom of Expression and the Internet" (n. 25), para. 130.

[71] *Cf. Artavia Murillo et al. (In Vitro Fertilization) v. Costa Rica* [2012] IACtHR, Ser. C No. 257, para. 143.

[72] 'Freedom of Expression and the Internet' (n. 25), paras. 188–190.

[73] "Freedom of Expression and the Internet" (n. 25), para. 131.

violation of the right to privacy. In this regard, the link between the right to *privacy* and *freedom of expression* is close: if repressive States deploy surveillance for unlawful purposes, the internet can be used to silence or undermine the protection of journalism and dissent, penalize criticism, and crack down on the provision of independent information, as well as the sources of such information.[74] For the UN Special Rapporteur on Freedom of Expression, the problem is so serious that he has recently called for:

> an immediate moratorium on the global sale and transfer of the tools of the private surveillance industry until rigorous human rights safeguards are put in place to regulate such practices and guarantee that Governments and non-State actors use the tools in legitimate ways.[75]

5. Concluding Remarks

In Advisory Opinion 5/85, the Inter-American Court held that freedom of expression is a:

> cornerstone upon which the very existence of a democratic society rests. It is indispensable for the formation of public opinion. It is also a *conditio sine qua non* for the development of political parties, trade unions, scientific and cultural societies and, in general, those who wish to influence the public. It represents, in short, the means that enable the community, when exercising its options, to be sufficiently informed. Consequently, it can be said that a society that is not well informed is not a society that is truly free.[76]

In recent years, the internet has become a part of the fundamental scaffolding upholding modern democratic systems. Public discourse and the free flow of information—which the Court highlighted as essential to democracy in its first decision on this right—are increasingly taking place through this decentralized network. The communications ecosystem that has emerged as a result represents a paradigm shift in the communications order, and this shift is having a direct impact on that discourse.

From this perspective, I submit that the bodies of the Inter-American System need to reaffirm their extensive jurisprudence on freedom of expression for at least three reasons. First, the paradigm shift brought about by the internet has

---

[74] Ibid., para. 21.
[75] SR/UN, *Surveillance and Human Rights*, para. 2.
[76] "Compulsory Membership in an Association Prescribed by Law for the Practice of Journalism" (n. 3), para. 70.

called into question many of the principles on which this jurisprudence is based. Faith in free, open, robust, and uninhibited debate seems to be giving way to demands for greater control and censorship in a deeply problematic regulatory approach that amounts to a repudiation of the principles and standards of the Inter-American System.

Second, new actors in the communications world have emerged with a variety of roles. Thus, the principle that limits the legal liability of intermediaries for third-party content does not mean that they do not play a fundamental role in the flow of information online, and this can be addressed legitimately through approaches that respect freedom of expression.[77] It seems clear that the larger internet platforms function as private curators of public debate. To the extent that they do in fact play this role, it is vitally important to reflect on the principles that should guide them. When operating as public forums, the principles of freedom of expression and transparency developed here should guide these private actors in their roles as moderators. At the same time, we need to ensure that there is sufficient democratic, citizen oversight of these forums and how they operate in practice.

The unlawful surveillance that has proliferated on the internet—often of journalists, activists, opposition figures, dissidents, and others exercising their right to freedom of expression—has at times led to various forms of retaliation by States. These surveillance activities are conducted against a backdrop of weak democratic controls on the purchase and transfer of technology to governments with repressive policies toward journalists and human rights activists. The issue of targeted and mass surveillance must be addressed by the System's bodies from the perspective of States' human rights law obligations and the related responsibilities of the companies that manufacture these technologies.

Third, and finally, democratic institutions throughout the world seem to be experiencing a moment of crisis and doubt in terms of their capacity to deliver effective responses to citizens' demands. Freedom of expression and protection from both mass and targeted surveillance, while guaranteeing public discourse (essential for democracies to function) has emerged as a fundamental right on the path toward addressing these challenges. Therefore, the principles must be updated and applied to the ever-changing reality of the world around us in order to guide us, once again, in the search for regulatory solutions to the novel problems we face.

---

[77] Cf. *Fontevecchia and D'Amico v. Argentina* (n. 48), para. 44, stating: "Social media platforms play an essential role as vehicles for the exercise of the social dimension of freedom of expression in a democratic society, which is why it is indispensable for them to encompass the most diverse information and opinions. As essential instruments of freedom of thought and expression, these media must exercise their social function responsibly."

PART III
OPTIMIZING THE IMPACT OF THE INTER-AMERICAN SYSTEM

III.1
Proposals for the Improvement of the Work of the Inter-American Commission on Human Rights

By Joel Hernandez García

1. Introduction

For over sixty years the Inter-American Commission on Human Rights (IACHR) has supported member States of the Organization of American States (OAS) and their civil societies in a broad endeavor to protect human rights.[1] Meaningful steps have been taken in the Western Hemisphere to build a world where all human beings are free and equal in dignity and rights. The IACHR has played a fundamental role in the democratization of American societies and its impact has been transformative. To a lesser or greater degree, the standards developed by the Commission have been incorporated into the domestic legal orders of American States. For example, the rule of law has been strengthened in many countries by internalizing recommendations made by the IACHR through its various mechanisms.

However, the Commission can and should do more. In a complex world, the Commission needs to remain effective and be more efficient. This could be achieved by improving some of its working methods, which would assist it in facing current challenges. This chapter, therefore, will provide a general analysis of the Commission's impact on the construction of an inter-American legal order. From there I will present some proposals to improve the Commission's continued work of complementing national efforts in the protection and promotion of human rights.

---

[1] This text was written in July 2020 and last revised in October 2021. This version has been approved by the author and editors.

2. A Robust Inter-American Human Rights System

The construction of international human rights law has experienced great progress in the Americas since the foundation of the OAS and the adoption of the American Declaration of the Rights and Duties of Man (American Declaration) in 1948.[2] The region has been able to develop a solid body of international human rights law, which is interpreted and applied by the IACHR and the Inter-American Court of Human Rights (IACtHR). The international order that emerged as a response to the horrors of World War II had a fundamental orientation toward the respect for human dignity. Indeed, the OAS was founded in order to promote the values of the new postwar international order. The commitment of the founding member States to the full respect for human rights appears in various sections of the OAS Charter. In accordance with the Preamble of that instrument, "the true significance of American solidarity and good neighborliness can only mean the consolidation on this continent, within the framework of democratic institutions, of a system of individual liberty and social justice based on respect for the essential rights of man."[3]

However, the action of the international community in the defense of human rights was gradual. Initially, that action was marked by the principle of nonintervention in domestic affairs, which limited any expression of concern by the international community to events that arose in the countries of the region. What happened within a State remained the exclusive competence of that State. Today, no State can argue that issues related to human rights are a matter of domestic competence as the international community has a vested interest in the promotion and protection of human rights at a global level.

The milestone that initiated the change in the international community's approach to human rights issues was the Fifth Meeting of Consultation of Ministers of Foreign Affairs, held in August 1959 in Santiago, where the foundations of the Inter-American System were laid down.[4] The Santiago Declaration contains two fundamental decisions of the foreign ministers: (1) to begin negotiations on a "human rights convention" and (2) to establish a Commission on human rights in charge of "promoting respect for such rights."[5] Ten years later, in 1969, the American Convention on Human Rights, the Pact of San José, was adopted.[6] The

---

[2] Organization of American States (OAS), "American Declaration of the Rights and Duties of Man," adopted at the Ninth International Conference of American States, Bogotá, Colombia, 1948.

[3] OAS, "Charter of the Organization of American States," Preamble, para. 4.

[4] Information on the evolution of the Inter-American Human Rights System, https://www.oas.org/en/iachr/mandate/Basics/intro.asp#_ftn6 (accessed November 2, 2021).

[5] See the complete text of the Declaration of Santiago, Chile, adopted at the Fifth Meeting of Consultation of Ministers of Foreign Affairs, Santiago, Chile, August 12–18, 1959, Final Act, Doc. OEA/Ser.C/II.5, 4–6, https://www.oas.org/consejo/MEETINGS%20OF%20CONSULTATION/minutes.asp (accessed November 2, 2021).

[6] OAS, American Convention on Human Rights, "Pact of San José," Costa Rica, November 22, 1969. Treaty Series No. 36.

Commission immediately began its work without waiting for the conclusion of the American Convention.

Sixty years later the region now enjoys a robust Inter-American Human Rights System (IAHRS) with two fully operational and complementary institutions, the Commission and the Court. The awareness that human rights and human dignity are inherent to human beings is commonly understood. More so, there is a widespread acceptance that the defense of human rights on the continent is a collective responsibility of all OAS member States and that no State authority can abandon its international responsibility in cases of human rights violations under the argument that human rights are matters that fall within the domestic arena. The impact that the Commission and the Court have had on the continent is undeniable, both generally in the construction of democratic societies respectful of human rights and individually through the reparation of human rights violations.[7]

The IAHRS works on the basis of three pillars. Firstly, the Commission has developed a strong human rights monitoring system directed at the thirty-five member States of the OAS through a toolbox of mechanisms. Secondly, the Commission provides technical assistance to States and civil societies to enhance national capacities. Nonetheless, the Inter-American System is largely known by the third pillar: its system of cases and petitions. Through the adjudication process, generally accepted legal standards have been established. The merits reports of the Commission and the sentences of the Court set obligations upon States to repair human rights violations committed against individuals. They have a reparatory objective and, therefore, a direct impact on victims. In addition, those decisions also have a general effect on the concerned State's population when measures of nonrepetition are ordered. These kinds of measures impose obligations to adopt laws, regulations, or policies with the purpose that the wrong committed by State agents is not to be repeated.

Inter-American legal instruments and the interpretation thereof by the Commission and the Court have developed standards on the human rights obligations of member States under thresholds established by those bodies. Even though State practice is an element in the creation of international law rules, inter-American human rights law has been advanced by the decisions of the

---

[7] Panlo Saavedra, "Algunas reflexiones en cuanto al impacto estructural de las decisiones de la Corte Interamericana de Derechos Humanos," in Armin von Bogdandy et al. (eds.), *Ius Constitucionale Commune en América Latina. Textos básicos para su comprensión* (IECQ y MPIL, Querétaro 2017), 457–502; Flávia Piovesan, "Ius Constitutionale Commune latinoamericano en derechos humanos e impacto del Sistema Interamericano: rasgos, potencialidades y desafíos," in Armin von Bogdandy, Héctor Fix Fierro, and Mariela Morales Antoniazzi (eds.), *Ius Constitutionale Commune en América Latina. Rasgos, potencialidades y desafíos*, (IIJ-UNAM-MPIL-IIDC 2014), 61–84; Ximena Soley, "The transformative dimension of inter-American jurisprudence," in Armin von Bogdandy et al. (eds.), *Transformative Constitutionalism in Latin America: the emergence of a new ius commune* (Oxford University Press 2017), 337–355.

Commission and the Court by moving States beyond literal interpretations of the norms they are bound by.

The most evident impact of the Inter-American System lies in the progressive development of international human rights law. The standards developed from the decisions of the Commission and judgments of the Court are part of an American *corpus juris* that nourishes their work. Through an evolutionary approach each precedent set by those organs serves as a source of law to continue developing the norms in subsequent decisions.

The IACHR and the IACtHR have thus adopted an evolutionary interpretation of the American Convention when developing standards. In this regard, the Court has established that the interpretation of the Convention "must consider the changes over time and present-day conditions."[8] It has also observed that the interpretation of other international norms cannot be used to restrict the enjoyment and exercise of a right. Furthermore, the interpretation must contribute to the most favorable application of the provision whose interpretation is sought. To that end, the Inter-American System has relied on the general provisions of interpretation set forth in the Vienna Convention on the Law of Treaties, in particular the principle of *pacta sunt servanda*: every treaty in force is binding upon the parties to it and must be performed by them in good faith.[9]

The Inter-American System is inherently victim-oriented. The adoption of human rights instruments, the establishment of the organs of the Inter-American System, and the development of their jurisprudence with far-reaching standards have the ultimate goal of preventing human rights violations and, where those violations have been committed, effective reparations to victims.

Victims, who in pursuit of justice denied by the State, are empowered to bring cases before the Commission in an expeditious manner and through a simple procedure. Even though it is the Commission's prerogative to bring cases against the State before the Court, since the reform to the Court's rules of procedure adopted in 2000 the victim enjoys *ius standi* in all the tribunal's proceedings.

We come, therefore, to the inevitable issue of the ways and means to guarantee a State's compliance with its international obligations. If the State remains inactive in relation to the decisions of the Commission or the Court and no reparation is given to the victim, as a basic principle of law, the State incurs international responsibility and shall be subject to consequences provided by international law. However, if the ultimate goal is the protection of the victim and the prevention and reparation of human rights violations, the question is how the Inter-American System can improve its effectiveness. Beyond the general issue of

---

[8] IACtHR, "The Right to Information on Consular Assistance in the Framework of the Guarantees of Due Process of Law," Advisory Opinion OC-16/99 of October 1, 1999, Ser. A No. 16, paras. 113–114.

[9] UN, *Vienna Convention on the Law of Treaties*, May 23, 1969, UN Doc. No. 18232, art. 26.

the efficacy of international law, the organs of the Inter-American System must work according to the understanding that the cooperation of the State is needed under all circumstance in order to have a positive impact on victims and society at large. How to secure the cooperation of States, therefore, is key and obliges the Commission to examine the way it performs its work, crafts its decisions, and designs its mechanisms with a view of obtaining compliance. The effectiveness of the system depends on the cooperation provided by States. If such cooperation is not obtained, their decisions run the risk of remaining without effect.

We must not lose sight of the fact that the development of the Inter-American System, like any other development of international law, stems from the willingness of States. A sovereign decision by twenty-one States allowed the adoption of the American Declaration in 1948. The States established the organs of this System and initiated the negotiation of the American Convention by a sovereign decision. The individual will of each State later allowed the adoption of and adherence to the American Convention and the recognition of the contentious jurisdiction of the Inter-American Court. However, once conventional agreements are adopted, States are obliged to fulfill them under the principle of *pacta sunt servanda*. Thus, we face a dichotomy between States accepting the human rights commitments arising from the American Declaration and the American Convention as a voluntary act and the duty to abide by the decisions of the Commission and the Court according to the nature of each organ and the terms of adherence by that State to those human rights instruments.

Taking into account the consensual nature of the international system and the standing obligations of States under inter-American human rights law, proposals for improving the work of the Commission contained in this chapter are made while also recognizing that, in order to have an impact on the protection of victims, State compliance with the decisions of the Commission is essential. In what follows, three proposals are put forward to improve the work of the Commission: strengthening national capacities (section 3), advancing standards through the selection of cases to remedy structural situations (section 4), and promoting compliance with the decisions of the Commission (section 5).

3. Strengthening National Capacities

We must proceed from two basic assumptions. First, States have the primary obligation to respect fundamental rights and freedoms and ensure their free and full exercise to all persons under their jurisdiction. Second, the Inter-American System has a subsidiary role and complements national judicial systems. The interplay between national systems and the Inter-American System provides victims with the widest degree of protection. The Court has long prescribed the obligation of States to establish their jurisdiction over human rights violations and reaffirmed the principle of complementarity. In the case of *Andrade Salmon v. Bolivia*, the Court affirmed:

> [T]he Inter-American human rights system consists of a national level, through which each State must guarantee the rights and freedoms provided for in the Convention and investigate and, where appropriate, try and punish the offences that are committed; and that if a specific case is not resolved at the domestic or national stage, the Convention provides for an international level in which the main organs are the Commission and the Court.[10]

In addition, the Court has also indicated "that when a matter has been resolved in the domestic order, according to the clauses of the Convention, it is not necessary to bring it before the Inter-American Court for its approval or confirmation."[11]

Each State should have the necessary legislation in place and the competent authorities to respect and ensure the full exercise of the rights and freedoms recognized in their constitutions and by international human rights law. As per Article 2 of the American Convention, States parties are to adopt such legislative or other measures necessary to give effect to those rights or freedoms. In order to afford the highest level of protection, national legislation should be drafted in accordance with the highest international standards. In fact, a number of countries in Latin America have given constitutional hierarchy to norms of international human rights in order to guarantee that laws and regulations, and the acts derived thereof, are consistent with those international standards.

The strengthening of national capacities should follow a two-prong approach. On the one hand, States have a duty to improve their normative framework and judicial systems in order to comply with their primary obligation to respect and ensure the full enjoyment of human rights. On the other hand, the obligations derived from the decisions of the Commission and the judgments of the Court have the effect of harmonizing policies and laws to meet international standards. Strong national systems with laws, regulations, and institutions within democratic societies prevent violations of human rights. In turn, when violations occur, those national systems have a greater capacity to remedy grievances. The adherence of national legal and institutional frameworks to inter-American standards is fundamental for a case to be concluded at the national level. Recourse to the Commission can only be by exception.

---

[10] *Andrade Salmón v. Bolivia* [2016], IACtHR, Ser. C No. 330, para. 92 (author's translation).
[11] Ibid.

The core of the system of petitions and cases is its complementarity. It is triggered when remedies at the national level have been exhausted in accordance with a general rule of international law contained in the American Convention. Only those cases that are likely to characterize a violation of rights contained in the instruments under the competence of the Commission would be admitted for consideration.[12] The purpose of the Inter-American System is not to provide a judicial review; it is not at the cassation level of a complaint. As the system of petitions and cases has the sole purpose of establishing a State's international responsibility for violations of Inter-American instruments, its complementarity means that its decisions and recommendations are aimed at correcting the wrongs not fully repaired at the national level. Once international responsibility is established, the State in question should repair those violations within the framework of its national laws and procedures. At the compliance level, the concerned State must internalize the decision or judgment.

As a consequence of the nature and functioning of the Inter-American System, it is in the best interest of victims to find protection at the national level, as the system of petitions and cases inevitably delays the reparation due to the victim. As explained in the next section, the number of cases in the Commission's docket makes the process long and, sometimes, cumbersome. Moreover, compliance with the Commission's decisions or the Court's judgments requires the activation of follow-up mechanisms, which in turn require additional efforts that prolong satisfactory reparation.

However, the need to strengthen national capacities to implement human rights focused public policies that generate concrete impacts for the enjoyment and exercise of human rights and effective means of reparation is a persistent hemispheric challenge. The Commission has played a vital role in promoting the adoption of constitutional reforms, laws, and public policies with a focus on human rights in accordance with inter-American standards. Its recommendations have led States to eliminate discriminatory laws, policies, and practices to provide reparations to victims, to prevent the repetition of human rights violations, and to strengthen their protection.

One of the main activities of the Commission is to promote knowledge and the implementation of inter-American standards in normative frameworks, national instruments for the protection of human rights, and in the formulation of public policies. In the present moment, strengthening national capabilities constitutes the basis for the realization of rights. Therefore, it is in the interest of the Commission to contribute proactively to the development of the sorts of objective conditions inside States that are conducive to transforming inter-American standards into concrete reality.

---

[12] Art. 34 American Convention on Human Rights.

The Commission has taken the responsibility for promoting the strengthening of national capabilities in Strategic Objective 3 (SO3) of its Strategic Plan 2017-2021.[13] SO3 aims to promote democracy, human dignity, equality, justice, and fundamental freedoms based on an active strengthening of State institutions and public policies with a human rights approach, in accordance with inter-American norms and standards, and to develop the capacities of social and academic organizations and networks to act in defense of human rights. In order to implement SO3, the Commission has developed a range of specific programs, including training and promoting human rights focused ideas and cultures; collaborating with Central American and Caribbean States; technical cooperation on institutionality and public policies with a human rights approach; and programs on social participation, as well as contributing to the capacity-building of social and academic organizations and networks acting in defense of human rights.

Over a five-year period, the Commission has implemented various actions to implement SO3 programs. The deployment of technical assistance has included training stakeholders, technical assistance for drafting bills, and supporting the development of public policies and preparing thematic reports on various topics that contain guidelines on inter-American standards.

As the Strategic Plan 2017-2021 comes to an end, the Commission must assess its achievements and the opportunities that exist to continue strengthening national capacities. In order to work more intensively on strengthening national capacities, future efforts of the Commission should address the issue of reaching out more actively to a larger number of actors. The common goal should be the internalization of inter-American standards in national laws and their dissemination among national autonomous institutions, legislators, and justice operators for their application in the performance of their duties.

One possibility could be the development of inter-American networks of national autonomous institutions directly involved in the defense and protection of human rights. These networks would then promote inter-American standards and liaise with the Commission. In previous paragraphs, we have highlighted the responsibilities of States to protect and respect rights and freedoms and to ensure their free and full exercise. Within each State there are actors who play a major role in the national justice system by means of defending or representing victims. As part of their work, they promote inter-American standards and compel national authorities to abide by those norms. Within this group, national human rights institutions (ombudspersons), national mechanisms for the prevention

---

[13] IACHR, "Strategic Plan 2017-2021," April 28, 2017, <https://www.oas.org/en/iachr/media_center/PReleases/2017/054.asp> (accessed November 19, 2021).

of torture, and public defenders, among others, have developed a general practice to promote the highest international standards in their defense work. The Commission could support those national actors by creating inter-American networks. These kinds of networks could be the basis for coordinating activities among their members, including the exchange of best practices, the development of common methodologies of work, the training of personnel, and the dissemination of inter-American standards. The ultimate purpose would be to support these national actors, whose work in the pursuance of justice has the effect of strengthening national capacities.

A second possibility is to develop cooperation programs with selected countries or regions. The Strategic Plan 2017–2021 established a cooperation program with Central America and the Caribbean. The program has achieved meaningful results in matters relating to monitoring and capacity-building. However, the Commission must intensify the promotion of these activities if it wants to have a greater impact, especially in countries with specific needs. Chapter 4.B of the Commission's Annual Report provides a general assessment of progress and challenges for each country in the region. This evaluation of the state of human rights in the region allows the Commission to identify specific areas to be jointly addressed with countries.

As part of this proposal for extended cooperation, the Commission could start working closer with key actors, including legislators and justice operators, for a broader dissemination of inter-American standards. Within this group, it is possible to identify parliamentary advisers, prosecutors, judges, and councils of the magistracy, among others. This would entail developing country-strategies to identify actors and subjects of work. Those strategies should aim at providing technical assistance in two aspects: first, by supporting legislative work that elaborates laws and regulations implementing inter-American standards, and second, by joining national efforts for training justice operators in the interpretation of those international standards. The combination of legislative and judicial technical assistance will have the effect of directly promoting the highest levels of protection to be afforded by national authorities, which in turn will allow an effective prevention of human rights violations and adequate reparation in cases of infringement.

As established previously, the second prong in the interplay between national systems and the Inter-American System has to do with the internationalization of decisions of the Commission and judgments of the Court with the effect of harmonizing national legal frameworks with international standards. Thus, the Inter-American System has an overarching impact stemming from single complaints that are brought into the system of petitions and cases. The following sections deal with proposals to advance the impact of cases in strengthening national capacities.

4. Advancing Standards through the Selection of Cases to Remedy Structural Situations

Despite the influence that the Inter-American System has had on the region in promoting the highest standards of protection, the Commission's continued impact and effectiveness faces significant challenges. One of the weaknesses of the Commission has been the longstanding procedural backlog. This backlog is explained by the increasing number of petitions and the limited resources available to the Commission to face the procedural burden. As reported in detail in the 2020 Annual Report,[14] the number of petitions lodged with the Commission has exponentially increased in recent years. Last year the Commission received 1,990 petitions.[15] The case backlog has resulted in significant delays. Once a petition is filed, the average time for an admissibility report is seven years, and the average time for a merits report is twelve years and seven months.

To address this situation, the Strategic Plan 2017–2021 established as one of its objectives the Special Procedural Delay Reduction Program. Before the adoption of the Strategic Plan, the Commission approved sixteen merits reports in 2016. Thereafter, there has been a gradual increase. In 2017, the number increased to thirty-five merits reports; in 2018, forty-three reports were adopted, in 2019 the Commission approved a total of forty-seven, and in 2020, sixty-seven reports were adopted.[16] The result is a 400 percent increase in merits reports compared to the reports adopted in 2016. With regard to cases referred to the Court, the number has also increased. In 2016, sixteen cases were sent to the Court; in 2017, there were seventeen cases; in 2018, eighteen cases, in 2019, thirty-two cases, and in 2020, twenty-three cases. This translates into a 100 percent increase compared to 2016. These numbers are a positive sign that the procedural backlog is declining. However, the Commission still maintains a substantive docket. The 2020 Annual Report presents a portfolio of 3,089 petitions and cases. At the end of 2020, there were 1,685 petitions at the admissibility stage, and 1,404 cases at the merits stage.[17]

The system of petitions and cases has given the Inter-American System its most representative feature. Therefore, the procedural burden must be tackled quantitatively, in order to attend to all those who have approached the system seeking redress, and qualitatively, in order to continue generating standards that guide the action of States. Addressing the significant number of cases, both quantitatively and qualitatively, raises a dilemma. Should the Commission continue taking action on all petitions that meet the admissibility requirements provided

---

[14] IACHR, "Annual Report 2020."
[15] IACHR, "Annual Report 2020," para. 14.
[16] IACHR, "Annual Report 2020," para. 30.
[17] IACHR, "Annual Report 2020," paras. 217–218.

in the Convention and its Rules of Procedure or should it instead adopt admissibility criteria in order to address paradigmatic cases that will produce structural changes in States?

Under the first option, petitions would follow the current procedure as established in the Commission's instruments. The Executive Secretariat of the Commission would continue to study and process petitions that fulfill the requirements set forth in Article 28 of the Rules of Procedure—mostly the provision of certain information, including the alleged violation of any of the human rights recognized in the American Convention and other applicable instruments. Once the petition has been lodged, the Commission would take the decision on its admissibility at a later stage and, if applicable, on the merits. Timely and efficient reparations to victims would depend on the extent to which the Commission has significantly reduced the case backlog. Undoubtedly, the advantage of this option is to keep the System open to any cases that involve alleged violations of the American Convention and other inter-American human rights instruments. The downside is that cases that would likely have an impact on remedying structural deficiencies in national legal systems would not be prioritized.

Under the second option, the Commission would have to adopt admissibility criteria to prioritize cases that may have an impact in addressing structural impairments to the enjoyment of human rights in a given State. This option would have the advantage of speeding up decisions with an impact both on reparations to victims of violations and on strengthening national capacities via structural recommendations. The downside of this option is that petitions that have been lodged before the Commission in recent years would receive limited attention. In addition, this option would establish additional criteria for admissibility, which would also require an amendment to the Rules of Procedure. Any such amendment entails a complex process of negotiation and requires a wide consultation to take into account the views of all interested parties. Therefore, amendments to the Rules of Procedures are possible only in exceptional circumstances.

A proposal for improving the current situation may address this in two simultaneous ways. On the one hand, the Commission must make additional progress in reducing the existing case backlog. The Special Procedural Delay Reduction Program should continue its implementation. On the other hand, the Commission should pay special attention to cases with a higher severity threshold and that are paradigmatic for the development of inter-American standards. A possible solution would be to make more frequent use of criteria contained in Article 29(d) of the Regulation in order to expedite the evaluation of a petition during the initial processing stage in the following situations: when the decision could have the effect of remedying serious structural situations that have an impact on the enjoyment of human rights, or when the decision could promote changes in legislation or State practices and avoid receiving multiple petitions on the same matter.

The Commission should continue exploring other ways, in consultation with States and civil societies, to achieve a greater impact and efficiency in its system of petitions and cases. For instance, a possible way to advance cases to remedy structural issues could be to extend criteria for the expedited study and initial processing of petitions currently contained in Article 28 of the Rules of Procedure to the admissibility and merits stages. However, this action would require an amendment of the Commission's Rules of Procedure, entailing the aforementioned complexities.

In the end, the Commission needs to engage in deep reflection and embark on a wide consultation process on measures to advance cases with an impact in remedying structural situations. As stated throughout this chapter, the Inter-American System of cases and petitions has contributed to the development of standards not only to repair violations of human rights committed against individuals but to avoid the repetition of violations. The challenge the Commission is facing is to continue to have an impact in strengthening national capacities without losing its transformative character due to its case backlog. It is imperative, therefore, that the Commission starts a dialogue on how to advance cases that may contribute to remedying structural situations.

5. Promoting Compliance with the Decisions of the Commission

As with any other human rights body, a State has to comply with the Commission's decisions in order for victims to be protected. The effectiveness of the IAHRS is largely based on States complying with the decisions of the Commission and the judgments of the Court. Both bodies have implemented their own monitoring mechanisms. Although the duty to comply with the decisions and judgments of the Commission and the Court is fully established, the cooperation of States is determinant. It is not sufficient to exhaust proceedings at the level of the two organs to repair the victims. A significant number of measures remain unfulfilled, and in various cases compliance processes take considerable time. This situation is extremely worrisome because the effectiveness of the System is placed in question when a victim's rights are not restored in a satisfactory and timely manner. The general objective of the Strategic Plan 2017–2021 is "to stimulate the effectiveness of the Inter-American Human Rights System as a pillar and common commitment of the Americas."

At times, State structures are complex and compliance with decisions depends on several domestic actors. Federal States pose a special challenge as international responsibilities may arise from different levels of government and the federal authorities must embark on internal procedures to respond to the Commission's requests. However, it is an established rule of international law that the conditions within a State do not exempt it from fulfilling its international obligations.[18]

The Commission resorts to various tools to obtain compliance with its decisions. Public hearings or private working meetings in the framework of its periods of sessions are used to make a situation visible and to present recommendations to the parties that might encourage compliance. In such meetings, members of the Commission meet with concerned parties to review compliance levels with precautionary measures, merits reports, and friendly settlement agreements. In addition, other measures are being taken to buttress compliance. For example, the Commission has made progress in the systematization of its recommendations and the development of special follow-up mechanisms to move State authorities to give effect to their decisions. One landmark has been the recent launching of the Inter-American System to Monitor Recommendations, also known by its acronym in Spanish as the Inter-American SIMORE.[19] The Inter-American SIMORE is an online tool that systematically collects all recommendations made by the IACHR through its various mechanisms. In particular, it is a platform to exchange and receive information concerning efforts to monitor the Commission's recommendations.

The Inter-American SIMORE plays two main roles. First, it enables users to conduct specialized searches for various recommendations, such as published merits reports, friendly settlement agreements, country reports, resolutions, and recommendations of the Commission's Annual Reports. At the same time, it also gives registered users the opportunity to submit information concerning efforts to monitor the recommendations made by the IACHR in the user's country and thematic reports and its resolutions. The Inter-American SIMORE will be an essential tool to support the work of the Impact Observatory of the IACHR. The Observatory is a platform established by the Commission by Resolution 02/19 of September 22, 2019 with the objective of reflecting, systematizing, and making visible the impact of its actions in the defense and protection of human rights in the region and in collaboration with States, civil society organizations, international organizations, and academia.[20] The Commission has also developed special mechanisms to follow up its recommendations, namely, MESENI (Nicaragua), MESA for the *Ayotzinapa* case (Mexico), and MESEVE

---

[18] Art. 27 Vienna Convention.

[19] See IACHR Press Release 132/20, "Inter-American SIMORE," June 10, 2020, <https://www.oas.org/en/iachr/media_center/PReleases/2020/132.asp> (accessed November 15, 2021).

[20] IACHR, "Impact Observatory," Resolution 02/19, <https://www.oas.org/en/iachr/decisions/pdf/Resolution-2-19-en.pdf> (accessed November 15, 2021).

(Venezuela). The purpose of these special mechanisms is to closely monitor the situation in those countries so as to make recommendations both focused and timely. In addition, the Commission and the government of Honduras established a collaborative mechanism to provide technical assistance to implement the recommendations made by the Commission in its country report of 2019.[21]

However, the Commission must make additional efforts. Notwithstanding that the Commission's recommendations are contained in various instruments now systematized in the Inter-American SIMORE, emphasis must be placed on the system of petitions and cases—due to its transformative impact. Some proposals to obtain a higher degree of compliance could include a revision to the contents of the recommendations, a more strategic use of the Court, and a greater political dialogue with States and petitioners.

With regard to the contents of the recommendations, the Commission has a duty to apply the concept of integral reparation, as developed by the Inter-American System. The concept of integral reparation, derived from Article 63.1 of the American Convention, includes the accreditation of damages in the material and immaterial sphere and the granting of measures such as the investigation of the facts; the restitution of rights, goods, and liberties; physical, psychological, or social rehabilitation; satisfaction, through acts for the benefit of the victims; guarantees of nonrepetition; and compensation for material and nonpecuniary damage. The measures for integral reparation are contained in the merits reports issued by the Commission in accordance with Article 50 of the American Convention. Redressing human rights violations depends on adequate reparation. Therefore, the recommendations in the merits reports must ascertain that measures are ordered in relation to the damage infringed upon the victim. In order for these recommendations to be effectively complied with, they must be drafted in clear and precise wording that indicates the measure to be implemented. Finally, the recommendation must be measurable and subject to follow-up procedures.

In the case of States that recognize the contentious jurisdiction of the Court, the Commission will always be able to initiate a procedure when States do not comply with the recommendations contained in the merits report and victims express their consent to proceed in that way. The Rules of Procedure of the Commission prescribe a presumption in favor of sending cases to the Court when the State has not complied with the recommendations. Article 45 of the Rules of Procedure establishes that if the State in question has accepted the jurisdiction of the Court and the Commission believes the State has not complied with the recommendations of the merits report, it shall refer the case to the Court,

---

[21] IACHR, "Situation of Human Rights in Honduras," August 27, 2019, OEA/Ser.L/V/II. Doc. 146, <https://www.oas.org/es/cidh/informes/pdfs/Honduras2019.pdf> (accessed November 15, 2021).

unless there is a reasoned decision by an absolute majority of the members of the Commission to the contrary. In addition, at the request of the State concerned, Article 46 permits the Commission to consider suspending the three-month time limit for cases to be referred to the Court, as established in Article 51.1 of the American Convention, so long as the State demonstrates that it is willing and able to implement the recommendations included in the merits report through the adoption of concrete and adequate measures of compliance. To this end, the Commission may take into account several factors, most importantly the position of the petitioner.

Referrals to the Court have a powerful impact on reparations of human rights violations and on the development of inter-American standards, especially for structural remedies. Before taking that decision, the letter and spirit of the Convention and the Rules of Procedure require the Commission to take measures to obtain compliance with recommendations contained in the merits reports. Thus, the Commission is entrusted with the difficult decision of determining whether the merits reports has been complied with; if the Commission decides that compliance has not occurred, then the case has to be sent to the Court. Article 46.2 of the Rules of Procedure provides several factors, among others, to be taken into account during the referral decision: (1) the position of the petitioner, (2) the nature and seriousness of the violation, (3) the need to develop or clarify the case law of the System, and (4) the future effect of the decision within the legal systems of member States. It is in the interest of victims to obtain full satisfaction and a duty of the Commission to obtain compliance with its merits report. The possibility of a referral to the Court serves as leverage to that purpose. However, the Commission has to make all efforts to fulfill its mandate. There could be situations where the Commission sees no possibility of fulfillment and a referral to the Court is the only possibility. Nevertheless, other cases might be better resolved at the level of the Commission, for instance, when there are procedural handicaps at the Court stage. Either way, the Commission is bound to give due consideration to the position of the petitioner.

Keeping dialogic channels open with States is an important part of the Commission's work of obtaining the cooperation of States. Indeed, the Commission's practice has been to maintain a permanent dialogue with States. This dialogue is even more important when seeking compliance. In recent years, the Commission has started to convene working meetings with the parties in cases with merits reports that might be referred to the Court. These meetings have proved to be efficient at assessing the possibility of State cooperation and at determining the best ways to obtain compliance. Beyond the system of petitions and cases, political dialogue with States and civil societies is needed. Civil societies play a fundamental role in beneficially shifting a State's position. As users of the System, civil society organizations represent victims, and their legitimate expectation is to have a more efficient Inter-American System. In turn, dialogue with member States fosters a common understanding on the regional challenges to achieving the full enjoyment of human rights.

6. Concluding Remarks

Sixty years after its foundation, the Inter-American Commission on Human Rights remains the patrimony of the Americas. The Inter-American System serves as an example of a multilateral construction of norms and standards guided by the practical pursuit of having a direct impact in the lives of the men, women, and children living in the region. The Commission has largely assisted in building a common understanding of human rights values. It is in the interest of all actors involved to keep the System in force in order to contribute to the strengthening of national institutions and to protect victims of human rights violations. It is also in the interest of the Commission to continue its permanent strengthening process in order to adjust to new challenges and to update its methods of work to achieve the full enjoyment of rights and fundamental freedoms for all.

III.2
A Broader Look at the Transformative Impact of the Inter-American Court of Human Rights' Decisions

By Pablo Saavedra Alessandri

1. Introduction

A fascinating feature of the Inter-American Court of Human Rights (the Court, or IACtHR) is how it can produce a truly transformative impact on the protection of human rights in the Americas,[1] despite its operating budget's constraints,[2] and the low number of cases presented before[3] and resolved by[4] the Court annually.[5]

The IACtHR issues decisions with a high degree of impact and relevance that we might call transformative decisions. The IACtHR decisions' impact and

---

[1] See Armin von Bogdandy et al. (eds.), *Transformative Constitutionalism in Latin America, The Emergence of a New Ius Commune* (Oxford 2017). Armin von Bogdandy, Mariela Morales Antionazzi, and Eduardo Ferrer Mac-Gregor (eds.), *Ius Constitutional Common* (Institute for Constitutional Studies of the State of Queretaro 2017). Javier García Roca and Encarna Carmona Cuenca (eds.), *Towards a Globalization of the Dertechos. The Impact of the Sentecias of the European Court and the Inter-American Court* (Thomson Reuters Arazandi 2017). Edgar Corzo Sosa, Jorge Ulysses Carmona Tinoc, and Pablo Saavedra Alessandri (eds.), *Impact of the Judgments of the Inter-American Court of Human Rights* (Tirant 2011). Javier García Roca et al. (eds.) *The Dialogue between the European and American Systems of Human Rights* (Thomson Reuters 2012).

[2] At its Forty-ninth Ordinary Session held on September 26, 2019, in Medellin, Colombia, the General Assembly of the Organization of American States (OAS) approved a US$ 5,296,100 budget for the IACtHR in 2020. Additionally, the IACtHR receives voluntary contribution from OAS member States and other actors throughout international cooperation. See IACtHR, "Annual Report 2019," 152–158, <https://www.corteidh.or.cr/docs/informe2019/espanol.pdf> (accessed February 5, 2022).

[3] In 2005, only 10 cases were brought to the IACtHR. However, after this date the number of cases began to increase (14 cases in 2006 and 2007, 9 cases in 2008, 12 cases in 2009, 16 cases in 2010 with, 23 cases in 2011, 12 cases in 2012, 11 cases in 2013, 12 cases in 2012, 11 cases in 2013, 19 cases in 2014, 19 cases in 2015, 14 cases in 2015, 16 cases in 2016, 2017, and 2018, and 32 cases in 2019. See IACtHR, "2019 Annual Report," 46, <https://www.corteidh.or.cr/docs/informe2019/espanol.pdf> (accessed February 5, 2022).

[4] The IACtHR issued 9 sentences of preliminary exceptions, merits, and reparations in the year 2010. In 2011, the Court issued 18 sentences; 21 in 2012; 16 in 2013; 16 in 2014; 18 in 2015; 21 in 2016; 14 in 2017; 28 in 2018; and 25 in 2019.

[5] I would like to thank Attorney Elizabeth Jiménez Mora for her support and comments in preparing this chapter.

transcendence can be seen from the perspective of the victims[6] and from the transformation of social reality stance. Thus, the Inter-American Court, on the one hand, provides a window of hope for victims of human rights violations in their quest for justice, truth, and reparation, and, on the other, it is a conduit to drive structural changes in spaces where human rights are not yet effectively guaranteed or a barrier to avoid human rights setbacks is not yet in place.

It is important to pause briefly to explain three different but concatenated concepts: (1) compliance and implementation of a judicial decision, (2) its impact, and (3) its significance.

According to the IACtHR rules and procedures, compliance and implementation are assessed by the Court's supervision and monitoring procedures which evaluates the concrete measures adopted by the State to comply with the set of reparations ordered by the Court in its judgment.[7] In this chapter, I analyze questions such as what are the mechanisms or institutional tools that the Inter-American Court has to supervise its sentences. How do these institutional mechanisms operate? Are these mechanisms effective? How does a State comply with the reparations that were ordered? Are the State bodies in charge of enforcing each of the reparations that were ordered? Are there internal mechanisms in the States to comply with reparations? How long does it take for a State to comply with reparations? What happens if a State does not comply with a sentence? What role do the victims play in the implementation and compliance with the decisions? Can other external actors help to comply with the judgments of the Inter-American Court? How is the interaction between victims and the State regarding compliance? What are the obstacles and resistances to achieving effective compliance with decisions?[8]

When we talk about the impact of a judgment, we have generally focused on a structural change perspective that focuses on the changes it may bring to the interior of a State. These changes are normally conveyed through guarantee of nonrepetition measures ordered by the Court to prevent facts similar to those known to the Court from happening again.[9] It is important to draw attention

---

[6] Carlos Martin Beristain, *Dialogues on Repair. Experiences in the Inter-American Human Rights System* (Inter-American Institute for Human Rights 2008), Tome I and Vol. II.

[7] The Sentence Compliance Oversight Unit within the IACtHR Secretariat assesses the compliance of each measure of redress that the Court ordered in its final judgment by conducting strict scrutiny of the execution of its various components, as well as for reparations to materialize with respect to each of the victims benefiting from the measures, with most cases being multiple victims. IACtHR, "2019 Annual Report," <https://www.corteidh.or.cr/docs/informe2019/espanol.pdf> (accessed February 5, 2022).

[8] IACtHR, "Learn About Oversight Compliance with Judgment," official website, available at <https://www.corteidh.or.cr/conozca_la_supervision.cfm> (accessed February 5, 2022). IACtHR, "Sentencing Compliance Supervision" (official website), <https://www.corteidh.or.cr/supervision.cfm?lang=es> (accessed February 5, 2022).

[9] Pablo Saavedra Alessandri, Guillem Cano Palomares, and Mario Hernández Ramos, "Repair and Supervision of Sentecias," in Javier García Roca and Encarna Carmona Cuenca (eds.), *Towards a Globalization of the Dertechos. The Impact of the Sentecias of the European Court and the*

to the fact that so far the literature has only analyzed the transformative impact through judgments arising from contention cases, leaving aside whether the other jurisdictional functions of the Inter-American Court, such as advisory opinions and provisional measures, may also have a transformative impact, as well as avoid structural setbacks in the effective protection of human rights on a given social reality.

Finally, I do not refer to the "significance" of a decision as the fulfillment of reparations or structural impact, but taking into account the knowledge, acceptance, and empowerment that a decision provokes in the different social actors according to their interests or communities of practice. Knowledge, acceptance, and empowerment become the necessary engine to drive changes in social reality or to prevent setbacks against the exercise and enjoyment of human rights. Acceptance and empowerment occur through the dissemination of judicial activity and the creation of spaces for dialogue and interaction with different social actors.

In this chapter, we would like to expand the concept of structural impact to include advisory opinions and provisional measures in its analysis, in addition to contention cases. We will first take up the concept of structural impact of the IACHR's judgments through nonrepetition guarantees from two recent cases of different natures and include a brief reflection on whether other forms of reparation could have had similar impact. Secondly, we will look at the Court's advisory role and look at one of its last rulings, which clearly illustrates the transformative impact on social reality that advisory opinions can have. Finally, we will look at provisional measures and see how they can aid preventing structural setbacks or providing structural protection to certain groups.

2. Structural Impact of Contention Cases

2.1. General Considerations about Reparations

The Inter-American Court of Human Rights is the international court that has developed and deepened the most on the right to comprehensive reparation for victims of human rights violations.[10] In its jurisprudence, comprehensive

---

Inter-American Court (Thomson Reuters Arazandi 2017). Victor Abramovich, "From mass violations to structural patterns. New approaches and classic tensions in the Inter-American System" [2009] 63 *Journal of the Faculty of Law of the Pontifical Catholic University of Peru* 95,138.

[10] Sergio García Ramírez and Marcela Benavides Hernández, *Reparations for Human Rights Violations. Inter-American Jurisprudence* (Ed. Porrúa 2014). Carlos Martin Beristain, "Dialogues on Repair. Experiences in the Inter-American Human Rights System" [2008] 1 *Inter-American Institute for Human Rights*. Andrés Javier Rousset Siri, "The concept of comprehensive reparation

reparation has various manifestations, depending on the nature of the case and the dimension of the damage it seeks to repair. We could classify or regroup reparations in six categories: compensation, restitution, rehabilitation, satisfaction, investigation of the facts and sanction when appropriate, and guarantees of nonrepetition. In turn, each of the categories of reparation can have a range of modalities, depending on the violations declared by the Court and their consequences.

With regard to guarantees of nonrepetition, the Court may order a State to adopt legislative reforms, public policies, or change of practices in cases where the legal rule or absence thereof, the implemented public policy or its deficit, the existing practice or the absence thereof were the ones that served as the basis for the violation generated.[11]

The reparation that entails regulatory change, such as the adoption of public policies or change of practice, seeks to ensure that a structural failure that allowed or served as the basis for the violation and consequently the international responsibility of the State is transformed or disjointed in order to prevent acts of the same nature from happening again in order to effectively guarantee the enjoyment of the rights and freedoms protected in the American Convention. This type of reparation necessarily has a public scope or impact and is aimed at solving structural problems by benefiting not only victims of the case but also other members and groups of society. That is to say, they have general effects and in turn acquire a dimension of prevention.[12]

In multiple cases, the Court has ordered the adoption of nonrepetition guarantees that have resulted in structural reforms. This has happened, for example with the reform of Chile's Political Constitution on freedom of expression so that film censorship was eliminated and changed to a cinematic rating regime;[13] the declaration of invalidity and lack of legal effects of Peru's amnesty

---

in the jurisprudence of the Inter-American Court of Human Rights" [2011] 1 *International Journal of Human Rights*. Laurence Burgorgue-Larsen (coord.), *Human rights in context in Latin America. The Impact of the Inter-American Human Rights System on States Parties (Colombia, Ecuador, Haiti, Mexico, Nicaragua, Peru, Dominican Republic, Uruguay and Venezuela)* (Tirant lo Blanch 2016).

[11] Principle 23. Non-repetition guarantees should include, as appropriate, all or part of the following measures, which will also contribute to the prevention of events similar to those that caused the violation. See United Nations Organization, "Basic principles and guidelines on the right of victims of manifest violations of international human rights standards and serious violations of international humanitarian law to bring appeals and obtain reparations," Resolution 60/147, December 16, 2005.

[12] Pablo Saavedra Alessandri, Guillem Cano Palomares, and Mario Hernández Ramos, "Repair and Supervision of Sentecias," in Javier García Roca and Encarna Carmona Cuenca (eds.), *Towards a Globalization of the Dertechos. The Impact of the Sentecias of the European Court and the Inter-American Court* (Thomson Reuters Arazandi 2017).

[13] Case *"The Last Temptation of Christ" (Olmedo Bustos and others) v. Chile* [2001] IACtHR, Ser. C No. 73.

laws; the adequacy of terrorist legislation from both a procedural and substantive perspective; ensured access to issues of public interest through the establishment of a procedure for this purpose in Chile; creation of an effective mechanism for demarcation and reclamation of ancestral lands of indigenous communities in Nicaragua; legislative reforms to ensure the right to appeal a criminal ruling in Costa Rica; restricting military jurisdiction for cases of human rights violations in Mexico; criminalization of the crime of enforced disappearance in Bolivia; modification of the provision of the penal code that refers to the concept of danger of the agent in relation to the crime of murder in Guatemala; establishment of a simple judicial remedy to control the decisions of the highest electoral body affecting human rights in Mexico; restriction of military service for minors in Paraguay; leaving the amnesty law in El Salvador, a reform on the regulations of insult and slander in Argentina; and non-imposition of the mandatory death penalty in Barbados.[14]

I would like to dwell on two sentences of a very different nature and relatively recent enforcement that show the transforming impact of the IACHR's judgments on the social realities of countries.

2.2. Authorization and Access to In Vitro Fertilization— Transforming the Hope of Having Children

The case *of Artavia Murillo and Others ("In Vitro Fertilization") v. Costa Rica* originated from a decision issued by the Constitutional Chamber of the Supreme Court of Justice in 2000 when it declared unconstitutional the decree regulating the technique of in vitro fertilization (IVF) and therefore prohibiting the practice of IVF in Costa Rica. The IACHR found[15] that the State was internationally responsible for violating, among others, the rights to private and family life and

---

[14] *Case Barrios Altos v. Peru* [2001] IACtHR, Ser. C No. 75. *La Cantuta v. Peru case* [2006] IACtHR, Ser. C No. 162; *Case Norín Catrimán and others (Leaders, Members and Activist of the Mapuche Indigenous People) v. Chile.* [2014] IACtHR, Ser. C No. 279; *Case Claude Reyes and others v. Chile* [2006] IACtHR, Ser. C No. 151; *Mayagna Community (Sumo) Awas Tingni v. Nicaragua* [2001] IACtHR, Ser. C No. 79; *Herrera Ulloa v. Costa Rica case. Preliminary Exceptions, Fund, Repairs and Costs* [2004] IACtHR, Ser. C No. 107; *Case Radilla Pacheco v. Mexico* [2009] IACtHR, Ser. C No. 209. *Case Fernández Ortega and Others v. Mexico.* [2010] IACtHR, Ser. C No. 215. *Rosendo Cantú case and another v. Mexico.* [2010] IACtHR, Ser. C No. 216; *Trujillo Oroza v. Bolivia case* [2000] IACtHR, Ser. C No. 64; *Fermín Ramírez v. Guatemala case* [2005] IACtHR, Ser. C No. 126; *Castañeda Gutman v. Mexico case* [2008] IACtHR, Ser. C No. 184; *Case Vargas Areco v. Paraguay* [2006] IACtHR, Ser. C No. 155; *Case Massacres of El Mozote and surrounding places v. El Salvador* [2012] IACtHR, Ser. C No. 252; *Kimel v. Argentina case* [2008] IACtHR, Ser. C No. 177; *DaCosta Cadogan v. Barbados case* [2009] IACtHR, Ser. C No. 204. *Boyce case and others v. Barbados* [2007] IACtHR, Ser. C No. 169.

[15] Judgment No. 2000-02306 of March 15, 2000 issued by the Constitutional Chamber of the Supreme Court of Justice, File No. 95-001734-007-CO.

sexual health, as well as the principle of equality and nondiscrimination to the detriment of eighteen people.[16]

As a result, the Court ordered that Costa Rica, among other reparations: (a) take measures to stop the prohibition of IVF practices and ensure that people who wish to have access to that reproduction technique do so without encountering impediments to the exercise of their rights; (b) regulate the implementation of IVF and establish inspection and quality control systems of qualified institutions or professionals developing this type of technique; c) include IVF within infertility programs and treatments in its health service.[17]

Costa Rica initially terminated the IVF ban and subjected its implementation to the approval of a law from the Legislative Assembly. At least three bills had been presented, and none had made progress in the corresponding legislative procedures. At the same time, representatives of the victims and other persons interested in accessing the IVF technique filed various appeals for amparo before the Supreme Court to annul the prohibition, so that the judgment of the Inter-American Court would be complied with. These remedies were rejected, it was argued, among other reasons, that it was not up to the Supreme Court to "order the execution" of the judgments of the Inter-American Court or to "supply the supervision of compliance with them."[18]

As no progress had been made in complying with these reparations, the Court convened a public Compliance Oversight hearing. At that hearing, the State represented by its executive branch reported that it had drawn up a draft executive decree authorizing and regulating IVF in order to comply with the

---

[16] *Case Artavia Murillo and Others (Fecundation in Vitro) v. Costa Rica* [2012] IACtHR, Ser. C No. 257.

[17] *Case Artavia Murillo and Others (Fecundation in Vitro) v. Costa Rica* [2016] IACtHR, Sentencing Compliance Supervision. Resolution of the Inter-American Court of Human Rights of February 26, 2016, 114, 115.

[18] The three bills were: (1) No. 18,057 "Law on Fertilization *in vitro* and transfer of fertilized eggs"; (2) No. 18.738 "Law on In Vitro Fertilization and Embryonic Transfer"; and (3) No. 18.824 "In Vitro Fertilization Framework Law." Both representatives of the victims filed amparo appeals in 2013. "Representative Boris Molina filed two appeals for protection on behalf of twelve of the eighteen victims of the present case, for the 'non-compliance' of the judgment issued by the Inter-American Court. In addition, that representative brought another appeal for protection on behalf of two other persons who are not victims of[l] case but who 'suffer infertility and given their status are candidates for in vitro fertilization', and in 'against the Costa Rican Social Security Box' in order that 'the judgment of the Inter-American Court gives them that reproductive right'. Representative May Cantillano filed an appeal for 39 people who are not victims of the present case, and 'against the Ministry of Health, the Ministry of the Presidency, the Legislative Assembly and the Costa Rican Social Security Box' by the 'incumplimiento' of the Judgment issued by the Inter-American Court and in order to 'enable and respect the fundamental rights of persons suffering from infertility disease.'" Cfr. Case Artavia Murillo and Others (Fecundation in Vitro) v. Costa Rica [2016] IACtHR, Sentencing Compliance Supervision. Resolution of the Inter-American Court of Human Rights of February 26, 2016; Judgment No. 69-2014 issued by the Constitutional Chamber on January 7, 2014; judgment No. 2014-001424 issued by the Constitutional Chamber on January 1, 2014; judgment No. 2014-02413 issued by the Constitutional Chamber on February 21, 2014, and judgment No. 2014-3968 issued by the Constitutional Chamber on March 19, 2014.

judgment. The Court welcomed this State initiative as it sought to comply with its judgment, as well as allowing and regulating the practice of IVF.[19]

A few days after the decree came into force, an unconstitutionality appeal was filed against it for the alleged " 'violation and/or threat to [the] fundamental right to life' of the 'conceived unborn', and a '[v]iolation of the principle of reserve of law' " that it represented. On February 3, 2016, the Constitutional Chamber issued its decision by majority vote, declaring the appeal of unconstitutionality valid, for violation of the principle of reservation of law. The Constitutional Chamber ordered the annulment of the decree. With this decision of the Constitutional Chamber, the prohibition of IVF was maintained, and it became an obstacle for the effective fulfillment of the judgment of the Inter-American Court.[20]

The Inter-American Court issued a Judgment Compliance Oversight decision and noted that with the decision of the Constitutional Chamber, the only specific measure taken by a State authority and body to comply with the judgment was voided. It was noted that this inaction had a negative impact "considering the passing of time without eliminating the IVF ban affected the possibility of people undergoing this treatment in Costa Rica to have biological children, mainly those who tried other treatments to deal with infertility or for those who had only that option to procreate." The Court recalled the immediate and binding effect of its rulings and noted that the IVF ban should be understood as manifestly inconsistent with the American Convention, cannot produce legal effects or constitute an impediment to the exercise of the rights protected in the Convention. As a result, it indicated that the practice of IVF should be understood as authorized in Costa Rica.[21]

The IACHR carried out an analysis of the decree and established that it was intended to comply with the judgment, and therefore positively valued the measure taken by the executive branch. Because of all of the preceding, the Inter-American Court provided that the decree be kept in force with the aim of preventing the right to access the IVF technique and compliance with its judgment from being illusory.[22] As can be seen, the IACHR gave validity[23] and revived the decree that

---

[19] Decree No. 39210-MP-S called "Authorization for the realization of the assisted reproduction technique of fertilisation in embryonic transference," issued by the President of the Republic and the Ministers of the Presidency and Health (hereinafter "the Decree"), published in the Official Journal La Gaceta No. 178, Year CXXXVII of September 11, 2015.

[20] IACtHR. *Artavia case Murillo and others (Fecunadation in Vitro) v. Costa Rica*. Sentencing Compliance Supervision. Resolution of the Inter-American Court of Human Rights of February 26, 2016, para. 18; Constitutional Chamber of the Supreme Court of Costa Rica. Resolution No. 2016-001692 issued on February 3, 2016.

[21] *Case Artavia Murillo and Others (Fecunadation in Vitro) v. Costa Rica*. Sentencing Compliance Supervision. Resolution of the Inter-American Court of Human Rights of February 26, 2016, paras. 20, 25, 26.

[22] Ibid., paras. 33, 35.

[23] Ibid., para. 36.

the Constitutional Chamber had declared invalid. This measure resulted in the beginning of the practice of IVF technique in Costa Rica. The State first authorized two private establishments to implement the IVF technique. In 2019, the Ministry of Health granted qualification to the High Complexity Reproductive Medicine Unit of the Costa Rican Social Security for the realization of the practice of IVF.[24]

This sentence transformed the social reality of Costa Rican men and women and especially of those who saw IVF practice as the last hope for biological children. Now they have access to it in their own territory, until before the judgment of the IACHR they could not do so. Today dozens of children have been born in Costa Rica thanks to IVF both through the public and private health system.[25]

2.3. Ensuring Effective Recourse—Transforming Access to Justice for Those Convicted by Councils of War

The *Maldonado Vargas case and others v. Chile* originated from the Supreme Court's refusal to review the convictions issued against twelve members of the air force by the Councils of War during the military dictatorship in Chile. In 2001, the victims filed an appeal for review of the convictions handed down by the Councils of War before the Chilean Supreme Court, arguing that evidence obtained under torture in those processes had been taken into account in order to convict them.[26] The appeal was rejected. The Inter-American Court condemned the Chilean State for the violation of the right to legal protection by not providing victims with an effective remedy that would allow them to review and be able to leave without effect convictions of trials carried out by Councils of War during the military dictatorship in Chile.[27]

The Inter-American Court ordered Chile, among various measures of reparation: (a) to make available to the victims in this case an effective mechanism to review and/or annul the conviction sentences; and (b) adopt

---

[24] *Case Artavia Murillo and others (Fecundación in Vitro) and Caso Gómez Murillo and others v. Costa Rica.* Sentencing Compliance Supervision. Resolution of the Inter-American Court of Human Rights of November 22, 2019, para. 11; CCSS News, "CCSS puts at the service of the modern population 'in vitro' fertilization unit" (July 17, 2019), <https://www.ccss.sa.cr/noticias/servicios_noticia?ccss-pone-al-servicio-de-la-poblacion-moderna-unidad-de-fertilizacion-in-vitro> (accessed February 5, 2022); see *Case Artavia Murillo and others (Fecundación in Vitro) and Caso Gómez Murillo and others v. Costa Rica.* Sentencing Compliance Supervision. Resolution of the Inter-American Court of Human Rights of November 22, 2019.

[25] La Nación. "71 babies conceived 'in vitro' have been born in Costa Rica since return from IVF" (February 20, 2018), https://www.nacion.com/el-pais/salud/71-bebes-concebidos-in-vitro-han-nacido-en-costa/QBNL6C4NGVELBDN3UAR5K3M5TY/story/ (accessed February 5, 2022).

[26] *Maldonado Ordóñez v. Guatemala case* [2016] IACtHR, Ser. C No. 311.

[27] *Maldonado Vargas case and others v. Chile* [2015] IACtHR, Ser. C No. 300, para. 120.

legislative, administrative, or any other measures to make available to other persons sentenced by courts martial an effective mechanism to review and annul the convictions that were handed down in processes that could take into account evidence and/or confessions obtained under torture. The Inter-American Court gave Chile a wide margin of maneuver to seek an ideal mechanism to guarantee effective access to justice for the victims of the case, as well as for all those who had been convicted by the Council of War.[28]

The presidency created a study group to analyze the best way to comply with the Court's structural reparations.[29] The result of the study led the Judicial Prosecutor of the Supreme Court to present before it an appeal for review to nullify the judgments of the Councils of War. In October 2016, the Second Chamber of the Supreme Court annulled the indicated judgments.[30] It is interesting to note that in its decision, the Supreme Court changed its previous jurisprudence on the matter, noting that the appeal for review was the procedural route and therefore the ideal tool for those who were convicted by court-martial and want to challenge those decisions.[31]

This Supreme Court ruling clearly exemplifies a constructive dialogue between Courts (Inter-American and national) for effective protection of human rights and the important role that national courts can play in assisting in the effective enforcement of Inter-American Court's rulings.[32] Thus, the Supreme Court's reinterpretation of the grounds of origin of the review appeal allowed victims of the case to be guaranteed effective access to justice and to be able to give effect to the convictions obtained in spurious proceedings. The review appeal also became the appropriate structural mechanism for other people who had been convicted in the same circumstances.

The Second Chamber of the Supreme Court of Chile, in 2016, changed its interpretation and admitted the appeal for review, giving great weight to the judgment of the Inter-American Court as an element of conviction to configure and expand the grounds for review raised. The Supreme Court noted:

---

[28] Ibid., paras. 132, 133, 167, and 170.
[29] Ibid., para. 25.
[30] Ibid.
[31] It's an important point out that in 2011, in a similar case, Chile's Supreme Court again rejected an appeal for review brought against convictions of the War Councils, arguing at that time that the appeal could not be admitted because the occurrence or discovery of a new event or the appearance of a document to allow the recourse to be accepted under the Code of Criminal Procedure had not been verified. C*fr. Maldonado Vargas case and others v. Chile* [2015] IACtHR, Ser. C No. 300, paras. 52 and 135.
[32] Judgment issued by the Second Chamber of the Supreme Court of Chile on October 3, 2016, in the case identified with role cause No. 27, 543-2016, caratula Chilean Air Force against Bachelet and others.

> [...] attending to the content and resolution of the ruling of the Inter-American Court, is unavoidable in this case, given the mandate contained in said statement to the State of Chile, this implies that the interpretation and application of the procedural provisions that regulate the action of the revision that has been proposed, contemplated in the Code of Military Justice and in the Code of Criminal Procedure, should be carried out this time trying to adjust to the reasoned and decided by that international court, in order to protect the right to judicial protection that is considered violated by the absence of resources to review the conviction sentences handed down by the Courts of War in the process Rol No. 1-73 and, ultimately, make possible the effective and fast mechanism to review and be able to annul those sentences that said ruling provides.[...][33]

Likewise, it is important to note that the Supreme Court of Chile in its judgment recognized the fundamental role that domestic courts have, within the framework of their competences, in the compliance or implementation of the judgments of the Inter-American Court and the importance of exercising control of conventionality so as not to incur in breach of its international commitments. In this sense, it indicated:

> It should not be forgotten that, as is typical of international law, States must comply with their commitments in good faith, that is, with the will to make them effective (this principle of international law emanates from the Vienna Convention on the Law of Treaties, Article 26) and that in addition—or as a consequence of the foregoing—, non-compliance with the ruling brings with it the international responsibility of the State of Chile, in accordance with Articles 65 and 68 No. 1 of the Convention, so that all of its organs—including this Court, it goes without saying—in the scope of its powers—they must take into consideration these obligations, so as not to compromise the responsibility of the State. Thus, in the interpretation and application of the norms that deal with the review action, especially the invoked grounds for invalidation, it should not be pretended that what is at stake is not only the resolution of a specific case, but also the responsibility of the State of Chile in case of opting for a restrictive reading of human rights and, in particular, of the right to an effective and rapid mechanism to review and be able to annul the sentences handed down as a corollary of an unjust process—as will be demonstrated—by the Councils of War summoned in the process Rol N° 1-73.[34]

---

[33] Ibid. Considering eleventh.
[34] The Supreme Court of Chile pointed out that "however, it should be noted that, even if it had not been delivered in the referred ruling by the C[orte IDH] in the case 'Omar Humberto Maldonado

It is interesting to acknowledge Chile's political goodwill in complying with the sentence. The same remedy that had been denied to the victims of the case and to others in equal situations was the appropriate mechanism for complying with it and ensuring access to justice. This is a good reflection of what we could call the harmonious and constructive *pro persona* dialogue between national and international jurisdictions. This dialogue, on the one hand, transformed the grounds for the judicial review appeal and, on the other, guaranteed access to justice for a group of uniformed men.

2.4. Additional Reflections on the Transforming Impact of Contention Cases

We have so far analyzed the transformative impact of the sentences through comprehensive reparation in its dimension of guaranteeing non-repetition. It would be convenient to begin to explore, if it is necessary to broaden the concept of structural impact, to also include those symbolic reparations that in their content carry a transforming dimension of social reality through acts of various kinds. On many occasions, the Court in its judgments has ordered the creation of a monument. Through this type of symbolic reparation expressed in an artistic work, in addition to repairing the victim, it is sought to transform the citizen who is the spectator of the artistic work of those spaces and experiences that are dehumanized, collectively stigmatized, historically discriminated, and invisible and that were known to the Court. With the artistic dimension of symbolic reparation, it is sought that in the spectator citizen an awareness is created about the events or social problems that have occurred, in order that they do not happen again. The sum of these spectating citizens allows us to create new and collective imaginary spaces, of a "never again."[35]

In this chapter, I do not intend to delve deeper into this point. Nonetheless, it is necessary to state it in order to begin to reflect on the matter and to be able to

---

Vargas and others versus Chile', likewise, this Supreme Court should seek to adopt an interpretation of national procedural rules leading to the result indicated in that ruling (...). In this order, the courts have an obligation to attempt an interpretation of national standards affecting human rights that is harmonious with the international obligations of the State in this field, even if those internal rules themselves do not comply with the Convention..., to which it can be added that, in accordance with the particularities of fundamental rights in a constitutional rule of law such as ours, those rights must be interpreted according to certain criteria, and one of these, is the principle *pro person*, according to which the rule or interpretation that gives greater effectiveness to the protection of human rights should be preferred."

[35] Yolanda Sierra León (ed.), *Symbolic Repair: Jurisprudence, Singing and Fabrics* (Universidad del Externado de Colombia 2018). Carlos Martin Beristain, "Dialogues on Repair. Experiences in

understand in its real dimension, the transformations of social reality that come with the judgments of the Inter-American Court of Human Rights.

3. Consultative Opinions and Their Transformative Impact

3.1. General Considerations

The IACHR has an advisory function where it is called upon to unravel the meaning and scope of international human rights standards that are submitted for the Court's consideration.[36] The advisory function allows the Court to interpret any rule of the American Convention by virtue of being the ultimate interpreter of the American Convention[37] as well as "other treaties concerning the protection of human rights in the American States" of what is its primary object or may be parties thereof, States outside the Inter-American System.[38] In addition, the Court has noted that consultative opinions aim to "assist Member States and OAS bodies in fully and effectively complying with their international human rights obligations." We can see that consultative opinions have a dual purpose or function, on the one hand, to determine the meaning and scope of

---

the inter-American human rights system" [2008] Inter-American Institute for Human Rights, Tome 1. *Case of the "Children of the Street" (Villagrán Morales and others) v. Guatemala* [2001] IACtHR, Ser. C No. 77, para. 103. IACtHR, *Moiwana Community Case v. Suriname* [2005] IACtHR, Ser. C No. 124, para. 218. *Case of the "Mapiripán Massacre" v. Colombia* [2005] IACtHR, Ser. C No. 134, para. 315. *La Cantuta v. Peru case* [2006] IACtHR, Ser. C No. 162, para. 236. *Ticona Estrada case and others v. Bolivia* [2008] IACtHR, Ser. C No. 191, paras. 164 and 165. *Case González and others ("Campo Algodonero") v. Mexico* [2009] IACtHR, Ser. C No. 205, paras. 271 and 272. *Case of the Massacre of Las Dos Erres v. Guatemala* [2009] IACtHR, Ser. C No. 211, para. 265. *Case Radilla Pacheco v. Mexico* [2009] IACtHR, Ser. C No. 209, paras. 355 and 356. *Cepeda Vargas v. Colombia case* [2010] IACtHR, Ser. C No. 213, paras. 228 to 230; Yolanda Sierra León (ed.), *Symbolic Repair: Jurisprudence, Singing and Fabrics* (Universidad del Externado de Colombia 2018).

[36] Article 64.1 of the American Convention states that: "Member States of the Organization may consult the Court on the interpretation of this Convention or other treaties concerning the protection of human rights in American States. It may also be consulted, as far as they are responsible, by the bodies listed in Chapter X of the Charter of the Organization of American States, as a matter for them, as a matter of view, by the Buenos Aires Protocol."

[37] *Almonacid Arellano case and others v. Chile* [2006] IACtHR, Ser. C No. 154, para. 124; Consultative Opinion OC-21/14, para. 19, Consultative Opinion OC-22/16, para. 16, and *Chinchilla Sandoval case and others v. Guatemala* [2016] IACtHR, Ser. C No. 312, para. 242.

[38] *Cfr.* "Other Treaties" Subject to the Court's Advisory Function (art. 64 American Convention on Human Rights). Consultative Opinion OC-1/82 of September 24, 1982. Ser. A No. 1, decisive point first. IACtHR, "Rights and guarantees of children in the context of migration and/or in need of international protection," Consultative Opinion OC-21/14 of August 19, 2014. Ser. A No. 21, para. 23. IACtHR, "Ownership of legal rights in the Inter-American System of Human Rights (Interpretation and scope of Article 1.2, Articles 1.1, 8, 11.2, 13, 16, 21, 24, 25, 29, 30, 44, 46, and 62.3 of the American Convention on Human Rights, as well as Article 8.1A and B of the San Salvador Protocol)," Consultative Opinion OC-22/16 of February 26, 2016. Ser. A No. 22, para. 26.

an international standard and, on the other, to assist States in better guaranteeing and protecting human rights.[39]

The interpretation produced in an advisory opinion is binding for States. The Court has pointed out that when carrying out a conventionality check, account must be taken of what is stated by it both in the exercise of its consultative competence and what has been developed in its contentious[40] competence. In this way, the issuance of an advisory opinion "constitutes a guide to be used to resolve issues relating to the respect and guarantee of human rights within the framework of protection (...) and thus prevent possible human rights violations."[41] In this way, we could say that consultative opinions are binding as soon as they are judged to be interpreted.[42]

As of the date of writing this chapter, the Court had issued twenty-six advisory opinions.[43] The Inter-American Court does not monitor their advisory opinions and thus is not able to measure their real impact on American States. In my view, the time has come for the Court to start monitoring the impact of its advisory opinions. This monitoring should be different from what the Court does in contentious cases, since it is not about monitoring compliance with the reparations ordered but the change and good practices generated by an advisory opinion and whether and how it can empower different actors according to their particular interests.

To illustrate the transformative impact that advisory opinions may have, I will draw on the advisory opinion requested by Costa Rica on two issues related to the rights of LGBTIQ+ people. The first concerns the recognition of the right to gender identity and in particular the procedures for processing applications for name change on the account of gender identity. The second issue concerns the economic rights of same-sex couples.[44]

---

[39] IACtHR, "Gender identity, and equality and non-discrimination to same-sex couples. State obligations in relation to name change, gender identity, and rights arising from a same-sex relationship (interpretation and scope of Articles 1.1, 3, 7, 11.2, 13, 17, 18 and 24, in connection with Article 1 of the American Convention on Human Rights)." Consultative Opinion OC-24/17 of November 24, 2017. Ser. A No. 24, para. 22.

[40] IACtHR, "The Effect of Reservations on the Entry into Force of the American Convention on Human Rights." Consultative Opinion OC-2/82 of September 24, 1982. Ser. A No. 2, para. 29. IACtHR, "Rights and guarantees of children in the context of migration and/or in need of international protection". Consultative Opinion OC-21/14 of August 19, 2014. Ser. A No. 21, para. 31.

[41] Cfr. IACtHR, "Rights and guarantees of children in the context of migration and/or in need of international protection." Consultative Opinion OC-21/14 of August 19, 2014. Ser. A No. 21, para. 31.

[42] Juan Carlos Hitters, "Are the pronouncements of the Commission and the Inter-American Court of Human Rights binding? (control of constitutionality and conventionality)" [2008] 10 Ibero-American Journal of Law Constitutional 131.

[43] Official website of the Inter-American Court of Human Rights, Consultative Opinions, <https://www.corteidh.or.cr/opiniones_consultivas.cfm> (accessed February 5, 2022).

[44] The questions resolved by OC-24 were: 1. "Taking into account that gender identity is a category protected by Articles 1 and 24 of the CADH, in addition to the provisions of numerals 11.2

3.2. The Consultative Opinion on Nondiscrimination against LGBTIQ+ People

3.2.1. The Context Situation

It is important to note that the Court, before going into discussion of the questions posed in the request for consultative opinion, conducted a brief context analysis on the situation of the LGBTIQ+ population in the region and warned that these people have historically been victims of structural discrimination, stigmatization, various forms of violence, and violations of their fundamental rights.[45] This context analysis highlighted a structural problem of vulnerability and lack of recognition of the rights of the LGBTIQ+ population in the Americas.

In light of the structural problems experienced by the LGBTIQ+ population, the Court pointed out the importance that this advisory opinion will have in the region since "it will make it possible to specify the state obligations in relation to the rights of LGBTI persons within the framework of their obligations to respect and guarantee the human rights of everyone under its jurisdiction. This will lead to the determination of the principles and specific obligations that States must comply with in terms of the right to equality and non-discrimination." In other words, this advisory opinion became a mechanism to assist the States in effectively guaranteeing the protection of the rights of LGBTIQ+ persons and a tool to promote changes where situations of discrimination still exist.[46]

Regarding the rights of same-sex couples, the Inter-American Court concluded that the American Convention, based on the right to equality and nondiscrimination, protects the family bond that may derive from a relationship between same-sex couples, and it should be done on the same terms as those

---

and 18 of the Convention does that protection and the CADH provide that the State must recognize and facilitate the re-name of individuals, in accordance with the gender identity of each person?"; 2. "If the answer to the above consultation is yes, could it be considered contrary to the CADH that the person interested in changing his first name can only go to judicial proceedings without administrative proceedings?"; 3. "Could it be understood that Article 54 of the Costa Rican Civil Code should be interpreted, in accordance with the CADH, as meaning that persons wishing to change their first name on the basis of their gender identity are not required to submit to the judicial process contemplated there, but that the State must provide them with a free administrative procedure, fast and accessible to exercise that human right?"; 4. "Taking into account that non-discrimination on the grounds of sexual orientation is a category protected by Articles 1 and 24 of the CADH, in addition to the provisions of numeral 11.2 of the Convention does that protection and the CADH provide that the State recognizes all economic rights arising from a same-sex link?"; and 5. "If the above answer is yes, is it necessary for a legal figure to regulate same-sex links, so that the State recognizes all the economic rights arising from this relationship?" IACtHR, "Gender identity, and equality and non-discrimination to same-sex couples. State obligations in relation to name change, gender identity, and rights arising from a same-sex relationship (interpretation and scope of Articles 1.1, 3, 7, 11.2, 13, 17, 18 and 24, in connection with Article 1 of the American Convention on Human Rights)." Consultative Opinion OC-24/17 of November 24, 2017. Ser. A No. 24, para. 3.

[45] Ibid., para. 33.
[46] Ibid., para. 21.

that are done with respect to heterosexual couples relationships. This protection transcends economic rights and extends to "all the rights and obligations recognized in the domestic law of each State that arise from the family ties of heterosexual couples." This means that the States must guarantee access to all existing concepts in domestic legal systems to ensure the protection of the rights of families made up of same-sex couples. According to the Court, it may be necessary for the States to modify the existing concepts, through legislative, judicial, or administrative measures, to extend them to couples constituted by persons of the same sex.[47]

Regarding the name change of trans people, the Court indicated that the nonrecognition of gender identity constitutes a structural problem that reinforces acts of discrimination against people who perceive themselves as having a gender regardless of their assigned sex at birth. The name of a person is an attribute of his or her personality that is essential for his or her free development and for the realization of his or her right to identity. The prohibition of changing the name according to self-perceived gender identity implies an impairment of the rights of transgender people by not being able to be freely recognized according to the person's self-perception, since their official documentation does not match their identity, being exposed to a situation of permanent revictimization. This also creates practical problems in exercising rights. It increases their situation of vulnerability by exposing them to situations of discrimination and generalized violence. In this sense, the Court pointed out that the States are under the obligation to recognize, regulate, and establish simple procedures or procedures for the change of name, the adaptation of public records and identity documents in accordance with the self-gender identity—perceived by each person. It indicated that the administrative and notarial procedures are the ones that best suit these elements.[48]

This interpretation of the Court gave rise to the activation of historical lawsuits in various countries to allow marriage between same-sex couples. In this sense, it is worth highlighting the impact of the advisory opinion regarding equal marriage in Costa Rica and Ecuador. As we will see in both countries, their constitutional courts advanced an evolutionary interpretation based on the aforementioned advisory opinion to allow marriage between same-sex couples

---

[47] Ibid paras. 191, 198, 228; Unconstitutionality actions accumulated and processed in files No. 15-013971-0007-CO, 15-017075-0007-CO and 16-002972-0007-CO. View Constitutional Chamber of Costa Rica. Resolution No. 12782-2018 (August 8, 2018), <https://nexuspj.poder-judicial.go.cr/document/sen-1-0007-875801> (accessed February 5, 2022).

[48] Organization of American States, "Guidelines for the implementation of Consultative Opinion No. 24 in the Framework of the Legal Recognition of Gender Identity. Implications of the Resolution of the Inter-American Court for Civil Registration and Identification Institutions" (May 2020), 21; ACT, "Towards the effective guarantee of the rights of children and adolescents: National Protection Systems" November 30, 2017, para. 299; IACtHR, Consultative Opinion OC-24/17, para. 116.

in their respective countries. This is an example of the transformative impact that advisory opinions can have on social realities and how they serve to empower various actors. On the other hand, with regard to the name change of trans people in various countries, important steps have been taken to facilitate the name change procedure, on this point we will see what happened in Costa Rica.[49]

3.2.2. Costa Rica

In August 2018, the Constitutional Chamber of the Supreme Court of Costa Rica ruled in favor of same-sex couple marriage as a result of various appeals alleging the unconstitutionality of Article 14(6) of the Costa Rican Family Code.[50]

The Constitutional Chamber harmoniously interpreted the national legal system with the OC and declared Paragraph 6 of Article 14 of the Family Code—which indicated that the marriage between same-sex persons was legally impossible—unconstitutional. In this sense, it pointed out:

> In accordance with the criteria of the Inter-American Court of Human Rights that (advisory opinion OC-24/17), and in view of the power that the Chamber has to graduate and measure the effects of its unconstitutionality judgments (ordinal 91 of the Law of Jurisdiction Constitutional), the Legislative Assembly is urged, in the use of its constitutionally assigned legislative function, to that within 18 months, counted from the full publication of this pronouncement in the Judicial Bulletin, adapt the national legal framework with the purpose of regulating the scope and effects derived from couple relationships between people of the same sex, in the terms set forth in this judgment. Consequently, subsection 6 of numeral 14 of the Family Code remains in force for up to the aforementioned period of 18 months.[51]

In accordance with what was ordered by the Constitutional Chamber, the union between people of the same sex had to be regulated by the Legislative Assembly by May 26, 2020, otherwise, marriage between couples of the same sex would be allowed. The Legislative Assembly during the period of eighteen

---

[49] Organization of American States (OAS), "Report on the Overview of the Legal Recognition of Gender Identity in the Americas" (May 2020). OAS, "Report on Guidelines for the Implementation of Consultative Opinion No. 24 in the Framework for the Recognition of Gender Identity. Implications of Inter-American Court of Human Rights for Civil Registration and Identification Institutions" (May 2020).

[50] Article 14.6 of the Family Code provided:
ARTÍCULO 14. Marriage is legally impossible: [. . .] 6) Between people of the same sex; Constitutional Chamber of Costa Rica. Resolution number No. 12782–2018 (August 8, 2018) <https://nexuspj.poder-judicial.go.cr/document/sen-1-0007-875801> (accessed February 5, 2022).

[51] Constitutional Chamber of Costa Rica. Resolution No. 12782–2018 (August 8, 2018), <https://nexuspj.poder-judicial.go.cr/document/sen-1-0007-875801> (accessed February 5, 2022).

months granted by the Constitutional Chamber did not legislate and, as a consequence, from the indicated date, same-sex marriage was allowed. On May 27, marriage between same-sex couples became lawful in Costa Rica.

Regarding the name change of trans persons, the Inter-American Court answered one of the questions posed by Costa Rica regarding Article 54 of the Civil Code of that country and indicated that its current wording would be in accordance with the provisions of the American Convention, only if it is interpreted, in the sense that the procedure established by that norm can guarantee that people who wish to change their identity data so that they are in accordance with their self-perceived gender identity, is a materially administrative procedure. In this sense, it indicated that Costa Rica, in order to more effectively guarantee the protection of human rights, may issue a regulation by which it incorporates the aforementioned standards to the procedure of an administrative nature which can provide in a parallel way, of conformity to what is stated in the previous paragraphs of this opinion.[52]

As a consequence of the advisory opinion, the Supreme Electoral Tribunal (TSE) of Costa Rica has become the State institution in charge, among others, of the civil registry. On the occasion of OC-24, an Internal Commission of the Supreme Electoral Tribunal issued a series of recommendations to adjust its regulations to those established by the Court. The foregoing resulted in the Reform of the Regulations for the Civil Status Registry and Regulations for the identity card with new characteristics, through which the procedure called "name change due to gender identity" was created through a simple administrative procedure. Previously, it was a relatively cumbersome judicial procedure. This allowed people who required rectification of their name due to gender identity to do so easily. Likewise, the Costa Rican authorities decided to eliminate the reference to sex/gender from the identity card. The TSE approved in 2019 "the Guidelines for Respectful and Equal Treatment, which compile mandatory compliance criteria for respectful and equal treatment of LGBTI persons, both for the Court officials and for those who come to request services."[53]

As observed, the advisory opinion has had a transformative impact on the Costa Rican social relationship since, as a consequence of this, marriage between same-sex couples was allowed and the change of names of transgender people was also made more expeditious and simple. It is noteworthy how much

---

[52] Ibid., para. 171.
[53] Official page of the Supreme Court of Elections of Costa Rica, <https://www.tse.go.cr/el_tse.htm> (accessed February 5, 2022); OAS, "Overview of the Legal Recognition of Gender Identity in the Americas" (May 2020), 47; Supreme Court of Elections of Costa Rica. Decree No. 6-2011. Regulations on the Registry of the Civil State and Regulations on the Identity Card with new features (reformed by Decree No. 7-2018), Articles 52–56, <http://www.pgrweb.go.cr/scij/Busqueda/Normativa/Normas/nrm_texto_completo.aspx?param1=NRTC&nValor1=1&nValor2=86510&nValor3=112246&strTipM=TC> (accessed February 5, 2022).

the constructive dialogue among the Inter-American Court, the Constitutional Chamber of the Supreme Court, and the Supreme Electoral Tribunal strengthened the protection of the rights of LGBTIQ+ people in Costa Rica.

3.2.3. Ecuador

On June 12, 2019, Ecuador's Constitutional Court recognized same-sex marriage under Sentences 10-18-CN/19 and 11-18-CN/19.[54]

In Case No. 10-18-CN/19, the Constitutional Court heard the constitutionality inquiry on Articles 81 of the Civil Code and 52 of the Organic Law on Identity Management and Civil Data. The Civil Judicial Unit queried the refusal of the Ecuadorian Civil Registry to register the marriage of a same-sex couple based on the aforementioned articles, since they only recognized the marriage between a man and a woman.[55]

In its ruling, the Constitutional Court recalled that according to the Ecuadorian Constitution, international human rights treaties that are more favorable to the Constitution itself prevail over any other legal norm or act of public power. With this in mind, it recognized the importance of following the interpretation of the Convention made by the Inter-American Court in its advisory opinion for four reasons: (1) the Inter-American Court itself has established the obligation to take into account, as part of the conventionality control, its jurisprudence and precedents or guidelines; (2) the Court is the ultimate interpreter of the American Convention; (3) the Court [IDH] has the rational requirement to universalize the future of its *ratio decidenci*; and (4) the Inter-American Court

---

[54] Constitutional Court of Ecuador. 10-18-CN/19 Case No. 10-18-CN (Marriage between same-sex persons) Concerning the constitutionality consultation of Articles 81 of the Civil Code and 52 of the Organic Law on Identity Management and Civil Data. Article 428 Ecuador's Political Constitution states that if a judge or judge, ex officio or at the request of a party, considers that a rule of law is contrary to the Constitution or international human rights instruments establishing rights more favorable than those recognized in the Constitution, will suspend the processing of the case and forward in consultation the file to the Constitutional Court, which within a period of no more than forty-five days, will rule on the constitutionality of the rule; Constitutional Court of Ecuador. 11-18-CN/19 Case No. 11-18-CN (Equal Marriage) Relating to the consultation issued by the Court of the Criminal Chamber of the Higher Court of Justice of Pichincha About compatibility between Article 67 of the Constitution and Advisory Opinion OC-24 of the IHR.

[55] Constitutional Court of Ecuador. Official Register, Constitutional Edition. Year III No. 96, Quito, Monday, July 8, 2019; Article 81 of the Civil Code provided:

> Art. 81. Marriage is a solemn contract by which a man and a woman come together in order to live together. Procreate and help each other; Article 52 of the Organic Law on Identity Management and Civil Data Established:
>
> Art. 52. Authority before whom marriage is celebrated and registered. Marriage is the union between a man and a woman and is celebrated and registered with the Directorate-General for Civil Registration, Identification and Cedulation. Outside Ecuadorian territory, it is held and registered with the diplomatic or consular agent, if at least one of the counteryents is Ecuadorian.

is the competent court to establish the responsibility of a State party for the violation of the Convention.[56]

Taking into account the preceding and AO-24, the Ecuadorian Constitutional Court recognized same-sex couples' right to marriage and the State duty to legislate this right, otherwise it would be "parliamentarily unfair" and "would provoke the international responsibility of the Republic of Ecuador before the Inter-American Human Rights System." Accordingly, the Constitutional Court declared the expression "a man and a woman" of both provisions and the term "procreate" in Article 81 unconstitutional. The Constitutional Court established with *erga omnes* effect the substitutionary and subtractive unconstitutionality of the terms mentioned so that the provisions would read as follows:

> Article 81.- Marriage is a solemn contract by which two people come together in order to live together and help each other.[57]
> Article 52.- Authority before whom marriage is celebrated and registered. Marriage is the union between two people and is celebrated and registered with the General Directorate of Civil Registry and Identification. Outside of Ecuadorian territory, it is celebrated and registered with the diplomatic or consular agent, if at least one of the parties is Ecuadorian.[58]

The Constitutional Court urged the National Assembly to "comprehensively review the marriage legislation to include same-sex couples as spouses, with the same treatment as that granted to different-sex couples."[59]

To the important contributions of the aforementioned judgment, what is established in the framework of Case No. 11-18-CN/19 is added. The Court of the Criminal Chamber of the Superior Court of Justice of Pichincha asked the Constitutional Court about the compatibility between Article 67 of the Constitution, which establishes that marriage is between a man and a woman, and the advisory opinion OC-24 of the Inter-American Court.

The Constitutional Court analyzed the legal nature of an advisory opinion of the Inter-American Court, concluding that it is "an authoritative" interpretation by a supranational body: the Inter-American Court, whose jurisdiction stems from an international treaty to which Ecuador is a party, and that Ecuador has the obligation to comply in good faith, without being able to "invoke the provisions of its internal law as justification for the breach of a treaty." Based on the preceding, the Constitutional Court concluded that "[t]he rights and

---

[56] Constitutional Court of Ecuador. Official Register, Constitutional Edition. Year III No. 96, Quito, Monday, July 8, 2019, 25.
[57] Ibid., 30.
[58] Ibid., 30, para. 98.
[59] Ibid.

guarantees that derive from the authentic interpretation of the Inter-American Court of Human Rights, which appear in the advisory opinions, are part of the Ecuadorian legal system and have to be observed in Ecuador by any public authority within the scope of its competence." In addition, the Constitutional Court recognized advisory opinions as part of the constitutionality block and established their binding character.[60]

Based on this important conclusion and drawing upon AO-24 in its analysis, the Constitutional Court established that marriage is a constitutional right that allows the exercise of the right to family and therefore Article 67 of the Constitution complements the regulation and interpretation of the ACHR, made by the Court through Advisory Opinion OC24/17, which recognizes marriage between persons of the same sex. The Constitutional Court found that instead of being contradictory, the domestic law and the American Convention (as interpreted by the IACtHR) are complementary. As such, the Constitutional Court concluded that neither a constitutional reform nor a legislative reform of Articles 81 of the Civil Code and 52 of the Organic Law on the Management of Identity and Civil Data were necessary, as these provisions should be interpreted in light of the Court's sentence No. 11-18-CN/19.[61]

In the present case there is evidence of what we could call a constructive and harmonious dialogue between the Constitutional and the Inter-American Court to guarantee the rights of same-sex couples. This dialogue was based on the advisory opinion, which caused domestic courts to formulate a query to the Constitutional Court on the basis of Article 428 of the Constitution, since the Inter-American Court's interpretation of the American Convention, in principle, was more beneficial to same-sex couples than the norms of the Ecuadorian legal system. The interpretation given by the Constitutional Court shows the transformative impact that advisory opinions can have on a social reality.

4. Provisional Measures: Avoiding Structural Setbacks, Providing Structural Protection

The American Convention, in Article 63.2, expressly empowers the Inter-American Court to adopt provisional measures in cases of extreme gravity and urgency and, when necessary, to avoid irreparable harm to persons. The Inter-American Commission on Human Rights is the competent body to request provisional measures before the Court when a case is under the Commission's procedures. However, when a case is brought before the Court, either in the

---

[60] Ibid., paras. 80, 130, 300.
[61] Ibid., paras. 112, 130.

merits stage or in the supervision of compliance with the judgment, in addition to the Commission, the victims and their legal representatives are competent to request provisional measures before the Court.[62]

According to the jurisprudence of the Inter-American Court of Human Rights, provisional measures may be of a precautionary nature, to ensure the outcome of the proceedings,[63] or of a protective nature, to protect the rights of persons.[64]

Recently, the Inter-American Court issued two important resolutions on provisional measures in the framework of cases that were in the phase of supervision of the sentence and that have had a structural impact. One of them refers to the order to file an amnesty bill in Guatemala that affected compliance with several cases with regard to the duty to investigate serious human rights violations that occurred during the internal armed conflict. The other resolution refers to the situation of extreme vulnerability in which a group of migrants found themselves as a result of the restrictive movement measures ordered by Panama and the closure of borders in the framework of the COVID-19 health emergency.

4.1. Archivor Amnesty Bill: Avoiding Structural Retracement

Within the monitoring compliance framework of the case of *Members of the Chichupac Village and neighboring communities of the Municipality of Rabinal v. Guatemala*, the victims' legal representatives requested provisional measures because the legislative process of a draft amnesty law was underway. It was indicated that if it were approved and turned into law, the judgment of the Court regarding the duty to investigate the events that occurred in the case would be made illusory and that impunity would be caused in this and other cases.[65]

---

[62] As regards gravity, for the purposes of provisional measures, the Convention requires that it be "extreme," i.e., to be at its highest or highest degree. The urgent nature implies that the risk or threat involved is imminent, which requires that the response to remedy them be immediate. Finally, as regards irreparable harm, there must be a reasonable likelihood that it will materialize and should not fall on goods or legal interests that may be repairable; Article 27.2 of the Rules of Procedure of the Court IDH states: "The case of matters not yet before it, the Court may act at the request of the Commission"; Article 27.3 of the Rules of Procedure of the Court provides: "The court's contention cases, victims or alleged victims, or their representatives, may submit directly to the Court a request for interim measures, which shall relate to the subject matter of the case."

[63] Cfr. *Herrera Ulloa case for Costa Rica* [2001] IACtHR, Provisional Measures. Resolution of the Inter-American Court of Human Rights of September 7, 2001, Considering 4, and *People of the Miskitu Indigenous People's Communities of the North Caribbean Region with respect to Nicaragua* [2018] IACtHR, Extension of Provisional Measures. Resolution of the Inter-American Court of Human Rights of August 23, 2018, Considering 3.

[64] *Case Members of the Chichupac Village and neighboring communities of the Municipality of Rabinal, Caso Molina Theissen and 12 other Guatemalan Cases v. Guatemala* [2019] IACtHR, recital 5.

[65] *Case Members of the Chichupac Village and neighboring communities of the Municipality of Rabinal v. Guatemala* [2016] IACtHR, Ser. C No. 328. In that judgment, the Court had ordered

After the public hearing, the Court analyzed the amnesty bill taking into account the impact that its approval could have in that and other prior Guatemalan cases where the State international responsibility was already established. In those cases, the Court held that Guatemala has the duty to investigate the facts and apply the corresponding sanctions to those responsible. This is how the analysis was made in the case *Members of the Chichupac Village and neighboring communities of the Municipality of Rabinal* and another twelve cases that were in the stage of supervision of compliance with the judgment.[66]

The Court observed that the amnesty bill sought to reform the National Reconciliation Law by repealing its Article 8 and declaring "amnesty or total extinction of criminal responsibility for all crimes committed" in the internal armed confrontation. In addition, in Article 5[67] the draft noted:

> [...] Any person who has been tried and is in compliance with a sentence or in criminal proceedings and measures of coercion were decreed, [...] must be ordered amnesty and dismissal in their case, and their freedom ordered by the court corresponding within twenty-four hours. The judicial, ministerial, police or penitentiary authority that does not comply with this rule will incur the crimes of Malicious Retardation, Denial of Justice and Illegal Detention.[68]

The Court established that the approval of this law would have a negative and irreparable impact on the victims' right of access to justice. It would contradict prior sentences ordered against Guatemala regarding the impossibility of applying amnesties to those responsible for serious crimes and violations of human rights. The bill would also be incompatible with Articles 8 (Judicial

---

that all obstacles, de facto and de jure, should be removed and that impunity should be effectively investigated enforced disappearances, forced displacement, alleged torture, extrajudicial executions, sexual rape, and forced labour, as well as allegations of crimes against humanity, war crimes, and/or genocide. The Court expressly noted that in order to comply with this obligation, no amnesty laws or limitation provisions, or purported exclusions from liability, may not be applied, which are in fact a pretext for preventing the investigation.

[66] *Case Members of the Chichupac Village and neighboring communities of the Municipality of Rabinal v. Guatemala* [2016] IACtHR, Ser. C No. 328, paras. 316 and 318; *Case Members of the Chichupac Village and neighboring communities of the Municipality of Rabinal, Caso Molina Theissen and 12 other Guatemalan Cases v. Guatemala* [2019] IACtHR, Provisional Measures and Sentencing Compliance Supervision. Resolution of the Inter-American Court of Human Rights of March 12, 2019, paras. 28 and 55.

[67] In its jurisprudence with respect to several Guatemalan cases, the Court has emphasized that the National Reconciliation Act expressly provided, in Article 8: "The termination of the criminal liability referred to in this law shall not apply to crimes of genocide, torture and enforced disappearance, as well as those crimes that are imprescriptible or non-extinguishing of criminal liability in accordance with domestic law and international treaties ratified by Guatemala."

[68] Initiative that provides for the approval of reforms to Decree No. 145-96 of the Congress of the Republic, Law on National Reconciliation. Registration Number 5377, Article 5.

Guarantees), 25 (Judicial Protection), and 2 (Duty to Adopt Provisions of Domestic Law) of the American Convention and the Court's solid jurisprudence. On the other hand, the Court pointed out that what is indicated in the bill regarding the release of convicted and accused persons within a period of twenty-four hours and expose judicial operators who question the law or their release to a possible criminal penalty. It affects judicial independence by having a chilling effect that prevents an autonomous exercise of the judicial function. This put pressure on judges and other judicial operators who wanted to carry out a control of conventionality of the referred law, if they were exposed to criminal sanctions.[69]

In this way, the Court concluded that it was facing a serious, urgent, and potentially irreparable situation, since the passing of the bill would by itself constitute a serious breach of Guatemala's obligations regarding the case of *Members of the Chichupac Village and neighboring communities of the Municipality of Rabinal* and twelve other cases that are in the stage of monitoring compliance with judgment. Likewise, the victims' access to justice would be illusory since a mechanism of structural impunity would be being created with respect to serious human rights violations, crimes against humanity and genocide, an issue that also openly contravenes the established jurisprudence of this Court, the American Convention on Human Rights and other instruments of international human rights law. In view of the foregoing, the Court expressly ordered the State to interrupt and archive the aforementioned bill.[70]

Making an analogy to certain developments in constitutional matters, such as the unconstitutional state of affairs, what the Court did was to prevent an unconstitutional state of affairs from being created in Guatemala by attempting to create a scaffolding of structural impunity regarding serious human rights violations, a question that is manifestly antagonistic to the American Convention and the repeated jurisdiction of the Court. It is worth recalling the jurisprudence developed by the Inter-American Court in the *Barrios Altos* case where it declared that Peru's amnesty law lacked validity and legal effects.

It is clear that the bill directly affected all Guatemalan cases in the compliance supervision stage that investigation concerning serious human rights violations had been ordered. Here the provisional measure had a precautionary dimension in the sense of ensuring compliance with the sentence. Moreover, the provisional measure acquired a tutelary dimension, in terms of protecting the right of access to justice for all victims, which prevented a structural setback and built a

---

[69] *Case Members of the Chichupac Village and neighboring communities of the Municipality of Rabinal, Caso Molina Theissen and 12 other Guatemalan Cases v. Guatemala* [2019] Provisional Measures and Sentencing Compliance Supervision. Resolution of the Inter-American Court of Human Rights of March 12, 2019, para. 46.
[70] Ibid., para. 52.

scaffolding of generalized impunity in Guatemala regarding the serious human rights violations from the country's internal armed conflict. Finally, the provisional measures helped to avoid that the State intimidated judges, since if the bill had been approved, judicial independence would be affected as judges that challenged or refused to apply the amnesty law would be exposed to criminal sanctions.

4.2. Immediate Protection and Adoption of Measures to Protect the Lives, Health, and Integrity of Migrants

The case of *Vélez Loor v. Panama* addresses the detention of Mr. Jesús Tranquilino Vélez Loor, an irregular migrant of Ecuadorian nationality sentenced to two years of deprivation of liberty. The Inter-American Court held that Panama was internationally responsible. Among other measures of reparation, the Court ordered as a guarantee of nonrepetition and with a structural nature that the State adapts the establishments destined to the detention of people for immigration reasons. According to the Court:

> The State must, within a reasonable period of time, adopt the necessary measures to have establishments with sufficient capacity to house the persons whose detention is necessary and proportionate in the specific case due to migration issues, specifically adequate for such purposes, offering material conditions and an appropriate regime for migrants, and whose staff is civilian and is properly qualified and trained.[71]

In the context of the crisis caused by the COVID-19 pandemic, the victims' representatives submitted to the Court a request for provisional measures in order to protect the rights to life, health, and personal integrity of all migrants held in the migratory centers in the Darien region of Panama as these were not adequate to meet the needs of migrants. The representatives requested the provisional measure based on the structural reparation ordered by the Court.[72]

The Inter-American Court observed that in Panama, as a result of the various measures adopted to prevent the spread of COVID-19, a critical situation was occurring in the migrant population. This is the result of the order to close the borders and the limitation of the right of movement to migrants on their

---

[71] *Vélez Loor v. Panama case* [2010] IACtHR, Ser. C No. 218, resolution point 15.
[72] *Vélez Loor v. Panama case. Provisional Measures* [2020] IACtHR; Adoption of Provisional Measures. Resolution of the Inter-American Court of Human Rights of July 29, 2020, visa 2; put urgent action, information and hearing, as well as the data provided by the Ombudsman's Office Group United Nations Inter-Agency on Human Mobility during the interim measures procedure.

way to the northern countries. This caused a situation of overcrowding in the Darien migration stations, making it difficult to adopt adequate measures of social distancing and hygiene recommended by the World Health Organization to avoid the spread of COVID-19, as well as the provision of health, water, shelter, and food. It was registered that there were infections with COVID-19 among migrants and State agents resident in the area.[73]

The Court concluded that Panama has a special position as guarantor of the rights of the people who are in its custody at the Immigration Reception Stations and that it was evident "the existence of a risk to the health, personal integrity and life of various people, whose severity warrants immediate intervention in favor of a group of people in vulnerable situations, such as migrants and other foreigners in the context of human mobility who may require international protection, a vulnerability that is increased by the pandemic."[74]

It is interesting to note that the Court ordered a wide and varied catalog of measures to Panama to address the urgent and serious situation of its migrant population. Among others, the Court pointed out that the State should reduce overcrowding; guarantee respect for the principle of non-refoulement of all foreign persons; adopt measures to prevent the risk of violence; establish protocols or action plans for the prevention of the contagion of COVID-19 and the care of infected migrants; provide migrants with free and nondiscriminatory access to healthcare services; provide pregnant women with free access to sexual and reproductive healthcare services as well as maternity care services, and provide adequate healthcare services for girls and boys; adopt the necessary measures to overcome language and cultural barriers that hinder access to health and information; continue with the free provision of masks, gloves, alcohol, and disposable towels, promote information on personal hygiene measures recommended by health authorities, provide sufficient food and drinking water for personal consumption, with special consideration of pre- post-natal nutritional requirements; guarantee access to the Migration Reception Stations of the Ombudsman's Office and other independent monitoring mechanisms, as well as international organizations and civil society; prevent the measures adopted from promoting xenophobia, racism, and any other form of discrimination.[75]

In the situation described, the adoption of the provisional measure arises from a guarantee of nonrepetition and acquires a protective dimension to give

---

[73] *Vélez Loor v. Panama case. Provisional Measures* [2020] IACtHR; Adoption of Provisional Measures. Resolution of the Inter-American Court of Human Rights of July 29, 2020, para. 8; the Court also finds the emergency requirement, as long as the State reported that, as of May 12, 2020, 58 positive cases of migrants had been detected in La Peñita, a figure that evolved from 158 to June 30, 2020 in Darien, including the contagion of officials.

[74] *Vélez Loor v. Panama case. Provisional Measures* [2020] IACtHR; Adoption of Provisional Measures. Resolution of the Inter-American Court of Human Rights of July 29, 2020, para. 23.

[75] Ibid., para. 35.

structural protection to health, life, and integrity to a group of migrants who were in a situation of aggravated vulnerability as a result of the pandemic.

5. Concluding Remarks

This chapter examined the structural impact of the Inter-American Court of Human Rights' decisions on the social reality of some States under its jurisdiction. Recognizing that the impact of a decision may well go beyond a merely State-centered transformation through the guarantee of nonrepetition, the decision's impact on the base of a broader construction of knowledge, acceptance, and empowerment within a broader community of practice as a whole will be of interest. Two very different judgments, the case of *Artavia Murillo and Others ("In Vitro Fertilization") v. Costa Rica* and the case of *Maldonado Vargas and others v. Chile*, were introduced to highlight how comprehensive reparation in its dimension of guarantee of nonrepetition has had a transforming impact on social realities. The jurisprudence of the Court has hence provided concrete content to the obligation to provide reparations by looking at the harm and impact that a human rights violation produces, both in an individual and collective dimension within diverse forms of social interaction. Such jurisprudence has led to the adoption of public policies, legislative modifications, and changes in State practices, among other things, and the adoption of new laws. Reparations turn the judgments into a living instrument.

Furthermore, the Court's social impact is also produced by the advisory opinions and provisional measures. The impact of both of them is reflected in good practices and in the empowerment of different actors according to their particular interests. It is also noteworthy that advisory opinions rest on democratic and participative elements, as there is an open participation for all Organization of American States member States, international organizations, civil society organizations, and academia, among others. They hence constitute a particular fruitful source of a collective construction of the law, which not only give rise to the Court's binding interpretations for States but which are also prone to be received by a broader community of practice that can amplify their impact.

Provisional measures are equally significant when talking about impact. These measures, adopted in cases of extreme gravity, urgency, and necessary to avoid irreparable harm to persons, avoid structural setbacks and provide structural protection. They can and in many cases should be included within the impact analysis, which by their nature can prevent structural setbacks and provide protection to certain groups.

Finally, a harmonious and constructive *pro persona* judicial dialogue between the national and inter-American courts is crucial when implementing the judgments of the Inter-American Court and giving life to the advisory opinions in the national legal systems. Likewise, it is important to highlight how other powers of the State can help provide the Inter-American Court's judgments with effectiveness and thus promote structural changes. The varied topics which the Court has addressed, in continuous contact with a broader community of practice, have strengthened the work of the Court itself and nurtured an inter-American legal system, with the interpretation of the American Convention and other treaties that form part of the inter-American *corpus iuris*.

III.3
Addressing Conceptual Challenges
Compliance and Impact

By Aníbal Pérez-Liñán, Kelly Morrison, and Luis L. Schenoni

1. Introduction

This chapter argues that time is a fundamental consideration to understand how States implement the orders of the Inter-American Human Rights System (IAHRS). Time is relevant not only to assess delays in legal outcomes but also to conceptualize variation in the causes of compliance. Given this premise, we propose a new set of criteria to assess levels of compliance and illustrate the use of those criteria with extensive evidence from the Inter-American Court of Human Rights (IACtHR). The proposed approach shows that compliance is sometimes at odds with broader transformative impacts, a point underscored toward the end of the chapter.

Our focus on the IACtHR allows us to place growing concerns about a crisis of compliance in proper perspective. The Court expects full compliance with its rulings for the sake of the victims of human rights abuses.[1] Reparations for victims may include State recognition of human rights violations, financial compensation, the prosecution of perpetrators, or institutional reforms to prevent abuses from recurring. Yet the Inter-American Court has few mechanisms to enforce such orders.[2] Although the Court issues annual reports and, in extreme cases, can invoke Article 65 of the American Convention of Human Rights (ACHR), the General Assembly of the Organization of American States rarely addresses compliance issues.[3] Member States also face a

---

[1] Antônio Augusto Cançado Trindade, "Compliance with Judgments and Decisions—The Experience of the Inter-American Court of Human Rights: A Reassessment." Lecture presented at the European Court of Human Rights, Strasbourg (January 31, 2014).

[2] In this chapter, we use the terms "compliance" and "implementation" as synonymous to avoid excessive repetition, although we understand that these terms may convey subtle differences. Similarly, we sometimes refer to reparation measures ordered by the Court as "orders," aware that the Court employs this English term to refer instead to supervision resolutions.

[3] See Cecilia M. Bailliet, "Measuring Compliance with the Inter-American Court of Human Rights: The Ongoing Challenge of Judicial Independence in Latin America" [2013] 31 *Nordic Journal of Human Rights* 477, 479. Article 65 of the ACHR establishes: "To each regular session of the General

variety of compliance hurdles, including a lack of political will and institutional capacity.[4]

Observers have lamented the ongoing crisis of compliance in the Inter-American System, which continues to cast doubt on its effectiveness.[5] As César Rodríguez Garavito and Celeste Kauffmann point out, though it is undeniable that the Court has made progress in promoting human rights, "it is equally evident that the implementation of reparation and non-repetition measures ordered by the Commission and the Court is scant."[6] Indeed, recent research suggests that noncompliance is widespread, particularly for reparations demanding institutional change. Damián A. González-Salzberg finds that implementation rates range between 3 percent and 31 percent for measures requiring prosecution or legislative changes.[7] Darren Hawkins and Wade Jacoby report compliance rates between 7 percent and 19 percent for similar measures. In recent years the Court itself implemented a strategic plan to overcome widespread "practices of impunity."[8]

In this context of perceived crisis, we focus on a technical issue with significant implications: the definition and measurement of compliance. We show

---

Assembly of the Organization of American States, the Court shall [report] cases in which a state has not complied with its judgments, making any pertinent recommendations." The Court has used this procedure as the last recourse to expose noncompliance.

[4] Ignacio Alvarez et al., "Reparations in the Inter-American System: A Comparative Approach Conference." [2007] 56 *American University Law Review* 1375, 1454. Courtney Hillebrecht, *Domestic Politics and International Human Rights Tribunals* (Cambridge University Press 2014). Sabrina Vannuccini, "Member States' Compliance with the Inter-American Court of Human Rights' Judgments and Orders Requiring Non-Pecuniary Reparations" [2014] 7 *Inter-American and European Human Rights Journal* 225.

[5] Jorge Calderón Gamboa, "Fortalecimiento del rol de la CIDH en el proceso de supervisión de cumplimiento de sentencias y planteamiento de reparaciones ante la Corte IDH" [2014] 10 *Anuario de Derechos Humanos* 105–116. Trindade (n. 1). Elise Mara Coimbra, "Inter-American System of Human Rights: Challenges to Compliance with the Court's Decisions in Brazil" [2013] 10 *Sur: International Journal on Human Rights* 57–74. Vittorio Corasaniti, "Implementación de las sentencias y resoluciones de la Corte Interamericana de Derechos Humanos: un debate necesario" [2009] 49 *Revista IIDH* 13–28. César Rodríguez Garavito and Celeste Kauffmann, "From Orders to Practice: Analysis and Strategies for Implementing Decisions of the Inter-American Human Rights System," in Camila Barreto Maia et al., *The Inter-American Human Rights System: Changing Times, Ongoing Challenges* (Due Process of Law Foundation 2016), 249–284. Mónica Pinto, "The Role of the Inter-American Commission and Court of Human Rights in the Protection of Human Rights: Achievements and Contemporary Challenges" [2013] 2 *Human Rights Brief* 34–38.

[6] Rodríguez Garavito and Kauffmann (n. 5), 251.

[7] Damián A. González-Salzberg, "The Effectiveness of the Inter-American Human Rights System: A Study of the American States' Compliance with the Judgments of the Inter-American Court of Human Rights" [2010] 15 *International Law: Revista Colombiana de Derecho Internacional* 115–142. Damián A. Gonzalez-Salzberg, "Do States Comply with the Compulsory Judgments of the Inter-American Court of Human Rights? An Empirical Study of the Compliance with 330 Measures of Reparations" [2013] 13 *Revisto do Instituto Brasileiro de Direitos Humanos* 93–114.

[8] *Strategic Plan: 2017–2021* (2017) Inter-American Commission on Human Rights. Darren Hawkins and Wade Jacoby, "Partial Compliance: A Comparison of the European and Inter-American Courts of Human Rights" [2010] 6 *Journal of International Law & International Relations* 35–85.

that existing metrics cannot give a full picture of aggregate levels of compliance within the Inter-American System. Most reports measure compliance by assessing the percentage of reparations implemented within a particular period of time. However, such measures cannot account for the time it takes for States to comply. Because the Court's caseload has increased in recent years,[9] it is difficult to discern whether rates of compliance have decreased over time, or whether more cases are now at the supervision stage.

We advocate an alternative approach, one that considers not only *whether* a State complies with a given reparation measure but also *how long* it takes them to do so. We describe this analytic perspective as a discrete-time approach, for reasons explained in the next section. Although a discrete-time approach can help scholars and practitioners evaluate levels of compliance more accurately, it has rarely been applied to an analysis of the Inter-American Court.[10]

The chapter proceeds through three sections. In section 2, we introduce the discrete-time approach for assessing rates of compliance then discuss the relevance of time as a crucial dimension of implementation before comparing two traditional (static) metrics of compliance against two discrete-time metrics. We introduce the concepts of a *yearly probability of compliance* and an *expected time for compliance* (ETC) and document their objective equivalence. Section 3 illustrates these concepts with data from all cases decided by the IACtHR until 2018. In addition to comparing Latin American States, this section shows that the implementation of Court orders follows a distinctive *life cycle*, as the yearly probability of compliance varies over time. There is a window of opportunity in which States tend to comply, but compliance becomes less likely the longer a reparation remains under supervision. The final concluding section 4 addresses the distinction between compliance and impact. Though it is true that the effectiveness of the Inter-American System rests "to a large measure on compliance with the decisions of its organs,"[11] we identify four distinct patterns of alignment between compliance and impact: direct transformative impact, indirect transformative impact, State resistance, and backlash.

---

[9] Nelson Camilo Sánchez and Laura Lyons Cerón, "The Elephant in the Room: The Procedural Delay in the Individual Petitions System of the Inter-American System" in Camila Barreto Maia et al., *The Inter-American Human Rights System: Changing Times, Ongoing Challenges* (Due Process of Law Foundation 2016).

[10] For a notable exception, see Francesca Parente, "Past Regret Future Fear: Compliance with International Law" (DPhil thesis, University of California 2019).

[11] *Annual Report: 2017–2021* (2018) Inter-American Commission on Human Rights 144.

2. Improving Inter-American Standards: Compliance in Time

Compliance with international court rulings necessarily involves a temporal dimension. States must adapt their behavior in order to conform to a norm or ruling,[12] and because any change in behavior is necessarily never immediate, time is a crucial dimension to consider when conceptualizing and measuring compliance. In this section, we compare two approaches to quantify compliance. The first, traditional approach calculates rates of compliance across cases (or reparation measures) at a particular point in time, offering a static "snapshot" of the situation. The second approach introduced in this chapter conceptualizes compliance as an event that takes place within discrete-time units (years), and thus allows for a dynamic analysis of the process.

To understand the difference between the two approaches, imagine a hypothetical case in which the IACtHR orders a State to comply with two reparation measures. Three years later, the Court issues a supervision resolution documenting that the State complied with the first order within two years of the decision but has yet to comply with the second order. The conventional procedure estimates the rate of compliance across orders at the time of the resolution. This "snapshot" of the situation would show that by the end of the third year, the State has complied with 50 percent of the orders (one out of two). In contrast, the discrete-time procedure records *every year* until an order meets compliance. In the previous example, the first order met compliance after two years, thus the annual rate of compliance is 1/2, that is, an event of compliance over a two-year period. The second order has not yet been met with compliance by the end of the third year, thus the annual rate for the second order is 0/3. We can easily aggregate this information across reparation measures. Overall, the yearly probability of compliance for the State is 1/5.

Why is the second approach necessary? The conceptual implications of the two approaches become clear if we imagine that the Court issues a new supervision resolution a decade after the decision. The new resolution reminds us that the State complied with the first order within two years but warns that the State has not complied with the second order *ten years after the ruling*. A decade after the ruling, the snapshot analysis would reiterate the initial conclusion: the rate of compliance remains at 50 percent. In contrast, the discrete-time estimate would penalize the State for the long delay in compliance. The annual rate of compliance for the first order is still 1/2, but the annual rate for the second order is now

---

[12] Jana von Stein, "The Engines of Compliance," in Jeffrey Dunoff and Mark Pollack (eds.), *Interdisciplinary Perspectives on International Law and International Relations: The State of the Art* (University Press 2013), 49. Oran Young, *Compliance and Public Authority: A Theory with International Applications* (Johns Hopkins Press 1979), 104.

0/10. Overall, the yearly probability of compliance for the State is now 1/12. That is, one event of compliance, on average, every twelve years.

3. Why Time Matters

Time is a relevant dimension of the concept of compliance for two reasons. First, as the previous hypothetical example illustrates, delays are relevant to characterize legal *outcomes*. Even if States conform to the orders of the IACtHR, they may display considerable divergence in how long they take to do so. Delays with compliance ultimately matter for the victims and for the Court's reputation. Second, time is relevant to understand the *causes* of compliance. Contextual variables that influence State behavior normally fluctuate over time. In the following sections, we discuss the reasons for this fluctuation and explain how the discrete-time approach allows us to improve our understanding of those issues.

3.1. Legal Outcomes

A good measure of compliance must take into account not only whether a State complied with a ruling but also how long it took to do so. States are unlikely to respond to Court rulings right away, and a variety of factors can impose delays. To treat equally cases in which a State complied after fifteen years with cases in which a State complied after fifteen months, for instance, would draw a false equivalence between two very different patterns of State behavior.

Consider, for example, the *Garrido y Baigorria v. Argentina* case. In response to the illegal detention and disappearance of Adolfo Garrido and Raúl Baigorria in 1990, the Court ruled that Argentina needed to compensate the families of both victims, pay the lawyers' fees for their work on the case, identify two extramarital children of Raúl Baigorria—in order to pay them reparations—and investigate and sanction the authorities complicit in the disappearances. Although these orders were issued simultaneously in 1998, Argentina's compliance record varied according to the reparation measure. A snapshot of this case in 2017 indicated that Argentina had complied with three-quarters of the reparation measures ordered by the Court. However, Argentina took nine years to comply with the first reparation, five years to comply with the second, and nineteen years to comply with the third. Because of this variance, the aggregate rate of compliance observed in 2017 (3/4) masks important information about Argentina's overall record and variation by type of reparation.

Conversely, time also matters for assessing noncompliance. A snapshot treats a lack of compliance at the end of the observation period (say, by 2017) as a negative outcome, irrespective of the time elapsed. Yet the hypothetical example introduced at the start of this section illustrates why this metric can be misleading. In *Garrido y Baigorria*, Argentina failed to comply with only one of four orders, but its lack of compliance with the fourth order deserved very different interpretations nineteen years after the ruling compared with two years after the ruling. Delays represent an important feature of a State's compliance record that scholars must consider when measuring levels of compliance.

3.2. The Causes of Compliance

The second reason to incorporate a temporal element is that compliance is not a static phenomenon. The contextual factors that influence a State's propensity to comply with a ruling evolve over time. For instance, changes in governments or regimes often affect the likelihood that leaders will recognize State culpability in past human rights abuses. Guatemala came into rapid compliance with a variety of historical obligations following the election of Óscar Berger in 2004.[13] A snapshot measure that encompasses this period would report a higher level of compliance for Guatemala but fail to account for the sudden increase associated with political change. Other contextual variables influence a State's propensity to comply over time. These include public opinion, the electoral calendar, economic conditions, and the political ideology of incoming governments.[14]

Even if these variables remain stable for several years, we may observe temporal fluctuations when we analyze the probability of compliance over time. As we discuss in section 6, compliance follows a distinctive life cycle. Compliance is unlikely in the wake of a ruling, becomes more likely after States have had time to implement the required measures, and it becomes unlikely again as reluctant States drag their feet. A good definition of compliance should allow us to document this life cycle.

4. Four Metrics of Compliance

We can now compare four different ways of conceptualizing and measuring compliance according to their capacity to address the two problems discussed previously. First, a static *rate of compliance* reflects the percentage of closed cases—or the percentage of implemented reparation measures—at the time of the snapshot, without acknowledging changing conditions. Scholars in this tradition

---

[13] Alvarez et al. (n. 4), 1454.
[14] Parente (n. 10).

look at a set of orders within a given period and simply calculate the proportion of reparations that were met with compliance.[15]

A second, less common approach reports the average number of years States take to comply. This measure tackles the first challenge discussed previously (delays) by reporting the *average time to compliance*. However, because the units of analysis are cases or reparation measures rather than discrete-time units, this measure cannot tackle the second problem (changing conditions over time). Moreover, the analyst is able to measure the time to compliance only if compliance has taken place by the end of the observation period. In the previous example of *Garrido y Baigorria v. Argentina*, an analyst taking a snapshot of the case by year nineteen would observe an average time to compliance of eleven years ((9 + 5 + 19)/3) without accounting for the fourth, pending measure. Thus, this approach presents the problem of selection bias, given that States are likely to comply with lenient measures first. To overcome the limitations of the snapshot approach, we advocate for the discrete-time approach introduced earlier. There are two possible discrete-time measures of compliance, one expressed as a yearly probability and a second expressed in terms of duration. Although they are expressed in different metrics, these expressions are mathematically equivalent.

The *yearly probability of compliance*, illustrated in section 2, reflects the likelihood that a State will comply with a given reparation measure at a given point in time. Because this third metric can vary from year to year, it is sensitive to changes in explanatory factors. For instance, the probability of compliance may be low in year t but increase substantially after a new government enters office in year $t + 1$. We show in section 6 that when we compare a large number of reparation measures this metric allows us to reconstruct the life cycle of compliance. Moreover, the yearly probability of compliance contains the necessary information to assess duration—a low probability of compliance in a given year suggests that the State will take long time to comply—but it is not a very intuitive metric to assess delays. Therefore, we need an alternative metric to convey this information.

For ease of interpretation, we propose a fourth measure: the expected time for compliance (ETC). The ETC represents the expected number of years until the State implements an order. We calculate the ETC in three steps. First, we record the number of discrete-time units (years) until we observe compliance. Returning to *Garrido y Baigorria*, for instance, there are nine time units for the first reparation measure, five for the second, nineteen for the third, and nineteen and counting for the fourth. Second, we estimate the yearly probability of

---

[15] González-Salzberg, "Do States Comply with the Compulsory Judgments of the Inter-American Court of Human Rights?" (n. 7).

compliance—the third metric discussed in the previous paragraph. The average probability of compliance per annum in *Garrido y Baigorria* is 3/52: three events of compliance in 9 + 5 + 19 + 19 time units. Third, we retrieve the ETC by taking the inverse of that probability. If the average probability of compliance is 3/52, the inverse of this figure provides the expected number of years (17, or 52/3) until the State honors an order.

Because the ETC is derived from the yearly probability of compliance, the discrete-time approach allows us to report the ETC and the estimated probability of compliance interchangeably. These two statistics are conceptually equivalent: an ETC of two years reflects a compliance probability of 0.50, while an ETC of ten years reflects a compliance probability of 0.10. We often prefer the ETC because of its intuitive interpretation: a high ETC means that the State will likely take many years to comply, while a low ETC indicates that a State is likely to comply promptly.

Before discussing our findings, it is important to note some caveats for the interpretation of our fourth metric. The ETC already accounts for the possibility that a State *will not comply* with a given order. The measure penalizes cases of noncompliance by reporting longer expected compliance horizons. Therefore, a very long ETC should not be interpreted as a specific prediction about the number of years until compliance but rather as an indication of unlikely compliance over the long run. For instance, an ETC of one hundred years does not imply that a State will wait a century to comply with a ruling but that noncompliance is likely over the long run—the yearly probability is just 0.01. In addition, because we normally report ETCs that summarize information for several years, this figure may mask important information about the implementation life cycle. Two States may have similar ETCs but vary in their propensity to comply at specific points in time following a ruling. Given this limitation, in the following section we report numerical information about ETCs to compare States, but also present graphical information about cycles of compliance.

5. Compliance with the IACtHR

We illustrate the four metrics discussed previously using evidence from the IACtHR. Between 1989 and 2018, the Inter-American Court ruled against States in 238 cases, ordering some 1,783 reparation measures. We compiled an original data set for these cases, documenting the year of each ruling and the year of the resolutions in which the IACtHR determined that the State had complied with the reparation measures. Because the Court's supervision resolutions identify two possible levels of compliance ("partial" or "full"), we calculate measures of compliance for two events: the first acknowledgment of any form of compliance whether partial or full, and the acknowledgment of full compliance, that is, the end of the supervision process for a particular order.

Table III.3.1 summarizes this information, comparing States along the two snapshot measures of compliance. The first four columns in the table identify the country, the number of cases in which the IACtHR ruled against the State, the number of cases that the Court has archived due to full compliance, and the number of reparation measures ordered in total. The following columns present conventional measures of compliance based on a snapshot at the end of 2018. The two columns under "Compliance (%)" compare rates of implementation across countries, using the conventional estimate for the percentage of reparations. The last two columns compare the average number of years elapsed between the Court's ruling and the moment when the Court acknowledges compliance.

The initial portrait presented in Table III.3.1 is admittedly dim, with only 33 out of 238 cases archived. This means the IACtHR has closed only 14 percent of the cases due to full compliance, while 86 percent of the cases still burden its supervision efforts. At the country level, it is also disappointing that no State has closed more than half of its cases. This evidence has played into the hands of critics who highlight the limited effectiveness of the Inter-American Human Rights System.[16]

The first three columns of the table also illustrate some problems with an analysis based on overall cases, which does not disaggregate rulings into specific orders. The column reporting the total number of cases makes it evident that we risk placing very different situations in the same category when comparing the rate of archived cases. For example, Uruguay, Colombia, and Venezuela had closed no cases by the end of 2018, yet Uruguay had only two cases pending, while Colombia and Venezuela had some twenty pending cases each. Moreover, the compliance rate for specific orders shows that the political will in Colombia and Venezuela has been quite different.

The remaining columns in Table III.3.1 compare levels of compliance based on individual reparation measures. To overcome some limitations of the analysis based on cases, legal scholars opted to break down cases into individual reparation.[17] The focus on individual reparations represented a considerable advance. States such as Bolivia, Ecuador, or Panama, which appear as noncompliant in most cases, are implementing most of the reparation measures ordered in the context of those cases even though the cases remain open. Perhaps most importantly, the literature analyzing compliance with specific reparation measures

---

[16] Carlos Villagrán and Fabia Veçoso, "A Human Rights Tale of Competing Narratives" [2017] 8 *Revista Direito e Práxis* 1603.

[17] Fernando Basch et al., "The Effectiveness of the Inter-American System of Human Rights Protection: A Quantitative Approach to its Functioning and Compliance with Its Decisions" [2011] 7 *Sur* 9. Bailliet (n. 3).

Table III.3.1 Conventional measures of compliance (by 2018).

Country	Cases Total	Cases Archived	Reparations	1. Compliance (%)* Any	Full	2. Average time† Any	Full
Argentina	15	4	90	61.1	48.9	4.2	4.0
Barbados	2	0	10	50.0	30.0	3.0	3.0
Bolivia	6	2	43	74.4	67.4	2.3	2.7
Brazil	8	1	58	31.0	24.1	2.5	2.5
Chile	9	2	54	66.7	61.1	2.4	2.4
Colombia	22	0	199	40.7	32.2	3.7	4.4
Costa Rica	4	2	24	37.5	33.3	3.1	4.8
Dominican Republic	4	0	38	7.9	7.9	3.0	3.0
Ecuador	20	9	111	73.0	64.0	2.9	3.4
El Salvador	6	0	66	53.0	39.4	3.3	3.5
Guatemala	27	1	226	41.6	36.3	2.9	3.0
Haiti	2	0	11	0.0	0.0	--	--
Honduras	13	2	93	41.9	32.3	3.2	2.4
Mexico	10	1	113	47.8	39.8	3.7	3.6
Nicaragua	5	2	31	32.3	22.6	3.5	3.1
Panama	5	1	31	71.0	64.5	2.5	2.8
Paraguay	7	1	70	42.9	35.7	4.4	5.8
Peru	43	3	302	37.7	27.5	4.5	4.2
Suriname	6	2	43	34.9	32.6	3.8	4.1
Trinidad and Tobago	2	0	14	0.0	0.0	--	--
Uruguay	2	0	14	35.7	35.7	2.0	2.0
Venezuela	20	0	142	4.9	4.2	6.3	6.5
TOTAL	238	33	1783	41.8	34.3	3.5	3.6

* Percentage of reparation measures with any form of *partial* or *full* compliance by the end of 2018.
† Average number of years from the ruling until IACtHR reported any form of *partial* or *full* compliance, *if* the State complied. Available only for reparations with compliance.

documented which type of remedies is more likely to be implemented. The evidence consistently indicates that States are more likely to honor monetary compensation measures and less likely to implement nonrepetition measures and orders addressing the State's obligation to prosecute perpetrators.[18]

The different rates of compliance across different types of reparation measures underscore the importance of treating compliance as a gradual rather than a discrete outcome. A gradual approach to compliance is especially important when it comes to orders that involve long-term processes and several domestic actors, such as guarantees of nonrepetition that demand changes in legislation. Specialists have argued for a flexible understanding of compliance, given that the Inter-American Court has a relatively expansive and maximalist jurisprudence.[19]

Fortunately, the IACtHR reports partial compliance—that is, demonstrated progress toward implementation—in its monitoring resolutions. Table III.3.1 illustrates the contrast between a strict definition of compliance, acknowledging only full implementation (with an average rate of 34%) and a broad definition including partial or full implementation (with an average rate of 42%). For complex orders that involve, for example, investigating, judging, and sanctioning perpetrators, specialists argue for an even more nuanced classification that goes beyond the two categories of partial and full compliance.

5.1. Rates of Compliance

The central columns in Table III.3.1 report rates of compliance as a percentage of reparations with any level of implementation (partial or full) or strictly in full compliance. We consider all reparations ordered by the Court from 1989 to 2018. The picture emerging from this analysis, based on individual reparation measures, is far more promising than the one based on individual cases. More than 40 percent of the reparations ordered since 1989 met with some degree of compliance, and over a third have been fully complied with. This might be a reasonable number for a Court credited with ordering high-bar reparation measures and sometimes at the cutting edge of human rights jurisprudence—something that other tribunals, like the European Court of Human Rights (ECtHR), do not aim for. As a point of reference, the ECtHR obtained a 55 percent implementation rate for its leading cases between 2009 and 2018.[20]

---

[18] Basch (n. 17), 24.

[19] Jorge Contesse, "Resisting the Inter-American Human Rights System" [2019] 44 *Yale Journal of International Law* 179.

[20] For the ECtHR, "leading" cases represent new legal issues, while "repetitive" cases represent later instances of the same issue. The Committee of Ministers closes repetitive cases when States comply with individual measures (e.g., monetary compensation), but only closes the leading cases once States comply with general measures (e.g., measures of nonrepetition). George Stafford, "The

5.2. Average Time to Compliance

The last two columns in Table III.3.1 report the observed time to compliance for the average reparation measure by country. The figures are somewhat surprising, with just three and a half years on average between the date of the ruling and the date when the IACtHR acknowledges compliance. However, these estimates exclude all reparation measures without implementation and thus present an overly optimistic picture. Countries with extremely low rates of compliance, such as the Dominican Republic (7.9%), may also display a prompt (three-year) execution of the few measures they actually choose to implement. Only a dynamic duration analysis is able to overcome this inferential problem.

In sum, Table III.3.1 illustrates the advantages and the limitations of snapshot measures of compliance. By moving from an analysis of overall cases to an analysis of specific orders (reparation measures), conventional statistics provide important insights. At the same time, however, they fail to effectively account for the role of time. A specific example will help convey this point: analyzing compliance in 2012, Cecilia Baillet noted that Mexico, which had at that time a zero percent compliance rate at the case level, behaved particularly well with regard to orders of investigation and punishment, complying with a remarkable 67 percent of those challenging orders.[21] Thus, the analysis of specific measures provides more nuanced information than the analysis of overall cases. However, nuance gained from comparing orders does not translate into nuance over time. The Court decided on four additional cases involving Mexico within five years of Baillet's study, issuing three of the four rulings in 2018. If we had conducted a similar analysis of decisions involving Mexico by the end of 2018, compliance rates at the reparation level would have dropped considerably because the State did not have enough time to implement the orders within a few months.

To overcome these limitations, Table III.3.2 displays discrete-time measures for the same cases. The central columns report the yearly probability of compliance, and the last two columns report the ETC for each member State. This ensures that countries with notable delays are brought to the forefront.

Implementation of Judgments of the European Court of Human Rights: Worse Than You Think—Part 2: The Hole in the Roof" (2019) *EJIL: Talk!*, <https://www.ejiltalk.org/the-implementation-of-judgments-of-the-european-court-of-human-rights-worse-than-you-think-part-2-the-hole-in-the-roof/> (accessed February 5, 2022).

[21] Bailliet (n. 3), 480.

Table III.3.2 Discrete-time measures of compliance (at 2018).

Country	Reparations	Yearly probability[‡] Any	Full	ETC (years)[§] Any	Full
Argentina	90	0.101	0.073	9.9	13.7
Barbados	10	0.067	0.034	15.0	29.7
Bolivia	43	0.147	0.122	6.8	8.2
Brazil	58	0.082	0.060	12.2	16.8
Chile	54	0.163	0.149	6.1	6.7
Colombia	199	0.069	0.047	14.6	21.4
Costa Rica	24	0.103	0.078	9.7	12.8
Dominican Republic	38	0.012	0.012	83.0	83.0
Ecuador	111	0.169	0.126	5.9	7.9
El Salvador	66	0.096	0.065	10.4	15.4
Guatemala	226	0.069	0.055	14.5	18.1
Haiti	11	0.000	0.000	--	--
Honduras	93	0.089	0.065	11.3	15.3
Mexico	113	0.097	0.078	10.3	12.8
Nicaragua	31	0.085	0.048	11.8	21.0
Panama	31	0.136	0.102	7.4	9.8
Paraguay	70	0.048	0.035	20.9	28.9
Peru	302	0.052	0.034	19.2	29.5
Suriname	43	0.055	0.049	18.1	20.5
Trinidad and Tobago	14	0.000	0.000	--	--
Uruguay	14	0.057	0.057	17.4	17.4
Venezuela	142	0.007	0.006	148.9	174.8
TOTAL	1783	0.069	0.052	14.5	19.4

[‡] Yearly probability of a first report documenting any form of *partial* or *full* compliance.

[§] Expected number of years until the IACtHR reports the first form of *partial* or *full* compliance. Undefined for countries that never complied with an order, i.e., ETC = ∞.

5.3. Yearly Probability of Compliance

The States most likely to comply with pending Court orders have been Ecuador, with an average yearly probability of partial or full compliance of 0.169, or 16.9 percent; Chile, with 16.3 percent; and Bolivia, with 14.9 percent. At the other end of the spectrum we find Haiti and Trinidad and Tobago, with no compliance events to date; and Venezuela, with a yearly probability of 0.007, or just 0.7 percent. Trinidad and Tobago and Venezuela denounced the American Convention in 1998 and 2012, respectively. As a result, the probability of Ecuador honoring a Court order has been twenty-four times greater than the probability of Venezuela doing so.

It is worth noting that the number of reparation measures pending is unrelated to the probability of compliance. Some States, like Haiti and Barbados, are confronted with only a few orders, but they are unlikely to comply with them. Countries like Ecuador and Mexico, however, confront a large number of orders but they display annual rates of compliance well above the mean. It follows that backlog is not the main explanation for annual rates of compliance. Causality could in fact flow in the opposite direction, as unresponsive States may discourage victims from appealing to the Inter-American System.

5.4. Expected Time for Compliance

For a more intuitive metric, the last two columns of Table III.3.2 display the ETC. Because the ETC figures incorporate information about noncompliance, the contrast with Table III.3.1 can be shocking. While the *observed* time for compliance for measures honored by the Dominican Republic is three years, the *expected* time for compliance for the country is eighty-three years.

To place those States in perspective, Figure III.3.1 plots the expected time until the first manifestation of partial or full compliance for all countries in Table III.3.2. The figure allows us to distinguish between two qualitatively distinct groups: noncompliers—the Dominican Republic, Haiti, Trinidad and Tobago, and Venezuela—and the rest. Noncompliers have zero probability of compliance in any given year or display unrealistic ETCs that indicate a probability effectively approaching zero. The remaining States present ETCs that range continuously between six and twenty-one years, as in the cases of Ecuador and Paraguay. Such a continuum suggests that States in this second group belong in the same category: their differences, although very significant, are a matter of degree. The figure shows that eight countries in this group are likely to comply with their reparation orders within a decade. These country averages, however, hide a

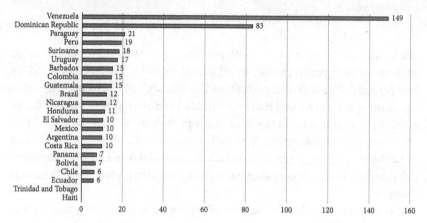

Figure III.3.1. Expected time for the first form of partial or full compliance in years

considerable amount of variance across types of reparation measures and over the life cycle of reparations, as we discuss in the following section.

Based on Table III.3.2. ETCs undefined for Trinidad and Tobago and Haiti.

6. The Compliance Life Cycle

The most important advantage of discrete-time measures is their capacity to track levels of compliance over time. Although Table III.3.2 reports the average probability of compliance for each State in a typical year, a State's propensity to comply naturally varies over the years. This variation in part reflects idiosyncratic conditions, for example, government changes, but it also reflects the nature of the implementation process. It is unlikely that States will comply with reparation measures immediately after a ruling because it takes time to address the Court's requests.

Even if most factors driving compliance remain stable, on average we observed temporal fluctuations when we analyzed compliance in time. Willing States will be unlikely to comply immediately, but they will do so within a few years. After willing States have complied within a reasonable period, only orders issued to reluctant States will remain in the analysis. Thus, the average probability of compliance should be low immediately after a decision (as willing States prepare to comply), will increase within few years, and then drop again when only reluctant States remain under supervision. While conventional measures of compliance (calculated for cases or reparation measures) are unable to track changes in the probability of implementation over time, discrete-time measures (calculated annually) allow us to document the life cycle of compliance with precise accuracy.

ADDRESSING CONCEPTUAL CHALLENGES 579

Figure III.3.2 documents the life cycle using data from the IACtHR. The horizontal axis reflects the number of years a measure has remained under supervision; the vertical axis reflects the probability of compliance by the end of the year. The series tracks the yearly probability of compliance for two outcomes: the first indication of compliance, whether partial or full, and indicated by the dotted line, and full compliance, indicated by the solid line. Annual probabilities are calculated for pending orders, that is, those without any implementation (dotted line) or those without full compliance (solid line). Thus, while the solid line in Year 1 reflects 69 episodes of full compliance for 1,607 pending orders, with a probability of 0.043, or 4.3 percent, a similar rate in Year 6 reflects 32 episodes for 734 pending measures, with a probability of 4.4 percent. Only 11 orders remain under supervision by year 20.

Although the average ETC reported in Table III.3.2 is more than fourteen years, the figure shows that this average hides an uneven historical trajectory: the probability of compliance increases consistently within the first three years of a ruling, as willing States prepare to implement the required measures. By the third year the probability of any form of compliance is about 16 percent, and the probability of full compliance is close to 11 percent. The likelihood of compliance declines in the following years, hitting a nadir by the end of the first decade.

In practice, this life cycle means that the cumulative probability of compliance, whether partial or full, approximates 50 percent within the first decade. The number of reparation measures monitored by the IACtHR therefore drops considerably after ten years. This pattern is hard to grasp from Table III.3.2, since the average ETC is prolonged by reluctant States and by a small percentage of measures without implementation. Figure III.3.2 therefore suggests that there is

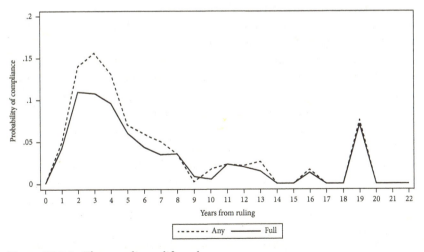

Figure III.3.2. The compliance life cycle

more room for optimism than commonly assumed. Moreover, the data tends to *overestimate* the time to compliance. Actual implementation takes place a year or two before the Court acknowledges State behavior. Most studies, including the one contained in this chapter, employ the date-of-supervision resolutions as the official time to compliance, but on average State actions precede those resolutions by at least eighteen months. Figure III.3.2 also suggests that compliance with lagging reparation measures appears to improve about two decades after a ruling. However, because very few measures remain open at this stage, this "surge" reflects the experience of only a very few cases (*Castillo Petruzzi v. Perú*; *Garrido y Baigorria v. Argentina* and *Suárez Rosero v. Ecuador*) and thus it is uncertain.

The study of life cycles introduces a dynamic perspective to the analysis. It provides a more encouraging outlook than the static comparison of compliance rates (as in Table III.3.1) or the comparison of ETCs across States (as in Table III.3.2). It also allows scholars and practitioners to identify the best window of opportunity to elicit State compliance. Given the large number of cases decided by the Court in recent years, it is hard to anticipate whether the observed life cycle will remain stable in the future.

7. Concluding Remarks

This chapter has shown that a dynamic analysis of compliance is able to sustain more reliable (and perhaps more optimistic) conclusions regarding how the Inter-American Human Rights System influences outcomes in Latin America. However, the longitudinal perspective also calls for a long-term distinction between *compliance* and *impact*. *Compliance* narrowly defines whether State actions align with the orders of the Inter-American System, while *impact* refers to the broader legal and social consequences of those orders.

An extensive literature has acknowledged that legal decisions have implications that transcend State behavior. For instance, Yuval Shany (2014) develops the idea of international court *effectiveness* to analyze whether tribunals are able to "attain, within a predefined amount of time, the goals set for them by their relevant constituencies."[22] Karen J. Alter, Laurence R. Helfer, and Mikael Rask Madsen (2018) conceptualize international court *authority* to understand "how the audiences that interact with international courts embrace or reject international court rulings."[23] We build on those distinctions to emphasize that

---

[22] Yuval Shany, *Assessing the Effectiveness of International Courts* (Oxford University Press 2014).
[23] Karen J. Alter, Laurence R. Helfer, and Mikael Rask Madsen (eds.), *International Court Authority* (Oxford University Press 2018).

over the long run compliance and transformative impacts may not coincide when it comes to expected outcomes. In the ideal-typical cases, State compliance leads to positive impacts, and a lack of compliance leads to negative human rights outcomes. However, observers can also identify "misaligned" instances in which a lack of compliance is followed by unexpected positive transformations or, by contrast, situations in which compliance triggers a backlash against the courts. We therefore close our discussion by identifying four potential patterns that link compliance and impact: direct transformative impact, indirect transformative impact, resistance, and compliance backlash.

7.1. Direct Transformative Impact

Compliance with human rights rulings often creates lasting consequences for society. In the domestic realm, iconic rulings, such as *Brown v. Board of Education* (1954) in the United States, have contributed to profound social transformations, even though compliance was achieved after considerable resistance. In the Inter-American System moreover, some decisions have transformative impacts beyond the original case and country. For example, when the Argentine Supreme Court nullified the 1987 amnesty law in 2005, it relied on the *Barrios Altos* case, an IACtHR decision referring to Peru (2001). This pattern of recursive interaction between domestic law and the Inter-American System led Armin von Bogdandy et al. to conceptualize "an original Latin American path of transformative constitutionalism," described as the emergence of an *Ius Constitutionale Commune* in Latin America.[24] This development "builds, far more than on neo-constitutionalism, on the Inter-American system of human rights, whose influence in the region the authors of the 1990s could not foresee."[25]

7.2. Indirect Transformative Impact

This type of pattern refers to surprising instances in which court rulings induce positive outcomes despite the lack of direct compliance. For example, although the two central measures ordered by the IACtHR in the 2006 *Almonacid Arellano y otros v. Chile* case—involving the State's obligation to investigate and sanction human rights violations—remain without compliance to this day, the Criminal Chamber of Chile's Supreme Court cited the decision within a few months in

---

[24] Armin von Bogdandy et al., "Ius Constitutionale Commune en América Latina: A Regional Approach To Transformative Constitutionalism" (2016) MPIL Research Paper Series No. 2016-21.
[25] Bogdandy et al. (n. 24), 21.

the *Hugo Vásquez Martínez and Mario Superby Jeldres* case to assert that crimes against humanity are not subject to statutes of limitations. This was not the first time that Chilean courts built on international law, but while "before *Almonacid* international law was mostly mobilized by parts of the Chilean judiciary as an interpretative tool, following the IACtHR ruling, international legal norms have also been deployed as distinctive legal criteria."[26]

7.3. Resistance

The evidence presented in previous sections shows that States too often resist the implementation of reparation measures. In some cases, however, passive resistance escalates into active defiance. Wayne Sandholtz et al. note that "noncompliance with, and even criticism of, the decisions of international human rights courts are normal forms of resistance to adverse rulings. But sometimes States strike at international human rights courts with more far-reaching forms of resistance."[27] States may cease to cooperate with the court, narrow the court's jurisdiction, limit access (standing) to the court, withdraw from the court's jurisdiction, and even—as in the case of the Southern Africa Development Community Tribunal—collectively terminate the court.

As mentioned before, Trinidad and Tobago (1998) and Venezuela (2012) have denounced the American Convention of Human Rights and withdrawn from the IACtHR's jurisdiction. The Dominican Republic has not taken this step, but its Constitutional Tribunal ruled in 2014 that the IACtHR's decisions are nonbinding. Sandholtz et al. discuss these cases as instances of backlash. However, we want to emphasize that those reactions were part of a deliberate strategy to avoid compliance. These preemptive forms of backlash are analytically distinct from the backlash triggered by compliance efforts discussed in the next section.

7.4. Compliance Backlash

We employ this term to refer to episodes in which actual or anticipated compliance with controversial rulings triggers unexpected negative consequences.

---

[26] Marcelo Torelly, "From Compliance to Engagement: Assessing the Impact of the Inter-American Court of Human Rights on Constitutional Law in Latin America," in Par Engstrom (ed.), *The Inter-American Human Rights System: Impact Beyond Compliance* (Palgrave Macmillan 2019), 124.

[27] Wayne Sandholtz, Yining Bei, and Kayla Caldwell, "Backlash and International Human Rights Courts," in Alison Brysk and Michael Stohl (eds.), *Contracting Human Rights: Crisis, Accountability, and Opportunity* (Edward Elgar 2018), 159.

For instance, in late 2017 the IACtHR asserted equal rights for same-sex couples in a consultative opinion (24/17) requested by Costa Rica. The Constitutional Chamber of the Costa Rican Supreme Court acknowledged the opinion and ultimately ruled against the Family Code in August 2018. However, the Inter-American Court's position triggered a political storm in the context of the 2018 presidential election campaign. A conservative public backlash against the decision bolstered mass support for presidential candidate Fabricio Alvarado, who railed against the Court and won the first round of the presidential election, though he was defeated in the runoff.

The Costa Rican experience illustrates a critical fact: compliance backlash is led by political entrepreneurs who exploit social reactions against unpopular rulings. We distinguish this pattern from instances of preemptive backlash discussed previously, in which State agents undermine human rights tribunals as part of a deliberate strategy to avoid compliance. Although the boundaries between the two categories are sometimes ambiguous, the distinction can help us differentiate between qualitatively different situations. For example, in the context of the European Court of Human Rights, the 2014 *Yukos* case resembles an example of preemptive backlash by Russia, while the 2005 *Hirst* case resembles an example of compliance backlash from the United Kingdom. Nevertheless, the distinction can be fluid: compliance backlash easily turns into a preemptive strategy when political actors leading the charge against human rights tribunals gain control of the national government or domestic courts. The complex relationship between compliance and transformative impacts underscores the importance of adopting a diachronic perspective when assessing State compliance with the orders of the Inter-American System. The discrete-time approach introduced in this chapter offers an effective strategy to address some of the major conceptual challenges created by such a diachronic perspective. Further development of this approach will therefore be crucial to advance consistent standards within the region's multilevel legal system.

III.4
Transformative Impact of the Inter-American Human Rights System
A Methodology to Think beyond Compliance

By Viviana Krsticevic and René Urueña

1. Introduction

The Inter-American Human Rights System (Inter-American System, or IAHRS) has made great contributions to the protection of the rights of victims, the development of legal standards, and the strengthening of democracies in Latin America. However, the low levels of compliance reported by the Inter-American Court of Human Rights (Inter-American Court, or IACtHR) and by some commentators could lead to the erroneous conclusion that the Inter-American System is of marginal importance in efforts to hold States accountable for human rights violations.[1]

The experience of most of the Inter-American Court's stakeholders suggests otherwise. The understanding that victims, litigants, and States have of its work seems to contradict the most critical assessments of the levels of compliance with IACtHR decisions and their impact on access to justice. From the perspective of these stakeholders, and also of the Inter-American Court itself, IACtHR judgments play a key role in ensuring State accountability.

This contradiction arises from the limits of compliance as an analytical category for assessing impact. This chapter extends the scope of analysis, arguing that compliance with international norms can be promoted through an institutional design and practice that considers their wider impact.[2] Ultimately, this chapter argues, there is a feedback loop between the wider impact of an international institution's order and compliance with that order. Compliance with international decisions is facilitated by the wider impact of such decisions, which

---

[1] See Armin von Bogdandy and René Urueña in this volume.
[2] Complementing this reading, see Armin von Bogdandy and René Urueña; and Stephania Yate Cortes and René Urueña, in this volume.

feeds into compliance processes. The Inter-American Court's jurisprudence on crimes against humanity illustrates this connection.

Most of the quantitative literature concerning compliance with IACtHR orders ignores this broader impact. Moreover, the scholarly work that does consider the Inter-American Court's wider impact nevertheless overlooks the connection between impact and compliance, instead framing them as two distinct categories. This chapter fills that gap in the literature, by proposing criteria to consider when assessing the impact of the Inter-American Court and by discussing how the IACtHR's wider impact affects compliance.

The second section of this chapter provides a more thorough review of the literature on compliance and the impact of the Inter-American Court and identifies its limitations. Next, the third section describes the institutional landscape for monitoring compliance at the Inter-American Court of Human Rights and emphasizes the dynamic nature of this process. Finally, the fourth section proposes that the following criteria be considered when assessing impact: (a) time; (b) quality of compliance; and (c) institutional impact.

2. Literature Review: Compliance with the Inter-American Court's Orders

The last decade has witnessed growth in the study of compliance with the Inter-American System's orders, and most commentators seem to agree that the IAHRS's work is characterized by extremely low levels of compliance. Both the Inter-American Court and recent scholarly work, however, have argued that these low levels of compliance do not necessarily mean that States are indifferent to the IAHRS, or that its work has no impact.[3] Nevertheless, most studies show a disappointing record of compliance with the Inter-American System's orders, especially when these orders are disaggregated by type and by the body adopting the order, either the Inter-American Court or the Inter-American Commission on Human Rights (Inter-American Commission, or IACHR).

One recent line of scholarship has measured the level of compliance quantitatively, finding that, while orders that have to do with economic compensation are often complied with, other orders that imply more politically costly action by the State seem to be less heeded. For example, Fernando Basch, Leonardo Filippini, Ana Laya, Mariano Nino, Felicitas Rossi, and Bárbara Schneider disaggregated by type of orders and found that those requiring economic and

---

[3] Annual Report of the Inter-American Court of Human Rights, 12; Damian A. Gonzalez-Salzberg, "Do States Comply with the Compulsory Judgments of the Inter-American Court of Human Rights? An Empirical Study of the Compliance with 330 Measures of Reparation" [2014] 13 *Revista do Instituto Brasileiro de Direitos Humanos*.

symbolic reparation have a higher level of compliance (total compliance of 47% and partial compliance of 13%), as opposed to orders requiring the investigation and punishment of perpetrators of human rights violations (total compliance of 10% and partial compliance of 13%).[4]

Following different classifications, Damian A. Gonzalez-Salzberg's study of orders issued by the Inter-American Court prior to 2011 similarly found that States are more likely to comply with orders requiring them to implement economic and symbolic measures, than with orders requiring the investigation and punishment of those responsible for the violation of rights: orders requiring payment of compensation, publication of the decision, and apologies to victims had a higher level of compliance (65% for compensation, 75% for publication, and 80% for apologies), whereas orders requiring the State to investigate or punish those responsible and to modify domestic law had lower levels of compliance (69% and 51%, respectively).[5]

These quantitative studies, though significant, have three crucial limitations.[6] The first concerns the notion of "partial compliance." Both quantitative and qualitative studies of compliance with inter-American orders adopt the three categories used by the Inter-American System: "compliance," "partial compliance," and "non-compliance," of which partial compliance encompasses, by far, the highest number of cases.[7] The category of partial compliance is too blunt, and studies that accept this category without further nuance fail to account for the differences among the many, varied actions that the IAHRS designates as "partial compliance."

Second, many quantitative studies of compliance arrive at counterintuitive conclusions regarding the relevance of the Inter-American System for the protection of human rights. These studies conclude that the Inter-American Court is ineffective, especially in ensuring accountability, based on low rates of compliance.[8] This conclusion ignores the reality that many orders with which States

---

[4] Fernando Basch et al., "The Effectiveness of the Inter-American System of Human Rights Protection: A Quantitative Approach to Its Functioning and Compliance with Its Decisions" [2010] 12 SUR—International Journal on Human Rights 9.

[5] Gonzalez-Salzberg (n. 3). For results in the same line, see Eduardo Bertoni, "El Sistema Interamericano de Derechos Humanos-SIDH-y La (Real?) Falta de Apoyo Regional" (2017) 20 Iuris Dictio. Eduardo Bertoni, "El Sistema Interamericano de Derechos Humanos—SIDH—y la (¿real?) falta de apoyo regional" [2017] 20 Iuris Dictio; Darren Hawkins and Wade Jacoby, "Partial Compliance: A Comparison of the European and Inter-American Courts of Human Rights' [2010] 6 Journal of International Law and International Relations 35; Alexandra Huneeus, "Courts Resisting Courts: Lessons from the Inter-American Court's Struggle to Enforce Human Rights" [2011] 44 Cornell International Law Journal 493; Open Society Foundations, From Judgment to Justice. Implementing International and Regional Human Rights Decisions (Open Society Foundations 2010).

[6] For a complementing critique of that body of literature, see Armin von Bogdandy and René Urueña; Stephania Yate Cortes and René Urueña, in this volume.

[7] See Hawkins and Jacoby (n. 5), 35.

[8] Bertoni (n. 5).

do not fully comply nevertheless generate significant societal change, including in the area of accountability. When the Inter-American Court classifies an order as partially fulfilled, it not only reveals but can also increase the effectiveness of the international system by acknowledging a State's progress, while at the same time enabling the IACtHR to continue to monitor and guide the State's efforts to achieve full compliance.[9] The Inter-American Court's extended period of attention to States' actions significantly increases the impact of IACtHR decisions on accountability processes at the domestic level, which are themselves often lengthy, as well as in other areas that are discussed later in this chapter's analysis of the case of *Barrios Altos v. Peru*.

Third, these studies' use of the IAHRS's categories not only oversimplifies institutional and social processes that respond to inter-American decisions but also presents a static analysis of those processes. Partial compliance, for example, can range from the opening of an investigation to a final ruling that has not yet been enforced. The broad spectrum of State actions that would fall into the category of partial compliance demonstrates the need to develop more dynamic and flexible categories that would better capture the effects of the System and how they vary in character and over time.

Clara Sandoval, Philip Leach, and Rachel Murray demonstrated this challenge in their study of the level of implementation of international obligations in nine countries.[10] According to them, "supranational bodies are doing more than monitoring the implementation of orders and recommendations despite a scarcity of resources."[11] Nevertheless, they note "an unused potential in the mandates of these supranational bodies as well as in their ability to bring other actors on board that cajole better implementation of reparation measures." They especially focus on how these bodies can open spaces for constructive dialogue, including the IAHRS's ability to organize hearings with States and victim's representatives.

Qualitative studies have emerged in response to this line of scholarship, seeking to understand the impact and the role of the Inter-American System in the protection of human rights in Latin America through changes in narratives, truth-telling, social behaviors, and more.[12] Alexandra Huneeus, for example, in

---

[9] This dynamic monitoring process is explored as an instance of "transformative constitutionalism beyond compliance" in Armin von Bogdandy and René Urueña, in this volume.

[10] The Human Rights Law Implementation Project, HRLIP, seeks to analyze the levels of compliance and implementation of nine countries in Arica, Europe, and America, regarding regional and international tribunals, https://www.bristol.ac.uk/law/hrlip (accessed November 9, 2021).

[11] Clara Sandoval, Philip Leach, and Rachel Murray, "Monitoring, Cajoling and Promoting Dialogue: What Role for Supranational Human Rights Bodies in the Implementation of Individual Decisions?" [2020] 12 *Journal of Human Rights Practice* 71–100.

[12] See, e.g., Stephania Yate Cortes and René Urueña, in this volume. Par Engstrom, *The Inter-American Human Rights System: Impact Beyond Compliance* (Springer 2018). For a similar perspective on IAHRS compliance that focuses on Colombia and combines quantitative and qualitative methods, see Sergio Anzola, Beatriz Eugenia Sánchez, and René Urueña, "Después Del Fallo: El Cumplimiento de Las Decisiones Del Sistema Interamericano de Derechos Humanos. Una

a study about the role of domestic institutions in the fulfillment of court orders, found that noncompliance is largely due to the inaction of domestic judges and prosecutors and a lack of coordination between State institutions. According to Huneeus, the higher the level of coordination between State institutions that is required, the lower the level of compliance with court orders will be.[13] Similarly, Courtney Hillebrecht recognized that there may be higher levels of compliance when the executive power of a government establishes coalitions with judges and legislators, although Hillebrecht considers the political will of the government to be the primary factor affecting compliance.[14] Cecilia Bailliet, on the other hand, analyzed States' degrees of compliance with eighteen IACtHR judgments and found that lack of judicial independence from military and security institutions has the effect of reducing compliance with orders to investigate those responsible for human rights violations.[15]

Scholars have also analyzed how various characteristics of domestic legal systems, and especially their differing approaches to the relationship between domestic and international law, affect State compliance with international court decisions. Huneeus, for example, has demonstrated that compliance with IACtHR decisions depends on the existence of a domestic legal community that envisions constitutional law as incorporating human rights standards, which forms alliances with relevant actors within the executive and legislative branches of the government.[16]

The Inter-American Court itself has observed that compliance with (and, relatedly, the effectiveness of) its decisions is linked to the integration of international law into domestic systems,[17] as illustrated by the "constitutional block" in Colombia as well as developments in constitutional law developments in Argentina and Peru.[18] Meanwhile, Jonathan Doak has proposed that the

Propuesta de Metodología," *Manual de Derechos Humanos y Políticas Públicas* (Universidad Pompeu Fabra 2012).

[13] Huneeus (n. 5), at 493.
[14] Courtney Hillebrecht, "The Domestic Mechanisms of Compliance with International Human Rights Law: Case Studies from the Inter-American Human Rights System" [2012] 34 *Human Rights Quarterly* 959–985.
[15] Cecilia M. Bailliet, "Measuring Compliance with the Inter-American Court of Human Rights: The Ongoing Challenge of Judicial Independence in Latin America" [2013] 31 *Nordic Journal of Human Rights* 477–495.
[16] Alexandra Huneeus, "Constitutional Lawyers and the Inter-American Court's Varies Authority" [2016] 79 *Law & Contemporary Problems* 179.
[17] *García Prieto et al. v. El Salvador* [2007] IACtHR, Ser. C No. 168, Voto concurrente del Juez García Ramírez, para. 11. See also Helio Bicudo, "Cumplimiento de las sentencias de La Corte Interamericana de Derechos Humanos y de las recomendaciones de La Comisión Interamericana de Derechos Humanos," in Antônio Augusto Cançado Trindade (ed.), *El Sistema Interamericano de Protección de Los Derechos Humanos en el umbral del siglo XXI* (Corte Interamericana de Derechos Humanos 2003), 229–234.
[18] See Jorge Ernesto Roa Roa, *Las antinomias entre las constituciones y La Convención Americana Sobre Derechos Humanos: El gran dilema del juez constitucional y convencional interamericano*

participation of civil society and victims in domestic criminal processes is a key factor in ensuring accountability for human rights violations.[19] Marcelo Torelly, on the other hand, has argued that compliance with IACtHR decisions depends less on the constitutional status of international law than it does on the legal culture of domestic judges.[20] And Sergio Anzola, Beatriz Eugenia Sánchez, and one of the authors of this chapter likewise demonstrated that, in the case of Colombia, compliance was not related to either the binding nature of IACtHR decisions in the Colombian judicial system or to the existence of a mechanism for compliance with reparation orders in such decisions. Instead, they found a positive correlation between compliance and the participation of victims in the reparations process, the direction of orders to the national government (as opposed to regional entities), and the type of nongovernmental organization (NGO) responsible for the litigation.[21]

Other qualitative work has studied the indirect impacts that IACtHR decisions have had on the protection of human rights. One of the most discussed topics has been the advancement of human rights through multilevel dialogue between domestic and international courts, which leads to domestic courts' reliance on inter-American standards and application of conventionality control,[22] a doctrine that requires domestic judges to apply the American Convention on Human Rights (American Convention, or ACHR) directly when exercising their domestic jurisdiction.[23] Tania Giovanna Vivas Barrera, and Jaime Alfonso Cubides Cárdenas, for example, have argued that conventionality control might

---

(Universidad Externado de Colombia 2015), 139–148; María Angélica Prada, "La integración del derecho internacional en el sistema colombiano," in George Rodrigo Bandeira Galindo, René Urueña, and Aida Torres Pérez (eds.), *Protección multinivel de derechos humanos* (Der Derechos Humanos and Educación Superior 2013).

[19] Jonathan Doak, "Victims' Rights in Criminal Trials: Prospects for Participation" [2005] 32 *Journal of Law and Society* 294–316.

[20] Marcelo Torelly, "From Compliance to Engagement: Assessing the Impact of the Inter-American Court of Human Rights on Constitutional Law in Latin America," in Par Engstrom (ed.), *The Inter-American Human Rights System: Impact Beyond Compliance* (Springer International Publishing 2019), 115–141

[21] Anzola, Sánchez, and Urueña (n. 12).

[22] See Víctor Bazán, "Corte Interamericana de Derechos Humanos y Cortes Supremas o Tribunales Constitucionales Latinoamericanos: el control de convencionalidad y la necesidad de un diálogo interjurisdiccional crítico" [2010] 16 *Revista Europea de Derechos Fundamentales/European Journal of Fundamental Rights* 15; Marcelo Neves, "Del Diálogo Entre Las Cortes Supremas y La Corte Interamericana de Derechos Humanos al Transconstitucionalismo En América Latina," in George Rodrigo Bandeira Galindo, René Urueña, and Aida Torres Pérez (eds.), *Protección Multinivel de Derechos Humanos. Manual* (Derechos Humanos y Educación Superior 2013). Eduardo Ferrer Mac-Gregor, "El Control de Convencionalidad Como Un Vehículo Para El Diálogo Judicial Entre La Corte Interamericana de Derechos Humanos y Los Tribunales de América" [2016] *Anuario de Derecho Constitucional Latinoamericano* 337.

[23] See Bazán (n. 22); Neves (n. 22); Mac-Gregor (n. 22).

encourage compliance with the Inter-American Court's decisions.[24] This line of scholarship also shows that judicial dialogue extends beyond the region to impact other legal systems, such as the European Human Rights System.[25] In this context, dialogue consists of an exchange of ideas and results in shared standards that provide a sense of common purpose that buttresses compliance[26] and enhances the prestige of the Inter-American Court, both regionally and globally.[27]

As can be gleaned from this overview, existing literature demonstrates the limit of focusing solely on compliance. A bridge is needed between the study of compliance and the study of the wider impact of the Inter-American System, which introduces more nuance into analyses of compliance and theorizes the confluence of compliance and wider impact.[28] Ultimately, work needs to be done to analyze the causal relations among institutional design, compliance, and impact beyond compliance.[29]

3. Dynamic Monitoring of Compliance

Crucial to rethinking compliance in the IAHRS is understanding the complex, iterative system the Inter-American Court uses to monitor its judgments.[30] The IACtHR has developed rich jurisprudence on reparations,[31] interpreting ACHR

---

[24] Tania Giovanna Vivas Barrera and Jaime Alfonso Cubides Cárdenas, "Diálogo judicial transnacional en la implementación de las sentencias de la Corte Interamericana" [2012] 8 *Entramado* 184–204.

[25] Laurence Burgorgue-Larsen and Nicolás Montoya Céspedes, "El Diálogo Judicial Entre La Corte Interamericana de Derechos Humanos y La Corte Europea de Derechos Humanos," in George Rodrigo Bandeira Galindo, René Urueña, and Aida Torres Pérez (eds.), *Protección Multinivel de Derechos Humanos. Manual* (Derechos Humanos y Educación Superior 2013).

[26] René Urueña, "¿Protección Multinivel de Los Derechos Humanos En América Latina? Oportunidades, Desafíos y Riesgos," in George Rodrigo Bandeira Galindo, René Urueña, and Aida Torres Pérez (eds.), *Protección Multinivel de Derechos Humanos. Manual* (Derechos Humanos y Educación Superior 2013).

[27] Burgorgue-Larsen and Montoya Céspedes (n. 25).

[28] See generally Oscar Parra, "The Impact of Inter-American Judgments by Institutional Empowerment," in Armin von Bogdandy et al. (eds.), *Transformative Constitutionalism in Latin America: The Emergence of a New Ius Commune* (Oxford University Press 2017), 357–376. See also Par Engstrom, "Introduction: Rethinking the Impact of the Inter-American Human Rights System," in Par Engstrom (ed.), *The Inter-American Human Rights System: Impact Beyond Compliance* (Palgrave Macmillan 2019), 1–22.

[29] Engstrom (n. 12).

[30] The following description of the monitoring process draws in part from Rene Urueña, "Compliance as Transformation: The Inter-American System of Human Rights and Its Impact(s)," in *Research Handbook on Compliance in International Human Rights Law* (Edward Elgar Publishing 2021).

[31] Dinah Shelton, "Reparations in the Inter-American System," in David J. Harris and Stephen Livingstone (eds.), *The Inter-American System of Human Rights* (Oxford University Press 1998); Sergio García Ramírez, "Las Reparaciones En El Sistema Interamericano de Protección de Los Derechos Humanos" [2008] Ciudad de México: UNAM. Viviana Krsticevic, "Diálogo para la consecución de justicia," in Armin von Bogdandy et al. (eds.), *Cumplimiento e impacto de las sentencias de la Corte*

Article 63.1 as granting it broad authority to order the measures necessary for a State to implement to provide redress to victims of human rights violations.[32] These reparations include monetary compensation, measures of satisfaction, and guarantees of nonrepetition.[33] For example, the Inter-American Court might order the investigation, prosecution, and punishment of those responsible for gross human rights violations and crimes against humanity; the training of public officials; the passage or reform of legislation; acts of recognition of responsibility; medical treatment; or education grants.[34] The wide range of reparations necessitates the cooperation of many different State actors for a judgment to be fully implemented. The IACtHR's detailed ordering of individual and general measures of reparation stand in stark contrast to the more restrained, declarative, and delegation practice of its European counterpart.[35]

The IACtHR's judgments set a timeline for compliance with different measures, which can range from one year to an undetermined period, or what might be considered a "reasonable time." The timeline for orders to investigate and punish those responsible for human rights violations is generally undetermined.

The Inter-American Court takes primary responsibility for monitoring compliance with its orders,[36] although compliance may also be reported to the General Assembly of the Organization of American States under ACHR Article 65 (which points to another difference between the Inter-American and European systems). Pursuant to IACtHR's rules of procedure, compliance with the judgments and other decisions of the Inter-American Court is monitored through a State's submission of reports, complemented by the victims' observations responding to those reports. The Inter-American Commission comments on both the State's reports and the victims' observations. The Court has also requested information from specific State institutions (e.g., the Prosecutor's Office and the Ombudsman's Office) during this phase, which sometimes prompts previously

---

Interamericana y el Tribunal Europeo de Derechos Humanos. Transformando realidades (UNAM 2019); Articles 67 and 68 ACHR provide that the Inter-American Court's judgments are final and binding.

[32] Shelton (n. 31).
[33] Gonzalez-Salzberg (n. 3), 5.
[34] Based on Article 63 ACHR, ICJ, and other provisions, the Inter-American Court has issued measures of cessation, compensation, nonrepetition, satisfaction, and rehabilitation.
[35] Hawkins and Jacoby call the European Human Rights System a system of "delegated compliance." We would call it, less optimistically, a system of optional compliance, since States decide what measures would suffice with minimal guidelines or input from victims, the European Court of Human Rights, or the Committee of Ministers of the Council of Europe.
[36] *Baena Ricardo et al. v. Panama* [2003] IACtHR, No. Ser. C No. 104, para. 72 ("[J]urisdiction includes the authority to administer justice; it is not restricted to stating the law, but also encompasses monitoring compliance with what has been decided. It is therefore necessary to establish and implement mechanisms or procedures for monitoring compliance with the judicial decisions, an activity that is inherent in the jurisdictional function. [. . .] To maintain otherwise, would mean affirming that the judgments delivered by the Court are merely declaratory and not effective.").

uninvolved actors to engage in the implementation of the orders. In 2008, for example, the IACtHR asked the Attorney General of Guatemala to produce a report on obstacles to the prosecution of human rights cases. Once the IACtHR has gathered all the information it requires, it proceeds to determine the level of compliance with its decisions and issue the relevant orders. The process of monitoring compliance thus primarily consists of soliciting written reports from the IACHR, the State, and the victims, a method which is, again, distinct from that of the European Human Rights System.

The Inter-American Court may not only rely on all these sources of information, but it may also convene a hearing with the State and the victims' representatives to monitor compliance. For some of these hearings, the Court has requested the presence of specific State institutions. These hearings are most often private but can be, in exceptional situations, public. Additionally, in 2015, the Inter-American Court began holding some of these hearings in the territory of the relevant States. On-site hearings have taken place in Panama (2015), Honduras (2015), Mexico (2016), Guatemala (2017), Panama (2017), Paraguay (2017), and Colombia (2019), among others. In 2020, the IACtHR convened a virtual hearing concerning provisional measures that were related to its work monitoring compliance with its decision in a case against Panama.[37] In exceptional circumstances, the IACtHR can also conduct an on-site visit to obtain firsthand information about compliance, as it did in the case of the *Massacres of El Mozote and surrounding areas v. El Salvador*, with the consent of the relevant State.[38]

As part of the monitoring process, the Inter-American Court issues additional resolutions in which it states which orders have reached full or partial compliance and which are pending compliance. The IACtHR also provides guidance to the State that will enable the latter to progress toward compliance with more complex measures of reparation, such as the investigation, prosecution, and punishment of individuals responsible for human rights violations. For example, a compliance resolution might determine that amnesties cannot be applied to crimes against humanity and should be considered void. Most of the cases the Court decided after 2001 were the subject of at least one monitoring decision within two years of the adoption of the original decision, as well as several decisions evaluating compliance and reorienting State action.[39] The vast majority of IACtHR cases are in the phase of compliance monitoring.

---

[37] This occurred due to COVID-19 travel restrictions. *Vélez Loor v. Panama* [2020] IACtHR, Provisional measures.
[38] IACHR, "Informe Anual 2018."
[39] IACtHR, "ABC de la Corte Interamericana de Derechos Humanos: El qué, cómo, cuándo, dónde y porqué de la Corte Interamericana" (San José, C.R./Corte IDH) 2018, at 10–11.

The Inter-American Court has also developed a strategy for jointly monitoring groups of similar cases. This method was first suggested by victims' representatives who had litigated cases against Colombia, all of which resulted in orders directing the State to fulfill the right to mental and physical health. Since then, the IACtHR has used this strategy of joint hearings and resolutions in several countries and on different issues to address structural obstacles to compliance.[40] For example, the Inter-American Court has jointly monitored cases that include orders concerning policies, laws, and practices that are critical for the investigation of gross human rights violations in Guatemala, Mexico, Peru, Colombia, and Honduras, among other countries.[41]

Moreover, compliance with the Court's orders changes over time. This crucial insight is missing from most research on compliance with inter-American decisions. Instead of viewing the IACtHR's orders as static in time, the IACtHR's stakeholders should take into account the changes that the Inter-American System introduces into its orders to make it easier to achieve compliance and, consequently, to have an impact.

The IACtHR is often aware of context and tailors its monitoring decision to make them more effective in often rapidly changing environments, with effects on the strategies of State and civil society actors. This is not to say that the Inter-American Court changes the substance of States' legal obligations established in the merits' judgment. Instead, as part of the dynamic process of monitoring compliance, the Inter-American Court's orders suggest various means through which a State can comply with its obligations, as laid out in the original judgment. Note that this process is distinct from the European Human Rights System's margin of appreciation doctrine, which the Inter-American System does not use to interpret the content of rights or obligations under inter-American law.[42]

In this monitoring process, relevant actors also change over time. Scholars of constructivist international relations have explored the idea that interactions between actors transform structures, which in turn triggers transformations in the interests and strategies of the actors.[43] The interests of the actors thus are not static but evolve through the interaction at the same time as they contribute to the transformation of other actors' behaviors, practices, and norms. These actors

---

[40] IACtHR, Informe Anual 2018, 69.

[41] IACtHR, Informe Anual 2018, 72–73.

[42] See Claudio Nash Rojas, "La doctrina del margen de apreciación y su nula recepción en la jurisprudencia de la Corte Interamericana de Derechos Humanos" [2018] 11 *ACDI—Anuario Colombiano de Derecho Internacional*.

[43] See Alexander Wendt, "The Agent-Structure Problem in International Relations" [1987] 41 *International Organization* 335; Emanuel Adler, *Communitarian International Relations* (Routledge 2005), 5–6. This section draws on René Urueña, "Interaction as a Site of Postnational Rule-Making: A Case Study of the Interamerican System of Human Rights," in Elaine Fahey (ed.), *The Actors of Postnational Rule-Making: Contemporary Challenges of European and International Law* (Routledge 2015), 133–159.

are not machines that merely collide or coexist, confront or coerce. Continual interactions transform the actors as well as the terms of engagement and the process.

This approach has the potential to improve analyses of the IACtHR's impact by exploring the Court's direct and indirect interactions with key domestic actors, including victims, civil society, governments, and perpetrators.[44] To assess both positive impacts and the negative resistance, it is critical to understand how compliance could be affected over time by the development of legal culture, the degree to which justice operators are open to implementing international standards, the involvement of civil society,[45] the obstacles imposed by governmental officials, policies, or interest groups, and more. This is important because one impact of the decisions of the Inter-American System is support for domestic institutions that aim to protect human rights,[46] which can lead to the consolidation and strengthening of civil society actors such as NGOs and social movements.[47]

This view of compliance contrasts with most quantitative studies' "realist" approach to compliance. The realist view considers international human rights institutions to have no ability to "pull" a State toward compliance; State compliance depends on the interests of the State, making human rights norms epiphenomenal.[48] According to this approach, compliance with a judicial decision is achieved by activating certain sociopolitical mechanisms (e.g., suing in a court of law) to "force" the addressee of the decision to do something (e.g., pay damages). Since international law, especially international human rights law lacks this kind of enforcement mechanism, the realist view considers compliance to be almost purely at the discretion of States.

Xinyuan Dai, on the other hand, observed that international institutions can influence States' compliance with international agreements through their interactions with domestic actors, including victims. According to Dai, States purposefully design monitoring arrangements for international institutions so that victims of human rights violations can help to monitor compliance. Most importantly, Dai observes that compliance is more a function of competing

---

[44] Engstrom (n. 12), 5.
[45] Par Engstrom and Peter Low, "Mobilising the Inter-American Human Rights System: Regional Litigation and Domestic Human Rights Impact in Latin America," in Par Engstrom (ed.), *The Inter-American Human Rights System. Impact Beyond Compliance* (Palgrave Macmillan 2019). Rossana Rocha Reis, "Transnational Activism and Coalitions of Domestic Interest Groups: Reflections on the Case of Brazil," in Par Engstrom (ed.), *The Inter-American Human Rights System. Impact Beyond Compliance* (Palgrave Macmillan 2019).
[46] Oscar Parra-Vera, "Institutional Empowerment and Progressive Policy Reforms: The Impact of the Inter-American Human Rights System on Intra-State Conflicts," in *The Inter-American Human Rights System* (Springer 2019), 143–166.
[47] Engstrom and Low (n. 45); Rocha Reis (n. 45).
[48] For example, Eric A. Posner, *The Twilight of Human Rights Law* (Oxford University Press 2014).

domestic constituencies than it is, as the realist view would suggest, of a monolithic national interest defined by the head of State.[49] Dai's approach fits the Inter-American Court's dynamic process of monitoring compliance. While not established by member States but rather by the international institution itself (and, often, against the desires of the States), the IACtHR monitoring system does create a continuum between the decision and the conditions for its implementation, which influence each other. The political leverage needed to achieve compliance changes over time and can be influenced by the very decision whose implementation is sought. Moreover, a range of domestic actors with competing interests can create or destroy the possibility of successful implementation of an IACtHR judgment.

4. A Methodology for Thinking beyond Compliance

The dynamic process of compliance monitoring makes it possible to open the black box of "partial non-compliance" and disaggregate the actions that States and civil society take to achieve compliance with IACtHR judgments. In doing so, it is possible to extend one's view beyond compliance, to analyze the wide range of direct and indirect effects that the Inter-American Court's decisions have on the protection of human rights—particularly through its interaction with various social and institutional actors. A dynamic approach makes it possible to identify more clearly not only progress toward compliance with IACtHR decisions but also resistance against these decisions and the wider impact of the Inter-American Court. Scholars must be careful not to create a narrative of progress according to which all interactions between the Inter-American System and domestic actors inevitably enhance the protection of human rights.[50] They must also account for resistance and backlash against the IAHRS that arise during the process of monitoring compliance.

4.1. Accounting for Change over Time

A dynamic process of monitoring means that the impact of a decision on the Inter-American System changes over time. Nevertheless, the temporal dimension is often ignored when assessing compliance with inter-American orders as well as their impact. For example, quantitative studies of compliance usually

---

[49] Xinyuan Dai, *International Institutions and National Policies* (Cambridge University Press 2007).
[50] On narratives surrounding the IACtHR, see Stephania Yate Cortes and René Urueña, in this volume.

ignore the year in which the respective decision was adopted, equating noncompliance with a decision adopted several years before their analysis with noncompliance with a decision adopted a few months prior to their analysis.

Neglecting to factor in change over time creates misleading results. Even in the absence of State resistance, it takes time to achieve compliance with international legal orders. A more accurate analysis would first define the normal amount of time needed for the implementation of an order, and only after this period of time had elapsed would it interpret noncompliance as resistance to the international decision. One strategy to account for the passing of time is to set expectations based on the stage of the proceedings at the international level. For example, studies could distinguish between domestic actions occurring: (1) when the petition is presented before the Inter-American Commission; (2) when the case is submitted to the Inter-American Court; (3) when the Inter-American Court issues a merits judgment; and (4) a set number of years after the merits judgment was issued (e.g., two, five, ten, fifteen).

This strategy provides a more accurate account of IAHRS proceedings over time and thus facilitates the study of impacts beyond compliance, the analysis of context, the application of impact measurement matrices, and more. Factoring in time also enables domestic action to be linked more easily to a specific IAHRS activity or stage of proceedings, so the effects of particular mechanisms or actions can be discerned. This approach also reveals the impact of international litigation and international decisions on domestic proceedings concerning individuals responsible for serious human rights violations by providing additional information that could establish correlations between international human rights proceedings and progress or setbacks in domestic criminal proceedings.

4.2. Improving the "Quality" of Compliance

The dynamic process of compliance affects the very nature of the act of compliance. Most literature concerning the impact of international legal proceedings on domestic criminal prosecutions adopts a dichotomic compliance/noncompliance approach. As such, this line of scholarship fails to register improvements in the "quality" of the State actions that constitute compliance.

Not all acts of compliance are the same in terms of truth, justice, and nonrepetition. For example, in the case of Court decisions that order criminal prosecutions for human rights violations, the prosecution of perpetrators with higher levels of responsibility (for example, those with command and control over the atrocities or who hold positions of political power) might have a wider impact to prevent impunity, than the prosecutions of lower-level perpetrators, who were simply following orders or were paid for committing their crimes.

While both prosecutions are a step forward in terms of compliance with the Court's orders, we suggest that prosecutions of perpetrators with substantial political or military decision-making power imply a better "quality" of compliance than prosecution at the lowest level of the criminal structure.

As will be described in this section, inter-American adjudication creates better outcomes in the administration of justice by contributing to prosecutorial and judicial action and by ensuring that those in power are less sheltered from prosecution. This is a remarkable achievement considering the Latin American context of impunity, particularly for individuals who have committed serious human rights violations.

The Inter-American Court's decisions can trigger specific actions in domestic criminal proceedings, including calling witnesses, hearings, indictments, and judgments. Consider the well-known case of *Barrios Altos v. Peru*.[51] In 1989, Peru's National Intelligence Service and Army Intelligence Service began to implement "Plan Ambulante," an operation monitoring residents of the Barrios Altos neighborhood in Lima, who were suspected of being part of the Shining Path (*Sendero Luminoso*) guerrilla group. On November 3, 1991, six armed individuals burst into a neighborhood fundraising party, or "pollada" as it is called in Peru, where they proceeded to kill fifteen people and wound four others. The victims filed a petition before the Inter-American Commission on June 30, 1995, and the Inter-American Court issued its judgment on the matter on March 14, 2001, six years after the initiation of proceedings before the IAHRS and ten years after the incident in question.[52]

Barrios Altos is a paradigmatic inter-American case because it constitutes the first IACtHR ruling on amnesty laws for serious human rights violations. In this case, the Inter-American Court found that Peru's amnesty laws were incompatible with the protection of fundamental rights recognized by the American Convention on Human Rights and that they consequently had no legal effects.[53] Additionally, and most importantly for this chapter, *Barrios Altos* illustrates how active engagement of victims and victims' representatives with the IAHRS can shape domestic judicial proceedings and how governments and judicial actors can prompt the IACtHR to suggest alternate methods for the implementation of its orders.

When *Barrios Altos* was submitted to the Court, then President Valentín Paniagua's transitional government moved to recognize the State's responsibility, and the IACtHR decided the case in March 2001. The Inter-American Court declared not only that the State was obligated to investigate the individuals

---

[51] Final Report of the Truth and Reconciliation Commission (TRC), Vol. VII, *Las ejecuciones extrajudiciales en Barrios Altos (The extrajudicial executions in Barrios Altos)*, 475–493.
[52] *Caso Barrios Altos v. Perú. Fondo* [2001] IACtHR, Ser. C No. 75, para. 2.
[53] Ibid., para. 18.

responsible for the human rights violations that had occurred but also that the amnesty laws releasing them from responsibility were "without legal effects," as the victims and the IACHR had requested.[54] A few months later, the victims' representatives asked the Inter-American Commission to file a request for an interpretation of the judgment, to clarify if the effects of the *Barrios Altos* decision were general or if they were limited to the particular case.[55] In September 2001, the IACtHR declared that "given the nature of the violation that amnesty laws No. 26479 and No. 26492 constitute, the effects of the decision in the judgment on the merits of the *Barrios Altos* cases are general in nature."[56]

Peru's Prosecutor's Office complied with the decision by ordering prosecutors to request that the amnesty laws not be applied. This enabled prosecutions concerning serious human rights violations to proceed domestically, without the need for a separate petition to the IAHRS.[57] These prosecutions included constitutional indictment proceedings against former President Alberto Fujimori for the extrajudicial executions in the neighborhood of Barrios Altos and for the kidnappings of Gustavo Gorriti and Samuel Dyer, among other individuals critical of his government.

Moreover, over the course of two decades, the IACtHR intervened at critical junctures in the decision's implementation to issue additional orders that guided all branches of the government toward the effective prosecution and sentencing of the individuals most responsible for the Barrios Altos incident and other similar cases.[58] The victims and their representatives requested these orders from the IACtHR and the State, especially the executive and the judiciary, implemented them. These interactions resulted in the Inter-American Court's determination that the human rights violations in *Barrios Altos* were crimes against humanity, which prevented the early release to Fujimori and others; its establishment of an obligation to extradite Fujimori in the case of *La Cantuta v. Peru*; and its prohibition that the application of pardons to Fujimori, with consequences for the executive and the judiciary, in a joint decision concerning *Barrios Altos* and *La Cantuta*.

---

[54] The organizations that represented the victims were Comisión de Derechos Humanos (COMISEDH); the Asociación Pro-Derechos Humanos (APRODEH); the Fundación Ecuménica para el Desarrollo y la Paz (FEDEPAZ); Instituto de Defensa Legal (IDL); Coordinadora Nacional de Derechos Humanos (CNDDHH); and the Center for Justice and International Law (CEJIL). Viviana Krsticevic, *El derecho común transformador: el impacto del diálogo del sistema interamericano de derechos humanos con las víctimas en la consecución de justiciar*, document submitted to the Max Planck Institute for International and Public Law, 2018.

[55] *Caso Barrios Altos v. Peru* [2001] IACtHR, Interpretation. Ser. C No. 83.

[56] Ibid, para. 18.

[57] Viviana Krsticevic, *Implementación de las decisiones del Sistema Interamericano de Derechos Humanos. Aportes para los procesos legislativos* (Centro por la Justicia y el Derecho Internacional 2007), 18.

[58] Most notably *La Cantuta v. Peru*, Fondo, Reparaciones y Costas, Inter-Am. Ct. H.R. (Ser. C) No. 162 (Nov. 29, 2006).

Barrios Altos demonstrates the impact that the Inter-American Court's process of monitoring compliance can have on domestic criminal proceedings and how such impact is characterized by both progress and setbacks. It also shows how, over time, the role of institutional actors can change: at first, the executive supported the IACtHR's decision in *Barrios Altos*, but later governments were reluctant to hold accountable the individuals responsible for the human rights violations in that case and even attempted to secure the early release of former president Fujimori from prison. Finally, *Barrios Altos* illustrates the importance of the participation of victims and civil society at the domestic and international levels for the development and implementation of international human rights law.[59]

The case of *Barrios Altos* provides a concrete example of how the Inter-American Court's process of monitoring compliance improves the quality of that compliance. Although Peru had punished some key perpetrators before this process began, the IACtHR's continued monitoring of domestic criminal proceedings kept the pressure on the State to investigate, prosecute, and punish the many perpetrators who had not been held accountable and to reject requests to exonerate the former president and others. Ultimately, all of the case's perpetrators, intellectual and material, were prosecuted, including high-ranking members of the government and military such as President Fujimori, his advisor Vladimiro Montesinos Torres, General Julio Salazar Monroe, General Juan Norberto Rivera Lazo, and General Nicolás de Bari Hermoza Ríos. Their sentences, twenty-five years in prison, were significant. This was also the first time in the world an elected president had been convicted of crimes against humanity. This is especially striking given that Latin America has had high rates of impunity in cases of serious human rights violations and Peru, prior to the IACtHR's intervention with a stronger accountability framework, was no different.

Analyses of the process of monitoring compliance should distinguish between types of perpetrators in orders concerning criminal prosecutions. In particular, they should distinguish between intellectual and material authors and between high- and low-ranking officials. Instead of considering only whether an IACtHR decision could increase the percentage of perpetrators held accountable overall, these analyses should also disaggregate based on the responsibility and rank of the perpetrators. This variable can then be cross-referenced to evaluate the impact of other factors on domestic criminal proceedings, such as the participation of the victims and civil society, the involvement of the press, and the attitude of the government toward the Inter-American System.

---

[59] See Krsticevic (n. 57).

This methodology will improve analyses of the types of perpetrators of human rights violations and the differentiated effects of the IAHRS on their investigation and punishment. The Inter-American Court has played an important role in promoting domestic criminal proceedings against those involved in human rights violations, including the prosecution of high-ranking authorities. Including this factor in analyses of compliance will help demonstrate and explain the impact of the IAHRS on these proceedings.

4.3. Institutional Impact

Many limitations of quantitative scholarship on compliance with inter-American orders are derived from a narrow understanding of the role of international judicial decisions in domestic politics. Some scholars have countered with a "beyond compliance" approach, which explores IAHRS impacts that do not fit within the compliance/noncompliance dichotomy.[60]

The Inter-American System has both direct and indirect effects on domestic legal systems. Direct effects are the result of decisions against the relevant State and can be equated with the concept of compliance. Indirect effects are triggered by the standards, if not the specific content, of orders against any State and can be equated with impact. Examining not only the relevant State's implementation of an IACtHR decision (direct effects) but also this decision's influence on other States (indirect effects) is the essence of the impact beyond compliance approach.

To understand the effects of the IACtHR's orders, it is necessary to understand each country's norms, institutions, practices, and attitudes.[61] In much of Latin America, receptiveness to international human rights law (e.g., the adoption of human rights standards by domestic courts, and the ability of civil society actors to mobilize for justice in different thematic areas)[62] is connected to the region's experience of dictatorships, conflict, and structural discrimination.[63] Nevertheless, the extent of this receptiveness varies significantly and can change over time for both government and civil society.

The following variables should thus be considered in analyses of the impact of the Inter-American System: (1) prosecution and punishment; (2) truth and

---

[60] See Dai (n. 48); and La Cantuta (n. 58).

[61] See Courtney Hillebrecht, "The Domestic Mechanisms of Compliance with International Human Rights Law: Case Studies from the Inter-American Human Rights System" [2012] 34 *Human Rights Quarterly* 959–985.

[62] See Engstrom (n. 12); on Brazil: Torelly (n. 20).

[63] Mariela Morales Antoniazzi, "El Estado abierto como objetivo del Ius Constitutionale Commune. Aproximación desde el impacto de la Corte Interamericana de Derechos Humanos," in Armin von Bogdandy, Mariela Morales Antoniazzi, and Héctor Fix Fierro (coords.), *Ius constitutionale commune en América Latina. Rasgos, potencialidades y desafíos* (UNAM 2014).

memory initiatives, both official (those carried out at the initiative of the State) and unofficial (those implemented at the initiative of civil society, victims, etc.); (3) domestic legal reforms in relation to the human rights obligations (whether positive or negative, that is, whether enhancing the protection of human rights or undermining it); and (4) impact of other factors on domestic proceedings.

5. Concluding Remarks

The Inter-American System conceives of compliance monitoring as part of a larger process of human rights protection. In accordance with this perspective, low levels of compliance should be understood in the context of broad social transformation through law. Thus, somewhat paradoxically, noncompliance can at times be more conducive to impact than full compliance.

Most of the mechanisms for monitoring compliance are less concerned with enforcing certain orders than with creating cognitive and political frameworks that will facilitate local pressure toward compliance, usually by a heterogenous set of institutional actors (such as ombudsman's offices or prosecutors' offices) as well as domestic NGOs and social movements. The Inter-American Court's process of monitoring compliance is thus directed toward the socialization of relevant domestic actors, a process "by which actors adopt the beliefs and behavioral patterns of the surrounding culture."[64] This socialization occurs as the IACHR and the IACtHR gather information, conduct on-site visits, and hold decentralized compliance hearings. The IAHRS uses compliance monitoring mechanisms as a tool to open spaces of dialogue and alter power dynamics with local stakeholders, working with civil society to create the conditions for compliance.

The inter-American approach to compliance blurs the lines between adjudication and compliance monitoring, rejecting the notion that the reparations ordered in the IACtHR's merits judgments are crystallized or carved in stone. These measures are often general, such that the precise contours of their domestic implementation will only become apparent through interactions with State authorities, victims and their representatives, and civil society. An IAHRS order thus defines the aim and scope of the measures a State must implement but sometimes leaves the details of implementation to domestic actors. The Inter-American System also challenges the notion that the context of compliance is static. The Inter-American Court's approach is, instead, a dynamic process of normative persuasion, that is, "a social process of interaction that involves

---

[64] Ryan Goodman and Derek Jinks, *Socializing States: Promoting Human Rights through International Law* (Oxford University Press 2013).

changing attitudes about cause and effect in the absence of overt coercion."[65] Nevertheless, the IACtHR maintains its role as the final authority on compliance, as evidenced in *Barrios Altos*.

This chapter began by discussing the contributions and limitations of current scholarship on compliance with and the impact of international decisions. It addressed the relationship between compliance and impact, thereby bridging a gap in the literature. It also proposed a methodology that complements and perfects other qualitative and quantitative approaches to evaluating the effects of international orders. Overall, it laid the foundation for an improved understanding of the various factors that interact to implement IAHRS decisions by suggesting changes to how compliance and impact should be assessed.

---

[65] Jeffrey T. Checkel, *Why Comply? Social Learning and European Identity Change* (International Organization 2001), 562.

III.5
Strategies of the Due Process of Law Foundation for the Promotion of New Standards and Expansion of the Impact of the Inter-American Human Rights System

By Katya Salazar and Daniel Cerqueira

1. Introduction

This chapter describes certain strategies of the Due Process of Law Foundation (DPLF) that aim to expand the impact of legal standards from the decisions of the Inter-American Commission on Human Rights (IACHR) and the Inter-American Court of Human Rights (IACtHR). Based on DPLF's experience as a regional civil society organization engaging with the noncontentious mechanisms of the Inter-American Human Rights System (IAHRS), such as monitoring and promotion activities (which excludes the system of petitions, cases, and precautionary measures), this chapter provides a detailed account, through some examples, of the joint action among DPLF, local and/or national organizations aimed at achieving and enhancing the impact of inter-American standards in the Americas.

The first section deals with the conceptual difference between compliance with the decisions of the organs of the IAHRS and the impact of inter-American standards as parameters for State action based on the decisions of these organs. The section stresses the fact that in spite of the low level of compliance with decisions pertaining to contentious cases, the impact of such decisions upon legislative processes, the design of public policy, and judicial practice in Latin America is irrefutable. The second section describes the institutional mission, strategies, and working methods developed by DPLF with the objective of raising awareness and disseminating information about the IAHRS's standards

---

Katya Salazar and Daniel Cerqueira, *Strategies of the Due Process of Law Foundation for the Promotion of New Standards and Expansion of the Impact of the Inter-American Human Rights System* In: *The Impact of the Inter-American Human Rights System*. Edited by: Armin von Bogdandy, Flávia Piovesan, Eduardo Ferrer Mac-Gregor, and Mariela Morales Antoniazzi, Oxford University Press. © Katya Salazar and Daniel Cerqueira 2024.
DOI: 10.1093/oso/9780197744161.003.0031

to ensure that these are properly used by State agents dedicated to the administration of justice in particular and legal agents more generally.

The third section explains how DPLF has tried to translate the demands of local and national civil society organizations into the development of new inter-American standards. To this end, we explain certain advocacy activities toward the IACHR prior to the development of new standards with regard to two specific topics: the extraterritorial responsibility of the countries of origin of transnational corporations involved in human rights violations, and the link between corruption and human rights. In our concluding remarks, we underline the role of civil society in the process of the creation of new standards and narratives by the organs of the IAHRS and in seeking to enhance the impact of IAHRS's decisions.

2. Impact of the IAHRS, beyond Compliance with Decisions Pertaining to Contentious Cases

One of the main challenges concerning the effectiveness of the IAHRS is State parties' low level of compliance with the decisions of its bodies. This challenge has been highlighted by the IACHR and the IACtHR. For example, the first Strategic Plan adopted by the IACHR for 2011–2015 established "promoting full compliance with its decisions and recommendations" as one of its strategic objectives.[1] In the same way, the Strategic Plan for 2017–2022 sets out twenty programs of work linked to five strategic objectives[2] that are integrated into a multidisciplinary "Special Program to Monitor IACHR Recommendations." In the words of the IACHR:

> While progress has been made and some States have, for example, introduced legislative reforms to enforce international decisions, the challenge of reaching

---

[1] IACHR, "Strategic Plan 2011–2015," 40, <https://www.oas.org/en/iachr/docs/pdf/iachrstrategicplan20112015.pdf> (accessed February 5, 2022).

[2] According to the Strategic Plan of the IACHR, these objectives are: 1. contribute to the development of a more effective and accessible system of inter-American justice in order to overcome practices of impunity in the region and achieve comprehensive reparations for victims through decisive measures for the strengthening of the petition and case system, friendly settlements, and precautionary measures; 2. have an impact on prevention measures and the factors that lead to human rights violations through the coordinated use of IACHR mechanisms and functions to achieve improved capacity for monitoring and coordinating relevant, timely, and appropriate responses; 3. promote democracy, human dignity, equality, justice, and fundamental freedoms based on an active contribution to the strengthening of State institutions and public policies with a human rights approach in accordance with inter-American norms and standards and to the development of the capacities of social and academic organizations and networks to act in defense of human rights; 4. promote the universalization of the Inter-American Human Rights System through coordinated initiatives with the Inter-American Court and to cooperate with other international, regional, and subregional human rights agencies and mechanisms; and 5. guarantee the human resources, infrastructure, technology, and budget necessary for full implementation of the Inter-American Commission on Human Rights' mandate and functions by means of results-based institutional management.

a level of implementation that ensures the effectiveness of the IASHR remains. Therefore, and as a central component of the Plan's strategy, the IACHR intends to develop a cross-cutting program in which it expects to initiate coordinated actions to follow up on recommendations using all available mechanisms (case reports, resolutions on precautionary measures, thematic and country reports, hearings, and monitoring of friendly settlement agreements).[3]

For several years now, the IACtHR has adopted the practice of issuing resolutions and convening hearings on compliance with the reparation measures contained in its judgments. This practice is regulated by Article 69 of its Rules of Procedure. In its annual reports, the Court has highlighted the necessity of overcoming the challenges linked to the low level of compliance with its judgments. In this regard, it has stressed the importance of the involvement of national human rights institutions, domestic courts, academia, and civil society organizations with the aim of contributing to the realization of the reparation measures contained in the judgments of the Inter-American Court.[4]

Expert studies have shown the low level of State compliance with reparation measures stipulated by the IACHR in its merits reports and by the IACtHR in its judgments. Based on a quantitative analysis, some of these studies indicate a particularly low level of compliance regarding reparation measures on the obligation to investigate and punish human rights violations. On the other hand, civil society organizations have participated in processes of dialogue with the IAHRS organs aiming at perfecting the mechanisms for monitoring compliance with its decisions.[5]

In the light of the extensively documented claim[6] about the low level of compliance with decisions, it is important to clarify certain concepts that will shape

---

[3] IACHR, "Strategic Plan 2017–2022," 62, <https://www.oas.org/en/iachr/mandate/StrategicPlan2017/docs/StrategicPlan2017-2021.pdf> (accessed February 5, 2022).

[4] IACtHR, "Annual Report 2018," 76–78, <https://www.corteidh.or.cr/sitios/informes/docs/ENG/eng_2018.pdf> (accessed February 5, 2022).

[5] For example, see the working document compiled by members of the International Network for Economic, Social and Cultural Rights (ESCR-Net) who are urging the IAHRS to adopt certain measures to bring about the improved monitoring of recommendations made in its final merits reports. ESCR-Net, "Implementation of decisions of the Inter-American Commission on Human Rights—discussion paper of ESCR-Net's Strategic Litigation Working Group" (2018), <https://www.escr-net.org/sites/default/files/201802-discussion-paper-of-escr-nets-strategic-litigation-working-group.pdf> (accessed February 5, 2022).

[6] For a more detailed paper on this topic, see Fernando Basch et al., "La Efectividad del Sistema Interamericano de Protección de Derechos Humanos: Un Enfoque Cuantitativo sobre su Funcionamiento y sobre el Cumplimiento de sus Decisiones" [2010] 7 *Sur*, <http://www.conectas.org/Arquivos/edicao/publicacoes/publicacao-201424165630161-76428001.pdf>, and Open Society Justice Initiative, "From Judgment to Justice: Implementing International and Regional Human Rights Decisions, Chapter II. The Inter-American Human Rights System" (2010), <http://www.opensocietyfoundations.org/sites/default/files/from-judgment-to-justice-20101122.pdf> (accessed February 5, 2022).

subsequent sections of this chapter. First, we need to make a distinction between the notions of "compliance with decisions of the IASHR" on the one hand, and the "impact of Inter-American standards" on the other. The first concept relates to the fulfillment of the reparation measures stipulated in final decisions on contentious cases. The second relates to the IAHRS's ability to create parameters for State action and to ensure that users of the IAHRS observe these parameters, especially State agents and institutions.

It is also important to clarify what we mean by the term "inter-American standards." The word *standard* denotes a behavior model required when complying with a certain obligation. Doctrine defines "Inter-American standards" as "behavioural guidelines for the State Parties to the Convention to be used as behavioural evaluation criteria and as legal rules whose content implies the establishment of specific obligations upon the States, whereby failure to comply shall bring about consequences relating to international responsibility."[7]

Another conceptual explanation necessary to enable a proper understanding of the inter-American standards' creation process is related to the IAHRS's protection, promotion, and monitoring pillars. For the purposes of this chapter, "protection" encompasses the ability of the IAHRS organs to recognize and pronounce judgment on petitions, cases, and requests for urgent (precautionary and provisional) measures. "Monitoring" refers to the supervision activities performed by the IACHR through its country and thematic reports, press releases, thematic hearings, and annual reports. Lastly, the pillar of "promotion" covers the thematic reports, training, professional development programs, and other initiatives of the IACHR for disseminating inter-American standards.[8]

Primarily, the inter-American standards emanate from the obligations contained in the American Convention on Human Rights (American Convention, or ACHR) and in the other instruments that form the normative framework of the IAHRS.[9] In Kelsenian terms, we could say that these

---

[7] Translation of quote by Manuel Quinche Ramírez, *Los estándares de la Corte Interamericana y la Ley de Justicia y Paz* (Editorial Universidad del Rosario 2009), 28.

[8] The responsibilities conferred upon the IACHR in its first Statute, adopted during the Fifth Meeting of Consultation of Ministers of Foreign Affairs in 1959, were restricted to the functions of monitoring and promotion, with no recognition of the power to receive petitions and contentious cases and to pronounce judgment upon them. In the light of the consolidation of mechanisms for individual petitions in the European and universal human rights context, the member States of the OAS decided to modify the Statute of the Commission during the Second Extraordinary Inter-American Conference, in 1965, which led to the IACHR beginning to pronounce judgment upon petitions and cases from 1967. For an explanation of the development of how the IACHR has prioritized the various working pillars since its creation in 1959 until 2015, see Daniel Cerqueira and Katya Salazar, "Las atribuciones de la Comisión Interamericana de Derechos Humanos antes, durante y después del proceso de fortalecimiento: por un balance entre lo deseable y lo possible," in Camila Barretto Maia et al., *Desafíos del Sistema Interamericano de Derechos Humanos—nuevos tiempos, viejos retos* (Due Process of Law Foundation 2016), 144–189.

[9] See IACHR, "Basic Documents in the Inter-American System," <http://www.oas.org/en/iachr/mandate/basic_documents.asp> (accessed February 5, 2022).

instruments establish rules of conduct for the State parties, whereby the failure to comply with these rules generates legal sanctions. We do not intend to delve into Hans Kelsen's account of international law in his *Pure Theory of Law*,[10] but to reinforce the premises upon which this chapter is based, we will employ the terminology used by Kelsen and the discrepancies between the two main theorists of legal positivism on the defining criteria of the effectiveness of law.

Kelsen distinguishes between the concepts of validity and efficacy of a legal norm, maintaining that while the former means that individuals must follow the conduct prescribed in the mentioned norm, the second refers to actual compliance of behavior with what has been established in the norm. To sum up, validity relates to the existence of obligations established in law and efficacy relates to the compliance of the behavior of the addressees of the obligations prescribed by law with the obligations themselves.[11]

Contrary to Kelsen, Herbert L.A. Hart moves away from the methodological dependence of the so-called primary norms that aim to prescribe behaviors and penalize their violation. Hart emphasizes what he terms secondary norms, which include the rules of change (creation of law), rules of adjudication (application of law), and rules of recognition (parameters for determining whether or not a norm belongs to a given legal system). For Hart, even if the compliance of individuals with the behaviors described in the primary rules is one of the essential objectives of any legal system, the efficacy of the system is based on the existence of a minimum level of agreement about the content of the secondary norms on the part of the operators of the law, that is, the persons upon whose conduct the very existence of the secondary rules depends.[12]

Without trivializing the theoretical depth of the two main authors of legal positivism, we draw upon their work in order to highlight the difference between compliance with decisions and the implementation of the standards of the IAHRS. Compliance requires State observance of the obligations prescribed in "inter-American law," defined here as the norms derived from the inter-American instruments and their interpretation by the organs of the IAHRS.

---

[10] According to Kelsen, law—in the sense of a legal system—comprises a coercive order of human conduct, supposed to be sovereign, that connects together certain facts determined by it as conditions of coercive acts determined by it. For the author, international law is in line with this definition in that it establishes specific sanctions for behavior that deviates from the prescribed norms. In the absence of a supranational entity authorized to impose sanctions on the States, in international law sanctions take the form of reprisals and wars, exercised by the States themselves, if they feel that their interests are affected by the failure of another State to comply with a rule established in a treaty or in another source of international law. See Hans Kelsen, *Pure Theory of Law* (University of California Press 1967), ch. VII.

[11] In accordance with the descriptive epistemology that characterizes legal positivism, Kelsen stresses that while the object of study of the philosophy of law is the validity of law, the efficacy of law is the object of the study of legal sociology.

[12] H.L.A. Hart, *The Concept of Law* (Oxford University Press 1961).

Above all, the analysis of compliance proceeds with an evaluation of the compliance of the actions of the denounced State with the specific reparation obligations prescribed by the adjudicatory organs of the IAHRS—the IACHR and the IACtHR. In Kelsenian terms, the analysis of compliance concerns the efficacy of the primary norms that make up "inter-American law" and whether the sanctions provided by the adjudicatory organs of the IAHRS are effectively respected by State parties, the addressees of the System's norms.

In turn, the impact of the standards of the IAHRS includes the existence of a minimum level of agreement about what "inter-American law" actually is, not only with regard to the content of the primary rules but also with regard to the integration between the norms (rules and principles) that make up "inter-American law" and the various domestic laws of States. In the current constitutional paradigm in most of this continent's countries, particularly in Latin America, the law applicable to a certain legal dispute encompasses both domestic and international rules, binding State authorities to base their decision on the rules that ensure the human rights at stake to the greatest extent possible. In light of this premise, the efficacy of the IAHRS depends on the integration of inter-American and domestic law via the minimum level of agreement on the part of legal professionals in the domestic sphere that lead them to base their decisions on inter-American standards.

One of the indicators of such agreement is, of course, the existence of fundamental judicial decisions in the inter-American jurisprudence. However, the efficacy of the IAHRS is not limited to respect or disrespect of the IACtHR's judgments and IACHR's recommendations. With regard to the rule of adjudication of "inter-American law," the dissemination of the doctrine of "conventionality control" among the domestic courts, the transconstitutionalism,[13] and the consolidation of a *ius constitutionale commune*[14] are expressions of the efficacy of the IAHRS. From our point of view, as an adjudicatory system that intends to adjudicate specific cases, the IAHRS has not been efficacious, given its inability to provide timely responses to the victims of human rights violations and the high level of noncompliance with the reparations stipulated in IAHRS decisions.[15] Nevertheless, as a source of legal standards that are capable of influencing the creation and interpretation of rules by the States parties of the IAHRS, its efficacy is demonstrable.

---

[13] Marcelo Neves, *Transconstitucionalismo* (WMF Martins Fontes 2009).

[14] Armin von Bogdandy et al., "Ius Constitutionale Commune En América Latina: A Regional Approach to Transformative Constitutionalism" (2016) MPIL Research Paper Series No. 2016-21.

[15] In this respect, see The Center for Justice and International Law (CEJIL), "Implementación de las Decisiones del Sistema Interamericano de Derechos Humanos—aportes para la administración de la justiciar" (2017), <https://cejil.org/en/publications/implementation-of-the-inter-american-human-rights-systems-decisions-only-in-spanish/> (accessed February 5, 2022).

There are various examples of cases in which, despite the fact that reparation measures arising from the judgments of the IACtHR are disrespected, these measures have influenced the actions of the denounced States and of other States parties of the IAHRS. This dualism can be verified on the basis of legal reforms, public policy design, and legal interpretations that are oriented toward the inter-American standards. Among others, we can mention two cases relating to the application of amnesty laws in the face of serious human rights violations. The judgment that opened up the jurisprudential development of the IACtHR in this matter—the *Case of Barrios Altos v. Peru* in 2001—is still in the compliance phase, and the IACtHR has periodically been called upon to decide upon measures adopted by the various bodies of the Peruvian State, which blatantly fail to comply with the reparation measures.[16]

The judgment in the *Barrios Altos* case is just one of the various judgments in which the IACtHR has ordered a State to revoke amnesty laws and in which the reparation measures remain in the compliance stage. Despite this, the impact that the rule derived from this judgment has had upon legislative and jurisprudential creation in the region is undeniable.[17] Various academic papers detail the impact that the rule on the prohibition of amnesty laws in the face of serious human rights violations has had on legislative and jurisdictional actions in the region.[18] Another matter addressed in judgments that are still in the compliance stage but whose rules have had a notable impact in different countries relates to the restriction upon the use of military proceedings to hear cases pertaining to violations of human rights and to try civilians. Since the first verdict dealing with this matter—the *Case of Castillo Petruzzi et al. v. Peru*[19]—the IACtHR has pronounced several judgments[20] reiterating the obligation to restrict the jurisdiction of military courts to the protection of legal interests linked to the actual functions

---

[16] See, e.g., *Case of Barrios Altos and Case of La Cantuta v. Peru* [2018] IACtHR.

[17] This rule establishes the obligation of the States to "refrain from resorting to amnesty, pardon, statute of limitations and from enacting provisions to exclude liability, as well as measures, aimed at preventing criminal prosecution or at voiding the effects of a conviction" in the case of serious violations of human rights. See, among other judgments, *Gutiérrez Soler v. Colombia* [2005] IACtHR, Ser. C No. 132, para. 97.

[18] See, e.g., Oscar Parra, "La jurisprudencia de la Corte Interamericana respecto a la lucha contra la impunidad: algunos avances y debates" [2012] 13 *Revista Jurídica de la Universidad de Palermo*, <https://www.palermo.edu/derecho/revista_juridica/pub-13/13JURIDICA_01PARRAVERA.pdf> (accessed February 5, 2022); and DPLF, "Digest of Latin American jurisprudence on international crimes" (2009) Vol. I, Chapter VI, Section 2, <http://www.dplf.org/sites/default/files/digestenglishs.pdf> (accessed February 5, 2022).

[19] IACtHR, *Case of Castillo Petruzzi et al. v. Peru*, Merits, Reparations and Costs, Judgment of May 30, 1999, Ser. C No. 52, para. 128.

[20] For a more detailed analysis of the matter, see Juan Carlos Gutiérrez y Silvano Cantú, "The Restriction of Military Jurisdiction in International Human Rights Protection Systems" [2010] 13 *Sur*, <https://sur.conectas.org/en/the-restriction-of-military-jurisdiction-in-international-human-rights-protection-systems/>.

of the armed forces.[21] Again, although most of the verdicts pronounced by the IACtHR are still in the compliance stage, there are many examples of reforms to military codes of procedure, laws, and jurisprudence relating to this matter, brought about through the implementation of inter-American standards.

We would like to stress the fact that in the two examples mentioned, the judgments of the IACtHR are part of a process in which the IACHR has played a fundamental role. For instance, since the start of the 1990s, the Commission has referred to the incompatibility of amnesty laws approved in Argentina[22] and Uruguay[23] with the obligations to investigate and to sanction serious violations of human rights as established in the American Convention. In its Annual Report 1996, the IACHR reiterated this stance in relation to the amnesty law enacted by Guatemala[24] and did the same in relation to every single one of the countries that has adopted amnesty laws in the region.

Thus, the rule established in the judgment in the *Case of Barrios Altos v. Peru* in 2001 was preceded by a decade of IACHR pronouncements based on final reports on the merits of cases and by pronouncements made in the context of monitoring and promotion activities.[25] It is worthy of note that, in the case of the amnesty law of El Salvador, the IACHR declared this law incompatible with the inter-American standards for the first time through a letter sent to the government of El Salvador on March 26, 1993, six days after the enactment of the said law. The concern shown in that case has been reiterated in the Report on the Situation of Human Rights in El Salvador in 1994[26] and in final reports on the merits of cases.[27]

Other examples of the development of standards on the basis of pronouncements upon cases, thematic reports, or country reports on the part of the IACHR that would subsequently be superimposed by jurisprudential

---

[21] The IACtHR has concluded that, under penalty of the violation of the "principle of the natural judge" and the guarantees of due process, ordinary justice is always competent to investigate, try, and punish the perpetrators of violations of human rights.

[22] IACHR, Cases 10.147, 10.181, 10.240, 10.262, 10.309, and 10.311 v. Argentina, Report No. 28/92 of October 2, 1992.

[23] IACHR, Cases 10.029, 10.036, 10.145, 10.305, 10.372, 10.373, 10.374, and 10.375 v. Uruguay, Report No. 29/92 of October 2, 1992.

[24] IACHR, "Annual Report 1996," Chapter V, Human Rights Developments in the Region— section on Guatemala.

[25] For an analysis of precedents in this matter on the part of the IACHR and of the obligation to leave without effect any domestic laws contrary to the obligation to investigate and sanctions serious violations of human rights, see the Chapter IV a) Par. 72 to 86 of the Annual Report of the IACHR of 2013, <http://www.cidh.org/countryrep/ElSalvador94eng/II.4.htm> (accessed February 5, 2022).

[26] IACHR, "Report on the Situation of Human Rights in El Salvador," Sec. I, OAS/Ser.L/II.85, Doc. 28 Rev., February 11, 1994, which quotes the letter sent by the IACHR to the Government of El Salvador on March 26, 1993.

[27] See, e.g., IACHR, "Report 1/99, Case 10.480, Lucio Parada Cea et al.," January 27, 1999, paras. 111–16; "Report 136/99, Case 10.480, Ignacio Ellacuría, S.J, Segundo Montes, S.J., Armando López, S.J., Ignacio Martín Baró, S.J., Joaquín López y López, S.J., Juan Ramón Moreno, S.J., Julia Elba Ramos, and Celina Mariceth Ramos, El Salvador," December 22, 1999, paras. 197–232.

rules of the IACtHR can be seen in relation to the incompatibility of contempt laws with the right to freedom of expression,[28] the legal definition as "torture" of sexual violence exercised during police or military operations,[29] and the protection of the lands of Indigenous people in the context of the right to collective property,[30] among others.

Beyond the endogenous process of the development of standards inside the organs of the IAHRS, we would also like to explain the exogenous process and, in this context, the role that a regional civil society organization (CSO) such as DPLF can play here. In the following we will address certain strategies with this objective, and we will explain the more relevant outcomes for the creation and impact of the inter-American standards, with a focus on two topics that DPLF has recently worked on: the extraterritorial responsibility of the countries of origin of transnational companies involved in violations of human rights, and the link between corruption and human rights.

3. DPLF's Strategies for Increasing the Impact of the IAHRS Decisions

DPLF is a regional, nongovernmental organization, whose mandate is to promote the rule of law and respect for human rights in Latin America. Founded in 1996 by former members of the Truth Commission of El Salvador, the organization was created following the peace accords that brought an end to the civil war in El Salvador between 1980 and 1992.[31] One of the main topics dealt with

---

[28] In 1995, the IACHR published a thematic report on this subject, ahead both in terms of time and depth of analysis of the first judgment of the IACtHR relating to a conflict between the criminal offense of contempt of court and the right to freedom of expression, viz., the *Case of Palamara Iribarne v. Chile*. See IACHR, "Report on the Compatibility of "Desacato" laws with the American Convention of Human Rights," OAS/Ser.L/V/II.88, Doc. 9 Rev., February 17, 1995, and *Case of Palamara Iribarne v. Chile* [2005] IACtHR, Ser. C No. 135.

[29] IACHR, "Report No. 5/96, Case 10.970, Raquel Martín de Mejía, Peru," March 1, 1996, Section B, Considerations on the substance of the case; this precedes the first case in which the IACtHR considered the legal status of sexual violence as a category of torture by several years. In this regard, see *Case of the Miguel Castro-Castro Prison v. Peru* [2006] IACtHR, Ser. C No. 160.

[30] IACHR, "Resolution 12/85, Yanomami Indians, Brazil," March 5, 1985, dealing with the obligation of the State of Brazil to demarcate, define, and protect the territory of the indigenous Yanomami people, this obligation being broadened with more detail decades later in the *Case of the Mayagna (Sumo) Awas Tingni v. Nicaragua* [2001] IACtHR, Ser. C No. 79.

[31] The Truth Commission for El Salvador was created in the light of the peace accords signed in 1991 between the government of El Salvador and the Farabundo Martí National Liberation Front, putting an end to the civil war. The Commission was headed by Thomas Buergenthal, former President of the Inter-American Court of Human Rights and the International Court of Justice, other members including Belisario Betancur, former President of Colombia, and Reinaldo Figueredo, former Minister of Foreign Affairs of Venezuela. See United States Institute of Peace, "From Madness to Hope: The 12-Year War in El Salvador: Report of the Commission on the Truth for El Salvador" (2001), <https://www.usip.org/files/file/ElSalvador-Report.pdf> (accessed February 5, 2022).

in the final report of this Commission was the role of the El Salvador judicial system during the war. Its lack of efficacy and independence enabled violence in the country to progress with complete impunity. Due to the need to make this situation visible and prevent similar events in the region, the members of the Truth Commission decided to create an organization aimed at strengthening the judiciaries of Latin American to make them more efficient and democratic.[32]

Over the years, the mandate of DPLF has adjusted to challenges in the way of the enjoyment of human rights and democratic governance throughout the hemisphere. At present, DPLF is a regional organization made up of professionals of various nationalities based in Washington, DC, with permanent personnel in Mexico, El Salvador, Peru, and Bolivia. The organization's strategy is based on the creation of knowledge, exchange of experiences and lessons learned, lobbying at national and international levels in coordination with its allies in the region, and the strategic dissemination of information.

During its twenty-three years of existence, DPLF has focused its work on countries with chronic situations of impunity and ineffective justice systems. In recent years, DPLF has also focused on countries that are moving toward a democratic transition, such as Venezuela, Nicaragua, and—most recently—Bolivia. At present, DPLF's programs are: (i) *Judicial independence*, which includes initiatives on the role of district attorneys in a democracy, transparent and meritocratic elections of high judicial authorities, elements of a democratic public security policy, and accountability and reparations for serious violations of human rights; (ii) *Impunity and Serious Human Rights Violations*, where DPLF looks in more detail at standards relevant for the reconstruction of judicial institutions in countries in transition and promote the exchange of experiences in order to address these challenges; (iii) *Human rights and natural resources*, where DPLF promotes the use of international law to defend the territory and natural resources of Indigenous peoples and rural communities; and (iv) *Strengthening the IAHRS*, where DPLF monitors and promotes reforms and transparent and participatory processes in the nomination and selection of members of the IACHR and IACtHR as well as other inter-American authorities.

The initiatives of DPLF deal with social phenomena with significance for the enforcement of the rule of law and human rights in matters where it feels that international law can make relevant contributions to the processes of political deliberation, the design of public policy, and the imparting of justice. Although

---

[32] "In time, our experience in El Salvador caused us to reflect upon the situation in other countries in the region and to understand that while the case of El Salvador was unique in many aspects, other countries in our region have suffered, to a greater or lesser extent, the effects of justice administration systems that are archaic, ineffective, oppressive, corrupt, and largely undemocratic, and which needed to be reformed...".—translation of the words of Thomas Buergenthal upon the formal inauguration of the activities of the DPLF. In *Reformas a la Justicia Penal en las Américas* (Fundacion para el Debido Proceso Legal 1999).

DPLF does not litigate before the IAHRS in the sense of submitting petitions or requests for protection measures directly to IAHRS organs, it is a user of its various mechanisms of monitoring and promotion.[33] Through the compilation of specialist studies, training activities, the observation of criminal trials,[34] and *amici curiae*[35] presentations to the organs of the IAHRS and domestic tribunals, DPLF hopes to encourage judges in the region to use inter-American standards in their decisions and to engage with the IACtHR and IACHR to develop new standards through their pronouncements. The mechanisms for monitoring and promotion, which include thematic hearings at the IACHR, allow DPLF to make the problems with which it is dealing visible at national and regional level and to require the States to comply with inter-American rules and standards in a multilateral and public forum.

In addition to case law, the advisory opinions, country reports, and thematic reports of the IACHR, which generally address more current and regional problems, are particularly useful for the work of DPLF. For this reason, the standards included in this document and those arising from the case system allow DPLF to disseminate and raise awareness of the Inter-American standards that are vital to its work. In this sense, DPLF has coordinated efforts with organs of the IAHRS and has compiled summary infographics of judgments,[36] advisory opinions, and instrumental thematic reports with the aim of bringing about a greater impact.

Another aspect of DPLF's work relates to the production of toolkits and reports that aim to more solidly define inter-American standards. By nature, these standards tend to establish general obligations for the States and lack the required effective force for direct implementation on the part of State operators. In the different programs and lines of work of DPLF, it has attempted to provide the various State organs and agents with clearer guidelines on how they should apply inter-American standards.[37] In order to contribute to the improved

---

[33] The DPLF has advised civil society organizations on the formulation of petitions and requests for precautionary measures before the IACHR, but, due to institutional policy, the DPLF has not directly pursued or invoked the system of petitions and cases or the protection mechanisms made available by the IACHR and the IACtHR (precautionary and provisional measures, respectively).

[34] For an example of the observation of an archetypal criminal trial by the DPLF, see Daniel Cerqueira and Katya Salazar, *La Sentencia sobre los Hechos de Violencia en la Curva del Diablo: comentarios a la luz de los estándares internacionales de derechos humanos* (March 7, 2017), <http://www.dplf.org/sites/default/files/bagua_v2.pdf> (accessed February 5, 2022).

[35] See the website of the DPLF, page on amicus curiae briefs presented in recent years, available at <http://www.dplf.org/en/resources/amicus_curiae> (accessed February 5, 2022).

[36] DPLF, *Folleto sobre la Sentencia de la Corte IDH en el Caso Ruano Torres y otros v. El Salvador*, <http://www.dplf.org/sites/default/files/folleto_agapito_web_v1.pdf> (accessed February 5, 2022).

[37] With regard to the inter-American standards on the right to prior, free, and informed consultation, for example, whereas the first regional report of DPLF aimed to state the applicable inter-American right and compare it with the regulatory framework of four Andean countries, the other publications on the matter deal with certain operational problems in the implementation of these standards on the part of the governments; problems derived from inadequate consultation processes and more concrete discussions on the pros and cons of adopting a regulatory framework with a

awareness of and use of inter-American standards, DPLF carries out applied research and disseminates it in shorter, more accessible versions through its institutional blog[38] and social networks. DPLF shares the latest developments of the IAHRS on the topics it works on and, if the case so deserves, it formulates opinions on current topics through press releases or public letters.

Having explained the institutional mission of DPLF and its way of working as a user of the IAHRS, we will now look at two examples of coordinated advocacy with partner organizations that aim at bringing about new narratives and the development of new standards on the part of the IACHR with regard to certain social phenomena and patterns of behavior by public and private actors that endanger the enjoyment of human rights in the region.

4. Specific Strategies for the Development of Standards on the Part of the IAHRS

4.1. Extraterritorial Responsibility of Countries of Origin of Companies Involved in Violations of Human Rights

Since the creation of a program dedicated to the study of the impact of extractive industries on human rights, in 2010, DPLF[39] has worked with CSOs, collectives, and other social movements that work with victims of human rights violations resulting from the intensive extraction of natural resources. A significant number

---

general scope as a model of the implementation of the right to prior consultation. Several of these reports were compiled along with other national and local organizations, allowing us to analyze the use and knowledge of the Inter-American standards in the light of the demands and needs of local groups. For more information about the publications of DPLF on the right to prior, free, and informed consultation, see <http://www.dplf.org/en/resources-topics/right-consultation> (accessed February 5, 2022).

[38] Entitled "Justicia en las Américas," this Spanish-language blog (BlogDPLF) is provided by the Due Process of Law Foundation as a space where staff and members of the board of directors of the organization, along with other persons and organizations dedicated to the enforcement of human rights in the Americas, can collaborate. The blog periodically publishes information and analyzes the main debates and events relating to the promotion of the rule of law, human rights, judicial independence, and the consolidation of democracy in Latin American. One important part of the articles published on the blog comprises analyses of decisions of the organs of the IAHRS and of draft laws or judicial decisions that are relevant because they conflict with or make progress toward the implementation of the inter-American standards. For more information on the BlogDPLF, see <https://dplfblog.com/> (accessed February 5, 2022).

[39] Some of the text contained in this section is an adaptation of a chapter originally published in a manual on holding States accountable for extraterritorial violations of human rights. See FIAN International and ETOS Consortium, *For Human Rights Beyond Borders: Handbook on How to Hold States Accountable for Extraterritorial Violations* (2017), 42–43, <https://www.etoconsortium.org/nc/en/main-navigation/library/documents/detail/?tx_drblob_pi1%5BdownloadUid%5D=204> (accessed February 5, 2022).

of these violations occur in contexts where transnational mining companies act with the political, diplomatic, financial, or other support from the countries where their parent company is registered or domiciled, so of their country of origin.

In Latin America, mining companies that are headquartered or registered in Canada and mining companies from other countries that are listed on the Toronto Stock Exchange account for more than 70 percent of all investment in mining projects from Mexico to Chile. In several of these projects, there have been reports of disputes over the lands of Indigenous and peasant communities, the criminalization of socio-environmental advocates, and a growing number of murders of people who oppose the presence of mining activities in their lands.

This reality is directly linked to the signing of investment and free trade agreements between Canada and certain countries in the region that include clauses facilitating mining concessions and that weaken socioeconomic safeguards. Particularly under the Stephen Harper administration (2006–2015), Canadian cooperation has been used as an agent for promoting Canadian companies' foreign investment in countries with which Canada has signed cooperation agreements.[40] Further, financial subsidies, fiscal extensions, and diplomatic support abroad have been expanded for Canadian mining companies without any proportionate advances in the creation of an institutional framework for accountability for human rights violations committed or tolerated by these companies in third countries.[41]

In this context, since 2011, DPLF has participated in initiatives with other CSOs, academic bodies, and social movements to increase visibility for the international responsibility of Canada. Based on the conclusion that the general standards of the IAHRS relating to the obligation to respect and protect human rights in the light of actions of private individuals are applicable to the States of origin of transnational companies,[42] DPLF coordinated a series of advocacy activities with the aim of causing the IACHR to issue specific pronouncements on the extraterritorial responsibility of the countries of origin of companies involved in violations of human rights.

In October 2013, a group of CSOs from various Latin American companies participated in a thematic hearing before the IACHR entitled *Situación de los*

---

[40] See MiningWatch Canada, *New Federally Funded Academic Institute a Tool to Support Mining Industry* (2014) at <http://www.miningwatch.ca/news/new-federally-funded-academic-institute-tool-su-pport-mining-industry> (accessed February 5, 2022).

[41] See, e.g., <http://www.dplf.org/en/news/over-180-organizations-urge-canadian-prime-minister-promote-effective-regulation-canadian> (accessed February 5, 2022).

[42] Daniel Cerqueira, "The Attribution of Extraterritorial Liability for the Acts of Private Parties in the Inter-American System: Contributions to the debate on corporations and human rights" (*BlogDPLF*, October 1, 2015), <https://dplfblog.com/2015/10/14/the-attribution-of-extraterritorial-liability-for-the-acts-of-private-parties-in-the-inter-american-system-contributions-to-the-debate-on-corporations-and-human-right/> (accessed February 5, 2022).

derechos humanos de las personas afectadas por la minería en las Américas y la responsabilidad de los Estados huéspedes y de origen de las empresas ("Human rights situation of persons affected by mining in the Americas and the responsibility of the host states and countries of origin of the companies").[43] In April 2014, after three years of research, organizations from Chile, Colombia, Honduras, Mexico, and Peru, along with academic centers from Canada and the United States, published a report on the impact of Canadian mining in Latin America and the responsibility of Canada.[44] The report examines twenty-two mining projects located in nine countries in the region and identifies a pattern of human rights violations and their underlying causes, above all in Canada, as the country of origin of the companies involved in the abuses.

The report was presented to the IACHR in April 2014 and played a part in the latter's statement in its end-of-session press release about "emerging issues such as corporate responsibility as regards the impact of extractive industries on the observance of human rights, especially the impact on certain groups such as Afro-descendants and indigenous peoples."[45] Eight months later, twenty-nine CSOs and Canadian academic entities participated in another thematic hearing before the IACHR dealing expressly with the role of Canada in abuses committed by mining companies in Latin America.[46] In the press release published a few days after this hearing, the IACHR urged the States to "adopt measures to prevent the multiple human rights violations that can result from the implementation of development projects, both in countries in which the projects are located as well as in the corporations' home countries, such as Canada."[47]

During the IACHR's 154th session, in March 2015, the extraterritorial obligations of the States were again addressed in a hearing coordinated by the DPLF on "Corporations, Human Rights, and Prior Consultation in the Americas."[48] At the end of the session, the IACHR stressed that it is "essential

---

[43] For more information about the hearing, see <dplf.org/es/news/nota-de-prensa-mineria-y-derechos-humanos-en-america-latina-los-estados-de-origen-de-las> (accessed February 5, 2022).

[44] Working Group on Mining and Human Rights in Latin America, "The impact of Canadian Mining in Latin America and Canada's Responsibility. Executive Summary of the Report submitted to the Inter-American Commission on Human Rights" (2014), <http://www.dplf.org/sites/default/files/report_canadian_mining_executive_summary.pdf> (accessed February 5, 2022).

[45] *IACHR Wraps Up its 150th Session*. Press release (Washington DC, April 4, 2014), <https://www.oas.org/en/iachr/media_center/PReleases/2014/035.asp> (accessed February 5, 2022).

[46] Available at <https://www.youtube.com/watch?v=OWYue8FP9ZY&feature=youtu.be> (accessed February 5, 2022). For a more detailed explanation of the effects of this hearing in Canada, see Shin Imai and Natalie Bolton, "El gobierno de Canadá no hace lo suficiente para abordar los problemas de las empresas mineras canadienses en América" [2015] 20 *Aportes DPLF* 24–26, <https://www.dplf.org/sites/default/files/aportes2020_web_final_0.pdf> (accessed February 5, 2022).

[47] *IACHR Wraps Up its 153rd Session*. Press release (Washington DC, November 7, 2014), >https://www.oas.org/en/iachr/media_center/PReleases/2014/131.asp> (accessed February 5, 2022).

[48] The video of the hearing is available at <https://www.youtube.com/watch?v=wFqc7ccS7Mw> (accessed February 5, 2022).

that any development project is carried out in keeping with the human rights standards of the Inter-American system."[49]

After four years of research, exchange of experiences and information, advocacy, and lobbying aimed at placing the extraterritorial obligations of the States on the agenda of the IAHRS,[50] in April 2016 the IACHR published its thematic report, *Indigenous Peoples, Afro-Descendent Communities, and Natural Resources: Human Rights Protection in the Context of Extraction, Exploitation, and Development Activities*.[51] One of the sections of this report deals with the obligation of the countries of origin of the companies to harmonize their domestic laws and public policies in order to prevent and mitigate human rights violations and to offer reparations for such violations. For the first time, the IACHR formulated specific rules on the obligations of the countries of origin of the companies in relation to human rights abuses committed abroad. The report finished with a list of recommendations for States to monitor, control, and supervise the activities carried out in other countries by companies headquartered or registered in their jurisdiction.[52]

With the aim of increasing the impact of the said report and disseminating its content, DPLF published an infographic summary in the four official languages of the Organization of American States (OAS), allowing more legal operators to become familiar with key standards concerning the obligations of the countries of origin of companies.[53]

The publication of the mentioned thematic report on the part of the IACHR was only a first step toward the incorporation of the extraterritorial obligation of the countries of origin of companies into the IAHRS's agenda, inspiring other future pronouncements of the Inter-American Commission itself and the approach of the IACtHR in its Advisory Opinion 23/17,[54] entitled "The Environment and

---

[49] *IACHR Wraps Up its 154th Session*. Press release (Washington DC, March 27, 2015), <https://www.oas.org/en/iachr/media_center/PReleases/2015/037.asp> (accessed February 5, 2022).

[50] For more information on the impact of the advocacy relating to the extraterritorial obligations of Canada in Canada and relating to the impact of Canadian mining in third countries, see Shin Imai, *Canadian Government Promises Stronger Monitoring of Canadian Companies Operating Abroad*, January 30, 2018, <https://dplfblog.com/2018/01/30/canadian-government-promises-stronger-monitoring-of-canadian-companies-operating-abroad/> (accessed February 5, 2022).

[51] IACHR, "Indigenous Peoples, Afro-Descendent Communities, and Natural Resources: Human Rights Protection in the Context of Extraction, Exploitation, and Development Activities," OAS/Ser.L/V/II. Doc. 47/15, December 31, 2015, <https://www.oas.org/en/iachr/reports/pdfs/ExtractiveIndustries2016.pdf> (accessed February 5, 2022).

[52] Ibid., 185. For a more detailed evaluation of the report of the IACHR, see D. Cerqueira and C. Blanco, *IACHR Takes Important Step in the Debate on Extraterritorial Responsibility and States' Obligations regarding Extractive Companies* (May 2016), <https://dplfblog.com/2016/05/11/iachr-takes-important-step-in-the-debate-on-extraterritorial-responsibility-and-states-obligations-regarding-extractive-companies/> (accessed February 5, 2022).

[53] DPLF, "Infographic summary of the report of the IACHR on 'Indigenous Peoples, Afro-Descendent Communities, and Natural Resources: Human Rights Protection in the Context of Extraction, Exploitation, and Development Activities,'" (March 30, 2017), <http://www.dplf.org/sites/default/files/ddhh_extractivas_digital_en_v1_0.pdf> (accessed February 5, 2022).

[54] IACtHR, "The Environment and Human Rights," OC 23/17 of November 15, 2017, Ser. A No. 23.

Human Rights." Adopted on November 15, 2017, this advisory opinion broadens the parameters developed by the IACHR in the aforementioned report, setting out clearer principles and rules on the attribution of State responsibility in the light of actions by private entities and the obligation of the countries of origin of companies that commit environmental harm abroad. Further, it establishes parameters for compliance with prevention and guarantee obligations relating to cross-border damage and enshrines—for the first time in the context of the IAHRS—the principles of precaution and prevention in relation to environmental damage. In accordance with these principles, the States must act if there are plausible indicators that an activity might bring about irreversible damage to the environment, even in the absence of scientific certainty.

The Inter-American Court of Human Rights clarified the circumstances in which the conduct of a State constitutes an exercise of jurisdiction, stressing that a State is internationally responsible for the violation of the right to a healthy environment and other associated rights, even if the environmental damage takes place on the territory of another country, if the State authorities concerned do not meet their prevention and guarantee obligations in relation to companies headquartered or domiciled in their jurisdiction.[55]

Again, due to the importance of the standards on the responsibility of countries of origin of companies contained in the advisory opinion, DPLF worked with the IACtHR and partner organizations to coordinate the compilation of an infographic on the fundamental principles and conclusions of the IACtHR's pronouncement.[56] This summary was published in the four official languages of the OAS and facilitated access to the content of the advisory opinion not only by users of the IAHRS but also by operators of law called upon to decide on disputes or to adopt decisions in the diverse spheres of State action in their respective countries.

Finally, in November 2019, the IACHR published the report "Business and Human Rights: Inter-American Standards," which expands the parameters relating to the obligations of countries of origin of companies beyond the context of extractive activities and environmental damage. Although the standards contained in this report are largely based on pronouncements of the United Nations' Human Rights Council, Special Rapporteurs, independent experts, and thematic committees, this is the most detailed document of the IAHRS in which parameters of State action toward the corporate sector are set out.[57]

---

[55] Ibid., para. 97.
[56] DPLF, "Infographic summary of Advisory Opinion 23/17 on the Environment and Human Rights" (September 2018), <http://www.dplf.org/sites/default/files/oc23_english.pdf> (accessed February 5, 2022).
[57] IACHR, "Thematic Report on "Business and Human Rights: Inter-American Standards," OAS/Ser.L/V/II, November 1, 2019.

4.2. Corruption and Human Rights

The connection between corruption and human rights in the narrative of the organs of the IAHRS is evolving, but the IAHRS organs have focused on identifying corruption as a direct or indirect cause of human rights violations that are not necessarily planned or foreseen. Nevertheless, the current reality in the region shows a much more complex scenario in which violations of human rights can be a key part of strategies designed by criminal networks comprising State and private agents who wish to fully or partly co-opt State institutional entities in order to take advantage of their resources to benefit the criminal network. To achieve their aims, these networks use increasingly deploying sophisticated strategies which, in many cases, include committing human rights violations in order to facilitate their objectives and ensure the impunity of the network.

In this context, the co-optation of justice institutions stands out. This can take the form of undue interference in and manipulation of selection processes—especially those of the highest authorities—in order to ensure the election of persons close to the criminal network, thereby ensuring impunity for illegal actions. This symbiosis between State institutional entities controlled by *de facto* powers (and therefore corrupt institutions) and manipulated judicial elections (which violate the inter-American standards governing them) also occurs with other human rights violations. Let's not forget paradigmatic cases such as the murder of the Indigenous leader and environmental activist Berta Cáceres in Honduras, whose activism brought to light a network of corruption operating in Honduras that then planned her murder in order to avoid the visibility caused by her demands and to ensure success in their activities with total impunity. Another case concerned the murder of defenders of territory in the Peruvian rainforest, whose defensive action and visibility work were obstacles to the lucrative illegal logging industry. There are also thousands of cases of missing persons in Mexico, many of them committed through organized crime networks, but many others linked to the activities of criminal networks fed by the authorities.

These are the new realities that have caused us to include a much broader contextual analysis in our work, including the role of large-scale corruption and the control of institutions by *de facto* powers, with the aim of better understanding the current patterns and trends in the violations of human rights committed on the continent. These aspects have also led us to ask ourselves if and how we could contribute to the fight against corruption through the promotion of human rights and the international justice systems. Was it possible to identify a "human rights perspective" in the fight against major corruption? Were new standards necessary for this objective, or were the existing standards sufficient? How can the various mechanisms of the IAHRS be used in this area?

For DPLF, this new type of analysis involves the tasks of learning and deepening knowledge of concepts, since at the international level, the fight against corruption and the defense of human rights have followed separate paths, with different audiences, narratives, and strategies, and attempts to connect them are relatively recent.

Within the United Nations, the treaty bodies and special procedures have indicated that when corruption is widespread, the States cannot meet their obligations relating to human rights.[58] Similarly, the Special Rapporteur of the United Nations on the Independence of Judges and Lawyers, in a report on corruption and judicial independence presented in 2017 to the UN Human Rights Council, indicated that the UN Convention against Corruption "should be also be seen as a fundamental international instrument for the protection of human rights, and it therefore warrants continued attention from the relevant competent bodies," since corruption has a devastating effect on the justice systems as a whole.[59]

At the inter-American level, in March 1996, the General Assembly of the OAS adopted the Inter-American Convention against Corruption, whose implementation is based on a process of scrutiny exercised by the States parties themselves, but neither the text nor the documents produced by the OAS Secretariat contain an approach to the impact of corruption upon the enjoyment of human rights in the region.[60] The narrative in the IAHRS on the links between human rights and corruption has developed primarily from the momentum arising from civil society organizations, which has been received with interest and concern by the IACHR. DPLF has actively participated in this process in the past years.

The IACHR made the relationship between corruption and human rights evident with the approval of Resolution 1/17 on Human Rights and the Fight against Impunity and Corruption, in which it indicated that "the establishment of effective mechanisms to eradicate corruption is an urgent obligation in order to achieve effective access to an independent and impartial justice and to guarantee human rights." One year later, it broadened its criteria with Resolution 1/18 on Corruption and Human Rights, stating that corruption is a complex phenomenon that often establishes structures that capture State entities, through different criminal schemes, and affects human rights in their entirety—civil,

---

[58] Committee on Economic, Social and Cultural Rights, "Consideration of reports submitted by States Parties under Articles 16 and 17 of the Covenant, Concluding Observations, Republic of Moldova," E/C.12/1/ADD.91, December 12, 2003, para. 12; and Committee on Rights of the Child, "Consideration of reports submitted by States Parties under Article 44 of the Convention, Concluding Observations, The Republic of the Congo," CRC/C/COG/CO/1, October 20, 2006, para. 14.

[59] Human Rights Council, "Report of the Special Rapporteur on the Independence of Judges and Lawyers," A/72/140, July 25, 2017.

[60] OAS, "Inter-American Convention against Corruption" (March 29, 1996), <http://www.oas.org/en/sla/dil/docs/inter_american_treaties_B-58_against_Corruption.pdf> (accessed February 5, 2022).

political, economic, social, cultural, and environmental—as well as the right to development, and weakens governance and democratic institutions, promotes impunity, undermines the rule of law, and exacerbates inequality. In this resolution, the IACHR emphasizes certain fundamental concepts and formulates recommendations that address the phenomenon with a human rights focus.

Subsequently, the IACHR addressed the topic in several country and thematic reports, stressing corruption as an aggravating factor in situations of exclusion and discrimination and as a direct or indirect cause of human rights violations—in particular ESCER, but also the right to access to justice and freedom of expression in cases where options for reporting acts of corruption are limited.[61] In the same way, in its most recent country reports on the situation of human rights in Honduras, Guatemala, and Mexico, the IACHR identified corruption as one of the factors having a bearing on impunity in cases of human rights violations in these countries.

In its turn, in the case of *Escobar v. Guatemala*, of 2018, the IACtHR stressed the negative consequences of corruption and the obstacles that it poses for the effective enjoyment of human rights along with the fact that the corruption of State authorities or private providers of public services affects vulnerable groups in a particular way.[62] The IACtHR indicated in its judgment that the impact of corruption (in this case, a network of illegal adoptions) reduces the confidence of the people in the government and, in time, in democratic order and the rule of law.[63]

The strategy established by DPLF for responding to initial questions and promoting a greater involvement on the part of the IAHRS in this field included an initial analysis, discussions, and the exchange of experience and information with other CSOs in the region with the same concerns, as well as disseminating information and lobbying the IACHR. These actions influenced the growing interest of the IACHR in the further development of the standards included in Resolutions 1/17 and 1/18 and, in line with the conclusions and recommendations of the heads of State of the continent at the 2018 Summit of the Americas,[64] in making a significant contribution in this field.

In this context, DPLF participated in various preparation meetings for the thematic report on the matter, during which it conveyed many of the concerns of its partners. In December 2017, DPLF participated in a closed discussion on corruption and human rights organized by the IACHR and the Office of the UN High Commissioner for Human Rights during the First Forum of the

---

[61] IACHR, "Democratic Institutions, the Rule of Law and Human Rights in Venezuela," OAS/Ser.L/V/II. December 31, 2017, para. 146.
[62] *Case of Ramírez Escobar et al. v. Guatemala* [2018] IACtHR, Ser. C No. 351, para. 241.
[63] Ibid., para. 242.
[64] 2018 Summit of the Americas, focusing on democratic governance against corruption.

Inter-American Human Rights System in Washington, DC.[65] Subsequently, in March 2018, it participated in a consultation meeting in Colombia during the 167th Extraordinary Period of Sessions in the presence of other experts on the matter.[66] In December 2018, DPLF organized a meeting in Washington, DC, with experts and colleagues from the region in order to discuss the advances of the IAHRS in this field and to make certain recommendations, which were also shared with the IACHR.

When the IACHR agreed to formulate a report on corruption and human rights, DPLF expressly supported this initiative and, in collaboration with groups with which it had been pondering this matter,[67] it organized meetings in six cities in the Americas with the aim of ensuring that the technical team of the IACHR, which was in charge of preparing the report, could gather relevant information. These meetings were attended by at least 150 organizations and took place in Argentina, Chile, Colombia, Peru, El Salvador, and Mexico.[68]

Subsequently, DPLF requested a IACHR thematic hearing on "Corruption and Human Rights: The role of justice systems in Latin America," which took place in Sucre, Bolivia, on February 15, 2019, with twenty-one organizations and experts in the field participating in the initiative.[69] During this hearing, DPLF provided relevant information on at least ten countries in the region and the role of their justice systems both as protagonists in acts of corruption and as the entities responsible for the criminal prosecution of this crime. Also, and more importantly, DPLF demonstrated regional patterns and made a series of recommendations for regional implementation.

At the same time, DPLF maintained a constant dialogue with its partners in the region, and whilst awaiting the IACHR thematic report, it established a strategy for the dissemination and—above all—the implementation of the new standards that the report would contain. The report was finally published on December 31, 2019, and DPLF planned presentations during 2020 in various capitals of the region. The report contains important advances, positioning the IAHRS as a relevant actor in the efforts of States and civil society to confront corruption and the violations of human rights that are usually derived from this phenomenon.

---

[65] IACHR, "Annual Report 2017," Chapter 1, at 43, <https://www.oas.org/en/iachr/docs/annual/2017/TOC.asp> (accessed February 5, 2022).

[66] Ibid.

[67] The events were mainly organized in collaboration with the Rule of Law Program of the Konrad Adenauer Foundation (KAS), the Latin American and Caribbean Network for Democracy (REDLAD), and Fundar.

[68] See IACHR, "Report on Corruption and Human Rights" (December 2019), 14.

[69] See <https://www.youtube.com/watch?v=ekAnMhacV3s&list=PL5QlapyOGhXuSrrN5AMHWWfm36AsMzrq0&index=14> and <http://www.oea.org/en/iachr/media_center/PReleases/2019/038A-EN.pdf> (accessed February 5, 2022).

Again, with the aim of contributing to the socialization of the content of the report and promoting the addressing of the phenomenon of serious corruption from the perspective of the human rights obligations of States, DPLF published an infographic summary on the main findings and conclusions relating to the justice systems.[70]

5. Concluding Remarks

The ideas expressed in this chapter intend to support the following hypothesis which, to a certain extent, guides the strategies, working methods, and initiatives of DPLF as a user organization of the Inter-American System. Despite the low degree of compliance with decisions issued by its organs, the standards of the IAHRS have guided the actions of State agents and operators of the law throughout the continent. Rather than proposing a methodology for proving this hypothesis, this chapter attempts to point out the way in which the DPLF and its partner organizations have tried to influence the development and dissemination of certain inter-American standards. Naturally, the experiences described here may well be different from those of civil society organizations engaged in activities of litigation and activism with a local or national scope of action or with institutional missions and strategies that differ from DPLF's own.

The use of two specific examples of the development of standards on the part of the IAHRS in order to consolidate the stated conceptual hypothesis is not intended to be an inductive demonstration in which the general premises can be shown through *specific* premises. Indeed, the examples cited in the last section of this chapter aim to support reflections on the role of civil society in the creation of standards in two processes of advocacy and lobbying in which DPLF was directly involved. The conclusion relating to the impact of the standards recently developed by the organs of the IAHRS requires a more specific evaluation of the way State actors and operators of the law on a domestic scale are shaping their actions on the basis of the standards, rules, and principles derived from the pronouncements of the mentioned supranational organs.

Although this chapter could be read as a self-referential exercise, our intention is to justify the premise that the impact of the IAHRS is directly correlated to the capability of the organs of the IAHRS to develop standards that respond to the demands of CSOs, as well as to their ability to ensure that these standards are better known and applied by operators of law and State agents at

---

[70] DPLF, "Independencia judicial y corrupción: Síntesis de los principales contenidos sobre justicia del informe 'Corrupción y Derechos Humanos' de la CIDH," <http://www.dplf.org/sites/default/files/info_corrupcion_digital_vf.pdf> (accessed February 5, 2022).

the national level. In the examples contained in this chapter, the development of new standards transcends the creation of legal rules in matters upon which the IAHRS has not previously made pronouncements, requiring the incorporation of new narratives about social phenomena which, in themselves, do not imply a violation of human rights but which nonetheless may be affecting the enjoyment of human rights and the normal functioning of the rule of law in the region.

III.6
Activism Strategies Involving the Inter-American System
Reflections for the Field of Action and Perspectives from National Human Rights Organizations

By Gabriela Kletzel

1. Introduction

The achievements of the Inter-American Human Rights System (IAHRS) are wide-ranging, diverse, and profound. Throughout its history, the IAHRS's mechanisms have taken an increasingly larger and unerring role in the fight against impunity for crimes against humanity in the context of civil–military dictatorships and armed conflicts. These mechanisms have also left their mark on efforts to defend the rights of groups who have historically been victims of discrimination. With the advent of democracy in the region, the IAHRS's agenda and actions have expanded to include work on the structural patterns of rights violations.[1]

In order to analyze the scope of the Inter-American System, it is useful to examine the dynamics between its different bodies and principal actors, specifically regional States, victims of violations that require intervention, and social organizations that channel the demands of victims. For the purposes of this chapter, I will focus on the work done by national human rights organizations. By understanding the potential of the Inter-American System, the organizations have not limited their actions to bringing cases of human rights violations to light but—in addition to providing assistance for specific situations that require redress—have also deployed diverse strategies to maximize the impact of the IAHRS and, therefore, have been a catalyst for structural transformations. At the same time, they

---

[1] See, in this respect, Victor Abramovich, "De las violaciones masivas a los patrones estructurales: Nuevos enfoques y clásicas tensiones en el sistema interamericano de derechos humanos" [2009] 6 *Sur* 7–37.

have also played a key role in aspects of the Inter-American System's substantive and institutional development by challenging and expanding the agenda of its bodies, safeguarding its composition, and generating and enhancing working tools, among other actions. To shed light on these roles, I will provide concrete examples of actors and interventions that have enabled material transformations in the observance of rights within States and, from an institutional perspective, the System itself.

To start, I think it is relevant to show that actions vis-à-vis the IAHRS ought to be considered as comprehensive strategies to fight impunity, with both national and international dimensions. I will support this claim by looking at the work done by historic organizations in Argentina that have developed themselves into successful interlocutors with the Inter-American Commission on Human Rights (IACHR) and the Inter-American Court of Human Rights (IACtHR). Secondly, I will discuss some of the contributions developed by domestic social actors from different countries in the region to bolster the actions of the IAHRS in institutional and substantive terms. I will prioritize recent strategies—based on their legitimacy and national experience—that social organizations have used to give momentum to the creation of intervention mechanisms in real time, to accomplish a proper integration of the System's bodies, and to push for a more complex account of the matters covered by the System's thematic agenda.

2. The Inter-American System as One Piece among More Complex Strategies

The logic behind actions taken before international bodies that protect and promote rights will be, without question, a determining factor in strategy-building around preventing or redressing human rights violations. The possibilities available to an actor putting forward a claim, the type of situations requiring intervention, and the specific response dynamic will impact the potential role attributed to the international authority and the way its effects are assessed.

The variety of competences held by the IAHRS, aside from assistance in cases that have not received an adequate response at the local level, allows its bodies to be seen as elements in a much larger machinery in the fight against impunity, especially in light of the structural deficiencies of many States in the region. In these scenarios, the actions of the IAHRS complement and, in many cases, reinforce the catalog of initiatives undertaken domestically and are in keeping with the logic of comprehensive strategy that must not be lost along the way. The persistent appeals to the IAHRS by human rights organizations seeking Memory, Truth and Justice in Argentina exemplify this particular dynamic.

Seeking justice for crimes against humanity committed during Argentina's last dictatorship has required the use of diverse tools and IAHRS standards in an ongoing and versatile legal battle that the country's historic human rights movement has sustained for decades. Within the framework of a claim that has managed to involve most of society and the political system, human rights organizations representing victims of State terrorism have used multiple strategies vis-à-vis the IAHRS to legitimize their struggle, keep their claims on the public agenda, develop new tools to reveal the truth, and move forward decidedly on the road to justice. At the same time, these efforts have fostered the development of standards and tools that have later benefited other struggles.

The *in loco* visit by the IACHR to Argentina in 1979,[2] and its 1980 Country Report in,[3] gave visibility and substance to the reports by the families of victims of systematic practices of mass arbitrary detentions, torture, and forced disappearances that characterized the extermination plan of the de facto military government in power between 1976 and 1983. In view of that precedent, human rights organizations have deployed a variety of actions vis-à-vis the IAHRS that have proven to be key factors at different moments in the fight against impunity.

With the return to democracy in 1983, both the work conducted by the National Commission on the Disappearance of Persons (*Comisión Nacional sobre la Desaparición de Personas*, or CONADEP)[4] and the details of the Trial of the Military Juntas[5] set out a path for truth and justice, which was abruptly interrupted with the passage of the Due Obedience (*Obediencia debida*) and Full Stop (*Punto final*) laws, as well as the presidential pardons of 1989. The Due Obedience Law created an irrefutable presumption that military personnel who

---

[2] In September 2019, the IACHR visited Argentina to commemorate the fortieth anniversary of its historic visit in 1979. See, in this respect, https://www.oas.org/en/cidh/prensa/comunicados/2019/226.asp (accessed November 13, 2021).

[3] IACHR, "Country Report on the human rights situation in Argentina," April 11, 1989, https://www.cidh.org/countryrep/Argentina80sp/indice.htm (accessed November 13, 2021).

[4] After the restoration of democracy, President Raúl Alfonsín formed the National Commission on the Disappearance of Persons (CONADEP) to investigate incidents related to the disappearance of persons during the civil–military dictatorship. CONADEP was presided over by writer Ernesto Sábato and twelve recognized figures from different areas of national life. CONADEP called upon dozens of volunteers and persons linked to the human rights struggle who spent just over nine months traveling across most of the country as part of their work to compile, organize, and establish a hierarchy of data on human rights violations. CONADEP produced a final report entitled "Nunca Más" ("Never Again"). More information at https://www.argentina.gob.ar/anm/oral/trabajadores-conadep (accessed November 13, 2021).

[5] The accused were members of the three military juntas: Jorge Rafael Videla, Emilio Eduardo Massera, and Orlando Ramón Agosti (first military junta, 1976–1980); Roberto Eduardo Viola, Armando Lambruschini, and Omar Domingo Rubens Graffigna (second military junta, 1980–1981); and Leopoldo Fortunato Galtieri, Jorge Isaac Anaya, and Basilio Lami Dozo (third military junta, 1981–1982). On December 9, 1985, the Federal Court issued its ruling confirming the existence of a systematic extermination plan by the military dictatorship that usurped power on March 24, 1976. In this regard, more details at https://www.telam.com.ar/notas/201512/129500-juicio-a-las-juntas-sentencia.html (accessed November 13, 2021).

had committed crimes had acted in due obedience, thus exempting them from criminal responsibility; the Full Stop Law set a term of sixty days for the termination of criminal legal actions; and the presidential pardons reversed sentences and trial procedures for persons accused of human rights violations who had not benefited from said laws.

This scenario led the families of victims—of whom many by then had set up a diverse range of human rights organizations—to intensify their strategies to fight impunity, resorting once again to multiple political and legal actions at the national and international level. This is the context within which the annual mass marches take place every March 24, marking the anniversary of the 1976 coup d'état, the multitudinous public denouncements (*escraches*) of "repressors at liberty," the commencement of trials in European countries for crimes committed against their own citizens, and the proceedings under universal jurisdiction by Spain's National High Court, as well as different initiatives brought before the IAHRS and the Universal Human Rights System.[6]

Among other actions, they submitted multiple petitions to the IACHR denouncing those laws and decrees as violations of the American Convention on Human Rights (ACHR) insofar as they obstructed the progress of criminal proceedings on grave human rights violations that occurred during the de facto government. By virtue of the material nature of the claims, as well as the legal nature of the issue, the Commission gave its decision on the entire set of petitions in its Report No. 28/92. In this report, the Commission ruled that the enactment of said laws and decrees had the effect of terminating any pending trials against people responsible for past human rights violations. The Commission concluded that this constituted a violation of the right to judicial guarantees, judicial protection, and the obligation to investigate, thus rendering said laws incompatible with the ACHR and recommended that Argentina adopt the "necessary measures to clarify the facts and individually hold responsible those who committed human rights violations during the last military dictatorship."[7]

Thus, after the Commission's visit to Argentina in 1979, domestic claims for justice were once again supported by international mechanisms, to the point that said laws and decrees were determined to be incompatible with Argentina's obligations within the framework of the American Convention. Nevertheless, given the limitations imposed by the political context, this international ruling did not result in the immediate reopening of judicial proceedings, but it did set

---

[6] Among other publications, see CELS, *Hacer justicia. Nuevos debates sobre el juzgamiento de los delitos de lesa humanidad en la Argentina* (Siglo Vientiuno Editores 2011), https://www.cels.org.ar/web/publicaciones/hacer-justicia-nuevos-debates-sobre-el-juzgamiento-de-crimenes-de-lesa-humanidad-en-la-argentina/ (accessed November 18, 2021).

[7] IACHR, "Report No. 28/92, Cases 10.147, 10.181, 10.240, 10.262, 10.309, and 10.311," October 2, 1992.

an inevitable precedent for the 2005 Argentine Supreme Court ruling on those instruments of impunity.[8] At the same time, it was a determining factor for organizations to continue insisting on their claims at the national and international level through an innovative proposal: truth trials (*juicios por la verdad*).

In 1998, the Inter-American Commission received a new petition against Argentina from Carmen Aguiar de Lapacó, sponsored by a number of human rights organizations.[9] The petitioner went to the IACHR after judicial authorities refused to properly channel her petition (based on the right to the truth and to bereavement) in order to determine what happened to her daughter Alejandra, who disappeared on March 17, 1977, after being detained by the authorities. They sustained the violation of their rights to judicial guarantees, to effective judicial protection, and the obligation to respect their rights under the American Convention.[10]

The demands made by the human rights movement, which came up against multiple sources of resistance at the local level,[11] finally found a proper conduit in the Commission. Through its framework a process of amicable resolutions commenced with the State agreeing to accept and guarantee the right to the truth and committing to take diverse measures to remedy alleged violations. Specifically, the government accepted that the right to the truth "consists of exhausting all measures to attain clarification as to what happened to disappeared persons . . . without any statutory limits" and determined that it would put in place a legal framework for National Criminal and Federal Correctional Courts throughout the country to have exclusive jurisdiction in all cases to ascertain the truth and final fate of persons disappeared before December 10, 1983. The government would also assign a corps of ad hoc prosecutors for all cases in the search for the truth and final fate of disappeared persons; they would also employ their specialized expertise in gathering and interpreting data and improve the centralization and circulation of information across dispersed cases.[12]

Among many other effects, including the effective commencement of the truth trials, this process of amicable settlement alongside the final report of the IACHR's *in loco* visit ended up being essential elements in the strategy to keep the public spotlight on the need to uncover acts of State terrorism committed by

---

[8] *Julio Héctor Simón y otros s/ privación ilegítima de la libertad, etc. (Poblete)* [2005], Argentine National Supreme Court, causa No. 17.768.

[9] Namely, *Abuelas de Plaza de Mayo, Asamblea Permanente de los Derechos Humanos* (APDH), CELS, *Centro por la Justicia y el Derecho Internacional* (CEJIL), *Familiares de Detenidos Desaparecidos por Razones Políticas, Liga Argentina por los Derechos del Hombre, Madres de la Plaza de Mayo—Línea Fundadora—Movimiento Ecuménico por los Derechos Humanos* (MEDH), and *Servicio de Paz y Justicia* (SERPAJ).

[10] For local precedents of international claims, see CELS, *La lucha por el derecho* (Siglo Veintiuno Editores 2008), 223.

[11] Ibid.

[12] *Carmen Aguiar de Lapacó v. Argentina* [2000], IACHR, Report No. 21/00, Case 12.059.

the civil–military dictatorship and prosecute them institutionally. Nevertheless, although knowing the truth was essential, the primary objective of the human rights movement was always justice. As such, the Center for Legal and Social Studies (*Centro de Estudios Legales y Sociales*, or CELS) and Grandmothers of the Plaza de Mayo (*Abuelas de la Plaza de Mayo*) did not miss the opportunity to specifically request the reopening of criminal cases on the grounds that the laws of impunity were unconstitutional. In this context, seeking recourse to the IAHRS was once again decisive. This time, however, it was achieved not through the impact of a petition (as in the Report No. 28/92 cases) or the implementation of an amicable settlement (like the *Lapacó* case) but through pushing for the application of international human rights law by domestic courts.

Consequently, along with Law 25779 repealing the Due Obedience and Full Stop laws, the precedents and standards set in other Latin American countries by the IAHRS on the incompatibility of pardoning crimes against humanity, such as *Barrios Altos v. Peru*,[13] were a cornerstone of the 2005 Argentine Supreme Court ruling in the *Simón* case,[14] which resulted in the definitive reopening of legal proceedings against all perpetrators.[15] Despite its transcendence, that decision would not be the end of the ongoing interaction between domestic and international law on the road to justice. On the one hand, human rights organizations have returned to the IAHRS through diverse routes in cases where trials have been hindered by the outdated dynamics of the Argentine justice system, which is ill prepared to handle the contingencies of these types of proceedings. In public sessions before the IACHR, these organizations have, among other actions, exposed the difficulties they have encountered, forcing the Argentine State to provide explanations.[16] Moreover, IAHRS standards were again essential to counteract a recent attempt to establish impunity through a significant reduction in the sentences sought in the Supreme Court ruling in the *Muiña* case.[17] This

---

[13] *Barrios Altos v. Perú* [2001], IACtHR, Ser. C No. 75.

[14] For a synthesis of the *Simón* case, see https://www.cels.org.ar/common/documentos/sintesis_fallo_csjn_caso_poblete.pdf (accessed November 15, 2021).

[15] The reopening of the justice process has meant that there are currently 226 court rulings throughout the country, in which 915 persons were convicted and 144 acquitted. Further information on the trials for crimes against humanity in Argentina at https://www.cels.org.ar/informe2019/lesa.html (accessed December 14, 2021).

[16] Among other instances, on March 6, 2007, there was a public hearing before the IACHR in the context of the "Monitoring compliance with Petition 28/92, Argentina, on the incompatibility of the laws of impunity with the American Convention" (*Seguimiento del cumplimiento del Informe 28/92, Argentina, sobre la incompatibilidad de las leyes de impunidad con la Convención Americana*). For an audio recording of the hearing, see https://www.cidh.oas.org/Audiencias/127/Seguimiento%20del%20informe%2028-92,%20Argentina.MP3 (accessed December 14, 2021).

[17] Argentine National Supreme Court, "Recurso de hecho deducido por la defensa de Luis Muiña en la causa Bignone, Reynaldo Benito Antonio y otro s/ Recurso extraordinario," May 3, 2007, https://www.cij.gov.ar/nota-25746-La-Corte-Suprema--por-mayor-a--declar--aplicable-el-c-mputo-del-2x1-para-la-prisi-n-en-un-caso-de-delitos-de-lesa-humanidad.html (accessed December 13, 2021). See, in this regard, CELS, *El fallo "Muiña" de la Corte Suprema de Justicia de la Nación*, https://www.cels.org.ar/web/publicaciones/fallo-muina/ (accessed December 2, 2021).

decision, in addition to receiving widespread domestic criticism,[18] prompted a reaction from the Inter-American Commission[19] and was ultimately dismantled under a new decision from the high court in the 2019 *Batalla* case.[20]

The capillary effect of the IAHRS's actions in this struggle for justice warrants a deeper analysis. Argentina's experience shows that the IACHR and the IACtHR can play a key role in political fights with long-term impacts. This will largely depend on the ability of social actors promoting the System's intervention to interlace their local strategies with the effects of international action. In this context, measuring the results of each intervention by regional organizations in the short term, in isolation or as an end in itself, could lead to a weakening of opportunities for action in which recourse to such intervention must be understood as merely a part of a much more complex approach.

3. Toward a Genuine Strengthening of the Regional Protection System

Throughout its history, the IACHR and the IACtHR have had to face serious risks to their mandates and fundamental competences. These risks arose in the context of severe questioning that arose from different alliances among States in the region, paradoxically presented as "strengthening processes." The latest of these episodes was a few years ago when Brazil, Colombia, Venezuela, and Ecuador pursued an agenda (on which we have already reflected[21]) that threatened not only the IACHR's autonomy, independence, and, in effect, its authority to rule on precautionary measures but also the work conducted by the Special Rapporteur

---

[18] In response to the decision on *Muiña*, the National Congress passed in record time Law 27.362 on the inapplicability of the 2x1 benefit for crimes against humanity. For further information, see http://servicios.infoleg.gob.ar/infolegInternet/anexos/270000-274999/274607/norma.htm (accessed December 2, 2021).

[19] The IACHR expressed that the Argentine Supreme Court's decision "departs from international standards for prosecuting grave human rights violations," and added that crimes against humanity differ from other crimes "because of the aims and objectives they pursue; they are based on the concept of humanity as victim. States, therefore, have an international obligation not to leave these crimes unpunished and to ensure the proportionality of the penalty. The application of the 'two for one' calculation or other benefits should not serve to undermine the proportionality of the penalty for persons responsible for crimes against humanity. Its application would render inadequate the punishment that was imposed, which runs contrary to inter-American human rights standards." IACHR Press Release No. 60/17, "IACHR Expresses Concern over Argentine Supreme Court Decision," May 15, 2017.

[20] Argentine National Supreme Court, "Batalla Rufino," December 4, 2018, https://www.cij.gov.ar/nota-32689-PENAL---Inaplicabilidad-del-beneficio-del-2x1-para-los-delitos-de-lesa-humanidad.html (accessed December 11, 2021). See, in this regard, https://www.cels.org.ar/web/2018/12/corte-suprema-de-justicia-de-la-nacion-no-es-aplicable-el-2x1-para-delitos-de-lesa-humanidad/ (accessed December 19, 2021).

[21] Camila Baretto Maia et al, *The Inter-American Human Rights System. Changing Times, Ongoing Challenges* (Colección Dejusticia 2015).

on freedom of expression, among other issues. Regrettably, these attacks have not tried to strengthen the bodies of the Inter-American System in terms of prioritizing the needs of victims of various and longstanding rights violations, despite how they were framed.

Luckily, as we will see, civil society has often picked up the gauntlet to bolster the issues, forms, and logic behind intervention by the Inter-American System in order to improve its impact. There are many examples, but the examples that I present here center on just three pivotal issues for the IAHRS: its devices, its composition, and the perspective on which it bases its standards.

I will first focus on the contributions made by domestic civil society actors toward creating working tools under a renewed logic of timely interventions. I will then take a look at the weight that civil society brings to bear on preserving the mandate of the regional protection system through its participation in the process of selecting IACHR and IACtHR members. This is happening in a context of concrete risks with regard to the profiles of candidates proposed by the region's governments. Finally, I will share the efforts of a group of organizations that have worked tirelessly for the development and consolidation of IAHRS standards on an issue of the utmost relevance: social protest and human rights.

3.1. The Role of Civil Society in Generating Disruptive Tools

After experimenting for years with the tools of the IAHRS, organizations have worked arduously to forge new instruments to provide more timely and effective responses to rights violations. In this context, an innovative intervention by some international experts in Mexico particularly stands out, as it invigorated the work being done by Mexican human rights organizations in the fight against systemic impunity. I am referring to the experience of the Interdisciplinary Group of Independent Experts (GIEI).

The GIEI was formed in the framework of precautionary measures granted by the IACHR in response to the disappearance of forty-three students from Ayotzinapa. The GIEI was an experiment without legal precedent,[22] prompted by Mexican human rights organizations that were mired in a struggle against systemic impunity. When the GIEI began its work, the Attorney General of the Republic of Mexico (*Procuraduría General de la República*, or PGR) had already publicly revealed the "true story" of the disappearances, according to which members of the Guerreros United cartel had incinerated the students in

---

[22] Silva Cabrera, Gabriela Ángel, and Gabriela Kletzel, "Ayotzinapa. La experiencia del Grupo Interdisciplinario de Expertos Independientes," in CELS (ed.), *Derechos Humanos en la Argentina, Informe 2017* (Siglo XXI editores 2017), 223–242.

a garbage dump and thrown their ashes into the river. The PGR had expressed its commitment to pursuing and punishing the alleged perpetrators. Without the intervention of human rights organizations, the case would have gone no further than that. However, a coalition of organizations prompted an innovative strategy. They proposed forming a team of institutionally recognized (by both the IACHR and the federal government) experts to provide technical assistance in real time to the investigations.

Three human rights organizations in particular—the *Centro de Derechos Humanos de la Montaña* (Tlachinollan), the *Centro de Derechos Humanos Miguel Agustín Pro Juárez*, and the *Red Guerrerense de Organismos Civiles de Derechos Humanos*—played a decisive role in coordinating this approach and forming the GIEI. Taking advantage of the political momentum that the case generated, they got the Mexican government and the IACHR to sign an agreement. One key objective was for the institutionalization of a Group of Experts to maintain social pressure on the government so as to prevent the *Ayotzinapa* case from falling into the tangled web of Mexican bureaucracy.

The most immediate results of the GIEI were two reports exhibiting the serious deficiencies in the methods of criminal investigation and recommending actions to improve institutional performance. These recommendations applied to the case at hand, but also made reference to structural problems in institutional responses to forced disappearances. In 2016, once the GIEI was dismantled by the government of then President Enrique Peña Nieto, the group was replaced with a system of direct monitoring between the IACHR and Mexican authorities.

At first glance the GIEI might seem like a strategy with only a limited scope. Years after their disappearance, the forty-three students have never been found. Moreover, impunity continues to be a serious problem in Mexico and the PGR continues to receive strong criticism from national and international organizations alike. However, a more complex assessment of this process requires more careful attention to the relationship between the GIEI, activists, the State, and society in general.

Despite being a technical body, the GIEI had strong ties to domestic social movements. This relationship was neither accidental nor natural but was built through the intermediation of human rights organizations that facilitated meetings, organized protests, and linked the GIEI's work to the most structural claims against impunity. The investigation became a benchmark in the search for truth in cases of disappearances and its strong political capital was useful for those groups leading the social movement around the *Ayotzinapa* case.

After a year and a half of work the GIEI had successfully discredited the official version of the story. It conducted a new, independent investigation that disproved the garbage dump fire theory and the disposal of the ashes in the river. At the same time, it showed evidence of State and federal police intervention, as well as army presence at the scene of the disappearances. Furthermore, it documented how a top government official actively participated in covering up the facts. It also revealed the existence of a bus that had not been included in the official investigation, along with indicators suggesting that it was loaded with drugs and heading for Chicago when the students boarded it. The GIEI formulated this hypothesis as a possible explanation for the wanton reaction by security agents who opened fire on the students before their disappearance.

Aside from the concrete impact on the *Ayotzinapa* case, the GIEI acted as a hub for leveraging energy around broader societal demands for justice. Its role in the investigation structured arguments that were later transformed into social mandates and set precedents for improving new strategies. In addition, in the course of its investigations the GIEI uncovered more than seventy mass graves in the State of Guerrero that were unrelated to the *Ayotzinapa* case. In conjunction with the conclusions on the case, these discoveries placed the problem of structural impunity in Mexico under intense public scrutiny and contributed to the organization and mobilization of a broad spectrum of social actors.

The GIEI's work involved the federal government in an uncomfortable discussion with international actors that led to the creation of ordinarily nonexistent instances of accountability. In addition, it provided tools for strengthening institutions like the Executive Commission for Attention to Victims and the National Commission on Human Rights.

The IACHR also played its part. It could have taken a legalistic position and refused to support this innovation. Nevertheless, aware of the need to take advantage of the scenario, the IACHR activated another of its legal tools and organized an *in loco* visit. This type of visit—which allows the Commissioners to travel to a country to interview officials, NGOs, and victims in order to assess the overall human rights situation—had not occurred in Mexico since 1998. By involving itself in the sociopolitical context created by the *Ayotzinapa* case, the presence of the IACHR invigorated discussions around the human rights crisis in the country and took it beyond the parameters of the specific case toward the severity and scale of the situation in general.

The work of the GIEI had such an impact that, three years after it was stopped, the government of President Andrés Manuel Lopez Obrador created the conditions to re-establish this mechanism and continue the search for the students and shed light on those responsible for their disappearance.[23] Furthermore, the IACHR has decided to replicate this logic of timely intervention in other contexts, such as Nicaragua, where, after visiting the country and

---

[23] See, e.g., Jannet López Ponce, "GIEI se reincorpora a búsqueda de 43 normalistas de Ayotzinapa" (*Milenio*, November 11, 2019), https://www.milenio.com/politica/ayotzinapa-giei-reincorpora-busqueda-43-normalistas (accessed November 11, 2021).

verifying the grave human rights violations occurring during the 2018 social protests, the Commission decided to establish a Group of Independent Experts and establish, at the same time, a Special Monitoring Mechanism (*Mecanismo Especial de Seguimiento para Nicaragua*, or MESENI).[24]

Through the GIEI, human rights organizations were able to devise a legal experiment to maintain the vitality of social movements, create a platform to show the magnitude of the crisis, and position proposals for structural reform that also reiterated the forms of intervention conceived within the IACHR itself. As with the process of Memory, Truth, and Justice in Argentina, this experience demonstrates that in the framework of more complex strategies international mechanisms can provide forums capable of generating innovative synergies to strengthen projects of institutional transformation driven from below.

3.2. Guardians of Mandate and Jurisdiction

A lack of transparent institutional and formal processes for nominating and selecting Commissioners and Judges to the IACtHR and who meet proper standards in human rights matters is a problem that can be a deciding factor for the profile and efforts of protection bodies.[25] This risk has escalated in recent years, with a number of States nominating candidates who are particularly unsuitable for the forum and whose positions are openly contrary to the standards of the Inter-American System.

In this context, civil society has played a fundamental role in safeguarding the composition of regional bodies. In addition to issuing specific proposals to regional States for the formalization of these processes following the analysis of candidate profiles—information that, not being made public until the process is well underway, may be difficult to get—various organizations have coordinated positions at the national and regional level to reject some candidates: they have produced joint statements from among hundreds of organizations requesting the removal of unsuitable candidates, prepared documents for foreign offices and missions to the Organization of American States (OAS), encouraged discussion-based meetings in embassies and in

---

[24] On the MESENI, see IACHR Press Release No. 135/18, "IACHR Launches Special Monitoring Mechanism for Nicaragua (MESENI)," June 25, 2018.

For an example of the impact of actions taken by the IACHR, see "CIDH anuncia liberación de 11 detenidos en Nicaragua" (*Voz de América*, July 7, 2018), <https://www.voanoticias.com/a/cidh-anuncia-liberaci%C3%B3n-de-11-detenidos-en-nicaragua/4473199.html> (accessed December 8, 2021).

[25] The IACHR and the IACtHR each have seven members from OAS countries who are elected by the Organization's General Assembly. To that end, the terms of the American Convention on Human Rights state that IACHR Commissioners should be persons of high moral authority and recognized as well versed in human rights matters.

Washington, created public discussion forums that have led to the formation of a panel prior to each election, and contributed to the construction of a system of evaluation for candidates by a group of distinguished scholars that is renewed after every selection process.

One concrete example of this work is the resistance to the election of Carlos Horacio De Casas, nominated to the Commission by Argentina in 2017. De Casas is a lawyer with hardly any human rights experience and a long history of defending corporate interests. He has openly positioned himself against reproductive and LGBTIQ+ rights, and has publicly supported the crime of contempt of court, which has been used to criminalize journalists, something the IACHR itself has condemned. After announcing his candidacy, De Casas even lied about the background of a military officer he represented who was accused of committing crimes against humanity during the civil–military dictatorship. The only interaction De Casas has had with the Inter-American System was to defend the executives of a company accused of financial crimes. Moreover, his law firm went before the IACHR to defend the interests of a mining corporation that severely damaged indigenous communities in Guatemala. His credentials could hardly have been worse.

In light of this significant risk to the composition of the IACHR, different civil society organizations joined forces to prevent De Casas from being elected by the OAS. This occurred first at the national level and was then extended to include organizations from other countries, as well as international organizations.

In Argentina, a diverse set of actors issued a formal objection to his candidacy: more than 130 Argentine organizations—human rights organizations, unions, rural movements, and associations working on justice issues, gender equality, the environment, LGBTIQ+ rights, and freedom of expression—asked the Minister of Foreign Affairs and the Secretary of Human Rights to revoke his nomination. These actors and organizations also informed the public on the problems his designation represented, taking advantage of social media platforms and coordinating with the *Abuelas de la Plaza de Mayo* and the *Ni Una Menos* groups to provide video testimonies in support of the campaign. These material expressions of concern and opposition to De Casas' candidacy were sent by organizations from different States to embassies of OAS member States in Buenos Aires and to the missions of OAS member States in Washington. Numerous meetings were also held with diplomatic personnel.

Meanwhile, in a public letter two former IACHR Presidents, Robert Goldman and Juan Méndez, urged the Argentine president to withdraw De Casas' candidacy. Finally, an international panel of independent experts sounded the alarm with regard to his credentials. Based on his CV, professional trajectory, and his previous publications, the panel expressed its concern about the candidate meeting the requirement of recognized competence in human rights matters. None of the other five candidates nominated to perform duties as Commissioners on the IACHR received this type of criticism. Finally, when regional elections were held, the campaign worked, and De Casas was not selected to the Commission.

Regrettably, this risk seems not to have gone away, as other inappropriate nominations have proliferated recently. Among other examples, in 2019 the Argentine government once again insisted on an openly "anti-rights" candidate,[26] and Colombia tried to designate a candidate that had expressly said "no to the peace agreement." In this context, organizations again coordinated strategically, deploying actions at the national and regional levels. In Argentina, the coordinated efforts of the human rights movement got the government to directly withdraw the nomination.[27] In Colombia, the filing of a lawsuit at the local level[28] and the regional disclosure of the candidate's professional background led to another victory and the Inter-American System's standards were upheld.

Both in Argentina specifically and in the region more generally, the work done by civil society organizations has thus had a hand in preventing the IACHR from incorporating persons who openly disdain the rights of women and girls, who defend companies that have violated the rights of rural and Indigenous communities, or stand against the most basic standards when it comes to fighting impunity. Indeed, after the last election and for the first time ever these efforts have contributed to making women the majority on the Commission, one of whom is an expert on gender issues.

This matter, which at times may seem far removed from the concrete dynamics of guaranteeing rights, is actually at the core of their effective safeguarding approaches. In addition to continuing to demand the formalization of transparent, participative selection processes and in keeping with suitability requirements, it is fundamental that there are more actors paying attention to these processes in order to preserve the role of international organizations in the promotion and protection of rights and the effective prevention and redressing of violations.

---

[26] Despite the De Casas fiasco, the Argentine government submitted another candidate in 2019 with positions that were openly contrary to IAHRS standards on sexual and reproductive rights, as well as State obligations regarding crimes against humanity.

[27] See Alejandra Hayon, "El antiderechos que se queda en casa" (*Página 12*, February 20, 2019), <https://www.pagina12.com.ar/175993-alfredo-vitolo-el-antiderechos-que-se-queda-en-su-casa> (accessed January 12, 2022).

[28] See Diego Camilo Carranza Jimenez, "Admiten acción contra la candidatura de exsenador para representar Colombia ante CIDH" (*Anadolu Agency*, May 22, 2019), <https://www.aa.com.tr/es/mundo/admiten-acci%C3%B3n-contra-la-candidatura-de-exsenador-para-representar-colombia-ante-cidh/1484939> (accessed November 13, 2021).

3.3. Broadening the Agenda and Scope

Experience has shown that anchoring and developing new issues on the IAHRS agenda is usually a long, stage-by-stage process, where the push from civil society plays a key role. Of the many possible examples, a useful one for our purposes has to do with the recent development of an agenda on social protests and human rights vis-à-vis the Commission. A group of organizations[29] in recent years have been working to encourage a much more systematic and complex approach by the IACHR to State responses to social protest. Rather than solely linking social protest to freedom of expression, their approach connects it to the lessons learned in different national contexts. Their goal was to cast a more complex lens on social protest, reclaim its legitimacy as a strategy, and place the focus on how different States react to its deployment.

After diagnosing the need for the IACHR to diversify its position on State reactions to public demonstrations, the organizations proposed a regional thematic hearing to address points of contact where protests and human rights overlap throughout the continent.[30] This hearing was accompanied by a closed working meeting with the Commission in which the organizations presented in detail the dimensions and perspectives warranting greater attention from the Commission.

This exchange led to the inclusion in the IACHR 2015 Annual Report of a specific chapter on the use of force and human rights in the context of protests[31]—for which the organizations were called upon to contribute. This was followed up with an ongoing study with the Commission that involved monitoring multiple

---

[29] American Civil Liberties Union (ACLU), United States Article 19, Brazil Article 19, Mexico, Asociación Pro Derechos Humanos (APRODEH), Peru, Canadian Civil Liberties Association (CCLA), Cauce Ciudadano A.C., Mexico, Centro de Derechos Humanos Fray Francisco de Vitoria, Mexico, Centro de Derechos Humanos Miguel Agustín Pro Juárez (Centro Prodh), Mexico, Centro de Estudios Legales y Sociales (CELS), Argentina, Centro de Justicia para la Paz y el Desarrollo (CEPAD), Mexico, Centro Nacional de Comunicación Social (CENCOS), Mexico, Colectivo de Abogados José Alvear Restrepo, Colombia, Comité de Familiares de Detenidos—Desaparecidos en Honduras (COFADEH), Comité de Solidaridad con los Presos Políticos (CSPP), Colombia, Conectas Direitos Humanos, Brazil, Coordinadora Nacional de Derechos Humanos, Peru, Corporación Humanas, Chile, Espacio Público, Venezuela, Fundar Centro de Análisis e, Investigación, Mexico, Instituto de Defensores de Direitos Humanos (DDH), Brazil, Instituto de Estudios Legales y Sociales del Uruguay (IELSUR), Instituto Mexicano de Derechos Humanos y Democracia (IMDHD), Mexico, Justiça Global, Brazil, Núcleo Especializado de Cidadania e Direitos Humanos de Defensoria Pública do Estado de São Paulo, Brazil, Observatorio Ciudadano, Chile, Programa Venezolano de Educación—Acción en Derechos Humanos (PROVEA), Venezuela, Propuesta Cívica, Mexico, Red de Apoyo por la Justicia y la Paz, Venezuela, Red Nacional de Organismos Civiles de Derechos Humanos "Todos los Derechos para Todas y Todos," Mexico, Servicios y Asesoría para la Paz, A.C. (SERAPAZ), Mexico.

[30] For an audio-visual recording of this hearing, see <https://www.youtube.com/watch?v=_NF0K33bkLI> (accessed December 12, 2021).

[31] IACHR, "Annual Report 2015," Chapter IV.A, Use of Force.

situations throughout the region, organizing national thematic hearings, and adopting informed positions articulated through public announcements. At the same time that the organizations published their own assessment,[32] the IACHR finally resolved to work on the matter in depth and committed itself to preparing a specific thematic report, which at the time of writing has yet to be published.[33]

The development of this line of work, encouraged by the initiative and push from domestic social actors, left the Commission in a better position to assess and respond to situations such as those taking place a few years ago in Ecuador, Chile, and Colombia.[34] It is worth noting that the contributions of civil society toward the development of this theme were decisive in the regional mechanism adopting a more comprehensive definition of protest while also identifying a series of positive State obligations for facilitating them, as well as looking deeper at legal and administrative restrictions, repression, the use of force, the criminalization of protest, and the impunity of police violence. Based on the road covered thus far, these organizations will surely also play a central role in implementing the key considerations arising from the Commission's new report, with a view toward generating effective material conditions to safeguard the right to protest.

4. Concluding Remarks

Throughout this chapter I have presented an overview of strategic interventions by social actors within the Inter-American System. Some show that our analyses of the Commission's impacts should not be focused on narrow or isolated actions, since its contributions are often in continuous dialogue with structural processes, national struggles, and transformations in which victims have displayed incredible levels of tenacity. The contributions of national stakeholders have demonstrated the value of having a deeper knowledge of the complex State networks operating in each context and re-signified the usefulness and specific role of international recourse. Others have shown the important role played by civil society in generating and renewing tools, safeguarding the integration of mechanisms, and proposing new outlooks on unresolved issues.

Fifty years after the American Convention on Human Rights was ratified, sharing the multiple but entangled roads taken can inspire other forms of activism

---

[32] In this respect, see CELS, "Latin American State Responses to Social Protest" (*CELS*, 2016), https://www.cels.org.ar/protestasocial_AL/en.html (accessed December 17, 2021).

[33] See <https://www.oas.org/es/cidh/expresion/showarticle.asp?artID=1160&lID=2> (accessed December 17, 2021).

[34] Among other statements, see https://www.oas.org/es/cidh/prensa/comunicados/2019/262.asp, <https://www.oas.org/es/cidh/prensa/comunicados/2019/270.asp>, and <https://www.oas.org/es/cidh/prensa/comunicados/2019/313.asp> (all accessed December 17, 2021).

to confront other debts when it comes to substantive and institutional challenges that, despite all its accomplishments, persist within the Inter-American System. Sharing experiences and lessons learned can function as a catalyst for developing new strategies to confront the broader challenge of upholding human rights on our continent, now and in the future.

Conclusion

By Armin von Bogdandy, Flavia Piovesan, Eduardo Ferrer Mac-Gregor, and Mariela Morales Antoniazzi

By developing the concept of transformative impact, this volume has brought the debate about the effectiveness of international human rights law in general, and of the Inter-American Human Rights System (IAHRS) in particular, beyond the narrow frame of compliance. It defined transformative impact as structural changes resulting from the Inter-American System's responses to human rights violations, which tackle systemic regional challenges by addressing the root causes and institutional enablers of violations, rather than focusing exclusively on their individual dimensions. The volume also connected the notion of transformative impact to transformative constitutionalism, in which law is responsive and even redistributive in the face of societal needs and structural inequalities.[1]

This collection of studies is a continuation to a decades-long scholarly conversation. It fits within the scholarship on *Ius Constitutionale Commune en América Latina* (ICCAL). As a concept, ICCAL describes a legal phenomenon that combines elements of inter-American legal orders into a regional system oriented toward the protection and advancement of human rights.[2] It is a form of transformative constitutionalism developed in Latin America as a regional project, a mutually supportive structure aimed at compensating national deficits in order to expand human rights.[3] It responds to structural challenges in the region, constantly adapting not only the issues it tackles but also developing procedural tools that are best suited to face them. Building upon previous ICCAL scholarship, the chapters have adopted a multidisciplinary methodology, anchored on legal principles and comparative analyses.

---

[1] See Armin von Bogdandy and René Urueña in Chapter I.1. of this anthology.
[2] Armin von Bogdandy et al. (eds.), *Transformative Constitutionalism in Latin America: the Emergence of a New Ius Commune* (Oxford University Press 2017), 4.
[3] Ibid.

The volume analyzed the unique characteristics of the Inter-American System that enable its transformative impact, emphasizing the system's victim-centric approach, community of practice, and institutional resilience. The Inter-American Commission on Human Rights (IACHR) and Inter-American Court of Human Rights (IACtHR)'s continuous, dynamic interactions with a variety of stakeholders facilitate both the diffusion of substantive human rights standards throughout the region and also the reinvention of the Inter-American System's procedural formulations to suit a particular time and place, thus maximizing the impact of inter-American law. The Inter-American System's influence on the region has the potential to increase as institutional innovations, capacity-building efforts, and educational programs draw more State actors, citizens, victims, and civil society organizations into the community of practice, with its shared understanding of and commitment to human rights.[4]

This community of practice, in turn, fosters institutional and social transformation. The community is constituted by a diverse group of stakeholders, including activists, academia, and public officials such as judges, prosecutors, and other government officials. These are the stakeholders who work to put inter-American standards and decisions into practice, ensuring that the changes envisioned by the Commission and the Court actually happen on the ground. The dynamic interactions between national actors and the Inter-American System strengthen them, providing tools and building momentum to overcome challenges that had been unsurmountable when left only to national systems. These challenges may involve active resistance by powerful groups (such as economic actors profiting from extractive industries that damage Indigenous lands, or military commanders seeking to avoid punishment for past crimes). At the same time, in many cases, the challenge to protect rights derives from indifference or prejudice against the victims, who are seen as unworthy of protection. Measures taken by the Inter-American System can contribute to overcoming these scenarios by shining light onto the violations, rallying social support and recognizing the legal value of the victim's claims. The actors seeking to protect human rights use such measures to strengthen their positions within domestic disputes (legal, political, or otherwise), reshaping the national equilibrium of forces in a way that favors victims who had been neglected or antagonized.

In addition to channeling implementation, the community of practice also fosters transformative impact and creates critical thinking. Constructive engagement enables improvement of the IAHRS institutions, identifying their shortcomings and indicating possible avenues to achieve better outcomes. The community of practice keeps ICCAL stakeholders aware of how their actions are—or are not—impacting the region, as well as of regional transformations that may require corresponding changes to the protection architecture. As

---

[4] See Mariela Morales Antoniazzi, Flávia Piovesan, and Júlia Cortez da Cunha Cruz in Chapter I.3 of this anthology.

the community of practice is diverse, ICCAL debates encompass different perspectives, multidisciplinary approaches, and creative takes. The community also generates interest for inter-American institutions and standards, disseminating knowledge about the system and drawing in new people and new actors, thus further expanding and strengthening the community of practice itself, as well as the human rights culture more broadly.

The Inter-American System thrives, in part, because of this environment. The Commission and the Court openly acknowledge the importance of the community of practice to their effectiveness, cultivating its engagement via a series of public participation initiatives, including capacity-building programs, holding IACHR and IACtHR meetings in places other than their headquarters to be closer to audiences throughout the region, and opening hearings and events to the participation of a broad range of actors. Fundamentally, the Inter-American System is open to continuous change in its focus, forms of action, tools, and procedure. This flexibility, which we describe as "institutional resilience," allows the System to feed on insight provided by the community of practice, continuously changing itself to respond to feedback and constructive criticism, as well as to new circumstances in the region.

At the center of the Inter-American System, as well as that of the broader ICCAL community, lies the victim-centric approach, especially as applied to comprehensive reparations. This means rights-holders are protagonists—institutions, standards, and procedures are oriented to recognizing victim's agency and to placing their claims front and center. The victim-centric approach is entrenched in every aspect of the System (indeed, the System itself is a testament to the rise of human rights as a driving force of international relations within the Americas): from the inter-American treaties that proclaim human rights in the region to the procedural rules that enable victims to participate in every step of IAHRS processes. In particular, the comprehensive reparations ordered by the Commission and the Court are a strong example of how the System takes the plight of the victims of human rights violations seriously, offering not only monetary compensation for their suffering but also restituting the fulfillment of their rights when possible (for example, freeing a person who has been arbitrarily detained or reinstating the job of a victim who had been wrongfully terminated), requiring rehabilitation measures (for example, the provision of mental health services for victims of torture), ordering symbolic measures directed at acknowledging victim suffering and changing social views on the violation (for example, via State apologies), determining the investigation, prosecution, and punishment of those responsible for the violation, and the adoption of measures of nonrepetition to prevent reoccurrence of the violations. This bold set of measures is a unique feature of the Inter-American System, one that recognizes the complex motivations and needs of a victim of human rights violations and places them at the center of the reparation process.

The victim-centric approach strengthens the Inter-American System and inspires engagement from victims of other violations as well as from agents who prize human rights progress in the region. In this perspective, the victim-centric approach is also a driver for growth in the community of practice. In turn, the community of practice contributes to implementation and to critical thinking on how to improve victim-centered outcomes. IAHRS institutions constantly transform themselves to ensure continued deliverance on human rights aims, responding to the needs of victims and proposals of the ICCAL community.

One can see that the three IAHRS elements highlighted by us—the victim-centric approach, the community of practice, and institutional resilience—are mutually reinforcing. They strengthen each other, generating positive feedback loops and an overall virtuous cycle. The success stories of the IAHRS and its track record of transformations in the region are built upon the continuous interaction of these elements.

The Inter-American System's victim-centered approach, the community of practice, and the institutional resilience have enabled the System to effectively change not only in spite of the lack of a robust enforcement mechanism but also in the face of State resistance.[5] In some cases, a State's resistance to a specific decision against it represents a form of good-faith engagement in a dynamic process of compliance.[6] Nevertheless, States have been known to engage in bad-faith efforts to weaken the community of practice and undermine inter-American standards by, for example, limiting the mandates and resources of the Inter-American Commission and Inter-American Court.[7] These kinds of challenges, which target the crux of the Inter-American System's effectiveness to date, alarm us far more than does the familiar, unnuanced observation that rates of compliance with the decisions of these bodies tend to be low.

To illustrate the transformative impact of the Inter-American System, its successes and shortcomings, the volume presented examples of how the Inter-American Commission and Inter-American Court have approached the rights of Indigenous and tribal peoples;[8] the rights of persons deprived of liberty;[9] economic, social, cultural, and environmental rights;[10] the rights of women;[11] reproductive rights;[12] the rights of LGBTIQ+ people;[13] rights of the

---

[5] See Rainer Grote in Chapter I.4 of this anthology.
[6] See Armin von Bogdandy and René Urueña in Chapter I.1. of this anthology, pp. 11 f..
[7] See Armin von Bogdandy and René Urueña in Chapter I.1. of this anthology; Rainer Grote in Chapter I.4 of this anthology; Claudio Grossman in Chapter I.2 of this anthology.
[8] See Gabriela C.B. Navarro in Chapter I.7 of this anthology; see Antonia Urrejola and Elsy Curihuinca Neira in Chapter II.3 of this anthology.
[9] See Clara Burbano-Herrera and Yves Haeck in Chapter I.8 of this anthology.
[10] See Eduardo Ferrer Mac-Gregor in Chapter II.1 of this anthology; see also Henry Jiménez Guanipa and María Barraco in Chapter II.2 of this anthology.
[11] See Julissa Mantilla Falcón in Chapter II.4 of this anthology.
[12] See Silvia Serrano Guzmán in Chapter II.5 of this anthology.
[13] See Chris Esdaile et al. in Chapter II.6 of this anthology.

child;[14] the rights of older persons;[15] the rights of migrants;[16] the right to defend rights;[17] the right to effective judicial protection;[18] and the right to freedom of expression.[19] The volume also examined the transformative impact of the Inter-American System in contexts of transitional justice[20] and impunity.[21] These examples both demonstrate the importance of the victim-centric approach, the community of practice, and institutional resilience to achieve transformative impact on the ground and highlight key elements of inter-American jurisprudence, such as evolutive interpretation, conventionality control, and comprehensive reparations, which provide the legal and theoretical basis for these real-world transformations.

They also shed light on a fundamental overarching point: transformative impact is the key to comprehending the successes of the Inter-American System. The project envisioned by the IAHRS architects was bold—even, some might say, utopian: in a region plagued by entrenched human rights deficits and, in many historical moments, run by governments that had no interest in solving these issues, how could one envision an architecture capable of generating positive human rights outcomes? The difficulties were compounded by the fact that international relations are dominated predominantly by States, and international human rights law defends the rights of individuals and groups against the States that have violated them. Like other international human rights institutions, the IAHRS has to overcome the challenge of relying on States to build and maintain a system that is used against them. In the twentieth century, human rights protection in the Americas faced the additional obstacle of a context where many Latin American States were, for a remarkable part of the century, authoritarian dictatorships that directly committed systematic violations of human rights.

Transformative impact is the bedrock that enabled the System to succeed in improving the protection of human rights despite such adverse conditions. By tapping into the human rights community, the System lets go of the fiction of the monolithic State and finds allies within national societies. Partnering with the IAHRS, such domestic allies use legal and political openings to lock in changes that yield long-term impact on the protection of human rights. Therefore, the System is able to, at the same time, respond to past human rights violations that would have gone unchecked and to mobilize against future wrongdoing. Its

---

[14] See Mary Beloff in Chapter II.7 of this anthology.
[15] See Aída Díaz-Tendero in Chapter II.8 of this anthology.
[16] See Elizabeth Salmón and Cécile Blouin in Chapter II.9 of this anthology.
[17] See Melina Girardi Fachin in Chapter II.10 of this anthology.
[18] See Carlos Ayala Corao in Chapter II.13 of this anthology.
[19] See Catalina Botero-Marino in Chapter II.14 of this anthology; see also EdisonLanza in Chapter II.15 of this anthology.
[20] See Christina Binder in Chapter II.11 of this anthology.
[21] See Oscar Parra Vera in Chapter II.12 of this anthology.

institutional resilience allows it to adapt itself to whichever format is more conducive of change in a particular time and place, acting within the realm of what is possible to reach true transformation. That is why the history of the IAHRS is marked by the issues it tackled as much as by the procedures it used to do so (standard-setting, reports, litigation, precautionary and provisional measures, follow-up mechanisms). In a way, the constant reinvention allows domestic and international actors to jointly hack whichever set of circumstances had been hampering change, and to skew structures of power in favor of victims of human rights violations and other disadvantaged groups.

Transformative impact also allows one to understand how a System with relatively few cases (if compared, for example, to the European System of Human Rights or to national institutions) and allegedly low rates of compliance has been able to not only last decades, but to affirm itself as a reference and a vanguard institution. Structural change and transformation that becomes embedded in national societies (either legally or culturally) are key to understanding the IAHRS legitimacy. They explain how the System is able to deliver on its mandate and maintain relevance even if its size is small when contrasted with the hundreds of millions of people it aims to protect.

The chapters in this volume should inspire future studies of the transformative impact of the Inter-American System that concern standards and contexts not covered in this volume, such as digital rights, climate change, and freedom from violence, including cyberviolence. Similarly, the volume identified and analyzed tools of the Inter-American System that merit study but whose impact could be further explored by scholars, including precautionary measures, provisional measures, and advisory opinions.[22] The volume also suggested that scholars deepen the methodological discussion on measuring compliance and impact, as well as their manner of theorizing the relationship between the two.[23]

Finally, the volume recommends changes that could increase the transformative impact of the Inter-American System. To be more responsive to societal needs and structural inequalities, for example, the Inter-American System could expedite cases that are most likely to address these problems and could prioritize developing inter-American standards in conversation with the society at large.[24] Then, to facilitate State compliance with its decisions and broad acceptance of its

---

[22] See Clara Burbano-Herrera and Yves Haeck in Chapter I.8 of this anthology; see also Pablo Saavedra Alessandri in Chapter III.2 of this anthology.
[23] See Aníbal Pérez-Liñán et al. in Chapter III.3 of this anthology; see also Viviana Krsticevic and René Urueña in Chapter III.4 of this anthology.
[24] See Joel Hernández García in Chapter III.1 of this anthology; see also Katya Salazar and Daniel Cerqueira in Chapter III.5 of this anthology.

standards, the Inter-American System could strengthen national capabilities and engage in continuous dialogue with State actors.[25]

The Inter-American Human Rights System has proved its ability to cause transformative impact. By opening a path for victims of human rights violations to address their grievances, it has contributed to face structural challenges in the region. It helps transform the pain of the victims into dignity, rights, and justice. The better the community of practice understands that impact, the better it can help transform.

---

[25] See Joel Hernández García in Chapter III.1 of this anthology; see also Gabriela Kletzel in Chapter III.6 of this anthology.

Index

For the benefit of digital users, indexed terms that span two pages (e.g., 52-53) may, on occasion, appear on only one of those pages.

Aarhus Convention, 240
abductions. *See* forced disappearances
abortion, 294–95
Abuelas de la Plaza de Mayo (NGO), 629–30, 636
access to information, 478, 479, 485–93
ACHPR. *See* African Charter on Human and People's Rights (ACHPR); African Commission of Human and People's Rights (ACHPR)
ACHR. *See* American Convention on Human Rights (ACHR)
ACtHPR. *See* African Court on Human and Peoples' Rights (ACtHPR)
activism strategies
　generally, 14, 625–26, 639–40
　complex strategies and IAHRS, 626–31
　impunity, 625–26
　in loco visits, 627, 629–30
　regional protection system
　　generally, 631–32
　　broadening of agenda and scope, 638–39
　　civil society organizations, 632–35
　　disruptive tools, 632–35
　　guardians of mandate and jurisdiction, 635–37
　social protest, use of force, 638–39
Additional Protocol to the American Convention on Human Rights in the area of Economic, Social, and Cultural Rights (Protocol of San Salvador)
　children's rights, 327, 328
　economic, social, cultural, and environmental rights, 218–19, 224, 225
　health, right to, 359
　healthy environment, right to, 242
　older persons, 359, 361
advisory opinions
　generally, 180–81
　LBGTQI+ rights, 550–56
　migration, 178, 181, 375t
　transformative impact, 548–49
African Charter on Human and People's Rights (ACHPR)
　generally, 76–77

adoption, 79–80
healthy environment, right to, 237–38, 238n.9
human rights defenders, 394
institutional reform, 93–94
life, right to, 290
living instrument doctrine, 81–82
older persons, 362n.41
remedial practice, 84–85
African Commission of Human and People's Rights (ACHPR)
　generally, 76–77
　creation, 79–80
　digital freedom of expression, 496
　future trends, 99
　healthy environment, right to, 238n.9
　human rights defenders, 394
　institutional reform, 93–94
　LGBTQI+ rights, 314, 316
　living instrument doctrine, 80–81
African Court on Human and Peoples' Rights (ACtHPR)
　generally, 76–77
　creation, 79–80
　documentation strategies, 194
　institutional reform, 93–94
　living instrument doctrine, 81–82
　noncompliance, 94
　remedial practice, 84–85
　standard-building function, 182
　withdrawal from jurisdiction, 91
African Moot Court Conference, 323–24
African Union
　Grand Bay Declaration and Plan of Action, 394
　human rights defenders, 393, 394
　institutional reform, 93–94
　LGBTQI+ rights, 314
　remedial practice, 85
Agosti, Orlando Ramón, 627
Aguiar de Lapacó, Alejandra, 629
Aguiar de Lapacó, Carmen, 629
Aguirre Roca, Manuel, 466–67
Alfonsín, Raúl, 627n.4

Alvarado, Fabricio, 582–83
American Convention on Human Rights (ACHR)
  access to information, 486, 492, 493
  Additional Protocol to the American Convention on Human Rights in the area of Economic, Social, and Cultural Rights (Protocol of San Salvador)
    children's rights, 327, 328
    economic, social, cultural, and environmental rights, 218–19, 224, 225
    healthy environment, right to, 242
    older persons, 349–50
  adoption, 78–79, 522–23, 525
  amnesty, 66n.80, 409, 413–15, 417–19
  Article 26, 242 (*see also* economic, social, cultural, and environmental rights)
  children's rights (*see* children's rights)
  claims, 35
  compliance, 564–65
  contempt laws, 481
  conventionality control (*see* conventionality control)
  criminal defamation, 483–84
  deprivation of liberty, 158
  digital freedom of expression
    generally, 496, 503
    hate speech, 512–13
    net neutrality, 506
    privacy, 515
  dignified life, right to, 108–9
  domestic courts, 114–15
  economic, social, cultural, and environmental rights (*see* economic, social, cultural, and environmental rights)
  embeddedness, 86–87
  evolutionary interpretation, 524
  family, right to, 292
  freedom of association, 403
  freedom of expression (*see* freedom of expression)
  fundamental rights, 597
  grievances of individuals against nations, 38
  healthy environment, right to, 239, 242, 246, 247
  human dignity, 155
  humane treatment, right to, 273n.13
  human rights community of practice, 18, 22, 25
  human rights defenders (*see* human rights defenders)
  impunity (*see* impunity)
  indigenous rights (*see* Indigenous rights)
  integral reparation, 534
  interpretation, 548n.36
  judicial independence (*see* judicial independence)
  legislative measures, 526
  LGBTQI+ rights, 314–15, 550
  life, right to, 290, 291–92, 341, 358–59
  maintaining human rights focus among dictatorships, 36–37
  migration, 371
  monitoring compliance, 142–43
  older persons, 349–50, 360
  personal liberty, right to, 292
  preventive detention, 159
  prison conditions, 158–59, 171–72, 173
  private life, right to, 292
  Protocol of San Salvador, 218–19, 224, 225, 242
  provisional measures (*see* provisional measures)
  rape, 157–58
  remedial practice, 83–84
  remedial provisions, 83–84, 83n.33
  sexual violence, 272, 273, 276, 279
  standards, 63, 64, 606–7
  transitional justice, 411–12
  in vitro fertilization (IVF), 285–86
  withdrawal, 87n.56, 88–90, 476–77, 582
American Declaration on the Rights and Duties of Man
  adoption, 78–79, 522, 525
  children's rights, 164n.62, 327
  claims, 35
  direct justiciability, 227, 228
  global human rights governance, 101–2, 103, 104–5
  healthy environment, right to, 241
  life, right to, 289, 290
  older persons, 349–50
  standards, 63
American Declaration on the Rights of Indigenous Peoples, 242
American Institute of International Law, 101–2
amnesty
  generally, 38–39, 39n.23, 66n.80, 409
  conventionality control, 417–19
  international human rights standards, 106–7
  jurisprudence of IACtHR, 412–19
    domestic reception, 419–22
    standards, 412–19, 423
  jus cogens status of law, 415
  nullification of laws, 416–17, 418–20
  past human rights violations, 409–11
  procedural legitimacy, 422
  transformative impact, 540–41, 557–60, 581, 609–10

INDEX 651

analytical framework for transformative impact
  generally, 10, 176–77, 196–98
  appropriation, 185–87
    communities of practice, 185–86
    compliance constituencies, 186
  documentation strategies, 192–96
    change in practices, 193–94
    change in social outcomes, 195–96
    change in structures, 194–95
  empirical approach, 197–98
  impact defined, 177–80, 197
  indirect effects, 178
  institutional response, 187–90
    academic curricula, 190
    domestic legislation, 188–89
    institutional design, 189–90
    jurisprudence, 189
    positive versus negative response, 187–88
    public policy, 189
  instruments, 180–85
    generally, 179
    adjudicatory instruments, 179, 180–81
    assisting function, 184–85
    directing function, 181–82
    documenting function, 184
    non-adjudicatory instruments, 179, 180–81
    positioning function, 182–83
    reframing function, 183–84
    standard-building function, 182
  rights effectiveness, 179
  transformations on ground, 190–91
  transformative sequence, 176, 180, 197
Anaya, Jorge Isaac, 627
Andean Tribunal of Justice, 18
Andrighi, Nancy, 501
Antigua and Barbuda, right to healthy environment, 249
Arab Spring, 99
Arellano, Almoncid, 431–32
Argentina
  access to information, 487, 489–91, 494
  amnesty
    compliance, 610
    transformative impact, 581
  transitional justice, 409–10, 410n.5, 410n.7, 412–13, 421–22, 421n.68, 423
  Center for the Implementation of Public Policies Promoting Equity and Growth (CIPPEC), 490
  children's rights, 340
  communities of practice, 23–24
  compliance, 28–29

Constitution, 95
constitutional law, 588–89
contempt laws, 481
controversial appointments to IACHR, 636–37
Country Reports, 184
COVID-19 pandemic, 62
crimes against humanity, 626–31, 631n.19
criminal defamation, 483–85, 540–41
democracy, declining support, 53–54
DPLF, 622
Due Obedience Law, 627–28, 630–31
extractive industries, 252
Federal Contentious Administrative Chamber, 384
Federal Correctional Court, 629
forced disappearances, 568–69, 626–31
freedom of expression, 28–29, 476, 480, 494
Full Stop Law, 627–28, 630–31
healthy environment, right to, 249, 252
human rights units, 115–16
human rights violations, 37
IACtHR, 95, 97–98
ICPHROP, 354
impunity, 424–25
indigenous rights, 151–52
LGBTQI+ rights, 322
Memory, Truth, and Justice, 626–31, 635
migration, 378, 382–83, 384, 387
militarization, 54–55
military reforms, 443
Ministry of Foreign Affairs, 636
National Commission on the Disappearance of Persons (CONADEP), 627–28, 627n.4
National Criminal Court, 629
National Emergency Decree No. 70/2017, 382–83
net neutrality, 508
prison conditions, 165
reparations, 568–69
Supreme Court of Justice, 151–52, 421, 489–90, 628–29, 630–31
Trial of the Military Juntas, 627–28
"truth trials," 628–30
assembly, right of, 404–5
association, freedom of
  human rights defenders, 403
  judicial independence, 459–62
asylum, 375–76
Austria, ECHR, 86
autonomous law, 19–20
average time to compliance, 570, 575

Bachelet, Michelle, 239
Bahamas
  access to information, 487
  healthy environment, right to, 249
Baigorria, Raúl, 568
Bangalore Principles of Judicial Conduct, 460–61
Barbados
  compliance, 577
  death penalty, 540–41
  healthy environment, right to, 249
  provisional measures, 161n.51
Basic Principles on the Independence of the Judiciary, 451–52, 453, 459–60, 461, 462
Bautista, Cristina, 265–66
"Beijing Rules," 330
Belize
  healthy environment, right to, 249, 250–51
  indigenous rights, 250–51
Benin, withdrawal from AFCtHR jurisdiction, 91
Benito, Odo, 322–23
Berger, Óscar, 569
Bernardino, Minerva, 103
Betancur, Belisario, 611n.31
Bogotá Conference, 103–4
Bolivia
  attempts to maintain human rights narrative, 40, 42n.38, 48
  children's rights, 340
  Code of Criminal Procedure, 364
  compliance, 572–74, 577
  Constitution, 482–83
  contempt laws, 481–83
  COVID-19 pandemic, 62
  DPLF, 612
  forced disappearances, 540–41
  General Law on Older Persons, 352, 364
  healthy environment, right to, 249
  human rights violations, 37
  ICPHROP, 354
  impunity, 433
  indigenous rights, 151–52
  migration, 373–74, 380
  militarization, 55
  older persons, 351–54, 361, 362, 363, 364
  Plurinational Constitutional Court, 151–52, 350, 351, 352, 354, 482–83
  Political Constitution of the Plurinational State, 364
Bolsonaro, Jair, 40
Brazil
  access to information, 487, 494
  anti-LGBTQI+ groups, 56
  attempts to maintain human rights narrative, 40, 42n.38

children's rights, 164–65, 336–37, 340
communities of practice, 23–24
Constitution, 25
contempt laws, 481–82
COVID-19 pandemic, 58, 62
Criminal Institute of Plácido de Sá Carvalho, 153–54, 155, 167–73, 174t, 175
democracy, declining support, 53–54
Fireworks Factory case, 207–9, 210, 212
freedom of expression, 494, 501
healthy environment, right to, 249, 251
human rights, 25
human rights defenders, 395
human rights units, 115–16
impunity, 438–39
indigenous rights, 97n.95
militarization, 54–56
Military Criminal Code, 55
National Policy of Protection for Human Rights Defenders, 395
National Program for the Protection of Human Rights Defenders (PPDDH), 395
net neutrality, 508
prison conditions, 163–65, 166–67, 171–73, 175
provisional measures, 153–54, 161n.52, 163–64
racial discrimination, 209n.35
reparations, 67n.83
Superior Court of Justice, 481–82, 501
Supreme Federal Court, 168–69, 171–73, 175, 494
threats to mandate of IACHR, 631–32
Brighton Declaration, 92
Buergenthal, Thomas, 611n.31, 612n.32
Bukele, Nayib, 40
Burkina Faso, AFCtHR jurisdiction, 91

Cáceres, Berta, 619
Canada
  extractive industries, 615–16
  extraterritorial responsibility, 615–16
Caribbean Court of Justice (CCJ), 250–51
Cartagena Declaration, 376, 376n.53, 380–82
Castro, Fidel, 36n.9
Cayapú, Alver, 265–66
Cayapú, Asdruval, 265–66
CEDAW. See Convention on the Elimination of All Forms of Discrimination against Women (CEDAW)
censorship, 478, 499, 509
Center for Justice and International Law (CEJIL), 400

INDEX 653

Center for Legal and Social Studies (CELS), 55
Centro de Derechos Humanos de la Montana (NGO), 633
Centro de Derechos Humanos Miguel Agustin Pro Juarez (NGO), 633
Centro de Estudios Legales y Sociales (CELS) (NGO), 629–30
César de Souza, Roni, 164–65
Chávez, Hugo, 230, 476–77
child pornography, 499, 509
children's rights
  generally, 11, 326–31
  child defined, 334–35
  evaluation of IAHRS, 346–33
  instrumentalization of child victims, 328
  international *corpus juris*, 329–34
  jurisprudence of IACtHR, 335–40
    child soldiers, 340
    communities, 340
    forced labor and trafficking, 340
    health, education, and special needs, 339–40
    individuals, 339–40
    institutional violence, 339
    juvenile justice, 339
    nondiscrimination, 339
  limits of IAHRS, 346–33
  possibilities of IAHRS, 346–33
  precautionary measures, 329–32
  provisional measures, 165, 329–32
  reparations, 337
  special protection measures
    best interests of child, 343
    detention, 342–43
    dignified life, right to, 341–43
    economic, social, cultural, and environmental rights, 342
    education, 341–42, 345
    family protection, 343–44
    forced disappearances, 344
    health, right to, 343
    indigenous people, 344
    institutional violence, 344
    life, right to, 340–43
    other rights, 343–46
    sexual violence, 346
    street children, 342n.103
  substance versus procedure, 331
  transformative impact, 327
child soldiers, 340
Chile
  abortion, 294–95
  access to information, 486–88
  amnesty, 409–10, 410n.5, 412–13, 414–15, 414n.30, 420–22, 423

anti-LGBTQI+ groups, 56
attempts to maintain human rights narrative, 40–41, 48
children's rights, 340
communities of practice, 23–24
compliance, 577
Constitution, 420n.64, 540–41
Constitutional Court, 487
Constitutional Tribunal, 294–95
contempt laws, 481–82
Councils of War, 544–47, 545n.31
Country Reports, 184
Decree Law, 431
DPLF, 622
freedom of expression, 475–76, 540–41
healthy environment, right to, 249
human rights violations, 36, 37, 65n.79
ICPHROP, 354
impunity, 424–25, 427, 429, 431–32
Inter-American SIMORE, 68
judicial independence, consequences of violations, 470–71
legislative reform, 188–89
LGBTQI+ rights, 315
migration, 378–80, 385, 387
militarization, 55
net neutrality, 507–8
older persons, 358–61, 360–61n.39, 362
reparations, 193
social protest, use of force, 639
Supreme Court, 182, 385, 420–21, 420n.64, 432, 545–46, 581–82
Truth and Reconciliation Commission, 432
civil society organizations (CSOs)
  DPLF, 613n.33, 621, 623–24
  healthy environment, right to, 240
  regional protection system, role in strengthening, 632–35
  sociopolitical dimension of IAHRS, 71
  standards, 611
climate change, 239–40
Coalition of African Lesbians, 314
Coalition of LGBTIQ+ Organizations of Latin America and the Caribbean, 310
Colombia
  access to information, 487, 492–93
  anti-LGBTQI+ groups, 56
  attempts to maintain human rights narrative, 40–41, 48
  Attorney General, 189–90
  children's rights, 340
  Civil Code, 294–95
  communities of practice, 23–24
  compliance, 572, 592

Colombia (*cont.*)
　Comprehensive System of Truth, Justice, Reparation and Guarantees of Non-Repetition, 189–90, 445
　Constitutional Court, 145, 151–52, 168–70, 171–72, 250, 252, 294–95, 323–24, 386, 444n.71, 445, 447, 492–93
　constitutional law, 588–89
　controversial appointments to IACHR, 637
　criminal defamation, 484–85
　DPLF, 622
　extractive industries, 252
　FARC guerrilla group, 189–90
　Final Peace Agreement, 265, 445
　forced disappearances, 224–25
　freedom of expression, 476, 500–1
　healthy environment, right to, 249, 249n.62, 250, 252
　human rights defenders, 395
　human rights violations, 37
　impunity, 427, 429–30, 434–38, 436n.46, 443–47, 444n.71, 444n.73
　Indigenous Guard, 265, 265n.40, 267
　indigenous rights, 151–52, 262–63, 264–66
　institutional response, 189–90
　investigations of human rights violations, 593
　Law of Justice and Peace, 445
　LGBTQI+ rights, 315, 323–24
　life, right to, 294–95
　migration, 378–80, 383, 386, 387
　militarization, 55
　military reforms, 443
　National Institute of Legal Medicine and Forensic Sciences, 189–90
　National Police, 492–93
　precautionary measures, 30–31
　prison conditions, 165, 166–67, 168–70, 171–72
　reparations, 30, 67n.83
　Search Unit for Presumed Disappeared Persons, 445
　Siona indigenous people, 261–62
　social protest, use of force, 639
　Somos Defensores, 395
　Special Jurisdiction for Peace (JEP), 189–90, 445–46
　Supreme Court of Justice, 249n.62, 430, 444, 444n.73, 501
　threats to mandate of IACHR, 631–32
　Unidad Nacional de Protección, 395
Colombia Diversa (NGO), 322, 324–25
Committee against Torture (CAT), 313
Committee on Economic, Social and Cultural Rights (CESCR), 313
communities of practice
　appropriation, 185–86
　human rights community of practice, 18, 22–26, 70–71, 642–43, 644
　narrative of human rights impact, 200–1
　transformative impact, 642–43
comparative analysis
　generally, 9, 76–77
　backlash against human rights jurisprudence
　　generally, 87
　　institutional reform, 91–94
　　noncompliance, 94–96
　　responses, 96–98
　　withdrawal from regional human rights systems, 88–91
　Cold War, expansion of human rights protection
　　generally, 77–78
　　diversification of remedial practice, 82–85
　　embeddedness, 86–87
　　institutionalization, 78–80
　　judicialization, 80–82
　future trends, 98–99
complementarity, 527
compliance
　generally, 8, 17–18, 32–33
　challenges, 45
　constructivist approach, 593–94
　conventionality control, 127–28, 589–90
　Country Reports, 533–34, 606, 610–11, 613, 621
　defined, 177–78
　dynamic monitoring, 590–95
　dynamic nature of decisions, 27
　dynamic nature of implementation, 28
　friendly settlements, 533–34
　hearings, 592
　human rights community of practice, 22–26
　IACHR monitoring, 97n.97, 113, 142–43
　IACtHR monitoring, 97n.97, 113, 142–43, 591–94
　impact versus, 30
　literature review, 585–90
　low levels, 4–5, 17, 18, 176, 584, 604–6
　measuring (*see* measuring compliance)
　Merits Reports, 533–36, 605
　partial compliance, 586, 587
　promoting, 532–36
　　dialogue, 535–36
　　integral reparation, 534
　　Inter-American SIMORE, 533–34
　　private working meetings, 533–34
　　public hearings, 533–34
　　referrals, 534–35

INDEX   655

qualitative studies, 587–90
quantitative studies, 585–87
realist approach, 594
Thematic Reports, 606, 610–11
traditional understandings, 27–28
transformative impact beyond
   generally, 13–14, 584–85, 595, 601–2
   amnesty, 609–10
   change over time, 595–96
   defining, 143–46
   IACtHR, 147–48
   improving quality of compliance, 596–600
   institutional impact, 600–1
   standards, 604–11
   transformative constitutionalism, 6, 29–32
   transformative practice, 26–29
compliance life cycle, 566, 578f, 578–80
Conference on the Human Environment, 237
"connection theory." *see* economic, social,
   cultural, and environmental rights
constructivist international relations, 593–94
contempt laws, 480–83
Convention against Corruption, 620
conventionality control
   generally, 9–10, 122–24, 136–37, 412n.13
   adjudication versus execution, 129–31
   amnesty, 417–19
   binding nature of decisions, 135
   categories, 132, 133–34, 136
   compliance, 127–28, 589–90
   defined, 125–29
   diffuse control, 122–23, 123n.2, 130–31, 136, 137
   diffuse versus concentrated control, 123n.2
   erga omnes, 132, 136, 137
   external versus internal control, 122–23, 122–23n.1, 130–31, 136
   flexibility, 32–33
   hypotheses, 123
   implementation as component, 132, 133
   indigenous rights, 151–52
   methodology, 124–25
   relaxing, 32–33
   res interpretata, 122–23, 129–36, 137
   res judicata, 122–23, 129–37
   targets, 128
Convention of Belém do Pará. *See* Inter-American Convention on the Prevention, Punishment and Eradication of Violence against Women (Convention of Belém do Pará)
Convention on Access to Information, Public Participation in Decision-Making and Access to Justice in Environmental Matters (Aarhus Convention), 240
Convention on the Elimination of All Forms of Discrimination against Women (CEDAW)
   CEDAW Committee, 269–70, 289–90
   direct justiciability, 228
   life, right to, 289–90
   sexual violence, 269–70, 272
Convention on the Rights of Persons with Disabilities, 228
Convention on the Rights of the Child
   child defined, 334–35
   child pornography, 499
   Committee on the Rights of the Child, 329n.8, 334
   direct justiciability, 228
   impact, 326–27
   indirect justiciability, 220–21
   international *corpus juris*, 329–30
   life, right to, 289–90
   nondiscrimination, 279
   ratification, 326–27
Coordinadora Nacional de Derechos Humanos (CNDDHH) (NGO), 305–6, 305n.8
Correa, Rafael, 476–77
corruption
   Country Reports, 621
   development of standards, 619–23
   rule of law, 52n.12
   Thematic Reports, 621–22
Corruption Perception Index, 51–52
Costa Rica
   access to information, 488
   Association of Doctors and Surgeons of Costa Rica, 300
   Centro FECUNDAR Costa Rica—Panama, 300–1
   Centro Fertilizacion In Vitro La California, 300–1
   Civil Code, 553
   Civil Status Registry, 553
   Constitution, 285–86
   Constitutional Chamber, 285–86, 287–88, 290, 298, 488, 543–44, 552–54, 582–83
   COVID-19 pandemic, 62
   criminal law, 540–41
   Family Code, 552, 582–83
   Guidelines for Respectful and Equal Treatment, 553
   healthy environment, right to, 249
   ICPHROP, 354
   Inter-American SIMORE, 68

Costa Rica (*cont.*)
  LGBTQI+ rights, 549–50n.44, 552–54, 582–83
  Ministry of Health, 300–1, 543–44
  name change for trans persons, 553–54
  same-sex marriage, 552–53, 582–83
  Social Security System, 189, 543–44
  Supreme Court of Justice, 296–97, 298–99
  Supreme Electoral Tribunal (TSE), 553–54
  Unit of Reproductive Medicine of High Complexity, 189
  in vitro fertilization (IVF)
    generally, 25–26, 189, 191, 223
    annulment of prohibition, 297–300, 542, 542n.18
    IACtHR decision, 285–87, 301–2
    inspection and quality controls, 300–1
    regulation, 300–1
    reparations, 295–96, 302
    reproductive rights, training judiciary, 296–97
    state healthcare system, 301
    transformative impact, 541–44
  Womens Hospital Dr. Adolfo Carit, 301
Côte d'Ivoire, withdrawal from AFCtHR jurisdiction, 91
Council of Europe (CoE)
  expansion, 78
  Recommendation of the Council of Europe on the Independence, Efficiency and Role of Judges, 463
Country Reports
  generally, 5–6, 26–27, 34–35, 36–37, 41–44, 47–48, 62–63
  compliance, 533–34, 606, 610–11, 613, 621
  corruption, 621
  freedom of expression, 475, 479–80
  human rights violations, 184
  impunity, 424–25, 627
  indigenous rights, 254–55, 266
  transformative impact, 177, 179, 182, 183, 184, 186, 197
Court of Justice of the Andean Community, 139–40
COVID-19 pandemic
  freedom of expression, 494
  healthy environment, and right to, 251
  migration, 560–61
  need for IAHRS, 57–62
  Rapid and Integrated Response Coordination Unit (SACROI), 46–47
crimes against humanity
  impunity, 431–32, 630–31, 631n.19
  pardons, 630–31

criminal defamation, 479, 483–85
Criminal Institute of Plácido de Sá Carvalho (Brazil), 153–54, 155, 167–73, 174t, 175
CSOs. *See* civil society organizations (CSOs)
Cuba
  healthy environment, right to, 249
  human rights violations, 36n.9, 37
cultural identity, right to, 255–56, 257
cybersecurity, 514–16

de Bari Hermoza Ríos, Nicolás, 599
De Casas, Horacio, 636–37, 637n.26
Declaration of Principles on Freedom of Expression
  generally, 474–75
  access to information, 485–86, 486n.87, 492–93
  contempt laws, 481
  criminal defamation, 483
  digital freedom of expression, 504
  public interest speech, 479–80
Declaration on Human Rights Defenders, 391–93
Declaration on the Elimination of Violence Against Women, 270
Declaration on the Right and Responsibility of Individuals, Groups and Organs of Society to Promote and Protect Universally Recognized Human Rights and Fundamental Freedoms, 391–93
Declaration on the Rights of Peasants and Other People Working in Rural Areas, 238–39
De-Justicia (NGO), 323–24
deprivation of liberty, 155–59, 161
Despouy, Leonard, 460–61
detainees, 157
dictatorships
  maintaining human rights focus, 36–37
  National Security Doctrine, 36
digital freedom of expression
  generally, 13, 495–97, 516–17
  challenges, 501–3
  digital divide, 505
  "digital footprints," 503
  principles
    generally, 503–4
    content blocking, 502, 509–10
    cybersecurity, 514–16
    disinformation, 512–13
    diversity, 505, 506
    filtering, 509–10
    hate speech, 512–13
    intermediary liability, 510–11
    net neutrality, 506–8
    nondiscrimination, 505–6

pluralism, 505, 506
privacy, 514–16
subsequent liability, 511–12
surveillance, 514–16
universal access, 504
private actors, 502–3
restrictions, 501–3
social media
  generally, 496, 517n.77
  abuse, 502
  hate speech, 512
  intermediary liability, 510
Thematic Reports, 496, 503
dignified life, right to, 108–9, 341–43
direct justiciability of ESCER. *See* economic, social, cultural, and environmental rights
discrete-time measures of compliance, 566, 576t
disinformation, 512–13
Dominica, right to healthy environment, 249
Dominican Republic
  access to information, 493
  anti-LGBTQI+ groups, 56
  children's rights, 340, 346–47
  compliance, 575, 577–78
  Constitutional Tribunal, 582
  healthy environment, right to, 249
  human rights violations, 37
  IACtHR decisions not enforced, 89–90
  Inter-American SIMORE, 68
  migration, 372–73, 374–75
  withdrawal from IAHRS, 90, 582
Dozo, Basilio Lami, 627
DPLF. *See* Due Process of Law Foundation (DPLF)
Due Process of Law Foundation (DPLF)
  generally, 14, 603–4, 623
  Blog DPLF, 614n.38
  civil society organizations, 613n.33, 621, 623–24
  corruption, 620, 621–23
  extraterritorial responsibility, 614–15, 616–17, 618
  programs, 612
  standards, 611–14, 613–14n.37
  strategies for expansion of IAHRS, 611–14

East African Court of Justice, 99
ECHR. *See* European Convention on Human Rights (ECHR)
economic, social, cultural, and environmental rights
  generally, 10, 217–18, 235–36

children's rights, 342
"connection theory"
  equality and nondiscrimination, 222–23
  groups in position of vulnerability, 221–23
  procedural rights, 221, 222
  substantive rights, 220–22
  violation of Article 26 alleged, 220–21
direct justiciability
  generally, 226–27
  education, right to, 225
  health, right to, 226, 231
  healthy environment, right to, 232
  indigenous rights, 232–33
  Lagos del Campo case, 227
  methodology, 227–28
  new model, 226–35
  Protocol of San Salvador, 225
  reparations, 234–35
  social security, right to, 232
  state obligations, 228–29
  trade unions, 225
  work, right to, 229–30
healthy environment, right to (*see* healthy environment, right to)
indirect justiciability
  education, right to, 220–21
  equality and nondiscrimination, 222–23
  forced disappearances, 224–25
  groups in position of vulnerability, 221–23
  indigenous rights, 220–22, 223–24
  procedural rights, 221, 222
  Protocol of San Salvador, 224
  reproductive rights, 222, 223–24
  sexual violence, 223–24
  substantive rights, 220–22
  trade unions, 224
  violation of Article 26 alleged, 220–21
  work, right to, 223–24
migration, 378
protection through civil and political rights
  generally, 218–20
  indirect justiciability, 220–23
  "rereading" of ESCER language, 223–25
Special Rapporteurship on Economic, Social, Cultural, and Environmental Rights, 217
Thematic Reports, 243, 247
Economic Commission for Europe, 240
Economic Commission for Latin America and the Caribbean (CEPAL), 235–36, 368–69
Economic Community of West African States (ECOWAS), 99

ECtHR. *See* European Court of Human Rights (ECtHR)
Ecuador
  attempts to maintain human rights narrative, 40–41, 42n.38, 48
  children's rights, 340
  Civil Code, 554n.55
  compliance, 572–74, 577–78
  Constitution, 25, 382–83, 554n.54
  Constitutional Court, 385–86, 554–56
  extractive industries, 250, 251
  freedom of expression, 476–77
  healthy environment, right to, 249
  Human Mobility Law, 380–82
  human rights, 25
  ICPHROP, 354
  impeachment of judges, 465–66, 467
  indigenous rights, 251
  LGBTQI+ rights, 315, 554–56
  migration, 371, 380–83, 385–86, 387
  Ministry of Interior, 386
  National Superintendency of Migration, 386
  same-sex marriage, 554–56
  social protest, use of force, 639
  threats to mandate of IACHR, 631–32
education, right to
  children's rights, 339–40, 341–42, 345
  direct justiciability, 225
  indirect justiciability, 220–21
effectiveness of international courts
  generally, 10, 138–39, 152
  compliance
    defining, 139–41
    evaluating compliance with IACtHR decisions, 141–43
    measuring, 139–41
  de facto authority, 145–46, 150
  functions, 143–45
  global governance, 145
  goal-based approach, 144
  ICCAL, 147
  indigenous rights, 148–52
  legal sociology, 145
  LGBTQI+ rights, 152
  transformative impact beyond compliance
    defining, 143–46
    IACtHR, 147–48
  women's rights, 152
elderly persons. *See* older persons
El Salvador
  access to information, 487, 488–89
  amnesty, 540–41, 610
  children's rights, 340, 346–47
  compliance, 592
  Constitutional Chamber, 488–89
  COVID-19 pandemic, 62
  criminal defamation, 484–85
  DPLF, 612, 622
  Farabundo Marti National Liberation Front, 611n.31
  healthy environment, right to, 249
  human rights violations, 36, 37
  ICPHROP, 354
  militarization, 54–55
  prison conditions, 166–67
  Supreme Court of Justice, 488–89
  Truth Commission for El Salvador, 611–12, 611n.31
Equal Rights Trust (NGO), 323–24
erga omnes, 132, 136, 137, 149–50
Escaleras Mejía, Carlos, 388–89, 399–400, 402, 403, 404, 406, 407
Escazú Agreement. *See* Regional Agreement on Access to Information, Public Participation and Justice in Environmental Matters in Latin America and the Caribbean (Escazu Agreement)
ESCER. *See* economic, social, cultural, and environmental rights
European Committee for the Prevention of Torture (CPT), 159n.37
European Convention on Human Rights (ECHR)
  compliance, 26–27, 593
  delegated compliance, 591n.35
  economic, social, cultural, and environmental rights, 218–19
  embeddedness, 86
  freedom of expression, 500
  institutionalization, 78
  institutional reform, 91–92
  LGBTQI+ rights, 311–12
  life, right to, 290
  Protocol No. 1, 95–96
  Protocol No. 11, 78, 91–92
  Protocol No. 15, 92, 96–97
  remedial practice, 82–83
  withdrawal, 91, 95–96
European Court of Human Rights (ECtHR)
  backlash, 583
  compliance, 26–27, 593
  contempt laws, 481
  delegated compliance, 591n.35
  digital freedom of expression, 503
  documentation strategies, 194

INDEX   659

duty to investigate, 308
effectiveness, 139
impunity, 431–32
institutionalization, 78
institutional reform, 91–92
judicialization, 80
LGBTQI+ rights, 311–12, 316, 321, 325
life, right to, 290–91
living instrument doctrine, 80–81
migration, 377
noncompliance, 94–95
prison conditions, 168–69, 171, 175
remedial practice, 82–83
reparations, 574
response to backlash, 96–97
standard-building function, 182
volume of cases, 646
European Court of Justice (ECJ)
effectiveness, 139
life, right to, 290–91
European Union, human rights defenders, 393
expansion of IAHRS
generally, 14, 603–4, 623–24
development of standards
corruption, 619–23
extraterritorial responsibility, 614–18
transformative impact beyond compliance, 604–11
DPLF strategies, 611–14
expected time for compliance (ETC), 566, 570–71, 577–78, 578f
expression. *See* freedom of expression
expression, freedom of. *See* freedom of expression
extractive industries, extraterritorial responsibility, 614–18
extradition, impunity, 428–30
extraterritorial responsibility, 614–18

fair trial, right to, 404
family, right to, 292
femicide, 107–8
Figueredo, Reinaldo, 611n.31
Figueroa, Ana, 103
forced disappearances
children's rights, 344
economic, social, cultural, and environmental rights, 224–25
human rights defenders, 402
impunity, 426, 428–29, 441–42
international human rights standards, 106–7
migration, 368–69
reparations, 568–69
sexual violence, 277

forced labor and trafficking of children, 340
France, ECtHR, 80
Franco, Marielle, 388, 395, 402, 403, 407
freedom of association
human rights defenders, 403
judicial independence, 459–62
freedom of expression
generally, 13, 473–74, 493–94
access to information, 478, 479, 485–93
collective dimension, 497–98
Country Reports, 475, 479–80
COVID-19 pandemic, 494
Declaration of Principles on Freedom of Expression (*see* Declaration of Principles on Freedom of Expression)
digital freedom of expression (*see* digital freedom of expression)
friendly settlements, 481
functions, 497
human rights defenders, 404–5
IAHRS legal framework, 497–501
IAHRS standards, 477–79
ICCAL, 474–77, 493
individual dimension, 497–98
judicial independence, 459–62
limitations
generally, 499
censorship, 478, 499, 509
child pornography, 499, 509
hate speech, 498–99, 512–13
war propaganda, 498–99
media regulation, 479
Merits Reports, 475
monopolization of media, 499–500
Office of the Special Rapporteur for Freedom of Expression (*see* Office of the Special Rapporteur for Freedom of Expression)
public interest speech
generally, 478, 479–80
contempt laws, 480–83
criminal defamation, 483–85
Leyes de Desacato, 480–83
rights and duties of public officials, 478
Thematic Reports, 474, 475, 479–80
threats or harm for exercising, 478
transformative impact, 474–77
friendly settlements
generally, 62–63, 65, 69–70, 80, 113, 115–16
compliance, 533–34
freedom of expression, 481
healthy environment, right to, 247–48
human rights defenders, 400–1
indigenous rights, 254–55

Fujimori, Alberto, 89–90, 182, 409–10, 413n.21, 419–20, 429, 442, 476–77, 598–99

Galtieri, Leopoldo Fortunato, 627
Gambia, AFCtHR jurisdiction, 91
Garcia Lucero, Leopoldo, 360–61n.39
Garrido, Adolfo, 568
Germany
  ECtHR, 94–95
  Federal Constitutional Court, 94–95
Ghana, AFCtHR jurisdiction, 91
Gini coefficient, 50n.3
global human rights governance, 101–5
global impact of IAHRS
  generally, 9, 100–1
  experimentalist approach, 120–21
  future trends, 118–21
  global human rights governance, 101–5
  international human rights standards, 105–11
    amnesty, 106–7
    dignified life, right to, 108–9
    femicide, 107–8
    impunity, 106–7
    indigenous rights, 109–11
    rape, 107–8
    reparations, 106–7
    transitional justice, 106–7
    violence against women (VAW), 107–8
  regional systems, 118–20
  transnationalized human rights implementation, 111–18
    domestic courts, role of, 114–15
    human rights actors, pressure from, 114
    states, engagement of, 115–16
Global Impunity Index, 52n.17
Goldman, Robert, 636–37
Gonzáles, Claudia Ivette, 275
Grenada
  criminal defamation, 484–85
  healthy environment, right to, 249
grievances of individuals against nations, 37–39
Grossi, Vio, 322–23
Group of Eminent International and Regional Experts on Yemen, 321
Guatemala
  access to information, 487
  amnesty, 416–17n.45, 557–60, 610
  attempts to maintain human rights narrative, 42n.38
  Attorney General, 591–92
  Chaab'il Ch'och' indigenous community, 263
  children's rights, 334–35, 340, 346–47
  compliance, 591–92
  Constitutional Court, 482
  contempt laws, 481–82
  corruption, 621
  criminal law, 540–41
  healthy environment, right to, 249
  human rights defenders, 405
  human rights violations, 36, 37
  impunity, 426–27, 432–33
  indigenous rights, 263
  Inter-American SIMORE, 68
  investigations of human rights violations, 593
  LGBTQI+ rights, 315
  militarization, 54–55
  National Reconciliation Act, 558, 558n.67
  prison conditions, 165
  sexual violence, 274, 281
Guidelines for the Prevention of Juvenile Delinquency ("Riyadh Guidelines"), 330
Guyana
  access to information, 487
  healthy environment, right to, 249

Haiti
  children's rights, 346–47
  compliance, 577–78
  healthy environment, right to, 249
  human rights violations, 37
  migration, 372–73, 374
Harper, Stephen, 615
hate crimes, 307, 309
hate speech, 498–99, 512–13
health, right to
  children's rights, 339–40, 344–43
  direct justiciability, 226, 231
  older persons, 356–57, 359–60
healthy environment, right to
  generally, 10–11, 237–40, 252–53
  access to information, 243, 247, 248
  civil society organizations, 240
  climate change, 239–40
  COVID-19 pandemic, 251
  direct justiciability, 232
  domestic level, 249–52
  friendly settlements, 247–48
  human rights, relation to, 237–39
  ICCAL, 252–53
  indigenous people, 243, 245, 246–48, 250–51
  protection, 240–46
    access to information, 243
    due diligence, 245–46
    indigenous rights, 243, 245
    individual and collective right, 244, 244n.37
    state obligations, 246

state obligations, 246, 253
transformative impact, 249–52
Herrera Monreal, Esmeralda, 275
Honduras
　access to information, 487
　children's rights, 340, 346–47
　compliance, 592
　contempt laws, 481–82
　corruption, 619
　dive fishing, 209, 211, 212–13, 213n.54
　Escalers Mejía case
　　legacy, 401–6
　　overview, 399–401
　healthy environment, right to, 249
　human rights defenders
　　generally, 388, 395, 397
　　Escalers Mejía case, 399–406
　　Kawas Fernández case, 398–99
　　Luna López case, 398
　human rights violations, 36, 37
　Inter-American SIMORE, 68
　investigations of human rights violations, 593
　Law on the Protection of Human Rights Defenders, Journalists, Social Communicators, and Justice Officials, 395
　LGBTQI+ rights, 316
　migration, 368–69
　militarization, 54–55
　Miskito Divers case, 207–8, 209–10, 211, 212
　prison conditions, 165
　sexual violence, 276
human dignity, 155
humane treatment, right to
　human rights defenders, 404
　sexual violence, 273n.13
Human Rights Committee
　dignified life, right to, 108–9
　judicial independence, 471–72
　LGBTQI+ rights, 312–13
　removal of judges, 462
human rights community of practice, 18, 22–26, 70–71, 642–43
Human Rights Council
　corruption, 620
　healthy environment, right to, 238–39
　LGBTQI+ rights, 321
human rights defenders
　generally, 12, 388–90, 406, 407
　autonomous right, 405–6
　defined, 391
　Escalers Mejía case
　　legacy, 401–6
　　overview, 399–401

　forced disappearances, 402
　friendly settlements, 400–1
　ICCAL, 390, 396, 397, 406
　jurisprudence of IACtHR
　　generally, 396–97, 401–2
　　assembly, right of, 404–5
　　Escalers Mejía case, 399–406
　　fair trial, right to, 404
　　freedom of association, 403
　　freedom of expression, 404–5
　　humane treatment, right to, 404
　　judicial protection, right to, 404
　　Kawas Fernández case, 398–99
　　life, right to, 402
　　Luna López case, 398
　　participation in government, right of, 403–4
　　rule of law, 397, 401, 402
　　standards, 389–90
　Merits Reports, 400
　multilevel approach
　　generally, 390
　　domestic systems, 394–96
　　global system, 391–93
　　regional systems, 393–94
　protection of rights, 392
　rights, 392
　transformative impact, 389, 397
　violence, 388–89, 395
Human Rights Law Implementation Project (HRLIP), 587n.10
hyper-presidentialism, 52

IACHR. *See* Inter-American Commission on Human Rights (IACHR)
IACtHR. *See* Inter-American Court of Human Rights (IACtHR)
IAHRS. *See* Inter-American Human Rights System (IAHRS)
ICCAL *See Ius Constitutionale Commune en América Latina* (ICCAL)
ICPHROP. *See* Inter-American Convention on the Protection of the Human Rights of Older Persons (ICPHROP)
immigration. *See* migration
improvement of IAHRS
　generally, 13, 521, 536, 646–47
　case selection standards, advancing to remedy structural situations, 530–32
　　admissibility criteria, 531
　　expedited petitions, 531–32, 646–47
　　Special Procedural Delay Reduction Program, 530, 531–32
　compliance, promoting, 532–36
　dialogue, 535–36

improvement of IAHRS (cont.)
    integral reparation, 534
    Inter-American SIMORE, 533–34
    private working meetings, 533–34
    public hearings, 533–34
    referrals, 534–35
  national capacities, strengthening, 525–29
    complementarity, 527
    cooperation programs, 529
    internationalization of decisions, 526, 529
    legislative measures, 526
    networks of national autonomous systems, 528–29
    normative frameworks, 526, 527–29
    Strategic Objective 3 (SO3), 528
    two-prong approach, 526
impunity
  generally, 12, 424–25, 447–48
  activism, 625–26
  Country Reports, 424–25, 627
  forced disappearances, 426, 428–29, 441–42
  institutional response, 189–90
  international human rights standards, 106–7
  in loco visits, 424–25
  need to investigate serious human rights violations
    generally, 426
    abuse of law, 432–33
    admissible weightings, 426–28
    crimes against humanity, 431–32, 630–31, 631n.19
    executions, 441–42
    extradition, 428–30
    extraordinary international supervisory mechanisms, 439–41
    forced disappearances, 441–42
    fraudulent *res judicata*, 426–28
    humanitarian pardons, 442–43
    ne bis in idem, 426–28
    penal military jurisdiction, 439
    prevalent classification, 433–34
    proportionality of punishment, 442–43
    state obligations, 428–30
    systemic crimes, 434–39
  transformative impact, 443–47
  transitional justice, 425, 434–39
  universal jurisdiction, 628
Independent Expert on SOGI, 321
India, transformative constitutionalism, 2
Indigenous rights
  generally, 11, 254–56, 266–67
  ancestral territory, 203–4, 204n.17
  challenges, 264–66
  conventionality control, 151–52
  coordinated effort, 267
  Country Reports, 254–55, 266
  cultural identity, right to, 255–56, 257
  direct justiciability of ESCER, 232–33
  effectiveness of international courts, 145–46, 148–52
  framing, 213
  friendly settlements, 254–55
  general standards, 256
  healthy environment, right to, 243, 245, 246–48, 250–51
  indigenous territory, 204n.17
  indirect justiciability of ESCER, 220–22, 223–24
  international human rights standards, 109–11
  lands and territories, 232–33, 255–56, 257–59
  life, right to, 358
  older persons, 355, 358
  participation in government, 255–56, 259
  poverty among indigenous peoples, 51n.4
  precautionary measures
    generally, 254–56, 260–61
    Chaab'il Ch'och' indigenous community, 263
    Siona indigenous people, 262–63
    "Tres Islas" indigenous community of Madre de Dios, 261–62
  progress, 264–66
  resources, 257–59
  sexual violence, 278–79
  Thematic Reports, 266
  violence, 267
indirect justiciability of ESCER. *See* economic, social, cultural, and environmental rights
in loco visits
  generally, 26–27, 41–43, 62–63
  activism strategies, 627, 629–30
  impunity, 424–25
Inter-American Commission on Human Rights (IACHR)
  accountability, ensuring, 584, 586–87
  analytical framework for transformative impact (*see* analytical framework for transformative impact)
  assisting function, 184
  authoritarianism as challenge, 47
  backlog of cases, 45–46, 119, 530
  challenges, 44–47, 48
  children's rights, 164–65
  controversial appointments, 636–37
  corruption, 620–22
  Country Reports (*see* Country Reports)
  COVID-19 pandemic, 58–61, 58–59n.48
  creation, 78–79

INDEX 663

Declaration of Principles on Freedom of Expression (*see* Declaration of Principles on Freedom of Expression)
digital freedom of expression (*see* digital freedom of expression)
documenting function, 184
economic, social, cultural, and environmental rights, 218–19, 236
Executive Secretariat, 531
Fifth Meeting of Consultation of Ministers of Foreign Affairs, 606n.8
friendly settlements (*see* friendly settlements)
healthy environment, right to (*see* healthy environment, right to)
human rights community of practice, 24–25, 643
human rights defenders, 394, 397
Impact Observatory, 69, 533–34
indigenous rights (*see* Indigenous rights)
informational requirements, 26–27
institutional dimension, 67
institutional elements, 50
institutional reform, 92–93
Inter-American System to Monitor Recommendations (Inter-American SIMORE), 68–69, 533–34
Interdisciplinary Group of Independent Experts (GIEI), 69–70n.92, 184–85, 439–40, 632–35
international human rights standards, 105–6
LGBTQI+ rights (*see* LGBTQI+ rights)
in loco visits
  generally, 26–27, 41–43, 62–63
  activism strategies, 627, 629–30
  impunity, 424–25
low levels of compliance, 4–5, 584, 604–6
Merits Reports (*see* Merits Reports)
MESEVE, 533–34
migration (*see* migration)
monitoring compliance, 97n.97, 113, 142–43
Office of the Special Rapporteur for Freedom of Expression (*see* Office of the Special Rapporteur for Freedom of Expression)
petitions, 42–44
positioning function, 183
precautionary measures (*see* precautionary measures)
Principles and Best Practices on the Protection of Persons Deprived of Liberty in the Americas, 156n.17, 168–69
prison conditions, 163–64
Procedural Delay Group, 45–46

Protocol of San Salvador (*see* Additional Protocol to the American Convention on Human Rights in the area of Economic, Social, and Cultural Rights (Protocol of San Salvador))
provisional measures, 160, 163–65, 556–57
public hearings, 62–63
Rapid and Integrated Response Coordination Unit, 46–47, 61–62
Rapporteur on the Rights of Human Rights Defenders and Justice Operators, 397
Rapporteurship on the Rights of Women, 271
referrals, 35
Registration Group, 45–46
Report on the Use of Pretrial Detention, 352–53
response to backlash, 97
role (*see* role of IACHR)
Rules of Procedure, 260, 530–31, 532, 534–35, 605
Second Extraordinary Inter-American Conference, 606n.8
selection of commissioners, 635n.25
sexual violence (*see* sexual violence)
Sistema de Monitoreo de Recomendaciones Internacionales de Derechos Humanos (Inter-American SIMORE), 68, 533–34
Specialized Academic Network of Cooperation, 69
Special Mechanism to Follow Up on the Ayotzinapa Matter (MESA), 266, 440, 533–34
Special Monitoring System for Nicaragua (MENESI), 69–70, 70n.93, 440–41, 634–35
Special Procedural Delay Reduction Program, 530, 531–32
Special Program to Monitor IACHR Recommendations, 604–5
Special Rapporteurship on Economic, Social, Cultural, and Environmental Rights, 217
Special Rapporteurships, 34–35, 42, 69
Special Study on the Right of Access to Information, 490, 493
standard-building function, 182
states, engagement, 115–16
Strategic Objective 3 (SO3), 528
Strategic Plan 2011–2015, 604
Strategic Plan 2017–2021, 528, 529, 530, 532, 604, 604n.2
Thematic Reports (*see* Thematic Reports)
transformative impact (*see* transformative impact)
victim-centric approach, 63
violence as challenge, 47
in vitro fertilization (IVF), 285–86

Inter-American Conference on Problems of War and Peace, 102, 103–4
Inter-American Convention against All Forms of Discrimination and Intolerance, 350, 354
Inter-American Convention against Corruption, 620
Inter-American Convention on the Prevention, Punishment and Eradication of Violence against Women (Convention of Belém do Pará)
　generally, 350, 354
　LGBTQI+ rights, 322–23
　sexual violence, 270–71, 272, 276, 283
　violence against women (VAW), 107–8
Inter-American Convention on the Protection of the Human Rights of Older Persons (ICPHROP)
　generally, 348, 350, 354–55
　adoption, 350, 354
　equality, 355–56
　health, right to, 356–57
　liberty, right to, 352
　life, right to, 356–57
　nondiscrimination, 355–56
　personal freedom, right to, 355–56
　proportionality, 353–54
　ratification, 354
　safety, right to, 356–57
Inter-American Convention to Prevent and Punish Torture, 282, 284
Inter-American Court of Human Rights (IACtHR)
　accountability, 584, 586–87
　advisory opinions
　　generally, 180–81
　　LBGTQI+ rights, 550–56
　　migration, 178, 181, 375t
　　transformative impact, 548–49
　amnesty, 66n.80, 106–7
　analytical framework for transformative impact (see analytical framework for transformative impact)
　assisting function, 184
　backlog of cases, 119
　children's rights (see children's rights)
　conventionality control (see conventionality control)
　corruption, 621
　Cotton Field case, 107–8, 207–8, 210, 211
　creation, 78–79
　Criminal Institute of Plácido de Sá Carvalho (Brazil), 153–54, 155, 167–73, 174t, 175
　deprivation of liberty, 155–56
　detainees, 157

digital freedom of expression (see digital freedom of expression)
dignified life, right to, 108–9
directing function, 181, 182
domestic courts, 114–15
economic, social, cultural, and environmental rights (see economic, social, cultural, and environmental rights)
effectiveness
　evaluating compliance with IACtHR decisions, 141–43
　impact beyond compliance, 147–48
embeddedness, 86–87
engagement of states, 115–16
extraterritorial responsibility, 617–18
Fireworks Factory case, 207–9, 210, 212
flexibility, 32–33
freedom of expression (see freedom of expression)
healthy environment, right to (see healthy environment, right to)
high levels of engagement, 18
human dignity, 155
human rights community of practice, 23–24, 25–26, 643
human rights defenders (see human rights defenders)
impunity (see impunity)
indigenous rights (see Indigenous rights)
inducing compliance, 26–29
institutional dimension, 67, 68–70
institutional elements, 50
international human rights standards, 105–6
judicial independence (see judicial independence)
judicialization, 80
LGBTQI+ rights (see LGBTQI+ rights)
life, right to (see life, right to)
living instrument doctrine, 80–81
low levels of compliance, 5, 17, 18, 584, 604–6
margin of appreciation, 97–99
migration (see migration)
Miskito Divers case, 207–8, 209–10, 211, 212
monitoring compliance, 97n.97, 113, 142–43, 591–94
narrative of human rights impact (see narrative of human rights impact)
noncompliance, 94–95
older persons (see older persons)
positioning function, 183
preventive detention, 159
prison conditions, 158–59, 163–64
provisional measures (see provisional measures)

INDEX 665

rape, 157–58
referrals, 35
reframing function, 183–84
remedial practice, 83–84
reparations, 29–30, 64–65, 64n.72, 106–7
response to backlash, 97–98
selection of judges, 635n.25
Sentence Compliance Oversight Unit, 538n.7
sentences, 180–81
sexual violence (*see* sexual violence)
Special Monitoring Mechanism for
  Nicaragua, 69–70, 70n.93
standard-building function, 182
standards, 64
transformative impact of decisions (*see*
  transformative impact)
transitional justice (*see* transitional justice)
victim-centric approach, 63
violence against women (VAW), 107–8
in vitro fertilization (IVF), 285, 286–87
Inter-American Democratic Charter (IADC),
  241–42, 459–60, 474–75
Inter-American Human Rights Network, 147–48
Inter-American Human Rights System
  (IAHRS). *See also specific topic or entity*
generally, 1, 9, 49–50, 74–75, 473n.2
amnesty, 66n.80
analytical framework for transformative
  impact (*see* analytical framework for
  transformative impact)
cases and petitions, 523
compliance (*see* compliance)
constructive engagement, 642–43
cultural dimension, 71–73
  academic institutions, 72, 73
  educational system, 72
  state action, 72–73
expansion
  generally, 14, 603–4, 623–24
  corruption, 619–23
  DPLF strategies, 611–14
  extraterritorial responsibility, 614–18
  transformative impact beyond compliance,
    604–11
First Forum of the Inter-American Human
  Rights System, 621–22
global impact (*see* global impact of IAHRS)
human rights community of practice, 23,
  642–43, 644
improvement (*see* improvement of IAHRS)
institutional dimension, 67–70
  implementation mechanisms, 67
  programs of cooperation, 68–69

institutional resilience, 642, 644, 645–46
key elements
  generally, 62–63
  reparations, 64–65
  standards, 63–64
  victim-centric approach, 63
monitoring pillar, 523, 606
need
  anti-LGBTQI+ groups, 56–57
  contemporary challenges, 53–57
  corruption, 51–52, 52n.12
  COVID-19 pandemic, 57–62
  democracy, declining support, 53–54
  hyper-presidentialism, 52
  militarization, 54–56
  populism, 53, 54
  rule of law, 51–52
  structural challenges, 50–52
  violence, 51
promotion pillar, 606
protection pillar, 606
robust IAHRS, 522–25
  cases and petitions, 523
  monitoring, 523
  progressive development of international
    human rights law, 524
  standards, 523–24
  technical assistance, 523
  victim-oriented nature, 524
sociopolitical dimension, 70–71
  civil society organizations, 71
  human rights community of practice,
    70–71
stakeholders, 642–43
standards
  generally, 63–64
  corruption, 619–23
  defined, 606–7
  extraterritorial responsibility, 614–18
  freedom of expression, 477–79
  migration, 384–87
  robust IAHRS, 523–24
  sexual violence (*see* sexual violence)
  transformative impact beyond compliance,
    604–11
technical assistance, 523
transformative impact (*see* transformative
  impact)
transitional justice (*see* transitional justice)
victim-centric approach, 63, 643–44
victim-oriented nature, 524
Inter-American Juridical Committee, 102
International Court of Justice (ICJ), 237

International Covenant on Civil and Political Rights (ICCPR)
  access to information, 492
  freedom of expression, 500
  hate speech, 513
  LGBTQI+ rights, 312–13
  life, right to, 289–90
  withdrawal, 87n.56
International Covenant on Economic, Social and Cultural Rights (ICESCR)
  Committee on Economic, Social and Cultural Rights (CESCR), 313
  direct justiciability, 228
  economic, social, cultural, and environmental rights, 218–19
  healthy environment, right to, 237–38
  LGBTQI+ rights, 313
International Criminal Court (ICC), 119–20
international human rights standards, 105–11
  amnesty, 106–7
  dignified life, right to, 108–9
  femicide, 107–8
  impunity, 106–7
  indigenous rights, 109–11
  rape, 107–8
  reparations, 106–7
  transitional justice, 106–7
  violence against women (VAW), 107–8
International Labour Organization
  child pornography, 499
  occupational safety and health, 235
International Network for Economic, Social and Cultural Rights (ESCR-Net), 605n.5
International Organization for Migration (IOM), 368–69
Internet. *See* digital freedom of expression
intersectionality
  narrative of human rights impact, 208–9, 210–11, 212
  older persons, 352, 352n.14, 362
  sexual violence, 277–80
in vitro fertilization (IVF)
  generally, 25–26, 189, 191, 223, 301–2
  Artavia Murillo case
    generally, 25–26, 189, 191, 223
    annulment of prohibition, 297–300, 542, 542n.18
    IACtHR decision, 285–87, 301–2
    inspection and quality controls, 300–1
    regulation, 300–1
    reparations, 295–96, 302
    reproductive rights, training judiciary, 296–97
  state healthcare system, 301
  transformative impact, 541–44
  IACtHR decision, 285–87, 301–2
  Merits Reports, 286
  new legal standards, 292–94
  transformative impact, 541–44
Iribarne, Palamara, 481–82
Istanbul Protocol, 443
Italy
  ECtHR, 80
  prison conditions, 171
Ius Constitutionale Commune en América Latina (ICCAL), 1–3. *See also specific topic or entity*
  generally, 473–74
  common law, 200–1
  cultural dimension of IAHRS, 73
  dimensions, 1–2
  effectiveness of international courts, 147
  freedom of expression, 474–77, 493
  healthy environment, right to, 252–53
  human rights defenders, 390, 396, 397, 406
  implications beyond Latin America, 2–3
  interplay between domestic law and IAHRS, 581
  narrative of human rights impact (*see* narrative of human rights impact)
  specific to Latin America, 2
  transformative constitutionalism, 4–7
    generally, 641
    actors, 6
    impact beyond compliance, 6
    tools, 5–6
  transitional justice, 408, 423
IVF. *See* in vitro fertilization (IVF)

Jamaica
  criminal defamation, 484–85
  healthy environment, right to, 249
  human rights violations, 87n.56
judicial independence
  generally, 12–13, 449–50, 472
  Basic Principles on the Independence of the Judiciary, 451–52, 453, 459–60, 461, 462
  consequences of violations
    generally, 467
    damages, 468–70
    judges, reparations for, 468–70
    parties, reparations for, 470–72
    reinstatement, 468–70
  disciplinary systems, 462–65
  elements
    generally, 453

external pressure, protection, 456–58
irremovability principle, 456–58
permanence in office, 454–56
political right of access, 454–56
selection and appointment of judges, 453–54
freedom of association, 459–62
freedom of expression, 459–62
impeachment, 465–67
individual dimension, 452–53
institutional dimension, 452–53
objective dimension, 452–53
obligation of effective judicial protection of human rights
essential content, 450
independent judges and tribunals, 451–53
provisional judges, 458–59
removal of judges, 462–65
subjective dimension, 452–53
judicial protection, right to, 404
jus cogens
amnesty, 415
migration, 370
justice, right to, 103
juvenile justice, 339

Kawas Curry, Jacobo Roberto, 398
Kawas Fernández, Blanca Jeannette, 398–99
Kawas Fernández, Carmen Marilena, 398
Kawas Fernández, Jacobo Roberto, 398
Kawas Fernández, Jorge Jesús, 398
kidnappings. *See* forced disappearances
Kimel, Eduardo, 476
Knox, John H., 238–39

labor unions
direct justiciability of ESCER, 225
indirect justiciability of ESCER, 224
Lambruschini, Armando, 627
Larreta, Eduardo Rodriguez, 103–4
Larreta Proposal, 103–4
Latinobarómetro, 53–54
legal norms, 606–7, 607n.10
legal positivism, 607–8
Leyes de Desacato, 480–83
LGBTQI+ Litigants Network of the Americas, 322
LGBTQI+ rights
generally, 11, 303–5, 325
anti-LGBTQI+ groups, 40n.26, 56–57
Azul Rojas Marin case
generally, 305–6
arbitrary detention, 306–7

background, 304
community impacts, 322–24
duty to investigate violence, 308
impact, 319–25
justice impacts, 320–21
legal impacts, 321–22
material impacts, 320–21
movement impacts, 322–24
reflections, 324–25
reparations, 309–10
torture based on sexual orientation or gender identity, 307
truth impacts, 320–21
effectiveness of international courts, 152
framing, 213
hate crimes, 307, 309
hate speech, 513
IACtHR advisory opinions
context, 550–52
Costa Rica, 552–54
Ecuador, 554–56
international protection
generally, 310–11
Africa, 314
cross-fertilization across systems, 316–17
Europe, 311–12
IAHRS, 314–16
UN, 312–13
name change for trans persons, 553–54
non-refoulement, 321
older persons, 356
same-sex marriage, 552–53, 554–56, 582–83
sexual violence, 280, 307
SOGI-based violence, 303–4, 310
strategic litigation, 317–19
attitude shifts, 318
community impacts, 318, 322–24
justice impacts, 318, 320–21
legal impacts, 318, 321–22
material impacts, 318, 320–21
movement impacts, 318, 322–24
policy and governance impacts, 318
social impacts, 318
truth impacts, 318, 320–21
transformative impact, 550–56
violence against LGBTQI+ persons, 303–4, 310
liberty, right to, 352, 360–61
life, right to
generally, 287–88, 291–92
children, 340–43, 342n.103, 343n.111
evolutive interpretation, 290–91
human rights defenders, 402

668 INDEX

life, right to (*cont.*)
  indigenous people, 358
  most favorable interpretation, 291
  older persons, 356–57, 358–59
  ordinary meaning of terms, 288
  systematic and historical interpretation, 288–90
  teleological interpretation, 291
living instrument doctrine, 80–82
Lopez Obrador, Andrés Manuel, 634–35
Luna López, Carlos Antonio, 398
Lutz, Bertha, 103

Maduro, Nicólas, 40, 476–77
Malawi, AFCtHR jurisdiction, 91
Mali, AFCtHR jurisdiction, 91
"Mandela Rules," 156n.11, 156n.17, 168–69
margin of appreciation, 97–99
Martin de Mejia, Raquel, 272–73
Massera, Emilio Eduardo, 627
Max Planck Institute for Comparative Public Law, 73
measuring compliance
  generally, 13, 564–66, 580–81
  average time to compliance, 570, 575
  backlash, 582–83
  compliance life cycle, 566, 578f, 578–80
  compliance versus impact, 580–81
  conventional measures, 573t
  direct transformative impact, 581
  discrete-time measures of compliance, 566, 576t
  discussion, 571–74
  expected time for compliance (ETC), 566, 570–71, 577–78, 578f
  indirect transformative impact, 581–82
  limitations, 586–87
  qualitative studies, 587–90
  quantitative studies, 585–87
  rate of compliance, 569–70, 574
  resistance, 582
  time
    causes of compliance, 569
    discrete-time measures of compliance, 566, 576t
    importance, 568
    legal outcomes, 568–69
    static "snapshot" approach versus, 567–68
  yearly probability of compliance, 566, 570, 577
media regulation, 479
Mejia Egocheaga, Fernando, 272
Méndez, Juan, 307, 424, 636–37
Menem, Carlos, 410n.7
Mercedes Gómez, Maria, 306–7

Merits Reports
  generally, 179, 180–81, 523
  case selection, 530
  compliance, 533–36, 605
  directing, 181
  freedom of expression, 475
  human rights defenders, 400
  migration, 369, 377
  in vitro fertilization (IVF), 286
Mestizo, Jesús, 265–66
metrics of compliance. *See* measuring compliance
Mexico
  access to information, 491–92
  anti-LGBTQI+ groups, 56
  Attorney General, 632–33
  children's rights, 340
  compliance, 575, 577, 592
  Constitution, 101–2
  corruption, 619
  Cotton Field case, 107–8, 207–8, 210, 211
  criminal defamation, 484–85
  democracy, declining support, 53–54
  DPLF, 612, 622
  Executive Commission for Attention to Victims, 634
  Federal Institute of Access to Public Information, 491
  Federal Law on Transparency and Access to Public Government Information, 491
  forced disappearances, 632–35
  freedom of expression, 476
  Guerreros United cartel, 632–33
  healthy environment, right to, 246, 249, 250
  human rights defenders, 395
  human rights violations, 540–41
  impunity, 439–40
  indigenous rights, 264
  Interdisciplinary Group of Independent Experts (GIEI), 69–70n.92, 184–85, 439–40, 632–35
  investigations of human rights violations, 593
  LGBTQI+ rights, 322
  migration, 369–70, 384–85
  militarization, 54–55
  military reforms, 443
  National Commission on Human Rights, 634
  National Human Rights Commission, 250
  National Institute of Transparency, Access to Information, and Protection of Personal Data, 491
  Protocol for the Adjudication of Cases with a Gender Perspective, 322
  reparations, 211

sexual violence, 275–76, 279, 281, 282–83, 284
Special Mechanism to Follow Up on the Ayotzinapa Matter (MESA), 266, 440, 533–34
Supreme Court of Justice, 322, 484–85, 491–92
violence against women (VAW), 107–8, 182–83, 207–8, 210, 211
migration
  generally, 12, 366–67, 387
  COVID-19 pandemic, 560–61
  defining migrant, 367
  economic, social, cultural, and environmental rights, 378
  forced disappearances, 368–69
  IACtHR
    advisory opinions, 370, 375–76, 375t
    asylum, 375–76
    contentious cases, 373t
    jus cogens status, 370
    non-refoulement, 369, 372–73, 375–76, 377, 380–82, 382n.74, 385–86
  IAHRS
    generally, 367–68
    development and expansion of standards, 372–77
    initial reactions, 369–72
    pending issues, 377–78
    recognition of standards, 384–87
    silence, 368–69
  Merits Reports, 369, 377
  sovereignty, 366
  transformative impact
    generally, 378
    normative frameworks, 378–83, 381t
    provisional measures, 560–62
    recognition of IAHRS standards, 384–87
  vulnerable group, migrants as, 372, 377
military courts, 55, 89–90
minors. *See* children's rights
Molina, Boris, 542n.18
Montaño Noscué, José Norman, 265–66
Montaño Noscué, Matias, 265–66
Montesinos Torres, Vladimiro, 599
Morales, Evo, 55

"naming and shaming," 115–16
narrative of human rights impact
  generally, 10, 199–200, 214
  cognitive categories, 201–4
    ancestral territory, 203–4
    defining problem, 208–10
    victims, 202–3

communities of practice, 200–1
  framing, 201–2, 204–6
narratives in practice
  generally, 207–8
  Cotton Field case, 107–8, 207–8, 210, 211
  defining problem, 208–10
  diagnosis of causes, 210–11
  Fireworks Factory case, 207–9, 210, 212
  impact, 212–13
  intersectionality, 208–9, 210–11, 212
  Miskito Divers case, 207–8, 209–10, 211, 212
  remedies defined, 211–12
National Security Doctrine, 36
Native Americans. *See* Indigenous rights
ne bis in idem, 426–28
net neutrality, 506–8
Nicaragua
  access to information, 487
  attempts to maintain human rights narrative, 40, 42n.38, 48
  children's rights, 340
  communities of practice, 23–24
  contempt laws, 481–82
  criminal defamation, 484–85
  DPLF, 612
  healthy environment, right to, 249
  human rights violations, 37
  indigenous rights, 150, 195–96, 540–41
  sexual violence, 279–80
  Special Monitoring System for Nicaragua (MENESI), 69–70, 70n.93, 440–41, 634–35
  thematic reports, 42–43
Nigeria, right to healthy environment, 238n.9
Ni Una Menos (NGO), 636
Nohlen, Dieter, 54n.28
nondiscrimination
  children, 274, 339
  digital freedom of expression, 505–6
  discrimination defined, 355n.26
  economic, social, cultural, and environmental rights, 222–23
  older persons, 355–56
non-refoulement
  LGBTQI+ rights, 321
  migration, 369, 372–73, 375–76, 377, 380–82, 382n.74, 385–86
  transformative impact, 561

OAS. *See* Organization of American States (OAS)
obligation to investigate, 38–39
Office for Democratic Institutions and Human Rights (ODIHR), 393

Office of the Special Rapporteur for Freedom of Expression
  generally, 474–75, 476–77, 477–78n.23
  access to information, 485–86, 490, 492, 493
  Annual Reports, 500
  content blocking, 509
  criminal defamation, 483, 485
  digital freedom of expression, 495, 496, 503
  filtering, 509
  intermediary liability, 511
  net neutrality, 506, 508
  privacy, 515
  public interest speech, 479–80
  subsequent liability, 511–12
  threats to mandate, 631–32
  universal Internet access, 505–6
Office of the UN High Commissioner for Human Rights, 621–22
older persons
  generally, 12, 348–51, 363–65
  IACtHR
    generally, 351, 358
    health, right to, 359–60
    indigenous people, 358–59
    liberty, right to, 360–61
    life, right to, 358–59
    security, right to, 360–61
  ICPHROP
    generally, 348, 350, 354–55
    equality, 355–56
    health, right to, 356–57
    indigenous people, 355
    integration of standards, 363–64
    LGBTQI+ persons, 356
    liberty, right to, 352
    life, right to, 356–57
    nondiscrimination, 355–56
    personal freedom, right to, 355–56
    proportionality, 353–54
    safety, right to, 356–57
    security, right to, 352
  intersectionality, 352, 352n.14, 362
  Latin America, 349n.9
  LGBTQI+ rights, 356
  long-term services, 356, 357, 357n.30
  preventive detention, 351–54, 361, 362, 363, 364
  Riffo Salinas case, 351–54, 361, 362, 363, 364
  social constructions, 348, 351, 361–63
Organisation of African Unity (OAU)
  generally, 76–77
  First OAU Ministerial Conference on Human Rights in Africa, 394
  human rights defenders, 394

Organization for Security and Cooperation in Europe (OSCE)
  digital freedom of expression, 496
  human rights defenders, 393
Organization of American States (OAS)
  generally, 34–35
  Charter, 101–2, 104, 227, 228, 241–42, 254n.3, 256, 522
  during Cold War, 78–79
  compliance, 564–65, 591–92
  corruption, 620
  economic, social, cultural, and environmental rights, 217
  elections, 56n.36
  extraterritorial responsibility, 617
  Fifth Meeting of Consultation of Ministers of Foreign Affairs, 522–23
  Follow-Up of Recommendations Section, 69
  healthy environment, right to, 241–42
  human rights defenders, 393–94
  indigenous rights, 254n.3
  Inter-American Model Law on Access to Public Information, 487
  LGBTQI+ rights, 310, 315–16
  Permanent Council, 92–93
  prison conditions, 168
Ortega, Daniel, 440–41
Oviedo Convention for the Protection of Human Rights and Dignity of the Human Being with regard to the Application of Biology and Medicine, 290–91

pacta sunt servanda, 524, 525
Pact of San José. *See* American Convention on Human Rights (ACHR)
Pan-African Reparation Initiative, 323–24
Panama
  compliance, 572–74, 592
  contempt laws, 481–82
  criminal defamation, 484–85
  healthy environment, right to, 249
  Immigration Reception Stations, 561
  migration a, 377, 560–62
Pan American Health Organization, 261
Paniagua, Valentín, 597–98
Paraguay
  access to information, 487, 488
  attempts to maintain human rights narrative, 42n.38
  children's rights, 340
  communities of practice, 23–24

INDEX 671

compliance, 577–78, 592
Country Reports, 184
health, right to, 359
healthy environment, right to, 249
human rights violations, 37
impunity, 428–29
indigenous rights, 151, 220–21, 358
Inter-American SIMORE, 68
LGBTQI+ rights, 57
life, right to, 358
migration, 371–72, 378, 379–80
Ministry of Education and Sciences, 57
older persons, 359, 361–62
Operation Condor, 428–29
Supreme Court of Justice, 488
partial compliance, 586, 587
participation in government, right of
  human rights defenders, 404–5
  indigenous people, 255–56
Peña Nieto, Enrique, 633
personal freedom, right to, 355–56
personal liberty, right to, 292
Peru
  amnesty
    compliance, 597–99, 609–10
    transformative impact, 540–41, 559, 581
    transitional justice, 409–10, 412–14, 413n.21, 413n.23, 419–20, 421–22, 423
  anti-LGBTQI+ groups, 56
  Army Intelligence Service, 597
  children's rights, 340
  Constitution, 419n.58
  Constitutional Court, 151–52, 419–20, 419–20n.60
  constitutional law, 588–89
  corruption, 619
  criminal defamation, 484–85
  direct justiciability of ESCER, 226, 227–35
  DPLF, 612, 622
  grievances of individuals, 38
  Grupo Colina, 38
  healthy environment, right to, 249
  IACtHR decisions not enforced, 89–90
  impeachment of judges, 465–67
  impunity, 429, 432, 442–43
  indigenous rights, 151–52, 261–62
  investigations of human rights violations, 593
  Lagos del Campo case, 227
  LGBTQI+ rights
    generally, 305–6
    arbitrary detention, 306–7
    background, 304
    community impact, 322–24
    duty to investigate violence, 308
    impact, 319–25
    justice, truth, and material impacts, 320–21
    legal impact, 321–22
    material impacts, 320–21
    movement impact, 322–24
    reflections, 324–25
    reparations, 309–10
    torture based on sexual orientation or gender identity, 307
    truth impacts, 320–21
  migration, 373–74, 380, 382–83, 386
  militarization, 55
  military courts, 89–90
  military reforms, 443
  National Intelligence Service, 597
  "Plan Ambulante," 597
  procedural rights, 221
  Prosecutor's Office, 598
  reparations, 67n.83, 309–10
  sexual violence, 272–74, 280, 282, 284
  "Tres Islas" indigenous community of Madre de Dios, 261–62
  withdrawal from IAHRS, 89–90
Peteche, Dora Rut Mesa, 265–66
Peteche Mensa, Crescencio, 265–66
Pew Research Center, 53–54
Piñera, Sebastián, 379–80
Pinochet, Augusto, 36, 65n.79, 379–80, 414–15
Poblete Cilches, Vinicio Antonio, 358–59n.33
precautionary measures
  generally, 30–31, 62–63
  adjudicatory instruments, 180–81
  challenges, 45
  children's rights, 329–32
  guardianship function, 261
  indigenous rights
    generally, 254–56, 260–61
    Chaab'il Ch'och' indigenous community, 263
    Siona indigenous people, 262–63
    "Tres Islas" indigenous community of Madre de Dios, 261–62
  precautionary function, 261
preventive detention, 159
Principles and Guidelines on the Right to a Fair Trial and Legal Assistance in Africa, 463
prison conditions, 158–59, 161, 162–67
private life, right to, 292
Promsex (NGO), 305–6, 305n.9, 322, 325
property, right to, 224–25
proportionality and impunity, 442–43

Protocol of San Salvador. *See* Additional Protocol to the American Convention on Human Rights in the area of Economic, Social, and Cultural Rights (Protocol of San Salvador)
provisional judges, 458–59
provisional measures
  generally, 10, 153–55, 175
  adjudicatory instruments, 180–81
  case study, 153–54, 155, 167–73, 174*t*, 175
  children's rights, 164–65, 329–32
  Criminal Institute of Plácido de Sá Carvalho (Brazil), 153–54, 155, 167–73, 174*t*, 175
  deprivation of liberty, 155–59, 161
  extreme gravity and urgency, 556–57, 557n.62
  legal basis, 160–61
  preventive measures, 160
  prison conditions, 158–59, 161, 162–67
  protective measures, 160
  transformative impact
    generally, 556–57
    amnesty, 557–60
    migration, 560–62
  transformative provisional measures, 161–63
  urgency, 161
public interest speech
  generally, 478, 479–80
  contempt laws, 480–83
  criminal defamation, 479, 483–85
  Leyes de Desacato, 480–83

Rabat Plan of Action, 513
Ramos Monárrez, Laura Berenice, 275
rape as torture, 107–8, 157, 282–83
rate of compliance, 569–70, 574
realist international relations, 594
Red Guerrerense de Organismos Civiles de Derechos Humanos (NGO), 633
REDRESS (NGO), 305–6, 305n.7, 317–18, 325
Regional Agreement on Access to Information, Public Participation and Justice in Environmental Matters in Latin America and the Caribbean (Escazu Agreement), 240–41, 240n.20, 248, 249, 252
reparations
  generally, 29–30
  children's rights, 337
  direct justiciability, 234–35
  economic, social, cultural, and environmental rights, 234–35
  forced disappearances, 568–69
  integral reparation, 534
  international human rights standards, 106–7
  in vitro fertilization (IVF), denial of right, 295–96, 302
  judicial independence, violations
    judges, 468–70
    parties, 470–72
  key element of IAHRS, 64–65, 64n.72
  low levels of compliance, 176
  non-repetition, 540–41, 540n.11
  transformative impact, 539–41
  violence against women (VAW), 211
repressive law, 19–20
reproductive autonomy, 293
reproductive rights
  generally, 11
  abortion, 294–95
  degree of interference in exercise of rights, 293–94
  family, right to, 292
  indirect justiciability, 222, 223–24
  life, right to
    generally, 287–88, 291–92
    evolutive interpretation, 290–91
    most favorable interpretation, 291
    ordinary meaning of terms, 288
    systematic and historical interpretation, 288–90
    teleological interpretation, 291
  new legal standards, 292–94, 301–2
  personal liberty, right to, 292
  private life, right to, 292
  reproductive autonomy, 293
  transformative impact, 287
  in vitro fertilization (IVF) (*see* in vitro fertilization (IVF))
res interpretata, 122–23, 129–36, 137
res judicata
  conventionality control, 122–23, 129–37
  impunity, fraudulent *res judicata,* 426–28
Responsibility to Protect, 104–5
responsive law, 19–21
Revoredo Marsano, Guillermo Rey Terry y Delia, 466–67
rights of the child. *See* children's rights
Rio Declaration on Environment and Development, 237
Rivera Lazo, Juan Norberto, 599
"Riyadh Guidelines," 330
role of IACHR, 34–35
  generally, 9
  overview, 47–48
  attempts to maintain human rights narrative, 39–42

INDEX   673

challenges, 44–47, 48
grievances of individuals against nations, 37–39, 47–48
improving inclusion and participation in political system, 42–44, 47–48
maintaining human rights focus among dictatorships, 36–37, 47–48
Rubens Graffigna, Omar Domingo, 627
rule of law
  human rights defenders, 397, 401, 402
  need for IAHRS, 51–52
Rule of Law Index, 51–52, 51n.10
Russia
  Constitutional Court, 94–95
  Council of Europe, 78
  ECtHR, 92, 94–95, 583
Rwanda, withdrawal from AFCtHR jurisdiction, 91

safety, right to, 356–57
Saint Kitts and Nevis, right to healthy environment, 249
Saint Lucia, right to healthy environment, 249
Saint Vincent and the Grenadines, right to healthy environment, 249
Salazar Monroe, Julio, 599
Santiago Declaration, 522–23
secondary norms, 607
Second World Conference on Human Rights, 270
security, right to, 352, 360–61
self-defence, 202n.10
sexual orientation and gender identity (SOGI)-based violence, 303–4, 310
sexual violence. *See also* violence against women (VAW)
  generally, 11, 268, 284
  children, 346
  forced disappearances, 277
  IAHRS standards
    generally, 272
    enhanced due diligence, 275–77
    gender stereotypes, 280–81
    intersectionality, 277–80
    recognition as violation of human rights, 272–75
    state responsibility, 282–83
    stringent due diligence, 275–77
  indigenous people, 278–79
  indirect justiciability, 223–24
  international human rights law framework, 268–71
  LGBTQI+ persons, 280, 307
  rape as torture, 107–8, 157, 282–83

social media
  generally, 496, 517n.77
  abuse, 502
  hate speech, 512
  intermediary liability, 510
social protest, use of force, 638–39
social security, right to, 232
Soria Espinoza, Carmelo, 193
Soto, James Wilfredo, 265–66
Soto, José Gerardo, 265–66
South Africa, transformative constitutionalism, 2
Spain
  National High Court, 628
  universal jurisdiction, 628
Special Rapporteur of the United Nations on the Independence of Judges and Lawyers, 620
Special Rapporteur on Freedom of Expression, 515–16
speech. *See* freedom of expression
Standard Minimum Rules for Non-custodial Measures ("Tokyo Rules"), 330
Standard Minimum Rules for the Administration of Juvenile Justice ("Beijing Rules"), 330
Standard Minimum Rules for the Treatment of Prisoners, 156n.11, 156n.17, 168–69
Stockholm Declaration, 237
street children, 342n.103
subsidiarity, 24–25
substantive equality, 7
Suriname
  healthy environment, right to, 249
  human rights violations, 37
  indigenous rights, 138
surveillance, 514–16
Switzerland, ECHR, 86

Tanta Marin, Juana Rosa, 306
Tanzania, withdrawal from AFCtHR jurisdiction, 91
Tasquinas, Rogelio, 265–66
Thematic Reports
  generally, 42–43, 47–48, 62–63, 105–6, 528, 533–34
  compliance, 606, 610–11
  corruption, 621–22
  digital freedom of expression, 496, 503
  economic, social, cultural, and environmental rights, 243, 247
  extraterritorial responsibility, 615–18
  freedom of expression, 474, 475, 479–80
  indigenous rights, 266
  social protest, use of force, 638–39

"Tokyo Rules," 330
Toronto Stock Exchange, 615
torture
　rape as torture, 107–8, 157, 282–83
　sexual orientation or gender identity, 307
trade unions
　direct justiciability of ESCER, 225
　indirect justiciability of ESCER, 224
transformative constitutionalism
　generally, 32–33
　flexibility, 32–33
　human rights community of practice, 22–26
　ICCAL, 4–7
　　generally, 641
　　actors, 6
　　impact beyond compliance, 6
　　tools, 5–6
　Latin America, 19–21
　substantive equality, 7
　transformative impact beyond compliance, 6, 29–32
transformative impact
　generally, 13, 65–67, 74–75, 537–39, 562–63, 644–47
　advisory opinions
　　generally, 548–49
　　LGBTQI+ rights, 550–56
　amnesty, 540–41, 557–60, 581, 609–10
　analytical framework (*see* analytical framework for transformative impact)
　beyond compliance
　　generally, 13–14, 584–85, 595, 601–2
　　amnesty, 609–10
　　change over time, 595–96
　　defining, 143–46
　　IACtHR, 147–48
　　institutional impact, 600–1
　　quality of compliance, improving, 596–600
　　standards, 604–11
　　transformative constitutionalism, 6, 29–32
　children's rights, 327
　Chilean Councils of War, 544–47
　communities of practice, 642–43
　contentious cases
　　generally, 547–48
　　Chilean Councils of War, 544–47
　　reparations, 539–41
　　in vitro fertilization (IVF), 541–44
　Country Reports, 177, 179, 182, 183, 184, 186, 197
　freedom of expression, 474–77
　future research, 646

healthy environment, right to, 249–52
human rights defenders, 389, 397
impunity, 443–47
LGBTQI+ rights, 550–56
migration
　generally, 378
　normative frameworks, 378–83, 381*t*
　provisional measures, 560–62
　recognition of IAHRS standards, 384–87
non-refoulement, 561
provisional measures
　generally, 556–57
　amnesty, 557–60
　migration, 560–62
reparations, 539–41
reproductive rights, 287
in vitro fertilization (IVF), 541–44
transitional justice
　generally, 12, 408–9, 422–23
　amnesty
　　generally, 38–39, 39n.23, 66n.80, 409
　　conventionality control, 417–19
　　domestic reception of IACtHR jurisprudence, 419–22
　　jurisprudence of IACtHR, 412–19
　　jus cogens status of law, 415
　　nullification of laws, 416–17, 418–20
　　past human rights violations, 409–11
　　procedural legitimacy, 422
　　standards, 412–19, 423
　defined, 408–9
　distributive dimension, 409, 413–14, 416, 423
　ICCAL, 408, 423
　impunity, 425, 434–39
　international human rights standards, 106–7
　multilevel legal system standards, 411–12
　past human rights violations, 409–11
　restorative dimension, 409, 413–14, 416, 423
　retributive dimension, 409, 413–14, 416, 423
transnationalized human rights implementation, 111–18
　engagement with states, 115–16
　pressure from human rights actors, 114
　role of domestic courts, 114–15
Transparency International, 51–52
Trinidad and Tobago
　compliance, 577–78
　healthy environment, right to, 249
　withdrawal from IAHRS, 88, 582
Tunisia, AFCtHR jurisdiction, 91
Twelfth UN Congress on Crime Prevention and Criminal Justice, 165

INDEX 675

2030 Agenda for Sustainable Development, 236, 240

UDHR. *See* Universal Declaration of Human Rights (UDHR)
Ukraine in Council of Europe, 78
UNICEF, 235
unions
  direct justiciability of ESCER, 225
  indirect justiciability of ESCER, 224
Uniscue, Eliodoro, 265–66
United Kingdom
  Brexit, 95–96
  ECtHR, 80, 92, 95–97, 583
  Human Rights Act 1998, 95–96
  Privy Council, 87n.56, 88
  Representation of the People Act 1983, 95–96
  withdrawal from ECHR, 91, 95–96
United Nations
  Basic Principles on the Independence of the Judiciary, 451–52, 453, 459–60, 461, 462
  "Beijing Rules," 330
  budget crisis, 119–20
  Charter, 102–3, 202n.10, 394
  Committee against Torture (CAT), 313
  Committee on Economic, Social and Cultural Rights (CESCR), 313
  Conference on the Human Environment, 237
  Convention against Corruption, 620
  corruption, 620
  Declaration on Human Rights Defenders, 391–93
  Declaration on the Rights of Peasants and Other People Working in Rural Areas, 238–39
  Declarations of the Rights of the Child, 330
  digital freedom of expression, 496
  Economic Commission for Europe, 240
  Group of Eminent International and Regional Experts on Yemen, 321
  Guidelines for the Prevention of Juvenile Delinquency ("Riyadh Guidelines"), 330
  Human Rights Committee
    dignified life, right to, 108–9
    judicial independence, 471–72
    LGBTQI+ rights, 312–13
    removal of judges, 462
  Human Rights Council
    corruption, 620
    healthy environment, right to, 238–39
    LGBTQI+ rights, 321
    human rights defenders, 394, 397
    Independent Expert on SOGI, 321
    LGBTQI+ rights, 312–13, 316
  "Mandela Rules," 156n.11, 156n.17, 168–69
  Office of the UN High Commissioner for Human Rights, 621–22
  "Riyadh Guidelines," 330
  Special Rapporteur of the United Nations on the Independence of Judges and Lawyers, 620
  Special Rapporteur on Freedom of Expression, 515–16
  Standard Minimum Rules for Non-custodial Measures ("Tokyo Rules"), 330
  Standard Minimum Rules for the Administration of Juvenile Justice ("Beijing Rules"), 330
  Standard Minimum Rules for the Treatment of Prisoners, 156n.11, 156n.17, 168–69
  "Tokyo Rules," 330
  Twelfth UN Congress on Crime Prevention and Criminal Justice, 165
  2030 Agenda for Sustainable Development, 236, 240
  UNICEF, 235
  Working Group on Arbitrary Detention, 306–7, 316
United States
  access to information, 494
  Brown v. Board of Education (1954), 20–21, 581
  Federal Communication Commission, 508
  freedom of expression, 494
  militarization, 54–55
  net neutrality, 508
  prison conditions, 170–71
  Supreme Court, 168–69, 170–71
Universal Declaration of Human Rights (UDHR)
  access to information, 493
  global human rights governance, 101, 103
  human rights defenders, 394
  life, right to, 289–90
  sexual violence, 268–69
universal jurisdiction, 628
Universal System of Human Rights, 386
University of Pretoria, 323–24
Uruguay
  access to information, 487
  amnesty
    generally, 39n.23
    compliance, 610
    transitional justice, 409–10, 410n.5, 410n.9, 412–13, 415, 422

Uruguay (*cont.*)
  children's rights, 340
  compliance, 572
  Country Reports, 184
  Expiry Law, 410n.9
  healthy environment, right to, 249
  human rights violations, 37
  ICPHROP, 354
  Inter-American SIMORE, 68
  migration, 382–83

VAW. *See* violence against women (VAW)
Vélez, Jesús, 371
Vélez Loor, Jesús Tranquilino, 560
Venezuela
  access to information, 494n.131
  attempts to maintain human rights narrative, 40, 41–42, 48
  children's rights, 340
  communities of practice, 23–24
  compliance, 572, 577–78
  Constitutional Chamber, 88–89
  criminal defamation, 485
  DPLF, 612
  freedom of expression, 476–77, 480, 494
  healthy environment, right to, 249
  IACtHR decisions not enforced, 89–90
  impunity in, 441–42
  judicial independence, consequences of violations, 470
  MESEVE, 533–34
  migration, 377, 382–83, 385–86
  precautionary measures, 88–89
  prison conditions, 165–66
  provisional measures, 161n.52
  sexual violence, 276–77, 283, 284
  threats to mandate of IACHR, 631–32
  withdrawal from IAHRS, 88–90, 166n.77, 476–77, 582
Videla, Jorge Rafael, 627
Vienna Convention on Consular Relations, 371
Vienna Convention on the Law of Treaties
  amnesty, 417–18
  life, right to, 287–89
  pacta sunt servanda, 524
Viola, Roberto Eduardo, 627
violence
  challenge to IACHR, 47
  children, institutional violence, 339, 342
  indigenous people, 267
  LGBTQI+ persons, 303–4, 310
  need for IAHRS, 51
  sexual orientation and gender identity (SOGI)-based violence, 303–4, 310
violence against women (VAW). *See also* sexual violence
  international human rights standards, 107–8
  narrative of human rights impact, 207–8, 210, 211
  positioning, 182–83
  reparations, 211
Vitonas Casamachin, Alexander, 265–66

war propaganda, 498–99
Watt Kawas, Jaime Alejandro, 398
Watt Kawas, Selsa Damaris, 398
Weeramantry, Christopher, 237
women's rights
  effectiveness of international courts, 152
  femicide, 107–8
  rape as torture, 107–8, 157, 282–83
  reproductive rights (*see* reproductive rights)
  sexual violence (*see* sexual violence)
  violence against women (VAW) (*see* violence against women (VAW))
work, right to
  direct justiciability, 229–30
  indirect justiciability, 223–24
Working Group on Arbitrary Detention, 306–7, 316
World Bank, 151–52
World Health Organization
  COVID-19 pandemic, 560–61
  indigenous rights, 261
"world of law," 200–1
Worldwide Governance Indicators Project, 51–52, 51n.9

yearly probability of compliance, 566, 570, 577
Yemen
  Group of Eminent International and Regional Experts on Yemen, 321
  LGBTQI+ rights, 321

Zimbabwe, LGBTQI+ rights, 314